RENEWALS 458-4574.

DATE DUE			
DEC 13			
MAY 09			
OCT 11			
GAYLORD			PRINTED IN U.S.A.

THE **MICROECONOMICS** OF
PUBLIC POLICY ANALYSIS

THE **MICROECONOMICS** OF PUBLIC POLICY ANALYSIS

LEE S. FRIEDMAN

PRINCETON UNIVERSITY PRESS

PRINCETON AND OXFORD

Published by Princeton University Press, 41 William Street, Princeton, New Jersey 08540

In the United Kingdom: Princeton University Press, 3 Market Place, Woodstock,

Oxfordshire OX20 1SY

LIBRARY OF CONGRESS CATALOGING-IN-PUBLICATION DATA

Friedman, Lee S.

  The microeconomics of public policy analysis / Lee S. Friedman

    p.   cm.

  Includes bibliographical references and index.

  ISBN 0-691-08934-5

  1. Policy sciences.   2. Microeconomics.   I. Title

H97 .F75   2002

338.5—dc21   2001051156

British Library Cataloging-in-Publication Data is available

This book has been composed in Adobe Times Roman and Futura

by Princeton Editorial Associates, Inc., Scottsdale, Arizona

Printed on acid-free paper. ∞

www.pup.princeton.edu

Printed in the United States of America

10 9 8 7 6 5 4 3 2 1

TO JANET, ALEXANDER, AND JACOB,
WHO BRING JOY TO MY LIFE

CONTENTS

(^{S} = Supplementary Section, ^{O} = Optional Section with Calculus)

PART TWO
USING MODELS OF INDIVIDUAL CHOICE-MAKING IN POLICY ANALYSIS

Chapter 4
The Specification of Individual Choice Models for the Analysis of Welfare Programs

79

Chapter 5
The Analysis of Equity Standards: An Intergovernmental Grant Application

124

PART THREE
POLICY ASPECTS OF PRODUCTION
AND SUPPLY DECISIONS

Chapter 9
The Cost Side of Policy Analysis: Technical Limits,
Productive Possibilities, and Cost Concepts   **317**

Chapter 10
Private Profit-Making Organizations:
Objectives, Capabilities, and Policy Implications   **373**

Chapter 20
Imperfect Information and Institutional Choices   724

ALTERNATIVE COURSE DESIGNS

The Microeconomics of Public Policy Analysis is used by people with diverse backgrounds in economics and diverse purposes for studying this subject. The book contains enough material to meet these diverse needs, but it is not expected that any single course will cover everything in the book. In many chapters, instructors teaching students with no economics prerequisite will spend more time on the basic theory and less on the detailed policy examples. Instructors and their students will also have different preferences for which policy areas or aspects of microeconomics they wish to emphasize. To help make these choices, the table below shows a suggested number of lectures to correspond to each chapter. Where a range such as 1–2 is shown, it suggests that the instructor should choose between partial and fuller coverage. Most instructors will choose a group that totals twenty-six to twenty-eight lectures for a standard course of thirty class meetings:

Chapters	Lectures
1	½
2	½
3	2
4	2
5	2
6	2
7	2
8	1–2
9	1–2
10	1–2
11	1–2
12	2
13	1–2
14	1–2
15	½–1
16	1*
17	1–2*
18	1–2*
19	1*
20	1*
Total	**24½–33**

*Chapter 15 provides an overview of the market (and government) failures that are the subjects of Chapters 16–20. Some instructors, after covering Chapter 15, may wish to pick only two to three of the latter chapters for intensive coverage.

PREFACE

THIS BOOK DEVELOPS AND BUILDS systematically upon intermediate-level microeconomic theory for a special purpose. That purpose is to develop the skills of microeconomic modeling and the principles of welfare economics used in policy analysis. No prerequisite is necessary, although the book can easily be used at a more advanced level by having one (more on this below).

A typical chapter begins by developing a few principles from intermediate-level theory and using them to construct and apply models, in some depth, to one or more policy issues. The issues selected are diverse, and they cut across the traditional applied fields of public finance, urban economics, industrial organization, and labor economics. Overall, the book illustrates how microeconomic models are used as tools to design, predict the effects of, and evaluate public policies.

Experts in many specific subject areas, such as welfare, housing, health, and environmental economics, will be, I think, pleasantly surprised by the coverage that their areas have received. As experts they will find most of these models simpler than the ones they construct or study in professional journals. Most subject area experts that I know find it easy to give examples of every conceivable reason for policy intervention, or for studying the harm from an intervention, right within their own sectors. Education economists, for example, have to account for monopoly schools, externalities in the classroom, the public good of having an educated citizenry, information asymmetries that make contracting for educational services difficult for all parties, and equity requirements for financing systems. This book, however, generally offers models with only one failure (of the market or of government) studied at a time. I believe that is the best way to explicate that type of failure carefully and to learn how to analyze alternative ways of responding to it. I hope that these experts will agree.

I have used this book as the primary text in one-semester courses offered both to undergraduates (primarily those studying economics or public policy) and to graduate students (from diverse disciplinary and professional fields). However, all material in the book cannot be adequately covered in one semester. I provide the short section "Alternative Course Designs" to suggest different ways of using the book to construct a standard semester-length course. Most of the time I use this book without intermediate microeconomics as a prerequisite. When I do so, I do not attempt to cover all of the applications, and I skip most of the supplementary sections denoted with the superscript "S." Sometimes, however, I offer a more advanced course in which I spend little class time on basic microeconomic theory and focus almost exclusively on the applications.

The chapters of *The Microeconomics of Public Policy Analysis* are sequenced to draw upon microeconomic principles in the same order that they are developed in most intermediate theory courses: individual decision-making, supplier decision-making, markets as organizations, and market and governmental failures. Exercises are included at the end of chapters, and I recommend use of them as a means to develop, practice, and test analytic skills.

The book has no special mathematical prerequisite, although it often has empirical illustrations of the models discussed. The illustrations have been kept numerically simple. There are optional sections and appendices in which differential calculus is used freely, and some of the exercises require calculus; all of these are denoted with the superscript "O." Other than in these instances, calculus is relegated to the footnotes. Readers who do or will use calculus as part of their professional training should benefit from these parts of the book.

I hope, in the end, that readers will appreciate the strengths while still recognizing the weaknesses of existing models and methods. I hope that they will be impressed with the breadth and depth of the contributions of microeconomics as an analytic tool for public policy. I also hope that exposing areas in which improvement in microeconomic models is needed will help to spur some of those improvements. I refer particularly to two areas important for a large number of policy issues: (1) the growing body of evidence that, in many situations, actual individual behavior departs substantially from standard utility maximization; and (2) the analytic difficulty of assessing alternative strategies (or institutions) for responding to market failures when all are imperfect. Although the book raises these challenges in considering models of particular issues, it does not dwell upon what has not yet been done or applied. Rather, the emphasis throughout is on successful "role" models: those that illustrate how microeconomics contributes constructively and importantly to policy analysis.

ACKNOWLEDGMENTS

THOSE INDIVIDUALS WHO have been graduate students in the Richard and Rhoda Goldman School of Public Policy at the University of California, Berkeley, have been a continuing source of inspiration for me. I doubt that my instruction will ever catch up to the level of their postgraduation accomplishments, but I do enjoy trying, and this book is a big part of my effort. I am grateful for their support and for their many constructive suggestions during this undertaking.

Colleagues at Berkeley, especially Eugene Bardach, Steve Raphael, and Eugene Smolensky, have made important substantive contributions, and I am grateful for their advice, wisdom, encouragement, and patience. Elizabeth Graddy of the University of Southern California, David Howell at the New School, Samuel Myers, Jr., at the University of Minnesota, and several anonymous referees offered invaluable, detailed feedback on draft chapters, and they have helped to improve this book enormously. Brave users of the evolving draft manuscript, including Joseph Cordes of George Washington University and Joseph DeSalvo at the University of South Florida, also alerted me to numerous opportunities for improvement.

My editor at Princeton University Press, Peter Dougherty, has done a wonderfully professional job shepherding this manuscript from review through design, copyediting, and production. I am grateful to him for his sound advice and encouragement, and for assembling a first-rate staff to produce this book. I am also grateful to the staff at the Goldman School for their careful and patient assistance with manuscript preparation: Merle Hancock, Kristine Kurovsky, and Theresa Wong.

Despite all of this able assistance, I accept full responsibility for any flaws in the content of this book. It has been a joy to craft it, and I hope that it will help to advance the field where microeconomics and public policy intersect.

PART ONE
MICROECONOMIC MODELS FOR PUBLIC POLICY ANALYSIS

CHAPTER ONE

INTRODUCTION TO MICROECONOMIC POLICY ANALYSIS

Policy Analysis and Resource Allocation

Policy analysis involves the application of social science to matters of public policy. The specific tasks of an analysis depend importantly on which aspects of policy are to be understood, who wants to know, and how quickly the analysis is needed. For many, the excitement of this discipline is in its often turbulent political application: the undertaking and use of policy analysis as a part of actual government decision-making. In that application the analysis is undertaken in order to advise; it is for the use of specific decision makers whose actions will depend on the analytic results. For others, the excitement is in rising to a more purely intellectual challenge: to create a more general understanding about how public policy is, and ought to be, made. The latter effort represents the more academic side of policy analysis. However, the same basic intellectual skills are used to conduct both types of analyses.

Microeconomic analysis is one of the fundamental skills of this discipline. It provides a critical foundation for both the design and the evaluation of policies. This is hardly surprising: *Most public policy involves resource allocation.* To carry out virtually any government policy either requires the direct use of significant resources or severely constrains the use of resources by economic agents (i.e., individuals, firms, or government agencies). These resources (labor, buildings, machinery, and natural resources such as water, oil, and land) are scarce, and different people will have different ideas about what to do with them. A proposed dam may mean economic survival for farmers needing water to grow crops, but may at the same time threaten destruction of a unique white-water river and canyon irreplaceable to the fish species that spawn there and to lovers of nature. A town may, through its powers of zoning, declare certain or all areas within it for residential use only—to the chagrin of a company that wants to build a small factory (which would employ some of the town residents and provide local tax revenues) and to the delight of estate owners adjacent

3

to the restricted area (who fear plummeting property values). As in these examples, public policy–making typically forces tough choices. *Microeconomics is the study of resource allocation choices, and microeconomic policy analysis is the study of those special choices involving government.*

Proficiency in policy analysis requires more microeconomics than is usually conveyed in a basic microeconomic theory course. Typically, most of the basic course is devoted to explaining and evaluating the operation of a private market system. By a private market we refer to the voluntary trading offers and exchanges made by independent, private, economic agents acting as buyers or sellers of resources, goods, or services. Public policy involves, by contrast, a *collective* decision to influence or control behavior that would otherwise be shaped completely by the private agents in a market. This does not imply, however, that public policy is antithetical to the use of markets. As we will see, much of the task of public policy analysis is to help create a proper blending of collective and market controls over resource allocation decisions. Thus microeconomic policy analysis requires a thorough understanding of the conditions that favor collective over individual action and the alternative collective or policy actions that might be taken, and it requires a means of evaluating the alternatives in order to choose among them.

To offer a brief preview of analytic thinking, we consider the following hypothetical and informal conversation:

Official: We have got to do something about the traffic congestion and pollution caused by commuting into the city. Why don't we make a toll-free lane for automobiles carrying four or more passengers?

Analyst: That's an interesting idea, and it has worked with some success in a few other areas. But may I offer an alternative suggestion? The four-for-free plan has two important disadvantages. One, it reduces revenues that we sorely need. Two, it provides no incentive for commuters to form car pools of two and three, nor does it encourage the use of mass transit systems. I've heard this system may actually worsen the problem in the San Francisco area because many people have stopped using mass transit in order to carpool for free!

Suppose instead that we raise the tolls during the peak commuting hours. The peak-toll plan would help solve our deficit problem. Furthermore, it would increase commuter incentives to form car pools of all sizes, to take mass transit rather than drive, and even to drive at off-peak hours for those who have that discretion.

In the above conversation, the analyst recognizes immediately that pollution and congestion are what economists call external effects (side effects of allocating resources to the activity of commuting). The analyst knows that economic efficiency requires a solution that "internalizes" the externalities and that the four-for-free plan deviates substantially from this idea. These same economic principles influenced the design of the alternative peak-toll plan.

Here is a second example:

Mayor: We have a big problem. Remember the foundation that pays for 4 years of nursing school for the top fifty low-income applicants from our public high schools?

The first of these groups is now in its third year of studies. A new report claims that the average cost of this education is $56,000 per nurse graduate, and that society only benefits from those who complete their degrees. These benefits, it seems, are only worth $48,000 per nurse. The foundation is not only considering pulling the plug on the program, but I'm told that it will terminate the groups that have already started.

Advisor: Yes, that is a big problem. I'll review the study for accuracy as soon as possible. But I believe that we can prevent the foundation from making one mistake.

Mayor: What is it?

Advisor: I think that we can make it understand, by its own logic, that it should not terminate the groups that have already started.

Mayor: What do you mean?

Advisor: The funds that have already been expended on the groups now in college are already gone. Nobody can put them to an alternate use. What matters is, right from today, the incremental costs of completing their educations compared with the incremental benefits from doing so. It will only cost about $14,000 for the last year of the oldest group. But that $14,000 will yield $48,000 in benefits from the nursing degree! Termination would therefore cause a net additional loss of $34,000. It would be criminal to pull the plug on those students now.

The same logic holds true for the other groups that have started. Even for the first-year group, the incremental benefits of $48,000 from graduating outweigh the incremental costs of about $42,000 for the remaining years. If the foundation is motivated by benefit-cost logic, the wise investment (not to mention public relations) is to let the groups that have started continue to completion.

In this second example, the advisor quickly identifies what economists call sunk costs, or costs that have already been incurred. It might be true, as the report claims, that it is a poor investment to start any new students down the path of the current program design. But the real costs to society of continuing those already in school are only the resources that could still be freed up for use elsewhere (the costs that have not yet been incurred). In this example, these are small in comparison to the benefits of completing the nursing education. It is fortunate that, in this case, the economic criterion suggests a course that would improve the foundation's public image under the circumstances.[1]

In actual settings, these conversations might lead to further consideration of alternative plans: the design of new alternatives, careful estimation of the consequences of the

---

[1] In other cases, economic criteria can suggest termination of a project that could be embarrassing to an organization that has incurred sunk but visible costs in it. The organization may prefer to spare itself embarrassment despite the poor economics. This is especially true when the organization does not bear the brunt of the economic loss. For example, the military may learn that the cost of completing an order for a new type of helicopter is far greater than what is economically reasonable. But owing to its sunk costs in prototype development, base preparation costs for training and maintenance, and prior lobbying to gain approval for the initial order, it may prefer to continue with the project rather than disappoint its supporters.

alternatives to be evaluated (e.g., the effect of specific tolls on the city's budget, benefit-cost calculations for the foundation of revised programs), and evaluation by a set of criteria wider than efficiency (e.g., fairness or equity, legality, and political and administrative feasibility). This book focuses on developing the microeconomic skills essential to applying this kind of analysis to a wide range of public policy problems.

The Diverse Economic Activities of Governments

To illustrate more concretely the specific subject matter of microeconomic policy analysis, let us take a brief tour of the many economic activities of government. This tour will serve the additional purpose of indicating the extensiveness of public controls over resource allocation. While we have already asserted that most public policy involves resource allocation, it is just as important that we understand the reverse relation: *All resource allocation decisions are shaped by public policy.* This shaping occurs in different ways: through direct government purchase or supply of particular activities, the regulation of market activities, the development and maintenance of a legal system, and the undertaking of redistributive programs. Let us consider each of these in turn.

In the year 2000 the total value of all measured goods and services produced in the United States—called the gross domestic product, or GDP—was about $10 trillion.[2] Roughly 17 percent of the total GDP, valued at $1.7 trillion, consisted of purchases by governments to provide various goods and services to citizens. The governments include federal, state, and local governments and regional authorities acting as collective agents for citizens. These different governments operate schools, hospitals, and parks; provide refuse collection, fire protection, and national defense; build dams; maintain the roads; sponsor research to fight cancer; and purchase a host of other goods and services that are intended to benefit the citizenry. What explains why these goods are provided through governments instead of markets? Why not let individual consumers seek them through the marketplace as they seek movies and food? What do we know about the economic advantages of doing it one way or the other?

Such questions are still quite general. Of the 17 percent of goods and services purchased by governments, approximately 11 percent was supplied directly through government agencies and enterprises (e.g., the Post Office) and the other 6 percent was provided through contracts and grants (e.g., a local government may tax its citizens to provide refuse collection and contract with a private firm to actually do the work).[3] When is it that a government should actually supply the goods, and when should it contract with private firms to supply them? If it does the latter, how should the contract be written to protect the economic interests of the citizens footing the bill? If a government actually produces the good or service itself, what mechanisms are there to encourage economy in production?

---

[2] *Economic Report of the President,* January 2001 (Washington, D.C.: U.S. Government Printing Office, 2001), p. 274, Table B-1.

[3] Ibid., p. 288, Table B-10. In 2000, $1.087 trillion of GDP was provided directly by the government sector out of $1.748 trillion in total government purchases, or 62 percent. The 11 percent in the text is approximately 0.62 of 17 percent.

To purchase all these services, governments must raise revenues. The overwhelming bulk of the revenues comes from taxes; a smaller portion comes from individual user fees (e.g., park admission charges). When should user fees be charged, and to what extent? If taxes must be collected, who should pay them and how much should each taxpayer be assessed?

The economic policy issues illustrated so far arise when governments have taken primary responsibility for providing goods and services. However, governments have great influence over a much wider range of goods and services through their regulatory mechanisms. In these cases, individual economic agents acting in the market still retain considerable decision-making power over what and how much to buy or sell of different commodities, although the available choices are conditioned by the regulations. Government regulatory mechanisms influence prices, qualities, and quantities of goods and services traded in the market as well as the information available to consumers about them.

Many industries are subject to price controls on their products. The form that such controls take varies. For example, some industries have their prices controlled indirectly through limits set by regulatory commissions on the return that producers are allowed to earn on their investments. Natural gas and electric utilities are common examples. Occasionally, rental housing prices are regulated through rent control policies; in the past, domestic oil prices have been controlled. Another form of price control operates through taxes and subsidies. These are common in the area of international trade; many countries have policies to discourage imports through tariffs and encourage exports through subsidies. Within the domestic economy, alcohol and tobacco products are taxed to raise their prices and thus discourage their use (and many countries are considering new taxes on carbon emissions to prevent global warming); disaster insurance and loans for small businesses and college educations are subsidized to encourage their use. Although it is difficult to give precise figures on the amount of economic activity subject to some form of price regulation, a reasonable estimate is that at least an additional 20 to 25 percent of GDP is affected by this type of public policy.

Price regulation may be the least common form of regulation. Product regulations controlling quantities and qualities are widely used, generally to provide environmental and consumer protection. Some of these regulations are highly visible; examples are automobile safety standards and the prescription requirements for the sale of medicines and drugs. Other regulatory activities, such as public health standards in food-handling institutions (e.g., restaurants, supermarkets, and frozen food factories) and antiflammability requirements for children's clothing, are less visible. There are standards for clean air and water, worker health and safety, and housing construction; there are licensing requirements for physicians and auto repair shops; and there is restricted entry into the industries providing taxi service and radio broadcasting. There are age restrictions on the sale of certain goods and services, notably alcoholic beverages. There are import quotas on the quantities of textile products that developed nations may receive from developing nations, under the Multi-Fiber Arrangement. Product regulations of one kind or another affect virtually every industry.

In addition to the product and price regulations, information about products is regulated. The Securities and Exchange Commission requires that certain information be provided to prospective buyers of new stock and bond offerings; lending institutions are subject to truth-in-lending laws; the Environmental Protection Agency tests new-model automobiles for their fuel consumption rates each year and publishes the results; tobacco products must be labeled as dangerous to one's health.

What are the economic circumstances that might make these regulatory public policies desirable, and are such circumstances present in the industries now regulated? How does one know when to recommend price, product, or information controls, and what form they should take? The social objectives or benefits of these policies may be readily apparent, but their costs are often less obvious. For example, when electricity production must be undertaken with nonpolluting production techniques, the cost of electricity production, and therefore its price, typically rises. Thus a decision to regulate pollution by utility companies is paid for through higher electricity prices. One task of microeconomic policy analysis is to consider costs and to design pollution control policies that achieve pollution reduction goals at the least total cost.

Another important area of public policy that greatly affects resource allocation is the activity of developing the law. The legal system defines property rights and responsibilities that shape all exchanges among economic agents. If there were no law establishing one's ownership, one might have a hard time selling a good or preventing others from taking it. Without a patent system to establish the inventor's ownership rights, less effort would be devoted to inventing. Whether or not the existing patent system can be improved is a fair question for analysis. An example of a policy change involving property responsibilities is the spread of no-fault automobile accident liability. Under the old system, the driver at fault was liable for damages done to the injured party. The cost of insurance reflected both the damage and the transaction costs of legal battles to determine which driver was at fault. These transaction costs amounted to a significant proportion of the total insurance costs. The idea behind the no-fault concept is to reduce the transaction costs by eliminating in some cases the need to determine who was at fault. To the extent that this system works, consumers benefit from lower automobile insurance premiums. These examples should illustrate that analysis of the law is another public policy area in which microeconomic policy analysis can be applied.

There is another very important function of government activity that can be put through the filter of microeconomic analysis: Governments undertake redistributive programs to influence the distribution of goods and services among citizens. Of course, all resource allocation decisions affect the distribution of well-being among citizens, and the fairness of the distribution is always a concern of good policy analysis; here the interest is in the many programs undertaken with that equity objective as the central concern. In 2000, of the $3.1 trillion collected in taxes and fees by the federal, state, and local governments (31% of GDP), $1.1 trillion was redistributed as transfer payments to persons.[4] Another common method of redistribution, not included in the above direct payment figures, is through "tax expenditures" that reduce the amount of taxes owed by persons qualifying for the special provisions (e.g., people who are elderly or who have disabilities).

---

[4] Ibid., p. 372, Table B-83.

Government redistributive programs include welfare, food stamps, Medicaid, farm subsidies, and Social Security, just to name a few. The programs generally transfer resources to the poorest groups in society from those better off. However, some programs might be seen as forcing individuals to redistribute their own spending from one time period to another: Social Security takes away some of our income while we work and gives back income when we retire. Other public policies, such as farm subsidies, grants to students for higher education, and oil depletion allowances, may redistribute resources from poorer to richer groups. As the success of redistributive programs generally depends heavily on the resource allocation decisions made by the affected economic agents, microeconomic policy analysis provides tools for both the design and the evaluation of such programs.

By now it should be clear that all resource allocation decisions are influenced, at least to some degree, by public policy. Governments shape resource allocations through their direct purchase and supply of goods and services, their regulations of specific economic activities, their development and maintenance of the legal system, and their redistributive programs. All the activities mentioned above illustrate the set of public policy actions that can be analyzed by the methods presented in this book. In undertaking such studies, it is important to consider the roles of analysis in a policy-making process and how the process influences the objectives of the analysis. The next section contains a general discussion of these issues.

Policy-Making and the Roles of Microeconomic Policy Analysis

Public policy-making is a complex process. Policy is the outcome of a series of decisions and actions by people with varying motivations and differing information. Policy analysis, when not done for purely academic purposes, may be used to aid any of these people—be they elected officials or candidates for elected office, bureaucrats, members of various interest groups (including those attempting to represent the "public" interest), or the electorate. Not surprisingly, these different people may not agree on the merits of particular policies, even if perfectly informed about them, because of differing values. Policy analysis cannot resolve these basic conflicts; for better or for worse, the political process is itself the mechanism of resolution.

It is important to recognize that the political process heavily influences the type of policy analysis that is done and the extent to which it is used. For that reason, anyone interested in learning the skills of analysis for the purpose of advising should try to understand the process. Such understanding yields a better perspective of the possibilities for contributions through analytic work as well as the limitations. We offer below the barest introduction (bordering shamelessly on caricature) to some of the rich thinking that has been done on this subject, and we strongly encourage a full reading of the source material.

Lindblom, in 1965, put forth an optimistic model of a democratic political process.[5] He described a system like ours as one of partisan mutual adjustment among the various

[5] Charles E. Lindblom, *The Intelligence of Democracy* (New York: The Free Press, 1965).

interest groups (e.g., unions, bureaucracies, corporations, consumer groups, professional associations) in the society. In his view, the political pulling and hauling by diverse groups (from both within and outside government) in pursuit of self-interest leads to appropriate compromises and workable solutions.

No one in this pluralist process ever sets national goals or identifies the alternative means available to achieve them.[6] Rather, progress is made by sequential adaptation, or trial and error. Legislation proposed by one group, for example, has its design modified frequently as it wends its way through legislative subcommittees, committees, the full legislative bodies, and executive branch considerations. At each stage, the modifications reflect the compromises that arise in response to strengths and weaknesses identified by the affected interest groups and the changes they propose.

After enactment and during implementation, the diverse interest groups continue to influence the specific ways in which the new legislation is carried out. These groups will also monitor the resulting government operating procedures. The procedures may not lead to the intended results, or someone may think of a better set of procedures. If enough support can be mustered for program modification, the groups can force renewed legislative consideration.

Lindblom argued that muddling through is better than any alternative process designed to solve problems in a synoptic or comprehensive way. For example, an attempt to specify goals in a clear way may permit a sharper evaluation of the alternative means, but it will also increase the political difficulty of achieving a majority coalition. Interest groups are diverse precisely because they have real differences in goals, and they are unlikely to put those differences aside. Instead, they will agree only to statements of goals that are virtually meaningless in content (e.g., "This legislation is designed to promote the national security and the national welfare.") and do not really guide efforts at evaluation. The groups affected by proposed legislation are concerned about the end result. It is easier politically to build a coalition around a specific alternative and worry later about how to describe (in a sufficiently bland way) the purposes it fulfills.[7]

Optimistic views of the "intelligence" of actual pluralistic processes are not widely held. Many people argue that the actual processes differ significantly (and perhaps inevitably) from the view Lindblom offered in 1965. For example, one obvious concern is whether an actual process is weighted unduly toward the "haves" (e.g., who can afford to employ high-powered lobbyists and analysts) and away from the "have nots." In a later book, Lindblom himself writes that "business privilege" in the United States causes "a skewed pattern of mutual adjustment."[8] Authors from the "public choice" branch of microeconomics, which studies the efficiency of resource allocation through political processes, have often called

---

[6] We refer to "national goals" for illustrative simplicity; the same logic applies to state, local, or other polities that use representative or direct democratic forms of government.

[7] Wildavsky also put forth this general view. See Aaron Wildavsky, "The Political Economy of Efficiency: Cost-Benefit Analysis, Systems Analysis, and Program Budgeting," *Public Administrative Review, 26,* No. 4, December 1966, pp. 292–310. See also D. Braybrooke and C. Lindblom, *A Strategy of Decision: Policy Evaluation as a Social Process* (New York: The Free Press, 1963).

[8] Charles E. Lindblom, *Politics and Markets* (New York: Basic Books, 1977), p. 348.

into question the wisdom of certain voting procedures or of industry regulatory processes that may protect the industry more than any other interest.[9]

Another important source of "skewness," argues Schultze, is that efficiency and effectiveness considerations are not explicitly brought into the political arena.[10] Schultze accepts the value of having a pluralist process and the inevitability that it will be characterized by special interest advocacy and political bargaining "in the context of conflicting and vaguely known values."[11] But he argues that *there is a crucial role for policy analysis in this process.* It improves the process's "intelligence." Analysis can identify the links between general values (in particular, efficiency and effectiveness) and specific program characteristics—links that are by no means obvious to anyone. Thus he offers this view of policy analysis:

> It is not really important that the analysis be fully accepted by all the participants in the bargaining process. We can hardly expect . . . that a good analysis can be equated with a generally accepted one. But analysis can help focus debate upon matters about which there are real differences of value, where political judgments are necessary. It can suggest superior alternatives, eliminating, or at least minimizing, the number of inferior solutions. Thus by sharpening the debate, systematic analysis can enormously improve it.[12]

Viewing a political process as a whole helps us to understand the inevitability of *analytic suboptimization:* The problem worked on by any single analyst is inevitably only a partial view of the problem considered by the system as a whole, and thus a single analyst's proposed solution is not necessarily optimal from the larger perspective. For example, during the Carter administration the president directed two independent analytic teams from the departments of Labor and Health and Human Services to develop welfare reform proposals. Not surprisingly, the team from the Department of Labor proposed a reform emphasizing a work component of the welfare system, whereas the team from Health and Human Services emphasized the cash assistance components. This not only reflects bureaucratic interests; it is a natural consequence of the expertise of each team.[13] Similarly, analysts for congressional committees or for varying interest groups would be expected to perceive the welfare problem slightly differently.

The inevitability of suboptimization has important consequences. It becomes clear that the intelligence of the process as a whole depends not only on how well each analyst does

[9] We consider many of these theories in various chapters of this book, e.g., bureaucratic behavior in Chapter 9, reasons for governmental failure in Chapter 13, and difficulties regulating industries in Chapter 16.

[10] See Charles L. Schultze, *The Politics and Economics of Public Spending* (Washington, D.C.: The Brookings Institution, 1968), particularly Chapters 3 and 4.

[11] Ibid., p. 74.

[12] Ibid., p. 75.

[13] This particular debate foreshadowed the important developments in welfare policy during the 1980s and 1990s, most notably the Family Support Act of 1988 and the 1996 Personal Responsibility and Work Opportunity Reconciliation Act. We analyze various aspects of current welfare policies at a number of points later on in the text.

the task assigned but also on the total analytic effort and on how cleverly the analytic tasks are parceled out. A certain amount of analytic overlap provides checks and balances, for example. However, excessive duplication of efforts may leave an important part of the problem unattended. Another pitfall is relying too heavily on analysis when the "true" social objectives are difficult to operationalize. For example, the problem of identifying an efficient national defense is not really soluble by analytic techniques (although certain important insights can be generated). If, however, it is decided that we should have the capability to gather a certain number of troops near the Alaskan oil pipeline within a certain number of days, then analysts may be able to reject methods that are too costly and help identify lower-cost alternatives.[14]

The line of thought concerning analytic contributions in a pluralist political process can be carried further. Nelson suggests that analysts can and should play important roles in clarifying the nature of the problem, the values that are at stake, and an appropriate weighting of those values to identify a recommended solution.[15] The idea is that the political process, without analysis, operates largely in the "intellectual dark" about efficiency and equity consequences. Thus both Nelson and Schultze appreciate the value of muddling through but think we can do it somewhat better with substantial analytic input to the pluralistic process.

Nelson goes on to suggest that it is also important for substantial analysis to go on *outside* the constraints of the current political environment. The industry of government, like any other industry, continually needs research and development to improve its products. Analysis from within the thick of government tends to concentrate on identifying incremental improvements to existing activities. Achieving those improvements is important, but analytic efforts in an environment that offers more freedom to reexamine fundamental assumptions and methods may be a crucial source of important new ideas.

The above general thoughts about the political process help us to understand **the roles of public policy analysis.** We enumerate them here in terms of four specific objectives. We have mentioned that **(1) analysis may help define a problem that is only dimly perceived or vaguely understood by participants in the policy-making process.** We have also mentioned that **(2) a crucial role of analysis is in identifying or designing new policy proposals.** Policy analysis also has these two important additional functions: **(3) identification of the consequences of proposed policies,** and **(4) normative evaluation of those consequences in terms of certain broad social goals.** Let us distinguish these latter two analytic objectives.

The third objective, identification of consequences, is a *positive* or factual task. It involves answering questions such as these: "If the bridge toll is raised from $1.00 to $2.00, by how much will that reduce congestion?" (Presumably, fewer automobile trips will be taken across the bridge.) "If we combine the two local schools into one larger one, how will that affect education costs?" "If we guarantee all adults an income of $9000 per year, how

---

[14] An excellent exposition of suboptimization with application to national defense is contained in C. Hitch and R. McKean, *The Economics of Defense in the Nuclear Age* (New York: Athenum, 1967).

[15] See Richard R. Nelson, *The Moon and the Ghetto: An Essay on Public Policy Analysis* (New York: W. W. Norton & Company, 1977).

will that affect the amount of work adults are willing to undertake?" These questions can rarely be answered with absolute certainty, but analysis can frequently provide reasonable estimates. With improved estimates of the consequences of proposed policies, policy makers can make better decisions about whether to support them.

The fourth objective, evaluation, is a *normative* or judgmental task. It involves the "should" questions: "Should the bridge toll be raised from $1.00 to $2.00?" "Should the nation have a policy that guarantees all adults $9000 per year?" The answers to these questions always depend on values. *There is no single, well-defined set of values that analysts must use in attempting to evaluate policies; the choice of criteria is discretionary.*[16] Nevertheless, in practice certain criteria are generally common to all analyses: efficiency, equity or fairness, political feasibility, and administrative feasibility. Efficiency and equity are commonly used criteria because almost all people care about them; since the insights of microeconomic analysis apply directly to these concepts, this book will emphasize them. Political feasibility is a common evaluative criterion because specific users of analyses are rarely interested in pursuing proposed policies, however efficient and equitable, if the policies cannot gain the necessary approval in the political process. In my own personal view, this criterion differs from the others in that it makes no sense to pursue it for its own sake: it is a constraint rather than an objective. While it may be naïve to recommend a policy that fosters certain social objectives without considering political feasibility, it is irresponsible to recommend a policy that is politically feasible without considering its effects on social objectives.

Although different individuals will have concern for political feasibility in accordance with their personal judgments, it should be made clear that analytic attention to political feasibility is very rational. If one is considering a policy that would need approval of the United Nations Security Council, but it is known that Russia is adamantly opposed to the policy and would exercise its veto power, then the only purpose of raising the issue would be to garner its symbolic value. At times, symbolism may be important; it may lay the groundwork for future action. Alternatively, one might make better use of the time by seeking policies that are both socially beneficial and politically feasible.

The point to emphasize here is that good policy analysis will generally include a diagnosis of the political prospects for the policies analyzed. Other examples of political analysis might question the prospects for passage in key legislative committees, whether any powerful lobbyist will work to pass or oppose the proposed policy, and whether the policy's potential backers will gain votes for such a stand in the next election. Economist Joseph Stiglitz, in writing about some successes and failures of good economic proposals made while he was chair of President Clinton's Council of Economic Advisors, reports on several important political obstacles that seem to recur. For example, he mentions the difficulty of government making a credible commitment to milk producers for a more economic alternative than the existing milk price supports, in a failed attempt to obtain their

---

[16] That is why this task is described as normative. If analysts did not have to rely partially upon their own values to choose criteria and did not have any discretion about how to operationalize them, then we could describe the evaluative task as positive from the perspective of the analyst.

political support.[17] General analysis of political feasibility is beyond the scope of this book, although a number of occasions on which microeconomic analysis provides political insight will be discussed. However, the reader interested in the use of policy analysis for other than academic purposes should undertake more complete study in this area.[18]

Administrative feasibility is also an important criterion. Similar to political feasibility, it is really a constraint rather than a desirable social objective in its own right. But policies that pass analytic scrutiny for efficiency, fairness, and political feasibility will not work right unless the agencies responsible for administering them implement them in a manner consistent with the other objectives. There are several reasons why divergence might occur, and good analysts will consider its likelihood as part of their work.

One set of reasons why divergence may occur is due to the fact that there are limits on any organization's capabilities in terms of information, calculation, and enforcement. An example that may illustrate this is a proposal for a tax on air pollution, as a means to discourage an unhealthy activity. An analyst ought to reject this proposal if it is not possible (or in some circumstances merely very costly) for the administrative agency to meter or otherwise know reliably the amount of pollution emitted by the different sources liable for the tax. This may seem obvious, but considerations like these are often ignored by excellent scholars who offer proposals without ever encountering responsibility for their implementation. Policy analysts, on the other hand, do bear responsibility for evaluating the administrative feasibility of proposals.

Another reason for divergence is that the implementing organization's objectives may differ from the objectives of those who design and approve the policy. That is, even if the agency has the capabilities to implement the policy efficiently and fairly, it may choose not to do so for other reasons. Suppose a state department of transportation is staffed primarily by individuals who like to build more roads. This department may participate in a federal grant program intended primarily to stimulate other transportation alternatives, but may nevertheless use the funds primarily to build more roads. The policy analyst will consider the consistency between the implementing agency's goals and the policy's objectives in evaluating administrative feasibility.

As with political feasibility, there is a rich literature on organizational behavior that is useful for policy analysts to study but it falls outside the scope of this book.[19] There are also may instances in which microeconomic analysis does make a distinctive contribution to understanding administrative feasibility, and this book includes applications to illustrate this.

In addition to the general criteria mentioned so far, other criteria may be important for particular issues. Some policies might be intended to enhance individual freedom or develop

---

[17] See Joseph Stiglitz, "The Private Uses of Public Interests: Incentives and Institutions," *Journal of Economic Perspectives, 12,* No. 2, Spring 1998, pp. 3–22.

[18] See, for example, John W. Kingdon, *Agendas, Alternatives and Public Policies* (New York: HarperCollins College Publishers, 1995) and Aaron Wildavsky, *Speaking Truth to Power: The Art and Craft of Policy Analysis* (Boston: Little, Brown, and Company, 1979).

[19] An introduction to this material that also includes a discussion of political feasibility is in David L. Weimer and Aidan R. Vining, *Policy Analysis: Concepts and Practice* (Englewood Cliffs, N.J.: Prentice-Hall, 1999), Chapter 13.

community spirit. Policies must conform to existing law (though in the long run, the law should conform to good policy!). Good analyses of these policies will, at a minimum, make these considerations clear to the users of the analyses. Because these aspects are only rarely illuminated by microeconomic analysis, little will be said here other than to note that one should be on the alert for them and remain open-minded about their importance.

Organization of the Book

The task of this book is to show how to extend and relate microeconomic theory to the design and analysis of public policies. A theme that will be emphasized throughout is that a solid understanding of the actual behavior of economic agents is essential to the task. Part of the understanding comes from learning about the individual economic agents: their motivations and capabilities and the effects of public policies on their economic opportunities. Once behavior at the individual level is understood, it is easier to consider questions of organization: how to design and evaluate alternative systems that influence the interaction among economic agents. Thus the book focuses on individual behavior first and organizational behavior second. It consists of five interrelated parts.

Part I, the introductory section, contains this chapter as well as two chapters to acquaint the reader with economic models that are commonly used in analysis. The second chapter introduces the concept of model construction as an analytic procedure and illustrates some of the issues that arise in using models. The discussion centers around a simple model of economic demand and supply and its use in understanding benefit-cost reasoning. The third chapter introduces normative concepts of efficiency and equity and develops the model of individual decision-making known as *utility maximization* to predict behavior and to evaluate the efficiency and equity consequences of that behavior. These chapters give an overview of the subject matter and a foundation for the methods of microeconomic policy analysis.

Part II focuses on the resource allocation decisions of individuals. Different aspects of the theory of individual choice are developed to show their uses and importance in policy analysis. We begin with standard aspects of individual choice theory—budget constraints, income, and substitution effects—and relate those concepts to the design of specific policies such as the Earned Income Tax Credit and intergovernmental grants. This involves some extension of ordinary theory to include models with a variety of restrictions on individual choices. We then introduce equity standards in some detail and consider how models of individual choice can be used in the design of school finance policies to achieve equity objectives.

Then the relation between individual choices and consumer demand functions is explored. The methodology of *benefit-cost analysis* is introduced, focusing initially on the use of demand functions for public policy benefit estimation. We then extend the model of individual decision-making to a variety of situations in which the outcome from a decision is not known at the time the decision is made (such as deciding how to invest one's retirement savings or what insurance policies to purchase). Connections among uncertainty, individual choice, and public policy are investigated through these different extensions, which include *expected utility maximization, game theory,* and the implications of *bounded rationality.*

Policy examples such as national health insurance and disaster insurance subsidies are used to illustrate these points.

Finally, we investigate individual resource allocation over time. We analyze *saving, borrowing,* and *capital creation by investing* and discuss the concepts of discounting used to compare resource allocations in different time periods. We consider index construction (such as the Consumer Price Index) and policies of indexation intended to reduce intertemporal uncertainty. All of the topics covered in Part II relate to individual behavior in pursuit of personal satisfaction or utility.

Part III concerns the efforts of economic agents to convert scarce resources into goods and services: the production task in an economy. The effectiveness of many public policies depends on the response of private profit-seeking firms to them; an example is the response of doctors and for-profit hospitals to the prospective payment system used by Medicare. Other public policies succeed or fail depending on the behavior of public agencies or private nonprofit agencies; an example is the effect of the pricing decisions of a public mass transit system on the number of people who will use the system.

The performance of an economic agent undertaking production is limited by the available technology, and policy analysis often has the task of uncovering technological limits through estimation of production possibilities and their associated costs. Potential performance can then be compared with actual practice or predicted behavior under a particular policy design. One must be careful in extending the ordinary method of *production and cost analysis* to the public sector, because of poor output measures and the possible lack of the usual duality relation that assumes production at least cost. Several examples of analyses involving these problems will be given.

Not only must the technological realities be understood, but predicting an agency's or a firm's response to a public policy requires an understanding of its motivations and capabilities. Different models used for these purposes are explained in Part III. For the most part, economic theory treats each production entity as an individual decision-making unit; for example, a firm may maximize its profits. However, this treatment ignores the fact that firms and agencies are generally organizations consisting of many diverse individuals. A discussion of the firm as an organizational means to coordinate individual decision-making helps to connect the analyses presented in Parts II and III with the organizational policy issues that are the focus of Parts IV and V.

Part IV focuses on the interaction of supply by competing suppliers and demand by many purchasers, in market situations referred to as perfectly competitive. We construct *models of the operation of* such *markets* in different situations, including markets for the consumer purchase of goods and services as well as markets for producer purchase of inputs or factors of productions. In the absence of specific policy interventions, the models predict that resource allocation will be efficient. But there are other reasons, usually ones of equity, that motivate policy interventions in some of them. The issues are the degree of public control of these markets that is desirable and the policy instruments that can be used to achieve varying degrees of control.

We begin Part IV with a review of the conditions for market efficiency, and then apply the conditions in a *general equilibrium framework* of perfect competition. We use that framework to illustrate how the effects of taxation can be predicted and evaluated. We demonstrate that taxation generally causes "market failure" or inefficiency. Then we look at a number of more specific markets. By using extended examples of price supports for agriculture, apartment rent control, methods of securing military labor, and gasoline rationing, we examine a variety of policy approaches to make the markets for specific goods more equitable and efficient. In these examples, the details of the administration and enforcement of policies bear importantly on the success of the policies—a lesson with continued importance in Part V.

Whereas Part IV is restricted to competitive market settings, Part V considers the circumstances that are normally called *market failures:* situations in which the attempted use of a competitive market process to allocate scarce resources results in inefficient allocations. We begin with a general review of the different reasons for market failures juxtaposed with a general review of reasons for governmental failures. In the attempt to reduce the extent of any market failure, a central idea is that all alternative methods of economic organization will have weaknesses that must be considered along with their strengths.

Successive chapters in this section focus on each of the different types of market failures. We consider the problem of providing a *public good:* a type of good that is shared by a collectivity of consumers, and we use television broadcasting and the role of public television as an example. We next consider the problem of *externalities,* or side effects of resource allocation. In an extended example, we analyze alternative ways that we might respond to the problem of air pollution (a side effect of much industrial production, car-driving, and other activities). Then we turn to problems of *limited competition* known as oligopoly and monopoly markets. We analyze in some detail alternative regulatory methods for limiting inefficiency in these markets, such as those used for telecommunications services and electric power.

The next market failures that we consider arise in allocating resources over time. These include the failure of capital markets to provide loans to those who wish to invest in their own higher education and secure a more productive future. They also include the failure of markets to account for the demands of future generations to reserve some of our exhaustible resources. Finally, we consider market failures that are due to important *information asymmetries* about the quality of a good or service. Examples include labor market discrimination that arises owing to the difficulty an employer has knowing the qualities of job applicants and the provision of child care for working parents who cannot directly observe the quality of care their children receive.

Each of the market failures is associated with a situation in which the private incentives of one or more market participants deviate from the ones necessary to generate efficient allocations. Well-established microeconomic theory is used to identify and explain these incentive problems. However, the methods available for designing, comparing, and evaluating the imperfect alternatives in all of these situations of market failure are still developing. Thus Part V includes in its extended examples a variety of different methods that have been used to compare different organizational ways of trying to solve or mitigate the failures.

These approaches include the use of "laboratory" methods for testing alternatives, a method for considering a choice of rules and enforcement procedures that focuses on identifying an appropriate level of decentralization, and a method known as *transaction cost economics* that helps identify appropriate contracting provisions. They also include simulation models, consideration of economic history, and use of an "exit, voice, loyalty" framework to identify economical ways to convey demand for goods and services with important multidimensional quality attributes. These methods can produce new ideas for organizational solutions to problems of market failure, as well as insight about the strengths and weaknesses of alternative solutions.

Conclusion

In this chapter we have had an overview of the relation between public policy analysis and the study of microeconomics. Public policy can often be analyzed and understood as a collective involvement in the resource allocation process. The intervention takes place to some degree in virtually all areas of the economy. Microeconomic policy analysis attempts to predict and evaluate the consequences of collective actions, and it can be used in the design of those actions as well as to identify areas in which public policy can be improved. Although there is no single well-defined set of evaluative criteria that must be used in policy analysis, this book will emphasize two criteria that are commonly used: efficiency and equity. By using and extending ordinary principles of microeconomic analysis, we will attempt to impart skills sufficient for the analysis of a wide range of public policies by those criteria.

CHAPTER TWO

AN INTRODUCTION TO MODELING: DEMAND, SUPPLY, AND BENEFIT-COST REASONING

TWO OF THE PRIMARY tasks of microeconomic policy analysis are prediction and evaluation. This chapter and the next illustrate, at a rudimentary level, how *models* constructed from microeconomic theory are used to help accomplish these tasks.

In actual practice, considerable skill is required to predict and evaluate the consequences of specific policy alternatives. Later chapters build upon microeconomic theory to develop more sophisticated modeling skills and illustrate their use in specific policy contexts. However, even when the predictions and evaluations are derived from the best practicable analytic methods, the possibility remains that the judgments are wrong. We try to clarify why analytic efforts are important despite the persistence of uncertainty about the conclusions.

The chapter begins with a general discussion of modeling. Then we turn to a somewhat unusual model: a story. One purpose of the story is to introduce basic economic concepts of *demand* and *supply,* in a way that also introduces the *benefit-cost reasoning* that is common in policy analysis. Each of these concepts will be developed more slowly, in more detail, and with more application in successive chapters. But it helps at the start to have a sense of where we are headed: the kinds of tools that we will develop and some introduction to their use. This story serves other purposes as well. It makes one think about modeling: the ease with which one can slip into making predictions and evaluations based upon a model and some of the informal ways that people use to judge a model. It will raise questions about the concept of value in economics. It will foreshadow some of the policy stakes that may depend upon the models that analysts use. The body of this book, in due course, will provide amplification, qualification, and clarification of these issues.

Modeling: A Basic Tool of Microeconomic Policy Analysis

A powerful technique used to predict the consequences of policies is *modeling*. A model is an abstraction intended to convey the essence of some particular aspect of the real world.

A child can get a pretty good idea of an airplane by looking at a plastic model of one. A science student can predict how gravity will affect a wide variety of objects, falling from any number of different heights, simply by using the mathematical equations that model gravity's effects. In the latter case the model equations represent assumptions based on a theory of gravity, and their implications can be tested against reality.

But can microeconomic theory be used to model resource allocation decisions accurately enough to help determine the consequences of proposed policies? The answer is a qualified yes. Economists have developed models with assumptions that seem plausible in a wide range of circumstances and whose predictions are frequently borne out by actual consumer behavior. As one of the social sciences, economics attempts to predict human behavior, and its accuracy, not surprisingly, is not as great as some models representing "laws" of the physical sciences. People do not all behave the same, and thus there is no ultimate model that we expect to predict each individual's economic decisions perfectly. Nevertheless, there appear to be strong commonalities in much economic decision-making. It is these commonalities that we strive to identify and understand through models and that we use to predict future economic decisions (such as those expected in response to a new policy).

Of course, predictions can be more or less ambitious. A qualitative prediction that "consumers will use less home heating oil as its price increases" is less ambitious than "consumers will reduce home heating oil consumption by 5 percent in the year following a price increase of 20 percent." The latter is less ambitious than one that adds to it: "And this will cause an efficiency decrease valued at $2 billion." Since the more precise predictions generally come from models that are more difficult to construct and require more detailed information to operate, the analyst must think about the precision required to resolve a particular policy question.

Although there is analytic choice about the degree of precision to seek in modeling, it is important to recognize from the start that all models only approximate reality. In general, the usefulness of a model to its users depends on the extent to which it increases knowledge or understanding (and not on how much it leaves unexplained). The plastic display model of an airplane is not considered a failure because it does not fly. Or consider the scientific models that represent the laws of aerodynamics. Earlier in this century, the models of those laws were used for airplane design, even though the same models predicted that bumblebees must be unable to fly! Without any loss of respect for science over this apparent model failure, airplanes (as well as bumblebees) flew successfully.

The perception that there is "something wrong" with a model does not necessarily deter us from using the model, as the above example illustrates. Analytically, we do not replace a partial success with nothing. Before replacing the earlier models of aerodynamic laws as applied to bumblebees, we required "something better."[1] The same is true of economic

---

[1] According to one expert: "It used to be thought that insect flight could be understood on the basis of fixed-wing aerodynamics, when in fact the wings of many insects, including bumblebees, operate more on the principle of helicopter aerodynamics." See Bernd Heinrich, *Bumblebee Economics* (Cambridge, Mass.: Harvard University Press, 1979), p. 39. Even this more refined model is imperfect: "when the wings flap, fluctuating or *unsteady* flow pattern must occur . . . but we are only beginning to understand the nature of the problem and how

models: "Good" models predict well enough to increase our understanding of certain situations, even though they may not predict them perfectly and there may be related situations in which the same models do not predict as well as expected.

If we predict, as in the last example, that average home heating oil purchases will drop by 5 percent, for some purposes it might be "unimportant" that some people reduce by only 2 percent while others reduce by 8 percent (as long as the average reduction is 5 percent). We expect to see a distribution of actual decisions around the predicted average. The model is more powerful, however, when the actual decisions cluster tightly around the model predictions (the model comes "closer" to predicting each person's decision correctly). To some extent, the power of a model depends on the analytic effort that goes into its construction (which in turn should depend on how valuable it is to have a more powerful model). However, human nature may be such that for some decisions, no model will make "powerful" predictions.

What is often more puzzling is when the central tendency or average predicted by a model is *systematically* different from actual behavior. If the model predicts that almost all home owners will invest in attic insulation (because its modest cost is quickly offset by lower fuel bills that save far more), but few actually do invest, that suggests that a different model might be more accurate. These kinds of unexplained imperfections in the predictions remain as "puzzles" that stimulate new research that leads (with luck) to better models. As in science, the process of improvement is continual.

Although all models are imperfect, not all are imperfect in the same way. Models vary in the variety of phenomena they can explain, as well as in their accuracy in explaining any particular phenomenon. In the economic example of the consumer response to a price increase for home heating oil, we suggested that alternative models can be constructed, models that attempt both increasingly precise estimates of the magnitude of the response (e.g., the specific percentage reduction in home heating oil usage) as well as broader implications of the response (e.g., the value of an efficiency increase or decrease associated with it). Even the simplest prediction illustrated—that consumers will purchase less home heating oil if its price rises—might be all that is necessary to resolve a particular issue.

For example, suppose the consumer price of heating oil has been increased by a tax in order to induce greater conservation of the supply. Imagine the problem now is to alleviate the increased financial burden of the tax on low-income families. It is not unusual to hear some policy proposals to reduce the price for these families only (e.g., exempt them from the tax). But this works in opposition to the primary objective.

Chapter 4 shows that such proposals are likely to be inferior to alternatives designed to provide the same amount of aid without reducing the price of heating oil.[2] This conclusion is derived from the model making the least ambitious predictions; it depends primarily on

---

animals make use of such unsteady flow." See Torkel Weis-Fogh, "Energetics and Aerodynamics of Flapping Flight: A Synthesis," in R. Rainey, ed., *Insect Flight* (Oxford: Blackwell Scientific Publications, 1976), pp. 48–72.

[2] Inferior in this case means that less conservation will be achieved for a given amount of tax relief. The conclusion is qualified for several important reasons explained in Chapter 4. For example, it is based on a model that does not consider the informational problems of identifying the tax burden on each family.

the qualitative prediction that consumers purchase less home heating oil at higher prices and more at lower prices. This model also is constructed without using any numerical data; it is based entirely on microeconomic theory.

On the other hand, suppose the policy problem is how to achieve a primary objective of reducing home heating oil consumption by 5 percent within a definite time period. We know from the simplest model that one way to do so is to raise the price, but by how much?[3] This question is easy to ask but difficult to answer. To resolve it, a model that makes specific numerical predictions is required.

Building this type of model requires empirical skills beyond the scope of this text; they are best acquired in courses on quantitative methods such as statistics and econometrics.[4] However, careful use of the empirical skills requires knowledge of the microtheoretic modeling skills that we do cover. Furthermore, models constructed from theory can often be applied directly to available empirical evidence (from past studies), as examples later on in the text will illustrate.

Each of the above two examples assumes that a policy objective is to reduce the consumption of heating oil. But suppose one wanted to consider whether that should be an objective at all. That is, suppose we asked a more basic question: Does the nation have an appropriate amount of heating oil relative to all other goods, or by how much should the price be changed (possibly increased or decreased) to remedy the situation?[5] Even if the only criterion is to choose a quantity that is efficient, the model is required to explain *two* phenomena: the price to charge that would lead to each possible quantity of heating oil and whether that quantity is efficient or not. Accurate predictions of the price-quantity combinations would be of little help if that information could not be linked to the efficiency consequences. It would be like needing the plastic model of the airplane to be of the proper scale and to fly as well.

One of the themes we shall emphasize throughout is the importance of **model specification: the choice of a particular set of abstractions from reality used to construct the model.** These building blocks are the model *assumptions*. For the plastic model of an airplane, the assumptions consist of the physical components included in the unassembled kit and the assembly instructions, as well as the way the model builder interprets or modifies them. In microeconomic policy analysis this set typically includes some representation of the policy objectives, the alternative policies under consideration, the motivations or objectives of the economic agents (people and organizations) affected by the policies, and the constraints on the agents' resource allocation decisions.

An important factor in model specification is the use of what has been learned previously about the phenomenon being modeled. This explains why many (but rarely all) of the spe-

---

[3] There are other policy alternatives for achieving this objective than simply raising the price. A fuller discussion of rationing methods is contained in Chapter 14, including an application to fuel rationing.

[4] See, for example, Robert Pindyck and Daniel Rubinfeld, *Econometric Models and Economic Forecasts* (Boston: Irwin/McGraw-Hill Book Company, 1998).

[5] To keep this example simple, we continue to assume that the only policy *instrument* is to determine the price. A policy instrument is a particular method that government can use to influence behavior, in this case the quantity of heating oil made available to consumers.

cific assumptions used in policy analysis are a part of conventional or neoclassical microeconomic theory. Models based on that theory have been very successful in predicting the direction of allocative changes made by economic agents in response to a wide variety of economic stimuli. Furthermore, they do not require inordinate amounts of information to predict the changes; the models are parsimonious. Therefore, a reasonable strategy for microeconomic policy analysis is to rely generally on conventional theory as a starting point and adapt it to account for the circumstances specific to each problem.

On the other hand, conventional theory is not so powerful that all of its implications deserve to be accepted uncritically. Indeed, the myriad roles of public policy in an economy such as those described in the previous chapter could not be scrutinized reasonably by fully conventional models. To get a sense of the limits of any theory, let us look at an example suggested by Milton Friedman.[6] He notes that an expert billiard player shoots *as if* he or she has an expert knowledge of physics. Therefore, by using calculations based on the laws of physics as the model, one can predict accurately the shots of the expert. This illustrates Friedman's proposition that a theory should be judged by the empirical validity of its predictions, not of its assumptions.

As long as the only purpose of this theory is to predict how an expert at billiards will direct the ball (or how a novice will fail to direct it), it does not matter that the assumptions are clearly inaccurate. However, theories are generally used to predict or explain a variety of phenomena. For example, suppose one proposed, based on the above theory, to evaluate applicants for jobs as physicists by their billiard scores (i.e., high billiard scores can be achieved only by individuals with an expert knowledge of physics). This method of predicting job success is not likely to do very well.[7] In other words, the substantial inaccuracy of the assumptions severely limits the variety of phenomena that can be successfully explained or predicted by the theory.

Few analysts think that the assumptions used in conventional microeconomic theory, which attribute a high degree of rationality to each economic agent, are highly accurate themselves. Sometimes an "as if" logic is used to justify the assumptions. For example, firms do not really know how to maximize profits (their assumed objective), but those that survive in competitive markets must behave *as if* they maximize profits.[8] Since the directional predictions made with the theory have been borne out over a wide range of phenomena, the assumptions seem quite acceptable for this purpose (at least until a better set of assumptions is developed). However, other uses of the theory may require more "faith" in the assumptions themselves.

For example, let us refer to the evaluative concept of efficiency. In order to have an efficient allocation, consumers must make the most rational choices available to them. (We

---

[6] See M. Friedman, "The Methodology of Positive Economics," in *Essays in Positive Economics* (Chicago: University of Chicago Press, 1953), pp. 3–46.

[7] The problem we are referring to is that those hired are not likely to perform well on the job. There is another problem: Some perfectly good physicists will be found unqualified for the job. However, the latter problem is not caused by the model assumptions. The model assumes that all experts at billiards are expert physicists and not that all expert physicists are experts at billiards.

[8] Firm behavior is discussed in Chapter 10.

review this shortly.) Conventional theory assumes that people make choices in this manner. But to interpret an allocation resulting from consumer choices as efficient, one must "believe" that the assumption is accurate.

However, consider the following analogy: Assume all billiard players are experts at the game, and accept the assumption because using it accurately predicts the direction in which players shoot. Then one is forced to interpret the poor shots of novices as misses on purpose. It may be that, for many types of choices, consumers rarely "miss." But surely there are some decisions that are harder to make than others (e.g., the purchase of complex insurance contracts, legal services, or used cars), and one should recognize that inefficiency can occur as a consequence of poor choice. Should we really assume, for example, that a consumer who maintains a savings account paying 5 percent interest while simultaneously carrying credit card debt at 18 percent is choosing wisely?

It is not enough to develop a sense of the strengths and weaknesses of any particular assumption. A fundamental analytic skill is to be able to identify plausible alternative specifications relevant to a particular policy analysis. The point is to understand how heavily a *policy* conclusion depends on specific assumptions. For example, the same conclusion may be reached over a wide range of reasonable specifications, in which case confidence in the policy conclusion is enhanced.

To build skill in model specification, each of the later chapters contains examples of alternative specifications relevant to the particular policy context. In addition to the specific lessons from each example, there are two general specification lessons to be learned from studying the range of examples. First, *policy conclusions are often quite sensitive to variations in the way the policy itself is modeled.* Therefore, the analyst must take care to understand the details of any specific proposal before deciding how to model it (or attempting to evaluate another's model of it). Second, *the reexamination of assumptions that are standard and appropriate in many contexts often becomes the central focus in a particular policy context.* Indeed it is their inappropriateness in particular contexts that, in the aggregate, helps us to understand the large and varied roles of public policy in an economy such as those described in the previous chapter.

Let us mention one final general modeling issue: the form that the model takes. Examples were given earlier of different forms that models might take: for example, the plastic model of an airplane and the mathematical model of gravity's effects. We will sometimes construct economic models from verbal descriptions, sometimes by geometric representation, and sometimes by mathematical equations. Models may appear in the form of short stories or other abstractions. What should determine the form that the model builder chooses? In the different forms of economic models mentioned, the essence of the underlying behavior can be the same. What purpose is served by presenting it in different ways?

We wish to note this distinction: Modeling is a way for the model builder to learn, but it is also a way to communicate with (or to teach) others. The main point of doing policy analysis is to learn: The analyst does not know the conclusion at the start and seeks to come to one by a logical procedure that can be subjected to evaluation by professional standards. Yet the form of a model used for learning is not necessarily appropriate as a form for communication. The latter depends upon the audience. If policy analysis is to influence policy, it is particularly important that it be communicated effectively.

As a general rule, policy analysis is done in a more technical format than that used to communicate it to decision makers. Analysts communicate their work to each other quite fully and efficiently through the presentation of technical models (such as those in professional journals). However, most public officials, administrators, and politicians with interest in a specific analysis prefer it to be presented in a concise, clear, jargon-free form.[9]

Most of the material presented in this book goes somewhat in the reverse direction; we expand and build upon technical concepts in order to see how microeconomic theory is used in policy analysis. By way of gentle introduction, the first model that we present is a story. The story is about beginning students of public policy in their first class. It will introduce some very basic economic concepts—the demand for and the supply of an economic good—and will emphasize the close relation between these concepts and the benefit-cost reasoning that is common in policy analysis. It will make you think substantively about the concept of value in economics. It will make you think about models: how to use them and judge them.

Demand, Supply, and Benefit-Cost Reasoning

Monday Morning, 6:45 A.M.

Barbara Blackstone was sleeping peacefully when the irritating sounds of normally sweet Mozart traveled quickly from her bedside radio to her ears and suddenly to her brain. Her eyes opened. Her hand snaked out from under the covers, desperately stabbing at the radio to turn it off before it truly woke her up. Too late. Her eyes rested, and the radio was silent, but she had lost, as she always did, in the struggle to preserve sleep against the onslaught of a new day. Her eyes opened again. This really was a new day. It was to be her first day of classes at the Graduate School of Public Policy.

For the past 2 years, since graduating from the University of Illinois and receiving her teaching certification, she had worked with enthusiasm and dedication in one of Chicago's tougher high schools (where the students fondly referred to her as Ranger Blackstone, a jokey reference to Chicago's infamous gang). She knew that, for at least some of her students, she

---

[9] The form of the analysis may be tailored for a specific user. An extreme example is offered by Richard Neustadt, who was asked by President Kennedy to analyze the decision-making process leading to a controversial decision in 1962 to cancel the Skybolt missile. The decision had unexpected and embarrassing foreign relations consequences, and the President hoped Neustadt could draw some lessons to improve future policy-making.

Neustadt felt that to understand the lessons from his analysis, Kennedy would have to read a lengthy document (which would have violated Washington's KISS rule: Keep it short and simple). But presidential schedules generally do not allow time for reading lengthy documents. This president was known to be a fan of Ian Fleming novels, and Neustadt therefore put his lengthy analysis in a format designed to appeal to such a fan. He sent the report to the President on November 15, 1963, and Kennedy finished it on November 17, 1963, suggesting that Neustadt's strategy was successful. This historical episode is discussed in Richard E. Neustadt, *Report to JFK: The Skybolt Crisis in Perspective* (Ithaca, N.Y.: Cornell University Press, 1999).

was making a difference. But she also knew that, for her, it was not enough. The whole system, with its layers of federal, state, and local rules, regulations, funding and curriculum restrictions, the power struggles between the administrative bureaucracy and union leadership, was an unbelievable, impenetrable morass that functioned every day to deaden and weed out any thoughts of teacher or student initiatives. Surely there must be a better way. How could our political leaders, our policy makers, our school officials do this to us?

Barbara was determined to improve the system. But she knew that she needed more equipment for this assault. She needed a better understanding of the economics of school finance, the politics of making change happen, the dynamics of organizations, and the numbers that were so often thrown in her face as an excuse for turning aside the suggestions she offered. Then one night many months ago, dining at a local trattoria (she recalled the calzone and excellent draft beer), her friend Susan described excitedly her environmentalist brother's new job.

Nate had done graduate work in public policy and was hired by the Environmental Protection Agency in Washington, D.C., to work on implementing something called a tradable permit system for SO_2 emissions, required by the 1991 Clean Air Act Amendments. Neither Susan nor Barbara really understood how trading pollution rights could be good for the environment, but they knew that Nate was enthusiastic about it. Nate said that without an economically efficient design, there was no way that pro-environmental forces could have overcome the powerful industry lobbyists to pass legislation mandating an annual emission reduction of 10 million tons. Economics, politics, public policy—suddenly, Barbara realized that Nate's skills seemed to be exactly what she was looking for. Almost a year later, following a lengthy application process and the agony of waiting to hear, she had been accepted and was ready to start the program. Actually, she would not be at all ready to start if she continued to lie there thinking. She got out of bed.

Monday Morning, 9:00 A.M.

Professor Weiss was standing in front of the class. He seemed to have friendly eyes. Well, probably friendly. Gentle, that was it. He was standing there patiently, waiting for the new students to amble in and settle down. After the expected role-calling, name mispronunciations and corrections, and barrage of handouts, he thought for a moment and began:

"In the next hour, I shall show you about 50 percent of what we'll be studying during the entire year. Of course, this will be a bit like showing someone a half-built model of a car. I don't really want to try and convince you that this particular car will be great. But I hope to get you interested in car-building."

What is he talking about, Barbara wondered. Am I in an auto mechanics class by mistake? But he turned to the whiteboard and wrote some of the economic buzzwords that had appeared in the school's literature—*market demand, market supply, efficiency and the benefit-cost principle*—and then went on.

"In the early days of President Clinton's administration, a decision was reached to rescind an executive order of former President Bush and reinstate a particular methodology known as 'contingent valuation', used for valuing environmental damage. The need for some methodology arises because in many cases, both inside and outside of government, the question comes up: how much are specific environmental resources worth? One study based on the contingent valuation methodology estimated that the oil spilled from the *Valdez* on the Alaskan coast created $3 billion in damages. This study was used by the government in its law suit against Exxon, a law suit that was later settled out of court with Exxon's agreement to pay $1 billion. Upon what basis could figures of these magnitudes—or any other—be derived?"

Professor Weiss did not seem to expect an answer, for he continued with barely a pause.

"I will not show you the specifics of contingent valuation methodology today. But I will talk about economic valuation in a more general way. I intend to plant the seeds of the connection between the money people are willing to pay for something and the broader efficiency principle for resource allocation that underlies much economic evaluation. I also wish to suggest that important observable information about a people's willingness to pay can often be found in the demand and supply curves that characterize economic activity in a market setting. That is, the same type of debate about value that was argued and resolved for the *Valdez* oil spill damages occurs as a matter of course, but through a quite different and impersonal process, for many other resources that are traded in markets. Good policy analysts learn how to take advantage of this information about value."

Professor Weiss then wrote on one side of the large whiteboard:

Lessons

1. Individual valuations connect to efficiency
2. Observable demand and supply curves reveal valuations

Reggie Thompson, a classmate on Barbara's left who had introduced himself just before class began, passed her a puzzled look. He was definitely interested in the oil spill example. But the professor seemed to be moving away from it. Where was he going? When would he get back to it?

"In analytic work, we use the concepts of demand and supply curves to characterize a market for the buying and selling of a good or service. These curves contain information relevant to evaluating efficiency. I'm going to draw some in a moment, define a market equilibrium, and evaluate its efficiency level. I'll also introduce the principle of *benefit-cost analysis,* and show how it can be used to measure changes in efficiency. These basic steps will be repeated a hundred different times throughout this course. Of course the activities we study will quickly become those that raise important public policy questions. In this first case we study an ordinary private good, but we shall also study public services such as schooling . . ." Barbara's eyes widened. Schooling? She was fully alert. ". . . and regulated activities such as electricity and environmental protection. Furthermore, the analytic methodology continually expands to take account of new wrinkles that are absent from this first case. Indeed, a totally firm grasp of economic concepts is just the beginning of what I hope you will learn. You must go well beyond this, to become proficient in the art and science of microeconomic modeling for policy analysis."

Professor Weiss turned to the whiteboard and began to draw (see Figure 2-1).

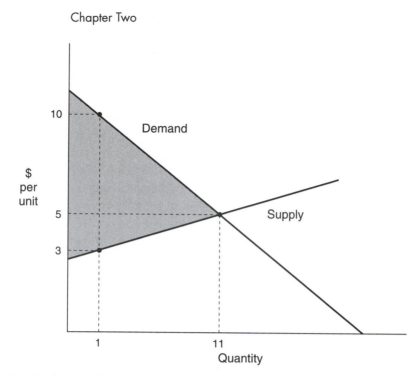

Figure 2-1. Market equilibrium and efficiency.

"Let us begin with the concept of demand. *The demand curve shows the quantity of a particular good,* measured on the horizontal axis, *that consumers will wish to buy at each possible price per unit,* shown on the vertical axis. It is drawn to be downward sloping: at lower prices, consumers will want more of it."

Here we go, thought Barbara. Would I fly back to Chicago more if airfares were lower? I suppose I would, my schedule permitting. Even if I don't, I guess other people would. Okay, so far this makes sense.

"Suppose that at any particular price each consumer buys or demands the quantity that best fits his or her circumstances. Then the demand curve reveals something important about how consumers value this good in dollar terms. To illustrate this, imagine that the demand curve only shows the demands of one consumer, Janet. It shows that at a price of $10 per unit, Janet only buys one unit of the good.

"This implies that the dollar value of a second unit to Janet, or her maximum willingness to pay for it, must be *less* than $10. If it were *more* than $10, say $12, then Janet would not be choosing the quantity that she feels best fits her circumstances. That is, if Janet were willing if necessary to forego $12—which could be used to purchase *other* goods—in order to get a second unit of *this* good, then she surely would forego only $10 to get the second unit. Since she does not do this, she must only value the second unit at something less than $10."

Barbara's hand shot up.

"Yes?" said Professor Weiss.

"Isn't it possible that Janet values the second unit at $12 or even more but simply doesn't have the money, perhaps because she is poor?"

"Excellent question!" replied Professor Weiss. "What is your name again?"

"Barbara Blackstone."

"Got it. The answer is no, because of the special way that economic value is defined. By willingness to pay, we mean from whatever resources Janet happens to have . . . how much she really is willing to give up of other things, given her actual budget or wealth level, in order to get a second unit. A person who is a clone of Janet except for being much richer would likely have a higher willingness to pay for the second unit. For all units, for that matter. But this demand curve, Janet's demand curve, tells us that Janet feels that there are more important things to spend $10 on then a second unit of this good."

Professor Weiss paused and looked around the classroom. "What does this imply?" he continued. "It implies that there may be nothing *fair* about the demands we observe. Janet *is* making the wisest choices possible, *given* the total dollars she actually has, but we do not have to like or approve of her wealth level. That is something we shall concern ourselves with throughout the course. But our concern will be expressed when we explicitly consider equity or fairness issues and not when we are evaluating efficiency."

What does he mean by "evaluating efficiency," Barbara wondered? But Professor Weiss was racing on.

"The demand curve also shows that Janet would buy eleven units at a price of $5. This implies, by the same logic as above, that the value of the eleventh unit must be *at least* $5 while the value to her of the twelfth unit must be *less* than $5. Extending this logic, we see that the value to Janet of each possible unit (the first, the second, . . .) is shown by the height of the demand curve above that unit. In economic terms, we say that *the height of the demand curve shows the marginal value or marginal benefit of each unit. An individual's demand curve is equivalent to a marginal benefit schedule for that individual.* The market demand curve may be interpreted similarly. That is, the market demand curve shows the quantity bought by all consumers at each possible price, and its height also reveals the marginal benefit associated with each unit, although not which particular consumer receives it.

"All we are doing so far is looking at the same line on the graph in two different ways. The "demand" interpretation is that the graph shows the quantity that would be bought, measured on the horizontal axis, at each possible price; the "marginal benefit" interpretation is that the graph shows the marginal benefit, measured on the vertical axis, of each possible unit of the good. Note that *the downward slope of the demand curve implies diminishing marginal value:* the first unit bought has the most value, and each successive unit has a value lower than the one preceding."

It all seems so reasonable, thought Barbara. Is he getting set to spring a trap?

"Next we introduce *the supply curve: the quantity of a particular good that producers will supply at each possible price.* We can show this on the same diagram," and he proceeded to add another line to his drawing. "Supply curves are often drawn as upward sloping: at higher prices, suppliers will increase their production levels and more quantity will be supplied to the market. This would be the case for the production of corn, for example. At low prices, only the most fertile land requiring the least tending would be used to produce corn.

Less fertile land would be unprofitable to farm: the cost of tending—irrigation, fertilizer, plowing, that kind of stuff—would be greater than the revenue from selling the crop produced. As the price of corn rises, farmers find it worthwhile—that is, profitable—to bring in the next most fertile land requiring slightly more tending, thus increasing the overall supply of corn."

Professor Weiss looked over the class. "I realize that this is a lot for those of you new to economics, and probably only somewhat familiar to those of you have majored in it. But we are getting there," and he continued.

"*The height of the supply curve shows the marginal cost of supplying each unit.* That is, the height above each unit—the first, the second, . . .—shows the cost to the producer of the resources used to make that unit. Assuming that producers act in their own best interests, we can think of this cost as the value of the resources in their best alternative use. Economists call this value the *marginal opportunity cost,* or simply marginal cost. Producers will supply a unit to this market whenever the extra revenue it brings there exceeds its marginal cost, defined as the maximum payment the resources could command if used in some *other* market."

I think I get the idea, thought Barbara. If I owned land—not with the balance in *my* savings account, that's for sure—and corn prices were low, I'd rather lease the land for grazing than grow corn. But if corn prices were high enough, I'd do better using the land for corn.

She began to wonder how this might be relevant to schools. But Professor Weiss was starting to draw again.

"Suppose at a price of $3 producers supply only one unit of the good. This implies that the marginal cost of the second unit must be *greater* than $3. At a price of $5, suppose eleven units are supplied. This means that units two to eleven have marginal costs *between* $3 and $5. Note that *an upward sloping supply curve corresponds to increasing marginal costs for successive units.*

"At this point, we introduce the concept of *market equilibrium: when the quantity demanded by consumers is just equal to the quantity supplied by producers.* This occurs at the intersection of the demand and supply curves—where the price is $5 and the quantity is eleven units. Suppose the market price is something other than $5, say $10. At this price consumers only demand one unit, but producers bring a large number of units to market.[10] The suppliers do not realize the profits they expect because consumers do not buy the goods. Since producers consider it better to get more revenue rather than less for the units they have produced, they will agree to sell the units for less than $10. As price falls, over time demand goes up while supply gets reduced. Price in the market will continue to change until the quantity *brought* is the quantity *bought.* Supply and demand are only equal where the two curves intersect: at a price of $5 with a quantity of eleven.

"Finally, let us relate this market equilibrium to the concept of efficiency. *Informally, think of efficiency as using resources to maximize the value to the economy's members of*

---

[10] Figure 2-1 does not extend the supply curve far enough to show the quantity supplied at the $10 level. Using the formula for the supply curve in the next footnote, we find this quantity to be thirty-six.

the goods and services produced. In this simple example, the market equilibrium is also an efficient allocation. The goods that are produced and sold are all those, and only those, for which the marginal benefit to consumers—the height of the demand curve—exceeds the marginal cost—the height of the supply curve. This maximizes value and is therefore efficient. Can anyone explain why?"

Professor Weiss looked around the class hopefully. So did most of the students. Just when the professor seemed about ready to give up, Reggie Thompson's hand managed to struggle a few inches above his head—it started up quickly, then retreated, then slowly rose to a level just marginally beyond ear-scratching height, and before the hand could retreat again Professor Weiss quickly nodded at him and said "Yes?"

"Reggie Thompson. Well, ten units can't be the maximum, although I don't know what the maximum value is. Above the eleventh unit, the demand curve is higher than the supply curve. That means its benefit is greater than its cost, or having it increases total value. Whatever the total value of ten units is, the total value of eleven is higher." Reggie stopped, uncertain if this was what the professor was looking for.

"Your observation is completely correct," Professor Weiss responded. "By the same logic, the total value of ten is greater than the total value of nine, and the total value of nine is greater than that of eight—in other words, total value is increasing at least up through the eleventh unit. By Reggie's logic, could we further increase value by producing the twelfth unit?"

Barbara was staring at the diagram on the whiteboard when, all of a sudden and somewhat involuntarily, a sharp "*No!*" erupted from her mouth.

"Why not, Barbara?" asked Professor Weiss.

"Because the cost of producing the twelfth unit—the height of the supply curve over it—is *more* than the benefit as shown by the height of the demand curve. Producing the twelfth unit would *reduce* total value. You would reduce total value by even more if you produced still higher quantities. You can't get total value any higher than it is at eleven!"

Professor Weiss nodded approvingly. "Yes, the only allocation where total value cannot be further increased by a change is at eleven units. There *the marginal benefit just equals the marginal cost, which implies that value is at its maximum and therefore the allocation is an efficient one.* Note that the allocation that has marginal benefit equal to marginal cost also identifies the intersection point of the demand and supply curves."

Another student's hand was waving. Melanie Garcia asked: "Are you saying markets are always efficient? I just don't believe that. Capitalist firms manipulate consumers for their own ends. Our national poverty rate is a disgrace. That's what markets give us. Is that part of your 'efficiency'"?

Professor Weiss raised his hand to his chin, wrapped in thought as he pondered how to respond to this challenge. Melanie clearly thought that a trap had been laid for them, and she was not going to fall into it. The students were looking at one another, perceiving that the stakes here were greater than they had realized.

"I love your question, Melanie, because of the connections you make between this simple model and the real world. I do not know if I can give you a satisfactory answer today, but let me try. Do you recall the analogy I made at the beginning of class, comparing this introductory discussion with showing someone a half-built model of a car? That I do not show it in order to convince anyone that this particular vision is desirable, but rather to get you interested in economic modeling? I meant that. As the course goes on, we will talk about markets a great deal. In some particular circumstances, I may well argue that a market or marketlike allocation process is better than some alternative. In other particular circumstances, I will argue that markets do not serve us well at all compared to government-guided allocation. In either case, I will tell you up front what I am going to argue and why.

"And no, I am not saying that markets are always efficient," he continued. "For example, and this is just my personal opinion with which any of you should feel free to disagree, I do not think the national labor market with an involuntary unemployment rate of 10 percent is very efficient—and this contributes to the poverty rates that distress many of us. The particular market in this *model* is efficient, but I have not claimed that the model is a good representation of any *real* market.

"I am glad that you are willing to entertain the idea that a model *can* represent a real situation. But every good analyst"—Professor Weiss paused here for several seconds, looking around the room to be sure that every student was responding to this implicit challenge with full attention—"has the responsibility for critically assessing the appropriateness of a particular model to a particular real situation. This is a matter of *evidence* and of *judgment.* Note that I have not offered you any hard evidence at all to suggest that this model might apply to some real situation. My bet is that many of you, unlike Melanie, have been accepting this model without thinking enough about why."

Now Barbara was truly puzzled. Rather than defending himself against Melanie's criticisms, he seemed to be agreeing with her. Am I guilty of accepting this model uncritically? Each part seems to have passed my own "tests" based on common sense; I did think about airfares and use of land for corn growing. And I want to *trust* this professor. Doesn't he want us to trust him? What is the point of this lesson, then, and why should I struggle with all the model's intricacies if it doesn't apply to anything real?

Professor Weiss continued as if he had been reading Barbara's mind. "In fact, I think there are many good reasons why you should understand this particular model backward and forward. For one, it is the model most commonly used in microeconomic policy analysis —even if you think it is inappropriate for a specific situation, you will have to persuade others of what is more appropriate. For another, different pieces of this model will often be useful, even if the model as a whole is not. Finally, I think there are situations in which the model as a whole is, in fact, better than other alternatives that analysts can reasonably contemplate.

"Getting each of you to the point where you have developed the skills necessary to make these assessments yourself will take some time. Therefore, I hope I can earn and maintain your trust in a limited way. I do not want you to trust me to tell you when a specific model applies; I want you to develop your independent critical abilities. I do hope that you will trust me to do my best to help you achieve mastery of microeconomic policy analysis."

With this, he stopped and looked directly at Melanie. She looked satisfied, at least for now. He looked around the rest of the room. All eyes were upon him. He stepped back toward the diagram. "There is one last conceptual point that I wish to add to the model we have developed so far. A very useful way to think about this or any other allocative process and its relationship to efficiency is in terms of *the benefit-cost principle*. Reggie and Barbara have already used it in our previous discussion. *An action that results in benefits being greater than costs increases efficiency, and one in which costs are greater than benefits reduces efficiency.* In our example, the action of supplying the first unit to the market increases efficiency: to the nearest dollar, the benefits of $10 exceed the costs of $3. The actions of supplying two to eleven units also increase efficiency, because each has benefits greater than costs. But the action of supplying the twelfth unit would have costs greater than benefits, and would reduce efficiency.

"We can measure the degree of efficiency. The shaded area in our figure shows the efficiency gain from using our resources to produce eleven units of this good compared to producing none of it at all. The benefits of the eleven units are represented by the entire area under the demand curve for those units, and the costs by the corresponding area under the supply curve. Benefits minus costs, or net benefits, are therefore the shaded area. Using some geometry, that area can be shown to equal $42.35."[11]

Professor Weiss went on to show this, and then announced that this was quite enough for one day and ended the class. Barbara and Reggie looked at each other, tired but smiling.

"That was some class, wasn't it?" said Reggie.

"You can say that again," Barbara replied. "I think this course is going to be *very* interesting. I just hope I can keep up with it. At times it seemed to be going too fast for me. I've never seen anything like this before."

Reggie grinned at her. "It sounded to me like you're going to do just fine."

Professor Weiss, who overheard the thrust of this conversation, smiled to himself as he left the room. They both will do just fine, he thought. This whole class will do just fine. I am lucky to have such good students. And with those private thoughts, he disappeared from view.

Summary

The most common analytic method for predicting the consequences of proposed policies is modeling. A model is an abstraction intended to convey the essence of some particular aspect of the real world; it is inherently unreal and its usefulness depends on the extent to which it increases knowledge or understanding. The accuracy and breadth of a model's predictions depend on its specification: the choice of a particular set of abstractions or assumptions used to construct the model. A fundamental skill of policy analysis is to be able to identify the alternative plausible specifications relevant to a particular policy analysis and to understand how analytic conclusions depend upon them.

---

[11] Assuming that the demand and supply curves are linear, the two points given on each determine their equations and thus their intercepts on the price axis. The demand curve has equation $Q = 21 - 2P$ and intercept $P = \$10.50$. The supply curve has equation $Q = 5P - 14$ and intercept 2.80. The line at $P = \$5.00$ divides the shaded area into two right triangles, each with a "quantity" height of eleven and "price" bases of $5.50 and $2.20 for the upper and lower triangles, respectively.

The chapter provides a story as a model. In the story, some fundamental concepts used in microeconomic models are introduced. One of these is the *demand curve,* a relation showing the demand or quantity of a good that a consumer (or some group of consumers) will wish to buy at each possible selling price for that good. Normally, consumers will demand greater quantities at lower prices. Another fundamental concept is that of the *supply curve,* a relation showing the supply or quantity of a good that a producer (or group of producers) will offer for sale at each possible selling price for that good. Typically, producers will supply greater quantities at higher prices. Both the demand curve and the supply curve are introduced as observable consequences of individuals trying to make the best choices, in their own judgments, from those available to them. A third fundamental concept is that of *market equilibrium:* when the quantity demanded by consumers is just equal to the quantity supplied by producers.

Also within the story, these three fundamental concepts are related to concepts of economic value in a highly specific way. The demand curve can be thought of as a marginal benefit schedule, interpreting its height as the maximum amount of money that someone would pay to receive each successive unit of the good. Similarly, the supply curve can be thought of as a marginal cost schedule, its height showing the minimum amount of money necessary to persuade a supplier to bring each successive unit to market for sale. The benefits and costs of bringing each unit to market can then be compared, and thus the story introduces the idea of *benefit-cost analysis.*

Furthermore, the story informally introduces the idea of *economic efficiency* as the use of an economy's resources to maximize the value to its members of the goods and services produced. In the story, efficiency varies with the quantity of the good that is produced (by suppliers using society's scarce resources) and then consumed. The degree of efficiency increases if allocative actions are taken that have benefits greater than costs, and decreases if actions have costs greater than benefits. The market equilibrium is shown to be the particular allocation of resources that *maximizes* benefits minus costs and is thus an economically efficient allocation.

Two important substantive questions of economics are raised by the students in the story. One is whether there is a conflict between seeking efficiency and seeking equity or fairness. This question arises when a student recognizes that a consumer's wealth influences his or her demand curve. This implies that wealth also affects the measured benefit of allocating a unit of output to one consumer as opposed to a different consumer, and thus wealth affects judgments about economic efficiency as well.

The other substantive question is about the efficiency of allocating resources through a market system. The model indicates that the market outcome is efficient. But one student objects, saying that market outcomes involve high unemployment and manipulation of consumers. The story does not attempt to resolve fully either of these important substantive concerns, although they will be addressed later in the book.

Finally, the story offers important insights about economic modeling. One of the students "tests" the plausibility of the downward-sloping demand curve by asking herself whether she would buy more of things she consumes if their prices were lower. In effect, she is testing the generality of the model by asking if it predicts her decisions accurately.

She makes a similar "test" of the plausibility of the upward-sloping supply curve. The objecting student mentioned above focuses on how the model evaluates efficiency and is concerned that it is intended to demonstrate the efficiency of real markets in general (which she disputes). The professor is pleased that his students are trying to understand how well the model might represent a real market. He reminds them that the "goodness" of a model can only be judged with respect to some particular purpose to which it is put. His primary purpose in presenting this model, he reiterates, was to get them interested in economic modeling.

Discussion Questions

1. What do you think of the economic concept of value as explained by Professor Weiss? What do you like and dislike about it? What do you think of the concept of efficiency offered? What do you see as its strengths and weaknesses as a public policy goal?

2. Do you think consumers buy the quantity of a good or service that best fits their own circumstances? What factors might make this difficult? If consumers buy things that do not best fit their needs, does this affect the value interpretation of the demand curve?

3. What is the relationship between the actions of a producer in the model and its profits? Can you think of circumstances that might cause producer behavior to be different?

4. How should the students in the class judge the usefulness of the model Professor Weiss has presented? What do you think of the factors used by Barbara to evaluate the model? Should you distinguish the predictive function of market behavior from the evaluative function of determining efficiency consequences?

CHAPTER THREE

UTILITY MAXIMIZATION, EFFICIENCY, AND EQUITY

IN THIS LAST CHAPTER of the introductory section, we first introduce a standard model of individual choice referred to as *utility maximization.* We do so in the context of an individual who is deciding what items to consume, but must do so within the limits of a budget constraint. This standard model, as well as alternative versions, will be used in later chapters to predict behavior as we increasingly make connections among individual behaviors, policies, and aggregate outcomes. But our primary use of it in this chapter is to introduce, at a rudimentary level, some central ideas about the normative goals of *efficiency* and *equity* used in policy analysis.

We introduce the concept of efficiency in a very simple setting where the only economic activity is the exchange of goods among different people. We illustrate how inferences about the efficiency of resource allocation can be drawn from the behavioral predictions of the utility-maximization model. We highlight that efficiency is evaluated with respect to the well-being of all individuals in an economy and that well-being is usually judged by the principle of *consumer sovereignty:* Each person is the judge of his or her own well-being. We emphasize that there are many different allocations of resources that are efficient and they vary widely in terms of how well-off specific individuals are with each of them.

We distinguish the concept of efficiency known as Pareto-optimality from the concepts of relative efficiency used to compare two (or more) specific resource allocations. The latter concepts can be controversial unless they are used in conjunction with standards for assessing equity or fairness. We introduce several concepts of equitable resource allocation and illustrate their relevance to evaluating the exchanges previously discussed. A supplementary section illustrates how efficiency and equity measures may be integrated in a form known as a social welfare function. In a brief appendix, calculus versions of the model of utility maximization and the conditions that characterize exchange efficiency are explained.

36

A Model of Individual Resource Allocation

Let us review here the most conventional and general assumptions about individual resource allocation choices. These assumptions form a model of human decision-making referred to as utility maximization. In later chapters, we will consider alternatives to this model, such as a model of bounded rationality (Chapter 7), and show that policy recommendations can depend in critical ways on which of the models is more accurate for the situation being studied. However, the utility-maximization model has proven to be insightful and useful in a wide range of situations, including the policy analyses that we will discuss in the next part of this book. Furthermore, understanding the construction of the most common model is a good way to begin to develop the skill necessary to construct and use less common models. The reader should be forewarned, however, that the utility-maximization model generally suggests that the individual is a highly competent decision-maker, and thus may not be very well suited for situations in which that competency is the key issue (e.g., for complex probabilistic situations, or at times of high emotional stress).

The model of utility maximization can be described in terms of four assumptions. We will introduce these verbally and then show graphical representations of them. **First, each consumer is assumed to have a preference-ordering.** This means two things. One is that the consumer can compare any two possible bundles or collections of goods and services and will prefer one to the other or be indifferent. (This rules out responses such as "I don't know" or "I can't decide.") The other is that the consumer is consistent: if bundle A is preferred or equal to bundle B, and B is preferred or equal to C, then A must be preferred or equal to C.

Second, each consumer is nonsatiable. Roughly speaking, this means that a property of the consumer's ordering is that more goods are preferred to less, other things being equal. The consumer is, of course, the judge of what things are "goods" as opposed to "bads." If a consumer does not like air pollution or street crime, then the corresponding good is clean air or safe streets. The consumer may consider charity to others as a good, and thus is by no means assumed to be selfish.

But is it not true that the consumer can be sated? Consider rare (but not raw) hamburgers as goods. You may like only one, and I may prefer two, and we both may know people who prefer more, but doesn't everyone have a limit? The answer is yes, of course: Consumers may commonly have limits for specific goods within any particular time period.[1] A precise way to state the assumption of nonsatiation that allows for these limits is as follows: There is always at least one good for which the consumer is not yet sated.

Practically speaking, individuals are constrained by their limited budgets from having consumption bundles that contain everything they could possibly want. Even very rich people might prefer more leisure time, an extra summer home, or making more philanthropic

---

[1] Obviously, the limit depends on the time period. The example is for hamburgers per meal; the limit would presumably be much higher for hamburgers per year. In general, economic activities must include a time dimension to be well defined. Since no particular period is required for many of our illustrations, the activities can be thought of simply as per period.

donations (if they did not have to give up something they already have). And, of course, most people would prefer to be able to afford more (in terms of quantity or better quality) of most goods they are currently consuming. A convenient generalization is to treat consumers as not sated with any of the specific goods in the alternative consumption bundles under discussion. We often use this version of the nonsatiation assumption (sometimes referred to as *strong monotonicity* in the professional literature), but we would not if the focus is to be on some good for which satiation is a distinct possibility (e.g., microeconomic policy analysis courses per semester).

The third assumption is that each consumer has strictly convex preferences or, stated informally, prefers diversity in consumption bundles. Suppose we know one consumer is indifferent between two bundles: one with much housing but little entertainment; the other with little housing but much entertainment. The third assumption asserts that the consumer would strictly prefer a third bundle formed by using any proportional combination (weighted average) of the housing and entertainment in the first two. For example, a bundle made up of one-third of the housing and entertainment in the first bundle plus two-thirds of the housing and entertainment in the second would be a proportional combination.

The idea is that the consumer would prefer a more "balanced" bundle to either of the extremes. This tries to capture the empirical reality that most people consume a diversity of goods rather than extreme quantities of only one or two items. Since nothing stops them from choosing less balanced bundles, it must be that the less balanced ones are not considered as desirable as the more balanced ones. Like the second assumption, this is simply an empirical generalization thought to be true in most circumstances but for which there are exceptions. (For example, someone might be indifferent to spending a one-week vacation in either of two places but think that half a week in each is worse.)

The fourth assumption is that each consumer makes resource allocation choices in accordance with his or her ordering. This implies that the consumer is both self-interested and informed (in terms of knowing which choice is the best one to make). Together, these four assumptions form the most common model of rational consumer decision-making. The first and fourth assumptions model rationality; the second and third assumptions are generalizations about preferences.

The first three assumptions of this model are often theoretically represented by an ordinal utility function, and the fourth assumption is equivalent to the consumer acting to maximize utility. Imagine that the consumer mentally considers all possible bundles of goods and lines them up in sequence from best to worst. Further imagine that some number (the utility level) is assigned to each of the bundles in accordance with the following rule: More preferred bundles get higher numbers than less preferred bundles, and equally preferred bundles get the same number assigned to them. This is an ordinal ranking because the numbers indicate nothing apart from the consumer's ordering.[2] Mathematically, we can write

---

[2] The ranking tells us which of two bundles is preferred, but not by how much. The distance between the numbers in an ordinal ranking has no meaning. A cardinal ranking, by contrast, reveals both the order and the distance between bundles (like temperature scales). However, to construct a cardinal ranking of an individual's preference would require more knowledge about the consumer than that postulated in the four assumptions discussed. In

the utility function as $U(X_1, X_2, \ldots, X_n)$, where there are n goods or services that can be in a bundle, X_i tells us how much of the ith good or service is in a bundle, and the value of the function tells us what utility level has been assigned to any particular bundle consisting of $X_1, X_2, \ldots, X_n$.

Note that since it is only the order or ranking of the bundles that the function reveals, a different function that, say, doubles all of the absolute levels $V(X_1, X_2, \ldots, X_n) = 2U(X_1, X_2, \ldots, X_n)$ represents exactly the same ordering. In fact, *any* transformation of the original function that keeps the bundles in the same order is representing the same preferences. The absolute levels of utility thus do not mean anything by themselves. The utility function is a conceptual construct that can neither be measured directly, nor be used to compare utility levels of two different consumers (since the level of the numbers is arbitrary). Nevertheless, it provides the foundation for a theory that has many practical applications.

We can also represent the consumer's preferences (or utility function) graphically by using indifference curves. Assume that consumption bundles consist only of two goods, meat M and tomatoes T and therefore that the utility level is a function only of them: $U(M, T)$. Any amount of meat and tomatoes can be represented by a single point in Figure 3-1a. For example, point A represents 5 pounds of M and 4 pounds of T, and point B represents 4 pounds of M and 3 pounds of T. **Define an indifference curve as the locus of points representing all consumption bundles that are equally preferred to each other (or equivalently, have the same utility level).** In Figure 3-1a, U_A shows all consumption bundles that have the same utility level as at point A, and U_B shows all bundles with the same utility level as at point B.

Point A, which has more of both goods than point B, must (by the nonsatiation assumption) represent a greater utility level ($U_A > U_B$). Thus the utility level increases as one moves upward and to the right on the diagram. One (and only one) indifference curve must pass through every point on the diagram. This follows from the assumption that the consumer has a preference-ordering. Each bundle (or point on the diagram) has some utility level (is on some indifference curve) that allows it to be compared with any other bundle to see if it has a higher, lower, or equal utility level. Thus there are an infinite number of indifference curves, one to represent each possible utility level.

Why is there *only* one indifference curve through each point? If two different indifference curves went through the same point and thus intersected (Figure 3-1b), it would violate the consistency aspect of the preference-ordering. It would imply that one bundle (the intersection point G) is indifferent to other bundles (points E and F) to which the consumer is not indifferent. To see this contradiction, note that point F has more of both goods than point E, and thus by the nonsatiation assumption $U_F > U_E$. If E and G are on the same indifference curve ($U_E = U_G$), then consistency requires that $U_F > U_G$—but then F and G cannot also be on the same indifference curve (implying $U_F = U_G$).

---

particular, it would require a measure of the magnitude of the psychological change in utility or pleasure that an individual derives from consuming any specific bundle of goods relative to some comparison bundle. Since we do not know how to do that reliably, it is fortunate (and a notable achievement) that most economic models do not require the information in order to fulfill their purposes.

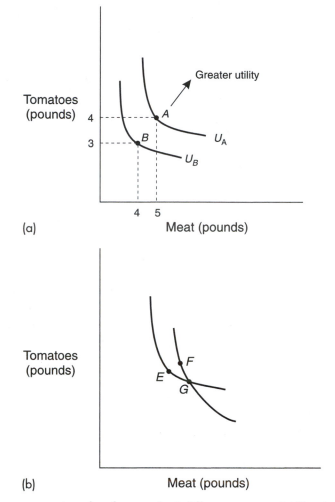

Figure 3-1. The representation of preferences by indifference curves: (a) The shape and location of indifference curves reflect the assumptions about preference orderings. (b) Indifference curves cannot cross ($U_G = U_F$ and $U_G = U_E$ means by consistency $U_F = U_E$ but by nonsatiation $U_F > U_E$).

The indifference curves are negatively sloped (they go downward from left to right). This is a consequence of the nonsatiation assumption. If the consumer begins in Figure 3-1a at A, and some meat is taken away, he or she is worse off. If we were to take away some tomatoes as well, the consumer would be still worse off. To bring the consumer back to U_A, we must *increase* the quantity of tomatoes to compensate for the meat loss. This results in the negative slope.

The marginal rate of substitution of a good M for another good T, represented by $\mathrm{MRS}_{M,T}$, is the maximum number of units of T a consumer is willing to give up in re-

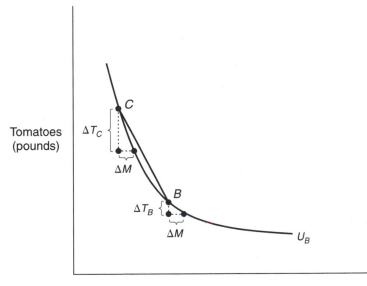

Figure 3-2. The diminishing marginal rate of substitution.

turn for getting one more unit of *M.* This is the number that keeps the consumer just indifferent, by his or her own judgment, between the initial position and the proposed trade. Note that, unlike the utility level, the $MRS_{M,T}$ is a measurable number that can be compared for different consumers. (We will make use of this aspect shortly.) **Formally, the $MRS_{M,T}$ is defined as the negative of the slope of the indifference curve** (since the slope is itself negative, the MRS is positive).

Note in Figure 3-1a that the *indifference curves are drawn to become less steep from left to right.* The MRS is diminishing: along an indifference curve, the more meat a consumer has, the fewer tomatoes he or she will be willing to give up for still another pound of meat. We illustrate this more explicitly in Figure 3-2.

At point *C*, a bundle with a relatively large quantity of tomatoes relative to meat, the individual is willing to give up ΔT_C tomatoes (Δ means "the change in") to get one extra unit of meat ΔM. But at point *B*, having fewer tomatoes and more meat, the individual will not give up as many tomatoes as before to get yet another unit of meat ΔM. This time, the individual will only give up ΔT_B tomatoes. We can refer to the (negative) slope of the indifference curve at one of its points as $\Delta T/\Delta M$, and the corresponding (positive) marginal rate of substitution $MRS_{M,T}$ is $-(\Delta T/\Delta M)$. The changing scarcity of one good relative to the other along an indifference curve provides an intuitive rationale for a diminishing MRS. Note that if we ask about the $MRS_{T,M}$ (i.e., we reverse the order of the subscripts), the definition implies this is $-(\Delta M/\Delta T)$ and therefore $MRS_{T,M} = 1/MRS_{M,T}$.

The diminishing MRS can also be seen as a consequence of the strict convexity assumption. Consider the two equally preferred bundles *B* and *C* in Figure 3-2. The set of bundles that represents proportional combinations of B and C corresponds to the points on the straight line between them.[3] By the strict convexity assumption, each of the bundles in this set is strictly preferred to B and C. Therefore, the indifference curve that connects any two equally preferred bundles, such as B and C, must lie *below* the straight line that connects them. This is possible only if the slope of the indifference curve becomes less steep from C to B.

Note also that with nonsatiation, the slope of the indifference curve does not become perfectly flat on its lower-right side nor perfectly vertical on its upper-left side. If it did, say, become perfectly flat on the right side, that would mean the $\text{MRS}_{M,T} = 0$. If no tomatoes must be taken away to hold utility constant after a small increase in meat, it means utility did not increase with the gain in meat. But this violates the nonsatiation assumption.

The indifference curves embody the first three assumptions of the utility-maximization model (preference-ordering, nonsatiation, and convexity). In order to illustrate the final model assumption, that an individual chooses in accordance with his or her preference-ordering (or equivalently acts to maximize utility), it is useful to introduce one final concept: a **budget constraint, which is the amount of money that an individual has available to spend.** When individuals make choices about what to consume, they are constrained by the size of their budgets. Suppose that one individual has $\$B$ to spend to buy meat at P_M per pound and tomatoes at P_T per pound. Given these fixed parameters, the individual can choose any amount of meat M and tomatoes T as long as its total cost is within the budget:

$$P_M M + P_T T \leq B$$

For illustrative purposes, we continue to assume that meat and tomatoes are the only two goods available, and the individual's problem is to choose the quantities (M, T) that maximize

---

[3] Represent B as the bundle (M_B, T_B) and C as (M_C, T_C). A proportional combination of B and C is defined, letting $\alpha(0 < \alpha < 1)$ be the proportion of B and $1 - \alpha$ the proportion of C, as follows:

$$M_\alpha = \alpha M_B + (1 - \alpha)M_C = M_C + \alpha(M_B - M_C)$$

and

$$T_\alpha = \alpha T_B + (1 - \alpha)T_C = T_C + \alpha(T_B - T_C)$$

We can show that the point (M_α, T_α) must lie on the line connecting B and C. The slope of the line connecting B and C is

$$\frac{\Delta T}{\Delta M} = \frac{T_B - T_C}{M_B - M_C}$$

The slope of the line connecting (M_α, T_α) and C is

$$\frac{\Delta T}{\Delta M} = \frac{T_\alpha - T_C}{M_\alpha - M_C}$$

Substituting the definitions of T_α and M_α in the equation directly above gives us

$$\frac{\Delta T}{\Delta M} = \frac{T_C + \alpha(T_B - T_C) - T_C}{M_C + \alpha(M_B - M_C) - M_C} = \frac{\alpha(T_B - T_C)}{\alpha(M_B - M_C)} = \frac{T_B - T_C}{M_B - M_C}$$

Since both (M_α, T_α) and B lie on a line through C with slope $(T_B - T_C)/(M_B - M_C)$, they must lie on the same line.

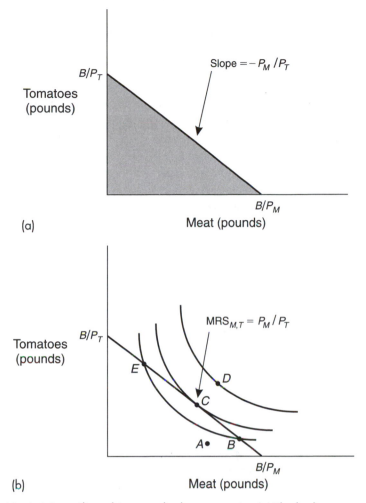

Figure 3-3. Maximizing utility subject to a budget constraint: (a) The budget constraint ($P_M M + P_T T \leq B$ limits choices to the shaded area. (b) A tangency point of an indifference curve to a budget constraint is a utility maximum (point C).

utility subject to the budget constraint. In Figure 3-3a, we represent the budget constraint graphically. If the entire budget is spent on meat, the individual could buy the bundle (M_B, 0) shown as the intercept on the horizontal (meat) axis, where $M_B = B/P_M$. If the entire budget is spent on tomatoes, the individual could buy the bundle (0, T_B) shown as the intercept on the vertical (tomatoes) axis, where $T_B = B/P_T$.

These intercepts are the extreme points of the line segment representing the different (M, T) bundles that can be bought if the budget is fully expended. To see this, we rewrite the budget constraint equation above to express T in terms of M:

$$T \leq -(P_M/P_T)M + B/P_T$$

At equality (when the budget is fully expended), this is the line with slope $-(P_M/P_T)$ and T-intercept B/P_T. Note for use below that *the slope of the budget constraint is determined by the ratio of the two prices.* Thus graphically the individual's budget constraint is shown as the shaded area: he or she can choose any bundle on the line or under it, but does not have enough money to afford bundles that are above the line.

In the context of this budget constraint, what does it mean for the individual to choose the most preferred bundle possible (or to maximize utility)? Which bundle will the individual choose? Might the individual choose a bundle under the line like point A shown in Figure 3-3b? Such a choice would be inconsistent with our model. Why? For *any* point under the line, there is a point on the line with more of both goods (like point B) and which, by the nonsatiation assumption, must have greater utility. Thus A cannot be the most preferred bundle attainable. The utility-maximizing bundle must be one of the points on the line rather than under it.

To see which point on the line is the utility maximum, we add several of the individual's indifference curves to the diagram. As drawn, we see that point B is not the maximum because point C is attainable and on a higher indifference curve. Point D has even greater utility than point C, but the individual cannot afford to buy the bundle at D. The key characteristic of point C that makes it the utility maximum is that the indifference curve at that point is just tangent to the budget constraint.[4] Recall that minus the slope of an indifference curve is the marginal rate of substitution, and that minus the slope of the budget constraint is the price ratio. Since tangency implies equal slopes, *at the utility maximum a consumer of both goods will have a marginal rate of substitution equal to the ratio of the prices:*

$$\text{MRS}_{M,T} = P_M/P_T$$

At any other point on the constraint such as point B where $\text{MRS}_{M,T} \neq P_M/P_T$, the individual can attain more utility from another bundle. To show this, suppose the price of meat P_M is \$4.00 per pound and the price of tomatoes P_T is \$1.00 per pound. If $\text{MRS}_{M,T} \neq \$4.00 \div \$1.00$, the consumer is not at a utility maximum. Suppose at point B the consumer has $\text{MRS}_{M,T} = 3 < P_M/P_T$, for example: indifferent between the current allocation and one with 3 pounds more of tomatoes and 1 pound less of meat. The consumer can forgo 1 pound of meat and save \$4.00, buy 3 pounds of tomatoes for \$3.00, and have \$1.00 left over to spend and thus increase utility over the initial allocation. In other words, from point B the individual can gain utility by moving along the constraint toward point C. From a point like E where $\text{MRS}_{M,T} > P_M/P_T$, the individual could also gain utility by moving along the constraint toward point C, in this case forgoing some tomatoes to buy more meat.[5] For utility to be maximized, any consumer of both goods must have $\text{MRS}_{M,T} = P_M/P_T$.

The four assumptions described in this section form a model of economic choice: an individual who has a utility function and acts to maximize it. We now wish to show (in a

---

[4] This illustration assumes that the maximum is not at either intercept. It is possible for the maximum to be at one of the intercepts (the individual chooses not to consume one of the goods at all), and in these "boundary" cases the tangency condition will generally not hold. We discuss these cases later in the text.

[5] Convince yourself this is possible by assuming that the $\text{MRS}_{M,T}$ at point E is 6 and identifying a way for the consumer to gain.

very simple setting) how this model can be used to draw inferences about efficiency. To do so, we must first explain the concept of efficiency.

Efficiency

The General Concept

Society is endowed with a limited supply of a wide variety of resources: for example, people, land, air, water, minerals, and time. A fundamental economic problem faced by society is how to use the resources. If the resources were not scarce, there would be no economic problem; everything that anyone wanted could be provided today, and infinite resources would still be left to meet the desires of tomorrow. But although human wants or desires may be insatiable, resource scarcity limits our ability to satisfy them. Scarcity implies that any specific resource allocation involves an **opportunity cost, or the value forgone from alternative opportunities for using the resources;** for example, if more resources are allocated to education, fewer resources will remain to be allocated to health care, food production, road construction, and other goods and services.

People differ in terms of their specific ideas for the use of scarce resources. However, we all generally agree that resources are too precious to waste. If it is possible, by a change in the allocation of resources, to improve the lot of one person without doing harm to any other person, then resources are currently being wasted. All efficiency means is that there is no waste of this kind: **An efficient allocation of resources is one from which no person can be made better off without making another person worse off.** Sometimes efficiency is referred to as **Pareto optimality** after the Italian economist Vilfredo Pareto (1848–1923), who first developed the formulation. Any allocation of resources that is not efficient is called, not surprisingly, *inefficient.*

To demonstrate the practical import of efficiency for policy, consider the resources devoted to national defense by the world's people.[6] In order to keep the illustration simple, let us assume that each nation, acting for its citizens, seeks only to produce "security" from military aggression by others. Then the efficient defense policy would be for the world to have no military resources at all: no person anywhere would face a military threat, and the freed-up resources could be devoted to increasing supplies of food, shelter, clothing, or other important goods and services.[7]

---

[6] For example, by a conservative definition the United States in 1999 spent about 4 percent of the GDP on defense. The federal government spent $365 billion on national defense out of a total federal product of $569 billion and total GDP of $9.3 trillion. Source: *Economic Report of the President,* January 2001 (Washington, D.C.: U.S. Government Printing Office, 2001), p. 288, Table B-10, and p. 298, Table B-20.

[7] The efficient level of national defense is substantially above zero for at least two important reasons that the illustration rules out: (1) some nations or groups may initiate aggressive military activities for offensive rather than defensive reasons, and (2) some nations may consider a military response appropriate to a nonmilitary threat (e.g., to enforce a claim to ownership of a natural resource such as land). Each possibility leads every nation to allocate some resources for national defense. Nevertheless, the reasons cited do not affect the point of our example, which is that defense expenditures can be significantly higher than necessary in order to produce the desired level of protection.

However, each nation is mistrustful of the others and allocates some resources to defense as a form of insurance. But that increases the threat perceived by each nation and leads to increases in national defense spending, which further increases the perceived threats, leads to more defense increases, and so on. In short, defense policies become the runners in an inefficient arms race.[8] Furthermore, efficiency is not achieved by a unilateral withdrawal: if the United States gave up its arms but no other nation did, many U.S. citizens would feel worse off, not better off. *This illustrates not only that efficiency is an important objective but that its achievement typically requires coordination among the different economic agents* (countries, in this example). This is the primary objective of negotiations such as the Strategic Arms Reduction Treaties (START I and II) between the United States and the states of the former Soviet Union and the chemical weapons disarmament treaty involving over 120 nations.

Efficiency with an Individualistic Interpretation

The definition of efficiency refers to individuals being either better off or worse off. To apply the definition to any practical problem, there must be a method of deciding whether someone's well-being has improved or deteriorated. One way to develop such a method is by using **the principle of consumer sovereignty,** which **means that each person is the sole judge of his or her own welfare.**[9] Based on that principle, economists have devised numerous analytic techniques for drawing inferences about whether individuals consider themselves better off or worse off under alternative allocations of resources.

Although the above principle is commonly used in the economic analyses of most western societies, it is not the only logical way of constructing a concept of efficiency that meets the definition given above. An alternative route is to let some other person (e.g., a philosopher-king) or perhaps a political process (e.g., democratic socialism or communism) be the judge of each person's welfare. Then efficiency would be evaluated by the values and standards of judges, rather than by those of the individuals affected.

In this text, we will always mean efficiency as judged under consumer sovereignty unless it is explicitly stated otherwise. If efficiency is not judged by that principle, one jeopardizes its acceptance in policy analysis as representing a value most people share. It is worth mentioning, however, that there are a number of situations in which deviations from the concept are commonly thought appropriate. Typically, they are those in which individuals have incomplete or erroneous information or are unable to process the available information.

One obvious example of such a deviation concerns children: Parents generally substitute their own judgments for those of their young children. Another example, and this one a matter of public policy, is that we do not allow suppliers to sell thalidomide, even though some

---

[8] The behavior described here may be thought of as a version of the Slumlord's Dilemma or Prisoner's Dilemma analyzed in Chapter 7. In that chapter, applications involving urban renewal and health insurance are discussed.

[9] The term "consumer" in the expression "consumer sovereignty" is a slight misnomer. The principle is intended to apply to all resource allocation decisions that affect an individual's welfare: the supply of inputs (e.g., the value of holding a particular job) as well as the consumption of outputs.

consumers might purchase it if they were allowed to do so. Certain medicinal drugs are legal to sell, but consumers can purchase them only by presenting physicians' prescriptions. In each of these cases, some social mechanism is used to try to protect consumers from the inadequacies of their own judgments.[10]

In using the consumer sovereignty principle, it is important to distinguish between consumer *judgments* and consumer *actions*. It is only the sovereignty of the judgments that we rely on for this definition of efficiency. Indeed, there will be many illustrations throughout this book of inefficient allocations that result from sovereign actions of well-informed consumers. The defense example given earlier is of this nature: The people of each nation can recognize the inefficiency of an arms race; but when each nation acts alone, the inefficiency is difficult to avoid. The problem is not with the judgments of people about how to value security, but with the mechanisms of coordination available to achieve it.

Efficiency in a Model of an Exchange Economy

To illustrate the analysis of efficiency, we will utilize a model of a highly simplified economy: *a pure exchange economy* in which there are only two utility-maximizing consumers and two different goods. In this economy, *we assume in addition to utility-maximizing behavior that there are no significant costs involved in negotiating, bargaining, or otherwise arranging trades—an assumption of negligible transaction costs.* By assuming for simplicity that *the goods are already produced,* we suppress the very important problems of how much of each good to produce and by what technical processes. Nevertheless, the basic principle of efficiency developed here holds for the more complicated economy as well. Furthermore, it highlights the critical connection between efficiency and the consumer sovereignty definition of human satisfaction.

The principle to be established is this: *The allocation of resources in an economy is efficient in exchange if and only if the marginal rate of substitution of one good for another is the same for each person consuming both of the goods.*[11] To see the truth of the principle, imagine any initial allocation of resources between two people, Smith and Jones, each of whom has a different $MRS_{M,T}$ and some of each of the two goods. Let us say that Smith has an $MRS_{M,T}^S = 3$ (i.e., $3T$ for $1M$), and Jones has an $MRS_{M,T}^J = 2$. Then imagine taking away 1 pound of meat from Jones and giving it to Smith and taking away 3 pounds of tomatoes from Smith. Smith's utility level is thus unchanged. We still have 3 pounds of tomatoes to allocate; let us give 2 pounds to Jones. Jones is now back to the initial utility level. Both have the same level of utility as when they started, but there is still 1 pound of tomatoes left to allocate between them. No matter how the last pound is allocated, at least one will be

---

[10] The fact that individuals may be imperfect judges of their own welfare does not necessarily imply that there is any better way to make the judgments. In later chapters we discuss several information problems such as these and analyze alternative responses to them.

[11] This is a slight simplification because it ignores consumers who are only consuming one of the goods. We show later in the chapter that for the consumer of only one good T, efficiency only requires that $MRS_{M,T}$ be no greater than the $MRS_{M,T}$ of individuals who are consuming good M.

made better off than initially and the other will be no worse off (in terms of their own judgments). Therefore, the initial allocation was inefficient.

Any time that two consumers of each good have different values for the MRS, there is "room for a deal," as illustrated above. On the other hand, if both consumers have the same value for the MRS, then it is impossible to make one of them better off without making the other worse off. Although the illustration involved only Smith and Jones, the same reasoning would apply to any pair of consumers picked randomly from the economy. Therefore, efficiency requires that *all* consumers of the two goods have the same $MRS_{M,T}$. Furthermore, there is nothing special about meat and tomatoes in this example; meat and fruit would work just as well, and so would fruit and clothing. Therefore, efficiency requires that the MRS between *any* two goods in the economy must be the same for all consumers of the two goods.

Now that we know what is required for efficiency in this pure exchange economy, recall that we have said absolutely nothing so far about any mechanisms that a society might utilize to allow its citizens to achieve an efficient allocation. If there are only two consumers, they could achieve an efficient allocation by bartering or trading.[12] Since trading can increase the utility level of each person, we predict that the two consumers will trade. Note that the value of the MRS depends on (all) the specific goods in a consumer's bundle, and it changes as the bundle changes through trading. We know that an "equilibrium" position of efficiency will be reached because of diminishing marginal rates of substitution. This is illustrated below.

In the example with Smith and Jones, Smith is gaining meat and losing tomatoes (and Jones the opposite). Smith will offer less than 3 pounds of tomatoes to get still more meat *after* the first trade, since tomatoes are becoming relatively more dear. Jones, with less meat than initially, will now demand more than 2 pounds of tomatoes to part with still another pound of meat. As they trade, Smith's $MRS_{M,T}^{S}$ continues to diminish from 3 while Jones's $MRS_{M,T}^{J}$ rises from 2 (or equivalently, $MRS_{T,M}^{J}$ diminishes).[13] At some point each will have precisely the same $MRS_{M,T}$ and then the two will be unable to mutually agree upon any additional trades. They will have reached an efficient allocation.

Note that knowledge of the marginal rate of substitution allows us to predict the direction of trade in the model. We have not had to decide whether Smith is more of a meat lover than Jones in terms of abstract utility.[14] All we compare is a relative and measurable value: the pounds of tomatoes each is willing to give up for additional meat *at the margin*. At the initial point, meat will be traded to Smith because Smith is willing to give up more tomatoes than Jones requires to part with an additional pound of meat. Smith may not like meat more than Jones in an absolute sense. Alternatively, for example, Smith may like tomatoes less than (and meat as much as) Jones in the absolute sense. Or they could both

---

[12] Recall that we assume that there are negligible transaction costs. In more realistic problems of policy, transaction costs are often significant and may play a major role in determining efficiency.

[13] Recall that at any point on a normal indifference curve $MRS_{M,T} = 1/MRS_{T,M}$.

[14] This would require not only a cardinal utility measure for each but also a method of making the interpersonal comparison between Smith utils and Jones utils.

have identical absolute preferences, but Smith might have an initial allocation with many tomatoes and little meat compared to Jones. Fortunately, efficiency requires only that we equate the comparable MRS values of each consumer at the margin; we do not have to know individual preferences in an absolute sense.

Efficiency may be achieved through a barter process when there are only two consumers and two goods, but what about the actual world that consists of a great many consumers and a very large number of different goods and services? What mechanisms exist to facilitate communication and coordination among the diverse economic agents? That general problem of organization will be the focus of Parts IV and V, but it is useful to introduce at this very early stage the idea of *price* as one simple coordinating mechanism that can help with the task.

Suppose each good has one price that all consumers either pay to buy the good or receive when they sell it. In this model of a pure exchange economy, each consumer can be thought of as having a budget constraint derived by multiplying the quantity of each good in the initial endowment by its price and summing over all the goods in the endowment. That is, the budget constraint is the market value at the given prices of each individual's initial endowment. As we have seen, the consumer will try to allocate his or her budget such that, for any two goods X and Y that are bought,

$$\text{MRS}_{X,Y} = \frac{P_X}{P_Y}$$

Since all consumers face the same prices, all try to achieve the same $\text{MRS}_{M,T}$. If they are successful, the resulting allocation is efficient. Thus prices can be a very powerful coordinating device.

Note that if consumers faced different prices for the same good and could buy the quantities of it that they wished, they would end up with different values for the MRS. This suggests a generalization (with exceptions to be uncovered elsewhere in the book) relevant to policy design: *If a policy results in at least one consumer of a good being charged a price different from that charged other consumers of the same good, the policy will generally be inefficient.*[15]

Are there policies for which this principle is relevant? One is the Robinson-Patman Act of 1936, which prohibits firms from engaging in price discrimination among their customers.[16] However, many policies cause different consumers to be faced with different

---

[15] The exceptions are typically based on one of three considerations: (1) It is only the price of the marginal unit purchased that must be the same for all consumers. (2) The consumer is unable or unwilling to alter the quantity purchased. (3) The policy offsets an inefficiency that arises elsewhere in the economy. When applying this generalization, it is important to make sure that the prices compared are for truly identical goods. For example, the price for a television with installation provided by the dealer need not be the same as the price for the same television at a cash-and-carry outlet. Differences in times of delivery, shipping costs, and guarantees also are common reasons for distinguishing otherwise identical goods.

[16] Price discrimination refers to the practice of a seller charging different prices for the same good. We consider this practice in Chapter 10.

prices. We will consider several of these in the next chapter when we discuss welfare programs. Programs to assist lower-income individuals often reduce the price of a good or service to recipients, and since only some people qualify for these reduced prices we might expect the result to be inefficient resource allocation. Alternative model specifications, taking program particulars into account, make this proposition a bit more complicated. Of course, one purpose of welfare programs is to help the poor and it is possible that achieving the equity objective is worth some efficiency cost. These questions can be raised about many programs that provide benefits to selected groups of people, for example, housing subsidies, food stamps, education benefits for veterans, Medicare, and Medicaid.

The main point of raising these issues here, even without resolving them, is to demonstrate the earlier claim that considerable insight into the efficiency consequences of policies can be achieved through modeling. We did not have to go around asking every (or even any) consumer how he or she would be affected by price discrimination. The conclusion that price discrimination is inefficient comes from applying the utility-maximizing model of behavior to the definition of efficiency. This type of reasoning, displayed in very elementary form here, can be extended to quite sophisticated forms of analysis.

All such analysis is subject to the same type of criticism: If the underlying model of consumer behavior is erroneous, then the analytic conclusion may be wrong. If some individuals are not utility maximizers, then making all individuals face the same prices will not necessarily result in each having the same MRS for any two goods. Finally, recall that models cannot be expected to be perfectly accurate. The relevant question, which is not addressed in this example, is whether the model is accurate enough. The answer depends, in part, on the alternative means of analysis with which it is compared.

The theoretical example of coordination through prices illustrates only part of the coordinating potential of a price system. It does not consider the problem of how to ensure that the total amount people wish to buy of one good, given its price, equals the total amount that other people will be willing to sell. (The only goods available are those in the initial endowments of the consumers.) If the price of one good is too low, for example, then the quantity demanded will exceed the quantity supplied. But prices can solve that problem as well: Raise the price of the goods in excess demand and lower the price of those in excess supply until the prices that exactly balance the demand and supply for each good are found. The *equilibrium prices* are the ones that will allow the consumers in the above example actually to achieve efficiency; any other prices will result in some consumers not being able to buy the quantities necessary to maximize their utility.[17]

---

[17] We should also note an important difference between two coordinating mechanisms mentioned: prices and START agreements. The price mechanism allows *decentralized* coordination: Consumers do not have to consult with one another about how much each plans to buy. START agreements are a *centralized* way of coordinating: Each party will agree only to "not buy" certain arms based on knowledge of what the other party promises to not buy. Thus, efficiency can be sought with both decentralized and centralized institutional procedures. One of the more interesting and subtle questions of policy design concerns the choice of centralized versus decentralized procedures. We focus on that choice in Part V.

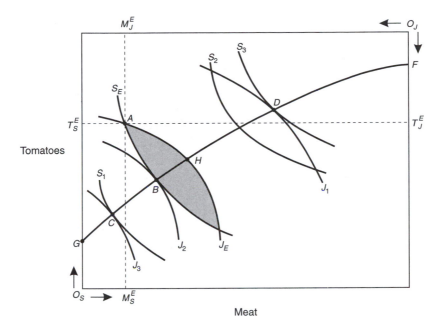

Figure 3-4. The Edgeworth box.

A Geometric Representation of the Model

The concept of efficiency in exchange can also be explained geometrically through the use of an Edgeworth box diagram. In our simple example with Smith and Jones, let $\bar{M}$ be the total amount of meat between them and $\bar{T}$ be the total amount of tomatoes. These amounts determine the dimensions of the Edgeworth box shown in Figure 3-4.

Let the bottom-left corner O_S represent the origin of a graph showing Smith's consumption. Point A shows Smith's initial endowment of meat M_S^E and tomatoes T_S^E. Let the upper-right corner O_J represent the origin of a graph showing Jones's consumption. The amount of meat consumed is measured by the horizontal distance to the left of O_J, and tomato consumption is measured by the vertical distance below O_J. Then, given the way the box is constructed, point A also represents Jones's initial endowment. Since the total quantities available are $\bar{M}$ and $\bar{T}$ and Smith starts with M_S^E and T_S^E Jones must have the rest:

$$M_J^E = \bar{M} - M_S^E$$

and

$$T_J^E = \bar{T} - T_S^E$$

In fact, every possible allocation of the two goods between Smith and Jones is represented by one point in the Edgeworth box. At O_S, for example, Smith has nothing and Jones has everything. At O_J, Jones has nothing and Smith has everything. Every conceivable trade between Smith and Jones can thus be represented as a movement from A to another point in the Edgeworth box.

We can also draw in the indifference curves to show each person's satisfaction level. Let S_E be the indifference curve reflecting Smith's level of satisfaction at the initial endowment (and thus point A lies on it). Higher levels of utility for Smith are shown by curves S_2 and S_3; a lower level of satisfaction is shown by S_1. The curves drawn are only illustrative, of course; for every point in the box, Smith has an indifference curve that passes through it.

The indifference curves for Jones are drawn bowed in the opposite direction because of the way the box is constructed, with Jones having more consumption at points away from O_J, and toward O_S. Let J_E be the indifference curve showing Jones's utility level at the initial endowment (and thus point A lies on it). J_2 and J_3 represent increasing levels of satisfaction; J_1 shows a lower degree of satisfaction.

Thus the Edgeworth box combines two indifference curve diagrams, each like figures we have drawn previously. Smith's preferences are represented like those in the earlier figures: origin at the bottom left, tomatoes on the vertical axis, meat on the horizontal axis, and higher utility levels upward and to the right. The same is true for Jones if the Edgeworth box is turned upside down.

Note that the shaded area between S_E and J_E represents all allocations of meat and tomatoes whereby *both* Smith and Jones would consider themselves better off than at the initial allocation. If we include the points *on* as well as those strictly between the indifference curves S_E and J_E, they represent the set of all possible trades that would make at least one person better off and no one worse off.

Consider the possibility that we could start the exchange economy (choose feasible initial endowments for each person) from any point in the Edgeworth box. From most points, there will be some trades that could make each person better off. For every point like A, through which the indifference curves *intersect,* improvements by trading are possible. But there are some points, like point B, where the indifference curves do not intersect but are just tangent to one another. Note that every single point that improves Jones's satisfaction over the level at B lies below the J_2 indifference curve (toward O_S). At each of these points Smith would be worse off than at B and so would not agree to any of the proposed trades. Similarly, Jones would not agree to move to any of the points that would make Smith better off. *Thus B is an efficient allocation: from it, it is impossible to find a trade that will make one person better off without making the other person worse off.* Further, as was claimed earlier, the MRS$_{M,T}$ is the same for Smith and Jones at B because the indifference curves are tangent there.

There are a few other efficient points, such as C and D, illustrated in Figure 3-4. (Although the MRS$_{M,T}$ may be different at B, C, and D, at any one of the points the two consumers will have the same MRS$_{M,T}$.) Imagine finding each of the efficient points. **Define the set of exchange-efficient points as the contract curve;** the curve is drawn as the line through the Edgeworth box connecting O_S and O_J. *The contract curve illustrates that there are many possible resource allocations that are efficient.*

Of course, if Smith and Jones are initially at point A and can trade with one another, utility maximization implies they will trade within the shaded area. Their trading will continue until they reach a point on the BH segment of the contract curve. (We cannot predict which

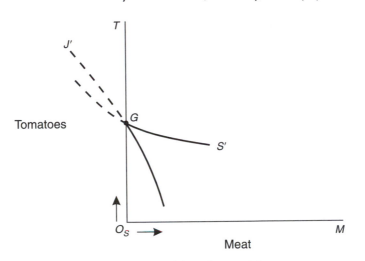

Figure 3-5. Efficient allocations at a corner of the Edgeworth box.

point without further assumptions.) Furthermore, we can see that Smith will be gaining meat and losing tomatoes, whereas Jones does the opposite.[18] In other words, the behavior in our previous verbal description of trading between Smith and Jones can be seen in the Edgeworth box diagram.

Note that some of the points from the entire contract curve lie on the boundaries of the box. These segments, $O_S G$ and $O_J F$, do not meet the same tangency conditions as the efficient points interior to the boundaries. Although the points on the boundary segments are efficient, Smith and Jones are not each consuming both of the goods. Careful examination of these points is interesting because it suggests why consumers do not purchase some goods at all, although they have strictly convex preferences. The reason is simply that the price is considered too high.

In Figure 3-5 the bottom left corner of the Edgeworth box is blown up a bit to see this more clearly. At G, Smith has utility level S' and Jones J'. The solid portions of each indifference curve are in the feasible trading region (within the boundaries of the box). The dashed extension of J' shows the consumption bundles that would give Jones the same utility level as at G, but there is not enough total meat in the economy to create these bundles. (Also, the points on this dashed segment do not exist from Smith's perspective, since they would involve negative quantities of meat!)

Although the indifference curves J' and S' are clearly not tangent at G, there are no mutually satisfactory trades that can be made from that point. Smith has only tomatoes to trade, and $MRS^S_{M,T,} < MRS^J_{M,T}$. This means that Jones will only part with another pound of meat for more tomatoes than Smith is willing to offer. Smith considers the meat price (in terms of tomatoes) demanded by Jones to be too high, and Jones feels similarly about the price (in terms of meat) for tomatoes.

---

[18] The slopes of the indifference curves at point A reveal that $MRS^S_{M,T,} > MRS^J_{M,T}$.

As with the other points on the contract curve, every point that makes Jones better off (those below J') makes Smith worse off, and vice versa. Thus G is efficient, although the tangency conditions are not met. This is explained by the limits imposed by the boundaries (along which at least one of the consumers is consuming only one of the two goods).

This analysis, of two consumers and two goods, generalizes to the many goods, many consumers economy just as before. Efficiency requires every pair of consumers to be on their contract curves for every pair of goods. Thus, we may use the Edgeworth diagram to represent metaphorically exchange efficiency for the entire society.

Note that we have examined the concept of efficiency with both a verbal and a geometric model of a pure exchange economy. The verbal model provides an intuitive grasp of the motivation for trading and how the trading process leads to an efficient allocation characterized by the equality of the MRS among traders. The geometric model makes clear that there are normally an infinite number of allocations that are efficient. The efficient allocations vary widely in terms of how well off each of the different traders is at any one of them. A third common form of this model of a pure exchange economy, using mathematical equations and calculus, is contained in the appendix.[19]

Relative Efficiency

The Pareto concept of efficiency is an absolute one: Each possible allocation is either efficient or inefficient. It is often useful, however, to evaluate **relative efficiency: a comparison of the efficiency of one allocation with that of another.** That is, we wish to know whether one allocation is *relatively* more efficient than another or whether an allocative change *increases* efficiency.

Measures of relative efficiency have been devised and are frequently used in policy analysis. They are controversial and more complex than the absolute standard of Pareto optimality, and we defer most formal exposition of them until Chapter 6. Below, we briefly introduce the general ideas that underlie measures of relative efficiency.

There is a natural extension of the Pareto rule that can be used to make some judgments about relative efficiency. **One allocation is defined as Pareto-superior to another if and only if it makes at least one person better off and no one worse off.** In Figure 3-6, the axes show utility levels for Smith and Jones. Point A in Figure 3-6 shows Smith with a utility level of S_E and Jones with a utility level of J_E (chosen to correspond with the utility levels of their indifference curves through point A in Figure 3-4). The shaded quadrant represents the set of all utility levels that are Pareto-superior to those at point A.

For reference, we also draw in Figure 3-6 the **utility-possibilities frontier: the locus of utility levels associated with the Pareto-optimal allocations of the economy.** These levels correspond to the levels of the indifference curves passing through each point on the contract curve of Figure 3-4. The portion of the shaded area ABH in Figure 3-6 corresponds to the utility levels of the allocations in the shaded area of Figure 3-4. These are the Pareto-superior points that are feasible in the economy. Point R in Figure 3-6 is Pareto-superior to

---

[19] Recommended for graduate students.

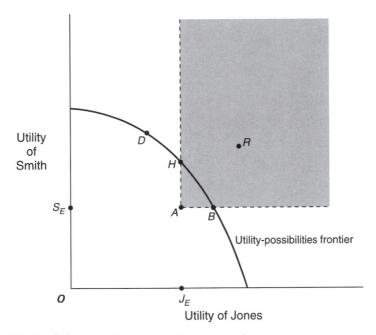

Figure 3-6. The shaded area is Pareto-superior to point A.

point A, but it is not feasible if the amounts of meat and tomatoes available only equal the dimensions of the Edgeworth box in Figure 3-4. Given the resources of the economy, the efficient allocations are those from which no Pareto-superior change can be made.

The concept of Pareto superiority is not itself controversial. However, it can become controversial if one proposes to use it normatively as a criterion for policy-making. For example, suppose one thought that all policy changes should be required to be Pareto-superior. That would restrict the pursuit of efficiency from point A to the allocations in the shaded area of Figure 3-6.

The problem with this proposed rule is that it eliminates all the changes whereby some people are better off (perhaps many people are much better off) and some are worse off (perhaps a few are slightly worse off). But in an actual economy most allocative changes, and especially those caused by public policy, are characterized precisely by these mixed effects. Inevitably, evaluating these changes involves interpersonal comparisons that the concepts of Pareto optimality and superiority try to avoid.

For example, the government may be considering building a new highway that bypasses a small town in order to increase the ease of traveling and the conduct of commerce between two or more cities. Benefits or gains will accrue to the users of the new highway and to those who own land adjacent to it that may be used to service the new traffic. But the owners, employees, and local customers of the service stations, restaurants, and motels in the small town may well experience losses because of the reduction in traffic. However, if the gains to the gainers are great enough and the losses to the losers are small enough, collectively the society might think the change justified.

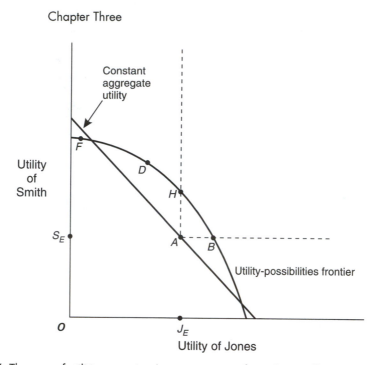

Figure 3-7. The sum of utilities at point *A* as a measure of its relative efficiency.

Allocative changes whereby some people gain and others lose certainly raise questions of equity or fairness. Suppose, however, we try to put these questions aside for the moment and consider whether some objective statements about relative efficiency can be made in these circumstances. Consider, for example, a change like the one from point *A* to point *D* in Figure 3-6. This clearly moves the economy from an inefficient allocation to an efficient one, and we might think that any objective measure of relative efficiency should indicate that the change is an efficiency improvement.

Note that the test for efficiency or Pareto optimality does not depend on whether someone *has* been made worse off (Jones in the above example); it depends only on whether it is *possible* to make someone better off without making anyone else worse off. Efficiency is a matter of whether there is room for improvement, and one might wish that measures of efficiency indicated only the scarcity of the available room for improvement (e.g., closeness to the utility-possibilities frontier). Then we would say that one allocation is more efficient than another if there is relatively less room for improvement possible from it. For any given initial allocation the set of more efficient allocations would include not only the Pareto-superior ones but others as well.

An example of a measure that avoids the restrictiveness of the Pareto-superiority criterion is the aggregate (or sum) of utilities.[20] In Figure 3-7, the line through point *A* with a

---

[20] This somewhat unusual example is chosen because it is easy to explain and because the most common measures (based on the Hicks-Kaldor compensation principle) can be seen as simple variations upon it.

slope of -1 is the locus of points with constant aggregate utility equal to the level at point *A*. Any point above this line has higher aggregate utility and by that measure would be considered relatively more efficient. All allocations that are Pareto-superior to point *A* have a higher aggregate utility level (since at least one person's utility level is higher and no one's utility level is lower), and thus are considered more efficient by this test. We can see that point *D,* which is efficient but not Pareto-superior, also is considered more efficient than point *A*. Therefore, this test is less restrictive than the test of Pareto superiority.

However, there are also problems with this measure. As we have pointed out before, utility is neither measurable nor comparable among persons. Therefore, the measure is not very pragmatic. Later in the text, we shall review methods of constructing related indices that solve the measurability problem. Indeed, the benefit-cost reasoning in Chapter 2's story is based precisely on such a construct.[21] Then we must face the remaining problem: The implicit interpersonal judgments in this measure (and the related measures discussed later) are arbitrary from an ethical viewpoint.

Consider, for example, point *F* in Figure 3-7. Like point *D,* point *F* is Pareto-optimal, but it is considered relatively *less* efficient than point *A* by the sum-of-utilities test. Why? One reason is that the test is defined independently of the utility-possibilities frontier. Unless the shape of the test line is geometrically identical to the shape of the utility-possibilities frontier, the different Pareto-optimal points will not receive the same relative efficiency ranking. Rather than an attempt to measure the distance *to* the frontier, the aggregate utilities test is better thought of as measuring distance *from* the origin; how far we have come, rather than how much farther there is to go. Since better use of resources does move us farther from the origin, a measure of this distance can be interpreted as an index of efficiency.

If we accept the notion of measuring distance from the origin, the aggregate utilities test still imposes an interpersonal judgment: To hold relative efficiency constant, a 1-util loss to someone is just offset by a 1-util gain to another. But why should this judgment be accepted? Why can the social judgment not be something else, for example, that losses are more serious than gains, so that perhaps 2 utils of gain should be required to offset each util of loss? Then a quite different set of allocations would be considered relatively more efficient than point *A.*

The point of this last illustration is to suggest that, normatively, measures of relative efficiency can be controversial if one does not agree with the implicit ethical judgment in them. Rather than leave such judgments implicit, the strategy recommended here is to make equity or fairness an explicit criterion in policy analysis and evaluate policies on both efficiency and equity grounds. Standardized measures of relative efficiency can then be very useful, but they take on normative significance only when looked at in conjunction with some explicit ethical perspective. To illustrate that, we must introduce the criterion of equity or fairness.

---

[21] A *weighted* sum of utilities, where the weights are the inverses of each individual's marginal utility from an additional dollar, is equivalent to the Hicks-Kaldor rule for benefit-cost analysis (measurable in monetary units). This is demonstrated and explained in Chapter 6.

Equity

It is clear from the earlier Edgeworth analysis that there are many efficient allocations of resources. These allocations, represented by the points on the contract curve, *dominate* all other possible allocations. That is, for any allocation not on the contract curve, there is at least one point on the contract curve that makes one or more persons better off and no one worse off. Thus if a society could choose any allocation for its economy, it would certainly be one from the contract curve. But which one?

Recall that efficiency is but one social objective. Another important objective is **equity: fairness in the distribution of goods and services among the people in an economy.** However, no unique concept of equity is widely regarded as definitive for public policy-making. We shall use the term to refer collectively to all the various concepts of fair distribution, and later in the text we shall introduce specific concepts (e.g., strict equality or a universal minimum) to compare and contrast their implications in the analyses of particular issues.[22] At this stage we wish primarily to make the point that diverse concepts of equity deserve analytic consideration.

Equality of Outcome Is One Concept of Equity

Although all the points on the contract curve of Figure 3-8 are efficient, they differ in the distribution of well-being. In fact, *the contract curve offers a continuum of distributional possibilities.* As we move along it from O_S to O_J, Smith is getting an increasing share of the total goods and services and is becoming better off relative to Jones. One way in which equity is sometimes considered is in terms of these relative shares. Intuitively, distributions in the "middle" of the contract curve represent more equal outcomes than those at the extremes, and for that reason they might be considered preferable on equity grounds. According to this interpretation, *equality* of relative shares is the most equitable allocation.

Using the equality of relative shares as a standard, we must still confront the question "shares of what?" If equality of well-being or satisfaction is the objective, then it is the shares of *utility* that should be of equal size. But since utility is neither measurable nor interpersonally comparable, in practice we usually fall back on proxy measures such as income or wealth.

For example, point *A* in Figure 3-8 is the allocation that gives each person exactly one-half of the available wealth (meat and tomatoes). Without being able to measure or compare utility, making this the initial endowment may be the best we can do to ensure equal relative shares. This necessarily ignores the possibility that one of the two people, say Smith, simply does not like meat or tomatoes very much, and might require twice the quantity given to Jones in order to reach a comparable utility level. Furthermore, it would be difficult to distinguish on equity grounds any of the efficient allocations that the two might then reach by voluntary trading from point *A:* the *BC* segment of the contract curve. Some objective

---

[22] Most of the specific concepts are introduced in Chapter 5. The concept of *a just price* is not introduced until Chapter 13 in order to permit prior development of the workings of price systems.

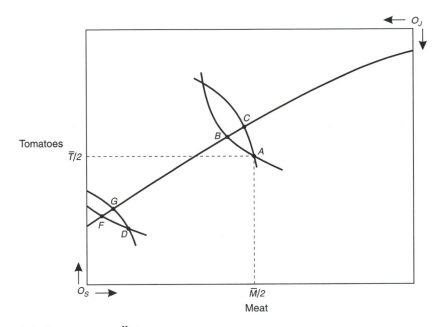

Figure 3-8. Equity versus efficiency.

standard for weighing the equity of the meat and tomato exchange between Smith and Jones would be necessary.[23]

Equality of Opportunity Is Another Concept of Equity

Some people do not feel that equality of outcomes should be a social goal of great importance. An alternative view is that only the process must be fair. One specific principle of this type, for example, is that all persons should have equal opportunity. We illustrate this view below.

The equal endowments at point A might be considered equitable if we were starting an economy from scratch, but in reality we always start from some given initial allocation such

---

[23] To understand why such a voluntary exchange might change the equity of the distribution, consider the move from point A to point B. Since the allocations at point A are perfectly equal by definition and at point B Jones's welfare has increased but Smith's welfare is the same, we must conclude that Jones is now better off than Smith. Obviously there must be some point on the BC segment that has the same equity as at point A, but the problem is whether it can be identified in any objective sense. One possible method is to use prices as weights. If the trading were done through a price system using the equilibrium prices, the market values of the endowments and the final consumption bundles would be equal (since no one can spend more than his or her endowment, and anyone spending less would not be maximizing utility). Thus we might define these equilibrium final-consumption bundles as the ones that keep the equity of the allocations identical with those at point A and use the equilibrium prices to evaluate the relative values of *any* allocations in the Edgeworth diagram. The important feature of these prices is that they are the ones that achieve an efficient equilibrium when starting from a perfectly equal allocation of the goods available in the economy.

as that at point D. Let us say that at point D it is obvious that Jones is richer (Jones has both more meat and more tomatoes than Smith). Consider whether your own sense of equity is affected by why we are starting at point D.

Suppose that Smith and Jones have equal abilities, opportunities, knowledge, and luck but that point D is the result of different efforts at production. That is, Jones obtained the initial endowment by working very hard to produce it, whereas Smith was lazy. Then you might think that the distribution at D is perfectly fair and that some allocation on FG reached through voluntary trading is equally fair. Furthermore, you might think that any policies aimed at redistribution toward equality (point A) are inequitable.

Alternatively, suppose you feel that we started at point D because of past discrimination against Smith. Jones was sent to the best agricultural schools, but Smith's family was too poor to afford the tuition and no loans were made available. Or the best schools excluded minorities or women, or there was some other reason for denying this opportunity to Smith that you think is unfair. While both worked equally hard at production, Jones knew all the best ways to produce and Smith did not. In this case, you might think that some re-distribution away from point D and toward point A improves equity. Your sense of the fairest distribution depends on how responsible you think Jones should be for the past discrimination.[24]

These two examples of different principles of equity (equality of outcome and equality of opportunity) are by no means intended to exhaust the list of equity concepts thought relevant to public policy and its analysis. They are intended to illustrate that diverse concepts of equity can be used as standards and that quite different conclusions about the fairness of policies can be reached as a result. They reflect real problems of equity that any society must confront. To be influential, analytic evaluation of equity consequences must be sensitive to the different principles of equity that will be applied by those involved in the policy-making process. Methodology for doing this will be illustrated later in the book in the context of specific cases.

Integrating Equity-Efficiency Evaluation in a Social Welfare Function[S]

Suppose that we are currently at the efficient allocation point G (Figure 3-8) but that the allocations near point A are considered more equitable. Suppose also that some constraints in the economy prevent us from achieving any of the efficient allocations on BC but that point A itself can be achieved.[25] Which of the two is preferable? To decide, a trade-off must be made between efficiency and equity.

---

[24] This example provides another illustration of why allocative changes should not be restricted to those that are Pareto-superior to the starting point.

[25] This approximates the situation when considering programs of income maintenance: Every method for transferring resources to the worst-off members of society causes at least some inefficiency. Income maintenance is discussed in Chapter 4. The inefficiency of taxes, used to finance income maintenance as well as other public expenditures, is discussed in Chapter 12.

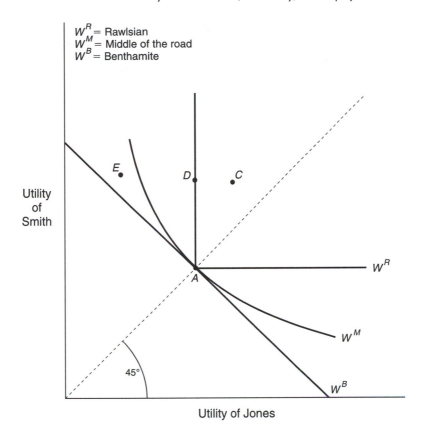

Figure 3-9. Alternative social welfare functions.

Making such a trade-off of course requires a social judgment; it is not a factual matter to be resolved by policy analysis. However, analytic work can clarify the consequences of alternative ways of making the trade-off. One approach for doing so, which we introduce here, rests on the concept of a **social welfare function: a relation between a distribution of utility levels among society's members and a judgment about the overall social satisfaction (the level of social welfare) achieved by that distribution.** Mathematically, we denote such a function by

$$W = W(U^1, U^2, \ldots, U^m)$$

where U^i is the utility level of the ith individual, with $i = 1, 2, \ldots, m$ individuals in the economy.

To clarify the meaning of a social welfare function, consider the Smith-Jones two-person economy. Social welfare is then a function of the utility level of each:

$$W = W(U^S, U^J)$$

Figure 3-9 displays three *social indifference curves* through point A, each representing a different social welfare function. The axes show the utility levels for Smith and Jones;

assume for illustrative purposes that we can measure them in comparable units. The social indifference curves represent social welfare functions with differing ethical choices about how to trade off the aggregate of utilities (used here as a measure of relative efficiency) versus the equality of their distribution (used as a measure of equity). Each curve illustrates a different conception of the set of Smith-Jones utility combinations that yield the same level of social welfare as that at point A.

The line denoted W^B comes from a social welfare function that considers relative efficiency but is indifferent to the degree of equality. The representative social indifference curve is a straight line with a slope of -1. The shape implies that the transfer of units of utility between Smith and Jones (thus holding the aggregate utility level constant) does not affect the level of social welfare, whether or not the transfer increases or decreases the equality of the distribution. Any increase in the aggregate sum of utility improves social welfare by the same amount no matter who receives it. This is sometimes called a *Benthamite social welfare function* after Jeremy Bentham. In 1789 Bentham proposed *maximizing the sum of satisfactions* as a social objective.[26] Mathematically, the Benthamite social welfare function is simply $W = U^S + U^J$. A move from point A to point E, for example, would increase social welfare (lie on a higher social indifference curve, not drawn) by this function.

The curve W^R represents a very egalitarian function. The representative social indifference curve is in the shape of a right angle with its corner on the 45° line. Starting from the equal distribution at point A, social welfare cannot be increased by giving more utility to just one person. The only way to increase social welfare is by raising the utility level of both people (e.g., point C). Starting from any unequal distribution (such as point D), *social welfare can be increased only by raising the utility level of the worst-off person* (Jones).

Sometimes W^R is called a Rawlsian function after the philosopher John Rawls. It was Rawls who suggested that inequalities in a society should be tolerated only to the extent that they improve the welfare of the worst-off person.[27] Mathematically, the *Rawlsian social welfare function* is $W = \min (U^S, U^J)$.[28] Note that a change such as the one from point A to point E improves welfare by the Benthamite function, but decreases it by Rawlsian standards because the minimum utility level, that of the worst-off person, declines.

The curve W^M represents a middle-of-the-road function that lies between the Benthamite and Rawlsian ideals. The social indifference curve has the shape of an ordinary indifference curve, and its changing slope takes on the value of -1 at the point on the 45° line. It implies that, for any given level of aggregate utility, social welfare increases with greater equality.[29] However, a big enough increase in aggregate utility can increase social welfare even if it makes the distribution less equal. The change from point A to point C illustrates

---

[26] Jeremy Bentham, *An Introduction to the Principle of Morals and Legislation* (London: Oxford University Press, 1907).

[27] John Rawls, *A Theory of Justice,* Rev. Ed. (Cambridge: Harvard University Press, 1999).

[28] The function $\min (X_1, X_2, \ldots, X_n)$ has a value equal to the minimum level of any of its arguments $X_1, X_2, \ldots, X_n$. For example, $\min (30, 40) = 30$ and $\min (50, 40) = 40$.

[29] The locus of points with constant aggregate utility is a straight line with slope of -1. The maximum social welfare on this locus is where the social indifference curve is tangent to it, which by construction is on the 45° line.

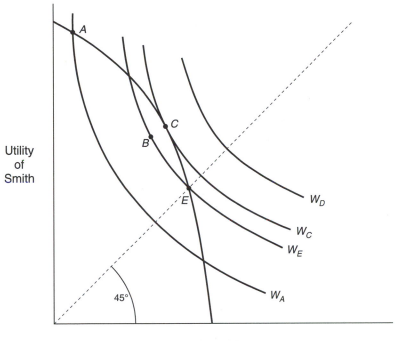

Figure 3-10. Social welfare and the utility-possibilities frontier.

the latter. However, the change from point *A* to point *E* is a social welfare decrease by this function; the increase in aggregate utility is not big enough to offset the reduction in equality.

To see how a social welfare function makes a combined equity-efficiency judgment, let us examine Figure 3-10, which is a graph of a utility-possibilities frontier representing the Pareto-optimal utility levels possible in the economy. Now let us return to the question posed at the beginning of this section: How do we choose an allocation from among them?

In Figure 3-10 we have also drawn some social indifference curves, each representing a different level of social welfare according to one underlying middle-of-the-road welfare function. The level of social welfare rises as we move upward and to the right on the graph. For example, if the economy is at the efficient point *A,* the level of social welfare is W_A. However, the inefficient point *B* is one of greater social welfare than point *A:* this reflects the social importance of the greater equality at *B*. The maximum social welfare that can be achieved is shown as point *C,* where the social indifference curve is just tangent to the utility-possibilities frontier. Higher levels of social welfare, such as W_D, are not feasible with the limited resources available in the economy.

Note that, as drawn, the maximum possible social welfare is not at a point of equality, that is, it is not on the 45° line. This happens even though, other things being equal, the society prefers (by this welfare function) more equality to less. The explanation lies in the shape of the utility-possibilities frontier. For illustrative purposes, we chose one that has

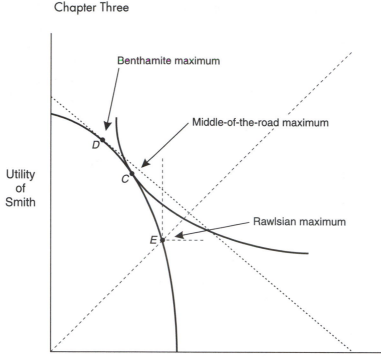

Figure 3-11. Maximum welfare as judged by alternative welfare functions varies in the degree of inequality that results.

this characteristic: With the available resources and the preferences of Smith and Jones, it is easier for the economy to increase Smith's happiness than that of Jones (e.g., Jones may not like meat or tomatoes very much). The best attainable point of equality is the allocation at point *E*, but society considers that the gain in aggregate utility at point *C* more than compensates for the loss in equality.

One final comparison of the three different illustrative social welfare functions is shown in Figure 3-11, which reproduces the utility-possibilities curve from Figure 3-10 and shows the maximum welfare associated with each of the different social welfare functions. The highest social indifference curve attainable for each welfare function is drawn. The middle-of-the road maximum is at point *C*, the same as in Figure 3-10. But the Rawlsian maximum is at point *E*, where the 45° line from the origin crosses the utility-possibilities frontier and thus the utility of Smith equals the utility of Jones.[30] On the other hand, the

---

[30] For any interior point above the 45° line, Jones is the worse-off person and any change that moves to the right within the area is a Rawlsian improvement. The furthest to the right that one can get without crossing the 45° line is point *E*. Similarly, for any interior point below the 45° line, Smith is the worse-off person and any changes that move upward within the area are Rawlsian improvements. The most upward that one can get is point *E*. Therefore, no matter where one starts, point *E* will be the highest attainable welfare by the Rawlsian social welfare function.

Benthamite social welfare function has its maximum at a more unequal distribution of utilities than at point *C,* shown as point *D* on the utility-possibilities frontier. We explain this below.

Since the Benthamite social indifference curve is a straight line with constant slope of −1, its tangency with the utility-possibilities frontier occurs where the slope of the frontier is also −1. We know the slope of the utility-possibilities frontier at point *C* exceeds (is steeper than) −1, since the slope of the middle-of-the-road social indifference curve tangent to the frontier is −1 where it crosses the 45° line and gets steeper along the way to point *C*. Therefore the point on the utility-possibilities frontier that has a slope of −1 must lie on the portion that is flatter than at point *C,* or to its left.[31]

There are important limitations to the use of social welfare functions in policy analysis. One obvious problem is that since utility is neither measurable nor interpersonally comparable, it is not possible to identify empirically the relative satisfaction levels of each individual. However, there are some situations in which the construction of social welfare functions is useful anyway. Typically they are those in which policy affects individuals on the basis of some observable characteristic (e.g., income level). All individuals with the same characteristic are to be treated alike, regardless of their individual preferences (e.g., all pay the same tax). We provide an illustrative example in Chapter 5 as part of the analysis of school finance policies.

A second problem, more conceptual than empirical, is that there is no agreement or consensus on what the "proper" social welfare function is: Each individual in the society may have his or her own view of what is proper. We have already illustrated that there are many possible social welfare functions (e.g., Rawlsian and Benthamite) concerning how society should trade off aggregate utility and equality. But other efficiency and equity concepts are not reflected by those formulations of social welfare, and they deserve attention as well.

For example, note the independence of the social welfare function and the utility-possibilities frontier. In Figure 3-10 it is apparent that the level of social welfare associated with an allocation does not depend on the location of the utility-possibilities frontier (i.e., the social indifference curves are drawn without knowledge of the frontier). But it is only the latter that represents the efficient or Pareto-optimal allocations (corresponding to the contract curve of an Edgeworth diagram). Thus the level of social welfare does not reveal whether there is room for more improvement (i.e., if we are interior to the utility-possibilities frontier). However, knowing whether an alternative is or is not Pareto-optimal is important because it may raise the possibility that a new and superior alternative can be found.

Similarly, the equity concept of equal opportunity is not reflected in the social welfare functions we illustrated. Indeed, it is a practical impossibility to have it otherwise. Knowledge of the utility level outcomes is not enough: One must decide the fairness of the process that

---

[31] The above result depends on the shape of the utility-possibilities frontier, but a similar result of increased inequality compared to the other two social welfare functions would obtain if the frontier were drawn so that it is possible to give Jones far more utility than Smith. The middle-of-the-road function would have its tangency to the right of the Rawlsian maximum, with slope flatter than −1. The portion of the frontier where the slope equals −1 (and thus would contain the tangency to the Benthamite social indifference curve) would have to lie further to the right where the slopes are getting steeper.

determined the starting point as well as the fairness of the processes associated with each way of making a specific change in outcome levels. That is, a change may make Smith better off relative to Jones for quite different reasons. Perhaps, for example, Smith worked harder than Jones and earned an extra reward or Jones was unfairly denied an opportunity that by default then went to Smith. One needs to know both the outcomes and the fairness of the process that explains them in order to incorporate an equal opportunity standard of equity into a social welfare function.

These problems illustrate that despite the appealing neatness of integrating social values in one social welfare function, the approach will not generally substitute for explicit evaluation by the general criteria of efficiency and equity separately. The diversity of specific concepts of efficiency and equity should receive attention. Given the lack of any predetermined social consensus about which of them apply and how to integrate those that do apply, policy analysis can usually best help users reach informed normative conclusions by clearly laying out its predictions and evaluating them by the different normative elements (e.g., efficiency, relative efficiency, equality, equal opportunity). Certainly, nontechnical users will find each of the elements more familiar or at least easier to understand than the concept of a social welfare function. Thus only occasionally will it be useful to combine some of the elements in the form of a social welfare function.

In the following chapters, we will build more thoroughly upon the general concepts introduced here in order to develop skills of application in specific policy contexts.

Summary

Because of the limits on obtainable data, a central task of the economics profession is to develop tools that allow the analyst to infer important consequences accurately and with a minimum of data. This chapter introduces one of these tools, the utility-maximization model of individual decision-making, which is used in many economic policy analyses. The model consists of these assumptions: Each individual has a preference-ordering of possible consumption choices that is consistent, convex, and nonsatiable, and makes choices in accordance with that preference-ordering.

The preference-ordering and choice-making can be represented as an ordinal utility function that the individual acts to maximize. While utility is neither measurable or interpersonally comparable, we can observe and measure an individual's marginal rate of substitution $MRS_{i,j}$—the amount he or she can forgo of one good j in order to obtain an additional unit of another good i and remain just indifferent. The $MRS_{i,j}$ varies with the mixture of goods that the individual consumes—it depends not only on the preference-ordering, but also on the relative abundance or scarcity of each item in the consumer's consumption bundle. We illustrate that utility-maximizing individuals, when subject to a budget constraint, will choose a mix of goods such that the $MRS_{i,j}$ of any two goods i and j that are in the bundle will equal the ratio of their prices P_i/P_j.

The assumptions used in the model are not intended to be literally true; they are intended to yield accurate predictions of many decisions. The analyst always retains discretionary judgment about whether the model works well for the particular decisions a policy might affect. While we will see many different uses of the utility-maximization model as we proceed, our primary use of the model in this chapter is to introduce the important normative concepts of efficiency and equity.

Efficiency, or Pareto optimality, is defined as an allocation of resources from which no person can be made better off without making another person worse off. Equity refers to the relative distribution of well-being among the people in an economy. The use of both concepts in policy analysis involves predicting how policies will affect each individual's well-being, or overall satisfaction, or utility level. In making these evaluative predictions, we typically follow the principle of consumer sovereignty: Each person judges his or her own well-being. On the basis of predictions using this principle, the analyst tries to infer whether existing or proposed policies are efficient and equitable.

We began to explore efficiency and equity concepts in the context of a pure exchange economy populated by utility-maximizing consumers and negligible transaction costs. The principal result is that efficiency (in exchange) requires that all consumers of any two goods in the economy must have the same MRS for those two goods. We illustrated that two individuals in a barter economy, starting from an inefficient allocation, can reach an efficient allocation by the voluntary trading of goods; this happens as a result of each individual attempting to maximize utility and that the resulting trading causes the MRS of each to converge. We also showed that, with a price system, each utility-maximizing individual will equate his or her MRS for any two goods consumed to the ratio of the prices for those two goods. Thus, it may be possible, by having one set of prices that apply to all individuals, to achieve efficiency in a complex economy with many individuals and many goods.

Whether this is desirable depends on whether equity can be simultaneously achieved. By using the Edgeworth box diagram, it becomes clear that an infinite number of efficient allocations are possible; each point on the contract curve is efficient. These efficient allocations differ from one another in equity: The relative well-being of each individual can vary from extremes at which one person has everything and the others nothing to more "balanced" allocations in which the goods are more evenly distributed among individuals. If one can pick any allocation within the Edgeworth box, it is at least theoretically possible to achieve both efficiency and equity of outcomes.

A source of analytic difficulty is that there are no universally agreed upon principles that allow one to draw the inference that one allocation is more equitable than another: Different individuals, with full and identical information about an allocation, may disagree about its "fairness." This becomes apparent when we recognize that an economy is always currently at some particular point in the Edgeworth box and that a policy change is equivalent to a proposal to move from that point to another one. What is considered fair may depend not only on where the initial location is but also on why it is the initial location; for example, to what extent does it represent a past characterized by "just rewards" or plain luck or unfair discrimination? We illustrated how two different principles of equity, equality of outcomes and equal opportunity, can lead to conflicting judgments about the fairness of a change.

The definition of efficiency as Pareto optimality is not very controversial because the set of efficient allocations spans a very wide distributional range and thus causes little conflict with notions of equitable allocations. However, public policy changes inevitably involve making some people better off and others worse off. Measures of relative efficiency and the construction of social welfare functions are analytic techniques that have been developed to help clarify some normative consequences of those changes, but they do involve equity judgments at some level. Although there may be some policy issues in which equity does not play a major role in the analysis, the analyst must be sensitive to equity's potential importance as a social goal and its impact on political feasibility.

Exercises

3-1 In a two-person, two-good pure exchange economy, Adam has an initial endowment of 15 flawless 1-caret diamonds ($D_A = 15$) and 5 gallons of drinking water ($W_A = 5$). Beth has no diamonds ($D_B = 0$) but 20 gallons of drinking water ($W_B = 20$).

a In explaining his preferences, Adam says that he prefers ($D_A = 5$, $W_A = 10$) to his initial endowment. He also says that he is indifferent to ($D_A = 5$, $W_A = 10$) and ($D_A = 12$, $W_A = 5$). Are these preferences consistent or inconsistent with the standard assumptions of the utility-maximization model?

b What are the dimensions of the Edgeworth box that represents the possible allocations in this economy? Draw it.

c Show the point on the Edgeworth box that represents the initial endowments. Is it possible for these initial endowments to be an efficient allocation?

3-2 Consider an economy of two people who consume just two goods X and Y. Person 1 has an endowment of $X_1 = 30$ and $Y_1 = 120$. Person 2 has an endowment of $X_2 = 180$ and $Y_2 = 90$. Their utility functions are, respectively,

$$U_1 = X_1 Y_1 \quad \text{and} \quad U_2 = X_2 Y_2$$

a Graph the Edgeworth box corresponding to this economy.

b What are the equations for the indifference curves of persons 1 and 2 that go through the initial endowments? Plot the curves. [*Hint:* How does total utility change along an indifference curve?]

c Shade in the locus of points that are Pareto-superior to the initial endowments.

d What is the equation of the contract curve in this economy? Graph it. [*Hint:* Recall that a marginal rate of substitution can be expressed as a ratio of marginal utilities, and that the marginal utility of a good is the increase in the utility level caused by a one-unit increase of that good.] (Answer: $Y_1 = X_1$.)

e Identify the boundaries of points on the contract curve that are Pareto-superior to the initial endowments. (Answer: $X_1 = Y_1 = 60$, $X_1 = Y_1 = 82.7$.)

f○ Suppose a secretary of the market announces that all trading must take place at $P_X = \$1$ and $P_Y = \$2$. Furthermore, the secretary takes away each person's initial endowment and replaces it with its cash value. The secretary instructs each person to order the quantities of X and Y that maximize utility subject to the budget constraint: (1) What quantities will persons 1 and 2 order? Can the secretary fill these orders with the endowments collected? (Answer: No.) (2) Go through the same exercise with $P_X = \$2$ and explain why the outcome is feasible and efficient.

APPENDIX

CALCULUS MODELS OF CONSUMER EXCHANGE°

It is useful to see the exchange principles covered so far in a mathematical form. Actual empirical application often involves mathematics, so that the ability to consume, criticize, and conduct analysis requires some facility with mathematical procedures. However, some prior background in calculus is necessary in order to understand the mathematical material presented.[32]

Let $U(X_1, X_2, \ldots, X_n)$ represent a utility function for a consumer in an economy with n goods. For mathematical ease, we assume that this function is smooth and continuous and that the goods are infinitely divisible. The assumption that more is better (strong monotonicity) can be expressed as follows:

$$\frac{\partial U}{\partial X_i} > 0 \quad \text{for all } i$$

The left-hand term is a partial derivative. It represents the marginal utility from a small increment of good X_i to the bundle, holding all the other Xs constant. The expression says that the marginal utility of this increment is positive or, equivalently, that total utility increases as X_i consumption becomes greater.

We have defined an indifference set (a curve if there are only two goods and a surface if there are more than two goods) as the locus of all consumption bundles that provide the consumer with the same level of utility. If $\bar{U}$ represents some constant level of utility, then as the goods $X_1, X_2, \ldots, X_n$ change along the $\bar{U}$ indifference surface, it must always be true that

$$\bar{U} = U(X_1, X_2, \ldots, X_n)$$

As the Xs are varied slightly, the total differential of the utility function tells us by how much utility changes. If we consider only changes in the Xs along an indifference surface,

---

[32] Basic courses in calculus that cover derivatives, partial derivatives, and techniques of maximization and minimization are usually sufficient background for understanding the optional material presented in this book. Two compact expositions of the most relevant aspects of calculus for economics are W. Baumol, *Economic Theory and Operations Analysis,* 4th Ed. (Englewood Cliffs, N.J.: Prentice-Hall, Inc., 1977), Chapters 1–4, pp. 1–71, and W. Nicholson, *Microeconomic Theory,* 7th Ed. (Hinsdale, Ill.: The Dryden Press, 1998), Chapter 2, pp. 23–65.

then total utility does not change at all. Suppose the only changes we consider are of X_1 and X_2, while all the other Xs are being held constant. Then as we move along an indifference curve,

$$d\bar{U} = 0 = \frac{\partial U}{\partial X_1} \, dX_1 + \frac{\partial U}{\partial X_2} \, dX_2$$

or

$$-\frac{dX_1}{dX_2}\bigg|_{U=\bar{U}} = \frac{\partial U/\partial X_2}{\partial U/\partial X_1}$$

The term on the left-hand side of this equation is simply the negative of the slope of the indifference curve; we have defined it as the marginal rate of substitution MRS_{X_2, X_1}. The term on the right-hand side is the ratio of the marginal utilities for each good. Therefore, the MRS_{X_i, X_j} at any point can be thought of as the ratio of the marginal utilities $\mathrm{MU}_{X_i}/\mathrm{MU}_{X_j}$.

Efficiency requires that each consumer of two goods have the same MRS for the two goods. Here we wish to show that this condition can be mathematically derived.

Consider Smith and Jones, who have utility functions for meat and tomatoes $U^S(M_s, T_s)$ and $U^J(M_J, T_J)$. Let $\bar{M}$ be the total amount of meat in the economy and $\bar{T}$ be the total amount of tomatoes. We will be efficient (on the contract curve) if, for any given utility level $\bar{U}^S$ of Smith, Jones is getting the maximum possible utility. To achieve this maximum, we are free to allocate the available goods any way we want to between Smith and Jones, as long as we keep Smith at $\bar{U}^S$. We will find this maximum mathematically and show that the equations that identify it also imply that Smith and Jones must have the identical MRS.

Note that, in the two-person economy, knowledge of Jones's consumption of one good allows us to infer Smith's consumption of that good; for example, $M_S = \bar{M} - M_J$. Thus we know that an increase in Jones's meat consumption (and similarly for tomatoes) causes the following change in Smith's:

$$\frac{\partial M_S}{\partial M_J} = \frac{\partial (\bar{M} - M_J)}{\partial M_J} = -1$$

We use this fact in the derivation of the efficiency proposition below.

The mathematical problem is to choose the levels of two variables, meat and tomato consumption, that maximize the utility level of Jones, which we denote as follows:

$$\max_{M_J, \, T_J} U^J(M_J, \, T_J)$$

With no other constraints and the assumption of nonsatiation, the solution to the problem is to choose infinite amounts of meat and tomatoes. But, of course, the real problem is to maximize subject to the constraints that total real resources are limited to $\bar{M}$ and $\bar{T}$ and that Smith must get enough of those resources to yield a utility level of $\bar{U}^S$:

$$\bar{U}^S = U^S(M_S, \, T_S)$$

The total resource constraints can be incorporated directly into the above equation by substituting for M_S and T_S as follows:

$$M_S = \bar{M} - M_J \quad T_S = \bar{T} - T_J$$

Then all these constraints can be represented in one equation:

$$\bar{U}^S = U^S [(\bar{M} - M_J), (\bar{T} - T_J)]$$

To solve the maximization problem with a constraint, we use the technique of Lagrange multipliers. We formulate the Lagrange expression $L(M_J, T_J, \lambda)$:

$$L(M_J, T_J, \lambda) = U^J(M_J, T_J) + \lambda\{\bar{U}^S - U^S [(\bar{M} - M_J), (\bar{T} - T_J)]\}$$

The first term on the right is simply the function we wish to maximize. The second term always consists of λ, the Lagrange multiplier, multiplied by the constraint in its implicit form.[33] Note that, when the constraint holds, the second term is zero and the value of L equals the value of U^J. Thus from among the (M_J, T_J) combinations that satisfy the constraint, the one that maximizes U^J will also maximize L.

In addition to the two variables that we started with, M_J and T_J, we make λ a third variable. How do we find the values of the variables that maximize the original function subject to the constraint? The solution requires taking the partial derivatives of the Lagrange expression with respect to all three variables, equating each to zero (thus forming one equation for each unknown variable), and solving the equations simultaneously.[34] We do

---

[33] The implicit form of an equation is found by rewriting the equation so that zero is on one side of it. If we have a constraint that says $F(X, Y) = Z$, we can always rewrite the equation as

$$Z - F(X, Y) = 0$$

and define the implicit function $G(X, Y)$:

$$G(X, Y) = Z - F(X, Y)$$

Then the constraint in its implicit form is

$$G(X, Y) = 0$$

This is mathematically equivalent to the original expression $F(X, Y) = Z$. That is, $G(X, Y) = 0$ if and only if $F(X, Y) = Z$.

[34] We try to explain this intuitively. Imagine a hill in front of you. Your object is to maximize your altitude, and the variable is the number of (uniform) steps you walk in a straight line. Naturally, you walk in a line that goes over the top of the hill. As long as your altitude increases with an additional step, you will choose to take it. This is like saying the derivative of altitude with respect to steps is positive, and it characterizes each step up the hill. If you go too far, the altitude will decrease with an additional step: the derivative will be negative and you will be descending the hill. If the altitude is increasing as you go up, and decreasing as you go down, it must be neither increasing nor decreasing exactly at the top. Thus at the maximum, the derivative is zero.

This extends to the many-variable case, in which the variables might represent steps in specific directions. Exactly at the top of the hill, the partial derivative of altitude with respect to a step in *each* direction must be zero. This analogy is intended to suggest why the maximum utility above can be identified by finding the points where all the partial derivatives equal zero.

Technically, we have only discussed the first-order or necessary conditions; they identify the interior critical points of the Lagrange expression. However, not all critical points are maxima; all the partial derivatives are zero at function minima also, for example. Most functions we use will only have the one critical point we seek. Some

the first two parts below, making use of the chain rule in taking the partial derivatives[35]:

$$\frac{\partial L}{\partial M_J} = \frac{\partial U^J}{\partial M_J} - \lambda \frac{\partial U^S}{\partial (\bar{M} - M_J)} \frac{\partial (\bar{M} - M_J)}{\partial M_J} = 0 \tag{i}$$

$$\frac{\partial L}{\partial T_J} = \frac{\partial U^J}{\partial T_J} - \lambda \frac{\partial U^S}{\partial (\bar{T} - T_J)} \frac{\partial (\bar{T} - T_J)}{\partial T_J} = 0 \tag{ii}$$

$$\frac{\partial L}{\partial \lambda} = \bar{U}^S - U^S[(\bar{M} - M_J), (\bar{T} - T_J)] = 0 \tag{iii}$$

Note that equation (iii) requires that the constraint be satisfied, or that Smith end up with a utility level of $\bar{U}^S$. This always happens with the Lagrange method; the form in which the constraint enters the Lagrange expression ensures it. Thus, when the equations are solved simultaneously, the value of $L(M_J, T_J, \lambda)$ will equal $U^J(M_J, T_J)$.

We can think of equation (iii) in terms of the Edgeworth box. It requires that the solution be one of the points on the indifference curve along which Smith has utility level $\bar{U}^S$. With this equation, the first two equations will identify the point on the indifference curve that maximizes the utility of Jones. To see this, recall that $M_S = \bar{M} - M_J$, $T_S = \bar{T} - T_J$ and that we pointed out earlier that

$$\frac{\partial (\bar{M} - M_J)}{\partial M_J} = \frac{\partial (\bar{T} - T_J)}{\partial T_J} = -1$$

Then equations (i) and (ii) can be simplified as follows:

$$\frac{\partial L}{\partial M_J} = \frac{\partial U^J}{\partial M_J} + \lambda \frac{\partial U^S}{\partial M_S} = 0 \tag{i$'$}$$

$$\frac{\partial L}{\partial T_J} = \frac{\partial U^J}{\partial T_J} + \lambda \frac{\partial U^S}{\partial T_S} = 0 \tag{ii$'$}$$

Subtract the terms with λ in them from both sides of each equation and then divide (i$'$) by (ii$'$):

$$\frac{\partial U^J / \partial M_J}{\partial U^J / \partial T_J} = \frac{-\lambda (\partial U^S / \partial M_S)}{-\lambda (\partial U^S / \partial T_S)} = \frac{\partial U^S / \partial M_S}{\partial U^S / \partial T_S}$$

---

functions, however, have both maxima and minima (as if, in our analogy, there were a valley between the start of our straight walk and the top of the hill). The second-order conditions to ensure that the identified values of M_J and T_J maximize L are more complicated. For a review of the second-order conditions, see H. Varian, *Microeconomic Analysis,* 3rd Ed. (New York: W. W. Norton & Company, 1992), Chapter 27.

   [35] The chain rule for derivatives is this: If $Z = G(Y)$ and $Y = F(X)$, then

$$\frac{dZ}{dX} = \frac{dz}{dY} \frac{dy}{dX}$$

The same rule applies for partial derivatives when $G(\ )$ and $F(\ )$ are functions of variables in addition to Y and X. In the economic problem above, the function $U^S(\ )$ plays the role of $G(\ )$ and the functions $(\bar{M} - M_J)$ and $(\bar{T} - T_J)$ play the role of $F(\ )$ in equations (i) and (ii), respectively.

or

$$\text{MRS}^J_{M,T} = \text{MRS}^S_{M,T}$$

That is, the first two equations require that Smith and Jones have the same MRS, or that their indifference curves be tangent. This is precisely the efficiency condition we sought to derive. We can also think of the first two equations as identifying the contract curve, and then, with them, the third equation identifies the point on the contract curve where Smith has utility level $\bar{U}^S$.

We also showed in the text that when a pricing system is used, each consumer will allocate his or her budget in such a way that the MRS of any two goods X_i and X_j equals the price ratio of those two goods P_i/P_j. This can be seen mathematically as follows, letting B represent the consumer's total budget to be allocated.[36] The consumer wants to choose goods $X_1, X_2, \ldots, X_n$ that maximize utility subject to the following budget constraint:

$$B = P_1 X_1 + P_2 X_2 + \ldots + P_n X_n$$

We formulate the Lagrange expression with $n + 1$ variables λ and $X_1, X_2, \ldots, X_n$:

$$L = U(X_1, X_2, \ldots, X_n) + \lambda(B - P_1 X_1 - P_2 X_2 - \ldots - P_n X_n)$$

To find the Xs that maximize utility, all of the $n + 1$ partial derivative equations must be formed. Taking only the ith and jth of these equations for illustrative purposes, we have

$$\frac{\partial L}{\partial X_i} = \frac{\partial U}{\partial X_i} - \lambda P_i = 0 \quad \text{or} \quad \frac{\partial U}{\partial X_i} = \lambda P_i \qquad (i)$$

$$\frac{\partial L}{\partial X_j} = \frac{\partial U}{\partial X_j} - \lambda P_j = 0 \quad \text{or} \quad \frac{\partial U}{\partial X_j} = \lambda P_j \qquad (j)$$

and upon dividing the top equation by the bottom one we see that

$$\frac{\partial U/\partial X_i}{\partial U/\partial X_j} = \frac{P_i}{P_j}$$

We have not yet noted any significance in the value of λ that comes from solving constrained maximization problems. However, from the above equations we can see that

$$\lambda = \frac{\partial U/\partial X_i}{P_i} \quad \text{for all } i = 1, 2, \ldots, n$$

This can be interpreted approximately as follows:

$$\lambda = \frac{\text{Marginal utility per unit of } X_i}{\text{Dollars per unit of } X_i} = \text{Marginal utility per dollar}$$

---

[36] If a consumer starts with an initial endowment of $X_1^E, X_2^E, \ldots, X_n^E$ then the total budget is

$$B = \sum_{i=1}^{n} P_i X_i^E$$

That is, λ can be interpreted as the amount of marginal utility this consumer would receive from increasing the budget constraint by one extra dollar. In general, the value of λ signifies the marginal benefit in terms of the objective (utility in the example) of relaxing the constraint by one increment (increasing the budget by $1.00 in the example). This is sometimes referred to as the *shadow price* of the resource causing the constraint, and it can be a useful way to estimate the value of that resource to its user.

A numerical example may help clarify the mechanics of constrained maximization. Suppose a consumer has a utility function $U = M \cdot T$. Suppose also that the budget constraint is $100, $P_M = \$5.00$ per pound, and $P_T = \$1.00$ per pound. How many pounds of meat and tomatoes should this consumer buy in order to maximize utility? The consumer wants to maximize $M \cdot T$, subject to $100 = 5.00M + 1.00T$. We formulate the Lagrange expression $L(M, T, \lambda)$:

$$L = M \cdot T + \lambda(100 - 5.00M - 1.00T)$$

Taking the partial derivatives and setting each to zero, we have

$$\frac{\partial L}{\partial M} = T - 5.00\lambda = 0 \quad \text{or} \quad T = 5.00\lambda \tag{i}$$

$$\frac{\partial L}{\partial T} = M - 1.00\lambda = 0 \quad \text{or} \quad M = 1.00\lambda \tag{ii}$$

$$\frac{\partial L}{\partial \lambda} = 100 - 5.00M - 1.00T = 0 \tag{iii}$$

On substituting 5λ for T and λ for M in equation (iii), we get

$$100 - 5.00\lambda - 5.00 = 0$$

from which

$$\lambda = 10 \quad M = 10$$

$$T = 50 \quad U = 500$$

That is, the consumer achieves the maximum utility of 500 by purchasing 10 pounds of meat and 50 pounds of tomatoes. According to this solution, the shadow price of the budget is 10 utils. This means that increasing the budget by $1.00 would allow the consumer to gain approximately 10 more utils, or achieve a utility level of 510. Let us check this. Suppose the budget is $101 and we maximize utility according to this constraint. Equations (i) and (ii) are unaffected, so we can make the same substitution in the new equation (iii):

$$101 - 5.00\lambda - 5.00 = 0$$

from which

$$\lambda = 10.1 \quad M = 10.1$$

$$T = 50.5 \quad U = 510.05$$

As we can see, the utility level has indeed increased by approximately 10 utils. As one last check on our original solution, it should be that

$$\text{MRS}_{M,T} = \frac{P_M}{P_T} = 5$$

From the utility function,

$$\frac{\partial U}{\partial M} = T = 50$$

$$\frac{\partial U}{\partial T} = M = 10$$

and therefore

$$\text{MRS}_{M,T} = \frac{\partial U/\partial M}{\partial U/\partial T} = 5$$

PART TWO

USING MODELS OF INDIVIDUAL CHOICE-MAKING
IN POLICY ANALYSIS

CHAPTER FOUR

THE SPECIFICATION OF INDIVIDUAL CHOICE MODELS
FOR THE ANALYSIS OF WELFARE PROGRAMS

IN THE INTRODUCTORY chapters we reviewed general predictive and evaluative aspects of microeconomic modeling. Now we wish to be specific. In this chapter, we develop skills of model specification useful for policy applications. The problems posed can be analyzed with models of individual consumer choice. The series of problems—chosen to be similar in some ways but different in others—is intended to create a facility with modeling that carries over to the analysis of new problems in new settings. The modeling emphasizes the role of the budget constraint and predictions based upon income and substitution effects. We also show how utility-maximizing behavior leads to consumer demand curves as well as labor supply curves.

All the analyses in this chapter are drawn from one policy context: government programs that provide means-tested welfare grants to individual families or households. Welfare assistance is an important function of governments at all levels. Its extent depends in part on the amount of poverty in the economy and in part on how the society responds to it. Some simple statistics can convey the magnitude of this subject.

In 1998 over 34 million Americans, almost 13 percent of the population, had incomes (excluding welfare assistance) below the official poverty level. In 1960 by contrast, almost 40 million were poor representing about 22 percent of the population. Thus, over this 38-year period, there was a reduction in the number and proportion of the poor population. However, progress in the reduction came to a halt in 1973, when approximately 11 percent were poor. The proportion did not change much during the mid-to-late 1970s, but increased to 14–15 percent for most of the 1980s and early 1990s. The population in poverty reached a peak of 39 million people in 1993 (15.1 percent of the population), and then declined slightly from 1993 to 1998. The exact causes of all of these changes are not yet well understood, but it is clear that some government programs to reduce poverty have had important effects.[1]

There is general consensus that great progress in reducing poverty within the *elderly* population has been made, largely through programs such as Social Security and Medicare that are not means-tested. There is also consensus, unfortunately, that *little progress has been made in reducing poverty among the nonelderly population.* The programs analyzed in this chapter focus largely on this latter group, and eligibility for them is restricted by means-testing. In 1998, federal expenditures on the major means-tested transfer programs came to $277 billion, and the states added $114 billion.[2] However, according to one study, the boost from all U.S. welfare programs is only enough to remove about 20 percent of the nonelderly poor from poverty status.[3] With so many resources expended, and so large a poverty problem remaining, it is clearly worthwhile to try and make every dollar spent be as effective as possible.

The skills developed here can be used to make a contribution to that goal. Throughout this chapter, we focus primarily on how to spend a given number of welfare dollars efficiently. We focus on the issue of policy design, and study features of particular designs that determine how well the policy works. Rather than presenting one model, we emphasize comparison among alternative models.

Each of the analyses presented involves thinking about different elements of *consumer choice* models and how to put them together. The elements include the nature of the constraints that limit an individual's utility and to some extent the nature of the utility function itself. We consider primarily various alterations in the budget constraints of welfare recipients owing to public policies, but also alterations in the form of the utility function in the model. We use these different specifications to make predictions about the responses of individuals to the policies and to evaluate the efficiency of the predicted responses.

We begin with a standard analysis that demonstrates that transfers in kind are inefficient. Then the real work of policy analysis begins. Actual policy designs typically include features not in the standard model, and it is important to understand how their inclusion changes the analysis. In order to extend our ability to analyze more features with more precision, we first discuss utility-maximizing responses to income and price changes known as *income and substitution effects.* Then we adapt the standard model to incorporate choice restrictions in the food stamp and public housing programs and examine the changes in predicted responses and their efficiency. Similarly, we review the standard microeconomics of *the labor-leisure*

---

[1] For a discussion of recent changes, which cautions that it is difficult to separate the effect of welfare reforms from the strong growth of the economy, see Rebecca Blank, "Fighting Poverty: Lessons from Recent U.S. History," *Journal of Economic Perspectives, 14,* No. 2, Spring 2000, pp. 3–19.

[2] Federal assistance consisted of 41 percent on medical benefits such as Medicaid, 27 percent on cash assistance such as the Earned Income Tax Credit and Supplemental Security Income, 12 percent on food benefits such as the Food Stamp Program, 10 percent on housing benefits, and lesser percentages for education, other social services, and energy aid.

[3] See Isabel V. Sawhill, "Poverty in the U.S.: Why Is It So Persistent?," *Journal of Economic Literature, 26,* No. 3, September 1988, pp. 1073–1119.

Table 4-1
Federal Expenditure for Selected Welfare Programs, 1989–1998 (Billions of 1998 Dollars)

Fiscal year	Food benefits	Housing benefits	Cash aid
1989	27,410	20,950	43,628
1990	29,803	21,909	45,502
1991	33,545	22,712	50,634
1992	38,142	25,486	56,635
1993	39,266	27,051	60,245
1994	39,739	26,574	69,774
1995	39,365	26,689	72,662
1996	38,622	26,497	72,758
1997	35,927	26,853	72,971
1998	33,451	26,897	73,872

Source: *2000 Green Book,* Committee on Ways and Means, U.S. House of Representatives, October 6, 2000, Table K-2, p. 1398.

choice to explain labor supply. Then we examine the relationship between welfare programs and work incentives, including aspects of the design of a cash assistance program—the Earned Income Tax Credit.

Standard Argument: In-Kind Welfare Transfers Are Inefficient

In the U.S. economy all levels of government are involved in providing welfare payments (through a variety of programs) to eligible low-income persons. These payments are transfers in the sense that they take purchasing power away from taxpayers and transfer it to welfare recipients. Some of the programs, such as the Earned Income Tax Credit and those supported by Temporary Assistance to Needy Families (TANF) grants, provide cash payments; other programs, such as food stamps, Medicaid, and housing allowances, provide transfers in kind (i.e., transfers that can be used only for the purchase of specific goods).[4] During the 10 years from 1989 to 1998, expenditures on the major means-tested programs shown in Table 4-1 rose 46 percent in real terms, and the in-kind expenditures for food and housing assistance exceeded the cash assistance until 1994.[5] In 2000, an average of 17 million low-income individuals (just over 6 percent of the population) participated in the Food Stamp Program each month.[6] Clearly the in-kind programs represent a very substantial

[4] The 1996 legislation ended the federal Aid to Families with Dependent Children and replaced it with state-run programs funded partially by federal block grants. While the states were allowed great discretion over the design of their programs, the federal legislation did mandate firm time limits on the time a family could be on welfare.

[5] The phrase "real dollars" means that the nominal number of dollars is adjusted to remove the effects of inflation. We review these procedures in Chapter 8.

[6] Food Stamp Program participation rates are available on the website of the Food and Nutrition Service of the U.S. Department of Agriculture at http://www.fns.usda.gov/pd/fssummar.htm.

portion of the federal response to poverty. Yet the conventional wisdom among economists has always been that transfers of this type are inefficient.

The proof of this proposition usually follows one of two closely related patterns: (1) For a given number of tax dollars to be transferred to the poor, the utility level of recipients will be higher if the transfers are in cash rather than in kind, or (2) to achieve given utility level increases among the recipients, fewer taxpayer dollars will be required if the transfers are in cash rather than in kind. Either argument suffices to demonstrate the inefficiency of in-kind transfers, since each shows the possibility of making one group better off with all others no worse off. We will demonstrate the proof of this by using the second of the two patterns.

In Figure 4-1a, let the line *AB* represent the budget constraint of a low-income individual who has $400 per month in income. The vertical and horizontal axes are each to represent quantities of a particular good. But to represent consumer possibilities properly on the diagram, all available spending choices must be shown. The "meat" and "tomato" axes used in the prior chapter are not appropriate if there are other goods such as clothing and oranges that the consumer could also choose. Thus the axes have to be defined carefully to divide all possible goods into one of two exhaustive categories, chosen to focus on the trade-off of concern to us.

In this case, let us say that we are interested in the trade-off between "food" (the horizontal axis) and "all other goods" (the vertical axis). We assume the consumer will make utility-maximizing choices across the two categories as well as within each and that we can think of the quantity units on each axis as $1 worth of "food" and $1 worth of "all other goods."[7] With these definitions, $OA = OB = \$400$. Recall that the slope of a budget constraint is equal to minus the ratio of the prices of the goods on each axis. In this special example, the "price" of an additional unit of each category is $1 so the slope of *AB* is -1.

Now suppose we introduce a food stamp program that allows eligible recipients to buy for their own use any quantity they wish of $1 stamps at a price of $0.50 per stamp. Grocers must accept the food stamps at face value for food purchases, and the government gives the grocer cash reimbursement for the stamps collected. From the individual's perspective, this changes the budget constraint from *AB* to *AC,* where point *C* represents $800 worth of food. That is, the consumer eligible for food stamps could take the whole budget, buy food stamps with it, and consume $OC = \$800$ worth of food—exactly twice as much as before. However, if the consumer buys only other things, the maximum that can be purchased is $OA = \$400$ worth, as before. Thus, the program, from the perspective of the eligible consumer, is equivalent to a price reduction for food (as if there is a sale in all participating

---

[7] Formally, the situation that allows us to treat these two aggregates of goods as if each were a single identifiable commodity is referred to as "Hicksian separability." This situation applies when there are no relative price changes within each group. The only price changes allowed are those that affect the price of each good within a category proportionately the same. As long as the individual food items included in the food category are all covered by food stamps, our analysis will meet the requirement for Hicksian separability. For a more technical discussion of separability, see Hal. R. Varian, *Microeconomic Analysis,* 3rd Ed. (New York: W. W. Norton & Company, Inc., 1992), pp. 147–150.

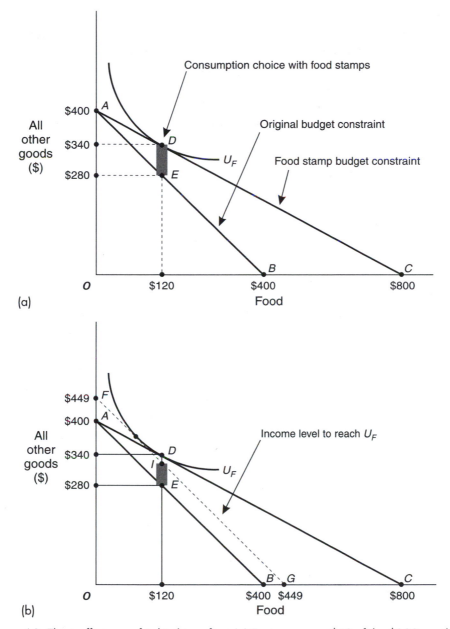

Figure 4-1. The inefficiency of in-kind transfers: (a) Taxpayers pay $60 of the $120 worth of food stamps used. (b) The $60 food stamp subsidy is like a $49 income supplement to this consumer.

food stores equal to one-half off the marked prices). The slope of the budget constraint changes from -1 to $-\frac{1}{2}$.

To maximize utility, let us say the consumer chooses the quantities shown at D, where an indifference curve is just tangent to the new budget constraint. The consumer is shown as receiving \$120 worth of food and \$340 worth of all other goods. In this example, the consumer pays \$60 for this food and the government pays the other \$60. This amount is represented on the diagram by the shaded line segment DE: the difference between the \$340 left for all other goods under the food stamp program and the \$280 that would be left after buying the same food at ordinary market prices. In short, taxpayers pay \$60 to bring this consumer to the indifference curve U_F.

To prove that this is inefficient, we must show that it is possible to make someone better off and no one worse off. Let us ask how many taxpayer dollars it would take to bring the consumer to utility level U_F with a cash welfare grant. We illustrate this in Figure 4-1b. With this type of grant, the recipient does not face any price changes. The slope of the budget constraint remains at the original slope of AB, but it is "pushed out" until it reaches FG, where it becomes just tangent to U_F. FA is the (unknown) dollar amount of the cash grant.

Now we will show that FA, while unknown, is less than \$60. First note that $IE = FA$ (because the vertical distance between two parallel lines is constant). On the diagram, it is clear that IE is less than DE (= \$60). But why does it come out this way? Note that the budget constraint FG, with slope determined by market prices, is steeper than the food stamp constraint AC. All points on U_F with steeper slopes than AC lie to the left of D; therefore, the tangency with FG occurs to the left of D. But then FG must go *through* the line segment DE—if it crossed above D, it would violate the tangency condition. This completes the proof: Since a cash welfare program could achieve U_F at a lower cost to taxpayers than food stamps, the food stamp program is inefficient.

It is useful to note a few characteristics of this result. First, it causes the individual to consume more food and less of other things compared to the lower-cost cash welfare program yielding the same utility. Second, we know the food stamp recipient is indifferent to a cash grant of IE or a food stamp subsidy costing the taxpayer DE. Therefore, we can say that the recipient values each taxpayer dollar spent on food stamps at IE/DE cents, or that the waste per taxpayer dollar spent on food stamps is $100 - IE/DE$ cents, or DI/DE cents. According to one study conducted in the early 1970s (before certain changes in the program discussed later), recipients on average valued each \$1 of food stamp subsidy at \$0.82.[8] Applying this figure to our diagram, we see that a cash grant of approximately \$49 would make the consumer just as well off as the \$60 food stamp subsidy.

The basic result of inefficiency should not be very surprising. Consider the MRS of food for "everything else." The recipient chooses a consumption point such that the MRS equals minus the slope of AC. But every consumer not eligible for the program chooses an MRS

[8] See K. Clarkson, *Food Stamps and Nutrition,* Evaluative Studies No. 18 (Washington D.C.: The American Enterprise Institute for Public Policy Research, 1975). One reviewer of this study argues that this waste estimate is exaggerated because of failure to measure recipient income correctly. See J. Barmack, "The Case Against In-Kind Transfers: The Food Stamp Program," *Policy Analysis, 3,* No. 4, Fall 1977, pp. 509–530.

equal to the ratio of the prices in the market, or minus the slope of *AB*. Therefore, the condition for exchange efficiency is violated, and we know there is room for a deal. The proof above simply illustrates one possible deal that would make some people (taxpayers) better off and all other people (food stamp eligibles) no worse off. The cash welfare program leaves all consumers (taxpayers and welfare recipients) facing the same market prices and thus, under the assumption of utility-maximizing behavior, leaves no room for a deal. By this reasoning, all in-kind welfare programs that cause recipients and nonrecipients to face different prices for the same good are inefficient.

Responses to Income and Price Changes

In order to expand our analytic ability, we examine an additional set of inferences that one can draw based upon utility-maximizing behavior and some modest empirical information.[9] These inferences concern an individual's responses to changes in prices and budget levels and are referred to as *income and substitution effects.*

Response to Income Changes

Let us refer informally to the budget level as "income."[10] In Figure 4-2a we show an individual's utility-maximizing choice for each of several different budget constraints representing different income levels. The constraints differ only in the total budget size; the identical slopes reflect the assumption that prices are constant. **The locus of the utility-maximizing choices associated with each possible budget level is referred to as the income-expansion path.**

For every possible income or budget level (at the given prices), we ask what quantity of the good *X* the individual would purchase. In Figure 4-2b that relation, called an **Engel curve,** is drawn.[11] The horizontal axis shows each possible income (or budget) level; the vertical axis measures quantity of *X;* and the curve shows **the quantity of *X* that would be purchased at each possible budget constraint or income level.** The one illustrated slopes upward and is for **a normal good: as income increases, the individual increases the quantity of the good purchased.** Some goods, such as spaghetti and potatoes, may have downward-sloping Engel curves (at least over a broad range of budget levels). These are called **inferior goods: the individual buys less of them as income increases.**

Note that a good that is normal for one individual could be inferior for another; it is simply a matter of individual tastes. Nevertheless, empirical observation reveals that some

---

[9] These are explained without calculus. A brief appendix at the end of the chapter contains the calculus version and explains the Slutsky equation for the income and substitution effects of a price change.

[10] Later in the text we shall consider more fully the determinants of an individual's budget constraint. If there were no borrowing, lending, or saving, then the level of an individual's budget constraint for a given period would equal that individual's income in the period (including net gifts and bequests). However, the existence of opportunities to save, borrow, or lend makes the determination of actual budget constraints more complicated.

[11] Sometimes it is more convenient to define the vertical axis as $P_X X$, the expenditure on *X*. This relation is called the Engel-expenditure curve.

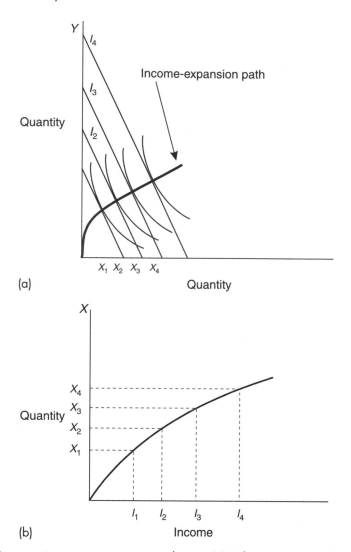

(a)

(b)

Figure 4-2. Consumption response to income change: (a) Utility-maximizing choices. (b) Engel curve.

goods are treated as normal by most people, and others are generally treated as inferior. This modest knowledge can be important in predicting the responses to policy changes.

In order to give a more precise measure to the sensitivity of X consumption to changes in income (holding all other factors constant), we introduce the important notion of an elasticity. **The elasticity of one variable X with respect to another variable Z, denoted $\varepsilon_{X,Z}$, is defined as the percentage change in X that occurs in response to a 1 percent change in Z.** In mathematical terms, we can write this as

$$\varepsilon_{X,Z} = \frac{\Delta X/X}{\Delta Z/Z}$$

where Δ means "the change in" and thus, for example, the numerator $\Delta X/X$ is the percentage change in X. This expression is often rewritten in an equivalent way[12]:

$$\varepsilon_{X,Z} = \frac{\Delta X}{\Delta Z}\frac{Z}{X}$$

Thus the elasticity of X with respect to income I is

$$\varepsilon_{X,I} = \frac{\Delta X}{\Delta I}\frac{I}{X}$$

The properties of normality and inferiority can then be defined in terms of the income elasticity: *a normal good is one whose income elasticity is positive, and an inferior good is one whose income elasticity is negative.*

Among normal goods, sometimes distinctions are made between *necessities* and *luxuries*. **A necessity is a normal good whose income elasticity is less than 1:** the proportion of income spent on it declines as income rises. Individuals often treat food and medical services as necessities. To say that food is a necessity means operationally that an individual spends a decreasing proportion of income on it as income increases (everything else held constant).[13] **A luxury good, on the other hand, is a normal good whose income elasticity is greater than 1.** For many people, sports cars and yachts are considered luxuries. One interesting good to mention is "everything"; it is normal with an income elasticity of 1, since the same proportion of the budget (100 percent) is always spent on it.[14] The reason for mentioning this is to suggest that the broader the aggregate of goods considered, the more likely it is to be normal with elasticity close to 1.

Empirical information about a good's normality or inferiority can be quite useful in predicting responses to changes in budget constraints (such as those caused by new policies). Figure 4-3 illustrates this for food consumption (in the home). A low-income family with a $10,000 annual budget is shown at point A initially spending $1800 on food. Suppose the family qualifies for an income supplement of $3000, shifting its budget constraint out so that the vertical intercept is now $13,000. What can we say about the effects of this change on its food consumption?

If we know that food is a normal good, then we know that food consumption will increase and therefore the utility-maximizing response on the new constraint will lie to the right of point B, or on the BC segment. If we know that "all other goods" is also normal, then its consumption must increase as well, and we can narrow our prediction to the segment BD, where both quantities increase.

---

[12] The elasticity definition may also be expressed in calculus terms: $\varepsilon_{X,Z} = (\partial X/\partial Z)(Z/X)$.

[13] Sometimes it is useful to speak of aggregates of certain goods; in fact, we have already done so several times. "Food" is not a single good but refers to an aggregate category of goods. How do we know whether an individual consumes more food? Typically, we measure the expenditures on food and calculate an Engel-expenditure curve.

[14] Saving is, of course, a legitimate possibility. It can be thought of as spending on *future-consumption goods,* so it is included as part of "everything."

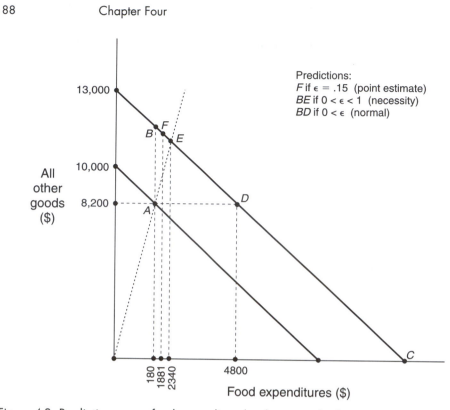

Figure 4-3. Predicting a new food expenditure level as a result of an income supplement depends on empirical knowledge about the income elasticity.

Suppose we have a little more information—say that food is a necessity. If the income elasticity were precisely 1, the straight line from the origin through point A would be the income-expansion path: It shows all bundles like A for which food comprises 18 percent of the bundle's value (at current prices). This line is thus the dividing line between necessity and luxury goods. It intercepts the new constraint at point E, where food expenditure is $2340 (= 0.18 \times 13,000)$. If food is a necessity, meaning its income elasticity is less than 1, then we can predict that the response must lie to the left of our dividing line, or on the BE segment.

Finally, suppose we have an estimate that the actual income elasticity for food in the home for this family is 0.15.[15] Then we could calculate a specific point estimate on the new constraint. Since income is increasing by 30 percent, we estimate that food spending will increase by $(0.15)(30) = 4.5$ percent, or to $1881 at point F. Of course we are rarely certain that we know an income elasticity precisely. Statistical methods can be used to calculate and report a "confidence interval" around the point estimate within which the "true" response

---

[15] This is the approximate estimate for average U.S. households in 1992, based on the author's calculations from more detailed estimates in the literature. See G. D. Paulin, "The Changing Food-at-Home Budget: 1980 and 1992 Compared," *Monthly Labor Review, 121,* No. 12, December 1998, pp. 3–32.

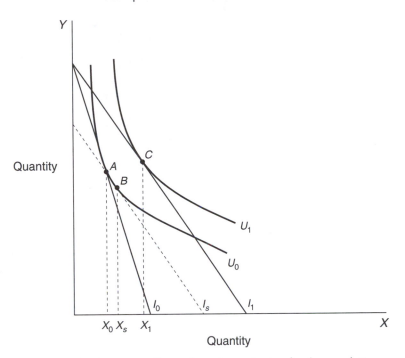

Figure 4-4. Income and substitution effects of a price reduction for the good X.

is highly likely to be found.[16] These examples illustrate how better empirical knowledge can be used to make more precise predictions.

Response to Changes in a Good's Price

Once the effects of income changes on consumption patterns are understood at a conceptual level, it is relatively easy to deduce the effects of price changes. *A price change can be understood as stimulating two different responses: a substitution effect and an income effect.* In Figure 4-4, assume an individual consumes two goods, X and Y, and is initially at A, with budget constraint I_0 and consuming X_0 of the good X. Then say that the price of X falls. This causes the budget constraint I_0 to rotate outward from the unchanged intercept on the Y-axis to I_1. The individual's new utility-maximizing point is shown at C with increased consumption of X (now at level X_1). Does this model always predict that consumption of a good will increase if its price falls? The answer is no, and the reasoning can be seen more clearly if we break the response into two effects. To do so, we *pretend* that the individual moves from A to C in two steps; first from A to B and then from B to C.

The first step, from A to B, shows **the substitution effect: the change in consumption $(X_s - X_0)$ that would occur in response to a new price if the individual were required**

---

[16] For example, a rule-of-thumb for statistically normal distributions is that a 95% confidence interval begins and ends approximately two standard deviations on each side of the mean or point estimate.

to remain on the initial indifference curve. The substitution effect is also called the *pure price effect* or the *compensated price effect* (because real income, or utility, is held constant). It is determined by finding the budget constraint that has the same *slope* as I_1 (reflecting the new price) but is just *tangent* to U_0. This is shown as the dashed line I_s, and thus the hypothetical compensation required to keep utility at the initial level is to take $I_1 - I_s$ dollars away from the budget.

The substitution effect of a price reduction for a good is always positive; the quantity consumed of that good increases. To show this, observe on the diagram that a price reduction for the good X always makes the slope of the new budget constraint less steep than the original one. This means that the tangency of the "compensating" budget I_s to U_0 must occur to the right of A (consumption of X increases), since all points on U_0 with less steep slopes than at A lie to the right of it (because of diminishing MRS). By analogous reasoning, the substitution effect of a price increase is always negative: The quantity of that good consumed decreases. *Thus the substitution effect on quantity is always in the opposite direction of a change in price for that good.*

The change in consumption associated with the second step, from B to C, is shown as $X_1 - X_s$. This is referred to as **the income effect: the change in the quantity of the good caused purely by a budget change that brings the individual from the initial to the new utility level** (holding prices constant). In this case, the changing budget level is from I_s to I_1.[17] We have already analyzed changes like this in deriving the Engel curve. The income effect (of a price reduction) will be positive if X is a normal good and negative if it is an inferior good. Since the change drawn on the diagram is positive, we have assumed that X is a normal good.

Thus *the total effect of the price change, including both the income and the substitution effects, is not clearly predictable without information about the good being analyzed.* If we know the good is normal, the income and substitution effects work in the same direction: Quantity consumed will change in the direction opposite that of the change in price. If the good is inferior, however, the substitution and income effects work in *opposite* directions. In these cases, it is typical for the substitution effect to outweigh the income effect, and thus price and quantity will move in opposite directions. But there may be a few goods, known as Giffen goods, such that the income effect predominates and we get the unusual result that price and quantity move in the same direction.[18]

At this point, a simple extension is to consider how an individual would respond to various possible price changes. The analogous question for pure income changes is used to derive the Engel curve; for price changes, one derives the demand curve. **The demand curve shows the quantity of a good an individual will consume at each possible price.** This is illustrated in Figure 4-5. Figure 4-5a shows how the utility-maximizing choices change as the price of X is successively lowered. Figure 4-5b is based upon these choices and shows the quantity of X that the consumer would choose at each possible price: the demand curve.

---

[17] Any change has an income effect if it results in an altered utility (or "real income") level.

[18] Sir Robert Giffen was an English economist (1837–1910), who observed that a rise in the price of potatoes in Ireland caused an increase in the quantity demanded.

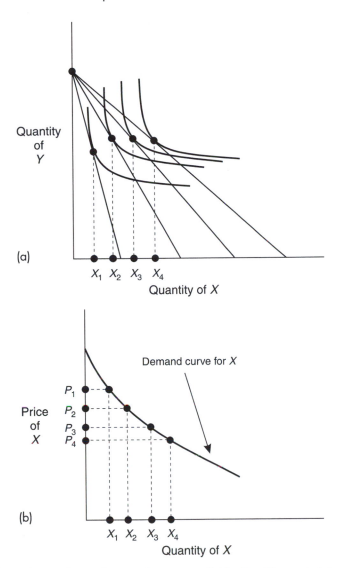

Figure 4-5. The ordinary demand curve shows an individual's utility-maximizing consumption choices in response to alternative prices.

Except for Giffen goods, the demand curve is downward-sloping or equivalently the ordinary price elasticity of demand is negative; for example, a 1 percent increase in price will reduce the quantity demanded. Note also that as the price of X falls, the individual's utility rises.[19]

[19] Closely related to the ordinary demand curve is a construct known as the *compensated demand curve*. It is derived analogously except that it is based only on the substitution effect as shown in Figure 4-3. Since the individual remains on the same indifference curve, utility is constant along the compensated demand curve. The

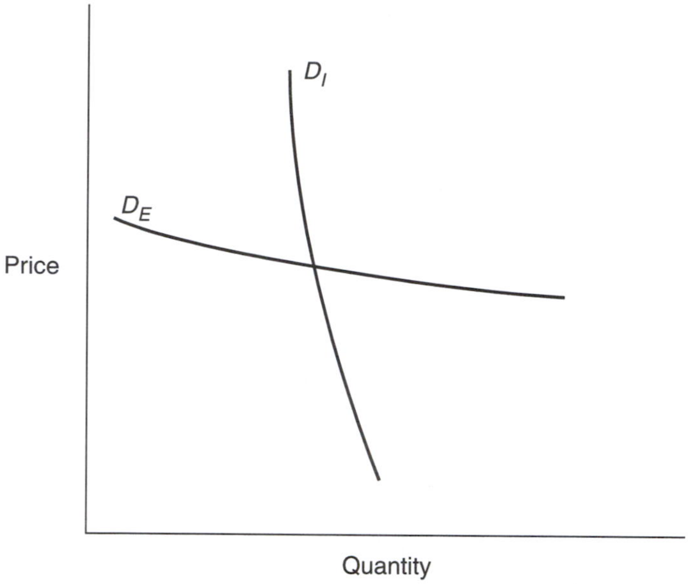

Figure 4-6. Demand curves may be elastic (D_E) or inelastic (D_I).

In Figure 4-6, we contrast two demand curves. Demand curve D_E is *elastic;* small changes in price are associated with large changes in quantity. *We call demand elastic when the price elasticity $(\Delta X/\Delta P)(P/X)$ is less than −1,* for example, −1.5 or −2. Demand curve D_I is inelastic: the quantity demanded does not change very much as price changes. *We call demand inelastic when the price elasticity is between 0 and −1,* for example, −0.1 or −0.7. Thus demand curves can take a variety of shapes, depending on individual preferences. We will make extensive use of demand curves in later chapters, but here we focus primarily on the workings of the income and substitution effects from which they derive.

Response to Price Changes of Related Goods

The above analyses concerned how the consumption of a good changes in response to changes in income levels and changes in its own price. However, the demand for a good is also affected by changes in the prices of related goods. These effects may again be thought of in terms of income and substitution effects, although the analysis is less straightforward. The reason for this is that the price that is changing might be that of either a *substitute* or a *complement,* and the effects differ.

Informally, substitute goods are those that can to some extent replace each other, like hamburgers and hot dogs. Complements are goods that go together, like mustard and hot dogs. If the price of hot dogs rises, then the consumption of hamburgers will go up but the

---

compensated price elasticity of demand is always negative. Compensated demand curves are developed and used in the supplementary section of Chapter 6.

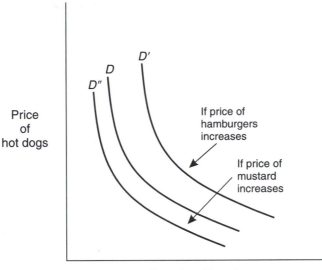

Figure 4-7. A price increase of a substitute (hamburgers) increases (hot dog) demand from *D* to *D'*, and that of a complement (mustard) reduces demand to *D''*.

consumption of mustard will go down (assuming ketchup and not mustard is used on the extra hamburgers).

A good *X* is defined as a gross substitute for another good *Y* if an increase in P_Y causes consumption of *X* to rise ($\Delta X/\Delta P_Y > 0$). Similarly, *X* is a gross complement to *Y* if an increase in P_Y causes *X* consumption to fall ($\Delta X/\Delta P_Y < 0$). These effects are illustrated in Figure 4-7 as causing *shifts* in an individual's demand curve *D* for hot dogs. If the price of hamburgers rises (all other things being equal), the demand for hot dogs shifts to the right at *D'*: at *any* hot dog price, more are demanded than when hamburgers were cheaper. If instead the price of mustard rises (all other things being equal), then the demand for hot dogs shifts from *D* to the left at *D''*: at *any* hot dog price, fewer are demanded than when mustard was cheaper.[20]

We can also express the definition in terms of the cross-price elasticity. *A measure of how much a good X responds to a change in the price of another good Y is its cross-price*

---

[20] A concept closely related to gross substitutability (or complementarity) is that of *Hicksian* or *net substitutability*. Two goods are Hicksian or net substitutes (complements) if the effect of a pure or compensated price increase in one is to increase (decrease) the consumption of the other. Thus gross substitutability includes any income effects of the price change, while Hicksian or net substitutability does not.

Under the gross definition, it is possible for good *X* to be a gross substitute for *Y* and at the same time *Y* could be a gross complement for *X*. If the price of coffee rises, less cream will be demanded: cream is a gross complement of coffee. But if the price of cream rises, the demand for coffee can increase if people simply drink it "blacker": coffee is then a gross substitute for cream. Under the Hicksian or net definition, there must be symmetry: if *X* is a net substitute for *Y*, then *Y* is also a net substitute for *X*.

elasticity $\varepsilon_{X,P_Y} \equiv (\Delta X/\Delta P_Y)(P_Y/X)$. Since the second term in this elasticity definition is always positive, for gross substitutes, $\varepsilon_{X,P_X} > 0$, and for gross complements, $\varepsilon_{X,P_X} < 0$.

Now let us return to the analysis of welfare policies.

Choice Restrictions Imposed by Policy

The earlier section suggests that considerable inefficiency may result from the use of in-kind welfare programs similar to the food stamp policy illustrated. The argument was based on a conventional model specification used in microeconomic analysis. But does this specification apply to actual programs? In this section, we are going to examine more carefully the nature of the budget constraint in our models. Alternate and more realistic model specifications of the budget constraint affect inferences about policy made with the model.

More specifically, we wish to highlight two general factors important to the design and evaluation of a policy: (1) the actual details of the policy design, and (2) the information and transaction costs necessary for the policy's operation and enforcement. Both factors can have important effects on the actual opportunity sets that individuals face, and thus they should be considered when model assumptions about the opportunity sets are chosen. We illustrate these factors with examples concerning the Food Stamp Program, public housing, and income maintenance programs.

Food Stamp Choice Restriction: The Maximum Allotment

The driving force of the inefficiency result in the standard model is the change in the price of food to food stamp recipients (but not others). This is what creates the room for a deal. But as presented, the model assumed that eligible individuals could buy all the stamps they wanted. A policy like that could easily lead to serious problems with illegal transactions—some individuals buying more stamps than they will use in order to sell them (at a profit) to others not legitimately eligible to obtain them. One way to resolve this problem is simply to limit the quantity of stamps to an amount thought reasonable given the family size. In fact, the actual Food Stamp Program sets a limit based on Department of Agriculture estimates for a low-cost nutritious diet. But then this changes the budget constraint in an important way.

In Figure 4-8 several budget constraints are shown. *AB* represents the budget constraint with no program; *AC* represents the unrestricted food stamp program as before; and *ARS* represents the restricted budget constraint. Under the last program, the individual can buy up to *OT* quantity of food with food stamps but above that limit must pay the regular market price for additional food. Thus from *A* to *R* the slope of the budget constraint reflects the food stamp subsidy, and from *R* to *S* the slope is identical with that of *AB*. The kink in the budget constraint occurs at the food stamp limit.

How does the individual respond to a restricted food stamp program? The answer depends on where the individual started (on *AB*) in relation to the limit *OT*. Suppose the individual was initially at point *U,* consuming over the program limit for food subsidy. Then the program has only an income effect. That is, given the quantity of food being consumed

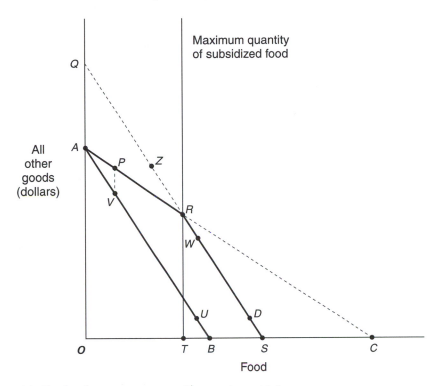

Figure 4-8. The food stamp program with quantity restrictions.

at U, there is no change in the price of additional food at the margin. Under the highly plausible assumption that food and everything else are normal goods, the individual's new utility-maximizing point must lie between W and D (points where the consumption of both goods increases). In that case, no inefficiency arises because of the food stamp program. The behavior is the same as if a cash transfer program with constraint QRS were implemented, the amount of the cash being QA, the size of the subsidy for the maximum allotment.

Suppose, however, that the individual was initially under the subsidy limit at a point like V. The new utility optimum must then be on the PR segment of ARS.[21] We explain this prediction below in two parts: first, that the individual prefers P to other points on AP and, second, that the individual prefers R to other points on RS. Together, these preferences imply that the individual's optimum point on ARS is on the remaining segment PR.

The first part is relatively easy. Since the price of additional food from V has been reduced, the substitution effect works to increase food consumption. Since food is a normal good, the positive income effect also works to increase food consumption. Both effects push in the same direction, so food consumption will increase from the level at V. Therefore, the

---

[21] This argument is affected by the choice of V, where the quantity of everything else is greater than at R. A related argument could be made for an initial point where the quantity of everything else on ARS must be at least as great as at the initial point.

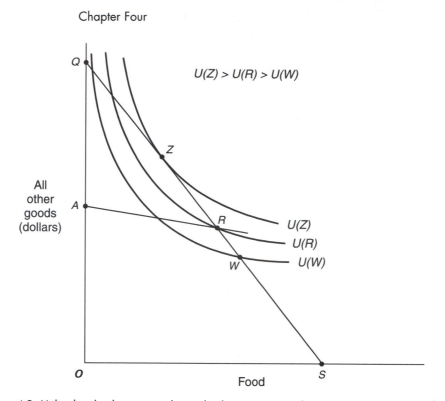

$U(Z) > U(R) > U(W)$

Figure 4-9. Utility levels along an ordinary budget constraint decrease with distance from the utility-maximizing point.

individual will choose a point on ARS that has more food than at V or is to the right of P. (The points to the left of P on AP are ruled out because they contain less food than at V.)

The second part is slightly trickier. The income effect on everything else is to increase it from V, since it also is a normal good. But the substitution effect is to decrease it. The effects go in opposite directions, and we do not know if the quantity of everything else will increase or decrease. However, even if it does decrease, it will not be less than the quantity at point R. This deduction follows from knowing the initial position V and that both goods are normal.

To see this, imagine that the individual had QRS as a budget constraint: a pure income increase compared to AB. Then, by the normality property, the utility-maximizing consumption choice would be some point on QR with more of both goods than at V, like Z. As we move downward and to the right from Z along QRS, the individual's utility level is steadily decreasing (Figure 4-9). Therefore R must yield greater utility than any other point on RS. Since the segment RS is feasible with the actual food stamp budget constraint ARS, if the individual is on this segment at all he or she will be at R.

Note also, in Figure 4-9, that the kink point R will be a popular choice among utility-maximizing individuals with budget constraint ARS. We have drawn the indifference curves to show R as the maximum utility for an individual with this constraint. It is not a point of tangency, but rather a "corner" solution. R will be the utility maximum whenever the slope of the indifference curve at R equals or falls between the slopes of the segments AR and RS. It is like a trap. The individual, when considering choices moving upward from S, wishes to go past R (to Z) but is unable to do so. The same individual, when considering choices moving rightward from A, wishes to continue past R but cannot do so. From either direction, things get worse when the corner is turned. Thus R will be the utility-maximizing point for a number of individuals (all those with a MRS at R equal to or between the absolute values of the slopes of AR or RS).

To sum up the general argument, the individual who starts at V and has a new budget constraint ARS will choose a point on the PR segment. The choices on AP yield less utility than P itself, and the choices on RS yield less utility than R itself. Therefore, the utility-maximizing point must be one from the remainder, the PR segment.

These examples imply that the efficiency of a food stamp program is higher when a limit is put on the quantity of food stamps available to a household. We explain this below. A household consuming a small quantity of food initially—meaning a quantity less than the limit—may choose a consumption point like the ones illustrated by line segment PR of Figure 4-8. For this household, inefficiency arises exactly as in the standard analysis: a cash grant smaller than the food stamp subsidy would allow the household to achieve the same utility level by purchasing less food and more of other things.

However, a household consuming a large quantity of food initially—meaning a quantity greater than the limit—treats the subsidy exactly like a cash transfer. For this latter household, the resulting allocation is efficient: There is no cheaper way for taxpayers to bring the household to the same utility level. *Thus the total impact of putting a limit on the food stamp subsidy is to increase efficiency overall: Low-food-consumption households are unaffected by the limit, and efficiency with respect to high-food-consumption households increases.* The program is still not as efficient as a pure cash grant, but it is closer to being so.

Let us reflect on this conclusion for a moment. If the only change in the program is a limit on the subsidy per recipient, the total taxpayer cost must be reduced. Recipients with low food-consumption levels end up with the same subsidy and same utility levels as without the limit. Therefore, high-food-consumption households must have reduced subsidies. True, the value to them of each subsidy dollar is higher. But these households must end up with lower utility levels than they would have without the limit. Without a limit they could choose the same consumption levels as with the limit; since they do not do so, it must be that the without-limit choices yield more utility than the limited choices. (This is clear in Figure 4-8, where the household initially at U would prefer some point on RC to any of the points on WD.)

How then do we make the statement about increased efficiency, if some people lose because of the limits (eligible households with high food consumption) and others gain (taxpayers)? Recall the discussion in Chapter 3 about relative efficiency. We have simply pointed out that the limits result in fewer potential deals among the members of the economy. (All potential deals are unaffected by the limits except those between taxpayers and high-food-consumption food stamp recipients, which are reduced.)[22] Whether one thinks

---

[22] Limiting the maximum allotment to each eligible family can provide gains to taxpayers (dollar reduction in food stamp expenditures) that exceed the losses to food stamp recipients (the dollar amount recipients would be

such a change is desirable depends as well on views of the equity of the change. In the latter regard, note that the high-food-consumption family still receives a greater subsidy than the low-food-consumption family.

But the desirability of such a change is not really the issue here. The issue is how to model the effects of food stamps. The actual Food Stamp Program does include limits on the subsidy available to any recipient family. Thus the model that takes account of these limits, and moves one step closer to reality, is more accurate. So far, it leads to a higher efficiency rating compared to the less realistic standard model.

This examination of the effect of subsidy limits illustrates that good analytic use of microeconomic theory requires consideration of the specific features of a policy's design. Because the subsidy limits for food stamps have important effects on the recipient's opportunity set, or budget constraint, they affect the efficiency of the program. A model that ignores this feature, like our first one, is misspecified.

Food Stamp Choice Restriction: The Resale Prohibition

Another source of specification concern involves the information and transaction costs necessary for the policy's operation and enforcement. The standard model does not explicitly consider them. Implicitly it is assumed, for example, that recipients obey the rules of the program. But recipients may not obey the rules; they have incentive to participate in the illegal resale of the stamps. Accounting for this results in another change in the budget constraint. We illustrate this below.

In Figure 4-10a, we draw the food stamp budget constraint *ARS* as before. The recipient family shown chooses $120 worth of food and $340 worth of all other goods, under a plan that sells each $1 food stamp for $0.50 and places a limit of $180 worth of food stamps as the maximum purchase. Thus the maximum subsidy is $90, although the family shown receives a $60 subsidy.

Consider what this household would do if food stamps were freely exchangeable among individuals. Because it has the privilege of buying a $1 stamp for only $0.50, it will always buy the maximum allowable. Any stamp that it does not wish to use for its own food consumption can be resold profitably at its market value. The market value is approximately $1, since anyone trying to obtain a deeper discount (say $.90) would be outbid by someone who would be satisfied with a very small discount that we will treat as negligible.

How does this new opportunity change the shape of the budget constraint? The segment *RS* is unchanged; the household uses all $180 of the stamps for itself and any food consumption beyond the maximum allotment must be bought at ordinary market prices. However, to the left of *R,* the constraint changes to the bold segment *QR*. By forgoing $1 worth of food from *R,* the consumer can resell one stamp and have $1 more to spend on all other goods. By forgoing $2 worth of food, the consumer can resell two stamps and have $2

---

willing to pay to prevent the imposition of the limit). This is a version of the Hicks-Kaldor test for relative efficiency explained in Chapter 6.

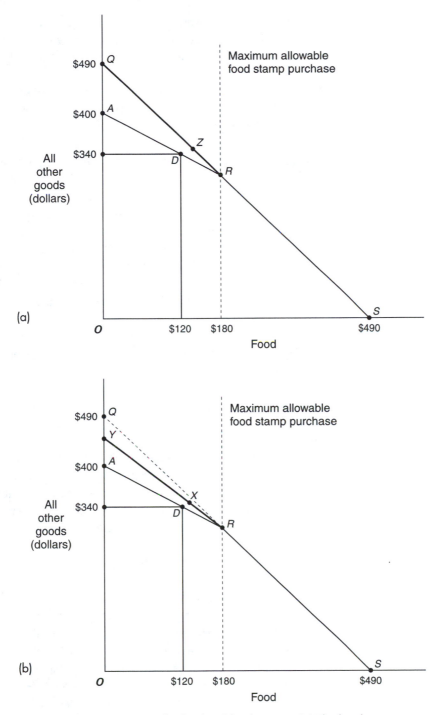

Figure 4-10. The incentive to resell subsidized food stamps: (a) The legal opportunity to resell food stamps would make recipients better off. (b) Illegal resale opportunities may tempt some recipients.

more for other things, and so on. But this is simply the ordinary market trade-off: The new constraint *QRS* is equivalent to the household receiving a cash grant of $90 (the difference between the face value of the maximum allotment and the household's subsidized cost for it).

Our illustrative household, initially at *D,* would now choose a point on the *QR* segment like *Z*. Point *Z* must have more of all other goods, since both income and substitution effects work in the same direction. Food expenditures could increase or decrease (income effect is to increase; substitution effect to decrease), but the new utility-maximizing choice must be on the portion of the *QR* segment that has $340 or more of all other goods.

Of course, food stamps are not freely exchangeable. It is, in fact, illegal for food stamp recipients to sell their stamps to others and for noneligible households to use them. Most people obey the rules out of respect for the law, but some will be tempted by the room for a deal. The food stamp recipient is tempted by any offer to purchase unused stamps for an amount greater than cost. A potential purchaser will not offer the full market value because of the risk of being caught but may well offer an amount greater than the seller's cost. Thus the effective budget constraint for the recipient will not be *QRS* but rather like *YRS* in Figure 4-10b: a price for illegal food stamp transactions yielding a slope between that of the normal subsidy constraint *AR* and the ordinary market value *QR*.

How do information and transaction costs enter the analysis? The slope of the budget constraint *YRS* is determined in part by the resources allocated to governmental enforcement efforts to prevent the illegal transactions. At one extreme, vigorous enforcement efforts lead to an effective constraint closer to *AR*. (A high probability of being punished or an inability to use illegally purchased stamps dries up the illicit market.) At the other extreme, little or no enforcement efforts lead to a constraint closer to *QR*. (Easy use of the stamps by ineligibles raises the illicit market price of the stamps.)

What are the implications of illegal trading possibilities? The eligible high-food-consumption household is unaffected: It prefers to use the maximum allotment for its own consumption, as before. However, the eligible low-food-consumption household may modify its behavior. Suppose it does engage in illegal trading and ends up with a point like *X* on *YRS*. Obviously, the buyer and seller consider themselves better off. Then we can say that the closer *X* is to *Z* (the choice if trading stamps were legal, as shown on Fig. 4-10a) the more the exchange inefficiency between taxpayers and eligible households is reduced. Why then should this be prevented?

One reason might be because of increased taxpayer cost. If the eligible household is on *AR* anywhere to the left of *R* itself, then illegal trading is accomplished by increasing its purchase of food stamps and thus taxpayer cost. However, if the eligible household is at *R* without any trading, then the resales occur at no additional taxpayer cost. (The full subsidy is used without illegal trading.) As a matter of equity, it is not obvious that households having identical eligibility should receive different subsidies dependent upon their food purchases. In fact, changes in the Food Stamp Program discussed below essentially obviate this concern, because they ensure that participating households with identical eligibility will all receive the maximum subsidy.

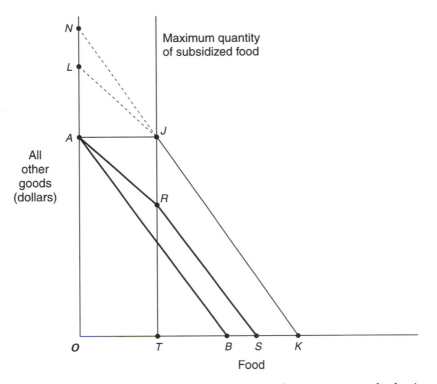

Figure 4-11. The household budget constraint with no purchase requirement for food stamps is *AJK*.

The model we have been discussing most closely represents the actual Food Stamp Program as it operated from 1964 to 1978, when participating families were required to purchase the stamps. However, the Food Stamp Act of 1977 eliminated the purchase requirement as of 1979. Each household is now given a free monthly allotment of food stamps based on its income and family size. Under these rules, we can make two inferences: (1) illegal resales of stamps do not increase taxpayer subsidies to recipients, and (2) illegal resales unambiguously reduce food consumption.

The effect of this on a household is illustrated in Figure 4-11. In the diagram *AB* is the original budget constraint. *ARS* is the budget constraint under the old Food Stamp Program, and *AJK* is the budget constraint under the revised Food Stamp Program with no purchase requirement. With *AJK* as the constraint, the household will always be on the *JK* segment. Starting from *A,* the household gives up nothing to increase its food consumption to *OT* at *J.* Since additional food increases utility, the household will always move at least to *J.* Thus all eligible households will always use the full allotment of stamps.

Think of the constraint *NJK* as an unrestricted cash grant. If the household prefers a point below *J* on the constraint, its behavior with respect to illegal trading of food stamps will be identical to that of the high-food-consumption household we analyzed previously. That is, it will prefer to use the full allotment for its own food consumption. But if the household has low preferences for food and prefers a point above *J* on *NJ*, then *J* is the best it can do under food stamps without illegal trading.[23] If *LJ* represents the illicit market opportunities, this household might take advantage of them and thereby reduce its food consumption. Under the revised Food Stamp Program, since all families use their full allotment, any family engaging in illegal selling of stamps must be reducing its food consumption. However, there is no extra subsidy cost to the government from this trading.

It is not known empirically exactly how much illegal trading actually occurs. However, its existence is not disputed. One study reported that 4.2 percent of supermarkets and 12.8 percent of small grocery stores were involved in illegal trafficking in 1995. The 902 trafficking investigations in fiscal 1994 involved in total $224,503 worth of food stamps sold for $124,779, implying a price of $0.56 per food stamp dollar.[24] Similarly, a newspaper description of illegal trading in Oakland, California, reported sellers receiving $0.50 for their food stamp dollars. According to this article, the buyers are middlemen who sell the stamps to supermarkets or grocery stores for a slight profit; these stores, in turn, trade them back to the government for their full value.[25]

The view of food stamps developed here is quite different from the first standard model, and it is worthwhile to summarize the differences. The standard model suggests that food stamps are inefficient relative to a cash grant essentially because of effective food price differences between participants and nonparticipants. This model does not get at the essence of *any* inefficiency caused by the modern food stamp program, because that program does not directly create the type of price differences analyzed by the model. Instead, we must focus on choice restrictions: the food stamp limits per family and the rules preventing recipients from selling them. Even when there are price differences caused by an "in-kind" program, the effective choice restrictions are usually key determinants of the program's efficiency.

The food stamp limit is a key determinant of efficiency. The potential inefficiency only arises for families with desired food consumption below the limit. The smaller the limit, the more families will have desired food consumption greater than the limit. These families fully utilize the stamps, pay ordinary market prices for their marginal consumption of food, and thus cause no inefficiency. Therefore potential inefficiency depends on the (statistical) distribution of food preferences among the eligible families relative to the limit (i.e., how many will wish to be below the limit, and by how much).

Given the potential inefficiency, its realization depends on the extent of illegal trading originating from these families. The more the illegal trading, the less the inefficiency! Since it is costly for the government to prevent illegal trading, one might wonder why any govern-

[23] This characterizes about 10–15 percent of food stamp recipients according to one estimate. See Thomas M. Fraker et al., "The Effects of Cashing-Out Food Stamps on Household Food Use and the Cost of Issuing Benefits," *Journal of Policy Analysis and Management, 14,* No. 3, Summer 1995, pp. 372–392.

[24] These figures are from notes 66 and 152 in E. Regenstein, "Food Stamp Trafficking: Why Small Groceries Need Judicial Protection from the Department of Agriculture (and from Their Own Employees)," *Michigan Law Review, 96,* June 1998, pp. 2156–2184.

[25] *Oakland Tribune,* "Local Black Market for Food Stamps Widespread," March 15, 1993.

ment effort should be made to prevent such trades (or why not simply allow recipients to sell the stamps if they wish?).

In fact, the efficiency implication above may still be drawn from too simplistic a model, despite accounting for the food stamp limits and illegal resales. The different model specifications we have discussed vary only in terms of the effective budget constraint for recipients. All these variants assume that recipients act in their own best interests (maximize utility) and that the utility of nonrecipients is not directly affected by the recipients' consumption choices. However, there are reasons to suspect that these assumptions should be open to question as well. Rather than presenting more formal analytical models at this point, we simply introduce these issues below.

To this point, we have used the terms "recipient," "household," and "family" interchangeably. Implicitly, we have assumed that the individual receiving the food stamps (e.g., a mother) acts in the best interests of those for whom they are intended (e.g., the mother, her children, and any other covered family or household members). We have assumed that there is such a thing as a "household" or "family" utility function representing the preferences of its members. But the formal economic theory of utility maximization is about individual behavior, not group behavior.[26] What if some recipients do not act in the best interests of their household members, for example, a parent who trades stamps for drugs and brings little food home for the children (and perhaps herself)? This concern offers some rationale for making the resale of food stamps illegal and enforcing the restriction.

In economics, **the problem of motivating one person (or economic agent) to act in the interests of another or others is called the principal-agent problem.** In this case, taxpayers through the government are the principal, the person receiving food stamps is the agent, and the covered members of the household are those whose interests the principal wants protected. Food stamp program regulations are the "contract" by which the principal and agent agree to do business. Presumably most of the agents do act in the best interests of their household members. Nevertheless, the "no resale" provision may be a reasonable one from the principal's perspective. However, this restriction could prevent actions that truly are in the best interests of the covered members, for example, careful economizing on food in order to free up some funds for special medical or educational needs. As analysts, we would want to know if the covered members achieve more gains than losses from the restriction.

Is there any other reason why our policy should prevent recipients from choosing a lower food consumption than the allotted amount? What happens if I and some of you say that our utilities depend on how recipients use their food stamps? If we are willing to pay eligibles specifically to increase their food consumption, then this creates room for a deal in which recipients increase their food consumption beyond the amount that they would choose if we did not care. In a supplemental section later in this chapter, we explore the significance of *interdependent preferences*. While its empirical significance remains an important issue for further research, it can in theory provide another rationale for one group subsidizing or penalizing certain consumption choices of another.

---

[26] For a survey on the economics of the family, see T. C. Bergstrom, "Economics in a Family Way," *Journal of Economic Literature, 34,* No. 4, December 1996, pp. 1903–1934.

There are other questions we could raise about food stamps; examples are the administrative costs and the difference between increasing food consumption and increasing nutritional intake. But keep in mind that our primary purpose is to develop skills in microeconomic policy analysis. We have used the food stamp issue to illustrate how alternative specifications of models of consumer behavior bear on policy analysis. Different model assumptions (the specific design features of a policy, the information and transaction costs relevant to a policy's operation, and the nature of utility functions) generated insights about how consumers will respond to the Food Stamp Program and how to evaluate that response.

Public Housing Choice Restrictions[S]

Another type of choice restriction can be seen in certain public housing programs. In these a family may be given a take-it-or-leave-it choice. In Figure 4-12a, we illustrate how such a choice affects the budget constraint. Let the original budget constraint, with no program, be AB and assume that the family initially maximizes utility at C, thereby consuming OG of housing. (Think of each consumption unit of housing in terms of a standardized quality, so higher-quality housing is measured as more of the standardized units.) The public housing authority then tells the family that it may have an apartment that is of the same size as its current one but of better quality (thus more housing) and, furthermore, that the rent is less than it currently pays (because the housing is subsidized). Thus the family's new budget constraint is simply the old one plus the single point E. (Note that the family can consume more of "other things" at E because of the reduction in rent.) By the more-is-better logic, the family must prefer E to C, and it will accept the public housing offer (remember that, by assumption, the quality really is better). Is this efficient or inefficient?

The argument we will make is that the take-it-or-leave-it choice is not necessarily inefficient. We will show the possibility that the indifference curve through E has a slope identical to the slope of AB, or (equivalently) that the individual at E could have a MRS equal to the ratio of the market prices. If that is so, there is no room for a deal and the public housing program is efficient.[27]

To make this argument, let us construct a hypothetical budget constraint AJ to represent an unrestricted housing subsidy program with the same percentage subsidy as at E. We will identify two points on AJ: one inefficient because it has too much housing (the slope of the indifference curve at that point is flatter than AB), and the other inefficient because it has too little housing (the slope of the indifference curve at that point is steeper than AB). As one moves along AJ from one of those points to the other, the slope of the isoquants through them is gradually changing. Therefore, there must be some point between them where the slope equals AB, and at that point there is neither too much nor too little housing. The point is efficient, and it could be E.

First, let us show that there is a point on AJ that is inefficient because it has too much housing. This point is an old friend by now: It is the utility-maximizing choice of the

---

[27] We ignore here the possibility of interdependent preferences discussed in a later section.

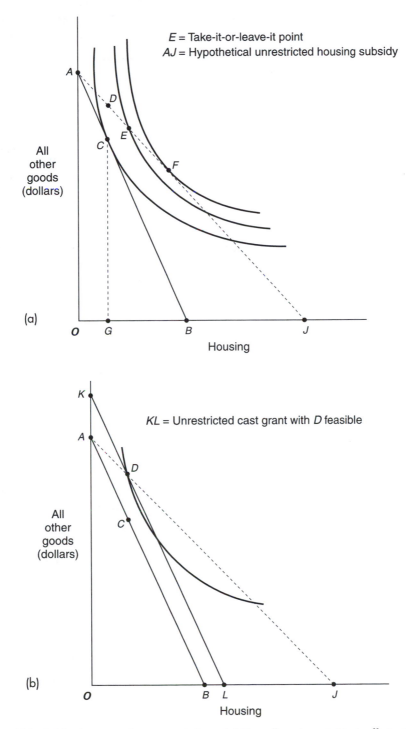

Figure 4-12. Public housing choice restrictions: (a) The allocation at F is inefficient with too much housing. (b) The allocation at D is inefficient with too little housing.

household free to choose any point on *AJ*. We label this *F* in Figure 4-12a, where the in-difference curve is tangent to *AJ*. This case is identical with the standard model of food stamps examined earlier. There is room for a deal because the household's MRS of other things for housing (the absolute value of the slope of the indifference curve) is *less* than that of ordinary consumers who buy at market (unsubsidized) prices. This household would be willing to give up housing for cash (other things) at a rate attractive to the nonsubsidized household; both could be made better off by trading. The point *F* is inefficient because the household has "too much" housing relative to other things, given the market prices.

Now let us examine another point. Suppose the housing authority simply offers to sub-sidize the current apartment (at the same rate as along *AJ*), which on the diagram is shown at point *D*. This point also is inefficient, but because it results in too little housing. To see this, in Figure 4-12b we have added a cash transfer program *KL* through *D*. Since the family started at *C*, it would choose a point from those on *KL* to the right and below *D* as long as both goods are normal.[28] Therefore, *D* is not the utility maximum on *KL*. As it lies above the *KL* maximum, the slope of the indifference curve through *D* must be *steeper* than the slope of *KL* (it equals the slope of *AB*, the market trade-off rate). The household at *D* would trade cash (other things) for housing at a rate attractive to nonsubsidized households; both could be made better off. Thus *D* is inefficient because it has too little housing relative to other things, given the market prices.

We have shown that the slope of the indifference curve through *F* at *AJ* is too flat for it to be efficient and that the slope of the indifference curve through *D* on *AJ* is too steep for it to be efficient. But as we move upward along *AJ* from *F* to *D*, the slopes of the indif-ference curves are gradually changing from the flat slope at *F* to the steep slope at *D*. There-fore, there must come a point between *F* and *D* where the slope of the indifference curve precisely equals the slope of *AB*, the market trade-off. This point is an efficient allocation. If the public housing authorities offer it as the take-it-or-leave-it choice, the public housing is efficient.

Whether actual public housing programs are or are not efficient is a matter for empiri-cal determination. The analysis we presented serves the function of raising the issue. Ac-cording to one study of federal housing programs, the degree of inefficiency is probably less than 5 percent (the average public housing recipient would require a cash grant of at least $0.95 to forgo a $1.00 housing subsidy).[29] As with food stamps, any inefficiency from too much housing might be offset by interdependent preferences. Meanwhile, we have seen that microeconomic theory can be used to analyze the take-it-or-leave-it choice, another type of budget constraint that is sometimes created by public policy.

---

[28] A slightly weaker version of this argument can be made without relying on the normality of the goods. Find the point at which the indifference curve through *C* intersects *AJ* (this will be to the left of *D*). At that point, too little housing is being consumed (the slope of the indifference curve is steeper than at *C* and therefore steeper than the cash transfer constraint *KL*). The rest of the argument is the same as above.

[29] For further discussion of this issue along with some empirical work, see H. Aaron and G. Von Furstenberg, "The Inefficiency of Transfers in Kind: The Case of Housing Assistance," *Western Economic Journal,* June 1971, pp. 184–191.

Income Maintenance and Work Efforts

The analyses so far have another source of oversimplification in their *partial equilibrium* nature. This means, roughly, that analytic attention is focused on only one of the resource allocation choices that is affected by a program. We have been focusing only on the analysis of exchange efficiency. Of course, the other questions of efficiency—whether the right goods are being produced and right resources are being used to produce them—are equally important. *General equilibrium analysis* requires that all the resource allocation choices affected by a program be considered. Although we shall continue to defer general discussion of these other efficiency issues until later chapters, it is convenient to introduce one element of them through analysis of the *labor-leisure choice* of recipients. All transfer programs affect and can cause inefficiency through this choice.[30]

The primary purpose of this section is to reinforce the usefulness of theory as a guide to policy design and evaluation. In particular, we build up to the idea of using the Earned Income Tax Credit (EITC) to provide aid and to encourage work efforts among low-income families. First, we review the general labor-leisure decision that all individuals face. Then we show how current welfare programs discourage work. Finally, we explain how the EITC can reduce the work disincentives of current programs.

The Labor-Leisure Choice

To this point we have referred to individuals having a budget constraint or an initial endowment without being very specific about where it comes from. The basic sources of individual wealth are gifts: material things, such as inheritances; childhood upbringing, such as schooling received; and natural endowments, such as intelligence. Individuals use these gifts over time to alter their wealth further, increasing it through labor or capital investments (the latter includes skill development or "human capital" investments, such as advanced schooling)[31] and decreasing it through consumption.

For now, we shall focus only on the labor market decisions of individuals as if they were the only source of wealth. One constraint individuals face in earning labor income is the wage offered to them, but the more important constraint is *time*. There is only so much time available, and a decision to use it to work means not using it for other things we will refer to here simply as *leisure*. Presumably every individual has preferences about how much to work, given the income that can be derived from the work and the *opportunity costs* of forgone leisure.[32]

---

[30] We note that taxpayer choices also are affected by transfer programs, because all methods of taxation cause distortions in prices that might be efficient otherwise. This is discussed in Chapter 12.

[31] This is discussed further in Chapters 8 and 19.

[32] For those of you thinking that individuals have little choice about how much to work (e.g., most jobs are 40 hours per week, and an individual can only take it or leave it), consider the many sources of flexibility. Many people work only in part-time jobs, and others hold two jobs simultaneously. Some jobs have more paid vacation than others. Sometimes the decision to pursue certain careers is heavily influenced by the time dimension, for example, most teaching jobs are for 9 to 10 months (and pay correspondingly). If one thinks broadly about work

We represent the labor-leisure choice in Figure 4-13a by using a diagram virtually identical to those we have been using all along. Leisure is measured on the horizontal axis, and
dollars for everything else on the vertical axis. The budget constraint is shown as *AB,* and
its slope equals minus the wage rate. (Since more work is shown on the diagram as a movement to the *left,* the budget size goes up in accordance with the wage rate as the individual
works more.) Thus the price per unit of leisure equals the wage. The location of the constraint depends upon the time framework selected by the analyst. If we select a 1-year period,
the maximum leisure must be 1 year, represented by *OB.* The dashed vertical line at *B* indicates that it is impossible to choose a point to the right of it. Point *C,* let us say, represents
the utility-maximizing choice of some individual.

Consider the response of an individual to a change in the wage rate, say an increase. This
changes the budget constraint to one like *DB.* How will the individual respond? This is clearly
a price change involving both income and substitution effects. The rise in wages is a rise in
the price of leisure (relative to all other things), and thus the substitution effect works to decrease leisure (or increase work). Real income increases because of the wage rise; if leisure
is a normal good, the income effect acts to increase its consumption (or reduce work).[33]
Thus the income and substitution effects work in opposite directions, and the net effect cannot be predicted on purely theoretical grounds.

**The labor supply curve of an individual is the locus of points relating the choice of
hours worked to each possible wage rate.** Empirically, it is often thought to be "backward-
bending" as in Figure 4-13b. That is, as the wage increases from a low initial rate, the substitution effect outweighs the income effect: The individual finds it more important to earn
income for basic necessities than to reduce work effort and live on almost nothing. But as
the wage rises past some point, the income effect begins to outweigh the substitution effect:
The individual may feel that he or she has earned the right to spend more time relaxing and
enjoying the fruits of a big paycheck.

Work Disincentives of Current Welfare Programs

Let us now consider the population of low-income and low-wealth individuals who are, or
might be, eligible for the various welfare programs we have mentioned: for example, TANF
(replacing the former AFDC), food stamps, Medicaid, and local housing assistance. Historically, many of these programs were designed in such a way that benefits available to recipients were reduced dollar for dollar in response to any increases in the recipient's earned
income. This created some bizarre incentives for the recipients.

---

during an individual's lifetime, there are important decisions about when to begin and when to retire. There are
decisions about how hard to seek new employment during a spell of unemployment. There are very subtle decisions such as how hard to work when working; some people prefer to take it easy on the job in full knowledge that
this usually slows down promotions or raises that come from working more. In short, there is a great deal of choice
between labor and leisure.

[33] Leisure is generally considered a normal good because it is a complement to a highly aggregated (and undoubtedly normal) good: consumption. More simply, it often takes more time to consume more (e.g., theater,
restaurants, shopping, vacation trips, reading).

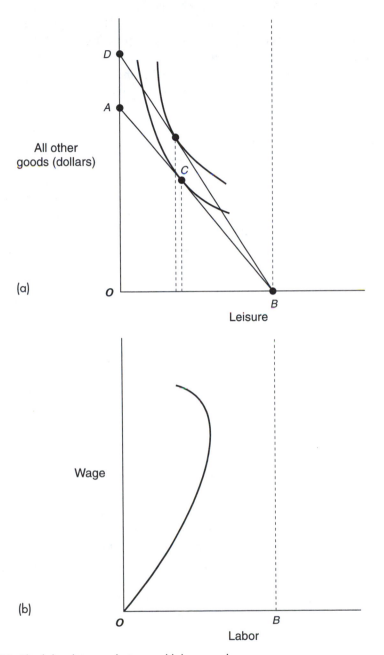

Figure 4-13. The labor-leisure choice and labor supply curve.

For example, consider a family receiving under the old system both AFDC payments and local housing assistance. If a part-time job were offered to one of the family members, not only would AFDC payments be reduced by the amount of the earnings, but so would the housing assistance; by accepting the job, the family could lose twice as much money as the amount earned! Needless to say, welfare recipients were hardly enthused by the moral encouragement of some to increase "self-reliance." Whereas most of the programs have been modified individually to allow some net increases in family income through earnings, as a group they still have close to a "100 percent tax" (i.e., for families eligible for several of them).

We can see the effects of this situation on a labor-leisure diagram. Figure 4-14a shows an ordinary budget constraint *AB* for a low-income family. With no welfare programs, the family might choose a point like *C*—where, say, the mother works part time but spends most of her time taking care of her two young children. Let us say that the current amalgam of programs can be represented by the line segment *DE*. This means that the family receives $7000 in annual benefits if the mother does not work at all, and net income stays at $7000 as work effort increases from *E* until *D* (net welfare benefits are reduced dollar for dollar by any earnings). At point *D*, welfare benefits have been reduced to zero and the family goes off welfare, thus retaining the full earnings from additional work effort from *D* until *A*.

It is hardly surprising that this family maximizes utility by completely withdrawing from the labor force, at *E*. Both the income and the substitution effects act to increase leisure. (Higher real income works to increase leisure; the lowered effective wage reduces the price of leisure, which acts to increase its consumption.) We thus know that the family will choose a point on the new effective constraint *ADE* with greater leisure than at *C;* this means it is on the *DE* segment. But although the slopes of indifference curves approach zero (the slope of *DE*) to the right because of diminishing MRS, they will not reach it if the nonsatiation assumption holds. The utility level increases as the family moves to the right along *DE*, but it never reaches a tangency position; instead, it runs into the boundary condition at *E*, which is the maximum attainable utility.[34]

The Earned Income Tax Credit (EITC)

The EITC is intended to reward work efforts of low-income families, as well as contribute toward the reduction of poverty. Originally adopted in 1975 to reduce the burden of the social security payroll tax on low-income working families, it was expanded significantly in the 1993 Omnibus Budget Reconciliation Act. The EITC covers all low-income taxpayers, including those without children (although the credit amount depends upon family size). For families with two or more children the EITC (as of 1999) provides a tax credit equal to 40 percent of earned income up to a maximum of $3816 (at an income level of $9540). The

---

[34] We note also that some families initially working with income *above* the welfare minimum will withdraw if the welfare plan becomes available to them. This will occur whenever the initial indifference curve crosses the welfare minimum height to the left of point *E:* If the family is indifferent to the initial position and the minimum income with *some* work effort, it must strictly prefer the minimum income and *no* work effort.

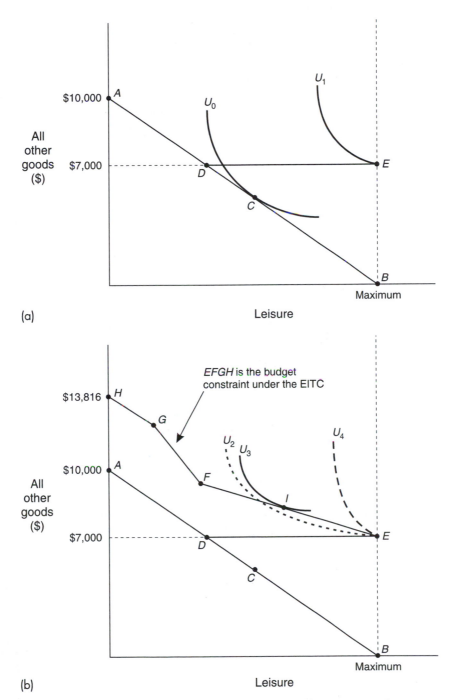

Figure 4-14. Welfare and work incentives: (a) Traditional welfare programs have poor work incentives. (b) The EITC increases work incentives for welfare families.

credit is gradually reduced at a rate of 21.06 percent for earned income above $12,460, until it is fully phased out at $30,580. The tax credit is refundable, which means that the government pays it whether or not the qualifying individual owes any federal income tax. Because this program is administered through the Internal Revenue Service like ordinary tax collection, it may not have the stigma associated with other welfare policies.[35]

The EITC budget constraint for a single mother, two-child family is shown as $HGFE$ in Figure 4-14b. As before, BE represents a welfare benefit level of $7000 in the absence of work, and welfare benefits are assumed to be reduced dollar for dollar for earnings up to $7000. However, the EITC provides a new credit of 40 percent of earnings. Thus as the mother begins to work, net income is not flat but rises above $7000. At $7000 earnings, welfare benefits are zero but the EITC is $2800 and total income is $9800 (point F). Leftward from F to G, total income is 140 percent of earned income (thus the slope of this segment is steeper than the no-program constraint AB). To the left of point G, where earned income reaches $9540 and the credit is at its maximum of $3816, additional work effort supplements income by the ordinary market wage rate and thus GH is parallel to AB.[36]

The EITC should, on average, increase work efforts for welfare families. However, whether or not any particular welfare family changes behavior depends upon its preferences. Consider two possible preference structures for a family that does not work under traditional welfare (i.e., initially at point E). One possibility is represented by the indifference curve U_2; its crucial characteristic is that its slope at point E is flatter than the EF segment under EITC. This family can reach a higher utility level by moving leftward along EF (i.e., by working) until it reaches the maximum at I on U_3.[37] However, the family may have a different preference structure represented by the indifference curve U_4 through point E; its crucial characteristic is that its slope at point E is steeper than EF. Its utility-maximizing point under the EITC would still be at E. Those families with slopes at E less steep than the slope of line segment EF will be induced to work; those with slopes greater than EF will still not work.

In sum, the EITC unambiguously increases work efforts among previously nonworking welfare families. The aggregate amount of this increase depends on two factors: (1) the strength of the EITC inducement (the steepness of the slope of EF) and, (2) the distribution of preferences (the number of families at E with MRS of leisure for other goods less than the slope of EF, as opposed to greater than that slope).

However, the EITC also affects the work incentives of families who are already working, and for many of these families the incentives are largely to reduce work. Families with earned income in the "flat" (GH) segment are induced to increase leisure through the income

---

[35] For more information about the EITC, see John Karl Scholz, "The Earned Income Tax Credit: Participation, Compliance, and Antipoverty Effectiveness." *National Tax Journal, 47,* No. 1, March 1994, pp. 63–87.

[36] The family shown does not reach the phase-out range even when working full time. For a family with a higher market wage than the one shown, the budget constraint would have an additional, flatter-than-market-wage segment for earnings above $12,460.

[37] The utility-maximizing work effort on EF will be less than that at point C: both income and substitution effects increase leisure. Thus the EITC will reduce work effort for some low-income nonwelfare families.

effect, and families in the phase-out range (not shown) face both income and substitution effects to increase leisure. It is not clear how the expected work reduction from these families compares to the expected increase in work effort from other affected families.[38]

The above analysis is but one illustration of many factors to consider in the design of welfare policies. Within the EITC framework it does not discuss, for example, the cost to taxpayers of offering the credit, the role of eligibility requirements to limit this cost and target its benefits, the effects of varying the subsidy and phase-out rates and ranges, or the overall antipoverty effectiveness of the credit. Of course, there are many other important welfare issues apart from the EITC and work incentives. For a greater understanding of the economics of welfare, one can refer to the extensive literature that is available.[39]

Note that throughout this discussion of labor market effects of policies, little attention was focused on resolving the efficiency issue. Rather, it was suggested that there was a problem with the current welfare system, and one alternative to alleviate the problem was explored. The problem was identified as poor work incentives, and we simply used knowledge about income and substitution effects to understand it and theoretically develop an idea that might mitigate it. If it is impossible to determine efficiency effects precisely (recall all the other determinants of efficiency we have discussed in regard to the same set of policies), the next best thing may be to suboptimize: take one piece of the larger issue where there seems to be consensus that it is a problem and try to do something about it.

Interdependent Preference Arguments: In-Kind Transfers May Be Efficient[s]

Another possible specification error in utility maximization models concerns the sources of utility: the arguments or variables of the utility function. The model of behavior as it is specified above has an implicit assumption of "selfish" preferences: The only sources of utility to individuals are from the goods and services they consume directly. There is nothing in the model of rational behavior that implies that people are selfish. It is perfectly plausible to have an **interdependent preference: where one individual's utility level is affected by another person's consumption.** You might feel better if you gave some food to a neighbor whose kitchen had just been destroyed by a fire. This act might please you more than if you gave the neighbor the cash equivalent of the food. People in a community might donate money to an organization created for the purpose of giving basic necessities to families who are the victims of "hard luck." This organization might be a church or a charity, but it might also be a government whose voters approved collection of the "donations" through taxes paid by both supporters and opponents of the proposal.

---

[38] See David T. Ellwood, "The Impact of the Earned Income Tax Credit and Social Policy Reforms on Work, Marriage, and Living Arrangements," *National Tax Journal, 53,* No. 4, December 2000, pp. 1063–1105; N. Eissa and J. Liebman, "Labor Supply Response to the Earned Income Tax Credit," *Quarterly Journal of Economics, 111,* No. 2, May 1996, pp. 605–637; and Scholz, "The Earned Income Tax Credit."

[39] See Rebecca Blank, "Fighting Poverty," and Isabel V. Sawhill, "Poverty in the U.S.," for good general introductions. For a general review of the incentive effects of welfare policies, see Robert Moffitt, "Incentive Effects of the U.S. Welfare System: A Review," *Journal of Economic Literature, 30,* No. 1, March 1992, pp. 1–61.

The use of government as the organization to make these transfers does raise an equity issue: What is the nature of the entitlement, if any, of the recipients to the funds being transferred? From the examples above, one might assume too quickly that initial entitlements rest fully with the donors and certain resources of their choice are granted to the recipients. The government is then used to effect these transfers as a mere organizational convenience. But the fact that some people are made to contribute involuntarily suggests that the transfer is enforced as part of a preexisting social contract. This latter interpretation affects the way we think about the extent of interdependent preferences.

In a social contract interpretation, all members of the society have contingent claims on their wealth (e.g., taxes) and contingent entitlements to wealth (e.g., transfers). A claim or entitlement is contingent upon an individual's future economic circumstances (e.g., tax payments if rich and transfers if poor). The magnitudes of entitlements and liabilities depend upon the rules of the social contract. These specifications are not necessarily reflected in the preferences expressed by citizens *after* they know their own levels of economic success. In fact, one might think that there is a specific bias after the "future" is revealed: The vast majority of people who end up with liabilities rather than entitlements would prefer to give less at the time of transfer than they would agree to be liable for before knowing who will be transferring to whom.[40] This helps explain why a legal system is sometimes necessary to be the "social umpire": to interpret contracts, to judge their validity, and to enforce them. Under the social contract interpretation, the appropriate interdependent preferences are those revealed when the valid contract is specified. This is presumably closer (compared to the pure donation interpretation) to the preferences that would be expressed when everyone is in the dark about who will end up "needy" and who will not.[41]

Whereas the size of the transfer is definitely affected by whichever of the above two situations is thought to be closer to the truth, interdependent preferences may exist in both cases. *If there are interdependent preferences involving the consumption of specific goods, then it is no longer efficient for each consumer to have the same MRS for any two goods consumed.*[42] Suppose we go back to our example with Smith and Jones (as two of many con-

---

[40] This is like asking people how much they are willing to pay for automobile insurance after they know whether they will be involved in any accidents.

[41] The legal problems of interpreting the contract vary with the policy area. For the provision of food stamps, congressional legislation like the original Food Stamp Act of 1964 may be the document of primary interest. For another in-kind good, the provision of legal defense counsel, the courts have ruled that important entitlements are contained in the Sixth Amendment to the Constitution of the United States.

[42] If the interdependent preferences are for general well-being, rather than for specific goods such as food or housing consumption, then no subsidization is required to sustain an efficient allocation. Ordinary prices will do. This result can be derived mathematically by following the format used in the appendix to Chapter 3. An efficient allocation can be thought of as one that maximizes the utility of Jones subject to keeping Smith at some given constant level of utility $\bar{U}^S$. We formulate the Lagrange expression as in the appendix to Chapter 3, noting the slight change in Smith's utility function due to the interdependent preference:

$$L(M_J, T_J) = U^J(M_J, T_J) + \lambda[\bar{U}^S - U^S(M_S, T_S, U^J)]$$

Recall that $M_S = \bar{M} - M_J$ and therefore $\partial M_S/\partial M_J = -1$ and similarly $T_S = \bar{T} - T_J$ and therefore $\partial T_S/\partial T_J = -1$. To find the values of M_J and T_J that maximize L requires the same procedure as before: taking the partial derivatives of L

sumers) consuming meat and tomatoes. For our purposes here, let us assume that Jones is quite poor relative to Smith and that Smith would derive some satisfaction (other things being equal) from an increase in Jones's meat consumption. This is equivalent to saying that Smith has a utility function

$$U^S = U^S(M_S, T_S, M_J)$$

where Smith's utility level increases as Jones's meat consumption rises.

Initially, suppose consumption of meat and tomatoes is such that each person has an $\text{MRS}_{M,T} = 4$ (4 pounds of tomatoes for 1 pound of meat). Smith, however, would also be willing to give up 1 pound of tomatoes in order to increase Jones's meat consumption by 1 pound ($\text{MRS}^S_{M_J, T_S} = 1$). After telling this to Jones, Smith and Jones approach a third consumer. They give the third consumer 4 pounds of tomatoes, 3 pounds from Jones and 1 pound from Smith, in exchange for 1 pound of meat. The third consumer is indifferent. Jones keeps the meat, so Smith is indifferent. But Jones is strictly better off, having given up only 3 pounds of tomatoes to get 1 extra pound of meat. Thus the initial position cannot be efficient, despite the fact that all consumers have the same $\text{MRS}_{M,T}$ in terms of their own consumption.[43]

Exchange efficiency requires, in this case, that the total amount of tomatoes consumers will give up to increase Smith's meat consumption by 1 pound equals the total amount of tomatoes consumers will give up to increase Jones's meat consumption by 1 pound. We can express this more generally if we think of M as any good for which there are interdependent preferences and T as any good for which there are none. Then for every pair of consumers i and j in an economy of m consumers:

---

with respect to M_J, T_J, and λ, setting them all equal to zero, and solving them simultaneously. However, writing down only the first two of these equations will suffice to show the efficiency condition:

$$\frac{\partial L}{\partial M_J} = \frac{\partial U^J}{\partial M_J} - \lambda \frac{\partial U^S}{\partial U^J} \frac{\partial U^J}{\partial M_J} - \lambda \frac{\partial U^S}{\partial M_S} \frac{\partial M_S}{\partial M_J} = 0 \qquad (i)$$

$$\frac{\partial L}{\partial T_J} = \frac{\partial U^J}{\partial T_J} - \lambda \frac{\partial U^S}{\partial U^J} \frac{\partial U^J}{\partial T_J} - \lambda \frac{\partial U^S}{\partial T_S} \frac{\partial T_S}{\partial T_J} = 0 \qquad (ii)$$

By moving the last term in each equation (after simplifying) to the other side and dividing (i) by (ii), we get

$$\frac{(\partial U^J/\partial M_J)(1 - \lambda \partial U^S/\partial U_J)}{(\partial U^T/\partial T_J)(1 - \lambda \partial U^S/\partial U_J)} = \frac{-\lambda \partial U^S/\partial M_S}{-\lambda \partial U^S/\partial T_S}$$

On canceling like terms in numerator and denominator and recalling the definition of MRS, we have

$$\text{MRS}^J_{M_J, T_J} = \text{MRS}^S_{M_S, T_S}$$

This is the usual requirement for exchange efficiency.

[43] Note that the existence of interdependent preferences does *not* interfere with consumer sovereignty. Each consumer is still attempting to use the initial resources to arrange voluntary trades that lead to maximum satisfaction by the consumer's own judgment. The claim that interdependent preference interferes with consumer sovereignty, sometimes seen in the literature, may mistake the equity issue for the efficiency one. If both parties believe they have the initial entitlement to the transfer, then each will feel the other has no authority to direct its allocation.

$$\sum_{k=1}^{m} \mathrm{MRS}_{M_i, T_k}^{k} = \sum_{k=1}^{m} \mathrm{MRS}_{M_j, T_k}^{k}$$

That is, the sum of tomatoes all m consumers will give up to increase i's meat consumption by 1 pound must equal the sum of tomatoes all m consumers will give up to increase j's meat consumption by 1 pound. In our specific example, in which the only interdependent preference among all m consumers is Smith's concern for Jones's consumption of meat M,

$$\mathrm{MRS}_{M_S, T_k}^{k} = 0 \quad \text{whenever } k \neq S$$

$$\mathrm{MRS}_{M_j, T_k}^{k} = 0 \quad \text{whenever } k \neq S \text{ or } J$$

Then the above efficiency condition collapses to

$$\mathrm{MRS}_{M_S, T_S}^{S} = \mathrm{MRS}_{M_j, T_j}^{J} + \mathrm{MRS}_{M_j, T_S}^{S}$$

where the last term reflects Smith's willingness to give up tomatoes in order to increase Jones's meat consumption.[44] The initial position can be seen to violate this condition:

$$4 \neq 4 + 1$$

This violation created the room for a deal that we illustrated.

It should be noted that this illustration is of a *positive consumption externality:* Smith derives pleasure or external benefits from an increase in Jones's meat consumption. In other situations the externality may be *negative:* For example, some people experience reduced pleasure or external costs when others consume tobacco products in their presence.[45] The "standard" case can thus be seen as the middle or neutral ground between positive and neg-

---

[44] To see this, let us use the model from the prior note but substitute M_j for U_j in Smith's utility function:

$$L(M_j, T_j, \lambda) = U_j(M_j, T_j) + \lambda[\bar{U}^S - U^S(M_j, T_j, M_j)]$$

Writing the first two equations for optimization as before, we get:

$$\frac{\partial L}{\partial M_j} = \frac{\partial U^J}{\partial M_j} - \lambda\left(\frac{\partial U^S}{\partial M_S}\frac{\partial M_S}{\partial M_j} + \frac{\partial U^S}{\partial M_j}\right) = 0 \qquad (\text{i})$$

$$\frac{\partial L}{\partial T_j} = \frac{\partial U^J}{\partial T_j} - \lambda\left(\frac{\partial U^S}{\partial T_S}\frac{\partial T_S}{\partial T_j}\right) = 0 \qquad (\text{ii})$$

This simplifies to:

$$\frac{\partial U^J}{\partial M_j} = \lambda\left(\frac{-\partial U^S}{\partial M_S} + \frac{\partial U^S}{\partial M_j}\right) = 0 \qquad (\text{i}')$$

$$\frac{\partial U^J}{\partial T_j} = \lambda\left(\frac{-\partial U^S}{\partial T_S}\right) = 0 \qquad (\text{ii}')$$

By dividing (i′) by (ii′) and recalling the definition of MRS, we get the result in the text:

$$\mathrm{MRS}_{M_j, T_j}^{J} = \mathrm{MRS}_{M_S, T_S}^{S} - \mathrm{MRS}_{M_j, T_S}^{S}$$

[45] Negative interdependent preferences may arise in many situations. For example, you may feel angry if your neighbor washes a car during a severe water shortage. Or you may simply be envious of someone else's good fortune.

ative externalities. In all cases of externalities, the key characteristic is that some agents cause costs or benefits to others as a side effect of their own actions.

In order to relate interdependent preferences to in-kind welfare programs, let us first consider whether efficiency can be achieved if all consumers independently buy and sell at the same market prices. With no mechanism for Smith to influence Jones's consumption, efficiency will not be achieved. Each will choose a consumption pattern that equates the MRS in terms of personal consumption to the ratio of the market prices, and thus each MRS will be the same and the interdependent efficiency condition above will be violated (since $\text{MRS}^S_{M_j, T_S} > 0$). This violation would continue even if a mechanism were created to transfer cash from Smith to Jones, since both would spend their new budgets in light of the market prices.

However, suppose we could create a situation in which Smith and Jones faced different prices. In particular, suppose P_M and P_T represent the market prices but that Jones gets a subsidy of S_M for every pound of meat consumed. Then the real price to Jones per unit of meat is $P_M - S_M$ and the chosen consumption pattern will be such that

$$\text{MRS}^J_{M_J, T_J} = \frac{P_M - S_M}{P_T} = \frac{P_M}{P_T} - \frac{S_M}{P_T}$$

Since Smith will so arrange purchases that $P_M / P_T = \text{MRS}^S_{M_S, T_S}$, the above equation implies

$$\text{MRS}^J_{M_J, T_J} = \text{MRS}^S_{M_S, T_S} - \frac{S_M}{P_T}$$

If S_M is so chosen that $S_M = P_T \text{MRS}^S_{M_J, T_S}$,

$$\text{MRS}^J_{M_J, T_J} = \text{MRS}^S_{M_S, T_S} - \text{MRS}^S_{M_J, T_S}$$

which is the interdependent efficiency requirement. This illustrates the possibility that in-kind transfer programs such as food stamps can be efficient if the subsidy rate is chosen correctly.

The correct subsidy rate in the example equals the dollar value of the tomatoes Smith will forgo in return for increasing Jones's meat consumption 1 unit (from the efficient allocation). This is necessary for the efficient allocation to be an equilibrium: At the real relative price each faces, neither has incentive to alter the consumption bundle.[46]

---

[46] In this example we are ignoring the problem of how to finance the subsidy. If we had to put a tax on Smith, it might alter the (after-tax) prices Smith faces and mess up the equilibrium. We discuss these and other effects of taxation in a general equilibrium framework in Chapter 12.

In a more general case with many "caring" consumers the correct subsidy rate to the ith consumer equals the sum of the dollars each other consumer is willing to forgo in return for increasing the ith consumer's meat consumption by one more unit. That is, to make an efficient allocation be a market equilibrium, the subsidy to the ith consumer must be as follows:

$$S^i_M = P_T \sum_{k \neq i} \text{MRS}^k_{M_i, T_k}$$

Of course, there may be other needy individuals besides the ith consumer, and presumably the willingness to donate to (or subsidize) one consumer depends on how many other needy individuals there are.

This example suggests that, in the presence of interdependent preferences for the consumption of specific goods (rather than general well-being), in-kind transfers may be efficient. Furthermore, cash transfers will generally be inefficient. Thus the standard argument depends on a particular specification of the factors that give individuals utility, namely, that no one has a utility function with arguments representing the consumption of specific goods by others.[47]

The above analysis raises several questions. First, do interdependencies involving specific consumption goods exist, and, if so, how large are they? Second, given the extent of interdependencies relevant to a specific good, do actual subsidies induce the efficient amount of consumption? These are currently unresolved empirical issues, although several analysts have suggested methods for estimating the answers.[48]

Finally, note that the use of theory in this section has not resolved an issue. It has raised empirical questions that otherwise would not have been asked at all. Sometimes this is one of the most important functions of analysis: to clarify and question the assumptions underlying a judgment about a policy.

Summary

This chapter uses models of individual choice for the analysis of government welfare programs. Each of the models assumes utility-maximizing behavior, although they vary in details of their specification. The predictions and efficiency conclusions drawn from these models depend on the particular specifications. The analyses presented are intended primarily to develop a facility with these types of models in order to be able to adapt and use them in other settings. In terms of conventional microeconomics, we have focused on the role of the budget constraint in limiting an individual's utility. We have seen that public policies can affect the shape of an individual's budget constraint in many different ways.

We began with a standard argument used to demonstrate the inefficiency of in-kind welfare programs involving price subsidies, like the Food Stamp Program from 1964 to 1978. Such subsidies create differences in the prices faced by program participants and other food consumers. In the standard model these price differences leave room for a deal and thus cause inefficiency. A cash grant, on the other hand, is efficient by this model. Every policy

---

[47] For more general reading on this subject, see H. Hochman and J. Rodgers, "Pareto Optimal Redistribution," *American Economic Review, 59,* No. 4, September 1969, pp. 542–557, and G. Daly and F. Giertz, "Welfare Economics and Welfare Reform," *American Economic Review, 62,* No. 1, March 1972, pp. 131–138.

[48] An empirical study suggesting the importance of interdependent preferences is A. Kapteyn et al., "Interdependent Preferences: An Econometric Analysis," *Journal of Applied Econometrics, 12,* No. 6, November–December 1997, pp. 665–686. However, another study concluded that they are unlikely to be important. See J. Andreoni and J. K. Scholz, "An Econometric Analysis of Charitable Giving with Interdependent Preferences," *Economic Inquiry, 36,* No. 3, July 1998, pp. 410–428. Earlier contributions include Henry Aaron and Martin McGuire, "Public Goods and Income Distribution," *Econometrica, 38,* November 1970, pp. 907–920; Joseph DeSalvo, "Housing Subsidies: Do We Know What We Are Doing?" *Policy Analysis, 2,* No. 1, Winter 1976, pp. 39–60; and Henry Aaron and George von Fursentberg, "The Inefficiency of Transfers in Kind: The Case of Housing Assistance," *Western Economic Journal, 9,* June 1971, pp. 184–191.

analyst ought to understand this important, general point. However, analysts also should understand that evaluation of the efficiency of actual policies is often more complex.

The standard argument does not account for certain choice restrictions typically imposed by in-kind welfare programs. These restrictions can have important effects, and they deserve analytic attention. To develop the capability for analyzing a broad range of choice restrictions that affect the shape of budget constraints, we explained the income and substitution effects that are used to analyze how an individual responds to changes in income and prices. An individual's consumption of a specific good varies with income in a relationship known as an Engel curve, and varies with the good's price in a relationship known as a demand curve. Consumption is also affected by changes in the prices of related goods that may be substitutes or complements. The degree of responsiveness of consumption to these changes is often summarized by the income, price, and cross-price elasticities, and the more empirical information we have about them the more precisely we can predict the response to a proposed change.

We then showed that some of the choice restrictions in welfare programs can prevent or reduce the inefficiency identified by the standard analysis. That is a characteristic of the food stamp allotment limits and the take-it-or-leave-it choice in public housing. We also analyzed the prohibition against food stamp resale transactions. The effectiveness of the prohibition depends on government efforts to enforce it. From the point of view of the standard model that treats a household like an individual, there is no reason for this prohibition: It is a choice restriction that reduces the utilities of recipients at no gain to anyone else. However, the standard model does not account either for the principal-agent problem of ensuring that the recipient acts in the best interests of the covered household members or for the interdependent preferences possibility (discussed in the optional section) that nonrecipients care about the food consumption of those participating in the food stamp program. It is an unresolved empirical issue whether or not there are benefits of these two types that might outweigh the costs of the resale prohibition.

We also considered the partial-equilibrium nature of the models used to focus on consumption and exchange efficiency. Such analysis can be misleading if it fails to call attention to other important effects of the same policies. Welfare programs affect not only consumption choices, but work efforts as well. We constructed a simple model of the labor-leisure choice that suggests that the work disincentive effects of the current mix of welfare programs can be strong on some participating families. We then showed that the Earned Income Tax Credit increases work incentives for nonworking welfare recipients, although it reduces work incentives for some other eligibles. Awareness of incentive effects such as these is important to the design of many public policies.

This chapter contributed in several ways to the development of analytic skill. First we developed familiarity with the logic of utility maximization subject to a budget constraint. Second, we emphasized that care in model specification is necessary in order to model any particular policy accurately. Third, we saw that public policies often change the incentives individuals face when making certain choices. Good analysts will not only recognize these in existing policies, but will also take account of them when designing new ones.

Exercises

4-1   Qualifying low-income families in a community receive rent subsidies to help them with housing costs. The subsidy is equal to 25 percent of the market rent.

a Draw on one diagram a qualifying family's budget constraint of $1000 for rental housing and all other goods. Show how the constraint is modified by the rental subsidy program.

b Suppose housing is a normal good and that, without subsidy, low-income families usually spend half of their income on rental housing. Find the point on your rental-subsidy constraint at which housing consumption (measured in dollar market value) equals the dollar consumption of all other goods. The values at this point are approximately $571 on each axis. Is this an equilibrium point for the subsidized family with the usual preferences? Explain whether it has just the right amount of housing, too little housing, or too much housing.

c For any point that the family might most prefer on the rental-subsidy constraint, how would you expect its housing consumption to change if the rental subsidy was replaced by an equal-size housing voucher (a certificate in dollars that can be used for housing only, similar to free food stamps).

4-2   The Earned Income Tax Credit (EITC) benefits millions of Americans with incomes below the poverty line and provides encouragement to work for those not currently in the labor force. However, it has different incentive effects for many families who work but whose incomes are still low enough to qualify for it. This problem set is designed to illustrate these latter incentives (in a simplified way). It is also designed to illustrate how every scrap of economic information can be used constructively to make "tighter" estimates of the policy's consequences.

Val is a member of the "working poor." She has a job that pays $8 per hour. She chooses to work 8 hours per day, 5 days per week, 50 weeks per year (i.e., 2000 hours per year), although her employer would hire her to work any number of hours per year. Because of the large family she supports, she does not owe any income taxes and would not owe any even if she increased her work effort by, say, 20 percent (and thus we will henceforth ignore ordinary taxes).

a Draw Val's budget constraint on a graph on which income per year is measured on the vertical axis and leisure per year on the horizontal axis (use 8760 total hours per year to be allocated to either work or leisure; OK to show leisure in range from 4500 up and income correspondingly). Label her current income-leisure choice as point *A*. What is Val's MRS of an hour of leisure for income at this point?

b Under a new EITC plan for Val's family size, there is a $1 credit for every $2 earned up to a maximum $4000 credit. The credit is reduced by 25 percent of all income above $12,000 (until the credit becomes zero). Draw Val's budget constraint under the EITC plan. At what point on this budget constraint is her income and leisure identical to what she could have with no plan (aside from zero work)? Label this as point *C,* the *break-even point.* (Answer: $28,000.)

c Can you predict how the EITC plan will affect Val's working hours? Note that at Val's pre-EITC hours, she is in the "phase-out" portion of the EITC plan. (Answer: It will reduce them.)

d Is it possible, assuming leisure is a normal good, that Val will choose a point at which the MRS of leisure for income is *not* equal to $6? (Answer: Yes.)

e The secretary of the treasury, in a draft of a speech on the EITC plan, calculated that Val's income will be increased by $3000 per year. Furthermore, with 20 million individuals exactly like Val, the annual cost to the government was estimated at $60 billion. The subsidy cost is based on Val's current working hours. Is this a good estimate of Val's annual subsidy? Explain. Assuming that leisure is a normal good, what is the range of possible annual costs to the government? (Answer: $60 to $80 billion.)

f In order to get a better estimate of the cost to the government of the EITC plan, a social experiment was undertaken. The experiment consisted of varying the amount of a fixed credit given to each family unit but always phasing it out at 25 percent of earnings above $12,000. The main thing learned was that, compared to no plan, families said they were equally satisfied with a maximum credit of $1440 and working 7 hours per day (5 days per week, 50 weeks per year). If there were no income effects on leisure in going from this plan to the actual proposed EITC, estimate the annual government costs.

g The second thing learned from the experiment was that, for these individuals, leisure is a necessity with income elasticity less than 0.5. Measure real income as the sum of the dollar values of any disposable income–leisure combination along the phase-out portion of the budget constraint (leisure is valued at its real price, the dollars of other goods and services that must be given up to get it). What leisure level would you expect on the actual proposed EITC if its income elasticity were 0.5?

h Use the answers to (f) and (g) to form a range within which the annual government cost of the proposed EITC plan must lie. (Answer: $70–$76.3 billion.)

APPENDIX

THE MATHEMATICS OF INCOME AND SUBSTITUTION EFFECTS°

For a given utility function we need to know the prices of all goods and the budget level in order to calculate the utility-maximizing choice. We know that individuals change their demands for a certain good X in response to changes in any of the parameters, for example, a change in price or income level as discussed above. The responses are summarized in an ordinary demand function:

$$X = D_X(P_1, P_2, \ldots, P_X, \ldots, P_n, I)$$

where the P_i represents the prices of each good (including X) and I is the income or budget level. The shape of the demand function depends, of course, on the individual's preferences. However, certain aspects of a demand function will appear for anyone who maximizes utility, independently of the particular preferences. It is those general aspects that we attempt to describe by the income and substitution effects.

The response to a unit increase in income is found by taking the partial derivative of the demand equation with respect to income $\partial X/\partial I$. A good is "normal" if this partial derivative is positive, and "inferior" if it is negative. The income elasticity is defined as

$$\varepsilon_{X,I} = \frac{\partial X}{\partial I} \cdot \frac{I}{X}$$

where $\varepsilon_{X,I}$ denotes the elasticity of the variable X with respect to the variable I. As I and X are positive quantities, the income elasticity has the same sign as the partial derivative $\partial X/\partial I$. Note that the magnitude of the elasticity does not have to be constant; it depends on the consumption point from which it is measured. As an obvious example, a good that is inferior at one income level must have been normal at some lower income level. (Otherwise, there would not be a positive quantity of it to reduce.)

The response to a unit increase in price is found by taking the partial derivative of the demand equation with respect to price $\partial X/\partial P_X$. *The decomposition of this total effect of a price change into its component income and substitution effects is described by the Slutsky equation:*

$$\frac{\partial X}{\partial P_X} = \frac{\partial X}{\partial P_X}\bigg|_{U=U_0} - X \frac{\partial X}{\partial I}$$

where the first term is the substitution effect (the utility level is held constant at its initial level U_0) and the second is the income effect.[49] Note that the overall size of the income effect is proportional to the individual's initial consumption level of the good X.

The price elasticity of demand is defined as

$$\varepsilon_{X,P_X} = \frac{\partial X}{\partial P_X} \frac{P_X}{X}$$

Except for a Giffen good, the price elasticity is negative (P_X and X are positive; $\partial X/\partial P_X$ is negative).

It is often easier, when doing empirical analysis, to work with elasticities because they are thought to be more "constant" than the partial derivatives over the changes in prices or income considered. The Slutsky equation can be rewritten in terms of price and income elasticities. Multiply both sides of it by P_x/X and the last term by I/I:

---

[49] Eugen E. Slutsky (1880–1948) was the Russian economist who first derived this equation. A short derivation of it, using the theory of duality that we introduce in the appendix to Chapter 6, is in Philip J. Cook, "A 'One-Line' Proof of the Slutsky Equation," *American Economic Review, 62,* No. 1/2, 1972, p. 139.

$$\frac{\partial X}{\partial P_X}\frac{P_X}{X} = \frac{\partial X}{\partial P_X}\bigg|_{U=U_0}\frac{P_X}{X} - X\frac{\partial X}{\partial I}\frac{P_X}{X}\frac{I}{I}$$

or

$$\varepsilon_{X,P_X} = \varepsilon_{X,P_X}^S \frac{P_X X}{I}\frac{\partial X}{\partial I}\frac{I}{X}$$

where ε_{X,P_X}^S is the "substitution elasticity, or

$$\varepsilon_{X,P_X} = \varepsilon_{X,P_X}^S - \frac{P_X X}{I}\varepsilon_{X,I}$$

Note that $P_x X / I$ is the proportion of income spent on the good X.

CHAPTER FIVE

THE ANALYSIS OF EQUITY STANDARDS:
AN INTERGOVERNMENTAL GRANT APPLICATION

THIS CHAPTER IS INTENDED to develop further skills of model specification and show how to use those skills to understand the equity consequences of proposed or actual policies. The equity or fairness of a policy is often difficult to evaluate because of a lack of social consensus on the appropriate standard. However, that does not mean that the analysis of equity consequences is left to the whims of the analyst. In this chapter we will introduce several equity standards and apply them in a discussion of school finance policy. These standards can be applied routinely to the analysis of a broad range of policies and are often used in legal and legislative settings.

The chapter is organized as follows. First, a number of principles of equity are introduced in a systematic way: strict equality, a universal minimum, equal opportunity, simple neutrality, conditional opportunity and neutrality, and horizontal and vertical equity. Some of these characterize the outcomes of a resource allocation process, and others characterize the fairness of the process itself. Next we turn to develop an application of these standards to school finance policies. We first go over some standard analyses of intergovernmental grants in general, and then review some grant policies for school financing that have caused public concerns. We relate these concerns to the equity standards and consider how intergovernmental grant programs can be designed to achieve the standards. In an appendix we present an exercise to illustrate the use of social welfare functions in evaluating school finance policies.

Equity Objectives

In general, *equity* or *fairness* refers to the relative distribution of well-being among the people in an economy. But although this identifies the topic clearly, it provides no guidance to what is equitable. There are a number of shared principles of equity that can serve as analytic guides, but in any particular situation the analyst must recognize that there may be no consensus about which one is most applicable.[1] Nevertheless, the analysts can describe the effects of proposed or actual policies in terms of the particular equity concepts thought most relevant.

The use of well-defined concepts of equity not only helps users of the analysis to understand policy consequences of concern to them but avoids arbitrariness in the analytic methodology. Even if the analyst feels that none of the better-known principles is applicable to a particular policy, those principles can still serve as a context for the analysis. By having to argue that some other concept is more appropriate than the better-known ones, this helps to produce a clarity of reasoning that might otherwise be absent.

The introductory discussion in Chapter 3 distinguished two broad categories of equity concepts: those that relate to outcomes and those that relate to process. **Outcome concepts of equity are concerned with the existence in the aggregate of variation in the shares that individuals receive. Process concepts of equity are concerned with whether the rules and methods for distributing the shares among individuals are fair.** Keep in mind that these are different standards by which to judge a system of resource allocation; a system can do well by one of these two broad concepts and poorly by the other. Furthermore, changes made to improve the system in one equity dimension can cause deterioration as judged by the other (and, of course, can affect efficiency as well). We will illustrate this for school finances shortly.

There is also an issue concerning the type of shares that should be scrutinized in the light of an equity norm. One position is that we are interested in how policies affect *general distribution: the overall distribution of utility in the economy, or measurable proxies for utility such as income or wealth.* A different position is that we are interested in *specific egalitarianism: the equity of the distribution of particular goods and services,* for example, medical care.[2] The underlying philosophy of specific egalitarianism is that although it might be fine to allow most goods to be allocated and distributed purely as the rewards of market forces, different rules should apply to a limited category of goods and services. The basic necessities of living (e.g., food, shelter, clothing, essential medical care) should be guaranteed to all, and civic rights and obligations (e.g., voting, the military draft, jury duty) should not be allocated purely by the forces of the market.[3] Most of the equity concepts discussed

---

[1] The framework in this section was first explicated in Lee Friedman, "The Ambiguity of *Serrano:* Two Concepts of Wealth Neutrality," *Hastings Constitutional Law Quarterly, 4,* 1977, pp. 97–108, and Lee Friedman and Michael Wiseman, "Understanding the Equity Consequences of School Finance Reform," *Harvard Educational Review, 48,* No. 2, May 1978, pp. 193–226. A comprehensive treatment of equity concepts for school finance is contained in Robert Berne and Leanna Stiefel, *The Measurement of Equity in School Finance* (Baltimore: Johns Hopkins University Press, 1984).

[2] See James Tobin, "On Limiting the Domain of Inequality," *Journal of Law and Economics, 13,* October 1970, pp. 263–278.

[3] Note that this can imply a rejection of utilitarianism. For example, we can imagine allowing the buying and selling of votes, which would increase individual welfare. Yet the laws prohibiting the transfer of voting rights suggest that the underlying norm of one person, one vote applies to the distribution of the voting right itself and not the individual utility that might be derived from it.

below can be applied either to the general redistributive effects or to the distribution of a specific good or service of concern.

Additionally, the concepts must be applied to a well-defined population. Often this is simply geographic, as to residents of a particular country, state, or city. However, non-geographic definitions can be used as well. For example, most of the legal debate about school financing applies to spending variation among *public school students* within a jurisdiction (and thus spending on students attending private schools is not considered). As another example, we might be interested in the equity of health services available to *veterans* (and thus a precise definition of veteran is required).

With clear definitions of the good or service and of the relevant population, we can turn to the different equity concepts that can be applied. There are two outcome concepts of equity that are commonly used: strict equality and a universal minimum. **The norm of strict equality means that all people should receive equal shares.** There are numerous ways of measuring the degree to which a system attains that standard. One common method is to graph a Lorenz curve and calculate its associated Gini coefficient.

A *Lorenz curve* shows the relation between two variables X and Y defined as follows:

X = the percent (from 0 to 100) of the measured population, ordered by and
   starting from those with the least amount of the good or service under study

Y = the percent (from 0 to 100) of the total amount of the good or service
   in the measured population that the X percent receives (or provides).

For example, one point on the 1997 Lorenz curve for U.S. household income is that 3.6 percent of total income accrues to the poorest 20 percent of the population (Figure 5-2, which we will discuss shortly). Every Lorenz curve begins at the origin and ends at the point where $X = Y = 100$ percent (the 100 percent of the population with the least amount of Y has all of it). When strict equality holds, the Lorenz curve is simply a straight 45° line (each X percent of the population has $Y = X$ percent of the good). If one person has all of the good or service and everybody else has none, the Lorenz curve is a right angle that coincides with the X-axis until it reaches 100 percent and then becomes vertical (to the height where Y equals 100 percent).

To illustrate, Figure 5-1 shows a hypothetical Lorenz curve for yearly jury duty. The percent of total population eligible for jury duty, ordered by and starting from those who served the least to those who served the most, is measured along the horizontal axis. The percent of total jury service provided (in terms of person-days on jury duty) is measured along the vertical axis. As drawn, 25 percent of the population provided no service, the next 25 percent provided 10 percent of jury service, the next 25 percent provided 15 percent of jury service, and the last 25 percent provided the remaining 75 percent of jury service.[4]

---

[4] Note that the shape of the Lorenz curve in this example might shift dramatically if we redefined the period of time considered, for example, 2 years instead of 1 year. Obviously this does not imply that the longer period is fairer; both are pictures of the same distribution and must represent equal fairness. The analyst must be careful to recognize the effect of choosing a particular definition of the units being distributed and to keep the units constant when making comparisons.

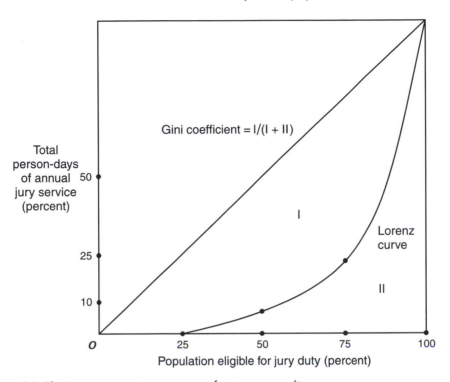

Figure 5-1. The Lorenz curve is a measure of outcome equality.

Sometimes it is useful to have an empirical measure of the degree of equality, and a common index used for that is the *Gini coefficient,* defined graphically by the Lorenz curve as the ratio of area I to area I + II as illustrated in Figure 5-1. Thus the further the Lorenz curve from the 45° line, the higher the Gini coefficient.[5] If each person in the population provided

[5] Mathematically, if $d_1, d_2, \ldots, d_n$ represent the days served as juror by each of the n people in the eligible population, the Gini coefficient equals

$$\frac{\sum_{i=i}^{n} \sum_{j=i}^{n} |d_i - d_j|}{2n^2 \bar{d}}$$

where $\bar{d}$ is the mean of the d_i.

As an illustrative example, suppose there are only four people and the jury days served by each (ordered from highest to lowest) are 75, 15, 10, and 0. Then there are a total of 100 days of jury service, and the average number of days per person is $\bar{d} = 100/4 = 25$. The denominator of the formula for the Gini coefficient is $2n^2\bar{d} = 2(4^2)(25) = 800$. The numerator is

$$\sum_{i=i}^{n} \sum_{j=i}^{n} |d_i - d_j| = |75 - 75| + |75 - 15| + |75 - 10| + |75 - 0| + |15 - 75| + |15 - 15|$$
$$+ |15 - 10| + |15 - 0| + |10 - 75| + |10 - 15| + |10 - 10|$$
$$+ |10 - 0| + |0 - 75| + |0 - 15| + |0 - 10| + |0 - 0|$$
$$= 460$$

The Gini coefficient is then $.575 = 460/800$.

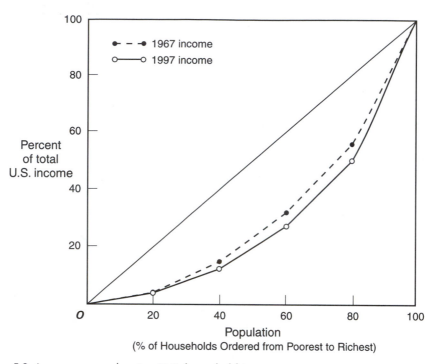

Figure 5-2. Lorenz curves showing U.S. household income.

the same jury service, the Lorenz curve would coincide with the 45° line, area I would shrink to zero, and the Gini coefficient would be zero. At the other extreme, if one person provided all the jury service, the Lorenz curve would coincide with the outer bounds of area II and the Gini coefficient would approach 1.[6] Thus the Gini coefficient is a measure of the degree to which strict equality is attained: zero if it is attained exactly, positive if there is any inequality, and approaching a maximum of 1 as the inequality worsens. If the Lorenz curve for one policy alternative lies strictly within the Lorenz curve for another policy alternative, the first is unambiguously more equal and will have a lower Gini coefficient.

A Lorenz curve can give a good visual picture of the degree of equality, and two or more of them drawn on the same diagram may be used to compare distributions (e.g., if jury service is more equal in New York than in Boston, or if jury service in New York is more equal in 1999 than it was in 1989). To illustrate this, let us leave the hypothetical and turn to an important real example. Figure 5-2 shows a Lorenz curve for household income in the United States for 1997 (the solid-line curve) and for 1967 (the dotted line).[7] The percent of total household population is measured along the horizontal X-axis, ordered and starting

---

[6] The Gini coefficient in this case is $(n - 1)/n$, which approaches 1 for large n.

[7] The data used in the discussion and to construct these curves were taken from pp. xi–xii of *Money Income in the United States: 1997,* Current Population Reports, Consumer Income P60-200 (Washington, D.C.: U.S. Bureau of the Census, 1998).

from those with the least income to those with the most. The percent of total U.S. income is measured along the vertical Y-axis. In 1997 the poorest quintile of households had only 3.6 percent of income, while the richest quintile had 49.4 percent. The Gini coefficient for 1997 was .459.

You may have noticed that the 1967 Lorenz curve lies entirely within the 1997 one: the distribution of income has become unambiguously *less* equal over this 30-year period. In 1967, the lowest quintile had 4.0 percent of income, and the richest quintile had 43.8 percent of it. The Gini coefficient for 1967 was .399; by this measure, income inequality in 1997 was 15 percent greater than in 1967. Many studies of U.S. income inequality have confirmed that inequality began to increase in the mid-1970s and continued to do so gradually until the mid-1990s; in the last few years (1997–2000), it has remained approximately constant.

This increase in inequality was not expected and is of concern to many. It was not expected because from the 1940s through most of the 1960s the economy had been growing rapidly while at the same time inequality was gradually lessening. The two main reasons generally offered for the long-term increase of the 30 years between 1967 and 1997 are that: (1) technological change during this period had a "bias" toward increased demand for higher-skill workers, resulting in greater earnings inequality among workers, and (2) the proportion of households headed by a single female increased significantly (from about 10 to 18 percent), and these households have less income than others because, on the one hand, there are fewer earners in them and, on the other, because women tend to earn less than men. Nevertheless, the causes of changes in income inequality are an unsettled matter for further research.[8]

In our example, the Lorenz curves did not cross. But they can cross, and two Lorenz curves that cross can have the same Gini coefficient: One curve will have greater inequality among the people in the lower end and the other greater inequality among those in the upper end. Like all single-parameter measures of the degree of equality, the Gini coefficient does not always reflect legitimate concerns about the location of the inequality.[9] Thus, one must be cautious about comparing two very different distributions by this or any other single-parameter measure. That is why it is often useful to display the Lorenz curves of the distributions being compared on a graph or, similarly, to construct a chart that shows what each

[8] A good overview of U.S. income inequality is provided in Chapter 5 of the *1997 Economic Report of the President* (Washington, D.C.: U.S. Government Printing Office, 1997). Interesting studies of this include Frank Levy, *The New Dollars and Dreams: The Changing American Income Distribution* (New York: Russell Sage Foundation, 1999), and Richard C. Michel, "Economic Growth and Income Equality Since the 1982 Recession," *Journal of Policy Analysis and Management, 10,* No. 2, Spring 1991, pp. 181–203. A review of inequality studies encompassing many countries is P. Aghion, E. Caroli, and C. Garæia-Penalosa, "Inequality and Economic Growth: The Perspective of the New Growth Theories," *Journal of Economic Literature, 38,* No. 4, December 1999, pp. 1615–1660.

[9] Another common measure is the coefficient of variation, which is defined as the standard deviation divided by the mean. It is zero at perfect equality and increases as the distribution becomes more unequal. For a general discussion of inequality measurement, see A. B. Atkinson, "On Measurement of Inequality," *Journal of Economic Theory, 2,* 1970, pp. 244–263.

quintile or decile of the population receives under the alternative distributions. Even the simple observation that the lowest quintile receives a smaller percentage does not necessarily mean that the households are worse off in an absolute sense: a smaller percentage of a bigger income pie can still be a larger slice.[10]

The other outcome standard of equity is the **universal minimum, which means that each person should receive a share that is at least the size of the minimum standard.** Unlike strict equality, application of this norm requires that a particular minimum standard be selected. During the Nixon administration, a proposal that was effectively a guaranteed minimum income was debated by Congress and did not pass, although a majority favored such a plan. The proposal, called a Negative Income Tax, was like an Earned Income Tax Credit with maximum credit occurring at zero work (and other income) and then gradual reduction. The maximum credit was thus a guaranteed minimum income. One part of the majority insisted upon a higher minimum guarantee than the other part would agree to support, so the majority became two minorities.

Once a minimum standard is selected, one can count the number or proportion of individuals below the minimum and the total quantity required to bring all those below up to the minimum. Often the analyst will pose several alternative minimum standards to discover the "equity cost" of increases in the standard. This exercise can be trickier than one might suspect.

One issue is whether the source of supplementation to those below the standard must come from those above it or whether other goods or services can be converted into the good or service of concern. For example, if minimum educational resources per child are the issue, one need not take educational resources away from those who have them in abundance. Instead, more educational services can be produced by doing with less of all other goods. On the other hand, a shortage of water in an emergency might require the redistribution of water from those who usually consume larger quantities (e.g., owners of swimming pools) to others. That is, the supply of water during the relevant time period may be fixed, or perfectly inelastic. When the good in question has positive elasticity of supply, it need not be directly redistributed. In the elastic case, it is not hard to show that the efficiency cost of achieving the minimum is lower with expanding production than with direct redistribution of the existing quantities.[11]

Not only does the cost bear on the method of achieving the minimum; it also bears on whether a minimum is more desirable than strict equality. For example, consider whether it might be appropriate to ensure strict equality in the distribution of the entire privately produced GDP. If all potential suppliers of resources (labor and nonlabor) to the market knew

---

[10] Unfortunately, this does not appear to be the case for the poorest segment in the United States during this 30-year period.

[11] Imagine assigning a tax to each person having more than the minimum standard so that the total tax will provide enough resources to bring all up to the minimum. Then give each taxpayer the choice of paying the tax directly from his or her existing stock of the good or by its cash equivalent. All the taxpayers will prefer to give cash, which is then used to produce additional units of the good. Thus it is more efficient to expand production (when it is elastic) than to redistribute directly.

that they would end up with the *average* share independently of their *individual* decisions (each having a negligible effect on the total), the incentives would be to supply very little and the GDP would plummet drastically. The achievement of strict equality does not seem to be a very pragmatic objective for a market-oriented economy with substantial individual liberties. However, this is not to say that moving closer toward it from where we are now is not important. Rather, past some point, the reduction in equality would not be worth its efficiency cost.[12] On the other hand, a reasonable universal minimum might be attainable well before the economy reaches its "most equal" overall distribution. Thus cost considerations might influence the choice of which equity standards to emphasize.

Of course, the choice of standards still comes down to a moral judgment about which is best. In the education example given above, a universal minimum was posited as the objective. But many people feel that is just not the relevant standard; they might insist that all children be educated equally. The responsibility of the analyst in this situation is to make clear that there are competing conceptions and to try to clarify the consequences of achieving the alternative standards.

Having discussed some issues relevant to the selection of an outcome standard of equity, let us turn to the process standards of equity. *Process standards become applicable when inequality of share sizes is explicitly permitted. The concern here is not with how much aggregate inequality exists but with whether the share that each person ends up with has resulted from a fair process.* There may be only one winner and many losers of a lottery, but if the entry conditions are the same for all and each entrant has an equal chance of winning, we might think that the distribution is perfectly equitable.

The economic agents in an economy might be viewed in an analogous way. When individuals make resource allocation decisions in an economic system, there is often uncertainty about what the outcome will be. For example, consider the sequence of decisions to invest in higher education by attending college, to choose a major subject, and to select a job from the jobs offered after graduation. These represent a series of contingent decisions that affect but do not completely determine the income streams of particular individuals. After all the decisions are made, we observe that, on average, those with college degrees have higher incomes than those without, those with certain majors have higher incomes than other college graduates, and those who accepted jobs in certain industries earn higher incomes than similarly educated people who went into other industries. Whether this whole process is thought fair depends upon the entry conditions to colleges, major subjects, and industries, as well as on how the payoffs are distributed within each part of the whole sequence. If, because of their sex, women are denied entrance to the best schools or are not considered for promotion within a particular industry, then one might think that this process of resource allocation is unfair.

There are several standards by which an attempt is made to capture the ideal of process equity. A fundamental one is **equal opportunity: Each person should have the same**

---

[12] Recall the discussion in Chapter 4 about the Earned Income Tax credit, which illustrated that welfare assistance reduced work effort more or less, depending on the design.

chance of obtaining a share of a given size. However, in practice it is virtually impossible to tell whether a particular person has been given equal opportunity. For example, periodically the government has a lottery, which any citizen can enter for a minimal fee, to award oil leasing rights on federally owned land. If a loser in the government lottery claims that his or her number did not have the same chance of being drawn as every other number, how can one tell after the fact? Because it is often the case that each person makes a specific decision only rarely (e.g., to enter the lottery), it may be impossible to know whether the outcome is explained by chance or by denial of equal opportunity. On the other hand, if a person made many sequential bets on the same roulette wheel, it would be possible by using statistical laws to tell whether the game had been rigged against the person.

Suppose that the oil lease lottery really was rigged to favor certain entrants. Could that be discovered through an examination of the results? If some identifiable group of entrants (e.g., private citizens as opposed to oil companies) does not win its fair share of leases, it may be taken as a strong indication of rigging.[13] But without group evidence of this kind, the rigging may go unnoticed. Thus, it may be necessary to fall back on tests involving a group of participants to substitute for the lack of multiple tests involving a single participant. If there really is equal opportunity for each person and if we divided the participants into two groups, each group ought to receive a similar distribution of share sizes.[14]

In fact, sometimes we simply substitute the concept of neutrality for particular groups instead of the more stringent concept of equal opportunity for each individual. That is, we may accept a resource allocation process as fair if it does not discriminate against selected groups of particular social concern. These groups usually become identified by suspicions that they have been discriminated against in the past. The courts, for example, often apply "strict scrutiny" in cases in which the alleged denial of equal opportunity or equal treatment arises by classifying people into groups by race or wealth.[15] This scrutiny was relevant to the findings that poll taxes are unconstitutional and that states must provide counsel to poor individuals accused of serious crimes. In both rulings, a key part of the arguments was that wealth was a suspect means of classification and that state action prevented poor people from having opportunity equal to that of others. Let us refer more loosely to the groupings thought to be of particular social concern as the suspect groupings and define **simple neutrality: The distribution of shares within a suspect group should be identical to the distribution of shares among all others.**

---

[13] The lottery for oil and gas leasing was temporarily suspended on February 29, 1980, by Interior Secretary Cecil Andrus. The government charged that some oil companies had cheated by submitting multiple entries for individual parcels, in violation of federal rules. See the articles in the *Wall Street Journal* on April 8, 1980 (p. 12, col. 2) and October 6, 1980 (p. 29, cols. 4–6). In January 1999, police in Italy arrested nine people for fixing the Milan lottery. According to newspaper reports, the investigation began 8 months earlier when police in Cinisello Balsamo noticed that an unusual number of locals were winning. See "Scandal Sullies Italian Lottery," *Associated Press Online,* January 15, 1999.

[14] In this manner, we use knowledge about the outcomes for the purpose of judging the process. Note that this is quite different from judgment by the outcome standards themselves.

[15] "Strict scrutiny" is a legal term for a particular type of judicial test for constitutionality. As the term suggests, it is more difficult for laws to withstand judicial examination with strict scrutiny than with other tests.

Whenever there is equal opportunity, there will be simple neutrality. If each person has the same chance as other persons of receiving a share of any given size, then any large grouping will be characterized by simple neutrality. Each group will receive approximately the same proportions of any given share size, and the average share size in each group will therefore be approximately the same.

However, simple neutrality with respect to one suspect group does not mean that there is equal opportunity. Overweight people, for example, can be systematic victims of discrimination and thus are denied equal opportunity. The discrimination will not affect neutrality with respect to race (the suspect group in this example) as long as each race has the same proportion of overweight people in it. Thus simple racial neutrality can hold while, at the same time, equal opportunity is not available to all. Simple neutrality is therefore a less stringent standard than equal opportunity.

One reasonable and common objection to the standard of either equal opportunity or simple neutrality is that there may be legitimate reasons for differences in share sizes. For example, excessive weight might be just cause for denial of employment as a police officer. Then weight is an *exceptional characteristic: a factor that is legitimately expected to influence shares.* All applicants might be considered equally, conditional upon being within the weight limits. To account for legitimate deviations from equal opportunity caused by exceptional characteristics, we define the standard of **conditional equal opportunity: Every person with identical exceptional characteristics has the same chance of obtaining a share of a given size.**

To continue with the police example, consider the question of neutrality by race. If applicants grouped by race have identical characteristics except that Caucasians are more overweight than others, then simple neutrality would not be expected to hold (a smaller proportion of Caucasian applicants would be offered employment). However, we would expect **conditional neutrality** to hold: **Among those with identical exceptional characteristics, the distribution of shares within a suspect group should be identical to that of all others.** Thus suspect factors are those that are not allowed to cause distributional differences, and the exceptional characteristics are factors that are allowed to cause those differences.

Whenever there are differences in exceptional characteristics across suspect groupings, simple and conditional neutrality offer different standards. (Both cannot be met by one system.) Conditional neutrality is less stringent than simple neutrality in the sense that it permits larger differences among the shares received by each group. Even if one finds that a system is conditionally neutral, it is wise to examine the effects of the exceptional characteristics. Exactly how much difference is to be allowed because of an exceptional characteristic depends upon the specific situation being analyzed.

The terms used to assess the fairness of differences allowed owing to exceptional characteristics are horizontal and vertical equity. The most common application of these is in evaluating the fairness of tax systems. In typical cases, the outcomes are the amount of taxes paid and one of the exceptional characteristics is before-tax income.[16] **Horizontal equity**

---

[16] Outcomes might alternatively be defined in terms of utilities. We provide an illustration in the appendix to this chapter.

means that likes should be treated alike. Since tax amounts are often determined by factors besides income (e.g., factors leading to deductions or exemptions, or use of a non-income tax base such as sales), the crucial equity issue is whether other exceptional characteristics in addition to income will be used to assess fairness. That is, are "likes" defined simply by their income levels or are there other characteristics that must also be the same for them to be truly "likes"?[17]

For example, consider two households with the same income and living in identical dwelling units and paying the same housing expenses. The only difference between these two households is that one rents the dwelling unit and the other is an owner-occupant. Under current federal law, the owner-occupant can deduct the mortgage interest charges from income and will pay lower taxes. Many economists feel that this difference, while long-established, violates the standard of horizontal equity. Other examples of differences recognized by the current federal tax code include age (extra deduction if over 65), medical expenses, and source of income (such as the exemption of dividend income from most state and local municipal bonds). These deductions and exemptions have consequences beyond their fairness: Each causes an increase in the tax rate necessary to raise a fixed amount of revenue, increasing the effect of taxation on other allocative decisions (as we saw in the labor-leisure choice example in the previous chapter).

One distinction deserving special mention is whether the benefit an individual receives from the government good or service is an exceptional characteristic. *Use of benefits as an exceptional characteristic is referred to as taxation by the benefit principle, whereas use of income is referred to as the ability-to-pay principle.* To the extent that governments raise revenue through user fees or other charges for goods and services provided, they are relying on the benefit principle. Gasoline taxes and cigarette taxes are often given the justification that they are collected from the people who most benefit from the roads and from medical services for smoking-related illnesses. The appropriateness of this distinction on grounds of horizontal equity is an important factor in the design of government financing systems.

Vertical equity means that there is a fair difference in shares among people with different levels of the exceptional characteristics. In the case of federal taxes, there is widespread agreement that people with higher income should pay higher taxes. In principle, taxation can be *proportional* (taxes rising proportionately with income), *progressive* (rising faster than income), or *regressive* (rising more slowly than income). To illustrate, suppose the tax on $10,000 income is $1000. Then the tax on $20,000 is proportional if $2000, progressive if more than $2000, and regressive if less than $2000.

Evaluations that attempt to measure the relative burdens on different groups caused by a tax are referred to as studies of *tax incidence.* Most evaluations of our federal income tax system have concluded that it is mildly progressive. Sales taxes and payroll taxes, on the

---

[17] In nontax applications, a measure of economic means such as income may not be an exceptional characteristic. For example, there are horizontal and vertical equity issues in criminal sentencing policy involving the relationships between the seriousness of crime and the penalty received.

other hand, are generally regressive. However, the study of tax incidence is quite complicated and the results subject to much uncertainty because of the phenomena of *tax-shifting:* The legal payers of the tax may not be the same as the individuals bearing its burden (e.g., if a landlord pays a property tax that is fully recovered through rents received, then the tax has been shifted to the tenants). We shall return to the tax-shifting issue in Chapter 12, and for now simply note that it complicates any efforts to assess vertical (and sometimes horizontal) equity.

The concepts of horizontal and vertical equity apply to many policy issues other than tax policy. For example, there are legal equity requirements concerning the provision of counsel to those accused of crimes and the appropriateness of the sentences given to the guilty. As another example, many people feel that health care should be based strictly on medical need and without regard to an individual's ability to pay.[18] In another area, Congress has ordered the Federal Communications Commission to find a way to ensure that women, minorities, and small businesses receive a fair share of licenses for use on the portion of the radio spectrum reserved for personal communications services.[19]

While equity judgments can be quite difficult to make, analytic review using the concepts covered here can greatly clarify the consequences of existing policies and proposed changes to them. Of course, there are many issues involving the use, measurement, and extension of equity concepts that are the subject of ongoing research.[20] However, let us at this point turn to issues in their practical application. We begin with some introductory analytics for intergovernmental grant programs, and then consider an ongoing equity issue involving intergovernmental grants for schools.

Intergovernmental Grants

In the fiscal year 2000 approximately $235 billion was provided through grants-in-aid from the federal government to state and local governments.[21] These funds were provided through a wide variety of programs, such as health care for the homeless, urban mass transit assistance, and community development block grants. States also fund grant-in-aid programs to local governments, most notably for school financing. About one-third of state

---

[18] An interesting debate on this issue was sparked by the article by Julian Le Grand, "The Distribution of Public Expenditure: The Case of Health Care," *Economica, 45,* 1978, pp. 125–142. See, for example, A. Wagstaff, E. Vandoorslaer, and P. Paci, "On the Measurement of Horizontal Equity in the Delivery of Health Care," *Journal of Health Economics, 10,* No. 2, July 1991, pp. 169–205, and in the same issue Julian Le Grand, "The Distribution of Health Care Revisited—A Commentary," pp. 239–245.

[19] See the article "U.S. Opens Air Waves to Women, Minorities," *San Francisco Chronicle,* June 30, 1994.

[20] See for example John E. Roemer, *Equality of Opportunity* (Cambridge: Harvard University Press, 1998); Edward Zajac, *Political Economy of Fairness* (Cambridge: The MIT Press, 1995); Amartya Sen, *Inequality Reexamined* (Cambridge: Harvard University Press, 1992); and William J. Baumol, *Superfairness* (Cambridge : The MIT Press, 1986).

[21] *Economic Report of the President,* January 2001 (Washington D.C.: U.S. Government Printing Office, 2001), p. 371, Table B-82.

spending consists of intergovernmental aid, and this spending is equal to about one-third of local revenues.[22]

Although these grants have diverse purposes, most economic rationales for them depend on either externalities or equity arguments. An example of an externality argument might be as follows. School districts do not have sufficient incentive to bear the costs of devising innovative educational techniques because the benefits of success will accrue primarily to schools external to the district boundaries (who will imitate for free). Thus, although the social benefits of research and development for the education sector might outweigh the costs, the private benefits to any single district may not justify the expense to the taxpayers within it.[23] As an attempt to ameliorate this problem the federal government sponsors the Elementary and Secondary Education Act, which provides grant funds to pay for innovative demonstration projects.

In the last part of this chapter we will consider the design of a grant program to achieve an equity goal: the "neutralization" of the influence of local wealth on local school finance decisions. Another grant program with a possible justification on equity grounds was the federal general revenue-sharing program for cities.[24] No single city can impose too progressive a tax system on its own, or those faced with high taxes might simply move outside the city boundaries. The federal government, on the other hand, has less need to be concerned about tax avoidance through locational choice. Thus the federal government might play the role of tax collector and, through revenue sharing, fund given services in a more progressive manner. Rivlin has proposed a system that could facilitate this, based on common shared taxes among the states, similar to the system used in Germany.[25]

Aside from strict economic rationales *for intergovernmental grants, political rationales may also be relevant.* For example, some people feel that individual liberties are threatened when too much decision-making power is left in the hands of the central government; they might favor more local control of spending even if revenues were raised by the central government.

Design Features of a Grant Program

In this section we will go over economically relevant *design features of an intergovernmental grant* program. They can generally be classified into three categories: *income effects, price effects,* and *choice restrictions.* Knowledge of these three features can then be com-

---

[22] See Helen F. Ladd, "State Assistance to Local Governments: Changes During the 1980s," *Economic Review, 80,* No. 2, May 1990, pp. 171–175.

[23] Under a private market system, these social benefits can often be captured by the innovating unit through the patent system, which "internalizes" the externality. In Chapter 17, we focus upon the analysis of externalities.

[24] This program was terminated during the Reagan administration in a reform movement that, somewhat inconsistently, consolidated a large number of specialized grant programs into a smaller number of broader ones. General revenue sharing is simply a further consolidation, but one that lacked special appeal to the politically organized interest groups at the time.

[25] Rivlin's primary focus is on productivity, but her proposal allows for progressivity for reasons similar to those for general revenue sharing. See Alice M. Rivlin, *Reviving the American Dream* (Washington, D.C.: The Brookings Institution, 1992).

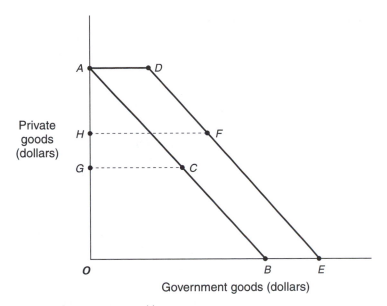

Figure 5-3. Nonmatching grants are like income increases.

bined with a model of the decision-making behavior of the recipient to predict the effects of the grant. Initially we will assume that the recipient community can be treated like a utility-maximizing individual; from that perspective, the analysis of intergovernmental grants is identical with the welfare policies analyzed in the preceding chapter. (Welfare payments also are grants, but to families rather than governments.) Then we will consider model variants of the decision-making process that challenge the "community utility-maximization" perspective.

Income Effects and Nonmatching Grants

Nonmatching grants, or block grants, are fixed amounts of funds given to an economic unit to spend. Typically these are given by a higher-level government to a lower-level one, and they may or may not be restricted to use for particular purposes. They affect the recipient primarily by altering the amount of funds available to spend on anything—a pure income effect. This can be seen in Figure 5-3, which shows the trade-offs faced by a community allocating its budget between government and private goods. Here government goods are any goods and services provided through the local government and financed by taxes. Private goods are goods and services that community members buy as individuals in the marketplace with their after-tax incomes. Both government and private goods are measured by the dollar expenditures on them; the sum of expenditures on them equals the community budget level.

Let *AB* represent the pregrant budget constraint, and say the community initially is at a point like *C*. Then let the central government provide general revenue-sharing funds to the community to be used for any local government goods or services.[26] The new budget constraint is then *ADE*. That is, the community still cannot obtain more than *OA* in private goods, can have government goods up to the amount at *D* (*AD* is the size of the grant) without sacrifice of private goods, and past *D* must sacrifice private goods to consume additional government goods. Since the grant does not alter the prices of either government or private goods, the *DE* segment is parallel to *AB* (as a pure income increase would be). If both government and private goods are normal, the community will increase its purchases of both, and it will move to a point like *F* on the new budget constraint.

Note that the grant described above, restricted to use for purchasing government goods only, has the effect of increasing the community's consumption of private goods. Observe on the diagram the dollar amount of expenditure on private goods *OG* at *C* and *OH* at *F*. The ratio *GA/OA* is the tax rate that the community used before the grant program, that is, the proportion of private wealth given up to have government goods. The ratio *HA/OA* is the tax rate after the grant program is introduced; it is *lower* than the initial rate. Thus the community meets the legal terms of the grant by using it for government goods, but it reduces the amount of its local wealth previously allocated to government goods.

To make sure the resulting allocation is clear, think of the community response as follows. Imagine that the immediate response to the grant is to reduce the tax rate so that exactly the same amount of government goods is being provided as before the grant. This meets the terms of the grant. But now the community can have the same private consumption as before and still have resources left over to spend on anything. The extra resources are just like extra income, and the community behaves as an individual would: It buys a little more of everything normal including government goods. Thus, the revenue-sharing grant to the community has allocative effects identical with those of a tax cut of the same size by the central government. Its net effect is to increase spending on government goods, but not nearly by the amount of the grant.

In this example the restriction that the grant be used to purchase only government goods did not play an important role; the grant size is small relative to the funds the community would provide for government goods without any restriction. Figure 5-4 gives an illustration of a *binding constraint:* The size of the grant is greater than the amount the community would freely choose to spend on government goods. This occurs when the grant size (measured along *AD*) is large enough to cross the income-expansion path *OCK*.[27] If *ADE* is the budget constraint with the grant, the community will choose *D* as its optimal point: more of the covered goods than it would choose if the grant were a pure income supplement.[28] This is unlikely to occur with general revenue sharing, but it becomes more likely

---

[26] Throughout this chapter, we will not consider the sources of central government revenues used to fund the grant program. The pregrant budget level of the local community is measured *after* central government taxes have been collected.

[27] Recall that the income-expansion path is defined as the locus of utility-maximizing consumption choices at each possible income level when all prices are held constant.

[28] Note that the MRS at *D* must be less steep than at *J* (the preferred point if the categorical constraint is removed). Starting from the utility-maximizing point along an ordinary budget constraint, the slopes of the in-

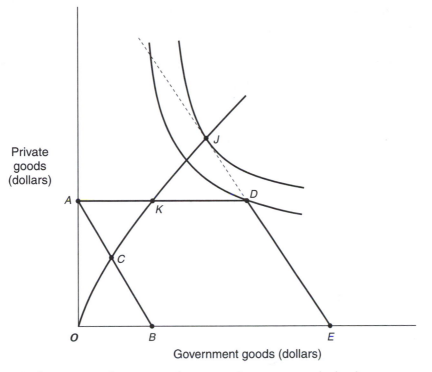

Figure 5-4. The categorical constraint of a nonmatching grant can be binding.

(for a given grant size) as the allowable uses of the grant are narrowed, as for new fire-fighting equipment. *A grant that restricts the recipient to spending it on only certain types of goods is called a categorical or a selective grant.*

Price Effects and Matching Grants

Analysis of the effect of matching requirements in a grant system is identical with the analysis of the Food Stamp Program. **A matching grant offers to pay a predetermined portion of a total expenditure level chosen by a recipient unit for the goods covered by the grant.** For example, under a program to develop mass transit facilities, the federal government will provide $9 for every $1 that is raised by a local jurisdiction for mass transit in that jurisdiction. The program has a matching rate m of 9 to 1. In other grant programs the matching rate may not be as generous; perhaps the donor government might offer only $0.10 for $1 raised by the recipient ($m = 0.1$). It is also possible for the matching rate to be

difference curves passing through the budget constraint become progressively less steep to the right and more steep to the left. The utility level becomes progressively lower as we move away from J in either direction. Thus D is the maximum attainable utility, and more grant goods are purchased than if the categorical restrictions were relaxed.

negative, which is a matter of taxing the local community for its expenditures on the specified good.[29]

To see how the matching grant affects the price of the covered goods from the recipient's perspective, imagine the recipient purchasing one additional unit. If the market price is P_0, then the local contribution plus the matching funds must sum to P_0. Let us call the local contribution per unit P_s and then the matching funds per unit will be mP_s. The equation summarizing this is as follows:

$$P_s + mP_s = P_0$$

or

Local funds per unit + Matching funds per unit = Market price per unit

Solving for P_s, we find the price per unit as perceived by the recipient to be as follows:

$$P_s = \frac{P_0}{1 + m}$$

Thus *a matching grant changes the terms of trade by which a community can exchange the good covered by the grant for other goods.* In the example used for food stamps in the preceding chapter, the program provided a match of $1 for every $1 provided by the recipient. Thus the matching rate was 1, which translates into a price reduction of 50 percent. The recipient had to give up only $0.50 instead of $1 worth of other things for each $1.00 worth of food.

Matching grants may either be open-ended or closed-ended. *In an open-ended grant there is no limit on the quantity the donor government is willing to subsidize.* An open-ended grant is shown in Figure 5-5 by *AC;* the pregrant budget constraint is *AB. In a closed-ended grant arrangement, on the other hand, the donor government will subsidize purchases only up to a certain amount.* In Figure 5-5 this is illustrated as budget constraint *AFG,* where the limit is reached at *F.* These two cases can be seen to correspond exactly with the food stamp analyses of the preceding chapter (Figure 4-8). The effect of closing the grant is either to reduce purchases of the grant good and the total subsidy (if the community prefers a point on *FC,* no longer attainable because of the restriction) or to have no effect (if the community prefers a point on *AF* that can still be attained).

To see the effect of the matching provision, let us compare an open-ended matching grant with a nonmatching grant of equivalent total subsidy. In Figure 5-6 the open-ended matching grant is *AC,* and let us assume that the community chooses a point like *F.* Then we construct an equivalent subsidy nonmatching grant (thus also passing through point *F*) shown as *ADE.* Note that point *D* must lie to the left of point *F* (*DE* is parallel to *AB*).

We will show by **revealed preferences** reasoning that the utility-maximizing choice from *ADE* cannot be on the segment *FE.* In general, **one bundle of goods and services** $X = (X_1, X_2, \ldots, X_n)$ **is revealed-preferred to another** $Y = (Y_1, Y_2, \ldots, Y_n)$ **if two condi-**

---

[29] The district power-equalizing proposal for financing local schools has this feature; it is discussed later in the chapter.

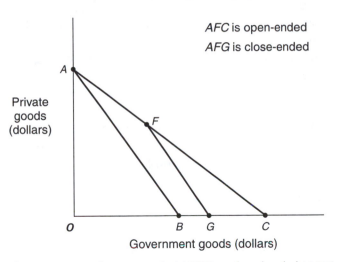

Figure 5-5. Matching grants can be open-ended (*AFC*) or closed-ended (*AFG*).

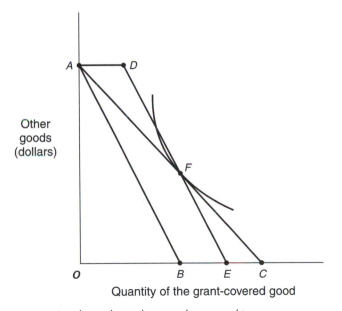

Figure 5-6. Comparing equal sized matching and nonmatching grants.

tions are met: **(1) *Y* is affordable given the budget constraint; and (2) *X* is the bundle actually chosen.** In terms of Figure 5-6, if the community preferred a bundle represented by some point on *FE* to the bundle *F* itself, it could have chosen it under the open-ended plan *AC*. Since it did not, *F* is revealed-preferred and must yield more utility than anything on *FE*. But point *F* is not itself the utility maximum on *ADE*: The indifference curve through it is tangent to *AC* and thus not to *DE*. Hence there are points on *ADE* that have greater utility than at *F*, and they cannot be on *FE*: They must be to the left of *F*.

If the categorical restriction is binding, *D* is the point of maximum utility; but since *D* is always to the left of *F,* it always implies a lower quantity of the grant-covered good than does the open-ended matching grant. Thus *the open-ended matching grant induces greater consumption of the covered good than an equivalent-subsidy nonmatching grant.* Therefore, there is also a matching grant with lower cost to the central government that induces the same consumption of the covered good as the nonmatching grant.

The above result suggests that matching grants have an advantage when the program's objective is to alter the allocation of some specific good. This objective characterizes grants to correct for externalities. Matching grants are generally considered appropriate for these cases because the matching rate alters the price to recipients and, if chosen correctly, internalizes the external costs or benefits of the recipient's allocative choice. (An example is the optimal food-stamp subsidy when there are interdependent preferences, discussed in Chapter 4.) Equity objectives may also imply altering the relative distribution of a specific good, such as the school financing issue discussed later in the chapter, and matching grants can be appropriate for those policy objectives as well. Nonmatching grants, on the other hand, are most appropriate for general redistributive goals.[30]

The Role of Choice Restrictions

We have already introduced several forms of choice restriction common to intergovernmental grants: the expanse of goods covered and the maximum quantity for which matching subsidies are available. Their importance depends not only on the allocative effects of the type we have been examining but also on institutional effects in terms of the information and transaction costs of grant administration and enforcement. We illustrate this by introducing *another common restriction: maintenance of effort. This means that the recipient community is eligible only for grant funds to supplement its prior spending on the covered goods.*

Figure 5-7 shows an example of how a nonmatching grant with maintenance-of-effort requirement achieves an increase in the government good at lower subsidy cost than an open-ended matching grant. The community initially has budget constraint *AB* and chooses *C.* Then a matching grant changes the budget constraint to *AD,* where the community chooses *E* (more of the grant good than if a cash-equivalent transfer had been made) at subsidy cost *EG.* The same quantity *OH* of the grant good can be stimulated with the less costly nonmatching grant with maintenance of effort represented by the budget constraint *ACFJ.*

The shape of *ACFJ* can be explained as follows. Imagine the community starting from point *A.* As it purchases units of the grant-covered good, it pays the ordinary market price and proceeds down the *AB* line until it reaches point *C.* At this point the quantity of the grant-covered good is *OK,* the amount that maintains the effort of the community in terms

---

[30] For a more detailed review of general economic policy issues concerning grants, see George F. Break, *Financing Government in a Federal System* (Washington, D.C.: The Brookings Institution, 1980), and Wallace Oates, "Federalism and Government Finance," in John Quigley and Eugene Smolensky, eds., *Modern Public Finance* (Cambridge: Harvard University Press, 1994), pp. 126–151.

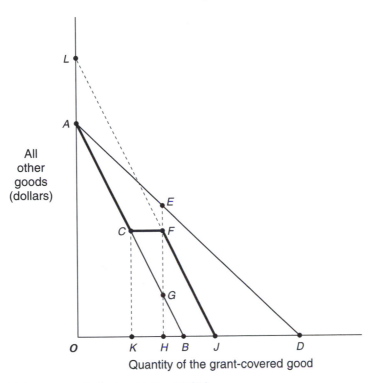

Figure 5-7. Maintenance-of-effort restriction (*ACFJ*).

of its past expenditure on this good. Additional units of the grant-covered good can then be had without sacrifice of other goods, because the community now qualifies for the grant and the grant funds pay for them in full. Thus the community proceeds horizontally and to the right from point *C* until it has spent the entire grant.

We have deliberately selected the grant that allows a maximum free purchase of *CF*, which would bring the community to *OH* consumption of the grant-covered good (the same quantity as would be chosen with the matching grant *AD*). The dollar cost of this grant is *FG*, less than the cost *EG* of the matching grant. Beyond point *F*, the community must sacrifice other goods at the market rate in order to further increase the consumption of the grant-covered good; thus, the slope of *FJ* is the same as that of *AC*.

With budget constraint *ACFJ*, the theory of individual choice predicts that the community will choose point *F*. If it chooses point *C* with constraint *AB*, point *F* is clearly preferable because it has more of one good and no less of any other good. How do we know that some point on *FJ* is not even better? Since the goods on each axis are normal, the community should increase the purchase of both goods as income increases. That is, the income-expansion path would cross *LJ* (the extension of *FJ*) to the left of *FJ*. Thus, point *F* is closer to the optimal point on *LJ* than any other point on *FJ* and therefore must be preferred. The community chooses *F;* its consumption is *OH* of the grant-covered good (as with the matching grant); and the cost to the donor government is less than the cost with the matching grant (*FG < EG*).

This highlights the strong impact of the restriction. However, it does not change our prior results about the greater inducement of matching requirements per subsidy dollar. That result holds as long as other things are kept equal (including the restrictions).[31] It does suggest that empirically one should not necessarily expect to find that matching grants have a more stimulative effect unless the restrictions are similar. However, it has been pointed out in the literature that the effectiveness of intergovernmental grant restrictions cannot be assumed; it depends upon the ability and effort made to administer and enforce the restrictions.[32] This caveat deserves further discussion.

Recall that whenever one consumer has a MRS for two goods different from that of another consumer, there is room for a deal. When economic agents make consumption (and production) choices, they usually do so in light of the prevailing market prices. However, a grant recipient subject to matching provisions or certain restrictions will typically have a MRS that is not equal to the prevailing market price ratio. Correspondingly, this creates incentives for deals. That is precisely what we saw in Chapter 4 in the discussion of individual food stamp grants and the illegal market for stamp resales. The recipient could increase utility by exchanging the food stamps at prevailing market prices. The income could then be used to purchase whatever goods maximize the recipient's utility.

The desire to exploit divergences in the MRS can be applied to communities as well as individuals. Any intergovernmental grant program that contains provisions causing divergences of this nature may fail to achieve its inducement objectives if the recipient community can find ways of making the potential deals. Thus the success of a grant program depends not only upon the allocative effects we have described so far but also on the administration and enforcement capabilities.

Consider a community offered a grant that requires maintenance of effort. It may keep its local budget size constant but change the composition of what is purchased with that budget. For example, a community may feel a pressing need to obtain more medical equipment for its local hospital but the only grant offered to it is for criminal justice with maintenance of effort required. It therefore decides to make its hospital security guards part of the police force. The grant funds are then used to maintain police services exactly as they were plus the hospital security guards, and the hospital finds its revenues unchanged but its costs decreased by the cost of the security guards. Thus the hospital buys the additional medical equipment with the grant, even though that is not the way it appears on the record.

If a grant program continues for several years, it may become harder to enforce choice restrictions. For example the maintenance-of-effort requirements may be clear in the initial year, but no one can know for certain what the community would have spent without any grants in successive years. If community income is growing, for example, one would expect expenditures to increase over time even without a grant program. Then the maintenance-

---

[31] To see this, it is left to the reader to compare the effects of matching versus nonmatching terms when both grants require maintenance of effort.

[32] See, for example, Martin McGuire, "A Method for Estimating the Effect of a Subsidy on the Receiver's Resource Constraint: With an Application to U.S. Local Governments 1964–71," *Journal of Public Economics, 10,* 1978, pp. 25–44.

of-effort restriction, if unchanged, becomes less important over time and the program effects become more like those of an unrestricted block grant.

The point of these examples is to demonstrate the importance of recognizing the incentives created by any particular grant design. *Part of any policy analysis of grant programs is to consider whether the administration and enforcement of its provisions can be accomplished pragmatically; otherwise, the overall objectives of the program can be jeopardized.* There is no standard answer as to whether enforcement is easy or difficult; it depends upon the nature of the good. Illegal markets may arise readily with food stamps because resales of the stamps are hard to prevent or detect; highways, on the other hand, are another matter.

Alternative Specifications of Recipient Choice-Making

To this point we have assumed that it is reasonable to treat a community as if it were an individual, as in having preferences or choosing a consumption bundle. But a community is not an individual. It is an aggregate of individual residents who have chosen to live in the area and can relocate if they wish. It also generally contains public and private agencies that may employ nonresidents and be owned by nonresidents; these people as well as the residents will be concerned about and affected by grant programs available to the community.

The community choice perspective we have been using is often given some theoretical justification by an appeal to the idea of the median voter, according to which local decisions reflect the median voter's tastes and preferences. Imagine, for example, successive voting on school expenditures: After each level is approved, a new and slightly higher level is voted on and the level selected is the last one to muster a majority. If the voters are then lined up in the order of the maximum school expenditures they approve, it becomes apparent that the median voter determines the total expenditure. In short, the community preferences can be represented by those of the median voter.[33]

Applied to local choices, the theory has been shown to be useful empirically in a number of studies.[34] However, it is important to recognize that over a period of time individuals and firms can choose their locations from among alternative communities in a given area. *Charles Tiebout hypothesized that the ability to "vote with their feet" creates pressure on the community to provide the most attractive possible bundle of public services (including taxes) lest its occupants go elsewhere.*[35] Of course, as people gradually relocate,

---

[33] This is offered only as a justification for why the community choice theory might predict collective decisions accurately. It is not intended to suggest that the choices are efficient; in fact, there is good reason to believe that no democratic voting procedure can be used to attain an efficient allocation of resources. See our later discussion in Chapter 15, and Kenneth Arrow, *Social Choice and Individual Values* (New Haven: Yale University Press, 1951).

[34] See Edward Gramlich, "Intergovernmental Grants: A Review of the Empirical Literature," in Wallace Oates, ed., *The Political Economy of Fiscal Federalism* (Lexington, Mass.: Lexington Books, 1977).

[35] See Charles Tiebout, "A Pure Theory of Local Expenditure," *Journal of Political Economy, 64,* No. 5, October 1956, pp. 416–424. For a test of this hypothesis and that of the median voter, see Edward Gramlich and Daniel Rubinfeld, "Micro Estimates of Public Spending Demand Functions and Test of the Tiebout and Median-Voter Hypotheses," *Journal of Political Economy, 90,* No. 3, June 1982, pp. 536–560.

this changes the characteristics of the median voter in any particular community. *Thus, competition among communities is an important additional determinant of community decisions;* its influence is undoubtedly greater in the long run than in the short run.

A second reason for questioning the community choice perspective comes from theories of bureaucratic behavior. The idea is that any particular grant-receiving bureau is like flypaper: The grant will stick where it hits. Let us go back to our earlier example of the community seeking funds for new medical equipment but offered only a criminal justice grant with maintenance of effort required. We suggested that the hospital security guards would be added to the police budget in order to meet the legal terms of the grant and the allocative effect would be to use the extra hospital funds (once used to pay for guards) to buy the new equipment.

However, what happens if the police chief does not like this idea? In particular, what happens when the police insist they need to use the grant funds to purchase helicopters? There may be no effective political mechanism to prevent the police from doing just that. It depends, of course, on the political power of the police department relative to other officials (who may or may not sympathize) and the public. Perhaps the public view will receive greater weight over a longer period of time (e.g., through new elections of officials who have the power to hire and fire the police chief). Thus the grant may in the short run, because of local bureaucratic support, have the effect its designers intended; in the long run there is more chance that the income conversion effect will predominate.

In fact, empirical research on the effects of grants offers strong support that something like the flypaper effect occurs and persists. According to Hines and Thaler, a pure income effect in most grant programs would increase spending on the covered goods in the long run by $0.05 to $0.10 for each $1.00 of a nonmatching grant. (The figures correspond to an income elasticity near unity.) But the actual estimated income effects are always substantially larger, between $0.25 and $1.00.[36]

Thus political and bureaucratic effects on grants can be significant and should be accounted for in making empirical predictions of a grant program's effects. The evidence, for example, contradicts the assertion based on individual choice theory made earlier that a nonmatching grant has the same effect on a community as a tax cut equal in size. The evidence suggests that a nonmatching grant stimulates greater expenditure on the covered good than an equivalent tax cut.

Equity in School Finance

In this section we apply both the theory of grants and the concepts of equity to the problem of public school financing. We shall focus primarily on the California system, which was declared unconstitutional by the state Supreme Court in its 1976 *Serrano vs. Priest* deci-

---

[36] See James R. Hines, Jr., and Richard H. Thaler, "Anomalies: The Flypaper Effect," *Journal of Economic Perspectives, 9,* No. 4, Autumn 1995, pp. 217–226, and Shama Gamkhar and Wallace Oates, "Asymmetries in the Response to Increases and Decreases in Intergovernmental Grants: Some Empirical Findings," *National Tax Journal, 49,* No. 4, December 1996, pp. 501–512.

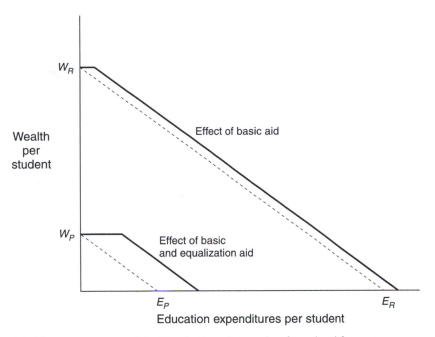

Figure 5-8. The unconstitutional California Foundation plan for school financing.

sion. The general problems considered then have been found to apply to many states, with good solutions being elusive. New York's system was declared unconstitutional by its Supreme Court in 2001, and a similar decision was reached about the New Hampshire system by its Supreme Court. The New Jersey Supreme Court declared its state system unconstitutional on grounds similar to *Serrano,* and in 1993 Texas voters rejected a wealth-sharing plan similar to some proposed remedies for *Serrano.* First we will review the system found defective in California and the equity requirements enunciated by the court, and then we will consider what system might meet those requirements.

The Equity Defects Identified in Serrano

In Figure 5-8 we represent the budget constraints of a "rich" school district (subscript R) and a "poor" school district (subscript P). Public school expenditures per child E are measured along the horizontal axis, and wealth for all other goods per child W is measured along the vertical axis.[37] The dashed lines represent a hypothetical school financing system that is purely

[37] Note that two districts can have the same budget constraint in this diagram but different total wealth, caused by differences in the number of children each has in attendance at public schools. The "per child" units are convenient for the analysis presented here, but one must be careful in their use: A community will respond to changes in its total wealth as well as to changes in the size of the school population, and accurate empirical prediction of the overall response may require more information than the proportion of the two. Consider two communities that are initially perfectly identical; one then experiences a doubling of real wealth while the other experiences a 50 percent drop in the public school population. Their new budget constraints on the diagram will continue to be

local; that is, one in which the state contributes nothing to the local school district. Under such a system, it would hardly be surprising to find the rich district spending more on education per child than the poor district; that will happen as long as public education is a normal good.

The actual system declared unconstitutional was not purely local. California, like many other states, had been using a system of school finance known as a foundation plan. Under it, every school district was entitled to some state aid. The amount of state aid received was an inverse function of the district property wealth per child.[38] All districts received at least $125 per child, an amount referred to as basic aid. This was the only aid received by rich districts. Poor districts received additional funds in the form of equalization aid, and poorer districts received greater amounts of equalization aid.

In Figure 5-8 the solid lines represent the budget constraints of the two representative districts including state aid. The grants are equivalent to nonmatching grants restricted to educational spending. The rich district is shown as receiving a smaller grant than the poor district. This plan should make spending in the two districts more equal, as the larger grant will have a bigger income effect (assuming nonincreasing marginal effects of budget increases). However, there is no reason to think that this system will lead to equal spending. The size of the grants received by poor districts would have to be very large for this to be so, as high-wealth California districts were spending more than four times the amount spent by low-wealth districts.[39] Note that this system of grants has no price effects and that we showed earlier that expenditure inducements for particular goods can best be achieved by matching grants (which make use of price effects). However, we have not yet discussed which equity standard is relevant in this case.

Why might a court find, as in the *Serrano* decision, that the system we have described denies "equality of treatment" to the pupils in the state?[40] The fact that there are differences

---

identical, but there is no theoretical reason to expect them to choose the same point on it. The choice depends on the respective wealth elasticities for spending on education versus other goods. For the purposes here, we are holding the number of children in the representative districts constant.

[38] Because the property tax is used almost universally to raise local funds for education, the measure of district wealth used by the courts and other government agencies is the total assessed valuation of property in the district. The appropriateness of this proxy measure is discussed later in the chapter.

[39] Grants of this magnitude would certainly cause recipient districts to select the consumption bundle where the restriction is binding. To see this, imagine a district that is very poor and is spending 10 percent of its wealth measured by property value (a very high proportion). If we gave the district a grant three times larger than its current expenditure, its wealth would be increased by 30 percent, that is, three times 10 percent. How much of that increase the district would spend on education if unconstrained depends on the wealth elasticity. Empirical research suggests it is inelastic. By a unitary elasticity estimate, the district would freely choose to spend 3 percent of the 30 percent wealth increase on education, for a total of 13 percent of the original wealth. But the grant restriction is that education expenditures must be at least 30 percent of original wealth (i.e., the size of the grant), so the restriction must be binding. The wealth elasticity would have to be something like 7 in this example for the constraint to be nonbinding. That is not plausible. It is more implausible given the unrealistically high proportion of spending on education assumed initially, and that a grant as small as three times the initial level would achieve equality if completely spent on education.

[40] It is important to note that the specific legal interpretation of phrases such as "equality of treatment" and "equal opportunity" can be quite different from their general definitions as analytic concepts. I know few who would

in expenditure levels from district to district is not what the court found offensive; the decision made it very clear that the court was not requiring strict equality. Nor did the court require a universal minimum, although it did express particular concern about the low expenditure levels typical for children attending school in low-wealth districts. Thus neither of the outcome standards was found applicable in this setting.

Instead, the court held that the state had created a system of school finance that violated wealth neutrality. Children living in low-wealth districts (the suspect class) had less money spent for their public education on average than children living in other districts. The court held that the education a child receives (measured by school expenditure per child) should not be a function of the wealth of his or her parents and neighbors as measured by the school district property tax base per child.

It is interesting to consider briefly this choice of an equity standard. It concerns the expenditure on a child in one district *relative* to a child in another. In theory, violations of this standard can be removed either by raising the expected expenditure level for those initially low or lowering the expected level for those initially high or both. The average expenditure level for the population as a whole is not restricted (no minimum has been held to be required), and there is no restriction on the overall distribution in terms of how much deviation from strict equality is allowed. The requirement is only that children in property-poor districts as a group have educational opportunities like those of children in all other districts.

Why should a neutrality standard be required as a matter of general policy? If we think back to our discussion of equity concepts, it is plausible to argue that a basic education is a requirement for modern-day life, much like food, clothing, and shelter. Argued more modestly, perhaps a basic education is one of those goods that we wish to guarantee to everybody. But this logic calls for a universal minimum; and since the supply of educational resources is elastic, there is no reason to be concerned about the relative educational expenditures on different children.[41]

Another reason for concern about equity in education is the belief that it affects the other opportunities available to an individual during the course of a lifetime and that there is a social responsibility to move toward process equality for those other opportunities. By this rationale education is seen as a means to an end; policies such as *compensatory education* might be derived from it. This concern does involve the relative expenditure levels for education, but it does not imply strict equality, equal opportunity, or neutrality as a requirement for educational expenditures. Requirements such as these can prevent the attainment

---

argue, for example, that the provision of a public defender ensures neutrality or equal opportunity as we have defined it. It may provide a universal minimum, but the court is satisfied that the public defender ensures "equal opportunity" by legal standards. To maintain these definitional distinctions, reference to legal meanings will be indicated by quotation marks or distinct terminology.

[41] An important issue not discussed here is the extent to which there is a relation between educational expenditures, real educational resources, and education absorbed by children. Most researchers in this area consider the linkages to be very weak. See, for example, E. Hanushek, "Assessing the Effects of School Resources on Student Performance: An Update," *Educational Evaluation and Policy Analysis, 19,* No. 2, Summer 1997, pp. 141–164; and "The Economics of Schooling," *Journal of Economic Literature, 24,* No. 3, September 1986, pp. 1141–1175.

of equal opportunity for other life opportunities (e.g., if compensatory education is necessary), although they may represent an improvement from the status quo.

A somewhat different rationale from the above focuses more on the importance of even-handedness by government, particularly when its actions bear on vital interests of the citizenry. That is, one could argue that education is a vital interest; and because the state influences the education provided by local governments within it, it must ensure that its influence is even-handed on all the state's children.[42] Since it is the state that defines local district boundaries and determines the financing rules that local districts face, it must choose the rules to ensure the same availability of educational opportunities to the children in each district.

Of course, the state may influence district behavior in many ways, and as a value judgment one might wish to apply the even-handedness rationale to all of the state influences. But the court expressed only the narrower concern about the opportunities affected by the wealth classifications (i.e., district boundaries) made by the state. Thus a rationale for a neutrality standard can be derived from an underlying concern with state even-handedness in regard to vital interests when they involve suspect classifications. It is concern of this type that is manifested as a matter of law in the *Serrano* decision.

The Design of Wealth-Neutral Systems

Now let us turn to the problem of designing a school finance system that meets the wealth-neutrality standard. Any state system that ensures equal spending, such as full-state financing, is wealth-neutral. However, local control of schools is an important value that makes that politically unattractive.[43] One could also redraw district boundaries so that all districts had equal wealth. There are two serious disadvantages to that approach: (1) It is politically unpopular because it threatens the status of many of the employees of the school system (e.g., district superintendents) and upsets families that have made residential choices partly on the basis of the school district characteristics. (2) In districts comparable in size with those now existing, the wealth of one relative to that of another can change significantly in just a few years (which would necessitate almost continuous redistricting). One could redistrict into much larger units, but then there are disadvantages similar to full state control.

As an interesting aside, the choice of residential location mentioned above suggests a Tiebout approach to wealth neutrality: If families really have free choice about where to locate, the system is wealth-neutral no matter how the state draws district boundaries or what grants are given to different districts. Obviously the court did not accept that reasoning, or it would have found the system free of state constitutional defect. Although few people

---

[42] Perhaps this could be interpreted with some flexibility. Certain circumstances might present sufficiently compelling reasons to allow exceptions to even-handedness, for example, compensatory education.

[43] Hawaii is the only state to have full-state funding financing, although New Mexico's system may be equivalent. (The state mandates a uniform spending level and a uniform tax rate that all localities must use.) One can separate the financing and uses of resource decisions, but most would still consider the move to state financing as a diminution of local control.

would argue that actual residential choices (in terms of school districts) are made independently of wealth (e.g., zoning restrictions that prevent construction of low-cost housing), another way to neutralize the influence of wealth is by open enrollment. That is, suppose each child had the option of choosing (at no additional cost) a school from alternatives in the area that represented a broad range of expenditure levels. Then one might consider such a system wealth-neutral. By the end of 1990, several states had introduced fairly broad open-enrollment programs. However, Odden reports a number of problems in achieving financial equity with these systems.[44]

We are left with alternatives that maintain the existing districts but attempt to neutralize the influence of wealth. At this point it is time to confront the issue of whether the required neutrality is simple or conditional. The court decision left the matter ambiguous, despite the fact that the differences between the concepts as applied to the remaining alternatives are great.[45] We construct simple models of school expenditure decisions and the effects of grants primarily to illustrate the difference between the equity standards. The actual design of grant systems to achieve either standard involves consideration of a number of important factors that are omitted from the simple models used here, and in the following section we will note a number of them.

Simple wealth neutrality requires that there be no functional relation between the wealth of a school district and its public school expenditure level on a per student basis. This implies that the expected expenditure of a district in one wealth class equals the expected expenditure of a district in any other wealth class.[46]

In Figure 5-9 we illustrate the aim of simple neutrality. The figure has two demand curves. Each represents the average demand of a group of districts: D_H for high-wealth districts, and D_L for low-wealth districts. With no grant system, all districts face a price of $1.00 per unit of educational spending.[47] The figure shows that districts spend, on average, $6300 per

---

[44] See Allan R. Odden, "Financing Public School Choice: Policy Issues and Options," in Allan R. Odden, ed., *Rethinking School Finance* (San Francisco: Jossey-Bass, Inc., 1992), pp. 225–259.

[45] The labels "simple" and "conditional" are simplifications used for convenience. There are a number of special sources of funds, such as federal funds for handicapped children, that could be included as part of the total expenditures and analyzed for their appropriateness in terms of exceptional characteristics. For purposes of the analysis here, we simply remove them from the expenditure base under examination and consider only the equity of general purpose funds. However, we could describe the same choice as between two alternative specifications of conditional neutrality by including the special purpose funds in the base. The equity of special purpose funds does deserve scrutiny; for some thoughts on the subject see Friedman and Wiseman, "Understanding the Equity Consequences of School Finance Reform."

[46] The earlier examples of simple neutrality were illustrated with dichotomous groupings, but the principle applies to a suspect classification into multiple groupings. In this illustration of district wealth classification, we treat each wealth level as a separate and continuous classification. The assumption here is that the court would be equally offended if middle-wealth or upper-middle-wealth districts were systematically handicapped relative to all other districts.

[47] The district demand curves are from the assumed functional form $E = 0.015P^{-0.4}W$, where E is educational spending per child, W is wealth per child, and P is the price per unit of education. This assumed form is used for ease of illustration. The price elasticity of -0.4 is realistic, although estimates of it in the literature vary between 0 and -1. A realistic wealth elasticity, based on the estimates available in the literature, would be lower than unitary

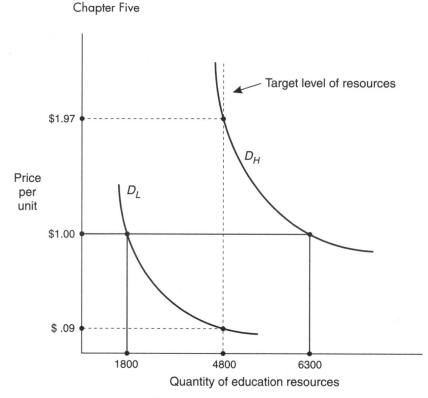

Figure 5-9. Achieving simple wealth neutrality through appropriate matching grants.

student for the high-wealth group and $1800 for the low-wealth group. It is important to understand that the figure only shows the group averages; we are not assuming, for example, that every single high-wealth district is spending exactly $6300.

To achieve simple neutrality between these two groups, the state can choose any average school expenditure level it wants as the target. The figure illustrates a target of $4800 per student. Then the state must design a grant system that causes each group to make choices that average $4800 per student. To achieve this, the figure shows that the low-wealth districts must face a price of $0.09 per unit of educational expenditure and high-wealth districts a price of $1.97.

The matching grant rates that will result in these prices are easy to identify from our earlier formula:

$$P_s + mP_s = P_0$$

---

and probably between 0.25 and 0.50. Hoxby, for example, reports an income elasticity of 0.54 for U.S. metropolitan areas, which probably proxies wealth closely since no separate measure of the latter was included. See Caroline M. Hoxby, "Does Competition Among Public Schools Benefit Students and Taxpayers," *American Economic Review, 90,* No. 5, December 2000, pp. 1209–1238.

For the low-wealth districts, this means:

$$0.09 + m(0.09) = 1.00$$

or

$$m = \$10.11$$

That is, the state offers low-wealth districts $10.11 for every dollar raised locally. This matching rate will cost the state $4368 per student ($4800 total per student, $432 raised locally). For the high-wealth districts, the formula requires:

$$1.97 + m(1.97) = 1.00$$

or

$$m = -0.49$$

That is, the state sets a negative matching rate! It requires that for each dollar raised locally for education, $0.49 must be returned to the state and only $0.51 is actually spent on local education. With this rate, the state will receive an average of $4611 per student in the high-wealth districts ($4800 total expenditure per student, $9411 raised locally).

Naturally the state, in determining the target level, will consider how much funding it is willing to provide out of general revenues to pay for the matching grants as well as how much it can feasibly recapture through negative matching rates. Furthermore, to reduce the uncertainty about finding the correct matching rates to achieve neutrality (since the actual demand functions by wealth are not known with confidence), the state can use choice restrictions such as those we have already discussed.

To this point we have illustrated only simple wealth neutrality. However, another possible interpretation is to require conditional wealth neutrality with the district tax rate choice as the exceptional characteristic.[48] That is, a court may define wealth neutrality to mean that those districts choosing the same tax rate should have the same expenditure level. This requires an equal percentage sacrifice of district wealth to buy the same amount of education everywhere. This interpretation is consistent with the California court's indication that a system known as district power equalizing (DPE) would be acceptable.[49]

---

[48] In California, a state initiative passed in 1978 and known as Proposition 13 limits local tax rates to 1 percent of assessed value. This effectively removes the option of choosing a local rate. California schools are now financed primarily through the state, with local property taxes contributing less than 25 percent of school revenues. In the 1980s the California courts concluded that the system was sufficiently wealth-neutral and the *Serrano* case was declared closed in 1989. In 1997–1998, the state reported that 97.91 percent of students were in districts in compliance with the *Serrano* wealth-neutrality standard. At the same time, according to *Education Week,* California ranked last among states in the nation for *adequacy* of educational resources, illustrating poignantly the difference between a wealth-neutrality standard and a universal minimum.

[49] Another way to reconcile the court's acceptance of DPE as a possible solution is if it is simply assumed (incorrectly) that simple wealth neutrality would result from using it. For more discussion of this issue, see Friedman and Wiseman, "Understanding the Equity Consequences of School Finance Reform."

Under a DPE plan the state would publish a schedule associating each possible expenditure level with a property tax rate. Any district that wanted to spend, say, $5000 per child would have to tax itself at the rate associated with that expenditure level on the state schedule, for example, 1 percent. If the district revenues collected at the 1 percent rate are not enough to provide $5000 per child, the state provides a subsidy to make up the difference. If the district revenues exceed the amount required to provide $5000 per child, the state recaptures the excess. But the only way a district can have an expenditure level of $5000 per child is to tax itself at the specified rate of 1 percent.

The advantage of the conditional neutrality interpretation is that it is relatively easy to design a system to meet the standard. As with the above illustration, no knowledge of district demand functions is required. But there is a cost to this interpretation as well. One must ask why the district tax rate choice should be an exceptional characteristic.

One rationale might be to rely purely on a notion of taxpayer equity. However, wealthy districts that wish to spend a lot on education incur a substantial financial burden in the form of revenues recaptured by the state, whereas equally wealthy districts that do not wish to spend as much escape the burden. Why should equally wealthy districts provide differing contributions to state revenues? Taxpayers might not consider this very equitable.[50]

Perhaps more importantly, wealth may remain as a significant determinant of educational spending on the children. That is, one might reject the taxpayer equity rationale and argue instead that the burden on high-spending wealthier districts is intended to protect children by neutralizing the influence of wealth on education-spending decisions. But there can be no assurance that it will do so.

To show this, Figure 5-10 illustrates the budget constraints that result from using a DPE system. Observe that if all districts tax themselves at 100 percent, all must end up at the same point on the horizontal axis. As a matter of policy, the state can select any point on the horizontal axis as the common point; the farther to the right, the greater the total expenditure—and state aid—will be. Under a very simple DPE system, the new budget constraints can be represented as straight lines that intersect the vertical axis at the district's own wealth level. This is equivalent to the state electing a common wealth base (the intercept with the horizontal axis) whereby educational expenditures in a district equal the districts' tax rate choice times the common base.[51] The important characteristic for our purposes is that the state schedule determines the new budget constraints (and thus prices and matching rates) for all districts.

Mathematically, the general DPE rule is that the expenditure per child (E) is a function of a state-determined formula $F(\tau)$ that depends solely on the tax rate choice (τ) of each local district:

$$E = F(\tau)$$

where $\Delta E/\Delta \tau \geq 0$.

---

[50] The taxpayer equity issue will also depend on how district wealth is defined. We discuss this issue later.

[51] The budget constraints need not be straight lines. For example, the state could increase or decrease the "common base" as the tax rate increases, making it nonlinear. Furthermore, it could restrict tax rates to be within a certain range (e.g., between 2 and 3 percent).

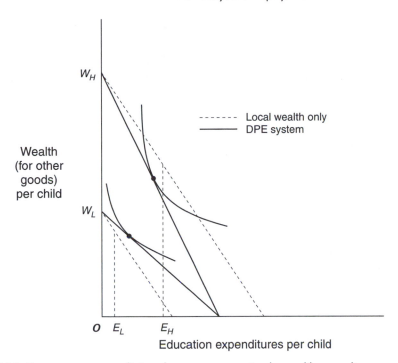

Figure 5-10. District power-equalizing does not ensure simple wealth neutrality.

The straight line constraints shown in Figure 5-10 have the particular mathematical form:

$$E = \tau W_C$$

where W_C is the state-chosen common wealth base. In actual practice, states using systems such as DPE choose more complex functional forms.[52] But with this simple form it is easy to show that the price per unit of education faced by a district with wealth i is[53]:

$$P_i = W_i / W_C$$

Thus the DPE rule determines a set of prices, but with *no* consideration of the demand functions that determine the prices necessary to ensure simple wealth neutrality. That is, requiring a DPE system in no way ensures simple wealth neutrality.

Suppose a state hopes to use a DPE system and achieve the same result with the districts from our earlier example: inducing districts of both wealth classes to average $4800 expenditure levels. Assume that the districts in the example have actual average wealth of

---

[52] The addition of a constant term to the formula would represent a nonmatching grant amount. This is common in practice, along with placing narrow limits on the choice of tax rate. Both of these features restrict the inequality in school spending.

[53] By definition, local contributions are $P_i E$ and the tax rate τ equals local contributions over local wealth or $P_i E / W_i$. Substituting this last expression for τ in the above equation, the Es cancel and the result is as shown.

$120,000 per child in the low-wealth group and $420,000 per child in the high-wealth group. We already know (from the demand curve of Figure 5-9) that the high-wealth districts will choose an average of $4800 per child on schooling if they face a price per unit of $1.97. The DPE schedule that has this price must use the following common wealth base W_C:

$$\$1.97 = W_H / W_C = \$420,000 / W_C$$

or

$$W_C = \$214,217$$

and therefore the state schedule must be

$$E = \tau^*(\$214,217)$$

With this DPE schedule, however, we know that the low-wealth districts will *not* average $E = \$4800$. To do so, they must face a price P_L of $0.09 (also known from Figure 5-9). But the schedule implies a price to them as follows:

$$P_L = W_L / W_C = \$120,000 / \$214,217 = \$0.56$$

This price is far too high. With it, they will choose an average expenditure level of $2270, far below the $4800 of the high-wealth districts.[54] The DPE plan will be inconsistent with simple wealth neutrality.

This example illustrates that a DPE requirement in no way guarantees simple wealth neutrality. It does not prove that there are no DPE systems that could achieve it, but in a real setting, that would be quite a difficult design task. The main point is simply that a school financing requirement of simple wealth neutrality is quite different from conditional wealth neutrality.

Other Issues of School Finance Equity

When the *Serrano* issues are being explained, it is common to illustrate inequities by describing the plight of children in low-wealth districts. However, it is also important to recognize that many children from poor families do not live in low-wealth districts. In California, for example, the majority of such children live in districts that are property-rich; an example is San Francisco, which has property wealth more than twice the state average. Under a plan meeting either neutrality standard and keeping average spending in the state at approximately the same level, these children could be made substantially worse off. It is important for analysts to think carefully about how to avoid or minimize this or other unintended harms when implementing standards such as those required in *Serrano*. Below are

---

[54] Calculated according to the hypothetical demand curve from note 47. In this example, DPE is weaker than simple neutrality requires. But if the demand for public education is price-elastic and wealth-inelastic, then DPE would induce lower-wealth districts to spend more than higher-wealth districts. See M. Feldstein, "Wealth Neutrality and Local Choice in Public Education," *The American Economic Review, 65,* No. 1, March 1975, pp. 75–89.

some suggested directions that an analyst working on the issue might explore; they are not intended to exhaust the range of equity issues that are encountered in school financing.

First, one dimension of a school finance plan that does not inherently interfere with neutrality is the proportion of funds derived from nonmatching revenues as opposed to matching grant arrangements. Earlier we suggested that full state financing meets both neutrality standards. It is possible to create a neutral system that maintains some degree of local choice but relies heavily on nonmatching revenues. For example, the state could provide $4000 to all students from general revenues and allow districts the option of adding up to $2000 to it by a matching grant system. This would reduce the stress owing to recapture placed on city budgets (assuming that the state general revenues are raised by broad-based taxes), at least as compared with a full matching grant system. Furthermore, by narrowing the range of expenditure variation that can occur as a result of local decision-making, it would make control of the variation easier. That can be an absolutely critical design feature if one is trying to achieve simple wealth neutrality, given the uncertainty about actual district price and wealth elasticities.

Second, the analyst should think carefully about what measure to use of a district's *fiscal capacity: its ability to generate tax revenues.* There is no law that requires the property tax base to be used as the measure of district wealth, nor is there any economic argument that maintains that total property value is the proper measure of a district's fiscal capacity. For example, most analysts think that the level of personal income in a district is an important determinant of true fiscal capacity. Thus, a wealth measure that depended on both property base and personal income could be constructed. It is no surprise that the hybrid measure would favor cities that have large low-income populations. One reason why the concern about them arises is the sense that property wealth alone does not give an accurate picture of fiscal capacity.

Another possibility is that commercial, industrial, and residential property should be weighted differently on the grounds that the ability to tax different types of property is different. For example, it may be less possible to impose taxes on industrial wealth than on residential wealth if industry is more likely to relocate; many communities offer tax breaks to new industries as locational inducements.[55]

Third, the nominal dollar expenditures may not be the best measure of the educational opportunities being provided through the schools. Although that remark could stir up a hornet's nest (e.g., when is one educational opportunity better than another?), there are some cost differences from district to district in providing identical resources. For example, to provide a classroom of 65° to 68°F in northern California during the winter costs a great deal more than in other parts of the state. Similarly, to attract a person with high teaching ability to an inner city school might require a higher salary than a suburban school would

---

[55] See, for example, Helen F. Ladd, "State-wide Taxation of Commercial and Industry Property for Education," *National Tax Journal, 29,* 1976, pp. 143–153. It is interesting to think about the effects of a *Serrano* solution on the willingness of communities to have industry locate within them. To the extent that expenditure levels are determined by the "common base" of a DPE plan, every community has less incentive to attract industry to it.

have to offer to obtain comparable talent. Thus it might be appropriate to adjust the expenditure figures to reflect differences in the cost of obtaining educational resources.[56]

Fourth, the student populations of equally wealthy districts may differ substantially in regard to the educational resources appropriate to each. For example, some districts might be characterized by high proportions of children from non-English-speaking families or of children who are mentally or physically handicapped or of children who are in high school. Thus one has to think carefully about how to best account for these differences. One approach, used in Illinois, is to develop a pupil-weighting system that gives a higher measure of enrollment in districts with students who are relatively expensive to educate.

Fifth, it is important to keep in mind that the long-run effects of any school finance reform may be substantially different from those observed in the short run. Over time, residents and firms may change their locations because of the reform. The use of private schools rather than public schools may change as the reform causes changes in the attractiveness of public schools. All of these factors result in changes in a district's preferences for public education and its wealth base, and thus one expects its response to any particular grant system to change as well. Thus it is important to consider analytic models that account for the long-run effects.[57]

Summary

To strengthen understanding of equity in general policy analysis, a number of important and competing concepts of equity must become part of the analytic framework. One conceptual distinction is the extent to which equity consequences refer *only* to effects on the general distribution of well-being (i.e., net effect on utility levels) or include specific egalitarian goals (e.g., equal distribution of jury service). In both cases, equity may be measured against outcome standards or process standards.

Outcome standards refer to the aggregate amount of variation in the shares (e.g., income, food) that individuals receive. Two common standards of this type are strict equal-

---

[56] For guidance on how to do this, see William Fowler, Jr., and David Monk, *A Primer for Making Cost Adjustments in Education* (Washington, D.C.: National Center for Education Statistics, Publication 2001323, 2001).

[57] There is an extensive literature on school finance equity that deals with the issues raised here as well as others. Examples include Robert Berne, "Equity Issues in School Finance," *Journal of Education Finance, 14,* No. 2, 1988, pp. 159–180; Thomas A. Downes, "Evaluating the Impact of School Finance Reform on the Provision of Public Education: The California Case," *National Tax Journal, 45,* No. 4, December 1992, pp. 405–419; W. Duncombe and J. Yinger, "School Finance Reform: Aid Formulas and Equity Objectives," *National Tax Journal, 51,* No. 2, June 1998, pp. 239–262; Caroline M. Hoxby, "Are Efficiency and Equity in School Finance Substitutes or Complements," *Journal of Economic Perspectives, 10,* No. 4, Fall 1996, pp. 51–72; Helen F. Ladd and John Yinger, "The Case for Equalizing Aid," *National Tax Journal, 47,* No. 1, March 1994, pp. 211–224; Andrew Reschovsky, "Fiscal Equalization and School Finance," *National Tax Journal, 47,* No. 1, March 1994, pp. 185–197. See also the symposium *"Serrano v. Priest:* 25th Anniversary," *Journal of Policy Analysis and Management, 16,* No. 4, Winter 1997, pp. 1–136, and the texts by David Monk, *Educational Finance: An Economic Approach* (New York: McGraw-Hill Book Company, 1990) and Allan R. Odden and Lawrence O. Picus, *School Finance: A Policy Perspective* (New York: McGraw-Hill Book Company, 1992).

ity and a universal minimum. One factor apart from moral feeling that influences the choice of the standards (as well as the methods for achieving them) is the elasticity of supply of the good(s) in question. The Lorenz curve and Gini coefficient illustrate methods of measuring the amount of outcome equality.

Process concepts of equity concern not the aggregate amount of variation but the rules and methods for assigning shares to individuals. These concepts become relevant once it is accepted that there will be inequality; the question is whether the share that each person ends up with has resulted from a fair process. A fundamental process standard is that of equal opportunity: Each person should have the same chance of obtaining a share of a given size. In practice it is often impossible to tell whether a particular individual had equal opportunity, and we sometimes try to test the implications of equal opportunity statistically by comparing the expected outcomes in a large group with the actual group outcomes.

In some instances, we substitute the less stringent concept of neutrality for particular groupings (the suspect ones) instead of equal opportunity for all. Simple neutrality means that the distribution of shares within a suspect group should be identical with the distribution of shares among all others. Often there will be exceptional characteristics that cause legitimate deviations from simple neutrality. (For example, the elderly will be overrepresented on juries if employment is a legitimate excuse from jury duty.) When deviations arise, the concept of conditional neutrality becomes appropriate: If the members of a suspect class have exceptional characteristics identical with those of all others, the distribution of shares within each group should be identical.

Whenever exceptional characteristics are relevant to process equity, it is appropriate to consider the additional concepts of horizontal and vertical equity. These concepts are used to assess the fairness of differences caused by the exceptional characteristics. Horizontal equity means that likes should be treated alike, and the question is the definition of the set of exceptional characteristics used to define who will be treated alike. In tax equity, for example, one question is whether the amount of income tax ought to depend upon the source of income (such as distinguishing wage income from dividend income). Vertical equity means that there is a fair difference in shares among people with different levels of exceptional characteristics. In the income tax case, the issue is the extra amount of tax due as income rises (the degree of progressivity).

Analysts contribute to public policy debate by examining the consequences of alternative equity standards. We illustrated this with an application to school financing. First we developed the basic theory of intergovernmental grants, relying primarily on the utility-maximization model developed earlier. Based upon the theory, a crucial distinction between grant types is whether there is a matching requirement: Grants with matching requirements have effects similar to those of price changes, whereas nonmatching or block grants have only income effects. However, this basic analysis must be modified to take account of the choice restrictions that are common design features of actual grant programs: the degree of selectiveness, whether the grant is open- or closed-ended, and maintenance-of-effort requirements. The effectiveness of these restrictions depends upon their administration and enforcement; the analyst should be aware that grant recipients have an incentive to convert a grant into its pure income equivalent.

One result that generally holds up within the context of these models is that a matching grant will induce greater spending on the covered goods than an equivalent subsidy non-matching grant (other things being equal). This suggests that matching grants are more likely to be appropriate when the grant's purpose is to correct an externality. Nonmatching grants are more likely to be appropriate when the purpose is general redistribution.

Other reasons for qualifying the predictions of these models are based upon the recognition that a community is not a single-minded maximizer. The Tiebout model makes us aware that individual locational choices influence community decision-making by changing the makeup of the community; policy changes may induce changes in locational patterns and thus affect prediction of the policy effects. The bureaucratic model suggests that decision-making power does not rest exclusively with residents or voters; a grant may stick like flypaper to the bureau receiving it and thus prevent or slow down its conversion into an income effect.

Armed with the theory of grants and some specific ideas about equity, we presented an application to school finance. The California foundation system of school finance, struck down as unconstitutional in the *Serrano* decision, is a nonmatching grant system that reduces aggregate inequality from the level that a purely local system would produce. However, the court was not concerned with the aggregate amount of inequality. It was offended because the state failed to provide a wealth-neutral system: Children in property-poor districts experienced much lower levels of school expenditures than did children in other districts. This same problem continues in numerous states.

The court was ambiguous as to requiring simple or conditional wealth neutrality; the ambiguity depends on whether the district tax rate choice is considered an exceptional characteristic. Several systems of school finance, for example, full state financing, can achieve both simple and conditional neutrality, but for political reasons it is likely that the existing districts in most states will continue to have at least some power over their individual expenditure levels. In these cases, either (but not both) of the neutrality standards can be met by a system of matching grants. Simple neutrality is harder to achieve because it requires knowledge of each district's demand curve. Conditional neutrality is easier to design but may result in substantial correlation between district wealth and expenditures.

A number of other issues must be considered in designing an equitable school finance policy. For example, a naïve application of the neutrality principle could substantially and unintentionally worsen the position of children of lower-income families living in the large cities, since those cities are considered property-rich. Careful thinking about the degree of state general funding versus matching grant funds, the measurement of a district's true fiscal capacity, the district cost variation of providing equivalent educational resources, the measurement of pupil needs, and the long-run consequences of reform can lead to a fairer system of finance and a reduction in unintended adverse consequences of seeking greater equity.

Exercises

5-1   The Minnesota legislature was debating how to give financial relief to the poor from higher heating bills expected in the future. One suggestion was that any increase in expenditure per household compared with the expenditure of the prior year be billed directly to the state. A second suggestion was to give each household a heating voucher (a nonmatching grant to be used only for heating the household) of an amount equal to the difference between last year's expenditure and the cost of the same quantity at this year's higher prices. Both suggestions would give each household more utility than it had last year, but only one would help conserve energy. Explain.

5-2   Sometimes the political implications of grants may not be what they seem. At one time, members of the liberal caucus in Congress introduced legislation to provide increased funding for local social services. It came as a great surprise when the caucus was approached by several conservatives with an offer of bipartisan support. These same conservatives had long attacked spending on social services as wasteful; now, however, they found that their voters perceived them as "heartless." Given the financial plight of local governments, they suggested dropping the matching requirement of the liberal version. This would allow them to take some credit for the legislation and to counteract their heartless image. The liberals readily agreed.

a Had these conservatives softened? Or can you offer an explanation for their behavior consistent with their long-standing objectives? [*Hint:* Use diagrams and assume some local community choice under a matching plan; then construct an equally costly nonmatching plan.]

b The answer to (a) was pointed out to one member of the liberal caucus. She chuckled softly, shook her head, and responded cryptically: "Never underestimate the tenacity of social service bureaucrats." What could the congresswoman be thinking?

5-3   The federal government has been providing a nonmatching grant of $1 billion to a community to provide training for the long-term unemployed (defined as those unemployed for 6 months or more). Before the grant program, the community had not been spending anything on training.

a Draw a diagram to represent the community's budget constraints and choices in the preprogram and postprogram periods.

b With new elections in Congress, the legislative mood shifted. More congressional members argued that the federal government should not tell local governments what to do. They proposed changing the terms of the grant so that it could be used either for training or public employment. The community already spends $25 billion for salaries of public sector employees out of its total budget of $250 billion. What effect do you think this proposal would have on spending for training? Use the standard theory of intergovernmental grants in answering.

c Suppose the proposal passed and you observed that spending on training programs hardly changed at all. What theory might explain this?

5-4   The district demand for public education expenditures per child E is $E = 0.03P_E^{-0.4}W$, where P_E is the price per unit of E and W is the district property wealth per child. Suppose that there are only two districts in the state and that they have property wealth per child of $20,000 and $70,000. Currently, school finance is purely local and $P_E = \$1$. If each district has the same number of children, identify a variable matching grant program that the state can introduce to make education spending equal with no net effect on the state treasury. [*Hints:* Recaptured funds must equal state subsidies. Use a calculator.] (Answer: Spending is equalized at $1618.92 per child with no net cost to the state when the state uses a matching rate of $-\$0.47818$ for the $70,000 district and $10.95883 for the $20,000 district.)

APPENDIX

AN EXERCISE IN THE USE OF A SOCIAL WELFARE FUNCTION AS AN AID IN EVALUATING SCHOOL FINANCE POLICIES°

The idea of using a social welfare function as a way of making evaluative judgments that combine equity and efficiency was introduced in Chapter 3. In this section we illustrate some of the mechanics of constructing a social welfare function for use in evaluating school finance grant systems. Realistic examples involve detailed empirical specifications, and the hard analytic work of choosing parameters carefully and cogently is essential to the success of any such analysis. Here we wish to keep the mechanics as transparent as possible and thus greatly oversimplify by building partially on the illustrative example of the chapter. However, it is strongly recommended that several actual applications be studied before use of this technique is attempted.[58]

Figure 5A-1, like Figure 3-9, displays three social indifference curves that represent different emphases on efficiency and equality (the Benthamite straight line W^B, the Rawlsian right angle W^R, and the middle of the road W^M). Although we know that there is no social consensus about an appropriate welfare function, it may be that individual politicians and interest group representatives have social preferences that are known to be closer to one function than another. Thus if policies could be evaluated with the functions representing the interests of the decision makers, such an analysis could be helpful to those decision makers in deciding what policies to support.[59] This is most likely to be useful when the

---

[58] The simple exercise presented here was inspired by a very thoughtful simulation study of school finance reform in New York. See R. P. Inman, "Optimal Fiscal Reform of Metropolitan Schools," *American Economic Review, 68,* No. 1, March 1978, pp. 107–122. An example using social welfare functions in another policy area is N. H. Stern, "On the Specification of Models of Optimum Income Taxation," *Journal of Public Economics, 6,* 1976, pp. 123–162.

[59] Policy conclusions from this type of analysis, and a defense of them, would have to be presented in a non-technical way. For example, the analyst might learn that when the matching rate in a certain grant plan goes above $2 for every local dollar, the ranking by the Benthamite criterion declines rapidly. The analyst would have to realize that the Benthamite criterion is most relevant to the large middle class (because each person's utility level is weighted

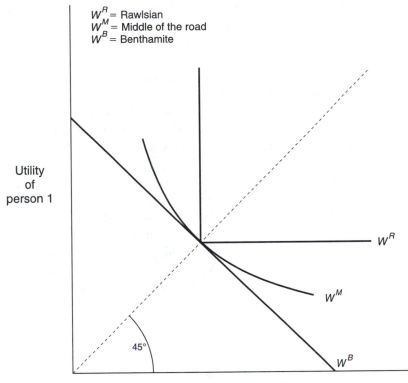

Figure 5A-1. Alternative social welfare functions.

consequences of adopting policies are complex: gains and losses of varying sizes distributed over different interest groups in a nonobvious way.

Social welfare functions can be constructed to take the basic shape of any of the social indifference curves shown in Figure 5A-1. For example, consider the family of social welfare functions represented by

$$W = \left(\sum_{i=1}^{n} U_i^\delta \right)^{1/\delta}$$

where $\delta \leq 1$. If we let $\delta = 1$, the social welfare function collapses to the Benthamite sum of utilities. As $\delta \to -\infty$, the function becomes more proequality and approaches the Rawlsian standard. Middle-of-the-road functions are generated by using values of δ between the extremes. The parameter δ simply specifies the weight to be given to each person; lower values of δ give greater weight to people with lower utility levels. Thus, once one knows the values of individual utility levels to enter as the arguments of the welfare function, one

---

equally). Then one can state a conclusion and explain it in language understood by policy makers, for example, "The matching rate should not be more than $2 for every local dollar. Otherwise, the state budget level would have to be raised and the crucial support of the Taxpayer's Association would be jeopardized."

can see if a policy proposal ranks favorably over a broad range of values for δ. (If it does, a potentially broad range of support for the policy is implied.)

How does one know what values of individual utility levels to enter? After all, utility is nonmeasurable and noncomparable among different people. Here we deviate from consumer sovereignty and seek to identify a way of making utility comparisons that reflect the social judgments of potential users of the analysis.

Typically, the assumption is that policy makers will count people who are identical in terms of certain observable characteristics as having the same utility. For the case of school finance, we will assume that each household's utility level can be fairly represented by a function $U(E, B_T)$, where E is the amount of education consumed by the household (measured by the educational expenditures on its children) and B_T is the after-education tax wealth that the household has available for all other goods (using the property tax base per child as a proxy variable adjusted for taxes paid). Both variables are observable, and households with the same E and B_T will be counted as having the same utility.

The specific functional form of the utility function is chosen to be common to all persons and to weight the observable characteristics in a manner that policy makers will judge reasonable. Here real-world statistics offer useful guidance. In the case of school finance for this exercise, we use the form

$$U = B_T^{0.985} E^{0.015}$$

This form implies that households will choose to spend 1.5 percent of their wealth on education.[60] This percentage is what we "observed" in the hypothetical prereform districts of the main chapter. That is, the average district with a $120,000 property tax base per child chose a $1800 school expenditure level (per child), and the average $420,000 district spent $6300 per child. In each case the ratio of expenditure to the tax base is 0.015 (= 1800/ 120,000 = 6300/420,000). The policy maker aware of the equality might reasonably conclude that households prefer the proportion, and might wish the analysis to penalize deviations from it caused by policy.[61]

Imagine that each district in our example is composed solely of homogeneous households with one child per household (this keeps the example as simple as possible). Then each household in a district will pay local taxes equal to the educational expenditure on its child (with no state intervention). If each of the households in one district has a pretax wealth of B_0, the behavioral demand function used in the chapter implies that it will spend 1.5 percent of B_0 on education. Since within a district all the households in our example are assumed to be homogeneous, they will unanimously agree as local voters to spend $1800 per child in the $120,000 district and $6300 per child in the $420,000 district.

---

[60] This form is a special case of the more general form $U = B_T^{\alpha} E^{1-\alpha}$, where α is the utility-maximizing proportion of the budget spent on B_T and $1 - \alpha$ for E. This function, called the Cobb-Douglas utility function, is discussed in Chapter 6.

[61] Like the analysis this exercise is modeled after, we forego complicating this socially chosen utility function further. It is not consistent with the price-elasticity assumptions used in the demand equations in the chapter, but then it is only used after the behavioral predictions have been made.

Table 5A-1
Simulated Effects of School Finance Reforms on Households

Districts	Prereform	School finance policies		
		Simple wealth neutrality (matching grants)	Conditional wealth neutrality (DPE)	Equal spending (full state financing)
Low-wealth district				
E	1,800	4,800	2,270	4,800
B_T	118,200	119,690	120,535	117,867
U	111,009	114,052	113,563	112,341
High-wealth district				
E	6,300	4,800	4,800	4,800
B_T	413,700	410,711	412,396	412,533
U	388,531	384,195	385,747	385,874

Now, we are almost ready to compare the three policies used in the preceding section's illustrations; do nothing, achieve simple wealth neutrality with target spending of $4800, and achieve conditional wealth neutrality with the high-wealth district spending $4800. First we must clarify some additional assumptions used in the calculations below.

We treat our two district types as if they were equal in population and made up the state. The state treasury always breaks even. The surplus generated by each reform (recaptures exceed state aid) is assumed to be distributed in equal payments to each household in the state (e.g., a tax credit for households with children in school). The redistributions have small income effects that we ignore. We continue to rule out household locational changes or the substitution of private for public education, so that the district responses to the reform remain as indicated in the main chapter.

The effects of the three previously discussed policies on the households are summarized in Table 5A-1. The positions of a low- and a high-wealth household with no reforms in effect are given in column 1. Since in this case a household's tax payment equals the district educational expenditure per child, B_T in the low-wealth district is $118,200 (= $120,000 − $1800) and in the high-wealth district it is $413,700 (= $420,000 − $6300). The utility level U is calculated (here and in the other columns) by substituting the levels of B_T and E in the utility function chosen earlier. For example, the utility of each family in the low-wealth district is

$$U = 118,200^{0.985} (1800^{0.015})$$

$$= 111,009$$

Columns 2 and 3 show similar calculations for the simple and conditional wealth neutrality proposals illustrated in the main chapter. The only entries that require explanation are those for B_T. Recall that the low-wealth district under simple wealth neutrality received $4368 in matching state aid and contributed only $432 of its own wealth to reach the $4800 expenditure level. The high-wealth district under this proposal raised $9411, of which the state recaptured $4611. Therefore, the state had net receipts of $243 (= $4611 − $4368) for every two households, or $121.50 per household. Under our assumption, the state rebates $121.50 to each household. Therefore, the after-tax wealth B_T of the household in the low-wealth district is

$$B_T = \$120,000 - \$432 + \$121.50$$

$$= \$119,689.50$$

Similarly for the high-wealth district,

$$B_T = \$420,000 - \$9411 + \$121.50$$

$$= \$410,710.50$$

The after-tax wealth figures for the DPE proposal used to achieve conditional wealth neutrality are similarly derived.[62] Note that in all cases the sum over both districts of educational expenditures and after-tax wealth for the two representative households is $540,000 (the joint budget constraint).

Column 4 of Table 5A-1 contains a new policy alternative not previously discussed: equal spending per child achieved by full state financing of schools with a statewide property tax. A uniform expenditure of $4800 per child is made with state revenues. This level is chosen for comparability with the simple wealth neutrality proposal. This means that the state tax rate τ applied to both the low- and high-wealth districts must raise $9600 in revenues for every two households:

$$120,000\tau + 420,000\tau = 9600$$

$$540,000\tau = 9600$$

$$\tau = 1.778 \text{ percent}$$

The low-wealth district makes tax contributions to the state of $2133 per household (= $0.01778 \times 120,000$), and the high-wealth district contributes $7467 (= $0.01778 \times 420,000$). These figures are used to determine the after-tax wealth in each district.

As we look across the columns, it becomes clear that no one of these proposals is obviously better than the others. Furthermore, their relative impacts on any single district are not obvious from the observable variables only. The DPE proposal, for example, barely increases educational spending in the low-wealth district compared to the increase under full state financing, but it is nevertheless ranked higher: The bigger after-tax wealth outweighs the lower educational spending.

The rankings are, of course, a consequence of the utility function chosen. Keep in mind that this choice has some justification: the observation that households across the wealth

---

[62] The exact demand of the average low-wealth district under DPE was calculated by using the demand curve $E = 1800P^{-0.4}$ at $P = \$0.56$.

Table 5A-2

Social Welfare Rankings of the Alternative School Finance Reforms (1 = Best, 2 = Second Best, 3 = Third Best, 4 = Last)

		School finance policies		
Districts	Prereform	Simple wealth neutrality (matching grants)	Conditional wealth neutrality (DPE)	Equal spending (full state financing)
Household utility levels[a]				
U_H	388,531	384,195	385,747	385,074
U_L	111,009	114,052	113,563	112,341
Social welfare functions[b]				
Benthamite	1	3	2	4
Middle of the road	4	2	1	3
Rawlsian	4	1	2	3

[a] H = high-wealth district; L = low-wealth district.

[b] The actual numerical scores for the alternative are not comparable across the different welfare functions because the functional form changes.

classes seem to prefer spending 1.5 percent of their wealth on education. The full-state-financing plan has the family in the low-wealth district spending 3.9 percent of its total after-tax wealth ($122,667 = $4800 + $117,867) on education, whereas under the DPE plan the percentage is 1.8.

Table 5A-2 shows the rankings of the four policy alternatives when evaluated by three different social welfare functions: Benthamite ($\Delta = 1$), Rawlsian (the utility level of the worst-off household),[63] and a middle-of-the-road function ($\Delta = 0.1$). Recall that the Benthamite function is simply the sum of the utility levels, and the middle-of-the-road function (using subscripts L and H for the households in the low-wealth and high-wealth districts) is

$$W^M = (U_L^{0.1} + U_H^{0.1})^{10}$$

On looking at the table, we see that a different alternative is ranked first by each of the social welfare functions. Although there is no consensus about what is best, *note that the full-state-financing proposal is dominated by both the simple and conditional wealth neutrality proposals* (i.e., the latter two are ranked higher than full state financing by all three evaluation rules). Thus, unless policy makers have a very strong social preference for equal

[63] When handling large amounts of data, it can be convenient to approximate the Rawlsian function. Even though the Rawlsian function is the limit as $\delta \to -\infty$, it turns out that $\delta = -10$ is usually approximate enough. This approximation applied to the data in this example is typically within 0.00006 percent of the exact number.

educational spending per se, we can eliminate this proposal from consideration.[64] Also, we can see that those with preferences other than Benthamite have some incentive to form a coalition to try to eliminate the prereform system. (They prefer any of the reform proposals to no reform at all.)

In a sense this exercise only begins to suggest how social welfare functions may be useful. A much more powerful use is in the design of the alternatives. We picked specific proposals rather arbitrarily: Why do we consider a full-state-financing proposal only at the $4800 expenditure level, for example, when some other level might rank much higher by one or more of the social welfare functions? It can be shown that the best full-state-financing plan by the Benthamite rule (indeed, any of the social welfare rules) is to set the expenditure level at $4050, with a statewide property tax rate of 1.5 percent, $U_L = 112,237$, $U_H = 385,964$, and $W^B = 498,332$.[65] With computer simulation one can identify the optimal financing plans of each type of reform according to various social welfare functions. Simulation with actual data can be a way to begin to clarify the most promising alternatives for serious policy consideration.[66]

---

[64] Recall that neutrality and educational equality are social values *in addition to* the social welfare criteria.

[65] For the full state plan, the sum of taxes from one household in each district must equal twice the chosen expenditure level (in order for the treasury to break even):

$$120,000\tau + 420,000\tau = 2E$$

$$\tau = \frac{E}{270,000}$$

The household in the low-wealth district therefore always pays $\frac{4}{9}E$ in taxes (= 120,000E/270,000), and the high-wealth household pays $\frac{14}{9}E$. The best Benthamite plan requires choosing E to maximize U_L plus U_H:

$$\text{Maximize} \left(120,000 - \frac{4E}{9}\right)^{0.985} E^{0.015} + \left(420,000 - \frac{14E}{9}\right)^{0.985} E^{0.015}$$

The solution to this is $E = \$4050$; in fact, it is the level for a statewide plan preferred by each district independently and would therefore be preferred if any of the social welfare functions were used.

[66] Inman, "Optimal Fiscal Reform of Metropolitan Schools," does precisely that. Similarly, Stern, "On the Specification of Models of Optimum Income Taxation," undertakes an exercise to determine the optimal income tax rates.

CHAPTER SIX

THE COMPENSATION PRINCIPLE OF BENEFIT-COST REASONING: BENEFIT MEASURES AND MARKET DEMANDS

ONE OF THE MOST important analytic tasks is to address questions of *relative efficiency*. For example, it was primarily analysts who argued for the deregulation of passenger air service because it was expected to *increase* efficiency. The analysts knew that some individuals would gain from the change and others would lose, but the analytic community was nevertheless virtually unanimous in advocating deregulation as an efficient change. The force of the analysts' arguments was largely responsible for the Airline Deregulation Act of 1978, which provided for the phasing out of the Civil Aeronautics Board by 1985 and return of the power to choose routes and set fares to the individual airlines. In fact, similar arguments were put forth with a high degree of consensus by analysts of the communications, energy, and other industries. In the period from 1977 to 1988, these led to a reduction in the portion of the U.S. economy that is fully regulated from 17 percent to 6.6 percent and resulted in efficiency improvements with estimated value of $36 to $46 billion annually.[1] While these examples happen to be of reduced government intervention, there are many other examples where relative efficiency is enhanced by an active government role. We consider in this chapter the shared concept of relative efficiency that led to this unusual degree of agreement.

We introduce the fundamental test of relative efficiency known as the *compensation principle*. Essentially, the principle involves considering whether it is possible for the gainers from a change to compensate the losers and still come out ahead. This principle not only helped lead to the substantial analytic agreement in the above example, but is the foundation for the important analytic technique known as *benefit-cost analysis,* which is used extensively throughout government. It was first required by the Flood Control Act of 1936 for

---

[1] See C. Winston, "Economic Deregulation: Days of Reckoning for Microeconomists," *Journal of Economic Literature, 31,* No. 3, September 1993, pp. 1263–1289.

use in estimating the economic value of proposed federal water resource projects such as dams, and its use has since spread to all types of expenditure and regulatory decisions.

For example, many analysts argue that regulatory standards such as those limiting water pollution or the use of hazardous substances were not originally designed with sufficient attention to relative efficiency. President Reagan issued an executive order directing regulatory agencies to use benefit-cost analysis when making new regulations and reviewing old ones. As his *Economic Report of the President* explains[2]: "The motive for incorporating benefit-cost analysis into the regulatory decision-making process is to achieve a *more efficient* allocation of government resources by subjecting the public sector to the *same type* of efficiency tests used in the private sector" (emphasis added). Indeed, we will introduce the compensation principle in a way that reinforces the analogy between the efficiency-seeking of a market and that of benefit-cost analysis.

But what does it really mean when we say that one allocation is more efficient than another or that an allocative change increases efficiency? Recall the introductory discussion of efficiency in Chapter 3. Efficiency or Pareto optimality is considered to be a neutral standard in terms of outcome equity implications, in the sense that there are efficient allocations characterized by virtually any relative distribution of well-being among individuals. However, this is an absolute concept rather than a relative one: It is either possible or not possible to make someone better off without making another person worse off. To determine whether one allocation is *more* efficient than another, we need a standard of *relative* efficiency.

Most allocative changes caused by public policy involve situations in which some people are made better off and others are made worse off. Standards of relative efficiency used to decide if a change is an improvement in efficiency make interpersonal comparisons in a specific way and therefore may be controversial on equity grounds. In this chapter we explain the fundamental test of relative efficiency—the compensation principle—in a way that makes its equity implications explicit.

There is a second theme to this chapter, in addition to explaining the compensation principle. To this point the theory that we have been using to understand policy consequences consists primarily of principles of individual choice. But the data most commonly available (or most readily attainable) for policy analyses are usually market statistics: information about aggregations of individual choices rather than the individual decisions themselves. For example, we are more likely to have estimates of a market demand curve than of all the individual demand curves that shape it. To understand the inferences that can be made from market observations, one often has to rely upon additional logical bridges to connect individual decisions with market observations. Good use of these logical bridges requires skill in model specification. We consider this problem in the context of applying the compensation principle: How and when can one use knowledge of market demand curves to make inferences about relative efficiency?

---

[2] *Economic Report of the President, February 1982* (Washington, D.C.: U.S. Government Printing Office, 1982), p. 137.

We begin by introducing the compensation principle. Then we illustrate its application in some simple settings that permit focus on the "demand" or "benefit" side (Chapter 9 introduces and focuses on cost-side issues). We define a specific benefit-cost component known as *consumer surplus,* and demonstrate how measurements of changes in consumer surplus are used in benefit-cost analysis. We consider whether or not the market demand curve contains the information we seek for benefit-cost analysis in three different policy settings: taxation, gasoline rationing, and consumer protection legislation. In the supplemental section, we consider three variants of the consumer surplus measure and the difficulty of applying them. We discuss their application through survey methods, with special attention to the method known as *contingent valuation* and its role in environmental issues. An appendix to the chapter goes over the mathematical relations between these measures and utility and demand functions, including concepts used in the dual theory of consumer choice.

The Compensation Principle of Relative Efficiency

The Purpose of a Relative Efficiency Standard

As we know, public policy alternatives will cause changes in the welfare of many people. Furthermore, it is virtually inevitable that every policy change will improve the lot of some but worsen the lot of others. As we recognize that the decisions are made through a political process, the problem we address is whether analytic input to the process can provide a useful judgment about the relative efficiency of each alternative.

In Chapter 3, we began discussing the analytic value of having a yardstick of some type. Neither the criterion of Pareto superiority nor that of Pareto optimality helps us to resolve whether the gains from a change might somehow be sufficient to offset the losses that it causes.[3] The criterion of Pareto superiority applies only to situations in which some gain but no one loses or no one gains and some lose. As a practical matter, this does not characterize the effects of actual policy changes. As an ethical matter, there is no compelling justification for trying to restrict policy changes to Pareto-superior situations. Aside from the practical impossibility of doing so, equity considerations could lead to a social preference for making some better off at the expense of others—as when, for example, the status quo is a consequence of unfair discrimination in the past.

Can we not simply rely upon Pareto optimality as the efficiency standard? If it were easy to attain and remain at a Pareto-optimal allocation, we might not have to be so concerned about our progress (or lack thereof) toward one. However, in complex and dynamic economies, the best that we can do is to strive toward this goal. Many different policy changes are considered each year by many different layers of governments, and each of them can bear in important ways on the populations affected. Should a new highway be built in a certain locality? With limited funds available for new equipment at a public hospital, what equipment would be most valuable to buy? Is it a good idea to require airlines to reduce

---

[3] Pareto superiority is an allocative change that makes at least one person better off with no one worse off, and Pareto optimality is an allocation from which it is impossible to make anyone better off except by making another worse off.

noise levels near airports? If we are fortunate enough to be able to reduce taxes, which taxes would it be the most beneficial to reduce? The people making these decisions try to resolve each by assessing the pros and cons of the different alternatives.

The purpose of the relative efficiency standard is to offer a systematic way of measuring the pros against the cons, or the benefits compared to the costs. The value of a consistent methodology is that it allows any particular application to be scrutinized for accuracy by any professional analyst. Furthermore, repeated use of the same measure helps users of analyses to understand the strengths and weaknesses of the measure. Because the measure will inevitably compare the gains to some against the losses to others, it is like using a particular social welfare function, and not everyone will agree that decisions should be made based upon it. In fact, our recommendation for its use is to treat it as an important but not sufficient indicator of an alternative's worthiness.

Two actual examples from the late 1990s illustrate the uses to which this standard is put.[4] Many federal agencies seek to make rules and regulations that they believe will improve the well-being of the citizenry. As we have seen, these agencies are required by Executive Order of the President to quantify benefits and costs of their proposed rules.[5] The Department of Energy (DOE), working to reduce fossil fuel consumption, imposed a ruling "Energy Standards for Refrigerators and Freezers." For each of eight classes of refrigerators (e.g., those with automatic defrost and top-mount freezers), DOE calculated the benefits and costs for at least twelve alternative performance standards in order to put forth the one with the greatest net benefits for each class. Based on its analysis, the standards implemented cost $3.44 billion per year, but generate benefits of $7.62 billion per year. The benefit estimates are derived from an analysis that begins by calculating physical benefits, such as the degree to which NO_x and CO_2 air pollution emissions will be reduced as a result of the standards and then putting monetary values on those reductions based on studies of the public's willingness to pay for them.

The second example is from the Health and Human Services Department (HHS). In April 1999, the Mammography Quality Standards Act became effective. This act mandates various quality improvements in mammography screening procedures for detecting breast cancer. As part of the analysis done to decide if such an act was beneficial, the Food and Drug Administration (FDA) conducted a benefit-cost analysis of the proposed standards. It estimated that the benefits of these higher standards were worth $182–$263 million per year, whereas the costs were only $38 million per year. The benefits come primarily from increased detection of breast cancers at an early stage, when treatment is most likely to be successful. Some of the benefits are that lives will be saved, and the monetary value of saving each of these "statistical" lives was estimated (based on other studies) at $4.8 million.[6]

---

[4] The examples are discussed in a 1998 report from the Office of Management and Budget entitled "Report to Congress on the Costs and Benefits of Federal Regulation."

[5] President Clinton continued this practice, mandating agencies to conduct benefit-cost analyses to the best of their ability and to the extent permitted by law. See his Executive Order 12866, "Regulatory Planning and Review."

[6] "Statistical" lives are saved when there is an increase in the probability of saving someone in a large population, even though no one can identify the specific individual. For example, if a new treatment applied to a

While the FDA assumed that the new standards would result in a 5 percent quality improvement, it noted that only a 2 percent improvement was needed for the benefits to exceed the costs.

In these cases the claim is not that the new standards achieve an "optimal" allocation of resources, but that they achieve a more efficient allocation. Many questions can be raised about the examples. How does anyone know the public's willingness to pay? If the benefits of the new mammography standards did not outweigh the costs, would this mean that they should not be imposed? Another federal agency that makes health regulations, the Occupational Health and Safety Administration, has been forbidden by a Supreme Court decision from assigning monetary values to human lives and suffering. How are such estimates derived, what are we to think of them, and why should some agencies be allowed to use them and others not? In order to begin to address any of these important issues (in this and later chapters), we have a more immediate task. Let us first understand carefully the principle that underlies our methods of measuring relative efficiency.

The Hicks-Kaldor Compensation Principle

The standard of relative efficiency that has come to be widely utilized in analytic work was first developed by the British economists John Hicks and Nicholas Kaldor.[7] The underlying concept, called **the compensation principle,** builds on the notion of Pareto superiority. The principle is as follows: **An allocative change increases efficiency if the gainers from the change are capable of compensating the losers and still coming out ahead. Each individual's gain or loss is defined as the value of a hypothetical monetary compensation that would keep each individual (in his or her own judgment) indifferent to the change.**

It is critically important to understand that the compensations are not in fact made. If they were, the change would then indeed be Pareto-superior. Thus the compensation principle is a test for potential Pareto superiority. Think of the gains from a change as its benefits and the losses from a change as its costs. Define net benefits as the sum of all benefits minus the sum of all costs. If a change increases efficiency, that is equivalent to stating that its net benefits are positive. **The analytic effort to examine whether or not changes satisfy the compensation principle is called benefit-cost analysis.** Often, benefit-cost analysis is used to compare mutually exclusive alternatives to identify the one yielding the greatest net benefits. Trying to maximize net benefits is thus the same as trying to maximize relative efficiency.

---

population of 1000 reduces the probability of death from a specific disease from 0.07 to 0.03, then we would expect only thirty rather than seventy people to die from the disease. The treatment is said to save forty statistical lives. The value of saving a statistical life is not necessarily the same as the value of saving particular identified individuals. For more information on valuing life and limb, see the review article by W. K. Viscusi, "The Value of Risks to Life and Health," *Journal of Economic Literature, 31,* No. 4, December 1993, pp. 1912–1946.

[7] See J. R. Hicks, "The Valuation of the Social Income," *Economica, 7,* May 1940, pp. 105–124, and N. Kaldor, "Welfare Propositions of Economics and Interpersonal Comparisons of Utility," *Economic Journal, 49,* September 1939, pp. 549–551.

Before illustrating some of the details of benefit-cost reasoning, it is important to discuss first the controversy about whether or not the pursuit of relative efficiency is equitable.

Controversy over the Use of the Compensation Principle

Most of the controversy over the use of compensation tests concerns the equity judgments implicit in them. Some analysts would like to ignore equity altogether and use the compensation test as *the* decisive analytic test. One rationale is the hope that a separate set of policies can be designed to take account of and amend the overall distributional effects. However, this view may underestimate the process equity concerns with particular policy changes and overestimate the ability of policy makers to change the outcomes once they are "done."

A second rationale for relying solely on the compensation test is the belief that concern for equity is simply unfounded: If a large number of policy changes are made in accordance with the compensation rule, then everyone will end up with actual gains. Even if correct, this argument has an implicit equity judgment that restricts redistributive concerns. (For example, perhaps some people should gradually be made worse off to allow others to become better off.) Putting that aside, let us consider the argument directly.

Think of the payoff to an individual from a policy change as arising from the flip of a fair coin: $2 if it is heads and −$1 if it is tails. On any one flip the individual may lose, but in the long run the individual will be better off. However, this reasoning depends heavily on the debatable proposition that gains and losses from policy changes are distributed randomly. If they are not, what have the losers (gainers) done to deserve the losses (gains)? At least in the author's judgment, the compensation test cannot substitute for explicit consideration of equity effects.

A third rationale focuses on the role of analysts in the policy process. This argument is that analysts are not needed to represent equity concerns because these concerns are appropriately represented by the other participants in the policy process (e.g., elected officials, lobbyists for interest groups); the need for analysts is to give voice to efficiency concerns that would otherwise be given no consideration at all. Acceptance of this rationale depends heavily on a view of the policy-making process in which the process (absent analytic input) is flawed in representing efficiency but not equity. Furthermore, the view implies that analytic input can give voice to important unvoiced efficiency concerns but cannot similarly give voice to important unvoiced equity concerns. In light of the importance of analytic contributions to the equity of issues such as school finance and criminal sentencing, this seems a strained argument at best.

Putting aside the arguments about whether to consider equity at all, some people argue that an implicit and unacceptable equity judgment is reflected in the money metric used. The principle implies that a $1 gain to one individual precisely offsets a $1 loss to any other. When the gainer is rich and the loser is poor, this would be a peculiar social welfare function to use as a rule. To clarify this, let us examine the compensation principle for small changes involving only two people.

Let us denote the hypothetical compensation as H_i for person i. For a small change, this may be expressed in utility terms:

$$H_i = \Delta U_i / \lambda_i$$

where ΔU_i is the change in utils and λ_i person i's marginal utility from an additional dollar. That is, the numerator is the total change in utils, and the denominator is the util value per dollar. Therefore the whole expression is the dollar equivalent of the utility change. For example, an individual who values a gain at $10 and whose marginal utility of a dollar is 2 utils can be thought of as experiencing a gain of 20 utils:

$$\$10 = 20 \text{ utils}/(2 \text{ utils}/\$)$$

The sum of hypothetical compensations in this two-person case is

$$H_1 + H_2 = \Delta U_1 / \lambda_1 + \Delta U_2 / \lambda_2$$

The above expression, in turn, can be expressed as the difference between the prechange and postchange utilities. Denoting A as the prechange utility and B as the post-change utility, and $\Delta U_i = U_1^B - U_1^A$ we can rewrite the above as

$$H_1 + H_2 = [U_1^B/\lambda_1 + U_2^B/\lambda_2] - [U_1^A/\lambda_1 + U_2^A/\lambda_2]$$

The bracketed terms in the above expression may be thought of as levels of a social welfare function. The social welfare function is simply the sum of the utility of each person, weighted by the inverse of the marginal utility of money. Viewed this way, objections to the compensation principle on equity grounds can now be made clear. If there is declining marginal utility of wealth, a 1-util gain to a poor person will be judged socially less worthwhile than a 1-util gain to a rich person!

In Figure 6-1, we illustrate this in terms of social indifference curves. Imagine that persons 1 and 2 have identical utility functions, so that all differences in their utility levels are due solely to wealth differences. We saw in Chapter 3 that the Benthamite W^B and Rawlsian W^R social welfare functions are usually considered the extremes of plausible social judgment. But the social indifference curve corresponding to indifference by the compensation principle W^c falls outside these extremes. It is bowed toward the origin. We explain this below.

The slope of any social indifference curve is $\Delta u^2/\Delta u^1$, where Δu^2 is the change in person 2's utility necessary to hold social welfare constant when person 1's utility changes by a small amount Δu^1; Indifference by the compensation principle requires that

$$\frac{\Delta u^2}{\lambda^2} + \frac{\Delta u^1}{\lambda^1} = 0$$

or

$$\frac{\Delta u^2}{\Delta u^1} = -\frac{\lambda_2}{\lambda_1}$$

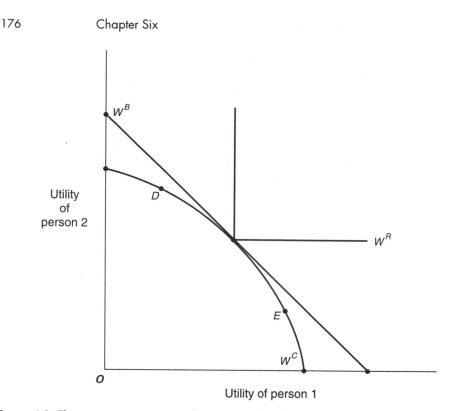

Figure 6-1. The compensation principle as a social welfare function is antiegalitarian.

At a point of equal utilities, $\lambda_2 = \lambda_1$ and the slope of the social indifference curve is -1. But as we move away from a point of equal utilities along the social indifference curve, λ declines for the gainer and rises for the loser. At point D, for example, $\lambda_2 < \lambda_1$ and the slope of the indifference curve is flatter or less negative $(-\lambda_2/\lambda_1 > -1)$. At point E, where person 1 is relatively well off, $\lambda_1 < \lambda_2$ and the indifference curve is steeper or more negative $(-\lambda_2/\lambda_1 < -1)$.

Thus, the social indifference curve associated with the compensation principle is bowed toward the origin. If the Benthamite welfare function is indifferent to equality, the compensation principle can be considered antiegalitarian. This explains why many analysts wish to assign different "ethical" weights to the utility changes (or, more practically, weights to their monetary metrics, dependent on each individual's wealth or income level).[8]

Of course, the equity objections to the compensation principle are primarily to proposals that the principle be used as a sufficient criterion for policy evaluation. We have suggested that it be used only in conjunction with other evaluative criteria of equity (and, indeed, Pareto optimality). Let us not forget that some consistent standard used to measure the size of the aggregate social pie is useful. Furthermore, in an important sense the compensation

[8] For examples of how to do this, see Anthony Boardman et al., *Cost-Benefit Analysis: Concepts and Practice* (Upper Saddle River, N.J.: Prentice-Hall, Inc., 2001), Chapter 18, and Edward M. Gramlich, *A Guide to Benefit-Cost Analysis* (Englewood Cliffs, N.J.: Prentice-Hall, Inc., 1990), Chapter 7.

test is a more demanding standard than simply asking if a change increases the value of the national product.

Actual measures of national product, such as the gross domestic product (GDP), are flawed in the sense that they exclude important goods such as leisure and bads such as pollution. Nevertheless, it should be clear enough that even the flawed measures are of great concern to policy makers. Increases in them are generally considered desirable and decreases undesirable. Even ignoring the flaws from omitting goods, the standard ways of measuring changes in national product have other flaws. For example, later on in the text we show that one extensively used national product measure is overly "optimistic," in the sense that the measure may go up even if all people are worse off.[9] However, the same change evaluated by the compensation principle would not have this flaw: It would indicate that relative efficiency has decreased. Thus *the compensation test is a procedure that, in principle, is more refined than the common methods used to measure changes in the aggregate social pie.*[10]

[9] See the explanation of the Laspeyre quantity index in Chapter 8. Figure 8-7 illustrates a case where the change affecting only one individual is positive by the Laspeyre index although the individual is worse off. By extension, the same result would occur if the change affected many people in the same way.

[10] For the case in which we can consider the national product to include all goods, we show that the following is true: If a policy change passes the compensation test, then national product valued at current prices must be increased by the change. The proof of this is not difficult, although it involves some mathematical notation that may not be familiar to all readers.

Let the vector X denote the aggregate amount of each good in the economy, using X_A for the amounts before the change, and X_B for the amounts after the change. A vector is simply a row or column of numbers. In our case, the vector X represents some specific quantity for each of n different goods $X_1, X_2, \ldots, X_n$ that form the consumption bundle. For example the row vector [2 4] would mean that there are two units of X_1 and four units of X_2. Let the vector P represent the price per unit for each of the goods $P_1, P_2, \ldots, P_n$, again letting P_A denote prices before the change and P_B prices after the change. The product of the two vectors PX is the total market value of the bundle $P_1X_1 + P_2X_2 + \ldots + P_nX_n$.

Mathematically our assertion is:

$$\text{If } \sum_i H_i > 0, \text{ then } P_A X_B > P_A X_A$$

If $\sum_i H_i > 0$, there is some allocation of the aggregate bundle of goods X_B among the consumers such that all consumers get at least as much utility as from the actual consumer allocations of X_A. Take the case in which X_B is hypothetically so allocated that each person is strictly better off. Now consider the ith person. Since we assume utility maximization, it must be true that

$$P_A X_B^i > P_A X_A^i$$

That is, it must be that the ith person could not afford the bundle of goods X_B^i before the change: Otherwise, the person could have increased utility by buying it (we assume each individual's hypothetical bundle is available before the change, though at that time the economy could not make these bundles available to all individuals simultaneously). Since the same is true for *every* person,

$$P_A \sum_i X_B^i > P_A \sum_i X_A^i$$

But the sum of allocations to each person must add up to the appropriate aggregate allocation:

$$\sum_i X_B^i = X_B \text{ and } \sum_i X_A^i = X_A$$

Therefore, we can substitute X_B and X_A in the above equation and get

$$P_A X_B > P_A X_A$$

Whatever one thinks about the desirability of using the compensation principle in policy analysis, it can be no more controversial than thinking that increases in national product are generally good.

In short summary, the Hicks-Kaldor compensation principle has come to be widely utilized as a guide for making this comparison: A policy change is considered an efficiency improvement if it is *possible* for the gainers to compensate the losers and still have something left over for themselves. Although there can be no strong ethical justification for it, such a principle is an attempt to capture a sense of which alternative allocation is considered to be the biggest social pie. It is a more refined measure of efficiency change than simply looking at the change in national product, and we know that many people are willing to use the latter as an efficiency indicator. Therefore, looked at as an indicator to be considered along with equity effects, it provides policy makers with useful information.

In actual policy use, the compensation principle may play an even more defensible role than can be argued on theoretical grounds alone. Its most common use is in the form of benefit-cost studies to compare alternative programs for approximately the same target populations of gainers and losers. We have already mentioned one example of this: the DOE study of alternative energy-efficiency standards for refrigerators. As another example, the Department of Labor sponsors or has sponsored different public employment programs aimed at youth (e.g., Jobs Corps, Supported Work, Neighborhood Youth Corps) and has commissioned or undertaken major benefit-cost studies of each. In those situations, the studies are more likely to influence decisions as to which of these programs will survive or grow rather than whether there will be any programs at all.

The relationship between policy process and policy analysis is very important and warrants serious reflection. To the extent that policy alternatives must be carefully designed and their consequences analyzed, there can be an important role for policy experts. This depends on whether the experts can perform their tasks with the confidence and support of the other participants in the policy process. If analytic work either cannot clarify what participants in the decision process wish to know or does not add to what they already know, it is of little use. An analyst attempting to use the compensation principle as a way of deciding among very divergent allocative alternatives may find the work ignored (like it or not).

The problem of deciding what to do may be solved quite "rationally" by breaking the problem into pieces and giving policy analysts responsibility for the pieces with which they can deal least ambiguously. Since the policy significance of a compensation test becomes less clear as it is used to compare broader and more diverse allocations, perhaps the test should be relied upon less. I know of no instance, for example, in which a compensation test was actually used to decide between the mix of flood control projects and urban renewal. But analytic work of that type is used regularly to help sort out which programs seem better within each category. Other types of microeconomic policy analysis may influence the broader allocative decisions; but when they do so, it is likely that the analysts involved have been successful in addressing the concerns of the other participants in the policy process.

Measuring Benefits and Costs:
Market Statistics and Consumer Surplus

There are a great many issues involved in actually measuring benefits and costs. In this section, we focus not on the possible problems but on the potential for success. At first, the information demands may seem overwhelming: How could any analyst find out the gains and losses experienced by each and every individual affected by a change? The answer is that, at least in some situations, essentially all the relevant information is contained in a few places where it can, in principle, be reasonably estimated through careful empirical investigation. In particular, much of the information is contained in market demand and supply curves.

We do not attempt to review the statistical issues involved in making reliable estimates of these curves. We do, however, emphasize that in many circumstances this hard task is at least feasible when the much harder task of obtaining similar information for each individual market participant is not. Our examples abstract from the statistical estimation problems by assuming that we have exact information about the demand curves, so that we can focus on the way benefits and costs are measured from them. We illustrate the relevant measurements using a simple model of an excise tax.

The value of benefit-cost analysis will depend on the accuracy of models relied upon for measurements. As we have seen, models do not have to be perfect to provide valuable information. Furthermore, models can handle considerably more complexity than that illustrated by this first benefit-cost analysis. Thus a task that may seem hopelessly insurmountable at first is not hopeless at all. Nevertheless, to conduct a good benefit-cost analysis in many situations requires considerable analytic ingenuity. In the following sections we explore several of the challenges that arise on the benefit side and some analytic approaches to them.[11]

Let us begin by going over the relationship between individual and market demand curves. Recall that *the demand curve of an individual shows the quantity of a good that the individual would purchase at each possible price, holding the total budget and the prices of all other goods constant.*[12] We saw in Chapter 4 that this relation is a consequence of utility maximization, using diagrams similar to Figures 6-2a and b.

Figure 6-2a shows the utility-maximizing quantities of milk and "all other goods" that an individual will purchase each year for several different budget constraints. These constraints are chosen to hold the total budget level and the price of "all other goods" constant (so that the vertical intercept is constant); the changes in the budget constraints represent

---

[11] We make no attempt to discuss comprehensively the nature of problems that may arise in doing benefit-cost analysis. Nevertheless, in the course of demonstrating the uses of microeconomics for public policy throughout the text, most of the major benefit-cost problems are discussed. This chapter highlights discussion of benefits, and the following chapter expands this to focus on the benefits of reducing uncertainty. Chapter 9 highlights discussion of costs. Chapters 8 and 19 emphasizes the role of time in economics and the importance of discounting to make benefits and costs that occur at different times commensurate.

[12] This is the definition of the ordinary demand curve. In a later section, we also define the compensated demand curve. The latter is a demand curve that also holds utility constant.

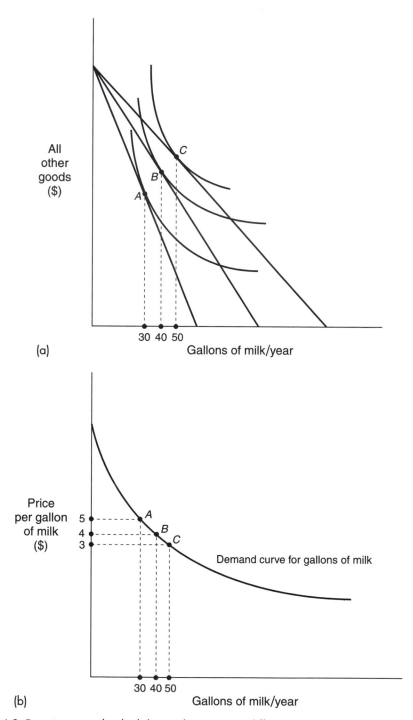

(a)

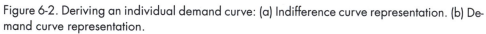

(b)

Figure 6-2. Deriving an individual demand curve: (a) Indifference curve representation. (b) Demand curve representation.

different assumptions about the price of milk (the cheaper the milk, the greater the horizontal intercept). Points *A, B,* and *C* show the utility-maximizing choice associated with each budget constraint. At lower milk prices, the individual would buy more milk.[13]

Figure 6-2b is constructed from the information in 6-2a. The vertical axis is the price of milk per gallon (the absolute value of the slope of the budget constraints in 6-2a). The horizontal axis remains the quantity of milk per year. Points *A, B,* and *C* in this figure are the prices (call them p_A, p_B, and p_C) and milk quantities associated with points *A, B,* and *C* in Figure 6-2a. If we imagine identifying the utility-maximizing quantity of milk at *every* possible price, then something like the curve shown passing through points *A, B,* and *C* in Figure 6-2b would result.[14] This curve is the individual's demand curve.

It is common to explain this curve as representing the quantity demanded at each possible price. However, it is equally true that *the height of the demand curve represents the dollar value of each incremental unit to the individual: the very most that he or she would be willing to pay to obtain it.* Consider point *B,* for example, where price (the height) is $4 per gallon and the individual buys 40 gallons. We know by the tangency condition of Figure 6-2a that the individual's MRS is precisely $4 at this point and that the MRS is by definition the largest amount of the other good (in this case, dollars) that the individual is willing to give up for the 40th gallon. Thus by construction, the height at each point on the demand curve shows the maximum willingness to pay in dollars for each successive unit of the good. In the normal case, the height diminishes as quantity increases: The value to the consumer of the fiftieth gallon is only $3.

In other words, **an individual's demand curve is also a marginal benefit curve, revealing the individual's maximum willingness to pay for each unit.** The demand interpretation focuses on quantity (the horizontal distance) as a function of price (the vertical distance). The marginal value interpretation focuses on marginal benefit (the vertical distance) as a function of quantity consumed (the horizontal distance). It is simply two different ways of looking at the same curve.

The marginal benefit interpretation, however, gives us an interesting way to measure the overall value of particular allocations to the consumer. Suppose we added the marginal benefit of each unit consumed. That is, when milk is $5 per gallon we add the marginal benefit from each of the thirty units consumed in order to get the total value to the consumer of these units. Geometrically, this is equivalent to calculating the area under the demand curve from the origin until $Q = 30$. We explain this below.

---

[13] The downward slope is expected for all goods except Giffen goods. Recall the discussion in Chapter 4 of the income and substitution effects that help to explain the shape of an individual's demand curve.

[14] Actually, the smoothness of an individual's demand curve depends on whether the particular good or service is of value only in discrete units (e.g., slacks, cameras) or a continuous dimension (e.g., gallons of gasoline, pounds of hamburger). A half of a camera is presumably of no value, while a half-pound of hamburger is of value. For discrete goods, the demand curve is a step function—looking like a series of steps descending from left to right—with the "rise" of the step generally declining with each successive unit of the good to indicate diminishing marginal value. If an individual purchases many units of a discrete good within a given time period, it is usually possible (and analytically convenient) to approximate the demand curve by a continuous function rather than the actual step function.

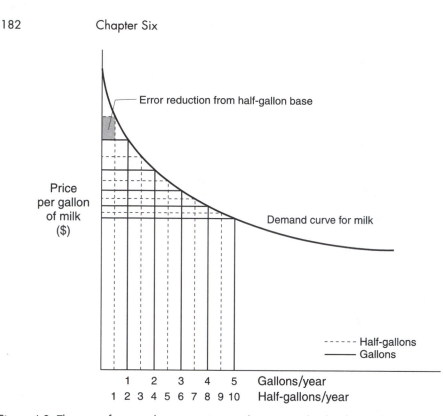

Figure 6-3. The sum of rectangles approximates the area under the demand curve or total consumer benefit.

In Figure 6-3, we show this idea by drawing in a series of rectangles with a common base. If the base is 1 gallon of milk, there would be thirty rectangles (only five are drawn) and we would sum their areas to get the total value to the consumer. However, our choice of gallons as a measure causes us to underestimate slightly. Within any single gallon, owing to diminishing marginal value, the value of the first drop to the consumer is higher than the second, and the second higher than the third, and so on until the end of the gallon is reached. But each of our rectangles has a height equal to the value of only the last drop in the gallon, thus underestimating slightly the value of the preceding drops in that gallon.

To reduce this error, we could simply use a smaller measure as the base: quarts rather than gallons would give 120 rectangles with smaller errors, and ounces rather than quarts would give 3840 very-small-base rectangles with further reduction in the degree of underestimation. Figure 6-3 illustrates this for the first gallon only, with the shaded area showing the reduced error by switching to a half-gallon base. As the number of rectangles (with correspondingly smaller bases) increases, the sum of their areas gets closer and closer to the exact area under the demand curve and the size of the error approaches zero. But then we may simplify: *total value to an individual, or equivalently the individual's maximum willingness to pay, equals the area under the demand curve for the units consumed.* This measure (as opposed to the sum of finite rectangles) will be the same regardless of the units chosen to measure consumption.

Figure 6-4. The consumer surplus is total consumer benefit minus consumer cost (triangle *AEB*).

In Figure 6-4, we draw a linear demand curve for the pedagogical purpose of making the calculation of the area easy and to illustrate one new concept. The area under the demand curve for the 30 gallons can be calculated as the simple sum of the rectangle *OABC* and the triangle *AEB*. The rectangle has area of $150 (= $5/gallon × 30 gallons), and the triangle $45 [= (½) × ($8–$5/gallon) × (30 gallons). Thus the total value to the consumer of the 30 gallons is $195.

This total value is not the *net* value or *net* benefit to the consumer, because it does not take account of what the consumer has to pay in order to obtain the goods. **The consumer surplus is defined as the total amount the consumer is willing to pay minus the consumer cost.** In this case, since the consumer pays $5 per gallon for the 30 gallons or $150 (the rectangle *OABC*), the consumer surplus is $45 (the triangle *AEB*). The surplus arises because the consumer is willing to pay *more* than $5 per gallon for the intramarginal units of milk, but obtains each for the $5 market price. Thus the area bounded by the horizontal price line, vertical price axis, and demand curve is usually the consumer surplus.[15]

Note also that 30 gallons is the precise quantity that *maximizes* the consumer's surplus when price is $5 per gallon. If the consumer chose only 29 gallons, where the height of the demand curve exceeds $5, surplus could be increased by the purchase of one more gallon. If the consumer chose 31 gallons, where the height of the demand curve is below $5, then the 31st gallon has reduced surplus (achieved marginal value lower than marginal cost),

---

[15] Examples in later sections and chapters will show exceptions, typically owing to nonuniform prices or non-price-rationing.

and the consumer could increase surplus by purchasing one unit less. Thus the surplus-maximizing choice is also the utility-maximizing choice. This suggests more generally that *maximizing net benefits is very much like the kind of maximization that economic agents try to achieve in a market setting.*

Recall that our primary motivation in this section is to understand how benefits and costs may be calculated or known in the aggregate. This requires us to move on from one individual's demand curve to the entire market demand curve. We focus on the benefit side here, and on knowledge about the market demand curve as a particular source of information. **A market demand curve, by definition, shows the sum of all individual quantities demanded for any given price.** Suppose we have a very simple two-person linear demand economy:

$$Q_1 = 80 - 10p$$

and

$$Q_2 = 160 - 20p$$

The market demand curve is then the sum of the individual demands:

$$Q_m = 240 - 30p$$

All three demand curves are shown in Figure 6-5a. This is obviously a special case used for illustrative purposes; the generality of it will be considered shortly.

If the market price is $p = 5$, then $Q_1 = 30$, $Q_2 = 60$, and $Q_m = 90$. The consumer surplus from this good for each person, the area enclosed by the individual demand curve, the price axis, and the market price line, is

$$CS_1 = \frac{1}{2}(8-5)(30) = \$45$$

$$CS_2 = \frac{1}{2}(8-5)(60) = \$90$$

Thus the actual total consumer surplus from this good (denoted CS) is \$135 (= 45 + 90). Now let us see whether the consumer surplus under the market demand curve (denoted CS_m) does in fact equal \$135:

$$CS_m = \frac{1}{2}(8-5)(90) = \$135$$

This illustrates the important result that the consumer surplus under the market demand curve, at least in some circumstances, equals the sum of the individual consumer surpluses.

Now suppose we consider this policy change: the imposition of a \$1 excise tax on each unit of Q purchased. Then the price that consumers face would equal \$6, and the quantity bought in the aggregate would equal 60.[16] This is illustrated in Figure 5-6b. How does this

---

[16] For simplicity we are assuming that the supply of the good is infinitely elastic. Explicit discussion of the relevance of supply conditions to the compensation principle is deferred until Chapter 9. Explicit discussion of tax incidence is in Chapter 12.

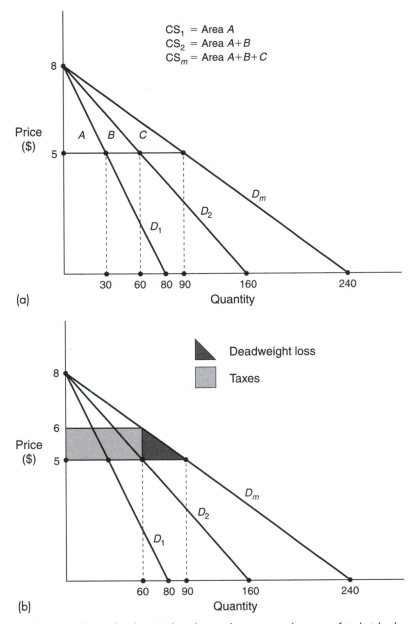

Figure 6-5. The benefits under the market demand curve are the sum of individual consumer benefits: (a) Individual and market consumer surpluses [CS_1, CS_2, CS_m]. (b) The deadweight loss from a $1 excise tax.

policy change fare by the compensation principle? To answer that question correctly, one must take account of all the changes that arise. That is, we must add up the change in each individual's consumer surplus across *all* markets. However, many of these changes will cancel each other out, and under certain conditions everything we need to know is contained in the information about this one market. In this market, the new consumer surplus under the market demand curve (CS'_m) is

$$CS'_m = \frac{1}{2}(8 - 6)(60) = \$60$$

Thus the aggregate loss in consumer surplus *in this market* is $75 (= 135 - 60)$. It is hardly surprising that these consumers are losers, but are there no gainers? There are two more effects to consider: What happens to the tax receipts, and what happens to the real resources that used to be used in this industry when $Q_m = 90$ but are not used here now that Q'_m is only 60?

We can see from Figure 6-5b that $60 in taxes are collected ($1 for each of the 60 units sold). Let us assume that the tax receipts are used entirely to provide cash to the needy and may be viewed as a **pure transfer: a redistribution of wealth from one set of people to another without any effect on the efficiency of real resource use.**

The idea is that this is just like taking dollar bills out of one person's pocket (the tax-payer's) and stuffing them into another's. By itself the pure transfer is assumed to have no significant effect on the efficiency of consumption or production; all real resources are still being used as effectively as before the transfer.[17] The $60 paid in taxes by the consumers in this market are given to some other people; the taxpayers would require $60 in compensation to be indifferent; and the recipients of the tax receipts would be indifferent if they received a compensating reduction of $60. Thus the sum of compensations is zero from this effect; $60 of the $75 loss in consumer surplus in this market is offset by the $60 gain to others from the tax receipts.

Now what about the remaining $15 loss? In Figure 6-5b, it is seen as the shaded triangle. This part of the loss in consumer surplus is referred to as **deadweight loss;** the idea is that it **is a loss for which there are no offsetting gains. The deadweight loss from a tax, sometimes referred to as its excess burden, can be defined as the difference between the tax revenues to the government and the loss the tax causes to others.** Under special assumptions, this is the end of the story. The resources that were used to produce units 61 to 90 have been released from this industry and are presumed to be in use elsewhere (e.g., other dairy products besides milk). The returns to the owners of the resources are assumed to be the same (their opportunity costs) in both cases, so no change arises in their budget constraints. Furthermore, the new products made with them generate no net change in aggregate consumer surplus; the assumption is that the released resources are spread evenly among the

---

[17] In actuality, programs that provide resources to the needy may improve their productivity through better health or education and to this extent would not be pure transfers. More generally a tax instituted to enable a specific reallocation of real resources (e.g., to build a public highway that would not otherwise exist) would not be a pure transfer.

many other production activities. Then the change in quantity of each good is small and at the margin of its market, where demand equals price. Thus the marginal change in the area between the demand curve and the price is negligible in each of these other industries.

Thus, under these special assumptions, we are able to calculate that the change in aggregate consumer surplus caused by the $1 excise tax is −$15. The remarkable aspect of this result is the parsimony of the calculation. The only pieces of information used are the price, tax, and market demand equation. Obviously, one is not required to make the assumptions that lead to this maximum economy in modeling. Indeed, it is completely irresponsible to do so if the analyst thinks an alternative model might be better. We will see in later chapters, for example, that the more common practice is to substitute the estimated supply curve for the assumption here that supply is at constant cost; this is easily incorporated into the compensation test through the concept of the producers' surplus.

However, not all of the assumptions made above are easily replaceable, and their accuracy depends on the context studied. As always, the true art and skill of microeconomic policy analysis is in constructing a model that captures the particulars of the phenomenon being studied accurately enough to improve decision-making. One should by no means underestimate the difficulty of carrying out an analysis that pins the number down within a range relevant to decision-making. The point of this parsimonious example is simply to dramatize that what might at first seem to be a totally hopeless quest (to discover all the necessary individual compensations) may be a useful endeavor after all.

To try to reinforce the preceding observations, let us point out an insight about taxation that follows directly from the illustration. One factor that determines the amount of deadweight loss is the elasticity of the demand curve: the more elastic it is, the greater the deadweight loss. Therefore, based on efficiency grounds, it may be preferable to tax goods that are more inelastic. On the other hand, goods that are characterized by inelastic demands are necessities. Since lower-income families spend greater portions of their budgets on necessities, such a tax is likely to be regressive in its incidence. Thus there can be a real tension between efficiency and equity in deciding how to raise taxes.

Now, putting aside other aspects of compensation testing, let us continue to focus on the information that can be extracted from the market demand curve. In the special case used earlier, we saw that the change in the sum of the individual consumer surpluses caused by an excise tax equals the change under the market demand curve. The more general principle is that this holds for a change in price levels applied uniformly to all. The easiest way to see this is to use the linear approximation to the change in consumer surplus experienced by one individual ΔCS_i in response to a price increase ΔP:

$$\Delta CS_i = \Delta P Q_i^1 + \frac{1}{2}\Delta P(Q_i^0 - Q_i^1)$$

where Q_i^0 is the initial quantity purchased and Q_i^1 is the quantity purchased after the price increase. The first term is the change in the consumer cost of the goods actually purchased after the price increase, and the second is the deadweight loss. We illustrate this in Figure 6-6 using the first consumer from our earlier example:

$$\$25 = (\$6 - \$5)(20) + (\tfrac{1}{2})(\$6 - \$5)(30 - 20)$$

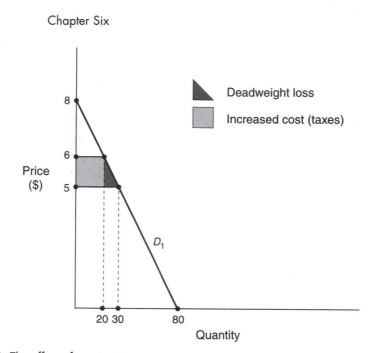

Figure 6-6. The effect of a price increase on consumer 1.

That is, the first consumer pays $20 in taxes (the change in consumer cost for the purchased goods), and has a $5 deadweight loss (the loss in consumer surplus from units 21–30, no longer purchased owing to the higher price).

If, in the more general case, we add up these amounts for all r consumers in the market,

$$\Delta CS = \sum_{i=1}^{r} [\Delta P Q_i^1 + \frac{1}{2}\Delta P(Q_i^0 - Q_i^1)]$$

$$= \Delta P \sum_{i+1}^{r} Q_1^1 + \frac{1}{2}\Delta P \sum_{i=1}^{r}(Q_i^0 - Q_i^1)$$

$$= \Delta P Q_m^1 + \frac{1}{2}\Delta P(Q_m^0 - Q_m^1)$$

These two terms are the areas under the *market* demand curve that are precisely analogous to the two relevant areas under each *individual's* demand curve. (In the earlier example they correspond to the $60 raised in taxes and the $15 deadweight loss.) Thus, for a uniform price change applied to all, the relevant areas under the market demand curve tell us exactly what we want to know about the total change in consumer surplus.

If a policy change can be characterized by the *uniform price change* effect, as is the case in the imposition of an excise tax, the market demand curve can be used to identify the net direct change in consumer surplus. But many policy changes are not that simple. If a policy change causes a direct shift in individual demands (as opposed to movement along a demand curve) along with a price change, then the change in the area under the market demand curves does not reflect the information we seek. If there is inefficiency in exchange either before or after the change, the same lack of correspondence can arise.

For example, when the gasoline shortages of the 1970s occurred, it was common in many areas around the country to introduce various ration plans such as 10-gallon limits per fill-up, no Sunday sales, and odd-even rationing so that a motorist could make purchases only every other day.[18] At the same time, the price of gasoline was rising. The combination of effects served the purpose: short-run demand was reduced. From empirical observation of aggregate behavior during those periods, careful statistical work can result in reasonable estimates of the ordinary demand curve (over the observed range) and even isolate the regulatory and price effects. But it is not possible, without disaggregated data, to make an unbiased estimate of the loss in consumer surplus.[19]

To see why this is so, let us use another simple two-person linear demand system, this one for the gasoline market:

$$Q_1 = 10 - 2p$$
$$Q_2 = 20 - 4p$$

and a market demand curve equal to the sum of the individual demands:

$$Q_m = 30 - 6p$$

We assume that the initial price per gallon is $2, and that government, in response to a shortage, mandates a price of $3 per gallon in the form of a $1 tax and $2 for the gas seller.[20]

Additionally, we add the regulatory constraint that no person can buy more than 4 gallons per time period. Because we know the individual demand equations, we know what quantity each person wishes to buy at the higher price:

$$Q_1 = 10 - 2(3) = 4$$
$$Q_2 = 20 - 4(3) = 8$$

But, because of the 4-gallon limit, person 2 can only buy 4 gallons. So the total quantity purchased in the market is 8 ($= 4 + 4$). Note that this total quantity is not a point on the "true" market demand curve (at $p = 3$, desired $Q_m = 12$) because of the regulatory constraint.

Figure 6-7 shows the demand curves that are discoverable from market statistics. The two market observations we have are the initial allocation ($p = 2$, $Q_m = 18$) and the final allocation ($p = 3$, $Q_m = 8$). One mistake to avoid is thinking that the change in quantity is due only to the change in price or, equivalently, that the ordinary demand curve passes through those points. If one has made that mistake and has estimated the change in consumer

[18] Rationing plans are the subject of Chapter 14.

[19] In this example the shortage will cause a loss in consumer surplus. The policy problem is to respond to the short-run shortage in a way that is fair and keeps losses at a minimum. The intention here is to illustrate only one aspect of evaluating a particular alternative.

[20] We are deliberately glossing over the supply conditions; as noted before, their relevance and importance will be studied in later chapters.

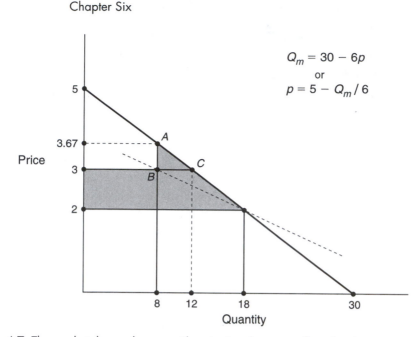

$$Q_m = 30 - 6p$$
or
$$p = 5 - Q_m/6$$

Figure 6-7. The market demand curve with rationing does not reflect the change in consumer surplus.

surplus by using the linear approximation to the erroneous demand curve (the dashed line), then

$$\Delta CS_M^L = 1(8) + \frac{1}{2}(1)(10)$$

$$= 13$$

A good analyst will realize that the dashed-line demand curve violates the usual *ceteris paribus* assumptions: Factors other than price are not being held constant; regulatory constraints have changed as well. After a bit of digging, it is discovered that the ordinary demand curve, which is shown on Figure 6-7 as the solid line, has been estimated previously and correctly.[21]

The next analytic pitfall is to think that the change in consumer surplus can be estimated on the basis of this perfectly accurate market picture. That is, it appears plausible to assume that the loss in consumer surplus is the shaded area in Figure 6-7. The area seems to consist of the two usual components: the extra cost of purchased units and the forgone surplus on the unpurchased ones. It differs from our original analysis of the excise tax by triangle

---

[21] It is common in policy analysis to review the existing literature in order to make use of prior empirical research of this type. However, many factors must be considered in evaluating the appropriateness and use of prior studies for a different context, and one must be careful. For example, the length of time used for a demand observation (e.g., a month, a year) should be commensurate, and the price sensitivity in one geographical area need not be comparable to that in another.

ABC. The extra triangle arises because of the regulatory constraint; without the constraint, four more units would be bought at a cost of $3 each (including the tax). To find the height at point *A,* we use the true market demand curve to find the price at which eight units would be bought:

$$8 = 30 - 6p$$

$$p = 3.667$$

Thus triangle *ABC* has the area

$$ABC = \tfrac{1}{2}(3.667 - 3.00)(12 - 8)$$

$$= 1.33$$

The rest of the loss under the market curve is $15.[22] Adding the two, we erroneously conclude that the loss in consumer surplus is $16.33.

The fallacy in the above analysis is that it assumes efficiency in exchange, but the regulatory constraint causes inefficiency in exchange. That is, the four-unit reduction owing to the regulatory constraint is *not* accomplished by taking the four units valued the least by consumers. At a price to consumers of $3.667 with no other constraints, $Q_1 = 2.67$ and $Q_2 = 5.33$ (and $Q_m = 8$). Since at a price of $3, $Q_1 = 4$ and $Q_2 = 8$, the efficient reduction is to take 1.33 units from person 1 and 2.67 units from person 2. The extra loss in consumer surplus caused by *this* change is the one that triangle *ABC* measures.

But the actual change results in $Q_1 = 4$ and $Q_2 = 4$, and it has a bigger loss associated with it. None of this information could be known on the basis of market statistics only. To calculate the actual losses, one needs information about the individual consumers. The actual individual losses are shown as the shaded areas in Figure 6-8a and b. Person 1, whose behavior is unaffected by the regulatory constraint, has a loss similar to the simple excise tax example:

$$\Delta CS_1 = 1(4) + \tfrac{1}{2}(1)(2) = 5$$

Person 2 loses more than in a simple excise tax case because the regulatory constraint is binding here; the extra loss is triangle *EFG.* The area of *EFG* is found analogously to the area of *ABC* in the above example; the height at point *E* must be 4, and thus the area of *EFG* is 2.

Person 2's loss in consumer surplus owing to the tax alone is 10 [= $(3 - 2)(8) + \tfrac{1}{2}(3 - 2)(12 - 8)$]. Therefore, $\Delta CS_2 = 12$ and the actual loss in aggregate consumer surplus is $17 with $8 as tax receipts and $9 as deadweight loss. In this case one knows that the area under the market curve must underestimate the true loss. Do not be misled by the small size of the underestimate in this example; in actual situations the error could be quite substantial.

---

[22] $15 = (3 - 2)(12) + \tfrac{1}{2}(3 - 2)(18 - 12)$.

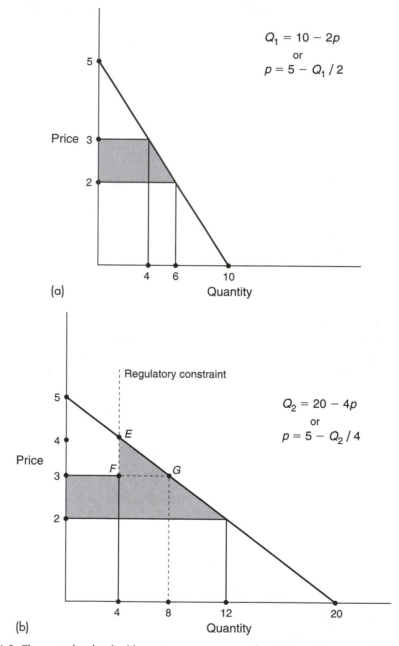

Figure 6-8. The actual individual losses in consumer surplus: (a) Loss for person 1. (b) Loss for person 2.

An Illustrative Application:
Model Specification for Consumer Protection Legislation[S]

One researcher attempted to estimate the value of consumer protection legislation for prescription drugs by the general methods we have been discussing. A brief review of the methodology is quite instructive.[23] In 1962 the Kefauver-Harris amendments to the Food, Drug, and Cosmetics Act added (among other provisions) a proof-of-efficacy requirement to the existing legislation. The primary objective of the amendments was to reduce the harm and waste that consumers experienced because of poor knowledge about the actual effects of drugs. In congressional testimony, numerous examples of manufacturers' claims that could not be substantiated were offered. It was hoped that the new legislation would not only improve the use of drugs on the market but would deter the entry of new drugs that did not offer any real improvements over existing ones.

Figure 6-9a illustrates, at a greatly simplified level, the conceptual framework used in the study. There are two solid-line demand curves on the diagram: the *uninformed demand* D^U and the *informed demand* D^I. Think of these demand curves as representing a physician's demands for a new drug for a particular patient. When uninformed, the physician-patient believes the drug will work miracles (perhaps like laetrile). Gradually the physician-patient learns (maybe by trial and error, or from other physicians, or published reports) that the drug does not work as claimed. Thus, over time, as the physician-patient becomes informed, the demand curve shifts inward.[24] For simplicity, we assume there are only two time periods: the uninformed period and the informed period.

Suppose we ask how much this consumer would value being perfectly informed from the start. In Figure 6-9a, the shaded area represents the value of the information. At price *OC,* the consumer buys *OB* units when uninformed. When informed, the consumer reduces the purchase by *AB* units to the quantity *OA.* The true benefits are always the area under the informed demand curve D^I, although the consumer is not aware of this when uninformed. (That is, when uninformed, the consumer misperceives the benefits.) Perfect information from the start would prevent the purchase of *AB* units; these units have costs (*AEFB*) greater than benefits (*AEGB*) by the amount *EFG.* Thus, the maximum amount of money this consumer would pay to be informed from the start is *EFG.* To find out what the aggregate value of perfect information is, we simply have to add up all these individual triangles.

---

[23] For a more detailed review of the methodology, the reader should refer to the debate in the professional literature. See S. Peltzman, "An Evaluation of Consumer Protection Legislation: The 1962 Drug Amendments," *Journal of Political Economy, 81,* No. 5, September/October 1973, pp. 1049–1091; T. McGuire, R. Nelson, and T. Spavins, "A Comment," and S. Peltzman, "A Reply," *Journal of Political Economy, 83,* No. 3, June 1975, pp. 655–667. Another important aspect to this debate, not discussed here, is whether or not the legislation causes delay in the approval of new medicinal drugs. The evidence suggests that it does, although the earlier studies overestimated the delay. See D. Dranove and D. Meltzer, "Do Important Drugs Reach the Market Sooner?," *RAND Journal of Economics, 25,* No. 3, Autumn 1994, pp. 402–423.

[24] There may be some situations in which the drug seems useful, so the demand curve does not necessarily disappear altogether.

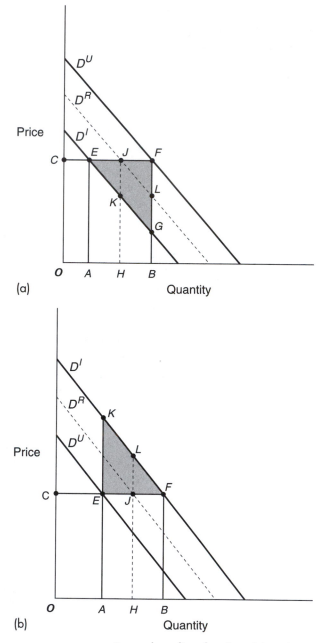

(a)

(b)

Figure 6-9. Some consumers overestimate benefits of a drug (a) and some underestimate them (b).

Of course, the new drug regulation did not purport to make information perfect. The idea was that it would cause the initial period to be one of *improved* information, so the first-period demand curve would be shown as the dashed line D^R.[25] As drawn, the consumer would purchase OH in the initial period, overbuying by AH, and then buy OA when fully informed. Thus the effect of the regulation is to avoid the mistake of buying HB in the initial period, which has costs $HJFB$ greater than benefits $HKGB$ by the amount $KJFG$. Thus $KJFG$ is the value to the consumer of the new drug regulations.

The study goes on to estimate the market demand curves corresponding to D^U, D^R, and D^I and report the area $KJFG$ under the *market* curves as the aggregate value to consumers. This last step is flawed and misestimates the information value by an unknown but perhaps extremely high factor. To see that, let us turn to Figure 6-9b. The demand curves in this diagram are those of a second physician-patient. They have been chosen to be identical to those in Figure 6-9a with one crucial twist: The uninformed and informed demand curves are switched around. Upon a moment's reflection, the existence of this behavior is just as plausible as that previously described. In this case the physician-patient is simply a cynic and skeptic. Having been misled by false claims in the past, the physician-patient initially tries new drugs only with great reluctance. However, the drug works better than the skeptic expected and over time the demand shifts outward.

In Figure 6-9b, the consumer initially buys OA when uninformed and then OB when perfectly informed. The true benefits are always the area under the informed demand curve for the quantity actually consumed. If perfectly informed from the start, this consumer would not make the mistake of underbuying AB units. These units have benefits of $AKFB$ but cost only $AEFB$, so the net benefit from consuming them is EKF, the shaded area on the diagram. The maximum amount this consumer would pay to be perfectly informed from the start is EKF. As before, the drug legislation is not expected to achieve perfection. With improved information represented by the dashed demand curve D^R, the consumer initially buys OH and thus avoids underbuying quantity AH. The value of the drug legislation is $EKLJ$.

If these are the only two consumers in the market, the aggregate value of the regulation is the *sum* of $KJFG$ in Figure 6-9a plus $EKLJ$ in Figure 6-9b. But now let us consider how the market demand curve hides those benefits. The clearest example can be seen if we assume that OH, the initial quantity bought by each consumer after the regulation is introduced, halves the errors (i.e., $AH = HB$ in both diagrams). In that case, the initial market quantity bought is

$$Q_m^U = OB + OA$$

After the regulation is passed, the initial market quantity bought is

$$Q_m^R = OH + OH$$

<hr>

[25] It could be argued, though probably not very plausibly, that the regulation actually worsens information. The idea would be that drug companies tell consumers what they really want to know and regulation prevents them from acting on the information. This argument does not affect the point of the discussion here: that information about shifts in the market demand curve does not include the information necessary to make a reasonable compensation test.

Since $AH = HB$, we can add and subtract them on the right-hand side:

$$Q_m^R = OH + HB + OH - AH$$

$$= OB + OA$$

That is, the initial market demand curve does not shift at all after the regulation is introduced! The reduction in overbuying by the first consumer exactly offsets the reduction in under-buying by the second. The researcher finds that the drug regulation has had no impact on consumer purchasing and measures the information value as *zero*, whereas it is obviously much greater. If we had 100 million consumers divided into two camps like those drawn of 50 million skeptics and 50 million optimists, the market demand curve would still be un-changed by the regulation. That is why the flaw is so serious; *savings in consumer surplus that should be adding up are being subtracted from one another.*

The seriousness of this flaw is not an artifact of the specific example chosen. The initial market demand curve will shift to the left if, preregulation, there are more optimistic pur-chases, to the right if there are more skeptical nonpurchases, and not at all should they happen to offset one another exactly. The point is that in all of these cases the shift in the market curve owing to the regulation shows what is left after one subtracts one group of benefits from another. For that reason the market demand curves simply do not contain the information necessary to make this compensation test.

The alert reader may have noticed a second flaw: The use of the market curves here is subject to the same flaw discussed in the gasoline rationing case. To illustrate it, let us put aside the last flaw by assuming that no consumers underbuy. A remaining problem is that not all consumers make the same size mistake. Consider a very simple example with only two consumers who make mistakes initially but do not make any after the regulation is introduced. Now contrast these two situations: (1) Consumers 1 and 2 initially overbuy by AH in Figure 6-9a. (2) Consumer 1 initially overbuys by AB, and consumer 2 makes no mis-takes at all. In both situations the amount of initial market overbuying is the same and the regulation prevents the errors, so the shift in the market curve owing to the regulation is the same.

But the benefits of preventing those errors are not the same. The regulation is more valu-able if it prevents the errors in the second situation. It is least valuable in the first situa-tion; use of the market curves is equivalent to assuming that the starting point is the first situation. In Figure 6-9a think of situation 1 as each consumer overbuying AH and losing area EJK; preventing both these errors is worth twice area EJK. Situation 2 can be thought of as one consumer overbuying AB (twice AH). *But the second unit overbought, HB, hurts more than the first.* Thus the total loss in situation 2 is greater than twice the area EJK.[26]

Market demand curves are so constructed that, for any price, the most highly valued units will be purchased. If a good is priced too low, there will be overbuying but only of the next

---

[26] As drawn, with all demand curves the same slope, it is exactly four times the area EJK; the triangle EFG has base and height each twice that of EJK. The actual error could be greater or smaller, depending on the shapes of the demand curves.

most highly valued units. This tends to minimize the aggregate error. But overbuying owing to consumer ignorance hardly guarantees that the least serious mistakes will be the ones made. Thus this second flaw also causes misestimation, to an unknown degree, of the consumer benefits from the regulation.

The main point of this extended illustration is, as always, to emphasize the importance of model specification. Careful thought about this approach to evaluating the drug legislation suggests that the available market statistics cannot be used to bound the uncertainty about the true benefits within any reasonable range. In other uses, as for taxation or estimating the harm from monopoly, the market demand curves may contain precisely the information sought. An important part of analytic skill is learning to understand when the appropriate linkages are present.

Before concluding this section, it may be useful to speculate about the interpretation of an accurate compensation test for drug regulation. That is, suppose we had no regulation and knew (which we do not) that passing the drug regulation would comfortably pass the compensation test. What significance, if any, might this knowledge have to an analyst? The parties primarily affected by the legislation are the demanders and suppliers of drugs. The benefits to consumers are likely to be spread over a fairly large population: all the people who have occasion to use prescription drugs. This is not the kind of policy change in which one narrow segment of the population is gaining at the expense of another narrow segment. The losers, if there are any, might also be widely scattered consumers: the lovers of laetrile (and other drugs whose efficacy cannot be proved). On the assumption that the gains comfortably outweigh the losses, and with no special reason to favor laetrile lovers over other consumers, one might rely heavily on the test as a reason for recommending that the regulation be passed.

An additional possibility is that the incomes of those on the supply side will be changed. Suppose the makers of laetrile will be forced to close up shop. Usually, such supply activities are geographically scattered and each is a small part of a local economy. If that is the case, the labor and capital resources may be quickly reemployed in other parts of the company or in other industries and suffer only small temporary losses (mitigated perhaps by unemployment insurance). Alternatively, all laetrile manufacturers might be geographically concentrated in one town whose entire economy is dependent upon laetrile manufacture. In that case it is more likely that some form of secondary legislation, for example, relocation assistance, would be passed to compensate the losers.

These speculative comments are intended only to suggest that an accurate compensation test could, in this case, have great significance for an analyst. Of course, actual analytic significance would require more detailed information and reasoning than can be provided here. Furthermore, most analysts would not wish to be restricted to a set of only two alternatives.

Problems with Measuring Individual Benefits

In the last section, we focused on when market demand curves contain information relevant to measuring aggregate benefits. In this section, we return for a closer examination of the underpinning: the measure of individual benefit. The one we have been using, the area under the ordinary demand curve, is actually an approximate measure. Now we will show two new measures, each exact but different from one another, because each uses a different initial reference point. We explain why the measure we have been using is an approximation of them. In most cases, the approximation is a good one because the two exact measures are themselves close and the approximation will be between them. However, we go on to discuss some circumstances in which a good approximation is difficult, if not impossible. The difficulties may arise in analyses of many policy areas, particularly in the environmental and health policy arenas.

Three Measures of Individual Welfare Change

We know that the area under an individual's ordinary demand curve reveals a good deal of information about the value of the goods and services consumed. However, along the ordinary demand curve, the utility level of an individual changes from point to point. For example, if the price of a good rises, the typical individual will buy less of it and end up with a lower utility level than initially. The compensation principle of benefit-cost analysis, however, requires that we find the compensation that makes the individual *indifferent* to the change (the price rise in this example). To do this, we introduce the concept of the individual's **compensated demand curve: a special demand curve that shows the quantity the individual would purchase at any price if the budget level were continually adjusted to hold utility constant at a predetermined level.**

Let us illustrate this graphically. In Figure 6-10a we have drawn one individual's ordinary demand curve for electricity, shown as AF. At the initial price p_0, the consumer buys q_0 and has utility level u_0. After the rate increase, the price is p_1 and the consumer buys q_1 and has a lower utility level u_1. Figure 6-10b is an indifference curve representation of the same consumer choices.

In Figure 6-10b let us identify **the compensating variation: the size of the budget change under the new conditions (price $= p_1$) that would restore the individual to the initial utility level (u_0).** Given the state of the world in which the consumer is at B (i.e., after the price change), how much extra income is needed to bring the consumer back to u_0? That is, keeping prices constant at the slope of DB, let us imagine adding income to move the budget constraint out until it becomes just tangent to u_0, which we have shown as the dashed line EC tangent to u_0 at C. The amount of income required is shown on the vertical axis as DE: this is the compensating variation. Note that it is the amount of income associated with the income effect $q_1 - q_1^c$ of the price increase.

To show the compensating variation in Figure 6-10a, we must first construct a compensated demand curve, which is simply an ordinary demand curve with the income effect removed. For example, let us construct the compensated demand curve associated with the utility level u_0 at point A. In Figure 6-10b, we have already located one other price-quantity combination that gives utility level u_0. It is at point C, where price is p_1 and quantity is q_1^c. We also show this as point C in Figure 6-10a.

In fact, all the price-quantity combinations for this compensated demand curve can be "read" from Figure 6-10b: For each point on the u_0 indifference curve, the quantity and

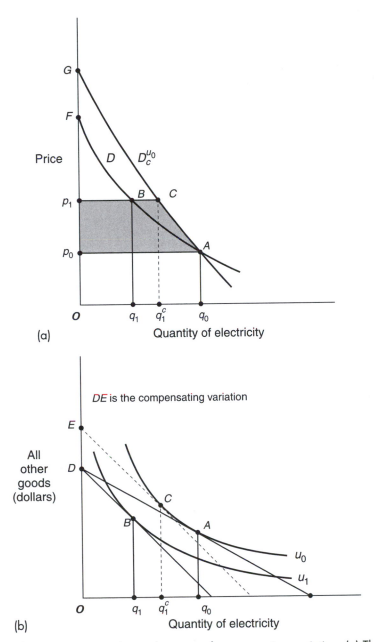

(a)

(b)

Figure 6-10. The compensating demand curve and compensating variation: (a) The compensated demand curve and compensating variation (shaded) for a price change from p_0 to p_1. (b) The indifference curve representation of the same consumer choices.

associated price of electricity (known from the slope of the curve) are points on the compensated demand curve. We have shown this as $D_c^{u_0}$ in Figure 6-10a. For a normal good (which we have illustrated), the compensated demand curve is steeper than the ordinary demand curve. If the price increases above p_0 the uncompensated consumer will, of course, end up with less utility. Compensation requires that the consumer be given additional income which, for a normal good, results in greater consumption than without the compensation. For prices below p_0 we would have to take away income to keep the consumer at u_0 utility level, and therefore the consumer would buy less than without the (negative) compensation.

Now consider in Figure 6-10a the consumer surplus associated with the compensated demand curve. This consumer surplus can be interpreted as a compensating variation. For example, suppose we forbid the consumer to buy any electricity when its price is p_1. The consumer then does not spend $p_1 q_1^c$ but loses the consumer surplus $p_1 GC$. The amount of money that we would have to give this consumer to compensate for the rule change (i.e., to maintain utility at the u_0 level in the new state of the world) is $p_1 GC$; thus this amount is the compensating variation.

Finally, what is the compensating variation for the price change from p_0 to p_1? Initially, the consumer surplus under the compensated demand curve is $p_0 GA$. When restored to the initial utility level after the price increase, the consumer surplus is only $p_1 GC$. Therefore, the amount of compensation necessary to restore the consumer to the initial utility level must be the *loss* in consumer surplus, the shaded area $p_0 p_1 CA$. This compensation plus the new consumer surplus equals the initial consumer surplus. Therefore, *the compensating variation for a price change is the area between the initial and new price lines bounded by the compensated demand curve for the initial utility level and the price axis.*

There is one last wrinkle that we must iron out. The compensating variation is measured under the assumption that the new higher price is in effect. However, we could ask the compensation question in a slightly different way. What is the most the individual would pay to prevent the price increase? This equals the size of the budget change at the original price that gives the individual the same utility as after the price increase. More generally, **we define the equivalent variation as the size of the budget change under the initial conditions (price $= p_0$) that would result in the same utility level as after the actual change (u_1).**

Figures 6-11a and b illustrate the equivalent variation, using the same ordinary demand curve and indifference curves as previously, with the individual initially at point A and then choosing point B in response to the price increase. In Figure 6-11b the equivalent variation is shown as the distance DK. It is the amount of income that can be taken away if the price is kept at its initial level (and thus the change is prevented) leaving the individual no worse off than if the change were made. We find it by moving the budget constraint parallel to DA and down until it is just tangent to u_1 shown at point J.

Note that DK is the income associated with the income effect $q_1^E - q_0$ of the price increase when the substitution effect is measured along the new rather than the original indifference curve. Recall that the compensating variation is the income associated with the income effect measured in the usual way. This explains why we stated earlier that the empirical difference between the compensating and equivalent variations is due to the difference in the way income effects are measured.

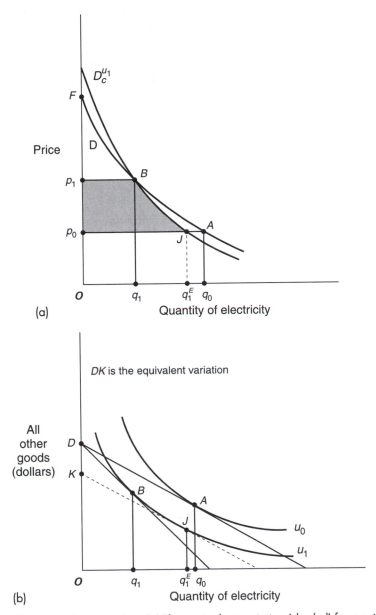

Figure 6-11. The equivalent variation: (a) The equivalent variation (shaded) for a price change from p_0 to p_1. (b) The indifference curve representation of the same consumer choices.

In Figure 6-11a we construct a compensated demand curve as before except that this time the curve is associated with utility level u_1.[27] It goes through point B on the ordinary demand curve, and price p_0 is associated with quantity q_1^E (from point J in Figure 6-11b). It is steeper than the ordinary demand curve by the same reasoning as before. Its height at any point is the amount of income that, if given up for an additional unit of electricity, just allows the consumer to maintain u_1.

The equivalent variation is the reduction in the initial budget level that reduces the consumer's utility from u_0 to u_1 when the price is at its original level. But note that the price change does not change the consumer's budget level. The consumer's budget when at point B is the same as when at point A. Thus, we can just as well ask what budget change from point B is necessary to leave the consumer with u_1 utility if the price is reduced to p_0. But as we have already seen, this is the change in consumer surplus under the compensated demand curve (area $p_0 p_1 BJ$). Thus, *the equivalent variation for a price change is the area between the initial and new price lines bounded by the compensated demand curve for the final utility level and the price axis.*

In Figure 6-12 we have drawn the ordinary demand curve and both of the compensated demand curves. It is clear from the diagram that, for a price increase, the equivalent variation is smaller than the compensating variation in absolute size. That is true for normal goods; for inferior goods the size relation is reversed.

Note that we have not given any reasons for preferring either the compensating variation or the equivalent variation. Both are exact measures of the welfare change; they just differ in whether the initial or final state of the world is used as the reference point. Sometimes it is argued that the compensating variation should be preferred because it is more plausible to assume that individuals have "rights" to the initial state of the world as a reference point rather than their positions after some proposed change. However, this clearly favors or accepts the status quo distribution, and one need not accept such reasoning. To actually calculate either of them requires knowledge of the (relevant) compensated demand curve. Since they are not observable in the actual uncompensated world, it can be difficult (but not impossible) to estimate them.

Fortunately, there is a third monetary measure that has two great virtues: It can be calculated directly from the ordinary demand curve, and it always has a value between the compensating and equivalent variations. It is simply the change in the consumer surplus under the ordinary demand curve (for short, the ordinary consumer surplus). In Figure 6-12 the ordinary consumer surplus at price p_0 is the area of triangle $p_0 FA$, and at price p_1 it is the area of triangle $p_1 FB$. The loss in ordinary consumer surplus caused by the price increase is the difference in the areas, or $p_0 p_1 BA$. It is more than the equivalent variation and less than the compensating variation.[28]

---

[27] Note that a whole family of compensated demand curves is associated with each ordinary demand curve (one for each utility level attainable).

[28] Note that if we now consider a price decrease from p_1 to p_0, the compensating variation for the price increase becomes the equivalent variation for the price decrease, and similarly the equivalent variation for the increase becomes the compensating variation for the decrease. The change in consumer surplus is the same, and it remains the middle-size measure.

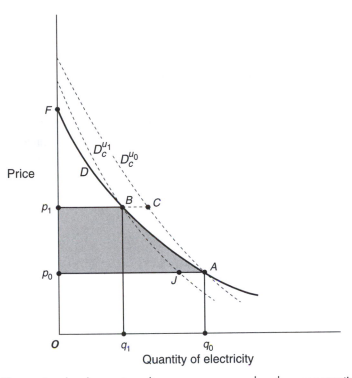

Figure 6-12. Comparing the change in ordinary consumer surplus, the compensating variation, and the equivalent variation.

In practice, the change in ordinary consumer surplus is probably used more frequently than either of the other two measures. Exactly how close together the different measures are depends upon the nature of the change. In an interesting article, Willig demonstrates that the measures are quite close except when the change involves goods that make up a large proportion of the consumer's budget or for which the income elasticity is unusually large.[29] This is because it is the income effects that cause the differences in the measures; if the income effects were zero for a particular good, all the measures would be identical.

To sum up this section briefly, we have presented three measures that represent monetary equivalents of the effect of a policy change on one individual's welfare: the compensating variation, equivalent variation, and change in ordinary consumer surplus. Although they differ slightly from one another, each is an attempt to reveal the change in general purchasing power that would make the individual indifferent to the main change. In the technical appendix, some illustrative calculations are presented after clarifying (by introducing the theory of duality) some linkages between observable phenomena such as demand and the theory of utility-maximizing choice. However, we now turn to the final

---

[29] R. D. Willig, "Consumer's Surplus without Apology," *American Economic Review, 66,* No. 4, September 1976, pp. 589–597.

section of this chapter to explore some actual situations in which the different measures give strikingly different results.

Empirical Evidence: Large Differences among the Measures

The above exposition focused on an economic change that is a relatively minor part of any one individual's well-being (the change in price of a common consumption good). Even so, it illustrated that there are two exact but different measures of the compensation necessary to hold the individual's utility constant and that the difference is caused by whether the prechange or postchange position is used as a reference point. However, one can imagine changes that might have a much more dramatic effect on an individual's well-being. In such cases, there is no reason to think that the alternative measures would necessarily yield similar monetary results.

Consider, for example, an individual whose life is threatened by disease and that person's right to a particular life-saving medical treatment. With no right to the treatment, the individual must pay to obtain it. The maximum willingness to pay is limited by his or her wealth, and for a poor individual, this may be an unfortunately small amount. However, suppose the individual in this example had a right to the treatment and could only be denied it if he or she sold the right to another. In this case, the minimum amount the individual is willing to accept to forgo the right might be infinite (i.e., no amount of money, no matter how large, will cause the individual to forgo the treatment).

The two differing amounts are a result of changing the reference point from which we are measuring. In the first case the poor individual does not own the right to treatment, and in the second case the individual has identical resources except that a (valuable) right to treatment has been added. The individual would have one (low) utility level without the treatment and another (high) utility level with the treatment. These two utility levels are the same no matter which reference point we use. But our measure of the amount of money necessary to compensate the individual for moving from one level to the other depends crucially on which position we use as the starting point.[30]

In cases with large differences between the measures, one can try to decide the appropriate one to use by a careful reading of the law (who does, in fact, have the right?). However, there are a number of cases in which ownership of the right may not be clear and there is no simple resolution of the matter. Some property, for example, is defined as common property and is not owned by anyone. Who, for example, owns the world's air, oceans, wild animals, or outer space? In these cases, there are often conflicts among humans about the uses of these natural resources. Should scarce wetlands be developed to provide more residential housing or should it be preserved as a wildlife habitat? Should new factories be

---

[30] The difference in these two amounts is simply the difference between the compensating and equivalent variations explained in the prior section. Without the right, the willingness to pay (for the right) is the compensating variation. The willingness to accept (the loss of the right) is the equivalent variation. If the right to treatment is assigned to the individual, the same measures switch roles: the willingness to pay becomes the equivalent variation, and the willingness to accept becomes the compensating variation.

allowed to add to air pollution in an area, in order to provide jobs and more consumer goods, or is it more important to improve air quality? If one consideration in resolving these issues is the magnitude of benefits and costs, and there are large differences in the benefit measures, then resolution is made more difficult.

There is an interesting and important psychological aspect to "problem" cases such as these. To some extent, it can be difficult to tell whether or not large observed differences between the two measures are real. In many cases, a substantial part of the difference may be due to difficulties that individuals have in truly understanding the implications of their responses. These difficulties are less likely to arise in choices that individuals make frequently where the consequences are clear, as with many ordinary goods and services that are purchased frequently in the marketplace. However, there are goods—such as the air quality in the above example—that individuals value but do not normally purchase directly. Analysts are often asked what, if anything, can be said about the value of these goods to the affected populations.

There are many clever ways that analysts use to discover how people value these non-market goods. For example, suppose one is interested in how residents value the quality of air surrounding their homes. Analysts have estimated this by examining the selling prices of homes that are comparable except for the fact that they differ in the air quality around them.[31] Other things being equal, we expect people to pay more for a home with "good" rather than "bad" surrounding air quality. Thus differences in home values can indirectly reveal the value of cleaner air. Similarly, we do not directly observe how much individuals are willing to pay for national parks, but we can study how much people pay in travel costs in order to get to the sites (and they must value the recreational benefit at least by that much).[32] Studies such as these, based on actual choices that people make, normally do not lead to unusually large differences between the benefit measures (e.g., the observed choices of a large sample of people are used statistically to infer ordinary price and income elasticities of demand, and then compensated demand curves can be approximated from them).

Nevertheless, there are some things that people value that do not get revealed either directly or indirectly by observable market choices. For example, you may value the existence of Yellowstone National Park even if you have no intention of going there yourself. As other examples, you may value the existence of Brazilian rainforests or the preservation of the spotted owl, even if you have no intention of visiting, seeing, or personally using either.

[31] I am oversimplifying for expositional clarity. The houses that are compared are typically dissimilar, and they are made comparable through statistical techniques. There are a great many factors that cause one home to have different value than another (e.g., size, quality of construction, neighborhood, quality of local public services such as schools), and it is a thorny statistical problem to control for all of these factors in order to isolate the effect of air quality alone. Nevertheless, there are numerous careful studies that provide estimates of this value. These estimates, while uncertain, do help us to understand what a plausible range for the true value might be. For a discussion of this and related approaches, see K. Ward and J. Duffield, *Natural Resource Damages: Law and Economics* (New York: John Wiley & Sons, Inc., 1992), pp. 247–256.

[32] For a review of some of these travel cost studies, see V. K. Smith and Y. Kaoru, "Signals or Noise? Explaining the Variation in Recreation Benefit Estimates," *American Journal of Agricultural Economics, 72,* 1990, pp. 419–433.

These values are sometimes referred to as "existence values" or "passive-use values." Understanding the magnitude of these existence values can bear on the policies adopted with respect to these natural resources. In order to get some idea of the magnitudes, economists have been developing procedures known as *contingent valuation surveys* in order to estimate them. The survey methodology involves asking people what they are willing to pay for various hypothetical government programs that would help preserve the resource. The methodology was used, for example, in a law suit by the State of Alaska to estimate that citizens across the nation valued the damage done to its coast by the *Exxon Valdez* oil spill at almost $3 billion.[33]

For a number of reasons, the validity of contingent valuation survey results has been a subject of intense debate. One simple argument against them is that, because no actual payments are required, those surveyed may not tell the truth (e.g., those liking the program may overreport willingness to pay, and those disliking the program may underreport). However, some experiments suggest that the survey answers may be surprisingly truthful.[34] A second argument is the psychological one: the results themselves reveal serious inconsistencies in individual responses, making it difficult if not impossible to give them a reasonable interpretation. In particular, there are often implausibly large differences between the two welfare measures we have been discussing. The surveys typically ask about the willingness to pay (WTP) for an additional program and the willingness to accept (WTA) a reduction in a program. When the addition in the WTP measure is the same marginal unit as the reduction in the WTA measure, then the measures are the compensating and equivalent variations.

One striking example of this inconsistency is found in the closely related work of psychologists Kahneman and Tversky.[35] They ask subjects, in two different ways as part of a controlled experiment, which of two programs they prefer. In their example, the lives of 600 people are threatened by a disease. One program saves 200 people but will not prevent the death of the other 400. The other program has a one-third chance of saving all 600, and a two-thirds chance of saving no one. When these programs are described in terms of lives saved, 72 percent of respondents favor the one certain to save 200. But when the same programs are described in terms of lives lost, 78 percent of respondents favor the program that might save all 600. The difference in responses is termed a *framing effect*, because it is due simply to the way the questions are asked. Because this is very similar to the framing difference between the equivalent and compensating variations—a willingness to pay for a *gain* of a good or service, as opposed to a willingness to accept a monetary amount for the

---

[33] The study is Richard Carson et al., "A Contingent Valuation Study of Lost Passive Use Values Resulting from the Exxon Valdez Oil Spill," report to the Attorney General of the State of Alaska, prepared by Natural Resource Damage Assessment, Inc. (La Jolla, Calif.: 1992). In 1991, Exxon settled the suit out of court, agreeing to pay $1.15 billion.

[34] See, for example, Peter Bohm, "Revealing Demand for an Actual Public Good," *Journal of Public Economics, 24,* 1984, pp. 135–151.

[35] Amos Tversky and Daniel Kahneman, "Rational Choice and the Framing of Decisions," in D. Bell, H. Raiffa, and A. Tversky, eds., *Decision-Making: Descriptive, Normative and Prescriptive Interactions* (Cambridge: Cambridge University Press, 1988), pp. 167–192.

loss of the same thing (assuming you start with it)—we might expect such framing effects to influence the results of contingent valuation studies.

In fact, this is confirmed by experimental research of economists. A study by Brookshire and Coursey is illustrative.[36] They wanted to study the differences between the WTP and WTA measures under three different elicitation procedures: the field survey methodology used in contingent valuation studies, a modified field method with monetary incentives to respondents to reveal their preferences honestly, and a laboratory setting with similar monetary incentives to the second method but with repetition of up to five elicitation "rounds" and discussion among participants allowed.[37] The difference between the first and second methods emphasizes the change in participant incentives, and the difference between the second and third methods emphasizes the role of learning from the opportunity to see the consequences and the chance to adapt behavior in response. The third method is also most like the purchase of ordinary goods in the marketplace, where consumers often can learn by trial and error.

The good in the Brookshire and Coursey study was the number of trees in a small public park, with artist renditions of the alternate proposals. The range of trees considered was from a low of 150 to a high of 250, with 200 as the "base" from which participants were asked to consider changes. The results showed considerable stability in the WTP measures across the three methods: for example, the average WTP for an increase of 50 trees was $19.40, $15.40, and $12.92 for the first, second, and third methods, respectively. However, the WTA measure was less stable, changing greatly with the third method: for example, the average WTA for a decrease of 50 trees was $1734.40, $1735.00, and $95.52. Furthermore, while there is no reason why the WTP and WTA measures should be equal to each other in this experiment (WTP values the change from 200 to 250 trees, WTA from 150 to 200), there is also no economic reason to expect differences as large as those observed. Even if we were to interpret the results of the repetitive laboratory method as the "truth" (i.e., a WTP of $12.92 and a WTA of $95.52, still a difference that seems too great a rise in marginal value to be the result of normal preferences), clearly the value difference resulting from the contingent valuation survey methodology (WTP of $19.40 and WTA of $1734.40) is substantially due to psychological phenomena such as framing effects and not true preferences.

The above should not be interpreted as implying that contingent valuation surveys are invalid. Indeed, the results of the one study reviewed above suggest that WTP measures derived from careful contingent valuation surveys may be reasonable indicators of value. The U.S. Department of Interior as well as other agencies make use of such studies. The conclusion of a blue-ribbon panel commissioned by the National Oceanic and Atmospheric Administration to review this methodology stated that contingent valuation studies "can produce estimates reliable enough to be the starting point of a judicial process of damage

---

[36] David S. Brookshire and Don L. Coursey, "Measuring the Value of a Public Good: An Empirical Comparison of Elicitation Procedures," *American Economic Review, 7,* No. 4, September 1987, pp. 554–566.

[37] We shall study the problem of honest revelation of preferences for public goods later on in the text.

assessment, including lost passive-use values."[38] Nevertheless, the use of such studies does remain controversial.[39]

To summarize, in some cases we may observe large differences between the equivalent and compensating variations. Sometimes these differences can be quite real, particularly when the nature of the change being studied is itself of great economic importance to the affected individuals. However, there are also cases where large differences must be viewed skeptically. These cases typically arise not from market observations but precisely in those areas where the "good" being valued is not normally bought or sold. The existence values to people of common-property natural resources fit this description, and these values are often studied through the use of contingent valuation surveys. Because these surveys involve asking people about complex economic choices that are hypothetical and abstract, their choices may not be the same as those that would be revealed in actual decision-making situations. Experimental evidence confirms the difficulty of making abstract choices as well as large differences between the two measures caused in good part by this difficulty. While the use of these surveys remains controversial, they seem most reliable when estimating WTP rather than WTA.

Summary

In this chapter we have reviewed one of the most commonly utilized analytic principles in making evaluative judgments: the Hicks-Kaldor compensation criterion. The criterion provides the foundation for the analytic technique of benefit-cost analysis. It is a test of *potential* Pareto superiority; it seeks to discover whether the gainers from a policy change *could* compensate the losers and still have enough left over to come out ahead. Because the compensations are only hypothetical, it is important to think carefully about whether, why, and when one might rely on such a principle. It is used because it captures an important element of social reality and no better operational criterion has been found to replace it.

The two relatively uncontroversial criteria of Pareto optimality and Pareto superiority generally do not characterize actual states of the economy either before or after proposed policy changes; this renders them of little use in making policy choices from among alternatives that make some people better off and others worse off. Nevertheless, there are many alternative allocations of this latter type, and there can be wide (if not unanimous) consensus that some of them are better because there is more product to go around. Viewed that way, analytic use of the compensation principle takes on more appeal. That is, we do not attempt to justify the principle as a rational decision rule that all reasonable people "should"

---

[38] The report is published in the Federal Register for January 15, 1993. The panel was chaired by Nobel laureate economists Kenneth Arrow and Robert Solow.

[39] A good general reference on contingent valuation methodology is Robert Mitchell and Richard Carson, *Using Surveys to Value Public Goods: The Contingent Valuation Method* (Washington, D.C.: Resources for the Future, 1989). The controversies and much of the literature are summarized in a symposium published in *The Journal of Economic Perspectives, 8,* No. 4, Fall 1994, pp. 3–64, with contributions by Paul R. Portney, W. Michael Hanemann, Peter A. Diamond, and Jerry A. Hausman.

follow. Consider it as an imperfect predictor of what informed social judgment on relative efficiency grounds would be. It does not purport to reflect equity judgments, and thus separate consideration of outcome and process equity issues would often be appropriate.

For changes involving only ordinary marketable goods, those that can pass the compensation test are a subset of those that would increase national product valued at the initial prices. This example suggests that the compensation test is no more controversial an indicator than measures of national product (which have flaws but are widely used). This comparison does not have much meaning if one is considering radically different resource allocations (so that prices also would be radically different), and thus the compensation principle should be expected to be of more use in comparing "smaller" changes. The most common use in practice is in comparing policy alternatives under the control of one agency that are similar in their target gainers and losers.

To carry out a compensation test, one must be able to measure the benefits to the gainers and the costs to the losers. A common measure used in such assessments is the change in the ordinary consumer surplus, which can be calculated from knowledge of the ordinary demand curve and the consumer cost. In a supplementary section, we relate this common measure to two exact monetary measures, called the compensating variation and the equivalent variation. The two exact measures seek to identify the hypothetical budget change necessary to make an individual indifferent to a policy change. The two differ only in the choice of a reference point. In most cases these two measures are close to one another. However, neither of them can be calculated directly from an ordinary demand curve. Since the change in ordinary consumer surplus always has a value between the two exact measures, in practice it is the one most commonly used.

Another supplementary section discusses problematic cases in which there may be large differences between the two exact measures. One type of case is when the change is of great importance to an individual, as in the provision of expensive medical treatments. Another type sometimes arises when goods and services are not normally traded in the market place and therefore no demand curve can be directly observed. For many of these, analysts avoid the potential problem and indirectly derive the demand curve (and then in turn the relative efficiency measure) from other activities that are observable: examples are using home values to estimate the value of cleaner air and transportation costs to give a (lower-bound) estimate of the value of recreational facilities such as lakes and parks. However, there remain some goods and services for which neither direct nor indirect measures are available.

The most prominent example of these are the existence values of common-property natural resources such as the oceans or various wildlife habitats. For the latter, contingent valuation survey methods may be used. These surveys are controversial and subject to a variety of difficulties. One is that psychological framing effects (rather than true preferences) can cause large differences between the equivalent and compensating variations. Nevertheless, carefully done contingent valuation surveys, particularly when used to estimate willingness to pay, may provide useful estimates.

The mathematical relations among utility functions, demand functions, and the above measures of individual welfare can be somewhat involved. In an optional appendix we derive them for the case of a utility function called the Cobb-Douglas function, and provide illustrative numerical calculations. We introduce the concepts used in the dual theory of consumer choice, the expenditure function and indirect utility function, and illustrate how welfare measures can be derived from them.

In this chapter no attempt was made to survey all the issues involved in carrying out a compensation test through benefit-cost analysis. Instead, we focused on one important part of it: utilizing information available from market demand curves. We saw that, under certain conditions, the market demand curve can reveal virtually everything necessary to calculate the sum of compensations. Under other circumstances, knowledge of the market demand curves is essentially useless for those purposes.

The most important point from these examples is the one that is emphasized throughout the text: The development of analytic skill depends heavily on understanding the implications of alternative model specifications. Linkages that are assumed to be universal in the context of purely private markets may be nonexistent in the particular policy setting being analyzed. In this chapter, for example, we showed that the link between individual consumer surplus and the area under the market demand curve is broken when consumers are misinformed and as a consequence make purchasing errors. But it is precisely in the areas in which consumer information is judged most seriously inadequate that public policy is likely to exist. The creators and users of policy analyses must be sensitive to the logical underpinnings of models in order to use the models and interpret them effectively.

Exercises

6-1   An Excise Tax

The diagram shows the demand (*D*) and supply (*S*) for passenger rail service between two cities. Initially the price per ticket is $4 and 1000 trips are made per week. An excise tax of $2 is placed on each ticket, which raises supply to *S'* and reduces the number of rail trips to 800.

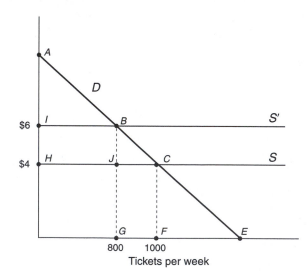

a Identify the area on the diagram that represents the tax revenue collected.

b What does "consumer surplus" mean? Identify the area on the diagram that represents the consumer surplus received by rail passengers *after* the tax has been imposed.

c Identify the area on the diagram that represents the deadweight loss (or equivalently the "efficiency cost") of the tax. Explain the meaning of this concept.

6-2 There are forty consumers in an economy who purchase a drug to relieve the pain of arthritis. They think that the only effective drug is Namebrand. However, the same drug can be bought by its chemical name acethistestamine, or ace for short. The drug costs $2 to produce no matter what it is called; any quantity demanded can be supplied at that price. The company producing Namebrand exploits consumer ignorance by charging $6 for each unit; that is, the consumers buy Namebrand at $6 per unit, not realizing that ace is a perfect substitute available for only $2.

The aggregate demand curve of the 40 uninformed consumers is $Q = 400 - 40P$.

a What would be the value to consumers of knowing that ace and Namebrand are identical? (Answer: $960.)

b How much is the deadweight loss due to the consumers' lack of perfect information? (Answer: $320.)

6-3 There are two and only two consumers, Smith and Jones, who buy a product of uncertain quality. When both are informed of the quality, they have the same demand curve:

$$P = 100 - Q/4$$

The market price is $P = \$50$. Suppose they are uninformed and have the following uninformed demand curves:

Smith:	$P = 125 - Q/4$	overestimates value
Jones:	$P = 80 - Q/4$	underestimates value

a Calculate the loss in consumer surplus to Smith from not having accurate information. Make a similar calculation for Jones.

b Calculate the uninformed market demand curve. Also calculate the informed market demand curve.

c What is the loss in consumer surplus as measured by the deadweight loss triangle between the market informed and uninformed curves? (Answer: $25.)

d What is the actual loss in consumer surplus from having poor information? (Answer: $2050.)

APPENDIX

DUALITY, THE COBB-DOUGLAS EXPENDITURE FUNCTION,
AND MEASURES OF INDIVIDUAL WELFARE°

The Cobb-Douglas function is a reasonably simple form of utility function that is often used in analytic work. For a two-good economy, its equation is

$$U = X_1^\alpha X_2^{1-\alpha}$$

where $0 < \alpha < 1$.[40] The ordinary demand curves derived from it are characterized by unitary price elasticity of demand, which is sometimes a good representation of actual behavior. The demand curves have the form

$$D(X_1) = \frac{\alpha B}{P_1}$$

and

$$D(X_2) = \frac{(1 - \alpha)B}{P_2}$$

where B is the consumer's budget. The budget elasticity of demand is 1. The proportion of this budget spent on $X_1 = a$ and that on $X_2 = 1 - a$. The demand curves can be derived by maximizing the utility function subject to a general budget constraint. We form the Lagrangian

$$L = X_1^\alpha X_1^{1-\alpha} + \lambda(B - P_1 X_1 - P_2 X_2)$$

To maximize utility subject to the constraint, we set the partial derivatives with respect to X_1, X_2, and λ equal to zero and solve the equations simultaneously:

$$\frac{\partial L}{\partial X_1} = \alpha X_1^{\alpha-1} X_2^{1-\alpha} - \lambda P_1 = 0 \qquad \text{(i)}$$

$$\frac{\partial L}{\partial X_2} = (1 - \alpha) X_1^\alpha X_2^{-\alpha} - \lambda P_2 = 0 \qquad \text{(ii)}$$

$$\frac{\partial L}{\partial \lambda} = B - P_1 X_1 - P_2 X_2 = 0 \qquad \text{(iii)}$$

To solve, first multiply both sides of equation (i) by X_1 and simplify:

$$\alpha X_1^\alpha X_2^{1-\alpha} - \lambda P_1 X_1 = 0$$

---

[40] For an n-good economy, $U = X_1^{\alpha_1} X_2^{\alpha_2} \ldots X_n^{\alpha_n}$, where $0 < \alpha_i < 1$ and

$$\sum_{i=1}^{n} \alpha_i = 1$$

or

$$\alpha U - \lambda P_1 X_1 = 0$$

or

$$X_1 = \frac{\alpha U}{\lambda P_1} \qquad (i')$$

Similarly, multiply both sides of (ii) by X_2 and simplify:

$$(1 - \alpha)X_1^{\alpha}X_2^{1-\alpha} - \lambda P_2 X_2 = 0$$

or

$$(1 - \alpha)U - \lambda P_2 X_2 = 0$$

or

$$X_2 = \frac{(1 - \alpha)U}{\lambda P_2} \qquad (ii')$$

Now substitute (i') and (ii') in (iii):

$$B - \frac{P_1 \alpha U}{\lambda P_1} - \frac{P_2(1 - \alpha)U}{\lambda P_2} = 0$$

or

$$\lambda B = \alpha U + (1 - \alpha)U = U$$

or

$$\lambda = \frac{U}{B} \qquad (iii')$$

Finally, substituting (iii') back in (i') and (ii') gives us the demand functions:

$$X_1 = \frac{\alpha U}{P_1}\frac{B}{U} = \frac{\alpha B}{P_1}$$

$$X_2 = (1 - \alpha)\frac{U}{P_2}\frac{B}{U} = \frac{(1 - \alpha)B}{P_2}$$

The unitary price and budget elasticities may be derived by applying their definitions to these demand equations. Note that by multiplying each side of the demand equations by the price, we see that expenditures as a proportion of the budget equal a constant α and $1 - \alpha$ for X_1 and X_2, respectively.

Much research effort has been devoted to developing easier ways to relate the theory of utility-maximizing choice to observable phenomena such as demand. One approach, which we introduce and use in this section, is based on the mathematics of *duality*. To convey the idea of the dual approach, note that we have formulated the consumer choice problem as maximizing utility subject to a budget constraint. An essentially equivalent way to formulate the problem is to minimize the expenditures necessary to achieve a certain utility level. In this dual problem we work with an expenditure function subject to a utility constraint, rather than a utility function subject to a budget constraint. Under certain fairly general conditions, knowledge of the expenditure function reveals the same information about the consumer as knowledge of the utility function would.[41]

To illustrate this dual approach, we define the concepts of an indirect utility function and an expenditure function. Then we use them in the Cobb-Douglas case to help calculate values of the welfare measures discussed in the preceding sections.

Sometimes it is convenient to use an **indirect utility function, which expresses the maximum utility a consumer can achieve as a function of prices and the budget level.** We denote it by $U = U(B_1, P_1, P_2)$ for the two-good case. For the Cobb-Douglas function, we find the indirect utility function by substituting the demand equations for X_1 and X_2 in the ordinary utility function:

$$U = X_1^{\alpha} X_2^{1-\alpha}$$

$$= \left(\frac{\alpha B}{P_1} \right)^{\alpha} \left[\frac{(1-\alpha)B}{P_2} \right]^{1-\alpha}$$

$$= \alpha^{\alpha}(1-\alpha)^{1-\alpha} B P_1^{-\alpha} P_2^{\alpha-1}$$

or, letting $\delta = \alpha^{\alpha}(1-\alpha)^{1-\alpha}$, we have

$$U = \delta B P_1^{-\alpha} P_2^{\alpha-1}$$

The indirect utility function can be rewritten in a form generally referred to as the expenditure function. **The expenditure function $B(U, P_1, P_2)$ shows the minimum budget or expenditure necessary to achieve any utility level U at prices P_1 and P_2.** For the Cobb-Douglas function:

$$B = \frac{U P_1^{\alpha} P_2^{1-\alpha}}{\delta}$$

From the expenditure function it is easy to find the compensated demand curves. Recall that a compensated demand curve shows the quantity of a good that will be bought at each possible price when the utility is held constant at some level $\bar{U}$. *Shephard's lemma* states that this quantity equals the partial derivative of the expenditure function with respect to price[42]:

$$X_i = \frac{\partial B(U, P_1, P_2)}{\partial P_i} \quad i = 1, 2$$

---

[41] The dual approach applies to the supply side as well as the demand side. We introduce duality on the supply side in the optional section of Chapter 8. A good introductory reference to the use of duality in economics is Hal R. Varian, *Microeconomic Analysis* (New York: W. W. Norton & Company, 1992). Additional references are contained in Chapter 9.

[42] A proof of this is sketched in the optional section of Chapter 9.

Applied to the Cobb-Douglas expenditure function:

$$X_1 = \frac{\partial B}{\partial P_1} = \frac{\alpha \bar{U} P_1^{\alpha-1} P_2^{1-\alpha}}{\delta}$$

$$X_2 = \frac{\partial B}{\partial P_2} = \frac{(1-\alpha) \bar{U} P_1^{\alpha} P_2^{-\alpha}}{\delta}$$

We will use these equations for the compensated curves below. We also note that it is easier to derive the ordinary demand curves from an indirect utility function than from an ordinary utility function. That is because of *Roy's identity,* which states[43]:

$$X_i = \frac{-\partial U(B, P_1, P_2)/\partial P_1}{\partial U(B, P_1, P_2)/\partial B} \quad i = 1, 2$$

For the Cobb-Douglas function we find the ordinary demand curve for X_1:

$$\frac{\partial U(B, P_1, P_2)}{\partial P_1} = -\alpha \delta B P_1^{-\alpha-1} P_2^{\alpha-1}$$

$$\frac{\partial U(B, P_1, P_2)}{\partial B} = \delta P_1^{-\alpha} P_2^{\alpha-1}$$

and therefore, by Roy's identity,

$$X_1 = \frac{\alpha B}{P_1}$$

This is, of course, the same result we derived earlier by solving a system of simultaneous equations.

---

[43] The following proof is from Varian, *Microeconomic Analysis,* pp. 106–107. It is true by identity that a given utility level $\bar{U}$ can be expressed by the indirect utility function

$$\bar{U} = U[P_1, P_2, B(\bar{U}, P_1, P_2)]$$

At any prices, that is, the consumer will achieve the $\bar{U}$ level if he or she is given the minimum expenditure necessary to achieve it. But then the derivative of this expression with respect to price must always equal zero:

$$\frac{\partial \bar{U}}{\partial P_i} = \frac{\partial U}{\partial P_i} + \frac{\partial U}{\partial B} \frac{\partial B}{\partial P_i} = 0$$

We can write this

$$\frac{\partial B}{\partial P_i} = \frac{-\partial U/\partial P_i}{\partial U/\partial B}$$

But from Shephard's lemma we know that the term on the left is X_1. This gives us Roy's identity:

$$X_i = \frac{-\partial U/\partial P_i}{\partial U/\partial B}$$

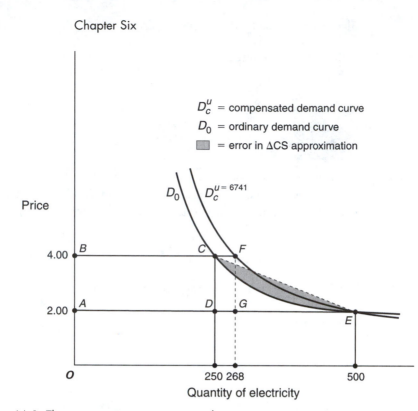

Figure 6A-1. The compensating variation and its approximations.

To illustrate some of the measures we have described, suppose an individual has this specific Cobb-Douglas utility function:

$$U = X_1^{0.1} X_2^{0.9}$$

and let us assume that the budget is $10,000, $P_1 = \$2.00$, and $P_2 = \$1.00$. Focusing on the first good, the consumer purchases

$$D(X_1) = \frac{0.1(10,000)}{2} = 500$$

Suppose the price of this good increases to $4.00. Then the consumer purchases

$$D(X_1) = \frac{0.1(10,000)}{4} = 250$$

We represent the initial situation and the change in Figure 6A-1. Let us find the change in ordinary consumer surplus ΔCS, the compensating variation CV, and the equivalent variation EV. The change in consumer surplus is area $ABCE$. Its exact area is[44]

---

[44] Note that the area $ABCE$ can be calculated by integrating over either the price or the quantity axis. Integrating over the price axis is more convenient in this case.

$$\Delta CS = \int_{2.00}^{4.00} [X_1] dP_1$$

$$= \int_{2.00}^{4.00} \frac{0.1(10,000)}{P_1} dP_1$$

$$= 1000(\ln 4.00 - \ln 2.00)$$

$$= \$693.15$$

In practice, the demand curves are always estimated from actual observations, so the ΔCS is also an estimate. Sometimes the only information available will be the initial and final prices and quantities. In that case, it is often assumed that the demand curve is approximately linear "over the relevant range." This assumption may be fine for small price changes, but it can lead to more serious estimation errors as the change considered gets larger. If we make the linearity assumption in the present case of a quite large price change (i.e., 100 percent), the area we calculate is still $ABCE$ but we treat the CE boundary as the dashed line shown in Figure 6A-1. In this case, using subscript L for linearity assumption,

$$\Delta CS_L = ABCD + CDE$$

$$= 500 + \frac{1}{2}(2)(250)$$

$$= \$750$$

Thus we overestimate the change in ordinary consumer surplus by 8.2 percent—not bad for such a large price change. Think of this error as being caused by uncertainty concerning the true demand curve.

Now let us turn to calculating the CV. One method requires two steps: (1) Find the relevant compensated demand curve. (2) Calculate the area of the CV by the method of integration used for the ΔCS. The relevant compensated demand curve is the one through point E in Figure 6A-1, where utility is held constant at its initial level. Since we know the utility function, we can find the initial utility level by plugging in the initial consumption amounts of X_1 and X_2 (or equivalently, by plugging in the budget level and initial prices in the indirect utility function). We know that X_1 is initially 500; X_2 is easily determined to be 9000 by substituting the known parameters $B = \$10,000$, $1 - \alpha = 0.9$, and $P_2 = 1.00$ into $D(X_2)$. Then

$$U_0 = 500^{0.1}(9000^{0.9})$$

$$\approx 6741$$

It is a simple matter to find the compensated demand curve associated with this utility level. We merely substitute in the compensated demand equation derived from the expenditure function:

$$X_1 = \frac{\alpha \bar{U} P_1^{\alpha-1} P_2^{1-\alpha}}{\delta}$$

$$= \frac{0.1(6741)P_1^{-0.9}(1^{0.9})}{0.1^{0.1}(0.9^{0.9})}$$

$$= 933.05 P_1^{-0.9}$$

This is the equation of the compensated demand curve through point E. When $P_1 = \$4.00$, $X_1 = 268$ if the consumer is compensated. This is shown as point F in Figure 6A-1 and the compensating variation is area $ABFE$. To calculate it,

$$CV = \int 933.05(P_1^{-0.9})\,dP_1$$

$$= 933.05\,\frac{P_1^{0.1}}{0.1}\,\bigg|_{P_1=4.00}^{P_1=2.00}$$

$$= \$717.75$$

Thus, the CV is only 3.54 percent bigger than the ordinary consumer surplus in this case. Note that if we use the linear approximation here, the estimated CV_L is

$$CV_L = ABFG + FGE$$

$$= 2(268) + \tfrac{1}{2}(2)(232)$$

$$= \$768.00$$

This method might be used if nothing is known except the initial and final positions and there is an estimate of the income effect used to approximate the location of point F. These empirical examples should help illustrate why, in many situations, abstract debate about which of the different measures should be used may not be worth the fuss; uncertainty about the true demand curve is often the dominating source of potential evaluative error.

The exact method of calculating the CV used above illustrated how to identify the equation for a compensated demand curve. But a little thought about the meaning of an expenditure function leads to an interesting shortcut. When the change in the state of the world concerns prices, the CV can be simply expressed:

$$CV = B(P_1^1, P_1^2, U_0) - B(P_1^1, P_1^2, U_1)$$

where P_j^i is the price of the ith commodity in period j and U_j is the utility level in period j. The first term is the minimum budget necessary to achieve the original utility level at the new prices, and the second is the actual budget in the new state of the world (i.e., the minimum expenditure necessary to achieve the actual utility level at the actual prices). The difference between them is precisely what we have defined as the CV.

Note that since price changes do not affect the size of the consumer's budget, the second term is equivalent to the following:

$$B(P_1^1, P_1^2, U_1) = B(P_0^1, P_0^2, U_0)$$

That is, the actual budget in the new state of the world is the same as the initial budget. Then we can substitute this in the expression for the CV:

$$CV = B(P_1^1, P_1^2, U_1) - B(P_0^1, P_0^2, U_0)$$

In our example where $P_1^2 = P_0^2$, this expression corresponds exactly to the change in consumer surplus under the compensated demand curve for $U = U_0$ when the price changes from P_0^1 to P_1^1. Rather than actually calculate this demand curve, one can compute the CV directly by using the Cobb-Douglas expenditure function and the above expression:

$$CV = \frac{U_0(P_1^1)^\alpha(P_1^2)^{1-\alpha}}{\delta} - \frac{U_0(P_0^1)^\alpha(P_0^2)^{1-\alpha}}{\delta}$$

On substituting the parameter values from our example, $\delta = 0.722467$, $U_0 = 6741$, $P_1^2 = P_0^2 = 1$, $P_1^1 = 4$, and $P_0^1 = 2$, we have

$$CV = \frac{6741}{0.722467}(4^{0.1} - 2^{0.1})$$

$$= \$717.75$$

Following the same reasoning, we can express the EV for price changes:

$$EV = B(P_0^1, P_0^2, U_0) - B(P_0^1, P_0^2, U_1)$$

The first term is the actual budget, and the second term is the minimum budget necessary to achieve the new utility level at the initial prices. The difference between the terms is what we have defined as the EV. Again, since price changes do not affect a consumer's budget, we substitute (this time for the first term):

$$EV = B(P_1^1, P_1^2, U_1) - B(P_0^1, P_0^2, U_1)$$

When $P_1^2 = P_0^2$, this expression corresponds to the change in consumer surplus under the compensated demand curve for $U = U_1$. For our example, we calculate $U_1 = 6289$ and by using the parameters above,

$$EV = \frac{6289}{0.722467}(4^{0.1} - 2^{0.1})$$

$$= \$669.62$$

as expected, this is less than the \$693.15 loss in ordinary consumer surplus.

CHAPTER SEVEN
UNCERTAINTY AND PUBLIC POLICY

IN THIS CHAPTER we will introduce models that have been developed to explain the effect of uncertainty on individual economic behavior. Increasingly, analysts have come to recognize that uncertainty is not just a curious oddity that arises in a few isolated instances. It is a pervasive phenomenon that explains a great deal about individual behavior and can be a major factor in the design of policies.

Consider the fear of crime and our individual and policy responses to it. As individuals, *we take actions to reduce the risk* of becoming victims. We put locks on our doors and windows. We may pay for door-to-door taxi service in some areas because we believe it exposes us to fewer hazards than alternatives that involve walking or waiting at a bus stop. We may pay a premium for housing located in a relatively "safe" neighborhood. We may purchase insurance that offers some reimbursement in the event of theft or other possible losses. None of these actions guarantees our safety and security. But they reduce the probability that we will experience losses, and *it is this reduction in uncertainty that many value* enough to make the protective expenditures worthwhile.

Our desire for more security from crime goes beyond individual actions. We have public policies in the form of police, prosecutors, courts, jails, and prisons to help keep our "streets safe." Other public policies can also be understood in terms of their risk reduction benefits, including social "safety net" programs such as unemployment insurance to protect against unexpected income loss, health insurance, programs to reduce environmental hazards, and license requirements for commercial airplane pilots. The value of these programs depends in part on how much people are willing to pay to avoid or reduce uncertainty and in part on how the cost of doing so through the programs compares to other methods. The examples illustrate why analysts must be able to assess the importance of changes in the level and cost of uncertainty associated with proposed policies.

220

To accomplish the assessment, we must develop a more general understanding of how individuals respond to uncertainty. We begin by reviewing the concepts of *expected value* and *expected utility* and consider the proposition that individuals act to maximize expected utility. The latter proposition, known as the *expected utility theorem*, is helpful in understanding the economic costs of uncertainty. We then consider some of the choice possibilities for responding to uncertainty, introduced in the section on risk control and risk-shifting mechanisms.

There are many situations in which individual responses to uncertainty do not seem to be modeled well by the expected utility theorem. Some situations may be better modeled by concepts from the *theory of games against persons*; we illustrate this with an urban housing problem known as the *Slumlord's Dilemma*; a similar situation may characterize certain issues in international trade. Behavior in other situations may be better modeled by concepts of *bounded rationality*; we consider this in the context of food-labeling requirements, federal policy to subsidize disaster insurance in areas that are highly flood-prone, and the allocation of a retirement portfolio between stocks and bonds. These latter models are discussed in the section on alternative models of individual behavior under uncertainty.

The response to uncertainty depends not only on how individuals think about it but also on the set of possible responses. The situations analyzed in this chapter are primarily those in which the individual does not alter the amount of uncertainty, but acts to reduce exposure to it.[1] An example is the uncertainty faced by the farmer planting now and concerned about crop price at harvest time. The farmer cannot change the price uncertainty, but he or she can reduce the risk from it by selling a futures contract (the sale of some portion of the expected future crop at a price agreed upon now).

There are a wide variety of social mechanisms that are designed to reduce the costs of risk. We do not pretend in this chapter to give an exhaustive description, but we mention and explain many of them at points convenient to their development. A *fundamental principle* behind many of them *is to shift the risk to where it is less costly.* Two basic procedures, *risk-pooling* and *risk-spreading*, are often used by individuals toward that end. Insurance, stock markets, and futures markets are examples of such mechanisms.

Some mechanisms of public policy, for example, limited liability and the subsidized disaster insurance mentioned above, are used to alter the distribution of risk. Other public policies are adopted in an attempt to control risk more directly through such means as occupational licensing requirements, consumer product safety standards, and health standards

---

[1] This is to allow focus on the value of risk-shifting. Individuals will also act to reduce uncertainty directly rather than simply shifting it. Protective expenditures in the form of fire extinguishers reduce the probability of damage from a fire. Fire insurance, on the other hand, changes neither the likelihood of a fire nor the damage that it will cause, but it does reduce the risk to the purchaser by shifting it to the insurance company. The chapter helps us to understand both of these types of actions. We defer some discussions until we have reviewed the functioning of markets and can develop perspective on the role of information within the markets. For example, credit lenders and employers can use resources to gather information about credit and job applicants before responding to their respective applications. Examples that emphasize information in markets are discussed throughout Parts IV and V.

in the workplace. The appropriateness of these policies is often a difficult question to resolve, in large part because of analytic uncertainty about how individuals respond to them relative to alternatives.

One interesting area of analysis involving uncertainty is health policy, particularly national health insurance or alternatives to it. In the section on medical care insurance later in this chapter, the cost spiral in the delivery of medical services is shown to be, in large part, an unintended consequence of insurance coverage. The insurance coverage that reduces risk simultaneously distorts individual incentives to conserve scarce resources. The chapter extends the analysis of this *moral hazard* problem with applications to the 1980s savings and loan crisis as well as the continuing problem of involuntary unemployment. An appendix illustrates several calculations of risk assessments, including an empirical method for estimating the value of risk savings from medical insurance.

Expected Value and Expected Utility

When an individual makes an economic decision, we often assume that each of the alternatives is known and understood with certainty. But in many, perhaps most, cases there is uncertainty about what the individual will receive as a consequence of any specific choice. For example, the decision to allocate time to reading this textbook is a gamble; it may not pay off for any particular reader.[2] New cars may turn out to be lemons; a job may be offered that exposes the worker to risk of injury. In each case the person making the decision simply does not know in advance what the outcome will be.

This type of uncertainty does not necessarily lead to any revisions in the ordinary theorems of demand and supply. For example, other things being equal, an increase in the price of a risky commodity would be expected to reduce the demand for the commodity. A reason for studying uncertainty on its own, however, is that we observe that the willingness to pay for a risky commodity depends upon the perceived likelihoods of possible outcomes. A potential buyer of a particular car will offer less as his or her subjective evaluation of the likelihood that it is a lemon increases. It is this phenomenon on which we wish to focus here: how individuals respond to changes in these perceived likelihoods and how social mechanisms can affect those perceptions.

Certain fundamental concepts must be clarified before we can consider alternative models of individual behavior under uncertainty. One is the set of alternative *states of the world: the different, mutually exclusive outcomes that may result from the process generating the uncertainty*. For example, if a coin is flipped, two states of the world may result: It can come up heads, or it can come up tails. If a single die is thrown, there are six possible states, one corresponding to each face of the die. The definition of the states depends in part on the problem being considered. If you are betting that a 3 will come up on the die, then only two states are relevant to you: 3 and not 3. An uncertain outcome of a university course may be any of the specific grades A−, B+, C+, and so on, for one student and pass or not pass for another, depending on which gamble has been chosen.

---

[2] Please note that the same thing is true of alternative textbooks.

Another fundamental concept is the *probability* that a particular state will occur. If an evenly weighted coin is flipped, the probability that it will come up heads is $\frac{1}{2}$ and the probability that it will come up tails also is $\frac{1}{2}$. If the evenly weighted die is thrown, each face has a probability $\frac{1}{6}$ of being up. If you bet on 3, then you have $\frac{1}{6}$ chance of getting three and a $\frac{5}{6}$ chance of getting not 3.

The relation between an *objective conception* of the states of the world with their associated probabilities and an individual's *subjective perception* of them is a subject of considerable controversy in many applications. It is a philosophical issue whether any events are truly random. If a coin is flipped in exactly the same way every time (for instance, by machine in a constant environment, e.g., no wind), it will land with the same face up every time: Under those conditions there is no uncertainty. Based on the laws of physics and given perfect information on how a coin is flipped and time to calculate, one can predict with virtual certainty what the outcome will be. Put differently, in an objective sense there is no uncertainty.

Why then do we all agree, for the usual case such as the coin toss at the start of a football game, that the outcomes heads and tails have equal probability? There are two parts to the answer. First, coins are not tossed exactly the same way, and we lack the information and calculation time necessary to predict the outcome with a model based on the laws of physics. Thus the *uncertainty is due to our own lack of information and/or information-processing ability*.

Second, we do have some information: historical evidence. We have observed that in a large number of these uncontrolled or irregular coin tosses, heads and tails appear with approximately equal frequency. We might say that when the actual determinants of the coin toss outcome are selected randomly (e.g., the force, speed, and distance of the flip), it is objectively true that the outcomes have equal probability. Furthermore, if we share the subjective perception that the football referee "chooses" the determinants of the toss randomly, we conclude that the probability of each outcome is $\frac{1}{2}$.

Recognizing that perceptions of probabilities depend heavily on the type of knowledge we possess, let us consider a distinction that Frank Knight proposed be made between "risky" and "uncertain" situations.[3] *Risky situations*, in his terminology, are those in which each possible outcome has a known probability of occurring. *Uncertain situations*, again according to Knight, are those in which the probability of each outcome is not known. The coin toss is risky, but whether there will be a damaging nuclear accident next year is uncertain. There is some risk of particular medical problems arising during surgery, but the consequences of depleting the ozone layer in the earth's atmosphere are uncertain. One of the factors that explains why we consider some situations uncertain is lack of experience with them; we do not have many trial depletions of the ozone layer, unlike our histories of coin tossing.

Let us now recognize that knowledge differences may cause the same situation to be perceived differently by different people. Before you started reading this book, you may

[3] In less formal usage common today, uncertainty is used to refer to all situations in which the outcome is unknown. Thus quotation marks are used here to denote the meanings assigned by Knight. See F. H. Knight, *Risk, Uncertainty, and Profit* (Boston: Houghton Mifflin Company, 1921).

have been uncertain about whether you would enjoy it. I may know the probability that you will enjoy it, based on surveys of past readers. But whether you will enjoy the rest of the book is perceived as risky by both of us. Furthermore, we will have different probability estimates, and yours will be based on better information (your own reactions so far) than mine. Thus our subjective perceptions of the probability will differ.

In most economic models *individual decision-making depends upon the subjective perceptions about the possible states and their likelihoods.* We made two points about those perceptions above. First, doubts about which state will occur are due to lack of knowledge. Second, because there are knowledge differences among people, subjective perceptions will often be different.

At this point we might inquire further about how subjective perceptions are formed. For example, individuals can alter their perceptions by seeking additional information, and they might decide to do so in light of the perceived benefits and costs. Different analytic assumptions about the formation of subjective perceptions lead to different predictions about behavior and can lead to quite different policy recommendations. However, we avoid those complications in this section by sticking to situations such as the coin toss; individuals perceive the world as "risky" and the subjective probability assessments coincide with the objective ones. Thus we can refer to "the" probability of an event in an unambiguous sense.

One other basic concept to be introduced is the *payoff* in each possible state of the world. Suppose that when a coin is flipped, you will receive $2 if the coin turns up heads and –$1 if the coin turns up tails. These payments or prizes associated with each state are referred to as the payoffs. Then we can define the *expected value* of a risky situation: **The expected value is the sum of the payoff in each possible state of the world weighted by the probability that it will occur.** If there are n possible states, and each state i has a payoff X_i and a probability of occurring Π_i the expected value $E(V)$ is

$$E(V) = \sum_{i=1}^{n} \Pi_i X_i$$

In the coin toss game, the $E(V)$ is

$$E(V) = \tfrac{1}{2}(\$2) + \tfrac{1}{2}(-\$1) = \$0.50$$

If all the states are properly considered, it will always be true that

$$\sum_{i=1}^{n} \Pi_i = 1$$

that is, it is certain that one of the states will occur. When we flip the coin, it must come up either heads or tails. (We do not count tosses in which the coin stays on its edge.)

If we agree to flip the coin 100 times with the same payoffs as above on each flip, then the $E(V)$ of this new game is $50 [100 times the $E(V)$ of one flip] because the result of any single flip is completely independent of the results of other flips in the game. Many people would be willing to pay some *entry price* to play this game. Suppose the entry price is $50, or $0.50 per flip. Then the entry price equals the $E(V)$ of playing the game, or the net expected gain is zero. **Any risky situation in which the entry price equals the $E(V)$ is called a fair game.**

It is common for individuals to refuse to play fair games. Let us go back to the simple game of a single coin toss with payoffs as above. For an entry price of $0.50, which makes the game fair, *risk-averse people* would not be willing to play. These people prefer the certainty of not playing, which has the same net expected value as playing, to the risky situation. Some people would be willing to take the risk, but if the payoffs on a single toss were changed to be $200 on heads and −$100 on tails and the entry price were raised to $50, fewer people would play. All three situations have the same net expected value, so it must be some other factor that explains why fewer people are willing to play as the stakes get raised. This other factor is the risk.

A crucial insight was offered by Bernoulli, a mathematician of the eighteenth century. He suggested that individuals value not the expected *dollars*, but rather the expected *utility* that can be derived from them. If individual utility functions are characterized by a *diminishing marginal utility of money,* then the expected utility of a *gain* of, say, $100 will be less than the expected utility of a *loss* of $100. The expected change in utility from accepting a gamble with these two outcomes equally likely would be negative: The individual would decline the fair gamble. Let us develop this idea more carefully.

We can define *expected utility* as follows: **The expected utility of a risky situation is the sum of the resulting utility level in each possible state of the world weighted by the probability that it will occur.** If we let W_0 equal the initial wealth, E_0 equal the entry price, and $U(W)$ represent the utility function, the expected utility $E(U)$ may be expressed as

$$E(U) = \sum_{i=1}^{n} \Pi_i \, U(W_0 - E_0 + X_i)$$

The expected utility theorem simply says that individuals choose among alternatives in order to maximize expected utility.[4]

As we discuss this theorem, let us keep in mind a distinction between positive and normative views. The positive question concerns the predictive power of the theory, the extent to which actual behavior is consistent with the implications of the theorem. The normative issue is whether people should behave in accordance with the theorem even if they do not.

---

[4] To derive the expected utility theorem from assumptions about behavior requires several assumptions about human decision-making in addition to those introduced in Chapter 2. For a full review see K. Arrow, *Essays in the Theory of Risk-Bearing* (Chicago: Markham Publishing Company, 1971). The original derivation of a utility measure to include risky situations was made by John von Neumann and Oskar Morgenstern in their *Theory of Games and Economic Behavior* (Princeton, N.J.: Princeton University Press, 1944).

Probably the most controversial of the additional assumptions is one that implies that an individual is indifferent to two lotteries that are identical except in one state of the world; in that state the prizes are different but are ones to which the individual is indifferent. If a person is indifferent between A and B, then the assumption is that

$$\Pi_A U(A) + (1 - \Pi_A)U(C) = \Pi_A U(B) + (1 - \Pi_A)U(C)$$

However, it is commonly found in surveys and experiments that individuals are *not* indifferent between these two lotteries. See, for example, Jacques Dreze, "Axiomatic Theories of Choice, Cardinal Utility and Subjective Utility: A Review," in P. Diamond and M. Rothschild, eds., *Uncertainty in Economics* (New York: Academic Press, 1978), pp. 37–57. See also Mark J. Machina, "'Expected Utility' Analysis without the Independence Axiom," *Econometrica, 50*, March 1982, pp. 277–323.

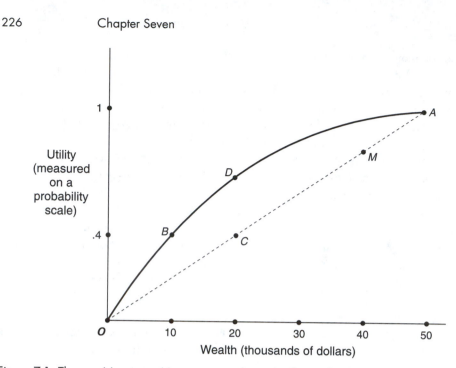

Figure 7-1. The von Neumann–Morgenstern utility index for evaluating risky situations.

That is, perhaps individuals do not always understand the consequences of their choices under uncertainty and they would be better off if they did act to maximize expected utility. Unless stated otherwise, we will generally take the view that increases in expected utility are desirable.

The main implication of this insight is that it offers an understanding of why people are willing to pay something to avoid risk. This, in turn, explains a great deal of behavior that cannot be explained by the effect on expected value alone, for example, the purchase of all forms of insurance, diversifying investment portfolios, and spending on safety measures beyond those that increase expected value. To illustrate the behavior implied by the theorem, we first construct a diagram illustrating how an expected utility maximizer evaluates risky choices.

Imagine for the moment that an individual can participate in a lottery with only two possible outcomes: winning $50,000 or nothing. Given a choice, naturally the individual would prefer a lottery with a higher rather than lower probability of winning the $50,000. The best lottery would be the one in which the probability of winning equaled 1, and the worst would have a probability of winning equal to 0. Let us arbitrarily assign a utility value of 1 to the best lottery (i.e., $50,000 with certainty) and 0 to the worst lottery (i.e., $0 with certainty).

In Figure 7-1 the horizontal axis shows the monetary payoff and the vertical axis shows the utility level. We graph the utility level and payoff of the two extreme lotteries, with point A as the best lottery and the origin as the worst. Using these two lotteries as reference points, we now construct a utility index specific to the individual. This index can be used to reveal the individual's preference ordering of all possible risky situations (with possible outcomes between the best and the worst), provided the individual is an expected utility maximizer.

Consider any amount of money between $0 and $50,000, such as $10,000, which we offer to the individual with certainty. Obviously, the best lottery is preferred to a certain $10,000. Similarly, the certain $10,000 is preferred to the worst lottery. Therefore, there must be some lottery with a probability of winning between 0 and 1 that the individual considers exactly as desirable as the certain $10,000.

We ask the individual to identify the probability. Suppose it is .4. Then we define the .4 probability as the utility value to the individual of $10,000 with certainty. This is shown as point B in Figure 7-1. If we follow this procedure for all monetary amounts between $0 and $50,000, we have a relation showing the individual's utility level as a function of wealth.[5] This is shown as the solid curved line. The height of the curve, or the utility level, equals the probability of winning necessary to make the individual indifferent to the lottery and the level of certain wealth shown on the horizontal axis. This construct is referred to, after its creators, as the *von Neumann–Morgenstern utility index.*[6]

The dashed straight line connecting the origin with point A shows, for each possible probability, the expected value of the lottery (on the horizontal axis) and the expected utility level (on the vertical axis). For example, the $E(V)$ of the lottery with a .4 chance of winning $50,000 is $20,000:

$$E(V) = .4(\$50,000) + .6(\$0)$$

$$= \$20,000$$

The expected utility of the lottery is

$$E(U) = .4U(\$50,000) + .6U(\$0)$$

$$= .4(1) + .6(0)$$

$$= .4$$

These are graphed as point C. Its height or expected utility level of .4 should not be surprising. The utility index was constructed in recognition of the individual's indifference between this lottery and the certain wealth ($10,000) assigned a utility level of .4. The lottery and its certain wealth equivalent should have the same utility level. Thus point C represents the expected value and expected utility from the .4 gamble. The expected values and expected utilities of gambles with higher probabilities of winning lie on the dashed line to the right of point C, and those with lower probabilities lie to the left.

---

[5] This is an *indirect* utility function; the utility comes not from wealth directly, but from the goods and services purchased with it.

[6] This index can be mistakenly interpreted as a cardinal utility scale. It is true that it is cardinal in the sense that it is unique up to a linear transformation. However, it does not measure preference intensity. For example, one cannot conclude that a risky situation with $E(U) = .2$ is twice as preferable to one in which $E(U) = .1$. All the index does is rank-order alternative risky situations. For a discussion of this, see William J. Baumol, *Economic Theory and Operations Analysis*, 4th Ed. (Englewood Cliffs, N.J.: Prentice-Hall, Inc., 1977), pp. 431–432.

The utility index can now be used to rank-order risky situations because it allows their expected utilities to be calculated and compared. Suppose the individual actually has $20,000 with certainty; thus the current position is shown at point D. We then propose a fair game: We will allow the individual to take a chance on the above lottery with .4 probability of winning $50,000 in return for an entry price of $20,000 (the expected value of the lottery). The individual refuses; the expected utility from the gamble (the height at point C) is less than the utility of the certain $20,000 (the height of point D). **An individual who refuses any fair gamble is said to be risk-averse.**

This does not imply that risk-averse individuals will refuse *any* gamble. Suppose, for the same $20,000 entry price, the individual could play a lottery that had a .8 probability of winning $50,000. This is shown as point M in Figure 7-1. It has an expected value of $40,000, and we can see geometrically that the expected utility from the gamble (the .8 height of point M) exceeds the utility of the current position at D. Thus the risk-averse expected-utility maximizer would accept this gamble. Its attraction is that it has an expected value sufficiently greater than the entry price (unlike a fair gamble). This suggests, for example, why even financially conservative people may invest in the stock market.

The risk aversion illustrated above is a consequence of the concavity of the utility function we drew. A (strictly) concave function is one whose values lie above the straight line connecting any two of its points (it is hill-shaped). This also means that its slope is diminishing. A utility function has a diminishing slope only if the marginal utility of money or wealth is diminishing. Thus anyone with a diminishing marginal utility of wealth has a concave utility function and is risk-averse. The greater the degree of concavity of the utility function, the greater the risk aversion. (We will provide a measure of this shortly.) We illustrate in Figure 7-2 several different utility functions that vary in the degree of risk aversion ($OBDA$, $OHEA$).

Of course, it is possible that some individuals are not risk-averse. We also show in Figure 7-2 a utility function $OGFA$ characterized by increasing marginal utility of wealth. This individual evaluates the utility of the fair gamble (the height at point C) as greater than the utility of a certain $20,000 (the height at point G). In other words, this individual would accept the fair gamble of participating in the lottery for an entry price of $20,000. **An individual who prefers to accept any fair gamble is a risk lover.** Similarly, the individual with the straight-line utility function OCA (constant marginal utility of wealth) is indifferent to our proposal; **an individual who is indifferent to any fair gamble is risk-neutral.**

One way to measure the strength of risk aversion to a gamble is to look at the *pure risk cost*. To understand the measure, we use the concept of the *certain-wealth equivalent*. **The certain-wealth equivalent is the amount of certain wealth that provides utility equivalent to the risky situation.** Geometrically it is the wealth level at which the height of the utility function equals the height measuring expected utility. Then **the pure risk cost is defined as the difference between the expected wealth of a risky situation and its certain-wealth equivalent.** To illustrate, we look at Figure 7-2 in a different context.

Suppose that each individual owns $50,000 in jewelry that has a .6 probability of being stolen. Think of the origin of the horizontal axis as an unspecified amount of wealth from other sources; the horizontal axis now measures the additional wealth from jewelry and is

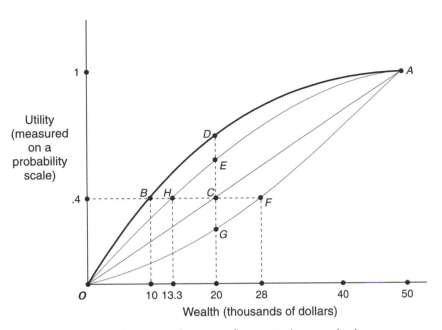

Figure 7-2. The curvature of the utility function reflects attitude toward risk.

dependent upon which state occurs (stolen or not stolen). On the vertical axis the utility level is measured; the scale is from 0 for the worst outcome (stolen) to 1 for the best outcome (not stolen) as before. Point *C* represents the expected wealth of $20,000 [= .4($50,000) + .6($0)] and the expected utility level of .4 [= .4(1) + .6(0)] of this risky situation; by design it is the same for each of the four different utility curves.

The certain-wealth equivalents for each individual are the wealth levels where their utility curves have a height of .4. These are different for each of the four utility functions. Consider first the individual with the utility curve *OHEA*. This person is indifferent to the risky situation with a $20,000 expected wealth (point *C*) and having a certain $13,300 (point *H*). Thus the pure risk cost is $6700 (= $20,000 expected value − $13,300 certain-value equivalent). That is, this individual will pay up to $6700 in terms of reduced expected value in order to avoid the risk.

Risk-averse persons will pay to reduce risk. The willingness to pay to avoid risk is a fundamental reason for the existence of insurance and other risk-reducing mechanisms that we will consider shortly. For example, this individual will pay up to $36,700 (the expected loss plus the pure risk cost) for full-coverage jewelry insurance; this ensures that the net wealth from jewelry (after insuring it) is $13,300 in both states of the world and thus eliminates all of the risk. If an insurance company can offer such insurance at or near the fair entry price of $30,000 (the expected loss), there will be room for a deal.

Recall that we stated earlier that the individual with the more concave utility function *OBDA* is more risk-averse. Now we can see that he or she evaluates the pure risk cost of the same risky situation at a greater amount than $6700; to be exact, $10,000 (= $20,000

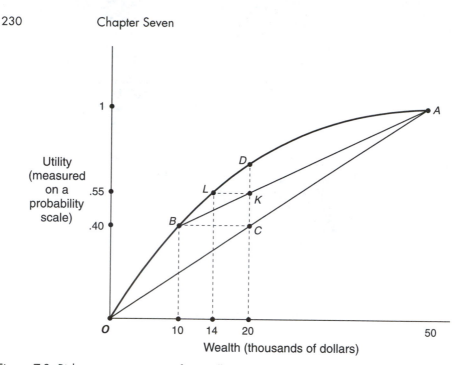

Figure 7-3. Risk-averse persons prefer smaller to bigger gambles.

expected wealth – $10,000 certain-wealth equivalent at point B). This person would be willing to pay up to $40,000 for full-coverage jewelry insurance. The risk-neutral person has no risk cost and will take no reduction in expected value in order to avoid the risky situation (i.e., is indifferent to purchasing insurance at the fair entry price of $30,000). The risk lover has a negative risk cost of $8000, since the certain-wealth equivalent (at point F) is $28,000. That is, because the latter enjoys the risk, the expected value would have to be increased by $8000 in order to persuade the individual to avoid the risk (the individual would decline insurance even at the fair entry price).

The above discussion shows that perceived risk cost is a function of risk preferences. Now we wish to illustrate the effect on one individual of varying the amount of risk. In Figure 7-3 we replicate the utility function $OBDA$ from Figure 7-2. Point C shows the expected utility and expected value from the jewelry as discussed above.

Let us contrast this with another situation, one in which only $40,000 of jewelry is at risk and the other $10,000 of wealth is safe. Thus, the individual will either end up at point B (the jewelry is stolen) or point A (not stolen). The straight line BA shows each possible combination of expected wealth (on the horizontal axis) and expected utility (on the vertical axis) that may result, depending on the probability of theft.[7]

Note that the line BA is above the line OA. This is because, in an important sense, the risk is lower in the new situation of BA: for any expected wealth the likelihood of ending

---

[7] Recall that both the expected value and the expected utility are weighted averages of their respective values at points B and A; the weights on each are the same and equal the probabilities of state B and state A.

up in positions "far" from it has been reduced (i.e., there is no chance wealth will end up at less than $10,000). Put differently, for any expected wealth the gamble represented by line *BA* is smaller than that of *OA*. *Two general implications for risk-averse individuals follow: (1) For any expected wealth (on the horizontal axis), the expected utility of a smaller gamble is greater than that of the larger gamble. (2) Similarly, for any expected wealth, a smaller gamble has a lower pure risk cost.*

Let us illustrate by assuming a specific probability of theft equal to .75, chosen to keep the expected value at $20,000 as in the prior situation. That is, the $E(V)$ of this new situation is

$$E(V) = .25(\$50,000) + .75(\$10,000)$$

$$= \$20,000$$

The expected utility can be calculated:

$$E(U) = .25U(\$50,000) + .75U(\$10,000)$$

$$= .25(1) + .75(.4)$$

$$= .55$$

This is shown as point K on line *BA*. The expected utility of the new situation (the height at point K) is greater than that of the initial situation (the height at point C), even though the expected value is the same. Furthermore, the risk cost of the smaller gamble is only *LK* or $6000, as compared with *BC*, or $10,000 for the larger gamble. This geometric illustration helps to clarify why, in our earlier examples of coin toss games with identical expected values but increasing stakes, individuals may become less inclined to play as the stakes become greater.[8]

It is often useful to be able to measure the level of risk in a way that does not depend on individual preferences (the pure risk cost does). There is no unique measure, and for any measure individuals need not respond to it similarly. Nevertheless, one common measure that goes a long way toward summarizing how dispersed the outcomes may be is the *variance*. **The variance Var(X) is defined as**

$$\text{Var}(X) = \sum_i \pi_i [X_i - E(V)]^2$$

where $i = 1, 2, \ldots, n$ possible states of the world, X_i is the outcome in the ith state and π_i its probability, and $E(V)$ is the expected value. For any given expected value, the variance is greater as the likelihood of ending up with an outcome "far" from the expected value increases. Furthermore, in the appendix we review a result that shows that the pure risk cost is approximately proportional to the variance.

To illustrate the calculation, the variance of our first jewelry example Var(1), when $50,000 is stolen with probability .6, is

$$\text{Var}(1) = .6(0 - \$20,000)^2 + .4(\$50,000 - \$20,000)^2 = \$600 \text{ million}$$

---

[8] Recall that risk-averse people will gamble if the gamble has a sufficiently high net positive expected value (i.e., is not fair).

The variance of the second example Var(2), when $40,000 is stolen with probability .75, is

$$\text{Var}(2) = .75(\$10,000 - \$20,000)^2 + .25(\$50,000 - \$20,000)^2 = \$300 \text{ million}$$

The variance of the second is lower than the first because it has greater probability of outcomes "closer" to the expected value.

Since the variance can get large, it is often convenient to report instead *the square root of the variance called the standard deviation*. In the above examples, the standard deviation is $24,495 of situation (1) and $17,320 of situation (2). In many situations with a large number of different possible outcomes distributed around the expected value, a useful rule of thumb is that there is approximately a 90 percent chance that the actual outcome will lie within two standard deviations of the expected value.[9]

In actual risky situations with many possible states of the world and different sources of risk, other measures may be used to convey the degree of riskiness. Corporate bonds, for example, are "letter graded" by Moody and Standard & Poor for their differing reliabilities in terms of making the payments promised to bondholders (interest and return of principal). In early 2000, for example, a bond terminating in 2008 and rated A+ by Standard & Poor had an annual yield to maturity of 7.24 percent, but a bond of similar maturity with the lower rating of BBB– was yielding 7.70 percent. The higher yield is the compensation for holding the riskier bond.

During the twentieth century, the average annual rate of return on stocks exceeded that of bonds by 5–6 percent. Are people who invest in bonds simply foolish? Not necessarily, because the risk associated with investing in bonds is generally lower. Typically, stock prices fluctuate much more than bond prices. The longer the holding period, the more likely the realized return on stocks will exceed that of bonds (e.g., over any 10 years, the U.S. stock market virtually always outperforms the bond market). But within shorter periods (e.g., 2 years or less), stocks performance may be much worse than that of bonds. Even though both investments are risky, within any interval the realized value of the bond investment is likely to be closer to its expected value than that of the stock. The higher average rate of return with stocks is the compensation for holding the riskier asset. In a later section we consider further the size of this differential. For now, we note that potential stock investors look at measures such as the standard deviation, Beta coefficient, and Sharpe ratio to gauge the magnitude of any individual stock's risk.[10]

As we have seen, the expected utility model allows for a diversity of risk preferences. But the above evidence, of higher rates of return for holding riskier assets, suggests that *empirically, risk-averse behavior is predominant*. Probably the most important evidence of

---

[9] This rule of thumb applies to situations that can be approximated statistically by the normal distribution.

[10] Among stock investments, the future price of stock for some companies may be much more volatile or uncertain than others (e.g., a new biotechnology company as opposed to a long-established water utility). The Beta measure compares a stock's price fluctuations relative to those of the Standard & Poor index of 500 stocks. The Sharpe ratio compares a stock's return given its standard deviation to that of a nearly riskless asset such as a 3-month U.S. Treasury bill. An introduction to financial investing, the importance of risk, and some of the measures used to assess it are contained in Burton G. Malkiel, *A Random Walk Down Wall Street: Including a Life-Cycle Guide to Personal Investing*, 6th Ed. (New York: W. W. Norton & Company, 1996).

risk aversion is that virtually all individuals diversify their portfolios. That is, wealth is not stored all in one asset but is spread among various stocks, bonds, real estate, savings accounts, pension funds, and other assets. We show in the following section that such diversification has the primary purpose of reducing risk. An individual with risk-neutral or risk-loving preferences would not behave in this manner.

As additional evidence, when individuals bear significant risk as a consequence of such factors as home ownership and automobile driving, they will usually offer others more than a fair price to bear the risk for them. Almost all insurance purchases are evidence of risk-averse behavior of this type, since the premiums are at least as great as the expected payout.[11] For example, most individuals who drive purchase more than the minimum insurance required by state regulations.

If risk aversion is so predominant, how do we explain the commonly observed willingness of individuals to participate in risky situations in which the odds are against them (i.e., the net expected value is negative)? For example, many people seem to enjoy an evening in Las Vegas or Atlantic City or a day at the race track. Apart from professional gamblers, this behavior is probably best understood for its direct consumption value. That is, people may receive utility directly from the process of gambling similarly to the consumption of any other good or service. The primary motivation for participation need not be the expected indirect utility from the wealth change associated with gambling.

Some individuals may engage in unfair gambles because of limited preference for risk, even though they are primarily risk-averse. That is, it is possible to be risk-averse over some range of wealth while simultaneously being a risk lover over another range. In Figure 7-4a we illustrate one such possibility.[12]

An individual is currently at a wealth level of $50,000. However, this wealth includes a $25,000 home that has some possibility of being accidentally destroyed by fire or natural disaster. The individual also has a chance to invest $2000 in a new "dot-com" company that, if successful, will return $10,000. The preferences indicated by the utility function in Figure 7-4a suggest that the individual is risk-averse concerning the bulk of wealth already in his or her possession but is willing to gamble small amounts "against the odds" if the prospects of wealth gains are large enough. As drawn, the individual will purchase actuarially fair insurance and may invest in the "dot-com" company even if the investment is less than a fair gamble.[13]

---

[11] We do not count employer-provided insurance as evidence of risk aversion. Private medical and dental insurance, when provided through an employer, is a form of nontaxable income. Roughly speaking, $50 of medical insurance provided in this way yields $50 of benefits to the individual in terms of expected medical services (ignoring risk costs). If the $50 is given to the individual as a taxable income, after taxes there will be only $25 to $40 (depending on the individual's tax bracket) left for consumption purposes. Thus, the favorable tax treatment can result in expected medical care benefits (apart from risk reduction) that exceed the individual's cost of the insurance (in terms of foregone consumption of other things).

[12] This was first suggested in M. Friedman and L. Savage, "The Utility Analysis of Choices Involving Risk," *Journal of Political Economy, 56,* August 1948, pp. 279–304.

[13] We have not specified the probability of success of the "dot.com" company. If it is a fair gamble, the individual will clearly invest because the expected utility exceeds the current utility. Therefore, the investment can be

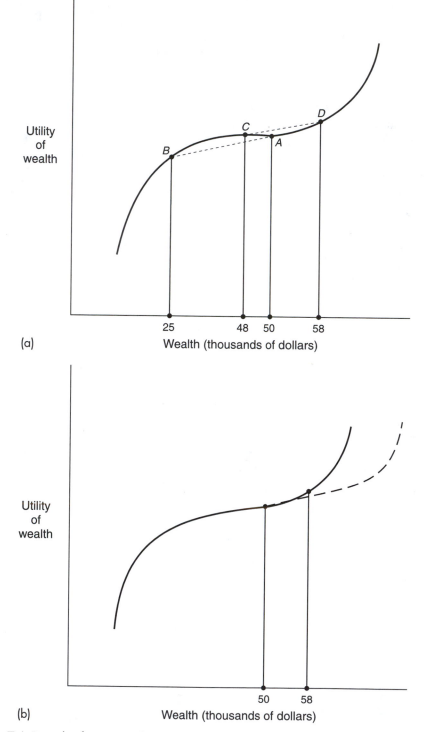

(a)

Wealth (thousands of dollars)

(b)

Wealth (thousands of dollars)

Figure 7-4. Do utility functions adapt to different situations? (a) An individual may both insure and accept unfair gambles. (b) An individual's utility function adapts to new wealth.

Although the shape of the utility function in Figure 7-4a does seem to explain some observed behavior, it raises other questions. In particular, suppose the "dot-com" investment wins in the above example and the individual now has a wealth of $58,000. To remain consistent with the behavioral idea of preserving wealth already possessed, the individual's utility function now has to shift to something like that illustrated by the dashed extension in Figure 7-4b. In most economic theory we typically assume that the utility function is fixed. But this example suggests that, for some situations, it may be important to consider the possibility of an *adaptive* utility function. (That is, the utility function depends on which state occurs.)

The above discussion is intended to suggest that, on balance, risk in our society is considered a social cost and not a social benefit. Thus, when public policy alternatives imply differing amounts of risk, those with more risk are disfavored unless other factors (e.g., sufficiently higher expected values) work in their favor. In the optional section later on in this chapter, we present an empirical method used to assess the risk costs of a change in policy (involving health insurance).

Risk Control and Risk-Shifting Mechanisms

Recognizing that risk is generally considered costly, we consider in this section mechanisms used to affect its costs. Two fundamental mechanisms used to reduce risk costs are risk-pooling and risk-spreading. We discuss them below and then turn to a discussion of public policies that affect risk costs.

Risk-Pooling and Risk-Spreading

Risk-pooling occurs when a group of individuals, each facing a risk that is independent of the risks faced by the others, agree to share any losses (or gains) among themselves. We develop the idea of risk-pooling informally here and provide more detail in the chapter's appendix. Imagine that each of many households has $5000 worth of property that is vulnerable to theft. Furthermore, suppose that each independently faces a .2 probability that the property will be stolen.[14] Let us consider what happens if an insurance company offers each household full-coverage insurance at the fair entry price of $1000, called an actuarially fair premium in the insurance industry. (That is, the premium equals the expected loss.) Unlike each household, the insurance company does not care whose property is stolen; its concern is that the total premiums it collects will (at least) cover the total cost of replacing all the property that is stolen.

---

at least slightly less than fair and the individual will still invest. However, the probability of success may be so low that the expected utility falls below the current level, and then the individual will not invest despite the preference for risk.

[14] Independence implies that the probability of theft in one household is unrelated to whether theft has occurred in any other household.

The statistical *law of large numbers* implies that, as the number of identical but independent random events increases, the likelihood that the actual *average* result will be close to the expected result increases. This is the same principle that applies to coin flips: The larger the number of flips, the more likely it is that the total proportion of heads will be close to $\frac{1}{2}$. For the insurance company it becomes a virtual certainty that approximately 20 percent of the insured households will have claims and that therefore it will face total claims approximately equal to the total premiums collected. Thus *by shifting the risk to the insurance company, where it is pooled, the risk cost dissipates.* As long as the pool is large enough, the risk cost to the insurance company becomes negligible and premiums equal to expected losses will be sufficient to cover the claims.

Let us give a simple example to illustrate how risk-pooling reduces risk costs. Suppose we consider two identical risk-averse individuals. Each has $50,000 in wealth, $5000 of which is subject to theft; each independently faces a probability of theft equal to .2. Initially, the two bear the risks independently, or they *self-insure*. There are only two possible outcomes: $50,000 with probability .8, and $45,000 with probability .2. The expected wealth of each is $49,000 [= .2($45,000) + .8($50,000].

Now suppose that these two individuals agree to pool their risk, so that any losses from theft will be evenly divided between them. Then there are three possible outcomes or states:

1. Neither individual has a loss from theft ($W = \$50,000$).
2. Both individuals have losses from theft ($W = \$45,000$).
3. One individual has a loss and the other does not ($W = \$47,500$).

Under this simple pooling arrangement, the only way they end up with $45,000 each is if both suffer theft losses. However, the probability of this occurring is only .04 = .2(.2). By contrast, this probability is .2 with self-insurance. Of course they are also less likely to end up with $50,000 each, since this only happens when neither suffers a theft loss. The probability of neither having a loss is .64 = .8(.8); this contrasts with the .8 chance under self-insurance. The remaining possible outcome, that each ends up with $47,500, occurs with .32 probability (the sum of probabilities for the three outcomes must equal 1).

As a consequence of this pooling arrangement, the probabilities of the extreme outcomes decline while the probability of an outcome in the middle increases. The expected wealth, however, remains the same:

$$E(W) = .64(\$50,000) + .04(\$45,000) + .32(\$47,500)$$

$$= \$49,000$$

With expected wealth the same and with the likelihood of ending up close to it greater, the risk is reduced. The standard deviation, for example, is reduced from $2966 under self-insurance to only $1414 with the two-person pool.[15] This illustrates how risk-pooling can reduce risk without affecting expected value.

---

[15] To the nearest dollar, $2966 is the square root of the variance of $8.8 million = $.8(50,000 - 49,000)^2 + .2(45,000 - 49,000)^2$, and $1414 is the square root of $2 million = $.64(50,000 - 49,000)^2 + .32(47,500 - 49,000)^2 + .04(45,000 - 49,000)^2$.

If we found more individuals to join this pool, we could reduce the risk costs even further. As the pool expands, the likelihood of outcomes near the expected value increases while the likelihood of extreme outcomes decreases. This is precisely the concept that underlies insurance: a large pool of people who agree to divide any losses among themselves. The insurance company in this concept is the intermediary: It organizes the pool, and it incurs the transaction costs of keeping track of membership and losses of insured property and making the necessary monetary transfers. A relatively simple way to do all this is to collect the expected loss plus a prorated share of the transaction costs from each member at the start and then pay out the losses as they arise. As the number of people in the pool gets large, the risk cost and often the transaction costs (both prorated) become smaller and in the limit may be negligible. Then the premium approaches the actuarially fair level (i.e., the expected loss).

When insurance is available at an actuarially fair premium, risk-averse individuals will of course purchase it. But for some items it may be that the transaction costs of operating the pool do not become negligible. Then the premium charged will be significantly higher than the expected loss to individuals, and many, depending on their degrees of risk aversion, will self-insure.

For example, low-cost items are rarely insured for the reason that the transaction costs of insuring them are large relative to the expected loss. Factors included in the transaction costs include determining the value of an item and the probability of its loss, verifying that an actual loss has occurred, and making sure that the loss did not arise through the negligence of the owner or someone else who might be held responsible. An interesting example of high transaction costs involves automobile insurance. When an accident involving more than one car occurs, substantial legal expenses are often incurred to determine if one party is at fault. (If there were no legal "fault," all premiums might be lower.)[16]

Another reason why risk-averse individuals may self-insure is government tax policy. Uninsured casualty and theft losses (above a minimum) are deductible when calculated for federal income tax purposes, provided the taxpayer elects to itemize rather than take the standard deduction. If an individual's marginal tax bracket is 31 percent, a $1 deductible loss from theft reduces the tax bill by $0.31. With private insurance, the $1.00 is recovered, but the $0.31 in tax savings is lost. Thus the next expected payoff from insurance is only $0.69, which is substantially below the $1 fair premium. In other words, government insurance, with benefits that increase in proportion to income, encourages individuals to self-insure.

We will explore other aspects of insurance later in the chapter. Now, however, let us return to the main point: to understand how risk-pooling and risk-spreading reduce risk costs. We have shown that risk-pooling is the essence of insurance. But it is just as important to recognize that the same principle operates in other institutional forms. For example,

---

[16] For an interesting theoretical analysis of this see Guido Calabresi, *The Cost of Accidents: A Legal and Economic Analysis* (New Haven, Conn.: Yale University Press, 1970). Some of the empirical issues and practical difficulties with the idea are explained in R. Cooter and T. Ulen, *Law and Economics* (Glenview, Ill.: Scott, Foresman and Company, 1988), pp. 463–472.

risk-pooling is a factor when firms in unrelated businesses merge to become conglomerates. By pooling the independent risks that each firm takes, the likelihood that the average return on investments will be close to the expected return is greater. This has the effect of lowering the cost to the firm of obtaining investment funds (because it is "safer"). Of course, this advantage must be weighed against the difficulty of managing unrelated business ventures.

The general principle of diversification of assets can be seen as an example of risk-pooling. That is, a portfolio of diverse investments that an individual holds is a pool much like the pool of theft insurance policies that an insurance company holds. Compare the expected utility of a risk-averse individual under two alternative arrangements: one in which the individual invests in one firm and the other in which the individual invests the same total amount spread equally among ten *different* firms facing similar but *independent* risks. (Note that firms in the same industry would not fully meet this criterion. While the success or failure of each is independent to some degree, presumably some of the uncertainty is due to factors that affect the industry as a whole.)

The same phenomenon that we described above applies here. It is like comparing ten coin flips each with the same relatively small bet against one flip (of the same coin) with stakes ten times greater. The expected value of both situations is the same (and for stock investments, presumably positive). However, the probability that the realized outcome will be close to the expected value increases with the number of flips (the standard deviation declines), and thus the risk is reduced. Any risk-averse investor will prefer smaller, more numerous independent investments of total expected value equal to that of one larger investment. A numerical example is given in the appendix.

At this point let us illustrate the advantage of risk-spreading. **Risk-spreading occurs when different individuals share the returns from one risky situation.** An obvious example of this is the diversification of firm ownership through the stock market. Through the issuance of common stock a single firm can allow many individuals to bear only a small portion of the total risk, and the sum of the risk cost that each owner faces is considerably lower than if there were a sole owner. This reduction in total risk cost is the gain from risk-spreading.

The easiest way to see the risk-spreading advantage is to make use of the result that we mentioned earlier (and that is reviewed in the appendix): the risk cost is approximately proportional to the variance. We will show that risk-spreading reduces the variance more than proportionately, and thus reduces the risk cost.

Suppose that one large investment is divided into ten equal-sized smaller investments. The expected value is the same either way. Now imagine that there are ten individuals with identical risk-averse preferences, each holding one of the small investments. If X_i represents the ith outcome of the large investment, then each of the ten individuals would receive $X_i/10$ in state i. The variance that each experiences is then

$$\text{Var}(X/10) = \sum \pi_i [E(X_i/10) - X_i/10]^2$$

Factoring out the $\frac{1}{10}$, this becomes

$$= (1/10)^2 \sum \pi_i [E(X_i) - X_i]^2 = (1/100)\text{Var}(X)$$

That is, when spread each individual receives $\frac{1}{10}$ of the expected value but only $\frac{1}{100}$ of the original variance—far less than a proportionate reduction of $\frac{1}{10}$. Since the risk cost is approximately proportional to the variance, the risk cost of the small investment is substantially less than $\frac{1}{10}$ that of the original one-owner investment. Put differently, ten times the sum of the spread investment's risk cost is significantly less than the one-owner risk cost. Or put still differently, the group of ten investors would be willing to pay more than any single one of them to own the one risky investment.

The risk-spreading strategy works as a consequence of diminishing marginal utility of wealth. We have seen that a risk-averse individual always prefers smaller gambles if expected value is held constant. For example, the risk-averse person prefers a fair coin flip with $1 at stake to the same coin flip with $2 at stake. The larger gamble represents not only a larger total but also a larger marginal risk cost. The expected utility gain from winning the second dollar is less than that from winning the first, and the expected utility loss from losing a second dollar exceeds that of losing the first—simply because of the diminishing marginal utility of wealth. Thus, the marginal risk cost increases as the stakes increase. Two similar individuals each bearing half the risk from one risky event have lower total risk costs than one individual facing the risk alone.

Another institution that facilitates risk-spreading is the futures market. For example, a crop grower may not wish to bear the full risk of planting a crop now to receive an uncertain return when it ripens next year. In the futures market the farmer can sell part of the future crop at a price specified now. Thus the crop grower, in selling now, gives up the possible gains and losses if next year's price turns out to be different. In return, certainty of income is achieved by the sale of the futures contract.

All these examples of insurance, futures contracts, and stock shares can be thought of as *contingent commodities: those whose values depend upon which state of the world occurs.* The theft insurance contract pays nothing if the state turns out to be no theft and pays the value of the insured article if there is theft. The buyer of crop futures faces a loss if next year's price turns out to be low and a gain if it is high. A share of common stock can be thought of as a claim on future value of the firm, and its value depends on which states of profitability arise.[17]

In theory, markets for a wide variety of contingent commodities are required to ensure optimal resource allocation in the presence of uncertainty. Yet we actually have very few of those markets developed. I might like to insure the value of my income against inflation, but there are as yet no futures contracts based on the level of the consumer price index. There are many reasons why such markets have not developed, but one reason relevant to policy analysis is that collective action may be required to create them, and we simply have not thought enough about how to do it. However, because uncertainty is so pervasive and costly, it is worth a great deal of time and effort to create efficient mechanisms for reducing risk costs.

---

[17] A nice survey of uncertainty and contingent commodities is contained in J. Hirshleifer and J. Riles, *The Analytics of Uncertainty and Information* (Cambridge: Cambridge University Press, 1992).

Policy Aspects of Risk-Shifting and Risk Control

In this section we give some brief examples of policies that have important effects on risk costs and their distribution. To do so, it is useful first to mention one important dimension of the relation between risk and resource allocation that we have so far ignored: Risk costs affect the amount of resources allocated to risk-taking situations.

In the pooling and spreading illustrations we accepted the total amount of risk as a given: The risk-creating events would be undertaken regardless of the risk-bearing arrangements. That is, the jewelry and other "unsafe" property would be bought whether or not insurance was available, and the risky high-technology firm would operate whether or not it was owned by a partnership. Those simplifying assumptions were made in order to emphasize this point: The risk costs of random events are not inherently determined by the events themselves; they depend importantly on the institutional arrangements that allow the risks to be moved from one economic agent to another. To be efficient, risks should be allocated in order to minimize their costs; otherwise, there will be room for deals like the ones illustrated. Institutions such as insurance and the stock market serve to reduce the risk costs from the initial allocation by allowing them to be pooled and spread.

However, another important aspect of risk-cost-reducing mechanisms is that they increase resource allocation to the risk-creating events. If no theft insurance were available, there would be less demand at any given prices for goods subject to theft. If firms were not allowed to spread their risks through the issuance of stock, the size of firms might be uneconomically restricted (e.g., that might prevent taking advantage of certain economies of scale). If people cannot insure against inflation, they will allocate fewer resources to activities whose value depends upon it (most notably investment).

The policy examples mentioned below are illustrative of other institutional ways in which risk costs are affected. These policies, like the pooling and spreading mechanisms, can have important effects on resource allocation. We note some of the effects, but our primary emphasis continues to be on increasing awareness of social mechanisms used to respond to risk.

An interesting risk-shifting mechanism created through public policy is *limited corporate liability*. That is, a corporation may be held liable only for amounts up to the net worth of the assets it owns. The assets of the corporation's owners, the shareholders, are not at risk. This limitation does not apply to unincorporated businesses, for example, a partner in an unincorporated business could be forced to sell his or her home to pay business debts. The limit on liability provides a strong incentive for firms to incorporate.

By limiting the liability of firm owners, part of the burden of the risks taken by the firm is shifted to others. In particular circumstances this may foster or hinder the efficient allocation of resources. For example, it may encourage new product development that has positive expected return but high attendant risk, depending on sales. Socially, such projects are desirable: Even though some may not work out, the average returns are positive and the aggregate risk from many such projects is negligible from the social point of view. However, those with the new idea may not think it worth their time if the profits must be spread through increased selling of stock. Limited liability combined with debt-financing (borrowing) may provide the right mixture of expected private return and risk to make the undertaking privately desirable.

On the other hand, liability that is too limited may encourage excessive risk-taking. Suppose a firm considers taking a risk, such as building a nuclear reactor, that may have catastrophic consequences for others. Decisions of that kind are made in light of the expected benefits and costs to the firm. The firm may know that there is some nontrivial probability of a catastrophic accident, but in that event it cannot be held liable for more than its own assets. Thus, the expected loss in the firm's calculation is less than the actual expected social loss, and the firm may cheerfully undertake risks that have negative expected social returns.[18] This will be relevant to our discussion later in the chapter of the savings and loan crisis of the 1980s.

In addition to risk-shifting mechanisms, risk creation can be and often is regulated through a variety of other controls. To take one simple example, legalized gambling on horse races is so designed that there is never any risk in the aggregate. Only individual bettors take risks. The track keeps a fixed percentage of the total funds bet and distributes the balance to the winning bettors in accordance with standard formulas. Thus there is no risk to the track of betting losses.[19] Similarly, the public policy of raising revenues through creating and selling risk in the form of state lottery systems is another example. These systems, which have negative expected value of about 50 cents per dollar, depend for their sales upon the less educated members of the public who are the primary buyers of lottery tickets.[20]

Another form of aggregate risk control that involves public policy concerns crime and *deterrence.* In our earlier example of theft insurance we took the probability of theft as given exogenously. But it may well be that the resources allocated to criminal justice activities in any area have an influence on the probability of theft. That is, the degree of street lighting, the frequency of police patrol, and the extent of citizen cooperation (as in the prompt reporting of suspected crimes) may influence the likelihood that potential thieves will actually attempt thefts.[21]

As mentioned in the chapter introduction, individuals may influence the probability of their own victimization by decisions such as to install burglar alarms to protect households

[18] This problem in this example is compounded by the Price-Anderson Act, which further limits the liability from nuclear reactor accidents. See J. Dubin and G. Rothwell, "Safety at Nuclear Power Plants: Economic Incentives under the Price-Anderson Act and State Regulatory Commissions," *Social Science Journal, 26,* No. 3, July 1989, pp. 303–311.

[19] This is a slight exaggeration. In most states the tracks are required to make payoffs of at least $0.05 on each winning $1.00. Occasionally, when a heavy favorite wins, there are not enough losing dollars to make the minimum payment and the track owners must make up the difference. That does not happen very often, however.

[20] See Charles Clotfelter and Philip J. Cook, "On the Economics of State Lotteries," *Journal of Economic Perspectives, 4,* No. 4, Autumn 1990, pp. 105–119.

[21] See, for example, D. Black and D. Nagin, "Do Right-to-Carry Laws Deter Violent Crime?," *Journal of Legal Studies, 27,* No. 1, January 1998, pp. 209–219; Hope Corman and H. Naci Mocan, "A Time-Series Analysis of Crime, Deterrence, and Drug Abuse in New York City," *American Economic Review, 90,* No. 3, June 2000, pp. 584–604; and H. Tauchen, A. Witte, and H. Griesinger, "Criminal Deterrence: Revisiting the Issue with a Birth Cohort," *Review of Economics and Statistics, 76,* No. 3, August 1994, pp. 399–412.

and to take taxis rather than walk to reduce exposure to street assault. Thus the decisions about how best to reduce risks are interrelated. That is, the least-cost way of achieving a given reduction in risk will typically involve a combination of public expenditure, private protective expenditure, and insurance.[22] In the example of health insurance to be presented, we will analyze some of the problems that arise from such interrelations.

Another policy form of risk control is *quality certification.* Imagine, for example, the medical care profession without licensing requirements. Anyone who wanted to be a doctor would simply hang out a shingle and offer medical services. An individual seeking services would then be very uncertain about the quality of care that might be received. Society imposes licensing requirements that require a demonstration of at least some medical training. That reduces the consumer's uncertainty in a particular way. It leaves some uncertainty about the quality of the care received, but it probably does have the effect of raising the average level of care by eliminating those who would be least competent to provide it.

Whether such licensing requirements have benefits greater than costs is another issue. Milton Friedman argues that they are inefficient.[23] Licensing requirements create a barrier to entry, which gives the suppliers of service some monopoly power and leads to higher prices and lower quantities than in an unregulated market. He further argues that competitive forces in an unregulated market would drive out the least competent suppliers, so that only competent ones would continue to have patients seeking their services.

Kenneth Arrow, on the other hand, suggests that the uncertainty costs of an unregulated regime may be great.[24] Because the primary method of consumer learning about quality is trial and error and because each consumer purchases medical services infrequently and often for different reasons each time, the competitive mechanism may be a very imperfect safeguard. Thus, substantial incompetence could persist, which would turn each decision to seek medical services into a risky lottery from the uninformed consumer's perspective.

These theoretical arguments do not resolve what is essentially an empirical question: whether the benefits of the reduction of uncertainty outweigh the costs of the supply restrictions.[25] Nor does actual policy debate about the medical care industry consider this question in such a broad form. The licensing issues that do receive serious consideration are more narrowly defined. For example, should licenses be required for the performance of specific kinds of surgery? Or should the medical knowledge of licensed doctors be periodically reexamined to ensure that physicians keep their knowledge current? Or should certain kinds of minor medical treatments be delicensed, or relicensed, to include paramedics and nurses as well as physicians?

These same issues can be raised with respect to all occupational licensure requirements: automobile mechanics, real estate agents, dentists, and teachers. They can also be applied

---

[22] This is discussed generally in I. Ehrlich and G. Becker, "Market Insurance, Self-Insurance, and Self-Protection," *Journal of Political Economy, 80,* No. 4, July/August 1972, pp. 623–648.

[23] See M. Friedman, *Capitalism and Freedom* (Chicago: University of Chicago Press, 1962), Chapter IX, pp. 137–160.

[24] See Arrow, *Essays in the Theory of Risk-Bearing,* Chapter 8.

[25] For an example of an empirical study of the issue, see W. D. White, "The Impact of Occupational Licensure of Clinical Laboratory Personnel," *Journal of Human Resources, 13,* No. 1, Spring 1978, pp. 91–102.

to safety requirements for products such as paint and microwave ovens. In each case it is not sufficient to analyze the number of substandard transactions that occur. One must remember to consider, for example, the pure risk costs that consumers bear because of the possibility of undesirable outcomes.[26] The chapter's appendix considers some methods for placing dollar values on the risk cost.

The above is a point worth emphasizing because ignoring it is a common error. Standards might raise the expected value of a service in a clear way. For example, suppose that certain automobile safety standards reduce automobile accidents. The quantitative reduction in accidents is a readily comprehended benefit, but the standard achieves far more: For *all* of us who drive, the pure risk cost of driving has been reduced. This latter benefit can be substantial.

Another issue to consider generally is that alternative policies can vary greatly in the extent of their coverage. A specific service can be restricted by licensure to a broad or narrow range of suppliers. Certification can be used as an alternative to licensure; it need not be required to supply the service (e.g., an accountant need not be a certified public accountant).

To get a better understanding of the analytic issues involved in considering policies such as these, we must broaden our own understanding about individual behavior under uncertainty. Until now, we have simply examined the idea that individuals behave so as to maximize expected utility; however, the extent to which actual behavior may be approximated by this model is disputed.

Alternative Models of Individual Behavior under Uncertainty

The Slumlord's Dilemma and Strategic Behavior

Most of the examples of uncertainty that we have mentioned so far are of the type Knight called "risky," that is, the probabilities of the different possible states of the world are known. However, in many uncertain situations that arise the probabilities are not known. One class of these situations may be referred to as *strategic games*, such as chess playing or even nuclear weapons strategies. Each of the players in the game chooses some strategy from the set of all possible strategies in the hope of achieving a desired outcome. The term "player" is roughly synonymous to "economic agent," in that the player may be an individual, a firm, a governmental unit, or any other decision-making entity. In the nuclear weapons case, countries are viewed as one-minded "persons" who attempt to deter nuclear attacks by choosing defensive capabilities that guarantee the attacker's destruction. Game theory is the scholarly attempt to understand strategic games.[27]

---

[26] This is sometimes referred to as the *ex ante, ex post* distinction. *Ex post* one can see the outcomes, but the risk is gone by that time. Social costs include the *ex ante* risk costs.

[27] For classic readings on game theory and strategic reasoning, see R. D. Luce and H. Raiffa, *Games and Decisions* (New York: John Wiley & Sons, Inc., 1957), and Thomas C. Schelling, *The Strategy of Conflict* (Cambridge: Harvard University Press, 1960). Modern treatments include Robert Gibbons, *Game Theory for Applied Economists* (Princeton, N.J.: Princeton University Press, 1992), and H. Scott Bierman and Luis Fernandez, *Game Theory with Economic Applications* (Reading, Mass.: Addison-Wesley Publishing Company, Inc., 1993).

		Slumlady Sally	
		Invest	Do not invest
Slumlord Larry	Invest	($5,000,$5,000)	(−$4,000,$6,000)
	Do not invest	($6,000,−$4,000)	($0,$0)

Figure 7-5. The Slumlord's Dilemma: The numbers ($A, $B) are net profits to Larry and Sally, respectively.

An interesting game of this type is known as the *Slumlord's Dilemma*.[28] Imagine that two slum owners, Slumlady Sally and Slumlord Larry, have adjacent tenements. Each owner knows the following: If both invest in improving their tenements, they will have the nicest low-rent apartments in the city and will earn high returns on their investments (say an extra profit of $5000 each). On the other hand, if, say, Slumlord Larry invests but Slumlady Sally does not, then Larry will lose his shirt but Sally will make out like a bandit.

The latter may happen because of externalities. That is, Larry will realize only a slight increase in the demand for his apartments because of a negative externality: His apartments are right next door to a slum. The increased rent is more than offset by the renovation costs, and Larry finds his net profit decreased by $4000. But Sally now finds her apartments in much greater demand, without having invested a penny, because of an external benefit: They are now in a nice neighborhood. Her profits go up by $6000. The opposite would be true if Sally were the only one to invest.

The situation is like that shown in the matrix in Figure 7-5. The question is, what will they do? Slumlord Larry might reason as follows: "If Sally invests, then I am better off not to invest ($6000 > $5000). If Sally does not invest, then I am better off not to invest ($0 > −$4000). Since I am better off not to invest in either case, I will not invest." Thus for Larry, not investing is a **dominant strategy: It gives the best outcome in each possible state of the world.** Sally goes through the same reasoning. She considers what will make her best off, and she concludes that the strategy of not investing is dominant for her.

Therefore, Sally and Larry end up with no change in profits, but they have obviously missed a golden opportunity to increase their profits by $5000 each. Why does this happen? Why do they not simply cooperate with each other and both invest?

---

[28] This version of the Prisoner's Dilemma was first proposed by O. Davis and A. Whinston, "Externalities, Welfare, and the Theory of Games," *Journal of Political Economy, 70,* June 1962, pp. 241–262.

The problem is that each owner has an incentive to be misleading, and the other knows it. If you were considering investing, say, $10,000 in renovating an urban slum but your success depended on what happened next door, would you trust that slumlord? That is, each player is *uncertain* about whether the other will really invest even if each agrees to do so. Imagine a more realistic example involving ten to twenty tenements owned by different individuals in which success depends on each owner making the investment. The inability to trust one another can lead to the uneconomic perpetuation of slums.

How can this problem be solved? Like all problems that arise from external effects, the solution involves internalizing the effects in some way. But how can the uncertainty owing to lack of trust be overcome? If there were only one owner of the adjacent tenements, then it is clear that the investment would be made. It is possible that one of the two original owners could be persuaded to sell to the other (there is, of course, room for such a deal). However, the more owners that must be coordinated, the smaller the likelihood that one owner will be able to buy out all the others. In these cases the government may wish to exercise its power of eminent domain and buy up all of the property. Then it can redevelop the property as a whole either itself or by selling it to a developer who will do so. The process is more commonly referred to as *urban renewal.*

Note that, in this game, no one is maximizing expected utility. No player knows the probability of each outcome. The analogous situation can be seen to arise in many different circumstances. When the game was first described, it was referred to as the *Prisoner's Dilemma.* A sheriff arrests two suspects of a crime, separates them, and urges each to confess. Each prisoner has a choice of two strategies: confess or do not confess. If neither confesses, each will get off with a light sentence for a minor offense. If both confess, each will get a medium-length sentence. But if one confesses and the other does not, the one who confesses will be let off on probation and the other will be sent away for life. Not trusting each other, each suspect is led by these incentives to confess.

This game is also thought to have some application in the important area of international trade policy. The most conventional economic analysis strongly supports the efficiency of free trade (based on logic quite analogous to that of allowing free trade among individual consumers in an economy). However, almost all countries make fairly extensive use of protective tariffs and export subsidies, and thus do not have free trade. Why? There may be many reasons of course, such as the political strength of a protected industry in one country (a good candidate particularly when the losses to that country's consumers outweigh the gains to its producers). But here we focus on an explanation that is rational in the sense of trying to achieve net benefits for the country.

Assume that the free trade solution maximizes net benefits in the world. If one (and only one) country adopts an import tariff (or an export subsidy), normally its consumers will lose but its producers and taxpayers will gain. In some circumstances, the gains will outweigh the losses and the country as a whole will be better off. However, other countries are harmed by the import tariff, and they may reduce their losses by imposing retaliatory tariffs of their own. The situation can easily be that of the Slumlord's Dilemma: no tariffs producing the highest welfare for all, but with individual countries having incentive for tariff adoption

		State A	State B
Larry	Invest	$5,000	−$1,000
	Do not invest	$2,000	$0

Figure 7-6. Larry's strategy depends on whether nature or a person chooses state A or state B.

and a net result of lower welfare for each country. Such a situation would of course provide a strong rationale for cooperative agreements to reduce or eliminate tariffs, such as the General Agreement on Tariffs and Trade (GATT).[29]

As a last example of this game consider what happens when a group of people go to a restaurant and agree in advance to divide the bill evenly. Then all participants have incentives to order more expensive meals than if each paid for his or her own. You may order Chateaubriand, since your share of the bill will go up by only a fraction of the cost of the expensive steak. Furthermore, your bill is going to be big anyway, because you have no control over the costs that will arise from the orders of the others. Thus the ordering strategy of choosing expensive dishes dominates the strategy of ordering normally, and the whole group ends up with a feast and a bill that nobody except the restaurant owner thinks is worth it.[30] We will see shortly that this identical dilemma is created by health insurance coverage and poses one of the most serious policy problems in the provision of health care.

To highlight the differences between games against persons and those against "nature," we assume a new set of possible outcomes for Larry in Figure 7-6. In a moment, we will discuss the "opponent." But first let us point out that Larry no longer has a dominant strategy. He is better off investing if state A occurs and not investing if state B occurs.

Consider how Larry might reason if state A or state B is to be consciously chosen by another person, the payoffs to the other person are identical with those to Larry, but the two people are not allowed to communicate.[31] Reasoning strategically, Larry will realize

---

[29] This example is a very simple one, and actual game-theoretic analysis of trade strategies and their implications is an important research area. See, for example, Frederick W. Mayer, "Domestic Politics and the Strategy of International Trade," *Journal of Policy Analysis and Management*, 10, No. 2, Spring 1991, pp. 222–246, and more generally Paul Krugman and Alasdair Smith, eds., *Empirical Studies of Strategic Trade Policy* (Chicago: University of Chicago Press, 1994).

[30] Not all people that agree to such bill-splitting think the results are suboptimal. Some may think the fun of the process is worth it; others may have a group relationship in which trust keeps all ordering normally. But the beauty of the example lies in recognizing the pressure that comes from the changed incentives and knowing full well that many people do become victims of this dilemma.

[31] This may occur when Larry and the other person each represent one of two firms in an oligopoly market and they are prevented by law from conspiring to act jointly as a monopolist would.

that the *other* person has a dominant strategy: State A is superior to state B no matter which strategy Larry chooses. The other person will choose A, and therefore Larry will decide to invest.[32]

Now let us change the opponent from a person to nature: State A or state B will be selected after Larry's choice of strategy and without regard to it. For example, state B could be an earthquake that damages Larry's building, and state A could be no earthquake. Or we could have states A and B determined by human events not directly related to Larry; for example, state B could represent a strike by public employees. The strike would interfere with refuse pickup whether or not Larry invested. That would impose greater cleanup costs on Larry and would also delay rental of the renovated units until city building inspectors returned to work. How would Larry behave in those situations?

One decision rule proposed for these situations is **the maximin rule: Choose the strategy that maximizes the payoff in the worst possible state of the world.** Since the worst payoff is \$0 if Larry does not invest and −\$1000 if he does, the strategy of not investing maximizes the minimum that Larry could experience.

The maximin strategy is one of extreme risk aversion, which does not depend in any way on Larry's subjective estimate of the probability that each state will occur. Suppose, for example, that Larry thinks the probability of no earthquake or no strike is .9. Then his expected profit from investing is

$$E(\Pi) = .9(\$5000) + .1(-\$1000)$$

$$= \$4400$$

His expected profit if he does not invest is substantially lower:

$$E(\Pi) = .9(\$2000) + .1(0)$$

$$= \$1800$$

As we have already seen, even a risk-averse expected utility maximizer could easily prefer the strategy of investing.

Let us consider one other strategy that might be available: the strategic decision to gather more information. We take a simple example. Suppose Larry, with time and effort, could find out with certainty whether the public employees will go on strike. How much would that information be worth? To an expected utility maximizer, *the utility value of perfect information is the difference between the expected utility of the current situation (with*

---

[32] A useful concept to understand this outcome is that of the *Nash equilibrium: an outcome from which no player's reward can be increased by unilateral action.* In this example, neither player can single-handedly increase the \$5000 reward by a change in strategy, so it is a Nash equilibrium. While the Nash equilibrium is the "best" outcome in this game, it need not be: The "Not invest, Not invest" outcome of the Slumlord's Dilemma is also a Nash equilibrium! Furthermore, while these two games each have exactly one Nash equilibrium, there are strategic games that have multiple Nash equilibria, and some that have none. Nevertheless, the usefulness of the concept is that it identifies good candidates for the game's outcome when *noncooperative* strategies are likely to prevail (owing to difficulties in securing binding cooperative agreements).

imperfect knowledge) and the expected utility of being able to choose the best strategy in whatever state arises. The monetary value of that information is simply the difference between the certain-wealth equivalents of the two expected utility levels.

To illustrate, suppose Larry currently has $45,000 in wealth and the following risk-averse utility function:

$$U = -e^{-0.0002W}$$

With imperfect knowledge, Larry will prefer to invest. The expected utility from this strategy is[33]

$$E(U) = .9U(\$50,000) + .1U(\$44,000)$$

$$= -0.0000559332$$

The certain-wealth equivalent of this is $48,956.76.

If Larry finds out whether there will be a strike, he can invest or not invest accordingly. The expected utility value from finding out is then

$$E(U) = .9U(\$50,000) + .1U(\$45,000)$$

$$= -0.0000532009$$

The certain-wealth equivalent of this is $49,207.17. In other words, Larry should be willing to spend up to $250.41 (= $49,207.17 − $48,956.76) to find out with certainty whether there will be a strike.

To follow the expected utility-maximizing strategy in the above example, Larry must have subjective perceptions of the probability of each state. Whether individuals have these perceptions, how the perceptions are formed, and whether the perceptions are acted upon are critical issues that we have not yet discussed. We will turn to them in the following section.

Bounded Rationality

When common decisions involving easily understood risks such as a simple coin flip game are considered, it is certainly plausible to entertain the notion that behavior is consistent with expected utility maximization. But as decision situations become more complex and are encountered only infrequently, actual behavior begins to take on quite a different cast. One way to explain this is to recognize that decision-making is itself a costly process and that individuals will allocate only a limited amount of their own resources, including time,

---

[33] The expected utility from not investing is

$$E(U) = .9U(\$47,000) + .1U(\$45,000)$$

$$= -0.0000867962$$

The certain-wealth equivalent of this strategy is $46,759.94.

to the activity of deciding. A somewhat different but related explanation is that there are bounds or limits to human rationality.[34] To illustrate this with a transparent example, let us consider the differences in decision-making that characterize playing the games of tic-tac-toe and chess. In tic-tac-toe it is not hard to become an expert player. Simply by playing the game a few times, it becomes apparent which strategies prevent losing and which do not. That is, a player becomes an expert by trial and error. The optimal choice of moves is not accomplished by mentally considering all the alternatives and their possible consequences (nine possible openings × eight possible responses × seven possible next moves, and so forth) and seeing which current move is best. Individuals do not have the mental capacity to make such calculations. Rather, a small set of routine offensive and defensive ploys must be *learned.*

For example, of the nine possible opening moves, it does not take long for the novice to realize that there are only three really different ones: the middle, a corner, or a side. Routine responses are developed as well: "If my opponent opens in the center, I will respond with a corner." Tic-tac-toe is simple enough that almost all people learn unbeatable strategies. Because virtually everyone can quickly become an expert at tic-tac-toe, observed behavior will correspond closely with the assumption that each player acts *as if* all possible alternatives have been considered and the optimal one chosen. For all intents and purposes, the players of this game may be thought of as maximizers or optimizers of their chances of winning.

The same limited calculating ability that prevents systematic consideration of all alternatives in tic-tac-toe applies *a fortiori* to the game of chess. No individual (nor as yet even our largest computer) is capable of thinking through all possible consequences of alternative chess moves in order to select the best one. People play chess the same way they play tic-tac-toe—by using routine offensive and defensive ploys that are learned primarily through the trials and errors of playing. That is, the same problem-solving procedure of trying to take a very complicated problem and breaking it down into manageable pieces (the standard routines) is followed.

However, an important difference between the two games is readily apparent. Although almost everyone finds optimal strategies for tic-tac-toe, no individual has ever found an optimal (unbeatable) strategy for chess.[35] Instead, individuals develop routines that *satisfice.* That is, they are satisfactory only when they are the best known to a player at a given time and do not seem to be the cause of losses. However, it is recognized that better routines can be discovered, and indeed most players strive to improve their routines over time.

Economic decisions run the spectrum of choice situations from those in which we as individuals have optimizing routines to others in which we have satisficing routines, and still

---

[34] Many of the ideas in this section are associated with the work of Herbert Simon. See, for example, Simon's "Theories of Decision-Making in Economics and Behavioral Science," in *Surveys of Economic Theory*, vol. III (New York: St. Martin's Press, 1967), pp. 1–28. See also Herbert Simon, *Models of Bounded Rationality*, vols. 1–2 (Cambridge: The MIT Press, 1982).

[35] It has been shown mathematically that such strategies must exist. See, for example, Herbert Simon, *The Sciences of the Artificial* (Cambridge: The MIT Press, 1969), p. 63.

others with which we are unfamiliar and for which we have no routines. When we buy meat, for example, it is not too difficult to discover whether the meat selections wrapped in a particular supermarket tend to have less desirable aspects (e.g., fat) hidden from view; and we have the opportunity to make frequent trials. Thus consumers may do pretty well at choosing their meat purchases from the alternative price-quality combinations available in their neighborhoods. To the extent that this is true, the meat choice game is like tic-tac-toe. There is no explicit calculation of all meat purchase alternatives every time one goes to shop; rather, a set of simplified routines for shopping becomes established. But the results may be the same as if an optimizing procedure had been followed.

On the other hand, certain aspects of meat choices may be relevant to consumers but very difficult to perceive when the choice is made. For example, the freshness of the meat may not be apparent. One could rely on competitive forces to keep unfresh meats off the market or to keep meats separated by their relative freshness. But competitive forces respond only to consumer choices. Consumer choice routines might be quite adequate to recognize and cause the failure of any supplier who systematically and frequently attempts to sell unfresh meat. But it is quite plausible that more clever suppliers would be able to get away with such abuses if they are not attempted too often.

In circumstances like this it may be possible for public policy to improve the workings of the market. A regulation requiring that all meat be labeled with a last legal day of sale, for example, might have benefits greater than its costs. For this to work, it is important that the regulation makers have better routines for evaluating freshness than consumers generally have. If the regulator thinks no meat should be sold after it has been cut and wrapped for two days but almost all consumers think that meat bought on the third day is fine, then the regulation can make consumers worse off. The gains from the reduction of unfresh meat sales can be outweighed by the losses from a reduced (and more expensive) supply of fresh meat.

Why not just have the labeling requirement in the above example but leave out the part about a last legal day of sale? This depends upon the sophistication and diversity of consumer choices. If consumers *only lack knowledge* about any specific piece of meat or *vary widely in their informed choices* about the time within which each would use it, *then the pure information policy may be best*. Since regulators lack information about individual consumer preferences, there is an efficiency gain from informing them but not restricting choice. On the other hand, consumers may have difficulty processing the information, that is, using it to make the decision. If many consumers simply do not develop their own standards for freshness (because they do not encounter substandard meat often enough), the legal-last-day-of-sale aspect could have net benefits rather than net costs.

One last meat example might be instructive. Suppose certain color-enhancing or taste-enhancing chemicals have been added to the meat and suppose further that they are carcinogenic, that there is some small probability that the intake of a given quantity will result in cancer in 20 or 30 years. This attribute is like freshness in that it is difficult if not impossible to perceive at the time of sale. But unlike freshness, individual consumers would not observe the consequences in time to consider different routines for making decisions. Even if informed about the facts in a dispassionate way, consumers have no experience in making such choices and may make them poorly.

It may be analogous to hearing a brilliant lecture by Bobby Fischer on how to play chess and then having your first and only opportunity to play. You are not likely to do well, particularly if you are facing a seasoned opponent. If the stakes of the game are important, the novice might well prefer to have Bobby Fischer play as his or her proxy. Similarly, potential consumers of food additives might prefer to have an expert make the decision for them. In this case a regulatory agency with the power to ban certain products may improve efficiency.

To the extent that rationality is bounded, the bounds are themselves the cause of uncertainty. In the last examples, often the consumer has all the information a supercomputer would need to solve for the optimum. The problem is that the consumer has not developed routines or programs that can process the information in order to identify the optimum. In such situations regulatory policies may have the potential to improve consumer satisfaction.

Of course, it is an empirical question whether actual consumer decision-making in any particular situation is improvable by public policy (and again this depends not only on there being some deviation from the consumer's optimum but also on the prospects for regulation actually reducing it). However, the existing empirical evidence on *individual* consumer choice suggests that actual behavior, even in simple choice situations, is often grossly inconsistent with expected utility maximization.[36]

One interesting study involved a household survey of consumer purchases of disaster insurance.[37] Approximately 3000 households in disaster-prone areas, half of them uninsured, were asked a variety of questions designed to determine their subjective estimates of the probabilities of a disaster, the resulting loss that they might experience in that event, and their knowledge of available insurance. While a large number of people indicated that they did not have the information, those offering the information appeared to deviate substantially from expected utility maximization. In this group 39 percent of the uninsured should have bought insurance (in order to maximize expected utility), whereas about the same percentage of the insured should not have bought insurance.

To give some policy perspective to the study's findings, less than 10 percent of the entire uninsured sample could be said to have rationally chosen to remain uninsured while living in the disaster-prone area. Over half of this group simply did not know about the availability of insurance, let alone that their flood insurance would be 90 percent federally subsidized. Many of the rest appeared to have unrealistically low expectations of the damage that would occur in the event of a disaster. Is there any policy problem here? If one simply takes the expected utility model on faith, then there is certainly no reason to subsidize the

---

[36] For an excellent survey of this and related literature, see Matthew Rabin, "Psychology and Economics," *Journal of Economic Literature*, 36, No. 1, March 1998, pp. 11–46. A fine example of experimental research from this literature is David M. Grether and Charles R. Plott, "Economic Theory of Choice and the Preference Reversal Phenomenon," *American Economic Review*, 69, No. 4, September 1979, pp. 623–638. The experiments in this paper reveal behavior inconsistent with preference theory in general, and not just expected utility maximization. Alternative models are tested in Lee S. Friedman, "Bounded Rationality versus Standard Utility-Maximization: A Test of Energy Price Responsiveness," in J. Fox and R. Gowda, eds., *Judgments, Decisions, and Public Policy* (Cambridge: Cambridge University Press, 2002), pp. 138–173.

[37] See Howard Kunreuther, "Limited Knowledge and Insurance Protection," *Public Policy*, 24, No. 2, Spring 1976, pp. 227–261.

insurance. In fact, the model suggests a good reason not to provide the subsidy: If individuals do not bear the true costs of their locational choices then they will overlocate in the subsidized areas.

But this model ignores a problem that the model of bounded rationality reveals. There may be many people living in these areas, because they do not have or cannot process the information about possible disaster, who will suffer serious loss in that event. Subsidized insurance probably does alleviate this problem to a small degree (depending on the price elasticity of its demand), but it can simultaneously cause the locational problem mentioned above.

A policy of compulsory unsubsidized insurance might be better. It solves the problem of the unprotected and provides essentially correct locational signals, except for the risk takers, who really would prefer no insurance. The best policies may be ones of information or even help with information processing, if consumer choice can be preserved but made more rational.

A final example is the *Equity Premium Puzzle* that returns us to a finding mentioned earlier: over the long run, the average annual rate of return on stock investments has exceeded that of bonds by 5–6 percent. The problem is that this differential seems too high to be the result of rational expected utility-maximizing preferences.[38] For it to be an equilibrium, that means on the margin investors must be indifferent to placing their last investment dollar in stocks or bonds. But with the rate-of-return on stocks so much higher, it implies an implausibly high average degree of risk aversion among investors: about 30 times greater than it has been found to be in other common situations.[39]

Thaler et al. put forth a more plausible explanation that depends upon two particular kinds of bounded rationality: *loss aversion* and *myopia*. **Loss aversion is the idea that people are more sensitive to decreases in their wealth than to increases.** A number of studies found that individuals weight losses more than twice as strongly as gains (far more than can be explained by diminishing marginal utility).[40] To illustrate, Thaler et al. suggest

---

[38] This was first pointed out by R. Mehra and E. Prescott, "The Equity Premium: A Puzzle," *Journal of Monetary Economics*, *15*, No. 2, March 1985, pp. 145–161. It has been studied more recently by R. Thaler, A. Tversky, D. Kahneman, and A. Schwartz, "The Effect of Myopia and Loss Aversion on Risk Taking: An Experimental Test," *Quarterly Journal of Economics*, *112*, No. 2, May 1997, pp. 647–661.

[39] Siegel and Thaler express the implausibility this way. Suppose an individual were subject to an uncertainty in which there was a 50 percent chance that wealth would double and a 50 percent chance that it would be cut in half (a positive expected change). The individual who is indifferent to the stock-bond choice on the margin is not only willing to pay to avoid the above gamble, but would be willing to forgo 49 percent of wealth to do so. Since the worst outcome of the gamble is to end up with 50 percent of wealth, 49 percent is an absurd amount of money to pay to avoid the risk. See J. Siegel and R. Thaler, "The Equity Premium Puzzle," *Journal of Economic Perspectives*, *11*, No. 1, Winter 1997, pp. 191–200.

[40] See Jack L. Knetsch, "Assumptions, Behavioral Findings, and Policy Analysis," *Journal of Policy Analysis and Management*, *14*, No. 1, Winter 1995, pp. 68–78. It may be a semantic issue whether this behavior should be described as a form of bounded rationality, but it does violate the assumption of having a unique preference ordering. One could see this as a consequence of it being too hard to know one's preferences in the abstract and easier to reform them in different situational contexts.

that such preferences could be represented by the following segmented utility function $U(\Delta W)$, where ΔW is the change in wealth from an initial level:

$$U(\Delta W) = \begin{cases} \Delta W & \Delta W \geq 0 \\ 2.5\Delta W & \Delta W < 0 \end{cases}$$

Such a utility function implies that the same individual would rank any given outcome (e.g., final wealth level $100,000) differently if evaluated from different starting points. Then, if offered the opportunity of an investment that has a net gain of $200 with probability .5 and a net loss of $100 with probability .5, the individual with this utility function would refuse.[41]

On the other hand, consider how the individual would respond if offered the investment opportunity to do this twice in succession (with the second result independent of the first). If the individual evaluates the whole sequence, there are three possible outcomes: win both times with .25 probability, lose both times with .25 probability, or win one and lose the other for a net gain of $100 with a .5 probability. The expected utility is positive and the individual would accept the offer:

$$U(\Delta W) = .25(400) + .25(2.5)(-200) + .50[100] = 25$$

On the other hand, the individual may reason myopically, calculate if the first investment is worthwhile, decide it is not, and thereby reject the sequence. **Myopia is the framing of a long-run decision in terms of its short-run consequences** (framing effects were introduced in the contingent valuation discussion of Chapter 6). Think of these two investments as "invest in the stock market this year" and "invest in the stock market next year." The individual who thinks of this choice as one sequence to be evaluated at the end of the second year will invest. However, the individual who thinks of this myopically will not invest.

Thaler et al. conduct an experiment and find that investors are indeed characterized by both loss aversion and myopia in deciding how to allocate an investment portfolio between stocks and bonds. Such behavior helps to explain the Equity Premium Puzzle, and is relevant to policies concerning individual control of retirement accounts. Furthermore, they also note that more information provision in this context (more frequent feedback on investment results) increases myopia, and thus that "more information" can be counterproductive.

Knetsch, accepting the validity of the valuations implied by these behaviors, argues that there are important consequences for many public policies of failing to account for them, for example, "activities with negative environmental and social impacts will be unduly encouraged . . . inappropriately lax standards of protection against injuries will be set."[42] These are not the kinds of implications that come from traditional economic models, and it

---

[41] The same individual starting with an initial wealth level that is $1000 lower and offered the choice between receiving an extra $1000 with certainty or a gamble that returned $1200 with probability .5 and $900 with probability .5 would accept the gamble. The possible outcomes here and likelihoods of each are identical to those in the text where the individual refused the gamble.

[42] Knetsch, "Assumptions, Behavioral Findings, and Policy Analysis," p. 74.

should serve as a reminder that it is healthy to remain open-minded about the models to be used in policy analyses.[43]

Moral Hazard and Medical Care Insurance

One of the more serious risky contingencies that each of us faces is the possibility of requiring expensive medical care. It is therefore not surprising that many people choose to purchase health insurance, which is so universal that it is usually provided as a fringe benefit of employment.[44]

Many people feel that a universal minimum of medical care should be guaranteed to all; thus it is not surprising that the government Medicare and Medicaid programs provide insurance for the elderly and lower-income individuals (primarily those on welfare). However, many people still "fall through the cracks" of these programs (e.g., the self-employed and the marginally employed), and legislation to extend health insurance coverage is the subject of continuing policy debate. It seems inevitable that some form of universal coverage will eventually be adopted, although exactly what that form will be is up for grabs.

A factor that has undeniably slowed the movement toward universal coverage is the dramatic increase in the costs of medical care. From 1965, when Medicare was getting started, to 1993, medical expenditures went from 6 percent of the GDP to 14 percent, where they have remained. At first, analysts thought that the cost increase was due almost entirely to the new demand from Medicare and Medicaid patients. But gradually, as medical inflation continued unabated and more data became available, the recognition grew that medical insurance coverage was itself an important factor. It was not simply that more people were being covered by a relatively inelastic supply; the level of real resources (labor and capital inputs) per capita approximately tripled from 1960 to 1990. During roughly the same period (1965–1991), insurance payments (both public and private) increased from 24 to 62 percent of total health care spending, and out-of-pocket spending declined from 46 to 20 percent.[45]

To understand why medical insurance has caused this problem, we return to fairly simple and traditional models of economic behavior. As we have already seen, the advantage of insurance is that, through risk-shifting and risk-pooling, the cost of risk is reduced. But in our earliest examples of theft insurance we assumed that the insurance company offered insurance at a premium approximately equal to the expected loss without insurance. This

---

[43] Other studies that have focused on policy implications of bounded rationality include C. Camerer and H. Kunreuther, "Decision Processes for Low Probability Events: Policy Implications," *Journal of Policy Analysis and Management*, 8, No. 4, Fall 1989, pp. 565–592; and Lee S. Friedman and Karl Hausker, "Residential Energy Consumption: Models of Consumer Behavior and Their Implications for Rate Design," *Journal of Consumer Policy*, 11, 1988, pp. 287–313.

[44] We noted earlier the tax advantages of receiving part of the wage in this form. The employer's contribution is nontaxable; but if the same money were included in the wage, the recipient would have to pay income taxes on it. Thus the public policy is similar to offering individuals (through their employers) a matching grant for medical care insurance when higher-income people receive more generous matches (the tax savings are greater).

[45] For more data and general discussion, see Chapter 4 in both the 1993 and 1994 issues of the *Economic Report of the President* (Washington, D.C.: U.S. Government Printing Office, 1993, 1994).

turns out to be a false proposition for medical insurance, as another version of the Slumlord's Dilemma makes its impact felt.[46] *The insurance changes the economic incentives that each individual faces, and this causes behavior to be different.*

The problem arises because medical care expenses, perhaps unlike the events of illness or injury themselves, are not random events. The quantity of medical care demanded by an individual depends, to be sure, on the random event of a medical problem. But it also depends on the income and tastes of the individual (or his or her doctor) and the price of the services. If I must be hospitalized, my decision to have a private or semiprivate room depends on the price. I may stay an "extra day" to be on the safe side if it is cheap enough, or I'll be particularly anxious to leave because of the high cost. If I am poor, the doctor may provide only the services that are essential to help keep my bill down; if I am well off, the doctor may provide "Cadillac quality" care.

How does this connect to insurance? The effect of full-coverage insurance is to reduce the price an individual is charged at the point of service from the ordinary market price to zero. Once insured, an individual receives all covered services "for free." Therefore, more medical expenses will be incurred by an insured person than would be incurred by the same person without insurance. A hospital, knowing most of its patients are insured (and absent any regulatory constraints), can buy any medical equipment no matter how expensive, use it as the doctor finds appropriate, and get reimbursed for the "necessary" expenses by the insurance company. Full-coverage insurance leaves the medical care industry without the usual mechanism of consumer demand as a cost control; in fact, it leaves the industry with virtually no method of cost control at all.

Full-coverage insurance can be offered only when the demand for the covered services is inelastic. To see this, let us look at Figure 7-7. Imagine that there are two states of the world: An individual is healthy or ill. If illness strikes (let us say with $\Pi = .5$) and the individual is uninsured, we might observe that 50 units of medical care are bought at the market price of $1.00 per unit. The expected cost to the individual is thus $25. Suppose that the demand for these services is completely inelastic (in this state), as if for every illness there is a unique, invariable treatment. Then the expected cost of insuring many individuals like this one is also $25, and every risk-averse individual will prefer to purchase the insurance that would be offered at this actuarially fair premium.

Now let us relax the assumption that the demand is inelastic; suppose the actual demand is *EAG* as drawn in Figure 7-7. The uninsured ill person behaves as before. But because the ill person with insurance faces a zero price at the point of service, 100 units of medical care will be demanded. The insurance company will receive a bill for $100, and thus its expected cost of insuring many people like this is $50 each $[= \frac{1}{2}(0) + \frac{1}{2}(100)]$. Thus the choice that the individual faces is to bear the risk and go uninsured with expected loss of $25 or to give up $50 with certainty in order to shift the risk. In this case, the individual might well prefer to remain uninsured.

---

[46] Mark Pauly was the first to point this out. See his "The Economics of Moral Hazard," *American Economic Review, 58,* 1968, pp. 531–537.

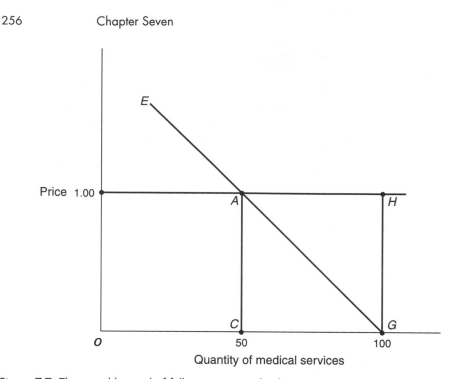

Figure 7-7. The moral hazard of full-coverage medical insurance.

Note the presence of the Slumlord's Dilemma here. The insurance company is still charging an actuarially fair premium: it breaks even. Every individual could perceive that his or her own excess use contributes to the rise in premium (from the inelastic case). Nevertheless, each individual controls only a negligible fraction of the premium costs. If I become ill and consider restraining my demands, the savings will not accrue to me but will be spread evenly over the entire insured population; and I will still be charged my share of the excess use by all the others. If I do purchase the excess units, the extra costs are spread evenly over the insured population and I pay only a tiny fraction. Thus I am better off following the strategy of demanding the "excess" services, even though every one would be better off if none of us demanded them!

To make sure that this last point is clear, let us return to Figure 7-7. Under full-coverage insurance, the social costs of units 51 to 100 can be seen to exceed their benefits. The area $CAHG$ indicates their cost of $50 (paid for through the insurance premiums) and the area under the demand curve ACG measures their value to the consumer of $25. Thus a risk-averse individual will purchase insurance only if the expected utility loss from consuming these marginal services, valued at $12.50 [$= \frac{1}{2}(25)$], is less than the value of the utility gain from the overall risk reduction; otherwise, he or she is better off remaining uninsured. On the other hand, we know that insurance with excess use forbidden would have the greatest value because it would provide the full risk-reduction benefits but *no* expected loss from the consumption of excess services. Thus, all risk-averse people would most prefer an insurance plan with some social mechanism to prevent excess use.

In fact, the problem extends to behavior beyond that of excess consumption when ill. It also includes actions that affect the probability of illness. The uninsured person would normally take some set of preventive health measures in order to ward off various states of illness. These could include the purchase of health services such as regular check-ups, as well as the avoidance (or reduced use) of "health-risky" goods such as alcohol or tobacco products. But again the fully insured person has less incentive to undertake these appropriate preventive measures, because the cost of any resulting illness is not borne by that individual but is spread over the entire insurance pool.

The problems of excess use and insufficient preventive measures are known in the insurance literature as *moral hazard*. A typical example used to illustrate the problem is arson: If the owner of a building could insure the property for any desired value, then he or she might buy a policy for twice the market value of the building and secretly arrange to have it "torched"! This example clearly identifies a moral hazard, but it is misleading in the sense that it downplays the pure role of economic incentives, morality aside. That is, we usually think that it is quite rational for individuals to increase consumption or investment in response to a lower price, and that is the temptation perceived by both those with medical insurance and the insured potential arsonist. Other examples are when the earthquake-insured fail to brace their homes the way they would without insurance and when the theft-insured fail to undertake the security measures they would choose in the absence of insurance.

Is there any way to solve the medical insurance problem? One method that might mitigate the problem, if not solve it, is the use of *deductibles* and *coinsurance*. A deductible requires the individual to pay for a certain amount of medical services before the insurance coverage goes into effect; it is designed to deter reliance on insurance to pay for "minor" illnesses. Coinsurance requires the individual to pay a certain fraction of each dollar spent: the coinsurance rate refers to the percentage paid by the individual. (For example, a coinsurance rate of 25 percent means that, for each dollar spent, the individual must pay 25 percent and the insurance company 75 percent.)

We can see the effect of each in Figure 7-8a. Suppose that the deductible is for the first 60 units and the insured individual becomes ill. It is not obvious whether the person will file a claim or not. One choice is simply to purchase the 50 units as would be done without insurance. The other choice is to file a claim, pay the full cost of the first 60 units, and consume the rest of the excess units (61 to 100) free.

Triangle AEF measures the net cost to the consumer of having to pay for the first 10 excess units, and triangle FGJ measures the net benefits of consuming the next 40 free. If $FGJ > ALF$, the individual will file the claim. In this particular example $FGJ = \frac{1}{2}(0.80)(40) = \$16.00$ and $AEF = \frac{1}{2}(0.20)(10) = \$1.00$, so the individual's behavior is unaltered by the deductible.

To understand the effects of deductibles in a more general way, imagine many possible states of illness from mild to severe and associate with each a demand curve that shifts progressively to the right as we consider more severe illnesses. This is illustrated in Figure 7-8b. Since the deductible remains as a fixed rectangle and the benefits of medical care increase steadily as the demand curve shifts to the right, it can be seen that one is less likely to file for the less serious illnesses and that past some point the deductible no longer deters filing.

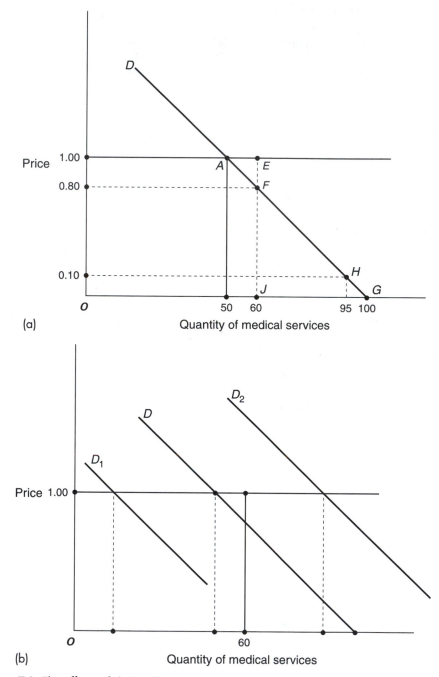

(a)

(b)

Figure 7-8. The effects of deductibles and coinsurance: (a) Deductibles and coinsurance can restrain use. (b) The deductible deters filing small claims.

To see the effect of coinsurance, suppose the coinsurance rate for the individual repre-sented in Figure 7-8a is 10 percent. If ill, the individual will then purchase ninety-five units of medical services (at point H). The smaller the price elasticity of demand, the smaller the restraining effect of coinsurance (and the less the moral hazard in the first place). Note that the existence of coinsurance can make a policy attractive to someone who finds full cover-age unattractive. Although it only partially shifts the risk (the amount depends upon the coinsurance rate), it does shift the more expensive portion (i.e., it prevents the losses where the marginal utility of wealth is greatest). Furthermore, it reduces the consumption of the least-valued of the excess units.[47] So it is quite possible that the risk-saving gains of partial coverage will exceed the expected costs from "excess" use, even if that is not true of full coverage.

The above analysis suggests that one direction to explore in an attempt to solve the medical cost problem is increased reliance on deductibles and coinsurance. When those ideas are integrated into national health insurance proposals, they are typically modified to be income-contingent. That is, it is recognized that lower-income families have limited abil-ity to meet even these partial payments.

However, this section is not intended as a recommendation of what to do; it is intended only to help clarify the nature of the medical cost explosion we have experienced. Although a full discussion of the normative implications that could be explored is beyond our scope, mentioning at least a few of them should help to keep this analysis in perspective.

First, the social benefits and costs referred to in the diagrams of this analysis cannot be easily estimated from observable data for a variety of reasons. Social cost, for example, is the value of what society gives up by allocating a resource to the provision of medical care. In perfectly competitive industries we can often approximate it by the market price. But in the medical care sector, unwarranted entry restrictions (such as limiting entrants to medical schools to a number less than the number of qualified applicants) may make observed cost greater than social costs. To the extent that is true, the optimal quantity of medical care should be greater than what uninsured people choose. In our diagram this might be equivalent to drawing the social marginal cost line at $0.80 rather than at the $1.00 observed price and calculating social benefits and costs on the basis of its relation to the demand curve.

But then the demand curves themselves are unreliable guides for social welfare. For one thing, very little is known about the relation between medical care and health; presumably it is health that people seek. This makes it extremely difficult to know whether delivered medical services are excessive. Disagreement among physicians about the appropriate care for a given patient is common. In addition, the specific equity concerns (about medical care) suggest caution in the use of compensation tests here; to the extent that a patient's income influences the location of the demand curve, the benefits and costs to people of different in-come groups might require separate analytic treatment.

---

[47] As drawn, for example, the coinsurance deters purchases of units 96 to 100. This reduces the expected cost of illness by $2.50, and reduces the expected consumer surplus from "subsidized" excess consumption by only $0.125 $[= (0.5)(0.5)(0.10)5]$. Thus, the consumer has an expected gain of $2.375, which is offset to some degree by the increased risk owing to having only partial insurance coverage.

Finally, much of the problem we have been discussing is exacerbated by the fee-for-service method of organizing the supply of medical services. A physician is supposed to be the consumer's agent and provide expert advice on how to further the consumer's medical interests. The need for an agent arises because of the generally accepted wisdom that consumers are not competent to choose their own medical treatments. But this puts the fee-for-service physician in an awkward position, because he or she is simultaneously a supplier of services to the patient and a receiver of income in proportion to the amount of services sold. There is a conflict of interest that may cause overpurchasing without insurance, and the presence of insurance only exacerbates the tendency.

An alternative to the fee-for-service system is a system of health maintenance organizations to which consumers pay annual fees in return for "free" health services as needed. That gives the suppliers incentive to conserve on their use of resources ("managed care"), and the forces of competition, as well as physician norms, work to ensure that appropriate treatments are supplied as required.[48] The use of such systems in the United States has grown dramatically, although 80 percent of the Medicare population still uses fee-for-service. Similarly, many hospital charges are no longer fee-for-service but are determined at admission in accordance with a schedule of "diagnostic related groups." Another alternative for medical services, much less politically feasible here, would be a national health service like that in Sweden or England.

These cautions about making normative inferences from the moral hazard analysis only hint at some of the complexities that are relevant to health policy. But the complexity does not make the achievement of the analysis presented here any less worthwhile. The medical cost problem continues to be of widespread concern, and the clarification of one of its sources is an important contribution. Furthermore, the same model generated some useful insights (the role of deductibles and coinsurance) for achieving policy improvement.

Information Asymmetry and Hidden Action: The Savings and Loan Crisis of the 1980s and Involuntary Unemployment

The previous section explained the moral hazard problem in the context of medical insurance. However, the moral hazard problem arises in many other policy contexts as well. *In order for moral hazard to be present, two conditions are necessary*. First, there must be an *information asymmetry* between two or more parties who wish to "contract" (i.e., enter an economic relationship). Second, the asymmetry must involve a *hidden action*: an outcome-affecting action taken by one of the parties *after* contracting. This implies that the outcome

---

[48] See, for example, D. Cutler, M. McClellan, and J. Newhouse, "How Does Managed Care Do It?," *Rand Journal of Economics*, *31*, No. 3, Autumn 2000, pp. 526–548. For a more extensive review of alternative reimbursement plans, see J. Newhouse, "Reimbursing Health Plans and Health Providers: Selection Versus Efficiency in Production," *Journal of Economic Literature*, *34*, No. 3, September 1996, pp. 1236–1263. Some problems with managed care are analyzed in S. Singer and A. Enthoven, "Structural Problems of Managed Care in California and Some Options for Ameliorating Them," *California Management Review*, *43*, No. 1, Fall 2000, pp. 50–65.

is determined by other additional factors that are also unknown (e.g., random events): otherwise, the action would be revealed by the outcome itself. Then **moral hazard can be defined as the situation where one party to a contract has incentive to undertake a hidden action with adverse consequences to another party to the contract.**

Think of the person taking the hidden action as the "agent" and the other person as the "principal." Then *moral hazard exists whenever there is a principal-agent relationship with hidden action.* In the health insurance case, the insurance company is the principal, the insured is the agent, and the hidden action is excess consumption of health services when ill (and the true degree of illness is a random event also unknown to the principal). The "split the bill" agreement at a restaurant, which creates incentives to overorder (the hidden action), is another moral hazard problem (with the group as the principal, the individual diners the agents, and true individual preferences also unknown to the group).

A very important moral hazard problem created by public policy was at least partially responsible for the savings and loan industry crisis during the 1980s, in which many deregulated institutions made unsound loans and became insolvent. During this period, regulators closed almost 1200 S&Ls at a taxpayer cost of over $100 billion.[49] In the case of a banking institution, think of depositors as the principals and the institution as the agent. The job of the agent is to earn interest for the depositors by lending out the deposited money, as well as keeping the balance secure. The hidden action is the lending of money by the institution to entities with credit worthiness unknown to the depositors; the principals do not know if a loan default is due to bad luck or excessive risk-taking.

In order for the agent to attract principals, it must convince them that their deposits will in fact be secure. For many years, federal deposit insurance played this role. However, such insurance also creates the usual kind of moral hazard: incentive for the insured institution to take greater risk than otherwise in lending funds. From the 1930s through the 1970s, this moral hazard was manageable because it was accompanied by restrictions on the types of loans allowed and interest rate ceilings on deposits that limited the supply of funds to the S&Ls.

Then in 1980 the United States enacted the Depositary Institutions Deregulation and Monetary Control Act. This act increased federal deposit insurance from $40,000 to $100,000 per account, removed many restrictions on the types of loans allowed, and gradually removed the rate ceilings that had moderated the competition for deposits. Not surprisingly, the institutions increased interest rates to attract more funds, and depositors did not worry much about the loans that were made (the hidden action) because of the deposit insurance. Banks that were not doing too well had every incentive to make unusually risky loans; they had an ample supply of deposits because of deposit insurance, few of their own assets to lose, and the hope that large profits from repayment of the risky loans could restore them to health. Thus the large number of insolvencies in the 1980s can be understood as a predictable response to the increased moral hazard from higher deposit insurance and

---

[49] *Economic Report of the President, 1993* (Washington, D.C.: U.S. Government Printing Office, 1993), p. 194.

deregulation. These insolvencies were stemmed, at least temporarily, by the passage of the 1989 Financial Institutions Reform, Recovery, and Enforcement Act.[50]

One last example of moral hazard is particularly interesting because of the importance of the problem: *involuntary unemployment*. In the most conventional microeconomic models, there is no involuntary unemployment (the market forces the wage to be at the level where demand equals supply). Yet the unemployment rate is one of the most closely watched measures of performance of a national economy, and all market-oriented economies go through periods where the extent of involuntary employment becomes a matter of serious national concern. While much of macroeconomic theory tries to explain this phenomenon at the aggregate level, it remains poorly understood and it is important to understand its microeconomic foundations.

One promising concept for explaining involuntary unemployment is that of the *efficiency wage*. This term refers to a wage that serves a dual purpose: to attract labor and to create incentives that increase labor productivity. It is the second purpose, motivated by the uncertainty about labor productivity, that relates to the moral hazard. The easiest way to explain this is by thinking about the *effort* that a single individual puts into work. Simplifying further, imagine that an individual chooses either "high" or "low" effort. This choice is the hidden action, recognizing that there are many cases in which it is difficult for the employer-principal to know just how hard any particular agent-employee is working (other factors unknown to the principal are also determinants of the outcome). If there were no penalty to "low" effort (e.g., no risk of being fired and unemployed, no reduction in promotion possibilities), many employees would prefer this choice.[51]

If the employee "caught" making a low effort was fired but hired immediately at the same market wage by some other firm (the "no unemployment" case), there would be no penalty to the low-effort choice. Employers, knowing this, would only offer a wage commensurate with low-effort productivity. If one views the market as offering each worker full employment insurance in case of job loss (i.e., an equivalent job immediately), then the moral hazard results in excess job losses and high insurance "premiums" in the form of lower wages (reflecting the low productivity). Everyone would prefer a high-effort, high-wage, full-employment equilibrium, but the cost of one individual's low-effort choice is not borne by that individual. It is spread out over all workers in the form of a small "premium" increase (i.e., market wage reduction). So, many workers make the low-effort choice resulting in the low market-clearing wage for all. It is another version of moral hazard that sounds similar to the Slumlord's Dilemma.

But suppose we introduce the equivalent of coinsurance: making the employee bear some portion of the cost of the low-effort choice. What if, upon firing, the worker was not instantaneously reemployed elsewhere but suffered a spell of unemployment? To an extent depending on the severity of the unemployment, this would increase the incentives of workers

---

[50] A great deal has been written about this issue. A good summary is contained in Frederic S. Mishkin, "An Evaluation of the Treasury Plan for Banking Reform," *Journal of Economic Perspectives*, 6, No. 1, Winter 1992, pp. 133–153.

[51] Employees who derive more *utility* from the high-effort choice will of course select it.

to avoid job loss, and fewer low-effort choices would be made. The number of "claims" would fall, and wages and average productivity would rise. The extent of the moral hazard would be mitigated. It gets ahead of ourselves to model fully the firm behavior that could lead to this "coinsurance" outcome. However, the gist of the argument goes like this. Starting from a low-wage, full-employment market position, any single firm has incentive to offer a wage that is above the going rate. Why? Because then its workers will suffer a loss if they are fired (the difference between the firm's wage and the market wage), and they will therefore increase their work efforts (and productivity) in order to avoid this. But as *all* firms start increasing their wages, the penalty disappears again. Firms continue to bid up the wage rate until it goes above the market-clearing wage, with demand for labor less than the supply, so that employees face an unemployment penalty for job loss and seek to avoid it. Even though there is unemployment, at some wage rate that sustains it each firm will be in equilibrium: while a firm could lower wages and hire additional workers from the unemployed pool, the gains from this would be precisely offset by the reduction in work effort of its current employees.[52]

Summary

Uncertainty is a pervasive phenomenon: It is present to some degree in virtually all economic choice situations. The sources of uncertainty are varied and many: nature, human interaction, lack of information, or complexity. Although different situations may not fit neatly into any one of these categories, the following examples should illustrate the sources of difference: the weather, labor-management bargaining tactics, buying a used car, and defending yourself against a lawsuit.

The presence of uncertainty is generally considered costly. As a matter of preference, most people simply dislike uncertainty and are willing to pay in order to avoid or reduce it. We call this *risk aversion*, and it can profoundly affect resource allocation to activities that generate risk. A good example of this is the impact of a high but uncertain inflation rate on the nation's aggregate savings and investment: Because this kind of inflation makes the real return from savings and investment more uncertain, it works to reduce them.

It is important to understand how people respond to the uncertainties they perceive, as well as how public policy can affect those perceptions. *The most widely used model of behavior under uncertainty is the model of expected utility maximization:* Individuals, when confronted with risky choice situations, will attempt to make the decisions that maximize their expected utilities. To understand this, we reviewed the concepts of probability and expected value.

---

[52] The best general reference on efficiency wages is George A. Akerlof and Janet L. Yellen, eds., *Efficiency Wage Models of the Labor Market* (Cambridge: Cambridge University Press, 1986). Two papers that provide empirical support for this concept are J. Konings and P. Walsh. "Evidence of Efficiency Wage Payments in UK Firm Level Panel Data." *Economic Journal*, *104*, No. 424, May 1994, pp. 542–555; and C. Campbell III, "Do Firms Pay Efficiency Wages? Evidence with Data at the Firm Level," *Journal of Labor Economics*, *11*, No. 3, July 1993, pp. 442–470.

Several examples of simple coin-flipping games were given to demonstrate that expected value is not a sufficient predictor of choice-making. Many people will refuse to take risks even when the entry price is fair. Such risk aversion is implied by a diminishing marginal utility of wealth, which leads naturally to the idea that people care about expected utility.

Because risk is costly, social mechanisms that can shift risk to where it is less costly are of great importance. Two methods of doing this are risk-pooling and risk-spreading. Risk-pooling is the essence of insurance; as a consequence of the law of large numbers, the aggregate risk cost to the insurance company from possible claims is much lower than the sum of risk costs when each individual bears his or her own. Risk-spreading, on the other hand, derives its advantage from the fact that one risky event has a lower total risk cost if different individuals share the risk. Dividing the ownership of a company among several partners or among many owners through the sale of stock is a good example of risk-spreading. Individuals also use futures markets for this purpose. For example, a farmer may not wish to bear the full risk of growing crops to be harvested in the future and sold at some unknown price. Instead, he or she may sell the rights to some of that crop now at a known price through the futures market.

The ability of insurance, stock, and futures markets to reduce risk costs is limited to coverage of only a few of the many risky phenomena. In later chapters we will see that other mechanisms of risk reduction are used in private markets: for example, the desire to be an employee rather than an entrepreneur can be understood as a way to reduce the risk. But in addition, many public rules and regulations can be understood as collective attempts to reduce risk costs.

Through the legal system we have the concept of limited liability, which forces certain risks to be shifted. This may not be desirable when the risks taken can have catastrophic consequences: A controversial example of this problem is the Price-Anderson Act, which specifically limits the liability of private producers from nuclear reactor accidents. Part of the function of the criminal justice system is to deter potential offenders from committing crimes and thus limit the risks of that type to be faced by the population. A whole variety of regulations involving product or service quality can be thought of in terms of risk-reduction benefits: examples are occupational licensure or certification, labeling requirements, and safety standards.

When we shift to policy considerations, it is important to recognize that risk is like other undesirable phenomena that we seek to avoid; the willingness to avoid these phenomena depends upon what we must give up to do so. A riskless society would probably be desired by no one, once it is recognized that either crossing the street or driving would have to be banned.

General cost considerations will be explored more fully in later chapters. In this part of the book we are concentrating on models of individual decision-making. Thus the next point emphasized in this chapter is that policy analysts must consider critically whether particular choice situations can be modeled successfully by the expected utility-maximization hypothesis. Some situations, as that of the Slumlord's (or Prisoner's) Dilemma, may be perceived as uncertain rather than risky. Choice-making may result from strategic reasoning rather than estimating probabilities of the various possible states. To the extent that this game-theoretic model applies to urban housing and international trade, it may provide a rationale for policies involving urban renewal and trade agreements to reduce tariffs.

A more general alternative to expected utility maximization is a model that assumes some type of bounded rationality. This type of model recognizes that there are limits to human information-processing abilities, such that the calculations required to maximize expected utility may be beyond them in some situations. This is not a statement that applies only to some people; it applies to all of us. No one has yet discovered an optimal chess strategy, even though we know that at least one exists. It is an empirical question whether particular decision situations we face are ones in which we are likely to find the optimum or, put differently, whether they are more like chess or tic-tac-toe. Most empirical evidence, however, suggests that people do not maximize expected utility in situations perceived as unfamiliar, even if they are quite simple.

Models with bounded rationality emphasize that people learn by trial and error and often develop strategies of problem-solving (or decision-making) that satisfice even if they do not optimize. With enough trials and errors and learning and ingenuity, people can solve incredibly complex problems. But in other situations, either because of complexity or the lack of trials to allow trial-and-error learning, human choice may be very poor. It is recognition that people can make quite serious mistakes that provides a potentially powerful rationale for many regulatory standards and other public policies.

The example of the purchase of disaster insurance in flood- and earthquake-prone locations illustrates this nicely. If people behave according to the expected utility maximization hypothesis, there is no public policy problem except possibly the lack of objective information. But survey evidence suggests that people do not make the coverage decision in that manner, that many people seem to choose purchase strategies that are inferior given their own preferences, and that public policies designed to take account of the bounded rationality in this situation may lead to better decision-making. Similarly, the Equity Premium Puzzle suggests that, owing to myopia and loss aversion, many people may not make good decisions when allocating funds such as those in retirement accounts across different financial assets such as stocks and bonds. One of the most important areas of policy-analytic research concerns more careful exploration of the differences in policy evaluations that arise from these alternative models of decision-making.

Mechanisms to reduce risk can have adverse side effects, as the moral hazard problem illustrates. This problem arises whenever there is a principal-agent contracting relationship with a hidden action information asymmetry; the principal does not know what outcome-affecting action the agent takes. In the case of medical insurance, the contract is between the insurance company (the principal) and the covered individual (the agent). The presence of insurance changes the incentives each individual faces when deciding on the purchase of medical services. Full-coverage insurance reduces the price at the point of service to zero, leading to a Prisoner's Dilemma in which everyone overconsumes medical services (the hidden action).

As a by-product of the desirable growth of medical care insurance coverage for the population, we created a system of medical care that lacked effective mechanisms of cost control. Fee-for-service physicians treating well-insured patients left little incentive to economize on services. This has been mitigated to some extent by reduced reliance on the fee-for-service system and increased reliance on prepaid systems such as health maintenance organizations. However, the vast majority of those covered by Medicare remain in the fee-for-service systems. We have also become more aware of the role of deductibles and coinsurance in limiting moral hazard in these and other insurance circumstances. The moral hazard problem also offers fundamental insights that help us understand the savings and loan crisis of the 1980s, as well as how involuntary employment can arise in a competitive market setting.

In the appendix several calculations are offered to illustrate various aspects of risk assessment. We consider the St. Petersburg Paradox of why those invited to play a game with very high expected value are unwilling to offer much of an entry fee. Measures of risk aversion are introduced and their use in estimating risk costs empirically is illustrated. In the prior section on moral hazard, we identified a trade-off between the amount of risk reduction and the amount of overconsumption of medical services. The calculation of the risk-reduction part of this trade-off is simulated in the appendix, albeit with a highly simplified model. By using boundaries for risk aversion derived by common sense and past experience, one can begin to get a feel for the magnitudes involved. Such an exercise can be very useful in policy analysis, as in the design of a plan for universal coverage.

Exercises

7-1   A consumer has a von Neumann-Morgenstern utility index for income Y:

$$U(Y) = 10Y - \frac{Y^2}{100,000}$$

Furthermore, if she becomes ill, her demand for medical care Q is

$$Q = 200 - 4P$$

where P is the dollar price per unit of medical care. The current price is $P = \$25$. The probability that she will become ill is .15. Her current income is \$10,000. To simplify this problem, assume that 100 units of medical care when the consumer is "ill" just restore the consumer to "healthy." Any medical care above that is considered as consumption of any ordinary good or service. Thus, the utility level in each state depends on the income level *after* medical expenses and premiums supplemented by any consumer surplus from medical care *above* the "healthy" point. (In this problem, the consumer will always choose at least enough medical care to restore her health.)

a What is the consumer's expected utility with no insurance? (Answer: $U = 95,316$.)

b Political candidate A proposes that fully comprehensive health insurance be provided to everyone. The proposed premium would be 10 percent above the actuarially fair level for this consumer (to cover transaction costs). What premium would be charged for this plan, and what expected utility level would it yield? (Answers: \$825; $U = 92,746$.)

c Political candidate B proposes a catastrophic insurance plan. It would cover all expenses above $2750, but the consumer would pay for all medical expenditures up to $2750. Again, the proposed premium would be 10 percent above the actuarially fair level. What premium would be charged for plan B, and what expected utility level would it yield? (Answers: Approximately $371; $U = 93,150$.) *Note:* Is there any difference in the medical service that would be received by this consumer under Plan A or Plan B? What causes the difference in expected utility?

d Political candidate C proposes a comprehensive plan with no deductibles but a 60 percent coinsurance rate (the consumer would pay $0.60 for each $1.00 of medical expenditure). The proposed premium would also be 10 percent above the actuarially fair level. What premium would be charged for plan C, and what expected utility level would it yield? (Answers: $231; $U = 94,821$.)

e Suppose a $50 preventive visit to the doctor lowered the probability of illness to .075. Would the consumer purchase a preventive visit when she is not covered by insurance? (Answer: Yes.) If covered by plan C, would the consumer purchase the preventive visit if the premium were adjusted to reflect the new expected costs plus 10 percent? (Answer: Yes.)

7-2 You are asked your opinion of a new plan proposed as federal unemployment insurance to cover a new group of workers. When uninsured, the *average* spell of unemployment per year per worker is 2 weeks, and the *maximum* time that any of these workers was unemployed was 52 weeks. The plan promises benefits equal to each worker's wage for up to 52 weeks of unemployment. It proposes to finance these benefits by a tax on the weekly wage, and estimates that a 4 percent tax is needed (4% × 50 weeks work per year on average = 2 weeks pay).

a What is moral hazard?

b What is the moral hazard in this proposed plan?

c Do you think the 4 percent tax will raise revenue equal to the expected payout? Explain.

d What do you suggest to reduce the moral hazard?

APPENDIX
EVALUATING THE COSTS OF UNCERTAINTY

In this chapter we have emphasized that uncertainty is costly. In this appendix we consider several different assessments of those costs. The first section reviews the St. Petersburg Paradox, in which we resolve the paradox not by its original resolution of expected utility calculation but by recognizing the strong effects of payoff constraints. The second section illustrates some explicit calculations of the value of benefits from risk-pooling and risk-spreading. The third section contains a method, albeit highly simplified, for estimating the order of magnitude of risk cost in a policy situation. It is intended to suggest that plausible boundaries can be placed on the increase in risk costs borne by the population because of an increase in the average medical coinsurance rate. This exercise could be useful in the design of national health policy.

Real Constraints and the St. Petersburg Paradox

A common but somewhat incorrect example often used to illustrate the point that expected value is not a sufficient predictor of decision-making behavior is the St. Petersburg Paradox. Consider the game in which an evenly weighted coin is flipped until it comes up heads, which ends the game. Suppose the winner receives $2 if a head comes up on the first flip, $2^2 = $4 if a head does not come up until the second flip, $2^3 = $8 if there is not a head until the third flip, and so on. If a head does not come up until the ith flip, then the payoff to the player is 2^i. Thus the payoff is relatively low if a head comes up "soon" but grows exponentially higher the more flips it takes before a head finally comes up. On the other hand, the probability is relatively high that the game will end "soon." There is a $\frac{1}{2}$ probability that the game will end on the first flip, $(\frac{1}{2})^2 = \frac{1}{4}$ probability that it ends on the second flip, $(\frac{1}{2})^3 = \frac{1}{8}$ probability that it ends on the third flip, and so on. The probability that the game continues until the ith flip is $(\frac{1}{2})^i$. Thus the game has the expected payoffs shown in Table 7A-1.

Since theoretically the game can go on forever, its expected value is infinite. That is,

$$\sum_{i-1}^{\infty} \Pi_i X_i = 1 + 1 + 1 + \ldots = \infty$$

But when people are asked what entry price they are willing to pay to play the game, the response is invariably a number below infinity; most people will not even pay a paltry $1 million to play this game. In fact, few people will offer more than $20 to play. This is the paradox: *Why should people offer so little to play a game with such a high expected value?*

This is where the idea of diminishing marginal utility of wealth enters. If the gain from successive tosses in the form of expected *utility* payoffs diminishes (unlike the constancy of the expected *monetary* gain), it could have a finite sum. Then it is perfectly plausible that individuals would offer only finite amounts of money for the privilege of playing the game.[53]

---

[53] For example, suppose the utility value of the ith payoff is $(\frac{3}{2})^i$. Then the expected utility $E(U)$ from playing the game is

$$E(U) = \sum_{i=1}^{\infty} (\tfrac{1}{2})^i (\tfrac{3}{2})^i = \sum_{i=1}^{\infty} (\tfrac{3}{4})^i = 3$$

This follows because the sum of an infinite series $a, ar, ar^2, \ldots, ar^n, \ldots$ equals $a/(1 - r)$ for $r < 1$. In the above equation $a = \frac{3}{4}$ and $r = \frac{3}{4}$. We have not yet discussed the monetary value of an expected utility increase of 3 utils to this individual, but it should be clear that there is no reason why it could not be a low dollar amount.

Since $X = 2^i$ and $U = (\frac{3}{2})^i$, we can take the logarithm of each equation and divide one by the other to deduce:

$$\ln U = \frac{(\ln X)(\ln \tfrac{3}{2})}{\ln 2}$$

Table 7A-1
A Game with Infinite Expected Value

Flip number	Probability	Payoff	Expected payoff
1	$\frac{1}{2}$	2	1
2	$\frac{1}{4}$	4	1
3	$\frac{1}{2}$	8	1
4	$\frac{1}{16}$	16	1
.			
.			
.			

However, the above reasoning does not explain why most individuals in fact will offer *low* dollar amounts to play the game, and in that sense the idea of expected utility maximization does not really resolve the paradox. The answer actually has nothing to do with diminishing marginal utility. The real answer is that no game operator has the assets to be able to make the larger payoffs.

For example, suppose the U.S. government guaranteed to pay prizes up to $10 trillion—roughly the entire annual product of the U.S. economy. That would enable payment of the scheduled prizes if heads came up on any of the first forty-three flips, but beyond that the prize could get no larger than $10 trillion. Thus the expected value of this game would be only $44. Since no plausible game operator could guarantee payments anywhere near that size, the expected value of the game with realistic prize limits is considerably below $44. If the maximum prize is $10 million, for example, the expected value of the game is approximately $24.

Calculating the Value of Risk-Pooling and Risk-Spreading

The chapter's text uses a simple example to illustrate how risk-pooling reduces risk costs. The example is of two identical risk-averse individuals. Each has $50,000 in wealth, $5000 of which is subject to theft; each independently faces a probability of theft equal to .2. Here we further assume each has a specific utility function of wealth W[54]:

$$U(W) = -e^{-0.0002W}$$

or

$$U = X^{0.58496}$$

We interpret this equation as showing the utility increase from additional dollars. When $U = 3$, the equation implies $X = \$6.54$. If the individual behaves in accordance with the expected utility theorem, then $6.54 is the most this individual would offer to play the game.

[54] This utility function is one with diminishing marginal utility of wealth. It is characterized by mild risk aversion: The individual is indifferent to receiving $900 with certainty or accepting a 50 percent chance to win $2000. This is explained further in the third section. The natural number $e = 2.71828$.

Using it, we can calculate certain-wealth equivalents and pure risk costs. When the two bear the risks independently, or self-insure, each has an expected utility of

$$E(U) = .2U(\$45,000) + .8U(\$50,000)$$

$$= .2(-e^{-9}) + .8(-e^{-10})$$

$$= -0.0000610019$$

We find the certain-wealth equivalent (W_c) by solving

$$-0.0000610019 = -e^{-0.0002W}$$

or

$$W_c = \$48,523.03$$

Since the expected wealth of each is $49,000 [= .2($45,000) + .8($50,000], the risk cost [$E(W) - W_c$] is $476.97. In other words, each would forgo as much as $476.97 of expected value in order to be rid of the risk from self-insurance.

If the two individuals agree to pool their risk, recall that there are three possible outcomes or states:

1. Neither individual has a loss from theft ($W = \$50,000$), with probability .64.
2. Both individuals have losses from theft ($W = \$45,000$), with probability .04.
3. One individual has a loss and the other does not ($W = \$47,500$), with probability .32.

The expected wealth remains at $49,000, the same as under self-insurance. What happens to expected utility? With expected wealth the same but with the likelihood of ending up close to it greater, the risk is reduced and expected utility increases (i.e., is a smaller negative number):

$$E(U) = .64U(\$50,000) + .04U(\$45,000) + .32U(\$47,500)$$

$$= -0.0000579449$$

The certain-wealth equivalent is found by solving as follows:

$$-0.0000579449 = -e^{-W_c}$$

whence

$$W_c = \$48,780.09$$

Thus, we can see that this simple risk-pooling arrangement increases expected utility because it reduces the risk cost per person from $476.97 to only $219.91. Another way to look at it is from the perspective of the compensation principle. That is, let us ask whether the change from self-insurance to risk-pooling has benefits greater than costs. Each individual values the initial situation at $48,523.03 and the risk-pooling situation at $48,780.09. Therefore, each would be willing to pay up to the difference of $257.06 in order to make the change.

The net benefits from making the change are $514.12, and, in this example, each person is strictly better off.

Recall that the general principle of diversification of assets can be seen as an example of risk-pooling. Let us use the utility function above to compare the expected utility of a risk-averse individual under two alternative arrangements—one in which the individual invests in one firm and the other in which the individual invests the same total amount spread equally among ten *different* and *independent* firms similar to the first firm.

Let one strategy be to invest $1000 in a risky, high-technology firm with a probability of .8 of being successful and returning $5000 and a probability .2 of failing and returning nothing. Assume the individual has $46,000 in wealth initially and thus utility:

$$U(\$46,000) = -e^{-9.2} = -0.0001010394$$

The proposed investment clearly has expected value greater than the entry cost:

$$.8(\$5000) + .2(0) = \$4000 > \$1000$$

We first check to see if making this investment would raise the individual's expected utility level (otherwise, the individual would not invest):

$$E(U) = .8U(\$50,000) + .2U(\$45,000)$$

This is the same expression we evaluated in the self-insurance example, where we found

$$E(U) = -0.0000610019$$

and the certain-wealth equivalent is

$$W_c = \$48,523.03$$

Thus the individual prefers this investment to no investment at all. The risk cost, as before, is $476.97.

Now we wish to see if the diversification of assets can reduce the risk cost. The second strategy is to divide the $1000 into smaller investments of $100 in each of ten different firms. We choose the firms to be similar in risk to the first: Each firm has a .8 chance of being successful and returning $500 and a .2 chance of losing the $100 investment. We choose diverse firms—ones such that there are no linkages between the successes or failures of any of them.[55] The expected value of each investment is $400 [= .8($500) + .2($0)]; since the investments are independent, the total expected value is simply 10 × $400, or $4000.

---

[55] When there is interdependence among some of the investments in a portfolio, the diversification is reduced. As an extreme example, suppose the profitability of building supply firms is determined solely by whether interest rates are low (which increases the demand for new construction) or high (which reduces the demand). Making small investments in each of ten building supply firms is then no different than investing the same total in any one: All ten firms will either be profitable or will not be.

Calculating expected value and utility is more complicated when there is interdependence among the assets in a pool. For a discussion of this in the context of energy investments, see P.S. Dasgupta and G. M. Heal, *Economic Theory and Exhaustible Resources* (Oxford: James Nisbet & Company, Ltd., and Cambridge University Press, 1979), pp. 377–388, especially pp. 385–387.

Table 7A-2
The Expected Utility of a Diversified Portfolio

Number of successful investments	Probability	Wealth level	Expected utility[a]
0	.0000	45,000	.0
1	.0000	45,500	.0
2	.0001	46,000	.0000000101
3	.0008	46,500	.0000000731
4	.0055	47,000	.0000004550
5	.0264	47,500	.0000019761
6	.0881	48,000	.0000059669
7	.2013	48,500	.0000123364
8	.3020	49,000	.0000167464
9	.2684	49,500	.0000134669
10	.1074	50,000	.0000048760
Sums	1.0000		.0000559069

[a] $U(W) = -e^{-0.0002W}$.

The numbers used to calculate the expected utility are shown in Table 7A-2. There are eleven possible outcomes, since the number of successful investments can be anywhere from zero to ten. The probability that any given number of successes will arise, given that each firm has .8 chance of success, is provided by the binomial probability measure.[56] We follow the usual procedure for calculating expected utility: we multiply the probability of each possible outcome by its utility level and sum.

From Table 7A-2 we see that the expected utility of the diversified portfolio is greater (i.e., less negative) than that of the undiversified portfolio. The certain-wealth equivalent of the expected utility level is found by solving

$$-0.0000559069 = -e^{0.0002W}$$

[56] When there are n independent risky events each with probability of success Π, the probability Π_r, that there are exactly r successes is given by the binomial probability measure

$$\Pi_r = \frac{n!}{r!(n-r)!} \Pi^r (1-\Pi)^{n-r}$$

The notation $n!$ means $(n)(n-1)(n-2) \cdots (1)$. For example, $4! = 4(3)(2)(1) = 24$. To illustrate the calculations for Table 7A-2, the probability that there are exactly 8 successes in the 10 investments is

$$\Pi = \frac{10!}{8!2!} (.8^8)(.2^2)$$

$$= \frac{10(9)(.00671)}{2}$$

$$= .30199$$

whence,

$$W_c = \$48,959.11$$

Thus the risk cost has been reduced from $476.97 to only $40.89 by diversifying the portfolio. Again, this risk-pooling strategy works because it reduces the probability of extreme outcomes and increases the probability of an outcome near the expected value. In this example the individual has a 96.72 percent chance of ending up with wealth in the range from $48,000 to $50,000.

Finally, we can see the advantage of risk-spreading easily through a reinterpretation of the empirical example we have just used. Suppose we characterize a risky high-technology firm by the $1000 investment with a .8 probability of returning $5000 and a .2 probability of returning nothing. Let us consider whether it is more efficient to have the firm owned by a single owner or by a partnership of ten. We assume for simplicity that potential owners are homogeneous and risk-averse and that each has preinvestment wealth of $46,000 and the same utility function we have been using.

We have already seen that a single owner would evaluate the certain-wealth equivalent of his or her position at $48,523. That is, an individual with the given preferences would be indifferent to receiving $2523 with certainty or owning the firm. Now let us show that a ten-person partnership would value the firm at a higher cash equivalency.

To raise the $1000 required to operate the firm, each partner would contribute $100, and so each would end up with either $45,900 (if unsuccessful) or $46,400 (if successful). The expected utility of this position is

$$E(U) = .8U(\$46,400) + .2U(\$45,900)$$

$$= -0.000095233$$

This has a certain-wealth equivalent of

$$-0.000095233 = e^{-0.0002W_c}$$

whence,

$$W_c = \$46,295.92$$

In other words, each partner would be indifferent to receiving $295.92 with certainty or owning the firm. But then in the aggregate the partnership values the firm at ten times that, or $2959, compared with only $2523 for the single owner. By the compensation principle, a change from single ownership to the partnership would increase efficiency: the partners could buy out the single owner at a price that would make everyone better off. The "social profit" is $436; it consists totally of the reduction in risk cost from $477 faced by a single owner to the $41 [10($46,300 − $46,295.92)] total risk cost of the partnership.

Methods of Assessing Risk Cost○

In the last section, we simply assumed a specific utility function in order to illustrate risk cost calculations. Now we wish to develop a somewhat more general method for estimating these risk costs. To begin with, we define two ways of measuring the degree of risk aversion:

1. *Absolute risk aversion:* $a(W) = -U''(W)/U'(W)$
2. *Relative risk aversion:* $r(W) = -WU''(W)/U'(W)$

Note that whenever an individual has a utility-of-wealth function characterized by risk aversion, $U''(W) < 0$ and, of course, $U'(W) > 0$. Thus, both measures of risk are positive when there is risk aversion. Also, the second measure $r(W)$ is simply the elasticity of the marginal utility of wealth. This corresponds to greater risk aversion when marginal utility is changing rapidly or, equivalently, when the utility function is more concave. A straight-line utility function, on the other hand, scores a zero on both measures ($U'' = 0$) and indicates risk neutrality.

To get a feel for the interpretation of these measures, we use an approximation suggested by Pratt.[57] Recall the risk cost definition: the difference between the expected wealth in a risky situation and its certain-wealth equivalent. Pratt shows that the risk cost C can be approximated by the following formula, which is derived from a Taylor series expansion:

$$C = \tfrac{1}{2} a(\bar{W}) \sigma_w^2$$

where $\bar{W}$ is the expected wealth and σ_w^2 the variance of wealth. Thus for individuals who have the same expected wealth and are faced with the same uncertainties, those with greater absolute risk aversion will pay more to avoid the risk. The absolute risk aversion is proportional to the absolute amount of money an individual will pay to avoid a fair gamble. Similarly, we can express the relative risk cost as the ratio of the risk cost to expected wealth:

$$\frac{C}{\bar{W}} = \tfrac{1}{2} a(\bar{W}) \frac{\sigma_w^2}{\bar{W}}$$

or

$$\frac{C}{\bar{W}} = \tfrac{1}{2} r(\bar{W}) \left(\frac{\sigma_w^2}{\bar{W}^2} \right)$$

where the term in parentheses on the right has a standard statistical interpretation: the coefficient of variation squared. This last equation shows that the share of wealth an individual will give up to avoid a certain risk is proportional to his or her relative risk aversion.

As we have seen in earlier chapters, simulation techniques may be profitably used when we do not have precise knowledge of certain parameter values but have some reason to believe the values are likely to lie within a given range. In this case we do not know the values of the risk-aversion measures for particular individuals. Nevertheless, common sense can be a useful guide.

[57] J.W. Pratt, "Risk Aversion in the Small and in the Large," *Econometrica, 32,* 1964, pp. 122–136.

Two parametric utility functions have been found to be useful for empirical exercises involving risk aversion. One of them is the function

$$U(W) = -e^{-aW}$$

where $a > 0$, which is characterized by constant absolute risk aversion equal to a. To see this we take the first and second derivatives:

$$U'(W) = ae^{-aW}$$

$$U''(W) = -a^2 e^{-aW}$$

Therefore, applying the definition of absolute risk aversion, we find

$$a(W) = \frac{a^2 e^{-aW}}{ae^{-aW}} = a$$

The other function of interest displays constant relative risk aversion equal to r:

$$U(W) = \frac{W^{1-r}}{1-r}$$

where $r > 0$, $r \neq 1$. To show this, we again take derivatives:

$$U'(W) = \frac{(1-r)W^{-r}}{1-r} = W^{-r}$$

$$U''(W) = -rW^{-r-1}$$

By applying the definition of relative risk aversion, we get

$$r(W) = \frac{rW^{-r}}{W^{-r}} = r$$

Now let us work with the constant absolute risk-aversion function and ask what values are reasonable for a. Imagine asking people what entry price they would require in order to make (be indifferent to) a bet with an even chance of winning or losing $1000. Casual observation suggests that a practical lower bound might be $50, in the sense that very few people would accept the bet for anything lower and the vast majority of people would demand more.

To see what degree of absolute risk aversion a this implies, we must solve the equations that indicate the utility equivalence of current wealth W with the gamble:

$$U(W) = \tfrac{1}{2}U(W + 1050) + \tfrac{1}{2}U(W - 950)$$

For the constant absolute risk aversion case:

$$-e^{-aW} = -\tfrac{1}{2}e^{-a(W+1050)} - \tfrac{1}{2}e^{-a(W-950)}$$

The initial wealth level drops out, and on simplifying we have

$$2 = e^{-1050a} + e^{950a}$$

This equation can be solved on a calculator, and we find $a \cong 0.0001$.[58] Suppose for an upper bound we use an entry price of $333; this makes a 50-50 chance of winning $1333 or losing $667 and is probably sufficient to attract most investors. Solving as above, this implies $a \cong 0.0007$.

To show how one could use these boundaries in a simulation of the effects of coinsurance on medical care insurance, a highly simplified illustrative calculation is done below. The major simplification is to assume that each household only faces two possible states of the world: healthy with $\Pi_H = .9$, and ill with $\Pi_I = .1$. In an actual simulation, one would use a standard statistical distribution to model the many real contingencies that households face.[59] We assume that the uninsured household would purchase $5600 worth of medical services if ill and that the price elasticity of demand is −0.5.

Let W_c be the certain-wealth equivalent that makes the "average" household indifferent to its current uninsured and risky state. That is,

$$U(W_c) = \mathrm{EU}(W) = .9U(W) + .1U(W - 5600)$$

or for the specific utility function

$$-e^{-aW_c} = .9(-e^{-aW}) + .1(-e^{a(W-5600)})$$

which can be simplified as follows:

$$e^{a(W-W_c)} = .9 + .1e^{a(5600)}$$

and, taking logs,

$$W - W_c = \frac{1}{a}\ln(.9 + .1e^{a(5600)})$$

By using our two bounds for a in the above equation, we find that

$$W - W_c = \begin{cases} \$723.83 & a = 0.0001 \\ \$2542.31 & a = 0.0007 \end{cases}$$

Since the risk cost of being completely uninsured is $W - W_c$ minus the expected medical care cost [$560 = .1($5600)$], we see it is between $163.83 and $1985.31 per household.

---

[58] For those not familiar with inelegant but remarkably practical ways of solving many problems by trial and error, here is how one might proceed for the above. Since we know a is positive when there is risk aversion, the answer will be greater than 0. The first term must be a fraction because of the negative sign in the exponent (the bigger a, the smaller the fraction. Since $e \cong 2.72$, any exponent larger than 1 makes the second term too big, or $a > \frac{1}{950} = 0.001$. Therefore, we have quickly realized that $0 < a < 0.001$. From here, one can achieve accuracy to any decimal point by trial and error. Take the halfway point in this interval, 0.0005, and try it on the right-hand-side terms, $0.59 + 1.61 = 2.20$, so 0.0005 is too big, and $0 < a < 0.0005$. Proceed in this manner until the difference between the two boundaries is negligible for your purposes.

[59] This exercise is a simplification of an actual one done by Martin Feldstein and described in his article, "The Welfare Loss of Excess Health Insurance," *Journal of Political Economy*, *81*, No. 2, part 1, March/April 1973, pp. 251–280. In the actual Feldstein simulation, the number of hospitalizations per household is assumed to resemble a Poisson distribution and the duration per hospitalization is assumed to resemble the gamma distribution.

Now, if each household purchased an insurance policy with a coinsurance provision of 50 percent, its members, when ill, would purchase more medical services. We have assumed $Q = 5600P^{-0.5}$, where $P = \$1.00$ initially. With coinsurance, P drops to $\$0.50$ and $Q = 7920$ (the moral hazard factor). Thus, in the event of illness, the insurance company and the household will each pay $\$3960$ to the hospital. The insurance company will charge $\$396$ for each policy, which the household loses in all states. To find the residual cost of risk to the household, we ask what certain wealth W_c^* would bring the same utility as is now expected:

$$U(W_c^*) = .9U(W - 396) + .1U(W - 396 - 3960)$$

or, using the same algebra as above

$$W - 396 - W_c^* = \tfrac{1}{a}\ln(.9 + .1e^{a(3960)})$$

Using our two bounds for a, we calculate:

$$W - 396 - W_c^* = \begin{cases} \$474.43 & a = 0.0001 \\ \$1308.44 & a = 0.0007 \end{cases}$$

As before, the residual risk cost is the difference between these figures and the household's expected out-of-pocket medical costs of $\$396$, so it is between $\$78$ and $\$912.45$. Therefore, the risk saving from taking out partial insurance coverage is between $\$85.40$ and $\$1072.87$ per household (the difference between the total and residual risk costs).

We emphasize that this exercise is intended to demonstrate a procedure for using risk-aversion measures in a simulation. To present an actual simulation would require more detail and more sensitivity testing than is appropriate for the purpose of this book. However, studying and understanding exercises like this one should provide the necessary courage to grapple with the existing work of this type, and perhaps improve upon it.

CHAPTER EIGHT

ALLOCATION OVER TIME AND INDEXATION

CURRENT ECONOMIC DECISIONS often have extremely important consequences for the future well-being of the individuals who make them (as well as society as a whole). For example, the decision to *invest* in schooling today can have a significant impact on an individual's future earnings profile. To do this, many students *borrow* funds to finance today's consumption and repay the loan later out of their future earnings. The amount someone chooses to *save* from current earnings when working has important implications for the amount of retirement or other income available to that person in the future. To make these decisions, an individual must somehow balance today's wants and opportunities against those of the future. In this chapter we consider some models that help us to understand and analyze these choices and some important public policies that affect them.

An investment is an increment to the capital stock, where capital refers to the durable resources that will be available to help produce a flow of consumption in the future. For example, raw materials, land, and labor can be allocated this year to the construction of a new factory. In the future, the factory will be used to make clothing. The creation of the factory is an investment that increases our total capital stock as well as the future flow of clothing available for consumption. Similarly, one can invest in people and increase the stock of "human capital." For example, an additional student in medical school is an investment that adds to the future stock of physicians and increases the future flow of medical services.

When a society invests, it is giving up current consumption in favor of future consumption. The medical student, for example, could be working in a restaurant producing meals instead of attending school. All of the invested resources could be used instead to increase current consumption. Any individual, in deciding whether to invest, must consider the current and future effects on both income and consumption. The medical student not only forgoes the restaurant income, but must be able to pay tuition and have enough left over for room and board. These costs must be weighed against the future benefits from becoming a physician.

Some investments will be undertaken only if the investor can *borrow* purchasing power today that can be repaid out of future earnings (e.g., a student loan). That is, the individual investor is not necessarily the one who defers current consumption in an amount equal to the invested resources. Others might be willing to *lend* or *save* some of their current purchasing power. Investment demands are bids to use real resources for future rather than current consumption (the student who pays tuition and expects teachers and classrooms to be provided in return), and savings supplies are offers of real resources for future use rather than for current consumption (the individual who offers himself or herself as a student). We will show that *the interest rate is the price that affects the investment demand* (a declining function of the interest rate) *as well as the savings supply* (an increasing function of the interest rate). To begin to understand the individual decisions that underlie the demands and supplies, we introduce a simple model that concludes that an individual will undertake all investments whose *present discounted values* are greater than zero at the given rate of interest.

There are many reasons why other models apart from this initial one may better explain actual decisions involving resource allocation over time. But our primary purpose is to introduce the importance of allocating resources over time, as well as the concept of discounting that is used to make comparisons across time periods. Our initial model illustrates these aspects clearly. We shall then review some of the evidence on actual individual behavior with respect to time allocation (we mentioned *myopia* in the last chapter). We shall also address in a limited way the problem of the uncertainty that individuals face in making intertemporal decisions.

One important source of intertemporal uncertainty is the degree of inflation, which makes the relationship between real future prices and current ones unclear. While an analysis of the causes of inflation is beyond our scope, we explain how various *indexing mechanisms* are used to adapt to inflation and to reduce an individual's uncertainty. After reviewing some principles of index construction, we consider a number of practical problems that arise in constructing and implementing the necessary indices. These problems have relevance in several policy areas such as government bond issuance, Social Security payments, and school financing. They may also be thought of as a special subset of the more general problem of linking decision-making to any social indicator (e.g., crime rates and health statistics).

Intertemporal Allocation and Capital Markets

For most people the timing of the receipts of income from their wealth does not match perfectly with the desired timing of their expenditures, or consumption. Although one could consider this problem over any period of time, it is most useful to think first about an average lifetime or life cycle. Figure 8-1 represents a family's income over a period of approximately 60 years and its consumption pattern over the same period. The most important feature to note is the relative evenness of the consumption pattern compared to the uneven income pattern.

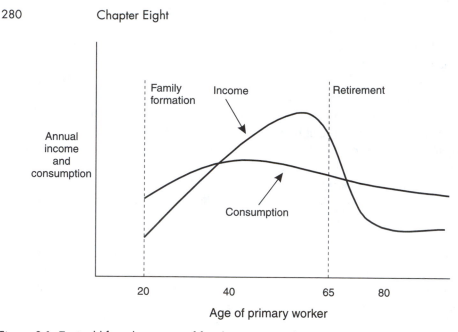

Figure 8-1. Typical life style pattern of family income and consumption.

The patterns in Figure 8-1 approximate facts we can observe. Incomes are typically low when the adult family members are in their 20s and may be in school or just starting their careers. They usually rise fairly steadily until they peak when these adults are somewhere in their late 50s or 60s, and shortly thereafter plummet sharply because of retirement. Meanwhile, consumption is likely to outpace income in the earlier stages: home-occupancy and child-rearing expenses, for example, are usually financed by borrowing that is paid back out of the savings that accrue during the middle stages of the family's life cycle. Similarly, the savings are used to help finance consumption during the low-income years of retirement. In other words, these facts suggest that a family prefers to consume at its "permanent" income level—roughly the average income over a lifetime—rather than have to alter consumption to fit the pattern of transitory annual income.[1]

[1] The difference between permanent and transitory income can often have a profound analytic impact on the evaluation of policies by equity standards. As one example, consider the degree of progressivity (or regressivity) of a tax such as the property tax. If the tax dollars paid by home owners are compared with their annual incomes, a regressive bias results.

To see this, recognize that many families living in homes with tax bills that are high compared with their low current incomes are at either the beginning or the end of their lifetime income stream. The tax bill as a proportion of permanent income for these families is much lower. Similarly, people in the equivalent homes but in the high-income stages of the life cycle will pay only a small portion of their high current incomes in taxes, even though their taxes are a much higher proportion of their permanent incomes. In other words, a tax that is proportional to home value is also approximately proportional to permanent income but will appear to be regressive in relation to current income. Thus, whatever the true incidence of the property tax, it appears more regressive if measured using current income as a base. Calculations showing the difference are in S. Sacher, "Housing Demand and Property Tax Incidence in a Life-Cycle Framework," *Public Finance Quarterly, 21,* No. 3, July 1993, pp. 235–259. This

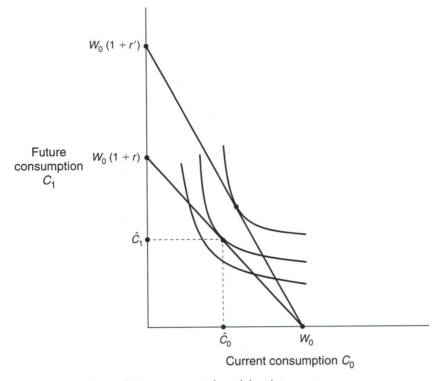

Figure 8-2. Savings $W_0 - C_0$ in a two-period model with interest rate r.

Individual Consumption Choice with Savings Opportunities

What we wish to do now is build up a more systematic model of individual desires to allocate resources over time and examine how capital market transactions can and do facilitate that allocation. We begin by imagining a consumer to have a fixed *wealth* endowment that can be allocated for consumption in one of two time periods. One important point of the present and successive models is to think more generally about the determinants of a consumer's budget constraint, and to recognize that it is not determined simply by the flow of current income but also by the stock that we refer to as wealth.

Figure 8-2 shows some indifference curves to represent the preferences of an individual for consumption in two different time periods: current consumption C_0 (the first half of life)

phenomenon was first noted in Henry Aaron, "A New View of Property Tax Incidence," *American Economic Review, 64,* No. 2, May 1974, pp. 212–221.

This does not mean that property taxes are no more of a burden to low-current-income families than to high-current-income families with the same permanent incomes. However, differences in burden are due to imperfections in the capital market. For example, an elderly couple may own a home that has greatly appreciated in value and on which the mortgage has long been paid off. This can leave them in the awkward position of being wealthy but with little liquid income. They might wish to pay their property taxes by giving up some of their home equity, but methods of lending to facilitate that (reverse mortgages) are not always available or are not at competitive rates.

versus future consumption C_1 (the second half). In this model the units of consumption are homogeneous except for time, and both are normal goods (think of them as little baskets each identically filled with a little of many different goods and services). The curves are drawn more bent than straight, with the corner near an imaginary line at an angle of 45° from the origin. This is to reflect the observation that many individuals have a preference for reasonably even consumption over time. (That is, over a wide range of possible slopes for the budget constraint, the tangency will be near the 45° line.)

The shape of our curves does depend on the idea of using generic, broad consumption units. There is no reason why in a model with more goods the time indifference curves for specific commodities cannot have quite different shapes from each other and from the ones drawn. Hearing aids might be strongly preferred only in the future period, whereas water skiing might be the opposite. But with our generic goods, the slope of the indifference curve is sometimes referred to as the *marginal rate of time preference*. It is nothing more, however, than a marginal rate of substitution and it varies along any indifference curve.

The wealth endowment is shown as W_0, where each unit of wealth can be used to purchase a unit of consumption today. However, we must determine the rest of the budget constraint; choosing $C_0 = W_0$ (and $C_1 = 0$) gives us only one of its extreme points. An extreme alternative to consuming all the wealth today is to defer consumption completely, saving all the wealth for future consumption. If that is done, the wealth can be put in a bank or in government bonds or in other savings instruments, where it will earn r, the market rate of interest.[2] Thus the maximum future consumption that is possible is $C_1 = W_0(1 + r)$, when $C_0 = 0$. Of course, the individual could choose any of the combinations on the line connecting the two extreme points; that locus is the budget constraint. At each point on the locus, **savings is simply the amount of deferred consumption** $W_0 - C_0$. The saved funds, after earning interest, are used to buy future consumption $C_1 = (W_0 - C_0)(1 + r)$. This is the budget constraint equation: any combination of C_0 and C_1 that for given W_0 and r makes the relation hold.

As usual, to maximize utility, the individual will choose the point on the budget constraint that is just tangent to an indifference curve. In Figure 8-2 the individual consumes $\hat{C}_0$ in the current period and saves $W_0 - \hat{C}_0$. Thus, the specific choice of how much to save depends not only on the initial wealth endowment and preferences but also on the interest rate, or the size of the return to savings. This brings us to the next important point of this illustration: *to interpret the interest rate as a relative price*. The slope of the budget constraint equals the (negative) ratio of the intercept levels on the vertical (future consumption) and horizontal (current consumption) axes:

$$-\frac{W_0(1+r)}{W_0} = -\frac{(1+r)}{1} = -\frac{1}{1/(1+r)}$$

Since we know that the slope of an ordinary budget constraint for two goods is minus the ratio of the two prices, it is only natural to interpret this slope similarly. The numerator

---

[2] We are ignoring regulatory constraints that may prevent banks from offering the market rate of interest. We are also referring to the "riskless" rate of interest; a range of interest rates exist at any one time in part because some vehicles for saving and borrowing are riskier than others.

1 is the price of a unit of current consumption. The denominator $1/(1 + r)$ is the price of a unit of future consumption. To see this, note that if we give up one unit of consumption today, we can buy $1 + r$ units of future consumption. To buy precisely one unit of future consumption, we must give up $1/(1 + r)$ units of current consumption, and thus that is its price. This latter number is sometimes referred to as the *present value,* or *present discounted value,* of a unit of future consumption. Think of it as the amount of money that must be put in the bank today (forgoing current consumption) in order to have enough to obtain one unit of consumption in the future. The rate r is then referred to as the *discount rate.* If the discount rate is 0.10, it means the present value of $1.00 worth of future consumption is $0.91 (the amount of current consumption forgone to get the unit of future consumption).

An alternative way to see the same point is to rewrite the budget constraint as if "solving" for W_0:

$$W_0 = 1 C_0 + \frac{1}{1 + r} C_1$$

This looks like any ordinary budget constraint,

$$W = P_X X + P_Y Y$$

where the prices and quantities in the time equation correspond as follows:

$$P_X = 1 \quad X = C_0$$

and

$$P_Y = \frac{1}{1 + r} \quad Y = C_1$$

In this form, *the budget constraint is any combination of C_0 and C_1 that makes the present discounted value of the consumption stream equal to the wealth.* (Note that only future consumption is discounted; current consumption is already in its present value.)

In this model an increase in the interest rate unambiguously makes the individual better off. It is equivalent to reducing the price of the future good, all other prices being constant. The budget constraint rotates outward from W_0, as shown in Figure 8-2, which means that the individual can reach a higher indifference curve. This result is due purely to the fact that the individual can only be a *saver* in this model: There are no opportunities for borrowing. C_0 must be less than or equal to W_0. An increase in the interest rate will unambiguously increase C_1; both substitution and income effects are positive. However, we do not know if savings will increase. The income effect on C_0 is positive, but the substitution effect is negative.

Individual Consumption Choice with Borrowing and Savings Opportunities

The unambiguous welfare effect of an interest rate increase disappears as we make the model more realistic and allow borrowing. To do so, we replace the wealth endowment by

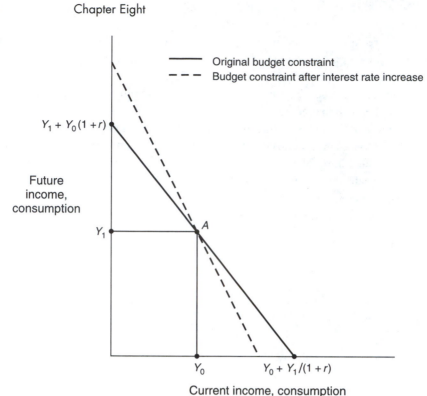

Figure 8-3. The budget constraint for allocation between time periods with savings and borrowing possible.

an income stream. The individual owns a *stock* of real resources that we refer to as *capital*. The capital produces a *flow* of services that earn income Y_0 in the current period and Y_1 in the future. **The individual's wealth is the value of the capital assets, which equals the present value of the income streams that they will generate.** Constrained by the value of those income flows, the individual must decide on a consumption pattern. We assume for now that current borrowing or lending (saving) of capital resources can be done at the market rate of interest. Thus this model takes r, Y_0, and Y_1 as fixed parameters that constrain the individual's choice of the two variables C_0 and C_1.

Figure 8-3 shows this slightly more sophisticated model graphically. The individual is initially at the point (Y_0, Y_1) and, of course, can choose $C_0 = Y_0$ and $C_1 = Y_1$. But what does the budget constraint look like? At one extreme, the individual could save every penny of Y_0 (i.e., choose $C_0 = 0$), put it in the bank where it returns $Y_0(1 + r)$ in the future period, and have $C_1 = Y_1 + Y_0(1 + r)$, which is the intercept level on the future consumption axis. At the other extreme, the individual can increase current consumption above the Y_0 level by borrowing against future income. The bank will lend the present value $Y_1/(1 + r)$ today in return for being paid back Y_1 next period. Current consumption can be made equal to the present value of the income stream. So when $C_1 = 0$, $C_0 = Y_0 + Y_1/(1+r)$. This is the intercept level on the current consumption axis. The budget constraint is thus the line that connects those two points and has this equation[3]:

$$C_1 = Y_1 + (Y_0 - C_0)(1+r)$$

You can think of this as saying that an individual can choose any future consumption level that equals future income plus the value of any savings. The second term on the right-hand side represents the future value of savings if $C_0 < Y_0$. But the individual might choose to borrow rather than save, which would make the second term negative, with $C_0 > Y_0$. In this case the second term simply represents the cost of borrowing: the reduction in future consumption that results from repaying the loan. The slope of the budget constraint is $-(1+r)$, as before.[4]

The budget constraint equation can be rearranged as below with the following interpretation: *The budget constraint is all combinations of C_0 and C_1 that make the present value of the consumption stream equal to wealth, the present value of the income stream:*

$$C_0 + \frac{C_1}{1+r} = Y_0 + \frac{Y_1}{1+r}$$

As noted an individual may be either a saver or borrower, depending upon personal preferences. Any point on the budget constraint to the *right* of point A represents borrowing ($C_0 > Y_0$), and any point to the left of point A represents saving ($C_0 < Y_0$). Suppose the interest rate now increases. That causes the budget constraint to rotate clockwise about point A, as shown by the dashed line in Figure 8-3: The present value of future income is lower (less can be gained by borrowing), and the future value of current income is higher (more can be gained by saving).

If the individual was a saver originally, he or she must be better off, since more of each good can be consumed than before. However, the person who was initially a borrower will be worse off unless the new savings opportunities outweigh the worsened borrowing prospects. Regardless of whether the person is a borrower or a saver, the substitution effect is to increase C_1 and reduce C_0. For the saver, income effects are positive and thus C_1 will increase and the change in C_0 is ambiguous, as before. For the borrower, we do not know if real income is increased or decreased and thus cannot predict the income effects.

---

[3] Let $C_1 = mC_0 + b$, where m and b are, respectively, the unknown slope and intercept of the budget constraint. From the point where $C_0 = 0$ and $C_1 = Y_1 + Y_0(1+r)$, we know that $b = Y_1 + Y_0(1+r)$. From the point where $C_0 = Y_0 + Y_1/(1+r)$ and $C_1 = 0$, we know that $m = -b/C_0 = -[Y_1 + Y_0(1+r)]/[Y_0 + Y_1/(1+r)] = -(1+r)$. Therefore, $C_1 = b + mC_0 = Y_1 + (Y_0 - C_0)(1+r)$.

[4] This is shown in the above note. We can also check this with calculus by taking the partial derivative:

$$\frac{\partial C_1}{\partial C_0} = \frac{\partial [Y_1 + (Y_0 - C_0)(1+r)]}{\partial C_0} = -(1+r)$$

Individual Investment and Consumption Choices

So far, we have shown that an individual may choose a consumption pattern over time by taking advantage of opportunities for borrowing or saving. Now we wish to add a third alternative: undertaking productive investment. To make this clear, let us go back to the start of the description of the last model: An individual can earn Y_0 in the current period and Y_1 in the future period. Let us say that the source of this income comes partly from labor (a return on human capital) and partly in the form of net rent from occupants in an office building that the person owns (rent minus any operating expenses).

One productive investment opportunity that might be available is education. Instead of allocating all current labor to employment, the individual can use some of it to enroll in school for the current period. This is an investment in human capital. It reduces current income, but it raises future income because of the better job that can then be obtained. Note that the primary cost of education may not be tuition, but the earnings forgone. The tuition payment further reduces the income available for current consumption. In Figure 8-4 this opportunity might be represented by a change in the income stream (available for consumption) from point *A* to point *B*.

A second productive opportunity might be to renovate the office building during the current period in order to make it more attractive to commercial occupants and thus receive higher net rents in the future period. This is an ordinary capital investment. Its cost includes the net rent forgone in the current period while the renovation work is being done. It also includes, of course, the cost of the labor and materials that go into the renovation. Since the owner must pay for them, they further reduce the amount of owner income available for current consumption. Graphically, this investment might be thought of as a move from point *B* to point *C*.

The idea in both these examples is that the individual controls an endowment of real resources that can be used for current production and earn up to the amount of the endowment flow of Y_0. He or she can also choose to withhold some of these real resources from use in producing current consumption goods and instead convert them to a different productive use for the future period.[5] Investment implies that a real resource spends *time* out of the most profitable use for current consumption and has a cost equal to the amount of forgone current consumption. The investment process is sometimes referred to as *real capital formation,* and the amount of investment is the increment to the existing capital stocks (e.g., human skills, buildings, and machinery).

Imagine someone facing a whole array of investment opportunities. For each unit of real resource, the individual considers removing it from production of current consumption (moving one unit to the left starting from Y_0) and allocating it to its best investment use (the

---

[5] In the formal model we use, each unit of real resource is homogeneous and thus there is no need for the individual to buy investment inputs in the market. Our examples add realism by having the individual produce current consumption but spend some of the proceeds on buying investment inputs. The net effect is the same: Equivalent amounts of real resources are withheld from use in current consumption, and equivalent amounts of income are available to purchase current consumption.

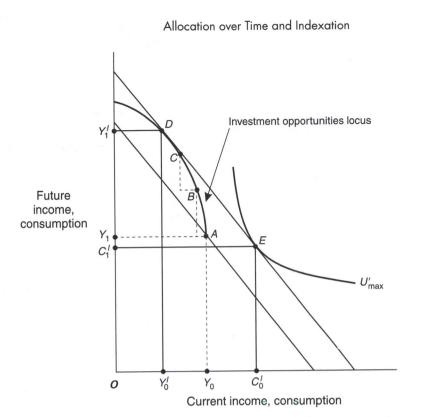

Figure 8-4. The effect of investment opportunities on intertemporal consumption choice.

largest possible gain to future income). This traces out the investment opportunities path in Figure 8-4, where the slope becomes flatter as we move closer to the future-period axis (the marginal investments are less lucrative).

Consider how these investment alternatives affect the individual's consumption possibilities. Any point on the investment opportunities path can be chosen, and then the budget constraint is determined precisely as in our last model. Naturally, the individual seeks the budget constraint with the best consumption possibilities: the one farthest out from the origin. Since the slope of the budget constraint is determined by the market rate of interest, the individual will choose the investment portfolio such that the budget constraint is just tangent to the investment opportunities path. We label this point D. Note that it is also the choice that intersects the axes at the farthest possible points. Thus we have the following result: *A necessary condition for utility maximization is to undertake the investment opportunities that maximize the present value of income calculated at the market rate of interest.*

The above rule is equivalent to undertaking all investments whose present values are positive at the market rate of interest. At point D, the slope of the investment opportunities locus is $-(1 + r)$. To the right of D the slope is steeper, and to the left it is flatter. If we undertook one additional investment project (and thus moved to the left), in absolute value

$$\frac{\Delta Y_1}{\Delta Y_0} < 1 + r$$

or , by rearranging,

$$\frac{\Delta Y_1}{1 + r} - \Delta Y_0 < 0$$

Since the expression on the left is the net present value of the incremental project, we can see that projects to the left of point D have negative present values and those to the right have positive present values.

Once the investment decisions have been made, an individual may choose any of the consumption possibilities along the budget constraint by using the capital market to borrow or lend claims to the current use of real resources. We draw the optimal consumption choice as point E, where the individual borrows $C_0^I - Y_0^I$. Note that it is arbitrary to label some portion of this loan for investment and another for consumption: the amount of borrowing or saving is jointly determined by the amount of after-investment income available for current consumption, the present value of future income, and consumption preferences. Put differently, we never actually observe the amount Y_0 that would allow us to divide the observable borrowing into one part $Y_0 - Y_0^I$ for investment and another $C_0^I - Y_0$ for consumption. The public policy that allows interest on home loans to be tax deductible (to encourage home consumption) but not the interest on brokerage loans causes individuals to borrow more against their homes in order to obtain (cheaper) funds to make stock market investments.

In this model, utility maximization is divided into two independent parts: the choice of investments to maximize wealth and then the choice of how to spend that wealth on a consumption path over time. This is sometimes referred to as the *separation property*. An implication of this property is that a hired agent can select and supervise the investments without having to know anything about the personal preferences of the owner: The agent's function is neither more nor less than wealth maximization. The purchase of a share of stock in a firm, for example, can be thought of as a delegation to the firm's managers of specific investment decision-making authority (e.g., which machinery to build). The investor-shareholder only has concern for the results (dividends plus stock price appreciation).[6]

The above separation property does not hold when the owner's utility is directly affected by the investments, so that some of the benefits and costs are "psychic" rather than monetary.[7] This is particularly true for human capital investments such as education, which do have the monetary benefits and costs that we have suggested but also have substantial direct effects on utility. That is why individuals generally do not give up control of their human

---

[6] In order to keep our intertemporal model as simple as possible, we have not considered uncertainty and its effects. Real firms cater to investors with a particular type of risk preference. For example, people generally are not indifferent to investing in a utility company with a long history of uninterrupted dividend payments or a brand new biotechnology company or Internet enterprise whose uncertain futures may be to earn either a fortune or nothing. A useful and accessible guide to stock market pricing is B. Malkiel, *A Random Walk Down Wall Street: Including a Life-Cycle Guide to Personal Investing* (New York: W. W. Norton & Company, 1996). For more discussion of financial markets, see H. Houthakker and P. Williamson, *The Economics of Financial Markets* (New York: Oxford University Press, 1996).

[7] In Chapter 14 we expand the concept of income to include both monetary and psychic, as it applies to labor market decisions.

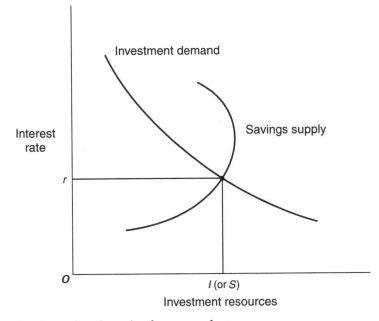

Figure 8-5. The demand and supply of resources for investment.

capital investments. Utility may also be affected directly by physical capital investments. A common example of this is preference for investing in "socially responsible" companies, although individuals may still rely primarily on agents to select these (such as the manager of a mutual fund specializing in the individual's desired type of investment). These complexities mean that many individuals will not choose investments simply to maximize monetary wealth (since direct utility effects may make other investments relatively more attractive), but they do not affect the basic ideas of discounting future effects to their current-value equivalents and the importance of interest rates to this process.

The Demand and Supply of Resources for Investment

It is not hard to see from the above discussion that, in the aggregate, the demand for investment resources increases as the interest rate gets lower. For any given interest rate, in our simplified model each individual chooses the point on the investment possibilities locus where the present value of an incremental project is zero. A higher interest rate means that the slope at the wealth-maximizing point is steeper, or closer to point *A* in Figure 8-4—less investment. The market demand for investment is simply the sum of all the individual demands at each possible interest rate, and thus it also is downward-sloping, as shown in Figure 8-5.

The supply of investment resources can also be understood from the individual behavior that we have discussed. However, the aggregate supply must be understood as a net amount from the amount saved by individuals (those who consume less than their current incomes) minus the amount dissaved by other individuals (those who consume more than their current incomes); this net amount is normally positive, although it does not necessarily have to be. In Figure 8-5 this supply curve is drawn as rising but backward-bending. As the interest rate increases, an individual perceives current consumption to be relatively more expensive than future consumption. Thus, the substitution effect works to reduce demands for current consumption or, put differently, increase the savings of savers and reduce the dissaving of dissavers (e.g., college students may cut consumption in order to borrow less). By itself, this suggests a normally rising supply curve of resources for investment.

The income effect is ambiguous, however. Many dissavers will be made worse off because of the interest rate increase and have income effects that go in the same direction as the substitution effect: to reduce current consumption (i.e., increase aggregate savings). But other individuals (savers) will be made better off: they will have income effects that increase current consumption (i.e., reduce aggregate savings). With more saving than dissaving, the net income effect on savings supply is likely to be negative. Will it outweigh the substitution effect? Recall that the magnitude of an income effect depends on the importance of the good in the overall budget. Then the probability of the investment supply response being negative (to an interest rate increase) is greater when aggregate savings are greater. That is why the supply curve is drawn as rising first and then bending backward, but whether and at what point this occurs is an unresolved empirical question.[8]

While Figure 8-5 illustrates a positive interest rate that makes demand equal to supply, this need not be the case. *There is no theoretical reason why the interest rate need be positive.* We can see this more clearly by referring for pedagogical purposes to a Robinson Crusoe economy (a one-person economy with no Friday, so that there is no one to trade with). Figure 8-6 shows Crusoe's productive possibilities for current and future consumption. Point A is the allocation where the slope is -1 or the interest rate r is zero (r is positive to the right and negative to the left as one moves along the frontier). One can draw Crusoe's indifference curves on the same diagram. To maximize utility, Crusoe must choose the point on this frontier that is just tangent to one of his indifference curves. There is no reason why it cannot occur somewhere to the left of point A, as at point B, where the interest rate is negative. The likelihood of this occurring depends on Crusoe's preferences and the shape of the transformation curve.

It is often thought that the real interest rate will be positive, and for much of our history that appears to be so. Reasons offered in explanation are: (1) as a matter of preference consumers are "impatient" and must be offered more than one unit of future consumption before they will defer a unit of current consumption, and (2) the productive possibilities for investments that yield more than what is put into them (in terms of consumption units) are

---

[8] Empirical studies of the interest elasticity of savings find that it is low, although the estimates range from near 0 to as high as 0.6. For example, Makin and Couch estimate that the interest elasticity of private saving is only 0.04. See J. Makin and K. Couch, "Saving, Pension Contributions, and the Real Interest Rate," *Review of Economics and Statistics, 71,* No. 3, August 1989, pp. 401–407. A number of these empirical estimates are discussed in H. Uhlig and N. Yanagawa, "Increasing the Capital Income Tax May Lead to Faster Growth," *European Economic Review, 40,* No. 8, November 1996, pp. 1521–1540.

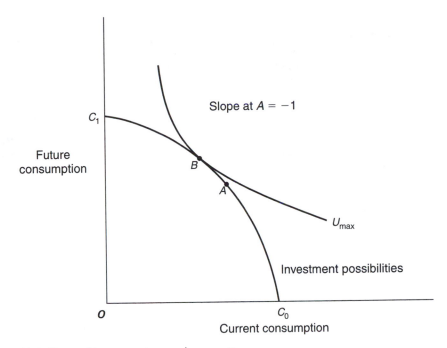

Figure 8-6. The real interest rate may be negative.

plentiful because time itself allows growth (e.g., the quantity of lumber in a growing tree).[9] As an empirical matter, however, positive interest rates do not always prevail. Occasionally we observe transactions at negative interest rates, as occurred briefly for certain short-term interest rates in Japan in 1998.[10] Most of the time the interest rates appear positive, but the real interest rate may be negative due to the effects of inflation.[11]

Table 8-1 looks at the nominal and real rates of interest on two savings instruments during the 1990s. The U.S. economy during this period experienced inflation of roughly 3 percent per year. This is shown in the table by the yearly percentage change in the Consumer Price Index, a measure of the change in the cost of living.[12] The two instruments we examine return fixed interest payments on a precise time schedule with very low risks of default: short-term six-month U.S. Treasury bills and long-term corporate bonds rated Aaa by Moody's.

[9] The first statement should be interpreted as applying to the marginal rate of time preference in the neighborhood of "even" consumption bundles on the indifference curve. If there were a stock of food that had to last for two time periods because the productive possibilities for making more food were scant, people would no doubt prefer to save a sizable portion even if half of the units saved were expected (statistically) to spoil.

[10] The *Financial Times* of London reported that Western banks were paying negative interest rates on interbank yen-denominated deposits in early November 1998.

[11] If an economy is experiencing deflation rather than inflation, meaning that the price of goods in general is falling over time rather than rising, then nominal interest rates could be negative while still offering a positive real rate of return. For example, an interest rate of −2 percent in an economy experiencing a price level drop of 5 percent is offering a positive 3 percent real rate of interest.

[12] This index and its construction are discussed shortly.

Table 8-1

Real Interest Rates (Nominal minus Inflation) Can Be Negative

| | | Annual interest rates | | | |
| | | Six-month U.S. Treasury Bills | | Corporate Aaa bonds | |
Year	Percent change in the CPI[a]	Nominal after-tax rate of interest[b]	Real after-tax rate of interest	Nominal after-tax rate of interest[b]	Real after-tax rate of interest
1990	5.40	5.38	−0.02	6.71	1.31
1991	4.21	3.95	−0.26	6.31	2.10
1992	3.01	2.57	−0.44	5.86	2.85
1993	2.99	2.26	−0.73	5.20	2.21
1994	2.56	3.36	0.80	5.73	3.17
1995	2.83	4.02	1.19	5.46	2.63
1996	2.95	3.66	0.71	5.31	2.36
1997	2.29	3.73	1.44	5.23	2.94
1998	1.56	3.49	1.93	4.70	3.14
1999	2.21	3.43	1.22	5.07	2.86

[a] Calculated as $(CPI_t - CPI_{t-1})/CPI_{t-1}$. The data are from *Economic Report of the President, 2000* (Washington, D.C.: U.S. Government Printing Office, 1999), Table B-60, p. 343.

[b] The numbers shown are 0.72 times the corresponding yields shown in ibid., Table B-73, p. 360.

Their nominal (not adjusted for inflation) and real (inflation-adjusted) rates are shown and explained below.

Because the earnings on these financial instruments are subject to federal income tax, individuals who invest in them and are in the 28 percent tax bracket (common at the time) get to keep only 72 percent of the interest earned (this ignores any state taxes). These after-tax earnings are calculated in Table 8-1. The difference between the after-tax rate of interest and the inflation rate is the real interest rate. During the period shown, the long-term bonds had positive real after-tax rates of interest generally between 2 and 3 percent per year. The T-bills also generally had positive rates of interest, but these were only rarely above 1 percent, and in a few years (highlighted in the table) the real after-tax interest rates were negative. The differential in real interest rates between these two instruments is typical because: (a) the corporate bonds are riskier (less reliable than the U.S. government for a given time length, and with a longer time period in which something could go wrong), and (b) the federal securities are exempt from state taxes.

Individual Choices in Multiperiod Models

The basic two-period model that we have used serves very well to introduce the principles of individual resource allocation over time. However, most people do not normally think of their lives as divided into a "current" half and a "future" half. Rather, we utilize common frames such as "years" over which to consider possible investment projects, and the most common interest rates we see are expressed on a yearly basis, such as those in Table 8-1. We review here economic calculations that involve multiple periods.

A helpful fact to keep in mind is this: A finite length of time can always be conceptualized as consisting of *any* number of intervals simply by choosing the length of the intervals. Of course, the definition of the interest rate must change accordingly, even though nothing real has changed. When viewed in that way, a many-period model is just a mathematically finer disaggregation of a "lumpy" two-period model. For example, the behavioral predictions of a model of many periods must "add up" to those for its equivalent two-period model.[13]

Let us review the mathematics of compounding and discounting over years. Define r as the simple interest rate for a 1-year period: \$1 saved in the bank now will yield \$$(1 + r)$ a year from now. Assume that borrowing and lending are done at the same interest rate r. Thus, a guarantee to repay \$1 in 1 year has a current loan value equal to the present discounted value of the future repayment: $\$1/(1 + r)$.

If the saver leaves the money in the bank for a second year and the interest rate remains constant, the money compounds (there is interest on the interest), and the amount A at the end of 2 years is

$$A = 1(1 + r)(1 + r) = (1 + r)^2$$

If the money is left in the bank for n years, the amount at the end of that period is

$$A = (1 + r)^n$$

Similarly, if the borrower is going to repay a \$1 loan 2 years after receiving it, the current loan value of that repayment is its present value (PDV):

$$PDV = \frac{1/(1 + r)}{1 + r} = \frac{1}{(1 + r)^2}$$

For example, \$0.83 is the present value of a \$1 repayment in 2 years at a 10 percent discount rate. If the \$1 is not repaid until n years, its present value is

$$PDV = \frac{1}{(1 + r)^n}$$

If someone offers a payment of \$$D$ in n years from now, its present value is

$$PDV = \frac{D}{(1 + r)^n}$$

---

[13] Note that this mathematical fact is distinct from the important idea that actual behavior may have to be modeled differently if one is considering allocation over a year versus over a lifetime. (For example, bounded rationality may cause lifetime choices to deviate substantially from expected utility maximization, whereas annual budgeting decisions may not.)

Finally, if someone offers a stream of payments over the years of D_0 (a down payment), D_1, $D_2, \ldots, D_n$, the present value of that stream is

$$PDV = D_0 + \frac{D_1}{1+r} + \frac{D_2}{(1+r)^2} + \ldots + \frac{D_n}{(1+r)^n}$$

This last equation is very important because it allows us to convert any stream of payments (or, in some applications, social costs or benefits) over time into one present value. For example, suppose someone buys a house and borrows $100,000 from a bank at 10 percent interest for 30 years. If the borrower wishes to make constant annual payments beginning in 1 year, what will those payments be? We have to find the annual mortgage payment M that makes[14]

$$100,000 = \frac{M}{1+0.10} + \frac{M}{(1+0.10)^2} + \ldots + \frac{M}{(1+0.10)^{30}}$$

$$100,000 = M\left(\frac{1}{1.1} + \frac{1}{1.1^2} + \ldots + \frac{1}{1.1^{30}}\right)$$

$$= M(9.4269)$$

or

$$M = \$10,607.92$$

Here is a second example. In the beginning of the chapter we discussed the concept of permanent income. Now we can define it precisely: **Permanent income is the stream of constant earnings whose present value is identical with that of the actual earnings stream.** For example, suppose someone works for 40 years, beginning at a salary of $30,000 that rises each year by 4 percent to $138,491 in the last year of work. If the discount rate is 10 percent, what is this individual's permanent income level? First we find the present value of the actual earnings stream:

$$PDV = \$30,000\left[1 + \frac{1.04}{1.10} + \frac{1.04^2}{1.10^2} + \ldots + \frac{1.04^{39}}{1.10^{39}}\right]$$

The term inside the brackets is a geometric progression with multiplier $0.94545 = 1.04/1.10$, and sums to 16.38857. Therefore the PDV = $491,657. To find the permanent income equivalent Y_p, we must have

$$\$491,657 = Y_p\left[1 + \frac{1}{1.1} + \frac{1}{1.1^2} + \ldots + \frac{1}{1.1^{39}}\right]$$

---

[14] In the calculation we use the formula for the sum of a geometric progression. If the progression is $a, ad, ad^2, \ldots, ad^{n-1}$ then the sum is

$$S = \frac{a(1-d^n)}{1-d} \quad \text{for } 0 < d < 1$$

In the above equation, $a = d = 1/1.1$, and $n = 30$.

Again the term in brackets is a geometric progression, this time with multiplier $0.90909 = 1/1.10$, and it sums to 10.75696. Therefore, Y_p is $45,706.

The calculation of present value extends easily to the case in which the stream of payments continues indefinitely. There are financial instruments that have this feature; perpetual bonds, called consols, are commonly sold in England, for example. If the bond issuer promises to pay $M each year in perpetuity and the market rate of interest is 10 percent annually, then the current market price of the bond is the present value[15]:

$$PDV = \frac{M}{1.1} + \frac{M}{1.1^2} + \ldots + \frac{M}{1.1^n} + \ldots$$

$$= \frac{M/1.1}{1 - (1/1.1)} = \frac{M}{0.1} = 10M$$

The general present-value formula for a constant, perpetual stream of payments M has the following simple form:

$$PDV = M/r$$

Suppose the annual payment on the consol is $10,607.92 (a number we use here only because of its relation to the mortgage example). Then the present value of the consol (at 10 percent annual interest) is simply $106,079.20. Note by how *little* the present value increases when we extend the stream of payments from 30 years in the $100,000 mortgage example to perpetuity in the consol example. That is because the present discounted value of payments that will not be received (or made) until the distant future is meager. For example, the present value of a payment of $10,607.92 made in the thirty-first year is only $552.66 and in the sixtieth year only $34.94.

However, it is also important to note that the discount rate can make a big difference in the calculation of present value for a stream that goes on over a lengthy period. For the consol that pays $M annually, the present value doubles to $20M if the market rate of interest drops from 10 percent to 5. At a lower rate of discount, each future dollar payment is worth more currently.

The extension of the basic model (with no inflation or uncertainty and the same interest rate for saving or borrowing) for choosing among multiperiod investments is straightforward. The rule for selecting investment projects (from along the multiperiod investment possibilities surface) applies as in the two-period case: All investments with positive present values should be undertaken (i.e., investments should be chosen in order to maximize wealth). Each independent possibility can be represented by the stream D_i of benefits and costs (net income per period) associated with it. This equation for investment value over multiperiods can be used not only for individuals, but in social (society-wide) benefit-cost analysis as well. While we will study cost concepts carefully in the next several chapters, let us illustrate this

---

[15] For an infinite geometric progression $a, ad, ad^2, \ldots$, the sum is

$$S = \frac{a}{1 - d} \qquad 0 < d < 1$$

calculation for a proposed public investment involving benefits and costs that occur at different time periods.

Suppose that the government is considering whether to construct (or approve the private construction of) a hydroelectric facility in a wilderness area. Suppose further that analysis has led to the following estimates of benefits and costs[16]: (1) The social benefits are that $1,400,000 worth of increased electricity output (above operating costs of production) will be available annually for 48 years starting in the third year from project initiation. (2) The social costs include $30 million for construction ($10 million in the first year, $20 million in the second year). (3) Social costs also include $800,000 in recreation benefits forgone annually (e.g., the facility interferes with the environment for fishing, hiking, and hunting purposes) for 50 years starting at project initiation. Does this project increase relative efficiency? That depends on whether the benefits outweigh the costs.

To calculate this, we must convert the stream of benefits and costs into a single present value, as suggested by the equation above. If the social rate of discount is constant and equal to 3 percent per year, then[17]

$$\text{PDV (electricity benefits)} = \frac{\$1,400,000}{1.03^2} + \frac{\$1,400,000}{1.03^3} + \ldots + \frac{\$1,400,000}{1.03^{49}}$$

$$= \$34,343,100 \tag{1}$$

$$\text{PDV (construction)} = \$10,000,000 + \frac{\$20,000,000}{1.03}$$

$$= \$29,417,480 \tag{2}$$

$$\text{PDV (forgone recreation)} = \$800,000 + \frac{\$800,000}{1.03} + \ldots + \frac{\$800,000}{1.03^{49}}$$

$$= \$21,201,330 \tag{3}$$

The net present value of the project is (1) − [(2) + (3)]:

$$\text{PDV (net)} = \text{benefits} - \text{costs} = -\$16,275,710$$

Thus, on efficiency grounds, the proposed project fails: The social costs exceed the social benefits by $16,275,710.

The examples in this section involve *simple* interest rates, but it is sometimes more convenient to work with *continuously compounded* rates over the same interval. We develop the mathematics of compound interest rates in the appendix to this chapter.

---

[16] This example is motivated by a highly regarded study in which considerable effort and ingenuity are used to derive actual estimates of a wide variety of benefits and costs. The study concerns the proposal to build a hydroelectric facility in Hells Canyon of the Snake River. See A. Fisher, J. Krutilla, and C. Cicchetti, "The Economics of Environmental Preservation: A Theoretical and Empirical Analysis," *American Economic Review, 62,* No. 4, September 1972, pp. 605–619.

[17] The formula used to sum these geometric progressions is explained in footnote 15.

Choosing a Discount Rate

There are many questions about resource allocation over time that we have not yet addressed. One of the most important is the choice of the discount rate to use in making present value calculations. The model suggests that there is a market rate of interest between any two time periods, and that individuals use this rate for any discounting that is to be done between these two periods. However, the model simplifies from the very large number of different market rates of interest that one can observe. Furthermore, there is a behavioral question about how individuals actually make these decisions—the whizzes of Wall Street and corporate financial experts may understand discounting perfectly, but ordinary people (without advisors) may not have much or even any familiarity with these concepts. The issues involved in trying to deal with these complexities are substantial, and here we address only two aspects briefly, saving the others for later chapters.

First, in terms of the large number of observable market interest rates, discount rates should be appropriate both for the time and degree of risk of the investment under consideration. Market rates are important because they represent the alternative opportunities available to investors. But what market opportunities are comparable? Comparable investments take place over a similar time period with a similar degree of risk.

We saw in Table 3-1 that short-term and long-term interest rates are generally different. Interest rates can be observed for periods as short as an overnight loan or as long as the perpetuity of a consol. For a riskless investment over a 20-year period, one might use the going interest rate on a U.S. government bond for the same duration (5.95 percent nominal in May 2001). For any given time frame, riskier investments are discounted at higher rates. For corporate bonds that mature in 20 years or more, the going nominal interest rate in May 2001 was 6.47 percent for those rated Aaa by Moody's, but 7.30 percent for those only rated A by Moody's. Riskier still are corporate equity investments (which have averaged roughly a 10 percent real annual return over quite long periods).[18] When the government considers investments such as new infrastructure projects (e.g., highways) or those required by regulation (e.g., air pollution controls), the federal Office of Management and Budget currently specifies that a 7 percent real discount rate be used.

In terms of actual behavior, research suggests that many people act as though they are using much higher discount rates than one might expect based on comparable market rates. For example, we witnessed one natural experiment during the 1990s when upon their separation from service over 60,000 U.S. military personnel were given the option of taking their

---

[18] It is only nondiversifiable risk, risk that cannot be eliminated by holding a diversified portfolio, that raises the discount rate. For corporate equities, the capital asset pricing model (CAPM) is often used to calculate the appropriate discount rate. This model uses a statistical measure, called β_i, which measures the extent to which the returns on the equity i correlate with the stock market as a whole—its nondiversifiable risk. Then using r for the riskless rate, r_m for the stock market as a whole, the discount rate r_i appropriate for a particular equity is $r_i = r + \beta_i(r_m - r)$. The second term in the equation is the risk premium that is added to the riskless rate. For the market as a whole, this has been about 8 percent historically ($r_m = 0.10$, $r = 0.02$). For more information about corporate finance models, see R. Brealey and S. Myers, *Principles of Corporate Finance* (New York: McGraw-Hill Book Company, 1999).

accrued retirement benefits in the form of a single lump-sum payment or as an annuity—a stream of constant monthly payments for a fixed period, in this case a period equal to twice the individual's years of service.[19] The benefits involved considerable sums of money, with the lump-sum values varying from a low of about $17,000 for enlisted personnel with 7 years or less service to a high of about $94,000 for officers with 15 years of service. Thus one might expect that the decision to take the lump-sum or the annuity would be made carefully.

The military provided information to each individual showing that the PDV of the annuity at a 7 percent discount rate was far greater than the lump-sum payment—always at least 50 percent greater and in most cases around 100 percent greater. A group of enlisted personnel with 12 years of service, for example, had the choice of a $35,549 lump-sum payment or an annuity with PDV of $72,710 using the 7 percent rate. We have already seen in Table 3-1 that high-grade long-term corporate bonds during this period were paying about 6 percent interest and that government-guaranteed annuity payments over a comparable period are safer. So the comparison the government provided to help with the decision—the PDV of the annuity at a 7 percent rate to compare against the lump-sum amount—was eminently reasonable. Yet 88 percent of the individuals chose the lump-sum payment. The discount rate that one would have to use to make the PDV of the annuity just equal to the lump-sum is 19.6 percent. In other words, *the 88 percent of individuals that chose the lump-sum payment were acting as though they were using discount rates in excess of 20 percent.*

Similar findings of high personal discount rates have been found in a number of other studies.[20] Why would individuals act this way? If they were planning on investing the funds, it is clear that the annuity offered a far more attractive return than comparable investments. Even investing in a broad stock market fund for 10 years or more, which is far riskier, only promises roughly a 10 percent average annual return. Might they have wanted to use the money to help buy a house or a car or attend college, so that they needed the cash? In most cases, they would have been able to borrow funds at a much lower rate than 20 percent (e.g., home mortgage rates were around 8 percent at that time). That is, they would have been better off opting for the annuity and borrowing funds.[21] To be sure, liquidity constraints could explain why some people preferred the lump-sum payment (i.e., some might have needed a large amount of cash and were not able to borrow it through conventional methods), but

[19] This natural experiment was analyzed in J. Warner and S. Pleeter, "The Personal Discount Rate: Evidence from Military Downsizing Programs," *American Economic Review, 91*, No. 1, March 2001, pp. 33–53.

[20] For example, relatively few people purchase energy-efficient appliances even though the extra cost of them is easily offset by reduced monthly energy bills when discounted at any rate close to market interest rates. But Hausman found that individuals used an average discount rate of 25 percent in considering this kind of decision. See J. Hausman, "Individual Discount Rates and the Purchase and Utilization of Energy-Using Durables," *Bell Journal of Economics, 10*, No. 2, Spring 1979, pp. 33–54. For a more general reference on individual choice over time, see G. Lowenstein and J. Elster, eds., *Choice over Time* (New York: Russell Sage Foundation, 1992).

[21] For example, suppose instead of taking the lump-sum payment an individual takes the annuity and then arranges for a home loan larger by the lump-sum amount. Further, let the term for the home loan match the annuity term (24 years in our example). The loan could be fully repaid with monthly payments that are only slightly more than half the monthly annuity income; the left-over portion is a pure economic gain.

this does not explain why practically everybody chose it. Thus it remains a puzzle for future research to explain why so many people made a choice that, by conventional calculation, seemed to leave them over $30,000 poorer.

Uncertain Future Prices and Index Construction

A major cost involved in intertemporal resource allocation is that of uncertainty concerning future price levels caused by inflation. A $5000 investment now may return $10,000 with certainty in 5 years, but how much consumption can be bought with $10,000 in 5 years? It depends on whether the inflation rate is low like the 2 percent average annual rate from 1993 to 1998 in the United States, or high like the 7.5 percent average annual rate from 1978 to 1983, or even higher like the 1990 to 1995 average rates of 18 percent for Mexico, 24 percent for Hungary, and 267 percent for Belarus.[22] The uncertainty makes intertemporal resource allocation choices very difficult. If real returns are highly uncertain, how can one decide how much to save or which investments to undertake?

One mechanism that is frequently used to respond to this type of uncertainty is **indexation.** Roughly speaking, this is **a method of adjusting a nominal number of dollars over time in order to hold their purchasing power constant.** For example, Social Security payments are indexed each year, as are the income brackets by which federal income tax rates are determined. Many other public and private programs have indexed payments; examples are food stamps, pension plans, labor contracts, and state grants to local public schools (to account for local variation in education costs). Indexed government bonds adjust nominal interest payments to maintain a positive real return, like U.S. Treasury "I" Bonds. All of these indexation plans make the real level of expected future receipts and expenditures more certain, thereby giving individuals a better sense of their own wealth and a clearer picture of the consequences of alternative intertemporal resource allocations.

Yet the construction of these indices is often controversial. For example, Social Security is adjusted in accordance with changes in the Consumer Price Index (CPI). But it is not clear that this index accurately captures the change in the cost of living experienced by retired individuals. Indeed, the U.S. Advisory Commission to Study the Consumer Price Index reported in 1996 that the CPI likely overstated inflation in general by about 1.1 percent per year, increasing the average federal deficit for the next decade by about $90 billion per year.[23] Since then, numerous changes in the index's construction have taken place. In this section we review some of the basic principles of index construction and then some of the problems that plague index construction in practice.

A starting point for understanding index construction is to look at the *Laspeyre and Paasche indices* as they apply to one person whose tastes do not change over time in a

---

[22] The U.S. rates are from the April 1999 *Survey of Current Business,* Table C-3, p. D-39. The Mexican and Hungarian rates are from the OECD *Hot File,* May 16, 1997, p. 34. The Belarus rate is from the United Nations *Monthly Bulletin of Statistics Online,* Table 50.

[23] The report is reprinted in D. Baker, ed., *Getting Prices Right: The Debate over the Consumer Price Index* (Armonk, N.Y.: Sharpe, 1998). This book also contains critical discussion of the report.

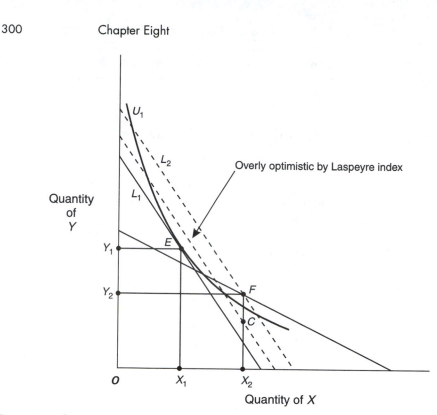

Figure 8-7. The Laspeyre quantity index.

two-good economy.[24] In Figure 8-7 we show at point E an individual's choice of goods X and Y in period 1 at prices P_{X_1} and P_{Y_1}. In period 2 we observe the individual at point F purchasing X_2 and Y_2 at prices P_{X_2} and P_{Y_2}. Can we estimate whether the person is better off or worse off in period 2 without knowing the exact location of the indifference curves?

The Laspeyre quantity index (price is fixed, quantity varies) can help us to make the comparison. Using period 1 prices as a base we compute

$$L_1 = P_{X_1}X_1 + P_{Y_1}Y_1$$

$$L_2 = P_{X_1}X_2 + P_{Y_1}Y_2$$

In other words, L_1 is the actual expenditure in period 1, and L_2 is how much the consumption in period 2 would cost if prices remained at those of period 1. We then define the Laspeyre quantity index:

$$L \equiv \frac{L_2}{L_1}$$

---

[24] These are also used in empirical work to estimate the "compensation" necessary to keep an individual indifferent to a change (i.e., to keep real income constant, which ideally means on the same indifference curve).

In Figure 8-7 we see that L_1 is the actual budget constraint when point E is chosen in the base period; L_2 is the budget constraint through period 2's consumption (point F) with the same slope (prices) as in the base period. A change is a welfare improvement by the Laspeyre test if $L = L_2/L_1 > 1$. This is clearly the case at point F, since L_2 is a "higher" budget constraint than L_1. However, Laspeyre indications of welfare improvements are overly optimistic, and they can be wrong. If period 2's consumption were shown at point C (still where $L > 1$), the change would be a welfare reduction (i.e., utility is lower). In the case in which $L < 1$ there is no ambiguity: Welfare is unambiguously decreased (the new allocation must be interior to the old budget constraint L_1).

The Paasche quantity index uses current prices (period 2) and has the opposite flaw. Changes that are Paasche improvements are unambiguous improvements; those that indicate a welfare decrease may be overly pessimistic. To see this, we compute

$$P_1 = P_{X_2}X_1 + P_{Y_2}Y_1$$
$$P_2 = P_{X_2}X_2 + P_{Y_2}Y_2$$

In this case, P_2 is the actual expenditure in period 2, and P_1 is what the consumption in period 1 (point E) would have cost if prices were those of period 2. We define the Paasche quantity index:

$$P \equiv \frac{P_2}{P_1}$$

This time, $P > 1$ means that the old bundle of goods must be interior to the new budget constraint P_2 and welfare must be higher in the current period. If $P < 1$, the Paasche test indicates a welfare decrease. This is the case drawn in Figure 8-8. The solid line through point F is the period 2 budget constraint, or P_2. P_1 is the budget constraint through point E with the same slope (prices) as in period 2; it lies further from the origin than P_2.

However, since the goods consumed during period 1 were those at point E, the budget constraint for period 2 allows welfare to increase (as at point F) even though $P < 1$. Thus, Paasche indications of welfare decreases are overly pessimistic and can be wrong, as in this case. Note that the change from point E to point F is judged an improvement by Laspeyre's method (Figure 8-7) and a welfare decrease by the Paasche method, so that the "truth" cannot be unambiguously determined in this case without knowledge of the indifference curves.

The same concepts apply in forming and using the Laspeyre and Paasche price indices (quantities are fixed, prices vary). In Figure 8-9 let us say a retired individual living on Social Security is initially (period 1) at point A. Price changes in the next period are such that the same nominal Social Security income leads to the budget constraint through point B (which the retiree would choose if necessary). However, the government wishes to compensate the individual for the increase in the cost of living. Using the period 1 quantities as a base, it calculates

$$L_1 = P_{X_1}X_1 + P_{Y_1}Y_1$$
$$L_2 = P_{X_2}X_1 + P_{Y_2}Y_1$$

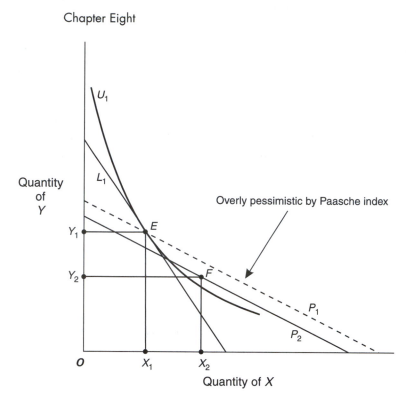

Figure 8-8. The Paasche quantity index.

and defines the Laspeyre price index as

$$L \equiv \frac{L_2}{L_1}$$

It then gives the retiree a Social Security payment of $L_2 = L \times L_1$—just the amount of money that enables the person to buy last period's quantity (point A) at the current period's prices.

This is overly generous, of course; the individual is at least as well off in the current period as in the previous one and must be better off if he or she chooses to spend the money differently. **A true cost-of-living index measures the percent change in nominal income required to hold utility constant at the base level.** It would give the budget constraint drawn in Figure 8-9 as L_T. Thus, the Laspeyre price index overestimates the increase in the cost of living. Similarly, the Paasche price index underestimates the cost-of-living increase.

The theoretical imperfections of these common methods of indexing are probably less significant than the practical problems of defining the goods and services that are included in an index and updating the index over time. We illustrated the method of index construction with just one person, two goods, and two time periods. But most indices are intended to include many people, goods, and time periods.

If the sum of the nominal budget constraints of several individuals is adjusted upward in accordance with the Laspeyre price index, there is no implication that each individual is now better off than initially. The welfare of the individuals within the group depends on how in-

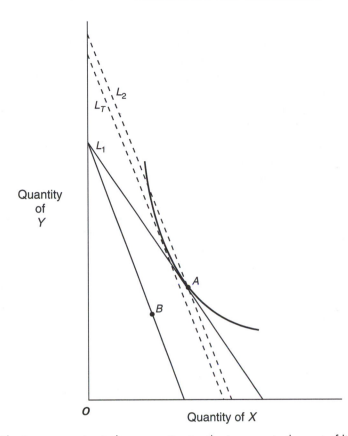

Figure 8-9. The Laspeyre price index overestimates the increase in the cost of living.

dividual budget constraints change over time, how the prices of specific goods in the aggregate bundle change, and the preferences of the individuals for the different goods in the aggregate bundle. When university faculty are told they will receive a 5 percent cost-of-living raise, some of the faculty will have had their apartment rents raised by 10 percent and others by only 2 percent. Senior faculty may have their salaries increased by 7 percent and junior faculty by only 3 percent. Which are the goods that should be used to determine this group's "average" cost-of-living change? How does one decide the components of the cost of living for the "average" retiree on Social Security or the "average" lower-income family? If one keeps track of the prices of the components over time, how often should their composition be reviewed?

The most familiar price index is the CPI calculated by the Bureau of Labor Statistics by using the Laspeyre method. Legislation at all levels of government ties annual increases in individual grants to the CPI; Social Security, food stamps, welfare payments, and government pensions are examples. U.S. Treasury "I" bonds are indexed to the CPI. Many private labor contracts tie wage increases to the CPI. This makes the details of the CPI computations important.

The CPI is a *fixed-weight index;* the weight on each price included in it is derived from an occasional survey of urban household expenditures. In 1997, the base period for the fixed weights was from 1982 to 1984. For example, the three item categories of residential rent, owner's equivalent rent, and housing at school comprised 27.3 percent in the CPI-U index.[25] While the prices for items in these categories are measured monthly, their collective weight in the overall index remains at 27.3 percent until the fixed-weights change as the result of a more recent survey. There are 206 different item categories in the CPI; the prices for items within each category are measured monthly in forty-four different urban areas and then aggregated, based on population weights from the last census, into the national index.

One problem with such a fixed-weight index is that the weights become more and more irrelevant to consumers over time. For example, beef prices may have increased significantly relative to other foods, but consumers respond by spending less on meat and more on poultry. This is an example of what we saw earlier in Figure 8-9: The cost of achieving a fixed utility level never rises as quickly as the cost of achieving it with the original bundle of goods and services. As consumers can achieve the original utility with less than the indexed amount by substituting other products for those that have become relatively more expensive, this source of overcompensation is known as "substitution bias." Being faithful to the concept of a *price index* over time works against the accuracy of the figure as a *cost-of-living index.*

One way to make a Laspeyre price index more useful as a measure of the cost of living is to have it *chain-linked.* For example, the CPI measures the change in prices from 1996 to 1997 by using the 1982–1984 weights, where P_iQ_j is short for the sum over the n goods in the index $\sum_{k=1}^{n} p_{ik}q_{jk}$:

$$L_{98} = \frac{P_{98}Q_{84}}{P_{84}Q_{84}}$$

$$L_{97} = \frac{P_{97}Q_{84}}{P_{84}Q_{84}}$$

$$\frac{L_{98}}{L_{97}} = \frac{P_{98}Q_{84}}{P_{97}Q_{84}}$$

But a chain-linked index would compute

$$\frac{L_{98}}{L_{97}} = \frac{P_{98}Q_{97}}{P_{97}Q_{97}}$$

$$\vdots \qquad \vdots$$

$$\frac{L_{85}}{L_{84}} = \frac{P_{85}Q_{84}}{P_{84}Q_{84}}$$

---

[25] CPI-U stands for the Consumer Price Index for All Urban Consumers, and is the version of the CPI that is used most commonly for indexation. The other version of the CPI, known as CPI-W, the Consumer Price Index for Urban Wage Earners and Clerical Workers, is used to index Social Security benefits.

This of course would require a method of identifying the changes in consumption patterns each year (bearing in mind that accurate surveys are expensive).

Beginning with 1998, the Bureau of Labor Statistics announced that new expenditure weights from the 1993–1995 period would be utilized. More importantly, it also announced that in 2002 it will utilize expenditure weights from 1999 to 2000 and thereafter update the expenditure weights every 2 years (e.g., the CPI in 2004 will be based on weights from 2001 to 2002). Thus in the future, the CPI will more closely approximate a chain-linked index rather than a fixed-weight index.

Another important change in the CPI that also works to reduce substitution bias became effective in 1999. Within any of the item categories of the CPI, such as "ice cream and re-lated products," the prices for specific items from a sample of different stores are measured monthly. These measurements, like the larger index, have historically been aggregated by using the fixed weights from the occasional expenditure survey. Starting in 1999, what is fixed for most categories is the *proportion* of expenditure spent on each item in the most recent expenditure survey. Thus if the price of a pint of ice cream goes up relative to a pint of frozen yogurt, the new method assumes that the quantity of ice cream purchased de-creases (and that of frozen yogurt increases) in order to hold its expenditure share constant at the base level. This method, known as the *geometric mean estimator,* does not require any new data but is in most cases a better approximation of how consumers as a group ac-tually respond to price changes among close substitutes. Note that the use of this method does not extend across item categories, but is only used within them.[26]

Another problem with any index is the difficulty of controlling for quality changes. Al-though we know inflation averaged almost 5 percent per year over the 27 years from 1972 to 1998, it is not obvious whether an individual with $2000 would prefer to spend it on the goods available in the 1972 edition of the Montgomery Ward catalog or the 1998 edition. Minarik cites an example of radial auto tires being more expensive than the older bias-ply style but lasting far longer.[27] Computer technology changes very rapidly, so that today's desktop com-puter is substantially advanced over those sold only a few years ago. Another example is controlling for quality improvements in medical and dental technology, such as the use of laser-based surgical tools and instruments. Quality also may decrease, as it undoubtedly did on certain airline routes following deregulation in 1984.[28] All these quality changes should be taken into account by the index, but that is usually not possible. One exception effective in

[26] The geometric mean estimator is used for categories covering about 61 percent of the CPI-U index. The major categories excluded from the new method are housing services, utility and governmental services, and medical care services. The first two are excluded primarily because consumer substitution within them is difficult, and the third is excluded based largely on low estimated demand elasticities for these services reported in the eco-nomics literature.

[27] See p. 18 of Joseph J. Minarik, "Does the Consumer Price Index Need Deflating?," *Taxing and Spending, 3,* Summer 1980, pp. 17–24.

[28] When price competition was prevented by regulation, airlines competed by offering nonprice benefits such as more space, more choice of travel time, and free in-flight movies. They are now able to offer lower prices as a more efficient means of competing.

1998 is the category "personal computers and peripheral equipment": an increase in quality of a major computer component such as a modem will be valued by an econometric method and deducted from the observed price.

The CPI is a very broad index, and it does not necessarily reflect the change in cost of living experienced by particular groups (e.g., families in a certain state or households with very low income). For example, in 1995 a report of the National Academy of Research suggested that it might be better to index the poverty line not to the CPI but to an index that concentrates on "necessities" such as food, clothing, and housing.[29] However, this is a controversial area. Studies that have attempted to construct a separate index for low-income households usually find that the CPI understates the changes in poverty, although others find the opposite.[30] Nevertheless, the idea that one might wish to use special indices for particular policy purposes is an important one.

Another example of an area in which special indices have policy use is education. In Chapter 5 we reviewed the problems of achieving equity in school finance. One of the problems mentioned was that nominal dollar expenditures of districts cannot always be compared directly. In California, for example, some school districts may have to spend considerably more dollars than other districts to provide reasonable temperatures in classrooms.

Suppose one is interested in the wealth neutrality of the real educational resources available to each child under a state financing plan. One must adjust the observable nominal dollar relations to account for the cost differences in obtaining real resources. But then one needs to have a comparison basket of educational resources. Furthermore, one must not confuse the observed price of each item in the district with the opportunity cost of the resources. For example, teachers' salaries may be high either because local demand for teachers is high or because previous grants were converted to higher salaries through the flypaper effect. Untangling these effects poses thorny statistical problems.[31]

One final point about the practical problems of index construction and use should be made: Political pressures to influence the index calculations are enormous. Analysts arguing for technical improvements (say, to better approximate a true cost-of-living index) must be aware that any proposed change will likely benefit some people and harm others, and thus ignite political forces seeking to protect their own interests. It is thus important to be very clear about the technical rationale for proposing any changes and mindful of the practical and political obstacles that are likely to be encountered. One political reporter opined that the improvements to the CPI that occurred in the late 1990s happened not simply because of analytic argument but at least partially because they were a convenient compromise be-

---

[29] National Research Council, *Measuring Poverty: A New Approach* (Washington, D.C.: National Academy Press, 1995).

[30] See, e.g., the studies mentioned on pp. 128–129 of D. Baker, "Does the CPI Overstate Inflation?" in D. Baker, ed., *Getting Prices Right* (Armonk, N.Y.: M. E. Sharpe, 1998); and those mentioned on pp. 21–22 of M. Boskin et al., "Consumer Prices, the Consumer Price Index, and the Cost of Living," *Journal of Economic Perspectives, 12,* No. 1, Winter 1998, pp. 3–26.

[31] For a study of these issues in New York State, see W. Duncombe and J. Yinger, "School Finance Reform: Aid Formulas and Equity Objectives," *National Tax Journal, 51,* No. 2, June 1998, pp. 239–262.

tween Democrats and Republicans seeking to agree upon a budget with greater revenues but less spending on entitlements.[32]

Summary

In this chapter we explored problems involving resource allocation over time. We reviewed the theory of individual choice as it relates to saving, borrowing, and investing. We motivated both saving and borrowing as responses to the uneven pattern in which income is accrued over a lifetime, in contrast to common preferences for a more even consumption stream. We motivated investment, the process of capital creation, as the response to opportunities to increase wealth. We saw that individuals can increase wealth not only by investing to create physical capital assets such as factories and office buildings, but also by investing in "human" capital through education. The benefit of investing is the extent to which it increases future income (or future utility directly), and its cost is that it reduces resources available for current consumption.

Because all of these decisions (saving, borrowing, and investing) involve some form of trade-off between current and future opportunities, a method of comparison across time periods is needed. Interest rates are the prices that guide these comparisons. We illustrated this in a simple two-period model. We saw that individuals generally want to invest more at lower interest rates, whereas low interest rates normally discourage the supply of savings available to meet the investment demand.

For any given market interest rate, we can think of individuals making their utility-maximizing intertemporal decisions by discounting, which is a way to convert any future amount into its current-value equivalent, called the present discounted value. Seen through the discounting perspective, individuals maximize their utility by undertaking all investments that have present discounted values of benefits greater than those of its costs. To the extent that the separation theorem applies—when the benefits and costs of an investment to an individual are all in dollar amounts as opposed to affecting utility directly—this is pure wealth maximization and it is relatively easy for individuals to hire agents with expertise to direct or carry out the investments (e.g., by purchasing stock or hiring an investment advisor).

Of course there are investments, particularly those involving human capital, such as education, that directly affect the utility of the investing individual (as well as his or her income stream), and then only the individual can factor in the nonmonetary benefits and costs. But in either case, the underlying model implies that the individual will discount future benefits and costs and strive to undertake the investments that maximize utility. Once the investments are chosen, individuals then choose the consumption stream that maximizes their utilities, subject to the budget constraint that the present value of the consumption stream can be no greater than the wealth.

---

[32] Ben Wildavsky, "Budget Deal May Still Hang on a CPI Fix," *National Journal, 29,* No. 12, March 22, 1997, p. 576.

This discounting perspective is useful when moving from the more abstract two-period model to models with more familiar time frames such as years. Individuals still follow the rule of undertaking all investments with net present value greater than zero. We illustrated use of the discounting rule with several different calculations, including one to illustrate that the same principle applies in benefit-cost analysis.

However, it is not clear to what extent individuals actually behave as if they are discounting as described above. Several studies suggest that individuals sometimes act as if they have discount rates that are far higher than market rates. For example, many thousands of individuals leaving the military during the 1990s had earned substantial benefits and were given a choice between receiving a lump-sum payment or an annuity with present value at market rates 50–100 percent greater than the lump-sum amount. The calculation of the annuity's present value was made for them and explained to them. But most chose the lump-sum payment, which means that they acted as if they had personal discount rates that exceed 20 percent (when market rates were at 7 percent). While some of these individuals may have needed a large amount of cash for which they had no alternative source, why so many people made a choice that left them about $30,000 poorer in conventional terms remains a puzzle.

If poor intertemporal choice-making is a legitimate public policy concern, then policies to simplify the problem might be quite valuable. We considered a set of policies that address one source of complexity for these choices: indexing policies to remove the uncertainty that inflation causes about the real purchasing power of future dollars. Social Security payments, many private pension plans, food stamps, and U.S. Treasury "I" bonds are all indexed to keep purchasing power approximately constant no matter what the inflation rate. We reviewed common methods of index construction used to achieve this objective.

A true cost-of-living index for an individual would measure the percent change in nominal income required to hold utility constant at a base level. To approximate this concept, Laspeyre and Paasche price indices can be constructed to estimate the change. The Laspeyre index calculates how much money would be needed to purchase the base period consumption quantities at the new period's prices. This overestimates the necessary monetary increase, because while the individual could then purchase the original bundle, at the new prices there will be a different bundle that yields more utility than initially. This overcompensation is sometimes referred to as a substitution bias because it does not account for the fact that the individual can and will substitute items that have become relatively less expensive for those that have become relatively more expensive. The Paasche index, which calculates how much more money it costs to purchase the new-period quantities owing to the price changes, has the opposite flaw and underestimates the money required to hold utility constant.

The theoretical imperfections of the Laspeyre and Paasche methods of indexing are probably less significant than the practical problems of defining the goods and services that are included in an index and updating the index over time. We consider these practical problems as they apply to the construction of one of our most important indices, the Consumer Price Index (CPI), which is the index actually used to adjust Social Security and many other nominal payments in the economy. These changes are very politically sensitive, because they affect the payments that millions of individuals receive.

The CPI is a fixed-weight Laspeyre index constructed by the Bureau of Labor Statistics. The weights are fixed by expenditure surveys, which the Bureau updates every 2 years in order to reduce substitution bias. The CPI is based on 206 different item categories; within each category the prices of specific items are measured monthly in many different urban areas and are then averaged to estimate a price change for each specific item. Again to reduce substitution bias, the Bureau assumes that the proportion of expenditure on each item (rather than its quantity) within a category remains constant. Finally, we noted that the index is imperfect because quality changes in many of the items surveyed do not get taken into account. Even if a computer this year costs the same as one last year, its quality is often substantially increased. While this remains a problem for most items, the Bureau is now using an econometric method to account specifically for quality changes in computers.

The allocation of resources over time has profound effects on economic growth. The more that we can understand about how individuals make these decisions and how public policies might improve them, the better off we will all be. The utility-maximizing model that we have used is a useful starting point to help us understand the important role of interest rates as well as the concept of discounting. The difficulty that many individuals may have with these decisions challenges us to improve our models as well as our public policies. To the extent that index construction is used to give individuals more certainty about their real entitlements to retirement benefits, it eases their task in deciding how much more to save. Index construction can also be used in many other ways, such as using an index of education costs in state aid formulas to ensure equity across districts.

Exercises

8-1 A house can be rented in an uncontrolled market for a profit of $20,000 this period and $20,000 next period. (There are only two periods.)

a If the market interest rate is 10 percent, what is the most you would expect a housing investor to offer for the house? Explain.

b Suppose the investor in (a) buys the house for his maximum offer and rent controls are then imposed, allowing the new owner to charge in each period only the operating expenses actually incurred plus $5000. Upset by the effect of rent controls on his profits, the new owner considers selling the house. What is the maximum a housing investor would now bid for it? (Answer: $9545.45.)

8-2 The secretary of labor is concerned about the human capital investments of young adults like Steven Even. Steven lives in an inner-city area that banks avoid and that discourages thoughts of higher education, but he is bright and full of potential. He is working now in a secure but low-paying job. His current income is $10,000 ($Y_0 = 10$), and his future income (Y_1) will stay at $10,000 unless he improves it by investing in himself through higher education. His productive opportunities locus is

$$Y_1 = 30 - 2Y_0^2/10$$

The market interest rate for borrowing or saving between the two periods is $r = 0.20$.

a Write down the numerical *equation* showing the present value of Steven's wealth if he stays in his current job. You do not have to calculate the value.

b Suppose Steven chooses the point on his productive opportunities locus where $Y_0 = 5$ and $Y_1 = 25$. Explain in what sense he is investing, and how much.

c Steven's consumption preferences are such that he prefers strictly even consumption ($C_0 = C_1$) at any interest rate. Given that no one will lend him any money, how much will he invest? [*Hint:* Draw a diagram including the given information, and think carefully about the shape of Steven's indifference curves. The answer is 0.]

d Suppose the secretary of labor stands ready to do what the market will not: lend money to people like Steven at the going interest rate. Now will he invest? [*Hint:* Note the slope of the productive opportunities locus at (10, 10) is −4.]

APPENDIX

DISCOUNTING OVER CONTINUOUS INTERVALS°

In this appendix we review the concept of a continuous stream of payments, which is often used in analytic calculations and requires some knowledge of integral calculus. We approach the idea by first distinguishing between simple and compound interest and then examining compound interest as the compounding period becomes shorter and shorter.

The examples in the chapter all involved *simple* interest rates, but it is sometimes more convenient to work with *continuously compounded* rates over the same interval. Imagine first that we deposit $\$P$ in a bank that pays r percent annual interest compounded semiannually. This is equivalent to keeping the money in the bank for two 6-month periods at a 6-month simple interest rate of $r/2$:

$$A = P\left(1 + \frac{r}{2}\right)^2$$

In other words, compounding holds the simple rate of interest constant but redefines the intervals to be shorter. The difference between this and the simple-interest case is that with compounding one earns interest on the interest. The interest earned after 6 months is $Pr/2$, and that is added to the account balance. Thus, during the second 6 months, one earns $Pr/2$ as interest on the original deposit plus interest on the first 6 months' interest $(Pr/2)(r/2) = Pr^2/4$. To check this, note that:

Simple interest: $A = P(1 + r) = P + Pr$

Compounded semiannually: $A = P\left(1 + \frac{r}{2}\right)^2 = P + Pr + \frac{Pr^2}{4}$

If we let the original deposit of $\$P$ earn compound interest for t years, we would have

$$A = P\left(1 + \frac{r}{2}\right)^{2t}$$

The more often interest is compounded (for a fixed simple rate), the more benefit to the saver. If the interest is compounded quarterly and held for t years,

$$A = P\left(1 + \frac{r}{4}\right)^{4t}$$

and if the savings are compounded n times per year and held for t years, the amount at the end of the period is

$$A = P\left(1 + \frac{r}{n}\right)^{nt}$$

Now what happens if we let n approach infinity, or compound continuously? To answer that, we first define the number e[33]:

$$e = \lim_{n \to \infty} \left(1 + \frac{1}{n}\right)^n \approx 2.718$$

This number can be interpreted economically as the yield on $\$1$ invested for 1 year at a 100 percent interest rate compounded continuously. If the simple interest rate is r rather than 100 percent, one must make use of the following limit to calculate the continuously compounded yield:

$$e^r = \lim_{n \to \infty} \left(1 + \frac{r}{n}\right)^n$$

Table 8A-1 shows the effect of the frequency of compounding or discounting on savings and borrowings.

Note that if $\$P$ is deposited and compounded continuously at annual interest r for a period of t years, the amount at the end of that time is

$$A = P(e^r)^t = Pe^{rt}$$

If one asks about the present discounted value of A dollars in the future, the answer expressed with continuous discounting is

$$PDV = Ae^{-rt} = P$$

We have already seen that the present value of a stream of payments is the sum of the present value of each payment. If one receives a payment A_t each year for n years, its present value using the continuously discounted rate is

$$PDV = A_0 + A_1 e^{-r} + A_2 e^{-2r} + \ldots + A_n e^{-nr}$$

---

[33] If mathematical limits are not familiar, try taking a calculator and experimenting. Compute the expression $(1 + 1/n)^n$ for $n = 10$ and then $n = 100$ to see that it approaches $e = 2.718$.

Table 8A-1

The Effect of Compounding on Yields and Present Values

Deposit $1 for 1 year at 10% annual interest	Formula	Yield	Equivalent simple interest[a]
(a) Simple	$1(1 + 0.10)$	1.1000	10.00
(b) Compounded semi-annually	$1(1 + 0.10/2)^2$	1.1025	10.25
(c) Compounded quarterly	$1(1 + 0.10/4)^4$	1.1038	10.38
(d) Compounded continuously	$1(e^{0.10})$	1.1052	10.52

Repay $1 in 1 year at 10% annual discount rate	Formula	Present value	Equivalent simple discount rate
(a) Simple	$1/(1 + 0.10)$	0.9091	10.00
(b) Discounted semi-annually	$1/(1 + 0.10/2)^2$	0.9070	10.25
(c) Discounted quarterly	$1/(1 + 0.10/4)^4$	0.9060	10.38
(d) Discounted continuously	$1/(e^{0.10})$	0.9048	10.52

[a] If r is the simple interest rate and r_c is the continuously compounded rate over a given time interval, they are equivalent if their yields are identical: $1 + r = e^{r_c}$ or $\ln(1 + r) = r_c$. This formula allows conversion from simple to continuous interest rates.

There is one last idea that is important to develop because of its analytic convenience. A payment at the rate of A_t per year could be sent in installments, just as annual rent is usually paid monthly; $100 per year could come in quarterly payments of $25, or weekly payments of $1.92, or at some other frequency. The frequency we wish to focus on is payment at each instant! An example of why we are interested in this may help. Suppose someone owns a tree and wishes to cut it and sell the lumber when its present value is maximized. The tree grows at its natural rate each instant; it adds more lumber as a stream of continuing payments and changes the present value. Or a machine may be thought of as *depreciating* continuously over time, that is, as generating a stream of instantaneous negative payments. The mathematics below is useful for finding the present value in these and similar cases.

Let us call $A(t)$ the annual dollars that would result if the instantaneous payment at time t continued for exactly 1 year. Let us call Δt the fraction of the year during which the payment actually does continue. Thus, the amount received is $A(t)\Delta t$, and its continuously discounted value is

$$\text{PDV} = [A(t)\Delta t]e^{-rt}$$

If we have a stream of instantaneous payments for T years, where the annual rate is constant within each small portion of the year Δt, then the present value of the whole stream

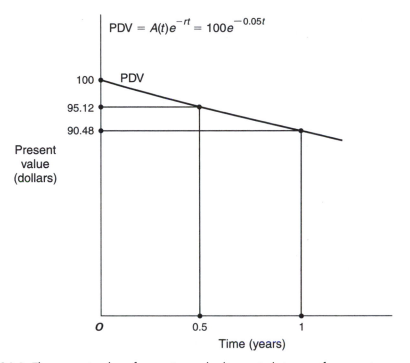

Figure 8A-1. The present value of a continuously discounted stream of payments.

can be thought of as the discounted sum of the payments during each Δt. The number of intervals being summed is $T/\Delta t$:

$$PDV = \sum_{t=0}^{T} [A(t)\Delta t] e^{-rt}$$

Now if we go to the limit where the size of the interval Δt approaches zero, the above expression becomes an integral:

$$PDV = \lim_{n \to \infty} \sum_{t=0}^{T} [A(t)\Delta t] e^{-rt} = \int_{t=0}^{T} A(t) e^{-rt} dt$$

To see what this means, let us use some numerical examples. Let $A(t) = \$100$. If it is paid in a single payment at the end of the year, $\Delta t = 1$. At an annual rate of 10 percent continuously discounted, its present value is

$$PDV = [A(t)\Delta t] e^{-rt}$$

$$= \$100 e^{-0.10} = \$90.48$$

If the $\$100$ is paid in two 6-month installments, $\Delta t = \frac{1}{2}$, so that $A(t)\Delta t = 50$ and there are two components to the present value:

$$PDV = 50 e^{-0.10(0.5)} + 50 e^{-0.10(1)}$$

$$= 47.56 + 45.24$$

$$= \$92.80$$

We can imagine paying the $100 in an increasing number of installments until the interval size is that of an instant. If the $100 is paid in equal instantaneous installments, its present value is

$$PDV = \int_{t=0}^{t=1} 100e^{-0.1t}\, dt$$

$$= \frac{100e^{-0.1(1)}}{-0.1} - \frac{100e^{-0.1(1)}}{-0.1}$$

$$= -904.84 + 1000$$

$$= \$95.16$$

We show the geometric interpretations of these calculations in Figure 8A-1. The downward-sloping line shows the present value of $100 (discounted continuously) at any point between the present and 1 year into the future. The single-payment calculation is the area of the rectangle using the height of the curve ($90.48), where $t = 1$ and with length $\Delta t = 1$. The two-payment calculation is the sum of two rectangles: Both have length $\Delta t = 0.5$, and the heights are the discounted values of the payments at $t = 0.5$ and $t = 1$, or $95.12 and $90.48, respectively. Note that the second calculation comes closer to measuring the whole area under the curve from $t = 0$ to $t = 1$. If we divided the intervals into 4, 8, and 16 payments, we would come even closer to measuring that whole area. In the limit of instantaneous payments at each infinitesimally sized interval, the area is the whole area. The integral is simply the way of calculating the area under the given curve for the relevant period ($t = 0$ to $t = 1$).

PART THREE

POLICY ASPECTS OF PRODUCTION AND SUPPLY DECISIONS

CHAPTER NINE

THE COST SIDE OF POLICY ANALYSIS: TECHNICAL LIMITS,
PRODUCTIVE POSSIBILITIES, AND COST CONCEPTS

IN THIS CHAPTER we examine concepts from the economic theories of production and costs. These theories are useful in deducing policy-relevant consequences from observable supply activities. First, they are crucial components of *predictive* models of producer behavior: understanding what outputs will be supplied by these organizations and what resources will be used to make the outputs. Second, they are important for the *normative* purpose of evaluating the efficiency consequences of supply activities. After presenting an overview of these uses below, we explain how the chapter is organized to develop skills by using several fundamental concepts from these theories.

In order to predict the behavior of a supplier organization, economic models provide specifications of the organization's objectives, capabilities, and environmental constraints. The latter are factors that are exogenous to the organization or outside its direct control: the technological possibilities for producing the product, the costs of the resource inputs used with alternative production methods, and the demand for the organization's product.[1] In this chapter we will develop familiarity with the supply constraints of technology and costs. In later chapters we will focus on specifying the objectives and capabilities of an organization and then linking them with the environmental constraints to predict the organization's behavioral response to proposed policies. However, we wish to clarify in advance that making deductions about technology and costs from empirical observations cannot be done in isolation from organizational objectives and capabilities.

Consider first the constraint of *technology,* the methods available for converting inputs into outputs. Obviously, one cannot expect an organization to produce more output than is

---

[1] When the supplier has monopoly or monopsony power, its own actions may affect the costs of its inputs or the demand for its product. We focus on these situations in later chapters. However, exogenous factors such as resource scarcity and consumer tastes still remain as important constraints.

technologically possible given the inputs it uses; therefore, understanding the constraint is useful for predictive purposes. Technologies that are efficient in an engineering sense (the maximum output for given inputs) are sometimes represented in models by a *production function*. Estimated production functions, based upon observations of supplier inputs and outputs, are used commonly in analytic work.

Understanding technological possibilities is easier for some activities than others. In agriculture, for example, it might be clear that one particular output is corn and that the inputs used to produce it are land, labor, fertilizer, capital, equipment, weather, and so on. Even in this relatively clear case there are difficulties in establishing the relation between inputs and outputs. Suppose, for example, that less fertilizer does not reduce the amount of corn produced but does reduce its sweetness. Then it would be a mistake to compare only the quantity and not the quality of the output and conclude that the process with less fertilizer is technologically superior. To corn lovers this is like comparing apples and oranges.

Imagine the difficulty of trying to understand the technology constraining some other important supply organizations. How does one define the outputs of a school, police force, or mental hospital, and what are the inputs that determine the outputs? One might think, for example, that the verbal and mathematical skills of children are intended as the outputs of schools and furthermore that they can be measured by scores on standardized tests. However, one community might emphasize learning about civic responsibilities as an important schooling objective, and that output would not necessarily be reflected in the standardized scores. Its schools might have smaller increases in the standardized scores of their pupils, but it would be wrong to conclude they were technologically inefficient compared with other schools with similar resource inputs: It is the objectives that differ, not the technological efficiency.

The other environmental constraint focused on in this chapter is *cost*. The supplier organization's choice of technology will depend upon its perception of costs. The monetary costs of inputs that we observe in the marketplace may or may not fully represent that perception. In the standard example of a profit-maximizing firm, the monetary costs are those perceived by the firm. For example, the firm will produce any level of output with whatever technology minimizes the monetary cost of its required inputs. In this case a relation known as the *cost function* can be used to predict the total costs of producing alternative output levels for any given input prices. Knowledge of the cost function can be useful for predicting how supplier organizations will respond to various policy changes such as those involving taxes or regulatory rules.

However, suppose the supplier organization is a public agency with a mandate to employ the hard-to-employ. It may prefer a labor-intensive technology to a capital-intensive one with lower monetary costs. That is, it may perceive forgone employment opportunities as a cost of using capital in addition to its monetary cost.

Some supplier organizations may produce in environments in which political costs are major expenses. A district attorney's office, for example, may require police assistance to obtain certain evidence. But the police have many important matters on their agenda and establish their own priorities. The district attorney's office may have to pay a political cost, such as agreeing to prosecute some other individuals arrested by the police promptly, in order to gain police cooperation in gathering the evidence.

The above examples demonstrate that understanding technological possibilities and costs is important for predicting the behavior of supply organizations; however, one must consider carefully how these constraints apply in specific situations. Now let us turn briefly to the normative use of concepts from the theories of production and cost. We discuss their relevance to the concepts of Pareto optimality and benefit-cost analysis.

We have not yet considered how the concept of Pareto optimality applies to a complicated economy in which decisions must be made about the outputs to be produced and the resource inputs to be used in making each output. Indeed, we defer most of this discussion until Chapter 12. Nevertheless, we shall sometimes point out when there is "room for a deal." For example, efficiency requires that each output be produced by a method that is technologically efficient: that is, one that achieves the maximum possible output with the inputs used. Otherwise, one could use the same inputs with an efficient technology and have more of that output with no less of anything else. The incremental output could be given to anyone and someone would be made better off with no one else worse off. Thus a necessary condition for Pareto optimality is that outputs be produced with technologically efficient methods.

Knowledge of the production function is useful for judging the technical efficiency of supplier organizations. We will illustrate this with an example from an evaluation of a public employment program. Partial knowledge of the production function is developed from empirical observations and used to judge changes in the technological efficiency of production over time.

All of the other normative illustrations in this chapter are applications of the benefit-cost principle. Whereas Chapter 6 focused on the "benefit" side of the principle, this chapter focuses on the "cost" side. The essential point is to demonstrate that knowledge of costs can provide a great deal of the information that can be used to find out if gainers from a change can compensate the losers. Once that is clear, we illustrate how the knowledge is obtained (and some of the difficulties that arise) through specific applications of benefit-cost analysis and the use of cost functions. We use examples from a public employment program, trucking deregulation, and peak-load pricing for public utilities.

The chapter is organized as follows: We begin with a review of the relation between technological possibilities and the concept of a production function. Both predictive and normative uses of the production function approach in a policy setting are illustrated from an analysis of a public employment program. We also provide an example to suggest how cross-sectional empirical data are often used to draw inferences about a production function, and we warn of a pitfall to avoid when the method is used.

Following the section on technological constraints, we compare and contrast concepts of cost: accounting cost, private opportunity cost, and social opportunity cost. We show how knowledge of the social opportunity cost can be used to test for relative efficiency by the compensation principle. The use of these different cost concepts is illustrated by benefit-cost calculations used in the analysis of the public employment program. The calculations illustrate both predictive and normative analytic tasks.

After reviewing cost concepts, we explore the relations between costs and outputs. The concept of a cost function is explained, and use of the function is illustrated in the evaluation of a regulatory reform concerning interstate trucking firms as well as in a public employment program. In a supplemental section, another type of cost-input relation known as the joint cost problem is discussed, together with its application to peak-load pricing of public utility services. In an appendix to the chapter, we use the mathematics of duality to clarify some of the relations between technology and cost functions and introduce some of the cost functions commonly used in empirical analysis.

Technical Possibilities and the Production Function

The Production Function Is a Summary of Technological Possibilities

The production function summarizes the various technical possibilities for converting inputs, or factors of production, into the maximum possible output. For example, if Q represents output, and the inputs are K for capital and L for labor, the production function may be expressed as

$$Q = F(K, L)$$

The idea is that the output may be produced by various combinations of the two inputs, and knowledge of the production function and specific quantities K_0 and L_0 allows one to infer the level Q_0 that is the *maximum* output that can be produced with that combination. Usually, more output can be produced if more of one of the inputs is available. In mathematical notation, $\Delta Q/\Delta K > 0$ and $\Delta Q/\Delta L > 0$.

Let us think of a single technology as a set of instructions for converting specified inputs into some output, exactly like the instructions that come with a model airplane kit, where the various parts are inputs and the model airplane is the output. Note that the economic meaning of "technology" is broader than its common interpretation as a type of machine; there can be technologies in which the only inputs are labor, and more generally, the variations in possible instructions to laborers can be an important source of technological change.

For example, suppose we imagine alternative processes of developing computer programs Q to sell to other firms (e.g., to keep track of their accounts receivable) and there are ten computer programmers L and five computer terminals K as the inputs available during a specified production period. There are many ways in which one could imagine organizing these inputs for production: Perhaps some programmers should specialize in drafting the program and others in debugging the drafts. We might instruct each programmer to develop a program from start to finish or perhaps some programmers should specialize in developing financial programs and others in inventory control. Two time shifts of labor might be developed to allow full utilization of the terminals. Each of these is a way to vary the technology of production.

If the production function for this example is represented as above, $Q = F(K, L)$, then the only information we have is on the maximum output that can be attained with the two types of inputs. On the other hand, we might consider the ten units of labor as divided into two different types of labor, for example, six programmers who make the program plan L_P and four who debug L_D, and represent the production function with three inputs as follows:

$$Q = F(L_P, L_D, K)$$

We could extend this to consider the morning M and evening E programmers:

$$Q = F(L_{P_M}, L_{P_E}, L_{D_M}, L_{D_E}, K)$$

Thus whether the effect of a technological variation can be identified from knowledge of the production function depends upon how the function is defined: the more aggregated the input definitions, the less information is revealed about technical variations.

Often an analyst is expected to be able to determine empirically some aspect of the technology of an actual production process. This typically requires statistical estimation of the production function. Although the statistical procedures are beyond the scope of this text, the theoretical and practical considerations that underlie the analysis can be illustrated.

One example arose in regard to the evaluation of the New York Supported Work experiment, a program of the nonprofit Wildcat Service Corporation, which hires ex-addicts and ex-offenders to deliver a wide variety of public services in the city. One group of employees was engaged in cleaning the exteriors of fire stations around the city, and the crews had been working for approximately 6 months. The question raised was whether the productivity of the workers was improving.

Answering this specific question actually had only a latent role in the overall evaluation of the experiment. This particular project was started before the formal experiment, and its participants were not randomly selected. However, the analyst hired to undertake the formal economic evaluation was not well known to the officials operating or funding the program, and they sought some early assurance that his work would be useful.[2] This project provided a low-risk opportunity to get some indication of the quality of the evaluation to come. That is, the resolution of the issue was to some degree a test of the analyst's skill and would be a determinant of the seriousness with which his future analyses and recommendations would be taken.

Accurate data were attainable on the inputs used to clean each building. This does not mean that the mass of data was all prepared, sitting and gathering dust on some desk while waiting for an analyst to walk in and have use for it. But the project managers, in the course of conducting routine activities, had maintained various records that the analyst could use in constructing a data set appropriate for this task. The project had several crews, which allowed them to work at different sites simultaneously. They kept track daily of attendance on each site for payroll purposes. For inventory control they kept daily track of the number of water-blasting machines assigned to each crew and the quantity of chemicals used by the crew. Furthermore, precise output data on the square footage of the surfaces cleaned, verified by site visits, were also available.

---

[2] All this is known to me because I was the analyst.

Efficiency, Not Productivity, Is the Objective

Let us consider for a moment what is meant by a productivity increase. Imagine a production process in which output Q is produced with inputs K and L. **The average product of labor AP_L is defined as output per unit of labor:**

$$AP_L = Q/L$$

This measure, output per worker, is what is usually referred to when productivity is discussed. Mayors often seek ways of raising the productivity of city employees. On a larger scale this measure applied to the aggregate private economy is often of great concern. For the 27-year period from 1947 to 1973, real productivity in the U.S. private business sector increased every single year. The rate of productivity increase averaged 2.91 percent per year. But from 1973 to 1980, average real productivity growth was only 0.58 percent per year, and in some years it was negative. Similarly, from 1980 to 1991 the average increase in the index was only 1.01 percent, and was again negative toward the period's end. The source of this 20-year slowdown in productivity is still not well understood, although it began to pick up in the 1990s and averaged 2.8 percent per year in 1995–1999 when the economy was once again growing at a healthy clip.[3]

Nevertheless, *maximizing productivity is not necessarily a wise or efficient strategy to follow.* To see this, we introduce standard diagrams of the total, average, and marginal product curves for one input. These curves show how output varies as the amount of one type of input changes, given a fixed level of all the other inputs. The curves for the input labor are shown in Figures 9-1a and b. If the amount of some other input such as capital increases, then all three of the labor product curves will usually shift upward. (Normally, the more capital each worker has available, the greater the output per worker.)

The total product-of-labor curve TP_L shows the total output level as a function of the different labor amounts possible, holding all other inputs constant at a fixed level. It is drawn in Figure 9-1a to increase rapidly at first (as enough laborers become available to use the capital stock) and then more slowly until L_T, where it actually begins to decline. (Too many workers jammed into one plant can become counterproductive.) The slowdown in the growth of total product is a consequence of diminishing marginal productivity. **The marginal product of labor MP_L is the change in output that results from adding one more unit of labor.** In Figure 9-1a it is equal to the slope of TP_L ($= \Delta TP_L/\Delta L$). It rises at first until it reaches a maximum at L_M and then declines; its graph is shown in Figure 9-1b.

The average product of labor AP_L in Figure 9-1a is the slope of the line drawn from the origin to any point on the TP_L curve (slope = height/base = total product/labor = AP_L); it reaches its maximum at L_A, where the line from the origin is just tangent to the TP_L curve. In Figure 9-1b the AP_L curve is constructed from the TP_L curve in Figure 9-1a.

---

[3] *Economic Report of the President,* February 1982 (Washington, D.C.: U.S. Government Printing Office, 1982), p. 278, Table B-40, and *Economic Report of the President,* February 2000 (Washington, D.C.: U.S. Government Printing Office, 2000), p. 362, Table B-47. Aggregate output in the tables is measured by the real gross domestic product in the business sector, and it is divided by the total hours of work of all persons in the sector.

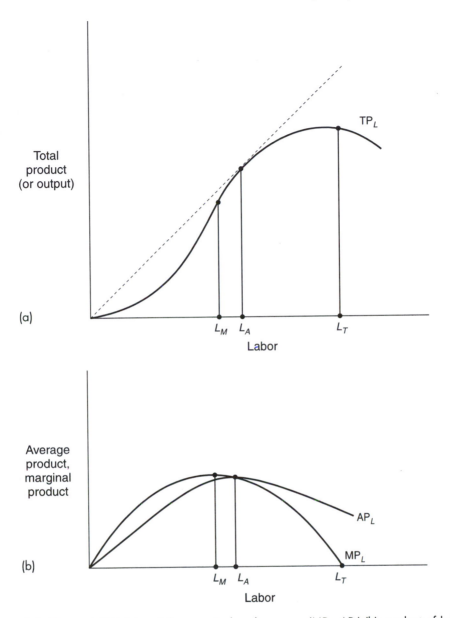

Figure 9-1. The total (TP$_L$) (a) and the marginal and average (MP$_L$, AP$_L$) (b) product of labor curves.

The MP$_L$ reaches its maximum before that of the AP$_L$ and it always passes through the maximum AP$_L$. This is shown in Figure 9-1b. That is, the marginal product pulls the average product up whenever it is greater (MP$_L$ > AP$_L$), and pulls it down whenever it is lower (MP$_L$ < AP$_L$). When they are the same, the AP$_L$ is neither rising nor falling; the slope of the AP$_L$ at this point is thus zero and the AP$_L$ is at a maximum.

From this analysis, we can see that maximizing productivity for a given stock of non-labor inputs implies that the quantity of labor used should be L_A. But is that desirable? In general, the answer is no. Imagine that the MP_L at L_A is three per hour, that labor can be hired at $6.00 per hour, and output sells at $3.00 each. Then hiring one more hour's worth of labor will cost $6.00 but result in $9.00 worth of extra output. It would be inefficient to forgo this opportunity, since there is clearly room for a deal (consumers and the extra laborer can all be made better off and no one worse off). *It does not matter whether productivity is decreasing. The relevant consideration is efficiency: If the value of the marginal product exceeds its cost, then efficiency can be increased by moving away from the maximum productivity.* In this example, labor should be hired until the MP_L declines to 2. That will be to the right of L_A, in general.[4]

One reason for pointing out the inefficiency of maximizing productivity (aside from its relevance to the public employment problem, to be discussed shortly) is that it can be a tempting mistake to make. Public managers, responding to their mayors' pleas to increase productivity, could decrease efficiency by utilizing too little labor with the available capital stock. Two people and a truck on a refuse collection route may collect 2 tons per day; three people on the same truck may collect 2½ tons per day and thereby cause "productivity" to decrease. But the relevant issue is efficiency: whether the extra cleanliness resulting from the marginal ½ ton of removed refuse per collection cycle is worth more than the cost of achieving it.

There are, of course, other ways to change the level of productivity: One can add to the nonlabor inputs such as the capital stock, or one can make technological progress (i.e., use a new technology that generates more output from a given set of inputs than the old technology). Like changes in labor quantities, neither method can be utilized for free. To generate an increase in the capital stock requires that people reduce current consumption in order to save more, and technical progress is usually a consequence of devoting resources to research and development. As with all economic activities, these methods should be pursued only to the extent that we (individually and collectively) are willing to pay the bills for doing so. Nevertheless, the relatively low 1973–1991 U.S. productivity was matched by similar sluggishness around much of the world, and the reasons for it, despite many studies, remain elusive. It requires further study to uncover whether this was because of "errors" in resource allocation or "bad luck" in research and development efforts, or simply due to living in a world in which it was truly "more expensive" to buy increases in productivity.[5]

---

[4] Take the case in which inputs and outputs have constant prices. To the left of L_A, where AP_L is increasing, average output cost is decreasing and profits per unit are increasing. Therefore, there is still room for a deal by employing more labor and expanding output. To the right of L_A, profits per unit begin to decrease, but very slowly at first whereas quantity is increasing at a constant clip. Thus total profits are still increasing. Eventually, profits per unit will decline enough that total profits do not increase; that will be the efficient production point.

[5] For an excellent introduction to this general problem, see Edward F. Denison, *Accounting for Slower Economic Growth* (Washington, D.C.: The Brookings Institution, 1979). Leading explanations for the worldwide productivity slowdown are the sharp energy price increase in 1973 (causing much of the energy-using capital stock to become inefficient), and data inadequacies that underestimate productivity gains through technical progress in the service sectors (e.g., the spread of computers). For analyses of the productivity slowdown, see the Symposium

How does this discussion apply to the supported work problem? First, what is the common sense meaning of wanting the workers to be "more productive"? In this case, it really refers to improving the contribution of the worker, all other things being equal. It means things such as better timeliness, better focus on the tasks to be accomplished, and more skill when undertaking the tasks. Productivity of the workers thus should not simply be defined by the AP_L at different times; this can change for too many reasons irrelevant to the real question of worker improvement (e.g., changes in the capital equipment available). We want to ask whether the supported workers, when utilizing any given quantity of nonlabor inputs, produce more output over time. One might think of this as a skill increase or an increase in "human capital": over time, each worker hour represents more labor. Alternatively, one could think of this as technical progress: The same inputs produce more output because the production process is becoming more refined. This case would be one of labor-augmenting technical progress.

Letting $a(t)$ represent a technical progress function (where t is time), we might hypothesize[6]:

$$Q = F[K, a(t)L]$$

The term $a(t)$ can be thought of as an adjustment to the nominal quantity of labor (e.g., hours worked) in order to account for changes in the effectiveness of labor over time. Now if we can estimate the production function, it may be possible to see if labor inputs produce more output over time, other things being equal. That is, we want to know, for $t_1 > t_0$ whether $a(t_1) > a(t_0)$. This would be true if $\Delta a/\Delta t > 0$, meaning that labor is more effective over time. For example, if $a(t_0) = 1$ and $a(t_1) = 1.2$, it means each hour of labor in t_1 has the same effect on output as 1.2 hours in t_0.

It is necessary to choose some specific empirical form for the production function. Theoretical considerations provide some guidance about the general shape of the function, but the specific numerical equation selected is then a matter of which fits the data the best. First we provide the theoretical background that helps us to understand likely shapes, and then we will turn to the empirical specifics.

Characterizing Different Production Functions

We begin with the idea of **an isoquant: a locus of input combinations that yield a given output level.** This is the production analogue to the indifference curves of utility theory. For example, in Figure 9-2 points A and B illustrate two of the many different input mixes that can be used to produce 30 units of output: point A uses $K = 10$ and $L = 5$, and point B

---

in *Journal of Economic Perspectives, 2,* No. 4, Fall 1988, pp. 3–97; and Zvi Griliches, "Productivity, R&D, and the Data Constraint," *American Economic Review, 84,* No. 1, March 1994, pp. 1–23. For a focus on measurement techniques, see R. Fare et al., "Productivity Growth, Technical Progress, and Efficiency Change in Industrialized Countries," *American Economic Review, 84,* No. 1, March 1994, pp. 66–83.

[6] Capital augmenting technical progress is represented as $F[a(t)K, L]$ and neutral technological progress as $a(t)F(K, L)$.

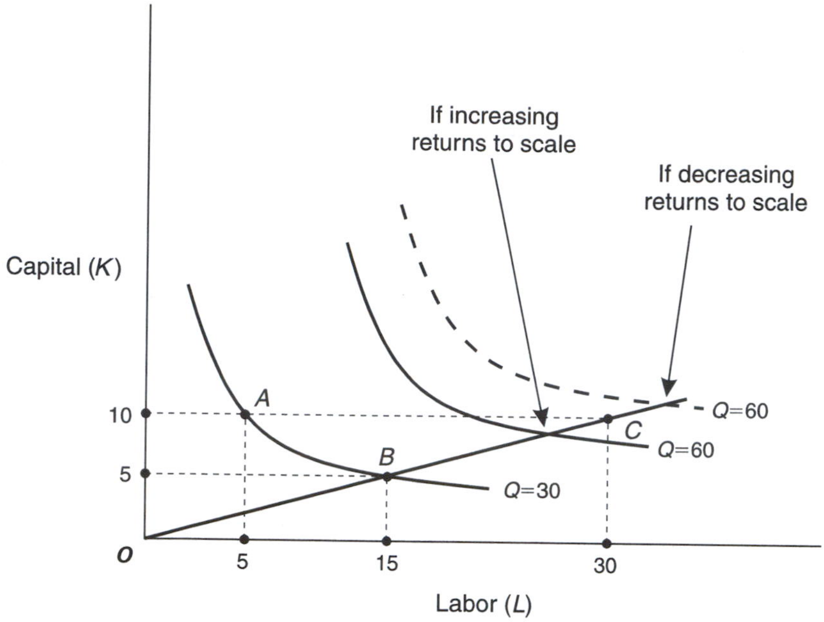

Figure 9-2. Returns-to-scale and production functions: If the isoquant for $Q = 60$ went through point C, the returns to scale would be constant.

uses $K = 5$ and $L = 15$. Because A uses more capital relative to labor than does B, we say it is the more "capital intensive" of the two. The isoquant generally has a negative slope: as less of one input (capital) is used, more of another input (labor) is needed in order to keep the output level constant. The absolute slope of the isoquant is called **the rate of technical substitution** (of labor for capital, given the axes definitions), or $RTS_{L,K}$, and its economic meaning **is the amount of an input (capital) that can be released when one extra unit of another input (labor) is added and still hold output constant.**

Generally, the $RTS_{L,K}$ diminishes as one moves from left to right along the isoquant. When capital is "abundant" and labor is "scarce" (the upper left portion of an isoquant), the marginal product of capital is "low" whereas that of labor is "high." So to hold output constant when an extra unit of labor is obtained, "many" units of capital can be released, thus implying that the slope is steep. The opposite is true on the lower-right portion of the isoquant, where capital is "scarce" and "labor" is abundant. Then an extra unit of labor has a "low" marginal product" whereas that for capital is "high." In this case, holding output constant when an extra unit of labor is added means that only "few" units of capital can be released, or that the slope is relatively flat.

The above reasoning suggests a relationship between the marginal products of the factors and the RTS, and indeed there is one. For any small change in the input mix, we can write the amount that output changes as follows:

$$\Delta Q = MP_K^*(\Delta K) + MP_L^*(\Delta L)$$

That is, the change in output is the sum of two effects. One effect is the amount output changes per unit change in capital (MP_K) times the number of units that capital changes (ΔK). The other effect is that owing to the changing labor: the amount output changes per unit change in labor times the number of units that labor changes. Now let this small change in input mix be a very specific type: from one point to another *on the same isoquant*. For such a change, ΔQ must be zero. Then the above equation becomes:

$$0 = MP_K*(\Delta K) + MP_L*(\Delta L)$$

or, rewriting,

$$-\Delta K/\Delta L = MP_L/MP_K$$

But the expression on the left-hand side of the equation is simply minus the slope of the isoquant, or what we have defined as the $RTS_{L,K}$. Therefore,

$$RTS_{L,K} = MP_L/MP_K$$

We will make reference to this relationship later on. But now we continue to explain aspects of production functions. Two important characteristics of production functions are the returns to scale and elasticity of substitution. Roughly, the returns to scale concerns just how much output changes when all inputs are increased. Normally isoquants for higher output levels will lie upward and to the right of some initial isoquant (more inputs allow production of greater output). **The returns-to-scale characteristic is whether a proportionate change applied to all inputs leads to an output change that is proportionately greater, the same, or smaller (corresponding to increasing, constant, or decreasing returns to scale, respectively).**[7] For short, we shall refer to these as IRTS, CRTS, and DRTS.

On Figure 9-2, the ray from the origin through point B shows all input combinations that have the same capital-labor ratio (the proportion K/L) as point B itself. We might wonder

---

[7] A production function $F(K, L)$ may be partially characterized by its scale coefficient ϕ, where returns are decreasing, constant, or increasing if $\phi < 1$, $\phi = 1$, and $\phi > 1$, respectively. ϕ is equal to the sum of the elasticities of output with respect to each input:

$$\phi = \varepsilon_{Q,L} + \varepsilon_{Q,K}$$

A quick derivation of this is possible with some calculus. Consider the total differential of the production function:

$$dQ = \frac{\partial Q}{\partial L} dL + \frac{\partial Q}{\partial K} dK$$

Divide both sides by Q:

$$\frac{dQ}{Q} = \frac{\partial Q}{\partial L} \frac{1}{Q} dL + \frac{\partial Q}{\partial K} \frac{1}{Q} dK$$

Note that the term on the left-hand side is the proportionate change in output. Now consider changes that are brought about by increasing all inputs by the same proportion α:

$$\alpha = \frac{dL}{L} = \frac{dK}{K}$$

how far out on this ray we would have to go to double the output level to $Q = 60$? Point C on the ray has twice the inputs of point B. If the isoquant for $Q = 60$ crosses the ray below point C, as is shown by the solid-line isoquant, then the production function is IRTS (output is doubled for an input increase that is less than double). If, alternatively, the isoquant for $Q = 60$ crossed the ray above point C, like the dotted-line isoquant drawn, then the production function would be DRTS. The CRTS case, not drawn, would be if the $Q = 60$ isoquant crossed the ray directly through point C.

The elasticity of substitution is a measure of the curvature of an isoquant. Denoting it as σ, it is defined as

$$\sigma = \frac{\%\Delta(K/L)}{\%\Delta RTS_{L,K}}$$

In English, it is **the percent change in the capital-labor ratio caused by a movement along the isoquant sufficient to change its slope by 1 percent.** This is illustrated in Figure 9-3. If the isoquant is sharply curved, then its slope is changing rapidly from point to point. Thus one does not have to travel too far along it (in terms of a changed ratio of K/L) to change the slope by 1 percent, or the elasticity is low. At an extreme, right-angle isoquants have zero elasticity.[8] On the other hand, relatively flat isoquants have very gradual changes in slopes; one has to travel a longer distance (in terms of the amount by which the ratio K/L changes) in order to change their slopes by 1 percent. Thus flat isoquants have high elasticities. In the extreme, a straight-line isoquant has infinite elasticity (no matter how large the change in the ratio K/L, it is not enough to get the constant slope of the isoquant to change by 1 percent).[9] Figure 9-3 illustrates both the right-angle and straight-line isoquants, as well as a "middle-of-the road" one that has $\sigma = 1$.

The greater this elasticity, the easier it is to substitute one type of input for another. Thus for the right-angle isoquants, which have zero elasticity, it is not possible to maintain an output level at the "corner" by increasing one output and reducing the other (substitution to maintain output is impossible). For the straight-line isoquants, however, one can maintain the output level indefinitely by substituting a fixed quantity of one input for a unit reduction in the other (until the axis is reached).

Divide both sides of the preceding equation by α or its equivalent:

$$\frac{dQ/Q}{\alpha} = \frac{\partial Q}{\partial L}\frac{1}{Q}L + \frac{\partial Q}{\partial K}\frac{1}{Q}K$$

But the term on the left is just the proportionate increase in output over the proportionate increase in input, or ϕ; and the terms on the right are the input elasticities. Therefore,

$$\phi = \varepsilon_{Q,L} + \varepsilon_{Q,K}$$

[8] A production function that has right-angle isoquants is called *fixed proportions* or *fixed coefficients* and has the mathematical form $Q = \min(aK, bL)$, where a and b are positive constants and "min" means the output level is the minimum of aK or bL.

[9] A production function with straight-line isoquants is called *linear* and has the mathematical form $Q = aK + bL$, where a and b are positive constants.

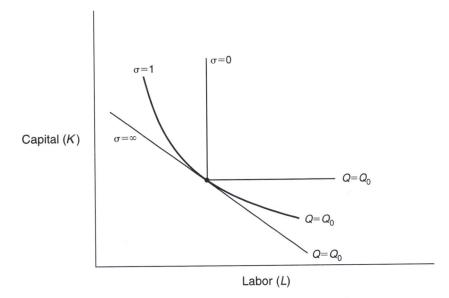

Figure 9-3. The elasticity of substitution characterizes the curvature of an isoquant.

While theoretically both the returns to scale and the substitution elasticity can change values at different production points, much empirical work assumes that these characteristics are approximately constant over the range of the production function examined. Production functions that meet these assumptions are called *constant elasticity of substitution* (CES), and have been used to approximate a broad range of production processes.[10]

How do we relate this to the problem of choosing a specific empirical form for the production function used by the Wildcat supported workers cleaning fire station exteriors? Site inspection of the supported work operations provided some basis for judging an appropriate form. Neither of the extreme elasticities of substitution σ seemed appropriate: The water-blasting machines could not operate themselves ($\sigma \neq \infty$), and there was substitutability between the factors because increased scrubbing of some areas could substitute for more water blasting ($\sigma \neq 0$). In terms of returns to scale, it would be surprising if the data revealed any large differences from the constant-returns case. Buildings large enough to use two crews simultaneously were not cleaned by following procedures very different from those for one-crew buildings.

---

[10] CES production functions have the form

$$Q = A[\delta K^{-\rho} + (1-\delta)L^{-\rho}]^{-\alpha/\rho}$$

where the elasticity of substitution $\sigma = 1/(1 + \rho)$ and the parameter restrictions are $-1 < \rho < \infty$, $A > 0$, $\alpha > 0$, and $0 < \delta < 1$. The returns to scale is determined by α, with $\alpha < 1$ being DRTS, $\alpha = 1$ being CRTS, and $\alpha > 1$ being IRTS. For further explanation and empirical studies of the CES function, see the following two references: K. J. Arrow et al., "Capital Labor Substitution and Economic Efficiency," *Review of Economics and Statistics, 43,* August 1961, pp. 225–250, and M. Nerlove, "Recent Studies of the CES and Related Production Functions," in M. Brown, ed., *The Theory and Empirical Analysis of Production* (New York: Columbia University Press, 1967).

The production function used to approximate the described features was *Cobb-Douglas:*

$$Q = AK^\alpha L^\beta \quad A > 0, 0 < \alpha, \beta < 1$$

The returns to scale of this function always equal $\alpha + \beta$, and it is often used in a more restricted form where $\beta = 1 - \alpha$ (i.e., constant returns). It has an elasticity of substitution equal to 1. (Use of a CES function did not provide significantly different results.)[11]

At this point it might seem fairly easy to apply standard statistical methods to determine A, α, and β by substituting the values of Q (the square feet of building cleaned), K (the number of machine-hours used in cleaning the building), and L (the number of worker-hours) observed for many buildings cleaned by the project. However, the most significant problem in applying that to the supported work setting was that not all buildings were equally easy to clean. Simply knowing the square footage cleaned did not reflect the difficulty of the task. The buildings varied in height from one to four stories, and the taller buildings required either extensive scaffolding to be erected or the rental of a large "cherrypicker" to carry the workers to the higher parts. Some of the buildings had a great deal of limestone surface, which was more difficult to clean and required special chemical treatment.

To get around the difference problem, it was hypothesized first that *standardized* (but unobservable) output Q^S was produced with Cobb-Douglas technology:

$$Q^S = AK^\alpha L^\beta$$

---

[11] To see these two points, note the equations for the marginal products in calculus form:

$$\frac{\partial Q}{\partial K} = MP_K = \alpha A K^{\alpha-1} L^\beta$$

$$\frac{\partial Q}{\partial L} = MP_L = \beta A K^\alpha L^{\beta-1}$$

We can use these equations to find the input elasticities:

$$\varepsilon_{QK} = \frac{\partial Q}{\partial K} \frac{K}{Q} = \alpha A K^{\alpha-1} L^\beta \frac{K}{Q} = \frac{\alpha Q}{Q} = \alpha$$

$$\varepsilon_{QL} = \frac{\partial Q}{\partial L} \frac{L}{Q} = \beta A K^\alpha L^{\beta-1} \frac{L}{Q} = \frac{\beta Q}{Q} = \beta$$

Since an earlier note showed that the scale coefficient is the sum of the input elasticities,

$$\phi = \alpha + \beta$$

Going back to the marginal product equations, let us divide the second one by the first:

$$\frac{\partial Q/\partial L}{\partial Q/\partial K} = RTS_{L,K} = \frac{\beta}{\alpha} \frac{K}{L}$$

Substituting this in the definition of σ gives us

$$\sigma = \frac{\Delta(K/L)/(K/L)}{\Delta RTS_{L,K}/RTS_{L,K}} = \frac{\Delta(K/L)/(K/L)}{(\beta/\alpha)\Delta(K/L)/(\beta/\alpha)(K/L)} = 1$$

Then it was assumed that the standardized output Q^S was a product of the observed output Q, in square feet, multiplied by several factors to correct for the degree of job difficulty.[12] The idea can be illustrated by assuming there is only one such factor D:

$$Q^S = Q(D)^{-\omega}$$

where ω is an unknown constant presumed to be less than 0 (the bigger D for a given Q, the higher Q^S should be).

Now the two equations can be combined to give an expression that is entirely in observable variables but which, when estimated statistically, will reveal the parameters of the production function (as well as some measures of how well the hypothesized form fits the data):

$$Q = AK^\alpha L^\beta D^\omega$$

Finally, recall that the motivation for undertaking this analysis was to see if the workers were improving over time. A convenient way to hypothesize a time factor t on labor is

$$Q = AK^\alpha L^{\beta + \delta t} D^\omega$$

where δ is the increment to β (the elasticity of output with respect to labor) per unit of time. If δ is positive, labor is becoming more productive over time.

We will not go into the details of estimation, but note what happens when the above equation is put in logarithmic form:

$$\ln Q = \ln A + \alpha \ln K + (\beta + \delta t) \ln L + \omega \ln D$$

The equation is linear, which allows it to be estimated by standard computer programs for multiple regression analysis simply by entering the logarithms of all the variables as the observations. In the actual estimation, there were twenty-five observations (buildings cleaned) and each was defined to be in one of two periods: $t = 0$ if the building was cleaned in the first 3 months of the project and $t = 1$ if in the second 3 months. The standardized production function was estimated as

$$Q = 50.217 K^{0.60} L^{0.45 - 0.07t}$$

where K was defined as machine-hours and L as labor-hours. The estimated returns to scale were close to 1, as expected. Note that the coefficient of t is *negative;* in the second time period, labor was *less* productive.[13]

This result did not come completely as a surprise. The raw data had revealed that the unadjusted AP_L had declined, but it was thought possible that the decline was due to taking

---

[12] A function like this is sometimes referred to as *hedonic,* which implies that the ordinary (output) measure may have a range of attributes about it that must be known to know its "value."

[13] All signs were as expected on the equation actually estimated. The R^2 was 0.81. There were three measures of job difficulty (per building): the number of stories high, the cherrypicker rental charge, and the proportion of limestone cleaning solvent to all solvents used. Of these, the cherrypicker variable had a significant coefficient (Student's t statistic >2). The two input variables and the time variable also were significant.

on tasks of increasing difficulty. However, the production function analysis ruled that out by controlling for the effects of job difficulty: *Other things being equal,* labor was less productive.

In the discussion of these results, two kinds of questions were asked of the analyst: (1) Does the equation predict realistically? (2) Could there be real job-difficulty factors that were omitted from the equation and cause the distortion of the results? To answer the first question, sample predictions were made, and they satisfied the project supervisor that each factor was predicted to have a reasonable (in his experience) effect. As for the second question, the project supervisor again played a key role: He could think of no other job-difficulty factors that were not included in the equation. Thus, the result was accepted in the sense that the decision makers were persuaded that the analytic work revealed to them something that had not been known before and which was of concern to them.[14] The analyst had passed the test.[15]

One of the obvious lessons from the supported work case is that the success or failure of the analytic task can depend crucially on the ability to take a neat concept from theory and figure out how to apply it in a meaningful way to a messy world. Theory can be credited with rejecting the typical productivity measures as unsuitable in this case and for pointing the way toward a form of input-output relation that allowed some substitution among the inputs. But to implement these concepts by taking the path from Cobb-Douglas functions to cherrypicker expenditures per building required learning in some detail about the nitty-gritty of the actual operations being studied.

Often the linkages assumed in ordinary uses of theory do not apply to empirical applications, and one must be careful to interpret the results accordingly. For example, the production function used in theory is one that summarizes all of the technologies that are efficient in the engineering sense (maximum output for the given inputs). But the function we estimated describes the relation between *actual* outputs and the inputs used. We have no reason to believe that the actual output is the maximum possible output. Nevertheless, we can infer something about the technical efficiency of the program.

How do we draw this inference? The observations during the first period ($t = 0$) give a lower-bound estimate of the true production function: maximum possible output must be at least as large as actual output. It is reasonable to assume that the actual skills of workers are not decreasing over time. Had the coefficient on labor increased during the second period ($t = 1$), there would be some ambiguity about whether the actual worker skills had increased or the program managers simply were able to increase the technical efficiency of the clean-

---

[14] Later it was discovered that not all of the crew members of the masonry cleaning project were receiving the same pay, and that had caused a morale problem during the second period. More careful hiring and promotion policies were instituted as a result.

[15] The clients of the analyst also passed a test by their acceptance of negative program results. Most public officials who operate programs or who have recommended funding for such programs wish the programs to be successful. Policy evaluation is not intended to fulfill their wishes; it is intended to be objective. Sometimes officials will resist this, which is one reason why good, truth-telling analysts follow this maxim: "Keep your bags packed!"

ing operations. However, the observed decrease in labor productivity must be due to lower technical efficiency, since skills are at least the same.[16]

In the above example the observations used to study technology came from one organization with considerable detail about the inputs and outputs. It is much more common to have observations derived from a cross section of organizations producing the same good and with less detailed knowledge about the inputs and outputs. For example, one might obtain data from the *Annual Survey of Manufacturers* undertaken by the U.S. Census Bureau, where output is reported as the annual dollar value per industry and an input such as labor is measured by the annual number of production worker hours in the industry. Even with these aggregated and less detailed data it is often possible to make inferences about technology.[17] However, caution similar to that in the supported work example must be exercised.

For example, a common assumption made when using aggregate (industry-wide) observations is that each organization comprising the aggregate is technically efficient. If that is not true, the estimated relation cannot be interpreted as the production function. To illustrate this concern, Table 9-1 presents two matrices containing data from two industries using highly simplified production processes. In each case we will accept as a given that the true production function is constant returns to scale with fixed coefficients (zero elasticity of substitution), sometimes referred to as Leontif technology[18]:

$$Q = \min (aK, bL) \quad a, b > 0$$

This function is for processes in which the inputs are always used in fixed proportion ($= b/a$), such as one operator per tractor. Suppose, for example, that $a = 4$ and $b = 4$, so that

$$Q = \min (4K, 4L)$$

Then if $K = 20$ and $L = 10$, the output is the minimum of (80, 40), or $Q = 40$. In this case we say that labor is "binding"; more capital will not increase output, but each extra unit of

---

[16] It might be argued that current program output (in terms of buildings cleaned) is not the only objective of the program, and what appears as reduced labor productivity might simply represent increased and deliberate program efforts to teach the participants skills that will have a future payoff. This argument is only partially correct. It certainly is true that the program is intended to produce both current and future benefits. However, the analysis above counts only the hours the participants were actually at work cleaning the buildings; furthermore, it controls for the amount of supervision given during those hours. Therefore, the conclusion that the reduced labor productivity is due to lower technical efficiency withstands this criticism. Later in this chapter we will discuss the future benefits as additional outputs of the program.

[17] An example of this is a cross-sectional study of pretrial release agencies in the criminal justice system. Agencies that used the technologies of point systems and call-in requirements were far more successful at producing outputs (released defendants who appear at trial as required). See Lee S. Friedman, "Public Sector Innovations and Their Diffusion: Economic Tools and Managerial Tasks," in A. Altshuler and R. Behn, *Innovation in American Government* (Washington, D.C.: The Brookings Institution, 1997), pp. 332–359.

[18] Wassily Leontif created an economy-wide model of production showing the flows of resources and goods across each industry. This has become known as input-output analysis. A characteristic of the model is that it assumes that inputs in each industry are always used in fixed proportions to one another (at the angle of a right-angle isoquant like that shown in Figure 9-3). See Wassily Leontif, *The Structure of the American Economy, 1919–1929* (New York: Oxford University Press, 1951).

Table 9-1
Industry Production Data

	Output	Capital	Labor
	Technically efficient suppliers		
Unobserved but factual			
Supplier 1	80	20	20
Supplier 2	160	40	40
Observed			
Industry	240	60	60
	Technically inefficient suppliers		
Unobserved but factual			
Supplier 1	40	20	20
Supplier 2	200	40	40
Observed			
Industry	240	60	60

labor from 10 to 20 will add 4 units of output. Note that a technically efficient organization will use inputs in only a 1:1 proportion with this technology; otherwise, it could produce the same output level with fewer resources. One could reduce K from 20 to 10 in the above example and maintain $Q = 40$.

Returning to Table 9-1, we imagine that the only data available for analysis are the industry totals and we are trying to deduce the unknown coefficients a and b of the Leontif technologies used by each industry. The example is so designed that the industry totals are identical for each industry, but the underlying production functions are not the same. In the top part of Table 9-1, we assume correctly that each of the two supplier organizations is operating at a point on its production function. This means that for each supplier (represented by subscripts 1 and 2),

$$aK_1 = bL_1 = Q_1$$

$$aK_2 = bL_2 = Q_2$$

and by addition we get the industry totals:

$$a(K_1 + K_2) = b(L_1 + L_2) = Q_1 + Q_2$$

Since we observe that $K_1 + K_2 = 60$ and $Q_1 + Q_2 = 240$, it must be that $a = 4$. By analogous reasoning, $b = 4$. Therefore, the production function is $Q = \min(4K, 4L)$, deduced from industry-level data and the assumptions we made.

If we apply the same reasoning to the suppliers in the lower part of Table 9-1, we reach the same conclusion. But in this case it is false. The truth (let us say) is that supplier 2 is operating on the production frontier with an actual production function of

$$Q = \min(5K, 5L)$$

Supplier 1 is simply operating with technologically inefficient procedures. If it were operating efficiently with inputs $K = 20$ and $L = 20$, it would produce 100 units. Thus the industry as a whole is producing only 80 percent of the output it could produce with the given inputs (240/300).

The aggregate data reveal only the *average* relations between inputs and outputs of the units comprising the aggregate. In the technically efficient case the average corresponds to the maximal output because each unit is attaining the maximum. But when the units are not operating at technically efficient levels, the aggregate data do not reveal the production function.

It is not easy to determine whether supplier organizations are technically efficient in actuality. The strongest arguments for assuming efficiency are generally made with references to firms in competitive, private industries. In this environment, it is argued, the only firms that can survive are those that produce at the least possible cost, and thus they must be technically efficient. However, not all economists think actual competitive pressures are strong enough to force this behavior or that firms have the capabilities to reach and maintain technically efficient production over time.[19] When one turns to different settings, such as production by public agencies, there is even less generalizable guidance. Thus to estimate the production function referred to in ordinary theory, methods that account for possible variation in technical efficiency may be very useful.[20]

It still can be useful to identify the actual average relations between inputs and outputs. The supported work example provides one illustration. If estimated with industry-wide observations, the average relations may be used to predict the output effects of a proportionate increase or decrease in resources to each supplier in the sector. But of course it also might be useful to try to improve the operating efficiency of the organizations, which is something one might overlook if a leap is made too quickly from knowing the inputs to inferring the production function.

Costs

The concepts of cost are absolutely fundamental to the comparison of alternatives: indeed, *the* most fundamental concept of an action, decision, or allocation being "costly" is that there *are* alternative uses of the resources. ("There is no such thing as a free lunch.") In this

---

[19] See, for example, Richard Nelson and Sidney Winter, *An Evolutionary Theory of Economic Change* (Cambridge: Harvard University Press, 1982): see also the debate between George Stigler and Harvey Leibenstein: G. Stigler, "The Xistense of X-Efficiency, *American Economic Review, 66,* March 1976, pp. 213–216, and H. Leibenstein, "X Inefficiences Xists—Reply to an Xorcist." *American Economic Review, 68,* March 1978, pp. 203–211.

[20] For a general review of techniques for measuring productive efficiency, see T. Coelli, D. S. Prasada Rao, and G. Battese, *An Introduction to Efficiency and Productivity Analysis* (Boston: Kluwer Academic Publishers, 1997), and H. Fried, C. A. Knox Lovell, and S. Schmidt, *The Measurement of Productive Efficiency: Techniques and Applications* (New York: Oxford University Press, 1993). One method that has been used in many public sector applications to account for variation in technical efficiency is *data envelopment analysis* (DEA); see, for example, Abraham Charnes et al., eds., *Data Envelopment Analysis: Theory, Methodology and Application* (Boston: Kluwer Academic Publishers, 1994).

section we will review different definitions of cost that the policy analyst encounters and must understand, and illustrate their use in a variety of predictive and normative applications.

In the first part of this section we introduce the normative concept of social opportunity cost and show how the concept is applied in benefit-cost analysis. In the second part we introduce the concepts of accounting cost and private opportunity cost and compare and contrast them with social opportunity cost. In the third we demonstrate both positive and normative applications of these concepts in the benefit-cost analyses of the supported work program. In the fourth we demonstrate some linkages between cost concepts and technology. One type of linkage is in the form of a cost function, and we illustrate the use of a cost function in an analysis of regulated trucking firms. Another type of linkage occurs when two or more outputs are produced with some shared input, and we illustrate how benefit-cost reasoning can be applied to this joint cost problem to identify the most efficient allocation of resources. An appendix illustrates the relations between production functions and cost functions by using the mathematics of duality and introduces some of the cost functions commonly used in empirical analyses.

Social Opportunity Cost and Benefit-Cost Analysis

The social opportunity cost of using resources in one activity is the value forgone by not using them in the best alternative activity. In Figure 9-4a we represent a simple society with a fixed amount of resources that can be devoted to producing two outputs: food F and shelter S. **The production-possibilities curve shows the maximum output combinations that are possible given the resources available and technological possibilities.** If all resources are devoted to shelter production and the best technology is used, S_M will be the maximum possible shelter output. The social opportunity cost[21] of producing S_M is F_M, the alternative output forgone.

More typically, we think of smaller changes like that from point A to B. If we are currently at point A (with outputs F_A, S_A), the opportunity cost of increasing shelter production by ΔS units of S is ΔF units of F. Thus, the opportunity cost per unit increase in S is simply $\Delta F/\Delta S$, and for a small enough change this can be interpreted as the negative of the slope of the production-possibilities curve at the current allocation. This number is called **the rate of product transformation ($RPT_{S,F}$): the minimum number of units of one output (food) that must be forgone in order to increase another output (shelter) by one unit.**

The bowed-out shape of the production-possibilities curve can be explained intuitively as follows. The economy is endowed with a stock of factors in a certain proportion K_0/L_0. The technically best proportion to use with each good is unlikely to coincide with the endowment. Let us say that food is best produced with a relatively labor-intensive technology (low K/L). Then at each end point of the production-possibilities curve (F_M and S_M), an "inferior" K/L ratio ($= K_0/L_0$) is being employed. If we insisted that each product be produced by using the ratio K_0/L_0, and assumed constant returns to scale, the production-possibility

---

[21] This is often referred to simply as the *social cost*.

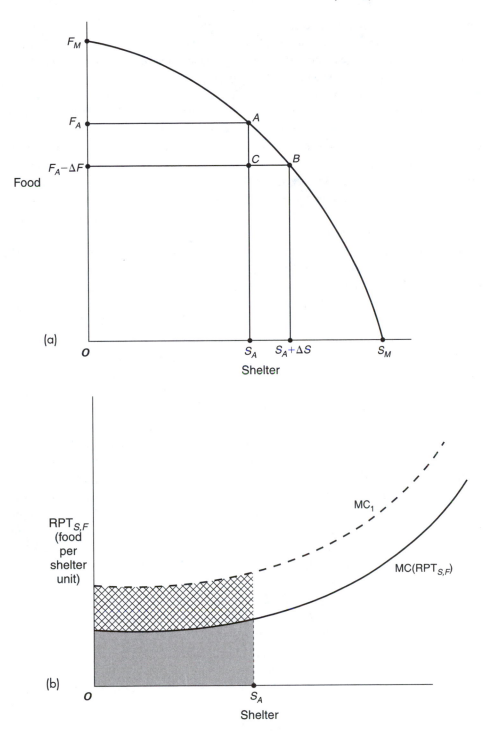

Figure 9-4. (a) Social opportunity costs and production possibilities. (b) The rate of product transformation (RPT) is the social marginal cost (MC).

frontier would be the straight line connecting the extreme points.[22] However, we know we can do better than the straight line by allowing each industry to use a capital-labor ratio closer to its technically best one: Only the weighted average of both has to equal K_0/L_0. Thus the frontier will be bowed outward.

An interesting interpretive point arises if we are currently at point C and ask, "What is the social opportunity cost of increasing shelter production by ΔS?" Point C is productively inefficient, either because some resources are currently unemployed or because the resources in production are not being used to produce the maximum possible output (for reasons of technological or input-mix inefficiency). The common interpretation is that there is zero social opportunity cost: Society need give up no unit of F, since it can move from point C to point B. However, the social opportunity cost concept seems to ask about the *best* use of the resources other than to increase S by ΔS. The best alternative is the one in the preceding example: to increase F by ΔF.

Both interpretations are correct; they simply answer slightly different questions. The first one answers the question, "What is the *change* in social cost associated with the resources used for S production at point C and point B, respectively?" Since the same $F_M - (F_A - \Delta F)$ units are forgone by being at either C or B, the change in social cost is zero. There is no increase in social cost because at C we have already paid for the ΔS units even though we do not receive them. The second answer is a correct response to the question, "What is the social cost of those ΔS units?" However, it is not a new cost generated by the move from C to B.

Another way to express the social cost is shown geometrically in Figure 9-4b. We keep the quantity of shelter as the horizontal axis, but the vertical axis measures the $RPT_{S,F}$: the number of units of food given up to obtain each additional unit of shelter. Thus the height of the solid curve drawn can be thought of as the least social *marginal cost* of each unit of shelter (in terms of food forgone). The area under the marginal cost curve up to a given quantity is the total social cost of that quantity, since it is simply the sum of the marginal costs of the units of shelter produced. For example, the shaded area in the diagram is the social cost of S_A units, which we know equals $F_M - F_A$ from Figure 9-4a. If inefficient production methods are used so that the economy is at an allocation like point C in Figure 9-4a, the observed marginal social costs (e.g., MC_I in Figure 9-4b) would be above the least marginal social costs, and the difference between them (shown as the cross-hatched area) would be the degree of production inefficiency.

Now we wish to integrate social cost considerations into the compensation principle of benefit-cost analysis. In Chapter 6, we avoided cost concepts by choosing examples in which the net change in consumer surplus revealed all that was necessary. In principle, this can always be done as long as all changes in individuals' budget constraints caused by the allocative change are taken into account. The earlier examples assumed these were held constant except for offsetting transfers. However, allocative changes will, in general, cause

---

[22] If there were continuing economies of scale without limit, under these assumptions the frontier would be bowed inward, since we lose the economies as we move away from the extreme points. However, constant or decreasing returns to scale are empirically much more likely at these (imagined) extreme uses of society's resources.

some nonoffsetting changes in individual budget constraints, and the question becomes how analysts find out about these.

It turns out that there are many circumstances in which knowledge of market prices and social costs give the analyst a neat summary measure of these budget constraint changes. This measure is called the *producers' surplus*. The more general statement of the compensation principle is that **a change is relatively efficient if the net change in the consumer surplus plus producer surplus is positive.** But this turns out to be identical to the difference between social benefits and social costs. Therefore, we can also state the compensation principle in this way: **A change in allocation is relatively efficient if its social benefits exceed its social costs.** In the simple model below we attempt to explain and clarify these concepts.

Figures 9-5a and b are similar to Figures 9-4a and b except for the addition of a *demand side.* Imagine as we did in Chapter 8 that we have a Robinson Crusoe economy with no Friday (i.e., a one-person economy). This allows us to draw Crusoe's indifference curves in Figure 9-5a. Crusoe has to choose a production point that, because there is no one with whom to trade, will also be his consumption point. The highest utility that he can attain is U_{max}, at point C, where the indifference curve is just tangent to the production-possibilities frontier. His optimal production and consumption are F_C and S_C. All we do below is explain this again using some new concepts that are important and useful for benefit-cost analysis in more complicated, many-person economies.

Since the two curves are tangent at point C, their slopes are equal and thus $RPT_{S,F} = MRS_{S,F}$ at Crusoe's utility maximum. This feature is often used in the many-person economy to identify how much of each good to produce. It is the condition for *product-mix efficiency,* and it is another necessary condition for Pareto optimality that we review more carefully in Chapter 12. We show here that the rule is essentially identical with choosing the allocation that *maximizes* social benefits minus social costs (or, equivalently, maximizes *net* social benefits).

To put this in the context of a benefit-cost analysis, we need a measure of the marginal benefit to Crusoe of each unit of shelter. Through each point on the production-possibilities frontier (his effective budget constraint), he has an indifference curve that crosses through it (such as the one labeled U_0 crossing point A). The slope of this indifference curve at the crossing reveals just how much food Crusoe is willing to forgo consuming in order to have one additional unit of shelter—the measure of marginal benefit that we are seeking. The MRS is high (the slope is steep) near F^*, and it gradually declines as we move along the frontier toward S^*. For example, the slope of the indifference curve at point B is much flatter than at point A.

Let us graph on Figure 9-5b Crusoe's $MRS_{S,F}$ at each point on the production-possibilities frontier. His marginal benefit (measured in units of food) declines as the number of units of shelter increases. We also graph the $RPT_{S,F}$ as before. It has a clear interpretation as the least marginal cost (in food units) to him of each unit of shelter. It is no accident that the marginal benefit curve crosses the marginal cost curve at S_C, since we know that is the point at which $RPT_{S,F} = MRS_{S,F}$.

Let us consider how Crusoe would reason as the sole recipient of benefits and bearer of costs. Imagine him starting at the upper-left end of the frontier at F^*, and considering

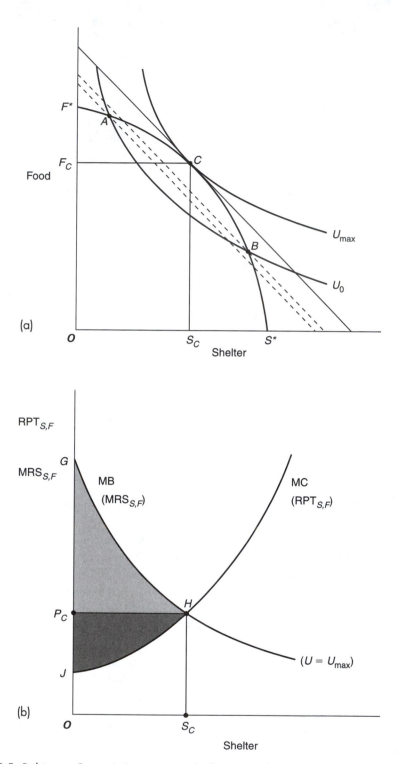

Figure 9-5. Robinson Crusoe's Pareto-optimal allocation of resources (a) is the same as his maximization of social benefits minus social costs (b).

whether marginal increases in shelter (moving rightward along the frontier) are worth the marginal decreases in food that would be required to achieve it. For each unit of shelter he would ask if its marginal benefit (the maximum amount of food he is willing to forgo—determined by the slope of the indifference curve) exceeds its marginal cost (the minimum amount of food he would have to forgo—determined by the slope of the production-possibilities frontier). He will choose to produce and consume each unit of shelter for which the marginal benefit exceeds the marginal cost and thus increases his net benefits. He will not go beyond S_C units of shelter, because these units have marginal cost greater than marginal benefit and would thus cause a reduction in net benefits. S_C *is the quantity that maximizes his net benefits,* which equal the area *GHJ.* Thus the marginal benefit–marginal cost reasoning simply reveals utility-increasing changes, and maximizing net benefits leads to the utility maximum (which, in this economy, is the Pareto-optimal allocation).

Let us extend this reasoning, by a two-step process, to the many-person economy. Crusoe still has the same production possibilities, but now imagine that the goods must be bought or sold in the marketplace, where shelter has a price (still measured in food units). This allows him to separate the production decision from the consumption decision. He will make production decisions to maximize his budget, which he can then use to choose his most preferred consumption bundle. Assume the market price is P_C—not accidentally the level at which the MRS = RPT.

Crusoe the producer will produce and sell to the "market" all the units that have opportunity costs below the market price: S_C units. One way to see this is on Figure 9-5a. Suppose he chose a point on the production frontier with fewer than S_C units of shelter, such as point *A.* Then his budget constraint in the marketplace would be the dashed line through point *A* with slope P_C.[23] Note that this is not tangent to the frontier. He could have a higher budget constraint by choosing a production point on the frontier to the right of point *A.* But at point *C,* the budget constraint is just tangent to the frontier. It is the highest one that he can reach. Any production point on the frontier where shelter exceeds S_C units, such as at point *B,* gives a budget constraint under the one through point *C.*

We can see the same logic in a slightly different form in Figure 9-5b. Producing the first unit of shelter means he forgoes producing *OJ* units of food (his opportunity cost), but then he can sell this shelter unit in the marketplace for P_C units of food (which is more than *OJ*). The difference between the market price and his opportunity cost $(P_C - OJ)$ is the "profit" or "surplus" that he gains by producing this shelter unit rather than food—an increment to his budget level.[24] He will find it similarly beneficial to produce each unit of shelter up to S_C, since each adds some "surplus" to his growing "buying power." But the opportunity cost of producing shelter units beyond S_C is too great (higher than P_C). Crusoe would forgo more food in production than he would regain by producing and selling the shelter; it would reduce his buying power. Thus again we see that S_C is the quantity that maximizes his purchasing power or budget constraint (which is necessary for maximizing utility).

---

[23] For any production choice (S, F) his budget level $B = P_C S + F$, where the price per unit of food is 1.

[24] His initial budget level (with no shelter production) is F^*. By producing one unit of shelter, he gains P_C but loses $RPT_{S,F}$ $(= OJ)$: $F^* + P_C - OJ$. So the net change in his budget is $(P_C - OJ)$.

As a producer, Crusoe receives **producer's surplus, or economic rent, defined as payments to the producer above opportunity costs.** *He makes the production decisions that maximize his producer surplus.* This is shown as the darker shaded area JP_CH. It is the increase in his budget constraint that results from producing S_C in the shelter market (and F_C food) instead of the next best alternative (0 shelter, F^* food). Note also that if Crusoe chose inefficient production methods (i.e., was not on his production-possibilities frontier), this would show up as a higher marginal cost curve (as we saw before) and therefore a lower producer surplus and lower budget constraint for consumption.

The consumption side in Figure 9-5b is already familiar. Crusoe the consumer buys from the market all units that have marginal benefit greater than the market price: S_C units.[25] Thus *he makes the consumption decisions that maximize his consumer surplus.* His consumer surplus is the lighter shaded area, P_CGH. The main point of this illustration is to see that his total net benefit GHJ can be seen as the sum of two components: his producer and consumer surpluses. **The net social benefit is the sum of the consumer and producer surpluses.** In social benefit-cost analysis it makes no difference whether a $1 change occurs in the consumer or producer surplus; both count equally.

Now let us move to step 2, where there are many people consuming and producing shelter (some people might do both, but others will participate only as demanders or suppliers). Here we simply reinterpret the marginal benefit (demand) and marginal cost (supply) curves as those applying to the many-person market and assume that there are no aggregation problems of the kind discussed in Chapter 6. Then *for a given market price the market demand curve reveals the sum of all the individual consumer surpluses* (from any quantity of shelter consumption), *and similarly the market supply curve reveals the sum of all the individual producer surpluses* (from any quantity of shelter production). The sum of the two surpluses is maximized at the quantity at which the market demand intersects the market supply (because it is also the quantity at which marginal benefit equals marginal cost).

In the above example with only two goods, the social cost of shelter is expressed in terms of food forgone. To apply the concept in a multiproduct economy, we measure the costs and benefits in terms of money. That is, the alternative to using resources for shelter is to use them for "dollars for all other things" (rather than simply food). This focuses just on the use of resources for shelter, and implicitly assumes efficient resource allocation *within* the "dollars for all other things" part of the economy. In later chapters, we shall consider a variety of ways analysts account for different complications that may arise. Nevertheless, knowledge of market demand and market supply curves can be used in many circumstances to assess the degree to which changes in resource allocation have benefits greater than costs

---

[25] This model differs slightly from the earlier one with no marketplace, in that it offers prospects of gains from trading with others. In this model, Crusoe has better consumption possibilities: the straight-line budget constraint lies everywhere above the production-possibilities frontier (which was also the consumption possibilities in the previous model) except at the tangency point C. However, we have deliberately constructed this example with the one market price P_C that does not offer him any gains from trade. Note for future reference that any market price $P \neq P_C$ would allow him to reach a higher utility level by consuming a bundle unattainable by his own production (i.e., trade increases welfare).

(i.e., increase the sum of the consumer and producer surpluses), or equivalently, increase relative efficiency according to the compensation principle.

The introduction of explicit accounting for social costs in the benefit-cost framework does not in any way alter the qualifications about its meaning introduced in Chapter 6. The same questions about the meaning of this aggregated definition of efficiency, as well as the equity implications of using it as a criterion in analysis, remain. *All that we have done here is show how benefits and costs are calculated when resource suppliers receive payments other than the least opportunity costs.* Each person in the society is a resource supplier as well as a consumer, and we must consider the effects on each side to know how any individual is affected by a change or how society in the aggregate is affected.

Accounting Cost and Private Opportunity Cost

All of the discussion to this point in the section has been about the concept of social cost. This is the concept of most evaluative use to the analyst, but do the available data on costs correspond to it? Often, recorded costs will differ from social costs because a different concept underlies each. **The accounting concept of cost is the bookkeeper's view: that which gets recorded on the financial statements and budgets of firms and agencies.** It is based on the actual price when purchased, sometimes modified by various conventions for depreciation (of durable goods). A number of examples illustrate important differences between the concepts.

When the nation switched to an all-volunteer army in the 1970s, it was recognized that higher wages and salaries would have to be offered in order to attract volunteers. Some people, thinking of the accounting impact that it would have on the government's budget, argued against the concept because it was "too expensive." But the change in accounting costs is in the direction opposite that of the change in social costs. The social costs of the army personnel are what they could earn in their best alternatives (reflecting the value of the forgone outputs) and forgone psychic incomes (the best alternatives may offer satisfaction in addition to pay). For draftees, the opportunity costs often exceeded their military wages by substantial amounts. Because many draftees would not choose to volunteer even at the higher wages of the voluntary army, it must be that the social cost of using a given number of draftees in the military *exceeds* the social cost of using the same number of volunteers. For volunteers, the total social cost cannot exceed the benefits to them of military employment: If a volunteer had a better alternative, he or she presumably would not have volunteered.

There are advantages to having military wage rates set at the social cost rather than below it: (1) The nation now has a more accurate picture of the true resource cost of providing national defense, which usually influences the amount of it sought. (2) The input mix used in the production of national defense has been biased in the direction of too much labor relative to capital, because labor appeared to be so cheap. That source of distortion has been eliminated. Of course, there are many other issues to consider in conjunction with the draftee-volunteer debate. For example, is it equitable for higher-income people to be more easily able to avoid the risk to life that might arise in the military, or is military service more properly viewed as a civic obligation incumbent on all citizens?

Other examples of differences in social costs and accounting costs involving labor abound. Jury duty, for example, is similar in this respect to the military draft: The social opportunity costs are greater than the wages paid jurors. Volunteers in hospitals, election campaigns, and other nonprofit activities may receive no wages, but that does not mean there is no social cost of using their services. In the same vein, an entrepreneur who could earn $30,000 elsewhere may draw no salary while operating a business that ends up with a $25,000 accounting profit. The economist, who defines economic profit as revenues above opportunity costs, would count this as a $5000 loss.[26]

A third cost concept, **private opportunity cost, is defined as the payment necessary to keep a resource in its current use.** This is very similar to and often identical with the social cost. Differences between private and social opportunity costs can arise when the prices of resources do not reflect the social costs. In the above examples of the army the private opportunity cost to the draftee is the same as the social opportunity cost. But the private opportunity cost of a draftee to the army equals the accounting cost. If the entrepreneur in the above example produces chemicals but pollutes the neighborhood while doing so (an externality), the social cost of the production exceeds the private cost to the entrepreneur (society not only forgoes alternative uses of the regular inputs to the firm; it also forgoes having the clean air it used to have).

In the above two examples, the private opportunity cost to the organization equals the accounting cost even though there is a divergence from the social cost. However, the private cost often diverges from the accounting cost; for instance, the divergence occurs in the example of the entrepreneur with a $25,000 "profit" and a $30,000 alternative employment opportunity. Another very important example, because it is quite general, is the treatment of capital resources such as machinery or buildings. The accountant uses the historical purchase price minus a certain amount of depreciation each year calculated according to a formula.[27] However, the historical purchase price is a *sunk cost,* and it is irrelevant to decision-making. The opportunity cost of employing a machine for a year is what is given up by not selling it now to the highest bidder (alternative user of the machine).

There are two components of this opportunity cost. One is the **true economic depreciation, which is the decrement in the selling price of the machine** over 1 year. This reduction occurs because there is "less" machine (it obsolesces over time). Sometimes the true economic depreciation can be roughly approximated by the accountant's method of depreciation. The second component is the forgone interest that could have been earned on the money from the sale; this is the opportunity cost of the capital in the machine at the start

---

[26] To the extent that these costs are borne voluntarily, they must have benefits to the participants that are at least as great. The hospital volunteer, for example, must consider the benefits of volunteering to outweigh the costs. If the entrepreneur claims to prefer operating the business to a higher-salaried opportunity, there must be nonmonetary benefits that more than offset the financial loss (e.g., pleasure from being the boss).

[27] Depreciation rules are somewhat arbitrary. For example, straight-line depreciation is one common method by which a reasonable life span of n years is estimated for a machine and then a fixed percentage equal to $1/n$ of the total cost is deducted each year until the cost has been fully deducted.

of the period.[28] (Together, these components are also the rental value of the machine: what someone would have to pay to rent the machine for a year.) The second component is not taken into account by the bookkeepers, although it is both a private opportunity cost of the firm using the machine and a social cost.

The latter point is of particular importance to policy analysts who use program budgets as one source of information about the costs of a government program. Unless the government agency actually rents (from other firms) all the capital it uses, the social costs of its capital resources will not appear in the budget. The analyst must impute them.

To summarize this discussion, the accountant's concept of cost is largely historical. It often differs sharply from the opportunity cost concepts, which refer to the value of the resource in its best alternative use. The difference between social and private opportunity costs is one of perspective. The social cost concept treats the whole society as if it were one large family, so that everything given up by the employment of a resource is counted as part of the cost. The private opportunity cost, the payment necessary to keep a resource in its current use, is the value in its next best alternative use from the perspective of the resource employer. Analysts are most interested in the opportunity cost concepts, because individual decision makers are thought to act on their perception of cost (the private opportunity cost), and the social costs are most relevant to efficiency considerations.

An Application in a Benefit-Cost Analysis

An early evaluation of New York's Wildcat Service Corporation in its experimental stage can be used to illustrate a number of points about the use of cost concepts. Four different organizational perspectives on costs (and benefits) are shown to have policy relevance.[29] In Table 9-2, *the social costs and benefits* of the program (those known by the end of the second year of the experiment) are summarized. This social benefit-cost calculation is equivalent to a compensation test: benefits and costs are simply a convenient way to organize and then summarize a variety of the effects of the program (the policy change). In making a social-benefit cost calculation, we are asking whether the gains to the gainers (benefits) outweigh the losses to the losers (costs) among all members of the economy.[30]

The benefits in Table 9-2 can be thought of as the value of the output of the program. The output consists of the goods and services actually produced as a part of the program

---

[28] The forgone interest is actually a monetary measure of what is being given up. The real change in resource use is that consumers must forgo some current consumption in order to devote resources to make the machine.

[29] The material in this section is drawn from Lee S. Friedman, "An Interim Evaluation of the Supported Work Experiment," *Policy Analysis, 3,* No. 2, Spring 1977, pp. 147–170.

[30] Interesting questions sometimes arise about who has "standing" in the social benefit-cost calculation. For example, should the preferences of convicted felons count equally along with those of average citizens? More commonly in the global economy, should Country X count equally the benefits and costs of its actions to people in Country Y? The classic reference article on this subject is by Dale Whittington and Duncan MacRae, Jr., "The Issue of Standing in Cost-Benefit Analysis," *Journal of Policy Analysis and Management, 5,* No. 4, Summer 1986, pp. 665–682.

Table 9-2
The New York Supported Work Experiment: Social Benefits and Costs per Year in the Experiment per Person

Benefits	
Value added by program to public goods and services	$4519
Post-program experimental earnings	1154
Savings from crime-connected costs	
System	86
Crime reduction	207
Drug program participation	—
Health	(285)
Total social benefits	$5681
Costs	
Opportunity costs of supported work employees	$1112
Staff and nonpersonnel expenses	2362
Total social costs	$3474
Net benefits	$2207

Source: Lee S. Friedman, "An Interim Evaluation of the Supported Work Experiment," *Policy Analysis, 3,* No. 2, Spring 1977, p. 165.

and the external effects of production. The measured external effects consist of the increase in the future (out-of-program) earnings stream of participants, the reduction in crime by participants, the reduction in drug treatment, and the change in health of the participants. In all cases the existence of the effects is measured by comparison with an experimental control group; individuals who were found qualified to be participants but were chosen by lottery not to participate. Without the control group it would be virtually impossible to know if the program was having any effect at all.

The listed benefits were measured in such a way as to underestimate their magnitude. For example, the out-of-program earnings increases included only the difference between the experimental and control groups within the first calendar year from the onset of the experiment. Presumably this difference persisted at least to some extent into the future, and thus the true benefit is higher than that measured. The reason for underestimating the benefits results from analytic judgment about how to handle the *uncertainty* of the exact level of benefits. If there were no uncertainty, there would be no need for this procedure.

Since the analysis indicates that the benefits outweigh the costs, confidence in this conclusion can be tested by deliberately making assumptions conservative (less favorable) to it. Since it still holds even with known underestimation of benefits, confidence that it is correct increases despite the uncertainty. Sometimes, small changes in the assumptions may lead to opposite conclusions, and then the analyst must report that it is really ambiguous whether the benefits outweigh the costs. Of course, an important part of analytic skill is learning how to convert available data into information that minimizes the range of uncertainty about the truth.

In Table 9-2 the costs are shown to be substantially less than the benefits. The component of the cost calculation relevant to the earlier discussion in the chapter is the opportunity cost to society of employing the participants in the program. The actual wages received were substantially higher than the $1112 opportunity cost. But that is irrelevant to the opportunity cost; we wish to know the value of whatever is forgone by the employment of participants in supported work. The traditional measure of this value is the earnings that would have been received otherwise. They are measured quite precisely by the actual earnings of the control group. The measure presumably reflects the value of the marginal product that would be added by this labor. In other words, one reason that the benefits easily outweigh the cost is that the costs are low: The control group members remain unemployed for most of the time, so society gives up little by employing them in the supported environment provided by Wildcat.[31]

A simple summary of the measurable social benefits and costs is generally inadequate as a basis for understanding or presenting the social effects of the program. Some decision makers might be more interested in one component than another and wish more detail. For example, the value of goods and services is discussed at length in the main analytic reports, and it might be of use to explore whether there are trade-offs between future earnings and in-program output. Or it might be interesting to find out if the participants are really more ill than the controls, or if they just consume more medical services in response to a given illness.[32] Other effects may be important but impossible to value in a meaningful way; an example is the effect of the program on the family lives of participants. However, our purpose here is to emphasize the effects of different perspectives on the cost and benefits.

Recall that the calculation of social benefits and costs reflects indifference in dollar terms of who is gaining or losing. However, society is not all one big family, and the costs and benefits to particular subsets of society's members can take on special importance. Through the political system, taxpayers have considerable influence on the spending decisions of

---

[31] This issue is more complicated than the above discussion reveals. There is another part to the opportunity cost: Participants forgo not only their alternative earnings but their leisure as well, which must have some value to them. If the unemployment of controls were voluntary, it could be argued that their wage rate (when actually working) applied to the time equivalent of full-time employment is the social opportunity cost. (This assumes that controls make an optimal labor-leisure trade-off.) However, most analysts accept the idea that much unemployment is involuntary because of imperfections in the labor market. Still, the analysis would be improved by an explicit accounting of that effect. Most evaluations of similar programs also have ignored the value of forgone leisure.

In this particular case, accounting for the value of forgone leisure would have been extremely unlikely to affect the conclusion. All the controls were revealed to prefer program participation to nonparticipation, implying that they would forgo their leisure for *less* than their net increase in tangible first year benefits of $1703. Although this excludes the fact that future earnings increases are part of the inducement, those must add more to benefits than to costs; furthermore, the participant is also forgoing the private returns to crime and perhaps better health (so all of the $1703 cannot be simply leisure's opportunity cost).

[32] The study assumed conservatively that the participants were more ill, based on data that indicate they averaged slightly more time in the hospital per year. However, this average was based on relatively few hospitalizations.

government. Thus we can ask, from the perspective of taxpayers, how does the Wildcat program look?

Table 9-3 shows the *major benefits and costs to taxpayers.* The primary difference between this perspective and the social perspective is that certain transfers that cancel out in the latter must be made explicit here. On the benefit side, the taxpayer will experience a reduction in welfare payments and a wider sharing of the tax burden as new taxpayers make contributions. These are not included in the social calculation because, at least as a first approximation, the payments are simply transfers of purchasing power (a dollar lost by the participant is offset by the dollar gained by the taxpayer). On the cost side, the actual wages paid the supported work employees are relevant to the taxpayer.

The taxpayer perspective is sometimes represented as the impact on the government budget. There is a difference between the concepts: The taxpayer perspective reveals private opportunity costs, whereas the impact on the government budget is measured by accounting costs. In this case, because capital assets of the program are very small, there is little difference. A more important simplification is treating taxpayers as a homogeneous group: Federal taxpayers in Ohio do not receive the public goods and services that accrue to the residents of New York City. One could further disaggregate the effects into New York taxpayers and other taxpayers; this might be useful in deciding how to share the costs of the program.

A specific example of *the perspective of a particular agency was offered as a third benefit-cost perspective in the analysis.* The New York City welfare department was one source of program funds. It provided $1.19 per participant-hour in supported work on the theory that this represented a payment it would have to make (to the participants) if the program did not exist. This added up to $1237 per year, and the department also provided certain direct benefits to the participants valued at $842 for a total of $2079. However, the welfare department had to pay out $2639 in benefits to the average control during the same period. Thus the department was getting a bargain: For every $1.00 put into supported work, it received $1.27 in reduced claims for welfare.

Finally, *a fourth important perspective on benefits and costs is that of the participant.* The change in disposable income was calculated. The average member of the experimental group received $3769 in program wages and fringe benefits and $1154 in out-of-program earnings, for a total of $4923. To receive this, he or she accepted a welfare reduction of $1797, increased taxes of $311, and forgone earnings of $1112, or $3220 total cost. Thus the increase in disposable income was $1703. This type of calculation is relevant to determining Wildcat wages. If it is large, taxpayers may be asked to transfer more than necessary to achieve the net social benefits. If the net benefit to participants is small or negative, then it will be difficult to induce those eligible for the program to apply.

Note that of the four benefit-cost calculations presented, only one has a specific normative purpose: The social benefit-cost analysis reveals whether the economy is made relatively more efficient by the program. The other three calculations can be thought of as summarizing the program's effects from the perspectives of various constituent groups. By calculating the benefits and costs from the perspectives of different constituencies, one can, for example, predict whether these groups will favor the program. Or one might use these calculations in

Table 9-3

The New York Supported Work Experiment: Taxpayer Benefits and Costs per Year in the Experiment per Person

Benefits	
Public goods and services	$4519
Welfare reduction	1797
Increased income tax collected	311
Savings from crime-connected costs	
System	86
Crime reduction	207
Total taxpayer benefits	$6920
Costs	
Supported work costs	$6131
Net benefits	$ 789

Source: Lee S. Friedman, "An Interim Evaluation of the Supported Work Experiment," *Policy Analysis, 3,* No. 2, Spring 1977, p. 167.

evaluating the equity of the program. The calculations also can suggest whether certain changes in the program will increase or reduce support from the various constituencies. In general, these benefit-cost calculations can be made for any program; they require judgment about which groups are the important constituencies.[33]

In this application, no linkage between the cost concepts and production function needs to be made. But in other applications, understanding such linkages can be a key point. In the next section, we illustrate this point.

Cost-Output Relations

In this section we will consider how opportunity costs (with private equal to social) vary as a function of the output level. Both producing agencies and analysts are often interested in least-cost production, and most of the standard cost curves are drawn on the assumption that production is or will be at least cost. However, actual observed costs in many situations are not the minimum possible.

Nevertheless, the attempt to identify consistent relations between observed costs and the production function is extremely useful. The primary reason is that it may be much easier

---

[33] During the 1970s one top federal analyst was reported to have directed all his associates to make at least two benefit-cost calculations: one from the social perspective and the other from the perspective of those living in Louisiana. The analyst was from the North, but the powerful chairman of the Senate Finance committee from 1965 to 1980, Russell Long, was from Louisiana.

An interesting study characterizes several different but common political perspectives that cause perceptions of benefits and costs to be skewed in particular ways. See A. Boardman, A. Vining, and W. G. Waters, II, "Costs and Benefits through Bureaucratic Lenses: Example of a Highway Project," *Journal of Policy Analysis and Management, 12,* No. 3, Summer 1993, pp. 532–555.

to obtain data on costs than on all the different input quantities. We give two examples of decisions that depend on determining aspects of the returns-to-scale characteristic of the production function. The first case involves trucking deregulation, and the second is concerned with the national supported work program. In both cases inferences about scale are made by estimating cost functions rather than production functions.

In the case of trucking the nature of scale economics in the industry bears on whether the industry ought to be regulated or not.[34] If there are increasing returns to scale over a large portion of the total demand for trucking services, then the way to meet that demand and give up the fewest resources in doing so is to have only a few firms or agencies as supply agents. However, if the supply were by private profit-maximizing firms, there would be little effective competition to ensure that the prices charged are close to the opportunity costs or that enough services are actually provided. The typical response to situations like this has been to regulate the prices charged by firms, as with utility companies. In 1994, 41 states regulated their intrastate trucking, and prior to 1980 the Interstate Commerce Commission (ICC) regulated the prices of interstate trucking. Federal legislation has largely done away with these practices.

Under federal regulation there were a large number of interstate trucking firms, not the small number associated with large economies of scale.[35] Proponents of regulation argued that the ICC has maintained prices just high enough for many firms to survive and compete, and that without regulation the industry would become extremely concentrated (i.e., have only a few firms) and would present the problems mentioned above. Opponents of regulation argued that there were no significant economies of scale, that a large number of competing firms would therefore continue to exist without price regulation, and that the result would be lower prices to consumers and services essentially unchanged. Under the assumption that these firms operated on their production frontiers (i.e., were technically efficient), knowledge of the returns to scale of the production function would reveal the expected degree of concentration. This knowledge was obtained without ever estimating the production function, simply by studying the cost functions of the firms.

Let us illustrate this point. In general, **the total cost TC of producing any output level is the sum of the opportunity costs of the inputs used to produce that level. The average cost AC is simply the total cost divided by the quantity of output. The marginal cost MC is the opportunity cost of the additional resources necessary to produce one additional unit of output.** Suppose we have a very simple production function $Q = F(L)$; that is, labor is the only type of input. Let us also assume that a firm can hire all the labor it wishes at the current wage rate w. Then the TC of producing any quantity is wL, and AC is simply:

---

[34] The behavior of monopolies will be treated in the next chapter and public policy with respect to natural monopolies will be treated in Chapter 18. Here we present only a bare-bones summary in order to motivate the cost analyst.

[35] According to Thomas Moore, there were 14,648 regulated trucking firms in 1974. See p. 340 in T. Moore, "The Beneficiaries of Trucking Regulation," *Journal of Law and Economics, 21,* October 1978, pp. 327–343.

$$AC = \frac{TC}{Q} = \frac{wL}{Q} = w\frac{1}{AP_L}$$

If the firm is technically efficient, this can be rewritten

$$AC = \frac{wL}{F(L)}$$

In this formulation the firm's average cost clearly varies inversely with the average productivity of the one and only factor. The quantity of output at which the AP_L is at a maximum must also be the quantity at which the average cost is a minimum. This illustrates that the output quantity at which the firm's average cost is minimized depends upon the shape of the production function (and technical efficiency).

The relation between a firm's average cost curve and the production function is more complicated when there is more than one input. However, the fact that there is a relation extends to the general case of many inputs. Suppose the inputs used are $X_1, X_2, \ldots, X_n$ with associated prices $P_1, P_2, \ldots, P_n$. Imagine three possible production functions that vary in their respective returns to scale. Using superscripts I, C, and D to indicate increasing, constant, and decreasing returns to scale and m to represent some positive constant, let us suppose that the functions are represented by

$$m^2Q = F^I(mX_1, mX_2, \ldots, mX_n)$$

$$mQ = F^C(mX_1, mX_2, \ldots, mX_n)$$

$$\sqrt{m}Q = F^D(mX_1, mX_2, \ldots, mX_n)$$

When $m = 1$, all three functions have the same output level. Since the inputs are the same, they have the same total cost (TC_0) and the same average cost (AC_0):

$$AC_0 = \frac{TC_0}{Q} = \frac{\sum_{i=1}^{n} P_i X_i}{Q}$$

But now let us ask what happens to AC if we expand production by multiplying all inputs by some m greater than 1. Then,

$$AC^I = \frac{TC}{m^2Q} = \frac{\sum_{i=1}^{n} P_i m X_i}{m^2Q}$$

$$= \frac{m\left(\sum_{i=1}^{n} P_i X_i\right)}{m^2Q} = \frac{AC_0}{m} < AC_0$$

Similarly,

$$AC^C = \frac{TC}{mQ} = \frac{\sum_{i=1}^{n} P_i m X_i}{mQ} = AC_0$$

and

$$AC^D = \frac{TC}{\sqrt{m}Q} = \frac{\sum_{i=1}^{n} P_i m X_i}{\sqrt{m}Q} = \sqrt{m}AC_0 > AC_0$$

Thus for a firm or agency that would produce at least cost for given input prices as the scale of operations increases, the AC increases, stays the same, or decreases depending on whether the production function is decreasing, constant, or increasing returns to scale.

One other related concept, crucial to understanding *multiproduct organizations,* is that of **economies of scope: when the cost of producing two (or more) products within one firm is less than the cost of producing the same quantity of each in separate firms.** If we denote the least total cost of producing outputs Q_1 and Q_2 in a single firm as $C(Q_1, Q_2)$, then we can say economies of scope are present if

$$C(Q_1, \ Q_2) < C(Q_1, 0) + C(0, Q_2)$$

Examples of scope economies are common: most automobile firms also produce trucks; most bakeries bake cakes, cookies, bread, and rolls; most computer software companies produce more than one software product; most police departments provide routine patrols as well as investigative services; most universities provide both teaching and research services. In all of these cases (presumably), the producers economize on some of their inputs (management expertise, ovens, programmers, knowledge of criminal behavior, professors) so that it is less expensive to provide multiple products through one organization rather than more.[36] One can also inquire, of course, about the presence of "size" economies in an industry composed of multiproduct firms (i.e., can "few" multiproduct firms produce at lower cost than "many" of them).

To relate this to the trucking issue, the size of the firm (measured by the quantity of output it produces) necessary for least-cost production depends on the returns to scale of the production function: The greater the returns to scale, the larger the firms in the industry should be. Furthermore, the observed relation between average cost and output level (for an organization that produces at least cost, and holding input prices constant), reveals the returns to scale: As firm quantity increases, the change in AC will vary inversely with the returns to scale. Therefore, we can look for evidence of the returns to scale by examining the cost-output relationship.

This is precisely what is done in a study by Spady and Friedlaender of the regulated trucking industry.[37] There are some problems in measuring the output of each firm—

---

[36] We can measure the degree of scope economies (ϕ_s) as

$$\phi_s = \frac{C(Q_1, 0) + C(0, Q_2) - C(Q_1, Q_2)}{C(Q_1, Q_2)}$$

For a good general reference on scope economies and related issues, see W. Baumol, J. Panzar, and R. Willig, *Contestable Markets and the Theory of Industry Structure* (San Diego: Harcourt Brace Jovanovich, 1988).

[37] See Richard H. Spady and Ann F. Friedlaender, "Hedonic Cost Functions for the Regulated Trucking Industry," *Bell Journal of Economics, 9,* No. 1, Spring 1978, pp. 159–179.

similar to those of the Wildcat example. The number of ton-miles carried is the unadjusted measure, but it must be converted into standardized ton-miles, which account for the length of a haul, the shipment size, and other quality factors that lead to differences in the effective output. For example, one firm may make one trip of 1000 miles on open highway, and another firm may make 1000 trips of 1 mile each. The ton-miles are the same, but the outputs are really quite different, and they should not be expected to have either the same value to consumers or the same costs. Similarly, a firm that handles shipment sizes that fill up the truck is producing a different output than one that picks up many small loads to fill the truck. Since these factors vary continuously, rather than each firm producing a small discrete set of different output types, one way to account for them is to create a continuously adjusted effective output measure (similar to the Wildcat example of adjusting the square footage of cleaned structures for job difficulty, so that one very tall building is not necessarily the same output as an equal amount of square footage in the form of two short buildings). An equivalent way to view their analysis is to think of it as estimating the cost function of a multi-product firm.[38]

The results of the Spady-Friedlaender analysis are shown graphically in Figure 9-6. The figure shows two alternative specifications of the AC function: one assuming that the output is hedonic (quality variable) and that its quality attributes must be included in the estimation procedure, and the other assuming that the unadjusted ton-miles measure is sufficient (the output is nonhedonic). The results of testing them statistically indicate that the nonhedonic specification is erroneous.

One of the crucial insights from the analysis is the importance of not making this specification error. Under the erroneous specification, it appears that there are significant economies of scale: The AC declines as firm size increases from its current average level to that of the largest firm. But under the maintained hypothesis (not rejected statistically as false) of the hedonic specification, the average-size firm is currently very close to the minimum AC and the lack of further scale economies would discourage expansion of firm size.

The Spady-Friedlaender analysis supported the policy arguments in favor of trucking deregulation. Of course, there are many other aspects of this policy that were considered. Our purpose is simply to illustrate the relevance of the cost-output relation to a policy decision. In 1980 the Motor Carrier Act was enacted, which removed regulatory entry barriers to the trucking industry and significantly reduced the rate-making (price-fixing) authority of the ICC.[39] In 1994, Congress passed further legislation barring the states

---

[38] We provide more technical details about cost functions in the appendix to this chapter.

[39] For one estimate of the efficiency gains from this decision, see J. Ying, "The Inefficiency of Regulating a Competitive Industry—Productivity Gains in Trucking Following Reform," *Review of Economics and Statistics, 72,* No. 2, May 1990, pp. 191–201. For a general review of the economics of trucking regulation, see W. Viscusi, J. Vernon, and J. Harrington, Jr., *Economics of Regulation and Antitrust* (Lexington, Mass.: D. C. Health and Company, 1992), Chapter 17. For an excellent analysis of the politics of this issue, including the role of policy analysts themselves, see Dorothy L. Robyn, *Braking the Special Interests: Trucking Deregulation and the Politics of Policy Reform* (Chicago: University of Chicago Press, 1987).

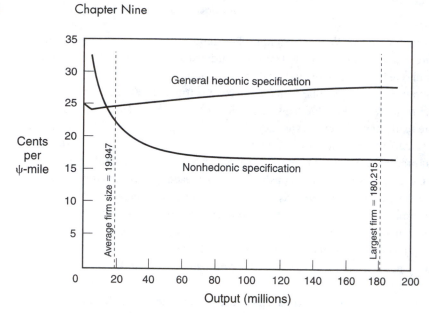

Figure 9-6. Average cost functions (from Richard H. Spady and Ann F. Friedlaender, "Hedonic Cost Functions for the Regulated Trucking Industry, " *Bell Journal of Economics, 9,* No. 1, Spring 1978, p. 172). Copyright © 1978. Reprinted by permission of RAND.

(effective in 1995) from regulating prices, routes, or services for all interstate trucking services except household moving.[40]

A second interesting application of a cost function bears on the Wildcat experiment and can be explained briefly. On the basis of the interim success of the New York program, a consortium of federal agencies decided to sponsor an expansion to fifteen cities known as the national Supported Work experiment. After the second year of the national program (when start-up costs were not a factor), the average cost per participant-year was significantly greater than in New York alone ($13,562 versus $9853). This was puzzling until analysts decided to look at annual costs in relation to the scale of each site as measured by annual participant-years.[41]

There turned out to be a clear cost advantage for larger sites, primarily because management expenses of a relatively "fixed" nature could be spread over the larger number of participants. Annual management expenses ranged from over $6000 per participant-year at smaller sites to under $3000 at the larger ones. Thus, many of the sites were not operating at the minimum of the average-cost curve.

In this example the analysts recognized that there are no obvious policy conclusions without further information. Perhaps most importantly, the output of supported work is not

---

[40] At least one study indicated that state regulations were responsible for raising rates above competitive levels. See T. Daniel and A. Kleit, "Disentangling Regulatory Policy: The Effects of State Regulations on Trucking Rates," *Journal of Regulatory Economics, 8,* No. 3, November 1995, pp. 267–284.

[41] See David A. Long and others, *An Analysis of Expenditures in the National Supported Work Demonstration* (Princeton, N.J.: Mathematica Policy Research, Inc., March 6, 1980).

measured by the participant-years, and it is possible that the social value of a participant-year at one site was quite different from that at another. This is simply another illustration of the need to control for quality when measuring output. Second, the number of participants desirable in each program is best thought of as determined by marginal benefit–marginal cost considerations. Even so, the analysis was useful because it provided some information on the cost side of this calculation and, more importantly, called attention to the issue.

To make sure this last point is clear, in Figures 9-7a and b we contrast the supported work example with the trucking discussion. In both cases it is desirable that each unit of output be produced if its marginal benefit (the height of the demand curve) exceeds its marginal cost. The optimal levels of output are denoted as Q_E in each diagram. In Figure 9-7a, representing supported work, the assumption as drawn is that it is more efficient for one agency to supply the demand in any location (a natural monopoly). This may be, for example, because there are only a limited number of potential employees for whom this kind of employment will lead to social benefits; this shows up in the diagram as a demand curve closer to rather than further away from the origin. Given that one agency has a cost structure like AC and MC, the most efficient level of output is determined by the intersection of the demand curve with the marginal cost curve.[42] Like our earlier productivity example of crew size on sanitation trucks, it does not matter whether AC could be improved by a different quantity: The value of any increase in output level from Q_E would not exceed its marginal cost.

In Figure 9-7b, representing trucking, the assumption is that many firms should supply the demand for trucks. Each U-shaped curve represents the AC over the quantity of output one firm can supply. As drawn, one firm would encounter significant diseconomies of scale well before it reached output levels that satisfied market demand. On the other hand, the industry can expand at constant AC simply by adding identical firms. Obviously the least-cost way of producing in this situation is for each firm to operate at the minimum of its AC curve. At the risk of oversimplification, the Spady-Friedlaender analysis was attempting to find out if the trucking cost structure looked more like Figure 9-7a or b.

Joint Costs and Peak-Load Pricing[S]

An additional cost-output relation that arises frequently in public policy analysis is that of *joint costs*. It occurs when two or more discrete outputs are made from some of the same inputs, and the problem is deducing whether the marginal cost of an output is greater or less than its marginal benefit. A standard example is that both wool and mutton are obtained from lambs. One may know precisely the marginal benefit of additional wool, but how is one to decide on the division of the marginal cost of a lamb between wool and mutton? The resolution lies in cleverly avoiding this question and instead comparing the sum of the two marginal benefits to the marginal cost.

---

[42] This is a simplification by which it is assumed that the total benefits outweigh the total costs and second-best arguments are ignored. The latter are discussed in Chapters 11 (Ramsey optimal pricing) and 15.

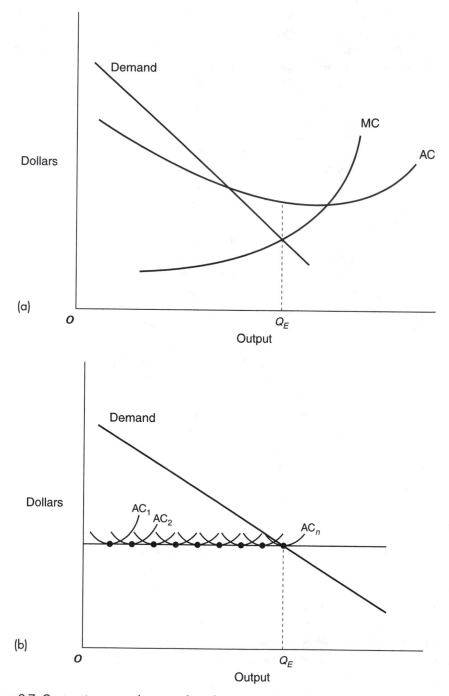

Figure 9-7. Contrasting natural monopoly with a competitive industry: (a) Supported work may be a natural monopoly. (b) Trucking may be naturally competitive.

From a public policy perspective, a more interesting example of the same problem is often referred to as *peak-load pricing*. We will illustrate this using as our joint input an electricity generating plant providing two discrete outputs: day electricity (the peak) and night electricity. These two products, because they are supplied by the plant at different times, are *nonrivalrous:* an increase or decrease in the amount of plant used to provide one (say, day electricity) does not change the amount of plant available to supply the other (night electricity). Given the demand for day and night electricity and the costs of building and operating the generating plant, what should we supply of each to make marginal benefits equal marginal costs? What prices should be charged so that demanders will utilize the supply?

Other similar examples of joint costs are roads, bridges, buses, airport landings, telecommunications and Internet lines, each providing nonrivalrous services to peak and off-peak users.[43] There are many uses of peak-load pricing principles in practice: for example, hotel rates for "in season" and "off season," higher telephone rates during weekdays compared to evenings and weekends. However, they are less common in the public sector. Interesting exceptions include peak tolls in Orange County, California, for a highway developed through a public-private partnership, tunnels in Marseilles and Oslo, and road use in Singapore.[44] It is unfortunate that the public sector does not make more use of this concept. In the California electricity crisis of 2000–2001, for example, the shortages that caused rolling blackouts were due in part to the fact that most consumers did not face higher peak period prices and thus had too little incentive to conserve and reduce their demands.

Let us assume for our electricity illustration that the (separable) operating costs per kilowatt-hour are 3 cents and the joint cost of providing each kilowatt-hour of capacity is 4 cents per day (the capital costs spread out over the life of the plant). The principle we follow is to provide to consumers all units of capacity the marginal benefits of which outweigh the marginal costs. To identify them, we must proceed in two steps. First, for each group we must find out how much willingness-to-pay per unit will be left after the operating ex-

---

[43] The nonrivalrous aspect is what distinguishes a joint cost from a *common cost*. A common cost is the cost of an input that is used to make several different products, such as a potato-peeling plant that provides the potatoes used for several different products (e.g., potato chips, instant mashed potatoes). The multiproduct firm that owns the plant has to decide how to allocate its costs to the different products. However, these services are rivalrous: if the plant is peeling potatoes for use in making chips, it must stop in order to peel potatoes for use in an instant food. In the normal case, efficiency requires a constant charge per use of the facility (e.g., per peeled potato) regardless of the product for which it is being used. The electricity plant has a common cost aspect to it. Utilities often think of themselves as selling residential, commercial, and industrial electricity (three different products), and have to decide how much of the generating plant to charge to each service. Like the potato-peeling plant, the generating charge per megawatt-hour *within a given time period* ought to be the same no matter which customer gets it. Unlike peeled potatoes, there are very distinct demands for electricity at different times (e.g., night and day, summer and winter). Thus, the electricity plant is a joint cost across time periods, and a common cost within time periods. Railroad tracks are somewhat like electricity plants in this respect: they are a common cost of freight and passenger service, but a joint cost across time periods (passengers have quite different demands for day and night service).

[44] The Singapore road pricing application has been the subject of several studies. See, for example, S. Phang and R.Toh, "From Manual to Electronic Road Congestion Pricing: The Singapore Experience and Experiment," *Transportation Research Part E—Logistics and Transportation Review, 33,* No. 2, June 1997, pp. 97–106.

penses are paid. For example, if a day demander is willing to pay (has a marginal benefit of) 10 cents for an incremental kilowatt-hour, then 3 cents of this must cover operating expenses and therefore 7 cents (= 10 − 3) is the residual willingness to pay that could be applied to cover capacity costs. Think of this 7 cents as the marginal benefit available for capacity. Second, we add together the willingness-to-pay for capacity for the day and the night demanders (since they can share each unit of capacity) in order to see if the sum exceeds the marginal cost and to identify the quantity of capacity at which this sum just equals the marginal cost. We illustrate this in Figures 9-8a and b by using the following two half-day-each demand curves for day D and night N electricity[45]:

$$P_D = 10 - \frac{1}{250} D \quad 0 \le D \le 2500$$

$$P_N = 8 - \frac{1}{250} N \quad 0 \le N \le 2000$$

Recall that a demand curve may also be interpreted as a marginal benefit curve, so we may express them as:

$$MB_D = 10 - \frac{1}{250} D \quad 0 \le D \le 2500$$

$$MB_N = 8 - \frac{1}{250} N \quad 0 \le N \le 2000$$

In Figure 9-8a, we graph the marginal benefit curves and the marginal operating costs (but not yet the joint capital cost). For each group, the marginal benefit available for capacity is the vertical distance between its (full) marginal benefit curve and the marginal operating cost. For example, the marginal benefit of the 750th kilowatt-hour is 7 cents for day users, and therefore the marginal benefit available for capacity is 4 cents (= 7 − 3). Similarly, the marginal benefit available for the 750th unit of capacity from night users is 2 cents (= 5 − 3). Since the 6-cent sum of these exceeds the 4-cent cost of capacity, it increases efficiency to provide the capacity used to produce the 750th kilowatt-hour for each group.

In Figure 9-8b we graph the marginal benefits available for capacity of each group (MB_D^C, MB_N^C). We also graph the vertical sum of those two curves to show the total marginal benefit available for capacity (MB^C). The amount of capacity to provide is thus found where the total marginal benefit available for capacity intersects the 4-cent capital cost per unit of capacity, or 1000 kilowatt-hours. We can find the same solution numerically. The individual equations are found by subtracting the 3-cent operating costs from the original marginal benefit equations, here denoting quantity as quantity of capacity Q^C:

[45] For simplicity, we make the unrealistic assumption that the demand during either time period is independent of the price in the other time period. This eases the exposition but is not necessary to illustrate how much costs bear on allocative decisions.

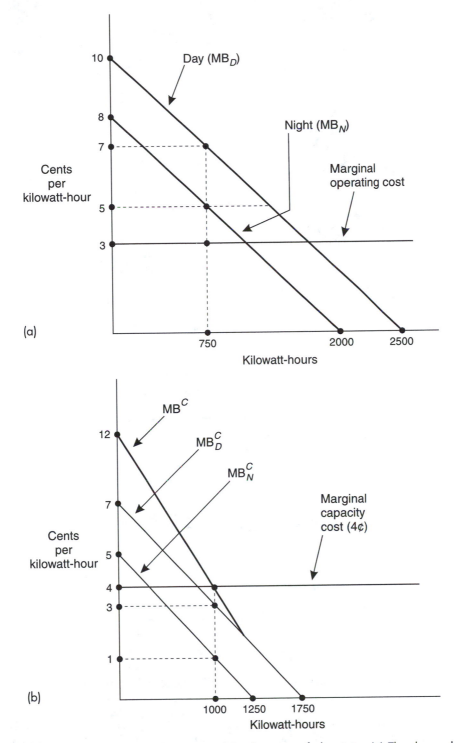

Figure 9-8. Efficiency with joint costs—peak-load pricing of electricity: (a) The demands for day and night electricity. (b) The most efficient capacity (1000) is where MB^C ($MB_D^C + MB_N^C$) equals the marginal capacity cost.

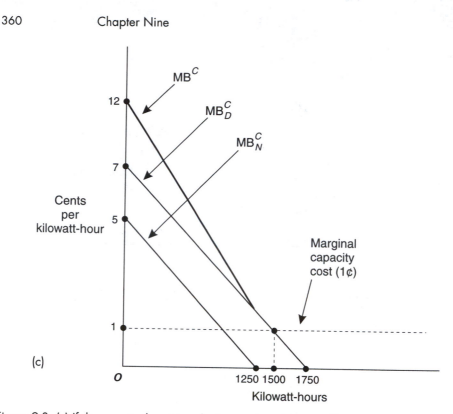

Figure 9-8. (c) If the marginal cost is only 1 cent, then the most efficient capacity is 1500.

$$MB_D^C = \begin{cases} 7 - \dfrac{1}{250} Q^C & 0 \le Q^C \le 1750 \\\\ 0 & Otherwise \end{cases}$$

$$MB_N^C = \begin{cases} 5 - \dfrac{1}{250} Q^C & 0 \le Q^C \le 1250 \\\\ 0 & Otherwise \end{cases}$$

We then sum these to find the total marginal benefit available for capacity (MB^C)[46]:

<hr/>

[46] Note that to add demand curves in the usual horizontal way, we have quantity on the left of the equation and a price expression on the right. We add to find the total quantity for a given price. To find the vertical sum, however, we write the equation so that price is on the left and a quantity expression is on the right. This gives us the total willingness to pay for an incremental unit at any given quantity. We do this only when different consumers receive benefits from the same resource.

$$MB^C = \begin{cases} 12 - \dfrac{2}{250}Q^C & 0 \le Q^C \le 1250 \\[2mm] 7 - \dfrac{1}{250}Q^C & 1250 \le Q^C \le 1750 \\[2mm] 0 & Otherwise \end{cases}$$

To find the quantity of capacity at which marginal benefit MB^C equals marginal cost, we use the part of the expression relevant for $MB^C = 4$ cents.[47]

$$MB^C = 12 - \frac{2}{250}Q^C = 4$$

whence

$$Q^C = 1000$$

Thus the most efficient capacity to provide is 1000 units. But how will it be utilized, and what prices should be charged? To answer these questions, we enter the 1000 unit capacity figure into our equations to solve for the other unknowns:

$$MB^C_D = 7 - \frac{1}{250}(1000) = 3$$

$$MB^C_N = 5 - \frac{2}{250}(1000) = 1$$

Note that by design these sum to 4 cents, the marginal cost of capacity. Continuing to work backward through the equations, note that if the marginal benefit available for capacity from a day user is 3 cents, then the ordinary marginal benefit (MB_D) must be 6 cents (adding the 3-cent operating cost back in) and similarly MB_N must be 4 cents ($= 1 + 3$). In the original demand equations, the corresponding prices P_D of 6 cents and P_N of 4 cents cause day and night demand each to equal precisely 1000 kilowatt-hours. Thus capacity is fully utilized both day and night, the (peak) day price is 6 cents, the (off-peak) night price is 4 cents, and when operating costs are subtracted this leaves capacity contributions of 3 cents from day users and 1 cent from night users. In this particular problem, because marginal capacity costs are assumed to be constant at 4 cents, these contribution shares exactly cover the costs.

An interesting insight can be had if we make a minor change in the problem. Suppose that the marginal cost of a unit capacity is only 1 cent rather than 4 cents (see Figure 9-8c). Then the relevant part of the market willingness-to-pay equation is the one in which night demanders have zero marginal willingness to pay:

$$MB^C = 7 - \frac{1}{250}Q^C = 1$$

[47] If one substitutes $MB^C = 4$ and uses the other line segment $7 - \frac{1}{250}Q^C$, one finds $Q^C = 750$. But this quantity is not in the range $1250 \le Q^C \le 1750$ where the segment applies. Thus, it is not a valid solution.

whence

$$Q^C = 1500$$

and

$$\mathrm{MB}_N^C = 0$$

That is, night demanders do not get allocated any portion of the capacity costs: The marginal capacity is there only because the day demanders are willing to pay for it. Of course, both groups must pay the marginal operating costs they impose, so $P_D = 4$ cents and $P_N = 3$ cents. Thus, the capacity is fully utilized during the day ($D = 1500$), but at night there is unused capacity ($N = 1250$).

Summary

In this chapter we examined the role of technology and costs as constraints on an organization's supply decisions. Policy analysts use these concepts in a variety of predictive and evaluative ways. One important way arises in considering technical efficiency in the public sector. For example, to discover if the skills or productivity of participants in a job-training program are improving, it may be necessary to estimate the observed technical relation between inputs and outputs in order to isolate the changing contribution of the trainee. To do this requires a theoretical understanding of production functions, a good working knowledge of the operations being studied, and certain statistical skills (not covered here).

We explained how production functions may be characterized in terms of their returns to scale and their elasticities of substitution. At a purely theoretical level it is helpful to understand the differences between concepts of efficiency and productivity. We illustrated this by examining the tempting mistake of maximizing productivity that a city manager or mayor might make.

Numerous practical difficulties stand in the way of discovering the empirical truth about input-output relations. One of these, discussed in the examples of masonry cleaning and trucking, is the importance of accounting for quality variations in the output. The hedonic method of accounting for these variations was illustrated at a simplified level. Another difficulty, common in the public sector, is having any good measure of output; we illustrated this with education but could raise the same question in other areas (e.g., how should we measure the output of public fire protection?). In looking at the relation between costs and participant-years in the national supported work experiment, analysts were able to identify the possibility of substantial managerial scale economies while being sensitive to the inadequacy of participant-years as an output measure.

The concepts of cost are fundamental to economic choice. They are used in virtually every policy analysis that considers alternatives. We explained how social costs are relevant to the compensation principle as embodied in social benefit-cost analysis. The important distinctions among social opportunity costs, private opportunity costs, and accounting costs were reviewed. The use of the different cost concepts was illustrated in the analysis of the New York supported work experiment; these included the social benefit-cost calculation (used to measure the change in relative efficiency) and other benefit-cost calculations from the perspective of different constituent groups that could be used to predict their responses to the program. The latter do not speak to efficiency, but can be very helpful in designing feasible and fair programs.

The opportunity cost concepts can have very important linkages to production functions. These linkages are most likely in environments where the supply organization produces at a technically efficient level. They are often assumed to hold for private, profit-making firms, such as those in the regulated trucking industry. Then the relation between a firm's cost function and its production function can simplify certain analytic tasks.

We illustrated this, at a simplified level, by showing how the Spady-Friedlaender study inferred the technical returns to scale of trucking firms from an analysis of their cost functions. The analysis, which indicated that no significant scale economies were available by expansion of the average firm, lent support to the arguments in favor of trucking deregulation. In the appendix, we provide more technical details about this duality relation between cost and production functions.

We also examined one other type of cost-output relation; the joint cost problem. We illustrated the most efficient solution to joint costs in the context of peak-load pricing problems, as might arise in utility pricing, bridge and tunnel crossings, commuter railroads, or roads. Benefit-cost reasoning was used to identify the solution.

Exercises

9-1 A public employment program in San Francisco for recently released ex-offenders paid each employee $225 per week. However, a study showed that each employee only caused output to go up by $140 per week. Therefore, the social benefits of the program are less than the social costs.

a Criticize the social cost measure.

b Criticize the social benefit measure.

9-2 The director of public service employment for a small city funded two different programs last year, each with a different constant-returns-to-scale production function. The director was not sure of the specification of the production functions last year but hopes to allocate resources more wisely this year. Production data were gathered for each program during three periods last year, and are listed in the accompanying table.

	Program A			Program B		
	K_A	L_A	Q_A	K_B	L_B	Q_B
1	24	26	48	25	25	50
2	24	28	48	25	36	60
3	24	22	44	25	16	40

a Program A operates with a fixed proportions production function. What is it? [Answer: $Q = \min (2K, 2L)$.] In period 3 what are the marginal products of capital and labor, respectively? In period 2 what is the elasticity of output with respect to labor? (Answer: 0.)

b Program B operates with a Cobb-Douglas production function. What is it? (Answer: $Q = 2K^{1/2}L^{1/2}$.) In period 3 what are the marginal products of capital and labor? In period 3 what is the elasticity of output with respect to capital?

c○ Suppose in the third period that the capital was fixed in each program but you were free to allocate the 38 labor units between the two programs any way you wished. If each unit of Q_B is equal in value to each unit of Q_A, how would you allocate labor to maximize the total value of outputs? (Answer: $L_A = 24; L_B = 14$.)

d○ Suppose you could use two Cobb-Douglas production processes (C and D) to produce the same output:

$$Q_C = K_C^{1/3}L_C^{2/3} \quad Q_D = K_D^{1/2}L_D^{1/2}$$

If you then had 100 units of capital and 105 units of labor, how would you allocate them between the two processes to maximize total output? (Answer: $K_C = 47, L_C = 67, K_D = 53, L_D = 38$.)

e○ Suppose your budget were large enough to employ 100 units of either labor or capital, and the cost of a unit of labor was the same as a unit of capital. The production function is $Q_D = K_D^{1/2}L_D^{1/2}$. Given that output must be at least 30, what is the maximum number of people you could employ? (Answer: $L = 90$.)

9-3   You are an analyst for a metropolitan transportation authority. You are asked if it would improve efficiency to buy more buses, and if so, how many more should be bought. Currently, there are eighty buses. The operating cost of a bus is $30 during the day and $60 during the night, when higher wages must be paid to drivers and other workers. The daily capital cost of a bus, whether or not it is used, is $10. The demands for buses aggregated over persons and stops during the 12 hours of day and night, respectively D and N, are

$$Q_D = 160 - P_D$$

$$Q_N = 80 - P_N$$

What is the efficient number of buses? What prices should be charged to induce efficient ridership? Will all the buses be in use at night? (Answer: 120 buses; $P_D = \$40$, $P_N = \$60$; no.)

APPENDIX

DUALITY—SOME MATHEMATICAL RELATIONS BETWEEN PRODUCTION
AND COST FUNCTIONS°

In this appendix we examine briefly some of the mathematical relations between production functions and costs when it can be assumed that the supplier will operate at least cost. This material is helpful for understanding (and undertaking) work such as Spady-Friedlaender analysis.

The problem of choosing the cost-minimizing inputs given a certain production function is usually explained by a diagram much like Figure 9A-1. Given a production function $Q = F(K, L)$ and input prices P_K and P_L, suppose we are told to produce an output of $Q = 30$ at the least cost. The isoquant for $Q = 30$ is shown in the figure. An isocost line is a locus of inputs such that $P_K K + P_L L$ is constant. This line has the slope $-P_L/P_K$. Thus, geometrically we wish to be on the lowest possible isocost line that reaches the isoquant where $Q = 30$. This occurs where the isocost line is just tangent to the isoquant. At that point the marginal rate of technical substitution ($\text{RTS}_{L,K}$, the negative of the slope of the isoquant) equals the input price ratio P_L/P_K.

Recall that the RTS is equal to the ratio of the marginal products at any point. To see this, remember that the change in output dQ along an isoquant is zero. That is,

$$Q = F(K, L)$$

and along an isoquant (taking the total differential)

$$dQ = \frac{\partial F}{\partial K}\, dK + \frac{\partial F}{\partial L}\, dL = 0$$

These terms can be so rearranged that

$$-\left(\frac{dK}{dL}\right)_{Q=\text{const}} = \frac{\partial F/\partial L}{\partial F/\partial K} = \frac{\text{MP}_L}{\text{MP}_K}$$

The term on the left-hand side is the negative of the slope of an isoquant, and thus it is by definition equal to $\text{RTS}_{L,K}$. Thus,

$$\text{RTS}_{L,K} = \frac{\text{MP}_L}{\text{MP}_K}$$

For the general problem of least-cost C input choice for the production of Q units of output, we may formulate it in calculus terms as

$$C = P_K K + P_L L + \lambda[Q - F(K, L)]$$

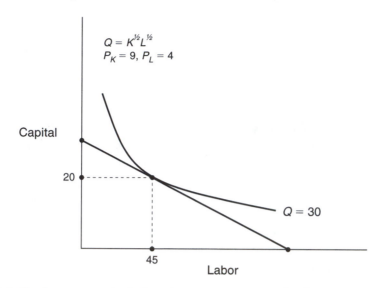

$Q = K^{\frac{1}{2}}L^{\frac{1}{2}}$
$P_K = 9,\ P_L = 4$

Capital

20

$Q = 30$

45

Labor

Figure 9A-1. The least-cost method of producing a given output level.

Thus, the first-order conditions for a cost minimum are

$$\frac{\partial C}{\partial K} = P_K - \lambda\,\frac{\partial F}{\partial K} = 0$$

$$\frac{\partial C}{\partial L} = P_L - \lambda\,\frac{\partial F}{\partial L} = 0$$

$$\frac{\partial C}{\partial \lambda} = Q - F(K,\ L) = 0$$

Dividing the second equation by the first after rearranging slightly gives us the calculus proof of the geometric argument:

$$\frac{P_L}{P_K} = \frac{\partial F/\partial L}{\partial F/\partial K} = \frac{\mathrm{MP}_L}{\mathrm{MP}_K} = \mathrm{RTS}_{L,K}$$

This simply reiterates that the least-cost input choice will be the point on the isoquant whose slope is minus the ratio of the input prices.

This reasoning allows us to find the cost-minimizing input choice given a specific production function, input prices, and a desired output level. For example, suppose the production function is Cobb-Douglas:

$$Q = K^{1/2}L^{1/2}$$

and $P_K = 9$, $P_L = 4$, and the desired output is 30.

We know the correct point on the isoquant will have slope $-4/9$. To find an expression for the isoquant slope in terms of K and L, let us find the marginal productivity equations directly from the production function and then combine them:

$$MP_L = \frac{\partial Q}{\partial L} = \tfrac{1}{2}K^{1/2}L^{-1/2}$$

$$MP_K = \frac{\partial Q}{\partial K} = \tfrac{1}{2}K^{-1/2}L^{1/2}$$

$$RTS_{L,K} = \frac{MP_L}{MP_K} = \frac{K}{L}$$

Thus K/L must equal 4/9, or $K = 4L/9$. Now we can substitute directly into the production function and solve for $Q = 30$:

$$30 = K^{1/2}L^{1/2}$$

$$30 = \left(\frac{4L}{9}\right)^{1/2} L^{1/2}$$

$$30 = \frac{2}{3}L$$

$$45 = L$$

$$20 = K$$

$$360 = C = P_K K + P_L L$$

Refer back to the general calculus formulation of this problem:

$$C = P_K K + P_L L + \lambda[Q - F(K, L)]$$

Note that $\partial C/\partial Q = \lambda$; that is, λ can be interpreted as the marginal cost of increasing the output level by one unit. We know from the first (or second) equation of the first-order conditions:

$$\lambda = \frac{P_K}{\partial F/\partial K}$$

Thus in our specific problem we can identify the marginal cost by substituting the correct expressions:

$$\lambda = \frac{9}{\tfrac{1}{2}(20^{-1/2})(45^{1/2})}$$

$$= \frac{9}{\tfrac{1}{2}(1.5)}$$

$$= 12$$

That is, it would cost \$12 to expand output by one more unit (in the least-cost way).

Now, one of the problems with the above method of solution, simply a calculus version of the usual geometric argument, is that it can be somewhat tedious. It certainly would be nice if there were a simpler way to find the answers. Economists using the mathematics of duality have associated a cost function with each "well-behaved" production function, from which it is often much simpler to find the answers to problems like the one just solved.

Of course, if one had to derive (as we will shortly) the cost function from the production function each time, there would be no gain. But the general equation for the cost function can be expressed just like the general equation for a production function. For example, it is no more difficult to remember (or look up) the Cobb-Douglas cost function than the Cobb-Douglas production function.[48]

Let us first give the general definition of a cost function: **A cost function $C(Q, P_1, P_2, \ldots, P_n)$ is a relation that associates for each output level and input prices the least total cost of producing that output level.**

Once a cost function is known, it is easy to derive the standard cost curves from it. For example:

$$MC(Q) = \frac{\partial C}{\partial Q}$$

and

$$AC(Q) = \frac{C(Q, P_1, P_2, \ldots, P_n)}{Q}$$

To get a better understanding of the cost function, let us derive it for Cobb-Douglas production technology:

$$Q = K^\alpha L^{1-\alpha}$$

To find the cost function, we must solve for the cost minimum in the general problem[49]:

$$C = P_K K + P_L L + \lambda(Q - K^\alpha L^{1-\alpha})$$

The first-order conditions are:

$$\frac{\partial C}{\partial K} = P_K - \alpha\lambda K^{\alpha-1} L^{1-\alpha} = 0 \tag{i}$$

$$\frac{\partial C}{\partial L} = P_L - (1 - \alpha)\lambda K^\alpha L^{-\alpha} = 0 \tag{ii}$$

$$\frac{\partial C}{\partial \lambda} = Q - K^\alpha L^{1-\alpha} = 0 \tag{iii}$$

---

[48] The dual approach on the supply side is analogous to the dual approach to consumer demand reviewed in the appendix to Chapter 6. The textbook by Hal R. Varian, *Microeconomic Analysis* (New York: W. W. Norton & Company, Inc., 1992) provides a good introductory approach. A more advanced reference is M. Fuss and D. McFadden, eds., *Production Economics, A Dual Approach to Theory and Applications* (Amsterdam: North-Holland, 1978).

[49] Note that this is the same formulation one would use to find the expenditure function associated with Cobb-Douglas utility function.

The solution requires that we express the cost C as a function of only the output level and the input prices (and the fixed parameters). Since $C = P_K K + P_L L$, we will use the first-order conditions to substitute for K and L in this equation.

By dividing (i) and (ii) after rearranging, we see that

$$\frac{P_K}{P_L} = \frac{[\alpha/(1-\alpha)]L}{K}$$

or

$$P_K K = \frac{\alpha}{1-\alpha} P_L L$$

or

$$K = \frac{[\alpha/(1-\alpha)]P_L L}{P_K}$$

Therefore,

$$C = P_K K + P_L L = P_L L\left(1 + \frac{\alpha}{1-\alpha}\right) = P_L L \frac{1}{1-\alpha}$$

Now we have only to rid ourselves of the L in the above expression. To do so, we use condition (iii), $Q = K^\alpha L^{1-\alpha}$. On substituting our expression for K derived from (i) and (ii), we have

$$Q = \left(\frac{\alpha}{1-\alpha}\right)^\alpha \left(\frac{P_L}{P_K}\right)^\alpha L^\alpha L^{1-\alpha}$$

$$Q = \left(\frac{\alpha}{1-\alpha}\right)^\alpha \left(\frac{P_L}{P_K}\right)^\alpha L$$

$$L = Q\left(\frac{\alpha}{1-\alpha}\right)^{-\alpha} \left(\frac{P_L}{P_K}\right)^{-\alpha}$$

Now we may substitute this in the expression for the cost:

$$C = P_L L \frac{1}{1-\alpha}$$

$$= P_L \left(\frac{P_L}{P_K}\right)^{-\alpha} \left(\frac{\alpha}{1-\alpha}\right)^{-\alpha} \left(\frac{1}{1-\alpha}\right) Q$$

$$= P_L^{1-\alpha} P_K^\alpha \alpha^{-\alpha}(1-\alpha)^{\alpha-1} Q$$

or, letting $\delta = \alpha^{-\alpha}(1-\alpha)^{\alpha-1}$,

$$C = \delta P_L^{1-\alpha} P_K^\alpha Q$$

Of course, this was tedious to derive, but the point is that the derivation need not be repeated: This expression is no more difficult to remember (or refer to) than the production
function itself.

Now let us resolve our problem, where we are given $Q = 30$, $P_K = 9$, $P_L = 4$, and $\alpha = \frac{1}{2}$ (δ
$= 2$). The least cost is obtained by simply plugging in the formula

$$C = 2(4^{1/2})(9^{1/2})(30)$$

$$= 360$$

But what are the inputs? They are simply the value of the partial derivatives of the cost function with respect to prices! That is, if we let $X_i (Q, P_1, P_2, \ldots, P_n)$ denote generally the optimal level of the ith input given output Q and input prices, we have *Shephard's lemma*[50]:

$$\frac{\partial C(Q, P_1, P_2, \ldots, P_n)}{\partial P_i} = X_i(Q, P_1, P_2, \ldots, P_n)$$

In other words, this simple derivative property of the cost function can be used to reveal the
derived demand curve for any factor holding the output level and other prices constant (i.e.,
it is a "compensated" derived demand curve).

To make this more concrete, let us apply Shephard's lemma to the Cobb-Douglas case:

$$L = \frac{\partial C}{\partial P_L} = (1 - \alpha)\delta P_L^{-\alpha} P_K^{\alpha} Q$$

$$K = \frac{\partial C}{\partial P_K} = \alpha\delta P_L^{1-\alpha} P_K^{\alpha-1} Q$$

These functions are the equations for optimal input demand conditional on the level of Q.
For our specific example, assume everything is given but P_L. Then the derived demand curve
(holding Q at 30 and P_K at 9) is

$$L = \tfrac{1}{2}(2)P_L^{-1/2}(9^{1/2})(30)$$

$$= 90P_L^{-1/2}$$

---

[50] A proof of Shephard's lemma offered by Varian, *Microeconomic Analysis*, p. 74, is instructive. Let $\hat{X}$ be
the vector of inputs that is cost-minimizing at prices $\hat{P}$ and output level Q. Now imagine considering other cost-
minimizing input vectors X that are associated with different prices P but the same output level. Define the cost
difference between the X and $\hat{X}$ input vectors at prices P as CD(P):

$$\text{CD}(P) = C(P, Q) - P\hat{X}$$

Since C is the minimum cost at price P, C is less than $P\hat{X}$ for all P except $\hat{P}$ (where they are equal). Thus this function CD(P) attains its maximum value (of zero) at $\hat{P}$, and its partial derivatives must all be equal to zero at that
point (the ordinary first-order conditions for optimization). Thus,

$$\frac{\partial \text{CD}(\hat{P})}{\partial P_i} = \frac{\partial C(\hat{P}, Q)}{\partial P_i} - X_i = 0$$

$$\frac{\partial C(\hat{P}, Q)}{\partial P_i} = X_i$$

This tells us the optimal level of L for any price P_L (conditional on the other factors). Thus, when $P_L = 4$, $L = 45$.

Similarly, we find the optimal K in our problem:

$$K = \tfrac{1}{2}(2)(4^{1/2})(9^{-1/2})(30)$$

$$= 20$$

We can also derive the standard cost curves for the Cobb-Douglas with about as little effort:

$$\text{MC}(Q) = \frac{\partial C}{\partial Q} = \delta P_L^{1-\alpha}P_K^{\alpha}$$

or for our specific function:

$$\text{MC}(Q) = 2(4^{1/2})(9^{1/2})$$

$$= 12$$

That is, the marginal cost curve associated with Cobb-Douglas technology is constant. Of course, this is always true for constant returns-to-scale production functions. The average cost must thus have the same equation:

$$\text{AC}(Q) = \frac{C}{Q} = \delta P_L^{1-\alpha}P_K^{\alpha}$$

In the main part of the text it was mentioned that most empirical studies of production assume Cobb-Douglas or CES technology. While these may often be good approximations, their use is due more to their ease of statistical estimation than to any strong belief that technology has constant elasticity of substitution. However, a new freedom arises with the cost function approach: Several functional forms that have been discovered are easily estimable statistically but are less restrictive in terms of the type of production function that might underlie them. Two will be mentioned briefly here. The first is the *generalized Leontif cost function.*[51]

$$C(Q, P_1, \ldots, P_n) = Q\sum_{i=1}^{n}\sum_{j=1}^{n}a_{ij}P_i^{1/2}P_j^{1/2}$$

where $a_{ij} = a_{ji}$. The a_{ij}'s are fixed parameters of the function.

For a two-factor technology this may be written

$$C(Q, P_K, P_L) = Q(a_K P_K + a_L P_L + 2a_{LK}P_L^{1/2}P_K^{1/2})$$

This generalized function is linear in the parameters, so it could easily be tested by statistical methods. It corresponds to the fixed-proportions Leontif technology when $a_{ij} = 0$ for $i \neq j$.[52]

---

[51] This was derived by W. Diewert, "An Application of the Shephard Duality Theorem: A Generalized Leontif Production Function," *Journal of Political Economy, 79,* No. 3, May/June 1971, pp. 481–507.

[52] The reader may wish to prove this as an exercise. It can be done by finding the two derived demand curves and using them to identify the relation between L and K. This is an isoquant, since the level of Q is constant and the same for each derived demand curve. The isoquant collapses to a right angle when $a_{LK} = 0$.

The second cost function of quite general use is the *translog cost function,* the one used by Spady and Friedlaender in their study of trucking:

$$\ln C(Q, P_1, \ldots, P_n) = Q\left(a_0 + \sum_{i=1}^n a_i \ln P_i + \tfrac{1}{2}\sum_{i=1}^n \sum_{j=1}^n a_{ij} \ln P_i \ln P_j\right)$$

where all the *a*'s are parameters and have the following restrictions:

$$\sum_{i=1}^n a_i = 1 \quad \sum_{i=1}^n a_{ij} = 0 \quad a_{ij} = a_{ji}$$

If it turns out that all $a_{ij} = 0$, the translog function collapses to the Cobb-Douglas.

CHAPTER TEN

PRIVATE PROFIT-MAKING ORGANIZATIONS:
OBJECTIVES, CAPABILITIES, AND POLICY IMPLICATIONS

THIS CHAPTER AND the following one are about the organizations that convert inputs into outputs: firms in the private profit-making sector, private nonprofit organizations such as certain hospitals and schools, public bureaus such as fire and sanitation departments, and public enterprises such as mass transit systems.[1] Each of these organizations must decide what outputs to produce, the level of each, and the technologies with which to make them. In the preceding chapter we reviewed the concepts of technological possibilities and their associated costs. These serve to constrain the organization's decisions. Similarly, the organization is constrained by the factors that influence its revenues: sales, voluntary donations, or government funding. For the most part we shall defer an examination of the sources of these latter constraints: they arise in part from consumer (including government) demand for the outputs and in part from the behavior of other producer organizations that supply the same or very similar outputs.

If we simply refer to all the external constraints on the organization as its environment, then we can say that the organization's behavior is a function of its objectives, capabilities, and environment. In this chapter our purpose is to examine the role of analytic assumptions about objectives and capabilities in modeling the behavior of the private, profit-making firm. We begin with models of the private firm because they have received the most attention in the professional literature and are more highly developed and tested than the models of other supplier organizations. The models of behavior we review here are useful for predicting the organization's response to such policy changes as taxes, subsidy plans, regulations, antitrust laws, and other legal requirements.

---

[1] The distinction between a public bureau and public enterprise is that the bureau receives its funds from government revenues and the enterprise receives its funds from sale of the output. In actuality most public supply organizations receive some user fees as well as government subsidies, so the distinction is really a matter of degree.

We begin with a discussion of the concept of a firm and emphasize the importance of uncertainty, information costs, and transaction costs to explain the formation of firms. Then we review the standard model of a firm: an organization whose objective is profit maximization and whose capabilities are sufficient to achieve that objective, subject to the environmental constraints. It can be difficult to predict the behavior of this standard firm, which we illustrate with an extended discussion of the firm's choice to price-discriminate. We consider different types of price discrimination, their normative consequences, public policy concerning price discrimination, and behavioral factors that determine when price discrimination will occur. In connection with the latter we emphasize the role of information flows and transactions between the firm and its customers.

In a supplemental section we turn to models that consider different firm objectives and capabilities. Holding the capabilities constant, we consider the effect of alternative objectives. In modern corporations, there is considerable information asymmetry between managers and the dispersed stockholder owners, and the managers may have goals other than profit-maximization that they wish to pursue. A model of revenue (or sales) maximization is discussed, and other objectives that may apply in particular situations are mentioned. We illustrate the policy relevance of these behaviors in the areas of taxation and antitrust and with regard to information disclosure requirements. Finally, we turn to capabilities and consider the idea that an organization may be boundedly rational: a satisficer rather than a maximizer. A simple rule-of-thumb behavioral model of markup pricing is presented. With it, we illustrate that in certain environments a satisficing firm may behave identically to a profit-maximizing one. However, this will not always be true, as we illustrate in the following chapter in regard to hospital behavior.

Each of these models may apply in particular circumstances. By studying the differences among them, we begin to appreciate the subtleties of designing or harnessing institutions to achieve particular goals. An analyst who is aware of these competing models will be considerably more sensitive about making policy inferences that depend on any one of them.

The Concept of a Firm

When the workings of a market economy are discussed, it is implicitly understood that individuals own all the resources that are potentially available for use in production and have legal authority over their use. We do not often ask why control over these resources frequently gets delegated to impersonal, intermediary institutions called firms that convert the inputs into outputs and array them in the marketplace for sale. Analogously, we do not often question why, on the demand side, such formal delegations of authority to intermediary institutions rarely exist.

It is generally assumed that each individual as a consumer makes perfectly decentralized decisions, that is, decides on his or her own which goods to purchase and makes the purchases from suppliers. We rarely take part of our consumption budget, voluntarily give up authority over it to some central consumption organization that makes purchasing decisions for the members, and then receive our share of the purchased goods.[2] Why then is it so normal for us to give up some control over the use of our labor by becoming an employee or give up control over the use of our capital by giving it to a firm in return for stock certificates or bonds? Why do we not supply as we buy, in a decentralized manner? Why do we voluntarily agree to more centralized decision-making by centralizing control in the institution known as the firm?

The answer that first comes to mind is economies of scale. Indeed, before the industrial revolution, we did supply as we buy. Many families were self-contained economic units that produced primarily for their own consumption. There was some specialization, of course, because some people were hunters, others dressmakers, and so forth. But it was not until the development of the factory that individuals began leaving their homes in large numbers to work in groups or teams elsewhere during the day. Much of this economic phenomenon was understood at the time. Adam Smith, writing in the eighteenth century, understood with remarkable clarity the advantages that could be had through the specializations made possible by large-scale enterprise.[3] For a given amount of labor and capital, total output is often greater if produced by assembly line rather than by many small shops.

Yet in an important way, this answer begs the question. To operate a large-scale enterprise, it may be that many individual resource units must be coordinated. But why is it common for this coordination to take place inside one firm rather than through arrangements made across firms? As a simple illustrative example, many firms use legal services from law firms. If one firm is assembling an airplane engine, different firms can assemble various components of it, or one firm can do the whole thing. These are alternative ways of organizing to carry out the same physical tasks. So the fact that resources need to be coordinated to produce the final output does not imply that the coordination should be accomplished within one firm.

At one extreme one could imagine that all parts of a production process are accomplished by single-individual "firms" controlling only that individual's resources: complete decentralization of decision-making for production. All coordination would take place through arrangements across firms. At the other extreme one could imagine that all the labor and capital resources of society are employed by one gigantic firm coordinating all activities internally: complete centralization of productive economic activities.[4] The common firm simply represents a voluntary choice about the degree to which production decisions should be centralized rather than decentralized.

The *key explanatory variables* that explain these choices have to do with the *information, transaction, and uncertainty costs that would arise under alternative organizational arrangements.* One may choose to become an employee rather than a self-employed

---

[2] There are, in fact, many instances in which we do allow organizations to spend part of our budgets for us. Governments are an obvious one. Families may be thought of as organizations whose members pool their resources and make joint consumption decisions (although for most purposes, economic theory treats the family as an individual). Other voluntary institutions—churches, consumer cooperatives, and social clubs—sometimes have these functions.

[3] See his description of the pin factory in *The Wealth of Nations* (New York: The Modern Library, 1937).

[4] In Chapter 17 we point out that there can be considerable decentralization within a firm and discuss the reasons why.

contractor because of a preference for greater certainty of income. An individual may delegate control over capital assets to a firm because it is too expensive for the individual to acquire the information necessary to direct the use of the assets in the most profitable manner. If a firm wishes to have certain intermediate products delivered on a variable but precisely timed schedule (e.g., engines to be installed in automobiles), the transaction costs may be cheaper if the intermediate products are made internally than if frequent new contracts have to be negotiated and arranged with an outside supplier. All of these examples remind us that market transactions are not costless. *It is the economies of scale from these sources that help explain why individuals choose to delegate some control over their resources to the centralized contracting agent known as the firm; it is also the diseconomies that arise from these factors* (past some point of internal growth) *that serve to limit the size of the firm.*[5]

One interesting point that can be made clearer through the realization that a firm is only an intermediary is that the concepts of outcome equity are not generally applied to firms. That is, firms do not enter as arguments in social welfare functions: only individuals count. The only concern for firm "welfare" arises indirectly through its effects on consumers and on the incomes derived by the individuals supplying resources to the firm.[6] That is also why, in Chapter 6, we described the compensation principle and illustrated benefit-cost calculations without reference to firms; all the relevant effects are counted by knowing (in each state) the available goods and each individual's budget constraint. The producer surplus introduced in the last chapter counts because it reveals increments to the budget constraints of individuals (resource owners). Thus when we discuss the effect of a policy on a firm's behavior, we must be able to trace the consequences through to individuals before the policy can be properly evaluated.

Additional importance to policy analysis of understanding the concept of a firm will become increasingly clear as the successive chapters in this volume unfold. At this stage let us simply point out that the role of policy in influencing economic organization is large and that deducing the consequences of alternative policies often requires perceiving the "transactional" impacts. We will illustrate, for example, that the design of policy to protect the environment from air and water pollution depends crucially on these concepts, and that can be said for the regulation of natural monopolies as well. But before we develop these applications, we must build up a number of other concepts relevant to understanding the pro-

---

[5] These issues were pointedly raised by R. Coase, "The Nature of the Firm," *Economica, 4,* November 1937, pp. 386–405; O. Williamson, *Markets and Hierarchies: Analyses and Antitrust Implications* (New York: The Free Press, 1975); and A. Alchian and H. Demsetz, "Production, Information Costs, and Economic Organization," *American Economic Review, 62,* No. 5, December 1972, pp. 777–795. Articles that discuss the ensuing research and its current status are in a symposium in the *American Economic Review, 91,* No. 2, May 2001: Michael D. Whinston, "Assessing the Property Rights and Transaction-Cost Theories of Firm Scope," pp. 184–188; George P. Baker and Thomas N. Hubbard, "Empirical Strategies in Contract Economics: Information and the Boundary of the Firm," pp. 189–194; and Sendhil Mullainathan and David Scharfstein, "Do Firm Boundaries Matter?," pp. 195–199.

[6] The individuals who work in firms may receive psychic as well as monetary income. We explain this in Chapter 14. Thus policies that affect how people feel about their workplaces matter, but they matter because of their effects on individual not firm welfare.

duction side of the economy. With this brief introduction to the nature of a firm, let us consider how the firm's behavior can be modeled in terms of its objectives and capabilities.

The Private Profit-Maximizing Firm

Profit Maximization Requires that Marginal Revenue Equal Marginal Coat

In standard uses of microeconomic theory, a firm in a private market is modeled simply by the objective function of profit maximization. That is, the firm is nothing more than a supercompetent clerk. It considers all production alternatives and chooses the one that will maximize its profit, subject to the constraints of factor prices and the demand for its output. Demand is modeled by a revenue function, $R(Q)$, which indicates what revenue will be brought in by an output level of Q. Costs are represented by the cost function $C(Q)$. **Profits $\Pi(Q)$ are defined as the difference between revenues and costs,** and the firm is assumed to pick the Q that maximizes

$$\Pi(Q) = R(Q) - C(Q)$$

Suppose Q increases by a small amount ΔQ. Then we can write the change in the equation as follows:

$$\Delta\Pi(Q) = \Delta R(Q) - \Delta C(Q)$$

In other words, the change in profit equals the change in revenue less the change in costs. We can express this as a change per unit increase in output if we divide both sides of the above equation by ΔQ:

$$\frac{\Delta\Pi(Q)}{\Delta Q} = \frac{\Delta R(Q)}{\Delta Q} - \frac{\Delta C(Q)}{\Delta Q}$$

Let us define $\Delta R(Q)/\Delta Q$ as the **marginal revenue: the change in revenue per unit increase in output.** We defined the marginal cost $\Delta C(Q)/\Delta Q$ in the previous chapter: the change in cost for a unit increase in output. The difference between them $\Delta\Pi(Q)/\Delta Q$ is the change in profit caused per unit increase in output.

At the profit-maximizing level of output it must be true that the change in profit for a unit increase in output is zero. Below the optimal level, increases in output yield positive incremental profits (make total profit larger). Past the optimal level, output increases yield negative incremental profits (make total profit smaller). So at exactly the optimal level, profits are neither increasing nor decreasing:

$$\frac{\Delta\Pi(Q)}{\Delta Q} = \frac{\Delta R(Q)}{\Delta Q} - \frac{\Delta C(Q)}{\Delta Q} = 0$$

or

$$\frac{\Delta R(Q)}{\Delta Q} = \frac{\Delta C(Q)}{\Delta Q}$$

In other words, *marginal revenue must equal marginal cost at the profit-maximizing level of output.*

Graphically, this is illustrated in Figures 10-1a and b. The revenue function is drawn as a straight line (Figure 10-1a), which is equivalent to assuming that the firm will sell each unit of output at the prevailing market price. In Figure 10-1b, we derive from the revenue function the marginal revenue $MR(Q)$ and the average revenue $AR(Q)$, defined as the total revenue divided by the quantity produced. The straight-line revenue function implies that $MR(Q)$ is constant at any output level and equal to the market price P_M, and therefore $AR(Q)$ stays equal to it. The cost function is drawn to reflect economies of scale up to a certain output level Q_A but diseconomies thereafter. Thus the range of output levels in which profits are positive $[R(Q) > C(Q)]$ is from Q_0 to Q_1. Profits at each output level are the vertical distance between $R(Q)$ and $C(Q)$, shown as the profit function $\Pi(Q)$ in Figure 10-1a. The maximum profit is at Q_Π, where the slope of the profit function $\Pi(Q)$ is zero (Figure 10-1a) and $MC = MR$ (Figure 10-1b).

The Profit-Maximizing Monopolist

In many applications of this standard model of firm behavior, the insights are derived by varying the external or environmental constraints on the firm's actions. For example, consider the situation where there is only one seller of a good: a monopoly. The predicted harm from monopoly can be easily illustrated through a simple extension of the analysis above. To see this, let us recognize that the demand curve for the *firm's* output[7] is simply the average revenue function: For any quantity produced, the average revenue is simply the price per unit. Thus the straight-line revenue function corresponds to the horizontal demand curve that each firm would face if it had many competitors selling the identical product (i.e., the firm is in a perfectly competitive market, discussed in Chapter 12). If the firm charged a price lower than the prevailing market price P_M, it would capture the entire industry demand (an amount so far to the right of the quantities shown on the axis that there is no apparent downward slope over the range shown). If it tried to charge a price higher than P_M, the demand would be zero, since consumers would buy the product from the competitors charging P_M.[8]

In the case of a monopoly the firm faces the entire downward-sloping market demand curve. To keep the example as simple as possible, Figure 10-2 illustrates the monopolist's choice assuming a linear demand (average revenue) curve and constant-returns-to-scale technology, so that the marginal cost is constant and the average cost is thus equal to it. The

---

[7] Note that this is not equivalent to consumer demand for the product generally; the consumer can buy the same product from other firms.

[8] It is sometimes easier to understand the geometry by first imagining that the firm's demand curve is not perfectly flat but is slightly downward-sloping: A small price increase from P_M leads to a large reduction in demand, and a small price decrease from P_M causes a large increase in demand. The more competitive the industry, the flatter the firm's demand curve. The demand does not actually become infinite for prices below P_M; it is just that the entire market quantity at that price is so great relative to the quantities shown that the curve is effectively flat over the diagram's range. The actual firm's demand curve in the perfectly competitive case equals the market demand curve for prices below P_M, is horizontal at P_M, and is zero above P_M.

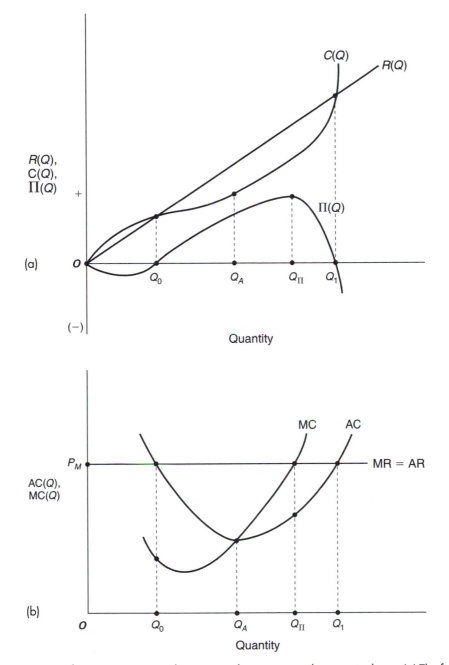

Figure 10-1. Profit-maximization implies marginal revenue equal to marginal cost: (a) The firm's revenue, cost, and profit functions. (b) Profit maximization occurs when marginal revenue equals marginal cost.

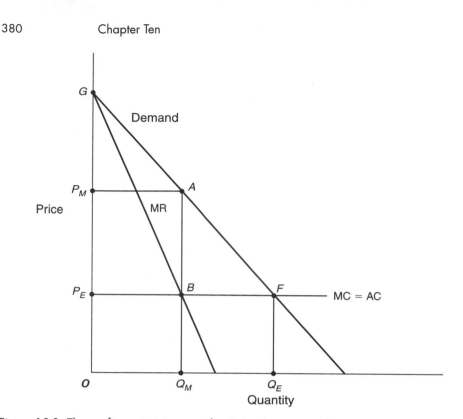

Figure 10-2. The profit-maximizing, nondiscriminating monopolist.

marginal revenue curve is lower than the demand curve, since to induce consumers to buy an additional unit requires lowering the price for all units.[9] Profit maximization implies that the monopolist will choose quantity Q_M (where MR = MC). The product will be sold at price P_M, and the monopolist's profits are shown by the rectangle $P_E P_M AB$ (the quantity sold times the difference between the price per unit sold and the average cost per unit).

The most efficient quantity to provide, however, is Q_E.[10] That is, assuming that the marginal cost curve measures the marginal social opportunity cost of production, units should be produced as long as the height of the demand curve exceeds the marginal cost. Recall that the height of the demand curve is a monetary measure of the benefit to the consumer of one additional unit: the maximum that someone will pay for that unit. The height of the marginal cost curve is the social opportunity cost of the resources used to make that unit, or the maximum that anyone will pay to use the resources *in some other way*. Thus there is

[9] $MR = \partial TR / \partial Q = \partial PQ / \partial Q = P + Q(\partial P / \partial Q)$. The first term, P, equals the height of the demand curve. The second term is negative whenever the demand curve facing the firm is downward sloping ($\partial P / \partial Q < 0$). The second term can be thought of as the reduced revenues on the first Q units caused by the price reduction necessary to sell one additional unit.

[10] Keep in mind that the distribution of resource ownership (wealth) influences the identification of the most efficient quantity by influencing both the demand and cost curves. We discuss this more explicitly in Chapter 12, on general equilibrium.

room for a deal if any output less than Q_E is produced, and therefore such an output level would be inefficient.

For example, consider the resources that could be used to produce one more unit of output above the Q_M level. In their alternative uses, they are worth only BQ_M (the marginal social cost). But there is a consumer willing to pay $AQ_M (>BQ_M)$ for the additional unit of output in this market. This consumer will offer an amount greater than BQ_M; the resource suppliers would be better off accepting the offer; and the alternative user is left indifferent (neither receiving the alternative output nor paying its cost). A related argument can be made about any incremental output levels greater than Q_E; in this case the alternative user values the resources more highly than the consumer in this market. Only at the output level Q_E is there no further room for a deal.

Thus *this type of monopoly behavior causes an inefficient allocation of resources: The quantity of the monopoly good that gets produced is too small.* The deadweight loss from this misallocation is the triangle *ABF*. The prediction follows simply from the assumptions about the objectives, capabilities, and demand curve the organization faces.

"Not so fast!" the experienced industrial organization analyst might cry out. There is a wrinkle (perhaps a gaping hole) in the above standard description of monopoly behavior, which can be understood from the earlier discussion of the concept of the firm involving information and transaction costs. The conclusions about the firm's behavior, as well as the inefficiency of the allocation, depend heavily on what is assumed about the organization's information and transaction costs. The most traditional assumptions are that the firm has perfect information and zero transaction costs. But if this is so, the monopolist will not behave as suggested. Under these conditions, the firm maximizes its profits by perfectly price-discriminating among the consumers (taking advantage of its perfect knowledge and its ability to bar resales costlessly). Put differently, it is in the monopolist's interest to exploit the room for a deal we have just identified.

Types of Monopolistic Price Discrimination

A perfectly price-discriminating monopolist could charge each consumer the maximum that consumer is willing to pay for each unit and thus extract the full area under the demand curve, produce Q_E, and make as profit the entire triangle P_EGF (Figure 10-2). Resource allocation would improve to the efficient level, although the monopolist would be hogging all of the gains from trade. Consumers buy the output, but their utility levels remain approximately unchanged[11]: The resource suppliers receive their opportunity costs so their income levels are constant, and the monopolist who costlessly organized these deals walks away with all the surplus. Note the consistency of this behavior with the MR = MC rule: we are simply asserting that the marginal revenue for each unit equals the height of the demand curve above it.

---

[11] This assumes that the consumer surplus under the ordinary demand curve is close to the compensating and equivalent variations (Chapter 6).

Perfect price discrimination, in which each unit is sold at a price equal to the full marginal value to the customer, is sometimes referred to as "first-degree" price discrimination. This might be a good description of an auction to purchase individual units of a homogeneous good, where the highest bidders win and pay the (differing) amounts that they bid. In 1994, for example, the Federal Communications Commission auctioned off rights to portions of the radio spectrum for Interactive Video Data Services. The two highest bidders in each metropolitan area paid their respective bids and received identical licenses. Of course, the use of the auction implies that the seller does not have perfect information about the willingness to pay of customers, and indeed the auction is a clever mechanism intended to obtain and make use of this information. Note that no one would bid "high" at this type of auction if the winners could resell the auctioned goods immediately afterward at the market-clearing price.[12]

Types of price discrimination other than first degree are more common. Models of them generally recognize from the start that the monopolist has imperfect information, faces costs to obtain increased information, and also faces transaction costs if it tries to prevent resales. These factors can deter the monopolist from discriminating at all, and their significance varies with the type of good or service. For example, it may be virtually costless to prevent the resale of electricity once delivered to a home, whereas it may be prohibitively expensive for the manufacturer to try and prevent the resale of ink cartridges for computer printers. Still, the profit-maximizing monopolist should be expected to price-discriminate whenever the costs of doing so are lower than the incremental profits to be derived.

Other types of price discrimination are usually classified as "second degree" or "third degree." **In second-degree price discrimination, the firm offers all buyers the same price schedule, but the average (and marginal) price varies with the quantity bought.** This is common with electricity and water. It sometimes occurs more subtly in what is called a "tie-in" sale, where a service such as copying is provided by a lease rate for the copying machine combined with an agreement to supply paper with a per-copy charge. **Third-degree price discrimination refers to a situation in which the seller segments the market into different groups, charging each group a different price.** A key factor in the monopolist's decision to segment, in addition to the ease of preventing resales across segments, is the difference in the elasticities of demand across the segments.

To see this, consider the monopolist's problem of how to select an output level and whether to divide it between two groups and charge each group a different price. To maximize profit, the monopolist must choose an output level and so divide it that the marginal revenue in each group is the same ($MR_1 = MR_2$) and equal to the common MC. If $MR_1 \neq MR_2$, more revenue (for the same cost) could be generated by moving some of the output

---

[12] The market-clearing price is simply the price at which supply equals demand. Under certain conditions, including unconstrained resale allowed, the expected revenue from the (attempted) price-discriminatory auction is no different from the expected revenue of an auction for the same goods to be sold at a uniform price. For further information about the economics of auctions, see Paul Milgrom, "Auctions and Bidding: A Primer," *Journal of Economic Perspectives, 3,* No. 3, Summer 1989, pp. 3–22.

to where the marginal revenue is highest. To see the implications of this, first we must derive a more general result that is itself of interest:

$$MR = P(1 + \tfrac{1}{\varepsilon})$$

where P is the price per unit and ε is the price elasticity of demand.

This equation is important in empirical work because it allows estimation of the MR from knowledge of the current price and the demand elasticity. Its derivation is fairly simple. In Figure 10-3 we show a demand curve with initial price of P and quantity Q. If we increase the quantity by ΔQ (and therefore price must decrease by ΔP) the change in total revenue ΔR is simply the difference between the two shaded rectangles[13]:

$$\Delta R = \Delta Q P - \Delta P Q$$

Dividing both sides by ΔQ, the left-hand side is then equal (by definition) to the marginal revenue:

$$\frac{\Delta R}{\Delta Q} = MR = P - \frac{\Delta P}{\Delta Q} Q$$

This can be rewritten as

$$MR = P\left(1 - \frac{\Delta P}{\Delta Q} \frac{Q}{P}\right)$$

or, recalling that the price elasticity is defined as negative,

$$MR = P\left(1 + \frac{1}{\varepsilon}\right)$$

Note that for this expression to be positive, the elasticity must be less than −1 (i.e., elastic, like −2). So *a profit-maximizing monopolist will locate at an elastic point on its customers' demand curve.* Now, to return to the discriminating monopolist and ignoring for the moment the costs of segmenting, profit maximization requires that $MR_1 = MR_2 = MC$, or equivalently,

$$P_1\left(1 + \frac{1}{\varepsilon_1}\right) = P_2\left(1 + \frac{1}{\varepsilon_2}\right) = MC$$

Thus, the monopolist would charge the same price to each group only if $\varepsilon_1 = \varepsilon_2$. Total revenues (for a given output level) can be increased whenever the entire market can be segmented into groups that have differing elasticities of demand. The higher price will be

---

[13] This derivation is an approximation. The first term on the right-hand side is actually $\Delta Q(P - \Delta P)$, and we are assuming that $\Delta Q \Delta P$ is approximately zero. This approximation is not necessary for the calculus derivation:

$$\frac{\partial TR}{\partial Q} = MR = \frac{\partial(P \cdot Q)}{\partial Q} = P + \frac{\partial P}{\partial Q} Q = P\left(1 + \frac{1}{\varepsilon}\right)$$

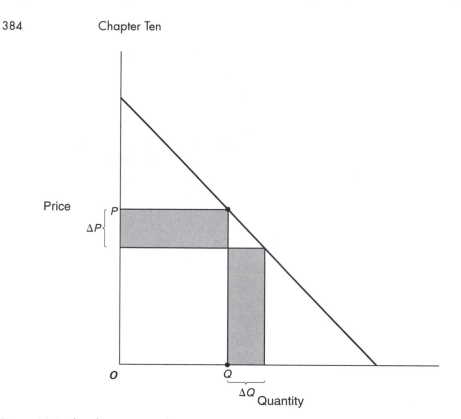

Figure 10-3. The change in total revenue owing to a quantity increase.

charged to the segment that has the least-elastic demand. The monopolist should be expected to do this whenever the increase in total revenues from the segmentation exceeds the cost of achieving the segmentation. Of course, by the same principle the monopolist could find it profitable to further segment the market, and in the limit this would be the perfectly discriminating monopolist.

Normative Consequences of Price Discrimination

To put these examples into a policy context, let us briefly explain some of the conventional normative reactions to price discrimination by organizations with monopoly power. Basically, price discrimination can occur in many different situations, and there is no general conclusion about its effects in terms of equity or efficiency (compared to monopoly with no price discrimination). We illustrate the reasons for this ambiguity below.

First let us consider equity. Price discrimination results in a transfer of income away from consumers to the owners of the monopoly: This is as we suggested in Figure 10-2, where the perfectly discriminating monopolist captures the entire consumer surplus. Furthermore, even the imperfect discriminator must capture more of it than the nondiscriminating monopolist: If profits were not higher, it would not discriminate. If the discrimination has negligible allocative effects (i.e., essentially the same consumers end up with the same quantity of goods), the equity of the outcome depends on who the monopoly owners are compared to the consumers with reduced surplus. For example, supposing a public utility providing electricity and natural gas charges residential consumers substantially more than the marginal cost of the service: This type of transfer is unlikely to be viewed as socially desirable. (The average utility shareholder is generally wealthier than the average household.)

On the other hand, often relatively wealthy consumers as a group are less price-elastic than others. For example, some airlines may have monopolies over certain routes. These airlines may engage in second-degree price discrimination by their pricing of first-class and coach tickets. Of course these are not the same goods—there are more comfortable, spacious seats and better food and drink service in first-class. However, think of first-class as simply "more service," or a greater quantity, than coach. If the price for traveling first-class is disproportionately higher than its marginal cost (compared to coach), this would be a form of price discrimination that primarily extracts surplus from those who are already relatively wealthy. If the owners of the monopoly route receive the surplus, and they are also relatively wealthy, then the income redistribution is occurring primarily within one wealth class rather than across different classes. Whereas there still may be social concern about this, it is presumably a lesser concern than the prior example.

If one considers cases in which price discrimination does have allocative effects (i.e., changes the quantity of the good purchased by consumers), society might actually favor the redistribution that occurs. Suppose, for example, that a physician in a rural town provides below-cost services to the poor (not covered by Medicaid) by charging fees above costs to the wealthier residents. If it were not for this price discrimination, the poor might not receive the medical services at all.[14] The same can be said for the provision of legal services to both rich and poor through price discrimination.

Let us turn to the efficiency consequences of price discrimination. As we shall see, it is difficult to generalize: Sometimes price discrimination will increase efficiency and sometimes it will reduce it. In the cases where price discrimination improves efficiency, the overall output level increases.[15] Our earlier example of perfect price discrimination was an efficiency-increasing case (compared to the nondiscriminating profit maximum). A more interesting case with a similar result is illustrated below.

In some situations, a good or service may be provided efficiently even if there is no single price at which it can be sold profitably. This sometimes arises when average costs decline over the range of output relevant to demand. Urban transit systems, for example, may fit this pattern: very large start-up costs followed by low operating costs and demand that is only moderate relative to the total costs. The rule that we use to evaluate situations like these is, of course, the usual one: *Producing the output improves relative efficiency if the total benefits minus total costs are positive, and the most efficient output level is the one that maximizes net benefits.*

---

[14] Note that it is primarily ill individuals that frequent the doctor. One might think it preferable to provide the subsidy from all wealthy individuals, not just ill, wealthy individuals.

[15] See R. Schmalensee, "Output and Welfare Implications of Monopolistic Third-Degree Discrimination," *American Economic Review, 71*, No. 1, March 1981, pp. 242–247.

For example, suppose it costs $600,000 to build a bridge, but once it is built bridge service may be provided at a constant marginal cost per crossing of $1 (say, to pay for maintenance). Then the average cost per crossing begins at $600,001 and declines as quantity expands. Suppose that the demand curve for bridge service is given by the following equation:

$$P = 21 - Q/5000$$

The demand and marginal cost curves are drawn in Figure 10-4, except that the initial $600,000 cost is omitted. The most efficient quantity is 100,000 crossings, where the demand (or marginal benefit) curve intersects the marginal cost curve. At this point, the consumer surplus of $1,000,000 [= ½(21−1)(100,000)] easily exceeds the $600,000 start-up cost, yielding positive net benefits of $400,000.[16] However, a firm that does not price-discriminate cannot provide this service profitably: In order to sell 100,000 crossings, it can charge no more than $1 and it will not recover any of its initial investment. Indeed, even if the nondiscriminating firm seeks its profit-maximizing solution, it will conclude that it is better off not building the bridge.

If it does build the bridge, then it identifies the profit-maximizing quantity by finding the intersection of its marginal revenue curve with the marginal cost curve. This is also shown in Figure 10-4. The marginal revenue curve is derived from the demand curve and has the following equation[17]:

$$MR = 21 - 2Q/5000$$

This is equal to the marginal cost of $1 at $Q = 50,000$. The (nondiscriminatory) price that must be charged to sell this quantity is $P = \$11$ per crossing (the height of the demand curve when $Q = 50,000$). However, at this price the firm only collects $500,000 above its marginal costs [= (11 − 1)(50,000)], still not enough to recover its $600,000 start-up cost. If this is the best operating alternative open to it, the firm will, of course, choose not to produce at all: zero profit is better than a loss. However, from a social point of view it would be more efficient to provide this output: the total costs of $650,000 (= $600,000 start-up + $50,000 maintenance) are less than the total benefits of $800,000 (the area under the demand curve up to 50,000 crossings). *Thus the private nondiscriminating firm will not supply any of this output despite the fact that the social benefits of its provision exceed the social costs.*

[16] If the net benefits were negative, it would be most efficient to forgo building the bridge.

[17] We already know that marginal revenue is the change in total revenue associated with the sale of one additional unit of output. In calculus terms, this is expressed as

$$MR = \frac{\partial P(Q)Q}{\partial Q} = P + Q\frac{\partial P}{\partial Q}$$

For any linear demand curve $P = a - bQ$, the marginal revenue curve is MR = $a - 2bQ$. To see this, note that $\partial P/\partial Q = -b$, and therefore

$$P + Q\frac{\partial P}{\partial Q} = a - bQ - bQ = a - 2bQ$$

In our example, $a = 21$ and $b = 1/5000$. This means the marginal revenue curve is MR = $21 - 2Q/5000$.

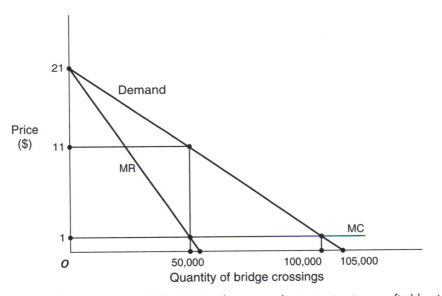

Figure 10-4. Profit-maximization (MR = MC) without price discrimination is unprofitable given high start-up costs (not shown).

In this situation price discrimination can lead to an improvement in the allocation of resources. For example, if the firm can perfectly price-discriminate, it will produce 100,000 crossings. Even if the firm can only imperfectly discriminate, it may be able to extract enough from consumers with less-elastic demand to make the operation profitable.

For example, suppose the demand for bridge crossings comes from two groups: trucks and cars. Note that it is easy to separate the market into these two groups, and that it is difficult to resell a crossing right.[18] In order to keep the example as simple as possible, let us assume that the demand for trucks is represented by the first 50,000 crossings demanded on the total demand curve, so that we already know that the profit-maximizing price for this segment is $11 and that it contributes $500,000 toward the start-up costs.[19] Then the demand from cars comes entirely from the portion of the aggregate demand curve with $Q >$ 50,000, and its individual equation is

$$P = 11 - Q/5000$$

The monopolist is now free to set a profit-maximizing price for cars only (thus increasing profits and total quantity provided over the earlier nondiscriminatory profit maximum).

[18] It is essentially impossible if the right is purchased by toll at the point of service. If rights may be purchased in advance (e.g., a monthly book with coupons for twenty crossings), then the monopolist must prevent resales across classes by some system such as differently sized and colored coupons or tokens (e.g., big and red for trucks, little and green for cars).

[19] This is an unusual assumption made for pedagogical reasons. Normally one would expect that any major subgroup in a market (like the truck subgroup) would have some additional demand as price continues to drop (in this case below $11). However, we are assuming that truck demand is completely exhausted after 50,000

Following the logic as before, the monopolist identifies the marginal revenue curve from cars and finds the quantity at which $MR = MC = 1$. The marginal revenue curve is

$$MR = 11 - 2Q/5000$$

and this becomes equal to $1 when $Q = 25,000$. The price associated with this quantity on the cars' demand curve is $6, and thus the monopolist will receive $125,000 above marginal costs from cars. But this means that the operation is profitable: A total of $625,000 is raised above the marginal costs, more than covering the $600,000 bridge-building costs. Compared to the "no bridge" solution without price discrimination, this price discrimination makes car drivers, truck drivers, and the bridge owner all better off.[20]

So far, we have only illustrated price discrimination that improves efficiency. However, it is easy to illustrate price discrimination that reduces efficiency, and there is no consensus about which type is empirically more common. One way that price discrimination reduces efficiency is by reducing exchange efficiency among the product's consumers. Without discrimination all consumers of the product have the same marginal rate of substitution, but with discrimination their rates will usually differ.[21]

To illustrate the inefficiency empirically, we use one final bridge-crossing example, making some minor changes in the problem. First, assume the start-up costs are only $450,000 (so that a nondiscriminatory profit-maximizing monopolist will find it profitable to build and operate the bridge). Second, we change the demand curves for trucks and cars as separate groups. The new demand curves are

$$P_T = 24 - \frac{Q_T}{2000}$$

$$P_C = 19 - \frac{Q_C}{3000}$$

When these two linear demand curves are added to identify the market demand curve, the result is a kinked demand curve as shown in Figure 10-5. This happens because for prices above $19, the demand from cars is zero and the market curve coincides with the truck demand. It is only for prices below $19 that both cars and trucks are demanding pos-

---

crossings, even if the price should fall below $11. Similarly, we are making the unusual assumption that no car driver will demand a crossing at any price above $11. These assumptions allow us to associate one portion of the market demand curve ($P > \$11$) with trucks and the other ($P < \$11$) with cars. In the normal case, there would be both truck and car demands in each segment.

[20] There are other organizational alternatives besides letting a profit-seeking firm price discriminate, and the example is not intended to suggest that allowing price discrimination is preferable to them. For example, later in the text we shall consider examples of public enterprises as well as public subsidies to private firms; both of these alternatives could be considered for the situation assumed here.

[21] An exception is first-degree or perfect price discrimination, because each consumer ends up with a marginal rate of substitution equal to marginal cost (each buys the same units as when the price is uniform and equal to the marginal cost).

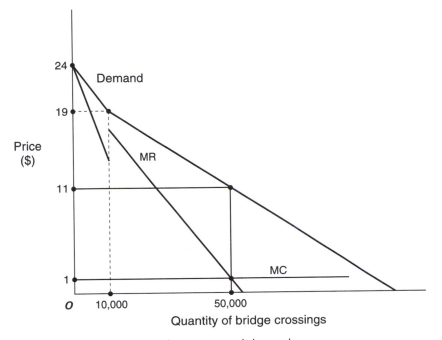

Figure 10-5. Profit-maximization with a segmented demand curve.

itive quantities that must be added; this lower portion of the demand curve coincides (by design) with the aggregate demand used previously. The marginal revenue curve also has two segments (shown in Figure 10-5), but the intersection with MC = $1 is at $Q = 50,000$ (26,000 trucks and 24,000 cars) and $P = \$11$ as before.

The cost of providing 50,000 crossings is now $500,000 ($50,000 operating + $450,000 start-up), so that the total benefits are $815,000 (not $800,000 as previously).[22] Therefore the social surplus (total benefits minus total costs) at the nondiscriminatory profit maximization is $315,000. We want to compare this to the solution with price discrimination.

The truck and car crossing demand curves, along with their corresponding marginal revenue curves (MR_T, MR_C) and the profit-maximizing solutions in each market segment are illustrated in Figures 10-6a and b. The MR_T becomes equal to $1 (the marginal cost) at 23,000 crossings, with trucks charged $12.50. At the $MR_C = MC$ solution for cars, they are charged only $10.00 and demand 27,000 crossings. The aggregate number of crossings remains at 50,000, and thus total costs remain at $500,000. However, the benefits (the areas under the two demand curves up to the quantity consumed) are $419,750 from truck

[22] Referring to Figure 10-5, we add the area under the demand curve for the first 10,000 units (the first segment) to the area under the second segment between 10,000 and 50,000 units. Each of these areas can be viewed as a right triangle atop a rectangle, and thus the total area of $815,000 is calculated as follows: $[\frac{1}{2}(24 - 19)(10,000) + (19)(10,000)] + [(\frac{1}{2})(19 - 11)(40,000) + (11)(40,000)]$.

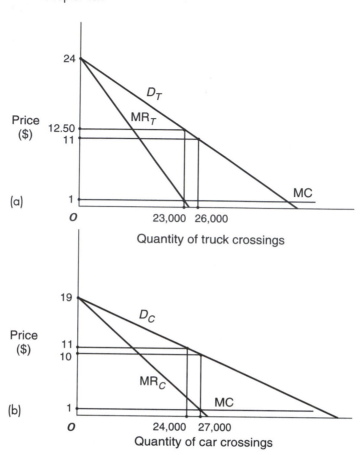

Figure 10-6. Profit-maximization with price discrimination can reduce efficiency: (a) The profit-maximizing truck crossing price is $12.50 (where $MR_T = MC$). (b) The profit-maximizing car crossing price is $10.00 (where $MR_C = MC$).

crossings and $391,500 from car crossings, or $811,250 total.[23] These benefits, $3750 less than from the nondiscriminatory solution, leave a social surplus of only $311,250. Thus the discriminatory solution has reduced relative efficiency.

Let us be sure that the cause of this result is clear. The 50,000 crossings provided are no longer being allocated to those who value them the most: More cars and fewer trucks get the crossings than under the nondiscriminatory solution. There are 3000 truckers beyond the 23,000 who are willing to pay at least $11.00 to cross the bridge, and there are 3000 car-crossers who value their crossings at no more than $11.00 (thus there is room to improve

---

[23] These benefits are calculated as follows, in each case viewing the relevant area in Figures 10-6a and b as a right triangle atop a rectangle:

$$\$419{,}750 = \tfrac{1}{2}(24.00 - 12.50)(23{,}000) + (12.50)(23{,}000)$$

$$\$391{,}500 = \tfrac{1}{2}(19.00 - 10.00)(27{,}000) + (10.00)(27{,}000)$$

Table 10-1
Price Discrimination Can Reduce Efficiency:
A Bridge Crossing Example

Net benefits	Uniform pricing	Discriminatory pricing
Monopolist's profits	$ 50,000	$ 57,500
Truckers' surplus	169,000	132,250
Car drivers' surplus	96,000	121,500
Total	**$315,000**	**$311,250**

exchange efficiency). The monopolist, however, worries about the marginal revenue: Lowering the truck price a little from $12.50 would attract more truckers, but it also means less revenue would get collected from the first 23,000. At the profit-maximizing discriminatory solution, the monopolist receives revenues of $557,500, and thus profits of $57,500. Thus the monopolist is better off by $7500 than without discrimination, even though net social benefits are reduced.

Table 10-1 summarizes the results of this last analysis in a slightly different way. The net benefits to each group (truckers, car drivers, and the monopolist) are shown under the profit-maximizing solutions with and without price discrimination. The big losers from the price discrimination are the truckers. Both the monopolist and car drivers are better off with price discrimination. Society as a whole loses: The loss to the truckers exceeds the gains to the others.

In a moment we will present a variety of actual situations in which price discrimination is observed in order to suggest some of the subtlety with which it occurs. But first let us emphasize a main analytic theme motivating this analysis. Predicting the actual behavior of an organization, even with total certainty about its objectives and capabilities and its market demand curve, is not simple. Major differences in behavior can arise because of variations in information and transactions costs under alternative marketing arrangements, and the latter are not easy to understand or recognize in advance. Nevertheless the effects of policies (and therefore their design and desirability) can depend on them. We are using an organization's decision about whether to price-discriminate as an example of this.

To clarify that it is information and transaction costs that are key determinants of the monopolist's decision about price discrimination, let us work through an additional example. In Figure 10-7, we consider whether or not a monopolist will implement a first-degree (perfect) price-discrimination strategy, with one new wrinkle: The cost of identifying each consumer's evaluation and preventing resale to other consumers (to be discussed further shortly) is constant per unit of output and raises the marginal cost curve to MC′. The monopolist will discriminate as long as it is profitable to do so, that is, if the profits with discrimination $P_D GH$ exceed the profits without discrimination $P_E P_M AB$:

$$P_D GH - P_E P_M AB > 0$$

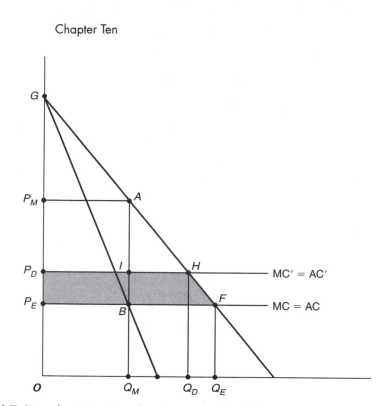

Figure 10-7. Price discrimination when it is costly (shaded).

Since these areas have the rectangle $P_D P_M AI$ in common, we can subtract it from both areas to get an equivalent expression:

$$P_M GA + IAH - P_E P_D IB > 0$$

Now let us compare this with the deadweight losses in each situation. We have already seen that BAF is the deadweight loss from a nondiscriminating monopoly. The deadweight loss from the discriminating monopolist is $P_E P_D HF$, assuming that MC reflects the least-cost method of production.[24] Thus, purely from the standpoint of relative efficiency, discrimination is preferable if it has a smaller deadweight loss:

$$BAF - P_E P_D HF > 0$$

Since these areas have $BIHF$ in common, we can subtract it from both to derive an equivalent expression:

$$IAH - P_E P_D IB > 0$$

Comparing this expression with the one that the monopolist uses in deciding whether to discriminate, we see that they are different by only one term, $P_M GA$. The monopolist may

---

[24] Society used to receive alternate outputs from the resources now being devoted to achieving the price discrimination. This use of them adds nothing of social value, and it is the bulk of the social loss.

choose to discriminate even though resource allocation may be more efficient under the nondiscriminating monopolist. This further illustrates why the efficiency effects of price discrimination (compared to a nondiscriminating monopoly) are ambiguous.

The Robinson-Patman Act and the Sherman Antitrust Act

With these theoretical examples in mind, let us consider public policy with respect to price discrimination. In Chapter 3 we mentioned that the Robinson-Patman Act of 1936 prohibits certain price discrimination. The act prohibits charging different prices to different purchasers for "goods of like grade and quality" where the effect may be to "lessen competition." The latter clause means this act does not usually apply to "natural monopoly" situations, where there is no competition. A natural monopoly occurs whenever the minimum cost of supplying market demand by one firm is lower than the minimum cost if supplied by multiple firms.[25] We earlier illustrated an unprofitable natural monopoly, although the profitable situations, such as for local delivery of electricity and natural gas, are probably more common. Generally local gas and electric companies do have rate structures characterized by price discrimination, but they are subjected to review by regulatory commissions and not challenged under Robinson-Patman.

The Robinson-Patman Act had its origins during the Great Depression, when skepticism about the effects of competition was particularly high. This was a time in which large retail chain stores were expanding, entering new markets, and underselling the existing small and independent stores. The intent of the legislation was really to protect the small firms from competition. A standard complaint of the small businesses was that suppliers would sell to the chain at a lower per-unit price, which enabled the chains to undersell the independents. However, to the extent that the lower prices were associated with reduced costs of supplying larger and perhaps more stable orders, preventing the lower prices would reduce efficiency.

Let us clarify this. We have been referring to price discrimination as charging different prices for the same good or service. In the models we have been using so far this definition has been satisfactory. But in the more complicated real world **price discrimination includes a variety of situations that may arise in which the prices a company charges for similar units of a good vary disproportionately with the marginal costs of supplying them.** In the chain store example above, lower prices owing to lower costs would not be discriminatory by the definition. Indeed, producing any given output level at a lower cost is an efficiency improvement. However, Robinson-Patman has often been applied to prevent these benefits from competition.[26]

---

[25] This is equivalent to the cost function being subadditive over the range of market demand.

[26] In a case brought by the Federal Trade Commission, cited by F. M. Scherer and D. Ross, the Morton Salt Company was found in violation of Robinson-Patman because it charged lower prices for bigger orders of its table salt. However, it did so primarily because of transportation economies. The Supreme Court in its decision noted that Congress was especially concerned with protecting small businesses. This policy interpretation fails to make the crucial distinction between harm to competitors and harm to the vigor of competition. For a more extensive

Let us consider another example. Suppose a company charges two customers a different price for the same item because the shipping costs to the customer farther away are higher than those to the customer nearby. This is not considered price discrimination by the analytic definition, nor is it a violation of Robinson-Patman. (The latter specifically exempts price differences owing to delivery cost differences.) If the company charges these two consumers the same price despite the delivery cost differences, that is price discrimination by the analytic definition. However, this practice also would fail to violate Robinson-Patman: One must first show a price *difference* before the claim of price discrimination will be heard.

Another situation that is considered price discrimination by the analytic definition but not by Robinson-Patman concerns quality differences. Suppose one company tries to segment its market by creating two slightly different products: a "premium brand" (perhaps heavily advertised) and a "regular brand." We earlier gave the example of airline services (first-class and coach); another example would be hardbound and paperbound editions of the same book. If the price differential is proportionate to the marginal cost differences of producing the two editions, there is no discrimination by our analytic definition. But if one edition is priced proportionately greater than its marginal cost compared to the other—as is often alleged for hardbound books—the publisher is trying to exploit the elasticity difference between the market segments by price-discriminating. However, this is unlikely to be viewed as a violation of Robinson-Patman because the law applies only to "goods of like grade and quality."

The charge of price discrimination is sometimes raised in the context of antitrust enforcement, where a firm may be accused of **predatory pricing** with intent to monopolize in violation of the Sherman Antitrust Act of 1890. This **refers to a firm strategy of charging a price that is below cost and intended to drive a competitor who is equally or more efficient out of business.** The link to price discrimination is that the alleged predator firm is often observed to charge a higher price for the same good in other locations.

Like the problems with the Robinson-Patman Act, it is very difficult to identify true predatory pricing in practice. First, there are common short-run situations in which competition and efficiency are enhanced by pricing below average total cost.[27] The courts have not always recognized this. Some scholars have tried to remedy this problem by advocating that average variable cost be used as the legal boundary (below which pricing would be predatory).[28] However, other scholars remain unconvinced that this would be an improvement.

---

discussion of this and other aspects of price discrimination, see F. M. Scherer and D. Ross, *Industrial Market Structure and Economic Performance*, 3rd Ed. (Boston: Houghton Mifflin Company, 1990), Chapter 13.

[27] The short run refers to a period of time in which a firm has certain fixed inputs for which it must pay (like plant depreciation). In Chapter 12 we review a standard microeconomic result that shows that a firm will choose to produce in the short run as long as it can cover its average variable costs, even if the average total costs are not covered (it loses money, but it would lose even more by shutting down production).

[28] This is sometimes known as the Areeda-Turner rule. See P. Areeda and D. F. Turner, "Predatory Pricing and Related Practices under Section 2 of the Sherman Act," *Harvard Law Review*, February 1975.

On theoretical grounds, one can construct models that suggest that predatory pricing is a good strategy for a firm. These models apply in particular situations characterized by information asymmetries and strategic uncertainty, and they deserve further investigation.[29] How commonly these theoretical circumstances are found in actual settings is an unanswered question. The only reason for a firm to accept the loss associated with predation is if it believes that the strategy will generate future profit that more than compensates for it. Future profits would seem to depend on deterring the entry of future competitors, a capability that is apparently lacking in the current competitive situation. Thus many economists suspect that situations in which predatory pricing is a rational temptation are rare. However, the U. S. Justice Department argued, and in April 2000 federal judge Thomas Penfield Jackson agreed, that the Microsoft Corporation pursued a strategy of predatory pricing in violation of the Sherman Antitrust Act; a main argument involved the short-run losses Microsoft incurred in order to enhance its Internet Explorer's share of web browser usage relative to its rival Netscape's Navigator.[30]

Predicting Price Discrimination

Let us turn to predictive matters. Where and how does price discrimination arise? First of all, a producing organization must have *market power, which generally means some ability to control the price in the market.*[31] That is why we discuss this in connection with monopoly; a firm in a perfectly competitive environment (i.e., one facing a horizontal demand curve) does not control the market price and therefore cannot price-discriminate. Lerner has suggested that market power M be measured as the following[32]:

$$M = \frac{P - MC}{P}$$

For the firm in a perfectly competitive environment, $P = MC$ (as in Figure 10-1b) and therefore $M = 0$. For the monopolist in Figure 10-2, $P > MC$. The measure has an upper bound of $M = 1$ unless some organization finds a way to produce at negative marginal cost. If the firm has constant-returns-to-scale technology, so that $MC = AC$, then this measure is simply profits as a percent of sales. For a profit-maximizing firm, $MR = MC$, and since $MR = P(1 + 1/\varepsilon)$

$$M = \frac{P - MC}{P} = -\frac{1}{\varepsilon}$$

[29] See Alvin K. Klevorick, "The Current State of the Law and Economics of Predatory Pricing," *American Economic Review, 83,* No. 2, May 1993, pp. 162–167, and David Roth, "Rationalizable Predatory Pricing," *Journal of Economic Theory, 68,* 1996, pp. 380–396.

[30] See *United States vs. Microsoft Corp.,* No. 98-1232 TPJ (D.D.C., April 3, 2000).

[31] Market power is discussed more extensively in Chapter 18.

[32] Abba P. Lerner, The Concepts of Monopoly and the Measurement of Monopoly Power," *Review of Economic Studies, 1,* June 1934, pp. 157–175.

This suggests that the more inelastic the demand, the greater the market power. Recall that this demand elasticity is for the demand curve facing the firm, not necessarily the whole market. Note also that, since $M \leq 1$, then $\varepsilon < -1$. That is, the monopolist must choose to operate on an elastic portion of the demand curve. This may be seen another way. The profit maximum cannot be on the inelastic portion. On that portion, one can raise the price and increase revenues while reducing output and costs, and thereby increase profit.

Two other conditions, in addition to market power, help explain when price discrimination may arise: the cost of segmenting the market in the first place and the cost of keeping it segmented (preventing resales from customers who buy at a low price to those willing to pay a higher price). These are the information and transaction costs to which we referred earlier.

One group of commodities that are not easily resalable is services: for example, health care, legal advice, accounting, taxi rides, restaurant meals, automobile fuel, and servicing stations. From the health insurance discussion in Chapter 7 it should be apparent that insured patients may be charged more than others for essentially the same services. As another example, compare the price of gasoline along limited-access highways with the price in suburban or urban areas (where there is more competition). Sometimes there is an interesting policy twist to this opportunity for price discrimination: The government may sell the right to operate a service station on its highway by competitive bid. What it is doing, in effect, is extracting from the supplier the value of the profits that will be made from the price discrimination. The consumers suffer either way. Of course, these government arrangements are more likely to arise when the motorists are not voting residents of the jurisdiction and do not have attractive alternate routes.

Another group of commodities that are not easily resalable includes utilities: telephone, electricity, water, and so forth. Large industrial users of electricity, for example, may be charged lower rates not because it is cheaper to serve them, but because they are able to use substitute sources of power and so have a more-elastic demand. An interesting variant of this group might be the recipients of such local government goods and services as police and fire protection, which are paid for through taxes. The tax assessor may charge industrial users less (i.e., assess the property at a relatively low proportion of its true market value) neither because they use less nor because it is a principle of just taxation, but simply because these users have more elastic demand for the services (i.e., are more likely to relocate elsewhere).

Ordinary durable goods are much easier to resell, so price discrimination is likely to be tied to something associated with the good. For example, in recent years some automobile manufacturers have offered interest rebates to consumers who finance their purchases through loans, and this lowers the price for one segment of the market demand. Some very clever schemes for price discriminating and simultaneously obtaining the information about the consumer's demand curve have been concocted. At one time, Xerox copying machines were leased rather than sold, which avoided the resale problem. Furthermore, the monthly charge was based on the number of copies made (far in excess of the actual marginal costs of the copies), and that allowed the company to extract more of the surplus from consumers with high willingness to pay. A similar result can be achieved with a tie-in sale if, as a condition of the lease, all copying paper must be bought from the same company. The Polaroid

Corporation, when its cameras were novel, could effectively price-discriminate as the exclusive supplier of film for the cameras.[33]

In the discussion to this point we have assumed that the organization both seeks and is able to maximize its profits. We have illustrated that some of the insights about such a firm's behavior are derived from very simple changes in the constraints of the model: The ordinary predicted monopoly behavior follows from a change in the shape of the demand constraint the firm faces (from horizontal in the competitive case to downward-sloping in the monopoly case). This leads to the conclusion that monopoly is inefficient. However, the very concepts that are used to understand why firms exist also indicate that predicting actual behavior is more complex than the simple model suggests. If there were no information or transaction costs, all monopolists would be perfect price discriminators. The fact that they are not suggests that the organizational costs are nontrivial, and it is closer examination of these costs that helps explain some of the observed variations in monopoly behavior (e.g., the extent of price discrimination). By developing this understanding, we increase our capacity to design policies that take this behavior into account. Now let us turn to another source of variation in organizational behavior: the objectives.

Alternative Models of Organizational Objectives and Capabilities[S]

In the preceding section we made the assumption that a firm's objective is to maximize profits. However, we did not include any discussion of why that should be. The simplest reason is that the firm is run in the interests of its owners. The owners are attempting to maximize their own budget constraints because that is what allows them to achieve the highest utility levels. Therefore, the owners are best served by operating the firm in such a way as to maximize profits.

However, this simple reasoning ignores a number of fundamental points, which we discuss below: (1) Because of information and transaction costs, the owners of a firm may not be able to exert perfect control over the behavior of its managers and other employees. Thus the firm's behavior may be influenced by the objectives of this latter group. (2) The owners of a firm may receive utility directly from operating the firm rather than purely from the dollar profit derived from it (e.g., pride in being the first with a new product). If that is so, the owners may seek to operate the firm in a way that trades off dollar profits for the activities that give them utility directly. (3) Because of organizational bounded rationality, which includes the limits of individual information-processing abilities as well as the information and transaction costs of communicating and coordinating within a firm, the actions of a firm may not be those required for profit maximization even if every participant in the firm strives for it.

---

[33] Tie-in sales may be prevented under Section 3 of the 1914 Clayton Act. For example, IBM once required those using its key-punch and card-sorting equipment to purchase IBM cards. However, the Supreme Court in 1936 ruled this a violation of Section 3.

Few students of organizations doubt the validity of this complexity of motivations and capabilities. The crux of the controversy within the economics profession over the acceptability of the profit maximization assumption concerns the range and accuracy of the predictions that can be made with it (compared to alternative models). The most powerful argument in its favor appears to be that it generates good predictions for firms in a competitive environment. The best explanation for why it makes good predictions is that the survival of a firm in that environment requires that the firm make decisions consistent with profit maximization.

However, many producing organizations are not in very competitive environments and therefore may have considerable degrees of freedom in making choices that allow them to survive. Thus, at a minimum, discussion of organizational intentions and capabilities enhances analytic skill in predicting behavior in these latter environments. We reinforce this in the next chapter with some examples of the behavior of nonprofit organizations and public bureaucracies.

Objectives Other than Profit Maximization

The first point made above that might cause behavior other than profit maximization has to do with the control of the organization. The control problem becomes significant in the larger firms, e.g., firms where there is separation between the owners (stockholders) and managers. Stockholders are often widely dispersed, and each may hold only a very small percentage of the firm's total equity. This makes it difficult for stockholders to be knowledgeable about the firm's alternative strategies, to express their desires about the firm's direction, or to build a sufficient coalition of owners in order to exercise effective command over management.[34]

The problem of owner control over firm managers is, of course, another example of *a principal-agent problem.* The owner-principals, recognizing their limited knowledge of the manager-agents' alternatives and actions, try to create incentive for the managers to want to maximize profit. Thus it is not unusual for managers to be partially rewarded through profit-sharing and stock bonus plans. This alleviates the problem but does not solve it; the manager's utility can still be greater from actions that do not maximize the firm's profit.

Owners have other means for trying to enforce their wishes. Dissident stockholders have been known to wage battles with management in solicitation of proxies from all shareholders to elect members of the board of directors. Furthermore, stockholders do observe the results (profits) from the firm's decisions, if not the reasons underlying them. Even if a stockholder cannot use *voice* effectively, management will be pressured by too much *exit,* that is, sale of stock by unhappy shareholders.[35] Exit puts downward pressure on the price

---

[34] A classic reference on managerial control is Oliver Williamson, *The Economics of Discretionary Behavior: Management Objectives in a Theory of the Firm* (Englewood Cliffs, N.J.: Prentice-Hall, Inc., 1964).

[35] The terms *exit* and *voice* were first used by Albert Hirschman. We will discuss them in a later chapter: The basic reference to them is Hirschman's *Exit, Voice, and Loyalty: Response to Decline in Firms, Organizations, and States* (Cambridge: Harvard University Press, 1970).

of the stock, which makes it more difficult for management to raise new capital (e.g., from the issuance of additional stock) and easier for others to take over the company by purchasing stock.

Nevertheless, these mechanisms of stockholder control are imperfect at best, and it should not be surprising to find management's objectives receiving attention at the expense of some profit. When asked, management personnel readily admit to other goals: maximizing revenues, market share (percent of total industry output it provides), growth, and anything else that sounds reasonable. The logical impossibility of maximizing these variables simultaneously does not faze them.[36] A number of scholars have noted that managerial salaries tend to rise with the total revenues of the firm, and they have therefore suggested that *revenue maximization (equivalently called sales maximization) may be the goal that best serves managerial interests.* We illustrate the implications of this goal, as well as its inconsistency with the rival goal of profit maximization, for the behavior of a firm facing a downward-sloping demand curve for its product.

In Figure 10-8a we assume that a nondiscriminating monopolist is a revenue maximizer. If there were no profit constraint on its behavior, it would continue to increase quantity from any level at which marginal revenue is still positive (total revenue is getting bigger). It would stop at the quantity level where MR = 0, shown as Q_R. This is clearly more output than the profit-maximizing monopolist would produce (shown as Q_Π). However, it is unrealistic to think that a private profit-making firm could not be held to some account by its stockholders. Therefore, *we assume that the firm maximizes revenue subject to earning at least some minimum amount of profit* (greater than at Q_R but less than at Q_Π).

Under these conditions, it is still unambiguous that *the firm will produce more output than the profit maximizer.* At Q_Π the marginal revenue is still positive, so total revenue can be increased by expanding output. This will reduce profit from its maximum level, and the firm will travel as far down the marginal revenue curve as it can until profits are reduced to the constraint level. This will occur somewhere between Q_Π and Q_R, shown as $Q_{R\Pi}$ in the diagrams. The shaded area shows the total profits, which are equal to the constraint level.

Can we say anything about the allocative efficiency of the sales maximizer? The most efficient output level is Q_E, the level at which net social benefits are maximized (where marginal benefit, the height of the demand curve, equals marginal cost). As illustrated, the sales-maximizing monopolist is more efficient than the profit maximizer: The deadweight loss is smaller (*BAE* is less than *FCE*). However, perhaps the sales maximizer may produce too much output, that is, a quantity greater than Q_E. With constant-returns-to-scale technology, this is not possible: Profits are down to zero at Q_E, so the profit constraint keeps output less than Q_E. But in Figure 10-8b, another case is illustrated[37]: The sales maximizer

---

[36] This is demonstrated shortly. A common phrase that is also a logical impossibility is "getting the maximum output for the minimum cost." You can produce a *given* output at minimum cost or you can maximize output for a *given* cost, but you cannot maximize and minimize simultaneously. It is always possible, for example, to reduce costs by reducing output.

[37] A necessary condition for this case is that MC >AC at the point where MC intersects the demand curve, which in turn implies that the firm is producing on the rising portion of its average cost curve (usually associated

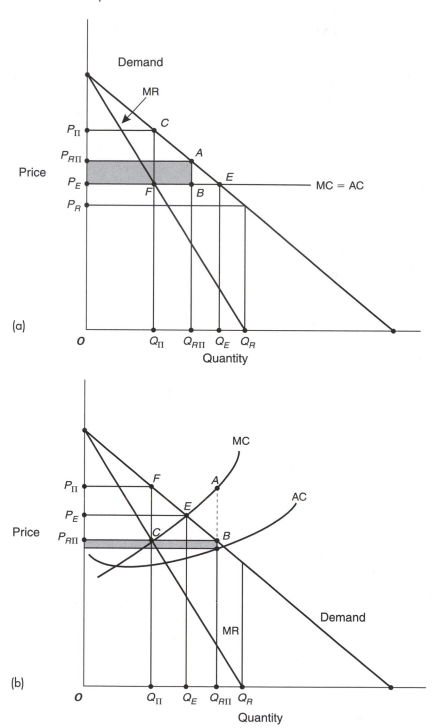

Figure 10-8. Revenue maximization with a minimum profit constraint: (a) The quantity is inefficiently low ($Q_{R\Pi} < Q_E$). (b) The quantity is inefficiently high ($Q_E < Q_{R\Pi}$).

will produce too much output, and the deadweight loss *EAB* can be greater than that of the profit maximizer *CFE*. Therefore, nothing in general can be said about the relative allocative efficiency of these two behaviors.

When we compare the equity of the two behaviors, it appears that consumers are better off if the monopolist is a sales maximizer. This happens because the sale of output levels greater than Q_Π requires that the price be lowered (from P_Π). Thus the total consumer surplus grows as quantity expands. The monopoly owners are being made worse off simultaneously, of course, but they are receiving economic profits in all cases.

Although managerial control may get exercised in ways other than the pursuit of sales maximization, any deviation from profit maximization should show up in reduced profitability of these firms compared to others. What evidence is there concerning variation in firm behavior under managerial versus owner control? The empirical evidence is somewhat mixed, although the bulk of it supports the idea that firm performance is affected by the degree of managerial control. For example, a review by Bolton and Scharfstein states (p. 109): "the most recent empirical literature suggests that internal capital markets do not work very well" and (p. 110) "Capital misallocation is more pronounced in conglomerates where management has small ownership stakes."[38] Relatedly, Scherer reviews the evidence from corporate takeovers and states: "In theory, tender offer takeovers provide a significant corrective against managerial departures from profit maximization. Careful scrutiny of the available evidence leads to a more skeptical assessment."[39]

What relevance has this to public policy and its analysis? Let us suggest briefly four types of applications. First and quite broadly, the antitrust laws of the nation—the Sherman Antitrust Act, the Clayton Act of 1914, and the Federal Trade Commission Act of 1914—are generally designed to promote competition and prevent monopoly and monopolistic practices. Considerable resources are spent every year by the government and by firms in the attempt to enforce these laws. In directing the enforcement efforts, it would seem sensible to allocate effort where it yields the greatest social return. By naively accepting one model of behavior when the empirical evidence is inconclusive, enforcement efforts can be misdirected. Enforcement is not going to wait for analysis to beco me definitive, but it is sensible to recognize that the social returns from one area of enforcement may be more uncertain than those from another (because of uncertainty about actual firm behavior) and to allow this uncertainty to influence the priorities of different enforcement possibilities.

A second area of policy that may be affected by these behavioral considerations is taxation. Figure 10-9 illustrates this point with a simple partial equilibrium analysis of the ef-

---

with diseconomies of scale). Monopolies can still be "natural" in this situation as long as the subadditive condition is met by the (least total) cost function: $C(Q) < C(Q_1) + C(Q_2)$, where Q is the monopoly quantity and Q_1 and Q_2 are production amounts of two separate firms with $Q_1 + Q_2 = Q$. This case arises when economies of scale characterize lower production levels and when they more than offset the diseconomies that set in at the higher level.

[38] Patrick Bolton and David S. Scharfstein, "Corporate Finance, the Theory of the Firm, and Organizations," *Journal of Economic Perspectives, 12*, No. 4, Fall 1998, pp. 95–114.

[39] F. M. Scherer, "Corporate Takeovers: The Efficiency Arguments," *Journal of Economic Perspectives, 2*, No. 1, Winter 1988, pp. 69–82.

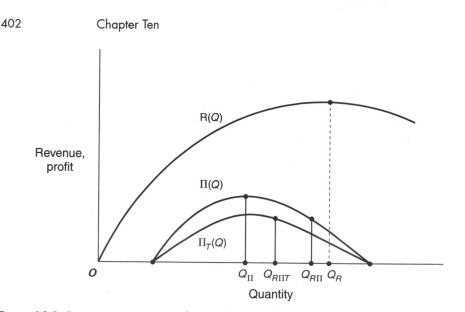

Figure 10-9. Firm response to a profits tax (Q_Π = profit maximum, $Q_{R\Pi T}$ = revenue maximum with profit constraint.

fects of a profit tax on the firm's output level. As before, we let Q_Π and $Q_{R\Pi}$ denote the profit-maximizing and sales-maximizing (with profit constraint) output levels, respectively (pretax). Now we imagine imposing a percentage tax (e.g., 50%) on the firm's profit. The after-tax profits curve is shown as $\Pi_T(Q)$. The tax does not change the quantity at which profits are maximized, so the behavior of the profit-maximizing firm is not affected (important general equilibrium effects are mentioned below). However, the revenue maximizer is no longer meeting its profit constraint at $Q_{R\Pi}$, since net profits have been reduced by the tax. Therefore, it will cut back on the output level until net profits once again satisfy the constraint, shown as $Q_{R\Pi}$.

This partial equilibrium analysis is not the end of the story about the effects of such a tax; it is only the beginning. In a general equilibrium model, we would, for example, consider investor reaction in terms of the supply of capital resources to the profit-maximizing firms. These investors might now prefer holding land to business equity and withdraw capital from the business sector. That, in turn, would raise the cost of capital to business, which would change cost curves and therefore choices of production techniques and levels. However, our purpose at this point is not to go into an in-depth analysis of taxation, but only to point out that the desirability of any particular tax policy can depend upon the firm's objectives.

A third example of the public policy relevance of this debate about firm objectives is in the area of corporate takeovers. In the United States during the 1980s, there was a takeover wave. While no single reason explains this wave, one factor was the increased use of debt financing instruments (including so-called junk bonds) to accomplish the takeover (the leveraged buyout). Since the takeovers engender considerable disruption and costly restructuring, often involving store or plant closings, job losses, and forced relocations, a number of states passed antitakeover laws to make them more difficult.

What do takeovers and their regulation have to do with managerial behavior? According to the standard theory of competitive markets, which we will review in Chapter 12, perfect competition among profit-maximizing firms results in an efficient use of resources. Yet virtually all researchers agree that in a competitive environment the managers of some firms at any particular time do not follow profit-maximizing strategies and are a source of inefficiency. Takeovers may be an important method of ensuring that managers will act to maximize profits: in an actual takeover, top managers are usually replaced, and simply the threat of such a takeover can deter managers from pursuing any goal other than profit-maximization. If this is so, then in a competitive environment the antitakeover laws that make takeovers more difficult can have the unintended effect of reducing efficiency. However, the empirical evidence on the efficiency effects of takeovers is mixed, and at least some researchers are concerned about motivations of the acquiring firms that are distinct from profit maximization.[40] In other words, the efficiency effects of takeover regulations depend on the managerial motivations in both the target and the acquiring firm.

These first three areas of policy relevance are potentially of great significance, but simple, pragmatic applications of how and when to use the behavioral uncertainty about firm objectives in analysis are not yet apparent. A fourth area is mentioned here because its practical significance for regulation can readily be identified. Some analysts have argued that the manager-controlled firm has greater incentive to misrepresent the firm's true economic performance to its stockholders (in the attempt to keep dissidence to a minimum and reduce the probability of takeover by others).[41] The owner-controlled firm has less incentive because the owners already know the truth and are less concerned (not unconcerned) about what others think.

An empirical test of this hypothesis does lend it some support.[42] The researchers examined the decisions of firms to implement accounting changes in the ways profits or losses are calculated. Often the motive is that the firm derives real economic benefits from the change, regardless of its control. But other changes, such as the decision to report an "extraordinary" gain or loss, have more potential for hiding true performance. Assuming that the stock market as a whole ferrets out the truth, which then gets reflected in the stock price and thus the actual returns to investors, the researchers looked for patterns in the differences between the actual and the reported stock returns.[43]

---

[40] A symposium on this subject appears in the *Journal of Economic Perspectives, 2,* No. 1, Winter 1988, pp. 3–82. Shleifer and Vishny think non-profit-maximizing behavior of the acquiring firm is central (see A. Shleifer and R. Vishny, "Value Maximization and the Acquisition Process," pp. 7–20). Scherer's empirical work on takeovers before the 1980s wave finds that they do little to improve operating efficiency (see Scherer [1988], "Corporate Takeovers"). However Jensen and Jarrell, Brickley, and Netter provide more sympathetic views of takeovers (see M. Jensen, "Takeovers: Their Causes and Consequences," pp. 21–48; and G. Jarrell, J. Brickle, and J. Netter, "The Market for Corporate Control: The Empirical Evidence Since 1980," pp. 49–68).

[41] See M. Jensen and W. Meckling, "Theory of the Firm: Managerial Behavior, Agency Costs, and Ownership Structure," *Journal of Financial Economics,* October 1976, pp. 305–360.

[42] See G. Salamon and E. Smith, "Corporate Control and Managerial Misrepresentation of Firm Performance," *Bell Journal of Economics, 10,* No. 1, Spring 1979, pp. 319–328.

[43] For the stock market to price the security correctly, only some investors must be well informed. But to change management of the firm requires the support of a majority of the common stock votes.

In the years in which accounting policy changes were made, the researchers correlated the estimated real returns with the reported results. They found less correlation between the two measures in management-controlled firms compared with owner-controlled firms, which supported the hypothesis that the former are more likely to attempt to misrepresent the truth. The second test was to examine the timing of accounting policy changes. They found that management-controlled firms were more likely to institute such changes in years of below-average stock performance, whereas owner-controlled firms were just as likely to make them in good years as in bad. This also supports the hypothesis of information misrepresentation, since the probability of stockholder dissidence and takeover is higher in below-average years.

This evidence is limited, but it does have relevance to the efforts of the Securities and Exchange Commission to ensure accuracy in the reporting of firm financial data. Not only does it tell the Commission where to look for likely abuses, but it also offers guidance on how to sample the financial returns for more intensive scrutiny.

In the beginning of this section, three reasons why firms might deviate from profit maximization were offered. We have discussed the first, the exercise of managerial interests, primarily through the sales or revenue maximization hypothesis. The second reason—that owners may receive utility directly from operating the firm—can be applied to the exercise of managerial control as well; either group may perceive its self-interest as affected directly by the firm's actions.

For example, newspaper firms, which often operate in environments of imperfect competition, may use their market power not to create additional profits but rather to pursue journalistic goals (such as allocating more resources to investigative reporting). To the extent that is true and corresponds with a positive externality (a better-informed citizenry), professional norms may serve as a countervailing power against the profit motive and in favor of efficient allocation.

Similarly, in the discussion of health care (Chapter 7), we suggested that prepaid health services plans may control the moral hazard problem better than fee-for-service arrangements. Under the latter arrangements both economic incentives and professional norms push inefficiently for Cadillac-quality care, and the abuses tend to be in the form of unnecessary operations. Under the prepaid systems, the economic incentives would be to conserve on health resources whereas the professional norms of doctors would still push toward high-quality care. If one gave no credence to the effect of professional norms on service delivery (e.g., assume the firm acts as a profit maximizer), that in conjunction with consumer ignorance could lead to prepayment systems no better than those based on fee for service. The influence of these professional norms is an empirical question, but the point of the illustration is that the norms may affect firm behavior and may be relevant to public policy formation.

In these two examples the utility that individual members of the firm's team derive from adherence to and furtherance of professional norms may be a positive feature. But it is unlikely that private utility-seeking within a firm would generally lead to benevolent outcomes. For example, managerial control of an ordinary firm may lead to the firm's using resources in a socially wasteful way. Just as the price-discriminating firm may waste resources in creating and maintaining price discrimination per se, so **a managerial firm can (with market power) choose to produce at greater than least cost** in order to pay, for instance, for various perquisites or more leisurely workdays. **This excess cost is sometimes referred to as X-inefficiency.** That is the name given it by Leibenstein, who is credited with highlighting its possible importance.[44]

Some analysts believe that X-inefficiency is a seriously underestimated harm from monopoly power. To see why, refer to Figure 10-10. Line LAC represents the least average cost of production. OAC represents the observed average cost of production, assumed higher because of management's use of monopoly power to purchase inputs that do not contribute to output but make working conditions more sybaritic.[45] The height of OAC compared with that of LAC is assumed limited by a "visibility" constraint; too much opulence in relation to output will be noticed.[46] Management is assumed to be interested in choosing the quantity of observed average cost that maximizes the area of its excess benefits, and we assume that, without further constraint, the maximum would be at Q_{MG} with excess benefits equal to area $P_E CAB$.[47]

However, management is also assumed to be subject to a profit constraint as before. Since the owners receive no profit at Q_{MG} this clearly does not meet the constraint. We assume that the profit-constrained managerial maximum is at Q_{HC} with managerial benefits area $P_E CFG$.[48]

The actual social loss in this situation cannot be identified precisely. There are two areas in the diagram that involve social losses. The first can be identified as the triangle *GHK*, which has the usual interpretation of deadweight loss. The second is the rectangle $P_E CFG$, but only part of it is a loss. As far as consumers and the firm owners are concerned, the use of these resources in production contributes nothing and the full value equal to their opportunity costs is lost. But this is offset to some unknown extent by the value of the resources to the managers (in terms of willingness to pay for them from personal, not corporate, budgets). For the fun of a crude calculation that we will make shortly, let us assume that one-half the area is a social loss.

Now let us consider what happens if one assumes that the observed average costs are the least costs. Then one would incorrectly measure the deadweight loss as triangle *HFA*. This

---

[44] See Harvey Leibenstein, *Beyond Economic Man* (Cambridge: Harvard University Press, 1976).

[45] It should be pointed out that certain managerial perquisites, which some might consider sybaritic, may also be consistent with least-cost production. A corporate jet, for example, may produce returns from increased business that are greater than its costs. Thus, above we are referring only to the cost of inputs beyond those necessary to achieve the output level.

[46] Without this constraint, management would simply go to the profit-maximizing solution and then convert part of the profits into perquisites.

[47] In some circumstances it is possible that the area could increase by continuing to expand output, even though this requires management to lower its excess benefit per unit. For that to happen, the marginal revenue must exceed the least average cost per unit. That is not the case as we have drawn it.

[48] There are some circumstances in which management could increase its profit-constrained maximum by lowering its per unit excess benefit and expanding output. The conditions are identical with those in the prior footnote—if marginal revenue exceeds the least average cost per unit. Again, that is not the case as we have drawn it.

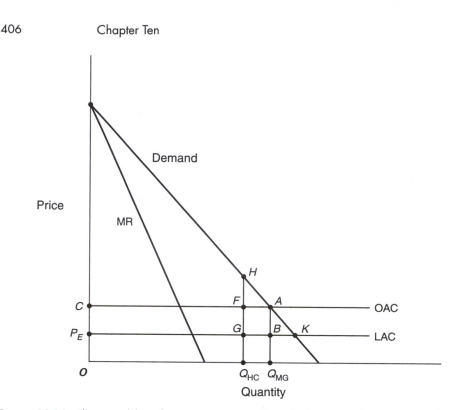

Figure 10-10. The social loss from excess-cost monopoly (OAC = observed average cost, LAC = least average cost).

is one of the criticisms made of empirical studies of the harm from monopoly.[49] At least as drawn, it appears that this can be quite a substantial error.

To get a feel for the magnitude of the possible error, we can make an illustrative calculation based on assumptions similar to those criticized in the actual studies. However, we simplify even further by treating the goods and services in the measured economy as if they were one product produced by a single, constant-returns-to-scale firm. This unrealistic simplification keeps the exercise simple; its true value is in demonstrating how actual estimates may be made with knowledge of a firm's revenues and elasticity of demand.

The 2000 GDP was approximately $10 trillion. Since that includes almost all goods, we can reasonably assume the price elasticity of demand for the aggregate is −1. If we imag-

[49] The original heroic effort is by A. Harberger, "Monopoly and Resource Allocation," *American Economic Review, 44,* May 1954, pp. 77–87. Harberger estimated that the loss from monopolistic restrictions in seventy-three manufacturing industries from 1924 to 1928 was under 0.1 percent of total sales, a surprisingly low figure. Cowling and Mueller, in a 1978 study revisiting this issue, estimated a much higher deadweight loss of approximately 4 percent and suggested that if other factors such as socially wasteful advertising expenditures were included, the total waste could rise to as much as 13 percent. See K. Cowling and D. Mueller, "The Social Costs of Monopoly Power," *Economic Journal, 88,* December 1978, pp. 727–748. Scherer and Ross, *Industrial Economic Structure and Market Performance,* Chapter 18, provide a good discussion of the empirical research relevant to this issue.

ine GDP as the product being produced, the average monopolistic price distortion of the order of 10 percent, and the aggregate technology as constant returns to scale, the loss L can be estimated by using the linear approximation for the triangle *HFA:*

$$L = \tfrac{1}{2}\Delta P\Delta Q$$

or

$$L = \tfrac{1}{2}(HF)(FA)$$

The derivation that follows is particularly useful for empirical work because it allows L to be estimated with knowledge only of initial expenditures, the demand elasticity, and the price change. Since the price distortion α can be thought of as $\Delta P/P,$ then

$$\Delta P = \alpha P$$

We will substitute the right-hand-side expression for ΔP in the above equation for the loss. Similarly, from the elasticity definition we derive an expression for ΔQ:

$$\varepsilon = \frac{\Delta Q/Q}{\Delta P/P}$$

or

$$\varepsilon = \frac{\Delta Q/Q}{\alpha}$$

and using the absolute value[50] of ε we have

$$\Delta Q = \alpha|\varepsilon|Q$$

Therefore, on replacing ΔP and ΔQ with their equivalent expressions in the equation for L we have

$$L = \tfrac{1}{2}\alpha^2\varepsilon PQ$$

$$= \tfrac{1}{2}(0.1^2)(1)(\$10 \text{ trillion})$$

$$= 0.005(\$10 \text{ trillion})$$

$$= \$50 \text{ billion}$$

As can be seen, this calculation leads to a low loss estimate of 0.5 percent of GDP. Now let us assume, alternatively, that the true waste arises from inefficient production of a comparable order of magnitude of 10 percent. Then for the triangular portion of the loss *GHK,* we approximate the price distortion as $2\Delta P/P = 0.2$. Simply substituting this in the formula for L gives us

$$L_T = \tfrac{1}{2}(0.2^2)(1)(\$10 \text{ trillion})$$

$$= \$200 \text{ billion}$$

---

[50] The bars around the ε in the formula stand for absolute value.

or about 2 percent of GDP. But the major source of loss is from the rectangular portion $P_E CFG$. By using our assumption that only 50 percent of the area is loss L_R, we get

$$L_R = \tfrac{1}{2}(0.1)(\$10 \text{ trillion})$$

$$= \$500 \text{ billion}$$

Therefore, our crude calculation puts the social loss from monopoly power at $700 billion, or 7 percent of GDP—fourteen times as great as our initial misestimate of 0.5 percent.[51] Percentage variations of this magnitude might be expected as a consequence of using this range of assumptions applied to any single monopoly.[52]

Limited Maximization Capabilities

In discussing the first two reasons why firms might be expected to deviate from profit-making behavior, we highlighted the difficulty of evaluating firm performance without knowing the behavior that leads to it. For example, observed firm costs may be least costs if firms maximize profits or sales, but the same observations can represent considerably more inefficiency if monopoly power is exercised on firm input selections. This makes the study of actual organizational behavior take on more importance if economic implications are to be drawn accurately. Among the researchers who have undertaken detailed studies of individual firms, there seems to be a near consensus that firm decisions are made primarily by rules of thumb rather than by anyone's careful optimization calculations.[53] That is, our third reason why firms might be expected to deviate from profit maximization is that, like individuals, they are boundedly rational.

What does it mean to say that a firm is boundedly rational? It is certainly no insult if we recall the discussion of individual bounded rationality. It is simply a recognition that the circumstances in which decisions are made are more like those in chess than in tic-tac-toe. (The author, at least, has more admiration for the winning chess player than the winning tic-tac-toe player.)

Firm decisions are typically made under conditions of uncertainty. When a firm decides to expand and build a new plant that will take years to complete, it is guessing that the future demand for its products will be large enough to make the investment profitable (let alone

---

[51] As an exercise, the reader may wish to redo this calculation by choosing the monopolistic distortion to make the initial misestimate be 0.1 or 1 percent of GDP and assuming the cost distortion is of similar magnitude. The revised social loss calculation should come out to approximately 2.6 percent of GDP on the low side and 11.1 percent on the high side.

[52] For further review of studies of X-inefficiency, see K. Button and T. G. Weyman-Jones, "Ownership Structure, Institutional Organization and Measured X-Efficiency," *American Economic Review, 82,* No. 2, May 1992, pp. 439–445; R. Frantz, *X-Efficiency: Theory, Evidence and Applications* (Boston: Kluwer Acadmic Publishers, 1988); and S. Borenstein and J. Farrell, "Is Cost-Cutting Evidence of X-Inefficiency?," *American Economic Review, 90,* No. 2, May 2000, pp. 224–227.

[53] See, for example, R. Cyert and J. March, *A Behavioral Theory of the Firm,* 2nd Ed. (Cambridge, Mass.: Blackwell Business, 1992); R. Marris, *Managerial Capitalism in Retrospect* (New York: St. Martin's Press, 1998); and Oliver Williamson, *Markets and Hierarchies: Analysis and Antitrust Implications* (New York: The Free Press, 1975).

optimal). In a world in which inflation might vary anywhere from (say) 0 to 15 percent over the period, that is a considerable risk. A superior technology might become available if the firm delays 2 years, but then again it might not. Competitors may or may not engage in a similar undertaking. If there is enough certainty about the possible states of the world, the firm may be maximizing expected profit. But given all the choices about the size, location, and technology of the investment, the firm may be like the chess player encountering a new situation in which the actual response is the player's best attempt to muddle ahead.

Not only is the external environment of the firm characterized by uncertainty about future factor prices, technological advances, demand, and competition, but there can be considerable uncertainty internal to the firm because of the costliness of communication and coordination among the members. The sales department of the firm, which generally is paid in accordance with sales, naturally goes full speed ahead for sales maximization. When production cannot keep up with sales, the sales division has fits. Conflict arises over the issue, and the firm must decide whether to speed up production or slow down sales. It can be difficult to know which decision is right. As a way to reduce this uncertainty and avoid some conflict, the firm creates inventories.

Although holding inventory is costly, it is less costly than miscoordination and continual conflict among the firm's divisions. There may be an optimal level of inventory to hold, but it can be difficult to know what that is; and the people in charge of inventory control receive salaries in proportion to the average inventory. If the optimal level is consistent enough over time, other members of the firm may notice excessive inventory costs on their profit and loss statements. The inventory people may claim that the fault lies not with them but with the firm's shipping department. The firm may hire other people to check periodically on the inventory-level-setting procedures. Rules of thumb tend to develop, such as that inventory should be kept at a fixed percentage of last year's sales during the coming period. The rule of thumb may be close to what is optimal for the firm, but it may also simply represent conflict and uncertainty avoidance that allows the firm to satisfice.

Let us summarize the gist of this discussion. Not all the different members of the firm's team have the same goal. Those with the best information cannot always be counted upon to use it for firm profit maximization, which creates internal uncertainty and thus the need for costly communication and coordination to reduce it. That in turn creates standard rules of thumb, such as "inventory should be about 5 percent of last year's sales," to which the inventory control manager must justify making exceptions. Everyone tends to work by standard operating rules rather than global optimization calculations for the firm as a whole, and it is only if one part of the firm begins to stand out in some way that the firm initiates search procedures that may lead to a change in the routines. At least as far as the members of the firm are concerned, the firm's performance either satisfices or it does not. Firm profit maximization is too complex to be an operational goal for the firm to pursue. That most firms try to follow the rule that profits should be higher this year than last year, nobody denies.

What does this behavioral model imply about the firm's performance? Given an environment that permits the firm to survive under a broad range of behaviors, as enjoyed by firms with monopoly power, the behavior is a product of the goals of each firm member and the various communicating, coordinating, and incentive devices that constrain each member's behavior. Presumably, power within the firm has something to do with how these constraints evolve. To the extent that firm members share an important goal, the firm as a whole may be understood as acting primarily to further that goal. As a firm grows in size and the shared goals become only a minor portion of each member's goals, one might expect production costs to rise above least costs as in the managerially controlled firm.

But then the same boundedly rational large firm in another environment may behave exactly like the profit maximizer, its denials to the contrary. This is a key concept that we find convenient to introduce here in a simple model of a behavioral firm. Let us assume that our behavioral firm follows a rule-of-thumb pricing strategy: It chooses the price that is simply a fixed percentage greater than its average costs. Practically all major firms claim to price that way. They are not sure what current marginal revenues or marginal costs are; and even if they did know the current figures, they would not be sure about the location of the demand curve and the effects of changes they might make. The system of markup pricing is much simpler, and the firms seem satisfied with it.[54]

Let us define the markup as

$$m = \frac{P - AC}{P} \quad 0 \le m < 1$$

It is easy to see, by rewriting, that price is a fixed percentage markup of average costs:

$$P = \frac{1}{1 - m} AC$$

How can such simplistic behavior be consistent with profit maximization? Recall that the marginal revenue always has the following relation with the price and elasticity of demand:

$$MR = P\left(1 + \frac{1}{\varepsilon}\right)$$

Since the profit maximizer always equates MR = MC, we can substitute

$$MC = P\left(1 + \frac{1}{\varepsilon}\right)$$

or, rewriting,

$$P = \frac{MC}{1 + 1/\varepsilon}$$

If a firm has constant-returns-to-scale technology or if it is operating at the minimum point of its average-cost curve, then MC = AC.[55] When we make the substitution, the profit maximizer can be seen to have the following price:

---

[54] One study uses a markup pricing model to investigate the incident of corporate tax shifting in Australia. See K. Daly and N. Hart, "Mark-Up Pricing and the Forward Shifting of the Corporate Income Tax," *Australian Economic Review,* No. 107, Third Quarter 1994, pp. 45–54.

[55] The marginal cost curve always crosses the average cost curve at its minimum. When marginal cost equals average cost, the marginal unit is neither pulling up nor pushing down the average. But this means the slope of the average cost at this point is zero: the minimum.

$$P = \frac{AC}{1 + 1/\varepsilon}$$

For this to be identical with that of our boundedly rational markup firm, all that is required is that

$$m = -\frac{1}{\varepsilon}$$

Let us try to summarize the substance of this result. Large firms are virtually unanimous in reporting a pricing procedure that is in the spirit of our markup model. However, every price, no matter how it is derived, will represent some percentage markup over average costs. A profit-maximizing firm with constant-returns-to-scale technology or at its average-cost minimum will have a markup that is the inverse of its demand elasticity: The more inelastic the demand, the greater the markup. How then do the markup firms determine the markups? Empirical observation generally confirms that the markups on the outputs of any single multiproduct firm do differ and do vary as the profit maximization hypothesis suggests: inversely with the product's demand elasticity.[56] The most likely explanation for this is that demand conditions do influence the markup and the profit maximization model can predict them, at least to some extent.

Let us conclude this section with a reminder about models and their purposes. Profit maximization as a model assumption is not the same thing as an assertion that firms have that motivation. Rather, it reflects the belief that by using the assumption, certain aspects of firm behavior can be predicted accurately enough for the purpose at hand. What makes for enough can be determined only in comparison with alternative models.

The strongest argument for maintaining the profit maximization assumption is that in many situations there do not appear to be alternative models that are "better." The complex behavioral models may be more accurate for individual firm decision-making, but so far their construction seems to require a tremendous amount of analytic effort for each occasion. Furthermore, not every problem requires an understanding of the response of a specific firm as opposed to the industry as a whole. In this chapter we have reviewed the behavior of firms in an environment in which profit maximization is generally thought weakest—the noncompetitive environment. All the alternative models we have reviewed are included because they may be the best models for particular analytic purposes.

Summary

In this chapter we examine the use of microeconomic models as aids to understanding the behavior of private, profit-making supply organizations. All the models are constructed by assumptions about the objectives of the organization, its capabilities, and its environmen-

---

[56] An early example is A. Kaplan J. Dirham, and R. Lanzillotti, *Pricing in Big Business: A Case Approach* (Washington, D.C.: The Brookings Institution, 1958). A more recent study of industry markups, using data from the United Kingdom, is I. Kaskarelis, "Inflation and the Mark-up in UK Manufacturing Industry," *Oxford Bulletin of Economics and Statistics, 55,* No. 4, November 1993, pp. 391–407.

tal constraints. We emphasize alternative assumptions about objectives and capabilities and leave the determinants of environmental constraints (those external to the organization) for later chapters. Because some environments may be very constraining on the firm's behavior (e.g., a perfectly competitive environment), most of the discussion assumes that the organizations are in settings that allow discretionary behavior: private firms with some degree of monopoly power.

The discussion begins by calling attention to the obvious differences in the way demand and supply are organized in our economic system. Individuals typically bring their demands directly to the marketplace, whereas they give their supply resources to intermediary organizations, known as firms, that, in turn, produce and bring finished goods to the marketplace. *This voluntary centralization of decision-making (from the individual to the firm) occurs primarily because of economies in handling uncertainty, information, and transaction costs.*

The first model of the firm we review is the standard one: an organization that seeks to maximize profits and has capabilities that allow it to do so. Two principal implications of the model are that the firm will equate its marginal revenue to its marginal cost and will use resources in production efficiently. However, given some degree of monopoly power (the ability to influence market price by its own actions), the assumptions are not enough to derive an empirical prediction of the firm's behavior.

The example we use to illustrate this is *price discrimination.* Analytically, we define price discrimination as charging, for similar units of a good, prices that vary disproportionately with the marginal costs of supplying the units. This practice can have large effects on the firm's output choice and the prices its consumers face. *Whether it occurs, however, depends on the information costs of finding which consumers have differing elasticities of demand and the transaction costs of segregating the consumers and preventing resales among them.* To the extent that the firm chooses to price-discriminate and incurs costs to do so, this invalidates the implication of production efficiency. It remains true that the firm equates marginal revenues and marginal costs, although these functions are different from those in the nondiscriminatory regime.

The efficiency and equity consequences of price discrimination depend upon the specific circumstances. Except for the empirically unlikely case of perfect (first-degree) and costless price discrimination (in which the firm captures the entire consumer surplus), price discrimination is unlikely to result in efficient allocations. However, the more relevant question is whether price discrimination improves the outcome from what it would be otherwise. It may do so in the case of goods and services for which the production levels are in the range of increasing returns to scale; these outputs might not be produced at all without price discrimination.

The Robinson-Patman Act of 1936 forbids price discrimination for "goods of like grade and quality" when the effects may lessen competition. However, the act is easily evaded even if the behavior does reduce competition. The law requires that a price *difference* exist to trigger scrutiny by Robinson-Patman; a firm may discriminate, for example, by charging the same price to two different customers even though the shipping costs to each (included in the price) vary substantially. Similarly, a firm can segment its market by producing similar goods of different quality levels and charging a price disproportionately higher than marginal cost in the market segment with more inelastic demand. Finally, a firm that is not price-discriminating in the analytic sense may be found in violation of Robinson-Patman: for example, it may charge one customer less than another because of cost differences in filling the orders but be unable to document the source of cost savings specifically enough to satisfy a court. For similar theoretical reasons and practical difficulties, prohibition of "predatory pricing" under the Sherman Antitrust Act of 1890 does not always work to enhance efficiency.

The supplementary section reviews alternative models. *Information and transaction costs also explain why some analysts think firms might have the objective of sales maximization rather than profit maximization.* Once the decision-making unit is a team rather than an individual, the goal that the team as a whole pursues can be unclear. The different team members have different individual interests (e.g., the income each derives from the firm), and there is no particular reason why being on the same team must lead to harmony (as on a basketball team perhaps) as opposed to the lack of it (traditional antagonism between management and labor).

The attempt of some team members to control others explains much about the incentive systems set up within firms (e.g., management bonuses as a function of firm profits). The power relations that determine who creates incentives for whom are an additional factor. Those with claim to the economic profit of the firm usually have the legal power to control the firm's contracts. (They are generally the suppliers of capital in the United States, but that need not be so. In some countries the labor-owned firm is common.) The sales maximization hypothesis arises from the idea that many dispersed owners (common stockholders) cannot effectively control management because of the high information and transaction costs that would be involved. Thus, much of the power of ownership gets effectively delegated to management, which runs the firm in its own interests. Since managerial salaries are observed to correlate with the size of a firm, size (total revenue) maximization (subject to a profit constraint) becomes the goal.

A closely related hypothesis is that the firm will maximize some weighted average of the utilities of its members. This is a more general version of sales maximization: The same problems of controlling firm members are assumed to exist, but the objectives of each member are thought of more broadly than sales. In particular, each member may wish the firm to purchase inputs that make his or her own job more enjoyable, which leads to inefficient use of resources in production. Owners may view the firm as their personal toy with which to play; managers may seek various perquisites such as oversized offices; and workers may seek more on-the-job "leisure." The waste of resources in this manner is known as *X-inefficiency*.

Sometimes the pursuit of utility through a firm can lead to social benefits rather than social costs. That is the case when journalistic norms correlate with positive information externalities from newspaper reporting, doctors place a patient's interest above that of the medical firm's profits, and day care centers are run with staffs that have the children's interests in mind more than the firm's profits.

The problem of organizational control, arising from information and transactional costs, may also be thought of as causing *bounded rationality of firms*. This can explain why a firm may pursue no single goal or even a consistent goal. It also explains why the firm may not be capable of achieving a certain goal even if all the members agree on it. Because it may be difficult for the "left arm" of a firm to coordinate, communicate with, or control the "right arm," the total result may at best be satisficing rather than optimizing.

Before one gets carried away with all the possibilities for understanding and predicting a firm's behavior, it is good to remember that *remarkably simple models sometimes do very well at explaining complex behavior.* Assuming markup pricing behavior of a boundedly rational firm is the "truth," we demonstrated that behavior may be perfectly consistent with what is predicted by profit maximization. The reason is that the firm's environment may be constraining enough that its survival depends upon taking actions like those a profit maximizer would take. Thus another analytic avenue, which we explore in later chapters, is to model the environments of firms rather than the firms themselves. However, the array of behavioral possibilities should be kept in mind when the environment is not so constraining.

Exercises

10-1 Answer the following questions with reference to the accompanying diagram and its labels. It shows the demand curve for a firm's product, the marginal revenue curve, and the constant marginal cost *OA* (= average cost).

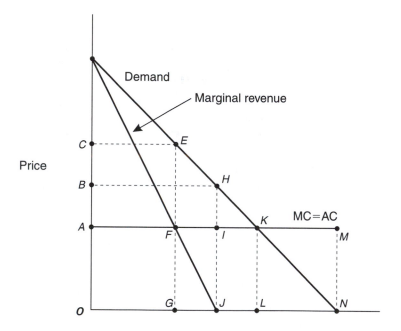

a Identify the price and quantity at the profit maximum. Explain why it is the profit maximum.

b Identify the price and quantity at the revenue maximum. Explain why it is the revenue maximum.

c Identify the efficient quantity. Explain why it is the efficient quantity.

d Explain which is more inefficient: the quantity in your answer to **a** or to **b?**

10-2[57] Suppose that daily airline service between two cities can be provided by only one of two types of airplane. Type 1 has seating capacity for 80 passengers and costs $3600 for each one-way trip. Type 2 is larger, with seating for 110 passengers, and costs $3900 for each one-way trip. The demand for air travel between the two cities has two components—business and leisure travel. There are 75 business travelers whose demand for daily trips, for our purposes, is perfectly inelastic. (They will fly at the lowest price available to them, no matter how high it is.) Leisure travelers are price-sensitive and have a demand curve

$$Q_L = 50 - P$$

[Note: After answering the questions below, you may wish to use the example to think about the desirability of airline deregulation.]

a Calculate the average cost of providing service to 80 passengers and to 110 passengers. What is the marginal cost per passenger of the increase in service from 80 to 110 passengers? Would you say that the technology in this range is one of increasing, decreasing, or constant returns? (Answer: Increasing.)

b Any firm that wishes to enter this market can do so with no special entry costs (e.g., airlines can shift planes now used on other routes to this route). This means that any firm actually providing service in this market must have zero economic profit. (Otherwise, another firm could enter and undersell it.) If a uniform price is charged per passenger, what will it be, which plane will be used, and how many passengers will travel? (Answer: Type 1.)

c How much are the social benefits associated with trips 81 to 110? The social costs? On social efficiency grounds, should these trips be provided? (Answer: Yes.)

d Suppose firms did not have to charge a uniform price and could charge a different price to each of the two groups (business and leisure travelers). Given entry conditions as in part (b), could a firm enter the market, offer each group of passengers a better deal than they have in part (b), and still break even? Illustrate with an example. Would this be more efficient? (Answer: This is feasible, and it would be more efficient.)

e○ The threat of competition (through entry) does not lead to a unique fare structure. For example, here are two possible outcomes that cannot be beaten by new entrants: (1) Use type 1 plane, charge 75 business travelers $48.00 per trip, and let 5 leisure travelers fly for free, (2) Use type 2 plane, charge business travelers $46.00, and let 35 leisure travelers fly for $12.86. Neither of these is an efficient outcome.

[57] This problem was motivated by an example given in an article by Robert Frank, "When Are Price Differentials Discriminatory," *Journal of Policy Analysis and Management, 2,* No. 2, Winter 1983, pp. 238–255.

Other outcomes are possible, where the price to business travelers can decline to a minimum of $43.67 (and the corresponding price to leisure travelers is higher than that in the above examples). Can you identify the range of fare structures that are possible market outcomes?

f° Of the range of possible market outcomes, there is only one fare structure that leads to an efficient solution. The other structures either involve wasteful excess capacity or are characterized by excess demand for leisure travel, which causes exchange inefficiency. What is the efficient fire structure? (Answer: Business price = $45.00.)

CHAPTER ELEVEN

PUBLIC AND NONPROFIT ORGANIZATIONS: OBJECTIVES,
CAPABILITIES, AND POLICY IMPLICATIONS

MUCH OF PUBLIC POLICY and its analysis concerns, quite naturally, the organizations that receive government funds. These organizations are often private but not for profit: examples are some hospitals, nursing homes, foster care agencies, and educational institutions. They also include public-service-providing bureaus or enterprises such as fire and police departments, mass transit systems, and highway departments. The general growth in government expenditures that we reviewed in Chapter 1 correlates with increased control over resources by these agencies. In this chapter we consider how analysis may be used to predict the behavior of public and nonprofit agencies and link the behavior to its efficiency consequences.

Normative analyses about how public and nonprofit agencies *should* behave have been much more common than studies of how the agencies *do* behave and the reasons for the actual behavior. Unless the actual behavior is serendipitous, the normative recommendations are not likely to have much impact. That is, to induce desired changes in actual behavior requires understanding the political, economic, and organizational forces that determine an agency's objectives, perceived production possibilities, and incentives for making particular choices.[1]

For example, as a policy matter we are concerned about growing Medicare and Medicaid expenditures. Suppose we learn that hospital services are produced inefficiently; for example, too many physician inputs are used relative to nonphysican inputs in providing the necessary treatments. If hospital administrators are made aware of this, are motivated to reduce hospital costs, and have the power to do so, they will respond in the appropriate way. But if hospitals are controlled by physicians who use them to maximize their own incomes

---

[1] Normative conclusions may also depend on recognition of these forces. For example, political constraints of democratic decision-making may cause an inefficient allocation of one good, but the inefficiency may be a small cost relative to larger benefits in terms of the maintenance of democracy.

the findings of production inefficiency may fall on deaf ears. To induce more efficient delivery of hospital services, analysts must understand not only what is inefficient about the services, but why the hospital selects the procedures it uses.

A better understanding of actual agency behavior can have substantial implications for public policy. Services can be delivered through alternative types of agencies, for example, public, nonprofit, or private profit-making organizations. Our expectations about the efficiency of each type should influence the choice. Or it may be possible to make great improvements in the efficiency of the public and not-for-profit sectors by restructuring the environments in which they operate (e.g., changing the nature of competition for the public funds, or the contract under which the funds are received, or the regulations that are to be followed).

For example, suppose we find that one public agency currently produces less efficiently than a comparable private agency, as when elementary education is provided by both types of organization. This does not imply that such relative performance is inherent. It may be that we have created an incentive system for the public agency that unnecessarily causes inefficiency; an example could be mandatory enrollment by geographic location of the child's residence, which gives each neighborhood school a captive audience. It is possible that public school production efficiency would increase significantly if parents could choose from among a number of the nearby public schools. Through the analysis of organizational behavior we may learn to improve organizational performance.

The models presented in this chapter, like those of Chapter 10, focus on the objectives and capabilities of the producer agency (rather than the determinants of the agency's environment). We show how one can deduce contradictory and empirically testable implications from alternative models of the same agency. It is through careful empirical analysis of those predictions that we learn which models are more accurate. Empirical testing also reveals areas in which no model makes good predictions and points the way toward the construction of new models to remedy the deficiencies. It is through the process of continual model improvement that we begin to understand how agencies in fact behave and why they behave that way, and we begin to develop predictive ability about how they will respond to proposed policy changes.

We also demonstrate how one can use models for normative purposes. Consider how public and nonprofit agencies ought to set prices for their services, since that will determine service allocation. Public and nonprofit agencies may be subject to constraints that prevent them from achieving efficient allocations. For example, we saw in the preceding chapter that organizations that produce in the region of increasing returns to scale may be unable to recover their costs. Public enterprises of this type receive costly subsidies from government sources to supplement revenues raised from its customers. We will present models that identify the most efficient allocations for enterprises subject to subsidy constraints and the prices that they ought to set in order to achieve these allocations.

The chapter begins with an analysis of nonprofit hospitals. We review the construction of three different models of hospital behavior. In the first two we focus on the objectives of the hospital; in the third we concentrate on the hospital's capabilities. We show how comparison of the models reveals contradictory predictions that can be examined through empirical research. One important policy area where this research is used is with respect to merger policy: for example, when should a proposed merger of two nonprofit hospitals be approved? We also illustrate how this research can generate policy implications by discussing possible changes in the Medicare Prospective Payment System.

After reviewing the analyses of nonprofit hospitals, we turn to models of public bureaus and public enterprises. We review the model of a budget-maximizing bureau. Then we consider an empirical test. The model is used to predict the pricing decisions of a public enterprise responsible for rail mass transit services in an urban area. The predictions are compared with those from two alternative models that emphasize the importance of external political influences; then all the predictions are compared with the actual pricing decisions.

Finally, we consider a normative model for the pricing of rail mass transit services. Given a passenger capacity constraint and a subsidy constraint, we derive the prices that will lead to the most efficient feasible allocation of the transit services. The pricing solution when there are subsidy constraints is referred to generally as *Ramsey optimal pricing,* and it has important implications in other policy areas, notably optimal taxation. The mathematical derivation of the Ramsey solution is contained in an appendix.

Nonprofit Organizations: Models of Hospital Resource Allocation

The nonprofit (and nongovernmental) sector of the economy consists of a wide range of organizations: charitable, educational, scientific and community service agencies, and associations such as labor unions, lobby groups, and organized religions. The most general definition of a nonprofit organization is one that is barred by law from distributing profits to the individuals that control the organization.[2] Public policies affect the formation, size, and performance of these organizations. For example, the nonprofit agency is generally exempt from federal (and usually other governmental) taxes.[3] Furthermore, many nonprofit organizations—the performing arts, for example, or hospitals—are heavily dependent on governmental subsidies. Government regulations often constrain the use of nonprofit resources; for example, a university's eligibility for federal subsidies depends on maintaining an appropriate affirmative action hiring program.

Our interest is in nonprofit agencies that are substantially involved in service provision or production; that is, we are focusing on schools, hospitals, and day-care agencies rather than on charitable foundations or trade associations. We wish to understand such matters as how effectively they use public funds and how their effectiveness can be improved. But then we must understand something about their behavior and the motivations that explain the behavior. If the motivation for their existence is not profit, then what objectives guide their decision-making?

---

[2] Hansmann refers to this as the nondistribution constraint. See Henry Hansmann, "The Role of Non-Profit Enterprise," *Yale Law Journal, 90,* 1980, pp. 835–901.

[3] One type of exception affects nonprofit agencies that participate in partisan political lobbying; they do not qualify for federal tax exemption.

Before turning to analysis of this issue, it may be helpful to point out several dimensions of the size of the nonprofit sector. One report estimates that nonprofits accounted for 12.4 percent of the gross domestic product in 1995, up from about 6 percent in 1975.[4] Over 1.5 million U.S. organizations claim tax-exempt status. According to Internal Revenue Service data, in 1995 nonprofits had $900 billion in revenues and owned assets worth $1.9 trillion. By any measure, the nonprofit sector uses a significant amount of the nation's resources in the production of its various goods and services.

The nonprofit sector has only received limited attention from analysts.[5] One area of non-profit activity that has been the subject of numerous modeling efforts concerns hospital behavior. Most hospitals are nonprofits and they provide most hospital care. In 1997, for example, 58.3 percent of short-stay hospitals were nonprofits.[6] According to one study, the nation's nonprofit hospitals handle approximately 70 percent of all inpatient cases in acute care hospitals.[7] Total hospital revenues in 1998 were $382 billion, about 33 percent of national health expenditures. Given the large public role in the financing of growing national health expenditures, it is not surprising that this area has attracted attention.[8]

Below we review some of the theoretical models proposed by analysts as predictors of nonprofit hospital behavior. In the first two we focus on the objectives of the hospital and in the third we concentrate on the hospital's capabilities. We illustrate some of the contradictory and testable implications of these models, as well as their bearing on some issues of policy with respect to hospitals.

One of the earliest economic models of a nonprofit hospital was constructed by Newhouse,[9] who reasoned that hospital decisions are made by its administrator in consultation with the staff. The principal decisions involve the quantity and quality of medical services to be provided.[10] The administrator prefers more quantity to less because that enhances his

---

[4] A. Meckstroth and P. Arnsberger, "A 20-Year Review of the Nonprofit Sector, 1975–1995," *Statistics of Income Bulletin, 18,* No. 2, Fall 1998, pp. 149–171.

[5] Good references are E. Boris and C. E. Steuerle, *Nonprofits & Government* (Washington, D.C.: The Urban Institute Press, 1999); S. Rose-Ackerman, ed., *The Economics of Nonprofit Institutions* (New York: Oxford University Press, 1986); D. Hammond and D. Young, eds., *Nonprofit Organizations in a Market Economy* (San Francisco: Jossey-Bass Publishers, 1993); and B. Weisbrod, *The Nonprofit Economy* (Cambridge: Harvard University Press, 1988).

[6] See p. 78 of the Health Care Financing Administration's *1998 Data Compendium* (Baltimore: U.S. Department of Health and Human Services, 1998).

[7] See Richard G. Frank and David S. Salkever, "Nonprofit Organizations in the Health Sector," *Journal of Economic Perspectives, 8,* No. 4, Fall 1994, pp. 129–144.

[8] In 1999, public sector health expenditures were $548.5 billion or 45 percent of the $1210.7 billion national health expenditures. See "1999 National Health Care Expenditures" of the U.S. Health Care Financing Administration (http://www.hcfa.gov/stats/nhe-oact). In 1979, by contrast, federal health expenditures were $68 billion and equaled 28 percent of national health expenditures. Hospital costs are the largest component of health care costs.

[9] See Joseph P. Newhouse, "Toward a Theory of Nonprofit Institutions: An Economic Model of a Hospital." *American Economic Review, 60,* No. 1, March 1970, pp. 64–74.

[10] For simplicity, think of the quantity of care as patient-days and the quality of care as the type of room, for example, a ward, semiprivate room, or private room.

or her own sphere of responsibility. Furthermore, higher quality is preferred to lower quality because of the prestige it wins for the hospital. Therefore, we can assume that the hospital is trying to maximize an objective function that consists of both quantity and quality of the outputs. This part of the model substitutes for the profit maximization assumption in the standard firm model.

The model also has these familiar constraints: demand, assumed to be downward-sloping (thus the hospital has some monopoly power), and technological possibilities with their associated costs. The remaining constraints follow from the nonprofit status: The hospital is not allowed to make a profit; and if it is to cover its costs, it must charge a price equal to its average cost.

Two implications of this model can be derived easily. First, the hospital will use inputs efficiently: For any given quality level, the hospital maximizes its objective function by producing the maximum quantity possible given demand. Or, put differently, it will produce any quality-quantity combination at least cost. (Otherwise, it could achieve a higher level of its objective function.) Second, the hospital will not provide all the services that are efficient to provide, but will be biased against "economy" care.

To see this, let us refer to Figure 11-la. Each of the average-cost curves drawn is associated with a different quality level: The higher the cost curve, the higher the quality. Also, the higher the quality, the more that will be demanded of it at any given price; thus the demand curves shift upward and to the right as quality increases. The zero-profit quantity for each quality is shown by the intersection of the demand curve with the average-cost curve (assuming no price discrimination). Presumably, there is some range of quality over which the break-even quantity increases, as in the movement from AC_1 to AC_2. However, past some quality level, demand begins to taper off and the break-even quantity starts to decrease, as in the movement from AC_2 to AC_3.

The hospital can, of course, produce several different quality levels in response to demand. Let us think of aggregate quantity as the sum, in terms of a constant unit (e.g., patient-days), of the quantities associated with the quality levels produced. Then the administrator perceives a quantity-quality frontier that is backward-bending, as shown in Figure 11-lb. If we draw in the indifference curves from the hospital's objective function—the combinations of average quality and quantity that produce the same satisfaction to the hospital—it is clear that, to maximize satisfaction, the administrator will choose the point on the frontier that is tangent to the indifference curve. Thus the hospital is productively efficient.

The second implication is that the nonprofit hospital will be biased against economy care. Efficient resource allocation requires that all qualities be produced up to the point at which the willingness to pay for a marginal unit just equals its marginal cost. But consider the hospital's perspective on this. Imagine an individual who is willing to pay the marginal cost of an additional unit of economy care. This expands quantity, which is a plus for the hospital, but it reduces the average quality. At some point along the quality spectrum, the hospital will not consider the unit quantity increase worth the cost in average quality reduction. Thus, some hospital care that can be provided efficiently will not be provided, and the forgone hospital care will be restricted to the lower quality ranges. This latter implication is important because it predicts a difference in the behavior of a nonprofit hospital rel-

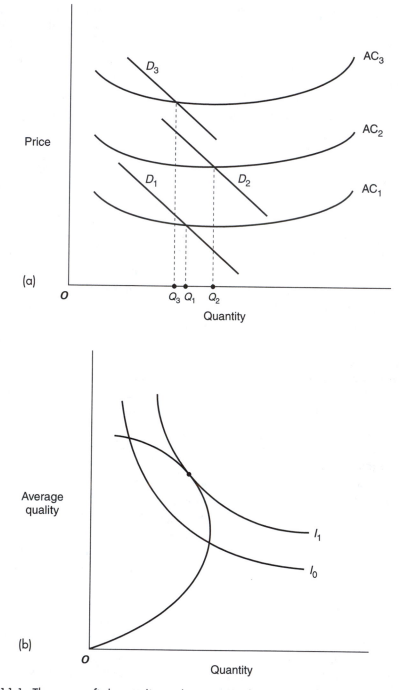

Figure 11-1. The nonprofit hospital's quality-quantity decision: (a) Quality-variable hospital services. (b) The hospital quality-quantity trade-off. (These drawings are similar to those in Joseph P. Newhouse, "Toward a Theory of Nonprofit Institutions: An Economic Model of a Hospital," *American Economic Review, 60,* No. 1, March 1970, p. 68.)

ative to a profit-maximizing one. The latter would produce all qualities, including lower ones, as long as they were profitable. Thus, there is some opportunity to test the model empirically.

Newhouse cites some evidence that the predicted quality bias is consistent with reality. For example, he points out that the nonprofit hospitals are much more likely than the proprietary hospitals to be accredited.[11] He also suggests that the tax laws favoring nonprofits and philanthropic contributions serve as barriers to the entry of proprietary firms that might attempt to fill the service gap. If the nonprofit is allowed to run at a deficit (made up by philanthropic contributions), it will simply provide greater quantity at each quality level, charge prices below average costs, and shift its quality-quantity frontier outward to the right. This puts the nonsubsidized profit-making hospital at a disadvantage.

A different model of the hospital has been proposed by Pauly and Redisch,[12] who argue that hospital administrators are primarily figureheads and that real control over the hospital's decision-making is in the hands of the staff physicians. Furthermore, staff physicians have the same economic motives as other people, and they will therefore operate the hospital in order to maximize their own net incomes.[13]

In Figure 11-2 we illustrate the physician staff size that maximizes the net income per physician. It is assumed that the hospital faces a downward-sloping demand curve and can purchase nonphysician inputs at given prices. Physicians divide up whatever is left over from the total revenues after paying for nonphysician inputs. For each possible physician staff size, there is an optimal amount of nonphysician inputs to use. Each nonphysician input will be bought until its *marginal revenue product* equals its cost. Otherwise, the physicians could increase the income pie by buying more (or less) of the nonphysician inputs. We explain this below.

The marginal revenue product of a factor or input (MRP) is the change in marginal revenue caused by using one more unit of that factor. The factor results in more output, and selling the additional output results in marginal revenue. Expressed as a formula, using labor to illustrate,

$$\text{MRP}_L = (\text{MR}_Q)(\text{MP}_L^Q)$$

If one extra person could conduct twelve additional hearing tests per day (holding constant the number of testing machines and other inputs available), and each hearing test brought in $30, then the marginal revenue product of that person would be ($30)(12) = $360 per day. Any enterprise that is trying to maximize its profit will expand the use of each input as long as its marginal revenue product exceeds its marginal cost (thus increasing the profit

[11] He reported that 62 percent of all short-term hospitals listed with the American Hospital Association in 1965 were accredited, but only 34 percent of the proprietary hospitals were accredited. See Newhouse, "Toward a Theory of Nonprofit Institutions," pp. 69–70.

[12] M. Pauly and M. Redisch, "The Not-for-Profit Hospital as a Physicians' Cooperative," *American Economic Review, 63,* No. 1, March 1973, pp. 87–99.

[13] An important general insight that follows from this reasoning is that nonprofit organizations, which most of us associate with benevolent undertakings, do not have to behave in an altruistic fashion.

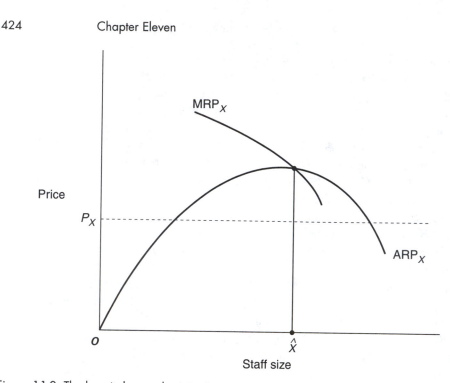

Figure 11-2. The hospital as a physician's cooperative. (From M. Pauly and M. Redisch, "The Not-for-Profit Hospital as a Physicians' Cooperative," *American Economic Review, 63,* No. 1, March 1973, p. 92, Fig. 1.)

level). *The profit-maximizing input quantity will be at the point at which the marginal revenue product just equals the marginal cost.* Our hospital will choose this quantity for each of the nonphysician inputs, in order to maximize the amount of revenue left over for the physicians to divide as payments to themselves (and thus ensuring that the hospital itself is nonprofit).

The only deviation from the profit-maximizing model arises with regard to the amount of physician inputs. Since each additional physician receives an equal share of the hospital's "profits" (the residual revenue after paying for all nonphysician inputs) in this model, the other physicians will want to know if one more physician will increase or decrease the share that each will receive. Thus they are interested in how additional physicians affect the **average revenue product (ARP), which is the sum of an input's marginal revenue products for each of its units divided by the number of units utilized.** As physician staff size X increases, presumably the hospital can take advantage of scale economies and elastic demand so that at first the MRP_X rises and then begins to decline (only the latter portion is shown in Figure 11-2). As the MRP_X rises, it is therefore above the ARP_X. Even when the MRP_X begins to decline, it is still above the ARP_X and thus continues to pull it up. It is only when the MRP_X drops below the ARP_X that it starts to pull the ARP_X down. Thus the maximum ARP_X occurs when it is just equal to MRP_X, as shown in Figure 11-2.

To see the relevance of this to the choice of the quantity of physician inputs to use, we must also consider the supply of physicians. Assume in an urban area that physicians have opportunity costs of P_X and are plentiful from the hospital's perspective. That is, the hospital can attract the number of physicians it wishes for any net income share above or equal to P_X. Past the staff size shown as $\hat{X}$ on the horizontal axis, average physician income begins to decrease. Thus, assuming the current staff controls its own size, it will not allow that size to exceed $\hat{X}$.[14]

Note that the output of this organization is *less* than that which the ordinary profit-maximizing monopolist (who hired physicians at their opportunity costs) would produce. *Total* hospital profit could be increased by expanding the number of physicians beyond $\hat{X}$—the MRP_X exceeds P_X at that point. On the other hand, the administrator-controlled model predicts behavior to be more like that of a sales maximizer for a given demand curve; it will produce more than the ordinary monopolist. Thus the staff-controlled hospital will produce less output than the administrator-controlled one, at least as predicted by these models. Furthermore, the staff-controlled hospital is not producing at least cost: More output could be produced for the same cost by buying slightly fewer nonphysician inputs and using the released funds to add to the physician inputs. Thus, there are at least two predictions that are different from the Newhouse model. These examples of contradictory predictions are crucial to empirical testing of the two theories, because researchers are given an opportunity to find out if one theory predicts actual behavior better than another.

So far, this task has proved to be difficult.[15] The empirical research is important nevertheless. We mention briefly two examples. The first one concerns policy with respect to allowing or disallowing particular hospital mergers. The concern is that a merger may result in a hospital that will have substantial monopoly power and choose to exercise it by restricting quantities of services in order to raise prices above marginal costs.[16] The number of hospital mergers has been substantial in recent years, as the health sector undergoes a major transformation in response to shifts in financing and technology. If the resulting hospital is organized as a nonprofit and behaves as the Newhouse model suggests, then it will not use any monopoly power to raise prices. However, if it behaves as suggested by the Pauly-Redisch model, then it will raise prices, and it may be wise to prevent the merger.

In a 1996 district court decision in Michigan, a judge allowed the merger of the two largest hospitals in Grand Rapids that together had 73 percent of the market. The judge wrote in his opinion that nonprofit hospitals behave differently than profit-making ones, and that nonprofits were unlikely to raise their prices—and the merged hospitals were to be

---

[14] This is very similar to maximizing productivity, as explained in Chapter 9. It is also the way one would expect a labor-owned firm to calculate. See, for example, B. Ward, "The Firm in Illyria: Market Cyndicalism," *American Economic Review, 48,* No. 4, September 1958, pp. 566–589. In many cases, this model predicts that the hospital will utilize even fewer physicians than $\hat{X}$, because each extra physician reduces the share per physician of any "profits" from the other inputs (the marginal physician's contribution of MRP_X must equal or exceed the sum of ARP_X plus its share of any net revenues from nonphysician inputs).

[15] Gulley and Santerre state: "Given the lack of any hard empirical evidence, researchers have been unable to pinpoint the main objective(s) motivating nonprofit hospitals." See O. Gulley and R. Santerre, "The Effect of Tax Exemption on the Market Share of Nonprofit Hospitals," *National Tax Journal, 46,* No. 4, December 1993, pp. 477–486.

[16] We discuss this general problem further in Chapter 17.

nonprofit. The judge cited one analytic, empirical study that found no evidence that non-profits raise prices in these situations, although profit-making hospitals do.[17] This behavior is consistent with the Newhouse-type of model and inconsistent with the Pauly-Redisch type. Since that decision, other analytic work based on more recent evidence finds that non-profits do raise prices following mergers and for any given level of market power the size of the price increase has been growing over time. The newer work does find that non-profits continue to charge lower prices than profit-making hospitals (other things being equal).[18] Thus the newer work suggests behavior similar to that predicted by the Pauley-Redisch model, although in a moderated form. It also suggests that proposed hospital mergers leading to substantial market power deserve scrutiny regardless of the type of ownership.

The second example is a work that focuses on estimating the degree of inefficiency in hospital production in a sample including public, proprietary, and nonprofit hospitals (using the econometric method of frontier cost estimation).[19] While the work does not resolve uncertainty about the motivations underlying the observed inefficiencies in each group, it does suggest a very useful policy proposal. Currently, Medicare uses a Prospective Payment System with payments based on the patient's diagnosis rather than the cost of the treatment actually provided. The amount paid for a given diagnosis is based on cost data from all hospitals, no matter how inefficient some of them may be. Since the methodology allows one to separate all hospitals into two groups, for example, the most efficient 75 percent and the least efficient 25 percent, the authors suggest that Medicare payments be based only on the costs that exclude the least efficient hospitals. This would make it harder for hospitals to remain inefficient, and thus should lead to increased efficiency.[20]

A third model of the hospital has been proposed by Harris.[21] He argues that a hospital's behavior cannot be understood without more explicit consideration of the information and

[17] The study is by W. Lynk, "Nonprofit Hospital Mergers and the Exercise of Market Power," *Journal of Law and Economics, 38,* No. 2, October 1995, pp. 437–461.

[18] See G. Melnick, E. Keeler, and J. Zwanziger, "The Changing Effects of Competition on Non-Profit and For-Profit Hospital Pricing Behavior," *Journal of Health Economics, 18,* No. 1, 1999, pp. 69–86; and, by the same authors, "Market Power and Hospital Pricing: Are Nonprofits Different," *Health Affairs, 18,* No. 3, May/June 1999, pp. 167–173.

[19] The work of Zuckerman, Hadley, and Iezzoni finds that a significantly higher proportion of the most inefficient hospitals are proprietary, rather than nonprofit. This is less surprising if the Newhouse model is more accurate than Pauly-Redisch, since the Newhouse model does not predict nonprofits to be productively inefficient at all. However, their results also show that the degree of inefficiency within the nonprofit portion of their sample is 11–12 percent, and this may well be consistent with the Pauly-Redisch model. There is no clear benchmark to separate a normal "transitional" amount of inefficiency to be expected in any dynamic industry from a more substantial amount caused by "permanent" systematic influences. Nor can one use the proprietary sector as the benchmark, if one expects some proportion of it to be substantially inefficient (although the standard profit-maximization model, which implies least-cost production, does not explain this either). See S. Zuckerman, J. Hadley, and L. Iezzoni, "Measuring Hospital Efficiency with Frontier Cost Functions," *Journal of Health Economics, 13,* No. 3, October 1994, pp. 255–280.

[20] This policy idea is discussed in J. Hadley and S. Zuckerman, "The Role of Efficiency Measurement in Hospital Rate Setting," *Journal of Health Economics, 13,* No. 3, October 1994, pp. 335–340.

[21] Jeffrey E. Harris, "The Internal Organization of Hospitals: Some Economic Implications," *Bell Journal of Economics, 8,* No. 2, Autumn 1977, pp. 467–482.

transaction costs of its operations—just as whether the monopolist will behave as a price discriminator cannot be understood without those considerations. In other words, Harris emphasizes the capabilities of the organization to produce, given the technical possibilities. He proceeds to the analysis and concludes that a hospital is really two firms in one: a physician firm and an administrator firm that are continually at war with one another.

Before explaining his reasoning, let us mention two implications of the analysis. First, the resolution of particular issues is often accomplished by letting the hospital get bigger and more complicated, which seems more like the size prediction of Newhouse than of Pauly-Redisch. Second, however, Harris predicts that policies that propose to limit the annual increase in hospital expenditures will be ineffective.[22] He points out the expenditures result primarily from the short-run decisions of doctors ordering various tests and treatments for all patients. A hospital administrator "responsible" for overall expenditures has no power to overrule specific physician decisions.[23] Thus the Harris model is more like that of Pauly-Redisch in terms of recognizing the important roles physicians play in the allocation of hospital resources.

The meat of the Harris model is not in the assumptions about the general objectives of the hospital decision makers, but rather in Harris's explanation of why certain standard procedural routines for decision-making arise in the hospital. The hospital is designed to solve a complicated decision problem: the diagnosis and treatment of illness. This requires an organization that can adapt rapidly to changing circumstances and new information. Suppose that for each patient's current state of illness there is a minimal acceptable level of various medical inputs; above that minimum may be considered higher quality.[24] But exceeding the minimum is not of the same concern as failure to reach it. In a world in which many of these decisions have to be made almost instantly, the doctor is the only one qualified to decide the minimal level quickly enough. Then production in the hospital must be organized as if every input received by the patient were potentially an absolute necessity.

To ensure that the inputs are available at the physician's command, hospitals develop split organizations. On the supply side the administrator oversees the ancillary services such as the blood supply and the number of operating rooms. On the demand side the medical staff has responsibility for ordering the ancillary services for their patients. The process of caring for a patient can be seen as a series of demands and supply responses, or transactions,

---

[22] For example, there was such a proposal during the Carter administration called the Hospital Cost Containment Act.

[23] In almost all hospitals a patient receives two bills: one from the hospital and the other from the physician. One way to evade the intent of hospital expenditure regulations is to have the doctor's bill include more of the test and treatment charges: this reduces (on paper only) the "hospital" expenditures. Another reason why such regulations may not work as intended is political: in the one proposed during the Carter administration, for example, employee pressure led the administration to exempt the wages of hospital employees. Since those wages are the bulk of what might really be controllable, the exemption emasculated the proposal. It never reached the floor of either house, however. For a brief history, see Henry Aaron, "The Domestic Budget," in Joseph Pechman, ed., *Setting National Priorities: The 1980 Budget* (Washington, D.C.: The Brookings Institution, 1979), pp. 99–159, especially pp. 106–112.

[24] Note that the patient's state of illness can change in a moment. Typically the patient does go through a number of states, including initial diagnosis, treatment during an operation, and postoperation recovery.

between the physician as patient agent who demands ancillary services and others in the hospital responsible for their supply.

Why does this split arise? The doctor must maintain considerable independence from the hospital in order to be free to act in the patient's best interest. But the doctor must also be closely linked to the supplies in order to make sure that they are available when demanded. The solution is for the patient to have independent contracts with both the physicians and the hospital. The physicians and hospital administrators work out a set of rules and procedures for sharing the hospital facilities and directing the internal resource allocations, which is like having two firms in one.

Why does this split arrangement encourage continual expansion of capacity? Each doctor always wants assurance that inputs are available for his or her patients. The hospital administrator will not add such new capital inputs as beds and test machinery unless the existing ones are in use up to capacity. But as the hospital approaches capacity, each doctor becomes more protective of his or her share of the inputs. Standard routines for giving priority—emergency requests for hospital services such as x-rays are filled before routine ones—break down as the doctors specify higher and higher proportions of requests as emergencies, and it is virtually impossible to interfere with the doctor's spot judgment. The easiest way out is to add capacity. Once available, it will be utilized as doctors exercise their discretion in giving their patients the "best" care. That sets off the protective instincts of each doctor over the remaining capacity and continues the spiral of increasing capacity.

Regulations that attempt to limit hospital expenditures can set off this kind of mad scramble for the resources, and the hospital administrator, who must enforce the regulations, cannot control the physicians who insist that they need a series of x-rays right away. The result could be an *increase* in resources used per case and a "need" for new hospitals as all the existing facilities are used to capacity with fewer patients. More likely, the regulations will be evaded in one way or the other. In either event there is little reason, in the Harris model, to think that they would achieve their intended purpose.

This review of nonprofit hospital models is intended to illustrate how the logic of microeconomic analysis can be used to understand the behavior of producing organizations that do not operate in ordinary markets. The insights come from applying the basic determinants of organizational behavior—objectives, capabilities, and constraints—to the new setting. Although all of the models have some intuitive plausibility about them, the strength of the methodology is that the models are explicit and empirically testable, or falsifiable. If, by contrast, one simply interviewed hospital administrators and physicians, any story that sounded plausible might be accepted as the "truth." One also might not realize the implications of the story for other situations or see that a simplification of complex reality (e.g., physician income maximization) can be useful for predictive purposes.[25]

The range and accuracy of hospital models such as those discussed above have not as yet been resolved. Nevertheless, the limited empirical evidence that we have suggests that

---

[25] These comments are not meant to disparage interviews as a source of information; indeed, they are often an invaluable source of information that would not otherwise be obtained, as well as ideas for improving empirical models.

the models are providing important insights. Furthermore, something is gained by going through the logic of the models in addition to deducing their implications. Perhaps it is best described as disciplined common sense. It is a way of achieving a heightened appreciation of how and why hospitals work as they do.

Public Bureaus and Enterprises

The application of economic decision-making models to public producing agencies, like that of the nonprofit models, is not highly developed. The best known theory of the type is Niskanen's *budget-maximizing bureau*.[26] This model assumes that the motivations of upper-level bureaucrats are like those of the sales-maximizing private-firm managers. That is, the bigger the bureau's budget, the higher the salaries of its top-level bureaucrats. If bureaucrats are interested in maximizing their salaries and prestige, one way to do so is to maximize the budgets of their bureaus.

Niskanen makes the further assumption that the bureau has the power of perfect price discrimination, argued in a novel way. There is a "public" demand curve for the bureau's output, and its height at any point shows the maximum willingness to pay for that unit. However, *that output is not sold directly to consumers—and this is what distinguishes it from the public enterprise, which does sell directly.* Rather, the legislature acts as the public's "purchasing agent" and decides the budget level to appropriate to the bureau. The legislature is assumed to know the public's demand curve and therefore the public's maximum willingness to pay for any given output level. But an information asymmetry is assumed: Only the bureau knows the curves of least-cost production. Therefore, the legislature is at the mercy of the bureau: The legislature will be led to accept any budget as long as the area under the demand curve for the promised output quantity is no less than the cost. The bureau will find that output level where the maximum it can extract—the area under the demand curve—just equals the least total cost of production. In other words, the Niskanen model predicts behavior equivalent to that of the perfectly price-discriminating sales maximizer with a break-even constraint.

To see this, let us look at Figure 11-3. We have drawn a linear demand curve and a constant marginal cost curve for simplicity. The economically efficient output level is denoted by Q_E. Clearly, the bureau will produce more than Q_E if it receives a budget equal to the area under the demand curve. At Q_E there will be a surplus of budget over least total cost equal to the triangle $P_E AB$; the bureau can get a bigger budget by expanding output and still stay within the break-even constraint. Since the budget keeps increasing as output expands, the bureau will expand until it bumps into the break-even constraint. For the linear demand, constant-cost case, this will be exactly twice the efficient output level, shown as Q_M.[27]

---

[26] William A. Niskanen, Jr., *Bureaucracy and Representative Government* (Chicago: Aldine-Atherton, Inc., 1971).

[27] This is true only if the demand curve is still positive in the range of Q_M. Should the curve hit the axis before reaching the break-even point (empirically unlikely), the budget is at its absolute maximum there and the

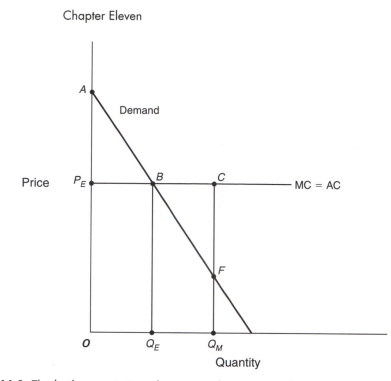

Figure 11-3. The budget-maximizing bureau produces too much output (Q_M).

The same kind of reservation can be expressed about this model as we indicated earlier by developing alternative models. We will simply summarize them here and then look at an application to the pricing decisions of a public enterprise. One type of reservation is that the underlying conception of self-interest that leads to the objective function is too much of a caricature of reality. Expressed in mild form, it can be argued that the bureaucrat might get more pleasure from inefficient production than from large budgets. That is, the bureaucrat might produce Q_E at a cost equal to the whole area under the demand curve, where bureaucratic benefits are garnered at the cost of excess resources $P_E AB$. That would result in the right quantity being produced, but the consumer loss in each case is the same.[28]

The same reservation expressed in stronger form is simply that the utility that individuals receive is influenced much more strongly by social norms of "doing a good job," or "behaving professionally," or "being honest" than those simple proxies for utility such as

---

bureau would not expand output further. Rather, it would use the excess budgetary resources inefficiently, departing from the least-cost production.

To see that the break-even point at Q_M is twice Q_E, note that the loss $\triangle BCF$ from the additional units past Q_E must equal the surplus $\triangle P_E AB$ from the first Q_E units. With a linear demand curve, these are similar triangles for any $Q > Q_E$. To be equal in area, they must have $P_E B = BC$ or $OQ_E = \frac{1}{2} OQ_M$.

[28] BCF is the consumer loss in the Niskanen model, compared to producing the efficient quantity Q_E and pricing at marginal cost P_E. $P_E AB$ is the consumer loss in this one, because it measures the opportunity cost of the excess resources. The losses are equal, since the triangles are similar and have equal sides ($P_E B = BC$). The social loss is the consumer loss minus the value of bureaucratic gains.

"salary" suggest.[29] That is, people for the most part behave in a socially responsible manner rather than an exploitative one because they receive more pleasure from living that way. This is not to deny that *some* people would try to exploit others maximally, and perhaps many people would engage in some selfish exploitation if they could get away with it. But social forces, in terms of, say, families, schools, and religion, act as very powerful constraints against exploitative urges. The bureau might seek to produce much more closely to Q_E and to minimum cost than the Niskanen model suggests.[30]

A second type of reservation about this bureaucratic model concerns the nature of the legislative constraints. A good argument can be made that the legislature knows far more about the cost curves than it does about the location of the demand curves (in terms of the population's true willingness to pay for additional outputs). Generally, there is no market mechanism for goods supplied by the federal and state governments that causes demand to be revealed. The main sources of legislative information about demand are elections, which express voter demand in a very crude aggregate manner, and special interest groups, which by definition represent special rather than general interests.

Records of expenditures and their purposes must be kept by the bureaus, and their procedures for making expenditures are constantly being examined. For example, most bureaus are required to obtain competitive bids from potential factor suppliers, and this bidding process is subject to regular scrutiny by watchdog agencies such as the federal Office of Management and Budget (OMB) and the General Accounting Office (GAO). Again, this is not to suggest that oversight committees have as much knowledge about costs as the agency has. But the difference may be of no greater consequence than is the differential knowledge of inventory costs possessed by a firm's inventory specialist and the rest of the firm: One side knows more of the details, but the other side can tell if costs get too far out of line.

Some bureaus, such as public schools, are controlled more directly by local voters. Although state legislators generally do play an important role in funding the schools, localities provide almost half of the school revenues and their citizens determine the budget by voting. It could be argued, within the bureau budget maximization framework, that these voters are as ill-informed as the legislature is assumed to be about the least-cost production possibilities. If that is so, the bureau may be able to extract the surplus of the median voter (Chapter 5). On the other hand, the Tiebout model suggests that public producing organizations such as schools are subject to competition from neighboring localities, which may

---

[29] See, for example, the theory and empirical work of D. McFadden. "Revealed Preferences of a Government Bureaucracy, Parts I and II," *Bell Journal of Economics, 6,* Autumn 1976, pp. 401–416, and *7,* Spring 1977, pp. 52–72. McFadden concludes that the routing decisions of the California Division of Highways are primarily explained by their net social benefits.

[30] Note that these forces are often ignored by economists without harm to predictions. That is because, for so many proposed economic changes, social forces are constant, that is, they exert approximately the same influence with or without the economic change. It also occurs because economic constraints often limit discretionary behavior. In the Niskanen model, in which there are few external economic constraints on behavior and the prediction involves the desired equilibrium (rather than, say, the response to a price increase), it is more important to consider the other social forces.

be another way in which the constraint on the organization deviates from the basic Niskanen model to limit the extraction of consumer surplus.

These latter reservations concerning the legislative and voter constraints do not involve alternative assumptions about the motivations or objectives of a bureau. Rather, in the extreme they suggest that the environment in which a bureau operates may be so constraining that the bureaucratic objectives become moot: The bureau must behave exactly as the legislature or the median voter wishes. In a less extreme version these reservations imply that there are constraints that limit the exercise of bureaucratic discretion substantially more than the bureau budget-maximization model suggests.

Empirical Prediction of Public Enterprise Behavior: The Pricing Decisions of BART

To demonstrate that the alternative theories of public supply organizations can be tested empirically, Cooter and Topakian analyzed the pricing decisions of a public enterprise.[31] They studied the Bay Area Rapid Transit District (BART), which operates the rail mass transit of the San Francisco Bay area. BART is subsidized by both federal grants and funds earmarked from local sales and property taxes; the rest of its costs must be covered by charging passengers fares, a break-even constraint.

Imagine a rail line with one end in the city center and the other in a distant suburb and with a number of stations for pickups and departures spread out along the way. BART must establish fares between all possible origin-destination pairs along the route. The question Cooter and Topakian consider is whether they can predict the fares that BART will set by using some of the theories we have discussed about decision-making in public supply organizations. The predicted (or actual) fares in relation to trip costs reveal which passengers (by station) receive the greatest subsidies.

One hypothesis that they use to formulate fare prediction is the bureaucratic one: The fare structure chosen will be the one that maximizes bureaucratic interests, and those interests are best achieved by maximizing the size of the enterprise. They suggest two measures of size: farebox revenues and total passenger-miles. Given their estimates of the elasticity of demand, they calculate the fares that maximize each of the alternative size measures.

Cooter and Topakian note that BART has a nine-member board of directors elected by the voters in each of the nine BART subdistricts. As an alternative to the bureaucratic view, they hypothesize that BART pricing decisions are effectively dictated by the political process. They suggest two versions of political control: (1) Subsidies will be distributed to maximize electoral votes, which implies maximizing the benefit of the median voter. (2) Subsidies will be distributed in accordance with the political power of various *interest groups,* whose identities are assumed to correlate with socioeconomic characteristics of the people in areas served by BART.

---

[31] R. Cooter and G. Topakian, "Political Economy of a Public Corporation: Pricing Objectives of BART," *Journal of Public Economics, 13,* No. 3, June 1980, pp. 299–318.

Because the actual Cooter and Topakian study is empirically quite complex, it may be useful to illustrate the different predictions of each model in a highly artificial but numerically simple setting. To do this, we use a setting similar to the one we used for the price discrimination example in Chapter 10. We will assume BART consumers may be separated into two groups (stations) with demand curves for passenger-miles as follows:

$$Q_1 = 10 - P_1 \quad \text{or} \quad P_1 = 10 - Q_1$$

$$Q_2 = 20 - P_2 \quad \text{or} \quad P_2 = 20 - Q_2$$

We also assume that the marginal cost per passenger-mile is constant and equal to $4, although BART incurred substantial initial costs to lay the track.

Let us first consider the two alternative bureaucratic objectives: *farebox revenue maximization* and *passenger-mile maximization*. If BART seeks to set prices that would maximize farebox revenues, it will, like a discriminating sales maximizer, identify the Q_1 with $MR_1 = 0$ and the Q_2 with $MR_2 = 0$. The marginal revenue curves for these demand curves (derived as those in Chapter 10) are

$$MR_1 = 10 - 2Q_1 = 0 \rightarrow Q_1 = 5$$

$$MR_2 = 20 - 2Q_2 = 0 \rightarrow Q_2 = 10$$

Then the prices charged are found by substituting the quantities $Q_1 = 5$ and $Q_2 = 10$ in the demand curves:

$$5 = 10 - P_1 \rightarrow P_1 = \$5$$

$$10 = 20 - P_2 \rightarrow P_2 = \$10$$

Thus BART charges district 1 commuters $5 and district 2 commuters $10 and collects the maximum farebox revenues of $125 = $5(5) + $10(10).

The above objective is quite different from maximizing passenger-miles ($Q_1 + Q_2$). With unlimited government subsidy, BART would simply set $P_1 = P_2 = 0$, and then $Q_1 = 10$ and $Q_2 = 20$. However, BART may at least be required to cover its operating costs of $4 per passenger-mile. With that constraint, it can be shown that BART would (approximately) set $P_1 = \$1$ and $P_2 = \$6$, which would lead to $Q_1 = 9$, $Q_2 = 14$, and BART revenues of $93.[32]

To understand how the political models would imply different solutions, suppose that the fares (P_1 and P_2) were determined by *majority vote,* that the number of voters equaled

---

[32] The solution equalizes the marginal revenue for an additional passenger-mile in each group. Otherwise, BART could get more total revenue for the same passenger-miles (and same operating costs). This would give it revenues above those required to meet the operating costs constraint, and it could subsidize additional passenger-miles.

Let us look at the problem in calculus form. In order to maximize $Q_1 + Q_2$ subject to the constraint, we form the Lagrangian expression

$$L = Q_1 + Q_2 + \lambda[P_1 Q_1 + P_2 Q_2 - 4(Q_1 + Q_2)]$$

10 in district 1 and 20 in district 2, and that the voters in each district represented the interests of their commuters. Of course, all voters could then agree to set $P_1 = P_2 = 0$ if there were no subsidy constraint (and the subsidy were provided by the federal government, not the taxpayers in each district!). But suppose BART had to cover its operating costs. That is, voters could approve any P_1 and P_2 as long as total revenues equaled total operating costs:

$$P_1 Q_1 + P_2 Q_2 = 4(Q_1 + Q_2)$$

Substituting $Q_1 = 10 - P_1$ and $Q_2 = 20 - P_2$, we rewrite this as

$$P_1(10 - P_1) + P_2(20 - P_2) = 4(10 - P_1 + 20 - P_2)$$

On simplifying, we are left with an equation for a circle:

$$10P_1 - P_1^2 + 20P_2 - P_2^2 = 120 - 4P_1 - 4P_2$$

or

$$14P_1 - P_1^2 + 24P_2 - P_2^2 = 120$$

This equation is the locus of all P_1 and P_2 combinations that satisfy the constraint, shown in Figure 11-4. Note that the equation applies only over the range of prices valid for the demand curves: $P_1 \leq \$10$ and $P_2 \leq \$20$. For $P_1 > \$10$, $Q_1 = 0$ and the constraint becomes $P_2 Q_2 = 4Q_2$, or P_2 must equal the marginal cost of $4. Similarly, for $P_2 > \$20$, $Q_2 = 0$ and P_1 must equal $4. The parts of the circle that have prices outside these ranges are not valid solutions and are drawn with dotted lines. The solid lines in Figure 11-4 show the fare combinations that satisfy the subsidy and price-range constraints.

Naturally, the voters in district 1 prefer the lowest feasible P_1 (and therefore a relatively high P_2), and the voters in district 2 prefer the opposite. If possible, the voters in district 1 would prefer that $P_1 = 0$. This would imply that

$$24P_2 - P_2^2 = 120$$

This has the two solutions shown below with the associated output levels and BART revenues (equal to the operating costs):

Then the first-order conditions are

$$\frac{\partial L}{\partial Q_1} = 1 + \lambda \left(P_1 + Q_1 \frac{\partial P_1}{\partial Q_1} - 4 \right) = 0 \tag{i}$$

$$\frac{\partial L}{\partial Q_2} = 1 + \lambda \left(P_2 + Q_2 \frac{\partial P_2}{\partial Q_2} - 4 \right) = 0 \tag{ii}$$

$$\frac{\partial L}{\partial \lambda} = P_1 Q_1 + P_2 Q_2 - 4(Q_1 + Q_2) = 0 \tag{iii}$$

We solve these equations simultaneously for Q_1, Q_2, and λ by substituting $P_1 = 10 - Q_1$ and $P_2 = 20 - Q_2$ and noting that $\partial P_1/\partial Q_1 = -1$ and $\partial P_2/\partial Q_2 = -1$. Q_1 is approximately 9.042, and Q_2 is approximately 14.042. Note that the expressions in equations (i) and (ii) following the λ are simply MR − MC. Since both these expressions equal $-1/\lambda$, they are equal to one another; and since MC = 4 in both cases, $MR_1 = MR_2$.

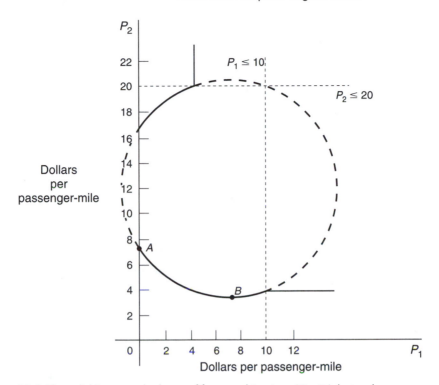

Figure 11-4. The solid lines are the locus of fare combinations (P_1, P_2) that make revenue equal operating costs.

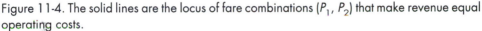

$$P_2 = \$16.90 \qquad Q_2 = 3.1 \qquad Q_1 = 10 \qquad TR = \$52.39$$

$$P_2 = \$7.10 \qquad Q_2 = 12.9 \qquad Q_1 = 10 \qquad TR = \$91.59$$

Obviously, of the two solutions district 2 would prefer $P_2 = \$7.10$ (as would BART management from the perspective of either revenues or passenger-miles). District 1 voters, hoping for the best, propose $P_1 = 0$ and $P_2 = \$7.10$ (shown as point A in Figure 11-4).

Of course, district 2 voters must prefer that $P_2 = 0$, which implies that

$$14P_1 - P_1^2 = 120$$

This is not feasible, however. As can be seen from Figure 11-4, there is no P_1 that could raise enough revenue to cover the operating costs of both the district 1 commuters and the 20 passenger-miles that are free to district 2 commuters.[33] Thus the best feasible plan from the perspective of district 2 voters will involve some $P_2 > 0$. It can be shown that the

[33] The quadratic equation $P_1^2 - 14P_1 + 120 = 0$ has the nonreal solutions

$$\frac{14 \pm \sqrt{14^2 - 4(120)}}{2} = \frac{14 \pm \sqrt{-284}}{2}$$

lowest feasible $P_2 = \$3.46$ with $Q_2 = 16.54$, which implies that $P_1 = \$7.00$ and $Q_1 = 3$.[34] This solution has BART revenues (equal to operating costs) of $78.23. Thus district 2 voters have a preferred solution of $P_1 = \$7.00$ and $P_2 = \$3.46$ (point B in Figure 11-4).

In this simple problem it is obvious that the voters in district 2 have a majority and can elect their preferred solution; then $P_1 = \$7.00$ with $Q_1 = 3$, $P_2 = \$3.46$ with $Q_2 = 16.54$, and BART revenues are $78.23. Note that this median voter solution differs substantially from either of the two solutions proposed to meet bureaucratic objectives. (BART could achieve $125 in revenues or 23 passenger-miles of service if not constrained by the voters.)[35]

Finally, a simple *interest group model* might be as follows: If district 1 residents are rich, powerful, and well-connected and district 2 residents are not, district 1 residents may be able to impose their preferred solution. Discreetly, they back a candidate to run as the head of BART's board of directors. The candidate makes campaign promises that appeal to everyone: for example, to keep BART safe, swift, sparkling clean, and subsidized. When elected, the candidate quietly imposes the fare structure preferred by district 1 residents.

These very simple examples are intended to illustrate why the four different models considered by Cooter and Topakian have different predictions. The authors tackled the diffi-

---

[34] We wish to choose P_1, P_2, and λ to minimize P_2 subject to the constraint that TR = TC. We formulate the Lagrangian

$$L = P_2 + \lambda(14P_1 - P_1^2 + 24P_2 - P_2^2 - 120)$$

and take the partial derivatives for the first-order conditions:

$$\frac{\partial L}{\partial P_1} = \lambda(14 - 2P_1) = 0 \tag{i}$$

$$\frac{\partial L}{\partial P_2} = 1 + \lambda(24 - 2P_2) = 0 \tag{ii}$$

$$\frac{\partial L}{\partial \lambda} = 14P_1 - P_1^2 + 24P_2 - P_2^2 - 120 = 0 \tag{iii}$$

From equation (i) we can see that $P_1 = \$7$ as long as $\lambda \neq 0$ (i.e., the constraint is binding). Equation (iii) then reduces to a simple quadratic:

$$14(7.00) - (7.00^2) + 24P_2 - P_2^2 - 120 = 0$$

or

$$P_2^2 - 24P_2 + 71 = 0$$

By use of the quadratic formula, this has the solution

$$P_2 = \$3.456$$

[35] This is a median voter solution in the following sense. We can describe the preferences of the voters in terms of the lowest P_1 they are willing to approve (since a relatively low P_1 corresponds to a relatively high P_2). If we order the thirty voters in terms of those preferences, ten will approve $P_1 = 0$ and the next twenty will require $P_1 \leq \$7$ for approval. If we imagine starting with $P_1 = 0$, voting on it, and raising it incrementally until sixteen voters (a majority) approve the plan, then no plan will be approved until $P_1 = \$7$.

cult question of numerically predicting the fares that BART would set if it behaved according to each model. Then they compared those predictions with the actual BART fares.

To test their hypotheses, the authors undertook a careful empirical study. They had survey data indicating the average trip length of riders originating at each of thirty-three stations along BART routes. The existing fares were, of course, known. Independent studies of the price elasticity of demand for BART riders had been calculated elsewhere, and the authors used a range of those elasticity estimates to predict how ridership would change in response to various fare changes.[36]

To calculate the subsidy received by the average rider at each station, one needs to know not only the fare charged but also the costs of the service. In a separate model Cooter and Topakian estimated the costs per mile from each station, again under a range of assumptions. Their methods led to a "best" estimate whereby the cost per passenger-mile is an increasing function of distance from the city center. This occurs primarily because the trains are more fully loaded nearer the center, and the fixed costs per person are therefore lower. With these estimates, they calculated the actual subsidies received by the average passengers at each station.

Figure 11-5 is a reconstruction of a diagram in the Cooter-Topakian article that displays the subsidy possibilities, the observed subsidies, and the ones predicted by the alternative models (except the interest group model, explained below). The subsidy possibilities are directly analogous to the locus of feasible P_1 and P_2 fare combinations in our simple illustrative example. Each subsidy possibility represents a set of fares (one for each station) minus the corresponding cost of service (from each station) that meets BART's break-even constraint.

This representation of the subsidy possibilities involves the following simplification. From each station there are actually numerous fares (and corresponding costs), one for each possible destination. However, Cooter and Topakian found that the fares could be approximated by a simple linear function of average trip length. That is, they calculated that a passenger from station j pays an average of P_j per passenger-mile and imposes average costs of C_j per passenger-mile, and therefore receives an average subsidy per passenger-mile of $S_j (= P_j - C_j)$. They also calculated the average trip length t_j from station j. They then found that this subsidy system (all S_j for $j = 1, 2, \ldots, 33$ stations) could be approximated accurately by a linear equation (with coefficients a_0 and a_1):

$$S_j = a_0 + a_1 t_j$$

They then suggested that alternative subsidy systems can be approximated with this equation by varying the coefficients a_0 and a_1. A positive a_1, for example, implies that stations with passengers taking the longest trips get the largest subsidies. For a fixed total subsidy, a higher a_1 implies larger subsidies to passengers with the longest trips and lower

---

[36] Over the whole system, the price elasticity estimate used was −0.3. The authors also had separate estimates of the price elasticities from each station, which averaged about −0.15. The second estimates were more inelastic because they were based on data from both BART *and* bus riders, so the only transportation alternative was automobile commuting.

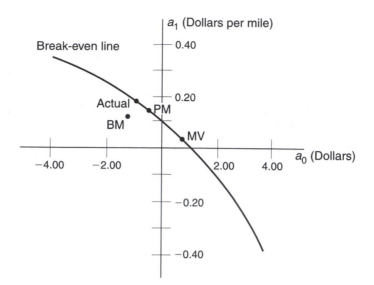

Figure 11-5. BART's subsidy possibilities: BM = budget maximization, PM = passenger-mile maximization, and MV = median voter. The best subsidy from each perspective is shown and compared with the actual subsidy. (From R. Cooter and G. Topakian, "Political Economy of a Public Corporation: Pricing Objectives of BART," *Journal of Public Economics, 13,* No. 3, June 1980, pp. 299–318, Fig. 3, with permission from Elsevier Science.)

subsidies to those with shorter trips. In Figure 11-5, the vertical axis measures a_1 and the horizontal axis a_0.

The solid line in Figure 11-5 shows all possible (linear) subsidy schemes that satisfy BART's break-even constraint. The actual subsidy is seen to favor riders with longer average trips. The budget maximization hypothesis implies that the coefficients on the subsidy equation should be those at BM; this is off the constraint on the assumption that the excess revenues would be converted into increased management expenses of one form or another. The alternative measure of size used was passenger-miles; it would be maximized at the point shown as PM. Both bureaucratic hypotheses are reasonably close to the actual subsidy system.

The median voter model, shown as MV, implies a subsidy structure quite different from the others. Although subsidies still increase slightly with average trip distance, those with shorter average distances are treated relatively more generously. The reason is not complicated. Voters have interests similar to those of the BART riders in their areas: The bigger the subsidies, the greater the number of BART riders and the less the pollution and congestion on the roads in the area. A high a_0 and a low a_1 favor the minority with the shortest trips and displease everyone else. It would be easy to oust the incumbents with a new subsidy proposal. Similarly, a low a_0 and a high a_1 favor the minority with the longest trips and displease everyone else. The only subsidy system that cannot be beaten by the formation of a new majority is the one in the middle.

However, the fact that the actual subsidy system does not look like the one predicted by the median voter model suggests that, in this case, there is no effective democratic voting control. If any control were exercised by this method, one would at least expect the actual system to lie between the bureaucratic preferences and the voter preferences in Figure 11-5. Instead, the actual system deviates from the bureaucratic preferences in a direction opposite to that which could be explained by pressure from the median voter. The median voter hypothesis is rejected in this context.

The other theory of political control, the interest group model, cannot be represented on the diagram. If some people have more clout than others, the areas in which they are concentrated would benefit relatively more than other areas. There is no reason to assume that these areas are geographically linear. The authors, by using regression analysis, attempted to see if they could explain the average subsidy at each station on the basis of the characteristics of people living there—average incomes, education, percent of riders who use BART regularly during the week, and so forth. The results did not provide much independent support for the hypothesis: The characteristics had little ability to predict the subsidy, except for those correlated with trip length.

Thus we are left with these conclusions: The median voter model is rejected. The bureaucratic models are "close" to the observed subsidies; but under the range of estimates used in their modeling, the bureaucratic predictions are not quite close enough to accept (or strongly reject) the hypothesis that bureaucratic objectives explain the actual subsidies. Furthermore, the bureaucratic interests correlate to some extent with the interest group characteristics correlated with trip length: income and education. Therefore, we cannot be certain about the extent to which these models explain the observed fare structure.

Of course, it is always possible that an untested model would be a better predictor than any of the models tested. Perhaps BART's objectives were to set the most efficient fares, for example. All the tested models focused on differing objectives or constraints that might be driving the system, and none of them considered the BART's capabilities to choose subsidies that meet any given set of objectives. It is possible, for example, that bounded rationality led BART to set its fares to be competitive with those on the existing bus routes, without thinking about which passengers get subsidies.

The above exercise illustrates a methodology for learning how to predict the behavior of a public supply organization. As with the nonprofit models, these are not easy exercises.[37] But if we had a better understanding of the pricing decisions of BART (and perhaps similar mass transit enterprises), we could predict the effects of changing subsidies (perhaps changing federal subsidies to many mass transit systems) on the fare structure and in turn on the usage of the system. Or we could predict how required subsidies would change in response to proposed standards for fare-setting. Or we might learn what inducement would be necessary to cause BART to allocate resources efficiently (and how this compares with

[37] For other examples, see E. Bertero and L. Rondi, "Financial Pressure and the Behaviour of Public Enterprises under Soft and Hard Budget Constraints: Evidence from Italian Panel Data, *Journal of Public Economics, 75,* No. 1, January 2000, pp. 73–98; and Dieter Bos, *Pricing and Price Regulation: An Economic Theory for Public Enterprises and Public Utilities* (New York: Elsevier Science, 1994).

other institutional forms). Such predictions, derived by a systematic, testable, and improvable methodology, would be substantially more reliable than those based on the untested impressions one might glean from direct observation alone.

A Normative Model of Public Enterprise Pricing: The Efficient Fare Structure

One question that the BART case study might raise is this: How should BART set its fares if its objective is to be socially efficient? Since prices determine the level of use, this is equivalent to seeking the optimal allocation of resources. The usual answer to such a question is to charge a price equal to the marginal cost, but that fails to illuminate the reason why BART is a public enterprise in the first place. Rail systems, bridges, utilities, and certain other segments of the economy are characterized by very high fixed or indivisible costs (e.g., laying the track, building the bridge) and low marginal costs. If these increasing-returns industries priced at marginal cost, they would be unprofitable since average cost is greater than marginal cost.

A review of this problem is illustrated in Figure 11-6. We assume there are fixed costs (not shown) and then constant marginal costs per unit of service; we further assume that total benefits exceed total costs over some positive range of output. As drawn, the marginal benefit of each unit up to Q_E exceeds its marginal cost of P_E; therefore, efficiency seems to require that Q_E units be produced. However, charging a price equal to the marginal cost implies that the enterprise will have *negative* profits equal to $P_E P_A AE$. No private firm would provide efficient service in those circumstances, and, in some cases, there might be no quantity at which operation without price discrimination is privately profitable. (This depends on whether the demand curve is ever higher than average cost.)

Given this failure of the private market, what kind of organization should provide the service? One suggestion is to have a regulated private firm do it. This could be made possible by a state-supplied *per unit subsidy* of $P_A - P_E$ (in Figure 11-6), with a requirement that the firm charge a price P_E. Another suggestion is to create a public enterprise, charge P_E, and let the government make up losses out of general tax revenues. The preferred organizational form depends upon the difficulty of controlling the behavior of each form. The considerations raised throughout this and the preceding chapter can be helpful in designing and evaluating specific organizational forms to fit specific problems.

But at this point, to get into the pricing question, we must introduce a new issue. It is that the government revenues raised to make up the deficit impose social costs elsewhere in the economy; therefore, the output level Q_E is not optimal after all. The first-best solution is to have the marginal net benefits be zero everywhere, but this turns out to be an impossibility. If they are zero in this sector (at Q_E), they will be nonzero for the activities taxed to provide the subsidy, and overall the resources will not be optimally allocated. We will not go into the problem of identifying the optimal level here, known as the second-best problem, but note that the government's determination of the subsidy level is an important part of solving the larger problem.

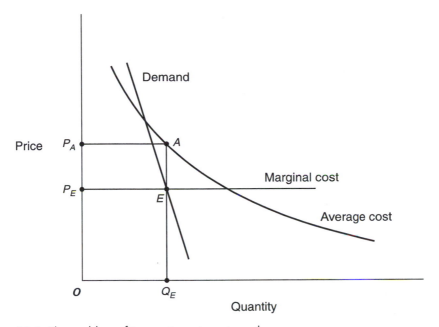

Figure 11-6. The problem of increasing returns to scale.

The problem we examine is a smaller one. We assume that the government has already set BART up as a public enterprise and announced the subsidy level. The tracks are laid and the capital equipment is purchased; in other words, the capacity of the system is "fixed" for the time period we are imagining.[38] We want to know *what prices will lead to the most efficient resource allocation, given the capacity, the break-even constraint (revenues must equal costs minus government subsidies), and demand for BART services.* This problem is sometimes referred to as the *Ramsey pricing problem,* after the man who posed and solved it in 1927.[39]

In the appendix we derive Ramsey's results and mention some other applications. Here we try to offer a more intuitive understanding of them and their implications for public enterprise pricing. To simplify matters, let us imagine that there is a BART line with only three stations: the Business District, One-Mile Island, and Two-Mile Island. (Owing to a nuclear accident, Three-Mile Island was shut down a number of years ago.) Demand is smooth all day (no peak-level problem), and it is the same coming into the city as going back. (All passengers are round-trippers.) We will refer to the daily demand for passenger-miles without worrying about the number of seats per car or scheduling problems. (The BART rolling stock

---

[38] Alchian has pointed out that nothing is ever "fixed." The expression implies that the cost of altering capacity (by any significant amount) within the time period being considered is too great to be economical. See A. Alchian, "Costs and Outputs," in W. Breit and H. Hochman, eds., *Readings in Microeconomics* (New York: Holt, Rinehart & Winston, Inc., 1971), pp. 159–171.

[39] F. P. Ramsey, "A Contribution to the Theory of Taxation," *Economic Journal, 37,* March 1927, pp. 47–61.

is flexible enough to handle these matters.) A main constraint is capacity: If BART stock rolls all the time, it can carry a maximum of 272 passenger-miles. The marginal cost of operating the train is a constant $1 per person per mile, up to the capacity. In addition, we assume that BART is required by the government to contribute $800 as its share of the fixed costs.

To make sure this model is clear, suppose that 40 people from Two-Mile Island wanted round-trips; this would take up 160 passenger-miles (2 miles each way per person). If 100 people also wanted round-trips from One-Mile Island, this would require another 200 passenger-miles and the total of 360 exceeds BART's capacity; there is no way that BART can provide this service. If only 50 people wanted round-trips from One-Mile Island, total demand would be 260 passenger-miles and within BART's capacity.

We are not worrying here about the details of assigning the number of rail cars on each run, the number of One-Mile Island runs, and so on. We assume that any enterprise smart enough to price efficiently is also smart enough to schedule trains properly. For example, BART might have two trains with a seating capacity of 25 each go to One-Mile Island only and have one larger train with a seating capacity of 40 be an express from Two-Mile Island. That would leave BART with 12 passenger-miles of unused capacity, and our assumption implies that the $12 marginal operating cost of the remaining capacity has been avoided. (One car sits idle all day, which saves the labor of moving and cleaning it.)

For further simplicity, we assume that the demand of One-Mile Islanders is completely inelastic (perhaps because they have no alternative such as a ferry service). Suppose that the demand curves for passenger-miles of One-Mile Islanders Q_1 and Two-Mile Islanders Q_2, respectively, are

$$Q_1 = 100$$

$$Q_2 = 268 - 32P_2 \quad 0 \leq P_2 \leq 8.375$$

In Figure 11-7a we show the sum of these demand curves as the market demand for BART passenger-miles Q_M:

$$Q_M = \begin{cases} 368 - 32P_M & 0 \leq P \leq 8.375 \\ 100 & 8.375 < P \end{cases}$$

We have also drawn in the line indicating a constant marginal operating cost of $1. In Figure 11-7b we illustrate each demand curve separately. Ignoring the capacity constraint, pricing at marginal operating cost would seem to imply $P = P_1 = P_2 = \$1$, where $Q_1 = 100$ and $Q_2 = 236$. This can also be interpreted as 50 round trips for One-Mile Islanders (2 passenger-miles each) and 59 round trips for Two-Mile Islanders (4 passenger-miles each). But we cannot do this for two reasons, which we deal with in the following order: (1) The "solution" provides 336 passenger-miles, which, given BART's capacity of 272, is impossible. (2) BART is extremely unprofitable; it covers only its marginal operating costs and thus does not contribute a cent toward its required payment of $800 to partially cover the fixed costs. It is the second problem that raises the Ramsey issue.

Under "first-best" rules (i.e., marginal cost pricing), we could point out that BART has the wrong capacity: it "should" choose the capacity that will provide service to all persons who are willing to pay at least the marginal cost (i.e., capacity "should" be 336).[40] The quotation marks are used to indicate that, because of the second problem, it is erroneous to apply first-best rules. There is an "optimal" capacity that would not turn out to be 336; however, its magnitude depends upon the "second-best" calculation of balancing the marginal efficiency loss caused by the tax used to provide the subsidy with the net gain from the marginal BART service it makes possible. We duck this complex issue and accept BART's current capacity of 272 as a constraint. How should BART price to ration the 272 available passenger-miles if it wishes to be efficient (still ignoring the second problem)?

The effect of the capacity constraint is shown in Figure 11-7a. Once one reaches the quantity of 272 passenger-miles, the marginal cost of providing one additional passenger-mile in the short-run (i.e., with fixed capacity) becomes effectively infinite. That is, the short-run marginal cost curve becomes vertical at the quantity 272. It is recognition of this feature that allows us to solve the first problem properly.

It can be seen from Figure 11-7a that the market demand intersects the short-run marginal cost curve on its vertical segment at a price of $3. In other words, the effective marginal cost is $3, consisting of the $1 marginal operating cost and a $2 cost of forgone surplus from denying service to an additional passenger. At this price $Q_1 = 100$ and $Q_2 = 172$, or One-Mile Islanders get 50 round-trips and Two-Mile Islanders get 43.[41] This is the short-run marginal cost pricing solution, once the effect of the capacity constraint on the short-run marginal cost curve is recognized. (If the demand curve crossed the short-run marginal cost curve on its horizontal segment, then the efficient quantity would be below capacity and the price would simply equal the marginal operating cost.)

At this stage of the problem, a $3 price per passenger-mile for all does lead to the "most efficient" allocation. Since we are at capacity, the only way to improve the allocation is if there is some nonrider who values riding more than some current rider does. All riders value their last passenger-mile at $3 or more. The only nonriders (with any demand) are on Two-Mile Island, but their willingness to pay for a passenger-mile is less than $3 (in Figure 11-7b, the nonrider demands are shown on the demand curve D_2 to the right of $Q_2 = 172$). There is no room for a deal; the allocation is most efficient given the capacity. This same reasoning leading to a price above the marginal operating costs applies to many other problems where there are important capacity constraints, for example, bridge pricing during peak periods, or electricity pricing when generators are already operating at their maximum capacity, or (perhaps someday) use of Internet capacity.

---

[40] We are assuming that total benefits exceed total costs (including the fixed ones) at this capacity; otherwise the first-best solution would be to incur no fixed costs and provide no service. This point was reviewed in Chapter 8. We are also assuming a very simple cost structure, in which the only differences between long-run and short-run costs (up to capacity) are the fixed costs used to determine capacity.

[41] As price increases from $1 to $3, Two-Mile Islanders reduce their demand for BART by a proportionately greater amount because their demand is more elastic.

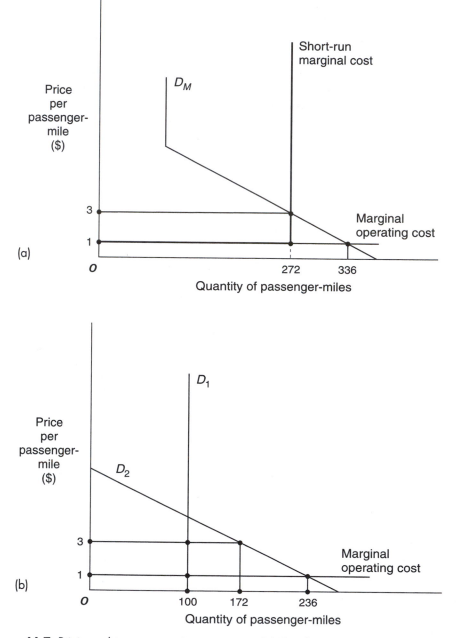

Figure 11-7. Pricing subject to capacity constraints: (a) The short-run marginal cost curve becomes vertical at the capacity of 272 and intersects market demand (D_M) at P = $3 per
passenger-mile. (b) One-Mile Islanders (D_1) demand 100 passenger-miles in the long run (P =
$1) and short run ($P$ = $3); Two-Mile Islanders ($D_2$) demand 236 in the long run and 172 in
the short run.

But we still have the Ramsey issue. BART's total revenues are $816, which exceed its operating costs of $272 by $544. The government insists that this is not a large enough contribution toward meeting the fixed costs—and it may be correct: Since taxpayers are making up the difference, the taxes used to raise the subsidy cause a wedge between the supply price and the demand price of each taxed commodity. For example, a sales tax T results in the consumer's marginal value of the taxed commodity being $P + T$, whereas the marginal opportunity cost of the resources used to supply it are only P. Being "myopically efficient" by marginal cost pricing in the BART sector causes an inefficiency in the taxed sector.

Since all conventional taxes create such wedges (discussed in Chapter 12), any increasing-returns activity that has deficits must balance its efficiency gains against the tax efficiency losses it creates. Thus there is an optimal deficit level, assuming optimal second-best pricing is followed everywhere. However, solving this very general "second-best" problem remains beyond our empirical abilities. For purposes here we assume that the government in its wisdom requires BART to contribute $800. Whether or not this is the correct level for optimal resource allocation, BART is stuck with it and must do the best it can from here.

Looking at Figure 11-8a, we might reason that the price per passenger-mile must be raised until $800 above operating costs can be collected. The lowest price per passenger-mile that will do this is (approximately) $4.64, which will result in 220 passenger-miles (50 round-trips for One-Mile Islanders and 55 round-trips for Two-Mile Islanders). The shaded rectangle in the diagram is the $800 contribution to fixed costs. The cross-hatched area is the loss in social benefits caused by this method of meeting the budget constraint requirement. This solution is equivalent to raising the price for round-trips from each location by the same proportion above its marginal costs.

However, there is another way to meet the budget constraint requirement that does not cause as big a social loss. Recall that there is a difference in the price elasticities of the One- and Two-Mile Islanders; the One-Mile Islanders are completely price-inelastic while the Two-Mile Islanders are not. Ramsey's principle, which we discuss below, suggests that we raise the price higher on the more inelastic product. Looking at Figure 11-8b, we can keep the price from Two-Mile Island at $3 per passenger-mile or $12 per round-trip (so that the residents continue to demand exactly 172 passenger-miles, or 43 round-trips), but charge $5.56 per passenger-mile or $11.12 per round-trip from One-Mile Island (where 100 passenger-miles or 50 round-trips continue to be demanded). The allocation is then exactly the same as when we charged $3.00 per passenger-mile from each island, fully utilizing the capacity and avoiding any loss in efficiency. Two-Mile Islanders contribute $344 above operating costs, and One-Mile Islanders contribute $456, for a total of $800 as required.

The above example is of an enterprise that has two products to sell (a round-trip from One-Mile Island and a round-trip from Two-Mile Island), and an overall budget constraint to meet (net revenue of $800). Any solution will cause some kind of departure from pricing each product at its marginal cost (after accounting for the capacity constraint, $6 and $12 are the respective marginal costs per round-trip). Our example was deliberately kept simple so that the most efficient pricing given the budget constraint would be transparent ($11.12 and $12 for the respective round-trips). While the exact solutions to less simple "Ramsey" problems are rarely transparent, general aspects of their features can be explained.

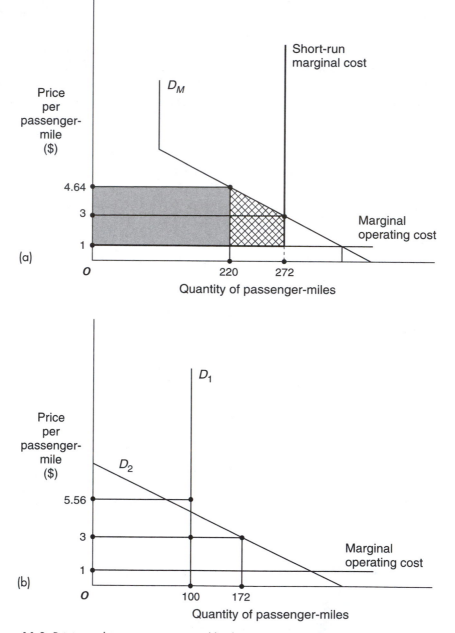

Figure 11-8. Pricing subject to capacity and budget constraints: (a) Raising the price the same percentage above marginal cost on both islands (to $4.64) meets the $800 budget constraint (shaded) but causes inefficient utilization (cross-hatched). (b) Ramsey pricing of $P_1 = \$5.56$ per passenger-mile and $P_2 = \$3$ per passenger-mile meets the $800 budget constraint and maximizes the efficiency of capacity utilization.

We have stated **the Ramsey pricing problem** thus: **How should an enterprise price its products to maximize efficiency when it is subject to an overall budget constraint? An analytically identical problem,** by the way, **is how to maximize efficiency when selecting tax rates for taxable goods and services in the economy given that total revenues of a certain amount are to be raised.**[42] Thus, solving the optimal enterprise pricing problem involves the same reasoning as solving for the optimal set of taxes. One version of the Ramsey solution, which applies to both, is known as **the inverse elasticities rule:**

$$\frac{P_i - \mathrm{MC}_i}{P_i} = \frac{k}{\varepsilon_i} \quad i = 1, 2, \ldots, n \text{ commodities}$$

where k is a negative constant (since ε_i is negative). In English, this says that **the percentage deviation of the price of a good from its marginal cost should be inversely related to its elasticity of demand.** This solution applies when the cross elasticities of demand among the goods subject to the budget constraint are zero.[43]

The reasoning underlying Ramsey's rule can be understood intuitively. If we cannot have the first-best allocation of resources because of a profit constraint that must be met, then presumably we wish to be as close as possible to first-best when we satisfy the constraint. Therefore, we raise the prices more on goods that are inelastically demanded because their allocations are least affected by the price increase.

We may be able to clarify this reasoning more precisely by looking at an equivalent expression of Ramsey's rule[44]

$$(P_i - \mathrm{MC}_i)\frac{\Delta Q_i}{\Delta P_i} = \delta\left[(P_i - \mathrm{MC}_i)\frac{\Delta Q_i}{\Delta P_i} + Q_i\right]$$

where δ is a constant. On the left-hand side, the first term in parentheses is the net benefit from consuming a marginal unit of Q_i. (P_i is the height of the demand curve and MC_i is the

[42] In fact, Ramsey actually solved the tax problem. Boiteux is generally credited with seeing the parallel to public enterprise pricing. See M. Boiteux, "On the Management of Public Monopolies Subject to Budget Constraints," *Journal of Economic Theory, 3,* 1971, pp. 219–242.

[43] When one takes account of cross effects, the solution is more complicated but it retains the same pricing tendency as the simpler case. This is shown in the appendix.

[44] It is easy to show the equivalence of the two expressions. Let us start with

$$(P_i - \mathrm{MC}_i)\frac{\Delta Q_i}{\Delta P_i} = \delta\left[(P_i - \mathrm{MC}_i)\frac{\Delta Q_i}{\Delta P_i} + Q_i\right]$$

Noting that the terms in parentheses on the right-hand side are identical with those on the left-hand side, we move them over:

$$(P_i - \mathrm{MC}_i)\frac{\Delta Q_i}{\Delta P_i}(1 - \delta) = \delta Q_i$$

or

$$P_i - \mathrm{MC}_i = \frac{\delta}{1 - \delta} Q_i \frac{1}{\Delta Q_i / \Delta P_i}$$

opportunity cost of the resources used to produce the unit.) The second term tells us by how many units Q_i decreases in response to a small price increase. So the whole left-hand side can be thought of as the dollar loss in benefits per unit increase in price.

On the right-hand side, ignoring the constant δ for the moment, we have the increase in "profit" (ignoring fixed costs) per unit increase in price. There are two components to it. The first terms after the brackets are identical with those on the left-hand side. They represent the loss in net revenue to the enterprise from the demand reduction owing to the unit price increase. But this is offset by the per unit increase in revenue on all the Q_i units that are sold. So the sum of everything between the brackets is the net increase in "profit" for a one-unit increase in price.

Therefore, the whole equation says the net loss in benefits for a unit price increase should be proportional to the net profit gained by it, or *the net loss in benefits for an extra dollar of profit should be the same for all commodities produced by the enterprise.* This is only logical. If social losses must be imposed (and they must), then following this rule will minimize them. If the marginal costs of obtaining an extra dollar of profit from any of the enterprise's products are not the same, then one could reduce the social loss by "giving back" $1 of profit where the loss is high and making it up where the loss is low.

Note that efficiency in the BART case, as implied by the Cooter and Topakian elasticity estimates, is to have the subsidies increasing as stations get farther away from the central business district.[45] Of course, this solution assumes no cross effects, and we have not considered equity. Let us mention a few considerations that are real, although outside our illustration.

There is good reason to think that One-Mile Islanders are relatively insensitive to changes in fares to Two-Mile Island. But Two-Mile Islanders may not be so insensitive to One-Mile Island fares. If, for example, fares were expensive from Two-Mile Island but cheap from One-Mile Island, Two-Mile Islanders might drive halfway and take the train downtown. Furthermore, if automobile congestion and pollution is an unpriced negative externality concentrated in the downtown area, then second-best pricing requires that its substitute (One-Mile Island rail trips) be made relatively cheaper. If it is thought appropriate to charge those with lower incomes less and those groups are concentrated close to downtown, that may be another argument to reduce (relatively) One-Mile Island fares. Since the actual differences in fare elasticity by station do not appear great, it is quite plausible that these additional considerations could reverse the direction of the subsidies implied by our illustrative model.

Dividing both sides by P_i gives us

$$\frac{P_i - \mathrm{MC}_i}{P_i} = \frac{\delta}{1 - \delta} \frac{1}{(\Delta Q_i / \Delta P_i)/(P_i/Q_i)}$$

and by letting $k = \delta/(1 - \delta)$ and recalling the definition of price elasticity ε, we get

$$\frac{P_i - \mathrm{MC}_i}{P_i} = \frac{k}{\varepsilon_i}$$

[45] Since prices are closer to marginal cost farther out, they are farther from average cost and thus the subsidy is increasing.

In practice, it is usually difficult to apply Ramsey pricing principles. One important attempt to do so involved the U.S. Postal Service, a public enterprise that sells a number of different products (e.g., first-class mail, express mail, bulk mail) and is required to meet an overall budget constraint. The courts declared illegal the Postal Service's attempt to set prices by using the Ramsey principles. Reasons cited were that knowledge of the necessary elasticity estimates was in doubt, as well as that statutory requirements mandated other rate-making factors apart from demand elasticities (e.g., educational and cultural values).[46] However, application in other areas such as hospitals, electric utilities, railroads, and telecommunications is sometimes recommended and implemented.

Some applications integrate equity considerations and unpriced externalities into the analysis. Harris, for example, considers how hospitals should price their products, given the distortion and inequities that exist in health insurance coverage.[47] He concludes that hospital prices "should" involve significant degrees of cross subsidization (some products above marginal costs, some below them) because to do so would improve social welfare.[48] Other empirical applications of the Ramsey principles are by Littlechild and Rousseau for a telephone company, Matsukawa et al. for Japanese electric utilities, and Cuthbertson and Dobbs for the United Kingdom Postal Service.[49] For those concerned about the complications of it all, there is some useful work on procedures that boundedly rational people can follow to find the right prices![50] In a later chapter, we return to public enterprises and utilities for a discussion of alternative solutions.

Summary

Two areas in which supply organizations may have degrees of freedom for discretionary behavior, aside from noncompetitive settings for profit-making firms, are the nonprofit and

---

[46] See William B. Tye, "The Postal Service: Economics Made Simplistic," *Journal of Policy Analysis and Management, 3,* No. 1, Fall 1983, pp. 62–73. Scott found that postal rates after the court decisions continued to be "fairly consistent" with Ramsey pricing. See Frank A. Scott, Jr., "Assessing USA Postal Ratemaking: An Application of Ramsey Prices," *Journal of Industrial Economics, 34,* No. 3, March 1986, pp. 279–290.

[47] J. Harris, "Pricing Rules for Hospitals," *Bell Journal of Economics, 10,* No. 1, Spring 1979, pp. 224–243.

[48] For other health care applications of Ramsey pricing, see Timothy J. Besley, "Optimal Reimbursement Health Insurance and the Theory of Ramsey Taxation," *Journal of Health Economics, 7,* No. 4, December 1988, pp. 321–336, and Gerard J. Wedig, "Ramsey Pricing and Supply-Side Incentives in Physician Markets," *Journal of Health Economics, 12,* No. 4, December 1993, pp. 365–384.

[49] S. C. Littlechild and J. J. Rousseau, "Pricing Policy of a U.S. Telephone Company," *Journal of Public Economics, 4,* No. 1, February 1975, pp. 35–56; I. Matsukawa, S. Madono, and T. Nakashima, "Ramsey Pricing in Japanese Electric Utilities," *Journal of the Japanese and International Economies, 7,* No. 3, September 1993, pp. 256–276; and K. Cuthbertson and I. Dobbs, "A Robust Methodology for Ramsey Pricing with an Application to UK Postal Services," *Journal of Industrial Economics, 44,* No. 3, September 1996, pp. 229–247.

[50] See C. Manski, "The Zero Elasticity Rule for Pricing a Government Service: A Summary of Findings," *Bell Journal of Economics, 10,* No. 1, Spring 1979, pp. 211–223, and M. Tam, "A Mechanism to Induce Ramsey Pricing for Natural Monopoly Firms," *International Journal of Industrial Organization, 6,* No. 2, June 1988, pp. 247–261.

public sectors. We reviewed several studies that develop models to use for predicting and evaluating the behavior of these organizations.

First, we examined three alternative models of nonprofit hospital behavior. The differences in model assumptions appear both in terms of objectives (e.g., whether doctors or administrators control the hospital's decision-making) as well as capabilities (e.g., the rapid life-and-death decision-making by physicians explains why hospitals are split organizations and why administrators may be unable to control hospital expenses). The implications of these models often differ, for example, in terms of hospital size or efficiency of input use, and it is these differences that empirical studies should focus on to test whether one model is more accurate than another.

Models of public bureaucracies and enterprises have also been constructed as a way to predict their behavior. The bureau budget-maximization hypothesis assumes that bureaucrats have a great deal of discretion and behave like sales maximizers. Other conceptions of the bureaucrat's self-interest, such as equating doing a good job with maximizing net social benefits, lead to quite different predictions. We also pointed out that the political environment may severely constrain bureaucratic objectives, no matter what they are.

The empirical work on BART (mass transit) pricing of Cooter and Topakian pits the predictions of a bureaucratic model against those that assume the bureaucracy is controlled by political forces (either the median voter or the interest group theory). The authors conclude that the prices predicted by the bureaucratic model come closer than those predicted by the other models to observed BART prices, although not close enough to make the size-maximization hypothesis statistically acceptable. The median voter hypothesis is rejected in this context. We mentioned briefly two other models that might explain BART's behavior: one of boundedly rational pricing (e.g., imitating bus fares) and another of pricing for social efficiency. Although empirical model construction and testing of this type is not mature, the future payoffs of continued modeling efforts can be great in terms of confidence in the design and evaluation of policy changes affecting these organizations.

To explain efficiency in the mass transit context (or increasing returns to scale), we develop the principles of *Ramsey optimal pricing*. These apply when a public enterprise must price its product to reach an overall profit (or maximum loss) constraint. First we review the effect of capacity constraints on pricing, and then we turn to the Ramsey principle. The best known version of this principle is the *inverse elasticities rule*, which states that the optimal deviation of price from the marginal cost of each good produced by the enterprise should be proportional to the elasticity of demand. This version does not consider the effects of cross elasticity of demand, nor does it consider distributional effects or the unpriced externalities of pollution and congestion from automobile commuting. More sophisticated versions do account for them. In the appendix we develop some of the mathematics necessary to calculate Ramsey optimal prices.

Exercises

11-1 The questions below are designed to provide practice in deducing the implications of alternative producer objectives.

A very small country has an economy consisting of 100 farms on which food is grown to support the population. Each farm owner can hire as much labor as she or he wants at a cost of $3000 per person per year, constrained only by the total labor force (= population) of 1000. The yearly crops are sold at the world price of $25 per bushel. The minimum level of food required per person for subsistence is 100 bushels per year. The farm owner is the first hired on each farm.

For any one farm, the yearly crop depends only upon the amount of labor used as shown in the accompanying table. *Note:* There is no simple function relating labor inputs to output levels.

Labor quantity	1	2	3	4	5	6	7	8	9	10
Bushels per year	125	300	500	725	925	1105	1225	1275	1175	1000

a If all farms are owned by profit maximizers, how many bushels will be produced in the economy as a whole? What will total employment be? (Other things being equal, farm owners prefer more workers to fewer.) (Answer: 122,500 bushels.)

b If all farms are owned by revenue maximizers, what will total output and employment be? Are wages a larger or smaller proportion of total income (wages plus profits) under this regime compared with (a)?

c Suppose farms are owned collectively by the country as a whole and the government directs each farm manager to hire labor in order to maximize productivity (output per worker). What are total output and employment? Do they reduce the starvation that has plagued the country under regimes (a) and (b)? (Answer: Starvation increases.)

d Suppose the farms are run as communes in which no wages are paid but output is divided equally among the workers: (1) If each commune admits members only if it is to the other members' advantage, how many members will each commune have? (2) Suppose members of communes were required to let other people join as long as the output shares did not fall below the subsistence level. How many members would each commune have, and how much starvation would there be? (Answer: No starvation.)

11-2○A utility company is a monopolistic supplier of energy to two types of customers: residential and commercial. Their demands for energy Q_R and Q_C, respectively, are

$$Q_R = 90 - \tfrac{1}{2}P$$

$$Q_C = 200 - P$$

The marginal cost of supplying energy is constant and equal to $20; however, the utility company must first incur substantial fixed costs equal to $6000.

a A profit-maximizing and price-discriminating utility would produce what output, charge what prices, and make what profit? (Answer: $H = \$5300$.)

b An attorney for the government has informed the utility company that its price discrimination was illegal, and the company has agreed to a cease-and-desist order. What uniform price will it charge now? Will the social benefits of this action outweigh the social costs? (Answer: $P = \$106.67$; no.)

c The community in which the utility company provided service has been upset by the price gouging it perceives under both (a) and (b). It decides to turn the utility into a public enterprise. As a public enterprise, it can charge different prices to the two consumer groups. The public enterprise maximizes total sales, subject to a break-even constraint. What prices and quantities result? Will the social benefits of this change from (b) outweigh the social costs? Will either consumer group be better off or will both groups be better off? (Answer: $P_R = \$90$, $P_C = \$100$; yes; both.)

d Newly elected officials in the community vow to institute fair prices and efficient service. If they are successful at making the public enterprise charge Ramsey-optimal prices, provide the service demanded at those prices, and still break even, what prices and quantities will result? Will either consumer group be better off compared with (c) or will both groups be better off? (Answer: $P_R \approx \$45.21$, $P_C \approx \$48.36$; both.)

APPENDIX

THE MATHEMATICS OF RAMSEY PRICING○

In this section we show how the usual Lagrangian techniques of calculus maximization can be used to see the structure of the Ramsey problem, as well as to provide specific empirical solutions. It is useful to begin with the first-best problem in the text—allocating BART resources subject to the capacity constraint of 272.

The expression "maximize social efficiency" is equivalent to maximizing the net benefits, or benefits minus costs, of the economic activities under consideration. It is equivalent to making a benefit-cost comparison of all alternative resource allocations within the scope of the problem and choosing the alternative that scores highest. The calculus techniques help to identify the best alternative with minimal effort. If we refer to Figure 11A-1, the benefits are represented by the area under the demand curve and the opportunity costs by the area under the marginal cost curve for the quantity of the good produced. Thus our problem is to choose quantities Q_1 and Q_2 that maximize the sum of the net benefits under each Islander's demand curve, subject to the capacity constraint that $Q_1 + Q_2 = 272$.

Let us solve the problem for any two linear demand functions:

$$Q_i = a_i - b_i P_i \qquad i = 1, 2$$

We shall substitute later the a_i's and b_i's for specific demand curves. It is convenient to note that the above equation can be rewritten:

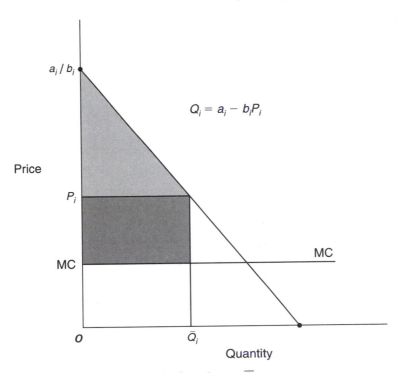

Figure 11A-1. The net benefits (shaded) of producing $\overline{Q}_i$ units.

$$P_i = \frac{a_i}{b_i} - \frac{Q_i}{b_i}$$

The term a_i/b_i is the value of P_i where the demand curve intersects the vertical axis (Figure 11A-1). We retain the simplifying feature that the marginal cost MC is constant and equal for both services. Then, for any level of Q_i, the net benefit NB can be written as the sum of the consumer surplus (a triangle) plus BART "profit" (a rectangle)[51]

$$\text{NB}_i = \frac{1}{2}\left(\frac{a_i}{b_i} - P_i\right)Q_i + (P_i - \text{MC})Q_i$$

This can be rewritten as

$$\text{NB}_i = \frac{1}{2}Q_i\left(\frac{a_i}{b_i} + P_i\right) - \text{MC}(Q_i)$$

Or substituting for P_i from the demand equation, we have

$$\text{NB}_i = \frac{1}{2}Q_i\left(\frac{2a_i}{b_i} - \frac{Q_i}{b_i}\right) - \text{MC}(Q_i)$$

[51] "Profit" is in quotes because we are ignoring the fixed costs. We refer to revenues above marginal costs as "profit" for purposes of this example.

Now we wish to maximize net benefits subject to the constraint. We form the Lagrangian

$$L = NB_1 + NB_2 - \lambda(Q_1 + Q_2 - 272)$$

The partial derivative of L with respect to Q_i (assuming no cross effects on demand) is

$$\frac{\partial L}{\partial Q_i} = \frac{a_i}{b_i} - \frac{Q_i}{b_i} - MC - \lambda = 0$$

Note that this is simply

$$P_i - MC = \lambda$$

In other words, the maximization requirement is that the price of each commodity minus its marginal cost be equal to the same number λ. This number is also interpreted as the marginal net benefit. The condition implies that each commodity has the same price (since each has the same MC in this case). If the two commodities in our problem have the same price, we can equate them:

$$P_1 = \frac{a_1}{b_1} - \frac{Q_1}{b_1} = \frac{a_2}{b_2} - \frac{Q_2}{b_2} = P_2$$

Let us illustrate with two specific demand equations, neither perfectly inelastic (and thus the Ramsey solution will not have the transparency of the text example, in which all of the constraint burden is placed on the perfectly inelastic good):

$$Q_1 = 112 - 4P_1$$

$$Q_2 = 268 - 32P_2$$

On substituting values from the above, we have

$$\frac{112}{4} - \frac{Q_1}{4} = \frac{268}{32} - \frac{Q_2}{32}$$

and on simplifying we have

$$Q_2 = 8Q_1 - 628$$

The remaining partial derivative of the optimization is the constraint equation

$$\frac{\partial L}{\partial \lambda} = Q_1 + Q_2 - 272 = 0$$

Now we have reduced the problem to two equations in two unknowns and can solve

$$Q_2 = 8Q_1 - 628 = 8(272 - Q_2) - 628$$

or

$$Q_2 = 172, P_2 = 3 \quad Q_1 = 100, P_1 = 3$$

This solved, let us now turn to the Ramsey problem. The government insists that BART have "profit" of $800, and we wish to know how to maximize social benefits subject to that constraint. (To simplify the mathematics, this problem was selected to ensure that the solution is within the capacity constraint.)

After a moment's thought it should be recognized that this problem looks very similar to the last one. Only the constraint is different. The new constraint is that total BART revenues minus operating costs equal $800. In other words, we wish to maximize

$$L = NB_1 + NB_2 - \lambda[P_1Q_1 + P_2Q_2 - MC(Q_1 + Q_2) - 800]$$

The partial derivative of this equation with respect to Q_i (again, assuming no cross effects on demand) is

$$\frac{\partial L}{\partial Q_i} = P_i - MC - \lambda\left(P_i + Q_i\frac{\partial P_i}{\partial Q_i} - MC\right) = 0$$

Note that the first two terms in parentheses are simply the marginal revenue from an increase in Q_i: The price P_i of the marginal unit plus the current quantity times the amount price on them is reduced. Therefore,

$$P_i - MC = \lambda(MR_i - MC)$$

which is one way to write Ramsey's result. Note that we can interpret the left-hand side as the marginal net benefit from an additional Q_i and the terms in parentheses on the right-hand side as the marginal "profit" to BART. Therefore, Ramsey's rule states: *The net social benefit forgone to obtain an incremental dollar of profit should be identical for each commodity produced by the enterprise.*

It is easy to show that this version of the rule is equivalent to the other versions we have seen. Recall that

$$MR = P\left(1 + \frac{1}{\varepsilon}\right)$$

We simply substitute in our last equation:

$$P_i - MC = \lambda\left(P_i - MC + \frac{P_i}{\varepsilon}\right)$$

Now we move a few things around:

$$(P_i - MC)(1 - \lambda) = \frac{P_i\lambda}{\varepsilon_i}$$

or

$$\frac{P_i - MC}{P_i} = \frac{\lambda}{1 - \lambda}\frac{1}{\varepsilon_i}$$

Since $\lambda/(1 - \lambda)$ is a number, we can call it k, and therefore

$$\frac{P_i - MC_i}{P_i} = \frac{k}{\varepsilon_i}$$

The above equation must hold for each product sold by the enterprise, as well as the final budget constraint equation obtained by taking the partial derivative with respect to λ:

$$\frac{\partial L}{\partial \lambda} = P_1 Q_1 + P_2 Q_2 - MC(Q_1 + Q_2) - 800 = 0$$

The simultaneous solution to these equations for our specific demand curves (as well as for those used in most actual empirical applications) is most easily obtained by computer.[52] It turns out to be approximately $P_1 = \$6.95$, $Q_1 = 84$, $P_2 = \$2.63$, and $Q_2 = 184$. Price is raised quite a bit more over the marginal operating cost for the more price-inelastic One-Mile Islanders. Despite their small share of the passenger-miles they contribute $500 to the fixed costs, whereas Two-Mile Islanders only contribute $300. The total passenger-miles of 268 almost fully utilizes the capacity. To show that Ramsey's rule is met, we check that

$$\frac{\varepsilon_1(P_1 - MC)}{P_1} = \frac{\varepsilon_2(P_2 - MC)}{P_2} = k$$

Since $\varepsilon_1 \equiv (\partial Q_1/\partial P_1)(P_1/Q_1) = (-4)(6.95/84) = -.331$ and $(P_1 - MC)/P_1 = (6.95 - 1)/6.95 = 0.856$, then $k = -0.28$ from the One-Mile Islanders equation. For Two-Mile Islanders, $\varepsilon_2 = (-32)(2.63/184) = -0.457$ and $(P_2 - MC)/P_2 = (2.63 - 1)/2.63 = 0.620$ and therefore, as expected, k also equals -0.28.

One last Ramsey result to show is when we allow cross effects among the commodities (i.e., they are substitutes or complements). The objective function and constraints are identical; it is only the partial derivatives that change, and they change because now we assume

$$\frac{\partial Q_j}{\partial Q_i} \neq 0$$

Thus the expanded partial derivative (with two commodities) yields this equation when set to zero:

$$(P_i - MC) + (P_j - MC)\frac{\partial Q_j}{\partial Q_i} = \lambda \left[(MR_i - MC) + (P_j - MC)\frac{\partial Q_j}{\partial Q_i} \right]$$

Note that the last term of the expression on the right-hand side is not exactly analogous to the first term (P_j rather than MR_j). The reason is that, in taking the partial derivative of the constraint, a part of the calculation is as follows:

$$\frac{\partial(P_j Q_j)}{\partial Q_i} = \frac{\partial P_j}{\partial Q_i} Q_j + \frac{\partial Q_j}{\partial Q_i} P_j$$

The first term on the right-hand side, $\partial P_j/\partial Q_i$, is zero: Price in the j market is constant; it is the demand curve that is shifting.

---

[52] MATHCAD was used to solve these equations.

Going back to the full expression, we can substitute $P_i + P_i/\varepsilon_i = MR_i$ and combine terms as before:

$$P_i - MC + (P_j - MC)\frac{\partial Q_j}{\partial Q_i} = \lambda \left[(P_i - MC) + \frac{P_i}{\varepsilon_i} + (P_j - MC)\frac{\partial Q_j}{\partial Q_i} \right]$$

$$(P_i - MC)(1 - \lambda) = \frac{P_i\lambda}{\varepsilon_i} + (\lambda - 1)(P_j - MC)\frac{\partial Q_j}{\partial Q_i}$$

and, using $k = \lambda/(1 - \lambda)$,

$$\frac{P_i - MC}{P_i} = \frac{k}{\varepsilon_i} - \frac{(P_j - MC)(\partial Q_j/\partial Q_i)}{P_i}$$

Thus the Ramsey rule with cross effects is similar to the less complicated rule. Note that $(P_j - MC)/P_i$ is always positive. Therefore, the Ramsey rule is, as before, modified by the degree of substitutability or complementarity of the two goods. If good j is a substitute for good i ($\partial Q_j/\partial Q_i < 0$), then the price of i should be higher than if there were no cross effects.

Suppose some of our BART riders live on houseboats between One- and Two-Mile Islands and are relatively indifferent to which station they use to board. BART increases its price for One-Mile Island fares, and we have already estimated the drop in demand at One-Mile Island. But now we must include the fact that demand increases at Two-Mile Island: We have lost fewer passengers and gained more revenues than we thought. This makes us favor greater price increases for One-Mile Island than we would without cross effects.

PART FOUR

COMPETITIVE MARKETS AND PUBLIC POLICY INTERVENTIONS

CHAPTER TWELVE

EFFICIENCY, DISTRIBUTION, AND GENERAL COMPETITIVE
ANALYSIS: CONSEQUENCES OF TAXATION

THE MOST COMMON MODEL of economic governance used by analysts is the perfectly competitive market. In this chapter we examine this model and distinguish sharply between its normative and predictive uses. For analytic purposes the predictive uses of such models have substantially firmer foundations.

Perhaps the two best known theorems of modern microeconomics, reviewed here, emphasize normative consequences of competition: (1) A perfectly competitive market allocation is Pareto-optimal. (2) Every Pareto-optimal allocation can be achieved by perfectly competitive markets, as long as costless redistribution of endowments is possible. These theorems suggest that there is something desirable about organizing economic activity through a system of perfectly competitive markets: With perfect information and costless transactions, such a system generates an *incentive structure* that leads economic agents to allocate resources optimally. We will show in this chapter that, because of taxation, the opposite result holds: Perfectly competitive markets in an economy with taxation generate incorrect incentives that lead economic agents to allocate resources nonoptimally.

Does the above nonoptimality conclusion imply that it is undesirable for an economy to utilize competitive markets? The appropriate analytic response is to ask, "Compared to what?" In later chapters we will emphasize that the assumption of perfect information and costless transactions must be relaxed to analyze these issues. There are many governance structures that can lead to optimal allocations (of those feasible) under these assumptions. The real analytic issues involve recognition that information is costly to produce, communicate, and process and that transactions are costly to organize and enforce; alternative governance structures (including the use of competitive markets) must be evaluated by the efficiency with which they perform these tasks. Thus the well-known twin theorems do not provide much normative insight about the desirability of competitive markets in an actual economy.

However, we do wish to show that the theory of competitive markets can be very useful as a predictive tool. With respect to taxation, we take note of Ben Franklin's remark: "In this world, nothing is certain but death and taxes." Taxation is an inevitable consequence of the wide variety of activities carried out by governments at all levels. Approximately one-third of the GDP is collected in taxes each year. Who bears the burden of a tax? We use the theory of competitive markets to predict tax incidence and show the difference between using models of partial and general equilibrium to analyze it. The main tax that we analyze is an excise tax, similar to the taxes on telecommunications services (that many think should be repealed).

We proceed as follows. First, we must review the necessary conditions for economic efficiency in economies with production (exchange, production, and product-mix efficiency); we emphasize that the concept of efficiency is totally independent of the type of economic organization that might be used to try and achieve it. It remains true, as was first illustrated in Chapter 3, that there are many possible efficient allocations with quite different distributional outcomes. Then we turn to one very special type of economic organization: the perfectly competitive market. We review the process and characteristics of resource allocation as they occur in a single competitive market. Next we turn to general equilibrium in markets and review the twin theorems that relate perfect competition and Pareto optimality.

Before turning to additional normative thought about general equilibrium, we consider how the models can be used in a predictive sense. We introduce concepts of tax incidence and contrast the analyses suggested by a partial and a general equilibrium model of an excise tax. We suggest that policies with large economic effects, such as those concerning taxes, are better modeled in a general equilibrium framework. However, for small sectors of the economy, partial equilibrium analysis may be sufficient.

We consider the efficiency of taxes briefly, primarily to point out that all the main taxes in use have distortionary allocative effects. This means that if an economy with taxation is characterized by markets that are perfectly competitive, it will generate incorrect incentives that will lead to inefficient resource allocation. Thus, although we can accept the predictive power of competitive models in certain situations, we have not yet established any normative conclusions concerning the desirability of competitive markets. To do so, we must first develop insight about how to compare alternative governance structures, a task we leave for the remaining chapters.

Economic Efficiency and General Competitive Equilibrium

Efficiency in an Economy with Production

We review the three basic necessary conditions for Pareto optimality in a production economy with many people and goods. These conditions are determined by the preferences of the individuals, the resources available, and the technological possibilities for converting the resources into goods and services. Thus the conditions are completely independent of the type of economy: They are required for efficiency in capitalist, socialist, or any other economic organization.[1] We assume that the satisfaction of those conditions is sufficient to ensure Pareto optimality.[2]

In Chapter 3 we reviewed the general definition of efficiency or Pareto optimality: *An allocation is efficient (Pareto-optimal) if and only if no person can be made better off without making another person worse off*. Logically, Pareto optimality in a many-person, many-good economy can be shown to require that certain relations hold among all the economic agents (individuals and producers). We have already seen some of those requirements, but we gather them here for general reference.

1. **Efficiency in exchange. An economy is efficient in exchange if and only if it is impossible to so reallocate the available goods that one person is better off and no one else is worse off.** For any two goods this requires that each consumer of both goods have the same MRS for the two.[3] This was proved in Chapter 3.

2. **Efficiency in production. An economy is efficient in production if and only if it is impossible to increase one output quantity without decreasing any other output quantity.** There are four requirements that producers must meet for this to hold[4]:

   (a) Technological efficiency. The maximum possible output is achieved with the inputs used by each producer.

   (b) All producers using both of any two factors must have the same RTS for the two: The proof of this is identical with the exchange efficiency proof that equal marginal rates of substitution are required. Suppose producer X has $\text{RTS}^X_{K,L} = 3$ (3 units of labor can be given up in return for 1 unit of capital without affecting the output level). Let producer Y have any different value, for example, $\text{RTS}^Y_{K,L} = 2$. Have X release 3 units of labor, and give 2 of them to Y. Take 1 unit of capital away from Y; thus, Y's output level is unaffected on balance. Give the 1 unit of capital to X and so restore X to the original output level. Both producers are at their initial levels, but we have one unused unit of labor left over that we can give to either. By doing so it is possible to increase one output without decreasing any other; therefore, the economy could not have

---

[1] In the discussion below we assume that the preferences are those of the individuals in the economy. However, as a logical matter, one could imagine alternative mechanisms for deciding preferences, and then the conditions described here would remain necessary and sufficient for achieving efficiency.

[2] Establishing this result is complicated. For an excellent in-depth exposition of the issues involved in this section, see the first essay in T. Koopmans, *Three Essays on the State of Economic Science* (New York: McGraw-Hill Book Company, 1957).

[3] This assumes that there are no consumption interdependencies, which would require the modifications discussed in Chapter 4. In addition, note that most individuals consume only a small fraction of the types of goods and services available. Let Q be a good that individual A does not consume but individual B does consume. If Z is any good that both A and B consume, efficiency requires $\text{MRS}^A_{Q,Z} < \text{MRS}^B_{Q,Z}$. This corner solution was demonstrated in Chapter 3.

[4] This assumes that there are no technological externalities, which would have effects directly analogous to those of consumer interdependency. We discuss them later in the book.

been productively efficient initially. Productive efficiency requires that the rates be equalized. Note that this condition applies regardless of whether X and Y are producing the same or different outputs.

This requirement is often the only one mentioned for production efficiency. It seems geometrically analogous to exchange efficiency; indeed, for a fixed supply of inputs, we will shortly construct an Edgeworth box for production, draw in isoquants for two goods, and use the tangency conditions to define a production "contract curve" that is equivalent to the production possibilities frontier. However, this construction is based on the assumption that society so arranges its producing units (i.e., for a particular good) that resources cannot be reallocated within the industry to increase output. The following two conditions are necessary for efficient resource allocation within industries:

(c) The marginal product of any single factor used by firms producing the same output must be identical in each of the firms: The proof of this is trivial. Suppose producer A has $MP_L = 2$ and producer B (of the same output) has $MP_L = 3$. Then, by taking 1 unit of labor away from A and giving it to B, we can increase the total output.

(d) When multiple-product suppliers produce at least two of the same outputs, each supplier's RPT of those outputs must be identical: Suppose supplier A has $RPT_{Q_1, Q_2} = 4$ and supplier B has $RPT_{Q_1, Q_2} = 2$. Then have supplier A reduce its Q_1 output unit by 1 and use the freed-up resources to produce 4 additional units of Q_2. Then have supplier B increase its production of Q_1 by 1 unit and thereby cause it to reduce Q_2 production by 2. Each firm is still using the same resources; total Q_1 production is unaffected; but there are now 2 more units of Q_2 than before.[5]

The conditions in (2) are designed to ensure that society is on its production-possibilities frontier. But it may not be on the right point of the frontier. For this, we need condition (3).

3. **Efficiency of the product mix. An economy has an efficient product mix if and only if it is impossible to choose an alternative product mix on the production-possibilities frontier (or transformation surface) and so distribute the new mix that one person is made better off and no one else is worse off.** For any two goods this requires that the MRS among consumers equal the RPT of the transformation surface: The proof is analogous to the preceding proofs. Suppose the condition is violated; for example, $MRS_{X,Y} = 3$ and $RPT_{X,Y} = 2$. Let a consumer order 3 fewer units of Y, in return for 1 more unit of X (thus remaining indifferent). A supplier, in order to produce the extra unit of X, must reduce Y production by only 2 units. An extra Y is left over, and we can give it to anyone and thereby increase one person's utility without decreasing the utility of another. Thus, the initial product mix could not have been efficient.

---

[5] This rule, incidentally, is referred to as the theory of *comparative advantage* when the "suppliers" are countries. It is used as an argument for specialization by country combined with free trade among countries.

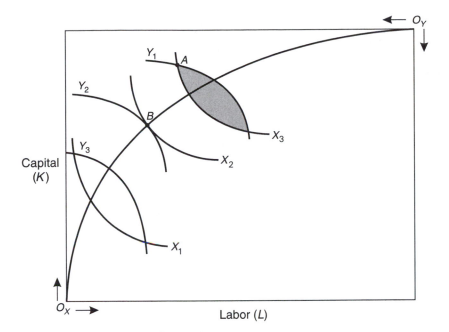

Figure 12-1. The Edgeworth box for production.

It may be useful to display the three basic conditions graphically. To do so, we illustrate them in a two-person, two-good economy that is endowed with given (fixed) amounts of labor and capital resources. We begin with production efficiency. In Figure 12-1, we draw an Edgeworth box of length L equal to the amount of labor available and height K equal to the amount of capital available. The lower left-hand corner of the box is the origin for the production of good X. Each point in the box represents an amount of labor L_X and capital K_X that are allocated to X production. Several isoquants X_1, X_2, X_3 are drawn to represent increasing levels of X production ($X_1 < X_2 < X_3$).

Analogously to the Edgeworth box for exchange, the origin for Y production is the upper right-hand corner of the box, with the amount of labor allocated to Y (L_Y) increasing as we move leftward from its origin and the amount of capital allocated to Y (K_Y) increasing as we move downward from its origin. Thus every point in the box represents an allocation of inputs to X production and to Y production, such that $L_X + L_Y = L$ and $K_X + K_Y = K$. We also draw several isoquants Y_1, Y_2, Y_3 to represent increasing levels of Y production ($Y_1 < Y_2 < Y_3$).

Thus every point in the diagram has two isoquants passing through it, one showing the level of X production and the other showing the level of Y. Most of these are like point A, with the isoquants crossing. Whenever we are at such a point, it is always possible to reallocate inputs to increase at least one of the outputs without reducing the other. The shaded area within the two isoquants through point A identifies these more efficient allocations. Recalling that the absolute slope of an isoquant is equal to the RTS, then $\text{RTS}^X \neq \text{RTS}^Y$ at the initial point A. However, there are some points in the diagram like point B, where the two isoquants are just tangent. At these points, it is impossible to reallocate resources in order to increase one output without reducing the other. Since the isoquants are tangent, that means $\text{RTS}^X = \text{RTS}^Y$ at point B. These are the input allocations that are productively efficient.

The locus of efficient production points is the production contract curve, drawn as the line connecting the two origins.[6] Note that as we move along this curve from the X origin toward the Y origin, the output level of X is increasing whereas the output level of Y is decreasing. On Figure 12-2, we show the same productively efficient allocations using output levels for the axes; that is, we graph the X, Y levels shown by the isoquants along the contract curve from Figure 12-1. The curve in Figure 12-2 is the *production-possibilities frontier* (sometimes called the *transformation surface*).

So far, we have only illustrated one of the three necessary conditions for Pareto optimality: production efficiency requires that we be at a point on the production-possibilities frontier, and not interior to it. Suppose we were to pick one of these points arbitrarily, such as point C. We could then ask, if the economy had exactly X_C and Y_C in the aggregate, how might it be allocated to our two consumers in order to be efficient in exchange?

In Figure 12-2, the rectangle with these dimensions is exactly equivalent to the Edgeworth box for exchange that we analyzed in Chapter 2. That is, think of the lower-left origin as the origin for person 1 and point C as the origin for person 2. By construction, each point in the box is a possible allocation of X_C, Y_C such that $X_1 + X_2 = X_C$ and $Y_1 + Y_2 = Y_C$. We already know that the exchange-efficient points are those where the indifference curves of the two people are tangent (or $\text{MRS}^1 = \text{MRS}^2$), shown as the usual contract curve in Figure 12-2. Given that we start from point C, the utility-possibility levels are those shown by the levels of the indifference curves through each point on the contract curve.

On Figure 12-3a, we graph these utility levels using axes that measure utility directly (this is conceptual, of course, because utility is neither measurable nor comparable). We label this utility-possibilities curve C_1C_2 to indicate that it comes from using point C from the production-possibilities frontier. If we are on C_1C_2, then we have satisfied two criteria: production efficiency and exchange efficiency.

But recall that point C was chosen arbitrarily. Suppose we chose a different point on the production-possibilities frontier, such as point D in Figure 12-2. We could go through the same exercise: construct a new Edgeworth box with the dimensions (X_D, Y_D), find the contract curve associated with it, and draw the resulting utility-possibilities levels D_1D_2 on Figure 12-3a. Each point on D_1D_2 would also satisfy the criteria of production and exchange efficiency.

When we compare C_1C_2 with D_1D_2, there are only two possibilities. As drawn, the two curves cross and we shall analyze this shortly. But the other possibility is that they do not cross. Unless they are completely coincident, this means that one curve dominates the other. This is illustrated in Figure 12-3b: for any utility level that person 1 may enjoy from the production choice of point D (i.e., on D_1D_2), person 1 can attain the same level from point

---

[6] As drawn, the contract curve goes from each origin directly into the interior of the box, rather than initially along the boundaries. This would be the case if, for example, neither output could be produced with only a single input. However, other production functions could result in some portion of the boundaries being part of the production contract curve.

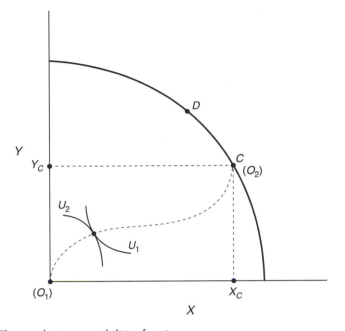

Figure 12-2. The production-possibilities frontier.

C (i.e., on C_1C_2) and person 2 can be made better off. For example, if we want person 1 to enjoy the level of utility U_1, this could be done on D_1D_2, where person 2 receives U_2^L, but it also could be done on C_1C_2, where person 2 receives U_2^H ($>U_2^L$). In other words, the product mix at point C leads to unambiguously better utility possibilities than the product mix at point D.

The other possibility, that C_1C_2 and D_1D_2 cross, is illustrated in Figure 12-3a. In this case, each curve is dominant for a portion of the possible utility levels. To the left of their intersection point, C_1C_2 dominates D_1D_2. But to the right of the intersection point, D_1D_2 dominates C_1C_2. Were the economy restricted to choosing only the product mix at C or at D, the best utility possibilities would be those shown by the envelope of the two curves, the thick line D_1C_2. For desired utility levels of person 2 less than U_2^*, it is better to use the product mix D because person 1 gets more utility than if product mix C is used. But for desired utility levels of person 2 greater than U_2^*, it is better to use product mix C.

Of course the economy is not restricted to choosing the production points C or D; these were arbitrarily selected from all of the points on the production-possibilities frontier (Figure 12-2). Imagine going through the following exercise. Consider each of the remaining points on the production-possibilities frontier one at a time, along with its associated possibilities for efficient exchange. Thus we are considering all possible product mixes, but restricting ourselves to allocations that are productively and exchange efficient.

To do this geometrically, on the same diagram as our envelope C_1D_2 draw the utility-possibilities curve associated with the first new point. If either curve dominates, discard the lower and save the higher to compare to the utility possibilities of the next new point. If the

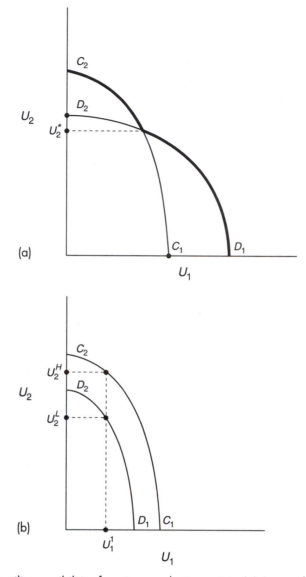

Figure 12-3. The utility possibilities from two production points: (a) An envelope (C_2D_1) of utility possibilities. (b) The utility possibilities from C are dominant.

utility-possibilities curve of the first new point crosses our envelope C_1D_2, discard the lower segments and retain the new envelope to compare to the utility possibilities of the next new point. Continue doing this until every point on the production-possibilities frontier has been considered. The result will be an envelope like that shown in Figure 12-4, the *grand utility-possibilities frontier*.

The utility levels shown on the grand utility-possibilities frontier are Pareto-optimal. By the method of constructing the envelope, we have found the allocations that give the high-

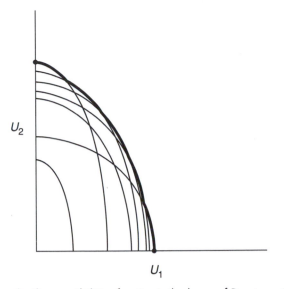

Figure 12-4. The grand utility-possibilities frontier is the locus of Pareto-optimal utility levels.

est possible utility for one person associated with any given level of utility for the other person. We restricted ourselves to allocations that are efficient both in production and in exchange, and then considered all possible product mixes to identify those that push the envelope farthest out. It must be, then, that the specific product mixes associated with the points on the grand utilities-possibilities frontier meet the necessary condition of product-mix efficiency (MRS = RPT). But we have not shown the latter.

Can we explain this geometrically? Starting from any arbitrary fixed allocation of X and Y to person 1, we will show that maximizing person 2's utility requires ensuring production efficiency and product-mix efficiency. This does not ensure Pareto optimality, for many of the allocations that result from each possible arbitrary starting point could be inefficient in exchange. But since the Pareto-optimal allocations must be a subset of this larger set, they will all be characterized by product-mix efficiency.

In Figure 12-5, we redraw the production-possibilities frontier from Figure 12-2. Recall that its (absolute) slope at any point is the RPT. Suppose that arbitrarily we agree to give person 1 the specific allocation shown at point E (i.e., person 1 receives X_E, Y_E), so person 1 enjoys the utility level U_1^* of the indifference curve through E. We now pick the production point that will maximize person 2's utility, given that person 1 is constrained to stay at E. The point will of course be on the production-possibilities frontier rather than interior to it (otherwise we could increase the amount of X and Y, and thus utility, given to person 2). We can consider all points on the production-possibilities frontier with $X \geq X_E$ and $Y \geq Y_E$ (which we label FG), and the "excess" $(X - X_E, Y - Y_E)$ is what is possible to give to person 2.

Geometrically, point E is the origin for measuring person 2's consumption (the "excess" here is $X = 0$, $Y = 0$) and FG represents the consumption possibilities available to person 2. Then one thing becomes clear: the maximum utility for person 2 occurs at a tangency of person 2's indifference curve (labeled U_2^*) with the FG portion of the frontier (labeled

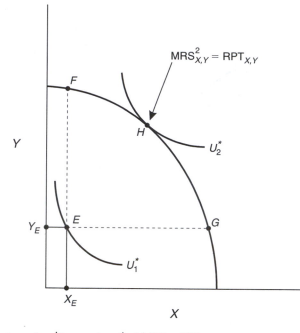

Figure 12-5. Pareto-optimality requires that MRS = RPT.

point H). So $MRS^2 = RPT$, the condition for product-mix efficiency from person 2's perspective. This property would hold for *any* arbitrary starting allocation to person 1 where person 2's utility-maximum includes some of each good. Of course we have not required that MRS^1, determined by the arbitrary choice of point E, be such that $MRS^1 = MRS^2$. So of all possible arbitrary allocations to person 1, the Pareto-optimal solutions to our problem would only be the subset of them where, after maximizing person 2's utility, $MRS^1 = MRS^2 = RPT$.

These conditions have a simplicity that may belie their importance. They apply to every sector of the economy, whether public, private, nonprofit, or anything else. They are necessary conditions: If there is a violation of them anywhere (and, of course, there always are violations), then resource allocation in the economy is not efficient. The conditions are based purely on technical possibilities and consumer tastes; we have no need to refer to prices, wages, incomes, or profits. To indicate the breadth of the requirements, let us suggest how the conditions determine the level of resource availability at any point in time.

Given the number of people in the economy, the supply of labor depends on how individuals make the labor-leisure trade-off discussed in Chapter 4. The efficiency conditions apply to this as well. They require that the rate of product transformation between leisure and any other good equal the marginal rate of substitution between leisure and that good. In other words, determining an efficient amount of leisure as part of the product mix is equivalent to determining an efficient amount of labor in the economy. If there is involuntary unemployment in an economy (above the amount necessary for efficient job-searching), then the efficiency conditions are violated.

The labor-leisure trade-off is assumed to take place within a specified time period. Society also faces resource allocation trade-offs that go across time periods, as we saw at the individual level in Chapter 8. Society begins with a natural endowment of land, minerals, and such that can be converted into consumption. Consumers have a marginal rate of substitution for a good today versus the same good in the future. As long as the economy does not use up all of the resources it has available today on today's consumption, it is saving some (the capital stock) for tomorrow.

Like all economic activities, the amount of savings required by the efficiency rules depends not only on preferences but also on the technical possibilities for converting consumption deferred today into consumption in the future. For each good, there is a rate of product transformation (that varies with production level) for transforming it from current to future consumption. Demand for snow skiing in the Vermont summers may be great, but few Vermont resort operators would keep skiers off the winter snow in order to try and preserve it until summer. On the other hand, through growth young trees can produce a large increase in tomorrow's lumber supply, although they embody only a small amount of lumber today. So it makes good economic sense to save the young trees, even if our only interest in them is lumber (and of course there are other reasons for not cutting trees).

Consider one final example: transforming fresh vegetables today into fresh vegetables in the future. Imagine we start with a very labor-intensive, capital-poor economy. We could slightly boost today's vegetable production by allocating additional labor and other resources to it. But those same resources could be allocated to building a tractor, which in the future will significantly boost the vegetable crop. The RPT of current for future vegetables is thus high, and let us assume higher than the MRS. As we imagine cutting back on increasing amounts of vegetables today in order to make more and more tractors, the marginal loss in terms of today's crop increases whereas the marginal gain in terms of future crops diminishes (thus the RPT is diminishing, whereas the MRS is increasing). At some point, the MRS of current for future vegetables will equal the RPT, and that is what determines the efficient number of tractors to build today.

This last example is important because it illustrates that we do not have to store or physically preserve current output in order to transform it into future output. Typically, we forgo some current production in order to free up the resources for a capital investment (the tractor) that will enhance production in the future. Thus the changes in our capital stock from period to period would also be determined by following the efficiency requirement: for every good and every time period, the MRS between time periods equals the RPT for those periods.

Competitive Equilibrium in One Industry

In this section we review the conditions that result in competitive equilibrium in one market and the characteristics of that equilibrium. First, we make a number of assumptions about the trading conditions in a **perfectly competitive market.** One is that we are discussing **a homogeneous good: Each firm produces the identical product.** On both the demand and supply side we assume that **consumers and firms are price takers: Each**

economic agent is too small (relative to the total number of agents in the whole market) to affect the market price by its own actions. (This rules out, e.g., firms characterized by increasing returns to scale.) **Each consumer is a utility maximizer, and each firm is a profit maximizer. We assume perfect knowledge and costless transactions.** These assumptions imply that the **law of one price** will hold: **All trades between buyers and sellers will be conducted at the market price.** (Otherwise, all buyers would flock to the seller offering the lowest price.) We assume there are **no barriers to the entry of firms to the industry or their exit from it.**

Under those conditions, how are quantity and price determined? The answer is usually divided into two cases by time: *the short run, in which it is assumed that the number of firms and their plant sizes are fixed,* and *the long run, in which all factors are variable and the number of firms varies in response to market forces.*

Short-Run Competitive Equilibrium

Let us consider the short-run case first. In Figure 12-6a we represent the short-run marginal, average variable, and average total cost curves of a representative firm (denoted MC, AVC, and ATC, respectively).[7] We have already seen (Chapter 10) that the firm in a competitive market faces a demand curve for its output perceived to be horizontal at the market price, and that profit maximization therefore requires that the firm choose the quantity at which its $MC = P$ (since $P = MR$ in the competitive case). If $P = P_1$, for example, the firm will supply q_1 (Figure 12-6a). **The firm's short-run supply curve thus corresponds to the upward-sloping portion of its MC curve, beginning at the point at which P = AVC.**[8]

In Figure 12-6b we depict the market demand curve (D_1) and the industry supply curve. Market demand, it will be recalled, is simply the sum of each individual's demand at each possible price. The market supply is derived similarly, but not exactly analogously. **Market supply is defined as the sum of each firm's supply at a given price.**[9] If the supply of factors to the industry is perfectly elastic, the analogy is exact. However, it may be that additional factors to the industry as a whole can be obtained only by bidding up their prices and thus shifting all the cost curves of firms in this industry. The market supply curve is upward-sloping in both cases. However, market supply cannot be derived solely from knowledge about each individual firm's supply curve; one must also know about the effects of changes in industry output levels on factor prices.

---

[7] Note that as quantity increases, the average variable cost approaches the average total cost; that is because the only difference between them is the firm's fixed costs (those assumed unalterable during the short run), which become a smaller and smaller contribution to average total costs as quantity increases. Letting FC stand for fixed costs, $ATC = AVC + FC/q$.

[8] For $P < AVC$, the firm is better off not to produce. As an exercise, the reader should explain why the firms will produce at a price like P_2 even though the firm is experiencing losses at that point.

[9] Some authors prefer to define the market supply curves in both the short run and the long run as the partial relation between the output quantity and its own price, input prices constant. With those definitions, the changes in input prices caused by changes in the industry output quantity are treated differently than we treat them below. These changes would cause shifts in the supply curves rather than movements along them. That is purely a descriptive difference; actual supply is the same function of input and output prices in either case.

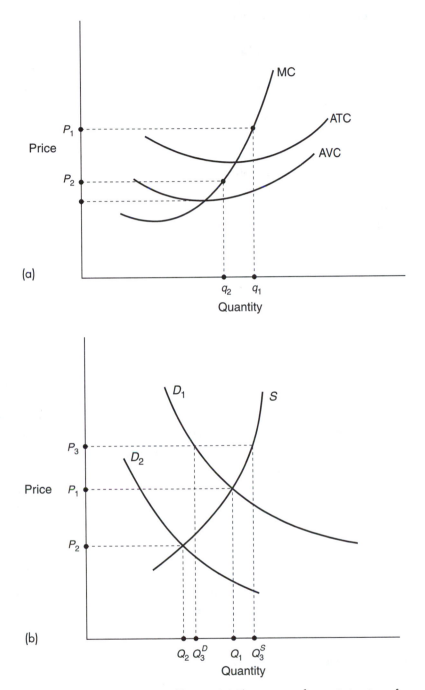

Figure 12-6. Short-run competitive equilibrium: (a) Short-run profit maximization of a competitive firm. (b) Short-run supply and demand.

Figure 12-6b shows the **equilibrium** point, **defined as a situation in which the market quantity demanded equals the market quantity supplied.** This occurs where the demand and supply curves cross, at price P_1 and quantity Q_1. At any other price-quantity combination, the market forces that would be set in motion would return the market to its equilibrium. If the price were $P_3 > P_1$, for example, the quantity supplied would exceed the quantity demanded ($Q_3^S > Q_3^D$). Suppliers would observe their outputs going unsold, and lowering the price would be the only way to sell the outputs. As the market price lowers, each firm adjusts its supply downward until all firms are in market equilibrium.

Note that the equilibrium may or may not be profitable in the short run. As we have drawn it, the representative firm is making economic profits at P_1, q_1. However, if the demand curve were D_2, crossing the supply curve at P_2, Q_2, each firm would be in equilibrium at P_2, q_2 and would be experiencing economic losses. Another possibility is that there is no "representative" firm: some might have lower cost curves than others, owing perhaps to natural advantages (think of farms producing the same homogeneous crop but with some fortunate enough to have fertile soil and natural water supply, while others have soil that needs much tending and purchased water). Then at a given price one could be profitable while the other is not. For simplicity, we will eliminate this latter case by assuming here that all firms are identical, although it is not necessary for any of the main results.[10]

Long-Run Competitive Equilibrium

In the long run, neither allocation would be an equilibrium. To see this, let us turn to Figures 12-7a and b, where we have drawn the long-run marginal (LMC) and average cost (LAC) curves. Recall that, in the long run, all factors are freely variable and firms are free to enter or exit the industry.

Suppose that we are initially at P_1, q_1, the short-run equilibrium where the representative firm is making an **economic profit—more than the "zero profit" level, that is, more than the normal market return on labor and capital inputs built into the definition of its cost curves.** Each firm in the industry will realize that it can increase profits by changing its plant and expanding output (since LMC < SMC at q_1); other firms will enter the industry in response to the existence of profits. Then the short-run supply curve will shift outward, which will cause the market price to fall until there are no profits left to be made by industry expansion. If the representative firm is making zero profit, it must be that $P = LAC$. Since each firm is assumed to be maximizing profit, it must be that $P = LMC$. Therefore, LAC = LMC, which occurs when the representative firm is at the minimum of its long-run average cost curve. It is only at this allocation, P_E, Q_E in Figure 12-7b, that **long-run equilibrium** is attained: **demand equals supply, and no consumers or firms have incentive to enter or leave the industry.**

What does the long-run supply (LS) curve look like? With perfectly elastic factor supplies it is simply the horizontal line at height P_E. That is, in the long run the market supply

---

[10] We will analyze in the following chapter a competitive equilibrium in an industry with variation in firm costs (the rental housing industry). The equilibrium results that are derived here will be shown to hold for the "marginal" firm in the industry.

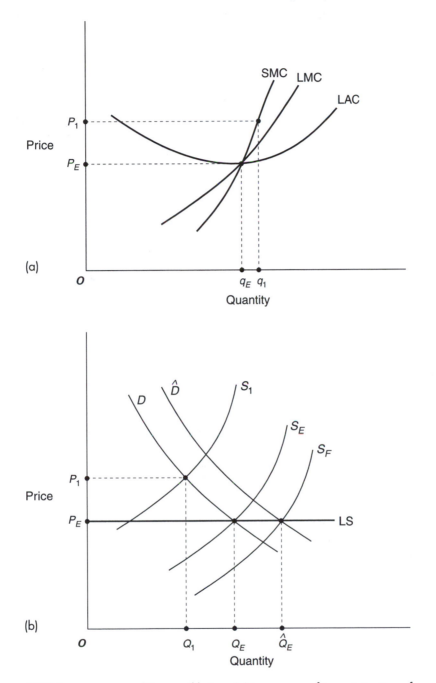

Figure 12-7. Long-run competitive equilibrium: (a) Long-run profit maximization of a competitive firm. (b) Long-run market demand and supply (constant-cost case).

will be met by firms identical with the representative one shown, each operating at the minimum of its LAC curve. The number of firms, Q_E/q_E, is determined by where the market demand curve crosses the P_E line. If, for example, demand shifted to $\hat{D}$, the firms would adjust to produce total quantity $\hat{Q}_E$. Each firm would continue to produce q_E; price would remain at P_E; but the short-run supply curve S_E would shift out because of the entry of new firms. This is the case of the *constant cost industry.*

If, because of economies of scale in their production, factors become cheaper as the industry expands, the LS curve will slope downward. That is shown in Figure 12-8b. The expansion will represent an external economy for all firms, because all firms will have their cost curves lowered as shown in Figure 12-8a. Such a situation is described as a *decreasing cost industry.* An example might be personal computers; they have come down in price as the market has expanded, in part because of economies of scale in producing their components. The last possible case is that of the *increasing cost industry,* the LS curve of which slopes upward (not drawn). But *in all three cases the conditions for long-run equilibrium, are the same: zero profit and profit maximization, which together imply that the representative firm produces at the minimum of its LAC curve.*[11]

A number of important insights arise from applying the logic of competitive analysis in various policy settings. To take an unusual example let us consider a policy to reduce the illegal use of heroin. During the Nixon administration, drug enforcement officials knew that Turkey was a main source of the illegal U.S. heroin supply. An arrangement was made with Turkish officials to ban the growing of the opium poppy from which heroin is derived.

In the short run the heroin supply in the United States was indeed reduced, but then the prospect of abnormally high profits enticed potential suppliers from elsewhere. The story might have been different if heroin cultivation required an unusual climate found in only a very few places. But a large number of countries have climates favorable to the cultivation of opium, and within a year several other countries were reported as the source of "major supplies" of heroin to the United States. A long-run solution to the heroin problem cannot be attained by a narrowly targeted supply strategy, when the relevant market for potential supply includes so much of the world. Furthermore, the United States is not capable of persuading all countries to ban (effectively) opium cultivation.[12] If there are opportunities for profits in a market, the competitive model indicates that new firms should be expected to enter. Kleiman reports that the Burma-Thailand-Laos "Golden Triangle," the Afghanistan-Pakistan-Iran "Golden Crescent," Mexico, Lebanon, and Colombia all grow poppies for the

---

[11] When there is variation in individual firm costs, it is only the marginal firm (rather than the "representative" firm) that makes zero economic profit at equilibrium. All lower-cost firms are also providing supply to the market, but the firm with costs just greater than the marginal one cannot profitably produce in this market and will not enter it.

[12] There may be circumstances in which a series of short-run disruptions add up to a long-run solution. In this case the strategy did not work, as was predicted by analysts before the Turkish policy was adopted. See John Holahan, with the assistance of Paul Henningsen, "The Economics of Heroin," *Dealing with Drug Abuse* (New York: Praeger Publishers, 1972), pp. 255–299.

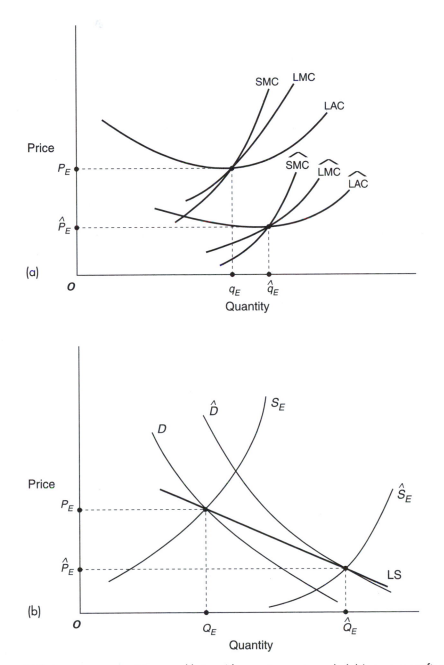

Figure 12-8. Long-run competitive equilibrium (decreasing-cost case): (a) Long-run profit maximization of a competitive firm. (b) Long-run market demand and supply.

illicit market. He concludes: "Heroin, even more than cocaine, must be addressed by domestic drug law enforcement."[13]

Before concluding this section, let us note the important roles of the price in a competitive market. First, price is created through the interaction of demand and supply in the market, which is *information* that all economic agents use in making their decisions. The price serves to *ration* the available supply among consumers. It also serves as a *signal* to producers, who use it in determining the output levels. In the short run, producer responsiveness to price is determined by the elasticity of the short-run supply curve. In the long run, price affects industry profitability, which in turn affects firm entry, exit, and investment decisions. The supply elasticity is greater in the long run than in the short run because of the greater time flexibility for adjustments.[14]

The Twin Theorems Relating Competition and Efficiency

With the above review of requirements for economic efficiency in an economy, it is easy to suggest why *any general competitive equilibrium is Pareto-optimal.* This proposition is the first of the well-known twin theorems relating efficiency and competition. The second theorem addresses distributional considerations: Assuming economic agents have well-behaved preferences and production technologies,[15] *any Pareto-optimal allocation of resources can be achieved as a general competitive equilibrium, as long as costless transfers of initial endowments are allowed.* The grand utility-possibilities frontier illustrates that there are many possible Pareto-optimal allocations in an economy; and as long as society can choose among them, (outcome) equity does not require the sacrifice of efficiency.

We shall not attempt to prove either of the two theorems rigorously, but simply review the logic behind them. A simple way to summarize the proof of the first is that: (1) all traders (individuals and firms) face the same prices in competitive equilibrium for the available factors and goods, which ensures that the required equality of all the marginal rates is satisfied (provided supply equals demand), and (2) market equilibrium ensures that supply equals demand. We clarify this below.

First, we must emphasize what we mean by a **general competitive equilibrium: that a full set of markets exists (for every good, including future goods), that each of these markets is characterized by the conditions we described for one competitive industry,**

---

[13] Mark A. R. Kleiman, *Against Excess* (New York: Basic Books, 1992), p. 370.

[14] The analytic framework of a short-run and long-run time frame is useful conceptually, but reality does not fit neatly into these two categories. Rather, the supply elasticity is a continuous, increasing function of time allowed for industry response. Researchers often will estimate specific numerical supply elasticities and refer to them as short run or long run, using judgment as to what real time frame for the industry being studied approximates the conditions of the two periods in the analytic framework. Sometimes a third analytic time period is specified, the "very short run," in which production levels are assumed to be unalterable and the only market activity is price-setting to make demand equal to the fixed supply.

[15] The phrase "well-behaved" is used to refer to the convexity requirements that rule out such problems as increasing returns to scale. For a rigorous review and proof of the theorems, see the essay by Koopmans cited earlier in the chapter.

and that each market is in long-run equilibrium. This implies that supply equals demand for all goods. Now all we have to do is show that the prices at the equilibrium lead to the correct marginal trade-offs.

First consider efficiency in exchange. For any two goods X and Y with equilibrium prices P_X and P_Y, each consumer of both (in order to maximize utility) will equate $\mathrm{MRS}_{X,Y}$ with P_X/P_Y. Since all consumers face identical prices, all will have the same $\mathrm{MRS}_{X,Y}$ and exchange efficiency will be satisfied.

There are four rules for efficiency in production. The first is technological efficiency. Firm profit maximization requires that this rule be satisfied: If more output can be produced with the same inputs, then more revenue can be produced for the same cost and the firm is not at the profit maximum.

The second rule requires equality of rates of technical substitution among firms using the same inputs, $\mathrm{RTS}_{K,L}^{X} = \mathrm{RTS}_{K,L}^{Y}$. But we know that each firm, to produce at least cost (necessary for profit maximization), must set

$$\mathrm{RTS}_{K,L} = \frac{P_K}{P_L}$$

This is the condition of tangency between a firm's isoquant (the slope of which is $-\mathrm{RTS}_{K,L}$) and an isocost line (the slope of which is $-P_K/P_L$), which is required if the output level represented by the isoquant is to be produced at least cost.[16] As all firms face the same prices for homogeneous factors, the RTS of all firms using them will be the same.

The third rule for productive efficiency is that the marginal product of a factor must be identical for each firm producing the same output. This can be shown to hold in competitive equilibrium as a consequence of profit maximization. If a firm hires one more factor, say, a unit of labor, the marginal cost of that action is P_L. The marginal revenue to the firm equals the marginal product times the price of the output P_X: $P_X \mathrm{MP}_L^{X}$. Profit maximization requires the firm to hire the amount of labor that makes

$$P_L = P_X \mathrm{MP}_L^{X}$$

This equation is sometimes referred to as the *marginal productivity theory of factor demand* (labor in this case), because for each possible wage rate (given the output price), the competitive firm will demand whatever quantity of labor makes the equation hold. A lower market wage rate, for example, will induce the firm to use more labor in order to lower its marginal product and restore the equality of the equation. The firm's demand is sometimes referred to as a *derived demand* because it is not based on tastes or preferences but is derived from doing what is necessary to maximize profit. We rewrite the equation as

$$\mathrm{MP}_L^{X} = \frac{P_L}{P_X}$$

Therefore, all firms in industry X will have identical marginal products, since all face the same prices P_X and P_L.

---

[16] This is shown graphically in the appendix to Chapter 9.

The fourth rule for productive efficiency is that the rate of product transformation between two goods must be identical across firms. In the Robinson Crusoe model of Chapter 9 we demonstrated that the $RPT_{X,Y}$ can be interpreted as the marginal cost of X in terms of Y forgone. If we wish to express the marginal cost in dollar terms, we have only to multiply by P_Y:

$$MC_X = RPT_{X,Y} P_Y$$

Competitive profit-maximizing firms always choose the output level where $MC = P$ ($= MR$); therefore, in competitive equilibrium

$$P_X = RPT_{X,Y} P_Y$$

or

$$RPT_{X,Y} = \frac{P_X}{P_Y}$$

Finally, since all producers of X and Y face the same prices P_X and P_Y, the $RPT_{X,Y}$ must be the same for all producers.

So far we have shown that, in the general competitive equilibrium, exchange and production efficiency are satisfied. The final condition, product-mix efficiency, follows trivially. We have already shown that $MRS_{X,Y} = P_X/P_Y$ for all consumers and that $RPT_{X,Y} = P_X/P_Y$ for all producers. Therefore, $MRS_{X,Y} = RPT_{X,Y}$ and the last condition is satisfied. A general competitive equilibrium is Pareto-optimal.

The second of the twin theorems states that any Pareto optimum can be achieved by a general competitive equilibrium (assuming preferences and technologies are well behaved). In other words, suppose we know where we wish to end up; the question is whether a competitive system can take us there. Consider any particular optimum. Since it satisfies all the efficiency requirements, we know the required marginal trade-off for each of them: for example, all consumers must have $MRS_{X,Y} = \alpha_{X,Y}$, where $\alpha_{X,Y}$ is some number. Therefore, we must choose prices P_X and P_Y such that $P_X/P_Y = \alpha_{X,Y}$.

Note that we have a degree of freedom: the efficiency conditions refer only to *relative* prices, not to each one singly. Therefore, we can pick any good to serve as a reference unit, called the *numéraire,* for expressing the relative values of all other goods. For example, we set P_X equal to any number we like. Since there is only one remaining unknown in each of the equations relating good X to every possible other good, this determines the prices of all other goods.[17]

Of course, we have not yet ensured that demand and supply will be in equilibrium at these prices. To achieve the equilibrium, we must assign to each individual an income that exactly equals the value of his or her optimal allocation at the prices identified above. Given that income and facing the specified prices, each consumer will be in equilibrium only when purchasing the bundle of goods and services (including leisure) that we initially identified

[17] In macroeconomics, it is often useful to think of the *numéraire* good as "money" and to consider how macroeconomic forces influence its level.

as the goal. We have simply assigned budget constraints (prices and income levels) that are tangent to each person's indifference curves at the desired allocations. Thus, as long as we can costlessly redistribute income, any Pareto optimum can be achieved through a general competitive equilibrium.

Some economists interpret this second theorem as a reason to avoid equity concerns. That is, as long as any optimal allocation can be achieved, the economist can simply assume that policy makers will assign the incomes to individuals that they think appropriate (e.g., through a progressive tax system or a welfare system). The economist can restrict his or her concern to the efficiency of the situation. This can have the added advantage of simplifying policy debate over specific issues.[18]

There are numerous counterarguments to this position, and those involving process equity and political limits on the use of a small number of policy instruments were reviewed in Chapters 3 and 5. An additional important argument that will be presented later in the chapter is this: *There is no costless method of redistribution,* and efficiency requires that any given redistribution be achieved through whatever policy instruments achieve it at least cost. In Chapter 14 we review more carefully some basic choices of instruments to achieve specific equity goals in particular markets.

General Competitive Analysis and Efficiency

Several times in the text we have cautioned that specific analytic effects that appear in *partial* equilibrium models may disappear or be quite different in *general* equilibrium models. **In the partial equilibrium model we allow variation in only the prices and quantities of one or several markets and assume that all other prices are held constant.** But depending on the source of the changes we consider, the assumption that other prices are unaffected may not be tenable. A tax on corporate capital, for example, may affect not only the price and allocation of capital through its direct effect on the corporate sector, but it may cause the relative price of capital to change elsewhere in the economy and thereby shift cost curves in other industries, which will affect allocation in them as well. This may cause further changes in the corporate sector because the other prices have changed.

In this section we attempt to clarify the importance of this difference with an illustration of partial and general equilibrium analyses of **tax incidence: the changes in the real income of individuals caused by the imposition of a tax.** However, the point we wish to emphasize is not the incidence in the specific illustrative model developed. The more important point is to develop analytic ability in understanding the reasons for differences between the two types of analyses and in beginning to judge the adequacy of one method versus the other in applications.

---

[18] Charles Schultze expressed concern that "equity" is an argument that can be used by any clever special interest group to tie up, change, or frustrate the attempt to improve the efficiency of the economy in specific areas, even if most people would benefit from the change. See his book, *The Public Uses of Private Interests* (Washington, D.C.: The Brookings Institution, 1977). Policy analysis that includes equity considerations should be able to address such arguments.

We begin the analysis with a partial equilibrium model and introduce the concepts of tax incidence and tax-shifting. Then we extend the analysis to general equilibrium in a two-sector model. We discuss each part of the *general equilibrium model* and then derive the competitive allocation by *ensuring that all markets are simultaneously in equilibrium (no prices are assumed constant)*. Then we look at the effects of the same tax examined in the partial equilibrium model and contrast the results. We conclude with a brief discussion of lump-sum taxes and efficiency in taxation.

Partial Equilibrium Analysis: The Excise Tax

Suppose, for our partial equilibrium model, that we are producing a product Q in a competitive market. The demand curve (expressed for convenience as a willingness-to-pay curve, i.e., with price on the left-hand side) is

$$P = 200/Q$$

The supply curve for Q is

$$P = 2$$

This perfectly elastic (horizontal) supply curve means that the industry will produce whatever quantity is demanded at a constant per unit price of $2. We draw the demand and supply curves in Figure 12-9a. The equilibrium quantity is $Q = 100$ at $P = 2$.

It matters neither for allocation nor distribution whether we legally collect the tax from the supplier or the demander, as long as the definition of the taxed activity remains the same.[19] The economic effects are determined by the tax amount, which causes a *difference* between the price demanders pay and the price suppliers receive. This result is quite general, applying to any situation in which the taxed activity can be appropriately represented with demand and supply curves. Many economists believe, for example, that the sometimes acrimonious political debate in the United States about proposals to change the traditional 50-50 split between employers and employees of the 12.4 percent social security tax is a red herring (because any split will lead to the same outcome). We explain this below.

For the excise tax of $0.67, the (partial equilibrium) effect is shown in Figures 12-9a and b. In Figure 12-9a, we draw the tax as if it is placed on suppliers. Since this is a new and unavoidable "cost" to them of supplying each unit, it raises the supply curve by $0.67 to S' (i.e., $P = 2.67$).[20] Taxing suppliers has no effect on the willingness to pay of consumers, so the demand curve D is not affected. The new equilibrium market quantity (equating D with S')

---

[19] There may be a significant difference in the transaction costs of collecting and enforcing a tax, depending on whether it is placed on the demand side or the supply side, and these factors should bear on the decision of where to place it. For example, a sales tax is virtually always placed on the seller (e.g., a grocery store) rather than the buyer (e.g., a household shopper) because the seller generally keep records of every sale anyway whereas the buyer does not.

[20] The tax is only a pecuniary cost, not a social cost; there are no additional resource inputs used to make the output.

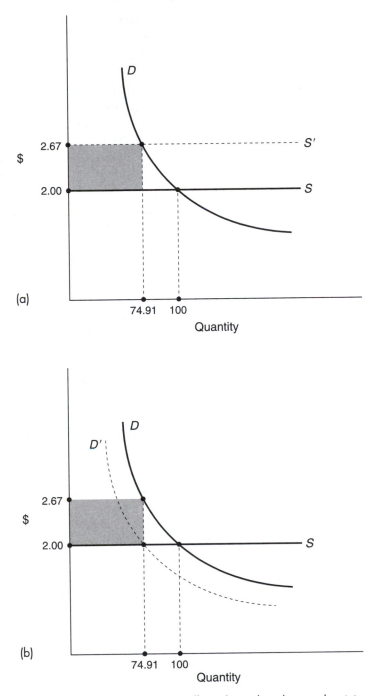

Figure 12-9. Tax allocative and distributional effects depend on the taxed activity and not from whom it is collected: (a) The tax is collected from the supplier (*S'* is the supply as perceived by the demander). (b) The tax is collected from the demander (*D'* is the demand as perceived by the supplier).

is shown as $Q_T = 74.91$ units, with $P = \$2.67$. The government collects $\$0.67$ per unit sold in tax revenues (the shaded rectangle of $\$50.19$), and suppliers have $\$2.00$ per unit left over to pay their nontax costs.

Before looking further at the consequences of the tax, let us turn to Figure 12-9b, where we place the tax on demanders. In this diagram, the supply curve is unaffected and remains horizontal at $\$2$ ($P = 2$). Consumers' willingness to pay suppliers, however, is now $\$0.67$ less than it used to be, since $\$0.67$ of the original willingness to pay per unit must go to the tax collector. So the demand curve (as suppliers perceive it) shifts down to D' or $P = (200/Q) - 0.67$. Once again, we see that the new equilibrium (equating D' with S) is $Q_T = 74.91$, with demanders paying $\$2.00$ per unit to suppliers but also $\$0.67$ per unit to the government, for a total of $\$2.67$ per unit. Thus it does not matter whether the tax is collected from suppliers or demanders; the final position of each economic agent is not affected.

Another way to see this is to note that in both Figures 12-9a and b, the new equilibrium can be identified from the original demand and supply curves and knowledge of the tax amount. The new equilibrium is at the quantity where the height of the demand curve D exceeds the height of the supply curve S by precisely the tax amount, in this case $\$0.67$. The height of the demand curve at this quantity is the gross price (inclusive of the tax) that demanders pay, and the height of the supply curve is the net price (exclusive of the tax) that suppliers receive. We draw this in Figure 12-10a, again shading the rectangular area representing the amount of tax collected. We also shade the triangular area to the right of the rectangle, the deadweight loss caused by the tax (roughly $\$8$).[21]

In this case, with perfectly elastic supply, the consumers bear the full burden of the tax. All of the tax payments (as well as all of the deadweight loss) come from a reduction in consumer surplus. If we had a sloping supply curve, as in Figure 12-10b, the incidence of the tax would be partially borne by both consumers (through the loss in consumer surplus) and producers (through the loss of economic rent). Thus, the more elastic the demand curve and the more inelastic the supply curve, the more the incidence of the tax will fall on producers (other things being equal). Of course, one cannot evaluate the equity of this unless one knows something about who the consumers and producers are.[22]

Another concept that is often used in the study of tax incidence is called **tax-shifting: the extent to which the legal payers of the tax escape its burden.** As we have already suggested, the economic agents upon whom the tax is levied may not be the full bearers of the tax. When they are not, we say that the tax has been partially shifted. If the tax in Figure 12-10a is imposed on the manufacturers, the partial equilibrium effect is to shift the tax fully *forward* to the consumers. The same tax imposed initially on consumers has an identical incidence but would not be considered shifted. Of course, the concept is intended to

---

[21] The amount by integral calculus is $\$7.60$. One can quickly approximate this by treating the shaded area as a right triangle and calculating $0.5(25.09)(0.67) \approx \$8.41$.

[22] The market could be for low-rent housing, in which it is likely that tenants are less well-off than apartment suppliers and the tax is a property tax. Alternatively, the market could be for expensive jewelry, in which the consumer may be at least as well off as the jewelry suppliers and the tax is an excise tax. Even these distinctions refer to specific groups, and there is sure to be variation of individual well-being within each group.

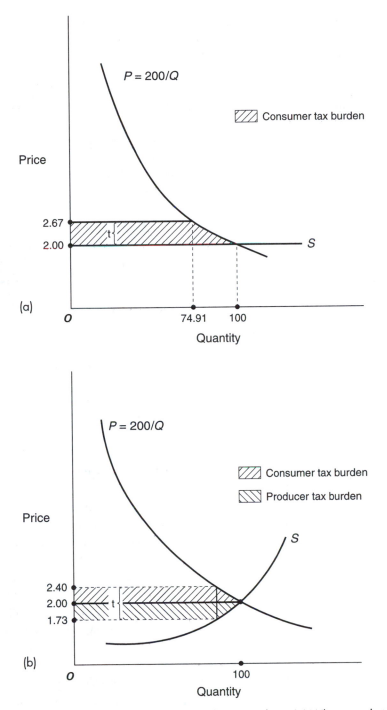

Figure 12-10. Excise tax incidence—partial equilibrium analysis: (a) When supply is perfectly elastic. (b) When supply is upward-sloping.

apply to more interesting cases such as that in Figure 12-10b: partially shifted forward if initially imposed on producers or backward if initially imposed on consumers. A tax may also be shifted *backward* to the factor suppliers (not shown).

General Equilibrium Analysis: Perfect Competition and the Excise Tax

Let us now look at the shortcomings of this analysis that are due to our considering only the partial equilibrium effects. To do so, we introduce a simple general equilibrium model. We assume that the economy is fully competitive with four different markets: two output markets (for goods Q_1 and Q_2), and two factor markets (for capital K and labor L). We represent the demand and supply curves for each market graphically in Figures 12-11a, b, c, and d, showing (in solid lines) the initial competitive equilibrium in each market. By design, the demand and supply for Q_2 shown in Figure 12-11b are identical to those used for the partial equilibrium analysis of the prior section (Figure 12-10a).

Suppose we introduce (again) an excise tax of $0.67 on output Q_2. What happens in the general equilibrium model? Before trying to be precise, let us present the idea intuitively. Initially, we can think as we did last time: In the Q_2 market, the new equilibrium output will be reduced to the quantity at which the height of the demand curve exceeds the height of the supply curve by $0.67. However, now we must take account of the fact that if the Q_2 output level is reduced, then the derived demand for factors by Q_2 producers must necessarily be reduced.

For simplicity, assume that Q_2 is produced only with labor. Then the derived demand curve for labor in Figure 12-11d must shift to the left to D_L'. In this particular model, because we have assumed a fixed (vertical) supply of labor, the new equilibrium wage rate will be lower than at the initial equilibrium. By way of contrast, the partial equilibrium model assumes that the shift has a negligible effect on the wage rate (an appropriate assumption for some circumstances).

The changed wage rate introduces a crucial new complication. Recall that all two-dimensional demand and supply curves are drawn with the *ceteris paribus* assumption: that all *other* prices are being held constant. If the wage rate goes down, this means that the cost of making any given quantity of each output is lower: *the supply curves for both outputs shift downward.* We draw the new supply curves as S_1' in Figure 12-11a and S_2' in Figure 12-11b.

Several effects of using a general equilibrium model to predict the consequences of the excise tax should begin to become clear at this point. Looking at Figure 12-11b, we see that the after-tax equilibrium in this model is different from that predicted by the partial equilibrium model. The equilibrium quantity, shown as $Q_2 = 87.80$, is higher than the partial equilibrium prediction of 74.91. The indirect effect of the excise tax—the wage reduction in the labor market—partially offsets its direct effect in the Q_2 market. Tax collections (about $59) are also higher than predicted by the partial equilibrium model (about $50). Furthermore, the tax has been at least partially shifted backward to labor throughout the economy: the tax causes a wage reduction that applies to labor used in both the Q_1 and Q_2 industries.

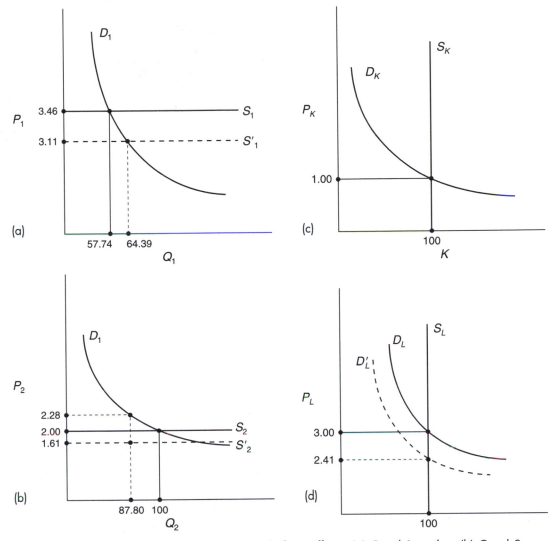

Figure 12-11. A general equilibrium model of tax effects: (a) Good 1 market. (b) Good 2 market. (c) Capital market. (d) Labor market.

There are other effects of the tax to worry about: for example, if labor income changes, the demand curves may change. So at this point it is useful to become more precise, and introduce in Table 12-1 the specific pretax demand and supply curves used in this example. In the appendix to this chapter, as a further exercise in competitive theory, these demand and supply equations are themselves derived from specific assumptions about production technologies, consumer tastes, and resource constraints.

The main aspect to note about Table 12-1 is that there are eight equations and eight unknowns (four unknown prices and four unknown quantities) and to identify the equilibrium

Table 12-1
Summary of the Two-Good, Two-Factor, Competitive Economy

Product markets
Sector 1

Demand	$Q_1 = \dfrac{\frac{1}{2}(P_L L + P_K K)}{P_1}$	(1)
Supply	$P_1 = 2P_K^{1/2} P_L^{1/2}$	(2)

Sector 2

Demand	$Q_2 = \dfrac{\frac{1}{2}(P_L L + P_K K)}{P_2}$	(3)
Supply	$P_2 = \frac{2}{3}P_L$	(4)

Factor markets
Capital

Demand	$K = K_1 + K_2 = P_K^{1/2} P_L^{1/2} Q_1$	(5)
Supply	$K = 100$	(6)

Labor

Demand	$L = L_1 + L_2 = P_K^{1/2} P_L^{-1/2} Q_1 + \frac{2}{3}Q_2$	(7)
Supply	$L = 100$	(8)

values one must solve the equations simultaneously.[23] One cannot, for example, simply use the demand and supply equations for Q_2 to determine the equilibrium P_2, Q_2; one first needs to know what values to use for P_L, L, P_K, and K. Indeed, and for the same reason, one cannot locate either the demand or supply curve for Q_2 on the usual price-quantity diagram. *After* the equations are simultaneously solved, one can then construct the usual two-dimensional demand and supply curves, on the assumption that the other variables are being held constant at their equilibrium levels. It is these (solid-line) curves that are shown in Figure 12-11, with their associated pretax equilibrium prices and quantities.[24]

[23] The mathematics of solving simultaneous equations, particularly nonlinear ones, goes beyond the scope of this book. In actual policy applications, computer programs are normally used to identify the solutions.

[24] For example, sector 2's partial equilibrium equations are found by substituting the equilibrium values for all variables except P_2 and Q_2 in equations (3) and (4) of Table 12-1 (discussed shortly):

$$Q_2 = \frac{\frac{1}{2}(300 + 100)}{P_2} = \frac{200}{P_2}$$

$$P_2 = \frac{2}{3}(3) = 2$$

One economic aspect of identifying the solution to the above equations should be pointed out. We know from theoretical considerations that only *relative* prices matter. That is, we can arbitrarily set the price of any one good (the *numéraire,* in this case $P_K = 1$) and measure all other prices relative to it. That will give us only seven real unknowns but eight equations. Does that mean there will be an infinite number of solutions to our problem? No, because *Walras' law* tells us that one of the equations is redundant anyway.

Walras' law states that the price-weighted sum of demands minus supplies for all quantities must be equal to zero, whether or not the economy is in equilibrium. Therefore, if demand equals supply in $n - 1$ of n markets, Walras' law implies that demand equals supply in the nth market as well.[25] In our model let us say we make sure that the solution equates supply and demand in the first three markets of Table 12-1. Then we do not have to bother equating the two sides of the labor market (although we must use one of the labor market equations to solve for the levels in the other three markets). Walras' law assures us that the market will be in equilibrium as a consequence of equating the first three.

Figure 12-11 shows the resulting equilibrium levels, but let us note a few other characteristics of the equilibrium[26]: $L_1 = 33.333$—share of labor in sector 1; $L_2 = 66.667$—share of labor in sector 2; $P_L L = 300$—labor's share of total income $P_K K = 100$—capital's share of total income.[27]

---

[25] A proof of this may be found in H. Varian, *Microeconomic Analysis* (New York: W. W. Norton & Company, 1992), pp. 317–318. The idea behind the proof is simple. Remember that firms are merely intermediaries. Each person has an endowment of goods and factors that may be supplied to the marketplace (e.g., through employment, the provision of capital to firms, or garage sales). The income received from these sources (e.g., wages, firm profits, and garage receipts) is the budget constraint, which is then spent entirely in order to maximize utility. Thus, for an individual, the price-weighted sum of demands (over all commodities) minus supplies (over all commodities) equals zero. But then the sum over all persons is zero, and that is Walras' law.

[26] In this economy it is particularly simple to illustrate the second of the twin theorems. Because of our assumptions, neither the aggregate supply of factors nor the aggregate demand for products is affected by the distribution of factor ownership. That is, no matter how the ownership of K and L is distributed, the equilibrium market prices and quantities will be as above.

Suppose there are only two people in this economy. Then the locus of Pareto-optimal allocations in the economy is simply any proportionate distribution of the two outputs. That is, for all $0 < \alpha < 1$, allocate αQ_2 and αQ_1, to person R and $(1 - \alpha)Q_2$ and $(1 - \alpha)Q_1$ to person S (Q_2 and Q_1 are the constant market quantities 100 and 57.74, respectively). To achieve any of these Pareto-optimal allocations, one simply redistributes income to give each person the appropriate budget size. Suppose each person starts with $K = 50$ and $L = 50$; then competitive markets will result in each earning $200 and will lead to the optimal allocation where $\alpha = 0.5$. If we want to achieve some other efficient allocation, say $\alpha = 0.6$, then we must take away the equivalent of $40 from S and give it to R. We could do that by taking 40 units of capital away from S and giving it to R. In this example competitive markets would then lead to all the same prices and aggregate quantities; R simply ends up with $40 more income and thus can purchase more. To make R very much better off than initially ($\alpha > 0.625$), we would have to assign R some of the fruits from the labor of S in addition to redistributing all 50 units of capital from S.

[27] The story would, of course, change if the government used the funds to demand different goods. Since that is what governments normally do with taxes, a word of explanation for our assumption may be helpful. The most common method of tax incidence analysis is called differential tax incidence. In this method two or more different taxes designed to be of equal yield are compared, the assumption being that the government's purpose for the funds does not change with the tax method. If we allowed the use of the funds to cause a change in our example

When the excise tax on Q_2 is introduced, the equations change somewhat. It is instructive to examine these changes and the reasons for them. First let us clarify some notation. Let us call the tax t, and let P_2 be the price the supplier receives and $P_2 + t$ be the price demanders of Q_2 pay.[28] Then the tax receipts will be tQ_2.

The model must take account of what happens to the taxes collected: Are they used to build a bridge, or to feed the hungry, or for some other purpose? We shall use the approach followed under the most common tax analysis called **differential tax incidence.** With this approach, the analysis is intended to focus on the pure effect of the tax itself, not to be confounded with the worthiness of whatever project is undertaken with the revenues raised. A common case is when the project to be funded is already agreed upon, but several different taxes could be used to raise the necessary revenue. Then analysts seek **to compare the effects of alternative taxes used to raise a fixed amount of revenue for a constant purpose.** To follow this spirit in our model, we make an assumption about the use of the tax proceeds that does not itself influence the results.

The assumption that will do the trick in this case is that the tax proceeds are simply redistributed to people in the economy. In this model (but certainly not in general), demand (as well as supply) is unaffected by which particular people receive the money. We explain this shortly, as we go through the changes the tax causes in the equations of our general equilibrium model.

In Table 12-1, three types of changes are necessary to make the equations represent the new situation with the tax. First, each instance of the demand price for Q_2 must be changed from P_2 to $P_2 + t$. In this particular model, there is only one instance of this: the denominator of equation (3). We do not have to change equation (4) because the P_2 in it represents the supply price.

Second, the redistribution to consumers of the tax proceeds introduces a new income source for which we must account. Income appears in this particular model in two places: the numerators of the demand curve equations (1) and (3). The original expression in parentheses $(P_L L + P_K K)$ is aggregate income in the economy; under the assumptions used to construct this simple model (explained in the appendix), aggregate income affects demand although its distribution does not. When we introduce the tax and redistribute the proceeds, a third source of income is introduced in addition to capital and labor income. So aggregate income is now $P_K K + P_L L + t Q_2$, and this term replaces the original in both equations.

Third, we have introduced a new variable t and therefore need another equation in order to be able to solve the entire system simultaneously. In this particular case, we add as equation (9) the simple expression $t = 0.67$. That is it. All factor market equations (5)–(8) are unaffected, and the product supply equations (2) and (4) are also unaffected. Thus our new system of equations is identical with the old except for these changes:

---

equilibrium, the analysis would not capture the pure tax effects. We are implicitly comparing our tax to a perfectly neutral one that does not change any allocation decisions and keeps income distribution the same.

[28] We could do this in the equivalent way, with P_2 defined as the demand price and $(P_2 - t)$ defined as the supply price.

$$\text{Demand } Q_1 = \frac{\frac{1}{2}(P_L L + P_L K + t Q_2)}{P_1} \tag{1'}$$

$$\text{Demand } Q_2 = \frac{\frac{1}{2}(P_L L + P_L K + t Q_2)}{P_2 + t} \tag{3'}$$

and

$$\text{Tax policy } \quad t = 0.67 \tag{9}$$

We can see without making any numerical calculations that the economy will remain productively efficient (factor suppliers face the same factor prices that factor demanders face). However, the economy will not be at the optimal point on the production frontier because

$$\text{RPT}_{Q_1, Q_2} = \frac{P_1}{P_2} \quad \text{for suppliers}$$

$$\text{MRS}_{Q_1, Q_2} = \frac{P_1}{P_2 + t} \quad \text{for demanders}$$

Therefore

$$\text{RPT} \neq \text{MRS}$$

The equilibrium values of the simultaneous solution to the modified equations with the excise tax are:

$$P_K = 1 \qquad K = 100$$

$$P_L = 2.41 \qquad L = 100 \qquad (L_1 = 41.42, L_2 = 58.58)$$

$$P_1 = 3.10 \qquad Q_1 = 64.45$$

$$P_2 = 1.61 \qquad Q_2 = 87.87$$

Tax collections $t Q_2 = 58.58$

Labor income $P_L L = 241$

Capital income $P_K K = 100$

Total income $= 399.58 \ (\approx 400)$

The striking aspect of this result is that the tax is borne fully by labor throughout the economy. Capital income is unchanged, as is total income. Labor income has gone down by the full amount of the tax proceeds. Why did that happen? It results from the special assumptions used to construct this model: that the supply of labor is completely inelastic and that we have taxed the labor-intensive industry.

Under less restrictive but still competitive model assumptions, we would find that an excise tax on the labor-intensive industry always makes labor worse off.[29] Capital may or may not be made worse off. Recall that under competition factors will be priced at the value of the marginal product $P_K = P_1 * MP_K$. The tax will cause capital's marginal productivity to rise (as labor flows from sector 2 into sector 1), working to increase capital's price, but this may or may not be outweighed by the fall in P_1.

We might also note that the consumer with average income is worse off than before the tax even though average income is the same. The reason for that is simple: We already know that the product mix under the tax regime differs from the optimal one. Under the tax regime prices, the consumer cannot purchase as attractive a bundle of goods for a given budget.

The deadweight loss (sometimes called the *excess burden* of the tax) in the economy is about $4.20, or about 1 percent of aggregate income. This may be calculated as the reduction in social (consumer plus producer) surplus from the information in Figures 12-11a, b, c, and d. There is no change in the capital market (Figure 12-11c). The change in the labor market (Figure 12-11d) is the loss in income to suppliers (approximately $59); labor demanders retain the same surplus (the lower marginal benefits as demand drops from D_L to D_L' are exactly offset by the lower labor costs).

However, turning to Figure 12-11b, we see that the $59 loss in labor income is exactly offset by the tax proceeds (the area between $1.61 and $2.28 bounded by the P_2-axis and $Q_2 = 87.80$ units); recall these are redistributed to the people in the economy. Producers of good 2 receive less for their goods, but this is offset precisely by their lower factor costs (they have zero surplus at both the initial and after-tax prices). Consumers of good 2, owing to the price increase they face, lose surplus of the area between the old price line (of $2.00) and the new one (of $2.28), bounded by the P_2-axis and the demand curve. This loss works out to $26.03.[30]

In Figure 12-11a, owing to the price reduction for good 1, consumers gain surplus of the area between the old and new price lines (from the P_1-axis to the demand curve). This gain works out to $21.82.[31] As with good 2, producers receive less revenue but this is exactly offset by the reduction in their factor costs (they have no surplus at either the initial or after-tax price). Thus the only effects that do not net out are the consumer loss of $26.03 from good 2, and the consumer gain of $21.82 from good 1. This leaves a net loss in social surplus of $4.21, slightly more than 1 percent of this $400 economy.[32]

---

[29] For more extensive review of the burdens and incidences of specific taxes, see standard texts in public finance, for example, Joseph E. Stiglitz, *Economics of the Public Sector*, 3rd Ed. (New York: W. W. Norton & Company, 2000).

[30] This may be calculated as the integral over the price axis, with limits that have one more significant decimal place than in Figure 12-11:

$$\int_{2.000}^{2.278} (200/P_2)\,dP_2 = 200(\ln 2.278 - \ln\ 2.000) = \$26.03$$

[31] The integral for this area, again with an extra decimal of significance in the limits, is

$$\int_{3.106}^{3.464} (200/P_1)\,dP_1 = 200(\ln 3.464 - \ln 3.106) = \$21.82$$

[32] Recall from Chapter 6 that the change in the social surplus is an inexact measure of the change in efficiency, usually close to the two exact measures called the compensating and equivalent variations. These latter two meas-

To return to the incidence of the tax, note that we cannot evaluate it further without knowledge of the distribution of factor ownership among the population. If each person owned one unit of capital and labor, the equity of labor bearing the full burden would be no different than if labor and capital shared it equally. On the other hand, if the ownership of capital is concentrated among the wealthy few and the labor is that of the poor majority, we say the tax is regressive in its incidence.

The comparison of this general equilibrium model with the earlier partial equilibrium one suggests very important differences in our understanding of tax effects. The latter completely missed the backward shifting of the tax to labor throughout the economy. In the matter of predicting government tax receipts, the partial analysis underestimated tax collection by 15 percent. Both models predict a deadweight loss owing to the tax, although its size (1% of total income) is overestimated (at about 2% of income) by the partial equilibrium model. Thus one might wonder if it is ever appropriate to do a partial equilibrium analysis; and as one ventures beyond the simplest models, what level of detail is appropriate?

Some general advice can be offered. First, there are many times when the partial equilibrium analysis is quite appropriate. Many changes are small relative to the rest of the economy and would not be expected to affect prices in other sectors. Second, the ability to construct workable general equilibrium models is limited by two factors: data availability and analytic constraints.

We may know that the aggregate national labor supply is highly inelastic (although not perfectly inelastic as in our simple model). But if we wish to build a model with, say, five to ten labor markets distinguished by various skill and expertise requirements (e.g., construction workers, retail workers, scientists) we may not be as certain about the supply elasticities in each sector. In other words, the larger and more disaggregated models require that many more parameters be empirically specified, and any advantage to constructing such a model depends in part on our confidence in the data available for it.

Furthermore, recall that our general equilibrium model assumed that *all* sectors are perfectly competitive. It is one thing to assume competition holds at least approximately in one sector and quite another to assume it holds economy-wide in economies with substantial public, regulated, and oligopolistic sectors and labor markets that are often characterized by high involuntary unemployment levels. One can certainly imagine general equilibrium models that do not assume competition throughout. However, computable general

---

ures can be calculated easily from the information in the appendix used to construct this general equilibrium model. In particular, the Cobb-Douglas utility function used to generate the demand functions has an associated expenditure function $B = (1/2)UP_1^{1/2}P_2^{1/2}$. The initial utility level is $U = 75.9836$, and the after-tax utility level is $U = 75.1928$. (In this model, because the utility function is linear homogeneous, we can treat the aggregate output as if it is all consumed by one person.) The compensating variation is the difference between \$400 and the budget necessary to achieve the initial utility level at the after-tax prices. Plugging in the initial utility level and the after-tax prices ($P_1 = \$3.106$, $P_2 = \$2.278$) to the expenditure function, we calculate that $B = \$404.23$, or that CV = \$4.23. The equivalent variation is the difference between \$400 and the budget necessary to achieve the after-tax utility level at the initial prices ($P_1 = \$3.464$, $P_2 = \$2.000$). Plugging the latter into the expenditure function, we get $B = \$395.83$ or EV = \$4.17. Note that the change in social surplus is between the two exact measures, as expected, and that all three measures are quite close to one another.

equilibrium (CGE) models normally cannot be used to solve for equilibrium prices and quantities in imperfectly competitive situations (where the allocation is not determined by the intersection of competitive demand and supply curves). Thus our ability to construct and implement general equilibrium models with noncompetitive sectors is sharply limited by the analytic methods available for calculating such an economy's equilibrium.

Taking these limiting factors as challenges to be overcome, general equilibrium models are increasingly being used for applied problems.[33] Harberger has pioneered the application of a two-sector model to the study of tax incidence.[34] He found, using a model no more complicated than ours, that a tax on corporate goods (the capital-intensive sector) is borne fully by capital. That tax is the corporate income tax. Furthermore, his findings are supported by the work of Shoven and Whalley, who pioneered the application of CGE models that expand the number of sectors and the range of demand and supply elasticities considered.[35] This type of work usually permits grouping of individuals by income classes, so that the burdens can be estimated by income class as well as by types of consumers or factor owners. In recent years, researchers have extended these models beyond the simple "static" equilibrium to include analyses of "dynamic" tax incidence: how the burden of a tax gets distributed over time as well as to which types of individuals.[36]

General equilibrium models can and have been applied to many other types of economic problems apart from tax incidence. Shoven and Whalley (1992) describe a number of CGE applications to predicting the effects of trade policies. Bergman has applied a CGE model to understand the effects of energy and environmental constraints on growth in Sweden.[37] Boyd, Doroodian, and Power construct a CGE model to analyze the effect of the U.S. sugar program.[38] However, at this point we return to taxation and our trusty model. We introduce one new tax in order to discuss further the efficiency effects of taxation.

Lump-Sum Taxes Are Efficient and Most Real Taxes Are Inefficient

The new tax that we wish to consider is, like Social Security, an employment tax that yields revenue equal to our excise tax. That is, in this regime the new price of labor to producers

[33] As a general reference, see V. Ginsburgh and M. Keyser, *The Structure of Applied General Equilibrium Models* (Cambridge: The MIT Press, 1997).

[34] See A. Harberger, "The Incidence of the Corporation Income Tax," *Journal of Political Economy, 70,* 1962, pp. 215–240.

[35] See J. Shoven and J. Whalley, *Applying General Equilibrium* (New York: Cambridge University Press, 1992). This book reviews general CGE methodology and a number of their applications including the Harberger model extensions.

[36] See, for example, D. Fullerton and D. Rogers, *Who Bears the Lifetime Tax Burden?* (Washington, D.C.: The Brookings Institution, 1993). See also the generational accounting framework developed in A. Auerbach and L. Kotlikoff, *Dynamic Fiscal Policy* (New York: Cambridge University Press, 1987).

[37] See L. Bergman, "Energy and Environmental Constraints on Growth: A CGE Modeling Approach," *Journal of Policy Modeling, 12,* No. 4, Winter 1990, pp. 671–691.

[38] R. Boyd, K. Doroodian, and A. Power, "The Impact of Removing the Sugar Quota on the U.S. Economy: A General Equilibrium Analysis," *Journal of Policy Modeling, 18,* No. 2, April 1996, pp. 185–201.

is $P_L + t$, although labor continues to receive only P_L as income. The striking aspect of this tax is that, in our model, it causes no allocative changes from the untaxed Pareto optimum. (The same thing would be true of a capital tax.)

Referring back to Table 12-1, let us consider the changes that must be made. They can be summarized with one instruction: Everywhere there is a P_L, substitute for it the variable $P_L + t$.[39] There is no distortionary wedge in the model because the labor supply equation is *fixed* at $L = 100$. If there were a variable labor supply, the equilibrium quantity of labor would be affected by any change in the real wage P_L and distorted by any difference between the price of labor to employers ($P_L + t$) and laborers (P_L). But since all the payments to labor (and capital) in this model are pure *economic rent* (payments *above* opportunity cost), no labor supply decisions are affected by the tax.

The only equation changes that may need further explanation are for the product demands. The new budget constraint is earned income plus tax proceeds:

$$B = P_L L + P_K K + tL$$

$$= (P_L + t)L + P_K K$$

It therefore comports with our single instruction for the necessary changes.

Thus we need not go through the solution again; it is essentially identical to our original solution. The only change is that instead of $P_L = 3$ we have

$$P_L + t = 3$$

What is t? To make the tax have equal yield to the excise tax, we have to collect $58.58:

$$tL = 58.58$$

$$t = \frac{58.58}{L} = \frac{58.58}{100} = 0.5858$$

$$P = 2.4142 \approx 2.41$$

In other words, the tax is fully borne by labor and the after-tax distribution of income is exactly the same as with the excise tax. However, *this tax is efficient:* The allocation of resources in the economy is identical with the no-tax Pareto optimum. The deadweight loss from taxation is zero. The general explanation for this result is as follows: *If the taxed entity cannot alter its tax liability, there will be no distortion in the allocation of resources.* Since we have postulated that the labor is fixed, the wage earner's labor-leisure trade-off has been assumed away. If the amount of labor L is fixed, then the tax liability tL cannot be altered (whether the tax is placed on the worker or on the firm). Furthermore, if the tax does not alter the demands or supplies for other goods (e.g., as it typically would through income effects), the incidence of the tax will be completely on the inelastic respondent to the taxed activity.

The catch to all this is that it is doubtful whether such taxes exist. In the real world, social security taxes and income taxes do affect labor-leisure trade-offs. Product taxes affect

---

[39] This would not be true if there were a P_L in the supply of labor equation.

consumer purchase decisions. A tax on all consumption distorts the consumption-savings decision. Property taxes affect decisions about the type of structure to build.

A tax (or a subsidy) that cannot be altered by the taxpayer's behavior, called a lump-sum tax (or transfer), is nondistortionary. Although theoretical exercises often make use of the idea of lump-sum transfers—note the importance in the second of the twin theorems of being able to redistribute income costlessly—there is no practical tax proposal, let alone an actual tax, that economists agree is lump sum and that could be used to raise all (or the bulk) of tax revenues. There may be some actual lump-sum taxes, but it is hard to identify any with confidence. Two common suggestions for lump-sum taxes are poll, or head, taxes and pure land taxes. Let us look at each briefly.

For the poll tax to be lump-sum, its magnitude must be totally independent of actions that individuals can take in response to it. Suppose we say that everyone must pay $4000 per year. That, in all probability, would be highly regressive.[40] If we made the tax contingent on income or wealth in any way, individuals would have incentive to alter their wealth statuses. That is a major pragmatic stumbling block.

Even accepting the regressivity, individuals can still immigrate or emigrate, and they can still control the number of offspring they have. (That is, there is a distortionary wedge between the general supply of people and the demand for them.) If this sounds of no practical concern, think of the arguments about the migratory flow of workers (both legal and illegal) from lower-wage Mexico to the higher-wage United States or the mobility of the poor from low-subsidy southern states to high-subsidy northern states. Similar behavioral responses can be engendered by people trying to avoid a high poll tax in one area by moving to a different area. Furthermore, what should be done about those who cannot or refuse to pay? The penalty must not be influenced by the behavior of the defaulter; otherwise, it will affect the number of defaults. In short, there may not be any socially acceptable way of creating a lump-sum poll tax.

Margaret Thatcher tried. She introduced a poll tax (called a "community charge") in Britain in 1990. Nine months later, Thatcher was deposed, with her successor John Major pledging to abolish it. The poll tax initially replaced a property tax, which returned when the poll tax was finally abolished in April 1993. During its brief existence, the tax was required by the central government, and set by local authorities at a fixed amount per adult (about $500), to pay for local services such as education, refuse collection, and street cleaning. While Thatcher intended the tax to shift burden away from the wealthiest, it made the median voter substantially worse off and caused substantial political and economic protest.[41] Many taxpayers resisted paying, and local authorities could not easily enforce collection, leading to large revenue losses.[42]

---

[40] The incidence of the tax may still be shifted through income effects, for example; thus there is slight uncertainty about its regressivity.

[41] See John Gibson, *The Politics and Economics of the Poll Tax: Mrs. Thatcher's Downfall* (West Midlands, U.K.: EMAS, 1990).

[42] The noncompliance rate was over 60 percent in some regions. See T. Besley, I. Preston, and M. Ridge, "Fiscal Anarchy in the U.K.: Modelling Poll Tax Noncompliance," *Journal of Public Economics, 64,* No. 2, May 1997,

How about the land tax? The idea is that land is fixed in supply and therefore any tax levied on it will not distort the allocation of resources. (The product mix may change because of income effects, but there will be no distortionary wedges.)[43] Furthermore, since the worst-off people do not own much land, the incidence is likely to be progressive.[44] However, the supply of land is not perfectly fixed owing to land reclamation activities. Furthermore, the tax cannot have anything to do with the quality of the land, since that is alterable by human effort. If those obstacles can be overcome, it may be possible to design a tax on acreage that is considered equitable and efficient.[45]

The principal conclusion that we wish to draw from this brief analysis of taxation and efficiency is as follows: *All, or virtually all, existing methods of generating tax revenues are distortionary.* The size of the distortions remains a subject of continuing research. The most common measure estimated is called the **marginal excess burden: the increase in deadweight loss caused by raising one additional tax dollar.** Different estimates of the marginal excess burden for particular taxes vary widely. Freebairn suggests that most studies report distortions of at least $0.20 per dollar raised.[46] Nor is there any consensus about the implications of these burdens for financing public expenditures. The most common suggestion is to have a stricter-than-usual benefit-cost test for public expenditures (e.g., that using the $0.20 estimate, benefits should equal at least $1.20 for every $1.00 of cost).[47]

---

pp. 137–152. For further information on the poll tax, see D. Butler, A. Adonis, and T. Travers, *Failure in British Government: The Politics of the Poll Tax* (New York: Oxford University Press, 1994).

[43] The idea that public expenditures should be financed completely through a land tax because it is non-distortionary is known as the *Henry George Theorem,* after its originator. See Henry George, *Progress and Poverty* (New York: Doubleday, 1914).

[44] In an interesting article, Feldstein has shown that a pure land tax may be shifted other than through ordinary income effects. Because land is an asset for savings, a reduction in its return will cause savers to increase their demands for produced capital (an alternative savings asset). The expansion of produced capital raises the marginal product of land and thus shifts part of the tax to capital owners. Even if capital were perfectly fixed as well, there would be shifting because of risk aversion: If the returns to land and capital are uncertain, the value of land initially falls in response to the tax. Land becomes a less risky part of the portfolio, and thus its price will rise above the "full burden" level. See M. Feldstein, "The Surprising Incidence of a Tax on Pure Rent: A New Answer to an Old Question." *Journal of Political Economy, 85,* No. 2, April 1977, pp. 349–360.

[45] Netzer reports another obstacle, namely that the value of land is an unrealized capital gain for many owners and that they may consider taxation of unrealized gains unfair. See Dick Netzer, "On Modernizing Public Finance: Why Aren't Property Taxes in Urban Areas Being Reformed into Land Value Taxes," *American Journal of Economics and Sociology, 43,* No. 4, October 1984, pp. 497–501. See also the discussion on pp. 1135–1140 in P. Mieszkowski and G. Zodrow, "Taxation and the Tiebout Model: The Differential Effects of Head Taxes, Taxes on Land Rents, and Property Taxes," *Journal of Economic Literature, 27,* No. 3, Sept. 1989, pp. 1098–1146.

[46] J. Freebairn, "Reconsidering the Marginal Welfare Cost of Taxation," *Economic Record, 71,* No. 213, June 1995, pp. 121–131.

[47] Kaplow argues against this, reasoning that incremental projects need not increase distortion at all. See Louis Kaplow, "The Optimal Supply of Public Goods and the Distortionary Cost of Taxation," *National Tax Journal, 49,* No. 4, December 1996, pp. 513–533. Feldstein, on the other hand, argues that the distortion exceeds $1 for every $1 raised, and would support a far stricter test. See Martin Feldstein, "How Big Should Government Be?," *National Tax Journal, 50,* No. 2, June 1997, pp. 197–213. An important earlier study, which finds more moderate distortions, is C. Ballard, J. Shoven, and J. Whalley, "General Equilibrium Computations of the Marginal Welfare Costs of Taxes in the United States," *American Economic Review, 75,* No. 1, March 1985, pp. 128–138.

Two important implications follow from this conclusion. One is the challenge to make the tax system *less* distortionary, and much public finance research is devoted toward this end. For example, many analysts believe that the actual excise taxes used by federal, state, and local governments on telecommunications services are inefficient and inequitable anachronisms from a much earlier era, which now interfere with the development and spread of valuable new telecommunications technologies.[48] As another example, one very important class of potential taxes may *improve* rather than worsen efficiency: taxes on externalities, such as pollution that contributes to acid rain or global warming. Substituting one of these taxes for one of the conventional-but-distortionary ones could yield a double efficiency gain![49] In April 2001 in this spirit, the United Kingdom introduced a Climate Change Levy (a tax on fossil fuels and electricity) and simultaneously reduced the rate on one of its payroll taxes.

However, there is little practical hope of totally replacing the current system of United States taxes (or other countries) with one that is nondistortionary. In the year 2000 the portion of our national income that became government receipts through the various taxes in our economy was 31 percent.[50] Even were one to cut this to, say, 20 percent of GDP (which is unlikely to be politically feasible or socially desirable), raising such a large amount of revenue requires a cumulative tax base that is proportionately much larger. Thus significant use of broad-based (and distortionary) taxes such as those on sales and income seems inevitable.

This brings us to the second important implication: the twin theorems, which suggest a reason why economic organization through competitive markets might be desirable, do not apply to economies with significant taxation (i.e., all real economies). Owing to the tax distortions we know that the resulting allocation will be inefficient, but we do not know how this compares with any other method of economic organization. It is an open question

[48] According to one study, these taxes distort prices by an average of 24 percent. Unlike tobacco excise taxes in which there may be a good reason for discouraging consumption, there is no analogous reason for discouraging the use of telecommunications services. Furthermore, the incidence of these taxes is significantly regressive, primarily for the simple reason that telecommunications bills are a much larger portion of the budgets of low-income than high-income households. See J. Cordes, C. Kalenkoski, and H. Watson, "The Tangled Web of Taxing Talk: Telecommunication Taxes in the New Millennium," *National Tax Journal, 53,* No. 3, September 2000, pp. 563–587.

[49] The central difference between externality taxes and conventional taxes is the efficiency of the pretax allocation. In the competitive models used throughout this chapter, we assume that the initial pretax allocation is efficient and that therefore any price distortion caused by a tax reduces efficiency. In the externality situation, we assume the initial pretax allocation is inefficient with too much of a negative externality (or too little of a positive externality), and that an externality tax will reduce the inefficiency. General equilibrium analyses that try to take account of the interactions between conventionally taxed sectors and an externality taxed sector caution that the externality tax is not as efficiency-enhancing as one might think based on partial-equilibrium reasoning. For example, Bovenberg and Goulder estimate that the most efficient environmental tax rate would be *below* the rate based on partial equilibrium analysis alone, even if the revenue raised is used to reduce other distortionary taxes. See A. Bovenberg and L. Goulder, "Optimal Environmental Taxation in the Presence of Other Taxes: General Equilibrium Analyses," *American Economic Review, 86,* No. 4, September 1996, pp. 985–1000.

[50] Tax receipts were $3.081 trillion and GDP $10.039 trillion. See the *Economic Report of the President, January 2001* (Washington, D.C.: U.S. Government Printing Office, 2001), pp. 274, 371.

whether or not methods of organization that rely more on active governmental guidance and less on the guidance of free competitive markets might enhance or reduce efficiency.

In later chapters, we shall see that there are many other factors apart from distortionary taxation that cause efficiency problems for competitively organized economies. As we consider each and what might be done about them, we shall increasingly focus on organizational features such as information costs, transaction costs, and degree of centralization or decentralization to provide analytic insight. An impressive feature of competitive organization is the decentralized way in which it achieves economic coordination. The actions of each independent agent on the demand or supply side in the aggregate create the market prices. These prices are the crucial information used by agents to adjust production and consumption until the coordination that we call equilibrium is achieved. They also are important stimulants to innovative activities that lead to technological progress, dynamically improving the equilibrium attainable at any given time.

Summary

In this chapter we discuss some general models of a competitive economy. We first review the standard description of the competitive process in one industry and then extend the model to consider characteristics of a general competitive equilibrium—one in which all markets are simultaneously in equilibrium. We summarize the twin optimality theorems of microeconomics: Every perfectly competitive equilibrium is Pareto-optimal, and every Pareto-optimal allocation can be achieved by a perfectly competitive economy with costless transfers of income. The marginal rules that characterize the optimality conditions, such as marginal cost pricing, have come to be used as the basis for judging efficiency in most "piecemeal" (single-sector) policy analyses.

We then turn to a predictive task. Competitive models are frequently used in the study of taxation. We examine analytic use of a two-sector general equilibrium model for the study of excise tax incidence, that is, determining who ends up paying the tax.

When the results are contrasted with the partial equilibrium model, they are seen to be quite different. The general equilibrium model reveals the extent to which a tax will be shifted either forward or backward. Furthermore, the general model can give more accurate estimates of tax revenues. The importance of using a general equilibrium model for predictive purposes depends on the size of the changes to the economy. Because taxes have large impacts on the economy, general equilibrium models are more appropriate for tax analysis.

After looking at tax incidence, we consider the efficiency of taxation. Lump-sum taxes, which do not depend on the taxpayer's behavior, are nondistortionary. However, they are more prevalent in the minds of theorists than in policy use. All major real-world taxes—income, sales, property, excise—do alter the allocative decisions of taxpayers and thus have an efficiency cost, called a deadweight loss, or an excess burden.

The simple fact of the existence of distortionary taxes, which are used to collect over 30 percent of the national income, implies that the economy is not at a first-best allocation (one that meets the conditions for Pareto optimality in all sectors). That is, the use of market governance in an economy with substantial taxation creates price signals that cause economic agents to allocate resources inefficiently. Contrary to the suggestion of the twin theorems, we have not yet uncovered any reasons why competitive markets in an actual economy might be a desirable method of resource allocation. Nevertheless, the competitive form of economic organization is a very important one. It is impressive as a highly decentralized method of organizing economic activity, and whether it compares favorably or unfavorably with alternative forms of regulation is something that we shall consider in more specific settings discussed in the remaining chapters.

Exercises

12-1 The diagram below shows the derived demand curve and the competitive supply curves for land in apartment use. The derived demand curve is

$$L_D = 60 - 5P_L$$

The competitive supply curve of land to apartment usage is

$$L_S = 10P_L$$

a What is a competitive equilibrium? For this example, what is the equilibrium price and quantity? Explain. (*Hint:* Answer is $P_L = 4$, $L = 40$.)

b Copy the diagram onto your answer sheet and shade the area that represents the social opportunity cost of the equilibrium quantity. Explain why economic rent is or is not included in this.

c Reconcile the existence of economic rent in the diagram with the zero-profit condition for long-run competitive equilibrium. That is, explain how the above diagram can represent a long-run competitive equilibrium even though many of the suppliers are making economic profit or economic rent.

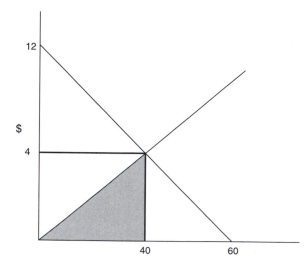

d Suppose a tax of $3 per unit of land in apartment use is levied on land *suppliers*. Using partial equilibrium analysis, determine what portion of the taxes raised will be borne by land suppliers.

e Suppose the same size tax was levied on the *demanders* of land for apartment use. How does this change their burden? Explain.

12-2 Local education finance equilibrium with interdependency among counties: A state is composed of two counties. All those who live in county R are rich, and those who live in county N are not rich. Within each county all families are homogeneous. In county R each family owns property assessed at $2000. In county N each family owns property assessed at $1000. There are 100 families in each county, and each family has one school-aged child. Educational achievements are measured completely and accurately by Q-scores on a standardized test. The demand for educational achievement as a function of the education expenditure per family is:

$$Q_D^R = 150 - E_R \quad \text{in county } R$$

$$Q_D^N = 100 - E_N \quad \text{in county } N$$

The supply of educational achievement as a function of expenditure per student is

$$Q_S^R = E_R \qquad \text{in county } R$$

$$Q_S^N = E_N - 10 \qquad \text{in county } N$$

a Suppose we treat decisions in each county as if they were independent or, equivalently, as if we had two partial equilibrium models. Assume the voters in each county set a property tax rate t to finance education expenditures. For each county what tax rate will the voters select, what expenditure per student will result, and what will be the educational achievement level? Is there any sense in which the families in county N can be said to be making a greater effort to provide education than the families in county R? (Partial answers: $t_R = 0.0375$; $E_R = 75 = Q_R$; yes.)

b A famous court decision allows each county to continue to set its own tax level but orders the state to collect the taxes and so distribute them (administrative costs are zero) that expenditures per pupil are equal throughout the state. This system causes demanders and suppliers in each county to perceive different prices for education, as with an excise tax. Furthermore, the interdependence of counties caused by this system makes general equilibrium considerations important. For each county what tax rate will be chosen, what will be the expenditure per pupil, and what will be the educational achievement level? (Partial answers: $t_N = 0.045$; $E = 65$; $Q_N = 55$.)

c° Suppose expenditures are fixed at $65 per student and are financed as in part (b). The state announces a new open enrollment plan. Assume there are only two schools, one in each county. Collectively, the families in the state are highly rational. Any individual family will always choose to have its child attend the school offering the highest achievement level. For each enrolled student in excess of 100 in a school, the achievement level of all students in that school slips down one unit (an overcrowding effect). For each of the first twenty-five rich students who attend the school in the non-rich county, the educational achievement of all students in that school is raised by one unit (a one-way positive integration effect). What educational achievement level do you expect in each county? Does this system improve the solution in any way compared with (b)? Is there a unique solution to the number of rich and nonrich in each school? Explain why the results are like those in the Slumlord's Dilemma of Chapter 7. (Answers: $Q_N = Q_R = 65$; yes; no.)

d° Suppose the families in each county are now free to set their own tax rates with both the spending rules from part (b) and the open enrollment plan in effect. Family motivations and capabilities are as assumed in part (c). What tax rates will be chosen; what expenditure level will result; and what achievement level will result in each county? How do these outcomes compare with those of the earlier parts? (Partial answers: $Q_N = Q_R = 62.5$; $t_R = 0.04375$.)

APPENDIX

DERIVATION OF THE COMPETITIVE GENERAL EQUILIBRIUM MODEL

In this appendix, we show how competitive model assumptions are used to derive the market demand and equations in Table 12-1, given consumer tastes, technology, and resource availability.

We assume that each individual has a utility function of the form

$$U = Q_1^{1/2} Q_2^{1/2}$$

As was calculated in the appendix to Chapter 6, this function implies demand curves for a budget of B as follows:

$$D(Q_1) = \frac{\frac{1}{2}B}{P_1}$$

$$D(Q_2) = \frac{\frac{1}{2}B}{P_2}$$

Thus each person will spend one-half of his or her budget B on, say, Q_1, independently of the budget level. This implies that the aggregate expenditure for Q_1 will always be one-half of aggregate income, and the aggregate quantity demanded for each good is not affected by the distribution of income in the economy. (More realistic models would relax that assumption.) It also means that there is zero cross-price elasticity, which keeps the consumption side "simple."

On the production side we also choose assumptions to simplify the analysis. We assume that the economy has a fixed (perfectly inelastic) supply of labor ($L = 100$) and capital ($K = 100$); thus we are ruling out changes in the total quantities of factors that might be caused by policies. (For example, a tax on labor income might in actuality reduce the labor supply, and this model would obviously not be a good one for analysis of that effect.) We also assume that each good has constant returns-to-scale (CRTS) technology:

$$Q_1 = K_1^{1/2}L_1^{1/2}$$

$$Q_2 = \tfrac{3}{2}L_2$$

Note that the second technology is the one used in the partial equilibrium analysis. At this point all the information necessary to determine the general competitive equilibrium has been given: We know tastes, technologies, and factor endowments. All that remains is to apply the logic of competitive analysis.

We first note one convenient implication of the assumptions we have made. The competitive environment and the CRTS technology imply that the output of each sector can be calculated as if all the factors were used by one big firm that behaves competitively.[51] This simplifies a number of the derivations that follow.

---

[51] We know competition ensures that each firm will choose the same $\text{RTS}_{K,L}$. For CRTS this implies that each firm operates at a point on its isoquant that is on the same ray through the origin (capital-labor ratio) as all other firms in the sector. Because there are neither economies nor diseconomies of scale, the sum of the outputs of all firms on this ray is the same as if one firm using the summed inputs produced the output.

To show that all competitive firms operate on the same ray requires use of Euler's theorem for homogeneous functions. A function $Q = F(X_1, X_2, \ldots, X_n)$ is homogeneous of degree s if, for any positive constant m,

$$m^S Q = F(mX_1, mX_2, \ldots, mX_n)$$

Euler's theorem states that, for any homogeneous function of degree s,

$$sQ = \frac{\partial F}{\partial X_1}X_1 + \frac{\partial F}{\partial X_2}X_2 \ldots + \frac{\partial F}{\partial X_n}X_n$$

Furthermore, the partial derivatives of a homogeneous function of degree s are themselves homogeneous of degree $s - 1$:

$$\frac{\partial F(mX_1, mX_2, \ldots, mX_n)}{\partial mX_1} = m^{s-1}\frac{\partial F(X_1, X_2, \ldots, X_n)}{\partial X_1}$$

All CRTS production functions are linearly homogeneous ($s = 1$). Thus if $Q = F(K, L)$ is CRTS, we have:

$$Q = \frac{\partial F}{\partial K}K + \frac{\partial F}{\partial L}L$$

$$= \text{MP}_K K + \text{MP}_L L$$

Since the marginal products are the partial derivatives of a linear homogeneous function, they are themselves homogeneous functions of degree *zero* (like demand functions). Multiplying K and L by any constant m does not change the value of the marginal products, but multiplying an initial K and L by any positive constant m defines precisely the locus of points along one ray from the origin in an isoquant diagram. Thus, all points on the ray have the same MP_K, MP_L, and $\text{RTS}_{K,L}$.

We begin with the derivation of the competitive supply curve for sector 2,

$$P_2 = \tfrac{2}{3}P_L$$

It is useful to derive it by using the cost function approach described in Chapter 7 (with technical details in that chapter's optional section). Recall that the cost function for a firm expresses total cost as a function of the input prices and output level. In this simple case, the only input is labor: to produce one unit of output requires two-thirds of a unit of labor, and therefore the cost per unit is always $\tfrac{2}{3}P_L$. Therefore, the (total) cost function C_2 associated with sector 2's production function is

$$C_2 = \tfrac{2}{3}P_L Q_2$$

The marginal cost of one more unit of Q_2 is, as noted,

$$MC_2 = \tfrac{2}{3}P_L$$

Profit maximization requires that the firm produce where marginal cost equals marginal revenue. Since in the competitive environment $MR = P$, we have

$$P_2 = \tfrac{2}{3}P_L$$

This is the supply curve for the firm. Because it is perfectly horizontal (i.e., does not vary with quantity), it is also the supply curve for the entire industry.[52]

What is the derived demand for labor in this sector? In the appendix to Chapter 9 we showed that the change in the cost function for a small (1-unit) change in the input price is the optimal input quantity (Shephard's lemma). That is, we consider the change in least total cost caused by a small factor price change while the output level is held constant. In the one-input case it is simply the amount of labor multiplied by the price change, since the same labor is required. If we think of the small change as being a 1-unit price change, the change in total cost is 1 multiplied by the optimal labor input, or simply the optimal labor quantity.

Thus, we use the cost function to identify the quantity of factors demanded. If we ask how sector 2's least total cost changes in response to a small (1-unit) change in the price of labor, the answer is

---

We have not shown that all points off the ray must have a different $RTS_{K,L}$, but that is not a problem. For any elasticity of substitution strictly within the interval $0 < \sigma < \infty$, the slope of each isoquant becomes continually flatter from left to right, so the locus of points with a constant slope must lie on one ray. (Otherwise, on some isoquants there would be two points with the same slope, which we have ruled out.) For the extreme case of $\sigma = \infty$, the slope of each isoquant is everywhere constant (i.e., the isoquant is a straight line). In this case the factors are perfectly substitutable and the competitive (and efficient) firm will use only one factor or be indifferent to any K/L combination (should the isocost line and isoquant have identical slopes). For the case of $\sigma = 0$, the competitive firm will produce at the right angle of the isoquant as long as factor prices are positive; CRTS implies that all these lie on one ray.

[52] In this case, the model does not determine how many firms there are. The costs would be identical if the industry's output were produced by one firm or by many, although the competitive assumptions imply the price-taking behavior associated with "many."

$$\Delta C_2 = \tfrac{2}{3}Q_2$$

But since that must equal the optimal labor input,

$$L_2 = \tfrac{2}{3}Q_2$$

This equation is the derived demand curve for labor, given any output level. In this case the answer may appear to be a trivial consequence of the production function, and one may wonder why we did not just assert that directly. Do not be misled; the cost function procedure is generally a means of simplification rather than complication.

Let us turn to sector 1, where the power of the cost function approach is more apparent. The cost function C_1 associated with our Cobb-Douglas production function is[53]

$$C_1 = 2P_K^{1/2}P_L^{1/2}Q_1$$

Then the marginal cost per unit of Q_1 is simply

$$MC_1 = 2P_K^{1/2}P_L^{1/2}$$

Note that, from the perspective of a firm, which regards P_K and P_L as fixed parameters, this is simply a constant. Since the competitive firm equates MC to product price, in equilibrium we have

$$P_1 = 2P_K^{1/2}P_L^{1/2}$$

This is the competitive supply curve for sector 1.[54] It is perfectly elastic for fixed factor prices (as expected for CRTS production).

In this sector both capital and labor are used. The derived demand curves are found by calculating the effect of a small change in the factor's price on the cost function[55]:

$$L_1 = P_K^{1/2}P_L^{-1/2}Q_1$$
$$K_1 = P_K^{-1/2}P_L^{1/2}Q_1$$

We have now described the equations for demand and supply in the product market and calculated the derived factor demands that (summed across sectors) must be equated to the (fixed) factor supplies. There is one last step to take before solving for the equilibrium: What budget level should be used in the demand equations?

The aggregate income in this economy is simply the sum of the payments to the factors:

$$B = P_K K + P_L L$$

---

[53] This was derived in the appendix to Chapter 9.

[54] Any one skeptical of the usefulness of the cost function approach in deriving the supply curve, and the factor demand curves that follow, is urged to derive the curves directly from the production function.

[55] These equations are found by taking the partial derivative of the cost function with respect to each factor price:

$$L_1 = \frac{\partial C_1}{\partial P_L} \qquad K_1 = \frac{\partial C_1}{\partial P_K}$$

That is, each person rents out his or her capital and labor, receives the competitive payments, and then uses the income to buy the two available products. We have already indicated that, in this simple model, the distribution of income does not affect the demand. However, how do we ensure that the model's equilibrium is one in which total income equals total spending? After all, it would be embarrassing to discover that our model calls for consumers to spend twice as much as they earn.

Fortunately, the competitive assumptions with CRTS technology imply that the factor payments add up to the total value of the output.[56] To show that, we made use of Euler's theorem (see earlier footnote) as it applies to CRTS (= linear homogeneous) technology, which implies that

$$Q_i = \text{MP}_K^i K_i + \text{MP}_L^i L_i \quad i = 1, 2$$

Multiply both sides of this equation by P_i and note that each term on the right-hand side contains the value of the marginal product ($P\text{MP}$):

$$P_i Q_i = (P_i \text{MP}_K^i) K_i + (P_i \text{MP}_L^i) L_i \quad i = 1, 2$$

In equilibrium, each firm hires factors until the value of the marginal product (the marginal benefit of an additional factor) equals the factor price (the marginal cost of the factor). Thus, we can rewrite the above equation by substituting P_K and P_L:

$$P_i Q_i = P_K K_i + P_L L_i \quad i = 1, 2$$

If we sum across both sectors,

$$\sum P_i Q_i = P_K \sum K_i + P_L \sum L_i$$

or

$$\sum P_i Q_i = P_K K + P_L L$$

In other words, aggregate consumer spending equals aggregate income. With that reassurance, we rewrite the product demand equations:

$$Q_i = \frac{\frac{1}{2}(P_L L + P_K K)}{P_i} \quad i = 1, 2$$

This completes the derivation of the equations in Table 12-1.

---

[56] This would hold for decreasing returns to scale as well. Competition ensures that each firm will be at the minimum of its average cost curve, and thus all firms are "locally" CRTS. However, the competitive model does not work with increasing returns to scale.

CHAPTER THIRTEEN
THE CONTROL OF PRICES TO ACHIEVE EQUITY IN SPECIFIC MARKETS

FOR A VARIETY OF REASONS, individuals in an economy will attempt through collective action to alter a specific market's distributional consequences. In earlier discussion (Chapters 3 and 5) we recognized specific egalitarian concerns, that is, a desire that the distribution of certain things, usually necessities, meet equity standards such as a universal minimum or strict equality (e.g., housing, food, jury duty). A somewhat different concern might be called *specific redistribution:* when consumers in a specific market believe that the payments they make to producers are unfairly high, or when workers in a specific market feel their pay is unfairly low. The cases of interest to us are those where public action is actually taken to address these concerns.

We will consider two cases of this type in this chapter. Both have in common that the specific markets examined can be treated as essentially perfectly competitive (except for the public actions). That is, here we are ruling out complaints about unfairness that depend upon imperfectly competitive markets, such as those that might arise owing to, say, a monopoly firm or racial discrimination in the labor force. Rather, at this point we wish to address fairness complaints about competition head on. In addition, these exercises with the competitive model strengthen and enrich analytic abilities to use it.

The two cases reflect important, contemporary policy debates. In 1996, the passage of the Federal Agriculture Improvement and Reform (FAIR) Act ensured substantial price supports to many farmers for at least 7 more years. This continues (with important modifications) a policy of support that has existed for over 65 years in the United States. In 1997, some 2.5 million New York tenants endured several months of anxiety when the rent control legislation that had been protecting them since World War II expired, replaced days afterward with a new but more modest set of protections. There has also been recent policy application of another form of rent control—the windfall profits tax. In 1997 the United Kingdom passed an $8.5 billion windfall profits tax on its newly deregulated and competitive utility companies, believing that these former state enterprises were sold too cheaply. We want to try and understand the equity concerns underlying these and similar policies and to focus particularly upon the effectiveness of the chosen policy instruments at addressing these concerns.

We begin with an analysis of federal price supports for agriculture.

Price Support for Agriculture

As economies industrialized, many agrarian segments experienced painful transitions despite overall rising standards of living. Increasing mechanization of farm production and labor-saving technological advances made it necessary for the size of farms to increase to achieve least-cost production. Within the farming sector large corporate farms grew, while the number of small family farms declined. Whereas 30 percent of the U.S. population resided on farms in 1920, only 1.8 percent did by 1992.[1]

For the people affected, these changes were not just marginal changes in economic organization. Families who had worked long hours on their farms day after day for years (in some cases generations) had more and more difficulty making ends meet. It did not seem just for such hard and honest work to receive economic hardship as its reward. Could we not do something to help preserve the small family farms?

Primarily as part of New Deal legislation following the Great Depression, policies of economic support were introduced that (despite many modifications) continue today. Wheat, cotton, rice, corn, soybeans, dairy products, tobacco, sugar, peanuts, and other crops all have different programs of support, although many have common characteristics.[2] In the aggregate, direct U.S. governmental support for farm crops was over $21 billion in 1999.[3] This does not include indirect supports such as supply restrictions that cost consumers many billions more.

Let us illustrate the effects of programs like these with an analysis of the peanut program. U.S. peanut growers produce a minority share of the world's peanut supply (India and China each produce more, and many other countries contribute to the aggregate supply). Nevertheless, U.S. growers are strong exporters; they easily produce quantities greater than domestic demand. For our purposes, we assume that U.S. exports are a small enough part of the rest-of-the-world supply that they do not affect world price. We focus on the domestic effects of our support policies. Each year, a national U.S. peanut "quota" for domestic producers is estimated based upon expected domestic food consumption of peanuts. The aggregate quota is then parceled out among states, who in turn parcel it out among counties and finally to farmers within the counties. U.S. farmers can only sell quota peanuts for

---

[1] See p. 177 in Bruce L. Gardner, "The Federal Government in Farm Commodity Markets: Recent Reform Efforts in a Long-Term Context," *Agricultural History, 70*, No. 2, Spring 1996, pp. 177–195.

[2] By contrast, fruit and vegetable growers have traditionally been left to fend for themselves, without any governmental support.

[3] This is the total payments to producers from Farm Service Agency programs, from Table 11-7 in *Agricultural Statistics, 2001* (Washington, D.C.: U.S. Government Printing Office, 2001).

domestic food use; all their other peanuts (called "additional" peanuts) are sold for export, crushed for oil or meal, or stored. Quota peanuts are supported at the rate of $610 per ton under the 1996 FAIR Act. Furthermore, imports for domestic consumption are severely restricted.[4] Additional peanuts do not have price supports, although subsidized loans are available for them.

The farmers who hold the quota peanuts may sell them directly in the marketplace or they may place their peanuts under loan to the United States Department of Agriculture (USDA). The USDA will sell the peanuts placed with it and pay the lending farmers the guaranteed support price. If the USDA cannot sell all of the peanuts for domestic food use at a price equal to (or greater than) the support price, then it is obligated to crush the remaining peanuts and sell them for (much lower-valued) oil or meal.

Figure 13-1 illustrates the effects of this program using numbers that correspond roughly to 1995 prices and quantities. The FAIR legislation specifies a support price of $610 per ton, and requires the USDA to set a quota equal to its estimate of domestic food-use demand at that price—1.3 million tons of peanuts. We show this as one point on the figure. Suppose that the USDA has a good estimate, so that this point is on the demand curve D. If a competitive market were allowed to operate without any government intervention, the $400 per ton world price of peanuts would determine domestic food-use demand, shown at a quantity of 1.4 million tons.[5]

What are the consequences of this policy in terms of economic welfare? Domestic consumption is reduced by 100,000 tons. The shaded rectangular area of $273 million[6] represents a transfer from consumers to peanut farmers. The cross-hatched triangle of $10,500,000[7] is a deadweight loss to consumers (the loss in consumer surplus due to restricting the quantity of their peanut consumption). Thus the total loss to consumers is $283,500,000. While the policy reduces domestic consumption by 100,000 tons, it does not affect the production levels of U.S. farmers: Peanut supply is simply shifted to export (all peanuts that can be produced for $400 per ton or less are still produced).[8] The diagram does not include the social cost of the USDA administering this program, which is roughly $5 million annually.

---

[4] The domestic food-use market exceeds 1 million tons of peanuts. Before the NAFTA and GATT trade agreements somewhat liberalized trade restrictions, imports were limited to a mere 1150 tons. In 1995, as the trade restrictions diminished, imports grew to 76,500 tons.

[5] This is a highly inelastic response. Studies of the price elasticity of domestic food-use peanut demand suggest that it is highly inelastic, in the range of −0.14 to −0.2. See the elasticity estimates in Table II.1 of *Peanut Program: Changes Are Needed to Make the Program Responsive to Market Forces* (Washington, D.C.: U.S. Government Accounting Office Report GAO/RCED-93-18, 1993).

[6] $= (610 - 400) \times (1,300,000)$.

[7] $= 0.5(610 - 400) \times (1,400,000 - 1,300,000)$.

[8] U.S. exporters to the rest-of-the-world market face a demand curve for their product that is essentially horizontal or perfectly elastic, analogous to the demand for one firm's output in a competitive market. Rucker and Thurman cite two export demand elasticity estimates of −20 and −32. See R. Rucker and W. Thurman, "The Economic Effects of Supply Controls: The Simple Analytics of the U.S. Peanut Program," *Journal of Law and Economics, 33,* No. 2, October 1990, pp. 483–515.

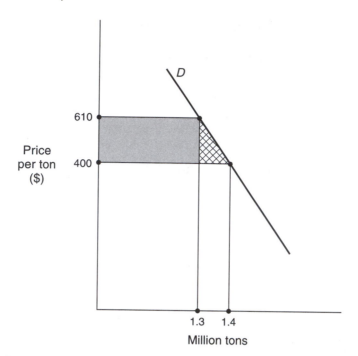

Figure 13-1. Peanut price supports transfer income to farmers (shaded) but cause inefficiency (cross-hatched).

In the above example, the policy may appear to be achieving its objective at a relatively small cost. For a total deadweight loss of $15,500,000 (including administration), peanut farmer income has been raised by $273,000,000. While this is a loss of 6 percent per dollar transferred, it is probably less than the loss that conventional taxation would cause to transfer the identical amount (recall the discussion of the inefficiency of most major taxes from Chapter 12). However, more realistic examples suggest substantially greater losses.

Note that in the example there is no need for the government to actually receive any peanuts or spend taxpayers' money on them! This is an important political aspect of the policy: It raises the same revenue as an excise tax of $210 per ton, but the government neither collects nor distributes revenues. All of the effects are "off budget." This illustrates why federal spending is a poor measure of the policy's cost.

In the example, USDA was assumed to set the quota quantity at precisely the amount that is demanded at the $610 support price. In actuality, the quota rarely corresponds to domestic demand.[9] In recent years, the quota has exceeded domestic demand so that the government actually pays for a significant number of quota peanuts. In 1995 about 300,000 tons of quota peanuts were placed with the government, and the expected disposal costs for this

---

[9] It is not clear to what extent this is due to inherent difficulties of estimating demand (e.g., to account for taste changes in the population, or the use of existing inventories), or to political pressures in setting the quota.

amount of peanuts is $101 million.[10] The government pays an average of $610 per ton and receives back an average of $272 per ton when the peanuts are sold for crush, for a net disposal cost of $338 per ton. Thus there can be "on budget" effects as well as "off budget" effects.

How does this change our calculation of the policy's effects? The $273 million increase in income to peanut farmers is unchanged (they still receive $610 per ton for the quota, rather than $400). However, it is transferred from different people. This is shown in Figure 13-2, in which we show the demand curve from Figure 13-1 as an (erroneous) estimated demand curve D_e. The true demand curve D is drawn with an identical (inelastic) slope but shifted linearly to the left.

Domestic peanut consumers provide less of the transfer, only $210 million, shown as the shaded area above the $400 world price for the 1.0 million tons of quota peanuts that they buy. For the next 300,000 tons, the government (i.e., taxpayers) pays $183 million ($63 million more than if purchased at the world price). The government recoups some of this when it disposes of these peanuts. However, it receives only $272 per ton, substantially less than the world price. The net taxpayer expenditure of $338 per ton or $101 million, shown with a grid pattern in Figure 13-2, increases farmer income by only $63 million. From the taxpayer perspective, this does not look like a very good deal: For every taxpayer dollar spent, farmer income only goes up by $0.62.

Welfare calculations also help to make the economic cost of this policy apparent. There is no misallocation for the first 1 million tons of peanuts. But there is substantial misallocation of the next 300,000 tons. Not only are domestic consumers denied the 100,000 tons that they would consume at the world price, but the 300,000 tons of peanuts handled through the government get allocated to crush, where their value is substantially lower than as exports.

Figure 13-3 highlights the difference between this and our previous welfare calculation, focusing on the quantity range from 1 to 1.3 million tons (those are the government-allocated peanuts). The triangular portion of the cross-hatched area represents the dead-weight loss to domestic consumers from restricting their consumption by 100,000 tons; this is $10,500,000, as it was in Figure 13-1. However, the rectangular portion reflects the fact that these edible-grade peanuts are crushed and used for lower-value oil and meal. The difference between these values is the difference between their competitive prices of $400 and $272, respectively, which is $38,400,000 for 300,000 tons of peanuts.[11] Thus the total dead-weight loss, including the $5,000,000 for administration mentioned earlier, is $53,900,000 or 20 percent of the amount transferred to farmers.

---

[10] See the *Oil Crops Yearbook* (Washington, D.C.: Economic Research Service, U.S. Department of Agriculture, 1996). In 1994, some 295,284 tons of quota peanuts were placed with the government and actual disposal costs were approximately $120 million or $406.39 per ton. Assuming similar disposal costs per ton in 1995, this would imply a total disposal cost of $122 million for 300,000 tons. However, our example uses the FAIR-mandated support price of $610 per ton, rather than the $678 in effect when these net disposal costs were calculated. Thus we must reduce our estimated per ton disposal costs by $68 ($678 − $610), to $338. This latter figure implies total disposal costs for our example of $111 million.

[11] From the U.S. perspective, the world markets for peanut oil and meal are large enough so that the U.S. government's supply to them has no significant effects on their prices.

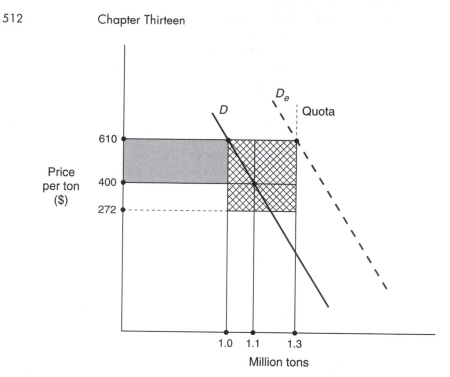

Figure 13-2. Setting the quota above demand at the support price means an increase in both consumer payments (shaded) and taxpayer expenditures (grid pattern).

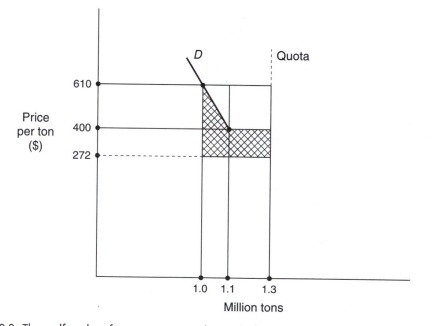

Figure 13-3. The welfare loss from government disposal of quota peanuts (cross-hatched) can be substantial.

Other welfare calculations to cover various different circumstances could also be made.[12] However, our last example is typical of the results of the actual analyses that have been done. The Government Accounting Office (GAO), for example, reviewed a number of actual studies including its own. These studies estimated social welfare losses from 13 to 29 percent of producer transfer costs.[13] It will be most useful if we turn to a different aspect of this policy: How successful has it been in terms of achieving its original equity goal of preserving small family farms? That is, we have seen the cost of transferring income to peanut farmers by this policy, but are they the "right" peanut farmers?

The changes in peanut farming have mirrored the changes in U.S. farming generally. According to the GAO, the number of peanut farms with quota has decreased from 172,981 in 1950 (the earliest data available) to 41,249 in 1991. Over this period, the average farm size has grown from 12 to over 49 acres. Total harvested acreage (including additionals) has remained approximately constant since the 1930s, but the yield per acre has gone up fivefold and the cost per ton has dropped steadily. Thus much bigger and more productive peanut farms have largely replaced smaller ones. Over 80 percent of the quota (and thus the transferred income) is controlled by 6182 producers, and the largest 409 of them hold nearly 20 percent.

What has happened over time is exactly what one would expect in a market with reasonably free entry and exit. Even when the small family farm can produce profitably (due to the support price), it is substantially *more* profitable to sell its quota rights to a larger grower who produces peanuts at much lower cost and thus even greater profit. For example, a small family farm may be able to produce at $500 per ton and sell for a profit of $110 at the $610 support price (as intended by the policy). But the large producer who can produce at $300 per ton can offer the small family farm well above $110—up to $310 per ton per year—for the right to its quota. So the large producers have largely replaced the small family farms, despite the existence of the support policy.[14]

One could imagine that if quotas were not transferable more small family farms would remain. Such a policy, however, would incur the enormous efficiency cost of forgoing the large productivity gains that have been made during this 60-year period. Many small farms would still exit the market, because at the price necessary to sustain these higher-cost farms both domestic demand and taxpayers' willingness to provide support would be reduced.

In short, I am not aware of any analytic study that suggests any good reason for the continuation of agricultural policies such as these, as they are very costly to consumers and to

---

[12] One of the more interesting is the case where the USDA underestimates demand, so that there remains excess domestic demand at the support price. In this case, a "buyback" provision of the policy allows additional peanuts held in grower pools to be sold at the support price. The peanuts placed in these pools are sold for crush if they are not "bought back." Individual growers receive an average price for the peanuts they place in the pool, weighted by the proportions "bought back" and crushed. This average pricing method causes inefficiency similar to our example: too few peanuts are exported and too many are crushed. See Rucker and Thurman (1990), "The Economic Effects of Supply Controls."

[13] See p. 42 of *Peanut Program: Changes Are Needed to Make the Program Responsive to Market Forces*.

[14] Before the 1996 FAIR legislation, quota sales were restricted to farmers within the same county as the seller. The FAIR legislation relaxes this to permit sales within a state. Geographical restrictions bound the location of potential beneficiaries, but prevent production from occurring wherever it is least costly.

taxpayers and fail to achieve their intents. Indeed, I can think of no area where there is greater analytic consensus about a policy matter. This raises a different issue: Why do the policies persist, and what does this say about the influence of public policy analysis?

Of course policies are made through a complex political process, with public policy analyses and their proponents only a small part of it. Still, in those instances in which analysts speak with one voice, it is reasonable to expect an impact over time. In the case of agricultural price supports, the jury is still out.[15]

Up through the mid-1980s when governmental support for agriculture reached over $20 billion per year, support had generally increased over time. But from 1986 to 1994, outlays declined by one-half. The 1996 FAIR legislation, while increasing outlays up through 2002 above those that would have occurred under the old legislation, makes significant pro-efficiency changes in many of the commodity programs. In peanuts, the support price was reduced from $678 to $610 per ton (reducing consumption inefficiency), and some sale of quotas is now permitted across county lines within each state (increasing production efficiency). For other agricultural commodities, more significant changes were made. For example, grain, cotton, and rice farmers have been granted much greater flexibility to respond to market forces in deciding what crops to plant. Furthermore, according to the 1997 *Economic Report of the President,* "once the 7-year payments run out, they are not expected to be renewed. At that time farmers will become subject to market forces."[16] However, only time will tell the accuracy of this forecast. By the end of the decade support payments to farmers had risen to new highs, and in the fall of 2001 Congress was debating new farm legislation that could reverse some of the efficiency gains achieved in FAIR.

Apartment Rent Control

Preview: Economic Justice and Economic Rent

Rent control ordinances exist in many cities, and they are intended to keep most apartment rental prices below market rates. Somewhat like agricultural price supports, the main concern is the fairness of market pricing. We might think of these policies as reflecting the thirteenth-century concern of Thomas Aquinas: Goods and services should trade at the "just" price. What standard determines the just price?

Aquinas believed that the values of goods and services were divinely determined: he thought, for example, that the just interest rate was zero. In discussing agricultural policies, we did not propose any specific principle for just pricing. In that case, it was sufficient to take account of the principles of efficient pricing (and their correspondence to the equilib-

---

[15] I investigated this for my presidential address to the Association for Public Policy Analysis and Management and found that, in agricultural policy, public policy analysts more than pull their weight in terms of effectiveness. See Lee S. Friedman, "Presidential Address: Peanuts Envy?" *Journal of Policy Analysis and Management, 18,* No. 2, Spring 1999, pp. 211–225.

[16] *Economic Report of the President, 1997* (Washington, D.C.: U.S. Government Printing Office, 1997), p. 229.

rium price in a perfectly competitive market) and the poor targeting of the redistribution. But for the discussion of apartment rent control, it will be useful to have a principle of justness in mind.

Suppose we think of the just price as the social opportunity cost of supply. Then payments above social costs, or economic rents, are unjust payments. That is, *we pose the issue of apartment rent control as a struggle between buyers (tenants) and sellers (landlords) over the distribution of economic rent.* Thus the problem is somewhat different than the agricultural one, although both stem from concerns about competitive market pricing. We are not starting with a specific needy population (like the small family farmers) and considering how well a policy addresses those needs, essentially an outcome equity issue. Rather, we are interested in the process equity of market-determined payments for a necessity good upon which most individuals spend a large fraction of their income. Several points are emphasized throughout the discussion. We list them here for convenience:

1. If controls only remove economic rent from sellers, the supply response in the short and long run will be identical with the uncontrolled market.
2. It can be very difficult to limit the effects of controls to economic rent because of the subtlety of some real opportunity costs to sellers and the administrative difficulties of accounting for them.
3. Many of the potential benefits to buyers as a collectivity can dissipate as individual buyers use other resources in the scramble to claim them.
4. Buyers who do end up with benefits may be an arbitrary subset of all buyers, rather than those who correspond to any reasoned definition of equity.

This discussion helps in the development of new and more general skills of policy analysis. The predicted outcomes of the processes we study depend on how individual economic agents are affected by the *joint* forces of the market and public policy and how the nature of the individual responses can lead to a new equilibrium. These responses depend heavily on the information economic agents have and the transaction costs of making and enforcing arrangements between agents. The details of the changes in legal specification of property rights and responsibilities associated with a specific policy can have substantial impact on individual behavior and thus also on the new equilibrium and predicted outcome. At a minimum, the analyst interested in the design of policies to alter specific market outcomes should appreciate why basic microeconomic insights about markets must be combined with careful specification of the new policy before the policy's effects can be predicted.

We proceed as follows. First, we discuss policy intervention in specific markets as a response to a sudden change in demand or supply that creates "unusual" *quasi-rents.* We illustrate with apartment rent control as an example, although similar issues can arise with other necessities, such as fuel for home heating and transportation or water. Then we consider the standard argument that suggests that rent control is inefficient. This argument does not illuminate either the possibilities for or the difficulties of rent control, so more detailed models of economic rent in housing markets are developed.

These more detailed models show the relation between rent control and the capitalized value[17] of the controlled property. They lead to the conclusion that, for rent controls to avoid adverse housing supply consequences, the capitalized value of the property in apartment rental use must remain greater than in any other use. The capitalized value depends not only on the formal control price but also, heavily, on how the exchange side of the market works (matching tenants to the available apartments). This in turn depends upon specific details of the rent control ordinances and their enforcement. We discuss this and show that the same details also explain why the individuals who receive benefits from the controls may be a fairly arbitrary subset of tenants.

Dissatisfaction with Market Pricing during Temporary Shortage of a Necessity

In this section we examine a special circumstance that causes many people to conclude that certain market prices are unfair. The circumstance occurs when the short-run market equilibrium price of a necessity is temporarily but substantially higher than the usual long-run price. It can arise owing to a temporary supply disruption, as when unusually low rainfall results in a severely limited water supply (as in Kenya in 2000) or when fuel supplies are very low (as in Nigeria in 1997 or during the 1973 OPEC oil embargo to the United States). It can also occur when there is a temporary surge in demand, as for medical services during an epidemic or after a natural disaster, or for apartments in New York City when the soldiers returned at the end of World War II. The feeling of unfairness is generated by the payments of *quasi-rents* to suppliers: payments *above* opportunity costs that would not persist in the long run. Such sentiments are a source of demand for policy intervention.

In Figure 13-4 we illustrate this type of market situation. We imagine that initially we observe an equilibrium quantity of housing (standardized to be of constant quality) Q_0 at a price P_0.[18] The long-run supply curve, which is drawn horizontally, represents the assumption that housing in the long run is a constant cost industry (to be modified later). In a world in which all population changes occur slowly, the equilibrium quantity would shift only gradually over time in response to demand—and the price to all current households would remain unchanged at P_0.

However, suppose there is a sudden surge in demand, as in New York City at the end of World War II. The demand curve shifts outward to D'. The short-run supply SS of housing

[17] *Durable* assets—assets that provide services over multiple time periods—have present discounted values or capitalized values. A house or apartment provides shelter over many years, for example. Not surprisingly, the capitalized value is a function of the rental rate: the price to use the asset for one time period.

[18] Apartments vary greatly in quality. Any simple measure of the quantity of housing, such as square footage, must be supplemented by measures that account for quality differences. For purposes of our analysis, we assume that an apartment of 1000 sq. ft. that is above average in quality can be considered equivalent to some number greater than 1000 sq. ft. of an average-quality apartment (e.g., 1230 sq. ft.). For an example of a study that looks at the effect of rent control on quality explicitly, see J. Gyourko and P. Linneman, "Rent Controls and Rental Housing Quality: A Note on the Effects of New York City's Old Controls," *Journal of Urban Economics, 27,* No. 3, May 1990, pp. 398–409.

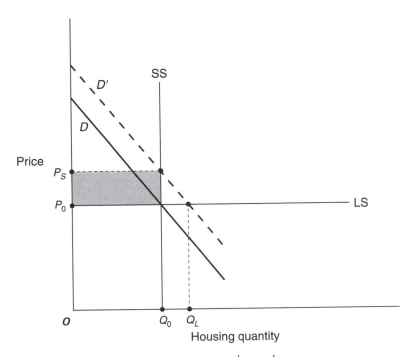

Figure 13-4. Short-run quasi-rents in response to a demand surge.

is *fixed* at Q_0. With more apartment seekers ready to pounce upon each vacancy that arises, the market price is driven up to P_s. As leases allow, landlords raise the rents for current tenants as well, since there are plenty of people who would pay P_s should the current tenants refuse. In other words, the landlord perceives a private opportunity cost of not raising the rent.

The final short-run allocation is efficient. There are no mutually profitable trades that could be made among any agents in this market. How has the market made room for the extra people, given that supply is fixed? By raising the price, each household is left free to respond in whatever way best suits its taste. Many who had been receiving a substantial consumer surplus make no changes and simply pay the higher rent, others look for smaller apartments, and still others take in roommates or boarders. Premarital engagements may even become shorter if it becomes too expensive to maintain separate apartments! Thus, the density of people per housing unit increases. Furthermore, the normal vacancy rate goes down: If the average unit used to be vacant 10 days per year, now it may be vacant only 3 or 4 days per year. *In short, each apartment is used more intensively with respect to both time and people;* and in the long run, of course, the supply expands to Q_L and the price returns to P_0.

What is wrong with this system, given that it allocates so well? The problem is the one perceived by the "initial" tenants: Why should they have to pay more when it is obvious that the landlord's operating costs have not increased by one penny? Think of some of the hardships imposed. For example, there are retirees on fixed incomes who have lived in the same apartments for 20 years. Should their lives be radically upset as a by-product of the "market" need for time to supply new housing? Is there no alternative by which the extra people could be housed without charging all the initial tenants more? After all, the short-run housing supply is fixed. A law that freezes rents at P_0 will leave the same total amount of housing available. Find another way of deciding how to house the new people.

In fact, the market might work almost as well under the rent freeze ordinance as under no ordinance; only this time the initial tenants would be the beneficiaries of the demand surge. They would receive offers from others to accept them as roommates or to give up apartments in return for lump sums of money. No initial occupant of an apartment receiving less surplus than $P_s - P_0$ would remain in the initial situation, because potential occupants would offer the initial one more surplus than that (in addition to the controlled rent to the landlord) for an alternative arrangement.

People could find each other through rental agencies, where initial tenants could list the "rent" at which they would take on a roommate or the "finder's fee" that they would charge for locating an apartment (their own). If you doubt that all this would happen, ask anyone who has looked for an apartment in New York. The final short-run allocation is as efficient and almost the same as under the "free" market,[19] and in the long run the supply expands to Q_L as before.[20]

Under the two simple alternatives, it should be clear that the majority of voters within one district would favor the latter plan (assuming apartment owners are a smaller percentage of voters than tenants).[21] In Figure 13-4 it can be seen that the net social benefit from housing under either plan is the area above LS and below D' up to the quantity Q_0. In the free-market plan, apartment owners receive the shaded area as quasi-rent. Under the rent freeze plan, the shaded area is distributed to tenants.

In this analysis the two alternatives are equal on efficiency grounds and differ in their equity implications. The main theoretical point illustrated is this: **Since economic rent is a payment to a factor above opportunity costs, its removal does not cause any distortions in resource allocation.** But in terms of coming to grips with actual apartment rent control, the model specification—the set of assumptions from which we draw inferences—is, at this stage, overly simplistic.

[19] Income effects will cause some difference in the final demand curve as compared to the prior example. For example, one would expect that some families who would have been forced to move because of higher prices (or who would have taken in boarders) will not do so under rent control. However, we do not show this in the diagram and use D' as the final demand curve for both situations, as if there are no income effects.

[20] For convenience, we assume throughout that producers will supply all goods and services for which they break even (i.e., earn the normal market rate of return on their capital, or zero economic profit). This should be understood as a limiting case. It is the prospect of positive economic profits (even if very small) that attracts more resources into an industry. For example, a very small increase in price may be all that is needed to lure additional single-family home owners to provide rental space within their homes.

[21] We might note that the population surge would also cause a substantial increase in price for potential home buyers. Similar arguments could be made about the inequity of this windfall gain to existing home owners at the expense of home buyers. However, the politics of this situation are very different: The number of existing home owners compared with home buyers in a jurisdiction is large, whereas the number of landlords relative to renters is small. Thus, local control of windfall gains in housing prices is politically unlikely.

A Standard Explanation of the Inefficiency of Rent Control

The preceding description is not the one that is usually given in explaining rent control policies. The usual one concludes that rent control is inefficient. This is illustrated in Figure 13-5. The only difference from the prior illustration is that the long-run supply curve LS is upward-sloping (an increasing cost industry).

The short-run analysis of this situation is unchanged; it is the long-run effects that are dramatically different. Under the "free-market" policy, long-run equilibrium is at P_L, Q_L, where both price and quantity are higher than the initial levels P_0, Q_0. The supply has expanded in response to the increase in demand, and the resulting allocation is optimal. However, the long-run effects of a policy that keeps rent at its initial level are deleterious. Although tenants demand Q_{DC} at the controlled price, suppliers provide only Q_0. The supply does not expand to the efficient quantity Q_L and there would be a perceived housing "shortage" of $Q_{DC} - Q_0$.

If this model captures the essence of rent control, there is always a net social loss in comparison with the uncontrolled market equilibrium. The long-run deadweight loss is shown as the shaded area OAL in Figure 13-5. Landlords lose the area $P_0 P_L BO$ because of lowered rent receipts from tenants, and they lose OBL in economic rent (or producer's surplus) because the units between Q_L and Q_0 are not supplied under rent controls. Thus, landlords are unambiguous losers from this policy (which is, of course, what is intended).

Tenants, on the other hand, may be net gainers or losers. Assuming that the Q_0 housing units are distributed efficiently among consumers (as in our short-run model), they gain rectangle $P_0 P_L BO$ but lose the consumer surplus ABL on the $Q_L - Q_0$ units that are not supplied. Tenants gain if $P_0 P_L BO > ABL$ and lose if the reverse is true. In either case the rectangle $P_0 P_L BO$ is a transfer between tenants and landlords and the area OAL is a deadweight loss (nobody gains it).[22]

Many analysts believe that rent control policies have another serious adverse effect: In the long run, rent control causes disinvestment in rental housing. Landlords are faced with rising bills for building maintenance, for example, but are unable to pass the costs on to tenants. So they respond by reducing building maintenance, which lowers the quality of housing and causes the housing stock to deteriorate more rapidly. This, of course, would be an exacerbation of the shortage we have already described.

Several empirical studies of rent control in New York City investigate these effects. An early RAND Corporation study reported that from 1960 to 1967 the inventory of sound housing grew by 2.4 percent while the inventory of dilapidated housing grew by 44 percent and deteriorating housing by 37 percent.[23] In the 3 years from 1965 to 1967, some 114,000

---

[22] An early study of this in New York concluded that the real income of occupants of rent-controlled housing was 3.4 percent higher than if there were no rent control and that poorer families received larger benefits. However, the cost to landlords was estimated at twice the benefit to tenants. See E. Olsen, "An Econometric Analysis of Rent Control," *Journal of Political Economy, 80,* No. 6, November/December 1972, pp. 1081–1100.

[23] RAND Corporation, "The Effects of Rent Control on Housing in New York City," *Rental Housing in New York City: Confronting the Crisis,* RM-6190-NYC, February 1970.

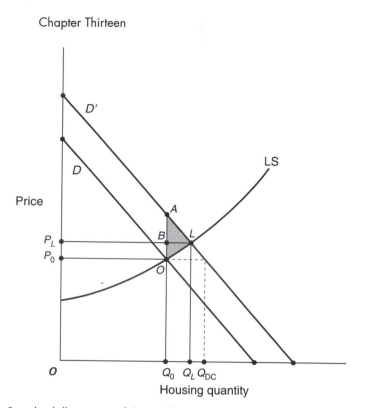

Figure 13-5. Standard illustration of the inefficiency of rent control in the long run (minimum social loss shaded).

housing units were withdrawn from the market (vacated and boarded up). A 1990 study by Gyourko and Linneman of these early data supports the interpretation that rent control was a significant cause of this deterioration.[24] However, a 1993 study by Moon and Stotsky using data from the 1980s finds little evidence that rent control contributed to housing deterioration during this latter period.[25] If disinvestment effects are in fact due to rent control policies, they constitute a serious, if not disastrous, problem with the policy.

Several good reasons why rent control might cause the disinvestment effects described above have been put forth in the literature. The problem with them, for our purpose, is that none of them apply analytically when used in conjunction with the standard economic model and the rent control policy we have described. That is, they all make some crucial assumption about behavior that is either not explicitly addressed by the model used in the analysis or is inconsistent with the actual policy. They may be insightful ad hoc rationali-

[24] Gyourko and Linneman, "Rent Controls and Rental Housing Quality."

[25] Choon-Geol Moon and Janet Stotsky, "The Effect of Rent Control on Housing Quality Change: A Longitudinal Analysis," *Journal of Political Economy, 101,* No. 6, December 1993, pp. 1114–1148. This study finds that rent control reduces somewhat the chances of quality improvement among low-quality units, but does not increase the chance of quality deterioration among sound units, and may even improve quality among those units that stay under rent control for extended periods. The latter may be due to good tenant care from long-term tenants.

zations, but we could not honestly say that they are predictions that an analyst would arrive at naturally by applying the standard models. We seek a method of analysis that leads to insight in advance of actually observing policy consequences. Let us briefly consider three common arguments put forth to explain disinvestment; our effort is to clarify why they are *not* proper deductions from the standard model applied to the rent control policy.

The first argument is that rent controls remove the incentive of owners to maintain their buildings. Without proper maintenance, the quality of the apartments deteriorates, and that leads to fewer units of standardized quality housing over time. Why do the rent controls remove incentives for maintenance? The assumption is that an apartment can continue to be rented at P_0, the legal rent ceiling, even if it is allowed to deteriorate, so that the owner receives the same revenue for lower cost, or at greater profit. Normally, competition would ensure adequate maintenance (a tenant could move to an equivalent but maintained apartment at the same price), but under rent control there is excess demand. Owners exploit the fact that potential tenants are willing to pay more per unit than the control price.

This argument depends upon assumptions about the behavior of the rent control board and other economic agents that have not explicitly been considered. The control price for an apartment is defined in terms of quality-adjusted units, and it should be lowered commensurately with any quality decrease in the unit. If that is so, there is no incentive to forgo maintenance. The argument is thus not a deduction of the standard model: it depends crucially on the notion that the rent control board will not adjust the control price as it should.

This is not to suggest that there is no insight here. Perhaps the board will not have the *information* necessary to keep the control price at the appropriate level for each apartment. Tenants, of course, have the incentive to inform the rent control board if maintenance is reduced. Nevertheless, this is an interesting question, and we shall return to the information issue later. Here the important point to note is that the disinvestment deduction depends upon an implicit assumption about imperfect decision-making of the rent control board, although the rest of the model assumes (e.g., under no rent control) that other agents have perfect information (and face zero transaction costs). Thus, although it may be true that rent control boards behave in this imperfect manner, it is a far cry from saying that the standard model explains the disinvestment effect.

A second approach used to suggest that rent control causes housing disinvestment is illustrated in Figure 13-6. This approach defines rent control broadly as an attempt to redistribute wealth from landlords to tenants (no surge of demand or cutoff of supplies is used to motivate the controls). The control price is drawn *below* the initial equilibrium price, and it is clear that suppliers will respond by withdrawing $Q_0 - Q_{SC}$ units from the market. The problem with this approach, for our purposes, is that it does not model a policy that attempts to control economic rent only (as most rent control policies do). The control price is set below the opportunity costs of supplying existing units, which is inconsistent with the rent control policy we are modeling.

In a sense this second approach makes the essential deduction of the standard model crystal clear: *If the control price is set below the opportunity cost, the unit will be withdrawn from the rental market.* However, the standard model provides *no* insight about why the control price might be set at such a level. Let us consider one final argument.

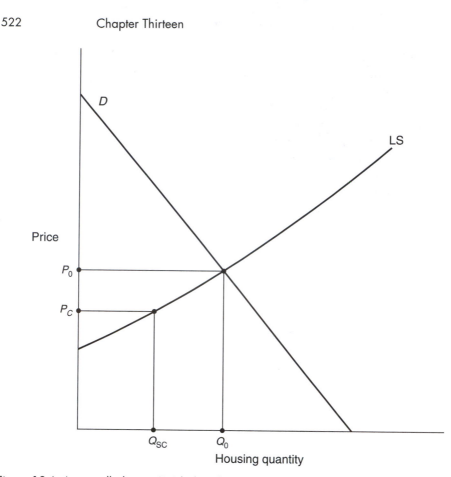

Figure 13-6. A controlled price (P_C) below the opportunity cost of existing housing (Q_0) causes disinvestment $(Q_0 - Q_{SC})$.

A third approach that leads to the disinvestment conclusion is shown in Figure 13-7. This is like the model in Figure 13-5, except that the long-run supply curve LS′ is assumed to shift upward gradually over time. The upward shift is based on the idea that the real opportunity cost per unit of housing rises over time (e.g., the real wage rates paid for building maintenance increase). Then, at the control price P_0, suppliers will respond in the long run by withdrawing $Q_0 - Q_{SC}$ units from the market.

The problem with this approach is similar to that of the second: The policy shown here allows the control price to fall below the opportunity costs of the existing units. This is inconsistent with the policy we said we are modeling. It equates rent *control* to a rent *freeze,* but actual rent control policies do allow periodic rent increases based upon increases in opportunity costs.

Do these long-run models offer any improvement over the short-run model? If so, by what analytic criteria? The empirical realities of the housing market and rent control administration determine how closely a model comes to identifying important aspects of the policy design. Our purpose is to illuminate those aspects. If we take the New York case as

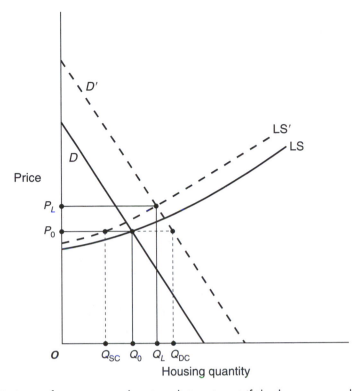

Figure 13-7. A rent freeze causes housing disinvestment if the long-run supply curve shifts upward.

evidence that rent control can cause shortages and disinvestment, the short-run model fails in calling that to our attention. The long-run models are better because they offer explanations for important empirical concerns. They are also better in calling attention to this aspect of political economy: Rent control may be introduced as a response to a *short-run* problem, but in New York the policy did continue into the long run. It is in the long run that the problems developed.

However, the long-run models are still too much of an oversimplification for our purposes. There are two significant problems with them. The first is that all of them are inconsistent with actual rent controls. Even the first long-run model (predicting a shortage but no disinvestment) equates rent control to a rent freeze and assumes that the frozen price applies to units as yet unbuilt. But most rent control policies, including New York's, specifically exempt new units and allow them to be rented at market-determined rates.

That is, most rent control policies attempt to control *economic rent only*. If successful, they would not affect opportunity costs or, therefore, supply decisions. Thus, the long-run models presented do not really offer a satisfactory explanation for shortages or for the observed disinvestment in New York. They may *predict* correctly, but they do not identify the *causal* mechanism. If we wish to know whether the same result should be expected elsewhere, we have to look more carefully at actual behavior.

A second problem with the analyses we have presented so far is that *transactions and their costs* have a much greater role than is yet apparent in determining both the allocative and distributive effects. The transactions among economic agents are a function of the *property rights and responsibilities* associated with the good or service to be traded, and rent control actually changes them. (For example, the landlord has a reduced right to the income generated by the property.) A thorough analysis of rent control must trace through the impacts of the changes, and the design of rent control policies must take careful account of the legal specifications.[26]

In ordinary market analysis we treat the legal specifications as constants and assume that the transactions that follow from them involve negligible costs of deal-making among economic agents. For example, we assumed that, under the free-market system, the cost of locating and matching demanders and suppliers (after the demand increase) is negligible. Thus, in the versions of rent control presented, we have made an analogous assumption: The cost of matching incoming demanders with initial tenants as suppliers is assumed to be zero.

But in neither case are transaction costs zero, and they are not likely to be of equal magnitude (with or without rent control). One must consider the legal changes and the transactional responses they induce in order to know how the benefits and burdens will be distributed. One must recognize that the policy problem includes the design of the legal changes; for example, enforced bans on finder's fees for initial tenants may cause benefits to be spread more evenly among all tenants. To understand rent control better, we present a simple but to-the-point model in the following section.

Rent Control as the Control of Long-Run Economic Rent

In this section we first develop an understanding of why economic rent may be a persistent part of total payments for urban apartments. We do this by presenting a very simple model of urban land rents in a special area known as Flat City. This model allows consideration of rent control as a long-run policy. It also explains the old real estate maxim: "The three most important aspects of real estate are location, location, and location!"[27]

Flat City is drawn in Figure 13-8. Its downtown area is at the extreme left, where all employment takes place. There is only one road into (and out of) Flat City, and all workers live with families in rental homes spaced at 1-mile intervals along the road. Family units have identical preferences and incomes. Sites along the road are restricted to residential use. (We relax this assumption later on; it makes an important difference.)

---

[26] Early examples that see this clearly are S. Cheung, "A Theory of Price Control," *Journal of Law and Economics, 17,* No. 1, April 1974, pp. 53–71, and "Rent Control and Housing Reconstruction: The Postwar Experience of Prewar Premises in Hong Kong," *Journal of Law and Economics, 22,* No. 1, April 1979, pp. 27–53.

[27] While location is indeed important, the maxim is silent on the many qualities that determine favorable versus unfavorable locations and on how these qualities may change and shift in importance over time. Real estate values depend on the possible uses of land and their desirability, and these change with technology and demographic shifts. The growth of Internet commerce, for example, reduces dependence on physical location for sales, and thus may affect the locational value of particular real estate parcels.

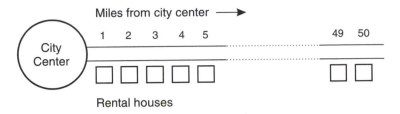

Figure 13-8. Flat City.

For a moment let us assume that the homes are costless to build and do not depreciate. They are competitively supplied at the long-run supply price of zero. Their size is determined by the common "satiation" point of all families. (Past some point, e.g., the disutility of cleaning a house outweighs the advantages of greater space.) Families would be completely indifferent about residences *except for the location* (the feature we seek to emphasize first). The cost of commuting to Flat City is $1 per mile (which includes the opportunity cost of the individual's time), and each occupied house has one worker who makes the trip each day (Flat City has no day of rest). The commuting cost is the *only* aspect of location that families care about. There are exactly fifty families (and one worker per family) in all. Under these obviously special conditions, what will the prices of the rental homes be to the families?

Consider the requirements for long-run equilibrium. Of course supply must equal demand (in this case, fifty sites with rental houses will be needed to fill the demands of the fifty families for them). On the supply side, the marginal rental house must earn zero economic profit to remove incentive for entry or exit. On the demand side, rental prices must be such that each family is content to stay where it is. Note that a rental price for each site equal to the competitive structure price (in this special case, zero) is not an equilibrium. It satisfies the supply-side condition of zero economic profit but not the demand-side condition. All families would strictly prefer the site closest to the city center (the house at 1 mile) to other sites because it has the least commuting cost.

For example, a family in the 2-mile house would be willing to pay up to $2 above the competitive structure price to move into the 1-mile house, because it would reduce its commuting cost by $2 (the commute is 1 mile less each way). But families further out would bid even more, because the reduction in their commuting costs would be even greater. A family in the 50-mile house would be willing to pay up to $98 more to move into the 1-mile house, because it would save that much from reduced commuting costs (49 miles less each way). It would also be willing to pay up to $96 more to move into the 2-mile house (its commute would be reduced by 48 miles each way), $94 more for the 3-mile house, and so on. In fact, the rent on *each* site is determined by the willingness to pay for it of the family at the *marginal* site.

Figure 13-9 shows the equilibrium rental rates and the commuting costs for each Flat City site. Because there are fifty families each of which prefers to be closer to rather than further from the city center, the last rental house supplied will be on the 50-mile site and its

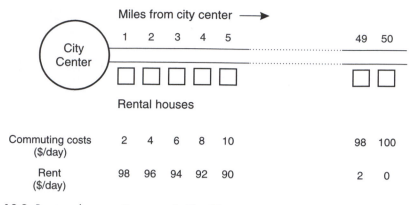

Figure 13-9. Rent and commuting costs in Flat City.

rental rate will equal the competitive structure cost of zero.[28] The forty-nine closer sites have rental rates above the competitive structure cost. The $100 cost of the marginal commute is crucial in determining these rates: At each site, the rent (above the competitive structure cost) plus the commuting cost equals the cost of the marginal commute. Put differently, the rent at each site is the maximum the marginal commuter would pay to live there (the savings in commuting costs). Thus the competitive rents are, starting from the first site, $98, $96, $94, . . ., $2, $0.

The rentals paid to live in each house are pure economic rents. They represent payments to the owner above opportunity costs, since the houses and land would be supplied for zero.[29] Even though the landlords of sites 1–49 make economic profit, new entry does not occur: Supply cannot be expanded at these sites (by the assumptions that we have made), there is no economic profit on the 50-mile site, and providing a rental house on the 51-mile site would be unprofitable. Note that no landlord can do anything to influence these rental rates, which arise as a consequence of the number of families and the locational preferences. That is why *economic rent is not a determinant of price; it is the marginal com-*

[28] None of the fifty families would prefer to be at the 51-mile site: The price cannot go below the competitive structure cost, the structure itself would be identical to the fifty other alternatives, and the commute would be worse.

[29] An important digression from our main purpose is to note that the pattern of urban rents in our model happens to *reflect* a real social cost—the cost of forgone commuting. It is generally true that urban rents will reflect the costs and benefits of all the attributes of that area: the quality of the housing itself, the available public services such as schools, the quality of the air, the convenience to employment and shopping, the property tax rates, the view, and so forth. We would expect a household to pay less rent if, for example, the air were bad, all other things being equal. Econometric studies have attempted to derive estimates of these implicit market values for each attribute as a way of isolating willingness to pay for various public goods and services (e.g., the value of making the air 10 percent cleaner).

A classic example is the article by W. Oates. "The Effects of Property Taxes and Local Public Spending on Property Values: An Empirical Study of Tax Capitalization and the Tiebout Hypothesis," *Journal of Political Economy, 77,* No. 6, November/December 1969, pp. 957–971. A survey of some of this literature is in V. Kerry Smith and Ju-Chin Huang, "Can Markets Value Air Quality? A Meta-Analysis of Hedonic Property Value Models," *Journal of Political Economy, 103,* No. 1, February 1995, pp. 209–227.

muting cost at equilibrium (less the commuting cost from each site) that determines economic rents.

It is useful to point out that the landlord is performing two economic roles simultaneously: one as a supplier of a factor, land, to the shelter industry and the other as a shelter supplier. Since the land at a particular location is fixed in supply, any payment toward it is pure economic rent. The landowner will rent the land to the highest bidder from among alternative users, which will ensure that the land is in its most valuable use. In Flat City we have restricted these bidders to residential users.

To use the land, *any* shelter supplier would bid up to the value of the profits (before land rental fees) from the home rental business (tenant receipts minus structure costs). Thus, the competitive shelter industry per se receives no net economic rent; it is the landowner that receives it. Even though it is typical for these agents to be the same person (apartment owners usually own the land and the structure), the distinction has allocative importance that will become apparent shortly.

The above model should clarify why economic rent is a persistent component of urban apartment rentals: Each apartment comes with a specific site, fixed in supply, that has a locational "attractiveness" completely determined by factors external to the landlord (the "attractiveness" of the marginal site). As families are willing to pay for it and bid against each other to receive it, this fixed attribute receives economic rent.

Let us now relax the assumption that houses are costless and do not deteriorate. We assume instead that structures are competitively supplied and maintained at a constant cost of P_H per unit, expressed for convenience in daily terms. By our assumptions about consumer preferences, the demands for structures and location are independent.[30] (Each homogeneous family will end up with the same net income after paying commuting and "location" costs; hence, the demands for structures are identical.) Figure 13-10 can thus depict a family's demand for home rental D_H (in terms of structure size, standardized for quality) exclusive of location. Each family will live in a structure of size H_E that the market supplies and maintains for a daily charge of $P_H H_E$. If for some reason the structure is not maintained, it will have fewer than H_E units. (How many fewer will depend on the depreciation rate.)

To gain the right to use the house on a particular site, families will bid up the price exactly as before. The total rental on the first site will be $\$98 + P_H H_E$, on the second site $\$96 + P_H H_E$, . . ., and on the last site just $P_H H_E$. This time, only part of the tenant's payment is economic rent (equal in magnitude to that of the last model). There is no room for a deal among any economic agents, so the allocation is efficient. The allocation is also an equilibrium, since at the market prices no economic agent has any reason to change his or her demand or supply decisions. Each of the homogeneous families would be equally happy at any of the locations, given their respective prices.

Now suppose we pass a rent control ordinance in Flat City. It states that no landlord may charge a tenant more than the competitive price for the structure and its maintenance. All

---

[30] A more realistic model would allow families to trade off the amount of site space and home size for locational advantages (e.g., more intensive use of the scarce land nearer to the center). However, this aspect of reality is an unnecessary complication in terms of illustrating the effects of rent control.

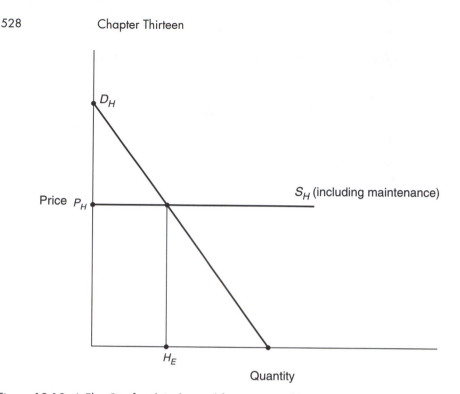

Figure 13-10. A Flat City family's demand for quantity of housing per site.

tenant payments are thus reduced (initially) to $P_H H_E$. We know that the initial allocation is Pareto-optimal. *If there is no behavioral response by any agent, the result is just like the quasi-rent model* in the first section: *a transfer of wealth from landlords to tenants with no harmful efficiency consequences. In this case it is long-run economic rent that is being re-distributed.* As long as landlords lose the economic rent, the policy transfers $2450 daily away from landlords to tenants.[31]

The Relation between Rent Control and Capitalized Property Values

It is likely that there will be behavioral responses to rent control. In truth, these cannot be predicted without specific knowledge of legal changes, enforcement efforts, and transaction costs faced by the agents in the market. Before we discuss them, we first clarify the important relation between rent control and the change in the value of the landlord's property.

This relation is of general importance because the economic logic applies to *all* policies that affect the earnings of *any* asset; examples are deregulation of trucking (removal of entry restrictions) and its effect on the value of trucking firm *operating rights,* construction

---

[31] The sum S_n of an arithmetic progression of n terms $a_0, a_1, \ldots, a_n$, where each term differs by a constant, is $(a_0 + a_n)n/2$. In this case, the sum of 0, 2, 4, 6, . . ., 98 = (0 + 98)50/2 = 2450.

of a new bypass road and its effect on the *land values* along the old route, and a change in the patent (or copyright) laws and its effects on the values of assets protected by *patents* (or *copyrights*). *The changes in value caused by forces external to the owner of the asset (such as policy changes) are often referred to as windfall gains or losses.*

In Flat City consider the original landowner that built a rental house on the first site, well before rent control. The (daily) cost of the house was $P_H H_E$ (including maintenance), and the (daily) rent of $P_H H_E$ + $98 came in like clockwork. Suppose this owner moved away, selling the property to the highest bidder from among those wishing to be new owners.

With no inkling that rent control was to come to Flat City, each potential bidder expected to receive a stream of $98 above daily costs in rental payments each day. Naturally, anyone who bid a sum less than the present value of that stream (referred to as the *capitalized value* of the property) was outbid by a competitor seeing the chance to make a small profit. The winning bid was therefore the one that exactly equaled the present value of the stream and produced zero net profit.[32] To keep this transparent, let us assume that the winning bidder financed the sum (given to the original owner) by a bank mortgage that required no money down and a $98 daily mortgage payment. This is obviously equal in value to the stream of rental payments above daily costs. We assume for convenience that the current value of this stream, or the capitalized value of the house, is $357,700.[33]

Now let us impose rent control in Flat City. Our initial effect is unchanged: The same amount of money is transferred to tenants, but note that it comes from *current* landlords. We have really devastated the new owner of the first site. If he or she tries to sell the property, the highest bid will be the value of the stream of future economic rents under controls. That is zero, as long as the controls work as intended. (More on this later!) The original owner captured all the profit by taking the expected future stream of economic rents (precontrol) and converting it by sale into cash on the table (the precontrol capitalized value). The new owner, who paid in advance for the privilege of receiving the economic rent, now

---

[32] We have simplified by assuming that the future "structure" payments by tenants $P_H H_E$ are exactly offset by daily "construction and maintenance" costs and so do not affect the expected stream of future net benefits. The purpose of this simplification is to keep the economic rent from the land in clear focus. However, it is more realistic to assume that the "construction" part of the "structure" payment (which has a corresponding opportunity cost) is not offset by any *future* cost. Therefore, it enters the expected stream of future net receipts, increasing the capitalized value and thus the sale price of the property.

This happens, under our competitive assumptions, because the current owner has already paid the structure costs. The increase in capital value merely repays the current owner for the structural services he or she has paid for (at the competitive price) but will not receive. The new owner (like the former owner) pays in advance and receives the rights to the remaining structural services that the asset produces in the future. Thus, each owner pays the opportunity costs and receives the benefits for the structural services supplied during the time of his or her ownership; the result is equivalent to our simpler model. This more realistic version does illustrate two important points: *Any durable asset (one that produces services over time) has capital value, and the concepts of capital value and economic rent are distinct.*

[33] If we assume that the $35,770 annual economic rent on this home will be paid continually and the annual simple interest rate is 10 percent, the present value of the home is $357,700 (annual rent/interest rate). This must be the size of the winning bid.

finds none coming in. All rental property owners at the time of the new policy announce-ment, whether they are new or old owners, suffer whopping *capital losses.*[34]

Thus the first point we are raising is whether the transfer of wealth from owners to ten-ants is equitable. It is common for assets (such as apartments) to be shifted from one owner to another through financial transactions (which do not necessarily affect the use of the as-sets). However, *any changes in the expected future earnings of an asset become instanta-neously capitalized into the asset's present or current value.* That is why, for example, a company's publicly traded stock price changes immediately with any news affecting the expected future earnings of the company. It is the asset owner at the time a future change is perceived who bears any burdens or receives any benefits.

In the initial illustration of this point we assumed that rent control strikes like a totally unexpected thunderbolt. In actuality, many potential changes are considered by investors as possible states of the world, and they affect the calculation of the expected present value and thus the amount bid for the asset. For example, suppose rent control was under discus-sion in Flat City at the time of the home sale on the first site. With no rent control, we sug-gested earlier that the house could sell for its capitalized value of $357,700. With rent con-trol, the selling price would be zero. If rent control was thought to have a 50-50 chance of passing, the expected value would be

$$EV = 0.5(357,700) + 0.5(0) = \$178,850$$

Because of uncertainty and risk aversion, the maximum bid of a single potential investor would be below the expected value.[35]

Obviously there are many sources of change in the expected future earnings from an as-set, and investors in such assets may be thought to understand the risks that they take.[36] One can argue, therefore, that it is tough luck on the part of the home purchaser when rent con-trol passes. He or she was aware of the possibility at the time of the sale, and the govern-ment need not be concerned with which of the two parties (buyer or seller) ends up the real winner. (If rent control were defeated, the original owner would feel that the sale at a price under $200,000 was a big mistake.)

Thus we make these observations. *The longer the time the economic rent has existed, the more unfair its "control" will seem to rent recipients.* That is because, through the transfer of assets, the current recipients of the rent are less likely to be reaping financial profit. (The

[34] The new owner may have no means of making the mortgage payments and may declare bankruptcy. In that case the ownership of the property will be assigned to the bank providing the mortgage (or similarly, the bank will foreclose on the mortgage). However, that does not change the zero value of the property, and the bank becomes the loser.

[35] Investment syndicates would be expected to form and outbid a single risk-averse investor because of the syndicate's lower risk cost (Chapter 7).

[36] Sometimes public policy action is taken to try to improve the information available to the investment com-munity. This may involve required disclosure of certain information by potential sellers, liability laws in case of failure to disclose certain facts, and the production of certain information that may be relevant to investors (and others) more generally, such as actual and predicted inflation rates and unemployment rates.

original owner is the one who profited.)[37] *Conversely, the best time to consider a policy of controlling economic rent is simultaneously with the event that is expected to cause the rent.*

A second consideration reinforces these observations: *It can be difficult, if not impossible, for an administrator or an assessor to determine accurately the amount of economic rent a landlord receives.* In homogeneous Flat City this task may not be overwhelming. However, real cities have virtually infinite quality variation among the apartment buildings in the housing stock and a multitude of factors that determine the attractiveness of the site itself. For example, apartment quality varies with building security, shared amenities such as a laundry room or swimming pool, parking facilities, and accessibility features such as elevators. Locational attractiveness depends not only on car commuting costs but on nearness to public transit, crime rates in the neighborhood, views from the site, and noise and air quality. Furthermore, there may be nonresidential bidders for the land (which we discuss shortly). One must be able to separate the total free-market price into the opportunity cost of all variable inputs (the structure, its maintenance, and any value of the land in an alternative use) and the balance as economic rent.

In practice, virtually none of the rent control ordinances attempt to control old economic rent. Rather, some events (e.g., a rapid population increase) cause unusual and visible increments to economic rent, and these increments trigger a political demand for rent control. Housing is particularly susceptible to these demands because: (1) it is a significant part of each consumer's budget; (2) moving to avoid higher monetary rents is itself expensive, both financially and psychologically; (3) land is a scarce input that earns long-run rents; and (4) the housing stock responds slowly to market pressure, which can result in significant quasi-rents on structures. *The most common way to implement rent control is to use the market prices existing at the start of the causative event as a base and thus control only part of the economic rent.* Then annual fixed percentage increases are usually allowed automatically (designed for normal increases in operating and maintenance costs), and there is an appeal mechanism for landlords claiming higher cost increases.

The Supply Response to Rent Control

So far we have not considered the behavioral responses of landlords to the imposition of rent control. We have seen that landlords, by making no changes, suffer large capital losses. Is there anything they can do to avoid those losses of economic rent? In particular, since it is now less profitable to supply rental housing, will the supply be reduced? Let us assume for the moment that rent control is administered as it is often intended: Initial control prices are no lower than the supply price (opportunity cost) for shelter, and the allowable annual rent increase is at least as high as the increase in optimal uncontrolled maintenance costs.

---

[37] Note that the previous owner is not necessarily the original owner. This whole line of argument extends backward *ad infinitum:* The previous owner had to buy the land from someone and presumably had to pay a price reflecting the value of expected rents. The first settler is the only one who receives private benefits greater than private costs. All others break even, except for the windfall gains and losses that arise.

Under those circumstances there are reasons to expect a supply reduction. One is condominium conversion (the occupant is an owner rather than a tenant). This is primarily a change in legal contract rather than in the actual quantity of housing units; thus, it is more significant to the frustration of the redistributional objectives than to the actual housing supply.

In the simple Flat City model with no rent control, each family is actually indifferent to owning its own home or renting. For example, the family in the first site pays $P_H H_E + \$98$ each day it rents. If it buys the property, it will pay the same amount. (Like our previous purchaser, the \$98 becomes a daily mortgage payment, or the family finances the purchase with any other method of equivalent capital value.)[38] Since the rent control ordinance does not change the demand for the first site (or any other site), condominium conversion is a way of making essentially the same deals as would be made without rent control. If that happens, there is no redistribution at all. Thus, most rent control ordinances include bans on condominium conversions.[39]

The more general reason for supply reduction (which includes condominium conversion as a special case) is as follows: If *the land has value in an alternative (and thus noncontrolled) use, the landowner may change the use of the land.* Think of rent control as an imperfect attempt to impose a lump-sum (nondistortionary) land tax. Each landowner pays the tax, which then gets redistributed to the landlord's tenants. However, the tax is not lump-sum because it is on one use of the land rather than on the land itself. The land and its location may be fixed, but its current use for residential rental purposes can be varied.

The Flat City model assumes this problem away by restricting the land to home rental uses. Zoning laws, if they are perceived as permanent, may justify such an assumption. But if there are alternative legal uses of the land, they are an opportunity cost of using the land for apartment provision. To see the effect of alternative uses, we develop a simple variant of the Flat City model. In this variant, the supply of land remains fixed as before. However, we locate this land in a doughnut-shaped ring of given radius from the city center. (If you insist, Fat City.) This is shown in Figure 13-11. The land in the ring is divided into equally sized plots, so that from a land-user perspective each plot is equally attractive (e.g., commuting time to the city center is the same from each).[40] Thus in equilibrium, each site will rent for the same price.

In Figure 13-12a we show the total supply of sites in Fat City as fixed at $\bar{L}$. Suppose the demand curve crosses the fixed supply at P_L; then this is the competitive price for the land,

---

[38] In actuality, imperfections in the capital market (imperfect information) cause ownership to be favored by temporally stable households. (The transaction costs of entering and terminating ownership agreements are high compared with rentals.) We discuss these imperfections in a later chapter. Unrestricted condominium conversion with rent control can result in an occupant population that is socioeconomically different from that under no controls.

[39] Condominium conversion bans generally apply when an owner of one building wishes to subdivide the ownership rights by dwelling units and sell them separately. They do not restrict the sale of the original structure to a new owner who may wish to occupy it rather than rent it. Thus, single-family homes (and duplexes in part) that were rented out can avoid controls by sale to an owner-occupant.

[40] If we made a series of such rings by drawing first a circle of 1-mile radius, then a 2-mile circle, and so on up to a 50-mile circle, the rent pattern as one moved to rings successively further from the city center would decline as in Flat City.

One land site in Fat City

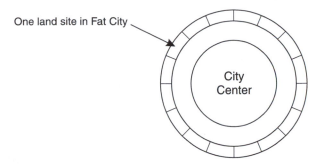

City
Center

Figure 13-11. The Fat City model (land sites equidistant from the city center).

and all payments toward it are pure economic rents. However, the demand curve is for all potential land users, and so the diagram shows all potential benefits and costs in the land market. If the only demands are for rental housing purposes, then imposing rent control in this situation would take away only economic rent. But now let us imagine that some of that demand is from nonapartment land users (e.g., dry cleaners, video rental stores, dental offices).

In Figure 13-12b we draw the demand and supply of this land *to the apartment industry.* The demand curve is shifted to the left from diagram (a) because we have removed all the nonapartment land demanders (thus, at any price, less quantity is demanded). However, *the nonapartment demands are the opportunity costs in the supply curve of land to the apartment industry.*[41] That is, the willingness of the landowner to supply a site for an apartment depends on how much others such as dentists or dry cleaners are willing to pay for the use of the same site. As drawn, all land is shown to have some alternative use.[42] However, the value of L_A units in apartment use exceeds the value anywhere else. Thus, L_A units are allocated for apartment rental purposes and $\bar{L} - L_A$ units for other purposes. The economic rent received by the units is shown as the shaded area.

The economic rent in Figure 13-12b is considerably lower than the amount of Figure 13-12a, which equals all payments. What explains the difference, and which one is relevant for rent control? One obvious difference is the definition of the market: The top diagram includes rent from both apartment and nonapartment land uses. However, even if we eliminated the rent payments of nonapartment users, the remaining rent, $P_L L_A$, would exceed that shown in Figure 13-12b. That is, the shaded area in Figure 13-12b is less than $P_L L_A$. The same units of land are shown receiving different amounts of rent. How can we reconcile the two diagrams?

Figure 13-12a shows the value of land in its best productive market use relative to the opportunity cost of allocation off the market. Figure 13-12b shows the value of land in its

---

[41] For any price, $\bar{L}$ minus the quantity shown on S_A is the precise demand for land in nonapartment use. That is, the supply curve S_A is also the mirror image of the nonapartment demand curve for land (with the price axis as the dashed vertical line and greater demands farther to the left away from $\bar{L}$).

[42] Alternative use may include an owner's personally using a room or unit and the land it is on, rather than renting it out. In some areas this type of apartment makes up an important share of the total rental housing market.

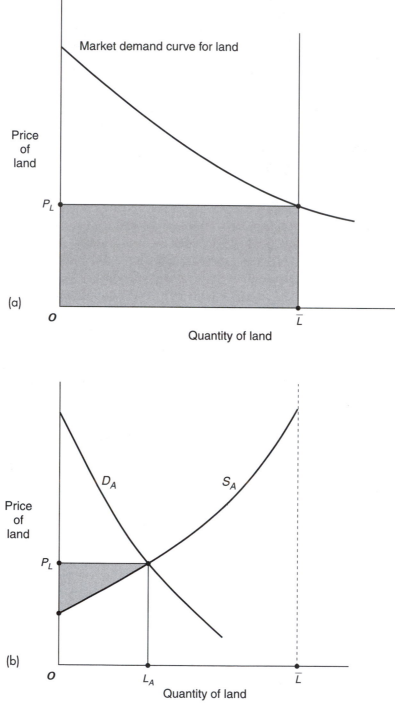

Figure 13-12. The demand and supply of land (economic rent shaded): (a) To all uses. (b) To the apartment industry only.

best apartment use relative to the opportunity cost of nonapartment allocation. These are simply two different ways of dividing the universe of possible land allocations. The latter is the one of concern to rent control policy, because it divides the land universe into units directly affected by the policy versus all others. To keep land in apartment use, it must command a payment greater than or equal to its value in alternative uses. One can only "control" the economic rent that *accrues to the apartment sector* without affecting resource allocation *to that sector.*

To express this point more generally, *economic rent is a relational concept,* defined as a payment above the opportunity cost. But "the" opportunity cost depends on how we divide the universe of possible allocations into two exclusive and exhaustive sets of uses and alternative uses. Thus "the" rent also depends on this divisional choice. A resource receives economic rent in use *X relative* to its employment in the best alternative from among the uses in not-*X.* If we change the definition of *X,* we change the definition of the alternatives, and thus the opportunity cost and economic rent. The employment of the resource is constant; it is only the way we look at it that changes.

For a different example, suppose it is true that all people will supply their maximum labor if the wage is at least $8 per hour. Then payments above that are economic rents to laboring relative to not working at all. We could remove them and cause no reduction in the aggregate labor supply. But this would cause havoc in terms of the allocation of labor to particular occupations (which normally have different wages, unlike land that has the same price to any type of demander). The wage of firefighters, for example, might be reduced by this policy from $20 to $8. While each individual may be willing to work at something for $8 per hour, that does not mean that each is willing to work at a *dangerous* something for $8 per hour. Such a change alters relative occupational wages *within* the labor market, and society is not indifferent to labor allocation among occupations.

To return to price control of rental housing, we were exploring how the rent control ordinance affects the supply decisions of landlords. The critical feature we have just discussed is that the landlord may find it profitable to change the use of the land, despite a rent control administration that allows all supply costs of housing and its maintenance to be passed along. This can happen if rent control continues into the long run. That is, we have assumed all land uses are optimal right before the event causing rent control, and the base prices are set to correspond to those prevailing in the free market at that time. Thus, problems of land use arise only if the reallocations that occur over time are different from those that would have occurred without rent control.

Imagine the causative event to be a rapid population surge resulting in a permanent increase in land rents as well as short-run quasi-rents for housing per se. The growth in population can easily stimulate an increased willingness to pay on the part of retail establishments to service it, for example, a gasoline station on the first site of Flat City. Suppose that, before the population surge, the station was not willing to offer the $98 land rent (now part of the control price) to obtain the use of the land. After the surge, the station might bid $120 because of the increased business. The true value of the land in housing might be still greater (say, $150), but the controls prevent apartment suppliers from bidding more than the $98 control price. Thus, the landowner will be able to avoid the full capital loss from controls by changing the use of the land. This is a misallocation of resources (which, in this model, results in residential displacement from near the city center to the "suburbs").

The seriousness of this as a problem with long-run rent control is not really known. For one thing, zoning laws that exist independently of rent control may rule out nonresidential uses in many areas. The zoning policies themselves probably improve resource allocation compared to a free market because of the rampant externalities involved in urban land-use decisions. Thus, land in apartment use may be earning substantial economic rent. Nevertheless, on the margins between zoned areas landlords may believe that there is a good chance a zoning change or exception will be granted. This chance may be further enhanced if the area becomes run down and the request is presented as part of a revitalization effort.

This suggests one explanation for the disinvestment in housing that can be associated with rent control. The capital value of the property in apartment use is restricted by rent control. Any property owner will seek ways to increase the value. If the restriction is only on economic rent, there will (by definition) be no alternative use that yields a higher value. *Allowed rent increases must be sufficient to keep the capitalized value of the property greater in apartment use than in any other use.* If not, the landlord has an incentive to change the use. *Rent control ordinances that allow only building costs and maintenance expenses to be passed on to tenants will generally cause inefficiency in the long run.* That is because the opportunity cost of the land in an alternative use may be growing over time as well.[43] Berkeley, California, had this type of rent control from 1979 to 1999, and from 1980 to 1990 U.S. census data show a decline of 12 percent in its rental stock (but no decline in ten nearby communities without rent control). A number of these units have been converted at minimal expense to medical, dental, and other professional offices.

We should also note that rent control will have similar effects on the supply of new housing. If uncontrolled (market) rent can be charged initially, then the supply of new rental structures will depend on expected future control board decisions analogously to the existing rental stock. *If the expected net capitalized value of building a new rental housing structure is greater than any alternative, the structure will be built; otherwise, the land will be used for an alternative purpose.* Often, rent control ordinances do not deter the construction of new condominiums (even if they prevent conversion of existing structures). In that case one would expect that the close substitutes with much higher capital values would largely displace any new rental units that would have been supplied if no rent controls were in effect.

In the discussion of the response of landlords to rent control we have assumed that the policy is successful in reducing the payments from tenants to landlords. That lowers the capital value of the property and causes landlords to seek alternatives to increase it.

---

[43] Several rent control studies have suggested that rent control administrators do not allow increases equal to the maintenance costs, which causes disinvestment. For example, in the RAND study of New York, cited earlier, it was found that, from 1945 to 1968, the rent control board allowed average increases of only 2 percent whereas the real annual cost of maintaining the apartments rose at 6 percent. The above argument suggests that it is difficult to establish the causes behind these statistics. Some landlords will choose to undermaintain their buildings, even if they can request and receive approval for a higher maintenance level, as a way of converting the property to a more profitable use (without throwing away the "free" benefits from the existing capital structure).

Nevertheless, "perfect" rent control could, in theory, affect only economic rents and cause no supply inefficiency even in the long run. The models of Flat City and Fat City illustrate the existence of this rent, as well as some of the difficulties of knowing how much of any payment is economic rent. Actual rent controls such as that in New York differ from the theoretical ideal and cause inefficient disinvestment in rental units in the controlled area. Now let us turn to the tenant side of this market and, in so doing, reexamine our assumption that rent control reduces tenant payments.

The Effects of Rent Control on Apartment Exchange

Rent control may or may not disturb the supply equilibrium (depending on whether only economic rent is controlled), but it *unambiguously creates disequilibrium in exchange.* Consider first the control of all economic rent in Flat City with all land use restricted to home rentals, so that all tenant payments are initially reduced to $P_H H_E$. Previously, each family was indifferent to its location. With the rent control prices in effect, each family strictly prefers the first site to the second, the second to the third, and so on. Each family will seek ways of obtaining a closer location and will be willing to pay up to the reduction in its own commuting costs for it.

Suppose for a moment that there is no behavioral response from tenants, and consider the resulting equity implications. The first family now has an increased daily income of $98, the second $96, and so on, and the last family is unaffected. But all these families are homogeneous with identical incomes and utility levels before rent control. Instead of redistributing the total savings equally among the families, the benefits go disproportionately to the families closer to the city center. Since all families are equally deserving of any redistribution, this appears to be a grossly arbitrary and unfair method. This illustrates another reason why the control of old economic rent can be inequitable.

However, the control of new economic rent may be thought more reasonable. To see this, let us assume that the population of Flat City surges from fifty to sixty homogeneous families. The additional ten families live in homes on sites 51 to 60 (we will not treat the short-run problem of home construction), making the cost of the marginal commute $120. Thus, the land rent on the first site increases to $118, the second $116, and so on; each of the original families must pay $20 more in economic rent. Outraged by this, the original families pass a rent control ordinance that freezes the rents at the level existing before the population surge (with new rental homes uncontrolled). The result is shown in Figure 13-13. Each of the original families saves $20, and the market rents on the new homes start at $P_H H_E$ + $18 for the fifty-first site and decline to $P_H H_E$ for the sixtieth site (the figure only shows the economic rent, which excludes the structure cost).

In this more reasonable case, there is still disequilibrium in exchange. The first fifty families are content; they see no alternative sites that they would prefer to their current ones (at the control prices). However, the last ten families strictly prefer any of the first fifty houses to their own and are willing to pay more than the controlled price for the right to occupy them. Each of these families would pay up to its savings in commuting costs. The sixtieth family, for example, would offer up to $P_H H_E$ + $ 118 for the first site.

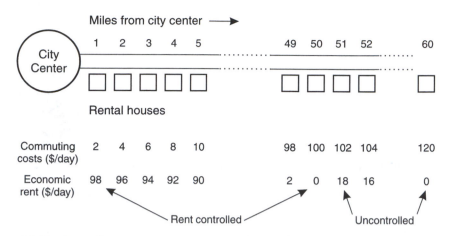

Figure 13-13. Controlling new economic rent in a larger Flat City.

The prediction of the behavioral responses to this disequilibrium, and the resulting distribution of benefits and costs, depends on the details of changes in legal specifications and their enforcement that accompany the rent control ordinance. The ordinance reduces the right of the landlord to receive income from the property, but it is not always clear who ends up with the right. Below, we describe a variety of behaviors that are commonly observed in rent-controlled cities.

If the rent controls apply to the rental unit rather than its occupant, then a waiting list system may develop. This will result in the original tenants getting most of the benefits, although new families will capture some benefits through turnovers. Those waiting for vacancies may hire an agent to watch for them—and so spend some of the potential gain in consumer surplus. That can happen for several reasons.

Landlords, for example, have no incentive to spend time tracking down people on the waiting list, and they may quickly cross off names of people who are "hard to locate" (i.e., do not answer the telephone by the second ring) in order to pass it on to someone more favored. An agent with enough clients can afford to monitor the waiting lists continually and be accessible to landlord calls. If waiting lists are not used and rare vacancies are pounced upon by whomever is there first, potential tenants may prefer to hire agents to search rather than pay the time costs themselves. All this is part of the cost of rent control: an over-allocation of resources to the agent industry and other search activities beyond the amount desired at market rental prices.

The above activities are usually legal, but there is also incentive to engage in bribes or side payments that may be illegal. We mentioned in the first section that original tenants can sometimes pass on their apartments to new tenants in return for some sort of finder's fee. A common way in which that occurs is for the original tenant to make a "permanent improvement" in the apartment that is truly valueless and sell it to the new tenant. In the limit the original tenant can capture the full capital value of the future stream of reduced rents.

Of course, landlords do not necessarily have to accept any particular incomers. Thus, they can try to extract the market rent in some other form similar to the sale of the worthless improvement. (When the landlords are absentee, building managers may get into the act.) Although these payments are almost always illegal, it is difficult to enforce a law against behavior that is engaged in voluntarily by both parties to the transaction. The original tenant has some incentive to prevent these transactions in order to get some of the surplus. Systems may evolve where the accepted practice is to split the gains in some way. On the other hand, one should expect many landlords and tenants to refrain from engaging in illegal side payments simply because they are law-abiding people (or at least are highly price-inelastic with respect to this behavior).

All these behaviors may arise when the rental unit is controlled independently of the occupant. A considerably milder form of rent control is tenancy-specific, sometimes called vacancy decontrol: Controls are in effect during a tenancy, but the landlord may charge market rates when filling a vacancy. Obviously, this version allows landlords to keep more of the economic rent than the other version does; the expected stream of rental payments is higher. It is thus less likely to interfere with opportunity costs and cause a disinvestment problem, although that still depends on how rates are controlled during a tenancy.

The tenancy-specific version also creates a somewhat different set of exchange incentives. Current occupants receive the same benefits as long as they remain in the apartment, but they no longer have any *transferable* value to their "squatter's rights."[44] An incoming tenant, faced with paying the market rent, will no longer be willing to pay for worthless improvements made by the current occupant. Thus there will be more of a tendency to keep the apartment "in the family," and this can cause increasing exchange inefficiency over time. (Even if a family's composition and income changes, it will tend to stay in an apartment that it would leave if charged the market price.)[45] Another change is that the landlord has a large incentive to evict tenants; in fact, it increases with each year of tenancy. Usually, tougher eviction laws accompany this kind of ordinance.

The primary beneficiaries of this type of ordinance are tenants who are occupants from the start and retain the apartment for a long period. Once the control rules are understood, the knowledge will drive up the market rents paid when vacancies are filled. To see this, let us go back to the Flat City model and imagine a steady population growth that would cause regular rent increases. Suppose a vacancy in the first site arises when the uncontrolled economic rent would be $98. Let the expected uncontrolled increase be $10 per time period and the controlled increase be zero.

A student coming to Flat City for a graduate program of two time periods will be willing to bid more than $98 for the apartment. That is, the student knows that offering more now is the way to obtain control benefits next period. Unfortunately for the student, someone who plans to be in the area longer than 2 years will make a higher bid. Thus, *tenants*

---

[44] Regulations regarding sublease clauses may affect this value. For example, the right to sublease indefinitely is a property right of transferable value.

[45] A similar inhibition to mobility has applied to California home owners since the passage of Proposition 13 in 1978. Proposition 13 keeps the assessed value of homes below their market value for the current owners, reducing property taxes. If the homes are sold, they are reassessed at the market value, which can result in property taxes that are substantially higher.

simply bid away their expected control benefits in order to get occupancy rights, and the landlord ends up with close to the equivalent of the uncontrolled market rents. Because there is uncertainty in advance about the actual length of a tenancy, risk aversion will cause the bids to be somewhat below the uncontrolled market value.[46] This uncertainty is itself an exchange inefficiency caused by rent control. (Both landlord and tenant would prefer a regime of uncontrolled prices with flexibility to recontract each year rather than this system of effectively paying too far in advance.)

In terms of equity, it is hard to argue that the long-term tenants who are here from the start are the people who are most deserving of benefits. For example, why should they pay substantially less than the long-term tenant of comparable income who moves in one period after the start of controls? (That is, why is the initial period an exceptional characteristic?) Why should families that suffer hardships such as divorce or death of a family member (events that often motivate changes of dwelling units) be the ones to lose benefits? Why are the poorest families not made the beneficiaries? The policy seems inequitable by both process and outcome standards.

Let us sum up the discussion. Exchange inefficiencies arise because the controls prevent economic agents from making trades that are mutually beneficial in both the short and long run. Under controls, this is necessary to keep landlord receipts below the market level. Tenants as a group are better off (assuming no supply inefficiency), but *many individual tenants have incentive to bid up prices to obtain another's apartment, and this sets forces in motion that work to reduce the net benefits that accrue to tenants.*

The reduced property right of the landlord to receive income creates a contracting problem. If the occupant were given all property rights except the right to receive controlled income, then tenants would only bid with each other, the rent control benefits would remain in the tenant class, and exchange would be efficient. However, this is a pure transfer of future wealth from landlords to occupants at the time of control, whether or not they remain occupants. Furthermore, no rent control ordinances give occupants these rights. Landlords retain rights of tenant selection and eviction.[47] Thus, potential occupants may make side payments to tenants, landlords, or building managers who influence the choice of new tenants, and they may pay extra search costs in looking for apartments. Of the potential gain in tenant consumer surplus from rent control, some finds its way back to landlords, some gets dissipated by search costs and by tenants remaining in nonoptimal apartments, and some portion becomes actual gain for tenants. The balance among these depends on more detailed aspects of the legal specifications and their enforcement.

We have also suggested that *the equity of rent control often seems arbitrary.* It is not targeted at specific groups identified by income levels, nor are the total benefits likely to be "evenly" distributed among those in the tenant class. We have roughly specified the

---

[46] Empirical support for this is provided by John Nagy, "Do Vacancy Decontrol Provisions Undo Rent Control?," *Journal of Urban Economics, 42,* No. 1, July 1997, pp. 64–78. He finds that new tenants under tenant-specific rent controls in New York City pay more for equivalent apartments than those in uncontrolled sectors.

[47] This is subject to tenant sublease rights.

equity objective for rent control in terms of the "just" price; tenants should not have to pay any "new" economic rents. But we have seen many subtle ways to circumvent this intent, so that only some arbitrary subset of tenants will make payments in accordance with it.

Recent Issues of Rent Control

In the next chapter we will discuss alternative policies to pure price controls that appear generally more attractive in both equity and efficiency terms. Nevertheless, one must keep in mind that apartment rent control is often a quick political response of a democratic electorate to a perceived problem. An example of this followed the passage, by statewide referendum, of California's Proposition 13 in 1978. This proposition rolled back all property taxes to 1 percent of the 1975–1976 level of assessed valuation in each local district. Furthermore, it limited annual increases to a small percentage of the base.

A fascinating aspect of this amendment is that many renters evidently expected to receive rebates from their landlords commensurate with the property tax savings. Perhaps this expectation came about because it was asserted repeatedly by supporters during the campaign. Anyone with a modicum of training in microeconomics would realize that *Proposition 13 has no effect on the market equilibrium price for rentals in the very short run: With a fixed supply, demand determines price.*

In another culture, perhaps, landlords might be severely dishonored for not providing rebates, and a very small minority did provide rebates in the "spirit" of the proposition. But the overwhelming majority of landlords provided no rebates and continued business as usual. Therefore, it is not surprising that outraged renters responded by passing rent control ordinances in many California cities, including Los Angeles, San Francisco, Santa Monica, Berkeley, and even Beverly Hills. A somewhat similar experience was repeated in Massachusetts in the 1970s, where rent controls were adopted in Boston, Brookline, and Cambridge after the passage of a state proposition limiting property taxes.

In all three places that we have mentioned (New York, Massachusetts, and California), major changes in the rent control laws were adopted in the 1990s, all designed to reduce the restrictiveness of the controls. In New York, the state legislature passed new rent control laws that would allow New York City landlords much larger rent increases for vacant apartments, as well as deregulating both high-rent apartments and apartments with high-income tenants. In Massachusetts, voters approved Question 9, which ended rent controls as of 1997 in the three cities that had them. In California, the 1995 legislative passage of AB 1164 (the Costa/Hawkins Rental Housing Act) phased in vacancy decontrol statewide during 1996–1999, exempts rented single-family homes and condominiums from controls, and forbids controls on new rental units. The California legislation affects almost all California communities with rent controls, including Berkeley, Los Angeles, San Francisco, and Santa Monica.

In a review of the economic literature on rent control, Richard Arnott refers to modified rent control laws such as those in New York and California as "second-generation" rent control, to be contrasted with the earlier and stricter "first-generation" controls.[48] Consistent with our analysis that explains the difficulty of "targeting" rent controls to an intended population, he does not find any support in the literature for either "generation" based upon equity objectives. He does report, however, that many jurisdictions (particularly in European cities) continue political support for rent controls for this purpose.

Interestingly, he reviews two strands of literature that offer some theoretical support for "second-generation" rent controls on efficiency rather than equity grounds. Each of these strands postulates a free rental market that is not perfectly competitive and is inefficient, with well-designed rent control reducing the inefficiency.[49] However, there is no empirical research as yet that estimates the presence or extent of these market inefficiencies nor the effects of the second-generation rent controls on them. This remains an interesting issue for future policy research.

A Windfall Profits Tax as Rent Control

Apartment rent control is hard to limit to economic rent because of the tremendous number of factors that determine an apartment's value relative to other uses and the difficulty of accounting for any changes in them over time. However, economic rent accrues to other goods or services, and in some situations identifying it may be less complex. Firm profits (the returns to a particular collectivity of assets) are sometimes a tempting target. To the extent that firm profits are in excess of those necessary to keep the firm in its current market, the excess is economic rent or what is sometimes called economic profit. It is interesting to discuss briefly two examples where governments have attempted to limit this economic rent through the passage of windfall profits taxes.

Note that in general the proceeds of a tax do not accrue to the consumers of the taxed good, so that judgments about fairness depend on who receives the benefits from these proceeds. Our comments below do not focus on this aspect, but on how the economic rent is identified. One example is quite recent: the 1997 imposition by the United Kingdom of a "windfall tax" on "excess" profits of its recently privatized utilities. The other is the "windfall profits tax" on oil in the United States in the early 1980s.

---

[48] Richard Arnott, "Time for Revisionism on Rent Control," *Journal of Economic Perspectives, 9,* No. 1, Winter 1995, pp. 99–120. See also the entire issue on rent control in *Regional Science and Urban Economics, 28,* No. 6, November 1998, pp. 673–816; and W. Keating, M. Teitz, and A. Skarburski, *Rent Control: Regulation and the Rental Housing Market* (New Brunswick, N.J.: Center for Urban Policy Research, 1998).

[49] In one, landlords are assumed to have monopoly power (they sell differentiated products in a market characterized by monopolistic competition), and well-designed rent control improves efficiency by reducing the exercise of this power. In the other, asymmetric information between landlords and tenants creates the problem. In the latter, landlords do not know before renting which tenants are "good" (e.g., take good care of the apartment) and which are "bad" (e.g., behave in a way that costs the landlord more money). When they find out by experience, they raise the rent for the "bad" tenants causing them to move to a new apartment (where they impose uncompensated costs on the new landlord who did not know they were "bad"), creating a cycle of frequent and inefficient turnover. Rent control can prevent the cycle by disallowing the rent increase that would spur it. See Arnott, "Time for Revisionism on Rent Control," pp. 107–108.

In the late 1980s and early 1990s, many United Kingdom public enterprises that had been providing electricity, natural gas, water, and telecommunications, rail, and airport services were privatized by the sale of stock. The Labor Party complained at the time that these enterprises were being offered at too low a price by the Conservative government then in power, and threatened a windfall tax on excess profits in the future. The future came in 1997, with the election of Labor led by Prime Minister Tony Blair. The tax, expected to raise over £5 billion ($8 billion), equals 23 percent of the difference between average company value during the first 4 years of privatization and the value at the time of privatization. It is a one-time tax.

Standard accounting rules limit to some extent the ability of public corporations to hide real profits. For any profit level that appears on the firm's financial records, there remains the issue of deciding whether any of this is *economic* profit. In the United Kingdom's tax, the measured profit (averaged over its first 4 years following privatization) is multiplied by nine to estimate a company's value (on the British stock exchange, nine was taken as the representative price-earnings ratio for firms most similar to the recently privatized ones). The excess subject to the 23 percent tax is then defined as the difference between this calculated value and the original value based on the price the government charged for the shares at the time of privatization.

The tax base was designed to be historical, a matter entirely of preexisting financial records. Once enacted, a firm could do nothing to alter the amount of tax due. Since the tax amount is independent of any future behavior of the firm, it is difficult to argue that enactment of such a tax will cause any inefficiency. However, it is less clear whether the *threat* of the tax *before* its enactment induced any firm behavioral responses.

To the extent that firms were put on notice by Labor that such a tax might be forthcoming, this changes the firm's expectations of how before-tax profits in particular time periods will translate into after-tax profits for shareholders. It may be that some firms found it advantageous to "move up" costs (inefficiently) that otherwise would have been incurred after enactment, in order to shift profits to the future and reduce what was then the "expected" windfall profits tax payment (and of course reduce the resulting redistribution). On the other hand, if firms believed that there might be additional windfall profits taxes enacted beyond the first one (i.e., that the tax is not really a one-time tax), then predicting their behavior and its effects is more complex. The incentive to shift costs forward is mitigated, but then so is the incentive to increase profits generally. It will be interesting to study the behavior of these recently privatized firms, to find out how successful this attempt to recapture economic rent has been.

The earlier windfall profits tax on oil in the United States was initiated by the Carter administration and enacted as the Crude Oil Windfall Profit Tax of 1980. It was criticized later by President Reagan and repealed in 1988. To its credit, it replaced a complex set of oil price controls that had two significantly perverse effects at a time when the country was concerned about its energy independence. The controlled prices actually subsidized very expensive imported oil from the Organization of Petroleum Exporting Countries (OPEC). They also discouraged the use of alternative energy sources and energy conservation. Allowing the domestic oil price to rise to its market level would solve these problems, but could this be done without the accompanying painful distributional consequences to U.S. consumers? At the time the windfall profits tax was enacted, the world price of oil was high. U.S. domestic producers, supplying two-thirds of the country' s consumption, would have received large windfall profits (estimated at $220 billion) if prices were simply decontrolled.

Crude oil is a fairly homogeneous product. There are several different grades, each with its own price. It seems safe to assume that wells that were being pumped at low oil prices would, if prices rose without any commensurate cost increases, then be receiving new economic rent. The windfall profits tax was designed to recapture 60–70 percent of any increase in revenues from these wells over the base (predecontrol) price. One complication is that the marginal cost of extracting oil from a well increases as the well becomes older. The legislation set base prices by the year of discovery of the well and had lower tax rates when certain expensive tertiary techniques were used for extracting the oil near the "bottom."

However, at least two features of the legislation were problematic. One was a provision to tax oil from *new* wells (at 30 percent of revenues above a base price of $16.55 per barrel). Clearly this discouraged seeking and producing oil from new wells that would have been supplied without the tax and violated the idea of controlling only economic rent. Some might think it is a good idea to discourage consumption of this exhaustible resource beyond what the market would do. (More on this topic later!) Note that this tax, however, artificially encourages other problematic fuel sources such as coal and nuclear energy to be substituted for oil. The second problematic provision was that Congress changed Carter's proposal for a permanent tax to be temporary, designed to operate for 10 years and then to be gradually phased out. The temporary nature of the tax meant it could be avoided simply by withholding production, distorting the oil supplied in particular years especially near the phase-out time. The effects of the latter were never observed, because unexpectedly in 1986 the world price of oil dropped substantially. There were few "windfall profits" after this time, and the tax was repealed in 1988.

Summary

This chapter presents analyses of the effect of price controls on competitive market processes. We suggest that the use of these controls stems from a concern over the fairness of the distribution of income in a specific market. One example we analyze is the peanut program, typical of agricultural subsidy programs initiated at a time when concern for the economic survival of small family farms was high. The other principal example is apartment rent control, seen as a struggle over economic rent. For purposes of our analyses, we assume that there are no problems in these markets other than the distributional ones. The principal issues are whether the policies used can fix the distributional problems and can do so without causing significant efficiency problems.

In the case of the peanut program, the price support and quota system fails to prevent the exit of small family farms from the market and causes considerable efficiency problems as well. The program does not change the fact that technology makes it possible for large farms to produce at much lower cost than small ones. Even though the supports may make it possible for small farms to produce profitably, *competitive forces encourage least-cost supply.*

It is *most* profitable for the small farms to sell out to large ones, and that is primarily what has happened. The price supports cause substantial inefficiency because they restrict the flow of peanuts to their mostly highly valued use in domestic consumption. The inefficiency is often multiplied several times over by quotas set at levels that do not correspond to demand at the support price, causing high-valued peanuts to be crushed and allocated to low-value uses such as oil or meal.

There is widespread analytic consensus that agricultural subsidy programs such as the peanut program are not in the public interest. Nevertheless, these programs have so far continued to survive the political process. The 1996 FAIR Act actually increases the amount of taxpayer support for agricultural subsidy programs. At the same time, however, it introduces a number of market-oriented reforms to reduce the extent of inefficiency and provides for declining support payments over time. Its intent is that in 7 years when the act has run its course, farmers will be largely left to market forces. However, Congress has since acted to increase support payments and is considering new agricultural subsidy programs, so only the future will reveal the fate of the market-oriented FAIR reforms.

The case of apartment rent control is analytically more complex. Seen as a struggle over economic rent, there is no inherent allocative reason to determine who should receive the rent. In theory, economic rent may be redistributed without causing any allocative efficiency in the short or long run; any further changes in resource allocation are due only to the income effects of the distribution.

Of course, it is a practical matter whether particular methods of intervention can achieve equity goals without adverse efficiency consequences. The standard supply and demand analysis of rent control suggests that it is inefficient in the long run because it prevents landlords from receiving payments equal to (or greater than) their opportunity costs. But this analysis is really of a rent freeze and does not identify the possible aim of the policy as the control of economic rent or the reasons why control might be difficult to accomplish.

We use the models of Flat City and Fat City to demonstrate that economic rent is a long-run as well as a short-run phenomenon in urban housing markets. The short-run rents are quasi-rents that exist because the supply of structures responds only slowly to demand pressure; they disappear in the long run as price settles to its long-run level. The long-run rents are primarily on the land when its long-run supply is inelastic to the rental housing industry (perhaps because of zoning laws). In all cases in which there is economic rent, it is important to remember that price determines economic rent and not vice versa. This is seen clearly in the Flat City model: The cost of commuting from the farthest dwelling unit in use determines the economic rent on all other dwelling units.

To understand the effects of rent controls on allocation, we first consider the landlord's position and how rent controls affect the *capitalized value* of the property. The capitalized value is the current worth of the asset based upon the stream of benefits and costs it is expected to bear in the future. Any policy that reduces the returns on a durable asset (such as housing) will create windfall losses for the owner and reduce the capitalized value correspondingly. However, if the reductions are only economic rent, then the capitalized value of the assets in their current use remains greater than in any alternative use, and no allocative changes will result.

When economic rent has been a significant part of the returns to an asset that has changed ownership, the current owner makes no profit because the purchase price included the economic rent. Therefore, it may not be considered equitable to control old economic rent; the best time to consider controlling it is simultaneously with the event that causes it. This is reinforced by the administrative difficulties of determining the amount of old economic rent. Thus, in practice, most apartment rent control attempts only to control the increment to economic rent associated with some change such as a population surge (as in New York City) or property tax rebates to landlords (as in California and Massachusetts).

For rent control to avoid adverse supply consequences (reductions in housing supply), the capitalized value of the property must be kept greater in its rental use than in any other use. If condominium conversion is allowed, many landlords will be able to evade the controls by making the legal change. (For stable households with access to credit markets, ownership may be essentially equivalent to renting the same structure at competitive rates.) In other words, the building stays the same but the tenant becomes an owner. If there is an alternative use of the land that has greater capitalized value than the rent-controlled apartments, the landlord will convert to the more profitable use (e.g., using the existing building for professional offices or constructing a new condominium or even retail stores). Thus, rent control ordinances that allow only current building costs and maintenance expenses to be passed on to tenants will generally be insufficient to prevent the change to an alternate use in the long run.

The degree to which rent control reduces the capitalized value of the building depends not only on the base level and the allowed annual increases but also on how the market for apartment exchange is affected. Since rent control does not affect demand, potential tenants will eagerly seek the benefits of controlled apartments. This may lead to side payments to current tenants or the landlord or both, depending on particular specifications of the rent control ordinance and its enforcement. For example, rent control that is tenancy-specific (uncontrolled rates may be charged to fill a vacancy) will lead to rents almost the same as without controls: Tenants simply bid away their future control benefits in attempting to obtain the apartment. Legislation passed in 1995 in California requires that any rent control ordinances within the state be of this type, and the 1997 New York rent control revisions move substantially in this direction. If the controls apply to the rental unit regardless of tenant, the incomers may bribe the landlord and the current tenant to gain the occupancy right.

To the extent that the landlord receives them, the extra payments keep the capitalized value up but only by defeating the distributive purpose of the controls. The distributive purpose is also defeated by the extra costs tenants bear in terms of searching for controlled apartments (e.g., hiring rental agents). To the extent that extra benefits do accrue without dissipation to the tenant group, their distribution can be quite arbitrary (e.g., the side payments to the initial occupants). There is little in the control process to lead one to think that the benefits are spread evenly among tenants or are targeted particularly to deserving groups. An open question about rent controls, particularly the less restrictive "second-generation" policies, is whether they create benefits by reducing market imperfections that have been suggested in theory but have not yet been documented empirically.

The final section of the chapter looks briefly at another example of controlling economic rent: windfall profits taxes. Profits to a firm that are above those necessary to keep the firm in its current market are simply another form of economic rent. The recently privatized utilities in the United Kingdom had a windfall profits tax of over $8 billion imposed on them in 1997. The tax is a one-time assessment based on past rather than future economic activity and is thus unlikely to affect future behavior (unless firms believe that high future profits will lead to further windfall taxes). However, because the passage of this tax was threatened at the time of privatization, firms may have inefficiently shifted costs into the period of the tax base in order to reduce their expected tax payments.

We also discuss briefly the 1980 Crude Oil Windfall Profit Tax in the United States, in effect until its repeal in 1988. This tax was designed to coincide with the removal of very inefficient price controls on oil. The idea was to allow the price of oil to rise to its market level (and thus encourage efficiency gains through energy conservation as well as the use of alternative energy sources), but to prevent the large redistribution of income that would arise as windfall gains to domestic oil producers. New economic rent would arise if oil from wells being pumped and sold at the control prices were then to be sold at the much higher market prices. In theory this rent could be controlled without distorting the oil supply, but the legislation imposed the tax on new oil as well as old (thus discouraging new supplies) and made the tax on old oil temporary rather than permanent (encouraging stockpiling until phase-out). The poor incentives were made moot by the large decline in the market price of oil in 1986. Little revenue was collected after this and the tax was repealed.

Exercises

13-1 The State of California is having a miserable time with its failing effort to restructure its electricity industry. It required its utilities to sell off generating plants that used to provide electricity at close to their average costs. These same plants, now owned by out-of-state companies, are receiving prices that are many multiples higher than before restructuring. The following problem is a highly simplified exercise to help understand this situation: There are four generating plants, each capable of producing 1000 megawatts of power but with different short-run average costs. For simplicity we assume the short-run marginal cost (SRMC) is constant and equal to the short-run average cost for each plant up to its capacity and that these costs are $10, $20, $30, and $40 per megawatt-hour. At plant capacity, the SRMC becomes infinite (or, on a graph, vertical).

a If consumers had full information at the time of consumption, their daily demand for electricity (the "informed" demand curve) would be $Q = 4300 - 10P$. If the electricity is supplied in a daily competitive market (even though there are only four suppliers) with the above demand, what will the equilibrium price and quantity be?

b In the long-run, new plants can be added and can produce at a constant long-run marginal cost of $25 per megawatt-hour. What is the LR equilibrium price and quantity given the above demand? How much output does the plant with SRMC = $30 produce?

c Unfortunately very few consumers know the daily price, and therefore the daily "uninformed" demand curve is much more inelastic than the informed one. The uninformed demand curve is $Q = 4100 - P$. With supply conditions as in (a), what will the equilibrium price and quantity be? (Partial answer: $P = \$100$.) Draw a demand and supply diagram representing this situation, and shade the loss in consumer surplus owing to being uninformed (you do not have to calculate this amount).

d The generators in the answer to (c) are receiving an awful lot of quasi-rent, primarily owing to uninformed consumer purchases. Compare two possible policy responses in terms of equity and efficiency: (1) The Federal Energy Regulatory Commission imposes a regional price cap of $70 per megawatt-hour (i.e., the maximum that any generator can receive is $70 per megawatt-hour). (2) California imposes a "windfall profits tax" of 80 percent on any generator revenues in excess of its average cost per megawatt-hour.

13-2 An administrator of a city's apartment rent control bureau wishes to determine initial control prices that remove all economic rent. Two landlords come into the office to register. Both charge the same market rents, have the same mortgage payments, and have the same annual maintenance expenses. Does this imply that both should have the same control price? Explain.

13-3 This problem is an exercise involving rents, externalities, and information in land values: The scene of the exercise is Flat City. Now there are 100 homogeneous two-person families who live in rental homes spaced 1 mile apart along the one road leading into and out of the city. All the homes are identical except for two characteristics: their distances from the center and the amount of pollution that envelops them. Each day, one member of each family leaves home to work in the center and returns later that day. The other member stays at home. Workers are paid the competitive wage of $6 per hour in Flat City. Each worker drives the family car and travels at 2 miles per minute. Each car emits one pollutant per mile. The pollutant lingers for several hours, and it is unpleasant wherever it is emitted. Assume that the only commuting costs are the time values involved and that the only other real cost is from the pollution externality. (The houses are costless to build and are nondeteriorating.)

a If there were no pollution, what numerical pattern of rents would you expect to observe? Explain by assuming constant marginal values of travel time equal to the wage rate. (Also explain why the value of travel time might be related to wage.)

b Suppose there is constant marginal harm whenever a family member is exposed to a unit increase in the *average* daily pollution level shown below. The observed pattern of rents and pollution in Flat City is shown in Table 13E-1.

Explain the observed pattern of rents. Why is the rent on the first house zero and that on the 100th house $4.95? What would be the value of totally eliminating air pollution? Assume that each person going to the city center suffers only from the pollution there, at the same harm per unit of average daily pollution as those who stay in the residences.

Table 13E-1
Rents and Pollution in Flat City

	City	House 1	House 2	House 3	House 99	House 100
Round-trip time (minutes)		1	2	3	99	100
Average daily pollution level	100	100	99	98	2	1
Daily rent ($)		0.00	0.05	0.10	4.90	4.95

[Note: The sum of a series $1 + 2 + 3 + \ldots + n = (1 + n)(n)/2$] (Partial answer: Eliminating air pollution is worth $2257.50 per day.)

c Someone has suggested that automobiles be banned and a large nonpolluting bus be put on the road to pick up each commuter. The bus could travel at only half the speed of cars. Would the people of Flat City as a group regard that as an efficient change? Would any families be made worse off? (Partial answer: The change would be efficient.)

CHAPTER FOURTEEN
DISTRIBUTIONAL CONTROL WITH RATIONS AND VOUCHERS

IN CHAPTER 13 we examined the use of price controls as instruments to achieve redistributive goals in a competitive market. A weakness of those instruments, aside from the difficulty of avoiding adverse efficiency consequences, is the lack of control over the benefit distribution. In this chapter we consider additional methods (ration coupons and vouchers) that allow more explicit distributional control.[1] We compare the various methods as they might apply to the rationing of military service and gasoline during a shortage, with brief mention of applications to salmon fishing, parking, and electricity. The methods are relevant to many other contemporary problems such as pollution control, traffic congestion, surgical organ transplants, and water allocation. We continue to focus upon aspects that can be understood in the context of a perfectly competitive market (and delay until later chapters discussion of the use of these policy instruments in other contexts).

While this chapter builds up substantive knowledge about these new rationing instruments, we are also integrating the skills of analysis covered earlier into a problem-solving approach. The ability to design alternatives and evaluate their effects depends on understanding and applying the concepts we have already reviewed, for example, transactions and their costs, equilibrium, and the efficiency and equity criteria. We use each of these skills in our consideration of alternative strategies.

This chapter is organized in the following manner. First, we introduce the method of ration coupons as a policy instrument to achieve specific equity and consider how it affects market functioning. Then we discuss the use of an alternative instrument, vouchers, to achieve similar goals. These two instruments may be used together as a combined ration-voucher ticket, which we also discuss.

---

[1] This chapter owes much to the general discussion of the instruments provided in James Tobin, "On Limiting the Domain of Inequality," *Journal of Law and Economics, 13,* October 1970, pp. 263–277.

After the general discussion, we turn to the problems of rationing military service and then gasoline during a shortage. The military service example, in which we compare conscription systems with all-volunteer systems, highlights both how rationing systems affect opportunity costs and distributional effects. The gasoline rationing example illustrates a policy-analytic comparison of a variety of alternatives. We evaluate the price freeze method that was adopted after the OPEC embargo of 1973, a nontransferable ration coupon plan, transferable rations, and an excise tax plan with rebates or vouchers. We also discuss the political pressures on policy design and suggest why awareness of those pressures should influence the analytic work. A final section briefly illustrates other policy areas where understanding the analytics of alternative rationing methods is important to policy design.

Ration Coupons

Ration coupons are likely to be used when the good being allocated is in short and *inelastic* supply: water during a shortage, food during wartime, or parking in a congested city (e.g., required residential permits). The only way to ensure a minimum to some or all in these situations is to prevent consumers who would exercise greater purchasing power in the marketplace from doing so. **A ration coupon has this crucial feature: Its presentation is a necessary condition for receiving the good.** The government controls equity by the initial distribution of ration coupons to consumers. **The coupons may or may not be transferable among consumers.**

The word "coupon" should not be taken too literally. In some cases, actual coupons might be printed but in other cases an individual's use of a rationed amount may be known in other ways. A water meter, for example, can track water consumption of households and businesses, and thus establish if a customer stays within an allotted usage. Purchases of a rationed good may be tracked by a central computer system that "knows" if the purchaser is within allotted limits. In some parts of China the number of children per family is strictly limited. Because exceeding such a limit is normally visually apparent, this system has some abhorrent effects when families take extreme measures to comply or escape detection.[2] The feasibility and effectiveness of any rationing plan will depend upon the ease of its administration and enforcement, and that may depend upon the "coupon" design.

Generally, individuals will still have to pay a money price to receive the rationed good. *If the rationing is at all effective, the money price (with competitive supply of the good) will be lower than with no rationing.* Consider first the nontransferable case. The demand at any given price is lower because some consumers who are willing to pay will not have a coupon that allows them to enter a bid. For example, someone willing to buy eight units at a price of $2 per unit may only have coupons authorizing the purchase of five units; thus this

---

[2] These include the drowning of infant females in the hope that future offspring will be male, as well as pregnant women fleeing home and hiding in the wilderness to escape forced abortions. See Su Xiaokang and Yuan Xue, "The Humanitarian and Technical Dilemmas of Population Control in China," *Journal of International Affairs, 49,* No. 2, Winter 1996, pp. 343–347.

individual's demand at a $2 price drops from eight units (before rationing) to five units (when coupons are required for purchase).

Figure 14-1a illustrates an example of this. The effective demand curve shifts downward and to the left (from D to D_{NT}), with the exact nature of the shift a function of the total number of coupons Q_C and how they are distributed. As drawn, demand is reduced from Q_0 to Q_C, price is reduced from P_0 to P_R, and all the coupons are used.

Figure 14-1b is an example of some of the coupons going unused. In this case we do not reach the aggregate coupon limit Q_C along the ration demand curve D_{NT} until *after* D_{NT} crosses the supply curve. Price is still reduced ($P_{NT} < P_0$), and the equilibrium quantity Q_R is less than the total number of coupons issued. The unused coupons $Q_C - Q_R$ are owned by individuals whose marginal value of one more unit of the rationed good is less then P_{NT}.

Nontransferable ration coupons usually cause inefficiency in exchange: The rationed supplies are not allocated to the consumers willing to pay the most for them. Suppose $2 corresponds to P_0, and recall the individual who would buy eight units if allowed but who has coupons for only five units. Another individual with five coupons uses all five at the lower price P_R (say, $1) under rationing, but would only buy three units if the price were $2. If these two consumers were allowed to trade freely, there is room for a deal. The high demander could offer at least $2 each to buy three units from the low demander, and the low demander would agree to sell at least two of the units. Both are made better off and no one is worse off. The nontransferability of the coupons, however, makes this trade illegal. If, on the other hand, the coupons are *transferable,* the resulting allocation will be exchange-efficient. "High" consumers simply purchase the coupons from those willing to part with them. **The total price per unit for the rationed good with transferable coupons is the money price for the good plus the opportunity cost of using (rather than selling) the ration coupon.**

In Figure 14-1a the demand curve under transferable rationing D_T is shown as coincident with the ordinary demand curve until it becomes vertical at the aggregate coupon limit Q_C.[3] The money price of the good P_R is unaffected by the transfer option, but the total price of the good $P_R + P_C$ includes the coupon price P_C.[4] Note that this is similar to pricing with an excise tax. To make both demand and supply equal to Q_C, the price received by competitive suppliers must be precisely P_R and the price to demanders must be precisely $P_R + P_C$; the coupon price P_C plays the role of the tax rate.

In Figure 14-1b the effect of making the rations transferable is slightly different. There will no longer be any unused coupons, and the money price of the good rises from the nontransferable level P_{NT} to P_T, the price that makes supply just equal to Q_C. Thus, when the

---

[3] This ignores income effects. Actually, positive income effects arise in the aggregate from the receipt of the coupons: Less money income is spent on acquiring the rationed good up to the quantity of the individual's coupon allocation. Thus, the demand curve with transferable rations would actually lie slightly above the ordinary demand curve (until the coupon limit is reached).

[4] These examples assume that supply of the good is competitive. A monopolist supplying the rationed good could charge $P_R + P_C$ and get away with it. Since the coupons are fixed in supply, their price is determined by the difference between demand for the good and the supply price at the margin. The coupon price is P_C under competitive supply of the good and zero under monopolistic supply.

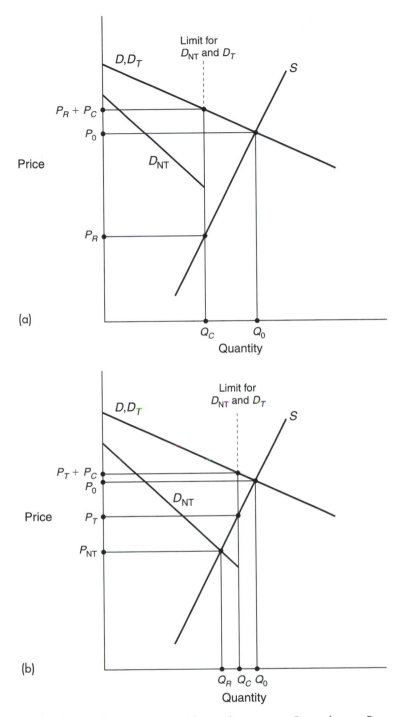

Figure 14-1. The effects of ration coupons (demand curves are D = ordinary, D_{NT} = with non-transferable coupons, D_T = with transferable coupons): (a) With binding constraint. (b) With nonbinding constraint.

coupon limit of the nontransferable solution is not binding (i.e., there are unused coupons), a switch to the transferable option causes increased consumption of the rationed good at a higher money price.

It is also important to note that the change in *individual* consumption caused by ration coupons (compared to no rationing) can be very substantial. This is true even when the coupons are transferable. Should our supply of oil imports suddenly be cut off, this could easily lead to a doubling of the U.S. gasoline price.[5] How might this affect a low-income family?

The pure income effect of the change may be great even if the pure price effect is highly inelastic. This is illustrated in Figure 14-2. The original budget constraint is B_0. After the price doubles, with no rationing and an unchanged budget level the family has constraint B_M and chooses to cut back substantially on gasoline; the dollars required for minimum food and shelter are unchanged. The total reduction in gasoline from Q_0 to Q_M includes both income and substitution effects.

Suppose we remove the income effect (approximately) in the following manner. Imagine a transferable rationing plan that gives this family a quantity of coupons equal to prior consumption. Let the real price of gasoline (which includes the market coupon price) that clears this market also be the doubled price, but let the money price of gasoline at the pump be the same as before the supply reduction. Then our family has constraint B_{TR}, parallel to B_M and through the point representing the original bundle (it is just affordable). As drawn, with constraint B_{TR} the family can and will consume quantities of goods that are almost the same as before, because its pure price elasticity is assumed low. Thus most of its gasoline cutback in response to a high price is due to income effects; a transferable rationing plan can mitigate these while maintaining the high price needed to reduce aggregate demand.

Another way to state this point is as follows: *If there were zero income effects from the transferable coupon distribution, each individual would have consumption identical with*

---

[5] The short-run (1-year) price elasticity of demand for gasoline is thought to be in the range of –0.2 to – 0.4. For example, Kayser estimates it at –0.23; see H. Kayser, "Gasoline Demand and Car Choice: Estimating Gasoline Demand Using Household Information," *Energy Economics, 22,* No. 3, June 2000, pp. 331–348. Using illustratively the rounder, more elastic figure –0.3 and assuming that the cutoff reduces gasoline supplies by 30 percent, we can make a back-of-the-envelope calculation follows:

$$\varepsilon = \frac{\Delta G/G}{\Delta P/P}$$

$$-0.3 = \frac{-.3}{\Delta P/P}$$

$$1 = \frac{P}{\Delta P}$$

Therefore,

$$\Delta P = P$$

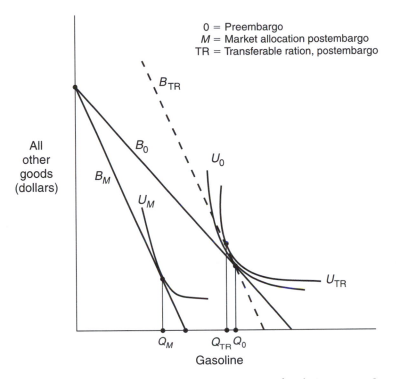

0 = Preembargo
M = Market allocation postembargo
TR = Transferable ration, postembargo

Figure 14-2. The effect of transferable rations on a low-income family (receiving Q_0 coupons).

that of the free-market solution. The only effect of the coupons would be pure income re-distribution. The actual change in individual consumption that occurs (compared with the free market) is due purely to the income effects on demand of the income redistribution. The change in an individual's income depends on the number of coupons received in the initial distribution and their value in the market. For a low-income family, the income ef-fects on demand can be substantial if the rationed good is a necessity.

Transferable rations have an administrative advantage when variation in individual consumption is permitted and is difficult to monitor. Not knowing which consumers will have high or low demand, administrators may issue too many nontransferable coupons in the aggregate and cause the rationed demand curve to cross the supply curve at a high price. With transferable coupons, however, one can simply issue the number of coupons equal to the available supply. The money price of the rationed good will always equal the supply price for that quantity.

To illustrate this advantage, first imagine rationing gasoline. This is a case in which con-sumers have diverse demands and administrators prefer a system that allows for the diver-sity. However, the administrators do not know which individual motorists (e.g., owners of all registered passenger vehicles) have high or low demands. Coupons are issued in equal amounts to all motorists, at least within broad categories. If they are nontransferable, the administrator must issue a high average share to enable those with high inelastic demands to obtain a reasonable portion. But this can cause effective demand to approximate ordinary demand, with the resulting high price.

Other goods may also be characterized by very diverse demands, but monitoring them may be easy. For example, residential heating oil or water use is metered and records of past consumption are available. It is much more feasible in these cases to issue nontransferable coupons as a fixed proportion (perhaps above some minimum) of past individual demand. There is still the exchange efficiency advantage of transferable rations, but it is not as severe as with gasoline because the initial distribution leaves individuals closer to their optimal quantities. Whether one uses the transferable option may depend upon the transaction costs of creating and operating the coupon market.

Finally, in some cases of rationing, the supply may be so scarce that diverse market demands must be ignored. If there is only just enough food or water for everyone to survive, the nontransferable rations will lead to the same outcome as transferable rations. (Presumably no one would sell his or her ration.) It might be better to ban transfers to protect against consumer ignorance. ("I sold them because I thought I could always get more.") The systems used to allocate heart and liver transplants to particular patients, based upon medical need, can be thought of as nontransferable coupon rationing.

As transferable rations are more efficient and often have administrative advantages, one might wonder about reasons other than strict scarcity why nontransferable rations are used. One reason is *external effects*.[6] For example special medical examinations (the rationed good) may be intended only for a population possibly exposed to an infectious disease (the "coupon" recipients), and not their hypochondriacal neighbors. That is, a voluntary exchange between the coupon recipient and the hypochondriac does not take into account the social interest in ensuring that the coupon recipient specifically is examined. As another example, in the British navy each sailor received one tot of grog that had to be consumed immediately. This was a strict way of precluding any transfers that might give rise to drunkenness (a negative externality).

A second reason for using nontransferable rations involves a judgment about *equity;* this could be considered a special case of external effects. In some situations, such as voting or jury duty or other civic rights and responsibilities, we might think that the equality or equal opportunity of their distributions specifically is what matters. In other words, even if one individual willingly wants to sell his or her vote to another (there is room for a deal between them), the rest of us would feel worse off (the externality) because of the greater inequality of distribution of the rationed good. In some cases, the problem of how to distribute coupons initially might cause an equity problem only if they are transferable: Visible coupon selling may lead to charges that government coupon distribution is arbitrary (i.e., not according to need) and provides undeserved and unearned windfall gains to the recipients.

A third reason is the significant transaction costs of coupon trading. A water company, we suggested above, may be able to monitor each metered user's consumption very easily to see whether it is within the ration allotment. However, the cost of keeping track of *traded* allotment rights may be prohibitive relative to the potential exchange benefits. A crucial

---

[6] These are the subject of Chapter 15, pp. 599–602, and Chapter 17.

part of a water-rationing policy analysis would be to try to design a simple, pragmatic method for accomplishing such transfers.

It should be mentioned that, while we have been focusing on rationing demand, ration coupons are also used to ration supply. In this case, we usually call the coupon a license (it is necessary to supply the service). The licensee may be required to meet certain qualifications, although the number of licenses issued is often below the number of qualified license seekers (e.g., permission to provide taxi service in many cities, permission to explore for oil or gas off of coastal areas, permission to sell alcoholic beverages). To the extent that the number of licenses issued is below the number of qualified license applicants, the rationing restricts supply and thus (for given demand) causes price to be higher than it would otherwise.[7]

The examples used suggest that one should not be myopic in terms of recognizing situations that are in effect coupon rationing. Similarly, one should be broad-minded about the market purchasing power that is being restrained by the coupons. For example, goods such as parking spaces in a company lot are normally allocated on a first-come, first-served principle. Special parking rights (coupons) may be issued to a privileged few, who can then arrive late and still be assured of a reserved and desirable space. One can imagine many methods of identifying the reserved spaces (e.g., painting them a special color, having a special entry) and the rights bearer (e.g., a special permit, the license plate). Again we see that the rationed exchange need not involve coupons literally. In this example, ordinary parking space consumers exercise purchasing power in the form of *time*. That is, one buys a better space by arriving early and paying the price of time wasted (or spent nonoptimally) before paid hours begin. The ration coupons alter the outcomes of the allocation-by-time process.

Recall that we have stated that, on the demand side, ration coupons are used when the supply is relatively inelastic. They cause a redistribution of the rationed good away from some consumers to those who receive the coupons. Because this lowers the money price, producers may not be getting the correct signals to expand supply. If the supply is elastic, then vouchers may be the more appropriate instrument.

Vouchers and Ration-Vouchers

A voucher is a grant that has value only for the purchase of a specific good; it is not necessary to have one in order to purchase the good. Again, the government controls equity through the initial distribution to consumers, and the vouchers may or may not be transferable among individuals. The effects of vouchers on individuals, depending on the rules for obtaining and using them, are simply the various grant effects that we have already analyzed in Chapters 4 and 5. They increase consumption of the good at least through a pure income effect and often through substitution effects or choice restrictions. Food stamps and Medicaid are examples of vouchers.

---

[7] Evaluating the social interest is not always clear when rationing supply. Indeed, many economists suspect that a good number of these cases are not in the public interest at all, but rather are an attempt by suppliers to create a form of monopoly power through the license requirement that restricts free entry.

An interesting proposal is to use vouchers for elementary and secondary education.[8] Under the current monopolistic system of public education, a minimum is provided but each child is a captive of the school to which he or she is assigned.[9] There do not appear to be particularly strong incentives to improve the quality of education, especially if diverse approaches are best suited for the diversity of students. If the state instead gave each child a voucher of a fixed dollar amount (or allowed the purchase of education stamps by family power-equalizing formulas analogous to the district power equalizing discussed in Chapter 5) and allowed the family to choose any licensed school it wished, this would create keener competition among schools and thus create incentives to improve quality.[10]

Another use of vouchers is in the form of housing allowances for low-income families. Such allowances have been the focus of major social experimentation at the national level.[11] One interesting part of these experiments was that the vouchers were made conditional upon the household living in units that met minimum quality standards. This constraint, if effective, would cause housing consumption to be different from a pure cash transfer of equivalent size. Analysis of the data suggests that the constraint had only a minor effect on housing: In Pittsburgh and Phoenix, housing expenditures under the constraint averaged 9 and

---

[8] See, for example Stephen D. Sugarman and Frank R. Kemerer, eds., *School Choice and Social Controversy: Politics, Policy and Law* (Washington, D.C.: The Brookings Institution, 1999), Paul E. Peterson and Bryan C. Hassel, eds., *Learning from School Choice* (Washington, D.C.: The Brookings Institution, 1998), and John F. Witte, *The Market Approach to Education: An Analysis of America's First Voucher Program* (Princeton, N.J.: Princeton University Press, 2000).

[9] One can escape only by expensive routes: private schools or residential relocation.

[10] Voucher proposals are controversial, and for good reason. In the first place, they may not work as intended because organized interest groups in the school systems will not let them; an early voucher experiment in Alum Rock, California, was not successful for that reason. Various interest groups within the organization (e.g., teachers, principals) were successful at preserving enough of their traditional powers to prevent some of the most important competitive mechanisms from working. For example, teachers insisted that there be no threat of firing under the voucher plan; this made it difficult for schools to improve their productive efficiency. See Elliott Levinson, *The Alum Rock Voucher Demonstration: Three Years of Implementation* (Santa Monica, Calif.: Rand Paper Series P-5631, April 1976).

Another argument against vouchers is that school officials and teachers are better motivated by their professional interests in child development. Under a system of financial incentives (and very limited ones, as high profits are unlikely to be tolerable politically), more attention may be paid to gimmicks that create the appearance of educational success by taking advantage of consumer ignorance and less attention to achieving real success. A still different argument is that public schools produce an important sense of community (local, state, and national), which would be absent in a voucher system.

There are interesting voucher experiments in Cleveland, Indianapolis, Milwaukee, New York, and San Antonio. Early research on these has not produced any consensus among analysts as yet. For contrasting views of the Milwaukee experiment, for example, see Witte, *The Market Approach to Education;* and Peterson and Hassel, *Learning from School Choice.* For a review of the European experience, see John S. Ambler, "Who Benefits from Educational Choice? Some Evidence from Europe," *Journal of Policy Analysis and Management, 13,* No. 2, Summer 1994, pp. 454–476.

[11] The experiments are reviewed in K. Bradbury and A. Downs, eds., *Do Housing Allowances Work?* (Washington, D.C.: The Brookings Institution, 1982). Housing allowances are used in a number of countries; see, for example, M. Steele, "Housing Allowances in the US under Section 8 and in other Countries: A Canadian Perspective," *Urban Studies, 38,* No. 1, January 2001, pp. 81–103.

27 cents, respectively, out of each subsidy dollar, compared with 6 and 9 cents out of each subsidy dollar with no constraint.[12] This suggests that the housing allowance in these programs worked primarily like income maintenance.[13]

The aggregate effect of adding vouchers to a particular market is to increase the equilibrium quantity and perhaps to increase the price. (If in a constant cost industry, no price increase will result.) We illustrate this in Figure 14-3, which contrasts the aggregate effects of nontransferable ration coupons R and vouchers V. Nontransferable ration coupons dampen demand (shown as D_R^{NT}) and vouchers enhance it. Transferable vouchers D_V^T compared to the same quantity of nontransferable vouchers D_R^{NT} result in a smaller increase in demand: They will be transferred until each person is affected only by a pure income effect, as in our earlier analysis of food stamps in Chapter 4.

It should be clear that when vouchers are used to ensure a minimum, the extra quantity of the good comes from expanding supply. When ration coupons are used, the intended additional consumption for some comes by taking the same good away from others. We argued in Chapter 5 that vouchers are more efficient when the supply is elastic. As Tobin points out, in that situation vouchers may be considered more equitable as well.

Consider the example of providing medical care to the poor when the long-run supply is elastic. If done by rationing, the effect will be, illustratively, to reduce the number of physicians who would become plastic surgeons in order to increase the number of general practitioners. But there are many other places from which the extra resources for general prac-

---

[12] See H. Aaron, "Policy Implications of the Housing Allowance Experiments: A Progress Report," in Bradbury and Downs, *Do Housing Allowances Work?*, pp. 67–112.

The figures above and those from other parts of the experiment led to a surprising but relatively unambiguous conclusion: The price and income elasticities of demand for these households are much lower (in absolute value) than had previously been thought. Based on earlier studies, it was thought that reasonable values for the price and income elasticities were −1 and 1, respectively. But according to the experimental data, the income elasticity is only 0.2 in the short run and 0.4 in the long run. Similarly, the price elasticity is only −0.2 in the short run and between −0.5 and −0.6 in the long run. Thus, neither price subsidies nor income subsidies should be expected to influence housing consumption greatly; they will be used primarily as rent relief. See E. Hanushek and J. Quigley, "Complex Public Subsidies and Complex Household Behavior: Consumption Aspects of Housing Allowances," in Bradbury and Downs, *Do Housing Allowances Work?*, pp. 185–246.

[13] Housing vouchers can also be considered as an alternative to rent control. From an efficiency perspective, this proposal probably has advantages on the exchange side: It does not reduce the apartment owner's legal entitlements to rental income as rent control does, and thus it does not set off the inefficient scramble among market participants to claim (or reclaim) the entitlements. However, housing vouchers may also create exchange inefficiencies such as the illegal markets for food stamps.

Whether vouchers have an advantage in terms of long-run housing supply effects depends on the method of financing them. For example, financing through a property tax (which may be likely on equity grounds) can induce a net reduction in the housing stock. This reduction could be greater or smaller than that caused by rent control; the latter depends on the degree of imperfection in administration.

The relative merits of the two proposals depend strongly on the equity objectives. If the objective is, for example, to target aid selectively to low-income families, housing vouchers given through an existing welfare agency may be a relatively easy way to ensure that the intended beneficiaries are the actual beneficiaries. If, however, the objective is to prevent tenants from paying and owners from receiving quasi-rents in the short run, then housing vouchers are probably counterproductive. (They increase demand, which raises price with a fixed short-run supply.)

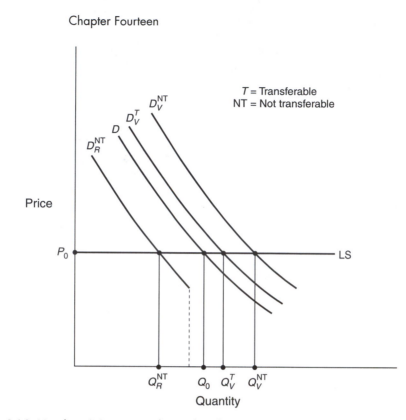

Figure 14-3. Vouchers (V) increase demand and ration coupons (R) reduce it.

tice can be drawn. Why should consumers who desire cosmetic surgery such as face-lifts and eye-tucks bear the main burden of supplying the poor, when the burden can be spread easily among the rich consumers of other things such as furs, yachts, and caviar?

Sometimes the two instruments may be used together, to form a *combined ration-voucher ticket.* This means that the ticket is necessary to obtain the good, and it also represents purchasing power. Depending on the number issued, their distribution, and the amount of purchasing power, the effect could be to move the equilibrium in any direction. This is because the ration element works to restrict demand, whereas the voucher element works to expand it.

Policy uses of the ration-voucher instrument are often associated with civic rights and responsibilities. The right to vote, for example, is a nontransferable ration-voucher distributed to each citizen 18 years of age and older. This ensures a perfectly equal distribution of voting rights and prohibits voluntary sales of votes for the good of the overall political process. As another example, we assign those of school age ration-vouchers that enable them to attend the public schools in their areas.

An interesting example of rationing a civic responsibility is jury duty. Demand for jurors is determined by the court system. In theory, court systems could announce a wage rate for jury service and see what supply results, but we normally do not allow such volunteers.

Instead, we pick at random from among the eligible citizens and require them to report for jury duty. Effectively, we are issuing a nontransferable ration coupon to those chosen (only those chosen can provide the service).

If there were no obligation to provide the service and those selected had to be enticed to serve, this system would cause the jury wage to be above that of the free market (because supply is restricted). However, *the obligation to serve is essentially a voucher in a negative amount (like a tax).* It *removes* purchasing power from the recipient, in an amount equal to the opportunity cost of the selectee's time while serving (less any remuneration for serving as a juror—usually a token amount). Thus jury service is provided by a nontransferable ration-voucher system.

A similar example mentioned by Tobin of the combined ration-voucher concerns military conscription. Let us work through an example of how this method compares to the all-volunteer system.

Rationing Military Service

In the United States today, all military service is provided voluntarily. In order to attract the 1.4 million active military personnel required to fulfill its defense plans, the wage (and other fringe benefits) must be sufficient to call forth this supply. In a number of other countries, military forces are provided by conscription. These systems are often the subject of great debate, and countries often change or revise them. Belgium and Holland, for example, recently ended conscription. As of a 1994 survey, thirty-five out of seventy-eight countries did not use conscripts, whereas forty-three did.[14]

Sometimes conscription takes the form of "universal" service whereby all eligible people participate (e.g., men in South Korea, China, the Netherlands, and Syria; men and unmarried women in Israel). In other cases, "selective" conscription is used. During the Vietnam War, for example, the United States used a lottery system to select a fraction of eligible men for conscription. It did the same thing during the Civil War, except that then the obligation was transferable: It was permissible for a selectee to pay another to take his place. Similarly, until recently Egypt and Jordan allowed conscripts to pay a fee in lieu of service.

Conscripting people to provide military service places a costly obligation or civic duty upon them (like jury duty). *Those conscripted have effectively received a ration coupon that is required to fulfill the draft obligation. Furthermore, the ration coupon is a voucher,* usually negative, as well. It requires the individual to provide labor for a given period, losing the earnings and leisure that he or she would have received if not conscripted (i.e., the opportunity cost) while receiving the (typically meager) pay provided to draftees. *The net voucher amount—opportunity cost less military pay—can differ vastly across the conscripts.*

---

[14] Thomas W. Ross, "Raising an Army: A Positive Theory of Military Recruitment," *Journal of Law and Economics, 37,* April 1994, pp. 109–131.

The Utility Value of Work

Let us clarify this divergence in individuals' opportunity costs of serving. Labor typically provides monetary income (in return for the goods and services produced).[15] But labor also typically provides "psychic" income or direct utility (e.g., pleasure from doing a job well). Some people may receive substantial psychic income from their jobs, whereas others receive more modest amounts and still others find that work directly reduces their utility. So the attractiveness of any employment opportunity depends on the *sum* of the monetary plus the psychic compensation (the latter may be positive or negative).

The same job can provide vastly different psychic incomes to individuals because of differing preferences. Military service is a high honor to some, and it may be a high enough honor to induce some to volunteer "for free" (even if it means forgoing substantial monetary income from nonmilitary employment). To others military service may be a distasteful, hazardous job, and it may be distasteful enough to prevent some from volunteering no matter how high the wage (even if little is forgone from the best nonmilitary alternative).

For any given distribution of preferences in the population, it is still normal for the aggregate supply curve of labor to a particular occupation (such as the military) to be upward-sloping: higher monetary pay (which includes the value of any benefits such as food or housing provisions) will attract a larger supply. The height of the supply curve at any quantity is sometimes called the *"reservation wage"*—the monetary pay necessary to just induce the marginal unit to participate in this market. It is the amount of money necessary to just compensate the individual for forgoing the next best alternative, and thus is the social opportunity cost. The individual considers the monetary pay of the alternative and the psychic factors of both jobs in determining a reservation wage. We can clarify it with the aid of an informal but transparent mathematical equation.

For a particular individual, let us refer to the value of monetary pay for any job as Y^W and the value of the job's psychic income (the dollar value of direct utility) as Y^U, so that the full value is $Y^W + Y^U$. Then if we are considering the value of the military job (M) relative to its next best alternative (A), we can ask if the benefits (the full value of M) exceed the costs (the full value of A):

$$Y_M^W + Y_M^U > Y_A^W + Y_A^U$$

Since neither psychic component is observable, we do not know what these are for individuals. What we are able to *observe* in the marketplace is the same equation with Y_M^U subtracted from both sides:

$$Y_M^W > Y_A^W + (Y_A^U - Y_M^U)$$

The left-hand side is the monetary military pay for a unit of labor (e.g., yearly pay). The right-hand side of this equation is the height of the observed supply curve (wherever this individual is positioned on it)—what we have called the reservation wage—and it is ob-

---

[15] Most commonly this is current income, but labor can also provide expected future income when its purpose is to earn a promotion or to train and learn a new job skill.

servable even if its individual psychic components are not.[16] The difference between the left- and right-hand sides of either equation is the same and equal to the individual's net benefits from M relative to A. The second equation simply uses a slightly different accounting convention from the first: In the second, any psychic income from M is counted not as a positive benefit but as a negative cost.[17]

Suppose, for example, Mark is indifferent to serving in the military for $10,000 (his reservation wage) and working in his best nonmilitary alternative for $50,000. This implies that Mark would lose $40,000 in psychic income if working in the nonmilitary alternative. Mark could be someone who thinks military service is a high honor; he could as well be someone who finds it distasteful but whose best nonmilitary alternative is extremely distasteful. We do not know the details of his tastes, but we do know the social cost. What is the social cost of his military service? Two things are given up by it. First, society gives up the $50,000 that is Mark's value to the employer in the alternate use. But second, it also avoids Mark's loss of $40,000 in psychic income. So the net opportunity cost is $50,000 − $40,000 = $10,000.

Recognizing the utility value of work is a key to understanding why wages may differ across jobs that have the same value to employers (i.e., the same demand for labor) and require the same skills. If one job of necessity takes place in an "unpleasant" or "hazardous" environment relative to the other (as judged by most workers), the supply curve of labor to the unpleasant or hazardous job will be higher by the amount each laborer values the negative psychic income—and thus the equilibrium wage will be higher than the other job. This wage difference is called a "compensating wage differential" precisely because it compensates the workers for choosing to work in the poorer environment.

Conscription versus the All-Volunteer Military

Now we wish to consider conscription versus the all-volunteer method of providing military service and show an interesting tension between political and economic costs. There are, of course, reasons other than cost for preferring one or the other system. For example, some people feel (and perhaps more so in wartime) that military service is a civic

---

[16] The reservation wage can also be defined by reference to the individual's utility function. Imagine that the utility of this individual in his best nonmilitary alternative (A) is $U(X_A, Y_A)$, where X_A represents the nonmonetary characteristics of labor in A and Y_A is monetary pay of A (think of it as the annual wage, or income). Thus the utility function measures both the direct, psychic rewards from labor in A as well as the indirect rewards from spending on all other goods and services. Then the reservation wage Y_R necessary to compensate this individual for serving in the military is the amount that just makes this equation hold: $U(X_A, Y_A) = U(X_M, Y_R)$, where X_M represents the nonmonetary characteristics of labor in the military. If the left-hand side is held constant, an individual who gets positive utility from military service ($\partial U/\partial X_M > 0$) will have a lower reservation wage than one who finds it distasteful ($\partial U/\partial X_M < 0$).

[17] Note that the accounting convention distinction is independent of our earlier observation that the psychic income itself may be either positive or negative. For cases where negative psychic income is more prevalent, it might seem more natural to account for it on the "cost" (right-hand) side rather than the "benefit" (left-hand) side of the equation.

obligation that all appropriate citizens ought to share equally.[18] It is interesting that in the selective (rather than universal) case, one would have to ban all volunteers to truly make each eligible have the same probability of serving. Otherwise, those with low opportunity costs (primarily those with poor alternative economic opportunities) would be much more likely to serve.

But there are also important political and economic cost aspects to the choice of a system. Because conscripts are *obligated* to serve, their pay can be and usually is set at quite low levels. Politically, this is attractive because it keeps the *budgetary costs* to the government low (relative to a volunteer force of equal size) and minimizes demands made upon taxpayers. However, the *social costs* of the labor go in the opposite direction: The conscripted force has greater opportunity cost than the volunteer force.

In Figure 14-4, we have drawn a simple linear supply curve of volunteers, chosen to have an elasticity of 1.[19] The eligible population is assumed to be 800,000 in number, of which 200,000 are needed for service. If 200,000 recruits must be induced to volunteer, the annual wage must be set at $20,000. The social cost of this service is shown as the shaded area under the supply curve (the sum of the first 200,000 "heights" or reservation wages), equal to $2 billion. By the nature of a voluntary supply curve, this is the labor with the minimum opportunity cost for the given quantity. The budgetary cost of meeting the payroll is greater—$4 billion.

Suppose instead that the 200,000 recruits were conscripted by fair lottery from among the 800,000 eligibles (with no volunteering allowed). This implies that the social cost of each conscript is also a random draw from the 800,000 eligibles comprising the supply curve. That is, it is equally likely that we conscript the 800,000th person (who has a social cost of $80,000), the 200,000th person (who has a social cost of $20,000) or the first person (who has a social cost of zero). The expected social cost for each eligible is 0.25 times his social cost if chosen, and in the aggregate it is 0.25 times the sum of all 800,000 individual social costs.[20] But this is simply 0.25 times the triangular area under the supply curve up to 800,000:

$$\text{Expected social cost} = (0.25)(0.5)(800{,}000)(\$80{,}000) = \$8 \text{ billion}$$

[18] The term "appropriate" begs the question of which persons should be subject to conscription. In the terminology introduced in Chapter 5, there are typically "exceptional characteristics" that cause some individuals to be treated differently than others. Many countries only conscript those within a certain age range such as 18–35. Most countries conscript only men. Virtually all countries grant exemptions to people with certain disabilities or medical conditions.

[19] Estimates of the elasticity of supply to the U.S. military range from 0.5 to 1.8 according to a study that summarizes them. See J. Warner and B. Asch, "The Economics of Military Manpower," in K. Hartley and T. Sandler, eds., *Handbook of Defense Economics* (New York: North-Holland Publishing Company, 1995). These estimates are best interpreted for the supply of volunteers over quantity ranges that we have actually experienced. However, they are unlikely to apply over the full quantity range including all potential conscripts, some of whom would surely be almost perfectly inelastic (i.e., would not volunteer even at very high salaries). Our assumption for simplicity of constant elasticity equal to 1, roughly the midrange of the available estimates, undoubtedly underestimates the opportunity costs at the right-hand tail of the full supply curve.

[20] This ignores the pure risk cost of the uncertainty that the lottery system introduces to the eligibles.

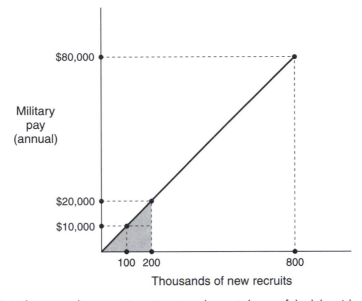

Figure 14-4. Voluntary military service minimizes the social cost of the labor (shaded).

Thus the social cost of the conscripts is four times greater than the social cost of the volunteers. What about the budgetary costs? Since the supply in no way depends on the wage set for the conscripted recruits, the wage could be set anywhere. There is no need to pay $20,000 as was necessary to induce the volunteers. Let us somewhat arbitrarily assume that the budgeted wage is $10,000 per conscript, so that the total budgetary cost is $2 billion (substantially less than for the volunteers).[21]

This is a case in which there appears to be a substantial conflict between efficiency and the equity goal (and the associated political expediency) of using conscripts.[22] What would happen if we used the lottery system but made the obligations transferable as in the Civil War? We wish to illustrate how a market for transferable coupons would work. We assume

[21] As an exercise, show that the social cost would drop to $5 billion if volunteers were allowed and a lottery used to choose the residual.

[22] One interesting caveat to this comparison is that we have not included any deadweight losses caused by the taxation necessary to pay the forces under either system. Because the voluntary system has higher pay, it will cause more deadweight loss from taxation. In the example, $2 billion more revenue is needed under the voluntary system. The extra deadweight loss caused by taxation of this size is likely to be within the range of $400–$600 million, according to estimates reviewed in Chapter 12. So accounting for this would not affect the thrust of the example, which is to illustrate the high social cost of using conscripts relative to volunteers. The importance of taxation to this calculation was first pointed out in D. Lee and R. McKenzie, "Reexamination of the Relative Efficiency of the Draft and the All-Volunteer Army," *Southern Economic Journal, 58,* No. 3, January 1992, pp. 644–654. They also point out that the tax distortions become more important in the calculation as the force size approaches that of the eligible population. An article by J. Warner and B. Asch, "The Economic Theory of a Military Draft Reconsidered," *Defence and Peace Economics, 7,* No. 4, 1996, pp. 297–312, extends this analysis to include productivity factors as well.

that this market, which will be characterized by a large number of buyers and sellers each representing an atomistic share of the aggregate, can be well approximated by the competitive, price-taking assumptions.

In Figure 14-5a, we divide the supply of recruits into three groups: Group 1 contains the 100,000 who would volunteer at the military pay of $10,000; group 2 contains the next 100,000, who would not volunteer at $10,000 but would serve at the $20,000 pay of the all-volunteer force; and group 3 contains the remaining 600,000 eligibles, who would not volunteer at $20,000. With a fair lottery giving each eligible a 0.25 chance of being chosen, we assume that 25,000 people are conscripted from group 1; 25,000 from group 2; and 150,000 from group 3.

Let us consider the willingness to pay of the conscripts to have others take their places (in other words, transfer the "coupon" that obligates them to serve to someone else). This will enable us to construct their demand curve for substitutes. To keep the example simple, we assume away income effects. This implies that the reservation wage of each individual (as represented in the supply curve of Figure 14-5a) is not affected by conscription. Each conscript is willing to pay the difference between his reservation wage and the military wage to avoid service. A simple example would be of an individual with no psychic income from either the military or his alternative. If the alternative pays $40,000, then he would be willing to pay up to $30,000 to persuade another to take his "coupon" and thus avoid serving for only $10,000 military pay.[23]

Those willing to pay the most to avoid serving are, of course, the conscripts with the highest opportunity costs: the 150,000 randomly chosen from group 3. Within this group, the maximum willingness to pay a substitute would be from the conscript closest to the right end of the supply curve, approximately $70,000 (= $80,000 opportunity cost − $10,000 military pay). It then declines linearly until it reaches the minimum. The minimum willingness to pay is from the conscript closest to the left end of group 3's supply, approximately $10,000 (= $20,000 opportunity cost − $10,000 military pay). We draw this on Figure 14-5b as the first 150,000 demands of conscripts for substitutes.

Following the same logic for the 25,000 conscripts from group 2, we see that the maximum willingness to pay for this group is approximately $10,000 and it declines linearly to a minimum of zero (at the left end of group 2's supply in Figure 14-5a, the opportunity cost of $10,000 just equals the military pay). We add these 25,000 demands for substitutes to our demand curve on Figure 14-5a. There are no other demands for substitutes, since no draftee in group 1 is willing to pay anything to avoid serving (they all prefer to serve and receive the $10,000 military wage, that is, to use the "coupons" themselves).

What is the supply curve of substitutes (people who will agree to accept a "coupon" and serve in the draftee's place) from among the 600,000 nondraftees? The most easily enticed would be the 75,000 from group 1 (the group with the lowest opportunity cost). In fact, all of these people are willing to serve for no more than the $10,000 military wage. That is, all of these people would agree to take a "coupon" from a draftee even if no draftee offered any

---

[23] If he had to pay $31,000, then he would end up with only $9000 and he would be better off serving in the military for $10,000.

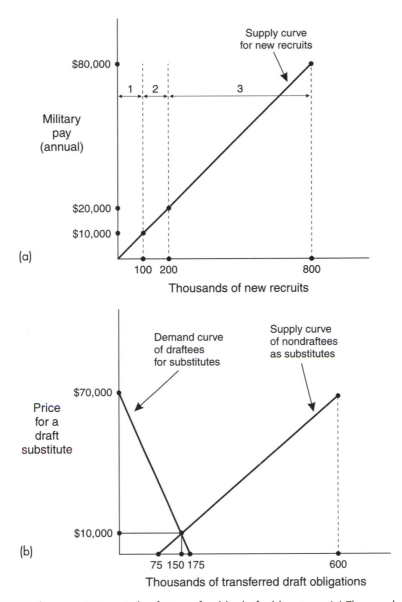

Figure 14-5. The competitive market for transferable draft obligations: (a) The supply curve of recruits from eligibles with low (group 1), medium (group 2), and high (group 3) opportunity costs. (b) The demand for substitutes and the supply of substitutes to fulfill draft obligations.

payment to them at all. So in Figure 14-5b the first segment of our supply curve of substitutes coincides with the quantity axis from zero to 75,000.

Consider next the 75,000 nondraftees from group 2. The least payment would be required by the individual with opportunity cost at the left-most end of this group's supply in Figure 14-5a. Since this opportunity cost is approximately $10,000, the military pay of $10,000 is just sufficient to cover it, and further payment from a draftee is not necessary. However, the opportunity costs increase linearly as we move to the right within this group, and the military pay by itself is no longer sufficient incentive to induce them to serve. A nondraftee at the right end with a $20,000 opportunity cost would require a $10,000 payment from a draftee before agreeing to serve for only $10,000 in military pay. So the second segment of our supply curve of substitutes in Figure 14-5b begins at price of zero and quantity 75,000 and rises linearly to a price of $10,000 and a quantity of 150,000. The final segment, from the 450,000 nondraftees in group 3, rises linearly from this last point until its end at a price of $70,000 and a quantity of 600,000 (the individual with the highest opportunity cost of approximately $80,000 would require $70,000 to take a conscript's place and receive only $10,000 in military pay).

As is now transparent from Figure 14-5b, the "coupon" equilibrium where supply equals demand is at a coupon price of $10,000 and a quantity of transfers equal to 150,000. Every draftee from group 3 pays this amount to every nondraftee from groups 1 and 2 to serve as a substitute. All 200,000 "coupons" (draft obligations) end up being held by the 200,000 eligibles in groups 1 and 2; the 25,000 in each group that receive them initially keep them, and the other 75,000 in each agree to be substitutes for the draftees in group 3. In equilibrium, there is no inefficiency from labor misallocation, and the voluntary transfers remove all the situations where there was "room for a deal." With the further assumption of no income effects, exactly the same people end up serving as with the all-volunteer method.

One of the subtler but most important points to understand is that all eligibles, whether or not they are conscripted, face the same price of $20,000 as an inducement to serve. The total inducement is the sum of the military wage plus the reward for holding the coupon that requires its owner to serve. For all eligibles, the military wage is $10,000. The tricky point to see is that for all eligibles, the coupon-holding reward is $10,000. This latter reward is received in one of two quite different ways, depending on whether or not an eligible individual is a draftee.

The draftee is the initial holder of the coupon (the obligation to serve) and must pay $10,000 out-of-pocket to induce another to take it. A reward for serving is that the draftee avoids paying this fee. The nondraftee's reward, on the other hand, is to receive a $10,000 positive payment for becoming a coupon holder (and serving as a substitute). Both receive rewards of $10,000 for holding on to a coupon, and thus the total inducement to each for serving is $20,000. This illustrates the earlier general statement about rationing with transferable coupons: The total price for a rationed good is its ordinary money price (the $10,000 military wage) plus the coupon price (the $10,000 that the draftee who serves avoids paying, or that the substitute who serves receives from a draftee).

It is the response to this $20,000 price that explains why all of group 2 ends up serving, whether or not they are drafted. Those drafted prefer to serve rather than paying the $10,000 necessary to get a substitute and missing the $10,000 in military pay. Those not drafted prefer to become substitutes rather than forgoing receipt of $10,000 from a draftee and $10,000 in military pay. But the income that each ends up with is, of course, quite different.

Consider the income distributional effects of the transferable ration plan, compared with the all-volunteer method. Congress and taxpayers get off easily—paying only half of the all-volunteer budget. The substitutes serving receive exactly the same pay as they would under the all-volunteer method. With Congress only paying half, the other half comes from those who have chosen to transfer their obligation to serve. Under the all-volunteer method, those who opt out pay nothing. Perhaps on equity grounds, the transferable lottery has some merit to it. On the other hand, there is considerable merit in having Congress face the social cost of using labor in the military, so that it will be discouraged from using too much of it.

There are other important income distributional effects. In particular, all conscripts (whether or not they opt out) are $10,000 poorer than under the all-volunteer system.[24] We have already mentioned that the conscripts who do opt out pay their substitutes $10,000 each, a charge that they would not bear under the all-volunteer system. Furthermore, the conscripts that choose to serve only receive military pay of $10,000 (rather than the $20,000 under the all-volunteer method). We show this comparison in Table 14-1.

The burden of the transferable lottery system that we have been discussing falls by far most heavily on those who are drafted. However, presumably their civic obligation to provide this service is no greater or smaller than those who are eligible but unpicked. Is it possible to design a lottery system that would burden all of the eligibles equally, whether or not they actually provide service?

Control of the definition of the coupon as well as its distribution gives policy designers important tools for placing the relative burdens. Suppose that the lottery coupon was transferable only before the drawing. That is, people could buy out of the lottery before the numbers are chosen, but not after. One would immediately encounter the problem that some multiple coupon holders might be picked more than once and could not simultaneously fulfill multiple obligations to serve. We solve this by requiring multiple coupon holders to exchange their independent draws for one draw at the sum of the individual coupon probabilities. If one coupon represents a 0.25 chance of serving, then two coupons mean the individual has a 0.50 chance of serving, and four coupons guarantee serving and are the maximum that one individual can hold.[25] How would this system work?

Using simplifying assumptions (of no income effects and risk-neutrality) with the same supply curve as before, we can quickly identify a trading equilibrium. From the government's point of view, the end result will still be 200,000 conscripts obligated to serve at any military wage it sets (which we will keep at $10,000). The equilibrium coupon allocation would be essentially the same as before: Groups 1 and 2 would now hold all 800,000 coupons, four per person, guaranteeing that each of them serve (and thus no lottery would actually be necessary). Group 3 would rid themselves of all 600,000 coupons. The equilibrium coupon price would be $2500.

---

[24] All eligibles face the uncertainty of the lottery before the conscripts are chosen, and at this stage the expected income for each is (0.25)($10,000) = $2500 less than under the all-volunteer system.

[25] Administratively, think of each coupon as bearing the social security number of the initial recipient. A buyer signs the back of the form, providing his or her social security number and certifying eligibility, which the seller submits to the government. The government then increases the probability by 0.25 of drawing the buyer's social security number and reduces to zero the probability of drawing the seller's. Any buyer who provides false certification could be subject to criminal penalties.

Table 14-1

All Individuals Forgo $20,000 if They Choose Not to Serve, but the Draftees Are Poorer by $10,000

	Individual income	
	Serve	**Do not serve**[a]
Drafted	$10,000	$(Y_A - 10,000)$
Not drafted	$20,000	Y_A
All-volunteer	$20,000	Y_A

[a]Y_A is the individual's income in the best nonmilitary alternative.

Rather than the draftees in group 3 bearing all of the buyout burden as before, this is now shared equally by all members of group 3. Furthermore, all members within groups 1 and 2 are treated alike (there is no categorization into draftees and substitutes). Finally, each eligible in the entire population has $2500 less income than under the all-volunteer plan, so in that sense they are sharing the burden equally.

Income Effects of Rationing Methods[s]

How does the assumption of no income effects bear on this example? It does not affect the general point that the social costs of conscripted labor are greater than the opportunity costs of the all-volunteer method. Nor does it affect the conclusion that transferable rationing, like the all-volunteer method, leads to an efficient supply of military labor. But it does affect the conclusion that the same people end up serving under the transferable rationing and all-volunteer methods.

Keep in mind that income effects have to do with individual propensities, rooted in their preferences, to purchase various goods and services as their income levels vary. The income variation we are discussing is that caused by the initial distribution of the transferable coupons. If the value of these coupons is only a tiny fraction of an individual's income, then we would not expect significant income effects at all. But in our example, the $10,000 value of the coupon means that its receipt causes quite significant income changes. (Note that in this case the government's setting of the military wage has a big influence on the coupon value, since the sum of the two must equal the market-clearing wage.) So it is reasonable to consider whether such changes could cause individuals to change their decisions about military service.

Even when a job is simply a source of money income, income effects will apply to the labor-leisure choice of how much to work. The best nonmilitary alternative to a draftee who would have to buy out is not necessarily the same as the best nonmilitary alternative for that individual if not drafted. Paying the buyout fee makes the draftee poorer. If leisure is a normal good, the draftee will want to work longer hours (i.e., reduce leisure) than if not drafted and facing the same nonmilitary job choices. Thus the reservation wage if drafted is not necessarily the same as if not drafted, and there will be some individuals for whom military service will be the best choice under one circumstance (e.g., if drafted) but not under the other (e.g., if not drafted).

Additionally, income effects bear on the psychic components of job pay. For a given job that has, say, pleasurable characteristics for an individual, that individual's willingness to pay for them (the Y^U variable in our equations) depends on his or her monetary wealth level. Suppose you consider a pleasurable job with $17,000 money pay equivalent to $20,000 in cash (i.e., you value the pleasure at $3000). If the same job pays only $7000 but its other characteristics are unchanged, you may now consider it equivalent to only $9000 (rather than $10,000) in cash. That is, your reduced monetary income affects your willingness to pay for these pleasurable characteristics (as well as all other goods), and if these characteristics are normal economic goods, then your willingness to pay for them is less (in the example, $2000 rather than $3000).

How does this bear on the comparison between the transferable draft and all-volunteer methods? Draftees are made poorer than nondraftees by the coupon price no matter which job they choose (in the volunteer system, all individuals are nondraftees). Thus their willingness to pay for pleasurable job characteristics, as well as to avoid unpleasurable job characteristics, may be affected. However, a switch in preferred job owing to these income effects would only occur when there is a strong impact on one job that is not matched by a similar impact on the other. In most cases (those where the psychic factors are normal goods), being drafted reduces the relative value of the job with the greater psychic effects. Interestingly, the income effects of being drafted will make one group of people more likely to serve, but another group less likely.

People that are more likely to serve if drafted than if not are those with meager pay in the nonmilitary alternative and a relative distaste for military service.[26] These people do not offer to serve if they can provide for necessities with their nonmilitary incomes.[27] But if conscripted, they find that paying for a substitute goes beyond their means. That is, as long as they can provide for their necessities, they may be willing to sacrifice considerable income in order to avoid military service. Being drafted puts them in a position where they will not have enough for necessities even if they can scrape up the money for a substitute.[28]

Conversely, the people who are less likely to serve if drafted than if not are those who enjoy military service (relatively) but have a somewhat better-paying alternative. If not drafted, these people place a high enough value on the psychic benefits of military service to volunteer. But being drafted means they will have $10,000 less money income no

[26] By relative distaste, we mean that the psychic effects of military service are more negative or less positive than those of the nonmilitary alternative.

[27] If the nonmilitary alternative is insufficient to provide for necessities, then military service that does will be preferable to most, even if distasteful.

[28] There is another caveat to this that has nothing to do with income effects. Many people may not have the cash in hand to pay for a substitute, even if they have the earning power to pay for it over time. In most circumstances they will be able to borrow the money and repay it, but imperfect markets for lending could cause some to serve when it is inefficient for them to do so. We discuss these important markets in detail in another chapter.

matter what they decide, and they may feel that the extra money from the nonmilitary alternative now outweighs the psychic benefits of military service.

In sum, the income effects of a transferable rationing system can cause some draftees to make different decisions about serving than they would under an all-volunteer system (or if not drafted). In cases where the coupon or buyout price is itself only a small fraction of income, we would expect these effects to be minimal. As the value of the coupon increases relative to income, income effects will become more pronounced. However, these effects do not all go in the same direction. Generally, we would expect draftees with relative distaste for the military to be more likely to serve than if not drafted, and draftees with relative preference for military service to be less likely to serve.

Rationing Gasoline during a Shortage

Let us turn now to a discussion of gasoline rationing in response to a sudden and large reduction in the short-run supply. This type of reduction actually occurred in October 1973, when OPEC ordered an oil embargo, and for approximately 10 years thereafter Congress mandated the president to have a rationing plan prepared. The purpose of this discussion is to illustrate the effect of alternative responses to one situation. We begin with a summary of the criteria. Then we present alternative strategies, including our actual policy response at the time, and analyze them with respect to the criteria.

It is helpful to specify criteria for evaluating the options. *It is useful to decompose efficiency into five mutually exclusive and together exhaustive categories: exchange, production, product mix, market transaction costs, and administrative transaction costs.* Among the three usual components of allocative efficiency, we emphasize exchange (i.e., goods are allocated to those most willing to pay for them) with some attention to product mix. We ignore production efficiency only because none of the alternatives discussed causes any deviation from least-cost production. Product mix efficiency (i.e., an additional unit of gasoline is valued by consumers at its marginal cost) is treated as less important than exchange because the inelasticity of the short-run supply allows for only small product-mix changes.

The two transaction cost categories capture other resource allocations that do not fit easily into the three usual ones. **Market transaction costs are costs to the agents in a market that are not included in price** (e.g., the time waiting in line to buy gasoline and the convenience of the selling hours). Efficient market transaction costs are those that cannot be lower and still be as effective in terms of the other criteria. Very long waiting times in lines or severely restricted selling hours would be inefficient if the same equity and allocative efficiencies could be achieved without them. **Administrative transaction costs refer to the government costs of administering and enforcing the policy** (e.g., printing and distributing coupons and enforcing coupon use). Efficient administrative costs are also those that cannot be lower and still be as effective in terms of the other criteria.

Equity concerns involve both the distribution of gasoline and the "after gas" incomes of individuals. Since Congress actually mandated the president to prepare a rationing plan, we make the presumption that quasi-rents should not accrue primarily to suppliers through high prices. A succinct but somewhat flexible way to summarize equity concerns that incorporate this aspect might be as follows: Each individual should be able to purchase a minimum share of gasoline at a price approximately equal to long-run rather than short-run marginal cost (i.e., eliminate quasi-rents to suppliers).

The flexibility comes in defining the ideal minimum share. One possibility, more likely in the event of a severe shortage, is to define the minimum as the same for all. An alternative definition of each person's minimum is some fixed proportion of past use. Mixtures of the two are possible. For example, the first 25 percent of supply could be allocated as an equal "lifeline" share to everyone and the rest allocated in proportion to past use. Or the federal government could allot shares to the states in proportion to past use and let the states make their own decisions about intrastate allocation (and some might choose equality).

There are many other equity issues that we do not treat here but that would be dealt with in a fuller analysis. One is the definition of the potential recipients: registered motor vehicles, licensed drivers, or some other category. Should two-car families receive twice the share of a one-car family, for example? Another concerns exceptional characteristics: The vehicle is, for example, an ambulance, police car, or fire truck. Although these are important issues, for the sake of brevity we restrict our attention to the capability of a proposed plan to meet the broader equity standard delineated above.

Another two criteria might be thought of as implementation considerations. One is the speed with which a plan can be put into effect. If it would take a year to print and distribute coupons, that would be a serious disadvantage. A second is the certainty that the plan will work at some tolerable or satisficing level. We take this to mean that we have the knowledge to set parameters so that the outcome is reasonably equitable and efficient: For example, if coupons are issued, we are reasonably certain about the number that will restrain demand to a quantity that approximates the available supply at a money price near the supply price. This keeps us from choosing an alternative that in theory could work beautifully but that, to implement, requires empirical knowledge that is not available.

Comments relevant to other important criteria such as political and organizational feasibility will occasionally be offered. These sparse thoughts should not be taken as a substitute for the more careful attention such criteria deserve in a full analysis. Let us now turn to the discussion of alternatives.

The initial U.S. response to the shock of the embargo was *to freeze the price of gasoline.* That is illustrated in Figure 14-6. The domestic supply curve of oil is assumed to be elastic at low quantities, but it becomes very inelastic past the point of current domestic production. The preembargo equilibrium is at price P_0 and quantity Q_0. After the embargo, the price freeze is announced. Demand remains at Q_0, but the available supply falls to Q_F; thus consumers perceive a shortage.

Long lines developed at gasoline stations, and the available supply was rationed primarily through time. Those gasoline consumers who valued their time the least had an advantage. For others, much of any potential consumer surplus (above the money price) was used up in waiting. Various regulations were passed in order to assert some priorities other than time. For example, weekend hours of service stations were severely restricted in order to reduce "unnecessary" pleasure driving. Also, a 10-gallon limit was placed on each purchase in order to increase the probability that everyone would get a minimum. These regulations

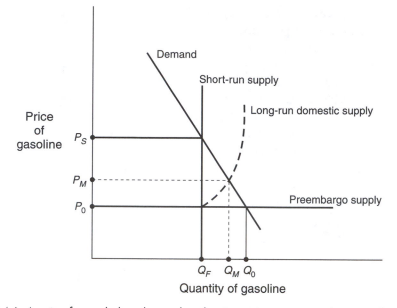

Figure 14-6. A price freeze below the market clearing price creates a shortage $Q_F - Q_0$.

imposed social costs because they reduced the flexibility of purchasing that consumers valued: For example, not only did the consumers have to wait, but for some it was more expensive (in terms of the opportunity cost of time) to wait during the week rather than on a weekend. Those with a willingness to pay that was high in cash but low in time would hire people to buy gas for them and thus partially evade the time-rationing system.

We can compare this briefly with the *hypothetical laissez-faire response.* The market-clearing price is P_S in the short run, and the allocation of gasoline is efficient.[29] Gasoline suppliers have a producer's surplus of $P_S - P_0$ on each of the Q_F units. We have already suggested that much of this pure transfer turns into a net cost under time rationing: Consumers pay more than P_0 because of the time cost of waiting and restrictions on the choice of when to wait, but producers receive only P_0. We think of this as a *market transaction inefficiency.*

---

[29] Sometimes an argument is made that *short-run* willingness to pay is not a reliable indicator of social value. For example, small businesses may operate profitably in the long run but be unable to absorb short-run losses because of the temporary high price. That may be true, but no social costs are incurred by shutting down the business *except* the transaction costs of reallocating the resources to their best short-run uses. If the owner had to bear them, the owner's decision on whether or not to close would still be the efficient one. However, the owner does not bear the social cost of the unemployed labor created by closing. Labor might be willing to work for a reduced short-run wage in order to prevent unemployment, but it is not clear whether labor markets work well in making such unexpected, short-run arrangements. In sum, the argument is that there are external costs to the short-run disruptions that might be caused by a large but temporary price increase. It follows that there is the potential for efficiency improvement by policy intervention that causes the externalities to be internalized (e.g., a special penalty related to the wage savings from firing labor during the period).

There is another efficiency disadvantage of the actual policy. Under the price freeze with time rationing, some of the demands from the portion of the demand curve between Q_F and Q_0 may be provided whereas other, "higher" demands (between 0 and Q_F) are not. Thus, the price freeze causes *exchange inefficiency.* Some consumers (e.g., busy executives) who do not get "enough" gas under the price freeze could (in theory) make a deal to buy gas from other consumers who get "too much" (e.g., low-income retirees) so that both would consider themselves better off. Of course, the laissez-faire method would not make the compensation: The higher willingness of the busy executives to pay becomes profit to the service station, and the retiree gets neither gas nor compensation.

The price freeze with time rationing, for all its inefficiency, does generally help the lower-income segments of the population. As an immediate and temporary response to an unexpected but urgent situation, it should not be judged too harshly. However, if the government were sufficiently prepared to have contingency plans ready to implement should a crisis arise, it is unlikely that a price freeze would be seen as the optimal policy. Let us review some additional short-run alternatives.[30]

Another strategy would be to issue *nontransferable ration coupons.* These could be issued to the registered owners of every licensed vehicle. The initial distribution could be made in any of a variety of ways: for example, equal coupons to all, more to commercial vehicles than passenger vehicles, more to states with heavier driving patterns (i.e., equiproportional coupons).

One large advantage of this plan over the price freeze is that it would remove the excess demand that causes long lines and the attendant transaction inefficiency. It would also remove some of the arbitrariness over who ends up with the available gasoline.[31] Furthermore, it would keep the price low, although not necessarily as low as the frozen price. This is illustrated in Figure 14-7, where Q_C is the quantity of coupons issued and P_{NT} is the price of gasoline under nontransferable rationing.

However, there are a number of disadvantages to this plan. One is that it is administratively costly, as it involves a bureaucracy to print and distribute the coupons. In itself, that is probably a small transaction inefficiency relative to the cost of the queues that would result from a price freeze. Another disadvantage is that there will still be exchange inefficiency: Some consumers who do not receive enough coupons would be willing to pay for more, and others who use their coupons would be willing to sell them. This can be seen in Figure 14-7. The value of gasoline to the marginal coupon user at Q_F is P_{NT}, but some other consumer values it at a minimum of P_S (the height of the ordinary demand curve at Q_F).

A third disadvantage, and an important one, is the uncertainty about how many coupons to issue in the aggregate. If too few are issued, the demand curve can cross P_0 before

---

[30] In all these cases we are not particularly concerned with the long-run effects because the policy is intended to be temporary and the short-run supply is inelastic. However, it is critical for analysts to be aware of how policies will affect the long-run supply response. A long-run price freeze, just as with apartments, would cause seriously deleterious supply reductions compared to the market-clearing price. Historically, unlike apartments, gasoline price controls have not been allowed to continue indefinitely (an interesting difference in political economy).

[31] Inevitable deviations from the equity standards are caused by the administrative need to classify diverse individuals into a limited number of categories for coupon distribution. We discuss that under transferable rationing.

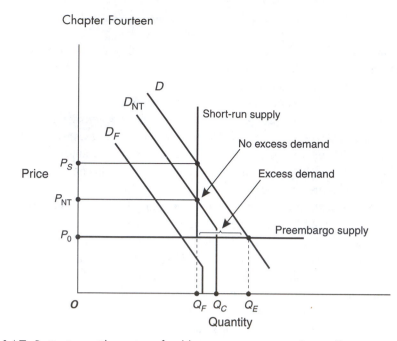

Figure 14-7. Rationing with nontransferable coupons removes the inefficient queues of the price freeze.

quantity Q_F, like D_F in Figure 14-7. This means that some of the available supply will go unused, and the public is not likely to be tolerant of such governmental bungling. If too many ration coupons are issued, the price and allocation will approach the free-market level and thus fail to meet the distributional objectives that motivate the policy. Other than making the number of coupons greater than Q_F, there is no obvious procedure (apart from trial-and-error learning, which should not be sneered at) for determining the right number of coupons.

Note that with fewer coupons distributed equally, the resulting gasoline distribution becomes more equal. The final result is always somewhere between the market solution as one boundary (too many coupons) and perfect equality as the other, with price lower toward the equality boundary. Why is this? It should be clear that a reduced number of coupons restricts market demand and thereby causes a lowering of price. In Figure 14-8 we illustrate that, for any given price, a lower coupon quantity tends to equalize consumption of the rationed good.

Consumption of the rationed good is measured along the horizontal axis, and consumption of all other goods (measured in dollars) along the vertical axis. Two budget constraints are drawn, one for a rich person B_R and one for a waif B_W. The optimal choices of both individuals with no rationing are shown as points R and W. When high numbers of coupons C_H are issued to each, both can and do continue to consume the unrestricted optimum (the market solution).

When medium numbers of coupons C_M are issued, the rich person can no longer attain point R; the effective budget constraint drops vertically down at point A. Point A, the kink in the budget constraint, yields more utility than any other feasible point. That is, point A has higher utility than any point on the original constraint to its left because utility along

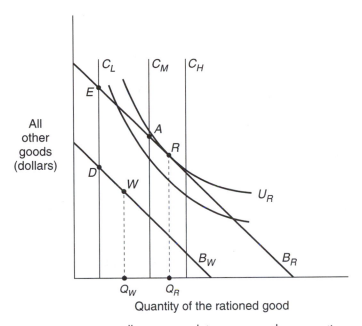

Figure 14-8. Lower ration coupon allotments result in more equal consumption.

the constraint systematically decreases as we move away from the optimum at *R*. (We have drawn in some indifference curves to illustrate this.) Point *A* also has more utility than any point directly under it, because more is better. Thus, the rich person with C_M ration coupons will choose point *A*. Since the waif still chooses point *W*, consumption is less unequal.

Now let the coupon limit C_L be low enough to restrict both individuals. By the same reasoning as above, both will choose the kink points on the respective budget constraints— point *D* for the waif and point *E* for the rich person. They use all their ration coupons C_L and have the same consumption level of the rationed good. Thus, as the number of ration coupons allotted to each person is reduced, we see two effects: Price is reduced, and consumption becomes more equal.[32]

It is also important to recognize that, for the same number of coupons, the outcome changes if the individual demands are distributed differently (even though aggregate demand is the same) or if the distribution of the coupons among individuals changes. If people were all homogeneous in their demands, there would not be nearly as much uncertainty about the effects of any specific ration plan, but then, the ration coupon solution would be identical with the free-market solution and the policy would achieve nothing but administrative waste.[33] It is precisely because people differ in their incomes and tastes that concern

[32] The example we gave is for a normal good, but it holds true for an inferior good as well. The only difference is that initially the waif would be consuming more than the rich person and would be the first to feel the effects of lowering the coupon quantity.

[33] For any coupon quantity greater than the available supply. For coupon quantities below the available supply, naturally the policy would cause underconsumption.

about how to ration arises in the first place. It is also those differences that create the inherent uncertainty about equilibrium in a nontransferable rationing plan.

To sum up, we have said that, compared with the price freeze, the nontransferable plan has these advantages: less transaction inefficiency and less arbitrariness about who ends up with available gasoline. Both plans cause exchange inefficiency. However, the nontransferable coupon plan involves substantial initial uncertainty about the number of coupons to issue and the price that will result. We should also point out that it would take longer to implement.

Another problem that arises when exchange inefficiency is caused by policy intervention is the potential for illegal markets. Under the price freeze plan, this is not a serious problem because the transaction costs of having an illegal market are high. Even if one consumer were willing to sell gas to another who would pay more for it, neither can get it without waiting in the queue, filling the tank to the regulated limit, and transferring the gasoline.

Under coupon rationing, however, all one has to do to make an illegitimate transaction is buy the coupons from someone else. This is illegal, but it is very difficult to prevent. It could be prohibitively costly to print coupons that are personalized, for example, pre-stamped with the license plate number. One could issue a coupon book to each consumer and require the whole book to be presented each time, but the station operator would still need to loosen and collect the coupons as proof that gas was sold only to those with coupons. Since the station operator has no particular incentive to hassle the customers about the validity of their coupons, it would be difficult to prevent illegal coupon sales.

Of course, this discussion forces us to ask what objectives we serve by preventing people from doing what they wish to do. Why not *allow the ration coupons to be transferable?* The exchange inefficiency disappears and the price at the service station remains low. The true price that each consumer faces (including the opportunity cost of forgone coupon sales) provides appropriate incentive to conserve. Perhaps most importantly, the uncertainties about both the number of coupons to issue and the resulting price level disappear.

One simply issues the number of coupons equal to the available supply, and all will be used. The initial distribution of coupons can be proportionately the same as in the nontransferable case. In fact, none of the three reasons given in our general discussion for preferring the nontransferable option—externalities, transaction costs of transfers, and a sense of equity among citizens that the redistribution can only be in kind—seems to be present here. A beauty of the transferable rationing plan is that policy makers can attempt to distribute a fair share of coupons to each person initially, and the market automatically corrects for exchange inefficiencies by compensating those who prefer to conserve (by more than their fair shares dictate).

Before we conclude that the transferable ration plan is ideal, recall that it does require an administrative bureaucracy and it may not be so simple to get legislative agreement on the coupon allocation.[34] Another proposal that could achieve an identical result is an *excise*

---

[34] Achieving legislative agreement under nontransferable rationing would presumably be more difficult because Congress would have responsibility for the greater constraints imposed. (For example, each lobby group cares more about its allocation when the coupons are nontransferable.)

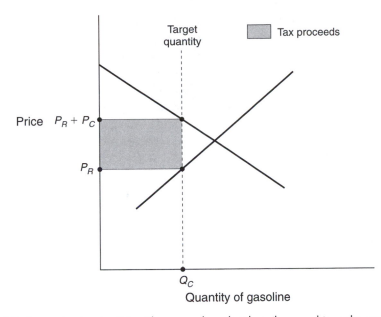

Figure 14-9. An excise tax (= P_C) with proceeds redistributed can achieve the same equilibrium as transferable rationing.

tax plan. To see this, we reproduce part of Figure 14-1a as Figure 14-9. This diagram shows
the demand and supply for gasoline under transferable rationing with Q_C coupons issued.
For supply to equal Q_C, the price at the pump must be P_R. For demand to equal Q_C, the
price to consumers must equal $P_R + P_C$ (the pump price plus the opportunity cost of using
a coupon). We noted earlier that the coupon price plays a role similar to an excise tax rate.
Now we develop that thought a bit further.

Suppose that instead of transferable rationing, we simply imposed an excise tax equal in
magnitude to P_C in this market. If we ignore income effects for the moment (so that the demand curve is unaffected), it is clear that suppliers receive exactly the same revenue ($P_R Q_C$)
as under transferable rationing. The tax proceeds are $P_C Q_C$, and what is to be done with
them? Suppose they are redistributed by the identical plan used for the initial distribution
of coupons. That is, for each coupon that an individual would have received under transferable rationing, we now provide instead P_C as a tax redistribution.

This leaves every individual with the identical budget constraint that he or she would
have under transferable rationing (since the tax rebate received equals the value of the
coupons received under rationing). But then there are no income changes that might cause
any income effects on demand. Since the consumer price of gasoline is the same under both
plans, and consumer budget constraints are the same, each consumer chooses exactly the
same quantity of gasoline (and quantity of all other goods) under either plan. The solutions
are identical not just in allocation but in distribution as well! *It is always possible to design
the two plans to have identical equilibrium.*

There is one clear advantage of the excise tax plan with rebate over transferable rationing. We can dispense with the entire administrative bureaucracy that would be needed to oversee coupon printing, distribution, and enforcement of coupon use at gasoline stations. To be sure, the excise tax plan would cause additional administrative costs but they would occur as small parts of existing operations. For example, there is already a federal excise tax on gasoline, and the machinery to collect the tax is in place whether or not we increase it.

Another difference between the two plans concerns the net redistribution that is likely to arise from each plan: Although it is possible to design the plans to be identical, political pressures will likely cause differences in the redistribution. Put simply, the transferable ration plan will give greater weight to gasoline "need" or past use in determining the redistribution, whereas the tax rebate plan will put more emphasis on ability to pay. However, the gainers and losers are not clearly predictable. This needs a little explanation.

When rations are transferable, the redistribution is not explicit but is proportional to the number of coupons received. All the political pressure for determining the initial distribution is based on perceived gasoline need, or past use. Commercial consumers can be expected to receive a large share of coupons, and passenger vehicles are likely to receive the same coupons regardless of the incomes of their owners. Consumers in states with heavier driving patterns will receive proportionately more coupons than other states.

One important inequity is involved in transferable rationing: Coupons will be allocated by broad classes, and within each broad class those who ordinarily use little gasoline will receive undeserved windfall gains. A high demander could be a person who ekes out a living by delivering milk by truck, and a low demander could be a wealthy individual who commutes to work by train. The low demander, whether rich or poor, may end up better off than before rationing. Thus, another blemish on the transferable rationing plan is that distributional benefits will accrue to many who do not deserve them on grounds of either high gasoline usage *or* ability to pay.

The excise tax rebates force policy makers to redistribute cash, and the political pressures here involve more attention to ability to pay rather than gasoline usage.[35] It is unlikely that commercial users will do as well, although certain deductions might be written into business income taxes. Individuals might receive rebates through income tax reductions. These could take so many forms that it is impossible to predict how the benefits would be spread, except again many low users of gasoline could receive large benefits. Deductions are of most benefit to the wealthy, who save the deductible amount times their higher marginal tax rates. Refundable credits would give the same to every taxpayer whether a driver or not. Another possibility is to give special fuel assistance payments through the welfare system, or some combination of these proposals.[36] In terms of redistributing a fixed total,

---

[35] Note that a policy to rebate the tax precisely according to usage is equivalent to the price freeze. In the transferable ration case, one receives cash in proportion to the coupons *not* used.

[36] Note that the fuel assistance payment can be in the form of vouchers. If the vouchers are given in proportion to usage, they tend to nullify or offset the price change caused by the tax.

it is difficult to see a clear equity advantage to either plan; it all depends on how one wants to weight gasoline usage versus ability to pay.

There is one advantage of the transferable ration plan over the excise tax with rebates. Consumers are more certain of avoiding the payment of quasi-rent. *For the excise tax plan to operate correctly, policy makers must set the correct excise tax rate.* But because the aggregate demand reduction is a large amount, there is a large uncertainty about the correct rate. Even the best demand elasticity estimates are reliable only in the neighborhood of the consumption observed. Although the total price will be that of the free market, the taxes may represent only a small portion of the quasi-rent. Political pressure to keep tax rates down works to reinforce this possibility. *With transferable ration coupons, policy makers only have to know the right coupon quantity; the market will determine price on its own.* This may be an important advantage.[37]

Table 14-2 summarizes the evaluative (and partially subjective) comments we have made on each of the plans discussed. The actual Carter administration plan was one of transferable rationing. It was intended to go into effect if the nation experienced a 20 percent or greater supply cutoff. Its initial design, rejected by Congress, was to give the same basic allotment to each registered vehicle in the country. This is the transferable plan that can be implemented most swiftly and with the fewest administrative errors.

To gain Senate approval, the plan had to be redesigned to base allotments on state driving patterns and give extra allotments to farmers and energy companies. The House demanded more special-interest categories and killed the Senate-approved version. To gain approval of the full Congress, the final plan had to allow for "supplemental" allotments to businesses based on past gasoline use, priority status for taxis, car rental companies, and certain other businesses, and 5 percent of each state's allocation to be at the discretion of the governor in order to handle certain "hardship" cases (e.g., handicapped drivers).

Each one of these exceptions would cause additional delay from the time of the shortage until the plan can operate, and each would lead to more errors, complaints, and confusion in the coupon distribution process, with individuals claiming that they have not been categorized properly. Since the coupons are transferable, the extra allotments to most businesses that Congress required are windfall gains that will have little allocative function. These provisions may reflect the congressional sense of what is equitable. They may also represent the clout that special-interest groups have in the political process.

In the 1980s, a waning energy crisis and a shift in political climate brought a new perception to the rationing plan. President Reagan, objecting to the storage cost of preserving the coupons that had been prepared for use, declared that the free market was his rationing

---

[37] For more theoretical reading about circumstances that cause quantity rationing to be preferred to price rationing, see the interesting article by M. Weitzman, "Prices vs. Quantities," *Review of Economic Studies, 41,* October 1974, pp. 477–491. Others have thought about why nonprice rationing sometimes arises in the marketplace; see, for example, R. Gilbert and P. Klemperer, "An Equilibrium Theory of Rationing," *Rand Journal of Economics, 31,* No. 1, Spring 2000, pp. 1–21.

Table 14-2

Summary of (Subjective) Evaluative Comments on Five Gasoline-Rationing Strategies

	Alternatives				
Criteria	Free market	Price freeze	Nontransferable rations	Transferable rations	Excise tax with rebate
Exchange efficiency[a]	Good	Poor	Poor	Good	Good
Incentives for long-run product mix efficiency (output level)	Good	Poor	Fair to poor	Poor	Fair to poor
Production efficiency (least-cost production)	Good	Good	Good	Good	Good
Market transaction efficiency	Good	Poor	Good to fair	Good	Good
Administrative transaction efficiency	Good	Good to fair	Poor	Fair to poor	Fair
Equity[a] (minimum share with no rent)	Poor	Fair	Good to fair	Good	Good to fair
Speed of implementation	Good	Good	Fair	Fair	Good to fair
Certainty of satisficing	Poor	Fair to poor	Fair to poor	Good	Good to fair

[a]Most heavily weighted in judging certainty of satisficing.

plan and ordered the coupons destroyed. With relatively stable and even declining energy prices since that time, the issue has not been reopened.

This case is another illustration of the importance of political feasibility to policy analysis. Policy designers should be able to anticipate the pressures that are likely to arise in gaining legislative approval and consider their worthiness and the best realistic designs that can gain approval. The best politically feasible transferable rationing plan should be compared with the best politically feasible versions of the other alternatives in making a recommendation. Thus, the basic design skills that come from microeconomics must be combined with other skills of policy analysis if one wishes to seek effective policy change.

Other Rationing Policies

There are many other areas of public policy in which knowledge of basic rationing methods is important for policy design. In this section, we mention a few issues briefly. In a later chapter on the economics of externalities, we will cover one of the most important areas involving the regulation of air and water pollution. The Clean Air Act Amendments of 1990 mandated a transferable permit system for sulfur dioxide (SO_2) emissions of U.S. electric utilities, and a similar system is frequently discussed for international regulation of carbon emissions that contribute to global warming.

Another important area for which rationing policies are required is that involving species preservation. It has unfortunately become fairly common in recent years to discover substantial threats to particular kinds of wildlife. On the west coast of the United States, for example, Chinook salmon have become increasingly scarce. The National Marine Fisheries Service has required very substantial cutbacks in the allowable oceanic salmon catches for commercial and recreational fishers. The most common way of implementing cutbacks like these is usually to shorten the allowed fishing season. Under any method, the economic survival of commercial fishing firms is severely threatened. Many of these firms are small, family-run businesses whose employee-owners could experience substantial personal economic hardship from rationing.

Let us accept the aggregate decision that there will be a substantial cutback on the catch and focus on the efficiency with which the reduced catch is harvested and allocated. There are, of course, inefficiencies of rationing by a substantial shortening of the season. With no actual limit on the catch itself, fishers have great incentive to fish much more intensively in the allowable part of the season. No matter how high consumers' willingness to pay, they will still be denied fresh fish over a substantial part of the year. If an aggregate allowed catch is also specified, that will worsen the "early" fishing incentive as each boat strives to fish as much as it can before the aggregate limit is reached. If a smaller catch were harvested over a regular-length season, fewer boats and less labor and other resources would be used each day. The released resources would have more time to establish alternative uses, and thus would have greater value than releasing the "full fleet" after a much-shortened season.

One Nobel economist, Gary Becker, suggested that a tax on the species be used instead of shortening the season.[38] The basic idea is, of course, that the tax will make the marginal cost of catching a fish align with its social value, and then the competitive market can do the rest of the work. The tax could vary by weight and size, in order to penalize the catching of small, young fish. A high tax would discourage but not prevent fishing each day. The least efficient fishing expeditions would not be undertaken, and the least efficient firms (and those with the best alternatives) would be the ones to leave the industry, whereas the more efficient ones would remain. Consumers would find fresh fish available for a longer period of time, more in accord with their preferences.

One shortcoming of the tax plan is the uncertainty about the appropriate tax rate to set. A different plan that might achieve the same goal would be to use transferable rations; in the fishing world, these are usually referred to as ITQs, or individual transferable quotas. Such systems are in use in parts of Europe and New Zealand, and thus known to be feasible. The total amount of ITQs is set equal to the aggregate allowable catch. Shares may be distributed in any number of ways (including selling them by auction), and then the recipients may trade them as they see fit. Perhaps organizations dedicated to wildlife preservation will purchase them and deliberately not use them. While no quota holder is forced to trade, the most efficient fishing firms will be able to bid amounts that make it most profitable for less efficient holders to accept them. Like the tax system, the firms that remain in production will be the most efficient ones.

The ITQ plan may have an advantage in preserving more small family-run fishing operations in an efficient way, although the advantage depends on how the ITQs are distributed and what is done with the tax proceeds. Under the ITQ plan, a small family-run business whose workers derive substantial "psychic" income from their work is not forced to sell any quota that it receives initially, and it may choose to continue to operate. Under the tax plan, however, the same business may be unable to cover the extra expense of the tax. In principle, the tax proceeds could be redistributed to it in an amount equal to (or greater than) the value of its quota under the transferable plan. However, political pressures are unlikely to lead to identical distributional results.

There may be enforcement differences between the two plans, although it would seem that the catch of each boat must be monitored similarly (either to assess the correct tax or to determine the amount of quota used). There also may be administrative differences in the cost of issuing and tracking quotas, on the one hand, and the cost of setting up and running a new tax collection system. But in this case, I suspect the big differences are: (1) the difficulty of setting the correct tax rate, as opposed to determining the aggregate amount of quota to issue; and (2) the political and administrative difficulties of coming to agreement on a feasible method for the initial distribution of ITQs.

There are many other policy issues to which the economics of rationing apply. Nontransferable parking permits are often issued to residents of certain areas, giving them the right to park there indefinitely while nonresidents may be limited to an hour or two only. This is inefficient, in the sense that some nonresidents will have a willingness to pay that is

---

[38] Gary S. Becker, "How to Scuttle Overfishing? Tax the Catch," *Business Week,* September 18, 1995, p. 30.

high enough to induce some residents to sell their permits—if it were allowed. Furthermore, inefficiency is caused by the lumpiness of the time unit for parking. Some nonresidents might have a high demand for, say, one additional hour of allowed parking per day while some residents might easily give up one of their permitted hours per day. If it were not for metering costs (both to the consumer and to the administering agency), the most efficient rationing method would be to charge the market price for each instant of parking time. Thus, designing an efficient parking system depends on how demand, supply, and the cost of making and enforcing parking transactions vary with different time units (e.g., days, hours, minutes).

In providing electric service, there are times when the demand for electricity temporarily exceeds the supply and service to some must be unfilled or interrupted. Some utilities arbitrarily distribute these "outages" among their customers (the California rolling blackouts of 2001), somewhat similar to being drafted in our military example. But other utilities offer "interruptible rates" so those customers who expect to be least inconvenienced by a brief outage can "volunteer" in return for a reduced regular rate. One method for doing this allows the utility to control a customer's air conditioning unit, so that should demand exceed supply in the area, the utility throws a switch that reduces power to the air conditioner (and causes room temperature to be slightly warmer than usual). Interruptible rates are a more efficient way of distributing the outage, and the potential efficiency gain depends on the degree to which technological advances (like the air conditioner example) can make interruptions less problematic for certain consumers.[39]

Similar to the parking example, there are potential efficiency gains to using less lumpy time units within which to make electricity transactions. In the limit, the price of electricity could vary instantaneously to keep demand and supply in balance (and then interruptible pricing would not be needed). However, the gains from allowing price to vary over shorter time intervals must be weighed against any extra transaction costs of making and enforcing demand and supply decisions. For example, most existing electricity meters in residences do not record the time at which electricity is used, and most residential consumers would not want to check rates every few minutes and calculate whether and how to adjust their consumption.

Finally, we mention briefly the problem of surgical organ transplantation. It is unfortunate but a fact of life that many people lose the functioning of an important body organ such as a kidney, the heart, or an eye. As medical technology has advanced, it has become increasingly possible to replace the dysfunctional organ with a functional one from a donor (often someone who has just died, but in some cases a living individual who will function without the donated organ). The question is: What system will be used to match demand with supply?

To many, the most natural system is to ration available supply in accordance with medically determined need. This is essentially a nontransferable ration system, with emphasis on medical objectivity as the primary criterion for distributing the coupons. Supply depends

---

[39] For more information on interruptible rates, see Lee Friedman, "Energy Utility Pricing and Customer Response: The Recent Record in California," in R. Gilbert, ed., *Regulatory Choices* (Berkeley, Calif.: University of California Press, 1991), pp. 10–62.

to a large degree on moral suasion and the goodwill of donors. This system largely ignores demander (patient) willingness to pay as well as supplier (organ donor) willingness to provide. Whereas there is no question that this problem raises very difficult ethical issues, it is also a fact that increased supply can result from higher compensation to donors. That is, a further ethical issue is that increased reliance on price-rationing, which may be distasteful to some, may allow many more patients to receive needed transplants.

Summary

To achieve redistributive goals in a specific market, the policy instruments of ration coupons, vouchers, or their combination may be appropriate. The resulting equity with all of these instruments is controlled by the initial distribution, which makes it less arbitrary than direct control of market price as in apartment rent control.

When ration coupons are used, they are necessary to purchase the good. They are most likely to be used when there is a shortage of an essential good in inelastic supply. The only way to guarantee a minimum for some or all is to forbid the exercise of the purchasing power that would result in an excessive share. Nontransferable rations restrict an individual's demand to the coupon allotment and thus cause market demand to shift inward and price to fall. This can allow those with coupons to obtain the good at a price near the supply price.

Transferable ration coupons also allow each bearer to purchase the good at a money price near the supply price. However, in this case use of the coupon entails the opportunity cost of not selling the right in the marketplace. Since an individual could sell all the coupons, the initial receipt of them is equivalent to an income grant. This grant can have a substantial positive income effect on the purchases of a rationed necessity by low-income families. The resulting allocation of the good is efficient in exchange; it differs from the free-market allocation only by the income effects. The other main difference from the free market is that suppliers receive little or no quasi-rent; the bulk accrues to the coupon recipients in proportion to their initial allotments.

Nontransferable rations are favored over transferable ones when the available supply is only enough to provide minimum essential quantities to each, if positive external effects are associated with the coupon recipient's consumption, if there are significant (external) transaction costs of coupon transfers, or if a prevailing equity judgment is that the redistribution must be in kind. Transferable rations are favored if there is a diversity of individual demands that administrators cannot easily know and the supply is sufficient to permit the exercise of diversity.

There are many markets in which supply is elastic, but it is nevertheless important to ensure a minimum consumption to all. This might characterize food, education, and medical care. In these cases use might be made of vouchers—individual grants that have purchasing power only for a specific good but are not necessary to purchase the good. Their effects on individuals have been analyzed in Chapters 3 and 4; their market effect is to increase the equilibrium quantity and perhaps increase the price if the supply is less than perfectly elastic. When supply is elastic, it is both more efficient and more equitable to use vouchers rather than ration coupons.

The two instruments are sometimes used together in a combined ration-voucher ticket, which has purchasing power and also is necessary to receive the good. Civic rights and obligations such as voting and jury duty may be seen as goods that are rationed in that manner. An interesting case of this type is military service. Many countries rely upon conscripts for this service, whereas others rely upon volunteer forces. The budgetary costs of conscripts are almost always substantially lower than for an equivalent number of volunteers, whereas the social opportunity costs of conscripted labor can be substantially higher than that of volunteers.

The social opportunity cost of conscription can be reduced to an efficient level if the obligation to serve is made transferable. In a simple model with no income effects, we show that no matter who is drafted, those who end up serving are the same individuals who would volunteer under an all-volunteer system. The principal difference is distributional (and this is reinforced in the optional section on income effects). Under the all-volunteer system, taxpayers bear the burden while those who do not volunteer bear none. Under conscription with transfers, taxpayers only bear the lower budgetary cost while the rest of the burden is borne by those drafted (whether or not they actually serve). We also illustrate a variant of this that spreads the burden equally over the entire draft-eligible population.

Under transferable rationing, government sets the official military wage administratively and typically at a low level since the supply is assured. This determines the share that will be borne by taxpayers. An advantage of the all-volunteer system, no matter how one evaluates the equity of it, is that it causes governmental decision makers to face the full social costs of employing military labor in considering how much of it to use.

Once the official wage is set, we illustrate how a competitive coupon price is established in the market. We identify the demand curve of draftees for substitutes and the supply curve of nondraftees as substitutes. The coupon price is established where the demand for substitutes equals the supply. The effective wage for military service is then the sum of the official military wage plus the coupon price. This is true regardless of whether an individual is drafted or not. The nondraftee who serves is paid both the actual military wage and the coupon price for being a substitute. The draftee who serves receives the actual military wage and, in addition, avoids paying the coupon price for a substitute.

Turning to a different example, we introduce a problem-solving approach by considering which of a variety of plans might be used to ration gasoline during a shortage. The criteria used account for efficiency, equity, and some implementation concerns. The free market is used as a benchmark, but at the time of the last shortage it was not seriously considered in light of the actual congressional mandate to find a more equitable alternative. A price freeze fails on almost all grounds except for speed of implementation: It may be a better response than doing nothing in the very short run because its equity is better than that of the free market. Nontransferable rationing would satisfy the basic equity objective, but it is cumbersome and causes unnecessarily large exchange inefficiency.

The two plans that are most capable of meeting the policy objectives are transferable rationing and an excise tax with rebate. In theory these two can always be designed to have identical equilibria. The differences between them are administrative and political. Transferable rationing requires greater administrative cost because of the coupons. The excise tax plan has an important administrative uncertainty: It can distribute the rent fully to consumers only if the administrator knows the correct tax rate to set.

Transferable rationing redistributes by classification of individuals into broad categories of prior use. Political pressures will be exerted on the definitions of these categories, as in the Carter administration plan. The excise tax is subject to political pressures to keep the tax rate low, and the funds that are rebated will be distributed in accordance with the special tax provisions made. A thorough political analysis is required to predict those pressures with any accuracy, which suggests why economic skills are only some of those needed by the working policy analyst.

In a final section, we briefly identify a number of other important policy areas where rationing arises and which could benefit from analysis of the type that we have introduced. These areas include species preservation with particular reference to oceanic salmon fishing, parking, electrical service during brief shortage periods, and surgical organ transplantation. Because ration coupons may take on such a wide variety of formats in application, sometimes the key to an interesting analysis begins with recognition of the connection between the theoretical instruments reviewed here and an actual situation.

Exercises

14-1 There is a drought, and the Hudson-Orlando Water District (H2O) has determined that only 50 percent of the available reservoir water should be consumed this year and the other 50 percent be saved for next year. The aggregate consumption will be 75 percent less than consumption in a normal year. Although that allows an average quantity per household above the life-essential level, the situation is nevertheless severe and it is very important that the targeted consumption level not be exceeded.

a In theory, any given quantity of water can be rationed efficiently among consumers by charging the correct price. Yet in this situation a serious problem could arise from trying to use this method. Leaving issues of equity aside, what is the problem with price rationing in this situation?

b One proposal is that H2O set a strict quantity limit per household (e.g., 20 gallons per household per day). Any household violating the limit would have a flow restrictor installed on its main water line. How would you evaluate this method as a means of meeting the aggregate objective and ensuring the efficient allocation of water among consumers?

c Another proposal is to use the method in (b) with one important change: The rights to each household's ration quantity are to be transferable. (For example, each household is to receive coupons for 20 gallons per day, is to be free to trade them, and must turn in enough coupons to cover its actual consumption.) Under this plan the price of a gallon of water to a household consists of more than the money price paid to H2O. Explain. Answer the same question asked in (b). If there are no income effects of this rationing plan, the equilibrium price of water in the plan is the same as the equilibrium price in plan (a). Explain. Thinking of your answer to (a), does plan (c) have any comparative advantage?

14-2 Last spring the university experienced a severe parking shortage. The university had fifty parking spaces offered at $10 each, but the students S needed forty and the faculty F needed twenty. What to do? After carefully considering the needs of each group, the university decided students should get thirty-four spaces and the faculty should get sixteen. The university recognizes that needs are diverse because of a study that indicated differing group price elasticities: $\varepsilon_S = -0.5$ and $\varepsilon_F = -0.25$.

a Even if the parking permits are allocated within each group to those who value them the most, the allocation is still inefficient. Prove this. [*Hint:* Recall that $\varepsilon \equiv (\Delta Q/Q)/(\Delta P/P)$.]

b Give a minimum estimate of the maximum expense worth incurring to change the situation and make it efficient. (Answer: $5, approximately.)

14-3 Charlie Canwalk has a demand curve for parking:

$$Q = 20 - 2P$$

where Q is the number of days per month he parks at work and P is the price of parking per day. Assume there are 20 days in 1 (working) month. The only available parking is in a municipal lot. Charlie only has one car.

a *Willingness to Pay.* Parking is only sold on a monthly basis (either you buy parking for the whole 20 days or you do not buy any). What is the most Charlie would be willing to pay for the monthly permit?

b *Rationing.* Suppose a municipal ordinance is passed that limits every vehicle's ability to park to 10 days by an odd-even license plate system (e.g., you can park on days 1, 3, . . ., 19 if the last number on your license plate is even; on days 2, 4 , . . ., 20 otherwise). Estimate the loss in parking value to Charlie caused by this ordinance. Explain your reasoning.

c *Bundling.* The ordinance is repealed. Monthly permits are sold for $60 and the true social cost of providing a parking space per working day is $3. What is the deadweight loss caused by the bundling of parking into a monthly permit rather than just selling it daily?

d *Municipal Motivations.* Give two reasons why the municipality might offer parking only on a monthly basis. One reason must have its roots in the self-interest of the municipal government; the other must have its roots in the public interest in efficiency.

PART FIVE

SOURCES OF MARKET FAILURE AND INSTITUTIONAL CHOICE

CHAPTER FIFTEEN

ALLOCATIVE DIFFICULTIES IN MARKETS AND GOVERNMENTS

IN PART FOUR we concentrated on models of perfectly competitive markets. In this chapter, we introduce problems that cause markets to depart from the competitive model and its allocative efficiency. We study them in more depth in the remaining chapters.

Careful thought about these problems can lead one to conclude that one or more of them are present in almost every market. As we consider them, keep in mind that it is easy to overlook the economic accomplishments of market-oriented systems. Without ever claiming to be in competitive equilibrium, real GDP per capita in market-oriented economies has multiplied many times over the centuries. Real markets have played a major role in the world's economic progress.

But the "market orientation" of many successful economies has been accompanied by crucial governmental institutions that limit or direct resource allocation in particular situations and in particular ways. For example, technological progress has been a hallmark of successful markets. Yet a substantial portion of this progress must be attributed to public policies in terms of patent and copyright laws that create incentives for firms to innovate. Government spending on basic research, which has provided many of the ideas and breakthroughs that have enabled progress in the marketplace, must be given credit as well. It is really the combination of government and market decision-making that explains an economy's progress. We seek to understand more about when and how they can be combined fruitfully.

In this chapter we identify weaknesses of various market and government controls as a means of coordinating economic agents in specific sectors. The specific equity issues that we have just examined were not inherently problems of coordination, although analyzing the proposed solutions did raise them (e.g., how to define transferable ration coupons to make trading and tracking ownership easy). Now we examine **market failures: situations in which ordinary market coordination does not lead to an efficient** (perfectly competitive) **equilibrium.**

In the perfectly competitive model, there is no failure. To achieve efficiency we never have to give a centralized public directive to anyone for anything. There need be no rules about what to buy, where or when to buy, how to produce, what to produce, or who should produce. Individuals, acting totally out of their own self-interests (i.e., utility maximization), find themselves coordinated by the impersonal forces of the marketplace. Production costs are kept at a minimum through competition, and demand ensures that the best possible products are made with the available resources. If all sectors of the economy met the perfectly competitive conditions, the role of government could be limited to achieving redistributional goals.

Obviously, this characterization assumes away many of the real problems of the economy, and these problems are ones that government is expected to solve. We have mentioned many of them before (e.g., monopoly, externalities), and in a moment we will summarize them. However, *even with all the problems* we will identify, it will remain true that *the market as a coordinating device is an incredibly effective mechanism.* That is one reason why "solutions" to problems often involve the public policy additions and deletions to *parts* of the market mechanism and leave the rest of the task to the same impersonal market forces.[1] There is a useful taxonomy of the specific problems that cause market failure.[2] Much insight into the economic functions of government has been gained from its use. However, the taxonomy does not pinpoint satisfactory government responses to the problems identified. Markets cannot be expected to function perfectly under all conditions, but then neither do government controls and operations. Thus following the section on market failures, we discuss **governmental failures: the systematic pressures within government that work against efficiency.**

The real problem is not to identify deviations from an ideal. The deviations represent good candidates for further scrutiny. The real problem is to identify the best organizational package from among the truly feasible alternative ways to coordinate economic agents in specific situations. These organizational alternatives are sometimes called **institutional structures: the frameworks or rules under which economic agents transact to produce and to purchase a good or service.** Institutional structure includes the applicable laws of property and contract, regulations and regulatory bodies, rules affecting government or nonprofit partici-

---

[1] This is true as well for economies that have "less" orientation toward capitalism. There is an important distinction between alternative views of who are the appropriate *owners* of capital (some societies favor more collective ownership of capital than do others) and what mechanisms a society should use to direct its *allocation*. As an illustrative example, pension funds own significant amounts of capital in the U.S. economy even though they rely on the financial markets to decentralize decision-making about specific allocations of the funds. One can imagine a pool of government-controlled pension funds owning the bulk of the capital and making allocative decisions in the same manner. Indeed, one of the reform ideas discussed for the U.S. Social Security system is to let the government invest Social Security funds like other pension funds. See Edward M. Gramlich, "Different Approaches for Dealing with Social Security," *Journal of Economic Perspectives, 10,* No. 3, Summer 1996, pp. 55–66, and Peter A. Diamond, "Proposals to Restructure Social Security," *Journal of Economic Perspectives, 10,* No. 3, Summer 1996, pp. 67–88.

[2] A classic reference article on this subject is F. Bator, "The Anatomy of Market Failure," *Quarterly Journal of Economics, 72,* 1958, pp. 351–379.

pation as a producer or consumer in the sector, and the cultural norms of the society. Each of these factors constrains and influences the behavior of the agents, and many of them can be chosen as a matter of public policy. *The design of an institutional structure to guide resource allocation in a specific sector requires analysts to understand the strengths and weaknesses of both markets and governments.* By identifying some of the generic problems in each, we increase our ability to undertake specific institutional analyses.[3]

Market Failures

We go through the taxonomy of market failure in order to understand the sources of problems in using the market as a coordinating device. For each market failure, we point out why the market deviates from first-best efficiency requirements.

Limited Competition Owing to Scale and Scope Economies over the Relevant Range of Demand

Limited competition is generally discussed in one of two categories[4]: *monopoly* (with only one provider) and *oligopoly* (with several providers). We refer only to limited competition that arises as a natural consequence of firm cost functions, wherein it is cheaper for one firm (in the case of monopoly) or a few firms (in the case of oligopoly) to supply the industry's output than for many firms to do so.[5] There are a large number of variants of these forms of imperfect competition, and a full discussion goes beyond the scope of this book.[6] We shall give most attention to the natural monopoly case, although we will discuss some oligopoly situations. Public policy intervention is traditional with natural monopolies and not as common nor as extensive in oligopolies.

We have already seen that increasing returns to scale can lead to a natural monopoly that is unprofitable despite the allocative efficiency of providing the product (Chapter 11). Since marginal cost is below average cost in this situation, marginal cost pricing is clearly unprofitable and the firm would not voluntarily choose it. If the market price to consumers does not equal the marginal cost of supplying the output, then the MRS of this good for any other will not equal the corresponding RPT and one of the necessary conditions for Pareto optimality will be violated. The common solution is to subsidize the enterprise; the enterprise itself may be either public (e.g., the Post Office, Amtrak, most subways) or private (e.g., some urban bus companies).

[3] For a survey that reviews how institutional constraints affect various economic pricing methods to deal with market failures, see Christopher Weare and Lee S. Friedman, "Public Sector Pricing: An Institutional Approach," in F. Thompson and M. Green, eds., *Handbook of Public Finance* (New York: Marcel Dekker, Inc., 1998), pp. 597–658.

[4] The qualification is to restrict our attention to cases in which the net benefits from production are positive.

[5] Thus we exclude from this definition monopolies or oligopolies that might be created by collusion among formerly competitive firms or by a government-granted exclusive franchise.

[6] Imperfect competition is generally the main focus of courses on industrial organization. It occurs in factor markets as well as product markets, and it may occur on the buyer side of the market as well as the seller side (e.g., if there is only one firm that employs all of the local residents).

A second version of the problem arises with profitable natural monopolies, such as public utility companies.[7] In this case, the monopolist is unlikely to allocate resources "correctly." (For profit-maximization, $P > MR = MC$, so the MRS of this good for another will not equal the corresponding RPT.) In addition, it may be able to charge consumers substantially more than marginal cost by exploiting its monopoly power. The standard solution, which we discuss further in a later chapter, is rate-of-return regulation.

It is difficult to generalize about cases of oligopoly because there are so many variants. However, inefficiency arises when one or more of the oligopoly firms has **market power: the ability of a supplier to charge a price greater than marginal cost.** We refer to such a supplier as a price maker rather than a price taker. The presence of market power means that the demand for the firm's product(s) has some downward slope to it (unlike the horizontal demand curve faced by a price-taking firm in a competitive market), and thus again $P > MR$. If the firm sets $MR = MC$ for profit-maximization, the consumer MRS of this good for another will not equal the corresponding RPT. In terms of public policy, both the Federal Trade Commission and the Antitrust Division of the Justice Department may refuse to allow a merger of firms if the result might be "too much" market power. A merger might have other efficiency-enhancing effects, for example, economies in terms of research and development of new products, or in marketing and distribution. It is often difficult to judge whether the efficiency-enhancing aspects outweigh the efficiency-reducing ones.

Public Goods

Until now we have generally assumed that a good is something that is consumed by one person only. Some goods, however, are jointly consumed by "everybody." National defense is the classic example. More common are *local* public goods that are consumed by "everyone in the area"; some examples are street lights, lighthouses, police patrols, weather forecasts, flood control projects, parks, and public health activities. Some public goods, such as the threat of street crime, are actually public "bads."

Public goods have at least one of two characteristics, and often both. One is that the goods are nonrival in consumption; my consumption of the weather forecast does not decrease the amount of it left for you. **The second is that the goods are nonexclusive:** Once a good is provided to one person, others cannot be prevented from enjoying its benefits (at least, without enormous expense). If I buy streetlights for my street, it is difficult for me to exclude those who use the street from the benefits of lighting. **Those who receive benefits without having to pay for them are called free-riders,** and they are an important reason why the market fails to provide public goods efficiently.

Pure public goods are both nonrival and nonexclusive, and for simplicity this discussion will concentrate on them. **Impure public goods are those for which only one of the characteristics applies.** An impure public good such as a zoo (nonrival at least up to a point of congestion) does not pose quite the same problem as a pure public good because individuals can be excluded with admission gates; a movie may be public up to the theater capac-

---

[7] This was mentioned briefly in the discussion of trucking deregulation in Chapter 9.

ity, but there is no problem excluding people. Different problems are posed by the oceans, for which exclusion of fishers is difficult even though fish consumption is rivalrous.

Efficiency requires, as usual, that we provide each unit of the pure public good when the marginal benefit exceeds the marginal cost. However, since everyone gets benefits from each unit, we have to *sum* the benefits to see if they outweigh the costs. Of course, not everyone will place the same marginal value on each unit. More formally, the Pareto-optimal allocation to the m consumers of a public good G requires that, for any private good X,[8]

$$\sum_{i=1}^{m} \text{MRS}_{G,X}^{i} = \text{RPT}_{G,X}$$

If their provision were left to the marketplace, public goods would be underallocated. The reason is that individuals have incentives to understate their own preferences in order

---

[8] Recall from our discussion in Chapter 9 (the Robinson Crusoe model) that the $\text{MRS}_{G,X}$ can be thought of as the marginal benefit of one more unit of G expressed in terms of units of X. The technical condition can be proved easily with a simple model using calculus. Imagine that we have a two-person economy and that we seek to maximize one person's utility U_1 while holding the other's $\bar{U}_2$ at a constant level. (This will therefore be one of the Pareto-optimal allocations.) There are two goods in the economy, one public G and the other private P. We are subject to a production-possibilities frontier as usual, which we will describe as $F(G)$, that is equal to the maximum number of units of the *private* good that society can produce, given that it is producing G units of the public good. Then the negative of the derivative (itself negative) $-\partial F/\partial G$ is the number of units of the private good that must be forgone for one more unit of G, or $\text{RPT}_{G,P}$. Note also that for any allocation between the two people

$$P = P_1 + P_2 \quad G = G_1 = G_2 \quad \text{(the public good is shared)}$$

Now the problem is to find the optimum of this Lagrangian expression:

$$L = U_1(P_1, G) + \lambda_1[U_2(P_2, G) - \bar{U}_2] + \lambda_2[F(G) - P_1 - P_2]$$

The first-order conditions with respect to P_1, P_2, and G simplify to:

$$\frac{\partial U_1}{\partial P_1} = \lambda_2 \qquad\qquad \text{(i)}$$

$$\lambda_1 \frac{\partial U_2}{\partial P_2} = \lambda_2 \qquad\qquad \text{(ii)}$$

$$\frac{\partial U_1}{\partial G} + \lambda_1 \frac{\partial U_2}{\partial G} = -\lambda_2 \frac{\partial F}{\partial G} \qquad\qquad \text{(iii)}$$

Let us divide both sides of equation (iii) by λ_2

$$\frac{\partial U_1/\partial G}{\lambda_2} + \frac{\lambda_1(\partial U_2/\partial G)}{\lambda_2} = -\frac{\partial F}{\partial G}$$

For the λ_2 in the first term on the left, substitute from equation (i). For the λ_2 in the second term, substitute from equation (ii):

$$\frac{\partial U_1/\partial G}{\partial U_1/\partial P_1} + \frac{\partial U_2/\partial G}{\partial U_2/\partial P_2} = -\frac{\partial F}{\partial G}$$

But by definition, this is

$$\text{MRS}_{G,P}^1 + \text{MRS}_{G,P}^2 = \text{RPT}_{G,P}$$

to avoid paying and free-ride on the demands of others. Thus, public goods provide one of the strongest arguments for government intervention in the marketplace: Not only can the market fail, but it can fail miserably.

Even in the case of a public good such that exclusion is possible, for example, a zoo, the market will not allocate properly. An entrepreneur will provide a zoo if admission fees generate revenues that equal or exceed total costs.[9] But since the marginal cost of admitting an extra person is zero, it is inefficient to deter entrance with admission fees. (This is similar to the pricing problem under increasing returns.)

However, there is also no perfect mechanism for government to use in deciding allocations. One of the most important uses of benefit-cost analysis is to estimate the proper quantity to provide of a public good. But taxpayers cannot be taxed in accordance with their true preference for the good (for the same reason that the market fails to reveal preferences honestly), and an optimal allocation may be disapproved by the voters because of the tax incidence (rather than the allocation).

Consider the provision of a simple public good, such as fire protection, where we know in principle that some quantity of protection and set of tax shares can make every person better off. But common tax systems, such as those proportional to property values, can assign a tax share that some individuals (even if not most) consider too high for the protection they receive. This may be because they are located further from the station, or because their residence is made of unusually fire-resistant materials, or simply because they do not have much fear of fire, or still other reasons. The only way around this is to have the tax shares set in accordance with the true willingness to pay of each individual, but this willingness is not known and individuals would have incentive to understate the truth. Thus there would be endless bargaining.

An important area of public policy research is the design of organizational mechanisms that are "incentive compatible" with the honest revelation of preferences.[10] A fascinating and practical example was the method of selecting programs to produce for viewing on the public broadcasting system (PBS). There are many affiliated PBS stations scattered throughout the country; and once a program is produced for one, it can be shown by all the others at essentially no extra cost. Thus, the consumption of programs by a local station is nonrival.

Originally, the decisions about which programs to produce were made by a central PBS authority in Washington, D.C. But the network found its choices subject to *political* pressures. With the avoidance of those pressures as motivation, the network designed a decentralized bidding system. Each affiliate was assigned a certain budgetary power, and it

---

[9] The entrepreneur may be able to make profits on food concessions and other activities "packaged" with the public good and thus avoid charging entrance fees. However, nonmarginal cost pricing of the concessions is inefficient.

[10] An important theoretical article on this subject is by T. Groves and J. Ledyard, "Optimal Allocation of Public Goods: A Solution to the Free Rider Problem," *Econometrica, 45,* 1977, pp. 783–810. A more comprehensive survey is found in J. Green and J.-J. Laffont, *Incentives in Public Decision-Making* (New York: North-Holland Publishing Company, 1979).

allocated its budget among the hundreds of proposed programs. The allocations were summed across affiliates, through several rounds of bidding, to see which programs had total bids that exceeded their costs.

For example, each of ten stations may have bid $5000 for program A on the first round, but the total cost of A was $100,000. The center informed all the affiliates that it "looked like" $10,000 each would be needed, and the affiliates reallocated their budgets among *all* the programs in light of the new information on expected costs. According to the research done on this system, the outcome was not "optimal" but was remarkably close to it. The discovery of this relatively efficient mechanism occurred as an unintended consequence of a political maneuver.[11] When the political need for the system dissipated, however, it was quietly abandoned (see Chapter 16 for more detail).

Externalities

We introduced in Chapter 3 the concept of an **externality: whenever the actions of one economic agent affect at least one other economic agent other than through prices.** Externalities occur among and between consumers and producers. In Chapter 3 we mentioned the interdependent preference, the type of consumption externality that arises simply because one person "cares" about some aspect of another person's activity. In many cases the externality is imposed, as when my neighbor's lawn becomes a junkyard or my house burns down because the house next door catches fire. Consumption externalities can be either negative or positive; that is, the external effect can have either net benefits or net costs to its recipients.

Externalities in production are common as well. A chemical plant that pollutes a waterway reduces the productivity of the local fishing industry; if the plant happens to leak fish food, it may bring a positive externality to the local fishing industry. If a malodorous glue factory locates near a residential neighborhood, there is an externality between a producer and many consumers; the same is true of an apartment builder who constructs a ten-story building that blocks views.

There are many other examples of externalities. The Slumlord's Dilemma in Chapter 7 occurs only because of externalities. Prostitution may involve negative externalities for the businesses located on sidewalks where solicitations occur (as well as for people simply offended by its practice). All the various kinds of pollution are externalities: air, water, noise, and visual. An automobile trip during rush hour imposes congestion externalities on others because it slows everyone down. One of the most important production externalities comes from basic research: When a really new idea is discovered, it often has thousands of applications. An example is Pasteur's discovery of the benefits of inoculation with a weakened agent of disease.

---

[11] For more details and an excellent analysis, see the work of J. Ferejohn, R. Noll, and R. Forsythe, "An Experimental Analysis of Decision-Making Procedures and Discrete Public Goods: A Case Study of a Problem in Institutional Design," in V. L. Smith, ed., *Research in Experimental Economics,* vol. 1 (Chicago: Johnson Publishing Company, Inc., Book Division, 1978).

The market fails to allocate resources properly to activities that generate externalities. The reason is that there will be a divergence between the private and social benefits and costs. When the apartment developer considers building a view-blocking structure, the developer weighs the cost of the land and the construction materials against the selling price of the finished product. The costs of blocking the view of others do not enter the developer's calculus. Why not?

Those whose views will be blocked have no right to prevent the construction, unless public policy creates such a right (which is one reason for zoning laws). Nor is there any mechanism for the surrounding inhabitants to "bribe" the developer to keep the new structure "low." Even if the inhabitants were willing as a group to offer such a bribe, there would be the free-rider problem in collecting it (and think of all the potential developers that would go into the bribe-collecting business). The market will produce too few of the activities that generate positive externalities (such as basic research), and too many of those that generate negative externalities (such as pollution).

The rule for efficient allocation of the activities involving externalities is similar to the rule for public goods. (The latter can be thought of as a special case of externality.) For each unit undertaken, the sum of the benefits to each agent affected should exceed the sum of the costs imposed on each agent affected. We explain the market failure for production externalities below.[12]

When there is an externality in production (between goods X and Y), competitive markets lead to inefficient output levels at which $RPT_{X,Y} \neq P_X P_Y$. To see this, recall that the $RPT_{X,Y}$ is the slope of the production-possibilities curve and represents the marginal cost to *society* of X in terms of Y forgone. This can be thought of as the ratio in money terms of the social marginal cost of X to the social marginal cost of Y:

$$RPT_{X,Y} = \frac{SMC_X}{SMC_Y} = \frac{\text{Dollars per unit of } X}{\text{Dollars per unit of } Y} = Y \text{ per unit of } X$$

When the marginal cost to society equals the marginal cost to each firm, competitive markets lead to $RPT_{X,Y} = P_X/P_Y$. However, *when there are production externalities, the social marginal costs do not equal the private marginal costs.* Suppose that the production of X (chemicals) has an external effect on the production of Y (fish). That is, the production function for Y is of a form

$$Y = F(K, L, X)$$

In other words, the amount of Y (fish) is a function of the amount of ordinary capital and labor inputs selected by the firm (boats and crew) but is also affected by the amount of X

[12] The exchange efficiency conditions when there are consumption externalities were derived in Chapter 3. Here we simply note that efficiency in the case of a consumption externality associated with good X requires that, for every pair of consumers i and j in an economy with m consumers of X and other goods Y,

$$\sum_{k=1}^{m} MRS_{X_i,Y}^k = \sum_{k=1}^{m} MRS_{X_j,Y}^k = RPT_{X,Y}$$

In normal market trading each consumer sets his or her own $MRS_{X,Y} = P_X/P_Y$, and the above condition will not be satisfied.

(say, because each unit of chemical produced is residual waste that enters the waterway where the fish are). If the externality is positive (the residual waste is fish food), $MP_X^Y > 0$. If the externality is negative (the residual waste destroys natural fish food), $MP_X^Y < 0$. The social marginal cost of an additional unit of X is thus

$$SMC_X = MC_X - P_Y MP_X^Y$$

The first term on the right is the usual marginal cost of X as perceived by its producer. The second term on the right subtracts the money value per unit of Y times the amount Y changes because of the extra unit of X (thus the social cost is less than the private cost for a positive externality, and vice versa for a negative externality). The rate of product transformation is therefore

$$RPT_{X,Y} = \frac{MC_X - P_Y MP_X^Y}{MC_Y}$$

As competitive firms will choose quantities that equate the private marginal costs to the market prices,

$$RPT_{X,Y} = \frac{P_X - P_Y MP_X^Y}{P_Y} = \frac{P_X}{P_Y} - MP_X^Y \neq \frac{P_X}{P_Y}$$

As each consumer will have $MRS_{X,Y} = P_X/P_Y$, we see that, when there are production externalities,

$$RPT_{X,Y} \neq MRS_{X,Y}$$

We shall look at some applications of this and focus on how to design solutions in a later chapter. The solutions proposed for externality problems vary, and here we only try to suggest the types of solutions. For the negative externality of automobile congestion, raise the price by imposing a commuting *tax*. In partial response to the external accident costs to others imposed by poor drivers, it may be efficient to design a uniform bumper height standard for automobile manufacturers. For certain kinds of pollution (e.g., factory air pollution) it may be efficient to assign property rights for the total permissible level and let economic agents trade them in the marketplace. If the externality involves only a few economic agents, as in the Slumlord's Dilemma, having one owner of both properties (merger) would solve the problem.

Every one of these solutions *internalizes* the external benefits or costs. The best way to do this often depends crucially on the transaction costs of the alternative remedies. It might be easy to meter and thus tax an automobile's contribution to congestion. Measuring the pollution level of the same car on each trip might be difficult, and a pollution standard might be a better policy.

Note the contrast between the perfectly competitive assumption of zero transaction costs and our statement indicating that good solutions often depend on the transaction costs associated with proposed alternatives. The discussion in Chapter 10 suggested that, in the market, transaction costs influence the formation of firms and the centralization of decision-making *within* them. Externalities cause market failure because of the high individual transaction costs of "internalizing" them *across* economic agents.

Imperfect Information

The perfect information assumption of the competitive model is one of the least satisfactory aspects of the model. The reason, as we began to emphasize in Chapter 7, is that the presence of significant uncertainties is more characteristic than its absence for a wide range of decisions, and behavior is changed because of it. That does not, by itself, imply any market failure. Suppose we think of uncertainty as hunger and knowledge as food that satisfies our appetites. We produce both food and knowledge in accordance with our preferences and our production possibilities; perhaps there is no problem.

However, we have good reason to believe that market failure occurs both in the production of knowledge and in the allocation of the residual uncertainty. For example, the price of a good has little meaning to a consumer unless the qualities of that good are known as well. The market does produce some information about qualities, as any subscriber to *Consumer Reports* knows. But these information markets fail because *information has public good qualities: Many people can "consume" the same information without reducing its supply.* Thus the market produces too little information, and that is one reason why government often acts to increase information by, for example, disclosure requirements and government testing of products.

More *problems arise because of imperfect information about future prices.* One of the most important social tasks involves the allocation of resources over time. Efficient market allocation requires a full set of futures markets to establish relative prices across time for all commodities. For example, decisions about how much oil to use today relative to electricity and other things depends not only on current relative prices but on future prices relative to today. Oil may be cheap relative to electricity today, but it could be worth saving if its value in the future will be much greater.

Futures markets do not arise for all commodities because of transaction costs. The existing futures markets are limited in the types of commodities included and the span of time. Even when there are partial futures markets, a difficulty is that future people are not here to articulate their share of demand.[13] Thus, the longer-term futures markets fail. This opens the door for a government role in preserving some of our important resources (e.g., oil, Yellowstone National Park), as well as influencing the aggregate savings-consumption trade-off. We focus on policy problems involving intertemporal allocation in Chapter 19.

Other information problems are caused by asymmetric information, such as can arise in hiring decisions. An employer may not know which of two potential employees has the higher marginal productivity and therefore may offer each an average wage. The better worker may invest in some signals, such as getting a college degree, simply to be identified

---

[13] To some extent, families may try to represent the wishes of their future descendants (although their information about the preferences of future descendants is surely imperfect).

initially as "better." (Thus, we are ruling out the consumption value of education in this example.) But if the degree does not itself improve productivity, society has lost. It has forgone output to pay for education and received no extra output in return; the distribution of income has also become more unequal.[14]

We have already discussed, in Chapter 7, many mechanisms for reducing the risk cost of uncertainty. One of the more important of these mechanisms—insurance—may fail because of *moral hazard* as well as *adverse selection.* The latter also involves information asymmetry and occurs when the insurer cannot separate better and poorer risks. The better risks find that the average premium is too high relative to their own expected costs. Accordingly, they drop out of the insurance market, which causes the premium to rise for everyone else. That, in turn, causes the best of the remaining insured to drop out, which further raises the premium, and so on, until no one has insurance.[15]

If one wishes to consider the implications of imperfect information that are due to bounded rationality, the problems can multiply. Nelson and Winter argue, for example, that the competitive mechanism may sometimes be a very weak instrument for ensuring least-cost production.[16] This is best illustrated when we recognize that economies are not static; they are dynamic and evolve.

If firms are boundedly rational, it will take them time to perceive profit opportunities in markets and more time to figure out by trial and error how to take advantage of the opportunities. For complicated technologies with long production times, as may characterize the airframe industry, the technology may change more rapidly than the ability of firms to keep up with it. There may be progress, but there may also never be least-cost production by any firm. The changes may involve big mistakes, with no competitors standing ready to knock the blunderers out of the business. It is possible that the imperfect knowledge caused by competition (firms protective of their knowledge) is more costly than a regime of less competition and more shared information. Bounded rationality on the part of individual consumers can also cause the market to fail. We discussed in Chapter 7 that "unsafe" products may be mistakenly purchased, and the possibility that government-imposed safety standards can improve the market by reducing these errors.

All these examples illustrate that different types of imperfect information can cause market failures in a broad range of markets, and understanding efficient responses to each is an enormous and difficult task. Some of the problems we examine in the following chapters (e.g., student loans for higher education, day-care provision) primarily involve policy responses to problems of imperfect information. The analyses illuminate and offer general insights about the efficiency implications of differing institutional structures for resolving them.

---

[14] See J. Stiglitz, "The Theory of Screening, Education, and the Distribution of Income," *American Economic Review, 65,* June 1975, pp. 283–300.

[15] See G. Akerlof, "The Market for Lemons: Qualitative Uncertainty and the Market Mechanism," *Quarterly Journal of Economics, 84,* 1970, pp. 488–500.

[16] See Richard R. Nelson and Sidney G. Winter, *An Evolutionary Theory of Economic Change* (Cambridge: Harvard University Press, 1982).

Second-Best Failures

There is one final source of market failure that we will mention, which only arises if there is some other deviation from the conditions for Pareto optimality in one or more parts of the economy. The other deviation might be due to, say, distortionary taxation used for redistributional programs (such as those comprising a social safety net) or other governmental activities. Or the other deviation might occur if any other sources of failure are not somehow fixed. *Given deviation from the necessary conditions for Pareto optimality in some sectors, a new failure arises from competitive market pricing in all of the other sectors.* This is because market pricing satisfies the first-best standard Pareto conditions (i.e., those reviewed in Chapter 12) in these other sectors, but the first-best conditions are no longer those appropriate for efficiency. The appropriate conditions are the second-best ones that take account of the distortions elsewhere in the economy that prevent achieving the first-best solution. The proof of this is called the "theorem of the second best"; second-best solutions, such as Ramsey pricing discussed in Chapter 11, depend upon the exact nature of the distortions that must be accepted as constraints.[17]

We illustrate the second-best problem with market pricing in Figure 15-1. Figure 15-1a contains a simple (solid-line) demand and supply curve for trucking services to carry goods from one place to another. Suppose that trucking rates are not set by the market at the competitive level, but are set imperfectly high by regulation (P_T^{Reg}). The usual first-best perspective is that this causes an inefficiently low level of service (Q_T^{Reg} rather than Q_T^C). Since trucking is a highly competitive industry, one solution to this problem would simply be deregulation. Price would fall to P_T^C and quantity would expand to Q_T^C.

The second-best perspective is brought in by looking at Figure 15-1b. This diagram shows the demand and supply curve for rail freight services, a close substitute for some (usually long-haul) trucking. It happens that rail rates are also regulated and also inefficiently high. But this has implications for the wisdom of the trucking deregulation plan.

The observed solid-line demand curve for trucking in Figure 15-1a takes the price of rails as constant at its (too high) regulated level. The true first-best solution is to deregulate both,[18] and then the demand for each service would shift inward as shown, say, by the dotted-line demand curves D_T' and D_R' (the prices of their substitutes have fallen). The first-best efficient allocations are shown as Q_T^E and Q_R^E for trucks and rails, respectively.

Consider again the wisdom of deregulating trucking. Note that the regulated quantities of both services are "close" to the first-best efficient quantities: the distortion introduced by regulating one service is, in this case, largely offset by similarly regulating the other. *If trucks are deregulated but rails are not, it can cause both allocations to move further from the true first-best allocations.* As drawn, trucking services expand (Q_T^C) to be even further

---

[17] See R. Lipsey and K. Lancaster, "The General Theory of the Second Best," *Review of Economic Studies,* *24,* 1956/1957, pp. 11–32.

[18] The example is kept simple for pedagogical purposes. There are "natural monopoly" reasons why deregulation would not result in efficiency along some freight rail routes, and "regulatory reform" would really be a more appropriate term than deregulation. Nevertheless, the example is motivated by regulated rail rates that were often set substantially above marginal cost.

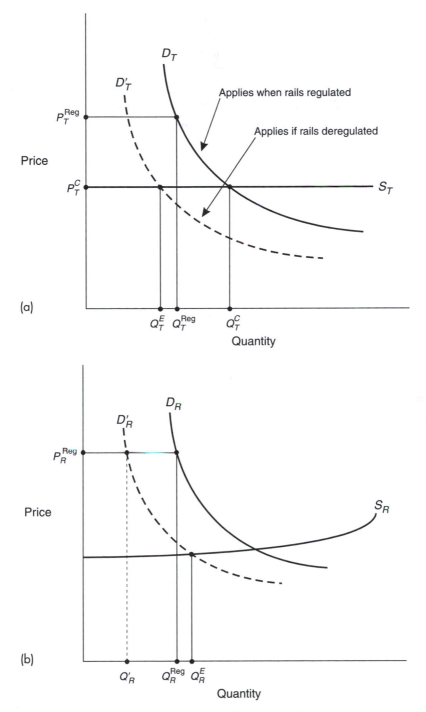

Figure 15-1. Market failure in a second-best world: (a) Rate deregulation in the trucking industry (Q_T^C less efficient than Q_T^{Reg}). (b) Rate regulation of a close substitute—the rail freight industry.

away from the first-best level than if no change is made. Regulated rail services contract (Q'_R) so that they too are further away from the first-best level than if no change is made. In this example, it would be more efficient not to deregulate trucking.

Let us restate the example to make sure the nature of the second-best market failure is clear. Suppose that we must take as a given that rail freight regulation will continue (in this case, presumably due to the political infeasibility of changing it). We know this implies that the standard first-best rule for efficiency is violated in this sector (price is above marginal cost). Are we better off following the first-best rule of marginal cost pricing in a sector where we can do so, namely by deregulating trucking? In this case, we are not. It is more efficient to allow the distortion caused by trucking deregulation to continue, because it largely offsets the rail distortion that we cannot alter directly.

How do we know when second-best considerations ought to influence our analysis? Unfortunately the answer is not always clear. As real economies have many sectors that deviate from first-best Pareto rules and as we know from our general equilibrium analyses that distortions in one sector affect allocations in others, we cannot be certain that following first-best allocative rules in one sector will be an efficiency improvement. However, just as we would not be so foolish as to concede a chess game simply because we are unable to deduce the optimal strategy, we must recognize the wisdom of doing our reasoned best.

Living in a second-best world creates uncertainty, not immobilization. Second-best considerations could just as well push us to a price either above or below marginal cost. The best practical advice, which I believe is followed by almost all analysts, is to assume that marginal cost pricing will in fact be most efficient unless there are known distortions in closely related sectors (e.g., those of close substitutes or complements). Known distortions in closely related sectors can be taken into account, just as we illustrated with the trucking and rail example.[19] This example was motivated by an actual analysis that the reader may examine for further detail.[20] It may be a difficult matter to know whether or not the "other" distortion should be accepted as continuing (e.g., will rail rates be reformed or not), but the analyst can draw attention to the importance of the issue.

Government Failures

While problems arise with reliance on markets as a coordinating mechanism, other problems develop from reliance on governmental mechanisms to address them. We discuss some reasons for "government failure" in this section, and organize the discussion in terms of problems of direct democracy, representative democracy, and public producers. The first two categories include problems that arise in expressing demand through the public sector, while the last category embraces supply problems. You will recognize some of these prob-

---

[19] Additionally, for some second-best problems, the Ramsey-pricing rules mentioned in Chapter 9 are appropriate.

[20] See Clifford Winston, "The Welfare Effects of ICC Rate Regulation Revisited," *Bell Journal of Economics, 12,* No. 1, Spring 1981, pp. 232–244.

lems from references to them in earlier chapters, but as with the market failure discussion it is useful to gather them in one place.[21]

There is no well-accepted formal model of government, analogous to the perfectly competitive model of economics, to suggest that ideal government will lead to (or closely approximate) an optimal allocation of resources. Nevertheless, as economists developed the theory of market failures, the implicit remedy was that government should intervene to fix them. Over time, a more cautious reaction has developed: not to oppose government action in general, but to consider more carefully the capability of government to effect an improvement. Systematic pressures within governmental systems sometimes work against achieving an efficient allocation of resources. The analyst who evaluates policy alternatives in cognizance of these pressures will better understand their consequences, and will be more able to design and propose attractive options. The discussion below reminds us of some of these pressures.

Direct Democracy

In thinking about possible institutions for allocating resources, one need not think about markets at all. We can certainly imagine making all resource allocations democratically through citizen voting. Of course, we would then face numerous questions about the design of the voting mechanisms. Which citizens would be entitled to vote on which resource allocation decisions? What would motivate them to exercise this entitlement? Who would decide precisely what issues to vote upon? How would the voters be informed about the alternatives and their consequences? Exactly what rules would be used to determine the decisions?

It would not be sensible for an economy with millions of citizens to use a procedure that required all citizens to vote on all resource allocation decisions. Many of the decisions would only effect a small geographical subgroup of the citizens, for example, so that one might expect some decentralization through the formation of different voting districts (e.g., federal, state, local). These districts might include responsibility for, say, those public goods whose degree of "publicness" best matches the district borders.[22] This could encourage efficiency because the voters are then the ones who receive the benefits and pay the costs of their own decisions. In addition, people with similar preferences can choose to locate in the same district. Then a community that prefers, say, very active and visible police patrol can choose it, whereas the community next door can choose a quieter, less visible approach to policing. Furthermore, the ability of dissatisfied citizens to exit one community in favor of another, or "vote with their feet," can ensure the responsiveness of the community's supply to the wishes of its citizens.[23]

---

[21] An interesting general reference on this subject is Charles Wolf, Jr., *Markets or Governments: Choosing Between Imperfect Alternatives* (Cambridge: The MIT Press, 1993).

[22] In the extreme, we could consider decentralization completely down to the individual level ("one person, one district"). This might be compatible with efficient decision-making for private goods, but it violates the spirit of collective decision-making that is our focus.

[23] We introduced these ideas in Chapter 5, when we discussed the median voter theory with respect to local school financing decisions.

However, any decentralization will cause its own problems. Of the myriad of goods to be allocated, the "borders" (in terms of citizens affected by its provision) for one will not correspond exactly with the borders for another. With separate districts for each, there would be an overwhelming number of polities. With a more limited number, the "deciders" for each issue will not match perfectly with the "beneficiaries" and "cost-bearers." Some decisions will therefore impose external benefits or costs on those affected outside of the district, so optimal provision decisions are unlikely to be reached. For example, a land parcel could have its highest value in public recreational sports use such as for soccer or baseball fields, but if some of the demand is from out-of-jurisdiction users who would not bear any of the costs, the project could be voted down locally. Other decisions will involve taxpayer-voters who may not benefit from a proposed public service but who would have to pay their share for it (e.g., an additional fire station on the other side of town). In cases of this type, a socially beneficial service may be underprovided. In other words, any realistic degree of government decentralization will result in imperfect resource allocation. As with any market failure, this government failure should be evaluated in light of the feasible alternatives.

Take the constellation of voting districts as a given, and ask within any single one what would motivate an individual to exercise the voting right? For most conventional types of elections with many voters, an expected utility maximizer would reason as follows: "The chance of my personal vote affecting the outcome of an election is close to zero. The benefit to me, even if I do change the outcome, is not that great. Therefore, the expected benefit to me from voting is also close to zero. When compared to the expected cost of voting, including informing myself about the issue or issues and the time lost actually casting my ballot, it is not worth it. Therefore I will not inform myself and I will not vote." By this logic, citizens would neither be informed nor vote.

Of course, not everyone reasons this way. Some people enjoy civic participation through informing themselves about the issues (and perhaps others who will listen) and voting. Others see voting as their civic obligation, although these voters will not necessarily take the time to become well informed on all voting issues. Despite the presence of some degree of civic engagement in the population, it is undeniable that many people do not exercise their rights to vote, and of those that do vote, many are ill-informed about the issues. *The outcome of an election is a public good to each voter, and each has incentive to free-ride upon the votes of others.* As a consequence, "too few" votes are cast, and those cast are done with "too little" knowledge. This is another reason why governmental decision-making is imperfect, or another source of government failure.

Taking the districts, actual voters, and their information about the issues as given, consider the following example of decision-making by majority vote. To make the example transparent, assume that there are only three voters: Kline, Lopez, and Williams. They are choosing the specific location of a bus route from three alternatives. Table 15-1 shows their individual preferences. Suppose we first vote on location A compared to B. Since both Lopez and Williams prefer B, it wins. Next we vote on location B compared to C. Since Kline and Lopez prefer C to B, C is chosen as the location.

Table 15-1
Majority Voting Is Intransitive:
B Beats A and A Beats C, but C Beats B
(1 = Most Preferred, 3 = Least Preferred)

| | Preferences | | |
Locations	Kline	Lopez	Williams
A	1	3	2
B	3	2	1
C	2	1	3

However, suppose we started by voting on location A compared to C. Both Kline and Williams prefer A, so A would be chosen. When we then decide between A and B, B wins as before. In this case, B is chosen as the location!

There are several lessons from this example. The first is that common voting rules such as majority vote do not necessarily identify a unique social preference. With the preferences in Table 15-1 the majority favors B over A, and A over C. One would hope that any social decision rule would be transitive: B should be chosen over C. But we have already seen that majority voting allows intransitivity: C is chosen over B. The second is that political power in determining the outcome is lodged in whoever determines the precise voting agenda. If, for example, Lopez controlled the agenda, he could ensure the outcome C by having the first vote on A versus B.[24]

The third lesson is that this voting process does not necessarily result in the selection of the most efficient alternative. With majority voting as well as other "one-person–one-vote" systems, the intensity of preferences is ignored. Suppose each individual in Table 15-1 had some willingness to pay for each of the three alternatives, with all dollar amounts less than $10 except that Williams would pay $50 for location B. Then the most efficient alternative would be B, but there is no reason to expect this outcome as a result of majority voting. If we changed the example slightly so that Kline had preferences identical to those of Lopez, then majority voting would always result in the choice of location C—even though the most efficient alternative would still be location B. Thus, government fails because there is no reason to think that common voting procedures will result in the selection of efficient outcomes.[25]

The above analysis is of choice from among fixed alternatives. The analysis becomes more complicated when we step back to ask what alternatives will be put before the electorate. Any inefficient alternative can be beaten by a Pareto-superior one, and so on until

---

[24] Condorcet first recognized this "paradox of voting" over 200 years ago. See Marquis de Condorcet, *Essai sur l'Application de l'Analyse à la Probabilité des Décisions Rendues à la Pluraliste des Voix* (Paris: Imprimerie Royale, 1785).

[25] Recall that we discussed majority voting procedures in other contexts. In Chapter 5, we discussed how the "median voter" in a majority vote system would determine the level of public school spending. In Chapter 11, we discussed why public transit subsidies might be allocated to maximize the benefits to the median voter.

the frontier of efficient allocations is reached. In the last example, Williams could propose a new alternative consisting of location B with a side payment of $10 or more to either Kline or Lopez (in order to achieve a majority).

With freedom to propose any allocation as an alternative, one might expect the final selection always to be efficient. The primary function of the voting process is then to make a distributional choice from among the many possible efficient alternatives (in our example, alternative sizes of the side payment and to whom it is given). Note also that with majority voting, there is nothing to stop a coalition from making someone worse off (e.g., Williams and Kline force Lopez to make the side payment). That is, one can move to a Pareto-optimal allocation without choosing it from among those few that are Pareto-superior to the starting point. However, there would still be an indeterminate choice, since a new majority coalition could arise from any current Pareto-optimal allocation and approve a change to one whose distribution it prefers.

The difficulty with the conclusion that only efficient alternatives will be selected lies in the failure to consider the transaction costs of discovering what alternatives are efficient and bargaining to form a majority coalition for one of them. Perhaps in our three-person example, these transaction costs would be surmounted. But with large electorates composed of people from widely varying circumstances, it is extremely difficult for anyone or any group fashioning an alternative to know whether a superior alternative (one that makes some better off, no one worse off) exists. It is hard enough to identify any alternative that will secure a majority, let alone worrying about finding one from which no improvement is possible. So practically speaking, the actual alternatives that get posed to voters are much more like the list of three in our example than the full set of allocations on the Pareto frontier. So we are back to our original conclusion: there is no reason to think majority voting will result in the selection of efficient allocations.

Majority voting is not, of course, the only voting rule that one could imagine. However, Arrow has shown that there are no "social decision rules" that can simultaneously satisfy a few very simple but desirable properties.[26] The properties include two explicitly ethical dimensions: (1) that the social decision rule be nondictatorial (the preferences of any one person can in principle be outweighed by the preferences of all others); and (2) that the social decision rule responds nonnegatively to each individual's preferences (your favoring a specific outcome cannot reduce the chance that it will be selected). The other properties may be thought of as desirable rationality attributes of the rule, although requiring them is also an ethical choice: (3) the rule can be used with any individual preferences; (4) its rankings are transitive; and (5) its relative ranking of any two alternatives will not be affected by the presence or absence of a third (irrelevant) alternative.

Much research has been done to try and avoid Arrow's negative result by specifying slightly different desirable properties of a social decision rule.[27] However, it appears that

[26] Arrow called this the "general possibility theorem," although it is commonly referred to as the "impossibility theorem." See Kenneth Arrow, *Social Choice and Individual Values* (New Haven: Yale University Press, 1951).

[27] For a review of this oriented toward economics, see Dennis Mueller, *Public Choice* (Cambridge: Cambridge University Press, 1979).

the result is quite robust. That is, avoiding the result seems to require giving up "too much" of the desirable characteristics sought. Of course, not all forms of voting are equally susceptible to the types of problems raised. For example, voting with a supermajority rule, such as requiring a two-thirds majority for passage, restricts the number of alternatives that can secure passage. Indeed if unanimity is required, then only Pareto-superior outcomes will be approved, and if an efficient outcome is reached, no further change will win approval (unlike majority voting).

Does the unanimity rule solve the problem? Let us change our choice in the bus route example slightly so that all three choices are Pareto-superior and on the Pareto frontier. That is, suppose each of the three routes compared to no bus route makes all three people better off, no side payments are possible so that each strictly prefers one, and there is no other alternative that dominates any of the three. There is no reason to expect unanimous agreement on any of the specific routes, since each of the three voters prefers a different route. They could discuss the three alternatives endlessly, each unwilling to agree unless his or her favorite route is selected. Indeed, these voters might prefer to make a decision by majority vote because it is better than making no decision at all! Buchanan and Tullock suggest that there is an "optimal constitution" (a voting rule requiring less than unanimity) that balances allocative and transaction cost efficiencies. That is, it balances the increased likelihood of inefficient allocations as one retreats from unanimity with the greater transaction cost efficiency of coming to a social decision.[28]

Of course the desirability of any voting rule depends upon other considerations apart from efficiency. Recall our discussions of the inevitability that policy changes will make some individuals better off and some worse off. We rely upon collective decision-making not only to consider efficiency, but to consider what is appropriate redistribution as well. A unanimity rule would not allow any redistribution from an individual unless it is agreed to by that individual. Thus, to the extent that we rely upon the voting rule as a mechanism for social judgment about distributional issues—not just pure redistribution, but the distributions implicit in defining property rights or choosing from among Pareto-optimal solutions—the argument for majority rule compared to unanimity becomes stronger. Different rules can be used for different types of decisions, but in practice there is no neat separation between "efficiency" and "distributional" decisions.

In sum, we have no reason to think that there are any methods of "direct democracy" that are feasible and ensure efficiency. Real voting is likely to result in some inefficiency because district boundaries cannot be perfect, because to some extent those with the right to vote will "free-ride" on others by either failing to vote or voting with too little information, and because no practical voting rule ensures efficiency even if all citizens are well-informed and participate. Real voting systems, like real markets, are imperfect.

Representative Democracy

Given the high transaction costs of direct citizen voting on an issue, it is not surprising that we try to economize by delegating some of our democratic authority to elected representa-

---

[28] J. M. Buchanan and G. Tullock, *The Calculus of Consent* (Ann Arbor: University of Michigan Press, 1962).

tives. That is, instead of us citizens deciding everything, we elect representatives and expect them to be expert on all of the public issues and to represent the preferences of their electorates.

Not surprisingly, representatives are only imperfect agents in terms of ensuring efficiency of resource allocations. Some of the reasons given in the direct democracy discussion apply here as well. For example, even if a mayor does perfectly represent the preferences of a town's citizens, he or she has at best imperfect incentive to account for spillover effects into other areas. As another example, a legislature of representatives that makes decisions by majority or supermajority voting, even if all representatives reflect their constituents' preferences perfectly, would still be subject to intransitivity and the selection of inefficient alternatives. Additional research on representative democracy has focused on representative behavior, voter behavior, and the nature of outcomes.

Most models of representative behavior assume that the representative wishes to maximize the chance of reelection, and thus perhaps has incentive to make decisions in accordance with voter preferences. If this is so, it is not clear that similar motivations would apply to those representatives who will be forced out of office by term limits. Even without term limits, it is not clear that the self-interest of elected officials would be served by remaining in office. Some may find that responding to a special interest, an action that might be opposed by the majority of district voters, offers a better future opportunity than staying in office.

When one considers the behavior of voters in a representative system, one of the more salient factors is the costliness to a voter of monitoring the representative. Recall that one good motivation for having representatives is for voters to avoid the high information costs of becoming well informed on a broad range of public issues. This same fact explains why it is difficult for voters to evaluate the work of their representatives. Indeed, it helps explain why so many voters want their representative to be a "leader"—someone they can trust to do what is "best" since on most issues they do not themselves know what is "best." This can give the representative considerable latitude, although it also may make him or her responsive to special rather than general interests (explained below).

On many issues there is an information asymmetry among the constituents that leads to a failure of representative government. A small number of constituents may be intensely concerned about a pending issue, while the vast majority of constituents may only be affected in minor ways. The small number intensely concerned will lobby the representative vigorously for their position, provide supporting material, and may hold out offers of campaign contributions, endorsements, or other rewards attractive to the representative. The diffuse individuals in the larger majority will not find it worth their time and effort to become informed, to organize, or to lobby. The problem occurs when the effects on the majority go in the opposite direction and collectively outweigh the effects on the successful lobbyist group.

One example is *rent-seeking:* when a lobbyist group such as an industry association or a union seeks legislation that will raise its earnings above the competitive level. Ordinances that limit taxi service to those with "medallions" illustrate this type of legislation. The existing owners and drivers may benefit, but the loss to taxi consumers is greater. The same logic applies not just in the legislature but in regulatory commissions, where elected or appointed commissioners decide the regulations and rates under which the (sometimes rent-seeking) regulated companies provide service to (often diffuse) consumers. A different example is *pork-barrel legislation*. In this case, a representative will seek a locally desirable project for the district paid for by state or federal funds, even though the social benefits do not outweigh the social costs. A coalition of representatives each seeking such a project can grow large enough to secure passage while still benefiting the coalition because a good portion of the cost is borne by the opposition.

In short, there is no reason to think that the outcomes of a representative government will be perfectly efficient. Representative government "fails" because it is subject to some of the same sources of failure as direct democracy, because citizens are imperfect monitors of their representatives, and because representatives often have strong incentive to respond to special rather than general interests. Again, keep in mind that our purpose is not to denigrate our democratic institutions. There may be better ones, but we have not suggested this. Rather, analogously to the theory of market failure, we are pointing out reasons why these institutions may fail in some cases to allocate resources efficiently.

Public Producers

We reviewed theories of bureaucratic behavior in Chapter 11. From this discussion, we know that government sometimes fails to provide goods and services at the most efficient levels or at the least cost. This occurs for a variety of reasons. For example, many of the goods and services produced by governments are not sold in the marketplace and are hard for anyone to value, such as national security forces or police services. Public producers are also often monopolists, not subject to direct competition from other suppliers of the same product or service. Both of these factors make for an environment that allows some latitude to agency managers. If the managers of these services have a strong belief in them and have more information about them than their public overseers, they may successfully argue for budgets that allow production at levels and costs beyond those required for efficiency. Thus, government may fail to produce efficiently.

Summary

This chapter reviews reasons why markets and governments often fail to allocate resources efficiently. Our purpose is to understand better the allocative strengths and weaknesses of governmental and market institutions in different circumstances. This understanding helps to develop skills of institutional design, or the construction of frameworks and rules under which economic agents will transact in specific sectors.

We begin with a review of the standard reasons for market failure: circumstances (unlike those of the perfectly competitive market) in which market allocation does *not* lead to the most efficient outcome. The reasons discussed are: limited competition owing to scale and scope economies, public goods, externalities, imperfect information, and second-best failures. Limited competition can take many forms (e.g., monopoly or oligopoly), and we are particularly concerned with those in which firms face downward-sloping demand curves for their own products. This means price will be above the firm's marginal revenue and thus also above the marginal cost at the profit maximum. Such an allocation violates one of the conditions for Pareto optimality reviewed in Chapter 10, namely that the MRS of consumers of this good for another (equated to the ratio of their prices) will not equal the RPT of this good for another (equated to the ratio of their marginal costs). In the case of monopoly, the most typical public policy responses to this market failure of inefficiently low output involve either regulation or production through a public enterprise. In the oligopoly cases, the most typical policy actions are uses of antitrust laws to limit the market power of individual firms (e.g., disapproving a proposed merger).

Public goods are those that are nonrival and usually nonexclusive in consumption, such as national defense and radio broadcasts. Nonrival means one person's consumption of the good does not reduce the amount of it left for others. Nonexclusive means that others cannot be prevented from enjoying the good, once it is provided to someone. Efficiency requires the provision of an additional unit of the public good whenever the benefits to all who will enjoy it exceed its cost. But the market underproduces public goods because an individual purchaser has no mechanism to prevent free-riding (force the others who will benefit to reveal their preferences honestly and to contribute appropriately to the purchase). Typical policy responses are to make governments responsible for the provision of public goods, with levels decided through voting, political, or bureaucratic decision-making (any of which may be informed by benefit-cost analyses).

Externalities are actions of an economic agent that directly affect the utility levels or production levels of parties who did not transact for them. They may be positive or negative: Your orchard may benefit from your neighbor's beehive, your ears may suffer from the same neighbor's loud radio, and your health may suffer from the air pollution caused by motor vehicles and some industrial plants. The market fails when there are externalities because the willingness to pay for receiving them (if good) or avoiding them (if bad) by the nontransacting parties does not enter the calculus of the agent causing them. The solutions to these problems involve internalizing the externalities. Solutions could involve mergers, a tax or subsidy on the external effect, the assignment of property rights, or regulation by the issuance and enforcement of required government standards. What is most efficient for a particular externality depends importantly on the transaction costs of using alternative types of solutions.

Imperfect information encompasses several different sources of market failure. One such source is the fact that information is itself a public good (your consumption of it does not reduce the amount of it available to me), and the market will underproduce it. Policy solutions may involve information disclosure requirements or government testing of products. An important variant of this is that imperfect information about future prices causes market failure in the allocation of resources over long periods of time, such as across generations. Other problems arise from information asymmetries between buyers and sellers. These can cause inefficient investment decisions, as well as failures owing to moral hazard and adverse selection. The insurance industry is often publicly regulated as a response to the problems of moral hazard and adverse selection in the markets for its products.

The final source of market failure that we discuss is the second-best failure. When there is at least one sector of the economy in which the usual first-best conditions for Pareto optimality cannot be met, then competitive market pricing in all of the other sectors will not maximize efficiency. We give the example of how trucking rate deregulation, which would lead to competitive market pricing in the trucking industry, could actually reduce efficiency because of distortions in the market for freight hauling by rail, one of its close substitutes. As actual economies are so complex with many distortions, it is very difficult to know the true second-best prices and they could be either above or below the products' marginal costs. As a practical matter, I believe almost all analysts assume that marginal cost pricing is the most efficient in a sector *unless* there are known distortions in closely related sectors for which they then account (e.g., through a version of Ramsey pricing, discussed in Chapter 11).

With all of these sources of failure, it is tempting to conclude that it is easy to improve upon market allocation through government intervention. But there are also many reasons for governmental failure. We discuss these under the headings of direct democracy, representative democracy, and public producers.

Direct citizen voting is unlikely to result in efficient outcomes because districts are imperfectly matched to their responsibilities, because those eligible to vote face incentives that discourage becoming informed and exercising the voting right, and because there is no reason to think that common voting procedures will result in the selection of efficient outcomes. Representative government "fails" because it is subject to some of the same sources of failure as direct democracy, because citizens are imperfect monitors of their representatives, and because representatives often have strong incentive to respond to special rather than general interests. Public production may be inefficient because the products may be hard to value, because the producing agency may be a monopolist without strong oversight, and because the agency managers may use the latitude in the environment to argue successfully for budgets that allow production at levels and costs beyond those required for efficiency.

It would, of course, be silly to conclude that "everything" fails. It would also be silly to ignore the great accomplishments that have been realized with our "imperfect" markets and governments. What is not silly is to strive for improvement and to use our understanding of the sources of weaknesses in markets and governments to help guide our institutional choices. We continue to develop skill in institutional analysis through our examination of specific problems in the remaining chapters.

Exercises

15-1 Any firm can produce a service at MC = $4 once it spends $380 for setup costs.

    a Using first-best rules, explain the efficient quantity of the service to provide if it is demanded by two consumers as follows:

$$Q_A = 40 - 2P$$

$$Q_B = 20 - P \quad \text{(Answer: 48.)}$$

b Explain the efficient quantity if demands are as follows:

$$Q_A = 30 - 2P$$

$$Q_B = 25 - P \quad \text{(Answer: 0.)}$$

c Could firms unable to price-discriminate survive by producing the efficient quantity under the demand conditions in (a)? Explain. How many firms are required technically to provide that quantity at the least social cost of production? (Answers: no; one.)

d Suppose the service is a pure public good, demands are as in (a), and we ignore second-best considerations. What is the efficient quantity to provide? What if the demands are as in (b)? (Answer: 32; 24.)

e Explain how second-best considerations might lead to the conclusion that the public good in (d) or the private good in (a) should not be provided at all.

f° Suppose the only way to finance the production of public good Q is through a sales tax on private goods. Let X be an aggregate good representing private goods, and suppose good X can be produced at constant marginal cost equal to $1 per unit. The demand for good X is

$$X = 3000 - 1000P_X$$

Assume for simplicity that the tax does not cause any shifts in the demand or supply curve for either good. What is the most efficient quantity of the public good Q to provide in this economy, under the demand conditions in (a), and what tax rate is used to finance it? [Note: Determining the exact answer to this question through Lagrangian techniques involves solving a cubic equation. An approximate answer may be obtained more simply by noting that: (1) the tax revenues must equal the cost of providing the public good, and (2) since four units of X must be sacrificed for each unit of Q produced, the marginal net benefit of Q must roughly equal four times the marginal net benefit of X.] (Answer: $Q \approx 30$; $t \approx 0.29.)

15-2 Given the preferences in Table 13-1, how would you structure a majority voting process to ensure that location A is selected?

CHAPTER SIXTEEN

THE PROBLEM OF PUBLIC GOODS

THIS CHAPTER IS ABOUT public goods, those that are nonrivalrous and (often) nonexclusive in consumption, such as national defense, lighthouses, and street lighting. We examine some of the allocative difficulties that arise because individuals do not have incentive to reveal honestly their preferences for these goods and some proposed methods for mitigating if not solving these problems. We focus primarily upon governmental actions, although there are also private market responses that arise in some cases.

We begin with a graphical treatment to review the efficient level of a public good and then explain the problem of poor demand revelation in the market. We consider a variety of procedures that have been proposed to overcome this problem. We review two practical applications: one method used in Sweden to decide if a public housing survey should be undertaken and the other used to decide what programs should be produced and shown on U.S. public television. The challenge to analysts is to make any of the procedures that are promising on theoretical grounds practical.

The Efficient Level of a Public Good

In Figure 16-1a, we draw demand curves that represent the demands of two different individuals for a good X. Recall that the height of these demand curves at any point may be interpreted as the maximum willingness to pay of the individual for an additional unit of the good, or equivalently the marginal rate of substitution (MRS) of the composite good "dollars for all other things" for X. For convenience, we label these curves MRS_1 (short for the more cumbersome notation $MRS_{X,\$}^1$) and MRS_2.

Now suppose that X is a pure public good, and that each unit provided will be enjoyed by both person 1 and person 2 (and, for simplicity, no one else). In Figure 16-1b, we show the marginal cost curve MC for providing this good, assumed to be constant at $6 per unit.

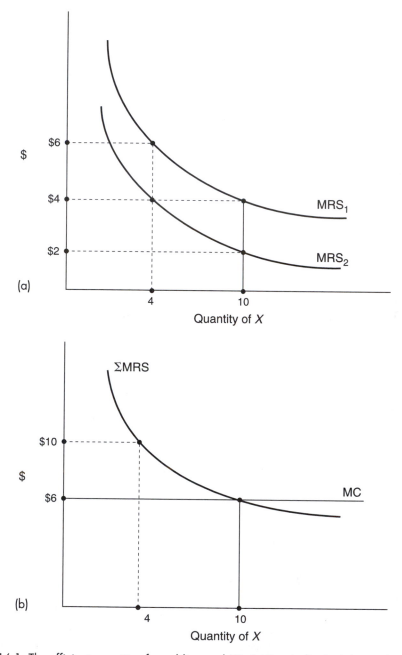

Figure 16-1. The efficient quantity of a public good (X): (a) Two individual demand curves for X. (b) The efficient allocation is where the vertical sum of the individual demand curves (ΣMRS) intersects the marginal cost curve (MC).

What is the efficient amount of the public good to provide? Since each unit yields benefits to both individuals, it is efficient to provide a unit as long as their *combined* willingness to pay for it exceeds its marginal cost. Their combined willingness to pay is shown in Figure 16-1b as the *vertical* sum of the two demand curves, labeled ΣMRS.

For example, at the fourth unit of the public good shown in Figure 16-1a, MRS_1 is $6 and MRS_2 is $4. Thus in Figure 16-1b, the height of the ΣMRS curve at the fourth unit is $10. Since this is greater than the marginal cost of $6, clearly it is efficient to provide at least four units. The efficient allocation is to provide all units to the point where the ΣMRS curve intersects the MC, shown at $X = 10$ in the diagram. Beyond this point, the marginal cost would exceed the combined willingness to pay of the two individuals. Recall that the MC curve can also be thought of as the rate of product transformation (RPT) of the good X for the composite good "dollars for all other things." Thus *at the efficient allocation, we satisfy the condition for Pareto optimality when one of the goods is public:* $\Sigma MRS = RPT$.

Note in Figure 16-1a that, at the efficient quantity of 10, MRS_1 is $4 and MRS_2 is $2. If person 1 faced a price of $4 per unit, he or she would wish to purchase exactly ten units; and if person 2 faced a price of $2 per unit, he or she would also wish to purchase exactly ten units. This illustrates an important general result. **Suppose each consumer i of a public good is charged a price P_i that equals his or her own MRS_i at the efficient allocation. Then the consumers as a group would all agree upon the quantity of the public good to provide, and it would be the efficient quantity. These special prices are known as Lindahl prices,** named after the Swedish economist who first explicated them.[1]

Not only would the Lindahl prices sustain agreement about the efficient allocation, but in the constant cost case they would also provide revenues just equal to costs. If a government used such prices, it would be an example of financing or taxing by the benefit principle rather than the ability-to-pay principle. However, Lindahl prices have not been used, in part because in practical application no one can determine what they are. Note also that, once the quantity of the public good is decided, any prices may be used to finance it without affecting the allocative efficiency (such prices are not being used to ration the good).

The Problem of Demand Revelation

How would anyone know the Lindahl prices? To know them requires knowing each individual's MRS (i.e., willingness to pay for an additional unit) at the efficient level of the public good. Suppose we imagine asking people to provide the government with their MRS curves. How might people respond to such a request? Let us assume for now that the individuals have actually thought through their demands for this good and are thus able to provide the information.

How people respond to the information request will depend upon how the government will actually finance the good. Suppose the government indicated that, after computing the ΣMRS curve and finding its intersection with the MC curve, it would in fact charge each

[1] See E. Lindahl, "Just Taxation: A Positive Solution," in R. Musgrave and A. Peacock, eds., *Classics in the Theory of Public Finance* (London: Macmillan, 1958), pp. 168–177.

person his or her marginal value. That gives individuals strong incentive to *understate* their true preferences. That is, with a large number of people, the quantity identified as efficient will be essentially independent of any one person's response (i.e., it will only change by a very small amount). The main personal consequence of the individual's response is in determining his or her own cost share, and clearly people wish this to be as low as possible (i.e., they hope to free-ride on the others). But with many people reasoning this way, the total willingness to pay for the public good will be substantially understated and too little of the good will be provided.

Suppose alternatively that the government asks for the information without mentioning financing or indicates that existing taxes will be used to cover any costs. Then there is no relation between an individual's response and that individual's tax payment. It is like asking "How much would you value one extra police patrol per day in your neighborhood? Two extra? Three extra?" In this case, the individual has incentive to *overstate* his or her true willingness to pay—free-riding on the payments of others.

Bowen considered a third alternative, in which the government states that each person will pay a proportional share of the cost and the quantity will be determined by majority voting.[2] Each individual will then prefer the quantity of the public good at which the personal marginal benefit equals the assigned cost share. Thus each voter will have a preferred quantity, with some favoring lower amounts and others higher amounts. A majority will approve the level preferred by the median voter; any other level can be outvoted in favor of the median.[3] There is no reason for individuals to vote falsely in this case. If your true preference is below the median, it does not change the result to vote as if your preference was even lower. Moreover, it would make you worse off to vote as if your preferred quantity was higher than the median, because then you would cause the outcome to be at a higher quantity. This voting equilibrium is sometimes called the *Bowen equilibrium*.

Except under particular circumstances, the Bowen outcome will not be efficient. Let us illustrate with the simple case of a public good that can be produced at a constant marginal cost (MC). Then each of the *n* voters has a cost share of MC/*n,* and the *i*th voter will prefer the quantity at which

$$MRS_i = MC/n$$

Suppose it happens that the median voter's marginal benefit at his or her preferred quantity is the *mean* of the marginal benefits to all voters at this quantity:

$$MRS_{med} = \Sigma MRS/n$$

Then (and only then) will the voting outcome be efficient. Since the median voter is like all other voters in equating the MRS to the cost share, the above two relations imply

[2] Howard R. Bowen, "The Interpretation of Voting in the Allocation of Economic Resources," *Quarterly Journal of Economics, 58,* November 1943, pp. 27–48.

[3] Imagine starting with a low level of the public good as a base, and then voting on successive increments as long as the previous increment has passed. All increments up to the median will pass, but none thereafter as a majority disfavors them.

$$\Sigma MRS/n = MC/n$$

Multiplying both sides by n gives

$$\Sigma MRS = MC$$

or, recalling that MC may be thought of as the rate of product transformation of the public good for the private good "dollars for all other things," we see the condition for Pareto optimality:

$$\Sigma MRS = RPT$$

Thus we get the efficient allocation if the median voter's marginal benefit happens to equal the mean marginal benefit in the voting population. This would happen if, say, the distribution of preferences was normally distributed. However, preferences are often skewed: for example, the mean will be above the median if those below the median prefer quantities close to it, whereas those above the median prefer quantities that are quite a bit higher.

In practice, most government public goods decisions are made with little attempt to link the amount explicitly to the preferences of the consumers. Instead, the judgments of elected officials and their appointees are used. The nature of police patrols, for example, is determined by the police chief. The chief will consult with his or her staff and perhaps other officials and various community groups. The decision will be constrained by the police budget, which is itself determined by the response of a mayor or city council to the police department's request. The practices of neighboring communities may be taken into account. In some cases, as part of this process, analysts may be asked to conduct benefit-cost studies of various patrol options. Benefits and costs may be estimated indirectly, as by reliance upon other studies that estimate the amount of crime deterrence with increased patrols and the monetary value of reduced crime.

The conventional processes for deciding public goods questions may work reasonably well. The institutional question is, "Compared to what?" Are there any practical methods for honest revelation of consumer preferences that might improve upon the conventional processes?

The Housing Survey Example

In some very interesting practical research, Peter Bohm took advantage of known biases in methods for asking people to reveal their preferences.[4] The policy question under consideration was whether it was worth undertaking a proposed housing survey in Sweden, a national census that would gather detailed information about all dwelling units in the country. Since the proposal was for a specific product at a fixed cost, the decision was discrete rather than continuous (either "do it" or "don't do it," rather than "how much" to do). The government wanted to know if the benefits outweighed the costs.

[4] Peter Bohm, "Revealing Demand for an Actual Public Good," *Journal of Public Economics, 24,* 1984, pp. 135–151.

The primary users of the survey, if it were conducted, would be the 279 local Swedish governments. They would then have access to data processing and data presentation tailored for them by the central government (this was in the early 1980s, before personal computers had become widespread). The central government wanted to determine if these local government units valued the survey at more than its cost. This is different from asking ordinary citizens how they would value it. Perhaps a good way to think of this is to consider the local governments the agents for their citizen-principals. The agents have the relevant expertise to value the survey, although they may be only imperfectly controlled by their principals.

Note that the good under consideration is nonrival, but exclusion is possible: The central government would not necessarily have to make the survey data available to all of the local agencies. Thus it is an *impure* public good, having only the nonrivalrous characteristic.[5] Other examples of this type are zoos and ballparks, which are nonrival (at least until a point of congestion), but consumers may be excluded by fences or walls. The efficiency condition for the exclusive-but-nonrivalrous public good is the same as for the pure public good, although in this case methods of financing that rely upon exclusion may be feasible.[6] Note, however, that it is inefficient to exclude someone from a nonrivalrous good when the marginal cost of including them is zero.

Bohm asked each local government how much it would be willing to pay for the survey (described in a brochure) and took care to explain why he was asking and the importance of answering honestly. He also explained that the survey would only be provided if the total willingness to pay (ΣWTP) exceeded the survey cost. However, one important aspect of the explanatory material was intentionally varied among the respondents. He divided the local governments into two roughly equal-size groups. Those in group I were told that if the survey is provided they will be charged a percentage of their stated willingness to pay (WTP) in order to cover the survey cost. This method gives the respondents incentive to *understate* their true WTP. Those in group II were told that if the survey is provided they will be charged a small fixed fee. As long as the true WTP is above the small fee, this method gives respondents incentive to *overstate* the truth.

The somewhat remarkable result was the closeness of the average WTP reported by the two groups. Group I reported an average WTP of SKr 827 (Swedish krona), while

---

[5] Recall the other type of impure public good is one that is rivalrous but nonexclusive, such as oceanic fishing. The inability to exclude consumers means that they may not face the marginal costs of their consumption. Efficient allocation requires that users face all of the marginal costs of their consumption, including any costs of their current consumption on the future supply. The latter is a major cost in oceanic fishing, because too much fishing may jeopardize the ability of the species to reproduce itself.

[6] In particular, the market may be suitable under certain conditions. Suppose an exclusive good is nonrivalrous only up until a congestion effect becomes important, such as viewing a movie in a theater. That is, the movie may be enjoyed by additional viewers at no extra cost to the first viewer up until the point that the theater becomes crowded. Because the number of people who can enjoy this good in a nonrival way is small relative to the overall demand for movie viewing in an area and because exclusion makes entry fees possible, many suppliers can compete to provide movies. The competition forces each supplier to charge entry fees that approximate normal costs, and encourages suppliers to provide theaters with different amenities to suit different tastes.

group II's average was SKr 889. Thus it must be, at least in this case, that the degree of understating (for group I) and the degree of overstating (for group II) are both small. By the research design, the true average WTP is highly likely to lie somewhere between these numbers. Since the survey cost only averaged SKr 717 per locality, the government decided to carry out the housing survey. Note that with substantial overstating or understating, the two estimates would be quite far apart, and it is much more likely that the answer to the motivating research question (whether the benefits outweigh the costs) would be indeterminate.[7]

Since the localities in group II only paid small fees, Bohm's method did not (and in general would not) raise revenues sufficient to cover costs. Nevertheless, more use of this method could reduce the revenues necessary from the central government's taxes. To extend the method to public goods enjoyed directly by citizens would raise other issues. For example, it would probably be sensible to ask only a small proportion of the affected citizens, in order to save on interviewing costs. But presumably all citizens should pay for the public good that they will enjoy. The fees collected need not be the same for everyone. For example, suppose one also determined the income level of those interviewed. If there is a correlation between the stated WTP and income, then this might be a justification for actual charges to all citizens that vary by income level.

Mechanisms of Demand Revelation

Bohm's clever method worked for the case of a discrete public good decision (do it or don't do it). Even in these cases, the analysis could be indeterminate if there were greater understating and overstating between the two groups. For the case of the public good that is continuously variable, where a specific quantity must be determined, the method might leave an unacceptable amount of uncertainty about the quantity itself.

Much research has been done to try to discover a method that will give people incentive to reveal their preferences honestly. Some mechanisms have been found that do have this property, and could in principle be used for the continuously variable case. They are sometimes referred to as *Groves-Loeb mechanisms,* or *Clarke taxes,* after their discoverers.[8] Practical impediments, however, pose a substantial challenge to their use.

These demand-revelation mechanisms are quite similar although not identical. They have this key feature: *the charge to an individual for a marginal unit of the public good equals the marginal cost of the good less the sum of the marginal benefits to all other users.* Note that this charge is exogenous to the individual; it does not depend on the individual's

---

[7] It is difficult to generalize about the extent of intentional misrevelation of preferences in response to a particular incentive structure. For further discussion, see Gareth D. Myles, *Public Economics* (Cambridge: Cambridge University Press, 1995), pp. 306–311.

[8] The Groves-Loeb mechanism was reported in T. Groves and M. Loeb, "Incentives and Public Inputs," *Journal of Public Economics, 4,* August 1975, pp. 211–226. Clarke taxes were reported by E. Clarke, "Multi-Part Pricing of Public Goods," *Public Choice, 11,* Fall 1971, pp. 17–33. An equivalent to the Clarke mechanism was described geometrically in N. Tideman and G. Tullock, "A New and Superior Process for Making Social Choices," *Journal of Political Economy, 84,* No. 6, December 1976, pp. 1145–1160.

own actions. Note also that when the individual wants the marginal unit provided (own benefit ≥ charge), it must be efficient to provide it (benefits to all ≥ marginal cost).

We can see this geometrically in Figure 16-2a, again for simplicity using a public good that can be produced at constant marginal cost (MC). Two willingness-to-pay curves are drawn. The lower one, denoted MRS_j, is as reported by the jth individual. The other is the total summed over the reports of all other people (everyone except j), denoted $\Sigma MRS_{i \neq j}$. The quantity Q_0 is the amount that would be efficient if there were no jth person. Now imagine considering increments to the public good beyond Q_0, following the rule described above: Person j will have to pay the difference between MC and $\Sigma MRS_{i \neq j}$ in order to convince the others to allow the increment. This amount is the vertical distance between the two curves. So geometrically, we are comparing this vertical distance (the charge to j) with the height of the MRS_j curve (the benefit to j).

At first the charge is quite small, as illustrated by the dotted line at Q_1. At Q_1 person j has an MRS_j that is clearly greater than the charge, and thus this increment will be provided. This will continue until Q_e is reached. At Q_e, the charge is just equal to MRS_j. Beyond this amount, such as at Q_2, the jth individual is unwilling to pay the amount necessary to convince the others to accept a further increment. Another representation of this same example is shown in Figure 16-2b. In this latter diagram, we have replaced the MC and $\Sigma MRS_{i \neq j}$ curves with their (positive) difference, which equals the charge to j (C_j) for each unit above Q_0. Again we see that the jth individual will pay to expand the output up to Q_e.

Given this system, does the jth individual have incentive for honest reporting of preferences? Yes. Underreporting would only lead to a quantity below Q_e, and overreporting would lead to a quantity above Q_e. Since Q_e is the jth individual's most preferred quantity for the given charge structure (determined by the reports of all others and the marginal costs), the only strategy that will secure it is honest revelation of preferences. If the same system is applied to each individual, all have incentive for honest revelation.[9]

One general problem with these mechanisms is that revenues and costs can diverge substantially. For example, the charges we have discussed apply only to units of the public good beyond Q_0. These may or may not produce revenue that exceeds the cost of these "incremental" units, but who will pay for the "base" units? A deficit could be made up from general taxes (or a surplus used to reduce general taxes), but then there are efficiency consequences of the tax change to consider. Alternatively, one can imagine assessing each individual in two parts: the charges already described plus some fixed amount (such as an equal share per person). It may be desirable on equity grounds to have the fixed assessment vary by income level.[10] Perhaps with some trial and error, the aggregate fixed fees

---

[9] This assumes that each individual acts independently. If collusion is not prevented, subsets of participants may be able to manipulate the system for their own benefit.

[10] A system of charges in which each purchaser pays both a fixed amount and per unit charges is called a multipart tariff. These are common in utility sectors such as electricity and natural gas. In the case where the per unit charge is constant, the system is called a two-part tariff. Friedman and Weare argue that this system is underutilized in public sector pricing because it often has desirable efficiency, equity, and administrative properties. See Lee S. Friedman and Christopher Weare, "The Two-Part Tariff, Practically Speaking," *Utilities Policy, 3,* No. 1, January 1993, pp. 62–80.

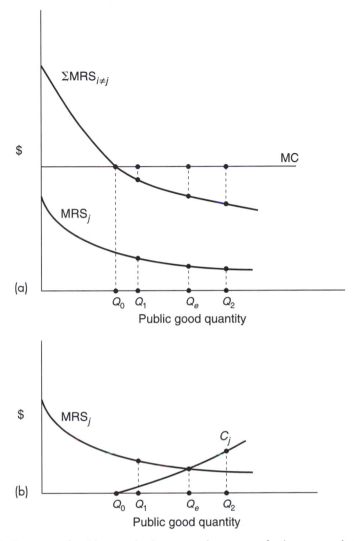

Figure 16-2. A system of public goods charges with incentive for honest revelation of preferences: (a) The charge to person j equals marginal cost (MC) minus the benefits reported by all other people ($\Sigma MRS_{i \neq j}$). (b) Given charges (C_j) only honest reporting of preferences (MRS_j) will result in person j's most preferred quantity (Q_e).

collected can approximate the difference between total costs and the revenues from the per unit charges.

If the budget-balancing problem were resolved, there would still be the question of whether or not individuals are willing to take the time to participate. In order for the method to work, individuals need a clear idea of the dollar benefits from various levels of specific public goods. Thinking this through as well as reporting it could take more time than most individuals are willing to give. Thus as with Bohm's method, it may be more practical to consider applications that rely upon population sampling techniques, or the equivalent of "authorized agents" for their "constituent-principals." Let us consider an actual application of the latter type.

The Public Television Example

Conventional radio and television broadcasts are particularly interesting examples of public goods. They are public goods because one person's reception of the broadcast does not reduce the amount of it left for others. One also cannot exclude people in the area of the broadcast from receiving it. What makes these goods interesting is that they are provided by the market despite their public features. Of course public goods theory only implies that too little of the good will be provided by the marketplace, not that there will be none. Are there too few television and radio broadcasts?

In the United States, radio and television stations have permits from the federal government that give them the right to broadcast on a particular frequency. Space on the conventional frequency spectrum is limited, so that the government only issues a relatively small number of permits per viewing and listening area. Historically these have been given away for free, although the government has begun to sell by auction the right to portions of the spectrum not utilized by the conventional technologies.[11] All of the permits for conventional television broadcasting are utilized fully in most broadcast areas, so it is hard to argue that there is too little conventional television (given the permit constraint). But how do the broadcasters market these public goods?

Of course most readers will know the answer to this question: The broadcasters are paid not by the consumers of their programs, but by the firms who pay enormous sums for the right to show their advertisements during the broadcasts. That is why we call it "commercial" television. The firms take advantage of the "captive audience" for a program and broadcast a second "show," their own commercial, in the belief that it will increase demand for the firm's products. The more people that watch a show, the more firms will pay to run their commercials during it. By bundling the program and the commercials together, the broadcasters use the market to provide a public good.

Despite the cleverness of this arrangement, a problem remains. There is no reason to think that the programs most desired by the viewing public are the ones that are actually produced and broadcast. If broadcasters are profit maximizers, they will produce and show the programs that generate the highest commercial value, that is, value to advertisers. As a hypothetical example, assume people who enjoy beer are particularly susceptible to advertisements that encourage their consumption of a particular brand. As this is a big market, beer manufacturers will pay healthy sums to sponsor a program that is attractive to beer drinkers (say, hypothetically, a football game). It may also be that they seek to entice the

---

[11] The design of the auction is an important institutional question, and one in which economic policy analysts played a substantial role. See J. McMillan, "Selling Spectrum Rights," *Journal of Economic Perspectives, 8,* No. 3, Summer 1994, pp. 145–162; and R. P. McAfee and J. McMillan, "Analyzing the Airwaves Auction," *Journal of Economic Perspectives, 10,* No. 1, Winter 1996, pp. 159–175.

same (susceptible) audience week after week. This does not mean that the total WTP for weekly football games (advertisers plus viewers) is greater than the total WTP for a quite different kind of show during the same time slots (e.g., a series of famous plays, or even unrelated shows with different audiences for each). The WTP of potential viewers does not enter into the broadcasters' profit equation because it cannot be captured by them. They only consider the WTP of sponsors.

This brings us to *public* television. The arguments for public television are quite consistent with this line of reasoning: There are shows of high social value that do not otherwise get produced. Some might take this a step further and argue that some shows should be produced and shown because they are **merit goods: goods that are underprovided in the market because their consumers do not understand their high value to them.** The prime examples from public television are educational programs for children. *Sesame Street* may have very high social value, but too many children and their parents may underestimate it as well. Public television can help fill this gap by providing such shows. Of course the difficulty with all of these arguments is how to distinguish between shows that truly do have high value and those that some group in power wants to impose on the rest of us.

This brings us to the central question of this section. Suppose we buy the argument that there is potential for public television to show programs of high value that would not otherwise be shown. By what process should we select the programs that are to be shown?

The Public Broadcasting Service (PBS) is the national distributor of programs to approximately 250 local public television stations. Starting in 1974, it used an institution known as the Station Program Cooperative (SPC) to select about half of the programs for production and national distribution. The other half were provided by corporate gifts, foundations, or government grants from the Corporation for Public Broadcasting (CPB). Stations could also acquire programs from sources apart from PBS, and did so primarily for regional and local coverage. We focus here on the programs from PBS. These are valued public goods from the perspective of each of the local stations (once a show is produced, it may be shown on one station without reducing the amount of it available for showing on others).

The PBS could have used a centralized method to select programs, similar to the British Broadcasting Corporation, but it preferred a decentralized system for two reasons. One was purely political: The PBS was concerned that centralized selection could be held hostage to political censorship or pressure against controversial programming. If a decentralized method were used, there would be no individual or board to blame if politicians did not like the programs chosen. The second reason was to allow local preferences as expressed by the 150 station managers (some responsible for more than one local station) to be the main determinants of the chosen programs.

The SPC was a 6-month process that worked in two stages. In the first stage, a catalog listing about 200 programs under consideration for production was sent to each local station. The local stations gave each proposed program a rating from 1 to 5, and the half with the highest scores continued on to the second stage. In the second stage, an interactive and iterative auction-type mechanism run through computers was used to select approximately thirty of the 100 remaining program candidates for production and distribution. Typically about twelve rounds or iterations over roughly a 3-month period were used to conduct and complete the second stage.

During the second stage, station managers were asked if they wished to pay for particular programs in order to have the right to show them. Here it is important to note that the programs are impure public goods: they are nonrival but stations can be excluded from broadcasting them. Without the exclusion feature, the SPC would not have been practical. The number of dollars a station had to pay for a particular program was a variable proportion of the total cost of the program. The proportion was determined by the station's "size" relative to the "sizes" of all other stations that wanted to purchase the program. The payment function defined "size" by each station's share of a Community Service Grant, a measure that correlated highly with the station's viewing population as well as its overall budget.[12] To show the function, we first introduce some notation. Let:

P_{ij} = the price in dollars to station i of purchasing program j
C_j = the total cost of producing program j
G_i = the size of the Community Service Grant received by station i
S_j = the set of stations that wish to purchase program j

Then the payment function may be written as[13]

$$P_{ij} = \frac{G_i}{\sum_{k \in S_j} G_k} C_j$$

The term with the G's is a weight or fraction that when used for each of the purchasing stations sums to one and assures that

$$\sum_{i \in S_j} P_{ij} = C_j$$

Thus the sum of the contributions will just equal the program's cost. If one station were to buy a program jointly with another twice its size, it would pay one-third of the program cost. If it bought the same program jointly with a station only half its size, then it would pay two-thirds of the cost. In practice, programs were shared by many stations. A station would not know what its cost share would be until the other purchasing stations could be identified. One way to see this uncertainty is to rewrite the above formula:

$$P_{ij} = C_j - \sum_{k \neq i} P_{kj}$$

Thus the price paid by station i for program j can be seen as a function of the program cost and the contributions of others (unknown initially). Since the station's WTP does not enter the formula, this would seem to foster honest revelation of preferences. Of course without any station's WTP in the formula, it is possible that allocations other than the efficient ones

---

[12] The Community Service Grant resulted from a congressional mandate to distribute a portion (about half) of the federal appropriation for public broadcasting directly to local stations.

[13] The symbol $\in$ means "is a member of." Thus the sum in the formula is over all of the stations that wish to purchase the program.

(those programs that maximize the sum of WTP over all stations less program costs) can satisfy this equation.

Although the payment function must hold in equilibrium, it does not say anything about a process that would bring the participants to an equilibrium. The process actually used was iterative and worked roughly as follows: The first five iterations were called bidding rounds. For the initial bidding round, the prices proposed to each station assumed that 80 percent of stations would choose to purchase each program. Then stations indicated which programs they would like to purchase at the initial prices (with no commitment at that point).

The center would then reestimate prices based on the number of stations indicating a willingness to purchase each of the programs. For those programs with few purchasers, the estimated price to purchasers on the next round would rise (and conversely for those programs with many purchasers). The bidding rounds did not involve actual commitments of stations. They did, however, eliminate programs with no more than one purchaser, and typically at least 50 percent of programs were eliminated during these rounds.[14]

Following the bidding rounds, the SPC entered elimination rounds. In these rounds, a station was committed to purchasing a program it chose as long as the price did not increase in successive rounds and some target proportion of stations wish to purchase it. New purchasers might join in and thereby lower the costs for the earlier purchasers. For other programs that did not meet these criteria, the target was lowered in successive rounds (increasing the probability that bids would become binding). Some programs lost their tentative purchasers and were eliminated. Finally, the SPC entered its third phase, called purchase rounds. In this phase, a program was purchased if its price did not increase for the next round. Typically these rounds involved some new stations joining in as purchasers for the surviving programs. The process ended when prices did not change for two consecutive rounds.

How can one evaluate the efficiency of a complex institution like this one? Theoretical insights are helpful (e.g., there are no apparent incentives for the misrepresentation of preferences), but in this case they do not resolve the issue. One fascinating approach is to conduct a formal "laboratory experiment." In this approach, the analysts try to replicate what they believe to be the "essence" of the institution in a controlled environment.

Ferejohn, Noll, and Forsythe did precisely that for the SPC.[15] Using California Institute of Technology undergraduates as subjects, they assigned them all "preferences" through a table that promised particular monetary payments if he or she joined in the group purchase of any subset of five proposed programs. Subjects had no knowledge of the preferences assigned to others. Each subject was also assigned a budget and a percentage cost share, told the total cost of purchasing each program, and told that his or her share of the total cost of

---

[14] For the sake of brevity, I am suppressing some of the details of the process. One of these details is that producers may choose to withdraw their proposed programs at any time, and do so if they believe there is nil chance of achieving the support necessary to cover costs.

[15] See J. Ferejohn, R. Noll, and R. Forsythe, "An Experimental Analysis of Decision-Making Procedures and Discrete Public Goods: A Case Study of a Problem in Institutional Design," in V. L. Smith, ed., *Research in Experimental Economics,* vol. 1 (Chicago: Johnson Publishing Company, Inc., Book Division, 1978).

a purchased program would be determined by a formula similar to the SPC. Then, like the iterative SPC, each member was given a starting price and indicated tentative purchasing decisions from which the center calculated new prices, continuing with successive rounds until prices stabilized.

The program costs and the payments in the tables, when aggregated over all the subjects in the group, also determined the subset of programs that were most efficient for the group to purchase. Thus the actual results could be compared to this. The experimenters had five different groups participate in the SPC experiment, and these groups achieved payoffs equal to 79 percent of the maximum possible. They also proposed an alternative to the SPC, one in which subjects were informed each round about tentative group purchase decisions and asked how much they were willing to pay for the various proposed programs. Without going into its details, eight different groups operated under the alternative procedures. The eight alternative groups achieved payoffs equal to 76 percent of the maximum possible. In terms of speed of convergence, the SPC procedure was superior (it converged by round 10 in all five groups, whereas the alternative did not converge by round 10 in any of the eight groups).

One important point of this case, from our perspective, is the potential of using "laboratory" settings to evaluate and compare alternative institutional designs. There are, of course, some weaknesses to this method—the student subjects do not have the same expertise and motivations as the actual station managers, and the "laboratory" environment may not replicate some of the real considerations that explain actual station manager decisions. Nevertheless, consider how new ideas are often tested by industry. Proposed new components for airplanes, for example, go through various stages of "laboratory" testing long before they are tried on actual airplanes (or, equally important, rejected for use on actual airplanes). The method is an important, relatively low-cost strategy for preliminary testing of promising new designs for economic institutions as well.

There is a postscript to this case, also quite important to students of institutional design. The SPC is no longer used by PBS as its method for selecting the programs to produce. A key criticism, as the SPC operated over the years, was that new, untried programs were rarely selected. Instead, the same programs that were produced in the previous year tended to be renewed for further production. By 1990, PBS abandoned decentralized decision-making and gave the decision-making power to the Executive Vice President of National Programming, commonly referred to throughout the 1990s as the "Program Czarina." Ironically, whereas a good part of the motivation for this change was to foster more innovative programs, the available funds were barely enough to cover the cost of public television's most popular series. Thus the desire to increase the stream of innovative programs has not been realized.[16]

The lesson of this postscript is not the particular result. It is to recognize economic performance over time as a key evaluative dimension of an economic institution. Even if the SPC were successful at realizing 100 percent of the "static" efficiency each year (choosing

---

[16] For more information about the political history of public television, see James Day, *The Vanishing Vision* (Berkeley, Calif.: University of California Press, 1995).

the most efficient programs from among those offered), it could still have poor "dynamic" efficiency if the "menu" did not keep pace with changing demands of the viewing public over time. However, there is no reason to blame this on decentralized decision-making. It would not be difficult, for example, to add a constraint that required SPC participants to allocate some small portion of their budget within a category of "innovative programs."[17] Evaluating performance over time is a complex problem that we shall return to in the remaining chapters.

Summary

This chapter reviews the theory of public goods, why it is difficult to achieve their efficient allocation, and some proposed methods for alleviating these difficulties. Pure public goods are those that are both nonrivalrous and nonexclusive in consumption (e.g., streetlights, police patrols, lighthouses, national defense). There are also impure public goods, and we discuss the type that is nonrivalrous but from which it is possible to exclude consumers (e.g., zoos). In both of these cases, efficiency requires that units of the public good be provided until the sum of marginal benefits from the last unit just equals the marginal cost. The sum of marginal benefits is taken over the population that could consume the good nonrivalrously, and thus ignores any artificial exclusion mechanisms that a provider might devise.

It is difficult to give consumers appropriate incentives for honest revelation of their preferences for particular public goods. In the ordinary marketplace, public goods are underprovided. Some consumers may, either on their own or by joining with others, purchase some units of a public good. But other consumers will try to free-ride on the purchases of others (when exclusion is not possible) or understate their true willingnesses to pay (WTPs) in order to lower their group cost shares. One advantage of using a government to purchase the public good is that it can require payment from all of the consumers. However, this will not solve the efficiency problem unless the government has some means of determining the truth about consumer preferences.

There is a set of prices, called the Lindahl prices, that would cause each consumer to demand the efficient level of the public good. This requires that the price to each consumer be equal to that consumer's benefit for the marginal unit. If such pricing were feasible (an example of public financing by the benefit principle), it might not be desirable on equity grounds. Different consumers would be paying different prices for the same good, and those paying the higher prices might not be those with greater abilities to pay. Once the efficient quantity is known, any prices could be used to finance its provision without changing the allocation (unlike ordinary goods in the marketplace). But this still begs the question of how anyone would determine the efficient level (or the Lindahl prices).

---

[17] For example, the SPC could require each station to allocate 10 percent of its budget for innovative programming and require that ten of the 100 proposed programs be in the innovative category. This centralized rule would result in the decentralized choice of two to four innovative programs each year of the thirty programs purchased.

The government could simply ask its citizens to write down their WTPs for given levels of the public good (perhaps through representative surveys when many people are involved). However, the answers will depend to some extent on perceived self-interest. If the government says that it will actually charge people according to their expressed WTPs, then individuals have incentive to understate them (as in market provision). If there will be no additional charges to the respondents, then they have incentive to overstate their true WTPs.

Peter Bohm took advantage of these two methods, with biases in different directions, to assist the Swedish government in making an actual public goods decision. The question was whether or not a proposed census of housing should be undertaken by the central government (recall information is itself nonrivalrous). The government decided that if Sweden's local housing authorities were collectively willing to pay more than the cost of the census, it should be provided. Bohm divided the local agencies into two groups, and gave one group incentive to underreport their WTPs and the other incentive to overreport. Somewhat remarkably, both groups reported similar WTPs, implying that the degree of any misrepresentation in each group must be small. Since the average WTP of each group exceeded the average cost of the census, the central government decided to provide it. Note that one cannot depend on there being small differences, and with large differences the method is much more likely to be inconclusive.

Other research has created methods for deciding upon the level of public goods that have incentive for honest revelation of preferences. These methods are sometimes referred to as Groves-Loeb mechanisms, or Clarke taxes, after their discoverers. Each of them works by making each consumer's payment equal to the difference between the marginal cost of the public good and the sum of marginal benefits to all *other* consumers. However, practical problems have so far been formidable obstacles to their use for actual decisions. These problems include the possibility of substantial divergence of costs and revenues raised, with attendant equity issues, and that from an individual's perspective the costs of participation may be high relative to benefits.

The closest practical example to a method like those above was the one used to decide what programs to produce for public television. Television programs are nonrivalrous, in that once produced they may be broadcast in many areas without reducing the amount of the program available for others. Most U.S. television is produced by commercial networks and satisfies the preferences of the sponsoring advertisers rather than viewers directly. Some of these programs may be among those most highly valued by consumers. However, there is no reason to think that the set of commercially broadcast programs coincides with the set of programs that would be most highly valued by viewers. Public television has the potential to offer the kinds of programs that are highly valued by viewers even if not by possible commercial sponsors. Furthermore, certain television programs, such as children's educational shows, may be merit goods: goods that are underprovided in the market because their consumers do not understand their high value. Public television may also provide these.

If public television has the potential to provide these valuable goods, can that potential be realized? The Station Program Cooperative, run by the Public Broadcasting Service, tried. Once a year in a 6-month process, the approximately 150 managers of public television stations across the nation would "vote" independently in order to choose collectively about thirty programs for production from an initial menu of 200. The SPC used an iterative method to calculate each station's cost share of a program and let station managers decide which of these programs they wished to purchase. The initial tentative purchase decisions ("votes") are used to recalculate cost shares, allow new tentative purchase decisions, and so on until a stable equilibrium is reached where cost shares do not change.

The actual SPC is a complex institution. In order to investigate its efficiency and compare it with an alternative institution that also features decentralized decision-making, Ferejohn, Noll, and Forsythe simulated the SPC in a laboratory experiment using students as the choosers. They found that both institutions operated at about the same efficiency level, with those programs chosen having 75–80 percent of the maximum benefits possible. This laboratory experiment method is very useful for evaluating institutional alternatives that either cannot be evaluated directly or are thought promising but do not yet exist.

The SPC operated from 1974 throughout the 1980s. However, in 1990 it was replaced by a more traditional centralized method (the "program czarina"). The main complaint about the SPC was that it failed to select new and innovative programs. Even though station managers themselves made this criticism, the independent "voting" method of the SPC made support of the "tried and true" more likely than agreement on any of the many innovative program proposals on the menu. There was little innovation under the program czarinas in the 1990s, at least in part because the budget was just sufficient to fund only the most popular of the PBS programs. The general lesson here is that the performance of economic institutions depends on both their static and their dynamic efficiency. Finding better practical methods for choosing public goods remains an important objective for policy analysis.

Exercises

16-1 Basic public goods:

    a For a nonrivalrous public good, how does the necessary condition for efficiency differ from the product-mix rule for ordinary goods?

    b Would you expect a private market to provide an efficient amount of public goods? Explain why or why not.

    c You want to know how much people value Yellowstone Park. You are considering conducting a survey and asking people how much they are willing to pay for it. Would you have any concern about the reliability of this method? Explain.

16-2 Fireworks: Two adjacent communities, on opposite sides of a river, both like to see fireworks displays for July 4th. They have the same population size and economic wealth. They both have equally wonderful views of any fireworks launched from the river between them. Skyrocket services can be bought in any quantity for $20 per skyrocket launch. Community A has the following July 4th demand curve for skyrocket launches:

$$Q = 120 - P_A$$

Community B's July 4th demand curve is

$$Q = 160 - 4P_B$$

a Why would the two communities have different demand curves, given that they have the same size, wealth, and view of a river fireworks display?

b What is the efficient number of skyrockets to launch on July 4th? (Answer: $Q = 112$.)

c What cost shares would be necessary to make the two communities agree upon the efficient number of skyrockets?

d What problems might prevent the two communities from reaching the efficient solution?

CHAPTER SEVENTEEN
EXTERNALITIES AND POLICIES TO INTERNALIZE THEM

THIS CHAPTER CONSIDERS some of the alternative methods available for internalizing an externality. Recall that an externality is a side effect—an effect outside of any transaction—of one economic agent's actions on another's utility or production level. In Chapter 15, we mentioned a number of different ways that externalities can be internalized through public policy. In this chapter we consider these methods further: taxes, subsidies, issuance of regulatory standards, and the establishment of tradable private property rights such as permits that allow for the production of a certain amount of the externality.

The analysis we present will revolve around the question of how to regulate the negative externality of air pollution. Thus it is directly relevant to issues such as the acid rain provisions of the 1990 federal Clean Air Amendments, or the problem of reducing Los Angeles smog, or the worldwide problem of global warming. The same type of analysis may be used for other externality issues, such as those involving health and safety in the workplace. Part of the analytic framework that we introduce may be useful in many problems where the degree of centralization or decentralization in the design of a policy institution is an issue.

In the first part of our analysis, we review the predominant form of environmental regulation—the issuance and enforcement of technical regulatory standards to control pollution—and some of the reasons why many economists think it is inefficient. Using standard models, we show that several alternative regulatory approaches can be efficient. In particular, we go over the Coase theorem concerning property rights and show that, in principle, either a pollution tax or (more surprisingly) a pollution-reduction subsidy can lead to an efficient solution. While this part of the analysis provides some good insight, it misses an important part of the real problem because it ignores information and transaction costs.

A key question for air pollution policy is how centralized or decentralized the recommended regulatory structure should be. Loosely speaking, the degree of decentralization refers to the amount of discretion or extent of choice given to the actual producer by the regulatory authority. The analytic framework that we introduce for this aspect focuses upon the role of information and transaction costs in institutional design. In principle, this framework for organizational design could be applied to quite different issues, such as the method for choosing a public good or the extent of services to be included in a monopoly franchise. Thus we first introduce it at a quite general level before turning to its application to air pollution policy.

Although no single theoretical framework has been accepted as the proper method for analyzing the range of issues that arise in designing a regulatory institution, the organizational design perspective offered by Kenneth Arrow yields good insights. Offering a way to clarify certain relations between the choice of governance structure and the information and transaction costs that result, Arrow's framework classifies an organization by the kind of operating instructions it issues (the "commands") and its rules for enforcing them (the "controls"). The "commands" may or may not give discretion to the agents who are to carry them out. The more discretion agents have, the more decentralized the institution. Indeed, free market organization or governance can be seen as a command and control structure that uses a particular form of decentralized decision-making.

Under the assumptions of perfect information and zero transaction costs, perfectly centralized as well as decentralized structures can lead to a Pareto-optimal allocation of resources. That is why these assumptions understate the importance of uncertainty (the absence of information) and its great influence on organizational design. As economic agents are confronted with much costly uncertainty, they seek a method of organization that efficiently reduces those costs. But that depends on the specific sources of uncertainty and the ability to reduce it (as by the creation, transmission, and use of information) or shift it (to those best able to bear it). In many situations, centralized rules are more efficient. In many other situations, decentralized rules have the advantage.

After explaining Arrow's organizational design perspective, we use it to consider alternative methods of air pollution control. Compared to the earlier standard analysis, we uncover new strengths and weaknesses of pollution taxes (a highly decentralized method) relative to the prevailing technical regulatory standards (a highly centralized method). Enforcement difficulties seriously limit the number of pollution sources that might be suitably regulated by the tax approach. Reasoning from Arrow's framework, we find motivation to explore other regulatory methods that depart from technical standards in order to relax the degree of centralization. We explore the modest relaxation that would be involved in the issuance of performance standards, and then the more substantial relaxation from a policy of marketable pollution permits. The analysis suggests that in this context the marketable permit approach largely dominates the performance standards approach and the tax approach.

The most promising direction for gaining efficiency over the technical standards approach, based upon this analysis, is through marketable pollution permits. The magnitude of this gain depends on the number and diversity of pollution sources that are included in the permit approach. High costs of monitoring emissions for permit compliance, relative to compliance with technical standards, is the main reason that certain sources should not be included. The chapter concludes with a discussion of a few other practical issues involved in operating a permit system, and a review of two actual permit trading programs: the national SO_2 (sulfur dioxide) permit market among electric utilities, and the RECLAIM (Regional Clean Air Incentives Market) program in the Los Angeles area to reduce both nitrogen and sulfur oxides.

A Standard Critique of Air Pollution Control Efforts

Air pollution is a case of negative externality in which there is interdependency among many economic agents, and the government is the central authority that must design some institutional way of internalizing it. The predominant form of control used in the United States is the setting of *regulatory standards*. For example, firms subject to federal requirements must use the "best available technology" to minimize pollution. The Environmental Protection Agency (EPA) then implements this rule by specifying the required technology for a particular firm and inspecting to make sure that the firm is using it.

Many economists have attacked regulatory standards for two reasons: (1) The standard requiring use of the "best available technology" implies that the harm from a marginal pollutant is always greater than any finite cost (even if high) of reducing it. (2) The costs of achieving a given aggregate pollution reduction are not minimized. The first criticism is surely just, although there is great uncertainty about what the "optimal" level of pollution should be. (For example, long-run damage may result from pollution levels that do not have deleterious short-run effects.) From any pollution level, the "best available technology" may make it feasible to eliminate more pollution. But the costs of doing so may greatly outweigh the benefits.

However, it is the second criticism that is more controversial and ties in directly to the analysis of this chapter. The usual reasoning behind it is approximately as follows. If an aggregate pollution reduction in an air basin has been achieved efficiently, the marginal cost to each polluting firm of the last unit reduced must be the same. Otherwise, there is room for a deal that leaves the aggregate pollution level unchanged. Suppose the last ton of pollution reduction from firm A has a marginal cost of $300 but the marginal cost to firm B for an equivalent reduction is only $200. Then firm A can save $300 by polluting one additional ton, but at the same time persuade firm B to cut back one more ton for a payment of, say, $250. Society is indifferent since total pollution in the basin is constant, but the owners of firms A and B are each better off by $50.

The next step in the usual reasoning is to argue that regulatory standards do not achieve this equalization of marginal costs. As interpreted by the regulatory agency, the "best available technology" required for one firm has no necessary relation to the requirements for another. One factory, for example, may be required to install and operate smokestack scrubbers. This may leave it in a position analogous to, say, firm B above. Furthermore, unbeknown to the regulatory agency, this same factory could reduce pollution further by substituting a more expensive chemical input for one it is currently using. A second firm in the same air basin may be emitting the same pollutant but, because it is a very different type of firm, it receives an order to reduce its pollution by a spraying process. It may be left in a position analogous to firm A above, and thus there is room for a deal between the two firms.[1]

The final step in the standard critique is to note that there are simple market mechanisms that would automatically eliminate the problem. Rather than rely on standards, a pollution tax could be imposed. In other words, firms could buy as much of the right to pollute as they wished, as long as they paid the tax price. We illustrate this below.

Imagine that within any single air basin there is a spectrum of polluting firms, with marginal cost for pollution reduction rising with the aggregate amount reduced. Think of clean air as an input that is demanded and used up (made dirty) by firms in their production processes. We measure the amount that is used up by the total amount of pollution emitted into it (e.g., tons of SO_2). Then the factor demand curve to use up clean air, illustrated in Figure 17-1, depends on the marginal cost to the firms of avoiding polluting. The curve has the normal shape, suggesting that the cost of avoiding some pollution is relatively low, but that it gets increasingly expensive to avoid successive increments.

At the unregulated supply price for using up clean air (i.e., zero), the firms emit Q_0 quantity of pollutants into the air. To achieve any desired pollution reduction, all we need do is set a tax rate corresponding to that level on the factor demand curve. For example, if we desire pollution to be reduced from Q_0 to Q_1 we simply impose a tax rate t_1 per unit of polluted air. Every polluting firm now prefers to reduce its pollution whenever its marginal cost of doing so is less than t_1 (otherwise, it would have to pay the tax). Thus on the margin, each firm has the same marginal cost of reduction (t_1), and there is no room for a deal among them. We reach the conclusion of the usual reasoning: Taxes are a more efficient method of pollution reduction than regulatory standards because they achieve the reduction at the least social cost.

The Coase Theorem

There is a quite important and interesting extension of this reasoning. A *subsidy* to reduce existing pollution (thus not available to any new pollution sources) has an allocative effect identical with that of the *tax*. That is, suppose each firm were offered t_1 for each unit of pol-

---

[1] In this example we have assumed that the regulatory standard is a *technological* one. Another form of regulation is the *performance* standard; for example, pollution can be no more than 500 particulates per minute. Performance standards have the same type of flaw as technological ones, at least by the reasoning we have been using so far. If it is assumed that firms have different cost functions for pollution reduction and that the assignment of standards does not take perfect account of that fact, the costs of achieving the aggregate reduction will not be minimized.

By the same reasoning, however, the performance standard enjoys a critical advantage over the technological one: The inefficiency must be of a lower degree. The proof of this is easy. Imagine replacing the technological standards assigned to each firm with the performance standard that requires the same reduction. The firm can certainly achieve it at no greater cost than is required by the technological standard, but it may be able to achieve its performance level more cheaply by using a different technology (e.g., chemical substitution rather than scrubber installation). Performance standards may also have a dynamic advantage over technical ones in terms of encouraging research and development of lower-cost methods to meet the standards.

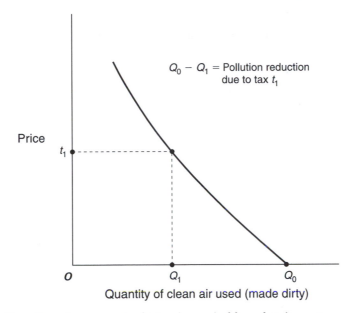

Figure 17-1. The effect of a tax on the factor demand of firms for clean air.

lution reduction. Whenever the marginal cost of reducing pollution is less than the offered subsidy, the firm increases its profits by choosing to reduce. Since that is true of all the units of air between Q_0 and Q_1, again the result would be to reduce pollution to Q_1![2] In both cases the opportunity cost of polluting is the same: The firm either forgoes a subsidy or pays an equal size tax for each unit of pollution it produces.

The allocative equivalence of the tax and subsidy policies is a special case of *the Coase theorem: With perfect knowledge, zero transaction costs, no income effects, and well-specified property rights, market allocation is the same no matter which economic agents have initial title to the property rights of the traded goods.*[3] In the above example, the good being traded is clean air. In the tax case, the government (as an agent for those harmed by pollution) can be considered to have the property rights to the air. If firms wish to use the air, they must pay its owner (the government) for the privilege of doing so. In the case of the subsidy, the polluters can be considered to have the rights to the air. If others (again acting through the government as agent) wish to have more clean air, they must pay the firms to provide it.

The underlying logic of the Coase theorem is that (under the assumptions) the assignment of property rights does not affect the net benefits from any specific allocation. Each agent has the same intrinsic value for consuming a particular quantity of the good, and the cost of doing so is either the price actually paid (if bought from another who holds the

[2] This assumes that there are no income effects on the aggregate demand for pollution reduction. Note the similarity between the equivalence here and those identified for various rationing plans in Chapter 12.

[3] See R. Coase, "The Problem of Social Cost," *Journal of Law and Economics, 3,* October 1960, pp. 1–44.

initial rights) or the equivalent opportunity cost (if one has the initial rights and forgoes selling them to another). Since the true price per unit of consumption is the same in either case, all agents buy the same quantities (again, assuming no income effects).

An additional implication of the Coase theorem is that the resulting allocation is efficient (even with income effects). As long as the property rights are well defined, there will be no externalities; all interdependencies get internalized. This result depends crucially on the assumption of zero transaction costs. In some cases of externalities, such as a case in which one firm causes an externality to only one other firm, the problem may be solved by a voluntary merger. The merged firm internalizes the externality by taking account of it on the combined profit level, and one would expect the merger to occur if the transaction costs of arranging it are low in relation to the increase in combined profits. In this latter case, the model's assumption of zero transaction costs approximates the actual situation. But in the air pollution example, the externality does not get internalized precisely because of high transaction costs. There are several reasons why the transaction costs are high; among them are the institutional specification of property rights and the bargaining costs of securing agreement among many economic agents. These are explained below.

Historically, air has been treated legally as common property. This means that no one has the exclusive rights to control the use of the resource; anyone, including polluters, can use the air for free. At that price, it is not surprising that the property gets overutilized. Since no economic agent has the authority to establish a positive price that others must pay to use the property, the external effects from each user on the others do not get internalized.

Imagine that those who dislike pollution costlessly band together and offer a subsidy to polluters to reduce emissions. Free entry to use the "commons" would be exploited by new sources as long as such entry is profitable (the marginal cost of making pollution is less than the offered subsidy). This would cause resource misallocation (no social value to the resources used in making the extra pollution), and would likely mean that the group offering subsidies would not be viable. The claimants to the offered subsidies would be essentially unlimited.

One could imagine trying to reduce transaction costs by changing the specification of property rights: making them private rather than common. Suppose each landowner is given the air rights above his or her property and anyone violating them is liable for damages. Then any one polluter would need to purchase permission to use the air from many independent landowners. But individual landowners could strategically hold out in order to bargain for larger payments, and those bargaining costs would prevent any agreement from being reached. The same problem arises if someone attempts to reduce the bargaining costs by offering to buy up all the land (thus giving one person all the air rights): The many independent landowners have the same strategic incentives to hold out and make the success of an attempted buyout unlikely.[4]

The bargaining costs could arise in another form if initially the private property rights are given to the polluting firms. Based upon true preferences, the many independent pollution sufferers could be willing to pay collectively an amount that would induce the pollut-

---

[4] This situation is similar to that of the slumlords in the Slumlord's Dilemma of Chapter 7.

ing firms to reduce emissions. But there would be a free-rider problem in trying to organize a collective offer: Each pollution sufferer has a strategic incentive to deny or understate his or her willingness to pay when contributions are solicited and thus enjoy the cleaner air purchased by the collectivity for free or at low cost.

Thus high transaction costs, relative to achievable allocative gains, explain why the externality of air pollution does not get internalized through voluntary market transactions. The natural question to ask next is whether there is some other institutional structure that could achieve allocative gains that exceed the organizational costs of operating the structure itself. But it is precisely that type of logic that is absent from the usual reasoning about the tax solution that we reviewed earlier. *The key fallacy in the standard reasoning is this: The "solution" is derived without taking explicit account of the information and transaction costs that create the problem and how to overcome them.* Note, for example, how the standard argument assumes that the EPA has imperfect information in setting the "best available technology" for control: If it were perfect (as the model purports to assume), then no firm could achieve its mandated reduction at lower cost, and no (low-marginal-cost) firm could further reduce its pollution to allow an increase in the pollution of another (high-marginal-cost firm). The result of the standard argument really arises because it assumes (without any justification) imperfect information in the setting of technical standards and perfect information in creating the tax solution. This does not necessarily mean that the solution is wrong, but it does imply that the analysis is unpersuasive.

Efficient Organizational Design and the Degree of Centralized Decision-Making

In this section we present a way of thinking about organizational design.[5] Striving for efficient resource allocation is often thought of primarily as an investment problem—a matter of choosing the economic activities that yield the greatest net social benefits. Yet the more one focuses on how to make the choices and appreciates the difficulties involved, the more one is drawn to expand the view of the problem to include organizational as well as investment terms. Rather than consider any specific decision, we focus here on how to organize a process of deciding, or how to create an organization that will make many decisions of the investment type.

Because information for decision-making is costly to produce and to communicate, there are often important economies in breaking decision problems up into pieces and assigning particular individuals (or subgroups) responsibility for each of the pieces. A firm, for example, may continually face the problem of what to do next in order to maximize profits. The large firm typically breaks the profit maximization decision down into pieces by creating separate marketing, sales, production, and planning divisions. Each division has

---

[5] The following discussion is based primarily on the chapter "Control in Large Organizations," in Kenneth Arrow, *Essays in the Theory of Risk-Bearing* (Chicago: Markham Publishing Company, 1971). Other references include J. Marschak and R. Radner, *The Economic Theory of Teams* (New Haven: Yale University Press, 1971); and R. Radner and C. B. McGuire, *Decision and Organization* (Amsterdam: North-Holland Publishing Company, 1972).

responsibility for developing its own expertise and making resource allocation decisions intended to contribute to the overall firm objective. Yet the attempt to organize in order to take advantage of the economies from specialized decision-making creates the problem of organizational control: How does one motivate the individual decision makers in each division to act in the interests of the organization as a whole?

To develop perspective on the problem of organizational design, we introduce the concept of a team. **A team is any organization of individuals sharing a common goal or goals.** The individual team members may have other interests in addition to the team goals, and the other interests may conflict more or less with the team purposes. To achieve its purposes, **the team must solve the general problem of organization: choosing the operating rules or instructions to command or direct certain behavior of the individuals involved and an enforcement mechanism (some form of incentive, either rewards or penalties) to control or induce the individuals to follow the operating rules.**

The concept of a team is one that should be quite broadly conceived. We could consider the organization of a sports team, school district, naval fleet, or department of motor vehicles. We have already suggested that we could think of a large firm as a team and consider its organization. One particularly important conception is to view the whole economy as a team sharing the common purpose of achieving an efficient and equitable allocation of resources. Then governments are seen as particular subgroups of the team (or smaller teams nested within a larger one). We will explain and apply this latter conception after we have introduced some general ways of thinking about alternative types of operating rules and enforcement mechanisms that can characterize the team organization.

We wish to place particular emphasis on the degree of centralization in the organizational design. **The degree of centralization refers to the amount of decision-making discretion left to the doer of an organizational task.** For example, an instruction to another of the form "do this task in this way," such as "tighten one nut to each bolt passing on the assembly line," is a centralized instruction. The recipient of the instruction is given no choice—or very little choice—about how to perform the task. Another instruction may be of the form "do whatever is necessary to maximize this objective function," such as "minimize the costs of assembling cars from these components." This is decentralized because it leaves the specific decisions about how to organize the assembly to the recipient of the instruction.

Of course, there are intermediate possibilities such as a rule book: "Determine which state of the world we are in and follow the specific procedures described for that state." Here the instructed person has some freedom to interpret which state of the world is relevant: "If the floor is dirty, mop it." Thus, the instructions that individuals receive may be more or less centralized; that is why we refer to the degree of centralization.

In a moment we will discuss circumstances relevant to the desired degree of centralization in the operating rules. One of the factors concerns which individual has the best information (or can obtain and process the relevant information most easily)—the doer of the task or the assigner of the role. However, these rules should be assigned with forethought to their enforcement as well.

Once an operating instruction is assigned, the organization must be able to identify whether it is obeyed. A centralized operating rule, for example, "do this specific task," may be relatively easy to monitor because obedience is a *"yes or no"* determination. Obedience to a decentralized rule, for example, "maximize this function," is a matter of whether the individual has done *more or less*. The same factors that push toward the use of the decentralized rule (e.g., the center or rule assigner has relatively greater costs of learning how to accomplish the maximization) also imply that the center has a more difficult monitoring task: How does it know how close the observed result is to the maximum? Therefore, use of decentralized operating rules is usually accompanied by enforcement mechanisms that reward team members for more or penalize them for less.

Now let us explore circumstances that explain the degree of centralization associated with the efficient conduct of economic activities. In a sense, it is interdependencies among economic agents that suggest that some degree of centralization may be efficient. We show this below in a very simple model of a team. But there is a caveat: The presence of an interdependency is only a necessary, and not a sufficient, condition for centralization to be relatively efficient. We also illustrate this caveat below.

We start with a simple example of a two-person team whose shared objective is to maximize the team profit. Each team member is given responsibility for, and has relevant knowledge about, one investment decision. Each strives to make the decision that most enhances the team profit. *However, each is uninformed about the other's knowledge unless some costly communication or coordination is undertaken.* Thus, we are assuming that there is some division of knowledge; no one person knows everything, and responsibility is allocated to the person with the most appropriate knowledge.

We stylize the individual choices and the possible outcomes in a very simple way. Each of the two team members must decide whether to take some action such as to go forward with an investment or to hold off. If person 1 invests, we represent this as $d_1 = 1$. If person 1 decides not to invest, we represent this as $d_1 = 0$. Similarly, $d_2 = 1$ if person 2 invests and $d_2 = 0$ otherwise.

Each individual, when deciding whether to invest, is assumed to have only *incomplete* information about the effect of investing on the team's profits (unless costly communication or coordination is undertaken). The information is incomplete because it ignores possible interdependencies. For simplicity, we assume that this incomplete information takes on one of three values (denoted Π_1 for person 1's investment and Π_2 for person 2's investment): \$10 if the investment looks good, \$0 if it looks neutral, and −\$10 if it looks bad. Person 1 knows the value of Π_1 when choosing d_1, but does not know d_2 or Π_2. Similarly, person 2 knows the value of Π_2 when choosing d_2, but does not know d_1 or Π_1.

Interdependencies in the team's decisions are reflected by the shape of the team profit function Π. Consider the following three possibilities:

$$\Pi = d_1\Pi_1 + d_2\Pi_2 \tag{1}$$

$$\Pi = (d_1 + d_2)(\Pi_1 + \Pi_2) \tag{2}$$

$$\Pi = (d_1 - \tfrac{1}{2})(d_2 - \tfrac{1}{2})(\Pi_1 + \Pi_2) \tag{3}$$

If the profit function is (1), no communication or coordination is necessary to maximize it. Each person has sufficient knowledge to decide which investments are profitable for the team (e.g., if $\Pi_1 = 10$, then person 1 knows to choose $d_1 = 1$) and which to reject as unprofitable (e.g., if $\Pi_2 = -10$, then person 2 knows to choose $d_2 = 0$). In fact, there is no reason for the two agents in this example to produce as a team rather than independently. Function (1) will be maximized if person 1 acts to maximize $d_1\Pi_1$ and, independently, person 2 acts to maximize $d_2\Pi_2$. This might characterize the local investment decisions of two franchises of the same company in different localities.[6]

However, the profit functions denoted by (2) and (3) contain interdependencies that the team will have to take into account. If the profit function is (2), then communication between the agents is valuable. Suppose, for example, that $\Pi_1 = 0$ and $\Pi_2 = 10$. Then person 1 should choose $d_1 = 1$ in order to achieve the maximum team profit of $\$20 = (1 + 1)(0 + 10)$. But if person 1 does not know the value of Π_2 and acts only on the knowledge that $\Pi_1 = 0$, he or she may choose $d_1 = 0$, and the team will end up with a profit of only $\$10 = (0 + 1)(0 + 10)$. This might characterize a situation such as the value to an electricity supplier of building an extra generating plant and an extra transmission line, with different divisions of the firm responsible for each. The transmission division might not build the line unless it is fully informed about the new generating plant.

A profit function like (3) gives value to both communication and coordination. Communication is valuable for reasons similar to the example in (2). One of the agents needs to know if the sum of Π_1 and Π_2 is positive, negative, or zero. With that knowledge the agents must coordinate their actions appropriately. If the sum is positive, for example, then maximizing team profit requires that both agents take the same action (either both investing or both not investing). If the sum of $\Pi_1 + \Pi_2$ is negative, then the agents must be sure to take different actions (if one invests, the other should not invest). To maximize team profit, communication must be undertaken so that one agent knows the sum of $\Pi_1 + \Pi_2$ and what action the other agent chooses, and the agent so informed must take the action that coordinates the team appropriately. This is a situation like the public television production choices of the Station Program Cooperative that we analyzed in the last chapter. Each station manager decides whether to invest in a particular program, and socially we want them to coordinate and communicate so that they invest only in those programs with the highest collective value.

Consider, as a different illustrative example, the mass production of an automobile engine that must fit into the automobile body and then meet given performance standards. There are hundreds of features of both the engine and body that must be designed to perform in harmony with one another. Not only does the engine construction require knowledge (communication) of the body design (and vice versa), but the designs must be chosen to fit each other (coordination). Furthermore, if the team is to do its job properly, the resulting product must be one that meets its performance standards at the least cost.

---

[6] We could add a constant term to the profit equation that would represent the value of the "name recognition" received by the franchises for belonging to the chain.

If the different activities of automobile engine and body construction are organized to take place under one firm, the communication and coordination problems are addressed through some centralization of the decision-making. Recall that Chapter 10 pointed out that activity within firms (as opposed to across firms) represents a centralization of decision-making. Within the firm, some directives of the "do this specifically" type are given (e.g., from managers to other employees). Thus communication and coordination problems can be addressed simply by directing one employee to communicate and/or to coordinate with another.

On the other hand, the interdependencies involved in communicating and coordinating need not necessarily be addressed by centralizing the decision-making within one firm. In the case of the automobile engine and body, it is also possible for separate firms to build the individual components. That is, *one can communicate and coordinate by contract through the market.* This method is a decentralized market transaction: A priced exchange between units that presumably is undertaken because each unit independently believes the exchange will further its objectives.

Agreement on exactly what is being exchanged requires specification of multidimensional aspects of the transaction: for example, the timing or flow of deliveries, dimensions of all the connecting parts, and the strength of various components. Suppose there needs to be some trial and error in construction before all these specifications can be known or agreed upon. Then it may be impossible to agree on price beforehand; there is too much uncertainty about what is to be produced. But the potential contractee may refuse to incur the costs of trials without a contract. Centralized construction within the firm may be a *more adaptable* and thus more efficient way to proceed in this case. On the other hand, if it is difficult for one part of the team *to monitor or know the least costs of production* of the other part, competitive contracting may have the advantage.

Recall that one of the key problems of organization is that the participating individuals do not necessarily share identical objective functions. The standard assumption that each individual is a utility maximizer does not in itself imply that team member behavior will be consistent with team objectives. Whatever operating instructions are issued, the team must be able to ensure that those instructions are obeyed. Within a firm, it is not always easy to monitor or measure the contribution of each of its subparts. This also makes it difficult to devise a decentralized self-monitoring plan of incentives that establishes an appropriate relation between rewards to the subpart and the subpart's contribution to the firm. In the automobile example, the adaptability advantages of centralized construction may be outweighed by the difficulties of motivating each subpart to attend to the team goals.

One solution may be to decentralize outside the firm (team) in the form of a contract arrangement with another firm. *Competitive bidding for the contract shifts some of the monitoring functions from the buyer to the competitors, and the latter may have better knowledge about what is least-cost production.* That is, the instruction "minimize the costs of production" may be best enforced by the decentralized monitoring of informed competitors rather than centralized monitoring by another part of the same firm.

Let us now broaden our view of an economic team to encompass more than one or two firms. It is important to be able to see an entire market economy as one large team, with smaller subteams like firms nested within it. In the market as an organization, the operating rules and the enforcement system are decentralized in a particular way. It is as if each consumer is "commanded" to maximize utility and each firm is "commanded" to maximize profit. Consumer demand and competition jointly provide the "controls" (determine the rewards or penalties) over the firm's choice of behavior.

If competitive enforcement is perfect, the observed centralization of decision-making within large firms (as well as observed contracting arrangements) must be efficient. Inefficient centralization (or contracting) by a firm would result in production above least cost, and the firm would be undersold by more efficient competitors. In other words, when the interdependencies are confined to small subsets of agents in a large market, perfect competition internalizes them efficiently.

However, competition as an enforcement mechanism is not perfect. It is crucially dependent on information, and information can be difficult to come by. We have seen many examples of imperfect consumer control that is due to a lack of information. Competitor firms also may have imperfect information. This is particularly true when one recognizes that conditions change over time and firms must learn about the new conditions. Some centralized procedure may improve the speed at which the industry learns.

In a competitive market, for example, individual firms may have little incentive to reveal certain (unpatentable) information about a new technique. But information is a non-rivalrous public good: once produced, it is not used up by giving it to others. The speed of diffusion of innovations may be slower than optimal. Thus, the efficiency of competitive enforcement depends on how quickly the "enforcers" receive relevant information. A centralized effort to diffuse new knowledge, perhaps like the USDA efforts to inform farmers of methods to improve productivity, may improve the overall organization for certain sectors. However, the effectiveness of such efforts can vary greatly with the type of economic activity. Both computer and farm technologies may change quickly, but competitors may find it easy to identify and imitate computer advances (e.g., by buying a computer and studying its parts) and the opposite for farming (e.g., studying another farmer's tomato may not reveal how it was produced, which is why USDA information may be valuable).

Another way to make and extend this focus on information-handling ability is to recall the debate between Lange-Lerner and Hayek over the merits of decentralized socialism.[7] We sketch this in oversimplified terms below. First, note that if all economic agents have perfect knowledge, a perfectly centralized authority can achieve resource allocation identical with perfect competition. (The central authority simply uses perfect knowledge to direct each resource to where it would be in the competitive regime.) Lange and Lerner place less burdensome demands on the central authority, but it is nevertheless their information assumptions that raise Hayek's ire.

In the socialist setting, the property rights to produced capital belong to the state as a whole rather than to individual "capitalists." The question naturally arises whether and how socialist economies can achieve an efficient allocation of resources. Lange and Lerner

---

[7] See, for example, Oskar Lange and Fred Taylor, *On the Economic Theory of Socialism* (New York: McGraw-Hill Book Company, 1964).

demonstrated that it can be done in theory by having central planners set prices and issue decentralized operating instructions to firm managers. Firms are instructed to produce at least cost and at the level of output where price equals marginal cost (the same task capitalist firms have). They can hire whatever labor and capital they wish at the state-determined prices. A state-operated bank rents out the available capital to firms demanding it. Individuals make consumption purchases and supply labor as in capitalist countries.

If demand exceeds supply for an activity, the central planning board simply raises its relative price (and vice versa if supply exceeds demand) until equilibrium is reached. When the board sets the prices that equate supply and demand in all markets, the allocation is Pareto-optimal. Therefore, Lange and Lerner conclude, decentralized socialism can be just as efficient as competitive capitalism. They have shown that a plausible price adjustment mechanism can be used to reach equilibrium.

The logic of the Lange-Lerner model fully supports its conclusion. Furthermore, the logic is essentially no different than that used to show the optimality of perfect competition. But does that prove the two systems are equally efficient? Hayek's vehement protests concern the information-generating properties of each system. He argues that competitive capitalism is associated with rapid and subtle price adjustments. These efficiently convey the information necessary to allow economic agents to adapt promptly to changing circumstances. He continues by suggesting that socialism, on the other hand, is characterized by sloppy and slothful price adjustments made by a cumbersome central planning board. By the time the board deduces the correct prices for this year, it will already be next year; the economy will be in constant disarray.

Our earlier discussion suggests that Hayek's focus on information is appropriate, although his response may underestimate some important interdependencies. We do not really have any established theory that evaluates the relative informational efficiency of markets versus other procedures.[8] For specific activities, which is our interest, centralized procedures are often more efficient than decentralized ones. Nevertheless, the Lange-Lerner–Hayek debate does reinforce the importance of considering the learning and coordinating processes associated with any institutional design to guide resource allocations. The method of organization clearly affects the demand and supply of information in both the short and the long run. We shall try to illuminate this more clearly, and show its relevance for policy analysis, in the following section.

Reconsidering Methods for the Control of Air Pollution

Let us reconsider the problem of air pollution and the proposed tax or subsidy solutions to it. We use insights from the framework of operating rules and enforcement mechanisms, although some other aspects of having imperfect information and costly transactions will be

---

[8] International empirical comparisons are also very difficult. There are no obvious generalizations about whether relatively "socialistic" countries (those with governments occupying a relatively large portion of the overall economy) do better or worse over the years than those that are more "market-oriented." It so happened that in 1999 Luxembourg with its per capita income of $34,200 was the only country that exceeded the $33,900 of the

taken into account. First, it should be noted that both solutions, as well as the regulatory standards approaches, involve the "appointment" of the government as a centralized bargaining agent to represent interests in pollution avoidance. This reflects a trade-off: a possible loss of allocative efficiency (the bargaining agent does not know the exact preferences of individuals for clean air) in order to gain transactional efficiency.[9]

We did not establish earlier any reason for preferring the tax to the subsidy solution or vice versa. By the standard logic, the two were allocatively equivalent. Of course, the distributional effects of the two plans seem quite different, and the public is likely to favor the tax plan (polluters pay) over the subsidy plan (although the actual distributional consequences may not support this position[10]). Additionally, operation of the two plans does not require equivalent information. In order to enforce the tax, the assessor must know the current level of pollution. In order to enforce the correct subsidy, the government must know both the current level *and* the prior or base level of pollution (in order to know the size of any reduction).

The additional burden of establishing a base level that is accurate for each polluter could be substantial, especially if that same base is to be used in successive years (and thus its level takes on greater financial significance for each firm). For example, when firms realize subsidies will be (or are likely to be) available for reductions, some may increase pollution levels in order to make their base higher. Inevitably, some firms will find it in their interest to contest the base level assigned to them by the government. The issue is not mitigated by modifying the base in successive years, because then the squabbling simply shifts to disputes over the new base.[11] Thus while both plans would involve some disputes over measurement of current levels, only the subsidy plan involves disputes and administrative expenses over the base.

There is one other economic disadvantage of the subsidy plan compared to the tax plan. The allocative equivalence of the two plans holds under unchanging economic circumstances, when the firms' demand curves to pollute remain constant. But of course in the actual world circumstances change, and firm demand curves shift over time. Suppose the two

---

United States; Luxembourg also has a significantly larger portion of its economy in government. Studies that try to control for the many factors that can explain differences in per capita incomes besides government and then analyze the independent effect of government size both across countries as well as over time within countries have been inconclusive. For a review followed by some discussion, see Joel Slemrod, "What Do Cross-Country Studies Teach about Government Involvement, Prosperity, and Economic Growth?," *Brookings Papers on Economic Activity*, No. 2, 1995, pp. 373–431.

[9] This is an interesting case because ordinary individuals may not know their own preferences, and thus any loss of allocative efficiency may be small. Scientists expert in this area, while in some dispute among themselves, understand far better than lay persons what actual risks are involved from exposure to air pollutants. However, they do not have expertise in regard to how ordinary individuals would want to respond to these risks. This may be a situation in which it is quite reasonable to let legislatures, upon hearing appropriate testimony from experts and other interested parties, make decisions about pollution reduction goals.

[10] For example, suppose the pollution tax is shifted backward to labor generally, and the pollution subsidy is similarly shifted to raise the wage of labor generally.

[11] In order to keep the equilibrium identical in both cases, a constant tax rate over time should be compared with a constant base and subsidy rate plan.

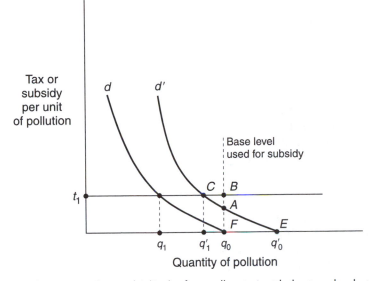

Figure 17-2. With growing demand (d'), the firm pollutes q_1' with the tax plan but q_0' with the subsidy plan (since $AEF > ABC$).

plans are initiated when a firm's demand curve is d in Figure 17-2. If q_0 is the unregulated amount of pollution (and the base for a subsidy plan), then a tax or a subsidy rate of t_1 will cause a cutback to q_1. But suppose the firm's demand curve shifts outward to d'? Under the tax plan, the firm would choose to pollute q_1': more than before, but less than if there were no tax. Under the subsidy plan, however, the firm does not qualify for any subsidy by marginal cutbacks from q_0' to q_0. If the willingness to pay for these emissions (area AEF) exceeds the gain from the available subsidy (area ABC), the firm will not reduce its pollution. It will emit q_0', more than the same firm under the tax plan.

There are different ways of trying to solve this last problem. For example, the government could raise the base level from q_0 to q_0' in response to the changed firm demand curve.[12] Of course, owing to the changed circumstances, the government may wish to change the tax or subsidy rates themselves. The feature that I wish to highlight here is that the tax plan automatically, without having to change policy at all, discourages some pollution under the changed circumstances whereas the subsidy plan does not. That is because the tax plan applies to all units of pollution, not just those below a base level. An interesting variant plan that would mitigate this problem is to offer subsidies for reductions below the base level, but to tax any units emitted above the base level. As long as the tax and subsidy rates are equal, this also keeps the price per unit of pollution constant for all levels! This variant would, however, still be subject to the other problems that arise from having

[12] This might be appropriate when circumstances really do change, but it also might give firms incentive to argue that circumstances have changed in this manner even if they have not. The latter could occur if there is an information asymmetry about this between the firm and the regulatory agency.

to define a base.[13] In light of the political and informational advantages of the tax plan over a subsidy plan, we will focus on comparing other alternatives to the tax plan.

The most interesting aspect of the tax (and subsidy) solution, compared to the regulatory standard approaches, is its use of decentralized operating instructions to firms: "Maximize profit, accounting for the tax cost (or subsidy) of pollution that you produce." This stands in contrast to the regulatory standards approach that uses centralized operating rules, for example, "Install this scrubber in your smokestack."

One question to consider is who has the better information. Do firms have better information than the central authority about how to control their own pollution? This must be asked not only in the static sense, based on current knowledge, but also in the dynamic sense: how quickly new techniques will be discovered and adopted. Since the use of particular techniques may be different under the centralized and decentralized alternatives, it would not be surprising if the efforts to improve the techniques (e.g., by would-be inventors) were different as well. Also, we have already noted that the speed of diffusion of new techniques may vary under these alternative regulatory systems.

Arguments can be advanced on various sides of the technical knowledge aspect. For example, often firms are likely to know best what substitute, pollution-reducing inputs they can use in order to remain productively efficient under pollution reduction constraints. This is particularly true of major polluters because of the high financial interest that they have in any control method (e.g., coal-burning electricity generators with substantial SO_2 emissions). Almost all polluting firms would be aided by factor suppliers who sell pollution-reducing inputs and who have every incentive to promote their products. The central government would have to become an expert on every product in order to possess the same range of information.

On the other hand, when there are a large number of relatively small, homogeneous firms that each pollute relatively small quantities, perhaps like dry cleaners, they may prefer to have the EPA tell them what to do. Otherwise, they would each face the transaction costs of figuring this out for themselves, and the combined transaction and pollution-control costs might be higher than under the centralized method. Furthermore, in some cases the decentralized adoption of particular techniques to reduce pollution may be invisible to other firms and result in slow diffusion of the techniques. That is, the innovating firm may hoard its knowledge (if not privately marketable) in order to gain a competitive advantage. A centralized authority might achieve a more rapid diffusion.

One might charitably assert that behind the suggestions for the tax (or subsidy) approach lies a belief that, on balance, the polluting firms have the advantage in terms of acquiring

---

[13] A variant like this was proposed for use on automobiles in conjunction with either sales taxes or annual registration fees. In both cases, government revenue was to be held constant. However, vehicles emitting more than average amounts of pollutants would be charged commensurately more than the normal sales tax or registration fee, and vehicles emitting less than the average amounts of pollutants would be charged commensurately less. See L. Levenson and D. Gordon, "Drive +: Promoting Cleaner and More Fuel Efficient Motor Vehicles through a Self-Financing System of State Sales Tax Incentives," *Journal of Policy Analysis and Management, 9,* No. 3, Summer 1990, pp. 409–415.

knowledge of pollution-reducing techniques. This advantage could extend to more development of innovative pollution control methods under the tax system, since firms could profit directly by adopting the innovations (under the technical standards, firms would have to convince the EPA to revise the standard applying to them). But these factors concern only the operating rules. What about the enforcement side? Is it possible to establish a system of rewards or penalties that leads to the intended result of achieving a given overall air quality at least cost? Therein lie the primary difficulties with the proposals.

In contrast to other inputs such as electricity or natural gas, the amount of pollution emitted by specific sources is not routinely metered. A tax on an input (or output) that is routinely metered is relatively easy to assess: one simply multiplies the tax rate by the known quantity. Even in this case one must solve the problem of knowing the right tax rate. (That is, it must give sufficient incentive to firms to achieve the desired aggregate reduction.) But for pollution this may require substantial trial and error, which would be prohibitive politically.

In addition, in the case of pollution, metering would have to be undertaken solely for the purpose of assessing the tax. It is not clear that we have the technology to meter all the different sources of the same pollutant at a reasonable cost; pollution is not as readily meterable as home electricity or gas. Emissions in a basin that originate from an immobile industrial smokestack might be relatively easy to monitor, whereas those that originate from the tailpipe of a particular automobile (which is not always driven in the basin) might be difficult or impossible to monitor. For tax assessments it is important that the quantity of pollution be accurately metered. The tax payments will be more or less, depending on the specific quantity.[14]

Some polluting firms may be metered continually, whereas others cannot be. In the latter case it may be feasible to sample a firm's pollutant levels randomly, but that must take account of the firm's ability to vary its pollution by the time of day. Sampling may not be considered a sufficient legal basis for assessing the firm's average tax for the tax period. Even if it is, there is an unfortunate incentive for corruption between the firm and the pollution level inspector: Who would know if the assessments were lower than the actual pollution level?[15] Thus, the difficulty or costliness of pollution-metering may be a serious drawback to the tax (and subsidy) approach.

By contrast, enforcing technological regulatory standards is a much easier task. Compliance is a "yes or no" rather than a "more or less" question. If firms are required to

---

[14] The accuracy required would be greater than that for performance standards. The latter involves answering only the "yes or no" question of whether the pollution level is higher or lower than the standard, and not by how much.

[15] It is easier to prevent corruption in the enforcement of regulatory standards; for example, it is easier to check up on the inspector if the inspection task is to see if the scrubbers are working. Corruption is influenced by the system for monitoring the inspectorate. For example, inspectors could receive a bounty for each pollutant they catch a source emitting, or one could randomly sample the inspectors' reported levels. But those enforcement systems might be enormously costly. For more on this subject, see Susan Rose-Ackerman, *Corruption: A Study in Political Economy* (New York: Academic Press, 1978). For an interesting example of how an inspectorate for regulatory standards might be used to simulate a tax, see John Mendeloff, *Regulating Safety: A Political and Economic Analysis of OSHA* (Cambridge: The MIT Press, 1979).

operate particular technologies such as smokestack scrubbers or cannot exceed certain pollution levels, random site visits are a highly plausible way of enforcing the rules. Catalytic converters can be required on all automobiles, with occasional inspections to verify their proper operation. To be sure, enforcement of standards would also be imperfect; for example, firms might not provide proper maintenance for the pollution control equipment. Nevertheless, this could be relatively easily observed on a random site visit and a penalty for noncompliance could readily be assessed.[16] The ease of checking compliance also makes it easier to spot-check the inspectors and reduces the likelihood of corrupt enforcement relative to the tax or subsidy plan.[17]

In fact, the enforcement problem makes it quite easy to understand why the tax solution to regulating air pollution has not been used in the United States. Even 20 years after the passage of the 1963 Clean Air Act, it would have been impossible. According to the Congressional Budget Office, by 1985 only 4 percent of the nation's 13,000 major stationary sources of air pollution were monitored by the "stack tests" necessary to assess emissions taxes; 60 percent were checked not for emissions but to see if special equipment was installed; and the remaining 36 percent were self-certified as complying (i.e., the firm sent a letter to the EPA stating that it was in compliance).[18] If the only choice were between a tax system and one of centralized technological standards, then the latter would be most efficient since the former was not even feasible.

What about other alternatives? As we noted earlier, regulatory standards do not have to be in the highly centralized form of specific technological requirements. They could, in principle, be in the form of a *centralized performance standard:* a requirement that a firm's emissions be no more than a given amount of pollution per time period, like 100 tons of SO_2 per year. This is a more decentralized solution in that it gives more discretion to the polluter about the method for controlling emissions (while the allowed emissions are still centrally determined). We mentioned earlier the standard argument that performance standards are always more efficient than technological standards that allow the same amounts of pollution: Firms can always use the technologies of the technological standards, but some will be familiar with and use less expensive ways to achieve the emissions limits.

We also mentioned earlier that the standard argument may be wrong when the costs of information and transactions are considered. A hospital patient with a fever of 103° wants to be restored to good health and does not want a doctor to say "do whatever is necessary to reduce your temperature to 98.6°." Rather, the patient seeks a centralized instruction such

---

[16] Note that if penalties are proportional to the seriousness of the violations, this begins to resemble a tax. Recognition of this is a key part of the analysis in Mendeloff, *Regulating Safety.*

[17] Recall the earlier footnote distinguishing technical and performance standards and reviewing the argument for favoring performance standards. Now we can see that this argument is subject to the same flaw as the usual pollution tax argument: It makes implicit assumptions about information and transaction costs that may be quite erroneous in certain circumstances. In particular, the enforcement of a performance standard (even though it is a "yes or no" question) may be much more difficult than a technical standard; measuring particular pollutants can be more difficult than checking scrubber installation.

[18] Congressional Budget Office, *Environmental Regulation and Economic Efficiency* (Washington, D.C.: U.S. Government Printing Office, 1985).

as "take this specific medicine every 4 hours until your temperature returns to normal." In this case, it is obvious that the doctor has better information than the patient. With reference to controlling pollution, we suggested earlier that some small establishments such as dry cleaners might prefer that the EPA set a technological standard for them, rather than requiring them to determine a solution themselves. A somewhat different example, which also illustrates the fallacy of assuming that more decentralization is necessarily better, is that automobile owners probably prefer emissions standards imposed at the factory to those placed on them directly (the automobile maker generally knows better than the future automobile owner how to choose an emissions control method).

However, suppose we grant the argument on the information side that most polluters do know better than the EPA how they can achieve specific emissions limits at least cost. If the performance form of operating rule is issued, how easy or hard would it be to enforce? Note that enforcing the performance standard requires answering a "yes or no" question: Is the firm within its allowed emissions limit? This is a harder "yes or no" question than the one associated with the technological standards because it requires some kind of on-site emissions testing. But it is less difficult than the "more or less" enforcement necessary for a tax system: Random site visits are probably acceptable in this case.[19] It is hard to know if the gains offered by the performance standard from the increased flexibility to the firm for controlling pollution outweigh the costs of the extra enforcement expenses necessary for its implementation.

Rather than pursuing this question further, it is more important to point out that there is probably a superior regulatory alternative to the centralized performance standard. Note that the centralized performance standard is equivalent to issuing nontransferable ration coupons necessary for emitting pollution. Why not make the coupons transferable? A *decentralized performance standard* is to issue *tradable emissions coupons*. Then each polluter is allowed the discretion to choose *both* the level of performance and the method of emissions control. The enforcement task for the regulatory authority is largely the same as with the centralized performance standard, except for the extra cost of keeping track of coupon trades.[20] However, a big advantage of this method is that it allows (indeed encourages) any sources with differing marginal costs of control to trade with each other, and thus reduces control costs.

A tradable emissions permit system provides the same incentives for efficiency as the ideal tax system (equalization of marginal costs of pollution across sources).[21] It relies on

---

[19] In another case of regulating externalities, Weil reports that compliance with safety standards is surprisingly high even when enforcement consists of a relatively small number of random site visits. See D. Weil, "If OSHA Is So Bad, Why Is Compliance So Good?" *RAND Journal of Economics, 27,* No. 3, Autumn 1996, pp. 618–640.

[20] To be sure this is clear, imagine that the initial distribution of the permits is identical to the assignments of the centralized performance standards. With no trading, enforcement costs of the two systems are identical. The only difference is that trades change the authorized performance levels of each polluter, so the regulator must know the number of coupons held after trading in order to verify that emissions are within the limit of these coupons.

[21] The tax (or subsidy) approach is sometimes referred to as Pigovian, after the economist Pigou, who first proposed solving the externality problem this way. See A. Pigou, *The Economics of Welfare* (London:

the market to set the permit price, and thus spares the regulatory authority the difficult task of setting an appropriate tax rate. Its enforcement is easier than a tax system because of a subtle difference. In terms of precise "more or less" measurement, it substitutes easy-to-identify coupon quantities for difficult-to-measure emissions quantities. Once the easy-to-identify coupon quantity is established, there is a second-step: the "yes or no" question of whether actual emissions are within the coupon limit. While this second step may still be difficult (or not feasible) for some sources, it is generally easier and more feasible than the one-step monitoring required for tax assessment.

Use of Arrow's framework for economic organization has left us focused on two alternatives for regulating air pollution: the technological standards that have been the predominant method in actual use and a tradable emissions permit system. We did not resolve whether or in what circumstances the realizable efficiency advantage of the tradable permit system outweighs its larger enforcement costs. Of course in actual practice, there is no restriction that only one type of system be used. It is quite possible to impose technological standards on those sources whose actual emissions cannot be monitored cheaply and to use tradable permits for the rest. The size of the efficiency gain through the permit system would then depend on the number and diversity of pollution sources that can be included.

Other practical issues about the tradable permit system would have to be resolved.[22] One is the initial method of distribution: Should the initial permit rights be given out according to EPA estimates of emissions under the best available technology (BAT) for control (as we assumed for convenience in the above discussion)? Or should they be "grandfathered" to sources in proportion to current pollution levels? Or should the government auction them off to the highest bidders (and if so, how should the auction be designed[23])?

A second issue concerns the duration of the permits. Should a permit authorize a given amount of pollution per year in perpetuity, so that the government would have to buy permits back in order to reduce aggregate emissions levels? Or should the permits be "recallable" at any time, perhaps at a predetermined price? Or should they simply be good for a fixed period, like one year (and if so, should it be for a specific year only or any year)?

A third issue concerns making the trading market work. As long as there are numerous buyers and sellers of a relatively homogeneous and well-defined product, the market may work well without any further government action. However, if considerations such as monitoring costs sharply limit the number of participants, then the market may be "thin"— either few buyers or few sellers. In this case, the government may wish to discourage the

---

Macmillan, 1920). Similarly, the issuance of tradable emissions coupons is sometimes referred to as a Coasian approach, after the economist Coase, who first proposed solving externality problems through the establishment of clear, marketable property rights. See R. Coase, "The Problem of Social Cost."

[22] Helpful references on this topic are: R. Hahn and R. Noll, "Designing a Market in Tradeable Emissions Permits," in W. Magat, ed., *Reform of Environmental Regulation* (Cambridge: Ballinger, 1982), pp. 119–146; and V. Foster and R. Hahn, "Designing More Efficient Markets: Lessons from Los Angeles Smog Control," *Journal of Law and Economics, 38,* No. 1, April 1995, pp. 19–48.

[23] For thoughts on designing auctions for emissions permits, see T. Cason and C. Plott, "EPA's New Emissions Trading Mechanism: A Laboratory Evaluation," *Journal of Environmental Economics and Management, 30,* No. 2, March 1996, pp. 133–160.

exercise of market power that might be expected in an unregulated market. One way to do this might be to require participation in a government-sponsored auction. For example, require all permit holders to submit their permits for sale at the auction and all bidders to submit a willingness-to-pay schedule for each permit on which they wish to bid (e.g., \$400 for the first, \$350 for the second, \$325 for the third, and so forth). Then rank order the bids, declare as the auction price the ranked bid that makes demand equal supply (e.g., if there are 100 permits in aggregate, then the 100th highest bid), and award the permits to the highest bidders (compensating the sellers at the auction price).

These quite practical issues of administration and enforcement help to explain why actual policy in the United States has relied so heavily on technological standards. However, policy analysts have been working steadily to try and create workable policies that allow market forces to achieve some cost reductions. The "offset" policy of the EPA was one of the first. Before the policy was introduced, air basins that had not met their pollution reduction targets were forbidden to allow the entry of any new pollution sources. Thus, the nonattainment areas had policies of no growth. That can be a very expensive policy, since the net benefits of new polluters are often greater than the net benefits from older polluters (of equivalent quantity). Under the offset policy, the new source may enter the area if it can induce (through the market) old sources to reduce their pollution by more than the amount the new source will cause. This is equivalent to distributing pollution rights to all the existing sources and allowing them to be transferred only to new sources.

There are now at least two regulatory systems in effect that make much broader use of tradable emissions permits. The 1990 Clean Air Act Amendments created an SO_2 emissions market among the 263 largest (and dirtiest) electricity generating plants in the nation, expanded beginning in the year 2000 to virtually all fossil-fueled electric generating plants. This market is intended to reduce the amount of annual SO_2 emissions by 10 million tons from 1980 levels. The other example is the RECLAIM program in California's South Coast Air Quality Management District, the most general emissions trading program implemented so far.

By all reports, the national SO_2 market seems to be evolving with considerable success.[24] The permits are called allowances, and each gives its owner the right to emit 1 ton of SO_2 into the atmosphere. Each allowance is dated with its year of issue, and may be used to cover emissions in that year or any future year (but not for prior years). The allowances are distributed annually for free to the participating sources in accordance with a complicated formula that gives more allowances to sources with historically greater emissions. These sources all have continuous emissions monitoring equipment for the measurement and reporting of actual SO_2 emissions.

---

[24] The development of this market is reported in Karl Hausker, "The Politics and Economics of Auction Design in the Market for Sulfur Dioxide Pollution," *Journal of Policy Analysis and Management, 11,* No. 4, Fall 1992, pp. 553–572. Evaluations include P. Joskow, R. Schmalensee, and E. Bailey, "The Market for Sulfur Dioxide Emissions," *American Economic Review, 88,* No. 4, September 1998, pp. 669–685; Robert N. Stavins, "What Can We Learn from the Grand Policy Experiment? Lessons from SO_2 Allowance Trading," *Journal of Economic Perspectives, 12,* No. 3, Summer 1998, pp. 69–88; and A. Denny Ellerman et al., *Markets for Clean Air* (New York: Cambridge University Press, 2000).

A small percentage of the allowances must be submitted for sale at an annual auction run by the EPA. In the market's first year of operation (1992–1993), some 280,000 allowances were sold (150,000 through the EPA auction). By the fifth year of operation (1996–1997), over 5,400,000 allowances were traded (300,000 through the EPA auction). Through the development of third-party allowance brokers, the market has grown considerably. According to one estimate, the SO_2 allowance trading (compared to issuing equivalent nontransferable allowances) has reduced costs by 25–34 percent.[25] An interesting aspect of the trading market is how wrong many of the initial planners were in terms of estimating market prices. The estimates centered around $500 per allowance (the range was $300–$700), whereas the actual allowance prices have been largely in the $100–$150 range. The best done of these estimates were closer to the mark, but sorting out which estimates are more or less reliable at the beginning is no easy task. It would be well to keep these estimation errors in mind if one is considering implementation of an emission tax system that requires advance estimation to set the tax rate necessary to achieve the reduction target.

The RECLAIM program operates in the southern California air basin that includes the Los Angeles area.[26] Tradable permits are issued for emissions of both sulfur oxides (SO_x) and nitrogen oxides (NO_x) to 329 sources emitting 4 or more tons per day of either pollutant. The program seeks to reduce emissions from these sources by 75 percent for NO_x and 58 percent for SO_x in its first 10 years (1994–2003). The permits, called RECLAIM Trading Credits (RTCs), were initially distributed for free, roughly on the basis of past peak emissions from each source over a 3-year period. These permits also depreciate according to a fixed schedule, to ensure the meeting of the reduction targets by 2003.

Among the innovative features of this system is that it allows the stationary sources to earn emissions reduction credits by paying for the removal of certain high-polluting automobiles in service in the basin. Early estimates of the expected savings from RECLAIM, compared to technological standards, are that it will achieve the reduction targets at 40 percent less cost. As of 1998, continuous emissions monitors were installed on sources emitting 84 percent of NO_x and 98 percent of SO_x. Emissions for the remainder are monitored with fuel-flow meters (an indirect method). By this time, there were 403 reported permit transactions, involving 28,662 tons of NO_x at an average price of $837 per ton and 13,305 tons of SO_x at an average price of $1428 per ton.[27]

[25] See p. 64 of R. Schmalensee et al., "An Interim Evaluation of Sulfur Dioxide Emissions Trading," *Journal of Economic Perspectives, 12,* No. 3, Summer 1998, pp. 53–68.

[26] Information about RECLAIM may be found on the web site of the South Coast Air Quality Management Board at http://www.aqmd.gov. Scholarly references include S. Johnson and D. Pekelney, "Economic Assessment of the Regional Clean Air Incentives Market—A New Emissions Trading Program for Los Angeles," *Land Economics, 72,* No. 3, August 1996, pp. 277–297; and J. Hall and A. Walton, "A Case Study in Pollution Markets: Dismal Science vs. Dismal Reality," *Contemporary Economic Policy, 14,* No. 2, April 1996, pp. 67–78.

[27] These averages hide the important fact that the price per ton of each pollutant has been increasing and is expected to increase significantly over time as the allowable aggregate quantity of emissions declines gradually to its target level. Note also that there is no necessary relation between the South Coast air basin prices, designed to meet its targets, and the prices for national SO_2 allowances. A source in the South Coast cannot meet its RECLAIM requirements by purchasing pollution reductions that take place outside of the air basin.

While these two programs are in operation, similar systems designed to regulate other pollution problems are under consideration. Perhaps the most important is a trading system to limit global carbon emissions. If such a system were put in place, it would represent an extraordinary degree of international cooperation.

Summary

Accounting for the information and transaction costs of making resource allocation decisions is often crucial to the identification of an efficient governance structure. These costs depend on the nature of the economic activity and on the governance structure used to guide the decisions of the economic agents. The significance of these costs explains why simple models in which they are assumed to be zero are unsatisfactory for comparing alternatives. With perfect information and no transaction costs, a centralized allocator does at least as well as the decentralized organization of a competitive market. Such a model specification hides the problem the governance structure is supposed to solve.

The trick is to develop a theoretical framework that quickly gets at the essence of information and transaction difficulties and provides remedies for them that maintain appropriate allocative incentives. Arrow suggests one approach when he defines a method of organization as a particular set of operating instructions and enforcement rules. Each may be more or less centralized, which is a matter of the scope of choice available to the agent responsible for doing the task.

We consider how to choose the degree of centralization in the context of regulating the externality of air pollution. Actual U.S. policy relies primarily on technical regulatory standards. These standards are a relatively centralized form of operating instruction, as the individual polluter is given little discretion or choice about the level of pollution or the method of control. Many economists have suggested that pollution taxes, a much more decentralized approach, would be an efficient way to internalize this externality.

To develop the argument, we first lay some basic groundwork for the analysis of externality problems. We demonstrate the "efficiency" of pollution taxes by using a standard model of economic behavior with perfectly informed agents and zero transaction costs. Using the same assumptions, we also show that the Coase theorem (market allocation of a good is independent of ownership, except for income effects) implies that a subsidy per unit of pollution reduction achieves the same result. But for those solutions to be better than well-intentioned regulatory standards, it must be that the standards are set with substantially less perfect knowledge or are substantially less enforceable.

The analysis of the operating rules, or the instructions given to polluting units on how to behave, is inconclusive. We interpret the usual argument for the tax approach as a judgment that the polluting units know best and can learn best how to reduce their own pollution and by how much. Given the subtle substitution possibilities that might characterize input choices of various products and the incentives of pollution-control equipment suppliers to develop and spread information about new marketable control techniques quickly, this judgment is not unreasonable.

It is on the enforcement side that the weakness of the tax or subsidy method becomes apparent. The amount of tax due is a more-or-less question that requires accurate metering of pollution by each source for assessment purposes. One must also know what tax (or subsidy) rate will lead to the desired aggregate reduction. Both pose very difficult information burdens on the taxing authority. Most pollution sources do not have their actual emissions measured. In fact, the cost of monitoring many air pollution sources to meet minimum legal requirements for taxation, so that the tax is not considered arbitrary or capricious, may be prohibitive.

The enforcement of technical regulatory standards, on the other hand, is a "yes or no" question that is open to dispute only in marginal cases. The achievement of aggregate reduction targets is more certain, since quantity is being rationed directly. Noncompliance is penalized by fines. Although the standards themselves are sure to be imperfect, they are at least reasonably enforceable.

The framework suggested by Arrow also helps us to think of alternative pollution control methods that may dominate either technical standards or the tax-subsidy approach. We consider the performance standard, which increases the degree of decentralization by allowing the polluter the choice of method to achieve a centrally determined pollution reduction. Enforcement of this requires answering a "yes or no" question: Is the source within its assigned emissions limit? This is harder to enforce than the technical standards (since some kind of emissions measurement is required), but easier than enforcing an emissions tax (e.g., in some cases random site visits may be acceptable and less expensive than continuous monitoring).

A better alternative in most cases is the tradable emissions permit, which is like the performance standard except that it decentralizes further by allowing each firm to choose its own emissions level (through the purchase or sale of emissions permits) and method of pollution reduction. For the modest extra enforcement cost of keeping track of the permit trades, it allows firms that can control emissions to substitute cheaply their extra reductions for those sources where control is more expensive. This system has the same allocative-efficiency advantages as the ideal tax system, but it is easier to enforce and does not require a very difficult tax rate estimation. This cost saving has been estimated at 25–34 percent for the national SO_2 emissions trading program among electric utilities.

RECLAIM in southern California, another emissions permit trading program for both nitrogen and sulfur oxides, is estimated to be achieving its goals for about 40 percent less than the cost of technical standards. Both RECLAIM and the national program cover only a fraction of the sources in the respective basins, primarily those that are clearly large enough to justify the extra monitoring expenses compared to technical standards. Greater inclusion of sources in trading programs can lead to further efficiency gains, providing that these are not offset by the marginal increases in monitoring costs. The most inclusive emissions trading program under discussion is a global market for carbon emission reductions to stem global warming. Extraordinary international cooperation will be necessary for it to become a reality.

Exercise

17-1 A large city wishes to reduce the amount of air pollution its businesses pour into the air. Two specific options have been proposed. One is a fixed dollar tax per unit of pollutant. The other is a quota system that would assign specific quotas to each individual firm. For example, all firms might be required to reduce pollution by 10 percent. The mayor has some specific questions about these two options:

a Economists have argued that a fixed pollution tax is an efficient solution. Administrative concerns aside, explain how such a tax promotes production efficiency in the jurisdiction.

b Business lobbyists like the idea of working through the tax system, but they have been arguing vigorously that the only fair approach is to offer a tax credit in return for each firm's pollution reduction. Still putting administrative concerns aside, would this approach be more or less efficient than the tax?

c The city is concerned about reducing pollution levels to an acceptable limit quickly. Even with perfect enforcement, might this be a weakness of the tax strategy?

d Given the concern for quickness as in (c), and still assuming perfect enforcement, is there any reason to think that the quota system would be better on this dimension?

e From the standpoint of productive efficiency, why might the quota system be undesirable?

CHAPTER EIGHTEEN

INDUSTRY REGULATION

IN THIS CHAPTER we consider industries that are characterized by substantial economies of scope or of scale—those that we usually refer to as "oligopoly" (few firms) or "natural monopoly" (one firm). Public policy aims to prevent the abuse of market power in such industries. Oligopoly is generally regulated through application of antitrust laws as a perceived need arises, while natural monopoly is generally regulated through some form of continuing public oversight. We discuss briefly an interesting example that at least during 2000–2001 seemed to fall between the cracks—the exercise of market power during the California electricity crisis. We review oligopoly first and then focus most attention on natural monopoly oversight.

We review the most widely used regulatory method for natural monopoly, known as rate-of-return regulation, and some of the criticisms to which it is subject. We also review a number of alternative types of regulation, including franchise bidding, performance contracting, incentive regulation, and partial deregulation. For part of our analysis, we introduce the framework of *transaction cost economics* that has been found useful for its insights about economic organization, including likely effects of different regulatory methods. Oliver Williamson, the principal developer of this framework, pointed out that certain governance structures such as ordinary rate-of-return regulation may be viewed as a particular form of contract between the regulatory authority and the regulated firm. Insight into a desirable form of governance is then derived by considering alternative ways to specify terms and arrange a contract between the government and a supplier.

We begin with a common model of oligopoly behavior referred to as the Cournot model. We use the model to suggest a link between the degree of *market power* and measures of the degree of *concentration* in an industry, and we discuss some of the observed behaviors of firms in concentrated industries, including the California electricity market. For the remainder of the chapter, we focus on natural monopolies and their regulation. Rate-of-return regulation is explained and compared with a suggestion that it be replaced by a market process: competitive bidding for an exclusive franchise to service an area's consumers. The latter suggestion is motivated in part by the hope that it can avoid the problem of *regulatory capture,* which is a theory that regulatory authorities end up being overly sympathetic to the industry position. The analysis shows that many of the features of ordinary regulation will also appear in the contract used to award the franchise. These features, which result from information and transaction costs present under either method of governance, are essentially those used to explain why capture occurs. Thus, there is little reason to think the franchising method is generally superior to ordinary regulation, although it may be superior in particular circumstances.

A case study of franchise bidding to provide community antenna television (CATV) services in Oakland, California, offers concrete examples in support of the above reasoning. Two other examples of this type of analysis, involving performance contracting, are discussed briefly. One involves Amtrak contracting for passenger rail service and the other relates to elementary education. We then discuss the form of incentive regulation known as price-cap regulation and its application primarily to telecommunication companies. Finally, we mention partial deregulation as another important strategy.

Oligopoly and Natural Monopoly

In this section, we consider market structures that range from perfect competition to pure monopoly. We have already seen the sense in which perfect competition leads to an efficient allocation of resources (Chapter 12), as well as the inefficiency of too little output that results from a profit-maximizing monopolist (Chapter 10). Of course, actual markets often do not approximate either of these extremes. The "in-between" situations are generally described as **oligopoly: a market structure in which a relatively small number of firms compete with one another. A key characteristic that distinguishes oligopoly from perfect competition is that one or more of the competing firms has some form of market power** (the ability to charge a price that is above marginal cost). In other words, in an oligopoly one or more of the firms is a price-maker rather than a price-taker.

An industry may be oligopolistic owing to economies of scale in the production of its outputs. That is, up to a point, larger firms may be able to produce more efficiently than smaller ones. A natural result of the competitive process in such a case is that the larger firms inevitably drive out the smaller ones, such that the "few" remaining firms are those capable of producing the industry's outputs at the least cost. Since our interest lies in the public policy implications, it may be useful to mention the term "*workable competition.*" Broadly speaking, the antitrust laws of the United States seek to prohibit the abuse of market power. *If in an oligopoly market there are no significant entry barriers and no firms are charging substantially more than marginal cost, then the situation may be considered "workable."*[1] However, industries in which some firms are charging substantially above

---

[1] This is a simplified definition of a complex concept. There is no widespread agreement on any particular definition, but more detailed definitions usually discuss aspects of the structure, conduct, and performance of the

marginal cost may be scrutinized by the Justice Department, the Federal Trade Commission, or state antitrust divisions. These agencies investigate whether a firm's actions violate one or more sections of the antitrust laws (e.g., mergers that substantially lessen competition, collusion in restraint of trade, predatory pricing, price discrimination, and deceptive advertising).

Some of the more visible cases in recent years include those against Microsoft (brought by the U.S. Justice Department joined by nineteen states) and Intel. Microsoft has a near-monopoly on the operating systems used by personal computers (although Apple, Unix, and Linux are other operating systems). It is not a violation of the law to be a monopoly, but the suit alleges that Microsoft has repeatedly used its market power to stifle competition (e.g., by integrating its Internet Explorer web browser into the operating system in order to disadvantage its main browser competitor Netscape's Navigator). The case against Intel, which has a near-monopoly on the central processor chips used inside personal computers (although Motorola, American Micro Devices, and Cyrix also supply some segments of this market), was narrower. The Federal Trade Commission alleged that Intel illegally withheld technical information from three computer makers (to disadvantage them in the personal computer market) as a tactic to force favorable resolution of patent disputes. The latter case was settled out of court in March 1999.

Not all cases are so visible, however. During 1999 in California, the state attorney general indicated that he was examining whether to challenge the proposed merger of two *nonprofit* hospitals in the Oakland area (the Summit Medical Center and Alta Bates). The charge would be that the merger would raise prices and reduce services in violation of the state's antitrust laws.[2] A key ingredient in a successful prosecution of cases like this and the ones mentioned above is the establishment of the existence of market power (a firm cannot abuse a power that it does not have). In the rest of this section, we provide a brief introduction to this aspect of the "industrial organization" branch of microeconomic policy.

There are a large number of different types of oligopoly structures and behaviors for which microeconomic models have been constructed. Unfortunately, there is no one "basic" model that captures the essence of behavior in oligopoly markets.[3] However, we introduce one model of oligopoly, referred to as the Cournot model,[4] that suggests a natural link between the degree of concentration in an industry and the market power of the individual firms. This helps explain why measures of industry concentration, such as the Herfindahl-Hirschman Index that we will introduce, are often calculated by the antitrust agencies as part of their investigations.

---

industry. For example, a structural aspect would be the number of firms compared to the number appropriate for the economies of scale, a conduct aspect would be whether or not price discrimination is practiced, and performance aspects would be profit levels and the industry's rate of technological progress. See F. M. Scherer and D. Ross, *Industrial Market Structure and Economic Performance,* 3rd Ed. (Boston: Houghton Mifflin Company, 1990), pp. 52–55.

[2] *San Francisco Chronicle,* "Dire Predictions about East Bay Hospital Merger," March 12, 1999, p. A19. This situation seems very similar to the 1996 Michigan case we discussed in the nonprofit section of Chapter 11.

[3] Many of the models can be framed with common game-theoretic terms.

[4] The model was first presented by Augustin Cournot in 1838.

The Cournot model assumes that each firm in the industry will choose its output level to maximize profit, assuming that the output from the rest of the firms in the industry stays fixed. We illustrate this behavior for a very simple case of a two-firm industry, or *duopoly,* in Figures 18-1a and b. Assume that firm 1 has constant marginal cost of $10 per unit and that the total market demand curve is

$$P = 100 - Q$$

Suppose firm 1 believes that firm 2 is going to produce zero output. Then the residual demand curve facing firm 1, which we will denote D_0, is the entire market demand curve. Firm 1 will thus choose the output level where the associated marginal revenue curve $MR_0 = MC$, or 45 units as shown in Figure 16-1a.[5] In other words, if firm 2 produces zero, firm 1 will produce 45.

Suppose, however, that firm 1 believes that firm 2 will produce 50 units. In that case, the residual demand curve D_{50} facing firm 1 will be the market demand less 50 units, or

$$P = 50 - Q_1$$

The associated marginal revenue curve MR_{50} will be

$$MR_{50} = 50 - 2Q_1$$

These curves are also shown in Figure 18-1a. In this case, the intersection of MR_{50} with MC occurs at $Q_1 = 20$. In other words, if firm 2 produces 50 units, firm 1's profit-maximizing choice is to produce 20 units.

Note that the quantity firm 1 will select declines as a function of the output level it believes firm 2 will select. **The reaction function shows a firm's profit-maximizing quantity for each possible level of output that the rest of the industry could supply.** Firm 1's reaction function, its best choice for each possible output level that firm 2 might choose, is shown in Figure 18-1b.[6] If we assume for simplicity that firm 2 has the same constant marginal cost as firm 1, then the former's reaction function on the same diagram will be symmetrical to that of the latter. *The Cournot equilibrium is the point at which the reaction functions intersect* ($Q_1 = Q_2 = 30$). *It is the only point that is a Nash equilibrium, meaning that from that point no firm has individual incentive to change its behavior.*[7] Put differently, it is the only point at which the output level of each firm triggers no reaction from the other.

---

[5] In Chapter 10, note 17, we showed that for any linear demand curve $P = a - bQ$, the marginal revenue curve is $MR = a - 2bQ$. Thus the marginal revenue curve MR_0 associated with D_0 is $MR_0 = 100 - 2Q_1$.

[6] The equation for the reaction function is found by equating firm 1's marginal cost curve with its marginal revenue function for any firm 2 output level. The marginal cost in the example is constant at 10, and the marginal revenue curve for any firm 2 output level Q_2 is $100 - Q_2 - 2Q_1$. Thus the reaction function is

$$100 - Q_2 - 2Q_1 = 10$$

or, by simplifying and rearranging terms,

$$Q_1 = 45 - Q_2/2$$

[7] We introduced the concept of Nash equilibrium in Chapter 7, note 32.

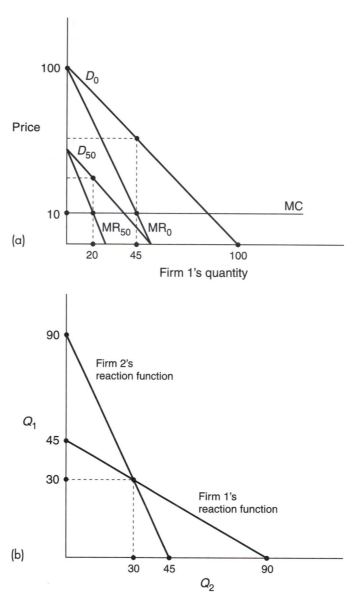

Figure 18-1. The Cournot model of oligopoly behavior: (a) Firm 1's profit-maximizing choice depends on firm 2's output level ($Q_2 = 0 \rightarrow Q_1 = 45$; $Q_2 = 50 \rightarrow Q_1 = 20$). (b) The firm reaction functions and Cournot equilibrium at $Q_1 = Q_2 = 30$.

Note also from Figure 18-1a that the industry output level of 60 (= 30 + 30) is more than what a single profit-maximizing monopolist would produce (MR = MC at $Q = 45$), but less than the efficient amount ($Q = 90$, where MC intersects the demand curve).

An interesting example of a policy problem in which Cournot-type behavior suggests considerable insight is the California electricity crisis of 2000–2001. California restructured its electricity markets during the latter 1990s to partially replace monopoly regulation with a competitive generation sector. To achieve this, it strongly encouraged its three investor-owned utilities to divest a substantial portion of their generating plants and barred them from entering into any long-term contracts. About 50 percent of their overall generating capacity, primarily those plants that run on fossil fuel, were divested to five different companies (out-of-state utilities that had substantial experience operating such plants). Essentially all of the power from these plants had to be purchased as needed on the daily spot market, since California consumers still received their power through the utilities, which were forced to obtain it without contracting. This complete bar on contracting was probably the single most important cause of the crisis.[8]

Because each of five companies controlled a substantial fraction of generation available to California, they each had market power. Figure 18-2 gives a very stylized version of profit-seeking firms in this kind of setting. Figure 18-2a assumes that in the short-run there are only four companies, each operating one good-size electricity plant that can generate 1000 megawatts of power. The plants each produce at constant marginal cost up to their capacity, but the marginal costs vary by plant: $10 per megawatt from the lowest cost plant, one at $20, another at $30, and the most expensive at $40 per megawatt. This is shown as the "stepped" supply curve S, which becomes vertical at 4000 megawatts (no greater quantity can be supplied at any price).

The aggregate demand for power D is also drawn on the diagram and is assumed to obey the following equation:

$$Q = 4100 - P$$

If this market operated in a perfectly competitive manner in the short run, then the price would be $100 per megawatt and the full supply of 4000 megawatts would be utilized.[9] Note that even this situation would upset consumers, who would know that the generators are receiving revenues far above their costs.

However, the point of this illustration is that the firms will not behave in a perfectly competitive manner. Consider the position of the fourth firm that has marginal cost of $40, for example, shown in Figure 18-2b. Suppose it uses Cournot reasoning and assumes that the other three plants will continue to supply 3000 megawatts. Then the residual demand that it faces (Q_4) will depend on the market price it makes (P):

$$Q_4 = (4100 - P) - 3000 = 1100 - P$$

---

[8] The rationale for forbidding long-term contracting was the concern that the newly divested utilities would prevent entry of other service providers by simply arranging long-term contracts for the full supply of power from the divested plants. This is a reasonable concern, but to address it does not require a total ban on contracting. One reason so few *new* sources of generation were developed was because the utilities could not contract for them.

[9] Actual user demand for electricity on the "spot" is uninformed and too inelastic; users in their homes and offices operating lights and air conditioners have no idea what the spot price is and are unresponsive to changes in it. The example does not attempt to deal with this problem, but mechanisms to improve demand-side responsiveness are also important in electricity markets.

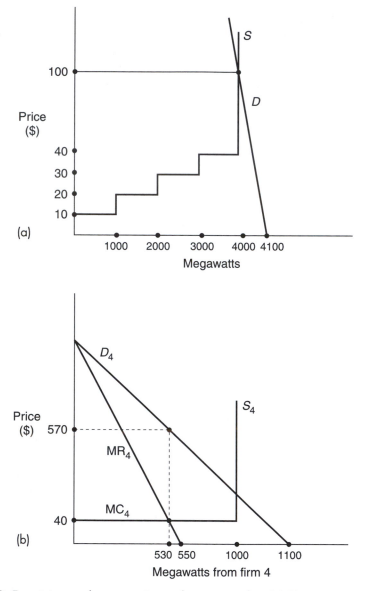

Figure 18-2. Exercising market power in an electricity market: (a) Short-run competitive equilibrium in the electricity market. (b) The exercise of market power by the Cournot firm with MC = $40.

or, equivalently,

$$P = 1100 - Q_4$$

This is shown as D_4 on Figure 18-2b. What is the firm's profit-maximizing price and quantity? It has to find the allocation where $MR_4 = MC_4$. The MR_4 curve associated with the above linear demand curve is[10]

$$MR_4 = 1100 - 2Q_4$$

Since we know that $MC_4 = 40$, we have to find the Q_4 that makes

$$1100 - 2Q_4 = 40$$

or

$$Q_4 = 530 \text{ and } P = \$570$$

In other words, Cournot behavior for firm 4 implies that *it will exercise market power by restricting its quantity in order to raise market price.* Instead of making a profit of only $60,000, it makes a better profit of $490,000.[11] It is interesting to note in this example that *imposing a public policy price cap at the competitive price level* ($100 per megawatt) *would increase short-run supply because it takes away the profit incentive to exercise market power by restricting supply.* There is some evidence that the behavior we have just illustrated mimics fairly accurately the behavior of the firms with divested generators in California's market during the summer of 2000, in which their generators operated at only 72 percent of capacity during times of high spot-market prices.[12] While price caps can be effective in the short-run, the best long-run solution is to ensure the entry of new, more efficient generators, which will both dissipate the market power possessed by generators during the transitional period and lower and lengthen the short-run supply curve.

At this point, we note that the Cournot model in general does not offer any very intuitive explanation of an adjustment process that might lead to its equilibrium. Furthermore, it is clearly a myopic kind of optimization on the part of each firm. We saw from our first illustration that a single monopolist would produce less than the duopolists and make more money.[13] Therefore the latter have incentive to collude and restrain output further (to act as if they were one monopolist and share the larger total profit).

---

[10] We use the formula for MR from note 5.

[11] Note that we have not calculated a Cournot equilibrium by assuming analogous behavior of the other firms; here we only wished to illustrate the exercise of market power.

[12] See Paul Joskow and Edward Kahn, "A Quantitative Analysis of Pricing Behavior in California's Wholesale Electricity Market during Summer 2000," January 15, 2001, unpublished paper available on MIT web site http://www.mit.edu/people/pjoskow/papers.html.

[13] The monopolist would produce forty-five units in total, charging the price on the market demand curve of $55 and thus making a profit of $2025 = 45($55 − $10). The Cournot duopolists produce sixty units in total, selling them at the market-clearing price of $40 and making $900 each.

Sometimes the oligopolists may try to form a **cartel: an association of independent producers who agree to coordinate activities in order to exploit the monopoly power of the collectivity.** Probably the best known cartel is the Organization of Petroleum Exporting Countries (OPEC), where the members are countries rather than the private producers themselves. From the mid-1970s through the mid-1980s, this cartel was quite successful at raising the world price of oil by imposing a series of coordinated export taxes on oil leaving each member country. However, the problem any cartel faces is in assigning and enforcing the market share (and thus profits) for each member. Any single member can increase its profits by cheating the cartel: cutting price (or export taxes) slightly and selling a quantity beyond its assigned cartel limit. But if all members do this, output expands, price falls, and the cartel collapses to the competitive solution. From the mid-1980s through the late 1990s, OPEC was unable to secure the cooperation of enough of its members to maintain the monopoly power it once exercised.

Cartels are illegal under U.S. law. They violate Section 1 of the Sherman Act, which prohibits "every contract, combination . . . or conspiracy in restraint of trade or commerce among the several states." In recent years the U.S. Justice Department has pursued the prosecution of international cartels for violating this law. For example, in 1999 it secured voluntary guilty pleas from one Swiss manufacturer and five U.S. executives for conspiring to fix prices and allocate sales of vitamins B_3 and B_4. The Swiss company agreed to pay a $10.5 million fine. Individual violators can be imprisoned for a maximum of 3 years, in addition to substantial fines. Since it is illegal for firms to collude in restraint of trade, one might expect them to seek other means of accomplishing the same ends. Much of oligopoly game theory explores other strategies and behaviors that might be more profitable than those implied by the independent decision-making of the Cournot model.

Nevertheless, the Cournot model can be used to show an intuitive relationship between the degree of concentration in an industry (the proportion of output supplied by the largest firms) and the market power of the oligopoly firms. First, recall from Chapter 10 that a firm's marginal revenue can be expressed as a function of the price of its output and the price elasticity of demand that it faces:

$$MR = P(1 + 1/\varepsilon)$$

where ε is the price elasticity of demand for the *firm*'s output. For a true monopolist, this is identical to the price elasticity of demand for the entire market. But the competitive firm, on the other hand, has a demand elasticity for *its* output that approaches $-\infty$ (the horizontal demand curve), so that for it the above expression collapses to $MR = P$.

Since the profit maximizer has $MR = MC$, we can also write

$$MC = P(1 + 1/\varepsilon)$$

By rearranging terms, we can show an interesting measure of monopoly power. We do this in two steps. First,

$$P - MC = -P/\varepsilon$$

Second, divide both sides by P:

$$(P - MC)/P = -1/\varepsilon$$

The term on the left is *Lerner's measure of a firm's monopoly power*.[14] It is zero for a competitive firm ($P = MC$) and can approach 1 as price gets far above marginal cost. The term on the right indicates that the firm's market power is the inverse of the price elasticity of demand for its output: The less the elasticity, the greater the market power.[15]

Recall also the definition of elasticity:

$$\varepsilon = (\Delta q/q)/(\Delta P/P)$$

where q is the firm's output level. Under the Cournot assumptions, we can relate one firm's demand elasticity to that of the entire market. Consider how a small change in one firm's output (Δq) affects market price (ΔP) when we make the Cournot assumption that the other firms do not react to this change (so that the change in market quantity ΔQ is equal to Δq). The market price changes in accordance with the market elasticity of demand ε_M:

$$\varepsilon_M = (\Delta Q/Q)/(\Delta P/P)$$

Since $\Delta Q = \Delta q$, we can substitute in the above equation:

$$\varepsilon_M = (\Delta q/Q)/(\Delta P/P)$$

Multiply both sides of the equation by Q/q to convert the right-hand side to the individual firm's demand elasticity:

$$\varepsilon_M(Q/q) = \varepsilon$$

If we assume for a moment that each firm in the industry is of equal size, then Q/q is simply the number of firms n. We can then see a simple relation between an individual Cournot firm's demand elasticity and that of the whole market in which it participates:

$$n\varepsilon_M = \varepsilon$$

That is, the price elasticity faced by an individual Cournot firm is simply the whole market elasticity times the number of firms in the industry. If there are four equal competitors in a Cournot industry facing a price-inelastic market demand of −0.9 for the industry's product, then each competitor faces a quite elastic demand for its own output of −3.6. If there are ten competitors, each would face an elastic demand of −9.0, and as n becomes large the individual firm elasticity approaches the perfectly competitive level of −∞.

Let us also use the above expression to substitute for ε in the market power equation:

$$(P - MC)/P = -1/n\varepsilon_M$$

---

[14] This is named after the economist Abba P. Lerner, who first suggested it. See Abba P. Lerner, "The Concept of Monopoly and the Measurement of Monopoly Power," *Review of Economic Studies, 1,* June 1934, pp. 157–175.

[15] Recall also from Chapter 10 that a profit-maximizing firm must be at an elastic point on the demand curve it faces. If $-1 < \varepsilon < 0$ in the above expression for MR, then MR will be negative.

The more inelastic the market demand for the product and the smaller the number of competitors the greater the individual firm's market power. For any market price elasticity, market power approaches zero if there are a large number of competitors.

Let us relax the assumption that the competing oligopolists are equal and define one firm's *market share* as $s \equiv q/Q$. There is still a simple relation between the price elasticity facing the individual Cournot firm and the market as a whole. Substitute $1/s$ for Q/q in the equation above relating firm to market price elasticity:

$$\varepsilon = \varepsilon_M/s$$

The smaller the market share of the firm, the more elastic the demand curve it faces. Using this expression in the market power equation, we get

$$(P - MC)/P = -s/\varepsilon_M$$

Thus market power increases directly with the share of the market controlled by an individual Cournot firm.

We can extend this relationship slightly further, to relate the average degree of market power in the industry with its degree of concentration. Concentration refers generally to the share of total market output that is contributed by the largest firms in the market. Sometimes this is measured (somewhat arbitrarily) as the market share of the four or eight largest firms. A measure that includes all of the firms in the market is the Herfindahl-Hirschman Index (H) defined as follows:

$$H \equiv \sum_{i=1}^{n} s_i^2$$

That is, the index would be 1 if one firm had 100 percent of the market, and approaches 0 as each firm has only a very small share of the overall market.[16] For a sense of how this index is used, consider that the Antitrust Division of the U.S. Justice Department reports that it is likely to challenge proposed mergers of firms in industries that have $H > .18$ and for which the merger would increase the index by .01 or more.[17] For example, an industry with six equal-size firms has $H = .17$, and a merger of any two would result in an $H = .22$ (and would thus probably be challenged).

Often the hardest part of any assessment using this index is the definition of the relevant market. It should include the production by all firms of "close" substitutes for the product being examined. It should not include firms producing the identical product but for a distinctly different geographic market. Firms producing glass containers, for example, probably face significant competition from those producing containers of plastic or lightweight metals such as aluminum. The cement industry in Los Angeles does not face much competition from cement firms in Chicago. Thus even though the index is reported for U.S. manufacturing in-

[16] It is common to calculate the measure using the market share percentage as a score from 0 to 100, so that a 100 percent share may be reported as $H = (100)^2 = 10,000$. The U.S. Department of Justice, for example, reports its calculations this way.

[17] See the Horizontal Merger Guidelines, U.S. Department of Justice, issued April 2, 1992, and revised April 8, 1997.

dustries in the U.S. Census of Manufactures, the Census Bureau does not attempt to define economic markets. It simply includes all of the U.S. firms with the same Standard Industrial Classification code (and, not surprisingly, excludes non-U.S. competitors).

Imagine we are in a well-defined Cournot oligopoly market with n firms of varying sizes and marginal costs. Denoting the market power equation above for the ith firm, let us first multiply both sides by its market share s_i:

$$s_i(P - MC_i)/P = -s_i^2/\varepsilon_M$$

Then let us add this expression over all n firms in the market:

$$\sum_{i=1}^{n} s_i \frac{(P - MC_i)}{P} = \sum_{1=1}^{n} -s_i^2/\varepsilon_M$$

Factor out the terms that are constant over the sums:

$$\frac{1}{P}\left(P\sum s_i - \sum s_i MC_i\right) = -\frac{1}{\varepsilon_M}\sum s_i^2$$

Note that the first term in parentheses reduces to P because $\Sigma s_i = 1$ and that the second term in parentheses is simply a weighted average of the marginal cost of each firm in the industry, which we will denote $\overline{MC}$. Also note that the last term on the right-hand side is simply the definition of H. Therefore the entire expression reduces to

$$\frac{P - \overline{MC}}{P} = \frac{H}{-\varepsilon_M}$$

In other words, the average amount of monopoly power in the industry is the Herfindahl-Hirschman Index divided by the market price elasticity for the industry's product. The more concentrated the industry, the greater the average market power of the firms in it.

Rate-of-Return Regulation

Let us turn now to the more extreme case of monopoly. The cost structure of a natural monopoly was introduced in the discussion of trucking deregulation in Chapter 9. Because of economies of scale over the relevant range of demand, competition can sometimes sustain only one firm in a market. In Figure 18-3 we illustrate such a situation.

The efficient output quantity to produce is Q_E, where the marginal cost curve intersects the demand curve. But a monopolist is unlikely to choose that output level. A profit-maximizing monopolist, for example, will produce at Q_M.[18] At that quantity, price P_M will be substantially above the marginal cost. Thus, consumers are being "exploited" (i.e., by the amount above marginal cost) and the quantity produced is below the optimal level.[19]

---

[18] Barring price discrimination.

[19] Note that the problem of the unprofitable natural monopoly will occur if the demand curve shifts far enough to the left. The usual response to this case, discussed in Chapter 9, is either to have a public enterprise or to subsidize a private firm. Of course, if the demand curve is too far to the left, there may be no positive output level at which the benefits outweigh the costs.

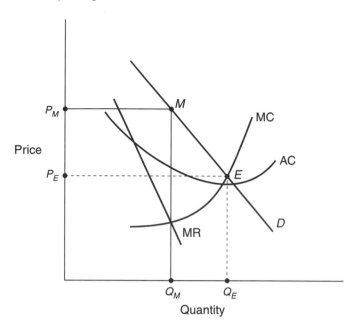

Figure 18-3. The profitable natural monopoly.

Historically, this market structure has been thought to characterize such activities as electricity, gas, and telephone services. It would be inefficient, for example, to have two sets of telephone poles when one is bad enough. The predominant response to these natural monopolies has been to subject them to rate-of-return regulation. Under that type of regulation, a regulatory commission determines a "fair" rate of return f on the company's net capital stock K. It then limits the price P charged per unit of service Q such that, after paying noncapital expenses (which we represent simply as the wage bill wL),

$$\frac{PQ - wL}{K} \leq f$$

Two quite different types of criticism are often voiced against this form of regulation. The first one is known as the *Averch-Johnson theorem,* relies on the ordinary model of firm profit maximization for its proof: *A profit-maximizing monopolist subject to rate-of-return regulation will produce its output with an inefficient combination of inputs. In particular, the firm will use too much capital relative to labor for any given output level.*

The complete proof of this theorem is somewhat tedious, and we present only an abbreviated, simplified version.[20] First assume that the firm finds the regulatory constraint bind-

---

[20] The original proof is in H. Averch and L. Johnson, "Behavior of the Firm under Regulatory Constraints," *The American Economic Review, 52,* December 1962, pp.1053–1069. A somewhat simpler geometric proof is offered by E. Zajac, "A Geometric Treatment of Averch-Johnson's Behavior of the Firm Model," *American Economic Review, 60,* March 1970, pp. 117–125.

ing (otherwise it could choose the ordinary profit maximum). With a convex production function, profit levels at production points where the constraint is not fully used up are strictly less than the maximum attainable. Also assume that the allowable rate of return f is greater than the competitive price per unit of capital. (That is, there will be some positive economic profit, as would characterize, for example, the efficient solution at point E in Figure 18-3.) We show below that, under these conditions, the firm cannot have an efficient input combination and simultaneously be at its equilibrium (i.e., constrained profit maximum). It can do better by finding another constraint point where it uses more capital relative to labor.

For convenience, we define the input units such that the price of a unit of capital equals the price of a unit of labor. Then if the firm is using an efficient input combination, $MP_L = MP_K$. If this is also a firm equilibrium, the regulatory constraint must be binding. But we will show a contradiction: The firm can make the same profit without running into its constraint (i.e., when the constraint is not binding), and therefore that profit amount cannot be the maximum.

Imagine that, from this hypothesized efficient equilibrium, we reduce labor and increase capital by one unit each in order to remain on the same isoquant. This marginal change holds output and total cost, and therefore profit, constant. The firm's rate of return, however, is now strictly less than f:

$$\frac{PQ - w(L-1)}{K+1} < \frac{PQ - wL}{K} = f$$

How do we know this? We multiply both sides of the claimed inequality by $K(K+1)$ and cancel like terms:

$$Kw < PQ - wL$$

or

$$0 < PQ - w(L + K)$$

But the right-hand side is simply the firm's profit, which we know is greater than zero from our initial assumptions. Since this shows that the firm can achieve the same profit level hypothesized as the maximum without running into the constraint, that profit level cannot be the maximum.[21]

---

[21] An informal calculus argument may be made along the same lines. Along an isoquant,

$$dQ = MP_K \, dK + MP_L \, dL = 0$$

Since the efficient point on that isoquant is one where $MP_K = MP_L$ (given our choice of units), it follows that at it the slope is -1, or $-dK = dL$. A movement from this point along the isoquant has the following effect on the rate of return:

$$df = \frac{\partial f}{\partial K} \, dK + \frac{\partial f}{\partial L} \, dL$$

$$= \left(-\frac{\partial f}{\partial K} + \frac{\partial f}{\partial L} \right) dL$$

Note that one cannot make the same argument by moving the opposite way along the isoquant, that is, by increasing labor and reducing capital. That would strictly violate the rate-of-return constraint. An intuitive explanation for this bias toward capital is as follows: Consider expanding output by using either a unit of capital or a unit of labor, either of which would increase profits by the same amount. The unconstrained firm would be indifferent about the input choice, but the regulated firm must consider whether the extra profit will be allowed, given its rate base. The extra unit of labor does not change the base, but the extra unit of capital expands it and thus allows greater profit. Thus, the regulated firm has some bias to favor capital relative to labor. In other words, when seeking marginal revenue, the firm considers both the ordinary marginal costs and the marginal cost of using up some of its scarce constraint.

In an important sense the Averch-Johnson theorem demonstrates government failure analogously to the examples we have seen of market failure. It shows that a particular way of regulating a specific activity (the natural monopoly) is imperfect. It does not say anything about the degree of imperfection; that depends on the actual behavior of the regulatory commission. (For example, will the allowed rate of return be generous or stringent?) Furthermore, it does not say anything about rate-of-return regulation in comparison with other alternatives (e.g., unregulated monopoly, public enterprise, and other forms of regulation).

Indeed, one of the strongest arguments against rate-of-return regulation is offered by those who believe in the **"capture theory": The regulatory commission acts in the in-**

Thus our claim that $df < 0$ in response to this change (where $dL < 0$) is equivalent to the claim that

$$0 < \frac{\partial f}{\partial L} - \frac{\partial f}{\partial K}$$

By definition,

$$f = \frac{PQ - wL}{K}$$

We take the partial derivatives, but for simplicity omit writing below the terms associated with the partial changes in the total revenue term PQ that later net out to 0 (because we are moving along an isoquant):

$$\frac{\partial f}{\partial L} = -\frac{w}{K}$$

$$\frac{\partial f}{K} = -\frac{PQ - wL}{K^2}$$

On substituting in the claimed inequality above, we have

$$0 < -\frac{w}{K} - \left(-\frac{PQ - wL}{K^2}\right)$$

By multiplying both sides by K^2 and rearranging, we get

$$0 < PQ - w(L + K)$$

Thus, the claim that f decreases is equivalent to the claim that firm profits are positive, and we know by assumption that the latter is true. Q.E.D.

terests of the firms in the industry it is supposed to be regulating.[22] This can happen in an unsubtle way if the commission members believe that the public interest coincides with unconstrained industry profit maximization (perhaps because they have been chosen by a governor hoping to receive substantial campaign assistance from the industry). Another method is to dangle the prospect of attractive industry jobs (or contracts, or other personal rewards) for cooperative commissioners when they leave public service. But the sophisticated version is that fair-minded commission members are subjected to heavily biased information channels, which leads to decisions that are "as if" the commission had been captured.

The last version follows from the assumption that the industry possesses an enormous information advantage. It knows its own cost structure and the demand for its products. Others, including the regulatory commission, must rely on the firms just to obtain basic information about the industry. The industry, however, has strong incentive to release and present information that is most favorable to its desired position. Thus, even if commission members truly seek to set a fair rate of return, the information used to determine the rate will be biased.

Commission hearings, in this latter view, are like court cases in which only one side gets to present its arguments (or more realistically, in which only one side has adequate representation). For any given real capital base, for example, the industry will invest considerable resources in maximizing the value of it accepted by the commission (and thus the fair "interest" which it is allowed to earn). Thus, fair-minded commission members, reacting to biased information, make decisions that are overly generous to monopolists.[23]

Figures 18-4a and b summarize in a simple way this discussion of rate-of-return regulation. First, we must mention that typical rate-of-return regulation includes the legal obligation of the regulated firm to provide service to all within its jurisdiction who demand it. This means that for any price actually charged, the firm will provide the quantity demanded at that price. In other words, the solution will be a point on the demand curve D. Additionally, we assume that the "fair" rate of return on capital is intended to be the normal market rate of return, so that the solution will also be a point on the average cost curve AC. But there is only one point that satisfies both conditions: the intersection of the demand curve with the average cost curve, shown as point R on Figure 18-4a (with price P_R and quantity Q_R). In this diagram, the regulatory solution implies a small inefficiency (shaded) from producing slightly less than the efficient quantity Q_E.

Figure 18-4b shows the effects of accounting for the Averch-Johnson effect and for regulatory capture. First, the Averch-Johnson effect implies that the observed average cost curve AC_{A-J} is everywhere higher than the least average cost curve AC, as the firm chooses inefficient input combinations (too much capital relative to labor) to produce any output level. Were this the only effect, the outcome would be at point J (with price P_{A-J} and quan-

---

[22] Typically one commission regulates several natural monopolies; for example, a state public utilities commission usually regulates electric companies serving various regions of the state.

[23] For a general review, see Paul L. Joskow, ed., *Economic Regulation* (Northampton, Mass.: Edward Elgar, 2000).

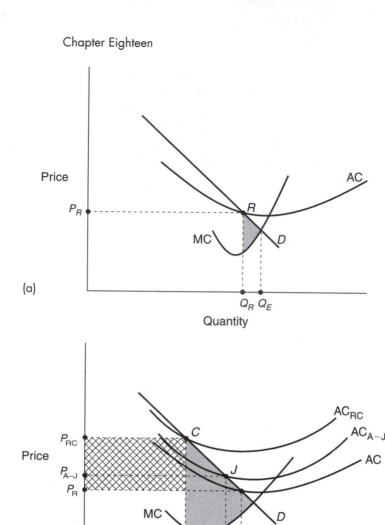

Figure 18-4. The outcome of rate-of-return regulation: (a) The "obligation to serve" combined with a "normal" rate of return implies a solution where demand equals average cost. (b) The Averch-Johnson effect (AC_{A-J}) and the effect of regulatory capture (AC_{RC}) increase inefficiency substantially.

tity Q_{A-J}) and the inefficiency would rise (produced output unnecessarily costly and output further reduced from the efficient level).

However, this does not yet include the effect of regulatory capture. To include this, we add the average cost curve as perceived by the regulatory commission AC_{RC}. This curve is shown as substantially higher than AC_{A-J}, as the commission has become convinced that the costs it perceives are "just and reasonable" and based on "prudent" decisions (even if most of the rest of us are not fortunate enough to have such large and well-equipped offices, generous expense accounts, and so many co-workers to help us with our tasks). The outcome is at point C, and the inefficiency is the sum of the cross-hatched (too costly) and shaded (unproduced) areas. This inefficiency is much larger than the inefficiency of "ideal" rate-of-return regulation shown in Figure 18-4a.

Franchise Bidding: The Case of Cable Television

A proposal that purports to do away with the regulatory process altogether is for the government to sell the right to operate the monopoly through a competitive bidding process.[24] Bidding processes are usually thought of as market arrangements: The transaction is priced, and the price is determined by the competitive bids. The regulatory commission, on the other hand, is a centralized price-setting agent with periodic hearings as an adjustment mechanism to keep the rate of return at its equilibrium ("fair") level. At least in some situations, the bidding procedure has the effect of removing the central agent's demand for information about the eventual supplier.

A simple example of bidding is the federal government's weekly Treasury bill auction, some of the revenue from which is used to finance government expenditure and refinance old debt. A Treasury bill is a promise to pay a certain amount to the holder at a specified future time, such as $10,000 to be paid 6 months from the date of issue. Suppose the government wishes to sell a certain number of these bills. It knows that individuals will be willing to pay only something less than $10,000 at the time of issue (since nominal interest rates are positive). If it sets a price by guessing, demand may not equal supply. In either direction the error is costly; either the government does not raise the revenue it desires (supply exceeds demand) or it forgoes revenue it could have collected (demand exceeds supply). Since interest rates vary substantially over time, there is no reason to think that the government can determine the right price after a few trial weeks.

On the other hand, competitive bidding solves the problem of finding the equilibrium price. Each potential buyer submits a bid that is the maximum price that buyer is willing to pay for a desired number of bills. The government orders all bids from highest to lowest and awards the bills to the top bidders. The cutoff point is determined by the total quantity offered, and each winner pays only the price at the cutoff point. Since there is no price discrimination, each bidder has incentive to offer the true maximum willingness to pay. (It costs nothing to be honest; and by understating true willingness to pay, one risks not buying a bill that is truly desired.)

A second bidding example brings us closer to using the process to prevent monopoly exploitation. Periodically, the federal government wishes to allow a small portion of its land to be leased for coal exploration and mining. The value of any particular land tract is very uncertain at the time of leasing, but the government nevertheless wishes to receive revenue near the true value for the use of the land. Furthermore, it wishes the land to be developed

---

[24] See, for example, H. Demsetz, "Why Regulate Utilities?," *Journal of Law and Economics, 11,* April 1968, pp. 55–66.

in efficient order—the least expensive coal sources first. The problem is how to organize the leasing process to obtain that result.[25]

One centralized way to approach the problem is to let geologists from the U.S. Geological Survey (USGS) examine the tracts in much the same way the geologists of any private mining company would. USGS routinely collects certain basic information relevant to estimating the tract value (e.g., average thickness of coal seams in the county), but it would have to collect a great deal more (e.g., sulfur content of the coal in a specific tract) to replicate private company procedures. If it did, the USGS analysts could estimate the fair market value for each of the tracts to be leased and the government would simply use the estimates to set the lease prices and identify the efficient tracts to lease (i.e., those with the highest value).

The problem with this procedure is that because there are many tracts, many mining firms, and realistic limits on the size of the USGS evaluative staff, the information at the "center" will almost always be worse than the information held by some firms for a particular tract. The lease prices for some tracts will be set too high, and the tracts will go unleased. For other tracts, the lease price will be too low and mining firms will receive economic profit at the expense of reduced government revenues.

So far, this does not sound too different from Treasury bills. But there is good reason to believe that competitive bidding for each tract will not solve the problem. That is because the true value of any specific tract will vary from firm to firm, depending on who owns adjacent land, operates a nearby mine, or has surface rights to the tract in question. In other words, the firm already in the area is the only one that can take advantage of these scale economies. Other firms, recognizing this, will not waste their time and exploration resources on preparing bids for such tracts. Thus, there will not be effective competition in the bidding, and the advantaged firms will be able to win at a price substantially below true value.

The ingenious solution to this problem is to have *intertract* competitive bidding. For example, the government announces that it will consider bids received within 6 months of an announcement on any of 100 specified tracts. It selects 100 "homogeneous" tracts to be open for bids based on the limited information available from the USGS. Furthermore, it announces that only ten tracts will be leased—the ten commanding the highest bids.

Thus, each firm in an advantaged position for a particular tract has incentive to bid the full value for it. That is, each firm recognizes that it is now competing against many other firms in situations similar to its own. The firm physically next to tract No. 12 may be the only firm that can achieve scale economies by producing on it, but it must bid higher than a similarly advantaged firm bidding on tract No. 37. Any bid substantially lower than the true value renders the firm at risk of forgoing an opportunity it would consider worthwhile.

The most important aspect of the process is the efficiency of its information structure. Economic agents, including the center, need no further information than what they already have. The government not only achieves its revenue objectives but does so in such a way

---

[25] A description of the problem and its proposed solution is contained in C. B. McGuire, "Intertract Competition and the Design of Lease Sales for Western Coal Lands," presented at the Western Economic Association Conference, Hawaii, June 25, 1978.

that the most efficient coal sources are utilized first.[26] (The highest bids are made for tracts where the coal extraction costs are lowest.)

Now, with these examples of bidding processes in mind, let us consider how competitive bidding might be used as a replacement for regulating a natural monopoly. One possibility would be to auction off the right to provide service in the area to the highest bidder. This has the advantage of allowing the government to collect all of the monopoly profit. (If competitive, any bidder offering less than the present value of expected monopoly profits will be outbid by another seeing the opportunity for gain.) However, this process would force the winner to produce and charge like the profit-maximizing monopolist (it is the only way to recover the purchase price). That is not allocatively desirable and is unlikely to be thought distributively fair.

Another suggestion is to award the franchise to whichever firm agrees to charge consumers the lowest price. That is, the bids are offers to provide service at a certain price to consumers, and the low bid wins. If the supplier must service all demanders at the bid price, then presumably the winning bid will be at the price at which the demand curve intersects the average cost curve (as in Figure 18-4a). This is not allocatively efficient, although it does keep the price low (in fact, the price is below the efficient price whenever the demand curve crosses the average cost curve to the right of its minimum, as in Figure 18-1).

Since all these bidding proposals are imperfect, it is not obvious whether the (diagrammed) solutions would be more desirable than those achieved through rate-of-return regulation. However, Williamson argues that the consequences of such competitive bidding in practice cannot be accurately deduced from models like those underlying the above analysis.[27] His method of analysis, which is now often referred to as *transaction cost economics,* highlights the effects of imperfect information and transaction costs and the importance of designing a natural monopoly solution that creates an efficient information structure. To illustrate these theoretical points, he presents a case study of the competitive bidding approach used by Oakland, California, to grant an exclusive franchise for the right to provide cable television services within the city.

In presenting the franchise bidding idea, we have described it as if there were one auction at which each bid submitted is a simple price per unit and the unit is a well-defined good that would be identical no matter which supplier provided it. This description ignores a number of real problems, for example, the franchise's duration and provisions to enforce its terms. The implicit assumption of the simplifying description is that these problems are complications that do not affect the essential validity of the model implications. But Williamson argues otherwise. He conducts an analysis by considering how one might specify the contract that the potential bidders are supposed to be seeking. The contract must take account of multidimensional aspects of time, price, and quality in specifying the operating

---

[26] In this bidding process, the government collects all the winning bids as revenues rather than charge the tenth highest bid to each of the winners. This may prevent firms from bidding their true willingness to pay because they can trade off a reduced probability of winning for increased profit.

[27] Oliver E. Williamson, "Franchise Bidding for Natural Monopolies: In General and with Respect to CATV," *Bell Journal of Economics, 7,* Spring 1976, pp. 73–104.

agreement. But those aspects of the transaction are often associated with costly uncertainties for each of the contracting parties, which can be reduced only by costly enforcement mechanisms. The result can easily be a contract with negotiation, arbitration, and inspection provisions that, if called by any other name, would surely be regulation.

In short, the original proposals for franchise bidding solutions to natural monopoly problems have the same analytic flaws as the original pollution tax proposals (discussed in Chapter 17). When the transaction costs are considered more carefully, Williamson concludes that substantial regulation is likely to be part of the franchise arrangement. Therefore, *the "market" solution and "regulation" are not really substitutes. In fact, traditional regulation can be viewed as nothing more than a particular form of contract (whether or not it is let by competitive bidding).*[28]

To derive these conclusions, Williamson considers whether the contract should be once-and-for-all, long-term, or one in a series of recurrent short-term contracts. In each case, the contract can be complete (if it specifies the response to all future contingencies) or incomplete (if it specifies mechanisms to resolve conflicting claims that may arise among the contracting parties). The complete once-and-for-all contract, for example, would have to specify the prices at which service is to be provided now and under every conceivable future condition. Since firms do not know how their factor prices might change over an indefinite future, they will certainly not agree to a price that is forever constant. Furthermore, since the possible states of the world extending into the indefinite future are infinite, it is too complex for the contracting parties to specify and agree on a price for each of them. Thus complete, once-and-for-all contracts are not written for services that are expected to be provided indefinitely.

Williamson argues that the incomplete once-and-for-all contract has essentially the same flaws as incomplete long-term contracts. With either of these or the complete long-term contract, the initial award criterion is obscure. How does one compare bids that represent different price-quality combinations, let alone bids that specify a whole vector of prices and qualities for the various services a company might provide? A local telephone company, for example, might have a basic monthly rate for one telephone, rates for additional telephones, installation charges, and a special rate for unlimited local calls. Furthermore, the quality of service can vary: The speed of installation, the frequency with which line repairs are needed, and the probability of receiving a busy signal are examples. Even if different companies submit bids specifying their price-quality offerings, it is not obvious how to compare them. Logically, one ought to pick the proposal that maximizes social welfare. But this task is a far cry from the simplicity of the auctioneer's decision rule.

A second series of problems is associated with the execution of a contract. Under incomplete contracts, for example, the parties may agree to some form of price-cost relation instead of price alone (because of the uncertainty of future cost conditions). The kind of incentive problems that arise are familiar to students of defense contracting.[29] Cost-plus con-

---

[28] This general point is made in Victor Goldberg, "Regulation and Administered Contracts," *Bell Journal of Economics, 7,* Autumn 1976, pp. 426–448.

[29] See, for example, Merton J. Peck and Frederic M. Scherer, *The Weapons Acquisition Process* (Cambridge: Harvard University Press, 1962).

tracts, for example, give suppliers incentive to maximize their costs. Under any price-cost arrangement, stringent auditing will be required by the government awarding the franchise. Note too that ordinary regulation can be described as a particular form of price-cost relation with attendant auditing procedures.

Another problem arising during contract execution is the enforcement of quality standards; even if the contract specifies exactly what the standards are supposed to be, the supplier may fail to meet them. Simply to inspect quality requires that personnel with relevant technical skills be part of the inspectorate. (Again, this resembles ordinary regulatory staffs.) The value of regular inspection depends, of course, on the technology used to deliver the service, as when continual maintenance is necessary to keep output quality at its contracted level.

It should also be noted that, once a long-term contract is let, it may be virtually impossible to enforce contract provisions strictly. The reason for this limitation is that there are opportunity costs to the government and the public of canceling the contract for reason of franchiser violations. Again, this is familiar from defense contracting, where "renegotiation" is almost standard. Government officials responsible for the contract fear that they will be held responsible for the supplier's failure, and thus they are not anxious to call public attention to any violations. Similarly, the officials will not be anxious to cause any disruptions in the services being rendered. Thus, it is often easier to renegotiate a contract and make its terms more favorable to the supplier.

In fact, the capture theory of regulatory behavior may apply with equal or greater force to the contracting process. Firms with high contracting expertise and low technical performance may be the ones that do best in this situation. That is, the contract may be awarded to a firm that deliberately bids an unrealistically low price, knowing that it has the political skills to renegotiate favorable terms at a later date and the ability to cut corners on its legal obligations. Thus it captures the government contract supervisors at all stages of the contract.

Many of these problems might be avoided if we consider short-term recurrent contracts instead of long-term ones. Such contracting encourages adaptive and sequential decision-making rather than complex contingency planning, and it may better suit the bounds of rationality. With short-term contracts, there is no need to create price-cost relations to deal with the various possible future states of the world. Potential suppliers simply take the actual changes into account in making bids during the next contracting period. Similarly, the government is in a stronger position to enforce quality standards: Firms that violate them can be barred from the next contracting period.

Gaining these advantages depends crucially on having parity among bidders during contract renewal. However, there are two good reasons why parity is elusive. The first concerns procedures to facilitate the transfer of capital assets from the former contractor to the new one. The second concerns the unique human capital skills developed in the process of providing the service. These are explained below.

In many of the natural monopolies, efficient service provision is associated with large investments in fixed-location, limited-alternative-use durable goods such as pipelines and large generating plants. The value of such assets is highly specific to their use in the intended market, a feature that Williamson refers to as *asset specificity*. That is, the investment cost is substantially greater than the asset's opportunity cost after the investment is made. In order to induce the contracting firm to undertake those investments, given that the contract period is much shorter than the useful lives of the assets, the firm must have assurances that it can sell the asset for its value in the current use in the event of a change of contractor. But this raises essentially the same issues that are involved in determining the annual rate base of a regulated firm.

The firm that wins the initial contract has incentive to exaggerate the size of its capital assets for the next round of bidding. There are two reasons for this: (1) The more other firms have to pay to take over the fixed assets, the higher will be the prices they propose to charge and the better the chances of the original contractor to have the winning bid. (2) If the original contractor loses the second round, it will naturally seek to receive the largest possible compensation. Therefore, other firms and the government franchiser will employ their own experts to inspect the physical plant and examine the records involving original costs and depreciation write-offs. The various sides will have divergent estimates of the transfer value, and some process will be required to reconcile them.

Since the valuation of these assets is a very uncertain task (unlike valuing goods that are commonly and frequently traded in the marketplace), there is no reason to believe any process will arrive at the correct value with certainty. But a process that is risky to the firm (because it might substantially undervalue the assets) will deter the investments in the first place. Moreover, if the process is biased to err in the direction of overvaluation, there may be little difference between it and rate-of-return regulation. In addition, such a process will favor the original contractor during the renewal bidding. (Other firms will have higher cost structures because of the inflated price of the assets they must purchase.)

Human capital can also lead to a lack of parity during contract renewal bidding. Although we often think of labor as interchangeable, that concept ignores the development of human capital quite specific to a particular workplace. There may be many idiosyncratic aspects of production within the firm: e.g., maintenance of certain machinery, development of informal communication networks across divisions, and relations with suppliers. A new firm is at a disadvantage because it does not possess any of these assets.

It can be terribly inefficient for a new firm to start developing the idiosyncratic human capital from scratch. If this is the only alternative open to them, new bidders are unlikely to be able to submit the winning bid (their cost structures are too high). Alternatively, they can try to arrange for the transfer of personnel as well as physical equipment from the original contractor.

In the case of employee transfer, one must consider whether the employees are likely to strike more costly bargains with their original firm or with potential competitors. Again, the cost of dealing with the familiar is generally lower than the cost of dealing with the unfamiliar. Informal understandings about wages, promotions, and working conditions are possible in a familiar, established context. But with a potential employer, employees are less likely to be trusting, harder to bargain with, and more demanding of formal guarantees. Thus, one would expect potential entrants to be at a disadvantage because of these human capital elements as well as the problems of transferring durable plant and equipment.

In sum, the low-price, low-cost advantages of competitive franchise bidding over ordinary regulation for a natural monopoly may be an illusion. The weakness of the analysis underlying the bidding suggestion is identical with that in the standard pollution tax argument. Since the problem is inherently caused by information and transaction difficulties, one cannot examine it through a model that assumes that information and transaction costs are negligible.

A more detailed analysis of the possible forms for the contractual agreement suggests that under both long- and short-term contracts the firm receiving the initial franchise has considerable information and bargaining advantages over the government and potential competitors. To counter this, substantial arbitration, negotiation, inspection, and auditing procedures would be necessary. But then the bidding arrangement looks much like ordinary regulation. Furthermore, to the extent that ordinary regulation is thought to fail because the regulators have an information disadvantage, it is possible that competitive franchising can fail for the same reasons. Thus, whether franchise bidding can be used to effect some improvement in natural monopoly supply will depend on the particular service in question. Improvement seems a more likely prospect when the durable assets of the firm are easily valued and transferable and when the amount of idiosyncratic human capital within the firm is low (e.g., local refuse collection).

All of the problems Williamson raised were apparent in his case study of the decision of Oakland, California, to award the right to provide CATV service by competitive bidding for the franchise. After holding preliminary discussions with interested potential suppliers, the city asked for bids to provide two types of viewer service: service A to consist of cable for local stations and FM radio and service B to include special programming services at the supplier's option. The city assumed that service A would be the predominant service, and the award criterion was therefore the lowest bid for providing that service. It turned out that 90 percent of the customers chose service B instead. The price charged for it was requested by the company on one day and approved as requested on the following day.

Construction of the system was not completed by the scheduled date. It went more slowly than expected; costs were claimed to be higher; and fewer households subscribed than had been anticipated by the company. The company appealed to the city to renegotiate the terms, which it did. The revised agreement allowed the company a reduction in the number of channels it had promised to carry, a reduction in the cable-laying requirement from dual to single cable, and substantially higher prices for providing cable to additional household televisions after the first.

After the service began operating, enough customers complained about its poor quality to make the city hire expert consultants to test for compliance with the quality standards in the contract. In renegotiating the dual-cable requirement, the revised terms also smacked of regulation: The city would require the second cable when the marginal revenues it would generate would exceed the company's gross investment cost plus 10 percent. In response to all these difficulties with the company, the city did consider contract termination but ended up accepting the poorer terms, and Williamson documents the city council's aversion to any service disruption and fears of expensive and extensive litigation.

In short, there is nothing in this case study to suggest that franchise bidding is superior to ordinary regulation. This conclusion follows from Williamson's investigation into the specific nature of the transactions being regulated: the degrees of asset specificity (making recontracting difficult), uncertainty (leading to price adjustment mechanisms similar to ordinary regulation), and incentives for opportunistic behavior (because contract cancellation is difficult and costly). The two main lessons to be learned are: (1) much of what is normally thought of as ordinary regulation became a part of the franchisee-franchiser relationship, and (2) the same information and bargaining problems that support the capture theory of regulation are evident in this example of franchise bidding as well. Thus, any differences between franchise bidding and ordinary regulation are a matter of degree and not of kind. Empirical studies that have been done since Williamson's original work have not found large differences in the performance of franchised versus regulated systems.[30]

Before concluding this section, we note that this same form of analysis can be applied to *performance contracting.* An alternative way of trying to maintain the quality of supply at a low price is to establish a price-performance (rather than price-cost) contractual relationship. According to some recent literature, the use of performance contracting by governments with both private and nonprofit suppliers has been proliferating.[31] Some earlier relevant experiences are instructive. One natural monopoly situation in which this has been briefly tried is Amtrak's passenger rail service. Another example of a brief trial, although not in the context of a natural monopoly, is an experiment with performance contracting for the education of children. We offer a few comments on these below.

Amtrak is a government corporation that sells rail tickets to passengers, contracts with private railroads to operate the trains, and receives subsidies from the federal government to make up the difference.[32] The traditional form of Amtrak contract with private suppliers is a flat fee derived from cost estimates of providing the service plus a fair return. Once the contract is written, the supplier has no incentive to care about the number of passengers carried or the quality of the service.

An incremental performance contract was tried briefly in the mid-1970s. It made the plus part of the flat fee into a plus-or-minus function dependent upon quality dimensions of actual service (trains on time, heated properly, clean, and so forth) and economy (the supplier could keep funds resulting from cost savings). The incremental aspect was due to the uncertainty about how to establish appropriate rewards and penalties under performance criteria; possibly, this resulted in *insufficient* incentives. The initial contracts placed heavy emphasis on punctuality at the expense of comfort. That might coincide with social value, but it happened because the availability of historical information on timeliness allowed more confidence among the contracting parties in determining a reasonable reward structure. However, Amtrak soon decided to abandon this experiment and reverted to its traditional

[30] This literature is included in a broader review by K. Crocker and S. Masten, "Regulation and Administered Contracts Revisited: Lessons from Transaction Cost Economics for Public Utility Regulation," *Journal of Regulatory Economics, 9,* No. 1, January 1996, pp. 5–39.

[31] See, for example, R. Behn and P. Kant, "Strategies for Avoiding the Pitfalls of Performance Contracting," *Public Productivity & Management Review,* 22, No. 4, June 1999, pp. 470–489.

[32] Before Amtrak, private suppliers were forced by the regulatory authorities to operate unprofitable passenger routes that were cross-subsidized by the suppliers' more profitable freight service. This is both inefficient (the benefits of the service do not outweigh its costs) and inequitable (the subsidies are paid by users of freight service rather than the general public). The creation of Amtrak is thought to alleviate the inequity.

contracting forms. It is not clear whether the abandonment resulted from inherent difficulties with performance contracting in this situation, implementation difficulties of defining an appropriate reward structure, or impatience.[33]

A brief trial also characterized the attempt at educational performance contracting. The experiment was motivated in part by the concern that ordinary public schools do not have sufficient incentive to improve the education that their children receive. The merit of performance contracting, in this context, is to create a profit incentive for improvement. To test it, the Office of Economic Opportunity (OEO) let performance contracts with six firms for 1-year periods. The rewards were made a function of the children's test scores. On average, the test scores of the subject children (compared with a control group) did not improve, and the experiment was terminated.[34]

The experiment did not test the long-run aspects of the new organizational relationship, which represent its most plausible source of gains. Unlike the railroads, there may be no obvious source for short-run gains in the schools. Ordinary schoolteachers and principals have a different set of motivations than railroad entrepreneurs. The latter may well know some ways to produce that are socially efficient, and it is not difficult to see how fixed-fee contracts create private incentives for the monopolist to diverge from efficient production. Improving the incentives for railroads can plausibly be expected to lead to observable service improvements in the short run.

But teachers are less likely to choose inferior techniques deliberately: They make no apparent profit by doing so, and it would be contrary to their professional principles. Some inefficiency may arise if teaching effort affects learning and if teachers under the existing systems are not motivated to put forth much effort. However, it would be surprising to observe performance contracting results that are, on average, substantially better than the usual ones, at least in the short run.

However, the long run is another matter. Even if one grants that ordinary teachers and principals are well motivated, it does not follow that the public educational system is organized in a way that best facilitates achieving educational goals. Consider improvements in teaching techniques that are largely unpatentable; that is, the source of the improvement is something like a different way of teaching. Private entrepreneurs might have incentive to develop these techniques if they could market them in a way that prevented imitation (perhaps like private speed-reading courses). But the regular public school system precludes such marketing: Once the method is taught to one district's teachers, there is little to prevent free imitation by others. Furthermore, the public school system may not have a very efficient screening mechanism to weed out the bad ideas; the rapid diffusion of the "new math," later discarded, may be an example.[35]

---

[33] For more information, see W. Baumol, "Payment by Performance in Rail Passenger Transportation: An Innovation in Amtrak's Operations," *Bell Journal of Economics, 6,* Spring 1975, pp. 281–298.

[34] For an account of this experiment, see E. Gramlich and P. Koshel, *Educational Performance Contracting* (Washington, D.C.: The Brookings Institution, 1975).

[35] In the criminal justice part of the public sector, I studied the production processes of pretrial service agencies nationwide, which were under no special performance incentives. I identified two specific procedures that

It is at least plausible that, in the long run, performance contracting provides a source of organizational improvement. The idea is to encourage suppliers to learn over time by trial and error in the context of a process that diffuses successes and halts failures. One attains these advantages by allowing the contractor to provide the service directly to the children, thus giving it more opportunity to preserve its valuable "technical" knowledge (perhaps like commercial speed-reading methods, which are largely unpatentable). Other firms will, of course, try to imitate, and improvements will come about by the growth of successful firms, the eventual success of imitators, the entry of new firms, and the demise of those unable to produce satisfactorily.

It is unlikely that any of these possible advantages could be observed in the one academic year OEO gave its six contracting firms. It could be that the most important observation about the experiment is that one of the six contractors did appear to have significant success. The average result may not seem very exciting, but a one-out-of-six success rate in the short run could translate into much wider success if the system were allowed to spread its success and weed out its failures. At least this is what one would hope for with performance contracting, but the opportunity to find out was foreclosed by the experiment's termination.

Other examples of performance contracting continue to be tried. For example, the state of Maine currently issues performance contracts to the private agencies that it hires to provide service to clients with substance abuse problems. According to one early study of this system, the performance contracts appear to be inducing more effective and more efficient treatment.[36] Another interesting example is the program used by the Department of Housing and Urban Development (HUD) to encourage energy efficiency in public housing. In 1995, more than 10 percent of HUD's budget went to pay for utility bills in public housing and assisted housing developments (over $2 billion per year). HUD now allows local housing authorities (LHA) to enter into energy performance contracts with private energy services companies. The LHA contracts with an energy service company to install improvements such as new boilers, setback thermostats, and window replacements to save energy. The performance incentive comes from HUD: it freezes the energy payments that it gives to the LHA at the preinvestment level and pays them for 12 years. Thus the LHA can "profit" by undertaking investments that have their costs outweighed by the present value of the reduction in energy bills that follow from them.[37]

---

made some agencies more efficient than others. I then studied the behavior of these agencies over time, finding that many improved their procedures although some became less efficient. Efficiency increased over time in the industry as a whole, both through the expansion of more efficient agencies (including new entrants) and the contraction of less efficient ones (including closure in some cases). I did not find clear "contractual" differences in the "regulatory environments" of these agencies that explained their relative success or failure. See Lee S. Friedman, "Public Sector Innovations and Their Diffusion: Economic Tools and Managerial Tasks," in Alan Altshuler and Robert Behn, eds., *Innovations in American Government: Opportunities, Challenges and Dilemmas* (Washington, D.C.: The Brookings Institution, 1997), pp. 332–359.

[36] See M. Commons, T. McGuire, and M. Riordan, "Performance Contracting for Substance Abuse Treatment," *Health Services Research, 32,* No. 5, December 1997, pp. 631–650.

[37] See S. Morgan, "Energy Performance Contracting: Financing Capital Improvements with Private Funds," *Journal of Housing and Community Development, 52,* No. 3, May 1995, pp. 25–27.

In this section we have tried to show how analytic insight concerning the design of a governance structure can be generated by posing it as a question of choice among alternative contractual forms. This offers a different way of "seeing" information and transaction costs than the framework of operating rules and enforcement methods used in the externalities chapter.

Incentive Regulation

An alternative to rate-of-return regulation that is being put into practice by many state public utility commissions is *price-cap regulation,* particularly for telecommunications services. Price-cap regulation is similar to performance-contracting in that it conditions the utility's rewards or penalties on a measure of the utility's performance. However, it is similar to traditional regulation in that no actual contracting takes place. It is one variant of a class of regulatory methods called *incentive regulation.*

The idea underlying incentive regulation can be illustrated with a simple example.[38] Suppose the firm is allowed to charge a price P_t that depends on two factors: the estimated average cost C_e (set in advance), and the actual average cost C_t at the time of service. Think of the estimated cost as set by a procedure somewhat similar to rate-of-return regulation and including a component representing the fair rate of return on capital. The formula used is

$$P_t = C_e + s(C_t - C_e)$$

where s is a constant between 0 and 1.

Suppose that $s = \frac{1}{2}$. For any cost estimate C_e, the firm maximizes its profit by arranging actual production at the least possible cost. If the firm's actual costs come in under the estimate, the firm retains half of this as "extra" profit (above the rate-of-return component already built in to the estimated cost). If the firm's actual costs turn out to exceed the estimate, then the firm will only be allowed to recover half of the difference (and thus receive less than the rate of return in the estimate, including the possibility of a loss). In either case, it does best by keeping actual costs as low as possible. Thus unlike rate-of-return regulation, the firm has incentive to minimize production costs. The firm will also do all it can to maximize the estimate C_e that goes into the regulatory formula (since for any actual cost C_t, profit increases with C_e).[39]

The parameter s is sometimes called the "sharing parameter." It determines how much of the risk (that actual costs will deviate from estimated costs) is borne by the firm and how much by customers. In the above example, customers also gain when actual costs are less than estimated (through lower prices) and lose when costs are more than estimated (through higher prices). If s equals 1, customers bear all of the risk. The formula collapses to a "cost-plus" arrangement from the firm's point of view that resembles regulatory capture. That is, the firm cannot make "extra" profit for any actual costs, and it is allowed to charge a price

[38] For greater detail on the theory of incentive regulation, see J.-J. Laffont and J. Tirole, "Using Cost Observations to Regulate Firms," *Journal of Political Economy, 94,* 1986, pp. 614–641.

[39] Of course the firm will not charge above the profit-maximizing price even if it is allowed to do so.

that recovers all of its costs, even if those costs are not the least-cost way of producing output. So s must be less than 1 for the firm to have cost-minimization incentive, and the lower s, the stronger the incentive. At the other extreme of $s = 0$, the firm bears all of the risk. This extreme is similar to a fixed-price contract. The firm keeps all "extra" profit if actual costs are less than estimated, but recovers none of the loss when actual costs exceed the estimates.

Consider the process for generating the initial cost estimate. The firm is better off with an overestimate, while consumers are better off with an underestimate. Suppose we assume that, initially, the same factors that cause regulatory capture also result in the regulatory commission's unwitting acceptance of an overestimate. In Figure 18-5, we depict the demand curve D, estimated average cost curve AC_e, and estimated price P_e at the obligation-to-serve quantity Q_e. We also show the least average cost curve AC, and the price P_R and quantity Q_R that would result if the least costs were known to the regulators. The relative positions of these curves are assumed to be identical to those in Figure 18-4b illustrating the effects of regulatory capture.

There are important differences between this case and that of capture. The first important difference is that, owing to the profit incentives under incentive regulation, the firm will prefer to produce at least cost. Thus for the quantity Q_e, there is no production inefficiency (saving the entire rectangle $P_R P_e AB$, compared to rate-of-return regulation with capture). This is the big gain, but there is also some gain in allocative efficiency. The actual consumer price P_t will be adjusted downward from P_e, the amount depending on the value of the sharing parameter s. If $s = \frac{1}{2}$ as in the earlier illustration, then P_t will be halfway between P_R and P_e, and the actual quantity consumed will be $Q_t > Q_e$. The degree of allocative inefficiency is shaded and less than it would be at Q_e.

The second important difference is what happens over time. In rate-of-return regulation with capture, there is no reason to think that the "capture" equilibrium will be any different in the future. Under incentive regulation, however, the firm reveals that it can produce along the curve AC. Therefore, while it might argue self-interestedly that there are reasons to expect future costs to be higher, the regulatory commission has powerful evidence to keep the estimated future price "near" AC. Thus over time one might expect consumers to be paying close to least average cost and the firm striving to find innovative ways (by adopting new technologies) to reduce costs further in order to receive additional profit.

The particular form of incentive regulation that is becoming commonplace in the regulated telecommunications industry is price-cap regulation. Its simplest version has the following form:

$$P_t = P_{t-1}(1 + \Delta CPI - X)$$

where ΔCPI is the annual percentage change in the Consumer Price Index and X is a factor that represents expected annual productivity gains (in percent). The intent is for X to be set in an infrequent regulatory proceeding and for the formula to remain fixed for a number of years (typically 4–5 years). For example, if X is set at 3 percent and ΔCPI is 4 percent, then the firm is allowed to increase its prices by a maximum of 1 percent during the next year. Thus the formula reduces real prices to consumers gradually over time, on the assumption

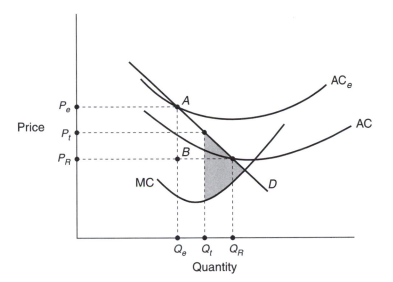

Figure 18-5. Incentive regulation can encourage production efficiency.

that the firm will continue to make productivity improvements that allow it to maintain at least a normal rate of return.

Note that this formula is just a special case of the general incentive regulatory approach. In this case, the price-cap formula specifies what the "cost estimate" will be, and the sharing parameter is set equal to zero. The firm can reap the full reward of costs less than revenues and bears the full risk of costs exceeding revenues. Given this formula, it maximizes profits by producing at least cost. If the "base year" price used to begin the process equals the (last) price under (the former) rate-of-return regulatory process with capture, then it may take quite some time before the price consumers pay approaches the least average cost. On the other hand, consumers do become better off immediately compared to the continuation of old-style regulation, and they become progressively still better off over time.

An interesting study by Mathios and Rogers offers the results of price-cap regulation as used by states for long-distance telephone service.[40] In the United States, telephone service is divided into 161 jurisdictions called Local Access and Transportation Areas (LATAs). During the 1983–1987 period of the study, local telephone companies were prohibited from providing inter-LATA service. AT&T was the primary provider of inter-LATA service within states, and thus each state could choose how it wished to regulate this long-distance service. Of the thirty-nine states with multiple LATAs within their boundaries, twenty-eight chose a form of price-cap regulation while eleven chose traditional rate-of-return regulation. After controlling for the many factors apart from regulatory method that explain variation in prices from area to area, they estimated that price-cap regulation itself caused rates

[40] See A. D. Mathios and R. P. Rogers, "The Impact of Alternative Forms of State Regulation of AT&T on Direct-Dial, Long-Distance Telephone Rates," *RAND Journal of Economics, 20,* No. 2, Autumn 1989, pp. 437–453.

to be 7–11 percent lower than they would be under traditional regulation. As AT&T also supported regulation by this method, it seems to be a win-win situation. Another study analyzing the period 1988–1993 also finds strong, positive effects of price-cap systems.[41]

While this work is encouraging, there are important limitations on the method that can affect its actual performance over time as well as its applicability to other services besides telecommunications. We will mention three.[42] One is the problem of exogenous costs. Another is the problem of multiple services with multiple prices. The third is the frequency with which the X factor is adjusted, particularly as a response to actual firm rates of return.

Many services are produced with inputs whose prices fluctuate substantially but are exogenous or outside the control of the firm. In producing electricity, for example, many generators require oil as a fuel. It is difficult to hold firm managers accountable for a firm's profit if it is primarily determined by forces outside of their control, such as the effect of changes in oil prices on the profits of an electricity utility. Even in telephone service, there are costs such as FCC-determined access charges and FCC-mandated accounting procedures that are beyond the control of the firm being regulated. One response to these situations is to try to divide costs into those that are "exogenous" and those that are "controllable," and treat these differently in the regulatory formula. The "simple" price-cap formula can be made more complex by allowing certain cost changes to be passed along to consumers and restricting the "incentive" part to those costs that are under the firm's control.

It can be difficult to add this feature of an "exogenous cost" pass-through mechanism without affecting incentives. In the case of oil for electricity generation, for example, one still wants the firm to have incentive to minimize both its short- and long-run costs of providing the levels of service demanded. To some extent it may do this through a mixture of long- and short-term fuel purchase contracts and through the availability of generators that utilize alternative fuels. But it would not have incentive to use (or to invest in having) the least-cost generators if the use of "expensive" oil in oil-based generators was just recaptured by the firm through a cost pass-through mechanism. Thus the method of adjusting for higher fuel prices must be based on some exogenous index of fuel prices (not the firm's actual expenditures), and a predetermined function to identify an appropriate (least-cost) quantity of fuel given the level of the fuel price index. This is feasible, but of course it makes the regulatory task quite a bit harder than the "simple" price-cap mechanism.

The second problem, that of multiple prices, is similar to the multiple prices that obscure the award criterion in franchise bidding. Because utilities have many services and prices, the price-cap typically applies to a large "basket" of services that are covered by the in-

---

[41] See S. Majumdar, "Incentive Regulation and Productive Efficiency in the U. S. Telecommunications Industry," *Journal of Business, 70,* No. 4, October 1997, pp. 547–576.

[42] These three as well as others have been mentioned in the professional literature. For a fuller discussion, see M. E. Beesley and S. C. Littlechild, "The Regulation of Privatized Monopolies in the United Kingdom," *RAND Journal of Economics, 20,* No. 2, Autumn 1989, pp. 454–472; John E. Kwoka, Jr., "Implementing Price Caps in Telecommunications," *Journal of Policy Analysis and Management, 12,* No. 4, Fall 1993, pp. 726–752; and Paul L. Joscow and Richard Schmalensee, "Incentive Regulation for Electric Utilities," *Yale Journal on Regulation, 4,* 1986, pp. 1–49.

centive contract. It is also typical, even for a regulated natural monopoly, that there is competition for some of the services offered. As competition in the long-distance tele-communications market has grown over the years, the need to regulate long-distance rates has decreased. So these rates may be unregulated and "outside" of the basket in some areas, whereas the rates for local calling (day, evening, night, weekend, measured, unlimited, commercial, residential), directory services, and connection charges may be within the price-capped basket.

To define how an overall cap of, say, 5 percent applies to an entire basket, the regulator must define a fixed weight on each included price. Typically, this would be the percent of last year's basket-item revenues that each specific service contributed. If there is some competition for any of the included items, the firm may be tempted to price them predatorily and make up losses on the noncompetitive ones. Some have argued that this is precisely what British Telecom did when regulated by this method and first subjected to long-distance competition from new entrant Mercury Communications. Regulators may respond with subconstraints to the overall cap, such as allowable "bands" for particular prices. In short, the multiplicity of services, prices, and the degree of competition for each substantially complicates the regulatory task of including basket definitions and subconstraints within the overall price cap.

The final problem we mention is the frequency with which the price-cap formula is reset. Suppose that both the firm and the regulatory authority agree to a formula that they believe will allow a 10 percent rate of return on average. If the firm realizes less than 10 percent in its first year, it may argue that the formula is wrong and that it must be adjusted to have a smaller X. Conversely, an actual rate of return that exceeds 10 percent may cause the regulatory authority to believe that it has erred with a too generous X, and it may seek to increase it. In either case, succumbing to the temptation of adjustment seems to signal that regulation will work to guarantee the target rate of return. But if the firm believes that, it loses the incentive to minimize costs. In order for the incentives to be real, the regulator must be willing to allow the firm's rate of return to deviate from normal in any given year and only adjust the formula very infrequently (every 4–5 years).

It will take more time to assess the performance of these incentive regulatory mechanisms, beyond the experiences that at least initially seem more successful than not. At the same time that these mechanisms have come into greater use, regulatory commissions have also been experimenting with partial deregulation. That is, they have been allowing and encouraging new entry into areas that have traditionally been serviced by only one natural monopoly firm. Telecommunications services, for example, have become subject to increasing competition (beginning with the deregulation of handset sales, then long-distance service, and now local service as well, including competition to provide Internet access and services). One of the most interesting experiments is the deregulation of electricity-generating services so that consumers can now buy their electricity from a number of power companies that arrange for delivery over the local (monopoly) distribution systems. This system seems to be working well in the United Kingdom and in Pennsylvania, whereas California has been having difficulty making its newly restructured system "workably" competitive.

In all of these deregulation cases, technological progress has been at least a partial stimulant to policy change.[43] The ability to transmit electricity over longer distances with less loss of power has helped to spur increased competition among generators, for example. The huge capacity of fiber optic cable for transmitting voice, data, and video services has allowed more competition between traditional telephone companies and cable television providers. It is also true, of course, that policy changes affect the pace of technological progress. Telephone handsets, for example, changed little during the traditional rate-of-return regulation that characterized most of the past century, but the availability of phones with a wide variety of new features followed quite quickly after handset deregulation. Partial deregulation also creates new difficulties for regulatory authorities, as one firm's costs often must be assigned either to the deregulated or still-regulated services. As with incentive regulation, a full assessment of deregulation's effects awaits more experience.[44]

Summary

An industry in which at least one firm has market power, or the ability to set price above marginal cost, is usually classified either as an oligopoly (if there are a few competing firms) or a monopoly (if there is only one firm). To some extent, such situations can arise as a natural result of competition when there are substantial economies of scale relative to the overall market demand (i.e., if the least cost way to supply market output is to produce it with only a few firms). Public policy in these cases is usually oriented toward preventing the abuse of market power. With oligopolistic industries, oversight is usually not continuous but occurs case by case through the enforcement of antitrust laws. With natural monopolies, oversight is typically continual through a regulatory commission (e.g., a state's public utilities commission).

Many economic models have been constructed to explain a wide variety of observed behaviors of firms in oligopoly situations, and no single model has become accepted as representing a "typical" oligopoly. It is typical, however, for market power to correlate with the degree of concentration in an industry. Concentration refers to the share of total market output that is contributed by the largest firms in the market. We introduce and use one common oligopoly model—the Cournot model—to illustrate the intuition behind this correlation.

The Cournot model assumes that the oligopoly firm will act to maximize profit given its belief that the output supplied by other firms in the industry will remain constant. The first use that we make of this model is to suggest how generating firms exercised market power during the 2000–2001 California electricity crisis. The crisis occurred during a transitional

---

[43] It should probably also be mentioned that, politically, the general success with the federal deregulation of interstate trucking and airline services to allow free entry and market pricing in both contributed to the pro-deregulation climate in the 1980s and 1990s. Neither of these industries, however, was ever classified by economists as a natural monopoly (although some circumstances of market power do arise, as with the unforeseen development of the hub-and-spoke system for airlines).

[44] For a thoughtful progress report, see Robert G. Harris and C. Jeffrey Kraft, "Meddling Through: Regulating Local Telephone Competition in the United States," *Journal of Economic Perspectives, 11,* No. 4, Fall 1997, pp. 93–112.

period in which California was attempting to move from a regulated natural monopoly structure to one of competition among many generators to supply electricity. During the transition, some 50 percent of the former monopolies' generating power was divested to five different companies, each of which then had market power in the newly formed market. Market power is exercised by reducing supply in order to raise price. Price caps could be an effective short-run strategy to prevent the exercise of market power and increase supply; this does not obviate the need for a long-run strategy to induce entry of new, more efficient generators to increase supply and lower costs as well as dissipate the transitional market power.

Using Lerner's measure of market power $(P - MC)/P$, we show that market power at the Cournot equilibrium increases as the number of (equal-sized) firms in an industry declines. Allowing for size variation among firms, we introduce the Herfindahl-Hirschman index (H) of industry concentration, which approaches 0 for unconcentrated industries and can reach a maximum of 1 for a pure monopoly. We show that average market power in the industry at Cournot equilibrium increases with greater concentration. This provides some intuition for policies such as the merger guidelines of the U.S. Department of Justice, which state that a merger that would increase H by .01 in an industry that has $H > .18$ is "highly likely" to be challenged.

We also review briefly the temptation for oligopolists to try and form a cartel—an association to coordinate their individual activities so that the group can act as if it were one large profit-maximizing monopolist. Cartels are illegal in most countries. Even in cases where they are not illegal, cartels are unstable economic institutions, as the individual members have incentive to cheat on the cartel agreements. Despite the illegality and instability, some firms nevertheless try different ways to form them. We mention as examples the cases of the Organization of Petroleum Exporting Countries (OPEC) and several international manufacturers of vitamins who pleaded guilty to violating U.S. antitrust laws.

Natural monopolies have traditionally been made subject to rate-of-return regulation. This regulatory method has been criticized for several different reasons. One is that it induces production inefficiency by encouraging the overuse of capital relative to other inputs for any given output level (the Averch-Johnson theorem). A second criticism, referred to as the capture theory of regulatory behavior, is that the method is overly protective of industry to the detriment of consumer interests. One suggestion for solving the "capture" problem is to substitute for regulation a competitive bidding process for the exclusive right to provide the monopoly service. The idea is that the market, through the bidding process, does away with the regulatory institution subject to capture. Competitive bidding is used successfully in many areas, including use by the U.S. government to sell Treasury bills and to allocate leases for oil and coal mining on government lands.

Williamson points out that it is not the bidding itself but the contract, the object of the bidding, that is to substitute for regulation. However, the services provided by most natural monopolies require a contract that is much more complex than that required to buy a Treasury bill. The focus upon the informational requirements and transactional details that he introduced is now often referred to as *transaction cost economics*. If the contract is long term, it will include provisions for arbitration, negotiation, auditing, and inspection. This begins to look like ordinary regulation. When one realizes that the supplier retains all the informational advantages it has in the regulatory case, the capture theory appears plausible in this context as well. This is supported by experience from defense contracting, in which cost overruns and contract renegotiation favorable to the supplier are not unusual.

The parallel of franchising to rate-of-return regulation is just as strong under short-term recurrent contracting. In this case, the transfer of fixed and durable assets at a fair price would be necessary to maintain parity among bidders at contract renewal times. But establishing a value for these specific assets is as difficult under franchising as it is under rate-of-return regulation. The supplier will use the knowledge asymmetry to exaggerate the value of these assets in this case, just as it attempts to inflate estimates of its rate base under ordinary regulation. Thus under either long-term or short-term franchising, the supplier of a complex product utilizing substantial fixed assets will retain considerable information and bargaining advantages.

Williamson's case study of cable television in Oakland supports these conclusions: Numerous difficulties resembling those of regulatory capture characterize what happened under the franchise contract. We also consider briefly two cases of performance contracting (passenger rail service and education) to suggest other applications of this form of analysis. Performance contracting substitutes a price-performance contractual relationship for the price-cost one. The two cases illustrate information difficulties with this idea as well, but it remains a promising contracting approach if these difficulties are taken into account. This leads us to the final substantive section of the chapter in which we consider another method for improving natural monopoly regulation, an extension of the "performance" approach known as incentive regulation.

Incentive regulation is similar to performance contracting in that it conditions a utility's rewards or penalties on a measure of its performance, although no actual contracting takes place. The utility commission establishes in advance a formula that will be used to determine the firm's prices (or revenues). A key attribute of the formula is that it penalizes the firm for high costs and rewards it for low costs. The formula may also have a sharing parameter so that a portion of gains and losses is allocated to consumers. One particularly simple formula that is being used in telecommunications regulation by many states is called price-cap regulation, in which the allowed price for the current period equals last period's allowed price minus a fixed factor for expected productivity gains, with an upward adjustment for inflation based on a national price index. Since the allowed price does not depend on the firm's actual costs, it maximizes its profit by producing the services it sells at the least cost. In this simple version, there is no sharing (all profits or losses accrue to the firm).

Results of price-cap regulation to date have been encouraging, although there are a number of caveats. One important study found that telephone rates were 7–11 percent lower under price-cap regulation than under traditional rate-of-return regulation (other things being equal). Problems that regulators must contend with under price-cap regulation include the following: (1) The price cap typically applies to a basket of services, and the regulated firm may be able to exercise monopoly power within the basket; (2) insulating a firm from certain costs that it cannot control by a pass-through mechanism may induce some unintended production inefficiency; and (3) too frequent adjustment of the factors in the fixed formula destroys the firm's incentive to minimize costs.

Another regulatory strategy that has been increasingly common in recent years is partial deregulation. This strategy recognizes that some of the services that have been provided as monopolies could be provided competitively, even if other services of the same firm remain natural monopolies. Such is the case with electricity, in which generation can be provided competitively even though local distribution remains a natural monopoly. In the telecommunications, electricity, and natural gas industries, many regulators have allowed deregulation and competitive entry for some services while they continue to regulate others as monopoly services. This creates additional complications, as one firm's costs must somehow be divided into the regulated and deregulated portions. It remains to be seen how well the regulatory strategies of incentive regulation and partial deregulation will work over time and in new areas.

Exercise

18-1 ○ Reaction Functions and Oligopoly: Two rival towns operate adjacent beaches during the summer months. The marginal cost of supplying the beaches is zero. They each charge the same beach fee because consumers (from anywhere) are indifferent between the two beaches. Each town wishes to maximize its beach revenues, since they use the fees to keep property taxes down for their own residents. Other things being equal, a town prefers to keep its beach as uncrowded as possible.

The total market demand for beaches is given by the function

$$P = 20 - \tfrac{1}{4}Q$$

where P is the beach fee, $Q = Q_1 + Q_2$, and Q_i is the number of people admitted to town i's beach:

a What is the marginal revenue function for Town 1?

b If town 1 wants to maximize revenues, express the Q_1 that it will supply as a function of Q_2 (this is its reaction function). What is the reaction function for town 2?

c What would the competitive output level be (total number of people admitted to both beaches)?

d If each town acts in accordance with its reaction function, what quantity will be supplied in the equilibrium? What are the total revenues to each town?

e If the two towns colluded to maximize joint revenues (splitting them evenly), what would revenues and output be?

f Why is it that the solutions to (d) and (e) are different? Show that the solution to (e) is unstable, according to the reaction function.

g In what sense is the behavior described by the reaction curves myopic? Is it like the Slumlord's (or Prisoner's) Dilemma?

CHAPTER NINETEEN

POLICY PROBLEMS OF ALLOCATING RESOURCES OVER TIME

MARKETS THAT ALLOCATE resources over time have important sources of failure. They impede the efficiency of factor markets by underdeveloping labor market skills and by over-utilizing exhaustible natural resources. In this chapter, we review the sources of these failures and consider some policy responses to them.

The failure in the labor market concerns the development of human capital through investing in higher education. The decision of an individual to invest in schooling today can have a significant impact on his or her future earnings profile, quality of life, and role in society. But exclusive reliance on the market would result in too little investment, especially for those coming from families of moderate means or less.

The failure in the exhaustible resource market concerns the amounts of the resource we conserve for future generations. The amount of oil used by the current generation determines how much, if any, oil will be left over for use in the future. But the representatives of the future generation are not here to stake their claims. The market failure is one of myopia, in which the tendency is to use up resources too quickly. This failure is compounded by the by-product of using oil as a fuel—the global warming that threatens our ecosystem. Clearly, an important task of any economic system is to enable decisions about the use of these scarce resources to be made wisely.

In both of these cases, one can describe how a perfect market system would operate to lead to efficient allocation over time. We review that idea briefly in the first section of this chapter. That is, the section reviews how perfect capital markets (for saving, borrowing, and investing real resources) would allow an economy to allocate resources efficiently between use for current and future consumption. One key concept is that *the interest rate is the price that equilibrates the investment demand with the savings supply. In equilibrium, total saving equals investment, and with perfect capital markets all investments whose net present values are greater than zero (at the market rate of interest) would be undertaken.*

There is wide agreement among economists that private capital markets are imperfect. For a variety of reasons they do not coordinate economic agents in a manner required for efficiency. Some of these reasons become clear when we extend the simple one consumption good, two-period model to a many goods, indefinitely long model. Perfect competition in the latter requires a myriad of prices: one for each good in each time period extending out for an indefinitely large number of periods. Actual markets fall far short of this ideal; this failure might best be thought of as one of "missing" markets. Thus, it may be possible to improve resource allocation through carefully designed public policies that compensate for the "missing" markets.

One problem that we discuss in a short section is the difficulty that the imperfections cause for choosing an appropriate discount rate to use in benefit-cost analysis. The basic reason for the difficulty is the divergence between the return on investment (or the opportunity cost of capital) and the marginal rate of substitution over time periods. Then the chapter focuses on two different applied areas in which actual capital markets are thought to have important "misses," and policy problems that arise in trying to compensate for them.

The first imperfection we consider is that *private markets lead to underinvestment in higher education by potential undergraduates.* This opportunity is one of the more important ways to enhance human potential, or human capital. There are two different reasons for the underinvestment: (1) Society may receive significant positive external benefits from an individual's undergraduate education. (2) The market "misses" providing loans to many individuals that would enable productive educational investments because of difficulties in ensuring repayment.

For investments in human capital generally, the market provides too few loans owing to substantial uncertainty concerning the repayment of funds and contract failures in insurance mechanisms that otherwise could reduce it. This second failure includes aspects of the information asymmetry failures that we focus on in the following chapter, but the problem as a whole is an important enough "miss" to warrant its inclusion here. The higher education market failures provide rationales for public policies that involve tuition subsidization as well as government-guaranteed student loans. We examine some of the problems that are perceived with these policies currently, including income-contingent loan repayment plans in use in the United States and Australia.

The second imperfection we consider is an intergenerational one: *the inadequate representation of future consumer claims on depletable resources.* We illustrate this in the context of the allocation of oil, a resource that is nonrenewable, at least with current technological knowledge. When a resource is to be rationed over a considerable span of time involving multiple generations, today's marketing decisions may not adequately represent the interests of future generations. Even speculators, who are popularly thought of as evil exploiters but often serve the useful social function of representing future interests, are likely to be too myopic to represent those interests optimally. Nevertheless, *the market does induce valuable technological progress* that economizes on resources that are becoming scarce.

We begin examining the allocation of natural resources by looking at models of a renewable resource—trees. Then we turn to an exhaustible resource—oil. We review how a perfect market would ration oil, and we consider briefly the use of simulation models to aid in the design of current energy policies. A depletable resource that is of greater current concern than oil itself is the world's ecosystem, which is threatened by the global warming that is an external by-product of burning oil and other fossil fuels, and is thus a significant aspect of the oil allocation issue.

Perfectly Competitive and Actual Capital Markets

Recall that we have already seen in Chapter 8 the derivation of the demand for investment resources as well as the supply of savings available to meet that demand. The demand for investment resources derives from the individual (or firm as agent) decisions on the investment-opportunities locus: weighing the value of holding or converting today's resources for future use against using them now for current consumption. The lower the interest rate, the more resources will be demanded for investment purposes.

The main social cost of investing is that it reduces current consumption, and those who agree to reduce consumption below their means are called savers. The supply of saved resources for investment comes from the utility maximization decisions weighing current versus future consumption. Normally we expect that the higher the interest rate, the greater the supply of savings because it reduces the price of future consumption relative to current consumption. Total resources minus the amount required to satisfy current consumption demand equals the supply left over for investment. These demand and supply curves are shown in Figure 19-1.

Note that in this two-period representation there is one unique interest rate r that makes demand equal to supply. This basic model (with no inflation or uncertainty) extends from the two-period case we have been using to many periods. As long as capital markets are perfectly competitive, the rule for selecting investment projects (from along the multiperiod investment possibilities surface) applies as in the two-period case: All investments with positive present values should be undertaken. Each independent possibility can be represented by the stream D_i of benefits and costs (net income per period) associated with it:

$$\text{PDV} = D_0 + \frac{D_1}{1 + r_1} + \frac{D_2}{(1 + r_1)(1 + r_2)} + \ldots + \frac{D_n}{(1 + r_1)(1 + r_2) \ldots (1 + r_n)}$$

In this more general formulation we allow for the possibility that the market interest rate varies from period to period.[1] There is nothing in the theory of perfect capital markets that requires that the price between periods j and $j + 1$ equal the price between periods $j + 1$ and $j + 2$ (or, for that matter, $j + k$ and $j + k + 1$). It depends simply on the demand and supply of resources for each period. There should be nothing surprising, for example, if interest rates in the United States respond to the changing life-cycle stages of its large and aging population segment known as "baby boomers" (now 45–55 years old). Now they are savers and real interest rates (r_{2002}) may be relatively low; 20 years from now they may be dis-

---

[1] We adopt the convention that r_i is the interest rate between period $i-1$ and i.

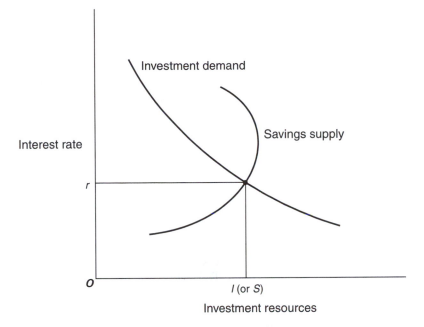

Figure 19-1. Intertemporal equilibrium in the capital market at interest rate r.

saving (shifting the aggregate supply of savings inward) which, other things being equal, would cause real interest rates (r_{2020}) to rise.

The determination of the market-clearing interest rates $r_1, r_2, \ldots, r_n$ in a multiple-period model is exactly analogous to calculating general equilibrium in the static model. Here we simply call the goods $C_0, C_1, \ldots, C_n$ with current prices $P_0, P_1, \ldots, P_n$. The relative price P_0/P_1, for example, is the number of units of C_1 that can be bought for one unit of C_0, or what we have seen earlier is $1 + r_1$. The relative price P_i/P_j, where $j > i$, is $(1 + r_{i+1})$ $(1 + r_{i+2}) \ldots (1 + r_j)$.

For each of these periods there is an investment demand function (a demand to invest within that period). It is the sum for each possible interest rate during that period of the optimal investment choices of each individual based upon his or her investment possibilities surface. The ordinary investment demand schedule is defined by allowing only that period's price (interest rate) to vary, all other prices (interest rates between other periods) being held constant at their equilibrium levels. For general equilibrium, we allow all the prices to vary simultaneously.

The investment (or savings) supply function for each period can be thought of as the residual from the consumption decision that would correspond to each possible interest rate during the period. That is, each person chooses consumption to maximize the intertemporal utility function $U(C_0, C_1, \ldots, C_n)$ given a budget constraint determined by intertemporal prices and after-investment income flows. For each possible interest rate during the period, the difference between the after-investment income for the period and the optimal consumption level, summed over all individuals, is the supply of savings for that period.

The ordinary savings schedule is defined by allowing only that period's price to vary, all other prices being constant at their equilibrium levels. For general equilibrium, all n prices in the savings function are allowed to vary simultaneously.

One could construct an even more general model in which we distinguish among the real goods available within a period. That is, instead of just having one good called "consumption," we have the usual m goods $X_1, X_2, \ldots, X_m$. If there are n time periods, each good must be identified by the time of its consumption; for example, X_{15} is the quantity of the first good that is consumed during the fifth period. Then individuals must maximize the intertemporal utility function:

$$\max U[X_{10}, X_{20}, \ldots, X_{m0}; X_{11}, X_{21}, \ldots, X_{m1}; \ldots; X_{1n}, X_{2n}, \ldots, X_{mn}]$$

In such a model there is no such thing as "the" interest rate between any specific periods. All goods have their own intertemporal prices as well as intertemporal cross prices with all other goods. There is no theoretical reason why the "own" interest rates should be the same across different goods. Technically, all these intertemporal prices have to exist in order for an economy to achieve a first-best Pareto-optimal allocation of resources. A further issue, which we will return to later in this chapter, is what determines the length of time (the number of periods) n over which all the resources are to be allocated. One common answer used by theorists is to let n approach infinity, so that the model has an "infinite horizon."

Perhaps, needless to say, few theorists think actual intertemporal markets approximate the requirements for perfectly competitive intertemporal allocation with infinite horizon. We have already observed in Chapter 8 that the intertemporal decisions of many individuals seem too myopic to be utility-maximizing. We can also observe that actual futures markets are limited to very short-time horizons, rarely offering any resources more than 20 years into the future. Furthermore, these markets exist only for a relatively small number of commodities. So there is reason to be concerned about how well actual intertemporal markets perform, given that there are so many "missing" components that are required for perfect competition.

The Social Rate of Discount

The substantial imperfections of actual capital markets create an important problem for choosing the discount rate in benefit-cost analysis. If these markets were perfect, the marginal return on investment would equal the marginal rate of substitution between current and future consumption, and the interest rate that equilibrates this market would be the appropriate social discount rate. However, because of the imperfections, and despite substantial research efforts, there is no agreement among professional economists on what discount rate should be used. This is a very complex subject: Many rules for choosing the rate have been proposed and justifications for them based on detailed analysis offered. Here we offer a highly simplified view that helps define the range within which the controversy lies.[2]

---

[2] An excellent discussion of these issues and the methods proposed for resolving them is contained in Chapter 10 of Anthony E. Boardman et al., *Cost-Benefit Analysis: Concepts and Practice,* 2nd Ed. (Upper Saddle River, N.J.: Prentice-Hall Inc., 2001).

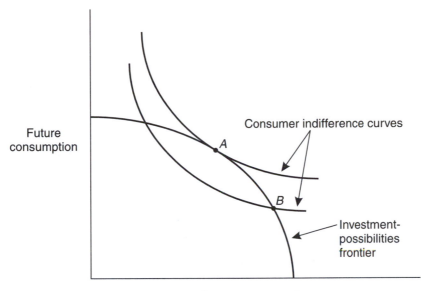

Figure 19-2. In the actual capital market, investment return (at *B*) exceeds the cost of deferring consumption.

Figure 19-2 gives a "Robinson Crusoe" view of the controversy. If there were no problem, society would be at point *A*, where the interest rate (and discount rate) is *r*. However, society is actually at some point to the right of *A*, like point *B*, where the absolute slope of the investment-possibilities locus $(1 + r_i)$ is greater than the marginal rate of substitution between current and future consumption $(1 + r_c)$. We will call r_i the return on investment (also called the opportunity cost of capital) and r_c the marginal consumer rate of time preference, with $r_i > r_c$. At this point we have too little investment (or too few resources being preserved for future generations).

One way to see why we are at a point like *B* is the effect of taxes and transaction costs.[3] Suppose $r_c = 0.03$. That means an individual buying a safe corporate bond for $1000 would demand to net $30. Suppose the corporation is able to earn $r_i = 0.10$ or $100 with the $1000. However, it must pay 35 percent corporate income tax on its earnings, so it can only give $65 to the bondholder. The bondholder must pay state and personal income taxes of, let us say, 50 percent on the interest earnings, leaving $32.50. Let us also say that the $2.50 just compensates the bondholder for the transaction costs of purchasing the bond and having a more complicated income tax to file. The bottom line is that the imperfections caused by taxes and transaction costs mean that r_i has to be 0.10 in order to yield r_c of 0.03 to the consumer.

If this situation crudely characterizes the actual capital market, then what discount rate is the right one to use for government projects? If all costs and benefits could be measured

---

[3] Boardman et al., *Cost-Benefit Analysis: Concepts and Practice,* suggested this type of example.

in terms of consumption forgone or gained, then the marginal rate of time preference would be appropriate. If all costs and benefits could be measured in terms of investment costs and returns, then return on investment would be appropriate. The difficulty is that even if we know numerical costs and benefits, we usually cannot know the extent to which these will represent changes in consumption or investment. The various methods that have been proposed to try to calculate this, such as estimating *the shadow price of capital,* generally produce some form of weighted average of the two rates.[4]

There is one further wrinkle that we shall mention here: the treatment of projects that have effects over long periods of time, such as projects to mitigate global warming or other long-term environmental issues. Different literatures support the idea of using discount rates that decline over time. One literature concerns actual individual behavior, in which the evidence suggests *hyperbolic discount rates: the use of high rates over short periods and relatively lower rates over longer periods.*[5] The other literature is concerned with future generations, which are not yet here to represent the claims on resources that they would like to make. This literature suggests lower discount rates for future generations for two reasons. The first is to compensate for the likelihood that per capita income will be higher in the future and thus, owing to diminishing marginal utility, a unit of consumption will be valued lower. The second is more controversial but simply follows the general logic of discounting the future: For two people who live in different time periods but are otherwise identical, weight the one closest to the current period more heavily.

The federal government's requirement to use a discount rate of 7 percent reflects a view that is weighted more heavily toward the return on investment (opportunity cost) perspective than on the marginal rate of time preference perspective. However, the guidelines mandating this do allow some latitude for making adjustments similar to using a lower discount rate for projects that span lengthy periods.[6]

Education as a Capital Investment

Let us turn to a particular dimension of intertemporal allocation with important policy implications: the development of human potential through higher education. Virtually everyone agrees that public policies are needed to help finance higher education, although there may be much disagreement about the quantity and form of assistance.

Education is somewhat analogous to making an improvement on a home. It results in a stream of consumption benefits over time: The educated person may derive more enjoyment from reading, skiing, discussing rent control with friends and landlords, or any of a

---

[4] See David Bradford, "Constraints on Government Investment Opportunities and the Choice of Discount Rate," *American Economic Review, 65,* No. 5, December 1975, pp. 887–899.

[5] See, for example, David Laibson, "Life-cycle Consumption and Hyperbolic Discount Functions," *European Economic Review, 42,* No. 3–5, May 1998, pp. 861–871; and George Ainslie and Nick Haslam, "Hyperbolic Discounting," in G. Lowenstein and J. Elster, eds., *Choice over Time* (New York: Russell Sage Foundation, 1992), pp. 57–92.

[6] See the "best practices" document issued by the Office of Management and Budget, *Economic Analysis of Federal Regulations Under Executive Order 12866* ("Best Practices Guidances"), January 11, 1996.

myriad of human activities. Just as home improvement can have positive external effects by improving the neighborhood, so can a more educated citizenry improve the community. In addition, education is an income-generating investment: By allocating one's time to taking courses and studying rather than indulging in leisure or current employment, future earnings can be enhanced. In other words, humans, like homes, can be viewed as durable goods that represent a form of savings and capital assets that may be invested. Education increases the stream of consumption and income benefits from human capital; it is a process of human capital formation.[7]

Human capital differs from other capital in important ways. One of the few noncontroversial public policies is the ban on the sale of human capital (i.e., slavery). This creates capital market inefficiency (!) despite the empirical likelihood that few informed adults would choose to sell themselves even if they legally could do so. The more important problem arises in financing human capital investments, since the asset invested cannot be used as collateral.

The Market Failures in Financing Higher Education Investments

Recall that a perfect capital market will lend the individual up to the present value of the future (investment-enhanced) earnings stream. But the lender is uncertain as to whether any loan will be repaid: Even with legal rulings that support the lender's right to be repaid, the borrower may have no tangible assets that can ensure the repayment. If one borrows to buy a house, the house can be claimed by the lender in the event of default. But if one borrows to finance an education and then spends the next 5 years as a part-time ski instructor in Europe, the lender may be just plain stuck.

Consider the equity implications of this issue. Recall that borrowing is used to buy the services of other inputs for the investment (tuition to pay for faculty, teaching assistants, and so forth) *and* to finance the desired level of current consumption. Those who are wealthy may have no need to borrow; they may have endowments with current income sufficient to undertake higher education by self-financing. Even if current income is not high, there may be other assets (e.g., a trust account) that can be used as collateral. But what about the bright individual from a not-so-wealthy family? The value of investing in one's education may be high, but the imperfect capital market will not provide the necessary current resources. (Note that a loan equal to the tuition costs may not be enough to meet current consumption needs as well.)

The obvious policy remedies are to provide or encourage some type of loans for students (which we discuss below). But this is not the only imperfection in the higher-education market. Many argue that there are substantial positive external benefits to the rest of society from higher (undergraduate) education.[8] If so, this could be internalized by giving a

---

[7] For a classic exposition of this view, see G. Becker, *Human Capital,* National Bureau of Economic Research (New York: Columbia University Press, 1964).

[8] For example, Bowen and Bok argue that ethnic minority college graduates often have community leadership roles and encourage other ethnic minorities to follow similar paths, generating positive externalities. See William

subsidy such that the cost of a marginal unit of education equals the sum of the private plus the external benefits. It is very difficult to quantify these external benefits (they are usually described as community leadership, increasing social mobility, and so on). Therefore, one of the main policy issues is to decide the extent of tuition subsidization and to treat the residual as a potential capital market problem.

Income-Contingent Loan Plans for Financing Higher Education

As part of President Clinton's successful 1992 election campaign, he proposed a national income-contingent loan plan to help students finance the cost of attending an institution of higher education. Congress approved the Student Loan Reform Act in 1993, a modified version of the Clinton plan that remains in effect today. In Australia, an income-contingent plan introduced in 1989 is also still in effect at its public sector universities. What are such plans intended to accomplish, and how effective are they?

No matter how one measures college enrollments, a very substantial portion of the young adult population does not enroll. In the year 2000, 43.5 percent of U.S. high school graduates 18–21 years of age were not enrolled in college.[9] Yet for those qualified, the economic returns to attending college far outweigh its costs. Kane and Rouse, for example, estimate that the increase in present value of earnings (using a 6 percent discount rate) from attending 1 year of a community college is between $15,600 and $25,000 after taxes while the costs to the student of attending (primarily opportunity costs) are only $9500.[10] In a separate work, Kane shows the impact of a family's financial means: among equally qualified youth, those from the lowest income quintile enroll at rates 12–27 percent lower than those in the highest quintile.[11] Thus the loans available to help finance these productive educational investments are highly important.

The income-contingent loan can be thought of as two products packaged into one: a loan that enables students to convert their uncertain future incomes into current cash and an insurance policy that protects the borrowers against the event of a relatively low future income. This is achieved by making the annual repayments not just contingent on the amount borrowed, but also an increasing function of the borrower's actual future income. Such plans are intended to encourage students to incur the debt necessary to invest in their own educations by reducing the probability that borrowers will be unable to make payments and thus have to default.

To be a true income-contingent plan, it is not enough simply to make repayments a function of income. During the Reagan administration, a pilot plan with this income-sensitive

---

G. Bowen and Derek Bok, *The Shape of the River: Long-Term Consequences of Considering Race in College and University Admissions* (Princeton, N.J.: Princeton University Press, 1998).

[9] There were 11,975,000 high school graduates of whom 6,768,000 were attending college. See Table 1, *October 2000 Current Population Survey* (Washington, D.C.: U.S. Census Bureau, 2001).

[10] See pp. 78–79 of Thomas Kane and Cecilia Rouse, "The Community College: Educating Students at the Margin Between College and Work," *Journal of Economic Perspectives, 13,* No. 1, Winter 1999, pp. 63–84.

[11] Thomas Kane, *The Price of Admission* (Washington, D.C.: The Brookings Institution and Russell Sage Foundation, 1999), p. 100.

feature was instituted among ten higher-education institutions. However, those repaying with low annual incomes still had to repay the full present value of their loans: They were assigned lower payments but had to pay for a greater number of years. Under a true-income contingent plan, the present value of repayments varies inversely with income. That is, those repaying but with low incomes will be discharged from further payment before they have repaid the full present value of their borrowing.

For example, under the U.S. plan in effect today a borrower never has to pay more than 20 percent of his or her discretionary income, and there is a maximum payment period of 25 years. Since discretionary income is defined (approximately) as ordinary income minus a poverty-level cost-of-living amount dependent on household size, those with income less than or equal to the poverty level pay nothing.[12] Of course if income rises sufficiently over time, then the individual will be required to make payments. If the full debt is not discharged before the end of the 25-year period, it is deemed fully discharged after 25 years.[13]

It is quite possible, in principle, to design such plans to be self-financing (the present value of all repayments equal to the present value of all borrowing). While low-income borrowers return less than the present value of their borrowings, this could be offset by high-income borrowers returning more than the present value.[14] Whether or not it would be appropriate to do this depends on circumstances. A private institution might have to do this as a necessity (i.e., if there is no other source to subsidize the program).[15] As a government program at the national level, it is a matter of equity. If the students as a group do not eventually fully repay their loans, then taxpayers make up the difference.[16] However, a more generous plan will attract more students and might target available subsidies better—to those among college students who end up with relatively low incomes over a lengthy period.

[12] For example, $10,610 is the poverty level cost-of-living for a household of two in the continental United States, so borrowers with annual income less than this have zero repayment amounts.

[13] The household must report any undischarged balance as income for income tax purposes.

[14] I do not mean to underestimate the difficulty of setting rates to achieve this balance. It requires predicting the number and income distribution of those making the repayments as well as defaults and the impacts of changes in interest rates, among other factors. An early and thoughtful analysis of this problem is provided in Marc Nerlove, "Some Problems in the Use of Income-Contingent Loans for the Finance of Higher Education," *Journal of Political Economy, 83,* No. 1, February 1975, pp. 157–183. Calculations along these lines are also provided in Alan B. Krueger and William G. Bowen, "Policy Watch: Income-Contingent College Loans," *Journal of Economic Perspectives, 7,* No. 3, Summer 1993, pp. 193–201.

[15] In the 1970s, Yale University briefly instituted a plan intended to be self-financing as an experiment. According to Hauptman, the plan was abandoned as federal student loans became more available in the late 1970s. See Arthur Hauptman, *The Tuition Dilemma* (Washington, D.C.: The Brookings Institution 1990), p. 49.

[16] Note that this is a separate issue from asking taxpayers to pay part of the costs of higher education on externality grounds. This issue is about paying that portion of costs that remain after accounting for externalities (the portion to be raised through student tuition and fees). In Australia, for example, Chapman reports (p. 739) that 1996 student charges were approximately 23 percent of costs. See Bruce Chapman, "Conceptual Issues and the Australian Experience with Income Contingent Charges for Higher Education," *Economic Journal, 107,* No. 442, May 1997, pp. 738–751. A comparable figure for the United States as a whole, recognizing it varies tremendously across private and public institutions, was 32 percent in 1995. See Table 1, p. 19, of Gordon C. Whinston, "Subsidies, Hierarchy and Peers: The Awkward Economics of Higher Education," *Journal of Economic Perspectives, 13,* No. 1, Winter 1999, pp. 13–36.

The U.S. plan is not intended to be self-financing. It has parameters that operate as follows: A single person with a $40,000 income and an average-size loan pays the normal amount that would discharge the loan in 12 years. Those with lower incomes make smaller payments but for longer periods (until the loan is discharged or the 25-year limit is reached). Those with higher incomes make larger payments but for shorter periods. For example, a single person with a $70,000 income is required to pay 25.77 percent more each month than the person with $40,000 income. However, instead of using any of the "extra" amount to subsidize low-income borrowers, the payment is fully credited to the retirement of that individual's debt and works to shorten the loan. In other words, no borrower in the U.S. plan pays more than the present value of the loan, but some will pay less.

The Australian plan also does not recapture more than the present value of the loan from any borrower. No payments are collected from individuals earning less than the average taxable income in Australia, and because the Australian policy is to charge a zero real rate of interest on the loans, all participants are receiving subsidies to some extent. However, this plan was introduced in Australia at the same time that tuition payments were being reinstituted, so that the net effect was to increase the proportion of higher education costs borne by the graduates. Chapman reports that there is no evidence to suggest that these new charges have deterred the access of the disadvantaged to the system, a result he attributes to the income-contingent nature of this plan.[17]

One of the major concerns with the development of any self-financing income-contingent loan plan is that of *adverse selection*. If the individual borrowers are able to predict their future incomes to some extent and more conventional loan programs are available, then those expecting relatively high future incomes will not participate. As they opt out and the plan rates are redesigned to be self-financing among those remaining, the group expecting the next-highest future income will realize that they also are better off with more conventional loans and decide not to participate. This can continue until all those able to utilize the more conventional loans opt out, leaving only those with the lowest expected incomes, the very group who cannot self-finance and whose needs motivated the system in the first place.

The adverse selection problem could be solved if participation were mandatory for all borrowers or if there were no more conventional alternatives. Of course since the actual U.S. and Australian plans do not try to recapture more than the present value of loans from those with high incomes, this incentive for adverse selection does not exist. However, the Australian system could move more easily toward self-financing should it be thought desirable: It is the only national system and all repayments are made through the tax system.

In the United States, there are many other student loan programs. Total student borrowing in fiscal 1996 was around $30 billion. Most loans (roughly two-thirds) are arranged through the private sector, backed by government guarantee of repayment in the event of default (the most common of these are Stafford loans). The income contingency option is

---

[17] For further information on the Australian system, see Chapman, "Conceptual Issues and the Australian Experience with Income Contingent Charges for Higher Education."

only available at the approximately 20 percent of the nation's higher-education institutions that participate in the federal government's direct loan programs.

Even within the set of loans made directly by the federal government, income-contingent loans are only used by about 9 percent of borrowers.[18] Almost 40 percent of these were placed in this program because they were in default under one of the private-sector programs. Thus it is not surprising that its default rate of about 5 percent is slightly higher than in the other direct loan programs; indeed it is possible that this program has been highly successful in achieving repayments that otherwise would not have been made. It is less clear why so few of the other borrowers participate in it, although it is difficult to understand and there are reports that financial aid counselors are not recommending it.[19]

Recall that the initial aim of the income-contingent program is to fix a capital market imperfection whereby people are deterred from making good educational investments owing to their uncertainty about future income and the ability to repay more conventional student loans. The U.S. plan still leaves much to be desired in terms of making such a plan widely available, easy to understand, generous enough in its subsidies for those most deserving, and resistant to adverse selection at a reasonable taxpayer cost.

We have identified two sources of market failure with regard to educational investments: inadequate borrowing opportunities and positive external benefits of the investments. We have centered the discussion on the first, not because it is more important but because it relates directly to the focus of this particular chapter on capital market imperfections per se. However, there are many other problems and policies involved in the provision of higher education. We have not touched upon the rationale for having a mixed public and private system, the important research roles of higher-education institutions, or other aspects of the supply side of this market.[20] Our point is to emphasize the policy relevance of understanding capital formation and capital markets by linking it in this section to problems of educational policy. In the following section, we turn to a quite different policy area—energy—to reinforce the same basic point.

The Allocation of Natural Resources

In perfect capital markets, investment choices will be made to maximize the present value of income. In this section we apply that logic to an analysis of the markets that allocate natural resources over time. There is a finite amount of oil in the world, for example, and we

---

[18] See the report by the Government Accounting Office, *Direct Student Loans: Analyses of Borrowers' Use of the Income Contingent Repayment Option,* Letter Report GAO/HEHS-97-155, August 21, 1997.

[19] To my knowledge, this has not yet been studied. However, a report in *The Chronicle of Higher Education* says "financial-aid officials in the direct-loan program have sold income contingency mostly as a 'last resort' option for needy students with sizable debts" (September 25, 1998, pp. A40–A41). The Department of Education brochure inappropriately named *All About Direct Loans* (March 1997) contains too little information about the specifics of the income-contingent plan for any prospective borrower to understand how present values under different circumstances would compare to other loan options.

[20] For more reading on these issues, see the Symposium on the Economics of Higher Education in *Journal of Economic Perspectives, 13,* No. 1, Winter 1999, especially the articles by Gordon Whinston, "Subsidies,

seek to understand how private markets allocate this oil. Why has it not been used up already? For how much longer can we expect supplies to flow? At what prices? Is there a danger that the world will plunge into a draconian darkness with no oil left for fuel and no substitutes to take its place? Although the issues involved in answering such questions and considering policy in relation to them are complex, the analysis reviewed here is basic to an understanding of them.

Thomas Malthus, writing in the early nineteenth century, predicted that the growth of the world's population would soon overwhelm the world's ability to produce food in enough quantity to sustain this population.[21] In this view the growth of the population accelerates the using up of the world's scarce resources, thus leading to rapidly declining living standards. A key unforeseen factor in the Malthusian scenario is technological progress: the ability over time to produce a unit of output with less of the scarce resources. He did not foresee, for example, the tremendous increases in agricultural productivity in the United States and elsewhere that would lead to far greater food output per capita despite tremendous growth in population and shrinking amount of land in agricultural use.

To modern day economists, technological progress and the conservation of scarce resources are natural consequences of a properly functioning price system. As any resource becomes scarcer its price in the marketplace will rise, and the price rise induces the use of substitute materials and stimulates efforts to find new resource-conserving technologies. This does not mean that there are no limits to growth, but they are not as severe as some authors have feared. In the modern day context, our concerns are less about running out of an essential conventional input such as oil and more focused on the ability of the global environment to sustain long-run economic growth. Will current levels of economic activity lead to devastating global warming or to the extinction of too many living species to sustain the ecosystem? The economic models introduced in this section help us to think about how markets allocate resources over time, some of their strengths and weaknesses, and policies that may improve their functioning.[22]

We begin with a very simple model of a renewable natural resource: when to cut trees in order to maximize the present value of lumber they provide. This model reinforces two general points: (1) One of the factors involved in the creation of capital is the time cost of de-

---

Hierarchy and Peers: The Awkward Economics of Higher Education," Thomas Kane and Cecilia Rouse, "The Community College: Educating Students at the Margin Between College and Work," and Ronald Ehrenberg, "Adam Smith Goes to College: An Economist Becomes an Academic Administrator," pp. 99–116. See also Charles Clotfelter, *Buying the Best: Cost Escalation in Elite Higher Education* (Princeton, N.J.: Princeton University Press, 1996); David W. Breneman and Chester E. Finn, Jr., eds., *Public Policy and Private Higher Education* (Washington. D.C.: The Brookings Institution, 1978); and J. Froomkin, D. Jamison, and R. Radner, *Education as an Industry,* National Bureau of Economic Research (Cambridge: Ballinger Publishing Company, 1976).

[21] T. R. Malthus, *An Essay on the Principle of Population* (London: J. Johnson, 1817).

[22] For general reference on this subject, see P. Lasserre, *Long-Term Control of Exhaustible Resources* (Philadelphia: Harwood Academic Publishers, 1991) and P. S. Dasgupta and G. M. Heal, *Economic Theory and Exhaustible Resources* (Oxford: James Nisbet & Company, Ltd., and Cambridge University Press, 1979). See also C. Kolstad, "Energy and Depletable Resources: Economics and Policy, 1973–1998," *Journal of Environmental Economics and Management, 39,* No. 3, May 2000, pp. 282–305.

ferred consumption, and (2) the amount of time that will be used to create capital varies with the interest rate. No profit-seeking supplier will make the investment without compensation for this time cost, and the compensation should not be thought of as economic rent.

Renewable Resources: Tree Models

Imagine that a small amount of labor is used to plant a tree and then to harvest its lumber when it is cut down. The price per board-foot of lumber is the same over time. Given that the tree is planted, when should it be cut? Let P be the price per board-foot and $Q(t)$ the quantity of lumber (which increases over time as the tree grows). If the cost of cutting down the tree is assumed to be zero for the moment, then the net value of the lumber at any time t can be described by the following equation:

$$F(t) = PQ(t)$$

The increase in the value of the tree from one period to the next is

$$\Delta F(t) = P\Delta Q(t)$$

One way to consider when to cut the tree (or equivalently, how much capital to create) is to think of the alternatives. At any time, one can simply let the tree grow. We have just seen that the increase in net value from this strategy is $\Delta F(t)$. Another alternative would be to cut the tree down, sell the lumber, and put the receipts in the bank, where they earn the market rate of interest r. In that case the increase in value is $rF(t)$. When the tree is growing rapidly [$\Delta F(t)$ is big], letting it grow (sometimes called capital deepening) is the better investment. Past a certain point, however, the tree's growth slows down and its natural increase in value will be less than the cut-and-bank strategy. In order to maximize the value of the tree investment, one should let the tree grow until just that point at which[23]

$$\Delta F(t) = rF(t)$$

or

$$r = \frac{\Delta F(t)}{F(t)}$$

Once the tree is planted, in other words, its present value is maximized at a time when the proportional growth in its value $\Delta F(t)/F(t)$ equals the market rate of interest. The

---

[23] In the calculus version using continuous discounting, the same result is easy to formulate. The present value of the investment at any time t is $PV = F(t)e^{-rt} - C_0$, where C_0 is the initial planting cost. To maximize this, we take the derivative with respect to t and set it equal to zero:

$$\frac{\partial PV}{\partial t} = \left(\frac{\partial F}{\partial t}\right)e^{-rt} - re^{-rt}F(t) = 0$$

By dividing both sides by e^{-rt} and rearranging, we have

$$r = \frac{\partial F/\partial t}{F(t)}$$

initial planting costs are not irrelevant to the decision, however; the maximum present value (given the tree is planted) could be a negative number. Thus, the result must be qualified: One should plant the tree only if there is at least one $t > 0$ at which the present value is positive. Provided the planting condition is met, the investment time is determined by the proportional growth rule.

It is easy to extend this model to the case when cut-down costs C are positive and, for simplicity, assumed to be constant.[24] The net value of the tree at any time is then

$$F(t) = PQ(t) - C$$

The increase in the value of the tree from one period to the next is independent of the cut-down and planting costs; it is the same as before:

$$\Delta F(t) = P\Delta Q(t)$$

This time the cut-and-bank strategy is not so profitable; after cut-down costs, only $F(t) - C$ can be put in the bank. Thus, the cut-and-bank strategy will yield $r[F(t) - C]$. Whenever $\Delta F(t) > r[F(t) - C]$, it is more profitable to let the tree grow rather than cut it down and bank the proceeds. In order to maximize the value of the tree, one should let it grow until

$$\Delta F(t) = r[F(t) - C]$$

If we divide each side of this equation by $F(t)$, we see that

$$\frac{\Delta F(t)}{F(t)} = \frac{r[F(t) - C]}{F(t)}$$

Since $[F(t) - C]/F(t) < 1$,

$$\frac{\Delta F(t)}{F(t)} < r$$

That is, when there are constant cut-down costs, the tree is at its maximum value when its proportional rate of growth is *less* than the interest rate: One lets the tree grow a little longer in response to an increase in cut-down costs.[25]

Finally, let us note that, so far, we have ignored *replanting*. The solutions we have discussed for the planting and cutting of trees are correct only if land is not scarce. But if land

[24] It is also easy to consider the case when cut-down costs are proportional to the value of the tree. In this case, the profit-maximizing rule is still to cut the tree when its proportional rate of growth equals the interest rate. This can be seen by following the same logic as for the constant cost case in the text, but replacing C by $kF(t)$, where $k < 1$ is a constant. Then the net value of the tree after cut-down costs is $(1-k)F(t)$, and the return if banked is $r(1 - k)F(t)$. The return from letting the tree grow is $(1 - k)\Delta F(t)$, and the return from each strategy is the same only when $\Delta F(t) = rF(t)$.

[25] This can be seen more precisely in the calculus version of this model with positive cut-down costs. The present value of the tree at any time t (with continuous discounting) is

$$PV = F(t)e^{-rt} - Ce^{-rt} - C_0$$

is scarce, efficiency requires us to use it to maximize the present value of the profits from it over *all* time. This changes the solution by reducing the time allowed for each tree to grow. Intuitively, the earlier solutions ignored the cost of pushing back the time at which profits from replanting would accrue. When that cost is taken into account, we cut the tree down a bit sooner.[26]

To maximize, we take the partial derivative with respect to t and set it equal to zero and thereby derive the equilibrium condition:

$$\frac{\partial PV}{\partial t} = \left(\frac{\partial F}{\partial t}\right) e^{-rt} - rF(t)e^{-rt} + rCe^{-rt} = 0$$

Dividing both sides by e^{-rt} and simplifying gives us

$$\frac{\partial F}{\partial t} = r[F(t) - C]$$

To see how the optimal t changes as C increases, we differentiate the above equilibrium condition totally:

$$\frac{\partial^2 F}{\partial t^2} \frac{\partial t}{\partial C} = r\left(\frac{\partial F}{\partial t} \frac{\partial t}{\partial C} - 1\right)$$

Solving for $\partial t/\partial c$ gives us

$$\frac{\partial t}{\partial C} = \frac{-r}{(\partial^2 F/\partial t^2) - r(\partial F/\partial t)}$$

Since $r > 0$, the numerator is negative. The denominator also is negative as long as the tree grows ($\partial F/\partial t > 0$), and the tree grows more slowly over time ($\partial^2 F/\partial t^2 < 0$). Thus, the whole fraction is positive; the optimal time to let a tree grow increases in response to increased cut-down costs.

[26] This point and its solution were first recognized by Martin Faustmann in 1849 (cited by Paul Samuelson, "Economics of Forestry in an Evolving Society," *Economic Inquiry, 14,* December 1976, pp. 466–492).

We show the Faustmann solution in a simple model in which we let $G(t)$ be the net value of the tree at time t (i.e., the value after paying cut-down costs). Then we wish to maximize the net present value of the yield from timber production over all time:

$$PV = G(t)[e^{-rt} + (e^{-rt})^2 + \ldots + (e^{-rt})^n + \ldots]$$

For positive r and t, the expression in brackets is an infinite series with a finite sum equal to $e^{-rt}/(1 - e^{-rt})$. Thus, we can simplify:

$$PV = \frac{G(t)e^{-rt}}{1 - e^{-rt}}$$

We maximize this by taking the partial derivative with respect to t and setting it equal to zero:

$$\frac{\partial PV}{\partial t} = \frac{[(\partial G/\partial t)e^{-rt} - re^{-rt}G(t)](1 - e^{-rt}) - re^{-rt}[G(t)e^{-rt}]}{(1 - e^{-rt})^2} = 0$$

Since the denominator does not equal zero, the numerator must. We can simplify the numerator by factoring out e^{-rt} from each term and dividing both sides of the equation by it. That leaves us with

$$\left[\frac{\partial G}{\partial t} - rG(t)\right](1 - e^{-rt}) - rG(t)e^{-rt} = 0$$

Moving the terms with $G(t)$ to the right-hand side gives us

The tree model is an example of a special type of investment sometimes referred to as *point input, point output,* where the terms refer to the technological fact that there is an initial outlay of resources and the output (and therefore income return) comes in one lump at the end. In such a model there is an important relation between time and the interest rate: The optimal time for the point input, point output investment is reduced by an increase in the interest rate.[27] This accords with the general rule that investment decreases with increases in the interest rate.

A Note on Investment Time and Interest Rates: Switching and Reswitching

One cannot generalize about the relation between the length of time of investments and interest rates. Under some circumstances, longer-term investments may substitute for shorter-term ones in response to a rise in interest rates. The basic reason for what may seem like a counterintuitive result is that the time cost depends on the quantity of resources diverted from current consumption, and this quantity can vary during the "life" of an investment.

To understand this, it helps to mention other investments apart from the point input, point output ones. Some crops may require continuous attention while growing and then yield output all at once (continuous input, point output). An oil well may have high initial drilling expenses and then return oil output over many periods (point input, continuous output, to

---

$$\frac{\partial G}{\partial t}(1 - e^{-rt}) = rG(t)$$

or, finally,

$$\frac{\partial G/\partial t}{G(t)} = \frac{r}{1 - e^{-rt}}$$

Since the denominator on the right is positive but less than 1,

$$\frac{\partial G/\partial t}{G(t)} > r$$

That is, the optimal time to cut the tree when replanting is considered occurs when the proportional growth in the tree's value is greater than the interest rate (or before the optimal time without considering replanting).

[27] We assume the technology satisfies the first- and second-order maximization conditions at a market interest rate r. Consider the simplest tree model. The first-order condition, equating the proportional growth in value of the investment to the interest rate, is a necessary one. To be sufficient, the second-order condition must be satisfied: The investment grows at a decreasing rate over time. Define $s(t)$ as the rate of growth at time t:

$$s(t) = \frac{F'(t)}{F(t)}$$

Then the second-order condition requires that $s'(t) < 0$. Otherwise, the investor is at a minimum (or a turning point), but not the maximum present value. Thus, in the neighborhood of the maximum, the rate of growth must be decreasing with time. This means that for a small decrease (increase) in the market interest rate r, the time to hold the investment must increase (decrease) if the first-order condition is to be satisfied.

an approximation). Many investments, such as building an airplane or a new modernized factory, may involve years of construction and provide years of output (continuous input, continuous output). To produce any given future output, there may be alternative investment opportunities of these different types that could be used. We use the criterion of maximizing present value to identify the economically most desirable ones.[28]

Suppose, for example, that we have two processes for aging wine quickly. In process 1 the wine is treated after crushing and then left to age for 2 years, at which time it is ready for sale. In process 2 the wine is crushed and aged "naturally" (with no costly treatment) for 2 years and is then processed and aged for 1 more year. Consumers, wine experts, and the FDA all agree that the outputs from the processes are identical. Suppose that the nominal values and times of the resources invested with each process are as shown in Table 19-1. Which process has the least cost (measured in dollars at the time the output is ready for sale)? We know that the costs (per unit of output) are calculated as follows:

$$C(1) = 100(1 + r)^2$$

$$C(2) = 43(1 + r)^3 + 58(1 + r)$$

If $r = 0.05$, then $C(1) = \$110.25$ and $C(2) = \$110.68$, and process 1 has the least cost. However, if $r = 0.15$, then $C(1) = \$132.25$ and $C(2) = \$132.10$, and process 2 has the least cost. It can be shown that cost-minimizing investors will switch processes when the interest rate rises above 10.58 percent.[29] But more startling is that they will *reswitch* if the interest rate rises above 21.98 percent. If $r = 0.23$, for example, then $C(1) = \$151.29$ and $C(2) = \$151.36$—the first process is cheaper again!

In this example, process 2 is the longer investment, in the sense that it takes 3 years to produce the output whereas process 1 requires only 2 years. But what is omitted from this usage of length is that the quantity of specific resources and the time they are invested differ in the two processes. Even though the quantity of physical resources each uses is fixed, we cannot judge which uses "more" resources without an interest rate to account for the time differences. Moreover, we have seen that the judgment varies with the interest rate. Finally, we have seen that there is no simple generalization of how investors will change the length of their investments in response to interest rate changes.

---

[28] In the presence of capital market imperfections, the use of this criterion may be difficult or even inappropriate. For example, suppose a firm cannot borrow unlimited funds at the market rate of interest and has a limited amount of capital to ration. The opportunity cost of that capital in one investment use depends upon the alternative internal investment opportunities, and the proper discount rate must be determined simultaneously with the optimal investments. This can be done by methods of integer programming, among others. For a discussion of this, see William J. Baumol, *Economic Theory and Operations Analysis* (Englewood Cliffs, N.J.: Prentice-Hall Inc., 1977), Chapter 25. In other situations, for example, when individuals face different interest rates for borrowing and lending, the separation property does not hold and they, like Robinson Crusoe, must go back to the basics of maximizing utility subject to the constraints. For some examples of this, see P. R. G. Layard and A. A. Walters, *Microeconomic Theory* (New York: McGraw-Hill Book Company, 1978), Chapter 12.

[29] Find the values of r that make $C(1) - C(2) = 0$; the equation can be solved by the quadratic formula.

Table 19-1

Two Technologies for Aging Wine to be Sold at Time _t_

Years before output	Treatment cost in each period		
	$t-3$	$t-2$	$t-1$
Process 1	0	100	0
Process 2	43	0	58

The Allocation of Exhaustible Resources Such as Oil

With these cautions let us extend the tree analysis to demonstrate the optimal pricing pattern for an exhaustible resource such as oil. The first question we will consider is how a perfect market would set prices to allocate the oil efficiently over a number of time periods.[30] Then we will consider some of the imperfections in the market.

Let the unknown price of oil at any time t be denoted $P(t)$. Suppose we start with an exceedingly simple model in which there are no extraction costs of pumping oil, there is a given total supply of oil in the ground, and the market rate of interest is r. We also assume that the oil should be rationed over a fixed period of time, which we denote T years, and that there are ordinary consumer demand curves for oil $D^t(P_t)$ within each of these years.[31]

Perfectly competitive suppliers will allocate their oil reserves during these T years in order to maximize present value. In an equilibrium, any supplier must be indifferent on the margin between pumping one more unit in the current period instead of in any future period. (The incremental contribution of each to present value must be the same.) In particular, the result we saw in the tree model must hold for this marginal unit:

$$\frac{\Delta P(t)}{P(t)} = r$$

or, equivalently,

$$\Delta P(t) = rP(t)$$

Note that in the second equation the term on the right can be thought of as the interest a supplier would earn in return for pumping and selling one more unit of oil today and "banking" the proceeds until the next period. The term on the left is the capital gain a supplier earns by leaving the unit in the ground and letting its price appreciate. Suppose the equation did not hold. If, for example, the sell-and-bank strategy were yielding a greater return, suppliers

---

[30] This analysis is a highly simplified version of work by William D. Nordhaus. See William D. Nordhaus, "Lethal Model 2: The Limits to Growth Revisited," _Brookings Papers on Economic Activity,_ No. 2, 1992, pp. 1–43, and his earlier paper "The Allocation of Energy Resources," _Brookings Papers on Economic Activity,_ No. 3, 1973, pp. 529–570.

[31] The demand curves are not assumed to be the same from one year to the next.

would sell more oil today. But all of them doing this would cause a reduction in the market price today relative to that of the next period and thus raise $\Delta P(t)$, until equality between the two terms was reached. When the equilibrium condition for intertemporal supply holds, each supplier is content with the quantity of oil being supplied in each time period.

The above condition implies (for discrete time periods) that the price path is a geometric progression. That is, it must have the form

$$P(t) = P_0(1 + r)^t$$

where P_0 is any constant greater than 0. If that is so,

$$\Delta P(t) = P_0(1 + r)^{t+1} - P_0(1 + r)^t$$

$$= (1 + r)P(t) - P(t)$$

$$= rP(t)$$

In other words, any geometric price path (i.e., P_0 is any positive constant) satisfies the one condition we have identified.[32]

The condition for intertemporal supply equilibrium is necessary but not sufficient to ensure a competitive equilibrium or an efficient allocation. Figure 19-3 suggests why. Figure 19-3a shows two different geometric price paths, one at a higher absolute level of prices than the other ($P_H^t > P_L^t$). Both have the property necessary for intertemporal supply equilibrium. But we have yet to account for consumer demands. Figures 19-3b and c illustrate the quantities of oil that consumers will demand in each of two periods, given the demand curves D^1 and D^2, dependent upon which of the two price paths is used. The lower price path leads to more oil being demanded over time than does the higher price path ($Q_L^t > Q_H^t$). For competitive equilibrium, we must find the geometric price path that is at just the right level to ensure that the total sum of oil demanded by consumers over time equals the total supply of oil reserves.

If the price path is such that the constant P_0 is too low, demand will be too great in the earlier periods and the oil will run out before $t = T$. If P_0 is too high, there will be unused oil at the end. Thus, only one value for P_0 will satisfy the terminal requirement that the oil demanded in all T periods add up to the total supply of oil reserves at the start. This is also the level that equalizes the present value of the willingness to pay for marginal consumption (i.e., the marginal benefit) in each year. Our two conditions determine the efficient price path. An allocation that meets them is Pareto-optimal: There is no way to reallocate the oil over time in order to make one person better off without making another worse off.

---

[32] In continuous time, the price path is exponential where $P(t) = P_0 e^{rt}$ and P_0 is any constant. This follows from the derivative property:

$$P'(t) = rP_0 e^{rt}$$

and therefore

$$\frac{P'(t)}{P(t)} = r$$

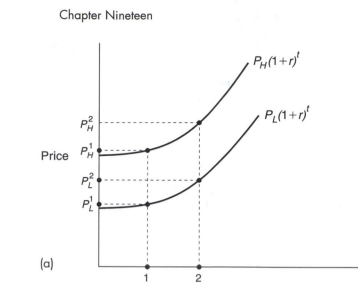

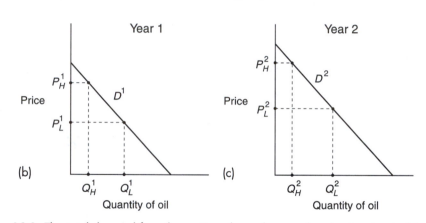

Figure 19-3. The total demand for oil over time depends upon the absolute level of the price path: (a) Two geometric price paths that differ by absolute price levels ($P_H^t > P_L^t$). (b and c) More oil is demanded in each year with the lower price path ($Q_L^t > Q_H^t$).

Let us illustrate this with a simple example. Suppose there are two periods, the interest rate is 10 percent, and there are available 100 units of oil competitively supplied with zero extraction costs. The demand for oil in each period is

$$Q(1) = 115 - P(1)$$

$$Q(0) = 90 - P(0)$$

The first condition for an efficient allocation is that the price path of oil makes suppliers indifferent on the margin between supplying or holding an additional unit of oil in the initial period:

$$P(1) - P(0) = rP(0)$$

Since $r = 0.10$,

$$P(1) = 1.1P(0) \qquad \text{(i)}$$

The second condition, or terminal condition, is that the sum of demands over time just equals the supply:

$$Q(1) + Q(0) = 100$$

Substituting from the demand equations gives us

$$205 - P(1) - P(0) = 100 \qquad \text{(ii)}$$

On substituting from (i) in (ii), we solve and find

$$2.1P(0) = 105$$

$$P(0) = 50 \rightarrow Q(0) = 40$$

$$P(1) = 55 \rightarrow Q(1) = 60$$

The prices in this model are sometimes called *royalties* because they arise from the scarcity value of the oil resources. All the price *increases* in this case reflect social opportunity costs: payments to oil owners for preserving the oil and thus forgoing the opportunities available from increased current income. However, the *level* of the price path P_0 is an economic rent that arises from rationing a fixed supply to meet the aggregate demand. (The identical intertemporal supply could be induced with any value of $P_0 > 0$.)[33]

Now let us add a small wrinkle to this simple model and allow extraction costs to be positive. Think of the price $P(t)$ as consisting of two components: a constant marginal extraction cost Z and a scarcity value or royalty $y(t)$. Thus

$$P(t) = y(t) + Z$$

Again as in the tree model, equilibrium requires that the price increase over time equal the interest that could be earned by the sell-and-bank strategy:

$$\Delta P(t) = r[P(t) - Z]$$

or

$$\Delta P(t) = ry(t)$$

and on dividing both sides by $P(t)$, we have

$$\frac{\Delta P(t)}{P(t)} = \frac{ry(t)}{P(t)} < r$$

---

[33] This is only in the simple model that ignores initial exploration and drilling costs. Even with no uncertainty as to location, P_0 must be high enough to make the present value of the oil minus drilling costs positive. This level would not be rent. Also, costly exploration to find oil will not be undertaken unless the costs can be recovered through oil prices.

The inequality on the right-hand side follows from $y(t) < P(t)$. In plain language, *the proportional increase in the price of an exhaustible resource along the efficient path is always less than the interest rate when there are positive extraction costs.*

Now let us extend the model in a deeper way. Recall that to this point we simply assumed that the oil would be allocated over an arbitrary T years. But how should T be determined, and what happens to the world when the oil has been used up and there is no more? If exhaustible resources such as oil (and coal, natural gas, and similar fuels) are the only way to provide energy, there is no finite horizon T beyond which we need not worry. But what if there is an alternative technology that produces energy using much less of any exhaustible resource? Nordhaus refers to this as the backstop technology: a technology such as solar, geothermal, or nuclear, which may be expensive in terms of the capital cost per British thermal unit (Btu) of safely produced energy but that runs on fuel resources that are for all intents and purposes unlimited and free (e.g., perhaps the sun).

Suppose that, as in our first model, oil is "costless" to produce but finite in quantity. The backstop technology is assumed to be very expensive at marginal cost of P_B per Btu equivalent, but it can be used to produce unlimited quantities of energy. How should society allocate its energy resources, given consumer demands? Of course, the free stuff should be used first. At some point the oil runs out and then we switch to the costly backstop technology. Let the time of this switch point, where oil is depleted and the backstop technology is brought into use, be denoted T_s. At that point, efficiency requires that the price of a Btu from oil equal the competitive price of obtaining the Btu with the backstop technology (otherwise there would be room for a deal):

$$P(T_s) = P_B$$

But now that we know the price of oil at one time T_s, we know the price at each time (by the equilibrium condition for intertemporal supply): It is simply the marginal cost of the backstop technology (the switch price) discounted back to the relevant period:

$$P(t) = P(T_s)(1 + r)^{-(T_s - t)}$$

or, equivalently,

$$P(t) = P_B(1 + r)^{-(T_s - t)}$$

This does not by itself answer the question of when the switch date should occur.

The switch date plays the same role as choosing the constant P_0 in the first model: It must be picked to balance the aggregate demand over time with the available reserves of oil. If it is too early, the price path necessary for intertemporal supply equilibrium (discounting backward from the proposed switch date) will result in too high a price today. Too little oil will be demanded currently and there will be unused oil at the switch point, which is inefficient. If the switch point is too late, the oil will be used up too quickly (before reaching the switch point). The efficient intertemporal allocation of oil requires that its exhaustion occur when the marginal willingness to pay for the last unit of oil just equals the marginal cost of using the backstop technology.

To sum up this analysis, *the efficient price for an exhaustible resource today should consist of its marginal production cost plus a royalty component. The size of the royalty component is determined by the cost of the backstop technology, the interest rate, and the switch date* (which ensures the aggregate balancing of demand and supply). *The more expensive the backstop and the earlier the switch date, the larger the royalty component of the current price.*[34]

Of course, reality is more complicated than any single exhaustible resource and any single backstop technology. Let us sketch the extension of this model to more than one exhaustible resource, so that we can recognize the role of other energy resources such as natural gas and coal. Let us also recognize that, for any single exhaustible resource, the marginal cost of extracting the reserve will rise because some portions of the reserve are more difficult to extract than others (e.g., sources that are in remote, difficult-to-access areas or the resources that are near the bottom of any single field such as the last barrels of oil from a well).

Imagine that we construct one supply curve of energy in Btu's from all of the different exhaustible resources that can provide it, starting of course from the lowest marginal cost and progressing to the highest. Each price in the price path is for 1 Btu of energy at a particular time. The condition for intertemporal supply equilibrium remains as before: Each supplier of each resource must be indifferent on the margin between supplying it in time period i or j (either choice contributes the same to the supplier's net present value). This time, we must match up the demands for Btu's over time with the supplies from all resources, and choose the switch date to the backstop technology (and thus the Btu price path) so that the last of the exhaustible resources is used exactly at the switch point.[35] This model extension suggests why an efficient allocation would have the production and use of different exhaustible resources in the same time periods.

Reality also includes far more uncertainty than in the simple models that we have illustrated. The cost of a backstop technology is not yet known. At any time there is a range of resource-conserving technologies under exploration, such as wind, solar, geothermal, and

[34] The effect of an interest rate change on current price is ambiguous, depending on the nature of the backstop technology. To see this, suppose the backstop technology is produced with capital as the only costly input (solar energy approximates this, in the sense that the sun's input is essentially free). Then we can think of $P_B = (r + \delta)K$, where K is the number of units of capital required to produce 1 Btu of energy and δ is the rate at which the capital depreciates (typically between 5 and 20 percent). We use the continuous time version of the efficient price path $P(t) = (r + \delta)Ke^{-r(T_s - t)}$ and differentiate:

$$\frac{\partial P(0)}{\partial r} = Ke^{-r(T_s)} - (T_s)(r + \delta)Ke^{-r(T_s)} = Ke^{-rT_s}[1 - T_s(r + \delta)]$$

Since K and the exponential term are positive, the whole expression is positive when $T_s(r + \delta) < 1$ (the switch point is near) and negative when $T_s(r + \delta) > 1$ (the switch point is a number of years away). For example, if $r + \delta = 0.2$, the current price would increase if the switch point was within 5 years and decrease if it was more than 5 years away.

[35] This assumes that the marginal cost of using the last of the exhaustible resource is still less than or equal to the marginal cost of the backstop. If the marginal cost of using some of the exhaustible resources exceeds that of the backstop technology, these resources will never be used.

nuclear energy sources, and we do not know in advance when and where breakthroughs will come in terms of the costs of relying upon them. A very important role of governments is to fund the public good of basic research in this area (once basic new knowledge is created, one person's consumption of it does not reduce the amount of it left for others). In turn, new basic knowledge can lead to private efforts to develop marketable innovations in energy production.

In addition, we do not know about the possibilities for technological progress involving the exhaustible fuels. There may be many valuable incremental advances over a fairly long period of time (perhaps a century or more) that have the effect of slowing up resource use and effectively buying us more time to find viable backstop technologies. Indeed, the evidence over the twentieth century has been that the real (inflation-adjusted) price of petroleum products has declined rather than risen, a good sign that there is *not* increasing scarcity. Indeed, the real prices of many exhaustible energy fuels, minerals, and agricultural land declined rather than rose over the century![36] Known oil reserves are far greater today than they were a century ago. As recently as 1973, proven world reserves were estimated at 600 billion barrels. But by the end of 1998 and despite 25 years of continued high consumption, this figure had risen to over 1 trillion barrels, primarily due to technological advances making it less costly to discover, drill, and recover oil from its sources.

Still, no one knows for how long into the future technological progress can prevent increasing scarcity of oil. But it is important to recognize the great significance of technological progress as a powerful conserving force, and that the amount of effort undertaken in the marketplace to create these improvements rises with any increase in the commodity's price. The more incentive there is for consumers to find less expensive substitutes for oil, the more the market will provide them. This does not mean that the market can stave off exhaustion, but it can greatly delay the time at which it will occur. Failure to account for this is why dire predictions about looming resource exhaustion in the past have thus far been erroneous.

Despite the relatively good performance of markets to date, there is little reason to think that we can rely upon them to keep us close to the efficient path for resource use over long periods of time. One source of market failure is the absence of long-term future markets and the myopia of economic agents. There is no economic agent today representing the prudent future demands for oil of citizens who will not be born until many years in the future. There is no mechanism, like a global planner, to ensure that the actual price path we are on is one in which the set of expected demands along it add up to the available supplies (with technological progress) for any reasonable (or safe) expectation of a switch point. What we observe is the outcome of market participants making investment decisions using their best estimates of energy prices in the near future.

If there is any near-term danger, it is that we do not fully understand how the use of these exhaustible resources may be straining the earth's ecosystem as a whole. That is, if we continue to burn fuel at current rates, to what extent will this contribute to global warming and what are its consequences? In the same vein, to what extent do the pesticides that contribute

---

[36] See Nordhaus "Lethal Model 2," pp. 22–28.

so greatly to increased agricultural productivity also contribute to the problems of reducing the number of diverse living species and to groundwater contamination? The market has not preserved the ecosystem as much as it has exhaustible fuels because the using up of the ecosystem has largely been an unpriced externality.

We do not know the answers to these important questions, but that does not mean that nothing can be done. Nordhaus, for example, has extended his theoretical analysis to construct simulation models of world energy markets as well as of climate change. In his studies done in the 1970s, based on estimated marginal production costs of all energy fuels and meeting then-existing environmental standards, he estimated that a backstop technology in the form of a breeder reactor would not become economic (reach the switch point) for 150–200 years. An implication of his work for U.S. public policy was that it would not have been sensible to engage in substantial nuclear energy production during the last part of the twentieth century (by coincidence, this study was published at a time when the country was reeling from the OPEC oil embargo and wondering what substitutes to rely upon). In his 1990s studies of climate change, he concludes that a global tax on carbon emissions would be an important positive policy step, but that an appropriate tax rate would be in the range of $5–$10 per ton and that the $100 rate proposed by the European Community would be worse than doing nothing at all.

Of course such studies are inherently complex and difficult, and no single one should be relied upon as a basis for policy. But the large uncertainties about the consequences of utilizing exhaustible energy resources and the unreliability of market allocation of these over long periods make it important as a matter of policy to continue vigorous study in this area in an attempt to make wise near-term decisions. By continuing to press the scientific limits of how far ahead we can project with some accuracy, we can improve the basis upon which we make policies today.

Summary

In this chapter we explored policy problems involving resource allocation over time. We first reviewed briefly the theory of perfect capital markets. The market rate of interest is determined by equilibrating the aggregate demand for investment with the aggregate supply of saving. This seems simple enough in the one consumption good, two-period model. But perfect capital markets must extend this to many consumption goods over an infinite horizon. Actual markets are missing many of these required components, and thus depart substantially from the ideal.

The chapter focuses on two specific types of intertemporal decisions in which the market seems to "miss" in important ways relevant to public policy–making. The first imperfection the chapter explores is the underinvestment of resources by private markets in the development of human potential, with particular reference to higher education. The market fails because there are positive external benefits from these investments and because there are insufficient loans to finance the investments (as a consequence of the lack of legal collateral and the borrower's uncertainty about future ability to repay). These lead to policies of tuition subsidization and guaranteed loans, respectively, although the proper mix between them is an unsettled and perhaps analytically unsolvable issue. The equity implications of these failures are particularly significant because individuals from families with relatively low current incomes are most likely to be unable to afford the current burden of investing despite its future payoffs.

A particularly interesting form of student loan is the income-contingent type. It differs from conventional loans in that its payback period can be quite extended (up to 25 years rather than 12 or under) and the amount paid back is an increasing function (up to a limit) of actual future income. Thus, the loan is also an insurance policy that protects the borrower against the event of a low future income. The insurance feature and the extended repayment period should, in theory, make this plan attractive to students. Plans of this type operate in both Australia and the United States. Neither attempts to recapture payments in excess of the original loan. In Australia, the plan was put into effect as part of a strategy to set tuition above zero and seems to be working successfully. In the United States, the plan may be successful in terms of achieving more repayments from students who have found it difficult to make repayments in other plans. However, the plan has not attracted very significant numbers of students, perhaps in part because its terms are unclear and in part because more conventional alternatives such as Stafford loans continue to be available.

A second imperfection in the markets that allocate resources over time is primarily an intergenerational one: the inadequate representation of the demands of future generations for current resources. We explore this in the context of the intertemporal allocation of oil. First we build up an understanding of the relation between wealth maximization and the supply of natural resources. Using trees as an example of a renewable resource, we show that the time at which trees are cut and replanted (to maximize their present value) depends on the growth rate of the trees, the planting and cut-down costs, and the market rate of interest. We then show that similar relations exist for exhaustible resources such as oil.

The efficient price path for the exhaustible resource, oil, should rise over time because its scarcity value increases (or, equivalently, because the compensation for holding it must increase with the length of the holding period). This royalty component, at any given time, is a function that increases with the cost of alternative energy sources and with the nearness of the switch date to an alternate source. It is also affected by changes in the interest rate. (An increase in the interest rate usually reduces the current royalty but may increase it if the switch date to a capital-intensive alternative is near.)

In the actual market for oil, there is no mechanism (like a global planner) to ensure that the price path is one that balances intertemporal demand with the recoverable supply of oil reserves. To the extent that future generations are not represented in the market place, there is understandable concern that exhaustible resources may be exhausted too quickly. However, even with an imperfect market, technological progress continually works to reduce resource scarcity. Proven oil reserves today, for example, are substantially higher than they were a century ago or even 25 years ago.

This does not mean that resource exhaustion can be prevented. It simply means that it takes far longer to occur than would be the case without technological progress. While the market does much of this on its own, it is important for governments to fund the public good of basic research that might lead to breakthroughs in the cost of using alternative technologies that do not rely upon exhaustible resources. (The lower the cost of a backstop tech-nology, the lower the level of the efficient price path for an exhaustible resource.)

In terms of other current day policy concerns related to the use of exhaustible energy re-sources, probably the major one is the extent to which this use strains our ecosystem (by causing acid rain, global warming, and other environmental problems). Simulation models can be used to estimate the optimal price path based on the best knowledge of reserves, es-timated future demand, environmental externalities, and the costs of alternative energy sources. Then current prices, and policies to affect them, can be considered in terms of the model implications. The work of Nordhaus, as an example, suggests that carbon taxes of $5–$10 a ton would be a valuable deterrent to environmental degradation, but that rates as some have suggested of $100 per ton would be worse than doing nothing. There is too much uncertainty in the results of such studies to rely upon any single one, but reasoned delibera-tion in light of a number of well-conducted studies may be the closest that we can come to the global planner that gives adequate representation to both current and future generations.

Exercises

19-1 Suppose 1000 units of oil are competitively allocated over three time periods. The oil is costless to extract. The demand for oil in each period is:

$$Q_0 = 900 - P_0$$

$$Q_1 = 1000 - P_1$$

$$Q_2 = 1100 - P_2$$

a If the interest rate is 8 percent, what are the prices and quantities at the competitive equilibrium? (Partial answer: $Q_2 = 381.42$.)

b Suppose the government imposes a $200 excess profits tax per unit of oil in the period in which the oil is consumed. Calculate the new equilibrium consumer prices and quan-tities. What is the efficiency cost (in present value terms) of this tax? (Partial answer: The efficiency cost is $219.21.)

c Suppose the excess profits tax is $200 in the current period and rises by 8 percent in each of the next two periods. Calculate the equilibrium prices and quantities. What is the efficiency cost of this tax? (Partial answer: $P_0 = 616.07.)

19-2○Suppose a tree costs $300 to plant and has a lumber content the net value of which (ex-cluding planting costs) after t years of growth is described by the following equation:

$$V = 60t - t^2 \quad 0 \le t \le 30$$

a The continuous discount rate is 5 percent. What would you do to maximize the pres-ent value? (Answer: $t = 13.94$; PV $= 19.80.)

b How would your decision change if the continuous discount rate were 10 percent? (Answer: $t = 0$, PV $= 0$.)

CHAPTER TWENTY

IMPERFECT INFORMATION AND INSTITUTIONAL CHOICES

WE HAVE SEEN THAT information and transaction costs often play an important role in explaining market problems as well as in evaluating remedies for them. In this final chapter, we introduce several additional methods that are used to illuminate the significance of these in particular circumstances. The relevant circumstances all involve problems that arise owing to asymmetric information, first introduced in Chapter 7. The first section reviews two general problems that asymmetric information can cause: adverse selection and moral hazard.

We describe adverse selection, discuss the signals that participants in the marketplace use to try to avoid it, and illustrate that it can also lead to labor market discrimination (by factors such as race or gender). We review the moral hazard problem and illustrate how a principal-agent analysis of contract design has been used to mitigate moral hazard in certain common managerial contract situations. We also review briefly the idea that nonprofit agencies may have efficiency advantages as suppliers in certain situations involving moral hazard. We then turn to a more extended analysis of a moral hazard problem, in which we consider the potential of different types of suppliers (profit-seeking, nonprofit, public, and cooperatives) to provide efficient service in this situation.

The application is an analysis of day-care services. Moral hazard is present in the delivery of this service because the parent is virtually never there to observe its quality. Under the 1996 federal welfare reforms, the combination of new work requirements and limited time on welfare will increase the demand for out-of-home child care. Many states will provide new forms of subsidies for working welfare mothers who utilize child care, and a question arises about what type of day-care facilities will qualify for this subsidization.

Two general analytic procedures, in addition to those previously discussed, are used here as a means of identifying strengths and weaknesses associated with particular governance structures. One is simply to review the economic history of the activity under consideration. This can provide insight about both demand-side and supply-side factors that are important for the efficiency of the service. The other is the exit-voice-loyalty framework of Hirschman, which is used to understand organizational responsiveness in markets for goods and services when quality is important. We explain briefly how this framework has been used to supplement the older view of unions as monopolistic labor suppliers with a newer view that recognizes their positive contributions to economic efficiency

We then present a plausible line of argument, based on insights from these frameworks, that suggests that subsidized day care for low-income families is likely to be provided satisfactorily in established nonprofit community organizations, perhaps more so than in many cooperatives, profit-making firms in a market, or public day-care centers. A key element in this argument is that parental uncertainty about the quality of the day-care service is high, and an efficient way to reduce it is for the service to be provided by someone the parent trusts. Nonprofit community organizations, it is argued, have a relative advantage in the trust dimension. However, the empirical evidence comparing these institutional forms in the day-care industry does not show large differences in quality across them. This may be explained by the effects of mixed-competition (across these sectors), an aspect worthy of further study. Nevertheless, the implication of the analysis is that on efficiency grounds nonprofit day-care centers seem worth including as eligible institutions to receive expanded public day-care subsidies.

Asymmetric Information

Earlier in the text two different problems that involved asymmetric information were introduced: adverse selection (Chapter 15) and moral hazard (Chapters 7 and 15). We review these and clarify that there can be important market failures caused by each. We also clarify that there are some mechanisms that arise naturally in the marketplace as mitigants to these problems. The resulting degree of market failure is an empirical question, as is the question of whether policy intervention of some kind can further reduce the degree of failure. We show that the problem of labor market discrimination can arise as a consequence of agents in a market trying to avoid adverse selection. Then, in the context of managerial compensation, we illustrate contract provisions in a principal-agent framework that can mitigate moral hazard. We also review the idea that, in some circumstances, nonprofit suppliers may be an effective way to mitigate moral hazard.

Adverse Selection, Market Signals,
and Discrimination in the Labor Market

Adverse selection can arise when quality variation in a market good or service is important, and one party to the transaction has more information about actual quality than the other. While both adverse selection and moral hazard involve asymmetric information, they differ in that there is no hidden action in the adverse selection problem. The asymmetric information arises only after contracting in the moral hazard case, but it exists before any contracting in the adverse selection case. In terms of an insurance example of the adverse selection problem, the individual seeking coverage may know more than the insurance company about his or her own (exogenous) riskiness. This is sometimes referred to as *hidden information.* How well or poorly the market functions in such a context depends on the distribution of risks in the population.

Suppose first that there are only two kinds of individuals, "low" or "high" risk but known only to themselves, and each type is equally likely in the population and mildly risk-averse. Say the expected cost is $200 for a "low" risk, and $400 for a "high" risk. An insurance company may offer a policy at a premium equal to the $300 average expected cost. But since individuals know their own types, those who are "low" risks will not purchase the policy (unless they are very risk-averse). Each insurance company, eventually recognizing the adverse selection that makes all of their customers "high" risks, will raise the premium to $400, at which point the market will be in equilibrium.[1] This is inefficient in that all the "low"-risk customers get no insurance, although they are all willing to pay somewhat more than the $200 social cost of providing it.

We can change the degree of market failure in the above situation by altering the distribution of risks. Suppose we add a third, equal-sized "very-high"-risk group with $600 expected cost to the example. If we imagine an initial insurance charge at the $400 average for this larger total population, at first both the "high"- and "very-high"-risk groups will participate. But then insurance companies will realize that their average costs are $500, not $400, and they will be forced to raise the premium in order to avoid losses. When the premium is raised to $500, the "high"-risk group will no longer be willing to purchase insurance. The new equilibrium will be at $600 and only cover one-third of the population. In the extreme case of a continuous distribution of riskiness within the population, the market completely unravels and will cover no one (the highest-risk person from the continuum does not have a group of equally risky people with whom to form a risk pool).

On the other hand, if the population is fairly homogeneous in its riskiness, the market may provide coverage to all despite some diversity. Suppose in the original example of two risk groups, the "high"-risk group is only 10 percent of the population. Then the average expected cost is $220 [= .9(200) + .1(400)], and the "low"-risk group may consider such a policy better than none at all (since they are mildly risk-averse). Everyone purchases insurance, and the result is efficient. Everyone is better off than if there were no insurance, and, even though the "high"-risk group is considerably better off, there is no room for a further deal.

To clarify that adverse selection is not limited just to insurance problems, here are two other examples. One, originally explicated by Akerlof, is the market for used cars.[2] Some cars are "lemons" and some are "normal," but only the sellers know for sure. "Lemons" have some value, but it is substantially below that of a comparable "normal" car. If buyers offer the expected value over the whole used car population, this may not be enough to induce "normal" car owners to sell. Then only "lemons" will be brought to market, and the expected value for "lemons" will be the going price.

---

[1] A company offering a $200 policy to serve the residual market will attract some "high"-risk customers eager to save on premiums, and thus be unprofitable.

[2] George Akerlof, "The Market for Lemons: Quality Uncertainty and the Market Mechanism," *Quarterly Journal of Economics, 89,* 1970, pp. 488–500.

The other example is in the labor market. Assume there are two types of workers, "high" skill and "low" skill, but employers do not know which applicants belong in which categories. If employers offer a wage at the expected skill level over the entire applicant pool, the response depends on the nature of the labor supply. One simple possibility is that workers have no alternatives other than unemployment, so that all will prefer to accept the job offers. This would be an efficient equilibrium, although "high"-skill workers are receiving less than their true marginal products and "low"-skill workers more.

Let us introduce a new dimension into the adverse selection problem. The general idea is *market signaling: it can pay market participants to acquire costly signals of the value of the good or service of uncertain quality.*[3] The "low"-risk applicant for life insurance may invest in a costly medical examination in order to provide a copy of the resulting report to the insurance company. The owner of a "normal" car may invest in a costly examination by an independent mechanic to certify the operability and quality of the car's components. While investing in signals will generally not remove all of the uncertainty about a product's quality, the signals may increase the market value of the product enough to make the investment worthwhile.

In our original insurance example above, suppose people can take a medical test that costs $40 and results for "low"-risk types in a report that makes the insurance company think the applicant is 95 percent likely to be "low" risk. Then the insurance company can offer such individuals insurance at the expected cost of $210 $[= .95(200) + .05(400)]$. Especially if the signaling cost only occurs once and the premium will apply for a number of years, "low"-risk individuals may find that the benefits to them (the discounted sum over time of the increase in annual consumer surplus from having this insurance) outweigh the signaling cost.[4]

Making signals is generally a socially costly activity (the labor of the mechanic to certify the car, the resources used to conduct the medical test). However, the signals do not themselves affect productivity (the car is no safer, the tested individual's risk type is unchanged). Thus they only increase efficiency if they bring about allocative changes of greater value than the cost of the signaling. The insurance example suggests a case where market signaling improves market efficiency (all individuals end up being covered). However, there are also cases where the use of market signals reduces efficiency.

Consider the labor market example above with both "high"-skill and "low"-skill workers employed and receiving the average wage. Suppose the "high"-skill workers can go to a school that certifies their "high" skills by a diploma (but the school does not affect their actual productivity). The "high"-skill workers will probably find this to be in their self-interest. The new market equilibrium will have two wages: a "high" one for those certified as "high" skill and a "low" one for the others. As long as the school cost is less than the present value of the wage increase, getting certified will satisfy the self-interest criterion. But labor output is unchanged from before, except that it is lower owing to the resources lost to schooling.

---

[3] See M. Spence, "Job Market Signaling," *Quarterly Journal of Economics, 87,* 1973, pp. 355–374.

[4] Note that in this example it does not matter which party pays for the test. If the insurance company pays the initial cost, then it will increase the annual premiums just enough to recover its present value over time.

Let us extend the simple labor market example to illustrate a real and quite important problem. For this example, imagine that within the labor supply individuals are characterized by a broad diversity of productive capabilities. Some of these productive capabilities may have been acquired through lengthy human capital investments that do affect productivity, such as those discussed in Chapter 17 (e.g., earning a college degree).

Employers are uncertain about the true productivities of job applicants. Both employers and employees will try to think of the least expensive ways that they can acquire signals of value to them. A trained word-processor may have a certificate from a school or a recommendation from a former employer. The prospective employer may ask job applicants to take a short (10-minute) test of word-processing skills. Even in this example, considerable uncertainty about true productivity remains. Prospective employers may place little weight on recommendations from someone unknown to them, or whose motives they question. The word-processing test does not indicate whether an applicant will, if hired, show up on time each day, work hard, be absent often, be likely to leave the firm in a short period, or work well with co-workers.

In other words, considerable uncertainty about true productivities may still remain even after examination of the signals mentioned above. Furthermore, while an employer could perhaps eventually determine these capabilities from on-the-job observation, we retain the idea that it is very costly to do so. The question to which we now turn is: Are there other indicators that an employer can use to reduce the uncertainty?

Under the circumstances described, an employer may fall back on indicators apparent from a job interview, such as race, gender, age, dress, speech, and other aspects of the individual. The prospective employer may well rely on stereotypical perceptions of these group classifications. While these generally will go unspoken, the employer may think that women are less likely than men to remain with the firm for long because of the possibility of following spouses to another job or leaving owing to pregnancies. Or a male applicant for a secretarial position may be presumed too risky in terms of getting along smoothly with the other (predominantly female) secretaries or to be less willing to make coffee. Members of racial minorities who apply for retail sales positions may be thought to make too many nonminority customers uncomfortable. In all of these examples, the prospective employer does not know the truth about the individual applicant, but uses subjective stereotypical judgments as a means of reducing the perceived uncertainty about productivity. This is sometimes referred to as *statistical discrimination.*

The use of these latter signals can of course be very frustrating to the individual applicant. Although the explicit use of them is for the most part illegal (violating antidiscrimination laws), the unstated use is hard to prove. Moreover, the effects of employer use of these signals go well beyond the hiring decision itself. Their use also affects the real efforts individuals will make to acquire desirable attributes. For example, assume that women know that their expected return from a business school education is lower than that of equally capable men (i.e., there is a "glass ceiling"). The natural response is for women to invest less in this type of education. The same can be said about the value of college degrees for certain racial minorities, if their returns from them are less than equally educated nonminorities. Thus discrimination as a means to avoid adverse selection can cause very harmful inefficiency.[5]

The problem of trying to avoid adverse selection when hiring labor of uncertain qualities helps to explain how and why discrimination can persist in markets with many competitors.[6] Public policies to prevent this type of discrimination exist at all levels of government. The major federal legislation is Title VII of the 1964 Civil Rights Act, which forbids discrimination in employment and is enforced by the Equal Employment Opportunity Commission as well as by private action in the courts. While these are imperfect mechanisms (because of the difficulty of obtaining the necessary evidence, as noted above) one careful study concludes: "Federal civil rights policy was the major contributor to the sustained improvement in black economic status that began in 1965."[7] Progress in reducing the gender gap has also been credited to this legislation.[8] There are also state and local antidiscrimination policies, although less is known about their effectiveness.[9]

Moral Hazard and Contracting

Let us turn now to a review of the other asymmetric information problem that can cause market failure: the moral hazard problem. We described this in Chapter 7 as a situation in which the outcome of a contract depends on an action taken by one of the contracting parties that is invisible to, or hidden from, the other. This implies that other factors besides the

---

[5] This point should make clear the empirical difficulty of separating earnings differences among groups into one part that is due to real productivity differences and another that is due to discrimination, since discrimination can cause real productivity differences. Reviews of these issues and the empirical studies are found in William A. Darity Jr. and Patrick L. Mason, "Evidence on Discrimination in Employment: Codes of Color, Codes of Gender," *Journal of Economic Perspectives, 12,* No. 2, Spring 1998, pp. 63–90 (see also the other papers and comments included in a symposium on discrimination in this issue), and T. D. Stanley and S. B. Jarrell, "Gender Wage Discrimination Bias? A Meta-Regression Analysis," *Journal of Human Resources, 33,* No. 4, Fall 1998, pp. 947–973.

[6] If there were not the asymmetric information problem, competitive forces would work to prevent discrimination. Suppose some or even most firms were run by individuals who wished to discriminate. Any laborer who is receiving less than the value of his or her marginal product could profitably be offered a higher wage by any firm that is nondiscriminatory, and the only stable equilibrium is the normal competitive one with all workers (regardless of race, gender, or other factors irrelevant to each individual's productivity) receiving the value of their marginal products.

[7] See p. 1641 in J. Donohue III and J. Heckman, "Continuous Versus Episodic Change: The Impact of Civil Rights Policy on the Economic Status of Blacks," *Journal of Economic Literature, 29,* No. 4, December 1991, pp. 1603–1643.

[8] See M. Gunderson, "Male-Female Wage Differentials and Policy Responses," *Journal of Economic Literature, 27,* No. 1, March 1989, pp. 46–72.

[9] One recent study of gay and lesbian earnings found no effect of state and local policies that prohibit discrimination based on sexual orientation on these earnings. This study, limited to individual and household incomes as reported by the U.S. Census, did not test for any increases in benefit levels that such policies may have caused. See Marieka M. Klawitter and Victor Flair, "The Effects of State and Local Antidiscrimination Policies on Earnings for Gays and Lesbians," *Journal of Policy Analysis and Management, 17,* No. 4, Fall 1998, pp. 658–686.

hidden action influence the outcome, for otherwise one could infer the action from the outcome. Examples of moral hazard that were discussed included the doctor-patient response to third-party health insurance coverage, the money lending decisions of deregulated banks using federally insured funds entrusted to them by depositors, and the effort that an employee exerts while earning the wage provided by an employer. These actions are hidden when the medical insurance company does not know to what extent a large bill is caused by medical need or doctor-patient overconsumption of services, the federal deposit insurers do not know to what extent loan defaults are bad luck or imprudent lending, and the employer does not know what portion of the firm's outcome to attribute to the work of a single employee.

Chapter 7 analyzed the consequences of moral hazard in the medical insurance case. We demonstrated that the result of moral hazard was a Nash equilibrium like that of the Slumlord's Dilemma.[10] Everyone would benefit from a lower premium if each individual would "restrain use" (meaning consume the same as he or she would without insurance). But each individual acting independently perceives the strategy "do not restrain use" as a dominant one, causing the equilibrium to be one of excessive consumption of medical services with the attendant excessive premium. We now recognize this as a market failure, because this market equilibrium is not a Pareto-optimal allocation.

A market with numerous competitor insurance firms could (and would) do better than simply provide full-coverage insurance. The firms can profitably mitigate (but not eliminate) the moral hazard problem by replacing full coverage with coverage limited by deductibles and coinsurance. Thus cleverness in the design of contracts may reduce the inefficiency from moral hazard in other contexts as well. The principal-agent framework that we also introduced in Chapter 7 has been used to consider ways of responding to moral hazards in other situations. Recall that in this general framework, the principal seeks to induce another person, the agent, to take some action that is costly to the agent but of benefit to the principal. The problem becomes interesting in that the principal cannot directly observe the actions of the agent, but may observe something that is partially but not fully determined by those actions.

A common example is one store in a chain in which the chain owners (for short, the chain) wants each store manager to maximize the profits of the store. The chain may observe the profit levels, but it does not observe exactly what the managers do to achieve them (the hidden action). It also does not know what factors outside the control of the manager might have worked to foster or hinder profits and whether or not the observed level is indeed the maximum that a manager could achieve. All stores may not be capable of making the same profit, because of, say, locational factors with effects also unknown to the chain. Other things being equal, the store managers may prefer not to make the strenuous effort necessary to take account of locational factors and maximize profit.

An additional factor that complicates the problem may be one of *hidden information:* The chain values learning something that the (effort-making) store manager knows. For ex-

---

[10] Recall that a Nash equilibrium is an outcome from which no individual can take independent action to improve his or her own position. A market equilibrium is thus also a Nash equilibrium.

ample, the chain may make certain products for distribution to its stores and needs an estimate of expected sales from the managers in order to make production decisions. Can the chain offer its store managers a contract that gives them incentive to maximize profits and reveal the information sought by the chain?[11]

For simplicity, let us assume that expected sales correlate highly with expected profits, so that an expected profit estimate from each manager is effectively just as good as a sales estimate. Suppose managers are asked to give expected profit estimates, and then, to motivate managerial performance, they are told that they will receive a bonus equal to 40 percent of any store profit above the target. This will motivate store profit maximization, but will also give each manager incentive to understate his or her true target estimate.

It is possible to provide correct incentives for both chain objectives. Consider, for example, the following bonus (B) plan as a function of target profit (Π_T) and actual profit (Π):

$$B = 0.1\Pi_T + 0.3\Pi \qquad (\Pi \geq \Pi_T)$$

$$B = -0.1\Pi_T + 0.5\Pi \qquad (\Pi \leq \Pi_T)$$

The top formula applies when profits exceed the target, and the bottom when profits are less than the target. If actual profits exactly equal the target, then either formula gives a 40 percent bonus. No matter which one applies, the bonus increases with an increase in actual profits so there is incentive to maximize store profits.

What about honest revelation of the profit target? Suppose profits are $100,000 and the target is underestimated at $70,000. Then the top formula applies, for a bonus of $37,000 (less than the $40,000 bonus if the target was on target!). For any target below actual profit, the bonus will be less than 40 percent (the greater the underestimate, the less the bonus). While the second term of the formula always equals 30 percent of actual profit, the first term is always *less* than 10 percent of actual profit (since $\Pi_T < \Pi$) and the amount declines with the stated profit target.

What if the target was overestimated at $120,000? Then the bottom formula applies, for a bonus of $38,000. For any target above the actual level, the bonus will always be less than $40,000 (the greater the overestimate, the smaller the bonus). While the second term in the formula always equals 50 percent of actual profit, the first term always subtracts *more* than 10 percent of actual profit (since $\Pi_T > \Pi$) and the amount subtracted increases with the size of the stated profit target. In short, the manager is always better off neither underestimating nor overestimating store profit, and thus has incentive to provide an accurate estimate.

The above formula works owing to the choice of the parameters. The illustration has the maximum profit percentage for the bonus at 40 percent (the sum of the two coefficients in

---

[11] A harder principal-agent problem is to specify the contract that meets the objectives above but at least cost to the chain owners. Such a problem goes beyond our scope. A good general reference on employment contracts is Paul Milgrom and John Roberts, *Economics, Organization and Management* (Englewood Cliffs, N.J.: Prentice-Hall, Inc., 1992). See also the chapters on information economics in David M. Kreps, *A Course in Microeconomic Theory* (Princeton, N.J.: Princeton University Press, 1990), and Hal R. Varian, *Microeconomic Analysis* (New York: W. W. Norton & Company, 1992).

each equation), although this could be pegged either lower or higher (presumably under 100 percent). This choice reflects the intensity of the incentive to maximize store profit.

Given the choice for the sum, the penalty for misestimating is then determined by the choice of the second coefficient in each equation. To ensure incentives for truthful revelation, the second coefficient in the top equation (underestimated target) must be positive and less than the maximum bonus percentage. Also, the second coefficient in the bottom equation (overestimated target) must exceed the maximum bonus percentage. The intensity of the penalty for misestimating depends on how far these coefficients are from the maximum bonus percentage. The closer either one is to the maximum percentage, the less a misestimate matters. If the coefficients for the top equation were 0.01 (on Π_T) and 0.39 (on Π), then the bonus on $100,000 profit with a $70,000 profit target would be $39,700 (the misestimate hardly matters). On the other hand, reverse these coefficients and the bonus would be only $28,300 (a much stiffer misestimation penalty).

The above illustration shows that managerial contracts can be designed both to provide incentives to combat moral hazard (the effort of the manager to maximize store profits) and to elicit hidden information from the manager that is needed for other decisions of the firm (the profit target that correlates with sales and is used to make production decisions). As the number of situations studied by principal-agent theory increases, the range of applications may increase as well. In the future, this approach may find application to numerous public sector problems, such as those of incentive regulation discussed in Chapter 18 or structuring bonuses for public schoolteachers or principals or for local postmasters.[12] At this point, however, we wish to turn to another dimension of the moral hazard problem: the type of supplier that can provide the most efficient response.

The Nonprofit Supplier as a Response to Moral Hazard

In an important article by Hansmann, the basic logic of the principal-agent problem is applied to explain a number of circumstances in which a nonprofit organization as agent may be advantageous from the point of view of the principal.[13] Most of these are moral hazard situations: The principal wants output and values its quality but either cannot directly observe or cannot directly evaluate quality, and the profit-seeking agent thus has incentive to deliver lower-than-demanded quality for any given price (the hidden action).

One situation is when there is separation between the purchaser and the recipient of the service. An example of this is a donative nonprofit organization such as CARE, which ships and distributes food overseas to the needy. Why will donors not give to a profit-making firm with the same mission? The reason is that the donors cannot observe the delivery of the food, and profit-making organizations have incentive to skimp or fail to deliver. The non-

---

[12] Baker discusses performance measures applied to employees. See G. Baker, "The Use of Performance Measures in Incentive Contracting," *American Economic Review, 90,* No. 2, May 2000, pp. 415–420.

[13] Henry Hansmann, "The Role of Nonprofit Enterprise," in Susan Rose-Ackerman, ed., *The Economics of Nonprofit Institutions* (New York: Oxford University Press, 1986), pp. 57–84.

profits, however, because they are barred from distributing any profits, do not have the same incentive.

Another situation is when the output is a complex personal service, such as nursing homes, hospital care (especially under fixed-fee reimbursement such as Medicare's diagnosis-related-group payments), or education. It is difficult for the principal to know if the services are adequately performed, and again profit-seeking enterprises may take advantage by skimping on quality.[14] Usually these services are provided by commercial nonprofits (those that provide services for fees) rather than donative ones. Common examples of these include many hospitals and universities. The problem is lessened somewhat when the principal is also the recipient of the service, and thus perhaps it is not surprising that profit-making firms may supply some of these services.

There are complex personal services that are typically provided by profit-making entities. Doctors, lawyers, and auto repair are examples. The transactions for these services are frequently small and discrete, and switching to another supplier is relatively easy. Other institutions arise to help, such as licensing boards. In these cases, the hidden action is more likely to be overcharging than not providing enough service. This distinguishes these problems from those like the nursing home problem, in which there is more incentive for profit-making entities to deliver less service than the purchaser desires.

Hansmann is not suggesting that nonprofit organizations solve the market failure that is due to the moral hazard problem. He also recognizes that, for various reasons, nonprofits may not operate efficiently. They may have other objectives, such as those discussed in Chapter 11, which cause them to sacrifice some efficiency. They have disadvantages in raising capital, since they cannot promise that its owners will receive any residual (i.e., profit) after other costs are paid. But there are some circumstances of moral hazard in which we observe consumers choosing to use nonprofit organizations. This suggests that whatever the imperfections of nonprofit supply, they are sometimes less serious from the purchaser's point of view than the imperfections of for-profit suppliers. Hansmann clarifies that nonprofits may have a relative advantage in mitigating the moral hazard problem at least in some circumstances.[15]

---

[14] Weisbrod reports on controlled comparisons between proprietary and nonprofit nursing homes. Patients with prescriptions for sedatives received four times as much of them in proprietary homes as nonprofit homes. The use of sedatives beyond medical necessity may be an inexpensive way to control patients, but many people regard this use as a hidden reduction in the quality of care provided. Similarly, controlling for price, size of facility, and other factors, Weisbrod reports that church-affiliated nursing homes compared to proprietary ones have more labor devoted to direct patient care (higher quality) and less to administration (less "profit" seeking). See Burton Weisbrod, *The Nonprofit Economy* (Cambridge: Harvard University Press, 1988), pp. 149–151.

[15] Nonprofit organizations also have tax advantages compared to profit-seeking firms. The tax advantage can foster inefficiency as, other things being equal, it allows the nonprofit to price below the profit-making entity even with some production inefficiency. This general advantage may be more than offset by general disadvantages such as the capital-raising difficulty and cumbersome entry costs into the nonprofit sector. A good general discussion of these and other strengths and weaknesses of nonprofits compared to other institutional forms is contained in Weisbrod, *The Nonprofit Economy*.

A question that we might ask is: To what extent can analysis identify strengths and weaknesses of different types of suppliers for delivering public or publicly subsidized services? In the following section, we consider this question as it arises for the provision of day-care services. Our context is that under the recent welfare reforms, the demand (and thus the supply) for day-care services is expected to increase. We consider four different provider types: profit-seeking, nonprofit, public, and parent cooperatives. In evaluating the strengths and weaknesses of the services likely to be provided by each, we consider whether or not they should be eligible for state subsidies (either directly from the state in return for caring for a given number of children or indirectly by vouchers given to a parent who will choose a day-care facility).

Nonprofit Organizations and the Delivery of Day-Care Services

In thinking about the type of organization that is appropriate for conducting specific economic activities, it is important that the analyst not be too limited in the alternatives considered. Most of our examples have concerned private profit-making firms and their governance, but we have also seen that public bureaus and nonprofit organizations can be used as agencies of production. In this section we offer an analysis that further considers the use of these latter institutions.

The purpose of this section is really twofold. First, we wish to illustrate in more detail that, in certain situations, there are economic rationales to suggest that nonprofit agencies will have advantages relative to the other supply institutions.[16] Second, we wish to demonstrate other analytic methods that help one to assess the relative strengths of these different institutions. We do this in the context of a specific example: public policy with respect to day care for small children.[17]

There are several reasons why day care is, at least in part, a public policy issue. One reason is that, owing to moral hazard in the provision of the service, there may be considerable inefficiency in an unregulated market. Day care is by definition a service that is rendered when the parent (who acts as the consumer agent for the child) is not present, and its quality level is generally considered quite important. Another reason is that, similar to public education, there may be some external benefits of well-cared-for children to society. A third reason is that, on equity grounds, the general population may wish to ensure adequate

---

[16] We do not wish to imply that there are no other economic rationales for nonprofit agencies than the one presented. Indeed, there are other very interesting rationales that have been identified in different settings. See Burton Weisbrod (1988), *The Nonprofit Economy,* and Susan Rose-Ackerman (1986), *The Economics of Nonprofit Institutions.* See also Burton Weisbrod in collaboration with Joel Handler and Neil Komesar, *Public Interest Law: An Economic and Institutional Analysis* (Berkeley, Calif.: University of California Press, 1978).

[17] This example is modeled after an earlier analysis by Richard R. Nelson and Michael Krashinsky, "Public Control and Economic Organization of Day Care for Young Children," *Public Policy, 22,* Winter 1974, pp. 53–75; and Dennis Young and Richard R. Nelson, *Public Policy for Day Care of Young Children* (Lexington, Mass.: Lexington Books, 1973). Another general reference on the economics of day care is David M. Blau, ed., *The Economics of Child Care* (New York: Russell Sage Foundation, 1991).

child care for its least well-off members. The last rationale has different strands: (1) regard for the children; (2) beliefs that working parents are preferable to welfare parents.[18]

We introduce two additional analytic methods, both of which happen to be useful for this particular illustration. The first can be stated simply: *Review the history of the provision of the activity from an economic perspective.* Economic theory by itself does not suggest the importance of history. But we have often seen that proper applications of theory require careful tailoring to account for the details relevant to a specific problem. To apply the theory, one must be able to identify the relevant details. One good way to learn about some of them is to review the economic history of how the activity has been provided, with an eye to the reasons why.

The second additional analytic method is the framework suggested by Hirschman. *His "exit, voice, and loyalty" framework provides insight into organizational responsiveness in markets for goods and services when quality is important.* Economic theory does not by itself focus attention on the many dimensions of product or service quality that may be important to a consumer. In a competitive setting, for example, theory simply asserts that competitive forces will result in outputs that have the quality dimensions that consumers demand. This is of small comfort, however, to those responsible for the qualities of outputs: How is one supposed to know or learn what qualities are important to consumers and ensure their provision? We describe Hirschman's framework briefly for its insights about how to learn about quality, and then turn to the consideration of day care.[19]

Hirschman asks how suppliers are supposed to learn, or become informed, about specific mistakes they are making. In most situations we assume consumers will not buy very much of an inferior product. If an automobile company introduces new models that consumers do not like, the company sales will fall. Consumers *exit* from the group of firm customers. But when the product has multidimensional quality attributes, this signal to the supplier is a *noisy* one. The exit decisions could be caused by many factors, and the supplier does not receive the information necessary to pinpoint the problem. The firm can and does learn through marketing research. But the firm's task might be made easier if the consumers exercise *voice*—if, rather than exit, they complain to the company and state directly what improvements they wish.

---

[18] An interesting fourth reason is taxpayer self-interest, if subsidies now can be more than repaid in the form of lower tax rates in the future (by inducing increased labor force participation of the parents of the subsidy recipients). For this argument, see Ted Bergstrom and Sören Blomquist, "The Political Economy of Subsidized Day Care," *European Journal of Political Economy, 12,* 1996, pp. 443–458.

[19] See A. Hirschman, *Exit, Voice and Loyalty: Responses to Decline in Firms, Organizations and States* (Cambridge: Harvard University Press, 1970). Hirschman's framework has been applied to a variety of problems. See, for example, R. Frydman, K. Pistor, and A. Rapaczynski, "Exit and Voice after Mass Privatization—The Case of Russia," *European Economic Review, 40,* No. 3–5, April 1996, pp. 581–588; K. Cannings, "An Exit Voice Model of Managerial Attachment," *Journal of Economic Behavior & Organization, 12,* No. 1, August 1989, pp. 107–129; R. Ogawa and J. Dutton, "Parent Involvement and School Choice—Exit and Voice in Public Schools," *Urban Education, 32,* No. 3, September 1997, pp. 333–353; G. Annas, "Patients' Rights in Managed Care—Exit, Voice, and Choice," *New England Journal of Medicine, 337,* No. 3, July 17, 1997, pp. 210–215; and S. Christensen and A. Rabibhadana, "Exit, Voice and the Depletion of Open Access Resources—The Political Bases of Property Rights in Thailand," *Law & Society Review, 28,* No. 3, 1994, pp. 639–655.

Exclusive reliance on either exit or voice by itself would not be very effective in most situations. If there is no exit, a firm has little reason to respond to voice. If there is no voice, the response may be extremely sluggish. An extreme case of this is the duopoly, in which customers of firm A exit to firm B while customers of firm B do the reverse; all customers are dissatisfied, but each company has constant sales and receives no signal. In an industry with more suppliers, consumers can still hop from one firm to another without signaling any single firm to change. Eventually consumers may exit from the entire industry (depending on the demand elasticity for the good), but this does not signal potential new firms to enter and correct the problem. Some firm may eventually figure out a way to stop the exiting, but there is no reason to believe that the process is one of efficient adjustment.

Thus, Hirschman suggests that in most situations there is some optimal combination of exit and voice. But how can it be achieved? A certain amount of firm *loyalty* may be a desirable means to that end. That is, the loyal customers accept an inferior product temporarily (rather than exit in the hope of finding a superior one) while they exercise voice and await the company's response. Presumably, the firm can create loyalty to some extent (e.g., through access to special sales or preferred service). Less loyal customers exit from the company and reinforce the voice signals. The combination of the two tells the supplier it ought to change and helps to pinpoint how to change. The net result is that the industry adapts efficiently, assuming that most firms in it adopt the strategy.[20]

It is instructive to mention briefly a particularly interesting application of this framework. Freeman and Medoff have used it to provide a nontraditional view of the economic functions of labor unions.[21] The traditional economic view of labor unions is that they try and act like monopolist suppliers of labor, for example, raising the wage above the competitive level, which then inefficiently reduces the quantity of labor used (union members benefit, but consumers and the other workers who would have been hired are made worse off by a greater amount). Freeman and Medoff point out, however, that there are many attributes of a workplace that are public goods to the collectivity of workers in that workplace: for example, plant safety, lighting, types of fringe benefits available such as health plan choices, layoff provisions, and seniority rules.

Just as with any public goods, there are incentive problems that result in these public goods being underprovided. Individual employees may know their own preferences, but they do not know the preferences of other workers and have little incentive to spend much of their time (and perhaps risk being fired) trying to determine them. When first hired, new employees are often not aware of the potential value to them of these public goods. As they

---

[20] Note that in this scenario loyal customers are not the same as uninformed ones. Sometimes the voucher idea for education is criticized on the ground that it will lead to a school system segregated by the degree of parental knowledge. The proposition is that the informed parents will have their children exit from inferior schools and the uninformed parents will leave their children in these schools. The inferior schools will then have no informed customer voices offering diagnoses of the problem.

[21] Richard B. Freeman and James L. Medoff, *What Do Unions Do?* (New York: Basic Books, 1984).

learn through experience about the value these public goods would have for them, they become disgruntled. The firm may recognize that it can gain through the provision of the efficient level of these public goods (workers will accept a trade-off of reduced money wages in return for these workplace public goods), but has difficulty determining what these are because of the honest-revelation-of-incentives problem.[22] However, once a union has formed to serve as the collective voice and agent for the workers, it can argue for the package of wages and workplace public goods that it thinks most suitable for its members.

Thus we now have two sharply contrasting views of unions. There is the traditional view of unions as monopoly labor suppliers that cause inefficiency through wage distortions, supply restrictions, featherbedding, and other practices. But there is also the newer view of unions fostering efficiency by serving as the voice that helps to overcome the free-rider problem for workplace public goods. It is a difficult empirical question to weigh the significance of each activity, although Freeman and Medoff concluded that the proefficiency forces slightly exceeded the antiefficiency ones. The more important benefit of their work may be the extent to which it helps target union voices and tune management ears to the more productive activities.

Let us turn to day-care services. First, it is helpful to provide some historical background about child care. Looking at its provision over 200 years in the United States, Nelson and Krashinsky offer insight into two of its features: (1) When the parents work, most child care has been provided by other family members. (2) Nevertheless, there has been a marked growth in the demand for extrafamily child care.

Their interpretation of this *economic history suggests a revealed social preference for child care to be undertaken by the most family-like institutions.* The key economic reason for this is that trust among agents in these institutions is relatively high, and *trust is an efficient mechanism for reducing the uncertainty costs that the agents would otherwise bear.* We explain this below. Then we consider alternative organizational modes that could be used to provide increased day-care services stimulated by public policy. We sketch the plausible argument that established nonprofit agencies should be eligible recipients of any increases in public subsidy funds, as they embody relatively more trust than the feasible alternatives and will be the preferred provider of child care by many parents. This line of reasoning is supported by some insights from the exit-voice-loyalty framework.

Over 200 years of U.S. economic history, activities that commonly were undertaken at home progressively shifted to specialized institutions such as the firm. Fewer households grow their own food, make their own clothes, or do their own ironing. This is a quite natural response to technical progress characterized by greater economies of scale (mass production). But child care has been much more resistant to this trend. Compared to other activities, there has been only a modest movement from at-home child care. In 1999, some 36 percent of mothers of children under 6 years of age were not in the labor force, and of those in the labor force, approximately 26 percent had their children cared for in their own homes

---

[22] An individual worker will exaggerate the value of these public goods if simply asked what they are worth and will underestimate their value if asked what wage reduction he or she will accept in return for their provision.

or in the home of a close relative.[23] What is there about this economic activity that explains its relative resistance?

Nelson and Krashinsky suggest a number of factors. Most obviously, child care is more than an ordinary chore. At least to some extent, it gives pleasure to parents and other close family members such as grandparents. It is a labor of love, as some would put it. Thus a simple preference for being with the child is one factor that explains the resistance.

There are as well certain "scale economies" to home care that work in its favor. One is that child care requires the full-time *availability* of an adult but is not necessarily a full-time activity. To some extent that varies with the child and with age; the adult can be engaged in cooking, cleaning, studying, or other activity. Thus, the time cost attributable to home child care is low compared with that of many activities that have shifted out of the home. Similarly, the space cost of home child care is relatively low: The family generally consumes housing of the same size even if it gives up home care.

In addition to these preference and economy factors, parents care a great deal about the ways in which their children are cared for. Child care does not necessarily require that all caregivers have expertise in the form of advanced degrees. It does require a sharp eye to make sure the child is comfortable, engaged in a suitable activity, and not in any danger.[24] To have real trust and confidence in the care one's child receives, there is nothing like providing it oneself. One simply does not know what happens if one is not there. Put differently, alternatives to family care introduce a good deal of costly uncertainty to the parents about the quality of the care. Thus, these three sets of factors (preferences, economy, confidence) help explain why child care has been maintained in the home while so many other activities have been shifting out of it.

Despite the factors that operate to keep child care in the home, there nevertheless has been growth in nonfamily care. This growth includes an increase in the number of larger, more formal day-care centers. As recently as 1977, only 13 percent of children under 5 years of age with employed mothers were cared for in organized child care centers. But by 1997, this figure had risen to 32 percent. Much of the reason for the trend is explained by demographic changes. In more recent years, increased public subsidies have added to the demand. We comment briefly on each.

Compared with families in 1800, today's families are smaller. Of course, out-of-home day care is relatively more affordable when there are fewer children who need minding. But there are accompanying changes to this reduction in family size that also bear importantly on the demand for day care. Child mortality rates are much lower. Those two factors combined help explain why the median age of a mother at last birth has dropped from the late 30s to the late 20s and why, as well, the median age of a mother at first birth has risen. Thus, the number of years of intensive child rearing has decreased while life ex-

---

[23] This information is contained in Section 9 of the *2000 Green Book,* Ways and Means Committee of the U.S. House of Representatives (Washington, D.C.: U.S. Government Printing Office, 2000).

[24] In a 1998 survey of 220 licensed child-care centers by the Consumer Product Safety Commission, two-thirds had at least one safety hazard. For example, 19 percent had cribs that contained soft bedding (which can result in suffocation).

pectancy has increased. That makes investment in career development much more attractive than it once was. Along with the loss of competitiveness for home-produced goods in general, these factors explain much of the increase in demand for day care. Additionally, during the past 30 years, there has been a large increase in the number of single-parent families.

It is important to recognize that decisions about day care are made under quite different circumstances for families of differing socioeconomic circumstances. For a two-parent, upper-middle-income family with one or two children, the choice is made without serious economic pressure. The issues that seem important are the value of career involvements and beliefs about what is best for the child. However, one- or two-parent families that have only low-income opportunities are confronted with a serious economic dilemma. The importance of achieving some additional money income is very high. But the only way to free up time in order to increase employment is to purchase day care, and the cost may well exceed the potential income from working. This raises the issue of subsidized day care.

The growth in subsidies is another factor that helps explain the increased reliance upon day care. There is a long history of subsidized day care in the form of settlement houses for children of poor families, particularly for immigrant families whose children receive acculturation benefits. A significant expansion of day-care subsidies starting in the 1960s has been rationalized in part by applying a similar argument: Poor and minority children might receive as well as generate external benefits if they are in socially and economically integrated child-care centers.

Another justification offered for subsidies is that of the work ethic—a belief that a welfare parent ought to work.[25] This value was prominent in the 1988 Family Support Act, which authorized more child-care assistance for welfare families and those families leaving welfare. It was even more prominent in the 1996 Personal Responsibility and Work Opportunity Reconciliation Act, which put firm limits on the time a family could be on welfare and further increased child-care funding.

There are arguments, of course, that subsidized day care should be made available to all families with small children. One line of reasoning is simply that day care is like elementary education: There is a social interest in the development and education of children that exceeds the private interest. A different argument is that it is beneficial to encourage women to work by making it easier and cheaper to find suitable places for their children.

In fact, there is a general subsidy available to most families for child care: the Dependent Care Tax Credit that is part of the federal income tax. This is a nonrefundable credit whose value depends both upon actual child-care expenses and family income.[26] The maximum value of the credit in 2000 was between $480 and $720 for one child. This compares with average annual expenditures of about $4000 for those families paying for the care of

[25] Note that this can be very expensive if the family is a large one.

[26] From 20–30 percent of the first $2400 in child-care expenses for one child (or $4800 for two or more children) may be credited toward any federal taxes owed. The percentage depends upon family income (the higher value for income no greater than $10,000; the lower value for any income above $28,000).

one child.[27] Of course this credit is of little or no use to the poorest families, who do not owe enough in taxes to make full use of the credit as an offset.[28] In 1998 approximately 6.1 million U.S. families claimed this credit, with an average claim of $433 and total value of $2.65 billion. We might think of this credit as a response to the general externality issue of child care.

Even with the growth in demand for nonhome care, the predominant form of child care is still in the home. In the mid-1990s, about 50 percent of mothers (mostly nonworking) had their preschool children cared for in their own homes and 9 percent in a relative's home. An additional 14 percent of parents cared for their children themselves while on the job. Care in a nonrelative's home was used by another 9 percent (so-called "family" day care, of which 80–90 percent is unlicensed and unregulated). This leaves 18 percent of mothers using organized day-care facilities.[29] The more informal methods, still the predominant form of nonparental care, are generally inexpensive, as they avoid the use of professional employees and do not require new facilities.

Of course the in-home day care does not include the formal education programs offered by some of the larger day-care centers. But it is important to point out that the larger day-care centers are very diverse in the type of care they do offer. Full-time care in these centers may cost anywhere from $3500 to over $10,000 per year, depending on the extensiveness of the facilities and the training and number of staff members. The more expensive ones are generally developmentally intensive. They have a highly educated, well-paid, and ample staff that may include one or more developmental psychologists, specialist teachers, and considerable resources for structured activities as well as play. The quality of care offered by the different types of centers varies enormously. Several studies conclude that their average level is below that considered developmentally appropriate.[30]

This concern about quality, and how to foster it, is the major focus of the continuing debate today. One expert puts it this way: "Over the past 15 years, a number of studies of the effects of varying levels of quality on children's behavior and development have reached

[27] The average weekly expenditure for families who pay was $66 for one child in 1993, according to the *1998 Green Book* (Washington, D.C.: U.S. Government Printing Office, 1998). The *2000 Green Book* reports 1995 average weekly expenditure of $82.74, but for all children. I used the $66 figure, adjusting for inflation to make it current and then rounding.

[28] Higher-income families can receive substantially greater tax benefits in lieu of the credit by taking advantage, if offered, of employer-sponsored plans for excluding up to $5000 in child-care expenses from taxable income. For a family in the 30 percent tax bracket, this has a value of $1500 in federal tax savings (and often another $500 in state income tax savings). However, there is also some risk to participants in these plans. They must specify the expected expenses a year in advance, which the employer then withholds, and they only receive reimbursement by the employer for actual expenses incurred. Someone who expects to spend $5000 in qualifying child-care expenses but who only spends $3000 will lose $2000 in income.

[29] Weisbrod indicates that nonprofits comprise 40 percent of the organized day-care industry. See Weisbrod, *The Nonprofit Economy,* pp. 84–85.

[30] See H. Naci Mocan, "Cost Functions, Efficiency, and Quality in Day Care Centers," *The Journal of Human Resources, 32,* No. 4, Fall 1997, pp. 861–891, and M. Whitebook et al., "Who Cares? Child Care Teachers and the Quality of Care in America," Final report of the National Child Care Staffing Study (Oakland, Calif.: Child Care Employee Project, 1990).

the same conclusion: *A significant correlation exists between program quality and out-comes for children.* Outcomes related to quality include cooperative play, sociability, cre-ativity, ability to solve social conflicts, self-control, and language and cognitive develop-ment." Yet this same expert concluded that "only 8 percent of infant classrooms and 24 percent of preschool classrooms were of good or excellent quality."[31] Similarly, economist James Heckman advocates increased investment in high-quality preschool programs, and cites approvingly the very high benefit-cost ratio of 8.7 for the Perry Pre-School Program, which has more extensive resources and staff than typical Head Start programs.[32]

Thus there appears to be a good case for increasing the resources that can be used to fos-ter high-quality child care, and especially for those families that are least able to afford this kind of care without assistance. We may all agree that such care is a good *investment.* But at least for the short term, even a generous increase in subsidy resources will not be enough to raise average expenditure levels to cover the fees of "upper-end" child care. Furthermore, it is not clear what resources are necessary to provide high-quality care. According to one study, if production were efficient a 10 percent increase in resources would be more than sufficient to increase average quality from mediocre to good.[33] But how do we ensure that production will be efficient? That is, what system will encourage making the most effec-tive use of any given level of resources available for child care?

In other words, all of the *organizational* questions remain. If increased subsidies are pro-vided for child care, who will be deciding what to do with them? What institutional mech-anisms will be used to help ensure that these funds are used wisely, rather than simply ex-acerbating the moral hazard problem? What kind of suppliers should be eligible to receive them? To what extent should the subsidies be given as vouchers to parents who will then choose a supplier? Or should the government select some suppliers to receive the subsidies directly, in effect channeling parents to the selected suppliers? What regulatory apparatus should be operating?

We consider one piece of the organizational question: the types of suppliers that should be eligible. Formal day care centers are run by a wide variety of institutions: private profit-seeking (proprietary) firms, public agencies, and private nonprofit agencies (some affiliated with religious institutions). The primary existing federal subsidy program, the Child Care Development Block Grant Program, currently allocates to states approximately $3.5 billion in funds per year.[34] In addition, states are free to use their welfare block grants for child-

---

[31] See John M. Love, "Quality in Child Care Centers," *Education Digest,* March 1998, pp. 51–53.

[32] See James J. Heckman, "Doing It Right: Job Training and Education," *The Public Interest,* No. 135, Spring 1999, pp. 86–107.

[33] Mocan estimates a short-run translog production function for child-care services based on a study of 400 day-care agencies. The average hourly variable cost per child in his sample is $1.65, and he concludes that only an additional $0.12–$0.16 cents per child-hour is needed to raise the average score on a highly regarded 7 point index of quality from the "mediocre" sample average of 4.01 to the 5.0 level considered "good" by child devel-opment experts. Since this is only 10 percent of the short-run costs, it is less than 10 percent of total costs. See Mocan, "Cost Functions, Efficiency, and Quality in Day Care Centers."

[34] This consists of about $1 billion in discretionary funds, and entitlement funds subject to some matching and maintenance of effort requirements, at $2.4 billion for fiscal 2000 and rising to $2.7 billion in fiscal 2002.

care services, and many contribute additional funds to supplement the federal sources.[35] Currently public agencies are the principal recipients of these subsidies, although some of them go to nonprofit agencies.

Let us use the historical review and the exit-voice-loyalty framework in a consideration of alternative modes of day-care provision. The general question is how to govern a system of day care so that it best satisfies the public interest given the resource constraints. "Govern" is used here to refer to both demand and supply—the blend of consumer (parent), professional, and government control over resource allocation to the agencies of supply. We will discuss four types of day-care supply (cooperatives, proprietary institutions, public provision, and nonprofit centers) and the problems of governing each.

One form of organization that might provide good-quality day care inexpensively is the *cooperative;* an example is five families sharing day care, each family providing one parent to mind all the children one day each week. These groups are formed voluntarily, usually by neighbors known to one another. Their attraction, in addition to the low cost, is that a relatively high degree of parental confidence is a consequence of the extensive family involvement. Public sector involvement is minimal, being limited to various kinds of organizational assistance such as information about how to set up a cooperative or a clearinghouse to help families in the same neighborhood identify one another.

Since the parent-suppliers can generally be trusted to act with the children's best interests in mind, heavy reliance on either the exit or voice option is not necessary. However, both mechanisms can be used: voice for the minor problems and exit (from the cooperative) if one family has a serious disagreement with the other families about the desired plan of care.

There are two serious drawbacks to relying on the cooperative as a primary method for delivering extrafamily day care. First, it requires the families to have jobs with arrangeable hours. (This is one reason why cooperatives are relatively popular in university communities.) Given current employment practices, this severely limits their potential use. The second drawback is that cooperatives are often unstable and unreliable. When one family has an emergency or illness or there is some other reason it cannot take its scheduled turn, one of the other families must be able to substitute or someone must be hired. Similarly, when one family leaves the cooperative, another must be found to take its place. These problems generally cannot be solved immediately and thus make the cooperative somewhat unreliable. The care may be fine in cooperatives that are stable, but reliable care for a large proportion of families will require reliance primarily on paid employees.

Let us consider another mode of supply: *proprietary institutions.* Perhaps we can rely upon self-interested profit-seeking to provide the desired services, as we do elsewhere. In this case we issue vouchers to families with children eligible for the day-care subsidy, and we let them be used wherever the parents wish. However, two problems must be confronted. One, already mentioned, is that the parent is not present and will therefore demand assurance of quality. The second problem, discussed briefly below, is that the parent is not always the best agent for protecting the child's interests.

---

[35] The states contributed $1.7 billion, about 50 percent of the federal contribution, in fiscal 1998. See Table 9-26 of the *2000 Green Book,* p. 621.

It is useful to raise the issue of the identity of the consumer of day-care services more explicitly. For the most part, we have not made a distinction between parent and child. But each has different benefits and costs from day care. As long as the parent acts in the joint interest of both, the second problem does not arise. But it is often suggested that many parents are not sufficiently concerned or knowledgeable about the welfare of their children. To some extent this may be a matter of disinterest or neglect, but it may also be a lack of understanding. For either reason there is an argument for professional as well as parental influence in governing extrafamily day care.

Consider how a market might respond to these problems. Leaving the role of professionals aside for a moment, recognize that it is the inherent absence of the parent that creates uncertainty about the quality of the service. Since the firm cannot change that, it might seek to create trust between itself and the parents. But private unregulated firms have a difficult time doing so. Consumers recognize that a firm can increase its profits by not fully providing promised services, as long as the consumers do not know. Given the information structure, the profit motive is itself a barrier to the trust that parents demand.

Note that there is plenty of opportunity for both exit and voice. However, neither is an effective mechanism because the consumer (parent) does not receive information to trigger either one. That is, the consumer generally does not know whether the service is as desired, and therefore he or she has little basis for making an exit or voice decision.

The market can respond to this quality uncertainty by putting some barrier between the profit motives of firms and the behavior of their employees. The common form of this is *professionalization,* as in the legal and medical services. The idea is that professionals act in the child's best interests even if it works against short-run profitability. This solution has the further advantage of dealing with both of the problems we mentioned: limited parental information and motivation concerning the quality of the service. Indeed, the more expensive types of day care currently available are provided on this professional model, for example, with licensed teachers and child psychologists on the staff. But that is exactly the problem with this solution: It is expensive. We are considering a context in which the available subsidy levels are not high enough to provide "deluxe" developmental day care for all.

Suppose we consider a third supply alternative: *direct public provision.* This could be made inexpensive by not relying upon the fully professional model. Nevertheless, professionals could be very influential at fairly high levels of the decision-making process, for example, in setting minimum standards for the government day-care centers. The problem with the alternative is the difficulty of achieving enough consumer sovereignty: Parents are unlikely to have sufficient choice about the kind of day care their children receive.

That is not to say that parents will have no powers of governance. They may be able to exercise voice through parental boards at each day-care center, or certain decisions could be decided by parental voting. But the exit possibilities, if this public service is like other public services, will be severely limited. As we saw earlier, that acts to mute the effectiveness of voice.

Note that public agencies, like private nonprofits, also face the nondistribution constraint. Does this work to develop trust in public agencies, as Hansmann argues for nonprofit ones?

This is a relatively unexplored question. It is true that profit-seeking is not the cause for concern in either. However, the motivations and constraints (other than nondistribution) will generally differ between the two kinds of entities. The behavioral models of nonprofit and public agencies discussed in Chapter 11 generally reflect assumptions of differences in their respective behaviors. It may be, for example, that nonprofits are more likely to be run and operated by individuals whose *raison d'etre* is to deliver good service (similar to the Newhouse model of hospital behavior). Of course there are many public managers who strive to deliver good service as well. But public sector agencies are also subject to a more intense variety of political pressures, and not all of them relate to pleasing the customers (recall also the government failure discussion of Chapter 15). Particularly with limited exit possibilities, moral hazard in terms of public employee effort may remain a problem.

One could consider a voucher system restricted to public day-care centers (such as open enrollment or a system of charter schools). An important advantage of such a plan is that it can respond to the heterogeneous preferences of the parental population: The public day-care centers could vary in terms of the nature of the care they provided. They could feature different hours, specializations, modes of parental participation, and other variations consistent with meeting or surpassing the required minimum standards. To work, it would require a substantial decentralization of public decision-making power: Each center must have significant authority to determine its own policies. Furthermore, the effectiveness of such a plan would depend on the motivation of centers to attract more children when there are no associated profit increases.

However, note that the system we are describing would be an exception to the usual provision of public service. While government-provided services may vary substantially across jurisdictional lines, within any jurisdiction there have always been very strong tendencies for governments to provide uniform service to all. To the extent that there are conflicts about what quality service means between parents and professionals, the professionals might find strength in traditional bureaucratic uniformity. One has to wonder whether the right diversity of services could be successfully produced with this type of institutional structure.

Finally, we come to the use of private, *not-for-profit* day care sponsored by various *established community organizations*. In principle, the more serious flaws that we have seen can be avoided. Parents are likely to have a relatively high degree of trust in the centers because the organizational objectives, compared with those of profit-making centers and bureaucratic ones, are more likely to be identified with the interests of children. To the extent that the latter is true, such centers can be expected to try to achieve the maximum quality care with their available resources. Day-care professionals can have effective voice in setting standards of eligibility to receive public funds, as well as through advisory roles to particular centers.[36]

There should be a reasonable diversity of day care offered, because the various community organizations within one area are generally independent of one another. Parents will thus have relatively effective exit options, and most established community groups depend

---

[36] One might suggest similar use of professionals as a control for private profit-making institutions. This idea has merit, although the profit incentive of the firms might cause substantial resistance to this form of control.

heavily on the exercise of voice by their members in making decisions. Budgetary costs to parents can be kept low by reliance in part on parent and community volunteers and in part on salaried employees.

Reliance upon the network of established community organizations is not without its problems. One such problem is the question of whether those with religious auspices will be legally excluded from eligibility for public subsidy in order to maintain the separation of church and state. Moreover, there is a resource allocation problem among centers: By what process will successful centers be allowed to expand and unsuccessful ones contract, so that the total supply balances with demand? If parents are to have choice, the subsidy must be in the form of vouchers. But then parents will require reliable information about each day-care center. Thus for any of the systems that we have discussed, some kind of regulatory mechanism must be part of the institutional structure.

Nevertheless, the point of this exercise should be clear. It is at least plausible that a preferred way of delivering subsidized extrafamily day care to many is through increased reliance upon nonprofit community institutions. The essential reason is the peculiar information structure of day care, which prevents the normal consumer-agent (the parent) from knowing the quality of service. Because of the obvious importance of quality to the parent, trust becomes the next best substitute for knowledge.

One can increase the level of trust from that of an ordinary market through professionalization, but that is expensive. One can generate trust cheaply through reliance on neighborhood cooperatives, but they are difficult to arrange and are unstable. Public provision may be too uniform with too little parental control to generate high consumer satisfaction, although it might be better than the other two alternatives. However, increased reliance on established nonprofit community organizations seems a promising way to provide the same economy benefits and public interest guarantees with a higher level of trust and, therefore, greater consumer satisfaction. To the extent that competition between public and nonprofit providers results in better public service with greater consumer choice, it could be that encouraging this mixed system through subsidies would be equally or even more effective than reliance upon either type alone. As important as this question of the value of mixed competitive systems might be, current theory is essentially silent on this issue.[37]

Empirical studies, on balance, probably reinforce the value of mixed systems. Several valuable studies have attempted to assess the quality of services delivered by nonprofit suppliers in situations of moral hazard. We have already referred to the studies suggesting that, other things being equal, quality is greater in nonprofit as compared to proprietary nursing homes.[38] Another study, comparing the quality of care in nonprofit versus for-profit health maintenance organizations, concluded that the patients of nonprofits receive better care.[39]

---

[37] Weisbrod writes: "Many industries are mixed—with for-profit, governmental, and private nonprofit organizations coexisting—but there has been little attention paid to why they are so, what the consequences are, and what public policy ought to be toward them." See Weisbrod, *The Nonprofit Economy,* p. 85.

[38] See Weisbrod, *The Nonprofit Economy.*

[39] D. Himmelstein et al., "Quality of Care in Investor-Owned vs. Not-for-Profit HMOs," *Journal of the American Medical Association, 282,* July 14, 1999, pp. 159–163.

However, the studies of organized day-care centers *per se* are less conclusive and do not find large quality differences (controlling for resources) by the type of agency. It may be that the combination of existing regulations and competition among public, nonprofit, and proprietary institutions works to minimize the problem of moral hazard in both the public and the proprietary ones.[40] These studies do not find that nonprofit agencies are any less effective than the others, and thus our conclusion that they should be able to participate in an expanded subsidy system stands.

The Value of Trust

A fitting note for the conclusion of this book returns us to the issue of public interest values. As we began the journey of microeconomic policy analysis, we mentioned briefly the importance of many social values such as liberty, democracy, and community. Our point then was to emphasize that this book's focus on efficiency and equity values is not meant to diminish in any way the social importance of the others. Rather, it is the comparative advantage of policy analysts in making meaningful assessments of efficiency and equity consequences, assessments that otherwise might be neglected or erroneous, that explains our focus.

For the most part, we have illustrated the use of microeconomic models in the contexts of quite specific policy issues. But we have also tried to emphasize that as skill develops and understanding of the specific models grows, a broader understanding develops of the forces that operate in our society and of opportunities to harness them constructively. Thus I would hope, for example, that the students using this book will have a fairly sophisticated understanding of strengths and weaknesses of market systems and of opportunities to harness market forces to serve the public interest.

I would like to conclude by returning to the broad values and suggesting two simple relationships. These relationships add economic supports to many other reasons for thinking that the values are important. The first is between individual freedom and efficiency. The presence of substantial individual freedom facilitates the operation of markets and enhances the efficiency with which they operate. If you and I are not free to make our own consumption choices and our own decisions about jobs and careers to pursue, it is hard to imagine how actions in our best interests would be chosen. *Liberty, a value integrally associated with democratic government, goes hand in hand with the use of markets to achieve economic efficiency.* Governments that uphold and encourage one of these values generally uphold and encourage the other. Once noted, this may seem obvious.

The second suggested relationship is less obvious and requires a little development. For me, it was stimulated by thinking about the moral hazard problem in the context of day

---

[40] For example, the study by Mocan concludes that "the hypothesis of for-profit centers taking advantage of the information asymmetry on quality is incorrect." This study is carefully done and has much to commend about it. Unfortunately for our purpose, it compares the proprietary group to a group that combines public agencies, publicly supported agencies, and private nonprofits. See Mocan, "Cost Functions, Efficiency, and Quality in Day Care Centers."

care. The importance of trust in the day-care context caused me to think about trust more generally.[41]

The available supply of trust from established nonprofit agencies is a scarce resource. One should not expect that it is easy to create more trust by, say, encouraging new nonprofit organizations to form. The legal form of a nonprofit agency—the nondistribution constraint—does not create trust by itself. Trust does develop with feelings of community within a group. We generally refer to the established nonprofits as *community* organizations. Trust gets developed in other organizational forms of communities: for example, families, school teams, social clubs. *Trust is a scarce resource that is produced at least in part by a sense of community.*

Trust is an economically valuable resource for many transactions, not just those involving moral hazard. Think for a moment of the complexity of many legal contracts and the cost of arranging them. To what extent could the cost of these be reduced if we had higher degrees of trust in the parties with whom we are transacting? To what extent could we reduce regulatory costs if we could simply trust the regulated party to report the truth (rather than requiring costly inspections or audits)? To what extent might we enjoy our economic lives more if our interactions took place with a higher degree of mutual trust? To what extent might there be new transactions and activities, ones that are forgone today owing to a lack of trust? *Trust is valuable because it reduces the cost of economic transactions and thus facilitates trade.*

Finally, let us put these thoughts together to see the second suggested relationship. Development of a strong sense of community is generally in the interest of members or participants in many social organizations, including governments. We can add any economy with voluntary transactions to this list of organizations because the trust that community engenders so greatly facilitates trade. *The value of fostering community goes hand in hand with the use of voluntary transactions to achieve economic efficiency.* The more that we in market-oriented economies can trust one another, the more able we shall be to raise the standard of living for all.

Those who choose to study microeconomic policy analysis often do so in part because they care about the world in which they live. They seek to improve it not just for themselves, but for the common good. They are aware of many social values that societies might rightly seek to foster. I hope that the study of this book has contributed in an important way to these worthy objectives and that it can be drawn upon in the future as readers act to realize them.

Summary

This chapter focuses on market problems involving asymmetric information. We described first the problem of *adverse selection*. This problem arises when there is important quality variation in a market good or service and one party to a potential transaction has more in-

---

[41] For thoughtful reading about trust, see Oliver E. Williamson, "Calculativeness, Trust and Economic Organization," in *The Mechanisms of Governance* (New York: Oxford University Press, 1996).

formation than the other about actual quality. How well or poorly the market functions in this context depends on the extent of quality variation (and thus the uncertainty owing to the information asymmetry) in the market.

We gave examples of adverse selection in markets for insurance, used cars, and the labor market. We illustrated how the fear of getting stuck with a "lemon" can result in the absence of any market for the nonlemons and in some cases no market at all. Thus the adverse selection is that the higher-quality commodities get driven out, leaving only the lower-quality ones in the market. These are inefficient outcomes, or market failures, because the willingness to pay of prospective buyers for the goods or services left out of the market generally exceeds their values in their current uses.

We then discussed a common market response to the threat of adverse selection called *market signaling.* This is when market participants acquire costly indicators of the quality of the good or service, such as hiring an independent mechanic to certify the condition of a car. This does not bring about any change in the car's condition (no new social value is created), but it may affect a buyer's expected value enough to enable a transaction that would be bypassed without it. Thus signals often work to reduce the extent of market failure.

There are cases, however, where signals increase the extent of market failure. One way this happens is when they affect distribution but not allocation, as when "high"-quality workers receiving an average wage incur a social cost for a signal that allows them to receive a higher wage. This may not affect employment but it will lower the wage of workers without the signals. Society has gained no new output, and it has lost output owing to the use of scarce resources simply to make the signals.

An important case of signals leading to worse outcomes arises in the labor market. Prospective employers have incentive to reduce their uncertainties about the productivities of individual job applicants. Some will apply stereotypical judgments based upon a cheap and visible "signal" such as an applicant's race, gender, or age, an unfortunate (and usually illegal) practice termed *statistical discrimination.* Of two people who have made the same productive investment in, say, a business school education, the one who is a woman may be offered a less important (and less remunerative) position because the employer believes women are less likely than men to stay with the company for the long haul. An important inefficiency caused by this practice is that its prospective victims, knowing that they will receive lower returns than others from the same productive investment (in education), will often forgo the investment in the first place. The major policy used to reduce this kind of discrimination is Title VII of the 1964 Civil Rights Act, which forbids discrimination in employment.

The second problem of asymmetric information is that of *moral hazard.* This occurs when the asymmetry arises after contracting, in the form of a hidden action taken by one party that affects the outcome to the other. A market failure arises because the individual choosing the hidden action does not face the appropriate social cost or benefit of the choice. A detailed illustration of this was provided in Chapter 7, showing how excessive consumption of medical services results from full-coverage medical insurance; a different example is the employee who chooses not to work hard because the employer cannot observe the choice or infer it from any visible outcome.

We also saw in Chapter 7 that there are market mechanisms that can mitigate (but not necessarily eliminate) the problem of moral hazard. We illustrated this by modifications in the medical insurance contract to include deductibles and co-insurance. In this chapter, we reviewed an application of principal-agent theory to consider how to motivate individual store managers of a large chain. The problem is how to induce them both to make the efforts necessary to maximize their stores' profits (the hidden actions) and to provide truthful information needed by the chain for production decisions. We illustrated the form of an incentive contract that would achieve these objectives.

We also reviewed the idea that, *in some cases of moral hazard, an efficient response can be to have the service provided by a nonprofit agency* rather than a profit-seeking firm. For some complex personal services, such as nursing-home care or hospital care under fixed-fee reimbursement, the profit-making firm has incentive to skimp on the quality and quantity of care actually provided. This decision is hidden from the purchaser when it is unobserved or when the purchaser lacks the expertise to recognize skimping. Because nonprofit agencies are barred from distributing any profits (the nondistribution constraint), they do not have the same incentive to skimp. Nonprofit agencies may have other imperfections as suppliers, but some circumstances of moral hazard will give them the relative advantage.

We introduced two additional procedures for identifying strengths and weaknesses associated with various institutional structures: reviewing the *economic history* of the activity under consideration and using *the exit-voice-loyalty framework* of Hirschman. These methods are applied in an analysis of another moral hazard problem: day-care services for small children.

The historical review of day-care provision highlights the important role of the family, extended family, and neighbors in the provision of day care. Trust is a key consideration of parents, who generally care a great deal about the quality of service (e.g., the degree of attention paid to the child) but are by definition not around to verify it. A second point from the historical review is that basic demographic changes in family structure help explain why the demand for day-care centers has grown. We then consider the problem of whether trustworthy centers can be had at a low cost.

We employ Hirschman's framework, which is used generally as a way of understanding organizational responsiveness in markets for goods and services in which quality is important. He suggests that an efficient way of learning usually involves a combination of exit and voice, where the latter is a direct complaint or suggestion for improvement to the firm. Firm loyalty can both induce the use of voice and give a firm time to adjust. This may lead to better industry performance than letting the original firm go bankrupt from exit while consumers wait for a new firm to take up the slack.

As a way of introducing the use of this framework, we review briefly an application by Freeman and Medoff to labor unions. Most economic analyses of unions regard them as monopolist labor suppliers that cause inefficiency through wage distortions and supply restrictions. Freeman and Medoff supplement this view by analyzing the efficiency-enhancing aspects of unions that serve as a collective voice and help overcome the free-rider problem for the provision of workplace public goods such as plant safety and available fringe benefits.

We then continue the analysis of the day-care industry. We consider how parents and, to a lesser extent, day-care experts can influence the behavior of day-care institutions. Experts play a voice role on the demand side as insurance for the child, since parents may not know enough (about child development) or sometimes may not act enough to ensure the child's best interests.

Several different supply modes for day care are considered in the context of a public policy that will increase limited subsidy funds primarily to help qualifying low-income families pay for day care. The voluntary cooperative is unsuitable for most families because it requires the parents to have jobs with arrangeable hours, and it is often unstable and therefore unreliable. Inexpensive private profit-making institutions are flawed by the lack of consumer trust: The parent knows that it is in the firm's interest to skimp on promised services when the skimping is hard to detect. The mechanisms of exit and voice are not very useful here, because the parent does not have the right information to trigger either one of them.

The market can attempt to remedy this problem by professionalization of the employees, which puts some barrier between the short-run profits of the firm and any behavior of employees that is not in the child's interest. But in the context of limited subsidy funds, the drawback of this response is its expense. The question arises whether there are more economical ways of providing the trust aspect that is important to quality.

Direct public provision of the service can probably be accomplished inexpensively and still allow for professional influence in setting minimum standards for government day-care centers. However, the degree of consumer sovereignty that can be exercised is likely to be very low. This means that the exit option cannot be used effectively, and that in itself tends to mute the effectiveness of voice. Although public agencies like private nonprofits are subject to the nondistribution constraint, differing motivations and constraints apply (such as uniformity of service within a jurisdiction). Thus students of public agency behavior have not hypothesized that these organizations should be expected to have the same high level of consumer trust that is expected of established community nonprofit agencies. While one could imagine a voucher system just for public agencies that could in principle encourage a diversity of supply to meet the diverse needs of parents, uniform service within jurisdictions is the norm in practice.

Finally, additional day-care service could be provided through private nonprofit established community organizations. These may enjoy the advantage of having a relatively high degree of consumer trust as compared with profit-making or bureaucratic institutions. Consumer voice is relatively effective here, and parents have exit options with some diversity of choice. Day-care professionals can exercise influence by setting minimum standards of eligibility for receipt of public subsidies; they can also influence the type of day care by serving on advisory boards to each institution. The budgetary costs to parents of these institutions should be relatively low, because the institutions, like cooperatives, can rely in part on parental volunteers and in part on salaried but nonprofessional employees.

Empirical studies to measure differences in quality between nonprofit and for-profit suppliers, expected because of the differing responses to the presence of moral hazard, have sometimes confirmed that nonprofits provide better quality for given resources. However, in the day-care context, large quality differences have not been found. It may be that the combination of existing regulatory mechanisms with competition across the different sectors works to even out their relative performances. It could be, for example, that the presence of known trustworthy nonprofit suppliers acts as a constraint to limit the effects of moral hazard on the other (for-profit and public) agencies. While the study of mixed competitive systems is a matter for further research, existing theory and empirical research would seem to support the inclusion of nonprofit agencies in any expanded subsidy system for day-care services.

We conclude with a reminder of the diversity of social values that should be fostered through our public policies. *The study of microeconomic policy analysis,* while it emphasizes the importance of efficiency and equity consequences, also has implications for other broad values. In particular, it *reaffirms the high value that societies should place on both liberty and community.* Liberty allows the freedom of choice and consumer sovereignty that is so important to achieving efficient outcomes in a market-oriented economy. Fostering community is a primary method of increasing the scarce supply of an invaluable resource— trust. Trust is important for many reasons, including the fact that it greatly facilitates all the voluntary transactions that are made in any economic system.

Exercises

20-1 Monopsony and Unions. The ordinary demand curve for labor (L_D) depends on the wage rate (W):

$$L_D = 120 - W$$

The ordinary supply curve of labor (L_S) also depends on the wage rate (W):

$$L_S = W$$

a Monopsony. Suppose a profit-maximizing monopsonist (the only demander) faced the above supply curve and valued labor in accordance with the above demand curve. It pays a uniform wage to all the workers it hires: (1) Draw a diagram to show conceptually its profit-maximizing choice. [*Hint:* Think about how its total wage bill changes if it wants to attract an additional worker.] ($2^\bigcirc$) Calculate the quantity of labor it will hire and the wage rate it will pay. (Answer: $40.)

b Minimum wage. If a minimum wage rate of $50 per day were imposed on the situation in (a), would that increase or decrease efficiency in this sector? Explain.

c Labor union (monopoly view). Suppose the demand curve was as above but that it came from the demands of many firms. A union controls the labor supply. The union's goal is to expand membership (= employment) as long as the increase in total wages equals or exceeds the opportunity cost of the marginal member: (1) Draw another diagram to show conceptually the choice that achieves this goal [*Hint:* This union is like a sales-maximizing firm.] ($2^\bigcirc$) Calculate how many laborers will be hired and the wage they will earn.

d Labor union (voice/response view). Give an example of how a labor union can increase efficiency by correcting a market failure that would otherwise persist in the workplace environment under competition.

20-2 For some economic activity, it may be that neither markets with profit-seeking firms nor government bureaus are the best institutional arrangements. Using hospitals as an example, could we argue that nonprofit, nongovernmental institutions might be the preferred structures for guiding the allocation of medical resources?

AUTHOR INDEX

SUBJECT INDEX

Page numbers for definitions are in **boldface.**